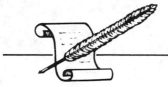

HISTORIC
DOCUMENTS
OF
1983

Cumulative Index 1979-83

Congressional Quarterly Inc.

Printed in the United States of America

Congressional Quarterly Inc.
1414 22nd St. N.W., Washington, D.C. 20037

The following have given permission to reprint copyrighted material: From *The State of Black America - 1983*, published by the National Urban League. From *The Code of Canon Law*, copyright © 1983 by the Canon Law Society of America. From Belton M. Fleisher, *Minimum Wage Regulation in the United States*, copyright © 1983 by the National Chamber Foundation. From "Nuclear Winter: Global Consequences of Multiple Nuclear Explosions" and "Long-Term Biological Consequences of Nuclear Winter," from *Science* magazine, 23 December 1983, Volume 222, Number 4630, pp. 1283-1299. Copyright © 1983 by the American Association for the Advancement of Science.

The Library of Congress cataloged the first issue of this title as follows:

Historic documents.   1972—
    Washington. Congressional Quarterly Inc.

    1. United   States—Politics   and   government—1945—   —Yearbooks.
2. World politics—1945— —Yearbooks. I. Congressional Quarterly Inc.

E839.5.H57   917.3'03'9205   72-97888
ISBN 0-87187-279-X

FOREWORD

Publication of *Historic Documents of 1983* carries through a twelfth year the project launched by Congressional Quarterly with *Historic Documents 1972*. The purpose of this continuing series of volumes is to give students, scholars, librarians, journalists and citizens convenient access to documents of basic importance in the broad range of public affairs.

To place the documents in perspective, each entry is preceded by a brief introduction containing background materials, in some cases a short summary of the document itself and, where necessary, relevant subsequent developments. We believe these introductions will prove increasingly useful in future years when the events and questions now covered are less fresh in one's memory and the documents may be difficult to find.

Conflicts in Central America and the Middle East continued to capture headlines in 1983. There was sharp debate over U.S. aid to the El Salvador government in its war with communist-backed guerrillas. The swift and unannounced U.S. invasion of the island of Grenada was among the most controversial of the Reagan administration's actions. The war in Lebanon intensified; its toll for the United States was tragically underscored by the terrorist bombing in Beirut that killed more than 240 Marines. On a global scale, the devastating effects of nuclear war were starkly delineated by an international group of scientists who described the "nuclear winter" that would follow such an exchange.

A number of domestic issues proved newsworthy in 1983. In a landmark decision with far-reaching repercussions, the Supreme Court declared unconstitutional Congress' use of the legislative veto, contained in scores of laws. A presidential commission found major flaws in America's schools and declared the "nation at risk." Although they continued to fault the administration for the so-called "gender gap," women's rights groups were encouraged by Court rulings that barred sex bias in pension plans and reaffirmed a woman's right to have an abortion.

Historic Documents of 1983 contains statements, Court decisions, reports, special studies and speeches related to these and other events of national and international significance. We have selected for inclusion as many as possible of the documents that in our judgment will be of more than transitory interest. Where space limitations prevented reproduction of the full texts, excerpts were used to set forth the essentials and, at the same time, to preserve the flavor of the materials.

Carolyn Goldinger
Margaret C. Thompson
Editors

Washington, D.C.
March 1984

Historic Documents of 1983

Editors: Carolyn Goldinger, Margaret C. Thompson
Contributors: Nancy A. Blanpied, Mary Ames Booker, Anne Chase, Carolyn H. Crowley, Suzanne de Lesseps, James R. Ingram, Jane Freundel Levey, Mary L. McNeil, John L. Moore, Patricia Pine, Patricia M. Russotto, Elizabeth H. Summers
Cumulative Index: Jodean Marks

Congressional Quarterly Inc.

Eugene Patterson   *Editor and President*
Wayne P. Kelley   *Publisher*
Peter A. Harkness   *Deputy Publisher and Executive Editor*
Robert E. Cuthriell   *Director, Research and Development*
Robert C. Hur   *General Manager*
I. D. Fuller   *Production Manager*
Maceo Mayo   *Assistant Production Manager*
Sydney E. Garriss   *Computer Services Manager*

Book Department

David R. Tarr   *Director*
Joanne D. Daniels   *Director, CQ Press*
John L. Moore   *Assistant Director*
Kathryn C. Suarez   *Book Marketing Manager*
Mary W. Cohn   *Associate Editor*
Michael D. Wormser   *Associate Editor*
Barbara R. de Boinville   *Senior Editor, CQ Press*
Nancy Lammers   *Senior Editor*
Nola Healy Lynch   *Developmental Editor, CQ Press*
Margaret C. Thompson   *Senior Writer*
Carolyn Goldinger   *Project Editor*
Mary L. McNeil   *Project Editor/Design Coordinator*
Patricia M. Russotto   *Project Editor*
Judith Aldock   *Editorial Assistant*
Andra Armstrong   *Editorial Assistant*
Mary Ames Booker   *Editorial Assistant*
Michael Horner   *Editorial Assistant*
Elizabeth H. Summers   *Editorial Assistant*
Nancy A. Blanpied   *Indexer*
Barbara March   *Secretary*

How to Use This Book

The documents are arranged in chronological order. If you know the approximate date of the report, speech, statement, court decision or other document you are looking for, glance through the titles for that month in the Table of Contents below.

If the Table of Contents does not lead you directly to the document you want, turn to the index at the end of the book. There you may find references not only to the particular document you seek but also to other entries on the same or a related subject. The index in this volume is a **five-year cumulative index** of Historic Documents covering the years 1979-1983.

The introduction to each document is printed in italic type. The document itself, printed in roman type, follows the spelling, capitalization and punctuation of the original or official copy. In some cases, boldface headings in brackets have been added to highlight the organization of the text. Where the full text is not given, omissions of material are indicated by the customary ellipsis points.

TABLE OF CONTENTS

January

February

March

April

May

June

July

August

September

October

November

December

HISTORIC

DOCUMENTS

OF

1983

January

BRITISH GOVERNMENT REPORT ON FALKLAND ISLANDS WAR

January 18, 1983

A British committee of inquiry officially cleared Prime Minister Margaret Thatcher's government of blame for Britain's failure to foresee or prevent the Falkland Islands War. The committee was established in July 1982 "to review the way in which the responsibilities of Government in relation to the Falkland Islands and their Dependencies were discharged in the period leading up to the Argentine invasion of the Falkland Islands on 2 April 1982. . . ." The 105-page report was released January 18.

For years Argentina and Britain had argued over sovereignty of the Falkland Islands in the South Atlantic. On April 2, 1982, Argentine forces invaded and quickly took control of the British-held Falklands. A 10-week struggle ensued, and in June Britain recaptured the islands. After the war, Britain increased its military presence on the islands to 4,000 men, from fewer than 100 before the struggle. (Falkland Islands War, Historic Documents of 1982, p. 283)

Argentina's invasion brought criticisms of the Thatcher government and its unpreparedness for the attack. A month after the British victory, the committee of inquiry was established and began its review of the period leading up to the war. Lord Franks, an Oxford don and Liberal Party member, chaired the panel. Two members of the governing Conservative Party, two members of the opposition Labor Party and a senior civil servant made up the rest of the committee. The group studied documents related to the conflict, including intelligence reports, and heard testimony from government officials and others.

Committee's Findings

The report included a review of the British-Argentine dispute over the Falklands from 1965 to 1982, with emphasis on the period immediately prior to the invasion.

In the main, the report was favorable to Thatcher's government. The panel concluded that the "invasion of the Falkland Islands on 2 April could not have been foreseen." And in response to charges that the government could have prevented the invasion, the panel wrote: "[W]e would not be justified in attaching any criticism or blame to the present Government for the Argentine junta's decision to commit its act of unprovoked aggression in the Falkland Islands."

The committee, however, criticized the government on several counts. The panel termed "inadvisable" the government's decision to announce in June 1981 the planned withdrawal of its ice-patrol vessel H.M.S. Endurance from the Falklands area. Argentina might have interpreted this announcement as a reduction in Britain's commitment to the islands. Lord Carrington, Foreign and Commonwealth secretary, repeatedly urged Secretary of State for Defence Sir John Nott to reverse the decision to withdraw the ship. (In fact, as the situation deteriorated, the Endurance remained in the South Atlantic.)

The panel also indicated concern over and recommended a review of the government's intelligence assessment facilities. The Joint Intelligence Organisation was "too passive in operation to respond quickly and critically to a rapidly changing situation which demanded urgent attention," the committee wrote.

Argentina's First Inroad

The committee studied in detail a bizarre incident that preceded the Argentine invasion. Constantino Davidoff, an Argentine scrap metal merchant, had a contract to take equipment from disused whaling stations on Britain's South Georgia Island, some 700 miles east of the Falklands. He made visits to South Georgia in December 1981 and March 1982. On both occasions Davidoff used Argentine naval vessels, disobeyed British instructions and landed illegally. Following Davidoff's March landing, there were reports of shots being fired and the raising of the Argentine flag. Despite British protests, some of Davidoff's party refused to leave the island and remained there with the Argentine government's knowledge. Uncertainties remained about the Davidoff incident, and there was no firm evidence that the Argentine government had planned the operations. But, the panel stated, better liaison among the British Foreign and Commonwealth Office, the British Embassy in Buenos Aires and the governor of the islands might have enabled Britain to deal with the situation more effectively.

Despite these criticisms, the report, with its general exoneration of the government, was a boost for Thatcher. The prime minister received the report on December 31, 1982, and on January 12 left Britain for a five-day visit to the Falklands. The trip outraged Argentina, and British Labor Party members criticized the tour as dangerous, provocative and politically motivated. The trip pleased Thatcher's Conservative Party, and the Falkland islanders welcomed her warmly. Thatcher assured the inhabitants that Britain would defend them "for a long, long time" and told reporters that "the islanders are absolutely emphatic — no negotiations on sovereignty with Argentina." The trip seemed to solidify Thatcher's hard-line resolve not to renew talks with Argentina on the sovereignty issue. Britain's victory in the Falklands and the favorable report on the war were significant factors in Thatcher's reelection in June.

Following are excerpts from Falkland Islands Review, *a report presented to Britain's Parliament by Prime Minister Margaret Thatcher and released to the public January 18, 1983.* (Boldface headings in brackets have been added by Congressional Quarterly to highlight the organization of the text.):

The Government's Discharge Of Their Responsibilities

260. In this Chapter we address the central issue of our terms of reference, the way in which the responsibilities of Government in relation to the Falkland Islands and the Falkland Islands Dependencies were discharged in the period leading up to the invasion. We have had to consider many questions, but two are crucial. First, could the Government have foreseen the invasion on 2 April? Secondly, could the Government have prevented that invasion? We deal with the first question at the outset of the Chapter. The second question is more complex and in our view cannot be answered until we have examined how the dispute became critical and how it was handled at various stages by the present Government. We consider the answer to this question at the end of the Chapter.

[COULD THE INVASION HAVE BEEN FORESEEN?]

261. We consider first the question whether before 31 March the Government had warning of the invasion of the Falkland Islands on 2 April. We have described in detail in Chapter 3 the events of the days leading up to the invasion and all the information available at the time, including all relevant reports from the intelligence agencies. We believe that our account demonstrates conclusively that the Government had no reason to believe before 31 March that an invasion of the Falkland Islands would take place at the beginning of April.

262.   All the information ... that has come to light since the invasion suggests that the decision to invade was taken ... at a very late date.

263.   Argentine naval forces were at sea between about 23 and 28 March, in the course of annual naval exercises, which included a joint anti-submarine exercise with Uruguay (press accounts of which the British Naval *Attaché* in Buenos Aires reported on 27 March). The Argentine news agency reported on 2 April that the fleet had sailed south from Puerto Belgrano on 28 March with a marine infantry battalion, an amphibious command section and troops embarked. The actual order to invade was probably not given until at least 31 March, and possibly as late as 1 April. Dr. Costa Mendez was subsequently reported as saying that the Junta did not finally decide on the invasion until 10.00 p.m. (7.00 p.m. local time) on 1 April. It is probable that the decision to invade was taken in the light of the development of the South Georgia situation; but it seems that the violent demonstrations in Buenos Aires on the night of 30/31 March were also a factor in the Junta's decision.

264.   It may be thought that, although the Government could not have had earlier warning of the invasion, they must have had fuller and more significant information of Argentine military movements. The fact is that there was no coverage of these movements and no evidence available to the Government from satellite photographs. We discuss these matters further below in the context of the arrangements made for gathering intelligence.

265.   We specifically asked all those who gave evidence to us — Ministers and officials, the British Ambassador in Buenos Aires and other Embassy staff, the Governor of the Falkland Islands, Falkland Islanders and persons outside Government with special knowledge of and interest in the area — whether at any time up to the end of March they thought an invasion of the Falklands was likely at the beginning of April. They all stated categorically that they did not.

266.   In the light of this evidence, we are satisfied that the Government did not have warning of the decision to invade. The evidence of the timing of the decision taken by the Junta shows that the Government not only did not, but could not, have had earlier warning. . . .

HOW DID THE DISPUTE BECOME CRITICAL?

267.   Before we consider the present Government's handling of the dispute, we need to examine the question: how did the dispute develop into such a critical state that a sudden and unforeseeable invasion took place? To answer it, it is necessary to look back at the main features of the dispute and the positions of the parties to it over a longer period.

The Positions of the Parties to the Dispute

268.   From 1965 the positions of the three main parties to the dispute — the Argentine Government, the British Government and the Islanders — remained constant.

269. First, for all Argentine Governments repossession of the 'Malvinas' was always a major issue of policy and a national issue. The dispute has not held the same place in the attention of British Governments or of the British people. Although it pressed its claims with greater force on some occasions than on others, Argentina never wavered in its commitment to recover the Islands. Whatever other issues were proposed for discussion, such as economic co-operation on fisheries or oil exploration, its overriding concern was with sovereignty . . . .

270. Secondly, all British Governments asserted British sovereignty over the Islands and the Dependencies, without reservation as to their title, coupled with an unchanging commitment to the defence of their territorial integrity. Although at the time of the first United Nations Resolution in 1965 the Government stated that sovereignty was not negotiable, from 1966 all British Governments were prepared to negotiate about sovereignty over the Islands, and to reach a settlement, provided that certain conditions were fulfilled and that it was capable of being carried in Parliament. The most important condition has always been that any settlement must be acceptable to the Islanders, and Ministers of successive Governments have made unequivocal statements to Parliament to this effect. This was also always made plain to the Argentine Government.

271. Thirdly, the Islanders always made it clear that they wished to remain British and consistently resisted any change in their constitutional relationship with the United Kingdom. On occasion they acquiesced in negotiations and later took part in negotiations; but they never apporved any proposals for a settlement of the sovereignty issue going beyond a lengthy freeze of the dispute. They were not prepared to agree even to the proposed scheme of joint scientific activity in the Dependencies worked out with Argentina in 1979, which they saw as a threat to British sovereignty in the area.

[Developments Affecting the Attitude of Argentina]

272. While the positions of the three sides in the dispute remained constant, circumstances in Argentina changed and British Government policy developed in several important respects.

(i) Developments in Argentina.

273. In Argentina itself the military takeover in 1976 was an important factor. The *coup* placed decision-making in the hands of a small group at the head of the armed services, and increased the influence of the Navy, which had always been the most hawkish of the services on the Falklands issue. It introduced a repressive régime, whose appalling human rights record understandably increased the Islanders' reluctance to contemplate any form of closer association with Argentina. There was also a danger that the Junta might at any time seek to divert attention from domestic

problems, particularly as economic difficulties grew, by appealing to Argentine nationalism to support an initiative on the Malvinas.

274. The other main issue in Argentine foreign policy over the period was its sovereignty dispute with Chile over three islands in the Beagle Channel. Argentina's concern is less with the islands themselves, which are occupied by Chile, than with their territorial waters and continental shelves, as it is strongly opposed to any extension of Chilean sovereignty into the South Atlantic. The relevance of this issue to the Falkland Islands dispute was that, if Argentina were preoccupied with the Beagle Channel dispute, it would divert its attention from the Falkland Islands: whereas, if that dispute were going in favour of Chile or reached deadlock, Argentina was more likely to seek a compensatory success in the Falklands.

275. In 1977 an International Court of Arbitration awarded the islands to Chile, but did not pronounce on the seaward extension of either side's claims. Argentina refused to accept the award, despite earlier agreement to adhere to the Court's findings, and the following year the two countries came to the brink of war on the issue. A Papal mediator was appointed, whose proposals again favoured Chile. Argentina delayed its response to his proposals, and early in 1982 announced its intention of abrogating a treaty with Chile, the effect of which would be to prevent the dispute being referred to the International Court of Justice. From Argentina's point of view the dispute had reached an impasse adverse to the Junta, and this was likely to focus its attention more closely on the Falklands.

276. A further development in Argentine foreign policy was its rapprochement with the United States from the time President Reagan's administration took office. . . . It seems likely that the Argentine Government came to believe that the United States Government were sympathetic to their claim to the Falkland Islands and, while not supporting forcible action in furtherance of it, would not actively oppose it. When initially asked to intervene, the United States did adopt an 'even-handed' approach, while using their good offices to attempt to find a solution.

277. Given the relative closeness of the Falkland Islands to Argentina, their distance from Britain and the absence of a substantial British deterrent force in the area, Argentina always had the capability successfully to mount a sudden operation against the Islands. Moreover, in recent years there was a substantial increase in Argentina's military strength in all three of its armed services, which must have increased its confidence in its ability to occupy the Islands and retain them.

(ii) Developments in British Policy

278. Argentina's growing military power coincided with an increasing concentration on the part of the United Kingdom on its NATO role and the progressive restriction of its other defence commitments. Even before the Defence Review published in 1966 the South Atlantic had not been a major area of deployment. . . . As the Argentine threat grew, in deciding to maintain only a token presence in the area, in the form of a small

detachment of Royal Marines and in the summer months *HMS Endurance*, successive Governments had to accept that the Islands could not be defended against sudden invasion. These decisions were taken in the light of wider strategic interests, but it is likely that they were seen by Argentina as evidence of a decreasing British commitment to the defence of the Islands. . . .

280.   There were other British Government policies which may have served to cast doubt on British commitment to the Islands and their defence. These included the Government's preparedness, subject to certain restrictions, to continue arms sales to Argentina (and to provide training facilities in the United Kingdom for Argentine military personnel); the decision not to implement some of the recommendations of Lord Shackleton's 1976 report, notably that relating to the extension of the airfield; and the failure in the British Nationality Act to extend British citizenship to those inhabitants of the Islands who either were not themselves patrial or did not have a United Kingdom-born grandparent.

281.   Finally, the 1981 Defence Review may have provided further reassurance to Argentina, in view of the planned reductions in the surface fleet, the sale of *HMS Invincible* and, more particularly, the decision, although it was never impelemented, to withdraw *HMS Endurance*. In short, as Argentine military power increased the British capability to respond to it became more restricted.

282.   The course of negotiations over the years was also itself an important factor limiting the Government's freedom of manoeuvre. As successive initiatives had been tried and failed, and with no signs of softening of either Argentine or Islander attitudes, the picture that the history of the dispute presents is one in which the negotiating options were progressively eliminated until only one — leaseback — was left that might eventually satisfy the aspirations of Argentina on the one hand and the wishes of the Islanders on the other.

283.   It is against that background that we examine the present Government's handling of the dispute. What stands out is the dilemma to which successive Governments were exposed by their policy of seeking to resolve, or at least contain, the dispute by diplomatic negotiation on the one hand and their commitment to the defence of the Falkland Islands on the other. This dilemma sharpened as the policy options diminished. The Islands were always at risk, and increasingly so as Argentina's military capability grew stronger; but a British decision to deploy to the area any additional warships, whose secrecy could not always be assured, also carried a risk, dependent on its timing, of frustrating the prospect of negotiation. This dilemma underlined the importance of the token defence presence, which we examine in the next section of this Chapter.

[Policy of Foreign and Commonwealth Office]

284.   Before coming to that, however, we first deal with the allegation that over the years Foreign and Commonwealth Office officials pursued a

policy aimed at getting rid of the Islands, irrespective of the views of Ministers. In our examination of the papers we have found no evidence to support this damaging allegation, and we believe it to be totally without foundation. . . .

[HOW DID THE GOVERNMENT HANDLE THE DISPUTE?]

Continuity of Policy and HMS Endurance

285. A chief responsibility of British Governments in relation to the Falkland Islands and the Falkland Islands Dependencies, as for any other part of British territory, is for their defence and security. As we have already explained, the policy of successive Governments on the defence of the Islands has been to maintain a token presence on the Falklands in the form of a small detachment of Royal Marines. This force was adequate to deal with sudden 'adventurist' incursions, which up to about 1975 were regarded as the main threat.

286. Although from that time the Argentine threat of military action increased, no Government was prepared to establish a garrison on the Falklands large enough to repel a full-scale Argentine invasion, or to provide an extended runway for the airfield, with supporting facilities. . . .

287. Throughout the period, in addition to the detachment of Royal Marines, a Royal Naval ice-patrol vessel, first *HMS Protector* and subsequently *HMS Endurance*, was kept on station in the area in the summer months. . . . We recognise the limited military value of this vessel; but, as the only regular Royal Naval presence in the area, her symbolic role was important in relation to Argentina. . . .

288. We conclude . . . that it was inadvisable for the Government to announce a decision to withdraw *HMS Endurance* and that, in the light of the developing situation in the second half of 1981, they should have rescinded their decision to pay off *HMS Endurance* at the end of her 1981/82 tour.

The Decisions of September 1981

289. As 1981 wore on, one of the most significant developments in the situation was the receding prospect of negotiating a leaseback solution. Mr. [Nicholas] Ridley's meeting on 30 June 1981 was held against the background of a general belief that time was running out and that Argentine impatience was growing. It reviewed the policy options and concluded that the only feasible option was leaseback preceded by an education campaign both in the Falkland Islands and at home. At his meeting on 7 September, however, Lord Carrington decided not to pursue that course of action, but to discuss the whole matter with Dr. Camilion in New York later in the month and to suggest to him that it would help if the Argentines were able to make constructive proposals for resolving the dispute. Lord Carrington told us that, in his view, there was no prospect of

'selling' leaseback at that stage. It did not have support in the Islands, in the House of Commons or amongst his own Ministerial colleagues in Government. So he saw this approach to Dr. Camilion as the best diplomatic tactic in the circumstances. The Government was thenceforth left with no resort other than attempting to keep negotiations going by some means or other, and they were in the position of having nothing to offer Argentina other than what the wishes of the Islanders dictated. . . .

290.   We conclude that the Government were in a position of weakness, and that the effect of Lord Carrington's decision was to pass the initiative to the Argentine Government.

291.   Lord Carrington also decided on 7 September not to present a paper for collective Ministerial discussion in the Defence Committee. Instead he circulated a minute to his Defence Committee colleagues on 14 September. This was one of a series of minutes . . . by which he kept the Prime Minister and Defence Committee colleagues informed of progress in the dispute up to the time of the invasion. We recognise that Cabinet Committees, such as the Defence Committee, usually meet to take decisions at the invitation of the Minister with proposals to put forward; and we have noted that, in September 1981, the propsect of further negotiations still existed on the basis of agreed Government policy. . . . Officials in both the Foreign and Commonwealth Office and the Ministry of Defence were looking to Ministers to review the outcome of the contingency planning they had done in view of a potentially more aggressive posture by Argentina. In the event, Government policy towards Argentina and the Falkland Islands was never formally discussed outside the Foreign and Commonwealth Office after January 1981. . . . There was no meeting of the Defence Committee to discuss the Falklands until 1 April 1982; and there was no reference to the Falklands in Cabinet, even after the New York talks of 26 and 27 February, until Lord Carrington reported on events in South Georgia on 25 March 1982.

292.   We cannot say what the outcome of a meeting of the Defence Committee might have been, or whether the course of events would have been altered if it had met in September 1981; but, in our view, it could have been advantageous, and fully in line with Whitehall practice, for Ministers to have reviewed collectively at that time, or in the months immediately ahead, the current negotiating position; the implications of the conflict between the attitudes of the Islanders and the aims of the Junta; and the longer-term policy options in relation to the dispute.

The View in the Foreign and Commonwealth Office At the Beginning of the Year

293.   At the beginning of 1982 there was evidence from several sources that Argentina, and particularly the new government of President [Leopóldo] Galtieri, was committed to achieving success in its Malvinas policy in a much shorter timescale than most previous Argentine Governments had envisaged. There were clear indications that it attached

particular significance to achieving a solution of the dispute on its terms, in which the sovereignty issue was the overriding consideration, by January 1983, the 150th anniversary of British occupation. These indications included General Galtieri's remarks in his speech in May 1981, intelligence about the attitude of different elements in the Argentine Government, the press comment at the beginning of the year and, definitively, the terms of the *bout de papier* at the end of January 1982, which called for serious negotiations with a timescale of one year, culminating in the recognition of Argentine sovereignty.

294.   The Foreign and Commonwealth Office recognised clearly that the situation was moving towards confrontation, as is shown by the advice they gave their Ministers at the beginning of the year, notably in connection with the Annual Report of the governor of the Falkland Islands. They believed, however — and their belief was supported by evidence — first, that Argentina would not move to confrontation until negotiations broke down; secondly, that there would be a progression of measures starting with the withdrawal of Argentine services to the Islands and increased diplomatic pressure, including further action at the United Nations; and thirdly — and the intelligence bore this out — that no action, let alone invasion of the Islands, would take place before the second half of the year.

Contingency Planning

295.   Nevertheless, in recognition of the deteriorating situation, the Foreign and Commonwealth Office had set in hand in 1981 contingency plans to provide alternative services for the Islands, and, at its request, the Ministry of Defence prepared a paper on the military options available in response to possible aggressive action by Argentina. A paper on civil contingency planning was also prepared in September 1981 in expectation of a meeting of the Defence Committee, at which Ministerial authority might have been obtained to take the plans further.... On the military side the absence of detailed contingency plans for responding to aggressive action by Argentina did not inhibit a very swift response once it was clear that an invasion was imminent, as can be seen from the remarkable speed with which the task force was prepared and sailed....

Foreign and Commonwealth Office Judgement
On How the Dispute Would Develop

296.   We believe that the view taken by Foreign and Commonwealth Office Ministers and officials early in 1982 of how the dispute would develop was one which could reasonably be taken in the light of all the circumstances at that time. In the event it proved to be a misjudgment, but not one in our view for which blame should be attached to any individual. There were, we believe, three important factors in the misjudgment: first, in underestimating the importance that Argentina attached to its timeta-

ble for resolving the dispute by the end of the year; secondly, in being unduly influenced — understandably and perhaps inevitably — by the long history of the dispute, in which Argentina had previously made threatening noises, accompanied by bellicose press comment, and indeed backed up its threats with aggressive actions, without the dispute developing into a serious confrontation; and, thirdly, in believing, on the basis of evidence, that Argentina would follow an orderly progression in escalating the dispute, starting with economic and diplomatic measures. Sufficient allowance was not made for the possibility of Argentina's military government, subject to internal political and economic pressures, acting unpredictably if at any time they became frustrated at the course of negotiations. The July 1981 intelligence assessment had warned that in those circumstances there was a high risk that Argentina would resort to more forcible measures swiftly and without warning.

[Response to Events Following New York Talks]

297. We acknowledge the skill with which Mr. [Richard] Luce and Foreign and Commonwealth Office officials handled the formal talks between the Argentine and British Governments in New York on 26 and 27 February.... The agenda for the talks was provided by the Argentine *bout de papier* issued on 27 January. They were held in a cordial atmosphere, and the general view of the British side was that they had gone somewhat better than they feared. A joint *communiqué* was agreed, and in the draft working paper on the negotiating commission reference to the frequency of meetings — an important element in the Argentine proposals — was avoided. At the same time, it had been clear even at the talks that the Argentine side's ability to manoeuvre was strictly limited. The Argentine Government were committed to the establishment of the commission, with negotiations being conducted at high level, at a much faster pace than in the past, and with a strict deadline of a year. They pressed strongly for a formal reply from the British Government to their proposal within a month, with a view to the first round of talks being held at the beginning of April.

298. The unilateral *communiqué* of 1 March instigated by the Junta marked an important change of attitude on the part of the Argentine Government. It in effect denounced the joint *communiqué* by making public the details of the informal working paper, and commended the proposals in the *bout de papier* for a programme of monthly meetings with the aim of achieving recognition of Argentine sovereignty within a short time; and, if those proposals were not effective, claimed the right to choose "the procedure which best accords with [Argentine] interests". Although Sr. Ros expressed regret about the *communiqué* and accompanying press comment, and Dr. [Nicandor] Costa Mendez assured the British Ambassador in Buenos Aires that no threat was intended, it indicated a hardening attitude on the part of the Argentine Government....

299. The increased seriousness of the situation was recognised by

Foreign and Commonwealth Office officials.... [T]hey discussed it with Lord Carrington at a short meeting on 5 March, at which several diplomatic initiatives were set in hand.

300.   This was also the occasion when they mentioned to him the previous Government's decision in November 1977 to deploy ships to the area covertly, though without recommending similar action at that stage. As it happens, 5 March was about the last moment at which, given that the invasion took place on 2 April, it would have been possible to sail a deterrent force to be in place in time. It would have taken nuclear-powered submarines approximately two weeks and surface ships approximately three weeks to reach the Falkland Islands. The evidence we received suggested to us that Foreign and Commonwealth Office officials did not press Ministers to consider deterrent rather than diplomatic counter-measures or prompt the Joint Intelligence Organisation urgently to update its July 1981 assessment because they believed that Argentina would not resort to military action before initiating diplomatic and economic measures....

302.   We believe that Foreign and Commonwealth Office officials did not attach sufficient weight at this time to the changing Argentine attitude at and following the February talks and did not give sufficient importance to the new and threatening elements in the Argentine Government's position. We conclude that they should have drawn Ministers' attention more effectively to the changed situation.

303.   We note that the Prime Minister reacted to the telegrams from the British Ambassador in Buenos Aires on 3 March reporting aggressive Argentine press comment following the New York talks, and called for contingency plans. We regret that the Prime Minister's enquires did not receive a prompt response. She also enquired of Mr. [John] Nott on 8 March about the timing of possible warship movements to the South Atlantic....

The Joint Intelligence Organisation

304.   The reports by the intelligence agencies and the assessments made by the Joint Intelligence Committee were a key factor in the judgments made by Ministers and officials in the period leading up to the invasion, which we have reviewed above.... For many years Argentina and the Falkland Islands were regarded as a priority for intelligence collection but were in a relatively low category.

Earlier Intelligence Assessments

305.   From 1965 the Argentine threat to the Falkland Islands was regularly assessed by the Joint Intelligence Committee, the frequency of assessment increasing at times of heightened tension between Britain and Argentina in the dispute on sovereignty, in the light of the internal political situation in Argentina and information about Argentine inten-

tions. The timing of assessments was often related to the rounds of formal negotiations between the British and Argentine Governments. In the period of the present Government a full assessment was prepared in November 1979. . . .

The Assessment of July 1981

306. A further full assessment, the last before the invasion, was prepared in July 1981. . . . This assessment was particularly important because, as was apparent from the oral evidence we received, it had considerable influence on the thinking of Ministers and officials.

Review of the 1981 Assessment

307. We were told in evidence that the Latin America Current Intelligence Group met 18 times between July 1981 and March 1982, but did not discuss the Falkland Islands on those occasions. They were, however, discussed on two occasions in that period at the weekly meetings held by the Head of the assessments staff; and on at least four separate occasions consideration was given by those concerned, who were in close touch with the Foreign and Commonwealth Office on this matter, to the need to update the assessment made in July 1981. These occasions were in November 1981, in preparation for the next round of talks, which were then scheduled for the following month; in December 1981; in January 1982, in the light of the proposals that it was known that Argentina would put forward before the February talks in New York; and in March 1982. On each occasion up to March it was decided that there was no need to revise the assessment.

308. We were told that the four principal factors that the assessments staff considered in assessing the Argentine threat were: the progress of Argentina's dispute with Chile over the Beagle Channel; the political and economic situation in Argentina; the state of inter-service rivalry there; and, most importantly, Argentina's perception of the prospects of making progress by negotiation. The information they received after July 1981 about Argentine intentions and the options open to them were regarded as consistent with more recent intelligence and therefore still valid.

309. In March 1982 it was agreed that a new assessment should be prepared, and work was started on it. It was thought, however, that it could most usefully be presented to Ministers in the context of a more general consideration of Falkland Islands policy, which they were expected to discuss at a meeting of the Defence Committee on 16 March. In the event, as we have explained, that meeting did not take place, and the new assessment was never completed.

310. The next assessment . . . was made at very short notice in the morning of 31 March and was concerned with events on South Georgia. In its conclusion it expressed the view that, while the possibility that Argentina might choose to escalate the situation by landing a military

force on another Dependency or on the Falkland Islands could not be ruled out, the Argentine Government did not wish to be the first to adopt forcible measures.

The Intelligence Agencies

311.   This assessment on the eve of the invasion relied chiefly on the information available from the intelligence agencies. . . . Throughout the period leading up to the invasion secret intelligence was collected, in accordance with the priority accorded to this target, on Argentina's attitude to and intentions in the dispute, in particular the views of its armed forces and Ministry of Foreign Affairs; on relevant internal factors in Argentina; and on its general military capability. In October 1981, following a general review of intelligence requirements in Central and South America and the Caribbean, the Joint Intelligence Committee notified the collecting agencies that, in view of the increasing difficulty of maintaining negotiations with Argentina over the future of the Falkland Islands, the requirement had increased for intelligence on Argentine intentions and policies on the issue. But additional resources were not allocated for this purpose. We were told in evidence that, for operational reasons which were explained to us, the deployment of additional resources would not necessarily have secured earlier or better intelligence of the intentions of the very small circle at the head of the Argentine Government where decisions were taken.

312.   If, as we believe, the decision to invade was taken by the Junta at a very late stage, the intelligence agencies could not have been expected to provide earlier warning of the actual invasion on 2 April. It might have been possible to give some warning of the military preparations preceding the invasion, if there had been direct coverage of military movements within Argentina in addition to coverage of its general military capability. But it would have been difficult to provide comprehensive coverage of these movements in view of among other things, Argentina's very long coastline and the distance of the southern Argentine ports from Buenos Aires. The British Defence *Attaché* in Buenos Aires told us that his section at the Embassy had neither the remit nor the capacity to obtain detailed information of this kind. By the time the diplomatic situation deteriorated at the beginning of March it would have been difficult to evaluate such information because of the absence of knowledge about the normal pattern of Argentine military activity.

313.   There was no coverage of Argentine military movements within Argentina, and no advance information was therefore available by these means about the composition and assembly of the Argentine naval force that eventually invaded the Falklands. There was no intelligence from American sources or otherwise to show that the force at sea before the invasion was intended other than for normal naval exercises. No satellite photography was available on the disposition of the Argentine forces. The British Naval *Attaché* in Buenos Aires reported the naval exercises when

he became aware of them, mainly on the basis of Argentine press reports.

314. We have no reason to question the reliability of the intelligence that was regularly received from a variety of sources.

[Effectiveness of Intelligence Machinery]

315. As to assessments, however, we were surprised that events in the first three months of 1982, in particular the Argentine *bout de papier* on 27 January, the unilateral *communiqué* on 1 March and the Prime Minister's comments on the telegram of 3 March reporting Argentine press comment, did not prompt the Joint Intelligence Organisation to assess the situation afresh. As we have explained, the assessments staff considered the need for a new assessment on several occasions in this period. Work was started on one early in March, but not completed because of the intention to link it to a meeting of the Defence Committee. It was decided not to prepare a new assessment before the beginning of March because of the view in the Joint Intelligence Organisation that the conclusions of a new assessment were unlikely to be significantly different from those of the July 1981 assessment. The assessment of 31 March 1982, although focused on the South Georgia incident, tends to support this view.

316. We do not regard the view taken by those concerned of the need for a new assessment as unreasonable in the light of the information available to them at the time. But in our consideration of the evidence we remain doubtful about two aspects of the work of the Joint Intelligence Organisation. First, we are not sure that at all important times the assessments staff were fully aware of the weight of the Argentine press campaign in 1982. As a result it seems to us that they may have attached greater significance to the secret intelligence, which at that time was reassuring about the prospects of an early move to confrontation. . . . Our second doubt is whether the Joint Intelligence Organisation attached sufficient weight to the possible effects on Argentine thinking of the various actions of the British Government. The changes in the Argentine position were, we believe, more evident on the diplomatic front and in the associated press campaign than in the intelligence reports.

317. We do not seek to attach any blame to the individuals involved. But we believe that these factors point to the need for a clearer understanding of the relative roles of the assessments staff, the Foreign and Commonwealth Office and the Ministry of Defence, and for closer liaison between them. The aim should be to ensure that the assessments staff are able to take fully into account both relevant diplomatic and political developments and foreign press treatment of sensitive foreign policy issues.

318. We are concerned here with defects in the Joint Intelligence machinery as we have seen it working in an area of low priority. As we have seen only the papers relevant to the subject of our review, we are not able to judge how the assessment machinery deals with areas of higher priority, but we believe that, in dealing with Argentina and the Falkland Islands it

was too passive in operation to respond quickly and critically to a rapidly changing situation which demanded urgent attention.

319.   We consider that the assessment machinery should be reviewed. We cannot say what the scope of such a review should be in respect of the machinery's wider preoccupations, but we think that it should look at two aspects in particular. The first, to which we have already referred, is the arrangements for bringing to the Joint Intelligence Organisation's attention information other than intelligence reports. The second is the composition of the Joint Intelligence Committee. On this, consideration should be given to the position of the chairman of the Committee: to the desirability that he or she should be full-time, with a more critical and independent role; and, in recognition of the Committee's independence in operation from the Government Departments principally constituting it, to the Chairman's being appointed by the Prime Minister. . . .

Impact of the South Georgia Incident

321.   If the Joint Intelligence Committee machinery had operated differently, we have no reason to believe that it would have increased the intelligence available to the Government about the operations of Sr. [Constantino] Davidoff, which led to the South Georgia incident preceding the invasion. There are still uncertainties about the full scope and character of those operations. The visits to South Georgia, by Sr. Davidoff himself in December 1981 and by his party in March 1982, were both made on Argentine naval vessels, and the Argentine Navy was no doubt aware of them. But there was no evidence at the time, and none has come to light since, suggesting that the whole operation was planned either by the Argentine Government or by the Navy as a follow-up to the occupation of Southern Thule. The intelligence available indicates that, when the incident grew more serious it was seized on to escalate the situation until the Junta finally decided to invade the Falkland Islands.

322.   We recognise that the response of Ministers had to take account of conflicting pressures at home, especially from Parliament, and from Argentina. The initial reports of the incident appeared alarming — shots having been fired and the Argentine flag run up — and it was a reasonable reaction to order *HMS Endurance* to sail to South Georgia to take the men off. Thereafter the Government went to great lengths to avoid exacerbating the situation and made every effort to offer constructive ways of enabling the Argentine party to regularise its position. These were all rejected by the Argentine Government, which by then were clearly intent on raising the temperature.

323.   Nevertheless we believe that, if Sr. Davidoff's operations had been more closely monitored from December 1981 onwards and there had been better liaison between the Foreign and Commonwealth Office, the British Embassy in Buenos Aires and the Governor in preparation for the second visit in March 1982, Ministers would have been better able to deal with the landing on South Georgia when it occurred.

The Possibility of Earlier Deterrent Action

324. We next examine whether the Government should have taken earlier military action to deter Argentina. We have considered two possible actions that the Government might have taken: the earlier despatch of a task force on a sufficient scale to defend, or if necessary retake, the Islands; and the deployment of a much smaller force in the form of a nuclear-powered submarine, either on its own or supported by surface ships.

325. We believe that it would not have been appropriate to prepare a large task force with the capacity to retake the Falkland Islands, before there was clear evidence of an invasion. As we have explained, this was not perceived to be imminent until 31 March. Sending such a force would have been a disproportionate, and indeed provocative, response to the events on South Georgia, and would have been inconsistent with the attempts being made to resolve the problems there by diplomatic means.

326. A smaller force might have been deployed, either overtly as a deterrent measure or covertly as a precautionary measure, whose existence could have been declared if circumstances required. There were three occasions when such a force might reasonably have been deployed: before the New York talks at the end of February; at the beginning of March in the light of evidence of increased Argentine impatience at lack of progress in negotiations; or later in March, as events on South Georgia moved towards confrontation. . . .

329. There was a stronger case for considering action of this nature early in March 1982, in the light of evidence of increasing Argentine impatience, culminating in the threatening *communiqué* issued on 1 March by the Argentine Ministry of Foreign Affairs and the accompanying bellicose Argentine press comment. . . . Lord Carrington was informed of the action taken in 1977 at the end of a short meeting on 5 March. Lord Carrington told us in oral evidence that the matter was mentioned only briefly. He asked whether the Argentines knew about the naval deployment, and, when told that they did not, he took the view that this reduced its relevance to the situation he faced. Lord Carrington also told us more generally that, although the situation had become more difficult, he did not believe that the prospect of continuing negotiations at that time was hopeless. In his view nothing had happened to trigger the sending of a deterrent force. He was concerned that, if ships were sent, the fact would have become known. This would have jeopardised the prospect of keeping negotiations going, which was his objective. With hindsight he wished he had sought to deploy a nuclear-powered submarine to the area at an earlier stage, but on 5 March it did not seem to him that the situation had changed in such a way as to justify such action.

330. We do not think that this was an unreasonable view to take at the time, but we believe that there would have been advantage in the Government's giving wider consideration at this stage to the question whether the potentially more threatening attitude by Argentina required some form of deterrent action in addition to the diplomatic initiatives and

the contingency planning already in hand.

331.   Finally, we consider whether earlier action should have been taken to deploy ships to the area in response to the developing crisis on South Georgia. In Lord Carrington's judgment a deployment involving surface ships was likely to carry too great a risk of becoming known at a time when the Government were concerned to avoid any action that might have appeared provocative. That could have provoked escalatory action by Argentina against the Falkland Islands themselves, which the Government had no means of resisting effectively. This objection would not have applied so strongly to sailing a nuclear-powered submarine, since there would have been more chance of keeping its deployment covert. The decision to sail the first nuclear-powered submarine was taken early on Monday 29 March.

332.   We consider that there was a case for taking this action at the end of the previous week in the light of the telegram of 24 March from the defence *Attaché* in Buenos Aires and the report of 25 March that Argentine ships had been sailed for a possible interception of *HMS Endurance*. We would have expected a quicker reaction in the Ministry of Defense to these two reports, which were the first indications of hostile activity by the Argentine Government. . . .

[Could the Invasion Have Been Prevented?]

335.   Finally we turn to the more complex question we posed in the opening paragraph of this Chapter. Could the present Government have prevented the invasion of 2 April 1982?

336.   It is a question that has to be considered in the context of the period of 17 years covered by our Report: there is no simple answer to it. We have given a detailed factual account of the period, and we attach special importance to our account of events immediately preceding the invasion. It is essential . . . to recognise, as we do, that there were deep roots to Argentina's attitude towards the 'Malvinas', and that the present Government had to deal with that within the political constraints accepted by successive British Governments.

337.   As to the Argentine Government — and this is quite apart from the influence on the Argentine Government of actions of the British Government — the Junta was confronted at the end of March 1982 with a rapidly deteriorating economic situation and strong political pressures at a moment when it was able to exploit to its advantage the developments in South Georgia. We have already stated at the beginning of this Chapter the reasons why we are convinced that the invasion on 2 April 1982 could not have been foreseen.

338.   The British Government, on the other hand, had to act within the constraints imposed by the wishes of the Falkland Islanders, which had a moral force of their own as well as the political support of an influential body of Parliamentary opinion; and also by strategic and military priorities which reflected national defence and economic policies: Britain's

room for policy manoeuvre was limited.

339. Against this background we have pointed out in this Chapter where different decisions might have been taken, where fuller consideration of alternative courses of action might, in our opinion, have been advantageous, and where the machinery of Government could have been better used. But, if the British Government had acted differently in the ways we have indicated, it is impossible to judge what the impact on the Argentine Government or the implications for the course of events might have been. There is no reasonable basis for any suggestion — which would be purely hypothetical — that the invasion would have been prevented if the Government had acted in the ways indicated in our report. Taking account of these considerations, and of all the evidence we have received, we conclude that we would not be justified in attaching any criticism or blame to the present Government for the Argentine Junta's decision to commit its act of unprovoked aggression in the invasion of the Falkland Islands on 2 April 1982.

Comments on Some Specific Assertions

There has understandably been much speculation about the causes of the Falkland Islands conflict and about whether it could have been foreseen and prevented. The truth of these matters is less simple than some commentators have asserted, and for an accurate and comprehensive account of the facts our Report needs to be read in full. In the detailed narrative of events and our comments on them we have answered explicitly or by implication many of the mistaken or misleading statements that have been made, but we think it right also to state for the record our view of some of the more important specific assertions which have been made, in order to clear up damaging misunderstandings.

1. *Assertion:* Ministers and officials secretly told Argentina that Britain was prepared to give up the Falkland Islands against the wishes of the Islanders.
   Comment: We have found no evidence to support this allegation. On the contrary, Ministers and officials made clear to Argentina on numerous occasions that the wishes of the Falkland Islanders were paramount, and that any proposals to resolve the dispute would be subject to approval by Parliament.
2. *Assertion:* Clear warnings of the invasion from American intelligence sources were circulating more than a week beforehand.
   Comment: No intelligence about the invasion was received from American sources, before it took place, by satellite or otherwise.
3. *Assertion:* On or around 24 March 1982 the British Embassy in Buenos Aires passed on definite information to London about an invasion and predicted the exact day.
   Comment: This assertion derives from newspaper interviews after the invasion. We have investigated these interviews. It is not our task to

come to any conclusion about what was or was not said to the journalists concerned or whether or not what was said was correctly interpreted. It is our task, however, to ascertain beyond doubt whether any such communication from the British Embassy in Buenos Aires predicting the invasion was in fact made. We have examined all the relevant telegrams and intelligence reports and interviewed the individuals concerned. We are satisfied that no such communication was in fact made.

4. *Assertions:* (i) Two weeks before the invasion the Cabinet's Defence Committee rejected a proposal by Lord Carrington to send submarines to the area;

(ii) The Government rejected advice from the Commander-in-Chief, Fleet, to send submarines soon after the landing on South Georgia on 19 March.

Comment: These assertions are untrue. We have described in detail the events of the weeks leading up to the invasion. The Defence committee did not meet at that time. The first discussion between Ministers about sending nuclear-powered submarines took place on Monday 29 March 1982 when the Prime Minister and Lord Carrington decided that a nuclear-powered submarine should be sent to support *HMS Endurance*. No earlier military advice recommending the despatch of submarines was given to Ministers. . . .

6. *Assertions:* (i) Captain [N. J.]Barker, the Captain of *HMS Endurance*, sent warnings than an invasion was imminent which were ignored by the Foreign and Commonwealth Office and the Ministry of Defence.

(ii) The Secretary of State for Defence saw Captain Barker and ignored his advice.

Comment: These assertions are untrue. Captain Barker reported his concern about events within his knowledge, but none of his reports warned of an imminent invasion. Both the Ministry of Defence and the Foreign and Commonwealth Office saw his reports and took them into account along with other intelligence material. Captain Barker confirmed to us that he never met Mr. Nott.

7. *Assertion:* On 11 March 1982 an Argentine military plane landed at Port Stanley to reconnoitre the runway. The incident was reported by the Governor as suspicious.

Comment: The emergency landing on 7 March of an Argentine Air Force Hercules transport aircraft was reported factually by the Governor to the Foreign and Commonwealth Office on 12 March but not as suspicious. He has subsequently confirmed that the landing was preceded by a 'May Day' call and that, after the aircraft landed, fuel was seen leaking from it. The Argentine Air Force would already have had detailed knowledge of the strength of the runway in consequence of its responsibility for operating the flights between Port Stanley and Argentina and of authorised landings by Argentine Hercules aircraft at Port Stanley on several occasions in 1981.

8. *Assertion:* The Argentine Government made a bulk purchase of maps

of the Falkland Islands in Britain before the invasion.

Comment: An investigation by the Foreign and Commonwealth Office found that no such bulk purchase was made. This has been confirmed by the agents for the sale of the hydrographic charts produced by the Royal Navy. It has also been confirmed by the Agents for the sale of the 1966 map of the Falkland Islands published by the Directorate of Overseas Surveys, copies of which were left on the Islands by the Argentine forces.

9. *Assertion:* There were massive withdrawals of Argentine funds from London banks shortly before the invasion, of which the Government must have been aware.

 Comment: We are satisfied that the Government had no information about such a movement of funds. The deposit liabilities of United Kingdom banks to overseas countries are reported to the Bank of England on a quarterly basis. The reporting date relevant to the period before the invasion was 31 March 1982, but, because of the complexity of the figures, they normally take several weeks to collect. Withdrawals by Argentine banks in March would therefore not have normally been reported until May. After the invasion the Bank of England asked banks for a special report, and this showed that around $1/2 billion of the original $1 1/2 billion of Argentine funds were moved out of London in the period running up to the invasion, much of it on 1 and 2 April. Since the withdrawals were in dollars, there would have been no effect on the sterling exchange rate to alert the Bank of England.

10. *Assertion:* On 29 March 1982 the Uruguayan Government offered the British Government facilities for Falkland Islanders who wished to leave the Islands before the Argentine invasion.

 Comment: Neither the Foreign and Commonwealth Office nor the British Embassy in Montevideo had knowledge at the time or thereafter of any such offer. The Uruguayan Government have also described this allegation as completely without foundation. They have confirmed that neither they nor their Navy had any foreknowledge of the Argentine invasion of the Falkland Islands.

PSYCHIATRISTS, LAWYERS ON INSANITY DEFENSE

January 19, February 9, 1983

In a position paper issued January 19, the American Psychiatric Association (APA) urged retention of the insanity defense in criminal trials but recommended a tightening of procedures and standards involved in the plea.

The insanity defense became the subject of intense debate and scrutiny following the trial of John W. Hinckley Jr. in the spring of 1982. Hinckley admitted shooting President Ronald Reagan and three other men in March 1981. A jury found Hinckley "not guilty by reason of insanity" on all counts. He was admitted to St. Elizabeth's, the federal mental hospital in Washington, D.C., and would be eligible for release if his mental condition improved. (Reagan shooting, Historic Documents of 1981, p. 351; Hinckley verdict, Historic Documents of 1982, p. 531)

The Hinckley verdict outraged the public, and calls came for the abolition or reform of the insanity defense. Some 20 bills dealing with reform of federal insanity defense rules were introduced in Congress, and many state legislatures took up the issue. The outcry following the Hinckley verdict led the APA, the major psychiatric organization in the United States, to study the issue and outline the group's position.

A four-member panel, headed by Dr. Loren Roth, director of the law and psychiatry program at Western Psychiatric Institute and Clinic and professor of psychiatry at the University of Pittsburgh, studied the insanity defense and drafted a position paper. In December 1982 the APA Board of Trustees approved a revised draft — the first comprehensive statement on the insanity defense by the APA in its 138-year history.

Psychiatrists' Recommendations

The APA paper presented a brief judicial history of the insanity defense plea, with a discussion of the legal standards used to determine a defendant's insanity. The paper touched on the impact of the Hinckley case, but the APA took no position on that verdict.

The principle behind the insanity defense was that an individual who has no understanding or control of his behavior should not be held criminally responsible for his actions. Because in its view "punishment for wrongful deeds should be predicated upon moral culpability," the APA recommended that the insanity defense be retained. However, the group proposed several reforms.

One suggestion dealt with the basic conflict between the legal and psychiatric approaches to insanity, with psychiatry focusing on the diagnosis and treatment of mental disorders and the law concentrating on the establishment of fault and the determination of responsibility. To avoid confusing juries, the APA suggested that expert psychiatric testimony be limited to discussion of a defendant's mental state and motivation at the time of the alleged crime. Psychiatrists should not be called upon to determine whether a defendant is sane or insane by the legal definition.

The APA also urged tightening insanity defense standards so that the plea is used only in cases of serious mental illness (on the order of psychoses) and not in less serious cases of "antisocial personality disorders."

Standards also should be tightened to make it more difficult for persons acquitted of violent crimes under the insanity defense to be released from mental institutions, the APA stated. The group suggested that a special board of psychiatrists and criminal justice professionals, acting as a sort of parole board, determine release and confinement decisions. Continued outpatient treatment should follow a person's release from a mental hospital, and if an individual no longer needs treatment in the hospital but still needs confinement, other facilities should be available.

Some states have adopted an alternative to the "not guilty by reason of insanity" verdict. Under this alternative verdict, a defendant may be found "guilty but mentally ill." The APA criticized this as an "easy way out" for juries to avoid tangled issues of guilt or innocence.

The APA did not take a position on where the burden of proof should lie in insanity defense cases. In all federal courts and in about half of the states, the prosecution had to prove the defendant was sane "beyond a reasonable doubt." (This was the case in the Hinckley trial.) In the other states and in the District of Columbia, the defendant must prove his insanity by a "preponderance of the evidence." Who bears the burden of proof can be important to the outcome of the case. The APA noted that "it is commonly believed that the likely effect of assigning the burden of proof . . . to defendants rather than to the state in insanity trials will be to decrease the number of successful defenses."

Lawyers' Proposals

At its midyear convention, the American Bar Association (ABA) on February 9 also endorsed changes in the insanity defense. In many states and in federal courts, the insanity defense involved a two-prong test: 1) could the defendant "appreciate the wrongfulness of his act" and 2) even if he could appreciate that, was he able to control his behavior. The ABA recommended eliminating the second part of the test, so that defendants who were aware of the wrongfulness of their acts would be held criminally responsible even if they later contended they were unable to control themselves.

The bar group further recommended that in states that use the two-prong test, the defendant should have the burden of proving his insanity. In jurisdictions where a defendant's insanity is based solely on his appreciation of the wrongfulness of his conduct, the prosecution should have the burden of proving the defendant's sanity. Finally, the ABA rejected the "guilty but mentally ill" verdict as an alternative to the "not guilty by reason of insanity" verdict.

> *Following are excerpts from the American Psychiatric Association's statement on the insanity defense, released January 19, 1983; and the recommendations on insanity defense adopted by the American Bar Association February 9, 1983. (Boldface headings in brackets have been added by Congressional Quarterly to highlight the organization of the text.):*

APA STATEMENT

Introduction

Long before there was psychiatry, there was the insanity defense. The idea that the insane should not be punished for otherwise criminal acts began to develop in the twelfth century as part of the more general idea that criminal punishment should be imposed only on persons who were morally blameworthy. In the thirteenth century, Bracton, the first medieval jurist to deal with the subject of insanity and crime stated, "For a crime is not committed unless the will to harm be present.". . .

In his treatise on the *History of the Pleas of the Crown* published posthumously in 1736, England's Lord Mathew Hale explained that the insanity defense was rooted in the fundamental moral assumptions of the criminal law:

> Man is naturally endowed with these two great faculties, understanding and liberty of will. . . . The consent of the will is that which renders human actions either commendable or culpable. . . . (I)t follows that, where there is a total defect of the understanding, there is no free act of the will. . . .

Thus it is a long-standing premise of the criminal law that unless a defendant intentionally chooses to commit a crime, he is not morally blameworthy, and he should not be punished. By singling out certain defendants as either lacking free will or, alternatively, lacking sufficient understanding of what they do, the insanity defense becomes the exception that proves the rule. In the law's moral paradigm, other criminal defendants, those who do not receive an insanity defense, are thus found blameworthy.

Despite these general premises in the criminal law, many questions have persisted about the insanity defense such as how best to define criminal insanity (what the legal test should be) and what should happen to criminal defendants once they are found "insane." The history of the insanity defense has been one of periodic revisions of standards, public debate, and contention. This has been the case especially when the insanity defense is highlighted by a case involving a defendant who has attempted to harm a well-known person.

The modern formulation of the insanity defense derives from the "rules" stated by the House of Lords in Daniel M'Naghten's case (1843). M'Naghten was indicted for having shot Edward Drummond, secretary to Robert Peel, the Prime Minister of England. The thrust of the medical testimony was that M'Naghten was suffering from what today would be described as delusions of persecution symptomatic of paranoid schizophrenia. The jury returned a verdict of not guilty by reason of insanity. This verdict became the subject of considerable popular alarm and was regarded with particular concern by Queen Victoria. As a result, the House of Lords asked the judges of that body to give an advisory opinion regarding the answers to five questions "on the law governing such cases." The combined answers to two of these questions have come to be known as M'Naghten's Rules.

> (T)o establish a defense on the ground of insanity, it must be clearly proved that, at the time of the committing of the act, the party accused was labouring under such a defect of reason, from disease of the mind, as not to know the nature and quality of the act he was doing; or if he did know it, that he did not know he was doing what was wrong.

M'Naghten quickly became the prevailing approach to the insanity defense in England and in the United States, even though . . . [it] was criticized often because of its emphasis on the defendant's lack of intellectual or cognitive understanding of what he was doing as the sole justification for legal insanity. M'Naghten's case was followed by a public response not unlike that of the public's response to the John Hinckley case.

Ye people of England exult and be glad
For ye're now at the will of the merciless mad...
For crime is no crime — when the mind is unsettled.
(*The Times*, 1843)

Over the last 150 years, legal formulations for insanity other than M'Naghten have, from time to time, been adopted in certain jurisdictions, e.g., the "irresistible impulse" formulation. Judge David Bazelon was midwife to the "product of mental illness" test for insanity employed in the District of Columbia from 1954 through 1972. However, the "product of mental illness" test was originally formulated in New Hampshire in 1869.

The alternative formulation for the insanity defense best known besides M'Naghten is that proposed by the drafters of the Model Penal Code during the 1950s, the so-called ALI (American Law Institute) test. Section 4.01 of the Model Penal Code provides:

> A person is not responsible for criminal conduct if at the time of such conduct as a result of mental disease or defect he lacks substantial capacity either to appreciate the criminality (wrongfulness) of his conduct to conform his conduct to the requirements of law.

This was the test employed in the Hinckley case.

The ALI (Model Penal Code) approach to insanity differs from M'Naghten in three respects. First, ALI substitutes the concept of "appreciation" for that of cognitive understanding in the definition of insanity, thus apparently introducing an affective, more emotional, more personalized approach for evaluating the nature of a defendant's knowledge or understanding. Second, the ALI definition for insanity does not insist upon a defendant's total lack of appreciation (knowledge) of the nature of his conduct but instead that he only "lacks substantial capacity." Finally, ALI, like the "irresistible impulse" test, incorporates a so-called volitional approach to insanity, thus adding as an independent criterion for insanity the defendant's ability (or inability) to control his actions.

Through court rulings, the ALI approach to criminal insanity has been adopted in all federal jurisdictions. It has been adopted by legislation or judicial ruling in about half the states. Some variation of M'Naghten is the exclusive test of insanity in about one-third of the states. A handful of states (6) supplement M'Naghten with some variation of the "irresistible impulse" test. Only New Hampshire continues to use the "product of mental illness" test. Montana and Idaho have abolished the insanity defense in recent years or at least that form of the defense that requires the defendant to meet one of the above-mentioned special legal tests or formulations for insanity.

Interestingly, the United States Supreme Court has never ruled whether the availability for defendants of an insanity defense is constitutionally compelled. Nor has the legislature of the United States (the Congress) yet adopted one or another of the traditional insanity defense formulations for use in the federal courts. Earlier in the twentieth century, three state courts (Washington, Mississippi, and Louisiana) ruled that recognition of the insanity defense was constitutionally required.

Despite the attention given to the insanity defense by legal scholars and the continuing debates about the role that psychiatry should play in the administration of defense, it should be noted that successful invocation of the defense is rare (probably involving a fraction of 1 percent of all felony cases). While philosophically important for the criminal law, the insanity defense is empirically unimportant. Making changes in the insanity defense will hardly be the panacea for reducing crime.

Historically, defendants who were found insane also did not usually regain their freedom. Instead, they often spent many years, if not their whole lifetimes, locked away in institutions for the criminally insane. Information also suggests that despite the prominence given the insanity defense through well publicized trials, the majority of such successful defenses (rather than being awarded by juries after criminal trials) occur, instead, by concurrence between the prosecution and defense. Thus, in many instances, the insanity defense functions in a noncontroversial manner to divert mentally ill offenders from the criminal justice system to the mental health system.

As has recently been summarized by persons testifying before Congress in the wake of the John Hinckley verdict, there is also a great deal that is unknown and not very well studied about the insanity defense. For example, contrary to popular belief, what little evidence there is suggests that the insanity defense is not solely or exclusively a defense of the rich. Nor is it a defense that is confined to defendants who are accused only of violent crimes.

During the last ten years, interest in abolishing or modifying the insanity defense has been renewed because of several factors. Public officials, speaking for a growing conservative consensus and a public understandably disturbed by the failures of the entire criminal justice system, have championed the cause that the insanity defense is one more indication that the country is "soft on crime." Thus, in 1973 President Nixon called for the abolition of the insanity defense noting that this proposal was "the most significant feature of the Administration's proposed criminal code."

A 1981 Attorney General's Task Force on Violent Crime proposed federal legislation to create a verdict of "guilty but mentally ill," similar to legislation that had been passed in a few states such as Illinois and Michigan.

The hardening of American attitudes about crime has not been, however, the only cause of concern about the insanity defense. Over the last decade, as a consequence of some civil libertarian-type court rulings that insanity acquittees may not be subjected to procedures for confinement that are more restrictive than those used for civil patients who have not committed criminal acts, the insanity defense became a more attractive alternative for defendants to plead. As noted by [A. A.] Stone, over the last decade and for the first time in history, a successful plea of insanity had "real bite." Modern psychiatric treatment, particularly the use of antipsy-

chotic drugs, permits the seeming restoration of sanity for many defendants, even if it cannot be known with certainty whether such acquittees
still remain dangerous.

The consequence of the aforementioned trends has been the rapid
release from hospitals for a segment of insanity acquittees in some states.
In Michigan, following the McQuillan decision, 55.6 percent of "not guilty
by reason of insanity" patients were discharged following a 60-day
diagnostic commitment. In contrast over ninety percent of insanity
acquittees are hospitalized in Illinois after the 30-day diagnostic hearing,
with their average length of hospitalization being 39 months. Once their
release is approved by the court, it is almost always under the condition of
participation in a mandatory, court-ordered outpatient program. The
exodus of insanity acquittees in some states has alarmed both the public
and the psychiatric profession which traditionally has been expected to
play some continuing role in the social control of persons found not guilty
by reason of insanity. The public's perception that a successful plea of
insanity is a good way to "beat the rap" contributes to a belief that the
criminal insanity defense is not only fundamentally unfair ("for after all,
he did do it") but also that insanity is a dangerous doctrine.

The Hinckley Verdict

The ruling of the District of Columbia jury in the John Hinckley case
catalyzed many of the above and related issues concerning the insanity
defense and its administration. Following the Hinckley verdict, some
twenty bills were under discussion or were introduced in the Congress that
would codify, for the first time, a federal approach towards insanity and
also restrict the defense. The debate has focused on the wording of the
insanity defense, its potential abolution, and on post-trial mechanisms for
containing the insane. The Reagan administration has proposed, in effect,
to abolish the traditional insanity defense and to substitute instead a
"mens rea" approach. A person would be found not guilty by reason of
insanity only if the person lacked "mens rea," the required mental state
that is part of the definition of a crime. Another approach proposed a
limited M'Naghten-type criterion to define insanity.

Other debates have focused upon procedural issues in the law of
insanity. In Mr. Hinckley's case, as is presently the case in about half the
states, the government had the burden of persuasion to prove the
defendant's sanity beyond a reasonable doubt. The other states include
insanity among the so-called "affirmative defenses," placing the burden of
proving insanity upon the defendant rather than making the government
prove sanity. One proposed change of the insanity defense is to shift the
burden of proof to the defendant, rather than to the state.

Another focus of discussion, both prior to and following Mr. Hinckley's
case, has been on the nature and quality of psychiatric testimony in
insanity trials. In particular, there has been criticism of psychiatric
testimony about whether defendants meet (or fail to meet) the relevant

legal test for insanity in a given jurisdiction. To some extent the public appears confused by the so-called "battle of the experts." Unfortunately, public criticism about the "battle of the experts" fails to recognize or acknowledge advances in psychiatric nosology and diagnosis that indicate a high degree of diagnostic reliability for psychiatry — 80 percent or so — so long, that is as psychiatric testimony is restricted to medical and scientific, and not legal or moral issues. Sanity is, of course, a legal issue, not a medical one. The "battle of the experts" is also to a certain extent foreordained by the structure of the adversary system. Experts often disagree in many types of criminal and civil trials. For example, other medical experts may disagree on the interpretation of X-rays, engineers on structural issues, and economists on market concentration issues. American jurisprudence requires that each side (defense and prosecution) makes the best case it can in the search for the just outcome.

The APA Position
[ABOLISH THE INSANITY DEFENSE?]

The American Psychiatric Association, speaking as citizens as well as psychiatrists, believes that the insanity defense should be retained in some form. The insanity defense rests upon one of the fundamental premises of the criminal law, that punishment for wrongful deeds should be predicated upon moral culpability. However, within the framework of English and American law, defendants who lack the ability (the capacity) to rationally control their behavior do not possess free will. They cannot be said to have "chosen to do wrong." Therefore, they should not be punished or handled similarly to all other criminal defendants. Retention of the insanity defense is essential to the moral integrity of the criminal law.

The aforementioned points do not, of course, mean that the insanity defense is necessarily "good for psychiatry," "good for all criminals" who invoke the plea, or even always "good for the public." In fact, the opposite may be the case. Psychiatrists, indeed even some psychiatric patients, might be less stigmatized, less susceptible to criticism by the media and the public were the insanity defense to be abolished. Thus the Association's view that the insanity defense should not now be abolished is not one that it takes out of self-interest. Only a minority of psychiatrists testify in criminal trials. Members of the American Psychiatric Association, however, recognize the important of the insanity defense for the criminal law, as well as its importance for genuinely mentally ill defendants who on moral and medical grounds require psychiatric treatment . . . rather than receiving solely custody and punishment.

To the extent that changes need to be made in the insanity defense, the Association, therefore, recommends consideration of some of the ideas discussed below concerning the legal definition of insanity, the burden of proof, the role that psychiatrists can or should play within the insanity defense, and the post-verdict disposition of persons found insane.

['GUILTY BUT MENTALLY ILL']

While some psychiatrists believe that the "guilty but mentally ill" verdict has merit for dealing with problems posed by the insanity defense, the American Psychiatric Association is extremely skeptical of this approach. Currently nine states are experimenting with a "guilty but mentally ill" verdict or its equivalent. They permit a "guilty but mentally ill" verdict as an alternative choice for jurors to the traditional insanity defense. Were, however, "guilty but mentally ill" to be the *only* verdict possible (besides guilt or innocence), this would be the abolitionist position in disguise. The idea of moral blameworthiness would be dismissed within the law. This does not seem right.

There are also problems with "guilty but mentally ill" as an alternative choice to the traditional insanity defense. "Guilty but mentally ill" offers a "compromise" for the jury. Persons who might otherwise have qualified for an insanity verdict may instead be siphoned into a category of guilty but mentally ill. Thus some defendants who might otherwise be found not guilty through an insanity defense will be found "guilty but mentally ill" instead.

The "guilty but mentally ill" approach may become the "easy way out." Juries may avoid grappling with the difficult moral issues inherent in adjudicating guilt or innocence, jurors instead settling conveniently on "guilty but mentally ill." The deliberations of jurors in deciding cases are, however, vital to set societal standards and to give meaning to societal ideas about responsibility and nonresponsibility. An important symbolic function of the criminal law is lost through the "guilty but mentally ill" approach.

There are other problems with "guilty but mentally ill." Providing mental health treatment for persons in jails and prisons has, over the years, proved a refractory problem. Yet the "guilty but mentally ill" approach makes sense only if meaningful mental health treatment is given defendants following such a verdict. In times of financial stress, the likelihood that meaningful treatment of persons "guilty but mentally ill" will be mandated and paid for by state legislatures is, however, slight. This has been the outcome in Michigan (the state that first embarked upon the "guilty but mentally ill" approach) where even though they have been found "guilty but mentally ill," felons have received no more treatment than they would have prior to the new law.

Alternatively, whatever limited funds are available for the treatment of mentally ill inmates may be devoted to "guilty but mentally ill" defendants, ignoring the treatment needs of other mentally ill but conventionally sentenced prisoners who require mental health treatment in prison.

The "guilty but mentally ill" plea may cause important moral, legal, psychiatric, and pragmatic problems to receive a whitewash without fundamental progress being made. We note that under conventional sentencing procedures already in place, judges may presently order mental health treatment for offenders in need of it. Furthermore, a jury verdict is an awkward device for making dispositional decisions concerning a person's need for mental health treatment.

[MODIFY LEGAL STANDARDS?]

While the American Psychiatric Association is not opposed to state legislatures (or the U.S. Congress) making statutory changes in the language of insanity, we also note that the exact wording of the insanity defense has never, through scientific studies or the case approach, been shown to be the major determinant of whether a defendant is acquitted by reason of insanity. Substantive standards for insanity provide instructions for the jury (or other legal decisionmakers) concerning the legal standard for insanity which a defendant must meet. There is no perfect correlation, however, between legal insanity standards and psychiatric or mental states that defendants exhibit and which psychiatrists describe. For example, while some legal scholars and practitioners believe that using the word "appreciate" (rather than "knowing" or "understanding") expands the insanity dialogue to include a broader and more comprehensive view of human behavior and thinking, this may not necessarily be so. Of much greater practical significance is whether the standard employed is interpreted by individual trial judges to permit or not permit psychiatric testimony concerning the broad range of mental functioning of possible relevance for a jury's deliberation. But this matter is not easily legislated.

The above commentary does not mean that given the present state of psychiatric knowledge psychiatrists cannot present meaningful testimony relevant to determining a defendant's understanding or appreciation of his act. Many psychiatrists, however, believe that psychiatric information relevant to determining whether a defendant understood the nature of his act, and whether he appreciated its wrongfulness, is more reliable and has a stronger scientific basis than, for example, does psychiatric information relevant to whether a defendant was able to control his behavior. The line between an irresistible impulse and an impulse not resisted is probably no sharper than that between twilight and dusk. Psychiatry is a deterministic discipline that views all human behavior as, to a good extent, "caused." The concept of volition is the subject of some disagreement among psychiatrists. Many psychiatrists therefore believe that psychiatric testimony (particularly that of a conclusory nature) about volition is more likely to produce confusion for jurors than is psychiatric testimony relevant to a defendant's appreciation or understanding.

Another major consideration in articulating standards for the insanity defense is the definition of mental disease or defect. Definitions of mental disease or defect sometimes, but not always, accompany insanity defense standards. Under Durham, the "product of mental illness" approach, a series of legal cases in the District of Columbia, suggested that (for purposes of criminal insanity) "sociopathy" or other personality disorders could be "productive" of insanity. It was assumed by the law that such disorders could impair behavior control. But this is generally not the experience of psychiatry. Allowing insanity acquittals in cases involving persons who manifest primarily "personality disorders" such as antisocial personality disorder (sociopathy) does not accord with modern psychiatric knowledge or psychiatric beliefs concerning the extent to which such persons do have control over their behavior. Persons with antisocial personality disorders should, at least for heuristic reasons, be held accountable for their behavior. The American Psychiatric Association, therefore, suggests that any revision of the insanity defense standards should indicate that mental disorders potentially leading to exculpation must be *serious*. Such disorders should usually be of the severity (if not always of the quality) of conditions that psychiatrists diagnose as psychoses.

The following standard, recently proposed by [R. J.] Bonnie, is one which the American Psychiatric Association believes does permit relevant psychiatric testimony to be brought to bear on the great majority of cases where criminal responsibility is at issue:

> A person charged with a criminal offense should be found not guilty by reason of insanity if it is shown that as a result of mental disease or mental retardation he was unable to appreciate the wrongfulness of his conduct at the time of the offense.
>
> As used in this standard, the terms mental disease or mental retardation include only those severely abnormal mental conditions that grossly and demonstrably impair a person's perception or understanding of reality and that are not attributable primarily to the voluntary ingestion of alcohol or other psychoactive substances.

In practice there is considerable overlap between a psychotic person's defective understanding or appreciation and his ability to control his behavior. Most psychotic persons who fail a volitional test for insanity will also fail a cognitive-type test when such a test is applied to their behavior, thus rendering the volitional test superfluous in judging them.

[THE BURDEN OF PROOF]

The case of John Hinckley brought renewed attention to who has the burden of proof in insanity cases. In the Hinckley case, the state had the burden to prove Mr. Hinckley's sanity beyond a reasonable doubt. This was a considerable burden for the state to overcome. Legal scholars believe that who bears the burden of proof in a legal case is a matter of considerable import. This is especially so when what is to be proven is inherently uncertain. And if anything can be agreed upon about criminal insanity, it is that insanity is a matter of some uncertainty.

At present about half of the states and all the Federal Courts require that once a defendant introduces into the proceeding any evidence of insanity, that state then bears the burden to prove the defendant was instead sane. An equal number of states and the District of Columbia, however, assign the burden of proof to the defendant who must then prove his insanity by "a preponderance of the evidence" or by an even higher standard of proof.

The American Psychiatric Association is exceedingly reluctant to take a position about assigning the burden of proof in insanity cases. This matter is clearly one for legislative judgment. For public policy, the issue is, in part, whether the rights of the individual or the rights of the state are to be given more or less weight in criminal insanity trials, or as is sometimes stated, which types of errors do we deem more or less tolerable in insanity trials. Given the inherent uncertainties involved in psychiatric testimony regarding the defense and the ever-present problems relating abstract legal principles to controversies of such emotion, who bears the burden of proof in insanity trials may be quite important. This is particularly so when what must be proved must also be proved "beyond a reasonable doubt." As suggested by the U.S. Supreme Court in the *Addington* case, usually psychiatric evidence is not sufficiently clear-cut to prove or disprove many legal facts "beyond a reasonable doubt."

It is commonly believed that the likely effect of assigning the burden of proof (burden of persuasion) to defendants rather than to the state in insanity trials will be to decrease the number of such successful defenses. This matter clearly requires further empirical study.

[PSYCHIATRIC TESTIMONY]

This area for potential reform of the insanity defense is one of the most controversial. Some proposals would limit psychiatric testimony in insanity defense trials to statements of mental condition, i.e., to statements of conventional psychiatric diagnoses, to provision of accounts of how and why the defendant acted as he did at the time of the commission of the act, to explanations in medical and psychological terms about how the act was affected or influenced by the person's mental illness. However, under this approach, psychiatrists would not be permitted to testify about so-called "ultimate issues" such as whether or not the defendant was, in their judgment, "sane" or "insane," "responsible" or not, etc. A further limitation upon psychiatric "ultimate issue" testimony would be to restrict the psychiatrist from testifying about whether a defendant did or did not meet the particular legal test for insanity at issue. Thus the law could prevent psychiatrists from testifying in a conclusory fashion whether the defendant "lacked substantial capacity to conform his behavior to the requirements of law," "lacked substantial capacity to appreciate the criminality of his act," was not able to distinguish "right from wrong" at the time of the act, and so forth.

The American Psychiatric Association is not opposed to legislatures restricting psychiatric testimony about the aforementioned ultimate legal issues concerning the insanity defense. We adopt this position because it is clear that psychiatrists are experts in medicine, not the law. As such, the psychiatrist's first obligation and expertise in the courtroom is to "do psychiatry," i.e., to present medical information and opinion about the defendant's mental state and motivation and to explain in detail the reason for his medical-psychiatric conclusions. When, however, "ultimate issue" questions are formulated by the law and put to the expert witness who must then say "yea" or "nay," then the expert witness is required to make a leap in logic. He no longer addresses himself to medical concepts but instead must infer or intuit what is in fact unspeakable, namely, the *probable relationship* between medical concepts and legal or moral constructs such as free will. These impermissible leaps in logic made by expert witnesses confuse the jury. Juries thus find themselves listening to conclusory and seemingly contradictory psychiatric testimony that defendants are either "sane" or "insane" or that they do or do not meet the relevant legal test for insanity. This state of affairs does considerable injustice to psychiatry and, we believe, possibly to criminal defendants. These psychiatric disagreements about technical, legal, and/or moral matters cause less than fully understanding juries or the public to conclude that psychiatrists cannot agree. In fact, in many criminal insanity trials both prosecution and defense psychiatrists do agree about the nature and even the extent of mental disorder exhibited by the defendant at the time of the act.

Psychiatrists, of course, must be permitted to testify fully about the defendant's psychiatric diagnosis, mental state and motivation (in clinical and commonsense terms) at the time of the alleged act so as to permit the jury or judge to reach the ultimate conclusion about which they, and only they, are expert. Determining whether a criminal defendant was legally insane is a matter for legal factfinders, not for experts.

[STATUS OF INSANITY ACQUITTEES]

This is the area for reform where the American Psychiatric Association believes that the most significant changes can and should be made in the present administration of the insanity defense. We believe that neither the law, the public, psychiatry, or the victims of violence have been well-served by the general approach and reform of the last ten years, which has obscured the quasi-criminal nature of the insanity defense and of the status of insanity acquittees.

The American Psychiatric Association is concerned particularly about insanity acquittals of persons charged with violent crime. In our view, it is a mistake to analogize such insanity acquittees as fully equivalent to civil committees who, when all has been said and done, have not usually already demonstrated their clear-cut potential for dangerous behavior because they have not yet committed a highly dangerous act. Because mental illness frequently affects the patient's ability to seek or accept treatment, we believe that civil commitment, as a system of detention and treatment, should be predicated on the severity of the patient's illness and/or in some instances on the metal patient's potential for perpetrating future violence against others. The usual civil committee has not, however, committed nor will he commit in the future a major crime. Most mentally ill persons are not violent. By contrast, the "dangerousness" of insanity acquittees who have perpetrated violence has already been demonstrated. Their future dangerousness need not be inferred; it may be assumed, at least for a reasonable period of time. The American Psychiatric Association is therefore quite skeptical about procedures now implemented in many states requiring periodic decisionmaking by mental health professionals (or by others) concerning a requirement that insanity acquittees who have committed previous violent offenses be repetitively adjudicated as "dangerous," thereupon provoking their release once future dangerousness cannot be clearly demonstrated in accord with the standard of proof required.

While there are no easy solutions to these problems, the following are some potential alternatives for the future.

First, the law should recognize that the nature of inhospital psychiatric intervention has changed over the last decade. Greater emphasis is now placed upon psychopharmacological management of the hospitalized person. Such treatment, while clearly helpful in reducing the overt signs and symptoms of mental illness, does not necessarily mean, however, that "cure" has been achieved — nor that a patient's "nondangerousness" is assured. Continuing, even compelled, psychiatric treatment is often required for this population once the patient is released from the hospital.

Although some insanity acquittees will recover in such facilities, there can be no public guarantee. Therefore, the presumption should be that after initial hospitalization a long period of conditional release with careful supervision and outpatient treatment will be necessary to protect the public and to complete the appropriate treatment programs. Unfortunately however, many jurisdictions have neither the trained personnel nor appropriate outpatient facilities and resources to provide for such close management of previously violent persons who are conditionally released. Where statutes provide for conditional release and judges allow it without these necessary resources, the public is subjected to great risk and the insanity acquittee is deprived of an opportunity for a necessary phase of treatment.

At any hearing that might order the conditional release of an insanity acquittee, the following questions must be answered affirmatively. Has a coherent and well structured plan of supervision, management, and treatment been put into place? Is this plan highly likely to guarantee public safety while maximizing the chances for rehabilitation of the insanity acquittee? Are the necessary staff and resources available to implement the plan? Is there in place a procedure to reconfine the insanity acquittee who fails to meet the expectations of the plan?

For some acquittees contingent release is not possible because of the risk to society, the lack of resources, or other relevant legal considerations. Yet because psychiatry has no more to offer the acquittee, continued confinement cannot be justified on therapeutic or psychiatric grounds. When there exists no realistic therapeutic justification for confinement, the psychiatric facility becomes a prison. The American Psychiatric Association believes this hypocrisy must be confronted and remedied. One appropriate alternative is to transfer the locus of responsibility and confinement for such acquittees to a nontreatment facility that can provide the necessary security.

The American Psychiatric Association believes that the decision to release an insanity acquittee should not be made *solely* by psychiatrists or *solely* on the basis of psychiatric testimony about the patient's mental condition or predictions of future dangerousness. While this may not be the only model, such decisions should be made instead by a group similar in composition to a parole board. In this respect, the American Psychiatric Association is impressed with a model program presently in operation in the State of Oregon under the aegis of a Psychiatric Security Review Board. In Oregon a multidisciplinary board is given jurisdiction over insanity acquittees. The board retains control of the insanity acquittee for a period of time as long as the criminal sentence that might have been awarded were the person to have been found guilty of the act. Confinement and release decisions for acquittees are made by an experienced body that is not naive about the nature of violent behavior committed by mental patients and that allows a quasi-criminal approach for managing such persons. Psychiatrists participate in the work of the Oregon board, but they do not have primary responsibility. The Association believes that this is as it should be since the decision to confine and release persons who have done violence to society involves more than psychiatric consider-ations. The interest of society, the interest of the criminal justice system, and the interest of those who have been or might be victimized by violence must also be addressed in confinement and release decisions.

In line with the above views, the American Psychiatric Association suggests the following guidelines for legislation dealing with the dispo-sition of violent insanity acquittees.

1. Special legislation should be designed for those persons charged with violent offenses who have been found "not guilty by reason of insanity."

2. Confinement and release decisions should be made by a board constituted to include psychiatrists and other professions representing the criminal justice system — akin to a parole board.

3. Release should be conditional upon having a treatment supervision plan in place with the necessary resources available to implement it.

4. The board having jurisdiction over released insanity acquittees should have clear authority to reconfine.

5. When psychiatric treatment within a hospital setting has obtained the maximal treatment benefit possible but the board believes that for other reasons confinement is still necessary, the insanity acquittee should be transferred to the most appropriate nonhospital facility.

In general, the American Psychiatric Association favors legislation to identify insanity acquittees who have committed violent acts as a special group of persons who, because of the important societal interests involved, should not be handled similarly to other civil committees.

Although efforts to treat mentally disordered offenders have met with limited success, we should also increase our commitment to developing and implementing new treatment approaches for those adjudicated insane.

There are practical as well as humanistic reasons for making this recommendation. A certain number of those who plead insanity will, whatever their disposition, eventually be released to society. To whatever extent their insanity is restored or their capacity to adhere to proper conduct is enhanced, the public will receive that much more protection from crime.

ABA RECOMMENDATIONS

The Standing Committee on Association Standards for Criminal Justice and the Commission on the Mentally Disabled recommend that the following policy positions be adopted:

Recommendation One

AND RESOLVED, That the American Bar Association approves the a defense of nonresponsibility for crime which focuses solely on whether the defendant, as a result of mental disease or defect, was unable to appreciate the wrongfulness of his or her conduct at the time of the offense charged;

Recommendation Two

AND RESOLVED, That the American Bar Association approves the following allocation of burden of proof in insanity defense cases: That in jurisdictions utilizing any test for insanity which focuses solely on whether the defendant, as a result of mental disease or defect, was unable to know, understand or appreciate the wrongfulness of his or her conduct at the time of the offense charged, the prosecution should have the burden of disproving the defendant's claim of insanity beyond a reasonable doubt; and, secondly, that in jurisdictions utilizing the ALI [American Law Institute] Model Penal Code test for insanity the defendant should have the burden of proving by a preponderance of the evidence his or her claim of insanity;

Recommendation Three

AND FURTHER RESOLVED, That the American Bar Association opposes the enactment of statutes which supplant or supplement the verdict of Not Guilty By Reason of Insanity with an alternative verdict of Guilty But Mentally Ill.

URBAN LEAGUE REPORT ON BLACK AMERICA

January 19, 1983

Black Americans, numbering approximately 26.5 million and about 12 percent of the population, ended 1982 "in worse shape than in 1981," reported the National Urban League in its eighth annual survey on the state of black America. "Two statistics are enough to tell the story," the report said. "Black unemployment was 15.5 percent at the end of 1981. Black unemployment was 20 percent at the end of 1982." The federal government's domestic spending cuts were largely responsible for the decline, the league stated.

Statistics from past years underscore blacks' declining economic status. From 1975 to the early 1980s unemployment rates for black adults had been twice the rate for white adults. In 1982 only 30 percent of black families, down from 32 percent in 1979, were in the middle class, compared with 56 percent of white families. (Report on employment, Historic Documents of 1982, p. 919)

To deal with long-term employment problems, the league recommended a public works/job training program. The recommendation called for a Universal Employment and Training System, a joint public/private effort, to rebuild the crumbling infrastructure of the nation: roads, bridges, railways and ports. The system would train the unskilled and unemployed and retrain displaced workers. The league also recommended a jobs creation program for the long-term unemployed. Congress, it said, should resist the Reagan administration's efforts to reduce funding for social service programs, such as food stamps and school lunches, that serve the poor and disadvantaged. The league also wanted the administration to restore funds cut from federal civil rights enforcement agencies.

Economic Problems

John E. Jacob, president of the Urban League, attributed the status of blacks to the 1980-83 recession and federal cutbacks in social services. In his introduction to the report, Jacob wrote, "The [Reagan government's] promised 'safety net' proved to be full of holes as the federal government continued the process of abandoning people-saving programs. The programs that were singled out for the deepest budget cuts by the Administration and a compliant Congress ... were those that most directly affected the poor."

The league reported that there were cuts in federal programs for the poor that amounted to $10 billion in 1982. They included the elimination of one million people from the welfare rolls, one million children from the federal school lunch program, one million fewer people on the food-stamp rolls, 600,000 children who lost Medicaid coverage and 900 school districts that were forced to cut back special education programs. These cuts resulted in one in three blacks living in poverty, compared with one in 10 whites.

"Sadly, the programs singled out for the most severe cuts were those programs that had proved to be most effective ... 1982 was not a good year — and of course no year is — to be black and to be poor in America," Jacob wrote. Hit hard by the federal budget cuts, blacks fared little better on the job. The median income earned by black families was only 56 percent of white families' income. (Congressional Budget Office report, p. 765)

James D. McGhee, the League's research director and one of the report's eight contributing authors, said black families always suffer most from recessions. He added that they may never recover from the recession of the early 1980s that was brought about, in part, by structural changes in American industry. Many of the blacks who were laid off from the auto manufacturing and steel-making industries, for example, would never return to their old jobs.

McGhee noted signs of major problems in the future for American cities. While poor blacks were moving into central cities, affluent whites were moving out. The impact of this trend blunted the political control blacks were assuming in many cities because the necessary financial resources were leaving with the more affluent citizens.

Social Problems

Writing on the mental health status of blacks, Harvard University professor of psychiatry Alvin F. Poussaint said that with unemployment rates of 20.2 percent for blacks and over 45 percent for black youth, the potential outcome for blacks was "ominous." He said institutional racism guaranteed high rates of unemployment and poverty for blacks. The record-breaking unemployment rates of 1982 indicated a surge in overall poverty levels, especially among blacks. A black child faced overwhelming odds of living in a poor household, Poussaint said. Because of the high divorce rate among black American couples, there was a high number of black households headed by women, he noted.

Approximately 84.9 percent of white children lived with both their parents, as opposed to only 42.6 percent of black children, increasing the odds of growing up in poverty. As a result of single-parenting, blacks were overrepresented among Aid to Families with Dependent Children (AFDC) recipients. They were overrepresented, too, in prisons. A black adolescent was seven times as likely to be involved in violent crimes as his white peers. While 51 percent, a bare majority, of prison inmates were white, 46 percent were black. This was nearly four times their proportion in the population of the United States.

Alcoholism and drug abuse, Poussaint said, were among the most serious mental health issues facing the black community. The mortality rate among blacks due to alcoholism was three times the rate of whites. The use of drugs among black youth, common even at the elementary school level, was cited as a contributing factor to underachievement at the secondary school and college levels.

Military Service and Higher Education

A weak economy generally encourages military enlistments and 1982 was no exception, Alvin J. Schexnider of Virginia Commonwealth University pointed out in his contributing paper. While constituting only 12 percent of the overall population, blacks made up 33 percent of the Army and 20 percent among all the armed services in 1982. The disproportionate percentage of blacks in the enlisted ranks did not transfer over to positions of authority: only 5.6 of all military officers were black. Military service could even hurt black men's chances for civilian employment, Schexnider said. Blacks were assigned in relatively higher proportions to combat specialities, precluding them from acquiring marketable skills.

In the area of higher education black undergraduate college enrollment had grown from 45,000 in 1940 to 926,700 in 1982, with 70 percent attending non-black colleges in 1982, up from 10 percent in 1940, reported Mary Frances Berry, history and law professor at Howard University. Recent cuts in education aid could make further growth difficult, especially in private colleges, she cautioned.

The National Urban League said in conclusion, "We aren't recommending a 'welfare state,' but certainly some better way has to be found to take care of our people than we presently practice. This is the challenge that the American people and their leaders face in 1983."

Following are excerpts from the introduction and conclusion of the National Urban League's annual report, dated January 19, 1983. (Boldface headings in brackets have been added by Congressional Quarterly to highlight the organization of the text.):

Introduction

Among the most heart wrenching commentaries on the nature of the past year were the reports from a number of department store Santa Clauses that during the holiday season many children were not asking for toys for themselves, but for jobs for their daddies. When the young are this aware of economic realities, we begin to understand that unemployment is more than a set of figures, it is the very human tragedy of people being unable to provide for themselves and their families.

And this was not the only sign of troubled times that we saw in 1982. People standing in line for hours to be handed a five pound block of cheese, just as people once stood in line to be handed a bowl of soup. We also saw something else that America has not seen since the 1930s — traveling bands of nomads in search of work. They packed what they could in their car, loaded up the family, and set out to find the job they could not find in their own hometowns.

They headed for where they believed opportunity still flourished, but many of them discovered they were chasing an illusion and at the end of the rainbow was a pot of nothing. Texas told them not to come and Alaska paid for an advertising campaign to deliver the same message. Other places did it in other ways, but the meaning was the same — there are no jobs. If the calendar did not say differently, these latter day nomads could have been the Joads of "The Grapes of Wrath" at the height of the Great Depression, except that they were not farmers fleeing from land laid barren by the forces of nature, but urban workers dispossessed by economic forces.

These are indeed troubled times, and trouble is magnified within Black America, just as it has always been. White America catches a cold. Black America develops pneumonia. As bad as things were for White America in 1982, they were worse for Black America. White America was stunned by an unemployment rate of 9.3%. Black America staggered under a 20.2% jobless figure. Median income of black families slipped to 56% that of white families. Among the last to be hired, blacks were among the first to be let go when the recession began to pinch.

The promised "safety net" proved to be full of holes as the federal government continued the process of abandoning people-serving programs.

The programs that were singled out for the deepest budget cuts by the

Administration and a compliant Congress — at least compliant until November 2, 1982 when the voice of the voter was heard — were those that most directly affected the poor. Those cuts went far beyond simple fat-trimming but slashed deep into the muscle. They seriously diminished our society's obligation to provide sustenance to the poor. . . .

Sadly, the programs singled out for the most severe cuts were those programs that had proven to be most effective. Medicaid made a real difference in the health of the poor. Aid to education improved basic skills achievement by poor children. Food stamps virtually ended the scandal of hunger in America. Job programs put the jobless to work. 1982 was not a good year — and of course no year is — to be black and to be poor in America.

[BLACK MIDDLE CLASS]

Most disturbing is what has happened to the black middle-class which is — as it is in all societies — a bastion of strength and a source of motivation within Black America. As the report, "A Dream Denied: the Black Family in the Eighties," issued by the National Urban League in 1982 disclosed, black middle-class families constitute only 30% of all black families as compared to 56% of white families and the position of many of these families is precarious. The report explained:

"The serious dilemma that many black families face is that many of them have not had enough good years to build a cushion against the bad years that are now upon them. In many cases, even a short interruption of family income due to lay-offs, furloughs or even the loss of a job can result in disaster for a family already living close to the edge."

After a long struggle to get a relatively modest number of black families into middle-class status (70% still exist on low incomes), it is tragic to contemplate the negative effects that a diminution in their ranks will have on Black America, in terms of sending a message to the poor, and especially the working poor, that being black and middle-class is now a virtually hopeless dream. The movement of blacks into the middle-class in any appreciable number should be understood as a fairly recent development. These families increased over the last two decades by some 18 percentage points, with 15 of these coming during the 1960s, and only three during the decade of the 70s.

Much of the growth was due in large measure to the Civil Rights Movement which stirred the conscience of the nation, and to the government's commitment to equal opportunity reflected most vividly in the programs of "The Great Society" that virtually created much of today's black middle-class by providing opportunities for education and employment that had not existed before.

Now these programs are under attack as being failures and they are being eliminated one after another for seemingly ideological rather than budgetary reasons, sending a clear signal that the nation is defaulting on its commitment to assure equal opportunity for all its citizens.

[REAGAN ADMINISTRATION]

If there is any doubt that this commitment is being rescinded, one only has to look at the actions of the U.S. Department of Justice over the past year, and specifically at those of its Civil Rights Division which has long been the centerpiece of federal civil rights commitment. Officially charged with coordinating and reviewing all civil rights policies and regulations of most federal departments, the Civil Rights Division has been accurately described as the barometer by which all federal agencies' efforts in this arena can be measured.

Over the past 20 years, through Democratic and Republican Administrations alike, the Division has been looked upon as being supportive of efforts to assure equality of opportunity under the law. This is no longer so.

What emerges from an objective examination of the division's record is a distinct pattern of the weakening of the government's civil rights mechanism and a studied effort to turn back the clock. Among others reaching this conclusion in 1982 was the Civil Rights Task Force of the Washington Council of Lawyers. In its report, "Reagan Civil Rights: The First 20 Months," the Council stated:

"The Administration has retreated from well established, bipartisan civil rights policies that were developed during both Democratic and Republican Administrations. At the same time, the Reagan Administration has failed to develop — and implement — cohesive and consistent civil rights policies, despite its promise to devise creative and innovative solutions to age old problems."

Black America is far from being monolithic, but there is a wide-spread and deeply rooted conviction that the Council's assessment of the Administration's approach to civil rights is correct, despite the President's assertion, made in a radio interview on December 19, 1982 that his Administration has the best record of all Presidential Administrations in actively pursuing violations against minorities.

There is also the strongly held conviction within Black America that the Administration is insensitive to the other problems of minorities and the poor. Taken together, these convictions have created a strong sense of alienation within Black America from the Administration, the like of which has not been seen in more than four decades.

One only has to talk to any of the people in any of the black communities in any city in the nation to discover this. The feeling ranges across all social and economic classes and should be of concern to the Administration, which so far has treated the matter as one involving public relations (i.e. the inability to get its message across to Black America), rather than as one of substance (i.e. Black America understands the message and is deeply disturbed).

We recall that in last year's "State of Black America" report we said:

"At no point in recent memory had the distance between the national government and Black America been greater than it was in 1981, nor had the relationship between the two been more strained." We erred only in that the gap apparently widened in 1982. We hold to our original contention made in 1981 that this alienation is not in the best interest of the American people and the Administration has to do more to bridge the gap, not with rhetoric but with its actions.

SOME POSITIVE DEVELOPMENTS

Despite the bleak economic situation, the cutbacks in funding for programs that served the poor, the general public coolness to programs and policies that would increase opportunities for minority groups, there were some developments in 1982 that impacted positively on Black America.

Of particular importance was the coalition that came together under the aegis of the Leadership Conference on Civil Rights to push for an extension of the Voting Rights Act as well as a strengthening of the measure. Composed of representatives from 160 major national organizations representing blacks, Hispanics, Asian Americans, labor, the major religious groups, women, the handicapped, the aged, minority businesses and professions, the Leadership Conference played a compelling role in the Voting Rights fight. It had been several years since such an effort had been mounted on behalf of any legislation, and the fact that it was successful indicated that under the right circumstances, the coalitions that were so effective in the past in advancing the causes of blacks, other minorities and the poor, can be mobilized again.

It is also important that even though the Administration dragged its feet on supporting the Voting Rights Act until the 11th hour, a bipartisan group of legislators in both Houses of Congress supported the measure and produced a strengthened piece of legislation.

Admittedly, Black America's victories were few in 1982, but among . . . [those that] should be counted are what we at the National Urban League view as reinvigoration of community concern at the grassroots level. Whether the forces of adversity have driven people closer together, or whether this concern has grown like Topsy — pretty much on its own — is relatively unimportant. What is important is that during the past year we found in city after city across the country, that the black community was looking more and more to itself to do those things that only it can do for itself.

Our discovery came about when we announced our Youth and Community Initiative program, identifying our young people, ages 11 to 25, as those individuals within the black community at greatest risk. While they are the future of Black America, they are being buffeted by a series of forces that if allowed to go unchecked can turn them into a lost generation.

Four areas were identified as being of primary concern. The first two — teenage pregnancy and female headed households — were chosen because every single analysis finds these two factors increase vulnerability to poverty. In addition, they are central to health, education and job problems afflicting the black community.

The second two — crime and voter education — were chosen because they deal with the alienation and community disintegration that must be reversed if black youth are to take their rightful places in society.

All four of these issues impact most heavily on youth. It is our young people who are most vulnerable to the pressures of poverty, who are disproportionately the victims as well as the perpetrators of crime, whose alienation from society keeps them out of the voting booth.

We operate under no delusions. We know that the basic problem of young people today is lack of jobs. Teenage unemployment rates of 50% and 60% do not exist just because of adolescent pregnancy, or low voter turnouts. Our society denies jobs to minority youngsters and young adults. It denies adequate eduational and skills training. It still discriminates against the black poor.

At the same time, we recognize that the black community can best address the four concerns raised above, thus providing a supportive system to our young people that will better prepare them for adult roles. We turned to other institutions within the black community for assistance — our churches, our press, our social and fraternal organizations and our many local citizen groups valiantly fighting to keep our communities whole and healthy. We found among them an extraordinary willingness to help build a stronger Black America. . . .

Conclusion and Recommendations

In this section of last year's "State of Black America," the National Urban League concluded:

"1981 was a difficult year inside Black America and 1982 threatens to be even more difficult particularly if the recession continues for any extended period of time, if further slashes are made in domestic programs, and if the millions of new jobs that the Administration's economic recovery program promised that the private sector would produce do not begin to develop fairly soon."

There is no satisfaction in reporting that the forecast proved to be all too accurate. The recession continued, the cutbacks in domestic programs proceeded apace, and the promised jobs never materialized. Black America ended 1982 in worse shape than in 1981. Two statistics are enough to tell the story. Black unemployment was 15.5% at the end of 1981. Black unemployment was 20% at the end of 1982.

We find it disturbing that in view of the overwhelming evidence that the economic recovery plan has not worked, and shows no likelihood that it will ever work, the Administration asks the American people to "stay the course." Consistency is to be admired, but there comes a time when prudence and objective reasoning demands [sic] that when Plan A is not successful, then directions have to be changed and new approaches formulated.

. . . [A] clear case has been made that a disproportionate share of the hardships now being experienced by this nation's people falls on the shoulders of black Americans and the poor. What is inescapable is the very real danger that those now being most adversely affected may never be able to recover what they are now losing.

In the past year, the programs that serve poor people have been cut by $10 billion. Those cuts have not lowered the national deficit but they have manifestly lowered the quality of life of the very poor. Nearly one million people have been cut from the federal welfare program. Over 600,000 children have lost medicaid coverage. Almost a million children no longer receive free or low-cost school lunches and about 150,000 poor working families have lost subsidized day care. A million people have been dropped from the food stamp program and some 200,000 pregnant women and infants have lost federal nutrition aid. Some 900 school districts have been forced to cut back special education programs. . . .

We are not recommending a "welfare state," but certainly some better way has to be found to take care of our people than we presently practice. This is the challenge that the American people and their leaders face in 1983.

We believe that the appropriate way to meet this challenge is to begin by halting the assault on the poor. They have been penalized much too much, and to inflict further hardship on them is unthinkable and indefensible.

Further, we most seriously recommend the establishment of a Universal Employment and Training System that would guarantee productive work to all of the jobless and training to the unskilled. As John E. Jacob, President of the National Urban League has said:

"This would not be a make-work, token program to lower social tensions or to counter dips in the business cycle. Nor would it be just a government hiring program.

"Instead, a Universal Employment and Training System would be a joint public-private effort that rebuilds our decaying infrastructure, meets the manpower needs of the nation, and draws into the mainstream the millions who have been relegated to the margins of our society. . . .

"The training component of the system would begin in the schools and extend to public support of private training for real jobs that would answer the nation's manpower needs for jobs that are now going unfilled such as computer technician, craftsmen and a host of other occupations. Our changing economy demands such a system if we are not to lose out to foreigners in the high tech fields of the future."

The pressing need for such a program is especially critical among the young. . . . [A]n observation made by the noted psychiatrist Dr. Alvin F. Poussaint in his paper, "The Mental Health Status of Blacks — 1983," is germane.

"The social costs of unemployment, inflation and poverty become apparent in a dramatic increase in the levels of physical and mental instability and crime in a given community. . . . With unemployment rates at 20.2% for blacks and over 45% for black youth, the potential outcome for blacks, particularly black males, is ominous."

Dr. Poussaint's concern about the human cost extracted by unemployment is rightfully placed. And to that should be added the economic cost. For every percentage point of unemployment above four percent the nation loses about $30 billion in lost taxes and higher social expenditures.

The examination of Black America contained in these pages has shown the dimensions of its problems. But it has also shown that some advances in securing parity have been made — albeit not enough — and there are road markers to indicate the distance that has been traveled.

Dr. Alvin J. Schexnider in the paper, "Blacks in the Military," points out that a large number of black men and women are fashioning successful careers in a truly integrated military, and that while there is still disparity in the ranks of officers, some 5% of the Army's generals are black. There are many graying veterans of World War Two and even Korea who can recall when segregation was a way of life in the military and black officers, of any rank, were rare indeed.

Dr. Mary F. Berry writing on "Blacks in Predominantly White Institutions of Higher Learning," describes and analyzes the difficulties that black students and faculty members face on the campuses of such institutions. This is a matter of major concern. But it is also important to note, as Dr. Berry does, that black college enrollment has grown tremendously over the past few years and the numbers of black professors and instructors have increased.

The paper authored by Dr. Lenneal J. Henderson, "Black Business Development and Public Policy," deals in detail with the difficulties black business people are facing in their efforts to survive in an ailing economy. At the same time, he reports that there are institutions within the black community that are devoting their considerable energies and talents to the building of a stronger black business community.

The fact is that many blacks are continuing to succeed against the odds. But all too many are not. To continue to exclude them from the mainstream robs America of human resources that could make it even stronger, even more secure.

Dr. Charles V. Hamilton expressed the hope of a large number of black Americans when, at the conclusion of his paper "On Politics and Voting: Messages and Meanings," he said: "Perhaps the felt experiences of whites will eventually lead them to perceive the stark reality so overwhelmingly experienced by blacks. And perhaps many white Americans will come to understand *their* interests as economically and politically compatible with those of many black Americans.". . .

Recommendations

EMPLOYMENT AND THE ECONOMY

1. A Universal Employment and Training System should be established that would guarantee the unemployed productive work and the skills training to get and hold a job. Such a system should be a joint public-private effort. It would include rebuilding the decaying infrastructure of

the nation such as its roads, bridges, rail systems and ports, as well as improving public services. The system would train the unskilled and the unemployed and retrain displaced workers for jobs in growth industries.

2. Congress should immediately implement a jobs creation program(s) whereby employment opportunities are made available to the long-term unemployed, especially in areas of the highest unemployment.

3. Congress should resist any further efforts of the Administration to reduce funding for those social service programs such as food stamps, school lunches, etc. that serve the poor and the disadvantaged.

4. The Department of Labor regulations implementing the Job Training Partnership act, which replaces CETA and gives the private sector a substantial role in local program development, should include a mandatory role for experienced and proven community based organizations at all stages and levels of the new system.

5. Defense spending must assume its share of the belt-tightening to which every other area of the budget has been subjected.

6. The private sector should be encouraged to develop creative approaches and programs for training and hiring the unemployed.

CIVIL RIGHTS

7. The budgets of the various civil rights enforcement agencies and offices within the executive branch of government should be restored to levels that will allow effective and adequate enforcement.

8. The Legal Services Corporation should be maintained and only those who demonstrate a firm commitment to administering legal services to the poor should be confirmed by Congress as board members.

9. "Court-stripping" legislation which attempts to restrict the authority of federal courts, should be rejected.

10. Private groups should continue to closely monitor the actions of the Civil Rights Division of the Justice Department and where those actions are not in the best interests of minorities, take appropriate action to oppose them.

AFFIRMATIVE ACTION

11. The principles of affirmative action should continue to be applied at both the state and federal levels, and there should be no retrenchment on the enforcement of these principles. This means that qualified minority applicants should be actively sought for job openings in every sector of the economy.

12. The Administration should reaffirm its commitment to those principles embodied in Executive Order 11246. In particular, the Office of Federal Contract Appliance Programs, its mandate, and its procedures must not be weakened. Requirements for the employer's compliance with the law must remain strong.

13. In order to uphold the principles of equal employment opportuni-

ties, Congressional attempts to weaken affirmative action laws should be opposed.

HOUSING AND COMMUNITY DEVELOPMENT

14. Housing assistance for low-income families must continue to be provided, in the form of subsidies, construction, and rehabilitation. Further, public housing operating subsidies must be continued at an adequate level.

15. The housing counseling program, a critical component of this nation's commitment to the shelter needs of the poor, must continue to be funded at an adequate level.

16. Housing and community development activities, particularly the Community Development Block Grant (CDBG) program, should be targeted to the low and moderate income community for whom they were intended. The federal government has a statutory responsibility to ensure this, and it must continue to exercise this authority.

EDUCATION

17. The President should make public the findings and recommendations of his Commission on Excellence in Education. Particular emphasis should be given to the commission's findings and background papers in determining a more equitable and effective approach to strengthening instruction in public schools.

18. In the wake of the report on the Armed Services Vocational Aptitude Test released by the Department of Defense — a moratorium should be placed on all assessment studies which do not equitably delineate and evaluate the roles, responsibilities and the performances of administrators and teachers as well as students.

19. A long term and consistent program of federal support for historically black colleges should be developed and be implemented through each and every department and bureau of the federal government.

20. Black students and black institutions of higher education have been particularly damaged by the impact of federal cut backs and the depressed economy. The President should re-constitute the National Advisory Committee for black colleges and universities and blacks in higher education. The committee which was dissolved this year has a proud record of documenting the status of blacks and historically black institutions. Continued documentation and oversight at the federal level continues to be needed.

21. Congress should give its approval to a major new investment in math and science education in order to respond to the needs of a high technology society. Such legislation should take into account the special needs of low-income and minority students.

22. Congress should give its approval to a bill that would re-establish the Emergency School Act, which has long been a vital component of this

nation's desegregation efforts. When the program was block granted in 1981, funding levels were seriously reduced, and the federal preclearance procedures which assured effective targeting were eliminated.

23. Legislation to grant tuition tax credits to parents who send their children to private schools should be opposed, regardless of antidiscrimination provisions, because they (tuition tax credits) will lead to further abandonment and underfinancing of the public schools.

SOCIAL SERVICES

24. There should be no effort on the part of the Administration to reduce Social Security benefits as a method of financing our Social Security System. Reduced payments will only cause more recipients to seek other forms of federally assisted programs that will impact the federal budget.

25. Consideration should be given to taxing half of the social security benefits of retired people whose incomes are above the median. The system should also be expanded by bringing in all workers including government employees and others currently excluded.

26. The Administration should refrain from block-granting any additional programs in the social services areas until such time that all the block grant programs have been thoroughly researched, studied and analyzed.

27. Congress should at a minimum reinstate Medicaid benefits to those who have lost them because of termination from the AFDC program.

HEALTH

28. The medicaid program should be federalized with the Federal Government assuming full cost. Ceilings on spending which have the effect of rationing care, i.e., limiting enrollment for eligible individuals and families, should be avoided.

29. Adequate resources should be made available to community-based organizations for the design and implementation of local programs in community health education, physical fitness and disease prevention.

30. The relationship between poverty and early teenage parenting is becoming increasing clear. Increased federal funding to support a variety of prevention, vocational and health related initiatives is needed. Special funds targeted to minority youth, so disproportionately represented among the unwed teen parent population, is a major need.

GOVERNMENT

31. The New Federalism proposals, which would shift various federal programs to the states, must be halted. The federal government cannot abdicate its responsibility for national needs, and the states' historical response to the plight of the disadvantaged has been uneven at best. This

record is insufficient to justify the states' assumption of these programs.

32. The Congress, the appropriate federal agencies, and the U.S. General Accounting Office should monitor the implementation of the block grants enacted in 1981, regularly and objectively. This is essential in order to guard against the possibility of misuse and abuse of federally appropriated funds, and to assure that the civil rights of blacks and other minorities are protected.

33. Efforts to streamline the regulatory process are commendable, but must be undertaken in a thoughtful manner . . . extensive citizen participation should be guaranteed, and rulemaking must not become so cumbersome as to thwart efforts to improve programmatic implementation and changes.

34. Universal on-site registration for federal elections should be instituted, to allow individuals with the proper identification to vote on election day. This system would bring into the electoral process many individuals now excluded because of cumbersome registration procedures.

35. Election day registration should also be encouraged for state and local elections.

SMALL BUSINESS

36. It is imperative that the federal minority business programs be perceived as economic programs and not as social welfare. To this end the following recommendations are made:

- The federal government must improve its delivery of services to the minority business community. Both technical and financial assistance must be provided to ensure its survival.
- The 8(a) program should continue to provide minority enterprises the opportunity to participate in government procurement activities, without the constraints of an unreasonable time limit on eligibility.
- Majority owned and operated enterprises should be encouraged to assist and use the services of minority businesses.

ENTERPRISE ZONES

37. Enterprise zones, a concept whereby certain inner-city areas are relieved of compliance with various regulations and provided tax incentives to lure businesses into a revitalization partnership, should be considered as a potentially important component of a comprehensive urban policy. Among the requirements needed to assure the success of this initiative are the following:

- The provision of job training for zone residents is essential to prepare them for employment with the entering businesses.
- Residents of the zones must not be displaced as businesses begin to enter the area.
- Local input and guaranteed citizen participation are essential to the

successful implementation of zone activities.
- Strong monitoring and accountability mechanism must be built into the legislation.

LAW ENFORCEMENT AND CRIMINAL JUSTICE

38. The federal government should adopt a national policy banning the importation, manufacture, sale and possession of handguns, except for legitimate and authorized purposes such as for use by law enforcement officials, the armed forces, authorized guards and firearm clubs that have been licensed and their guns appropriately registered.

39. The appointment of qualified blacks and women to the federal judicial system should be given high priority. Vigorous employment efforts should also be pursued by criminal justice policymakers and practitioners to assure the fair representation of both groups at all levels of the criminal justice system.

SOCIAL SECURITY REPORT
January 20, 1983

Rescuing the nation's massive, nearly bankrupt Social Security system had long been a pressing item on the legislative agenda, but it was not until a blue-ribbon National Commission on Social Security Reform issued its report January 20 that Congress enacted major changes in the 38-year-old retirement system.

The Social Security bill that finally cleared Congress March 25 and was signed into law (PL 98-21) by President Ronald Reagan on April 21 was in most respects close to the recommendations made by the commission. Like the commission plan, the new law involved an eclectic mix of tax increases, other revenue raisers, benefit cuts and adjustments and new accounting techniques.

The problems facing the Social Security system — a program that directly affected more than 60 percent of the U.S. population — were almost as immense as the program itself. But the statutory changes enacted in 1983 reaffirmed its role as the key source of income for the vast majority of U.S. retirees, regardless of their economic status.

Despite serious funding shortfalls in the 1970s and projections of more intractable problems in the next century, Congress and the joint executive-congressional National Commission on Social Security Reform endorsed the fundamental concept of Social Security. One of the commission's major premises was that "Congress ... should not alter the fundamental structure of the Social Security program or undermine its fundamental principles."

A Beleaguered System

Confidence in the Social Security concept was buttressed by the program's spectacular record in improving the economic status of America's elderly. By 1983 the system encompassed more than 90 percent of the retired population and had reduced the proportion of this group living in poverty by 50 percent over the preceding two decades.

In the mid-1970s, however, Social Security had become a victim of its own success and of uncontrollable economic factors. Over the years the system had built a large constituency of retirees who came to expect more and more in benefits. At the same time, Social Security was buffeted by economic developments that reduced the program's funds while increasing the cost of delivering benefits.

Social Security's severe financial position was hampered further by political obstacles that plagued efforts to forge a consensus on solutions or even to reach an agreement between Congress and the executive branch on the extent of the system's troubles.

In 1981 the Reagan administration made dire predictions about the system's future and called for cutbacks in benefits. Democrats said the administration was overstating the problem and charged that the president was trying to balance the budget at the expense of the elderly. A legislative standoff ensued, and the president in December established the National Commission on Social Security Reform to assemble a bipartisan package of changes to the system.

Social Security and the Economy

Public loss of confidence in the system was reflected in a January 1983 CBS/New York Times poll that found 63 percent of the population doubted they would ever receive Social Security benefits. The public's reaction reflected the extent to which millions of Americans had come to rely upon it at retirement. Any fundamental changes in the system would affect 36 million beneficiaries — one-seventh of the population — by 1983. Social Security paid out $206 billion in benefits and administrative costs in fiscal 1982. This amount constituted more than 25 percent of the federal budget for that fiscal year, equal to about 7 percent of the gross national product, as compared with 6 percent in the early years of the system. During the same period, about half the population — 116 million — contributed $183 billion to the system's trust funds through payroll taxes and health premiums. A large proportion of taxpayers — particularly those with low incomes — were paying more in Social Security taxes than in income taxes. Wage earners in 1982 paid an average of $971 in Social Security taxes; the maximum tax was $2,170.

The health of the system also had consequences for the national

*economy and the federal deficit. The Congressional Budget Office pro-
jected that Social Security would comprise more than 30 percent of the
federal budget by 1985.*

Previous Congressional Action

*Each time a Social Security crisis had arisen over the past few years,
Congress responded with a "Band-Aid" solution, juggling funds from one
trust fund to another. The system has three such funds:*

● *Old-Age and Survivors Insurance (OASI), which pays benefits to
retirees, their dependents and survivors.*

● *Hospital Insurance (HI), which pays Medicare benefits for the
elderly and the long-term disabled.*

● *Disability Insurance (DI), providing benefits for disabled workers.*

*Faced with a combination of recession and inflation, Congress in 1977
approved tax increases totaling $227 billion over the ensuing decade.
When the new taxes failed to solve the problem, Congress in 1980
temporarily reallocated taxes from the healthy disability trust fund to
OASI to avert a funding shortfall. In 1981, unable to reach agreement on
a more comprehensive package, Congress agreed to allow OASI to borrow
from the DI and HI trust funds until the end of the year.* (Carter plan,
Historic Documents of 1977, p. 377)

*But most Social Security experts agreed that time was running out on
such stopgap solutions. The huge pension system needed a quick infusion
of funds, and there was little surplus left in the other two trust funds to
bail it out again.*

National Commission Recommendations

*Unlike Social Security study commissions before it, the membership of
the National Commission included most of the key characters in the
debate, from seven members of Congress to powerful interest group and
business leaders. Chaired by Alan Greenspan, chairman of the president's Council of Economic Advisers from 1970 to 1974, members of the
panel included Lane Kirkland, AFL-CIO president; Alexander B. Trowbridge, president of the National Association of Manufacturers; and
Robert M. Ball, Social Security commissioner from 1962 to 1973.*

*By the end of November 1982, members of the commission agreed on
the scope of the problem: The shortfall through the 1980s could reach
$200 billion and the long-term deficit could be as high as 1.8 percent of
payroll tax. The panel decided not to recommend major structural
changes in the system, but instead called for some adjustments in
financing and benefit increases. The commission finally reached a
delicate compromise, endorsed by President Reagan and House Speaker
Thomas P. O'Neill Jr., D-Mass. As a comprehensive solution to Social*

Security's woes, the commission's recommendations could be challenged only piecemeal; no other group had been able to assemble a comparable package.

The commission's compromise agreement was termed an "extraordinary event" by Chairman Greenspan. After nearly a year of study and days of difficult last-minute negotiating between the White House and key members of the panel, the commission report had won bipartisan support from politically diverse members of the panel.

The compromise was intended to raise $168 billion for calendar years 1983-89 by a variety of controversial and innovative mechanisms, including a six-month delay in cost-of-living adjustments (COLAs, benefit supplements based on increases in the Consumer Price Index), a new, higher payroll tax schedule, the inclusion under the system of new federal civilian employees and all workers in non-profit organizations; and the unprecedented taxation of certain benefits for high-income retirees.

The balance between benefit cuts and tax hikes was the main issue among the 15 commission members, and the final plan called for both. About $40 billion was to come from the one-time delay in the COLA, but the greater part of the revenue would come from various tax hikes and the inclusion of new federal employees under the system. An increase in the basic payroll tax would yield $40 billion by 1990. The rate would be raised an extra .3 of a percentage point in 1984 to 7 percent and another .36 of a point in 1988 to 7.51 percent.

1983 Legislation

Public sentiment and the system's immediate financial crisis largely predetermined the direction Congress would take. It was tantamount to political suicide for members of Congress to propose benefit cuts for those already on the rolls. And with the high federal budget deficits projected for the rest of the decade, there was not much likelihood of siphoning off general revenues to help bail out the Social Security system.

Before Congress passed the new Social Security law late in March 1983, however, a number of adjustments and additions were made to the commission's recommendations. Most important among these was a provision raising the retirement age at which benefits could be received. To reduce the system's costs, Republican members of the commission unofficially had recommended that the retirement age be increased; Democrats called instead for an increase in payroll tax to increase revenues. The final bill gradually increased the retirement age from 65 to 67 by the year 2027.

The National Commission's recommendations — many of which ultimately were enacted into law — were acceptable to just over half the public, according to a poll made by Newsweek *in the spring of 1983. The 1983 legislation, while preserving the essentials of the system, signaled a period of retrenchment relative to the beneficence of preceding decades.*

While the 1983 changes would mean some hardship for many Social Security participants, some observers considered the funding crisis of the 1970s and 1980s a fortuitous exercise in preparing for more serious challenges to the system expected in the next century.

Following are excerpts from Chapter 2 of the report of the National Commission on Social Security Reform presented to President Ronald Reagan January 20, 1983. (Boldface headings in brackets have been added by Congressional Quarterly to highlight the organization of the text.):

Findings and Recommendations

The National Commission was assigned the critical job of assessing whether the OASDI [Old-Age, Survivors, and Disability Insurance] program has financing problems in the short run and over the long-range future (as represented by the 75-year valuation period) and, if so, recommending how such problems could be resolved.

The National Commission has agreed that there is a financing problem for the OASDI program for both the short run, 1983-89 (as measured using pessimistic economic assumptions) and the long range, 1983-2056 (as measured by an intermediate cost estimate) and that action should be taken to strengthen the financial status of the program. The National Commission recognized that, under the intermediate cost estimate, the financial status of the OASDI program in the 1990s and early 2000s will be favorable (i.e., income will significantly exceed outgo). The National Commission also recognized that, under the intermediate cost estimate, the financial status of the HI [Hospital Insurance] program becomes increasingly unfavorable from 1990 until the end of the period for which the estimates are made.

The National Commission makes the following recommendations unanimously:

(1) The members of the National Commission believe that the Congress, in its deliberations on financing proposals, should not alter the fundamental structure of the Social Security program or undermine its fundamental principles. The National Commission considered, but rejected, proposals to make the Social Security program a voluntary one, or to transform it into a program under which benefits are a product exclusively of the contributions paid, or to convert it into a fully-funded program, or to change it to a program under which benefits are conditioned on the showing of financial need.

(2) The National Commission recommends that, for purposes of considering the short-range financial status of the OASDI Trust Funds, $150-200 billion in either additional income or in decreased outgo (or a combination of both) should be provided for the OASDI Trust Funds in calendar years 1983-89.

(3) The National Commission finds that, for purposes of considering the long-range financial status of the OASDI Trust Funds, its actuarial imbalance for the 75-year valuation period is an average of 1.80% of taxable payroll.

The National Commission was able to reach a consensus for meeting the short-range and long-range financial requirements, by a vote of 12 to 3. The 12 members voting in favor of the "consensus" package were Commissioners [Robert M.] Ball, [Robert A.] Beck, [Barber] Conable, [Robert] Dole, [Mary Falvey] Fuller, [Alan] Greenspan, [John] Heinz, [Martha E.] Keys, [Lane] Kirkland, [Daniel Patrick] Moynihan, [Claude D.] Pepper, and [Alexander B.] Trowbridge; the 3 members voting against the "consensus" package were Commissioners [William] Archer, [William] Armstrong, and [Joe D.] Waggonner [Jr.].

The 12 members of the National Commission voting in favor of the "consensus" package agreed to a single set of proposals to meet the short-range deficit (with Commissioner Kirkland dissenting on the proposals to cover newly hired Federal employees). They further agreed that the long-range deficit should be reduced to approximately zero. The single set of recommendations would meet about two-thirds of the long-range financial requirements. Seven of the 12 members agreed that the remaining one-third of the long-range financial requirements should be met by a deferred, gradual increase in the normal retirement age, while the other 5 members agreed to an increase in the contribution rates in 2010 of slightly less than one-half percent (0.46%) of covered earnings on the employer and the same amount on the employee, with the employee's share of the increase offset by a refundable income-tax credit. . . .

PROVISIONS OF 'CONSENSUS' PACKAGE

Recommendations Nos. (4) to (16) describe the provisions of the "consensus" package. Table A presents the actuarial cost data for this package for both the short range (1983-89 in the aggregate) and the long range (the 75-year valuation period, ending with 2056). Table B gives the year-by-year actuarial cost data for the short-range period. The cost estimates underlying these figures are based on economic assumptions which have been developed in recent weeks and which assume significantly lower levels of both price and wage inflation than does the Alternative III estimate in the 1982 OASDI Trustees Report (and even somewhat lower than in the Alternative II-B estimate).

The "consensus" package would provide an estimated $168 billion in additional financial resources to the OASDI program in calendar years

Table A

Short-Range and Long-Range Cost Analysis of OASDI Proposals

Proposal	Short-Term Savings 1983-89 (billions)	Long-Range Savings (percentage of payroll)
Cover nonprofit and new Federal employees [3]	+$20	+.30%
Prohibit withdrawal of State and local government employees	+3	—
Taxation of benefits for higher-income persons	+30	+.60
Shift COLAs to calendar-year basis	+40	+.27
Eliminate windfall benefits for persons with pensions from noncovered employment	+.2	+.01
Continue benefits on remarriage for disabled widow(er)s and for divorced widow(er)s	−.1	—
Index deferred widow(er)'s benefits based on wages (instead of CPI)	−.2	−.05
Permit divorced aged spouse to receive benefits when husband is eligible to receive benefits	−.1	−.01
Increase benefit rate for disabled widow(er)s aged 50-59 to 71½% of primary benefit	−1	−.01
Revise tax-rate schedule	+40	+.02
Revise tax basis for self-employed	+18	+.19
Reallocate OASDI tax rate between OASI and DI	—	—
Allow inter-fund borrowing from HI by OASDI	—	—
Credit the OASDI Trust Funds, by a lump-sum payment for cost of gratuitous military service wage credits and past unnegotiated checks	+18	—
Base automatic benefit increases on lower of CPI or wage increases after 1987 if fund ratio is under 20%, with catch-up if fund ratio exceeds 32%	—	—
Increase delayed retirement credit from 3% per year to 8%, beginning in 1990 and reaching 8% in 2010	—	−.10 [1]
Additional long-range changes [2]	—	+.58
Total Effect	+168	+1.80

[1] *This cost estimate assumes that retirement patterns would be only slightly affected by this change. If this change does result in significant changes in retirement behavior over time, the cost increase would be less (or possibly even a small savings could result).*
[2] *Alternate methods for obtaining this long-range savings are presented in the Additional Statements of the members (in Chapter 4).*
[3] *Includes effect of revised tax schedule.*

NOTE: See text for complete description of the proposals.

Table B

Year-by-Year Short-Range Cost Analysis of OASDI Proposals

(in billions)

Proposal	1983	1984	1985	1986	1987	1988	1989	1983-89
Cover nonprofit and new Federal workers [1]	—	+$1	+$2	+$3	+$4	+$4	+$5	+$20
Prohibit withdrawal of State/local workers	—	*	*	*	+1	+1	+1	+3
Taxation of benefits for higher-income persons	—	+1	+4	+5	+6	+7	+8	+30
Shift COLAs to calendar-year basis	+$5	+5	+5	+6	+6	+6	+7	+40
Eliminate windfall benefits	—	*	*	*	*	*	*	+.2
Benefits for remarried widow(er)s	—	*	*	*	*	*	*	−.1
Index deferred widow(er)'s benefits by wages	—	*	*	*	*	*	*	−.2
Divorced spouse's benefits when husband eligible	—	*	*	*	*	*	*	−.1
Higher benefit rate for disabled widow(er)s	—	*	*	*	*	*	*	−1
Revised tax schedule	—	+9	*	—	—	+15	+16	+40
Revised tax basis for self-employed	—	+1	+3	+3	+3	+4	+5	+18
Credit trust funds for military wage credits	+20	−1	−1	*	*	*	*	+18
Total Effect	+25	+16	+13	+17	+20	+37	+41	+168

* Less than $500 million.
[1] Includes effect of revised tax schedule.

NOTE: See text for complete description of the proposals. Those having no short-range cost effect are not shown here. Totals do not always equal the sum of the individual items, due to rounding.

1983-89. This amount is very close to the midpoint of the $150-200 billion range stated in Recommendation No. 2. Actually, because the economic assumptions which are used for this package involve a lower inflation rate as to both prices and wages than those which had been used earlier in the deliberations, the resulting $168 billion of additional financial resources is really relatively near the upper end of the desired range.

   (4) The National Commission recommends that coverage under the OASDI program should be extended on a mandatory basis, as of January 1, 1984, to all newly hired civilian employees of the Federal Government. The National Commission also recommends that OASDI-HI coverage should be extended on a mandatory basis, as of January 1, 1984, to all employees of nonprofit organizations.

It is important to note that covering additional groups of workers such as those specified in this recommendation not only results in a favorable cash-flow situation in the short run, but also has a favorable long-range effect. The additional OASDI taxes paid on behalf of the newly-covered workers over the long run will exceed, on the average, the additional benefits which result from such employment, assuming that the program is in long-range actuarial balance.

The National Commission believes that an independent supplemental retirement plan should be developed for the Federal new hires, which would be part of the Civil Service Retirement system (just as private employers have plans supplementing the OASDI program). It is important to note that present Federal employees will *not* be affected by this recommendation (and that the financing of their benefits over the long run will not be adversely affected).

   (5) The National Commission recommends that State and local governments which have elected coverage for their employees under the OASDI-HI program should not be permitted to terminate such coverage in the future — specifically, termination notices now pending would be invalid if the process of termination is not completed by the enactment date of the new legislation.

   (6) The National Commission is concerned about the relatively large OASDI benefits that can accrue to individuals who spend most of their working careers in noncovered employment from which they derive pension rights, but who also become eligible for OASDI benefits as a result of relatively short periods in covered employment with other employers. Accordingly, the National Commission recommends that the method of computing benefits should be revised for persons who first become eligible for pensions from non-covered employment, after 1983, so as to eliminate "windfall" benefits.

The result of such a work history is to produce OASDI benefits that contain "windfall" elements — the benefits payable are relatively high compared to the proportion of time spent and the OASDI taxes paid during covered employment. This results from the weighted benefit formula, which treats these individuals in the same manner as if they were long-service, low-earnings workers. Specifically, the National Commission believes that these individuals should receive benefits which are more nearly of a proportionate basis than the heavily-weighted benefits now provided.

There are various methods of eliminating the "windfall" portion of benefits (while still providing equitable, proportional benefits). One method would be to modify the benefit formula for determining the Primary Insurance Amount by making the second percentage factor (32%) be applicable to the lowest band of Average Indexed Monthly Earnings (instead of the 90% factor), but the reduction in benefits would not be larger than the pension from non-covered employment. Another method would be to apply the present benefit formula to an earnings record which combines both covered earnings and also non-covered earnings in the future for the purpose of determining a replacement rate (i.e., the ratio of the benefit initially payable to previous earnings); then, that replacement rate would be applied to the average earnings based solely on covered employment. The short-range cost effect of these proposals — applied only prospectively for new eligibles — would be relatively small. The long-range cost effect would depend on the procedure used and on whether the recommended extension of coverage is adopted.

(7) The National Commission recommends that, beginning with 1984, 50% of OASDI benefits should be considered as taxable income for income-tax purposes for persons with Adjusted Gross Income (before including therein any OASDI benefits) of $20,000 if single and $25,000 if married. The proceeds from such taxation, as estimated by the Treasury Department, would be credited to the OASDI Trust Funds under a permanent appropriation.

It is estimated that about 10% of OASDI beneficiaries would be affected by this provision. The National Commission noted that a "notch" is present in this provision in that those with Adjusted Gross Income of just under the limit of $20,000/$25,000 would have a large total income (including OASDI benefits) than those with Adjusted Gross Income just over the limit. The National Commission points out the presence of this "notch" and trusts that it will be rectified in the legislative process.

(8) The National Commission recommends that the automatic cost-of-living adjustments of OASDI benefits should, beginning in 1983, be made applicable to the December benefit checks (payable early in January), rather than being first applicable to the June payments. The National Commission also recommends that the amount of the disregard of OASDI benefits for purposes of

determining Supplemental Security Income [SSI] payment levels should be increased from $20 a month to $50.

The increase in the CPI [Consumer Price Index] for purposes of the automatic adjustments for any particular year is currently measured from the first quarter of the previous year to the first quarter of that particular year. This procedure should continue to apply for the adjustment in benefit amounts for 1983 (payable in early January 1984). However, for subsequent years, the comparison should be made on a "third quarter to third quarter" basis.

The recommended increase in the amount of the disregard of OASDI benefits for SSI purposes is estimated to have an initial cost of about $750 million per year.

(9) The National Commission recommends that the following changes in benefit provisions which affect mainly women should be made:
   (a) Present law permits the continuation of benefits for surviving spouses who remarry after age 60. This would also be done for (1) disabled surviving spouses aged 50-59, (2) disabled divorced surviving spouses aged 50-59, and (3) divorced surviving spouses aged 60 or over.
   (b) Spouse benefits for divorced spouses would be payable at age 62 or over (subject to the requirement that the divorce has lasted for a significant period) if the former spouse is eligible for retirement benefits, whether or not they have been claimed (or they have been suspended because of substantial employment).
   (c) Deferred surviving-spouse benefits would continue to be indexed as under present law, except that the indexing would be based on the increases in wages after the death of the worker (instead of by the increases in the CPI, as under present law).
   (d) The benefit rate for disabled widows and widowers aged 50-59 at disablement would be the same as that for non-disabled widows and widowers first claiming benefits at age 60 (i.e., 71 1/2% of the Primary Insurance Amount), instead of the lower rates under present law (gradually rising from 50% at age 50 to 71 1/2% for disablement at age 60). Such change would not only be applicable to new cases, but would also be applicable to beneficiaries of this category who are on the rolls on the effective date of the provision.

(10) The National Commission recommends that the OASDI tax schedule should be revised so that the 1985 rate would be moved to 1984, the 1985-87 rates would remain as scheduled under present law, part of the 1990 rate would be moved to 1988, and the rate for 1990 and after would remain unchanged. The HI tax rates for all years would remain unchanged. The resulting tax schedule would be as follows:

Employer and Employee Rate (each)

Year	OASDI		OASDI-HI	
	Present Law	Proposal	Present Law	Proposal
1983	5.4%	5.4%	6.7%	6.7%
1984	5.4	5.7	6.7	7.0
1985	5.7	5.7	7.05	7.05
1986	5.7	5.7	7.15	7.15
1987	5.7	5.7	7.15	7.15
1988-89	5.7	6.06	7.15	7.51
1990 and after	6.2	6.2	7.65	7.65

For 1984, a refundable income tax credit would be provided against the individual's Federal income-tax liability in the amount of the increase in the employee taxes over what would have been payable under present law.

(11) The National Commission recommends that the OASDI tax rates for self-employed persons should, beginning in 1984, be equal to the combined employer-employee rates. One-half of the OASDI taxes paid by self-employed persons should then be considered as a business expense for income-tax purposes (but not for purposes of determining the OASDI-HI tax).

Under present law, self-employed persons pay an OASDI tax rate which is approximately equal to 75% of the combined employer-employee rate (exactly 75% for 1985 and after) and an HI tax rate which is 50% of the combined employer-employee rate. Also, under present law, self-employed persons cannot deduct, as business expenses, any OASDI-HI taxes paid. The reduction in income taxes payable by the self-employed during 1984-89 as a result of considering one-half of their OASDI taxes as a business expense is estimated to be about $12 billion.

(12) The National Commission recommends that the proposed OASDI tax rates should be allocated between the OASI and DI Trust Funds in a manner different from present law, in order that both funds will have about the same fund ratios.

(13) The National Commission recommends that the authority for inter-fund borrowing by the OASDI Trust Funds from the HI Trust Fund be authorized for 1983-87.

(14) The National Commission recommends that a lump-sum payment should be made to the OASDI Trust Funds from the General Fund of the Treasury for the following items:

(a) The present value of the estimated additional benefits arising from the gratuitous military service wage credits for service before 1957 (subject to subsequent adjustments if the experience deviates from the estimates).

(b) The amount of the combined employer-employee OASDI taxes on the gratuitous military service wage credits for service after

1956 and before 1983 (which were granted as a recognition of non-cash remuneration, and the cost of which is met, under present law, when additional benefits derived therefrom are paid). The payment would include interest, but would be reduced for any costs therefor which were paid in the past to the OASDI Trust Funds from the General Fund of the Treasury. In the future, the OASDI Trust Funds would be reimbursed on a current basis for such employer-employee taxes on such wage credits for service after 1982.

(c) The amount of uncashed OASDI checks issued in the past (which were charged against the trust funds at time of issue), estimated at about $300-400 million. (The problem of un-cashed checks in the future has been corrected as a result of changed procedures of the Treasury Department with regard to checks which are uncashed for a long time.)

(15) The National Commission recommends that, beginning with 1988, if the fund ratio of the combined OASDI Trust Funds as of the beginning of a year is less than 20.0% (except that, for 1988, the fund ratio to be considered would be that estimated for the end of that year), the automatic cost-of-living (COLA) adjust-ments of OASDI benefits should be based on the lower of the CPI increase or the increase in wages. If the fund ratio is 32.0% or more at the beginning of a year, payments will be made during the following year as supplements to monthly benefits otherwise payable to make up to individuals for any use of wage increases instead of CPI increases in the past, but only to the extent that sufficient funds are available over those needed to maintain a fund ratio of 32.0%.

This provision will serve as a stabilizer against the possibility of exceptionally poor economic performance over a period of time.

The increases in wages would be determined from the "SSA average wage index," the series used by the Social Security Administration in determining such elements of the program as the maximum taxable earnings base and the "bend points" in the formula for the Primary Insurance Amount. As an example, assuming that this new indexing method were applicable for 1995 (for the December checks), the COLA percentage would be the *smaller* of (1) the percentage increase in the CPI from the third quarter of 1994, to the third quarter of 1995 or (2) the per-centage increase in the "SSA average wage index" from 1993 to 1994.

(16) The National Commission recommends that the Delayed-Retire-ment Credit should be increased from the present 3% (for persons who attained age 65 after 1981) to 8%, to be phased in over the period 1990-2010.

Under present law, persons who do not receive benefits after age 65 (essentially because of substantial employment of any kind) receive increases in their benefit (and in their widowed spouse's benefit, but not in any other auxiliary benefit) at the rate of 3% for each year of delay in receipt of benefits from age 65 through age 71. Under the proposal, the Delayed-Retirement Credit for months in 1990 would be at the rate of 3 1/4%, those for 1991 would be at the rate of 3 1/2%, etc. until an 8% rate would be reached in 2009 and after.

COVERAGE OF PAYMENTS
UNDER SALARY-REDUCTION PLANS

(17) The National Commission recommends that, in the case of salary-reduction plans qualifying under Section 401(k) of the Internal Revenue Code, any salary reduction thereunder shall not be treated as a reduction in the wages subject to OASDI-HI taxes.

Section 401(k) of the Internal Revenue Code permits employers to install "salary-reduction" plans, under which employees may elect to forego a salary increase or have part of their pay set aside in a tax-sheltered fund. Such deferred salary is neither subject to Federal income tax currently, nor is it subject to the OASDI-HI tax. The National Commission believes that, for both OASDI-HI tax and benefit credit purposes, any salary deferred under a plan meeting the requirements of Section 401(k) should be considered in exactly the same manner as cash remuneration.

This proposal will not produce significant additional income to the OASDI and HI programs currently, because not many of these salary-reduction plans have yet been put into effect. However, if the recommendation is not followed, it is quite probable that many such plans will be instituted and that, in the absence of the action recommended, considerable decreases in OASDI-HI tax income to the trust funds and in benefit credits would result.

FAIL-SAFE MECHANISMS

(18) The National Commission believes that, in addition to the stabilizing mechanism of Recommendation (15), a fail-safe mechanism is necessary so that benefits could continue to be paid on time despite unexpectedly adverse conditions which occur with little advance notice. Several types of fail-safe mechanisms are possible other than the one currently being used — inter-fund borrowing; there is strong disagreement among the members as to which type of mechanism should be used. A combination of these types of mechanisms would, of course, be possible.

A number of mechanisms were considered. One would be to borrow, for a limited period, from the General Fund of the Treasury. Such limitation would prevent this procedure from being a part of the permanent method for financing the program. Another possibility along this line would be to permit the trust funds to issue their own bonds for sale to the general public.

A second mechanism would be to reduce, temporarily, the benefits payable. Alternatively, such a result could be accomplished indirectly, by reducing the amount of the next benefit increase which would occur as a result of the automatic-adjustment provision for benefits in eligibility status.

The third mechanism would be to increase, temporarily, the OASDI tax rates and/or the maximum taxable earnings base.

The National Commission makes a number of recommendations in addition to those discussed previously. Although these additional recommendations are of importance, they will not likely have any significant financial effects, on the average over the long run.

INVESTMENT PROCEDURES

(19) The National Commission recommends that the investment procedures of the OASI, DI, HI, and SMI [Supplementary Medical Insurance] Trust Funds be revised so that (1) all future special issues would be invested on a month-to-month basis (i.e., without fixed maturity dates, as under present law), at an interest rate based on the average market rate of all public-debt obligations with a duration of four or more years until maturity (not including "flower bonds"); (2) all present special issues would be redeemed at their face amount; (3) all "flower bonds" would be redeemed at their current market values; (4) all other current holdings would be held until maturity (unless disposed of sooner, if needed to meet outgo); and (5) only special issues would be purchased by the trust funds in the future.

There has been widespread public discussion about the investment procedures of the four Social Security trust funds. The view has frequently been expressed that the investments have not been made on a proper basis and that sufficiently high rates of return have not been obtained, because the *average* rate of return has, in recent years, been far lower than that on newly issued Government obligations. This is not a valid comparison, because it compares the *new-issues* rate with the *average portfolio* rate, which includes the effect of the lower interest rates on long-term obligations bought some years ago (at rates which were equitable and proper at that time). The same situation as to a higher interest rate on new issues than on the total portfolio, as of recent years, has also been present for private pension funds and insurance companies.

The National Commission believes that the investment procedures followed by the trust funds in the past generally have been proper and

71

appropriate. The monies available have generally been invested appropriately in Government obligations at interest rates which are equitable to both the trust funds and the General Fund of the Treasury and have not — as is sometimes alleged — been spent for other purposes outside of the Social Security program.

Nonetheless, the National Commission makes this recommendation in order to improve the level of public understanding of the operations of the trust funds. On the whole, and over the long-range future, it is likely that such a change in investment procedure will have little (if any) effect on the financial status of the Social Security program. It will probably result in a slightly higher average rate of return in the immediate future. The long-range effects are not determinable and, in any case, are not of great significance with regard to the overall financing of the program.

Although the National Commission has not considered the Medicare program in depth, it believes that the same investment procedures should apply for the HI and SMI Trust Funds as for the OASDI Trust Funds.

PUBLIC MEMBERS ON BOARD OF TRUSTEES

(20) The National Commission recommends that two public members be added to the Board of Trustees of the OASDI Trust Funds. The public members would be nominated by the President and confirmed by the Senate. No more than one public member could be from any particular political party.

The National Commission believes that increasing the membership of the Board of Trustees of the OASDI Trust Funds by including two individuals from outside the Executive Branch, on a bi-partisan basis, would be desirable from the standpoint of confidence in the integrity of the trust funds. The presence of such public members would inspire more confidence in the investment procedure (even though it is recommended that the procedure should be placed on a more or less automatic basis, as under the previous recommendation) and would help to assure that the demographic and economic assumptions for the cost estimates of the future operations of the program would continue to be developed in an objective manner. Although the National Commission is not generally making recommendations in connection with the Medicare program, it would seem reasonable that the same procedure of having two public members on the Board of Trustees should also apply for the HI and SMI Trust Funds.

SOCIAL SECURITY AND THE UNIFIED BUDGET

(21) A majority of the members of the National Commission recommends that the operations of the OASI, DI, HI, and SMI Trust Funds should be removed from the unified budget. Some of those who do not support this recommendation believe that the situa-

tion would be adequately handled if the operations of the Social Security program were displayed within the present unified Federal budget as a separate budget function, apart from other income security programs.

Before fiscal year 1969, the operations of the Social Security trust funds were not included in the unified budget of the Federal Government, although they were made available publicly and were combined, for purposes of economic analysis, with the administrative budget in special summary tables included in the annual budget document. Beginning then, the operations of the Social Security trust funds were included in the unified budget. In 1974, Congress implicitly approved the use of a unified budget by including Social Security trust fund operations in the annual budget process. Thus, in years when trust-fund income exceeded outgo, the result was a decrease in any general budget deficit that otherwise would have been shown — and vice versa.

The National Commission believes that changes in the Social Security program should be made only for programmatic reasons, and not for purposes of balancing the budget. Those who support the removal of the operations of the trust funds from the budget believe that this policy of making changes only for programmatic reasons would be more likely to be carried out if the Social Security program were not in the unified budget. Some members also believe that such a procedure will make clear the effect and presence of any payments from the General Fund of the Treasury to the Social Security program. (Under present procedures, such payments are a "wash" and do not affect the overall budget deficit or surplus).

Those who oppose this recommendation believe that it is essential that the operations of the Social Security program should remain in the unified Federal budget because the program involves such a large proportion of all Federal outlays. Thus, to omit its operations would misrepresent the activities of the Federal Government and their economic impact. Furthermore, it is important to ensure that the financial condition of the Social Security program be constantly visible to the Congress and the public. Highlighting the operations of the Social Security program as a separate line function in the budget would allow its impact thereon to be seen more clearly.

SOCIAL SECURITY ADMINISTRATION
AS AN INDEPENDENT AGENCY

(22) The majority of the members of the National Commission believes — as a broad, general principle — that it would be logical to have the Social Security Administration be a separate independent agency, perhaps headed by a bi-partisan board. The National Commission recommends that a study should be made as to the feasibility of doing this.

The Social Security Administration is now part of the Department of Health and Human Services. Its fiscal operations and the size of its staff are larger than those of the remainder of the Department combined.

The National Commission has not had the time to look into the various complex issues involved in such an administrative reorganization and, therefore, recommends that a study group should be formed to look into this matter. Issues involved include whether the leadership of such an independent agency should be assigned to a single individual or whether there should be a governing board of several members, selected on a bipartisan basis, and whether the operations of the Medicare program should be included in such an independent agency, or whether they should remain as a subsidiary agency within the Department of Health and Human Services, as at present.

[STATE AND LOCAL GOVERNMENT EMPLOYEES]

Although the National Commission believes that coverage of all persons who are in paid employment is desirable, some members do not favor mandatory coverage of employees of State and local governments.

A majority of the members is concerned about the constitutional problem of covering State and local government employees under Social Security on a mandatory basis because the Federal Government may not have the power to compel State and local governments to pay the employer share of the OASDI-HI tax. Other members believe that, regardless of the constitutionality question, the Federal Government should not do so because the two levels of government have equal roles and status. Some members point out that many State and local governments already have adequate, well-financed retirement systems for their employees, so that they do not need OASDI-HI coverage; others point out that many State and local systems have serious financing problems and that protection of the benefits under such systems against inflation (and often protection against other risks) is not as adequate as under the OASDI program.

[PROVISIONS PRIMARILY AFFECTING WOMEN]

In recent years, there has been widespread discussion as to whether the basic structure of the Social Security program should be altered in view of the changes in the role of women in our society and economy.

Some members of the National Commission believe that there should be a comprehensive change in the program to reflect the changing role of women, for example, by instituting some form of earnings sharing for purposes of the Social Security earnings record. Simply stated, earnings sharing means that all covered earnings received by a couple during the period of marriage would be pooled and half would be credited to each of their earnings records. Some other members believed that such comprehensive changes were outside of the scope of the charge of the National Commission.

SOCIAL SECURITY CARDS

The National Commission commends a recent decision of the Social Security Administration to use banknote-quality paper for new and replacement Social Security cards. The Senate Permanent Subcommittee on Investigations estimated in June 1982 that fraud involving identification cards, of which Social Security cards are the vast majority, cost the Federal Government between $15 and $24 billion per year.

STATE OF THE UNION ADDRESS

January 25, 1983

In his second State of the Union address, delivered before a joint session of Congress January 25, President Ronald Reagan said that the economy is troubled but "America is on the mend." Citing economic indicators such as increased housing starts and permits and reduced interest rates, the president noted that the economic recovery had begun but cautioned that without additional measures the nation could face the prospect of sluggish economic growth.

As though expecting strong opposition to his economic program, the president called repeatedly for bipartisanship in government and received a standing ovation when he proclaimed, "We who are in government must take the lead in restoring the economy." Reagan urged support for his plans to reduce long-term unemployment, to stimulate youth employment and to improve the educational system.

Without giving any details, the president alluded to a "New Federalism" plan scaled down from the one he had outlined in his first State of Union address. The administration was unable in 1982 to transfer dozens of federal programs to the states, and the president devised a more modest New Federalism proposal. The modified plan would eliminate part of the federal grant system and create more revenue sharing by consolidating 27 programs into three broad block grants to the states. The plan also would merge the community development block grant program into revenue sharing. (State of the Union address, Historic Documents of 1982, p. 73)

Economy and Unemployment

Reagan asked Congress to support his economic recovery plan, which hinged upon a one-year federal spending freeze. Unless runaway spending was brought under control, Reagan warned, "...the recovery will be too short, unemployment will remain too high, and we will leave an unconscionable burden of national debt for our children." Reagan stated that the deficit problem stemmed not from defense outlays or tax cuts but from uncontrolled domestic spending. In particular Reagan noted that automatic spending programs such as food stamps were the largest cause of the structural deficit problem. Yet, in a major policy shift and in line with the call for bipartisanship, the plan called for a standby tax in 1986 and a $55 billion saving in defense spending.

"The recovery program will provide jobs for most, but others will need special help and training for new skills," the president said in outlining additional legislation to reduce unemployment. His proposed Employment Act of 1983 included extended unemployment benefits, tax breaks for employers hiring the long-term unemployed, a summer youth subminimum wage and establishment of urban enterprise zones.

In addition to the economic recovery program, Reagan endorsed stronger free trade in American goods and agricultural products. In an attempt to reach out to women and minorities, Reagan called for an end to wage discrimination based on sex, extension of the Civil Rights Commission and enforcement of fair housing laws. Although Reagan spoke little of foreign policy, he urged passage of his Caribbean Basin Initiative and made clear that any arms agreements with the Soviet Union must be fair and verifiable.

Education

The president emphasized that "education, training, and retraining are fundamental to our success." His education program called for upgrading science and mathematics training through block grants to the states. The grants would provide additional teacher training in secondary schools. The plan stipulated three other measures: first, establishing education savings accounts in which earned interest and dividends would be tax exempt; second, enacting tuition tax credits legislation for parents who send their children to private or religious elementary and secondary schools; and third, passing a constitutional amendment permitting voluntary school prayer. Many Democrats considered the president's educational proposals inadequate. Gov. James B. Hunt of North Carolina, long identified with groups seeking to improve the quality of education, said, "We really need a kind of educational renewal in America ... better teacher training, a stronger emphasis on math and science, engineering, computer literacy, rigorous testing and a real *commitment to high standards and discipline."* (Education report, p. 413)

Reaction

Congressional reaction to the speech was mixed. Speaking for the Democrats in a nationally televised program following the address, Sen. Bill Bradley of New Jersey said, "There's no question we need a fairer tax system that everyone can understand and that will generate economic growth." The official response by Democratic National Chairman Charles Manatt was more biting. "When our nation needed careful, thoughtful restraint and pruning of federal spending," Manatt said, "this administration went on the warpath, attacking without foresight and without mercy every program and policy which offered educational opportunity, training for the jobless, decent nutrition for the needy or proper health care for the old, sick and poor." House Speaker Thomas P. O'Neill Jr., D-Mass., said, "President Reagan has taken the first, necessary step in putting America back to work. The next step is to present a program for action that goes substantially beyond those proposals mentioned by the President tonight."

Reaction among Republicans was generally favorable, but some warned of rough waters ahead. Senate Majority Leader Howard H. Baker Jr. of Tennessee foresaw a furious debate in Congress over defense spending. He and Kansas Republican Sen. Robert Dole, chairman of the Finance Committee, opposed Reagan's standby tax proposal.

> *Following is the text of President Ronald Reagan's nationally televised State of the Union address to Congress January 25, 1983. (Boldface headings in brackets have been added by Congressional Quarterly to highlight the organization of the text.):*

Mr. Speaker, Mr. President, distinguished Members of the Congress, honored guests and fellow citizens:

This solemn occasion marks the 196th time that a President of the United States has reported on the State of the Union since George Washington first did so in 1790. That's a lot of reports, but there's no shortage of new things to say about the State of the Union. The very key to our success has been our ability, foremost among nations, to preserve our lasting values by making change work for us rather than against us.

I would like to talk with you this evening about what we can do together — not as Republicans and Democrats, but as Americans — to make tomorrow's America happy and prosperous at home, strong and respected abroad, and at peace in the world.

As we gather here tonight, the state of our Union is strong, but our economy is troubled. For too many of our fellow citizens — farmers, steel and auto workers, lumbermen, black teenagers, working mothers — this is a painful period. We must all do everything in our power to bring their ordeal to an end. It has fallen to us, in our time, to undo damage that was a long time in the making, and to begin the hard but necessary task of building a better future for ourselves and our children.

We have a long way to go, but thanks to the courage, patience, and strength of our people, America is on the mend.

But let me give you just one important reason why I believe this — it involves many members of this body.

[Social Security Reform]

Just 10 days ago, after months of debate and deadlock, the bipartisan Commission on Social Security accomplished the seemingly impossible. Social security, as some of us had warned for so long, faced disaster. I, myself, have been talking about this problem for almost 30 years. As 1983 began, the system stood on the brink of bankruptcy, a double victim of our economic ills. First, a decade of rampant inflation drained its reserves as we tried to protect beneficiaries from the spiraling cost of living. Then the recession and the sudden end of inflation withered the expanding wage base and increasing revenues the system needs to support the 36 million Americans who depend on it.

When the Speaker of the House, the Senate majority leader, and I performed the bipartisan — or formed the bipartisan Commission on Social Security, pundits and experts predicted that party divisions and conflicting interests would prevent the Commission from agreeing on a plan to save social security. Well, sometimes, even here in Washington, the cynics are wrong. Through compromise and cooperation, the members of the Commission overcame their differences and achieved a fair, workable plan. They proved that, when it comes to the national welfare, Americans can still pull together for the common good.

Tonight, I'm especially pleased to join with the Speaker and the Senate majority leader in urging the Congress to enact this plan by Easter.

There are elements in it, of course, that none of us prefers, but taken together it performs a package that all of us can support. It asks for some sacrifice by all — the self-employed, beneficiaries, workers, government employees, and the better-off among the retired — but it imposes an undue burden on none. And, in supporting it, we keep an important pledge to the American people: The integrity of the social security system will be preserved — and no one's payments will be reduced.

The Commission's plan will do the job; indeed, it must do the job. We owe it to today's older Americans and today's younger workers. So, before we go any further, I ask you to join with me in saluting the members of the Commission who are here tonight, and Senate Majority Leader Howard Baker and Speaker Tip O'Neill, for a job well done. I hope and pray the bipartisan spirit that guided you in this endeavor will inspire all of us as we face the challenges of the year ahead.

Nearly half a century ago, in this Chamber, another American President, Franklin Delano Roosevelt, in his second State of the Union message, urged America to look to the future — to meet the challenge of change and the need for leadership that looks forward, not backward.

"Throughout the world," he said, "change is the order of the day. In every nation economic problems long in the making have brought crises of many kinds for which the masters of old practice and theory were unprepared." He also reminded us that, "the future lies with those wise political leaders who realize that the great public is interested more in Government than in politics."

So, let us, in these next 2 years — men and women of both parties, every political shade — concentrate on the long-range, bipartisan responsibilities of Government, not the short-range or short-term temptations of partisan politics.

[Economic Recovery]

The problems we inherited were far worse than most inside and out of Government had expected; the recession was deeper than most inside and out of Government had predicted. Curing those problems has taken more time, and a higher toll, than any of us wanted. Unemployment is far too high. Projected Federal spending — if government refuses to tighten its own belt — will also be far too high and could weaken and shorten the economic recovery now underway.

This recovery will bring with it a revival of economic confidence and spending for consumer items and capital goods — the stimulus we need to restart our stalled economic engines. The American people have already stepped up their rate of saving, assuring that the funds needed to modernize our factories and improve our technology will once again flow to business and industry.

The inflationary expectations that led to a 21 1/2-percent interest prime rate and soaring mortgage rates 2 years ago are now reduced by almost half. Leaders have started to realize that double-digit inflation is no longer a way of life.

I misspoke there. I should have said "lenders."

So, interest rates have tumbled, paving the way for recovery in vital industries like housing and autos.

The early evidence of that recovery has started coming in. Housing starts for the fourth quarter of 1982 were up 45 percent from a year ago, and housing permits, a sure indicator of future growth, were up a whopping 60 percent.

We're witnessing an upsurge of productivity and impressive evidence that American industry will once again become competitive in markets at home and abroad, ensuring more jobs and better incomes for the Nation's work force. But our confidence must also be tempered by realism and patience. Quick fixes and artificial stimulants repeatedly applied over decades are what brought us the inflationary disorders that we've now paid such a heavy price to cure.

The permanent recovery in employment, production, and investment we seek won't come in a sharp, short spurt. It will build carefully and steadily in the months and years ahead. In the meantime, the challenge of government is to identify the things we can do now to ease this massive economic transition for the American people.

[Federal Budget and Deficits]

The Federal budget is both a symptom and a cause of our economic problems. Unless we reduce the dangerous growth rate in government spending, we could face the prospect of sluggish economic growth into the indefinite future. Failure to cope with this problem now could mean as much as a trillion dollars more in national debt in the next 4 years alone. That would average $4,300 in additional debt for every man, woman, child, and baby in our nation.

To assure a sustained recovery, we must continue getting runaway spending under control to bring those deficits down. If we don't, the recovery will be too short, unemployment will remain too high, and we will leave an unconscionable burden of national debt for our children. That we must not do.

Let's be clear about where the deficit problem comes from. Contrary to the drumbeat we've been hearing for the last few months, the deficits we face are not rooted in defense spending. Taken as a percentage of the gross national product, our defense spending happens to be only about four-fifths of what it was in 1970. Nor is the deficit, as some would have it, rooted in tax cuts. Even with our tax cuts, taxes as a fraction of gross national product remain about the same as they were in 1970. The fact is, our deficits come from the uncontrolled growth of the budget for domestic spending.

During the 1970's the share of our national income devoted to this domestic spending increased by more than 60 percent, from 10 cents out of every dollar produced by the American people to 16 cents. In spite of all our economies and efficiencies, and without adding any new programs, basic, necessary domestic spending provided for in this year's budget will grow to almost a trillion over the next 5 years.

The deficit problem is a clear and present danger to the basic health of our Republic. We need a plan to overcome this danger — a plan based on these principles. It must be bipartisan. Conquering the deficits and putting the Government's house in order will require the best efforts of all of us. It must be fair. Just as all will share in the benefits that will come from recovery, all would share fairly in the burden of transition. It must be prudent. The strength of our national defense must be restored so that we can pursue prosperity in peace and freedom while maintaining our commitment to the truly needy. And finally, it must be realistic. We can't rely on hope alone.

[Four-part Plan for Recovery]

With these guiding principles in mind, let me outline a four-part plan to increase economic growth and reduce deficits.

First, in my budget message, I will recommend a Federal spending freeze. I know this is strong medicine, but so far, we have only cut the rate of increase in Federal spending. The Government has continued to spend more money each year, though not as much more as it did in the past. Taken as a whole, the budget I'm proposing for the fiscal year will increase no more than the rate of inflation. In other words, the Federal Government will hold the line on real spending. Now, that's far less than many American families have had to do in these difficult times.

I will request that the proposed 6-month freeze in cost-of-living adjustments recommended by the bipartisan Social Security Commission be applied to other government-related retirement programs. I will, also, propose a 1-year freeze on a broad range of domestic spending programs, and for Federal civilian and military pay and pension programs. And let me say right here, I'm sorry, with regard to the military, in asking that of them, because for so many years they have been so far behind and so low in reward for what the men and women in uniform are doing. But I'm sure they will understand that this must be across the board and fair.

Second, I will ask the Congress to adopt specific measures to control the growth of the so-called uncontrollable spending programs. These are the automatic spending programs, such as food stamps, that cannot be simply frozen and that have grown by over 400 percent since 1970. They are the largest single cause of the built-in or structural deficit problem. Our standard here will be fairness, ensuring that the taxpayers' hard-earned dollars go only to the truly needy; that none of them are turned away, but that fraud and waste are stamped out. And I'm sorry to say, there's a lot of it out there. In the food stamp program alone, last year, we identified almost $1.1 billion in overpayments. The taxpayers aren't the only victims of this kind of abuse. The truly needy suffer as funds intended for them are taken not by the needy, but by the greedy. For everyone's sake, we must put an end to such waste and corruption.

Third, I will adjust our program to restore America's defenses by proposing $55 billion in defense savings over the next 5 years. These are savings recommended to me by the Secretary of Defense, who has assured me they can be safely achieved and will not diminish our ability to negotiate arms reductions or endanger America's security. We will not gamble with our national survival.

And fourth, because we must ensure reduction and eventual elimination of deficits over the next several years, I will propose a standby tax, limited

83

to no more than 1 percent of the gross national product to start in fiscal 1986. It would last no more than 3 years, and it would start only if the Congress has first approved our spending freeze and budget control program. And there are several other conditions also that must be met, all of them in order for this program to be triggered.

Now, you could say that this is an insurance policy for the future, a remedy that will be at hand if needed, but only resorted to if absolutely necessary. In the meantime, we'll continue to study ways to simplify the tax code and make it more fair for all Americans. This is a goal that every American who's ever struggled with a tax form can understand.

At the same time, however, I will oppose any efforts to undo the basic tax reforms that we've already enacted, including the 10-percent tax break coming to taxpayers this July and the tax indexing which will protect all Americans from inflationary bracket creep in the years ahead.

Now, I realize that this four-part plan is easier to describe than it will be to enact. But the looming deficits that hang over us and over America's future must be reduced. The path I've outlined is fair, balanced, and realistic. If enacted, it will ensure a steady decline in deficits, aiming toward a balanced budget by the end of the decade. It is the only path that will lead to a strong, sustained recovery. Let us follow that path together.

[Employment and Trade]

No domestic challenge is more crucial than providing stable, permanent jobs for all Americans who want to work. The recovery program will provide jobs for most, but others will need special help and training for new skills. Shortly, I will submit to the Congress the Employment Act of 1983 designed to get at the special problems of the long-term unemployed, as well as young people trying to enter the job market. I'll propose extending unemployment benefits, including special incentives to employers who hire the long-term unemployed, providing programs for displaced workers, and helping federally funded and State-administered unemployment insurance programs to provide workers with training and relocation assistance. Finally, our proposal will include new incentives for summer youth employment to help young people get a start in the job market.

We must offer both short-term help and long-term hope for our unemployed. I hope we can work together on this, as we did last year in enacting the landmark Job Training Partnership Act. Regulatory reform legislation, a responsible clean air act, and passage of enterprise zone legislation will also create new incentives for jobs and opportunity.

One out of every five jobs in our country depends on trade. So, I will propose a broader strategy in the field of international trade — one that increases the openness of our trading system and is fairer to America's farmers and workers in the world marketplace. We must have adequate export financing to sell American products overseas. I will ask for new negotiating authority to remove barriers and get more of our products into foreign markets. We must strengthen the organization of our trade agencies and make changes in our domestic laws and international trade policy to promote free trade and the increased flow of American goods, services, and investments.

Our trade position can also be improved by making our port system more efficient. Better, more active harbors translate into stable jobs in our coalfields, railroads, trucking industry, and ports. After 2 years of debate, it is time for us to get together and enact a port modernization bill.

Education, training, and retraining are fundamental to our success, as are research and development and productivity. Labor, management, and government at all levels can and must participate in improving these tools of growth. Tax policy, regulatory practices, and government programs all need constant reevaluation in terms of our competitiveness. Every American has a role and a stake in international trade.

[Education and Status of Women]

We Americans are still the technological leaders in most fields. We must keep that edge, and to do so we need to begin renewing the basics — starting with our educational system. While we grew complacent, others have acted. Japan, with a population only about half the size of ours, graduates from its universities more engineers than we do. If a child does not receive adequate math and science teaching by the age of 16, he or she has lost the chance to be a scientist or an engineer. We must join together — parents, teachers, grassroots groups, organized labor, and the business community — to revitalize American education by setting a standard of excellence.

In 1983 we seek four major education goals: a quality education initiative to encourage a substantial upgrading of math and science instruction through block grants to the States; establishment of education savings accounts that will give middle- and lower-income families an incentive to save for their children's college education and, at the same time, encourage a real increase in savings for economic growth; passage of tuition tax credits for parents who want to send their children to private or religiously affiliated schools; a constitutional amendment to permit voluntary school prayer. God should never have been expelled from America's classrooms in the first place.

Our commitment to fairness means that we must assure legal and economic equity for women, and eliminate, once and for all, all traces of unjust discrimination against women from the United States Code. We will not tolerate wage discrimination based on sex, and we intend to strengthen enforcement of child support laws to ensure that single parents, most of whom are women, do not suffer unfair financial hardship. We will also take action to remedy inequities in pensions. These initiatives will be joined by others to continue our efforts to promote equity for women.

Also in the area of fairness and equity, we will ask for extension of the Civil Rights Commission, which is due to expire this year. The Commission is an important part of the ongoing struggle for justice in America, and we strongly support its reauthorization. Effective enforcement of our nation's fair housing laws is also essential to ensuring equal opportunity. In the year ahead, we'll work to strengthen enforcement of fair housing laws for all Americans.

[Problems Facing United States]

The time has also come for major reform of our criminal justice statutes and acceleration of the drive against organized crime and drug trafficking. It's high time that we make our cities safe again. This administration hereby declares an all-out war on big-time organized crime and the drug racketeers who are poisoning our young people. We will also implement recommendations of our Task Force on Victims of Crime, which will report to me this week.

American agriculture, the envy of the world, has become the victim of its own successes. With one farmer now producing enough food to feed himself and 77 other people, America is confronted with record surplus crops and commodity prices below the cost of production. We must strive, through innovations like the payment-in-kind "crop swap" approach and an aggressive export policy, to restore health and vitality to rural America. Meanwhile, I have instructed the Department of Agriculture to work individually with farmers with debt problems to help them through these tough times.

Over the past year, our Task Force on Private Sector Initiatives has successfully forged a working partnership involving leaders of business, labor, education, and government to address the training needs of American workers. Thanks to the Task Force, private sector initiatives are now underway in all 50 States of the Union, and thousands of working people have been helped in making the shift from dead-end jobs and low-demand skills to the growth areas of high technology and the service economy. Additionally, a major effort will be focused on encouraging the expansion of private community child care. The new advisory council on private sector initiatives will carry on and extend this vital work of encouraging private initiative in 1983.

In the coming year, we will also act to improve the quality of life for Americans by curbing the skyrocketing cost of health care that is becoming an unbearable financial burden for so many. And we will submit legislation to provide catastrophic illness insurance coverage for older Americans.

I will also shortly submit a comprehensive federalism proposal that will continue our efforts to restore to States and local governments their roles as dynamic laboratories of change in a creative society.

During the next several weeks, I will send to the Congress a series of detailed proposals on these and other topics and look forward to working with you on the development of these initiatives.

So far, now, I've concentrated mainly on the problems posed by the future. But in almost every home and workplace in America, we're already witnessing reason for great hope — the first flowering of the man-made miracles of high technology, a field pioneered and still led by our country.

To many of us now, computers, silicon chips, data processing, cybernetics, and all the other innovations of the dawning high technology age are as mystifying as the workings of the combustion engine must have been when that first Model T rattled down Main Street, U.S.A. But as surely as America's pioneer spirit made us the industrial giant of the 20th century, the same pioneer spirit today is opening up on another vast frontier of opportunity, the frontier of high technology.

In conquering the frontier we cannot write off our traditional industries, but we must develop the skills and industries that will make us a pioneer of tomorrow. This administration is committed to keeping America the technological leader of the world now and into the 21st century.

[America as World Leader]

But let us turn briefly to the international arena. America's leadership in the world came to us because of our own strength and because of the values which guide us as a society: free elections, a free press, freedom of religious choice, free trade unions, and above all, freedom for the individual and rejection of the arbitrary power of the State. These values are the bedrock of our strength. They unite us in a stewardship of peace and freedom with our allies and friends in NATO, in Asia, in Latin America and elsewhere. There are also the values which in the recent past some among us had begun to doubt and view with a cynical eye.

Fortunately, we and our allies have rediscovered the strength of our common democratic values, and we're applying them as a cornerstone of a comprehensive strategy for peace with freedom. In London last year, I announced the commitment of the United States to developing the infrastructure of democracy throughout the world. We intend to pursue this democratic initiative vigorously. The future belongs not to governments and ideologies which oppress their peoples, but to democratic systems of self-government which encourage individual initiative and guarantee personal freedom.

But our strategy for peace with freedom must also be based on strength — economic strength and military strength. A strong American economy is essential to the well-being and security of our friends and allies. The restoration of a strong, healthy American economy has been and remains one of the central pillars of our foreign policy. The progress I have been able to report to you tonight will, I know, be as warmly welcomed by the rest of the world as it is by the American people.

We must also recognize that our own economic well-being is inextricably linked to the world economy. We export over 20 percent of our industrial production, and 40 percent of our farmland produces for export. We will continue to work closely with the industrialized democracies of Europe and Japan and with the International Monetary Fund to ensure it has adequate resources to help bring the world economy back to strong, noninflationary growth.

As the leader of the West and as a country that has become great and rich because of economic freedom, America must be an unrelenting advocate of free trade. As some nations are tempted to turn to protectionism, our strategy cannot be to follow them, but to lead the way toward freer trade. To this end, in May of this year, America will host an economic summit meeting in Williamsburg, Virginia.

[Defense and Foreign Policy]

As we begin our third year, we have put in place a defense program that redeems the neglect of the past decade. We have developed a realistic military strategy to deter threats to peace and to protect freedom if deterrence fails. Our Armed Forces are finally properly paid; after years of neglect are well trained and becoming better equipped and supplied. And the American uniform is once again worn with pride. Most of the major systems needed for modernizing our defenses are already underway, and we will be addressing one key system, the MX missile, in consultation with the Congress in a few months.

America's foreign policy is once again based on bipartisanship, on realism, strength, full partnership, in consultation with our allies, and constructive negotiation with potential adversaries. From the Middle East to southern Africa to Geneva, American diplomats are taking the initiative to make peace and lower arms levels. We should be proud of our role as peacemakers.

In the Middle East last year, the United States played the major role in ending the tragic fighting in Lebanon and negotiated the withdrawal of the PLO from Beirut.

Last September, I outlined principles to carry on the peace process begun so promisingly at Camp David. All the people of the Middle East should know that in the year ahead we will not flag in our efforts to build on that foundation to bring them the blessings of peace.

In Central America and the Caribbean Basin, we are likewise engaged in a partnership for peace, prosperity, and democracy. Final passage of the remaining portions of our Caribbean Basin Initiative, which passed the House last year, is one of this administration's top legislative priorities for 1983.

The security and economic assistance policies of this administration in Latin America and elsewhere are based on realism and represent a critical investment in the future of the human race. This undertaking is a joint responsibility of the executive and legislative branches, and I'm counting on the cooperation and statesmanship of the Congress to help us meet this essential foreign policy goal.

[U.S.-Soviet Relations]

At the heart of our strategy for peace is our relationship with the Soviet Union. The past year saw a change in Soviet leadership. We're prepared for a positive change in Soviet-American relations. But the Soviet Union must show by deeds as well as words a sincere commitment to respect the rights and sovereignty of the family of nations. Responsible members of the world community do not threaten or invade their neighbors. And they restrain their allies from aggression.

For our part, we're vigorously pursuing arms reduction negotiations with the Soviet Union. Supported by our allies, we've put forward draft agreements proposing significant weapon reductions to equal and verifiable lower levels. We insist on an equal balance of forces. And given the overwhelming evidence of Soviet violations of international treaties concerning chemical and biological weapons, we also insist that any agreement we sign can and will be verifiable.

In the case of intermediate-range nuclear forces, we have proposed the complete elimination of the entire class of land-based missiles. We're also prepared to carefully explore serious Soviet proposals. At the same time, let me emphasize that allied steadfastness remains a key to achieving arms reductions.

With firmness and dedication, we'll continue to negotiate. Deep down, the Soviets must know it is in their interests as well as ours to prevent a wasteful arms race. And once they recognize our unshakeable resolve to maintain adequate deterrence, they will have every reason to join us in the search for greater security and major arms reductions. When that moment comes — and I am confident that it will — we will have taken an important step toward a more peaceful future for all the world's people.

[America's Noble Vision]

A very wise man, Bernard Baruch, once said that America has never forgotten the nobler things that brought her into being and that light her path. Our country is a special place, because we Americans have always been sustained, through good times and bad, by a noble vision — a vision not only of what the world around us is today but what we as a free people can make it be tomorrow.

We're realists; we solve our problems instead of ignoring them, no matter how loud the chorus of despair around us. But we're also idealists, for it was an ideal that brought our ancestors to these shores from every corner of the world.

Right now we need both realism and idealism. Millions of our neighbors are without work. It is up to us to see they aren't without hope. This is a task for all of us. And may I say, Americans have rallied to this cause, proving once again that we are the most generous people on Earth.

We who are in Government must take the lead in restoring the economy.

[Applause] And here all that time, I thought you were reading the paper. *[Laughter.]*

The single thing — the single thing that can start the wheels of industry turning again is further reduction of interest rates. Just another 1 or 2 points can mean tens of thousands of jobs.

Right now, with inflation as low as it is, 3.9 percent, there is room for interest rates to come down. Only fear prevents their reduction. A lender, as we know, must charge an interest rate that recovers the depreciated value of the dollars loaned. And that depreciation is, of course, the amount of inflation. Today, interest rates are based on fear — fear that government will resort to measures, as it has in the past, that will send inflation zooming again.

We who serve here in this Capital must erase that fear by making it absolutely clear that we will not stop fighting inflation; that, together, we will do only these things that will lead to lasting economic growth.

Yes, the problems confronting us are large and forbidding. And, certainly, no one can or should minimize the plight of millions of our friends and neighbors who are living in the bleak emptiness of unemployment. But we must and can give them good reason to be hopeful.

Back over the years, citizens like ourselves have gathered within these walls when our nation was threatened; sometimes when its very existence was at stake. Always, with courage and commonsense, they met the crises of their time and lived to see a stronger, better, and more prosperous country. The present situation is no worse and in fact is not as bad as some of those they faced. Time and again, they proved that there is nothing we Americans cannot achieve as free men and women.

Yes, we still have problems — plenty of them. But it's just plain wrong — unjust to our country and unjust to our people — to let those problems stand in the way of the most important truth of all: America is on the mend.

We owe it to the unfortunate to be aware of their plight and to help them in every way we can. No one can quarrel with that — we must and do have compassion for all the victims of this economic crisis. But the big story about America today is the way that millions of confident, caring people — those extraordinary "ordinary" Americans who never make the headlines and will never be interviewed — are laying the foundation, not just for recovery from our present problems but for a better tomorrow for all our people.

From coast to coast, on the job and in classrooms and laboratories, at new construction sites and in churches and in community groups, neighbors are helping neighbors. And they've already begun the building, the research, the work, and the giving that will make our community great again.

I believe this, because I believe in them — in the strength of their hearts and minds, in the commitment that each one of them brings to their daily lives, be they high or humble. The challenge for us in government is to be worthy of them — to make government a help, not a hinderance to our people in the challenging but promising days ahead.

If we do that, if we care what our children and our children's children will say of us, if we want them one day to be thankful for what we did here in these temples of freedom, we will work together to make America better for our having been here — not just in this year or in this decade but in the next century and beyond.

Thank you and God bless you.

REVISED CANON LAW CODE

January 25, 1983

Pope John Paul II approved January 25 a new set of laws to govern the Western rites of the Roman Catholic Church. The product of a 24-year effort, the code was the first revision of church laws since they were first codified in 1917. The revised code, which governed the religious practices of more than 735 million Roman Catholics, went into effect November 27. Although it was radically different from the 1917 code, many of the changes it contained already had been effected.

The new code was divided into six books and consisted of 1,752 separate laws (canons), about 700 fewer than the 1917 code. Because canon law governs procedures and is subordinate to dogma (that is, it spells out practices to implement the church's basic teachings), its statutes were open to varying interpretations.

The general thrust of the new code was to decentralize the church hierarchy by broadening the authority of bishops, widening the role of lay people in the church, eliminating a number of prohibitions and lessening the severity of punishments for violations of certain church codes. The revised law did not, however, change prohibitions on abortions, divorce, use of contraceptives, public office holding by clerics or the ordaining of women into the priesthood.

Background

Until the 20th century there was no single systematic code of laws governing the Western Roman Catholic Church. By the time of Vatican

Council I (1869-70) it had become apparent that the church's legislative activities were in considerable confusion. But it was not until 1904 that Pope Pius X ordered a complete codification of the numerous principles of law affecting church practices. The work took 13 years to complete; in 1917 Pope Benedict XV promulgated the first Code of Canon Law, which took effect a year later. Modeled after 19th century European civil codes, the work consisted of 2,414 canons divided into five books.

Although the pope indicated he would establish a body to update the code regularly, the group never was convened, and by the mid-century it was again apparent that revisions were in order. Responding to that need, Pope John XXIII in 1963 established a commission of cardinals to revise the law (he had announced his intention to do so in 1959). The bulk of the work was accomplished during the 15-year stewardship of Pope Paul VI, who succeeded John XXIII. The revisions were closely linked to the reform movement symbolized in the Second Vatican Council. Between the end of Vatican II in 1965 and Pope Paul VI's death in 1978, a number of reforms had become law, including major revisions in the liturgy, the formation and development of the Synod of Bishops as well as national conferences of bishops, and reorganization and decentralization of church power.

The 1967 world Synod of Bishops was asked to draw up norms for revising the code. The final plenary meeting of the code commission, held in October 1981, approved final revisions and submitted them to Pope John Paul II for approval.

Major Features of the Code

Because many of the reforms already had been introduced by church decree or were accepted practice as a result of Vatican II, "A document that would have been considered revolutionary 20 years ago actually contains very few surprises today," said Rev. Vincent O'Keefe, former president of Fordham University and a senior official with the Society of Jesus headquarters in Rome. "It's been talked about for nearly a quarter of a century, and now that it's here everyone is looking ahead to the unfinished work of Vatican II, the reorganization of the Curia and the intellectual and spiritual formation of seminarians." O'Keefe's remarks reflected the views of numerous other theologians and religious scholars.

The revised code reduced from 37 to seven the number of offenses that resulted in immediate and automatic excommunication. The remaining excommunicable offenses were abortion, violation of the confidentiality of a confession, absolution by a priest of a person who had committed a sin with the priest's assistance, profanation of the consecrated sacred communion host, consecration of a bishop without the Vatican's approval, a physical attack on the pope and heresy.

The law made it possible for lay people, both men and women, to take over some duties normally performed by priests in parishes where there was a shortage of priests. Lay people could be granted authority to manage a parish, serve on a parish council and on the diocesan synod, perform weddings and officiate at funerals. However, they were not authorized to say mass or hear confessions, duties that continued to be reserved for priests.

The code contained some advances for women's rights, although women remained excluded from ordained ministry, could not be formally installed in the lay ministries as lector or acolyte, or serve the priest at the altar for mass. However, women were allowed to become diocesan chancellors, auditors, assessors, financial administrators and seminary board members. They also were authorized to serve on diocesan annulment tribunals.

Among the restrictions dropped from the new code were laws against cremation, marriages with non-Catholic Christians and membership in the Masons.

A number of American bishops expressed concern about the code's requirement that all theologians must receive permission from their religious superiors before they could teach theology. The bishops argued that the requirement could produce a church-state relation that would bar government financial aid to an educational institution under the Constitution's Establishment Clause.

Another requirement troubling some American Catholics was one that would force the church to give up a simplified system of marriage tribunals for annulment. The code required a more complicated and time-consuming system whereby annulment cases would be reviewed by a church appeals panel following initial approval of the annulment by a church court.

Assessing the impact of the revised code, a number of theologians said that, more important than specific changes, was the more general thrust of the code; it emphasized human needs and conscience, appeared to place the church in a less authoritarian role and, by the same token, allowed more freedom of choice for laity and clergy alike. They pointed out that the revised code was not a fixed document and that the canons would be undergoing constant review.

Following are excerpts, arranged by subject, of some of the principal canons contained in The Code of Canon Law of the Roman Catholic Church (English translation prepared by The Canon Law Society Trust), approved by Pope John Paul II on January 25, 1983. (Boldface headings in brackets have been added by Congressional Quarterly to highlight the organization of the text.):

[Lay Participation]

Can. 129 § 1   Those who are in sacred orders are, in accordance with the provisions of law, capable of the power of governance, which belongs to the Church by divine institution. This power is also called the power of jurisdiction.

§ 2   Lay members of Christ's faithful can cooperate in the exercise of this same power in accordance with the law. . . .

Can. 227   To lay members of Christ's faithful belongs the right to have acknowledged as theirs that freedom in secular affairs which is common to all citizens. In using this freedom, however, they are to ensure that their actions are permeated with the spirit of the Gospel, and they are to heed the teaching of the Church proposed by the *magisterium,* but they must be on guard, in questions of opinion, against proposing their own view as the teaching of the Church.

Can. 228 § 1   Lay people who are found to be suitable are capable of being admitted by the sacred Pastors to those ecclesiastical offices and functions which, in accordance with the provisions of law, they can discharge.

§ 2   Lay people who are outstanding in the requisite knowledge, prudence and integrity, are capable of being experts or advisors, even in councils in accordance with the law, in order to provide assistance to the Pastors of the Church.

Can. 229 § 1   Lay people have the duty and the right to acquire the knowledge of christian teaching which is appropriate to each one's capacity and condition, so that they may be able to live according to this teaching, to proclaim it and if necessary to defend it, and may be capable of playing their part in the exercise of the apostolate.

§ 2   They also have the right to acquire that fuller knowledge of the sacred sciences which is taught in ecclesiastical universties or faculties or in institutes of religious sciences, attending lectures there and acquiring academic degrees.

§ 3   Likewise, assuming that the provisions concerning the requisite suitability have been observed, they are capable of receiving from the lawful ecclesiastical authority a mandate to teach the sacred sciences.

Can. 230 § 1   Lay men whose age and talents meet the requirements prescribed by decree of the Episcopal Conference, can be given the stable ministry of lector and of acolyte, through the prescribed liturgical rite. This conferral of ministry does not, however, give them a right to sustenance or remuneration from the Church.

§ 2   Lay people can recieve a temporary assignment to the role of lector in liturgical actions. Likewise, all lay people can exercise the roles of commentator, cantor or other such, in accordance with the law.

§ 3   Where the needs of the Church require and ministers are not available, lay people, even though they are not lectors or acolytes, can supply certain of their functions, that is, exercise the ministry of the word, preside over liturgical prayers, confer baptism and distribute Holy Communion, in accordance with the provisions of the law. . . .

Can. 463 § 1   The following are to be summoned to the diocesan synod as members and they are obliged to participate in it. . . .

§ 2   The diocesan Bishop may also invite others to be members of the diocesan synod, whether clerics or members of institutes of consecrated life or lay members of the faithful.

§ 3   If the diocesan Bishop considers it opportune, he may invite to the diocesan Synod as observers some ministers or members of Churches or ecclesiastical communities which are not in full communion with the catholic Church. . . .

Can. 511   In each diocese, in so far as pastoral circumstances suggest, a pastoral council is to be established. Its function, under the authority of the Bishop, is to study and weigh those matters which concern the pastoral works in the diocese, and to propose practical conclusions concerning them.

Can. 512 § 1   A pastoral council is composed of members of Christ's faithful who are in full communion with the catholic Church: clerics, members of institutes of consecrated life, and especially lay people. They are designated in the manner determined by the diocesan Bishop.

§ 2   The members of Christ's faithful assigned to the pastoral council are to be selected in such a way that the council truly reflects the entire portion of the people of God which constitutes the diocese, taking account of the different regions of the diocese, of social conditions and professions, and of the part played in the apostolate by the members, whether individually or in association with others.

§ 3   Only those members of Christ's faithful who are outstanding in firm faith, high moral standards and prudence are to be assigned to the pastoral council. . . .

[Bishops' Powers]

Can. 87 § 1   Whenever he judges that it contributes to their spiritual welfare, the diocesan Bishop can dispense the faithful from disciplinary laws, both universal laws and those particular laws made by the supreme ecclesiastical authority for his territory or his subjects. He cannot dispense from procedural laws or from penal laws, nor from those whose dispensation is specially reserved to the Apostolic See or to some other authority.

§ 2   If recourse to the Holy See is difficult, and at the same time there is danger of grave harm in delay, any Ordinary can dispense from these laws, even if the dispensation is reserved to the Holy See, provided the dispensation is one which the Holy See customarily grants in the same circumstances, and without prejudice to can. 291 [a dispensation from celibacy is granted solely by the pope]. . . .

Can. 88 The local Ordinary can dispense from diocesan laws and . . . from laws made by a plenary or a provincial Council or by the Episcopal Conference. . . .

[Ban on Holding Public Office]

Can. 285 § 1   Clerics are to shun completely everything that is unbecoming to their state, in accordance with the provisions of particular law.

§ 2   Clerics are to avoid whatever is foreign to their state, even when it is not unseemly.

§ 3   Clerics are forbidden to assume public office whenever it means sharing in the exercise of civil power.

§ 4   Without the permission of their Ordinary, they may not undertake the administrations of goods belonging to lay people, or secular offices which involve the obligation to render an account. They are forbidden to act as surety, even concerning their own goods, without consulting their proper Ordinary. they are not to sign promissory notes which involve the payment of money but do not state the reasons for the payment.

Can. 286   Clerics are forbidden to practise commerce or trade, either personally or through another, for their own or another's benefit, except with the permission of the lawful ecclesiastical authority. . . .

Ecclesiastical Universities and Faculties

Can. 815   By virtue of its office to announce revealed truth, it belongs to the Church to have its own ecclesiastical universities and faculties to study the sacred sciences and subjects related to them, and to teach these disciplines to students in a scientific manner.

Can. 816 § 1   Ecclesiastical universities and faculties may be constituted only by the Apostolic See or with its approval. . . .

§ 2   Each ecclesiastical university and faculty must have its own statutes and program of studies, approved by the Apostolic See.

Can. 817   Only a university or a faculty established or approved by the Apostolic See may confer academic degrees which have canonical effects in the Church. . . .

[Marriage]

Can. 1135   Each spouse has an equal obligation and right to whatever pertains to the partnership of conjugal life. . . .

Can. 1141   A marriage which is ratified and consummated cannot be dissolved by any human power or by any cause other than death. . . .

Can. 1124   Without the express permission of the competent authority, marriage is prohibited between two baptised persons, one of whom was baptised in the catholic Church or received into it after baptism and has not defected from it by a formal act, the other of whom belongs to a Church or ecclesial community not in full communion with the catholic Church.

Can. 1125   The local Ordinary can grant this permission if there is a just and reasonable cause. . . .

[Church Funerals]

Can. 1176 § 1   Christ's faithful who have died are to be given a Church funeral according to the norms of law.

§ 2   Church funerals are to be celebrated according to the norms of the liturgical books. In these funeral rites the Church prays for the spiritual support of the dead, it honours their bodies, and at the same time it brings to the living the comfort of hope.

§ 3   The Church earnestly recommends that the pious custom of burial be retained; but it does not forbid cremation, unless this is chosen for reasons which are contrary to christian teaching. . . .

[Excommunicable Offenses]

Can. 1364 § 1   An apostate from the faith, a heretic or a schismatic incurs a *latae sententiae* [automatically incurred on committing an offence, without the intervention of a judge or superior] excommunication. . . .

§ 2   If a longstanding contempt or the gravity of scandal calls for it, other penalties may be added, not excluding dismissal from the clerical state. . . .

Can. 1367   One who throws away the consecrated species or, for a sacriligious purpose, takes them away or keeps them, incurs a *latae sententiae* excommunication reserved to the Apostolic See; a cleric, moreover, may be punished with some other penalty, not excluding dismissal from the clerical state. . . .

Can. 1370 § 1   A person who uses physical force against the Roman Pontiff incurs a *latae sententiae* excommunication reserved to the Apostolic See; if the offender is a cleric, another penalty, not excluding dismissal from the clerical state, may be added according to the gravity of the crime.

§ 2   One who does this against a Bishop incurs a *latae sententiae* interdict and, if a cleric, he incurs also a *latae sententiae* suspension. . . .

Can. 1378 § 1   A priest who acts against the prescription of can. 977 [the cannon states that absolving a partner who sins against the sixth commandment of the Decalogue (thou shalt not commit adultery) is invalid, except in danger of death] incurs a *latae sententiae* excommunication reserved to the Apostolic See. . . .

Can. 1388 § 1   A confessor who directly violates the sacramental seal, incurs a *latae sententiae* excommunication reserved to the Apostolic See; he who does so only indirectly is to be punished according to the gravity of the offence. . . .

Can. 1390 § 1   A person who falsely denounces a confessor of the offence mentioned in can. 1387 [soliciting a penitent to commit adultery] to an ecclesiastical Superior, incurs a *latae sententiae* interdict and, if a cleric, he incurs also a suspension. . . .

[Can. 1387   A priest who in confession, or on the occasion or under the pretext of confession, solicits a penitent to commit a sin against the sixth commandment of the Decalogue, is to be punished, according to the gravity of the offence, with suspension, prohibitions and deprivations; in the more serious cases he is to be dismissed from the clerical state.]
Can. 1398   A person who actually procures an abortion incurs a *latae sententiae* excommunication. . . .

PRESIDENT'S BUDGET MESSAGE
January 31, 1983

President Ronald Reagan sent his annual budget request to Congress January 31, asking $848.5 billion in expenditures for the fiscal year beginning October 1, 1983. The budget anticipated a deficit of $188.8 billion even if $43 billion in budget savings recommended by the administration was adopted. But large as it was, the projected deficit was smaller than a shortfall of $207.7 billion that had been forecast for fiscal 1983.

The centerpiece of the president's fiscal 1984 budget was a spending "freeze" that, together with "structural reforms" in entitlement programs and other proposals, would hold fiscal 1984 spending to an amount only 5 percent (about the expected rate of inflation) over the previous year's spending. But the president's request for $238.6 billion for defense would boost the expenditures of that department in fiscal 1984 by 14.2 percent.

Striking a bipartisan note in his budget message, the president said his administration would work with Congress "to accommodate those special concerns of the legislative branch that have caused unnecessary strains in the past." The early reaction of many legislative leaders was to applaud what they said were the budget's realistic economic assumptions and sound projections.

Economic Assumptions

The president's budget predicted that an economic recovery from the worst recession since World War II would begin during the first half of

1983, "with greatest momentum during the year's second half." It estimated that real output as measured by the gross national product (GNP) would rise 3.1 percent from the fourth quarter of 1982 to the fourth quarter of 1983. Output was expected to grow only 4 percent in 1984, a small increase following a recession, as compared with historical patterns.

The budget forecast that both inflation and interest rates would continue to moderate. The consumer price index (CPI) was expected to rise 5 percent from the fourth quarter of 1982 to the fourth quarter of 1983 and another 4.4 percent in 1984. The rate on 91-day Treasury bills, 8.02 percent as the budget was released, was expected to average 8 percent in the fourth quarter of 1983 and 7.8 percent in the final quarter of 1984. Unemployment was seen as remaining at very high levels — averaging 10.7 percent in 1983 and 9.9 percent in 1984.

Defense Budget

After allowing for inflation, the Defense Department estimated that its fiscal 1984 request would provide a spending increase over the previous year's budget of 10.26 percent. The budget showed the fastest growing part of the defense program, in terms of real purchasing power, to be the nation's strategic nuclear forces. For strategic nuclear forces the request was $28.1 billion, up more than 30 percent over fiscal 1983.

The defense budget included $6.6 billion for the MX intercontinental missile. Of that amount, $2.8 billion was requested to build 27 of the missiles and $3.38 billion to continue development of the weapon, called Peacekeeper by President Reagan. (MX deployment, p. 365)

The budget recommended the procurement of 10 B-1 bombers costing $6.18 billion. It requested a secret amount to continue the development of a "stealth" bomber, intended to be more difficult than conventional bombers for Soviet radars to detect.

Four-Part Plan

The Reagan budget predicted triple-digit deficits for the next five years. The deficit would rise to $194.2 billion in fiscal 1985, it forecast, before beginning a gradual fall to about $117 billion in fiscal 1988. In order to "set the budget on the path that is consistent with long-term economic recovery," Reagan proposed a four-part plan designed to reduce spending over five years by $558 billion.

The first part of the savings plan called for a "freeze" that would affect non-defense discretionary programs, medical provider reimbursement and farm price supports. The second part of the plan would focus on "structural" reforms in entitlement and similar programs (entitlement *expenditures include items such as Social Security, welfare payments and food stamps). The third part would impose economies in the Defense Department anticipated to save $55 billion over the five-year period. The economies would, the budget said, "fully protect strategic programs and readiness. . . ." Finally, the fourth part would be a "contingency" tax plan designed to take effect in fiscal 1986 if federal deficits remained high.*

Congressional Reaction

While Reagan's fiscal 1984 budget was praised widely by legislators as a document they could work with, their reaction was sharply divided over its priorities. Senate Majority Leader Howard H. Baker Jr., R-Tenn., predicted that the budget ultimately would "look a lot more like Ronald Reagan's budget than anyone else's." Defending the Reagan budget, Sen. John Tower, R-Texas, chairman of the Armed Services Committee, said that senators who wanted to reduce the budget might suggest cuts that could be made on defense programs affecting their home states.

During a hearing held February 3 by the House Budget Committee, Rep. Leon E. Panetta, D-Calif., a committee member, cited $107 billion in social cuts compared with $300 billion in defense increases over the next five years. He asked David A. Stockman, the director of the Office of Management and Budget, "Where's the fairness here? Let's not kid the American people. You're cutting programs, you're cutting people."

> *Following are excerpts from the text of President Ronald Reagan's January 31, 1983, budget message to Congress.* (Boldface headings in brackets have been added by Congressional Quarterly to highlight the organization of the text.):

To the Congress of the United States:

Two years ago, in my first address to the country, I went before the American people to report on the condition of our economy, which had suffered from many years of seriously misguided policies. I made a strong commitment to change the traditional shortsighted view that had previously been taken on economic priorities so that we could achieve our goal of long-term prosperity. I stated that we had a massive job before us.

Government spending was taking a rapidly increasing share of national income, burdensome Government regulation had stunted productivity increases, and excessive tax rates combined with erratic monetary policy resulted in serious disincentives to investment and long-term real economic growth. Inflation was at double-digit levels. Interest rates were at record highs. Real growth and job creation had ceased. New investment, productivity, and personal saving were stagnant. Our economy was in the worst mess in half a century.

To make matters worse, our military strength had been allowed to run down relative to the aggressively expanding military might of the Soviet Union. We were in serious danger of becoming powerless to deter or counter Soviet aggression around the world.

The economic program that I proposed at that time focused on long-range real growth. My tax proposals were designed to provide badly needed private incentives to stimulate saving and productive investment. I supported the Federal Reserve in its pursuit of sound monetary policy. I worked with the Congress to reverse the growth of Government programs that had become too large or outlasted their usefulness. I worked to eliminate or simplify unnecessary or burdensome regulations.

The unprecedented buildup of inflationary forces in the 1970's, however, exacerbated in severity and duration the economic downturn of recent years. One of the key detrimental forces has been the growing Federal budget. Despite our success in reducing the rate of growth of nondefense spending in the last two budgets, spending in 1983 will exceed 1981 levels by 21%, reflecting continued increases in basic entitlement programs, essential increases in defense spending, and rapid growth of interest costs.

Thus, the full effect of the changes we have made is taking time to develop. Over-reactive short-term remedies are not the answer. What is essential now is that we continue to work together to rebuild this country — without losing sight of the four fundamentals of our economic program:

• Limiting tax burdens to the minimum levels necessary to finance essential Government services, thus maintaining incentives for saving, investment, work effort, productivity, and economic growth.

• Reducing the growth of overall Federal spending by eliminating Federal activities that overstep the proper sphere of Federal Government responsibilities and by restraining the growth of spending for other Federal activities.

• Reducing the Federal regulatory burden in areas where the Federal Government intrudes unnecessarily into our private lives or interferes unnecessarily with the efficient conduct of private business or of State or local government.

• Supporting a moderate and steady monetary policy, to bring inflation under control.

Two Years of Accomplishment

Over the past 2 years, dramatic improvements have been made in the way the Government affects our economy. The Congress joined with my administration in a cooperative and politically courageous effort to reverse a decade of runaway growth in spending and tax burdens, proliferation of unnecessary regulations and red tape, and erosion of our military strength.

Both the Omnibus Reconciliation Acts of 1981 and 1982 effected fundamental reforms in numerous Federal programs, and demonstrated a greatly heightened level of maturity and responsibility of the congressional budget process that has come to fruition with the help and support of this administration. Although I am disappointed that many administration spending-reduction proposals did not pass last year — which has resulted in higher deficits — I believe that the revitalized congressional budget process signifies a refreshing willingness on the part of the Congress to work with my administration to address squarely the many crucial, complex, and politically difficult budgetary dilemmas before us. The results have been impressive:

• Where the growth rate of spending was almost out of control at 17.4% a year in 1980, it is now declining dramatically — to 10.5% this year, and, with this budget, to 5.4% next year — which is no more than the projected rate of inflation; in effect, a comprehensive freeze on total Federal spending.

• Where spending growth totaled $220 billion from 1978 to 1981, a 48% increase, spending will rise by only 27% from 1981 to 1984, despite legislated cost-of-living adjustments and the needed defense buildup.

• For the first time since the Second World War, the Federal tax system has been fundamentally restructured. Income tax rates have been substantially reduced, greatly improving the climate for savings and investment. Excessive taxation of business income resulting from depreciation allowances rendered inadequate by inflation has been eliminated through depreciation reform. Tax loopholes have been closed, making the tax structure more equitable. Emphasis is shifting to financing programs through user fees commensurate with benefits and services provided.

• The excessive rates of growth of entitlement programs were curbed. Overly-broad eligibility criteria were tightened to limit benefit awards more to the truly needy, and eliminate or restrict unnecessary and costly payments of welfare-type benefits to those who are relatively well off and are, or ought to be, self-supporting. Overly-generous and unnecessarily frequent cost-of-living adjustments were pared back. Nonetheless, the growth of these programs has proven difficult to control and continues to be the primary cause of higher deficits.

• Limitation of Federal credit activity and off-budget spending is being achieved.

• The burgeoning growth of Federal regulations and red tape has been capped. The number of proposed new regulations has been reduced by one-third in the past 2 years. Unnecessary costs of Federal regulation to individuals, businesses, and State and local governments have been reduced by $6 billion in annual expenditures and $9 to $11 billion in capital costs. By the end of 1983, the time our citizens spend filling out Federal forms and reports will have been cut by over 300 million hours annually.

• Improvements in the management of Federal operations, such as better procedures for the collection of debts owed the Government and better cash-management practices, are being carried out. These improvements have helped reduce waste, fraud, and abuse in Government programs.

• And by the end of the 1982 fiscal year, the Federal nondefense workforce has been reduced by 91,300 employees since I took office.

During the past 2 years, we have also taken decisive measures to increase our military strength. At the same time, diplomatic approaches to increase our national security, such as arms reduction talks, have been vigorously pursued.

The improvement in our defense posture includes all of its major elements. Long-overdue modernization of our strategic forces is proceeding with new bomber-, submarine-, and land-based missile programs. Our conventional forces are also being modernized and strengthened, with new ships, tanks, and aircraft. Above all, successful recruiting and retention over the past 18 months have resulted in all of our armed services being more fully manned with capable, high-caliber men and women. The All Volunteer Force is now working well.

By any standards, these are accomplishments to be proud of. And I am proud of them. We have come far in restoring order to the chaos prevailing in our economy and Government affairs just 2 years ago.

This is not to say that we do not still face great problems such as excessive unemployment, slower than desired economic growth, and high deficits. During the past 2 years our Nation has labored to purge itself of the inflationary disease that for nearly two decades had progressively undermined the economy's ability to generate growth, capital formation, worker productivity incentives, and financial stability. Those inflationary fevers have largely subsided in the aftermath of my decision 2 years ago to redirect economic policy toward a more modest size and scope for the Federal Government, a series of tax rate reductions to reward productive investment and work effort, and a restrained monetary policy to sustain the purchasing power of individual savings and income.

Accompanying the marked progress in unwinding the damaging inflation spiral that plagued our Nation for so many years, financial markets in 1982 experienced their first sustained improvement in more than 5 years. Interest rates throughout the maturity spectrum declined substantially, and by yearend we can proudly report that key rates for home mortgages, consumer loans, and business investment were able to sustain their lower levels, indicating new confidence in administration policies and bringing much needed relief to the housing and auto industries, the farm community, and the export sector.

Inflationary pressures of the sort experienced during the past two decades extracted a heavy toll from our economy. We have learned that the problems we inherited were far worse than most inside and out of Government had expected; the recession was deeper and longer than most inside and out of Government had predicted. Curing those problems has taken more time and a higher toll than any of us wanted. Unemployment is far too high.

Fortunately, the long nightmare of runaway inflation is now behind us. Slowly, but steadily and unmistakably, our national economy is completing the transition from recession to recovery. The interaction of lower tax rates, reduced inflation, and falling interest rates has placed the consumer and the producer in a much strengthened position with respect to balance sheets, liquidity, after-tax income, and purchasing power.

There are numerous signs that the battered, sputtering inflation-warped economy that we found 2 years ago is on the mend, and that the dislocation and hardship we have suffered in the interim will prove to be a corrective interlude on the path of sustained recovery. But our confidence must also be tempered by realism and patience. Quick fixes and artificial stimulants, repeatedly applied over decades, are what brought on the inflationary disorders that we have now paid such a heavy price to cure.

In part as a result of the difficult period of disinflation, during the past year and one-half our projections of the Federal deficit have steadily risen. They have now reached very high levels, creating uncertainty in the financial markets and threatening to block the economic recovery ahead of us.

But before we consider what is to be done, we must review how we got here. And the truth is that as in the case of the social security fund, the looming gaps in our national budget are the consequence of both the inflation that got out of hand and the correctives that have been unavoidably applied to cure it.

During the 1970's, the share of our national income devoted to domestic programs and transfer payments soared by more than 50% — from 10 cents to 16 cents on every dollar produced by the American people. For a brief time, it appeared that we could afford all of this generosity because inflation badly misled us.

As inflation reached higher and higher peaks, the Treasury's coffers swelled from its take on inflated incomes and the upward creep of tax rates. For a time, we even financed our trillion dollar national debt on the cheap with interest rates that had not yet caught up with the spiraling inflation.

Meanwhile, defense spending grew at less than 60% of inflation, making room in the budget for extra domestic programs. The real purchasing power available to maintain our readiness, modernize our weapons, and maintain strategic nuclear safety declined by a startling 20%.

But it couldn't last — and it didn't. Today the Federal budget itself has become a major victim of the economic transition:

● The inflationary revenue windfall has dried up.

● Our staggering national debt until recently was being financed at the highest interest rates in peacetime history.

● The undelayable process of restoring our inflation-eroded military budgets and our decayed military strength has further strained our resources.

● Despite our great strides in reducing the spending growth over the last 2 years, the vast edifice of domestic programs remains significantly in place.

The social security system has also been a victim of our economic ills. First, the rampant inflation drained its reserves as Government tried to keep beneficiaries up with the spiraling cost of living that its own mistaken policies had created in the first place. Now the recessionary adjustments to disinflation have temporarily deprived it of the expanding wage base and growing revenues required to support commitments to the retired and disabled. As a result, for too long the specter of social security insolvency has haunted our Nation's elderly citizens and threatened to rupture the lifeline on which 36 million retired and disabled Americans depend.

But however obvious the threat of insolvency, one thing is certain: social security cannot and will not be allowed to fail the 36 million Americans who depend on it. With this commitment in mind, it is especially pleasing to me to join with the Speaker of the House and the Senate Majority Leader in urging the Congress to enact the bipartisan compromise plan developed by the National Commission on Social Security Reform.

There are elements in it that none of us prefers, but taken together it forms a package all of us can support. It asks for some sacrifice by all — the self-employed, beneficiaries, workers, new government employees, and the better-off among the retired — but it imposes an undue burden on none. And, in supporting it, we keep an important pledge to the American people: the integrity of the social security system will be preserved — and no one's payments will be reduced.

Toward Economic Recovery

To enhance prospects for sustained economic recovery and lower unemployment, I am proposing a sweeping set of fiscal policy changes designed to reduce substantially the mounting Federal deficits that threaten the renewal of economic growth. My plan is based on these principles.

It must be bipartisan. Overcoming the deficits and putting the Government's house in order will require the best efforts of all of us.

It must be fair. Just as all will share in the benefits that will come from recovery, all should share fairly in the burden of transition.

It must be prudent. The strength of our national defense must be restored so that we can pursue prosperity in peace and freedom, while maintaining our commitment to the truly needy.

Finally, it must be realistic. We cannot rely on hope alone.

With these guiding principles in mind, let me outline a four-part plan to increase economic growth and reduce deficits.

First, I am recommending a Federal spending freeze. I know this is strong medicine, but so far we have cut only the rate of increase in Federal spending. The Government has continued to spend more money each year, though not as much more as it did in the past. Taken as a whole, the budget I am proposing for the next fiscal year will increase no more than the rate of inflation. . . . That is far less than many American families have had to do in these difficult times.

I will request that the proposed 6-month freeze in cost-of-living adjustments recommended by the bipartisan National Commission on Social Security Reform be applied to other Government benefit programs. I will also propose a 1-year freeze on a broad range of domestic spending programs, and for Federal civilian and military pay and pension programs.

Second, I will ask the Congress to adopt specific measures to control the growth of the so-called "uncontrollable" spending programs. These are the automatic spending programs, such as food stamps, that cannot be simply frozen —and that have grown by over 400% since 1970. They are the largest single cause of the built-in or "structural" deficit problem. Our standard here will be fairness — ensuring that the taxpayers' hard-earned dollars go only to the truly needy; that none of them is turned away; but that fraud and waste are stamped out. And, I am sorry to say, there is a lot of it out there. In the food stamp program alone, last year we identified almost $1.1 billion in overpayments. The taxpayers are not the only victims of this kind of abuse; the truly needy suffer, as funds intended for them are taken by the greedy. For everyone's sake, we must put an end to such waste and corruption.

Third, I will adjust our program to restore America's defenses by proposing $55 billion in defense savings over the next 5 years. These are savings recommended to me by the Secretary of Defense, who has assured me they can be safely achieved and will not diminish our ability to negotiate arms reductions or endanger America's security. We will not gamble with our national survival. As a percent of GNP, the level I am requesting for defense spending in 1984 is less than the United States spent during the decade of the 1960's. As a percent of the total Federal budget it is far less than was allocated for national defense in those years. We are 2 years into the program to re-arm America. Sustaining the momentum of this program is essential if we are to avoid slipping back into the inefficient and counterproductive pattern of wildly fluctuating defense spending levels.

Fourth, because we must ensure reduction and eventual elimination of deficits over the next several years, I will propose a stand-by tax limited to no more than 1% of the gross national product to start in fiscal year 1986. It would last. no more than 3 years and would start *only* if the Congress has first approved our spending freeze and budget control program. You could say that this is an insurance policy for the future — a remedy that will be at hand if needed, but resorted to only if absolutely necessary.

In the meantime, we will continue to study ways to simplify the tax code and make it more fair for all Americans. This is a goal that every American who has ever struggled with a tax form can understand.

At the same time, however, I will oppose any efforts to undo the basic tax reforms we have already enacted — including the 10% tax break coming to taxpayers this July and the tax indexing that will protect all Americans from inflationary bracket creep in the years ahead.

This plan is urgently needed and is geared toward solving the problems of the growing deficits. But it naturally requires the cooperation of both branches of Government, both Houses, and both parties. Thus, our plan is aimed at bridging the institutional, philosophical, and political differences that separate us — which are not as important as the overriding common objective of economic recovery and sustained prosperity for America.

After 2 years of reducing much of the overspending, we have now reached the bone in many places — programs where we will not propose further reductions. My administration will now work with the Congress in an effort to accommodate those special concerns of the legislative branch that have caused unnecessary strains in the past.

Thus, we will propose $3 billion more for education programs than was proposed last year, and almost $2 billion more for employment and training. Proposals for new rescissions of already-enacted budget authority will be held to an absolute minimum.

This budget process must be a two-way street, for the problem of large deficits is very real. Even when all reasonable measures are applied to the vast detail of the budget, the resulting deficits are large and progress toward reducing them slow. The political risks entailed in these deficit-containment measures are considerable. But the risk of doing nothing at all due to partisanship or legislative stalemate is much greater. I therefore urge the Congress to join with my administration behind this common-sense strategy.

Meeting - and Reshaping - Federal Responsibilities

My administration seeks to limit the size, intrusiveness, and cost of Federal activities as much as possible, and to achieve the needed increase in our defense capabilities in the most cost-effective manner possible. This does not mean that appropriate Federal responsibilities are being abandoned, neglected, or inadequately supported. Instead, ways are being found to streamline Federal activity, to limit it to those areas and responsibilities that are truly Federal in nature; to ensure that these appropriate Federal responsibilities are performed in the most cost-effective and efficient manner; and to aid State and local governments in carrying out their appropriate public responsibilities in a similarly cost-effective manner. The Nation must ask for no more publicly-provided services and benefits than the private sector can ... finance.

EDUCATION

One of the high priorities I have set for my administration is the return to a more appropriate role for the Federal Government in the Nation's education systems and policies. We have slowed the alarming rate of growth of Federal spending for education, an area that is rightfully and primarily a family and State and local government responsibility. From

1974 to 1981, Federal spending for education increased by 172%. From 1981 to 1982, however, outlays declined by more than $1 billion. My administration has accomplished a major consolidation of small fragmented education programs into a flexible education block grant to States and localities. We have cut back on unnecessary regulation and Federal intrusion in local affairs.

The 1984 budget seeks to stabilize education spending, requesting $13.1 billion in budget authority for 1984. It reflects several important new initiatives to strengthen American education:

• Passing of tuition tax credits for parents who want to send their children to qualified private or religiously-affiliated schools.

• Establishing education savings accounts to give middle- and lower-income families an incentive to save for their children's college education and, at the same time, to encourage a real increase in savings for economic growth.

• Reorienting student aid programs to ensure that students and families meet their responsibilities for financing higher education, while making funds available across a wider spectrum of schools for the low-income students most in need.

• Allowing States or localities, if they so choose, to use their compensatory education funds to establish voucher programs to broaden family choice of effective schooling methods for educationally disadvantaged children.

• Helping States to train more mathematics and science teachers.

These initiatives represent the administration's continuing commitment to avoid improper Federal involvement in State, local, and family decisions, while preserving proper Federal support for key national policy goals such as supporting compensatory and handicapped education, facilitating access to higher education, and helping States improve science and mathematics education.

RESEARCH

My administration recognizes the Federal responsibility to maintain U.S. leadership in scientific research. Although support of basic scientific research represents a small share of the Federal budget, it is a vital investment in the Nation's future. Such research lays the foundation for a strong defense in the years to come, and for new technologies and industries that will help maintain our industrial competitiveness, create new jobs, and improve our quality of life. By carefully establishing budget priorities, my administration has been able to reinvigorate Federal support for basic scientific research. With my 1984 budget proposals, such support across the Government will have increased by more than 20% over the 1982 level.

HEALTH CARE

A major problem for both individuals and the Federal Government in meeting health care needs is the rapid inflation of health care costs. The rate of increase in health care costs is excessive and undermines people's ability to purchase needed health care. Federal policies have contributed significantly to health care cost increases. The budget contains several major initiatives to reduce cost increases. We must eliminate the tax incentive for high-cost employee health insurance programs. Savings from medicare cost controls will be used to protect the aged from catastrophic hospital costs. Incentives will also be proposed to slow the growth of medicaid costs.

AGRICULTURE

The administration seeks to move agricultural supply toward a better balance with demand by reducing farm production and Government program stocks. The budget proposes a four-part approach to solving the current surplus supply problem:

● establishing a payment-in-kind (PIK) program, under which farmers would receive surplus commodities now held for Federal loans, or owned by the Government, in return for reducing their production;

● freezing farm crop target prices at current levels;

● donating Government-held commodities through international humanitarian organizations for needy people around the world; and

● selling our agricultural produce abroad, both through commercial channels and through government negotiation.

Efforts are also continuing to identify surplus Federal land holdings for sale from those administered by the Departments of Agriculture and of the Interior. Planned sales total $500 million in 1984.

TRANSPORTATION

In the transportation area, my administration has made major strides in implementing one of the fundamental principles in my program for economic recovery: having users pay for program costs that are clearly allocable to them. During the past year, I signed into law two administration-backed proposals to increase excise taxes on aviation and highway users and thereby provide funding needed to revitalize and modernize these important segments of the Nation's transportation system. The 1984 budget reflects the administration's continued commitment to the "users pay" principle by again proposing user fees for:

● construction and maintenance of deep-draft ports;

● the inland waterway system;

● selected direct Coast Guard services; and

● nautical and aviation maps and charts.

Recognizing the importance of our transportation system in maintaining and contributing to the Nation's economic and social well being, my administration secured passage of legislation designed to rebuild the Nation's highway and public transportation facilities. This legislation substantially increased funds available to the States and local communities to complete and repair the aging interstate highway system, to rehabilitate principal rural and urban highways and bridges, and to improve mass transit systems.

Fully capable ports and channels are essential to make U.S. coal exports competitive in world markets. My administration will work with the Congress to provide for timely and efficient port construction. We propose a system of user fees for existing port maintenance and new port construction. Local governments would be empowered to set up their own financing arrangements for the immediate construction of facilities in their areas.

Reducing the Federal presence in commercial transportation, currently regulated by the Interstate Commerce Commission, the Civil Aeronautics Board, and the Federal Maritime Commission, will improve the efficiency of the industry. To this end, my administration will seek further deregulation of trucking, airlines and ocean shipping. Experience since the adoption of initial transportation deregulation legislation has shown clearly that both consumers and industry benefit from reduced Federal involvement in these activities.

ENERGY

The administration has significantly reoriented the country's approach to energy matters in the past 2 years. Reliance on market forces — instead of Government regulation and massive, indiscriminate Federal spending — has resulted in greater energy production, more efficient use of energy, and more favorable energy prices. For example:

● The U.S. economy today is using 18% less energy to produce a dollar's worth of output than it did in 1973 when energy prices first began to rise.

● The price of heating oil and gasoline has actually fallen in real terms by 12% in the past 2 years — confounding past theories that insisted that these prices could only increase.

Federal energy programs and policies have been refocused and made more productive:

● Wasteful spending on large, unprofitable technology demonstrations has been curtailed.

● At the same time, spending has increased in areas where the Government has a key role to play — for example, in supporting long-term energy research.

● The strategic petroleum reserve has more than doubled in size over the past 2 years.

CRIMINAL JUSTICE

My administration has also sought to strengthen the Federal criminal justice system by proposing major legislative initiatives, such as bail for sentencing reform, by attacking drug trafficking and organized crime, and by achieving a better balance among law enforcement, prosecutorial, and correctional resources. Twelve regional task forces will focus on bringing to justice organized crime drug traffickers. The administration will strengthen efforts to identify, neutralize, and defeat foreign agents who pose a threat to the Nation.

INTERNATIONAL AFFAIRS

Our foreign policy is oriented toward maintaining peace through military strength and diplomatic negotiation; promoting market-oriented solutions to international economic problems; telling the story abroad of America's democratic, free-enterprise way of life; and increasing free trade in the world while assuring this country's equitable participation in that trade.

● The security assistance portion of the international affairs program has been increased to assist friendly governments facing threats from the Soviet Union, its surrogates, and from other radical regimes.

● Development aid emphasizes encouraging the private sectors of developing nations and increasing U.S. private sector involvement in foreign assistance.

● A major expansion of international broadcasting activities aimed primarily at communist countries is planned, and a new initiative will be undertaken to strengthen the infrastructure of democracy around the world.

● Special attention is being given to assuring adequate financing of U.S. exports while my administration seeks to obtain further reductions in the export subsidies of other governments.

My administration will submit to the Congress a proposal to increase the U.S. quota in the International Monetary Fund and the U.S. obligations under the IMF's General Arrangements to Borrow, as soon as negotiations on these issues are completed. This is necessary to ensure that the IMF has adequate resources to help bring the world economy back to strong, noninflationary growth.

Although now less than 2% of the budget, international programs are critical to American world leadership and to the success of our foreign policy.

MINORITY-OWNED BUSINESSES

My administration will assist in the establishment or expansion of over 120,000 minority-owned businesses over the next 10 years. The Federal Government will procure an estimated $15 billion in goods and services from minority business during the 3-year period 1983-1985. It will make available approximately $1.5 billion in credit assistance and $300 million in technical assistance to promote minority business development during this period.

CIVIL SERVICE RETIREMENT

The 97th Congress made some improvements in the civil service retirement system. However, civil service retirement still has far more generous benefits and is much more costly than retirement programs in the private sector or in State and local governments. Accordingly, this budget proposes fundamental changes in civil service retirement designed to bring benefits into line with those offered in the private sector and reduce the cost of the system to affordable levels. Retirement benefit changes will be phased in over a period of years in order to avoid upsetting the plans of those at or near retirement.

Unemployment Demands Specific Attention

My administration seeks to provide appropriate assistance to the unemployed. There are three major groups who need help: the largest, those who are unemployed now but will find jobs readily as the economy improves; those whose jobs have permanently disappeared; and youth who have trouble finding their niche in the labor market.

Those in the first group need interim help because, historically, increases in jobs always lag in an economic recovery. Last year we provided a temporary program to give the long-term unemployed up to 16 added weeks of unemployment compensation, in addition to the up to 39 weeks available from our permanent unemployment insurance. This temporary program expires March 31, 1983. I propose to modify and extend the program for 6 more months, and provide an option for recipients to receive assistance in securing work through a system of tax credits to employers. This will give employers a significant incentive to hire the long-term unemployed, while workers will get full wages rather than the lower unemployment benefit.

Those whose jobs have permanently disappeared must be helped to find new long-term occupations. The Job Training Partnership Act, enacted last year, authorizes grants to States to help retrain such workers and assist them in locating and moving to new jobs. The Congress appropriated $25 million to start this new program in 1983. I am requesting $240 million to implement the program fully in 1984. In addition, I propose that the

Federal unemployment law be changed to allow States to use a portion of the unemployment taxes they collect to provide such retraining and job search assistance to their unemployed workers. Regulatory reform and passage of enterprise zone legislation will also create new incentives for jobs and opportunity.

Those youth who have problems finding jobs after they leave school are often condemned to a lifetime of intermittent employment and low earnings. The new Job Training Partnership Act is designed to help disadvantaged youth acquire the basic skills potential employers look for when they hire. I am requesting $1.9 billion for the block grant to States under that Act. The States must use at least 40% of that for youth.

One of the problems hampering youth is inability to get meaningful work experience during school vacations. Such experience is invaluable to demonstrate their qualifications to potential permanent employers. The budget provides for 718,000 public summer job opportunities for disadvantaged youth. But we must also make it possible for youth to experience work in the private sector. The minimum wage law now frequently prevents this. Inexperienced youth cannot produce enough of value to make it worthwhile for employers to pay them the full minimum wage during short periods of employment. I therefore propose that the minimum wage for summer jobs for youth be reduced to $2.50 an hour. Limitation of the reduced minimum wage to the summer months will make it unlikely that employers will substitute youths for older workers.

I remain adamantly opposed to temporary make-work public jobs or public works as an attempted cure for non-youth unemployment. There are several reasons for this. The cost per "job" created is excessive; we cannot afford major new programs, particularly in our current budgetary straits; the actual number of new jobs "created" is minimal; the jobs created tend to be temporary and of a dead-end nature; and most such jobs do not materialize until after recovery is well underway.

Improving the Efficiency of Government

The proposed freeze on program funding levels will compel program managers in every agency of the Government to find more efficient ways of carrying out their programs. For too long, costs of Federal operations have been mounting unchecked.

Good management has not always been a priority of the executive branch. I have been correcting that situation.

My administration has redirected programs to improve their efficiency and to achieve cost savings Government-wide. My administration is committed to improving management and reducing fraud, waste, and abuse. The President's Council on Integrity and Efficiency (PCIE), made up of 18 Inspectors General, reported that almost $17 billion has been saved or put to better use in the past 2 years.

In 1982, I signed into law the Federal Managers' Financial Integrity Act.

Under this Act, my Cabinet officers and other agency heads will report to me and the Congress annually on the status of their efforts to improve management controls that prevent fraud and mismanagement. A number of agencies have already begun to make significant improvements in this important area.

But the Government can go only so far with the seriously outdated and inefficient management/administrative systems that are currently in place. One-third of our large-scale computers, for example, are more than 10 years old. A comprehensive management improvement program was needed, so "Reform '88" was initiated. We intend to upgrade and modernize our administrative systems to make them more effective and efficient in carrying out the Government's business and serving the public.

We are already saving tax dollars by managing our almost $2 trillion yearly cash flow more effectively, collecting the Government's $250 billion of just debts, cutting Government administrative costs, modernizing Federal procurement systems, reducing internal regulations, controlling our office space and equipment more prudently, and streamlining the workforce in many departments and agencies. These cost-reduction efforts will continue.

Continuing Reform of Our Federal System

The overall efficiency of Government in the United States can also be improved by a more rational sorting out of governmental responsibilities among the various levels of government — Federal, State, and local — in our Federal system, and eliminating or limiting overlapping and duplication.

In 1981, the Congress responded to my proposals by consolidating 57 categorical programs into 9 block grants. In 1982, block grants were created for job training in the Jobs Training Partnership Act, and for urban mass transit in the Surface Transportation Act. The initiatives to be proposed this year will expand on these accomplishments.

Four new block grants will be proposed, with assured funding for major functions now addressed through categorical grants:

• A general Federal-State block grant covering approximately 15 categorical programs.

• A Federal-local block grant that would include the entitlement portion of the community development grant program and the general revenue sharing program.

• A transportation block grant.

• A rural housing block grant.

The administration is improving the management of intergovernmental assistance by providing State and local elected officials with greater opportunity to express their views on proposed Federal development and assistance actions before final decisions are made. Under Executive Order

12372, Intergovernmental Review of Federal Programs, which I signed in July 1982, Federal agencies must consult with State and local elected officials early in the assistance decision process and make every effort to accommodate their views. The Order also encourages the simplification of State planning requirements imposed by Federal law, and allows for the substitution of State-developed plans for federally required State plans where statutes and regulations allow.

Through the President's Task Force on Regulatory Relief and the regulatory review process, the administration is eliminating and simplifying regulations affecting State and local governments that are burdensome, unnecessary, and counter-productive. These changes have improved local efficiency and accountability and reduced program costs. Twenty-five reviews were completed during the past 2 years by either the Task Force or by various Federal agencies. Available data indicate that regulatory relief actions will save State and local governments approximately $4 to $6 billion in initial costs, and an estimated $2 billion on an annual basis. My administration is also simplifying selected, generally applicable crosscutting requirements that are imposed on State and local governments as a condition of accepting financial assistance.

Federal Credit Programs: More Selective

The administration continues its strong commitment to control Federal credit assistance, which has serious effects on the Nation's financial markets. . . . I propose a credit budget that reverses the . . . rate of growth in direct and guaranteed lending by the Federal Government. . . .

Federal intervention through guarantees and provision of direct lending misdirects investment and preempts capital that could be more efficiently used by unsubsidized, private borrowers. Because federally assisted borrowers are frequently less productive than private borrowers, large Federal credit demands must be reduced in order to improve prospects for economic growth.

Conclusion

The stage is set; a recovery to vigorous, sustainable, noninflationary economic growth is imminent. But given the underlying deterioration in the overall budget structure that has occurred over the past 2 years, only the most sweeping set of fiscal policy changes could help to reverse the trend and set the budget on a path that is consistent with long-term economic recovery.

If the challenge before us is great, so, too, are the opportunities. Let us work together to meet the challenge. If we fail, if we work at cross purposes, posterity will not forgive us for allowing this opportunity to slip away.

February

PRESIDENT'S ECONOMIC REPORT; ECONOMIC ADVISERS' REPORT

February 2, 1983

President Ronald Reagan and his economic advisers told Congress February 2 that the nation's economy would soon recover from the recession that had begun in July 1981. They predicted that the recovery would usher in a long period of sustained growth accompanied by low inflation.

In his annual Economic Report to Congress, the president supported the moderate-growth policy of the independent Federal Reserve Board and vowed to work against moves for protectionism at home and trade barriers abroad. The need to reduce unemployment and to increase business investment also were at the head of the president's agenda.

The Annual Report of the Council of Economic Advisers (CEA), transmitted to Congress with the president's message, hailed the "dramatic" reduction in the rate of inflation, calling it the major economic achievement of the previous year. At the same time, the advisers wrote that the high unemployment rate (10.8 percent in December 1982) was the nation's most serious economic problem. Although they declared that both "cyclical" and "structural" unemployment could be alleviated by sound public policy, they opposed public works programs as "counterproductive" and of limited capacity to fight "cyclical" unemployment.

The reports of the president and the Council of Economic Advisers were the first to bear the influence of Martin S. Feldstein, the second chairman of the CEA in the Reagan administration. Appointed August 6, 1982, Feldstein replaced Murray L. Weidenbaum as chairman of the three-member council.

Monetary Policy

Generally supporting policies adopted by the Federal Reserve Board, Reagan said he recognized the difficulties in controlling the growth of the nation's money supply. He said that he expected the Federal Reserve Board to "expand the money supply at a moderate rate consistent with both a sustained recovery and continued progress against inflation."

In their report, the president's advisers noted that it was in 1979 that the Federal Reserve Board had adopted new procedures that emphasized keeping the growth of money within target ranges. In earlier years, the economists wrote, the board had conducted monetary policy by focusing on interest rates. (Historic Documents of 1980, p. 159)

International Problems

Hoping to block moves in Congress designed to shield U.S. industries from foreign competition, Reagan said that widespread protectionist policies could hurt American consumers in the long run. "I am committed," he said, "to a policy of preventing the enactment of protectionist measures. . . ."

The president's economists sought to show that a major competitor, Japan, had not deliberately kept the yen undervalued to gain a competitive advantage. "There is no special yen issue, but the strong dollar does pose problems." They concluded that the "most effective strategy" the United States could pursue in the foreign trade sector was to get its "overall economic house in order — above all, by bringing budget deficits and real interest rates under control."

Forecasts

The Council of Economic Advisers forecast a "moderate, sustainable" economic recovery. The council also predicted that the lower rate of inflation in 1982 would continue in 1983 and that, after "stabilizing" at a high rate for several months, the unemployment rate would begin to fall. The president's advisers, however, conditioned those forecasts on enactment of the Reagan administration's 1984 budget proposals. (Budget, p. 101)

Following is the February 2, 1983, Economic Report of the President and excerpts from the January 31, 1983, Annual Report of the Council of Economic Advisers. (Boldface headings in brackets have been added by Congressional Quarterly to highlight the organization of the text.):

ECONOMIC REPORT OF THE PRESIDENT

To the Congress of the United States:

Two years ago, I came to Washington with a deep personal commitment to change America's economic future. For more than a decade, the economy had suffered from low productivity growth and a rising rate of inflation. Government spending absorbed an increasing share of national income. A shortsighted view of economic priorities was destroying our prospects for long-term prosperity.

The economic program that I proposed shortly after I took office emphasized economic growth and a return to price stability. My tax proposals were designed to encourage private initiative and to stimulate saving and productive investment. I have supported and encouraged the Federal Reserve Board in its pursuit of price stability through sound monetary policy. My Administration has slowed the growth of Federal regulation, strengthening the forces of competition in a number of economic sectors. And I have worked with the Congress to enact legislation that has reversed or limited the growth of government programs that have become too large or outlasted their usefulness.

Although the full effect of these changes in government policy will take time to develop, some of the benefits have already become apparent. The rate of consumer price inflation between December 1981 and December 1982 was only 3.9 percent, about one-third of the rate in the year before I took office. Interest rates are now lower than when I took office, and have fallen rapidly during the last 6 months.

The Administration will propose many additional measures over the next several years to strengthen economic incentives, reduce burdensome regulations, increase capital formation, and raise our standard of living. It is easy to lose sight of these long-term goals in a year, like 1982, when the economy was in an extended recession. I am deeply troubled by the current level of unemployment in the United States and by the suffering and anxiety that it entails for millions of Americans. The unemployment that many of our citizens are experiencing is a consequence of the disinflation that must necessarily follow the accelerating inflation of the last decade. Allowing the upward trend of inflation to continue would have risked even greater increases in unemployment in the future. In spite of the present high unemployment rate and the accompanying hardships, it is essential that we maintain the gains against inflation that we have recently achieved at substantial cost. Continuing success in restraining inflation will provide a stronger foundation for economic recovery in 1983 and beyond.

Reducing Unemployment

The Federal Government can play an important role in reducing unemployment. I believe, however, that the government should focus its attention on those groups that will continue to face high unemployment rates even after the recovery has begun. By helping them to develop their job-related skills, we will foster productive careers in the private sector rather than dead-end jobs. This emphasis on training and private sector employment is the focus of the Jobs Training Partnership Act that I supported and signed into law in 1982. I am proposing additional steps this year to strengthen Federal training and retraining programs and to help the structurally unemployed find lasting jobs.

It is understandable that many well-meaning members of the Congress have responded to the current high unemployment rate by proposing various public works and employment programs. However, I am convinced that such programs would only shift unemployment from one industry to another at the cost of increasing the Federal budget deficit.

Although programs to help the structurally unemployed are important, only a balanced and lasting recovery can achieve a substantial reduction in unemployment. There are now over four million more unemployed people than there were at the peak of the last business cycle. Nine million new workers are expected to join the labor force by 1988. Only a healthy and growing economy can provide the more than 13 million jobs needed to achieve a progressively lower level of unemployment over the next 5 years.

The Prospects for Economic Recovery

There are now signs that an economic recovery will begin soon. By December 1982 the index of leading economic indicators had risen in 7 of the last 8 months. Housing starts have risen substantially over the last year, and by December 1982 were 39 percent higher than 12 months earlier. Inventory levels have fallen sharply, so that increased sales should translate quickly into increased production and employment. Both long-term and short-term interest rates have fallen substantially. The Administration's economic forecast predicts that the gross national product will begin to rise in the first quarter of 1983 and will then rise more quickly as the year continues. Most private forecasters also predict a recovery in 1983.

Monetary policy will play a critical role in achieving a sound and sustainable economic recovery. If the monetary aggregates grow too slowly, the economy will lack the level of financial resources needed for continued economic growth. But if these aggregates are allowed to expand too rapidly, an increase in inflation and a short-lived recovery will result. I recognize the difficulties that the Federal Reserve has faced and will continue to face in guiding the growth of the money supply at a time when major regulatory changes have made it difficult to rely on old guidelines. I expect that in 1983 the Federal Reserve will expand the money supply at a moderate rate consistent with both a sustained recovery and continued progress against inflation.

Investment and Economic Growth

An economic recovery beginning in 1983 should bring not only a reduction in unemployment but also an increase in business investment over the next several years. A higher level of investment is an important ingredient in raising productivity and economic growth. The Accelerated Cost Recovery System that I proposed and that the Congress enacted in 1981 was designed to encourage a substantial expansion of business investment above the relatively low levels of the 1970s. Since that time the adverse effects of the recession have outweighed the positive effects of the new tax rules. As the economy turns from recession to recovery, however, incentives to invest will become more powerful. But business investment may not grow rapidly unless measures proposed by the Administration to reduce potentially large Federal budget deficits are enacted.

Federal borrowing competes with private investment for available savings. If the government continues to borrow large amounts to finance its deficit, the real interest rate will remain high and discourage private investment. This process of "crowding out" will tend to depress private investment in the years ahead unless the budget deficit is progressively reduced.

Fiscal Year 1984 Budget Proposals

It is important to distinguish the cyclical part of the budget deficit from the structural part, which would remain even at the peak of the business cycle. Approximately one-half of the 1983 budget deficit is due to the depressed state of the economy. With earnings and profits reduced, tax receipts have significantly decreased, and expenditures have increased. As the economy recovers, the cyclical part of the deficit will shrink. But cyclical recovery alone will not bring the deficit down to an acceptable size.

In the budget I am now submitting to the Congress, I am proposing the dramatic steps needed to reduce Federal budget deficits in future years. My budget proposals are designed to reduce the deficit by dealing directly with the rapid growth of the domestic spending programs (apart from interest payments) of the Federal Government. In 1970 these programs accounted for 10 percent of the gross national product and 48 percent of Federal spending. By 1980 these programs had grown to 14 percent of gross national product and 63 percent of the budget. I remain committed to the idea that we can reduce budget deficits without increasing the burden on the poor, without weakening our national defense, and without destroying economic incentives by counterproductive tax increases.

Rapid congressional enactment of the budget would provide clear and credible evidence that the Federal Government intends not to place heavy burdens on the capital markets in future years. Such reassurance should hasten the decline in interest rates, especially long-term interest rates on bonds and residential mortgages, and improve prospects for the recovery of the housing, automobile, and capital investment sectors of the economy.

I recognize the special importance of protecting the social security and medicare programs for aged retirees and their dependents. These programs now face very serious financial problems. The bipartisan National Commission on Social Security Reform has recently recommended a series of measures, which I have endorsed, to eliminate the cumulative deficiency of $150 billion to $200 billion projected for the social security system in the years 1983 through 1989. It is critically important at this time to make changes in the social security programs that will protect their solvency and financial viability for the years to come.

[Burden of Federal Regulation]

For many decades, the Federal Government has regulated the price and entry conditions affecting several sectors of the American economy. Much of this regulation is no longer appropriate to the conditions of the contemporary economy. Over time, most of this regulation — by restraining competition and the development of new services and technologies — has not served the interests of either consumers or producers. Since deregulation of some markets began several years ago, the experience has been almost uniformly encouraging. My Administration has supported these step-by-step efforts to reduce these regulations in markets that would otherwise be competitive. It is now time to consider broad measures to eliminate many of these economic regulations especially as they affect the natural gas, transportation, communications, and financial markets.

[Interest Rates and Trade Deficit]

The very high levels of real interest rates over the last several years are a principal cause of the sharp rise in the exchange value of the dollar relative to foreign currencies. This rise has reduced the ability of American exporters to compete in foreign markets and increased the competitiveness of imports in the domestic market. Largely as a result, the U.S. merchandise trade balance showed a substantial deficit in 1982.

Our current trade deficit is a reminder of the importance of international trade to the American economy. The export share of U.S. gross national product has more than doubled over the last three decades. American workers, businesses, and farmers suffer when foreign governments prevent American products from entering their markets, thus reducing U.S. export levels. While the United States may be forced to respond to the trade distorting practices of foreign governments through the use of strategic measures, such practices do not warrant indiscriminate protectionist actions, such as domestic content rules for automobiles sold in the United States. Widespread protectionist policies would hurt American consumers by raising prices of the products they buy, and by removing some of the pressures for cost control and quality improvement that result from international competition. Moreover, protectionism at home could hurt the workers, farmers, and firms in the United States that produce goods and services for export, since it would almost inevitably lead to increased protectionism by governments abroad. I am committed to a policy of preventing the enactment of protectionist measures in the United States, and I will continue working to persuade the other nations of the world to eliminate trade distorting practices that threaten the viability of the international trading system upon which world prosperity depends.

Trade in goods and services is only one aspect of our economic relations with the rest of the world. The international flow of capital into the United States and from the United States to other countries is also of great importance. The United States should play a primary role in preserving the vitality of the international capital market. Severe strains on that market developed in 1982 as several nations found it difficult to service their overseas debt obligations. In 1982, the Federal Government worked closely with debtor and creditor nations and the major international lending agencies to prevent a disruption in the functioning of world capital markets. Now, with the cooperation of a wide variety of creditors, countries with especially severe debt-servicing difficulties are establishing economic and financial programs that will permit them to meet their international obligations.

The Years Ahead

We are now at a critical juncture for the American economy. The recession has led to strong pressures from some members of the Congress and from others to abandon our commitment to a policy that is aimed at long-term economic growth, capital accumulation, and price stability. There are many who urge new government spending programs and forcing the Federal Reserve to raise monetary growth rates to levels that would rekindle inflation.

I am convinced that such policies would prove detrimental to the long-run interests of the American people. Our economy, despite the recession, is extraordinarily resilient and is now on the road to a healthy recovery. It is essential in the year ahead that the Administration and the Congress work together, take a long-term perspective, and pursue economic policies that lead to sustained economic growth and to greater prosperity for all Americans.

THE ANNUAL REPORT OF THE COUNCIL OF ECONOMIC ADVISERS

From Recession to Recovery and Growth

The major economic achievement of 1982 was a dramatic reduction of inflation to its lowest rate in a decade. The 4.6 percent increase in the gross national product (GNP) implicit price deflator between the fourth quarters of 1981 and 1982 was less than half the 10.2 percent rate of increase between the fourth quarters of 1979 and 1980. This decline in inflation has moderated the earlier widespread fears that inflation would accelerate. While some of this improvement in inflation was transitory, reflecting such special factors as the appreciation of the exchange value of the dollar, the largest share was almost certainly due to a decline in the underlying rate of inflation. The reduced rate of inflation is a major step toward the Administration's goals of full employment, healthy economic growth, and price stability.

The progress made in reducing inflation, however, was accompanied by a painful slowdown of the economy. Beginning in July 1981, the Nation suffered the second of two back-to-back recessions that brought the unemployment rate to 10.8 percent in December 1982. At that time, approximately 5 million more people were unemployed than in January 1980, when the first of the two recessions began.

The increase in long-term unemployment poses a particularly severe problem. In January 1980, about 550,000 people had been unemployed for more than 6 months. In December 1982 there were more than four times as many. Long-term unemployment is particularly serious in that it causes substantial financial hardship and is associated with a loss of job skills that may reduce future income significantly.

Some temporary decline in real economic activity was probably unavoidable in the process of reversing the upward trend of inflation. The United States entered the 1980s with a high rate of inflation and with widespread public expectations that the rate would remain high, and perhaps increase. As high inflation persisted, it became embedded in the plans and contracts of firms and workers, and lowering it involved a painful process. The decline of real GNP since early 1981 was in large part the price the United States paid for failing to control inflation in the late 1970s.

LEGACIES OF THE 1970s

In the 1960s, many economists believed that the Federal Government could keep unemployment down permanently by accepting a higher rate of inflation. Steady rises in productivity and living standards were taken for granted. During the 1970s these views proved to be incorrect. By the closing years of the 1970s, both the unemployment rate and the inflation rate were higher than they had been in the 1960s, and the rate of productivity growth was lower.

Why did unemployment, productivity growth, and inflation all worsen in the 1970s? These developments occurred in part because of factors outside the government's control, such as changes in the size and composition of the work force and rising world energy prices. But the economy also suffered from long-standing government policies that exacerbated inflation and distorted the incentives to work, save, and invest. . . .

Of all the economic problems that this Administration inherited when it came to office in 1981, the most urgent was the problem of rising prices. Double-digit inflation had created serious economic distortions. An equally serious concern was that the trend rate of inflation was rising over time.

From 1960 to 1970, the GNP deflator rose at an average rate of 3.0 percent per year. Between 1970 and 1973, the average rate of inflation by this measure was 5.3 percent. Then, aggravated by the sharp jump in world oil prices and other special factors, inflation reached 10.2 percent during 1974, but by 1976 it was down to 4.7 percent. In the next 4 years, which included the second oil price shock in 1979, inflation increased continually until it reached 10.2 percent again in 1980....

DISADVANTAGES OF INTEREST RATE TARGETING

From World War II until the mid-1970s the Federal Reserve, like most central banks, conducted monetary policy by focusing on interest rates and money market conditions. Over the 1970s, increasing emphasis was given to targeting monetary aggregates. More recently, under new procedures first adopted in October 1979, the Federal Reserve has given greater emphasis to keeping the growth of the monetary aggregates within pre-announced target ranges, even though it was recognized that this could result in greater variations in interest rates.

Since 1979 both long-term and short-term interest rates have proven more variable than in the past. Many critics attribute this change to the increased emphasis on monetary targets and the level of bank reserves as the operational basis for monetary policy. Although some have argued that the Federal Reserve should drop monetary targeting in favor of targeting interest rates, the Administration believes strongly that targeting interest rates, either nominal or real, would prove to be a serious error.

The *nominal* rate of interest is a very unreliable indicator of the thrust of monetary policy. The financial variable important to borrowers and lenders is not the *nominal* interest rate but a *real* interest rate determined by subtracting the rate of inflation from the nominal interest rate. Borrowers and lenders take into account the fact that the dollars repaid when a loan matures do not have the same purchasing power as the dollars originally borrowed. When inflation is expected, lenders insist that the nominal rate of interest include a premium to compensate them for the declining purchasing power of the dollar, and borrowers are willing to pay such a premium.

Although the real interest rate is more closely linked to borrowing and lending decisions than the nominal interest rate, the real interest rate is also not an appropriate target for monetary policy. There are several basic reasons for rejecting the policy of real interest rate targeting.

First, real interest rate targeting might well lead to an inflationary monetary policy. Any given real interest rate is compatible with a wide range of inflation rates. For example, a real interest rate of 2 percent could occur with a 5 percent nominal rate and a 3 percent inflation rate, or with a 12 percent nominal rate and a 10 percent inflation rate. Thus, achieving a real interest rate target would provide no assurance of price stability.

Second, the real interest rate that governs economic behavior is the difference between the nominal interest rate and the *expected* rate of inflation. Since expectations of inflation are not observable, the monetary authorities cannot as a practical matter measure or target the expected real interest rate.

A third reason why real interest rate targeting is not feasible is that the relevant interest rate is not merely the real rate but the real net-of-tax interest rate. Because net-of-tax rates of interest vary among individuals and businesses in different tax positions, there is no way for the monetary authorities to determine the relevant average real net-of-tax interest rate in financial markets. . . .

There is a final and even more fundamental reason for rejecting real interest rate targeting. Even if the expected real interest rate were measurable, there would remain the virtually impossible task of determining what level of that interest rate is actually compatible with noninflationary growth. The problem of identifying the equilibrium interest rate is made even more difficult by the interaction of tax rules and inflation. . . .

The Budget Deficit

The Federal budget deficit has become a major problem for the American economy. Without the savings proposed by the Administration in its budget plan for the years 1984 through 1988, the United States is forecasted to experience a series of deficits that would consume more than 6 percent of GNP in each of the next 6 years. Although budget deficits have been a nearly constant feature of our Nation's economic life for the past two decades, the prospective budget deficits that would result if no legislative actions were taken to reduce them would be far larger than those previously experienced in the postwar period. The economic effects of such deficits are beyond our previous experience.

The fiscal 1983 deficit is partially a result of the recession. Any recession reduces tax collections and increases outlays for unemployment benefits, retirement benefits, and certain other activities. A reasonable approximation is that the change in economic output associated with a percentage point change in the unemployment rate would raise the fiscal 1983 deficit by about $25 billion. The Administration forecasts that the unemployment rate for fiscal 1983 will average 10.7 percent. If the unemployment rate were 6.5 percent instead, the budget deficit would be about half the $208 billion now forecast for fiscal 1983. The cyclical component represents a similarly large share of the fiscal 1984 deficit.

Economic recovery and growth in the years ahead will reduce the cyclical component of the deficit. The Administration's forecast projects a decline in the unemployment rate by 4 percentage points between fiscal 1983 and fiscal 1988, leaving only a negligible cyclical component in the fiscal 1988 budget. Unless the Administration's proposals are enacted, a current services budget deficit of $300 billion is forecasted to materialize.

To see the origin of these large deficits, it is useful to compare the components of the 1988 current services budget with the same components for 1970. Between those years, taxes decline very slightly as a percentage of GNP, from 19.9 percent in 1970 to 18.9 percent in 1988. The defense share of GNP remains unchanged at 8.1 percent of GNP in both years. By contrast, nondefense activities excluding interest rise from 10.6 percent of GNP in 1970 to 13.6 percent in 1988, an increase of about one-fourth. In addition, the accumulation of previous deficits raise the net interest component of the budget deficit from 1.5 percent of GNP to 3.4 percent of GNP....

The Dual Problems of Structural and Cyclical Unemployment

Unemployment is the most serious economic problem now facing the United States. By December 1982 the number of unemployed had risen by more than 4 million since the beginning of the recession in July 1981. The unemployment rate was higher in December 1982 than at any point since the Depression, with over 12 million persons counted as unemployed. Even after the economy recovers from the recent recession, it is likely that the unemployment rate will reach a plateau between 6 and 7 percent.

This chapter analyzes the two major types of unemployment: cyclical and structural. The high level of cyclical unemployment now prevailing in the United States is a major problem, but it should prove transitory. Only a healthy and sustained recovery from the recent recession can effectively diminish cyclical unemployment. Even after full recovery, however, a serious structural unemployment problem will remain unless measures are taken to improve the functioning of labor markets. Reducing structural unemployment will require attacking the special problems of young people and the long-term adult unemployed....

THE RECENT RECESSION

The unemployment rate in December 1982 stood at 10.8 percent of the civilian labor force. Since the recent period of economic slack that began in January 1980, the unemployment rate has risen by 4.5 percentage points. During the recent recession, which began in July 1981, the unemployment rate rose by 3.6 percentage points. Historical experience suggests that the unemployment rate tends to increase for several months after the level of production bottoms out and it is possible that the unemployment rate will reach 11 percent at some point during 1983.

Beyond those officially counted as unemployed, the recent recession has prevented many Americans from working as much as they would like. In

December 1982 there were over two million persons involuntarily working part time. The Bureau of Labor Statistics also reported that there were over 1.8 million discouraged workers in December. These are individuals who have given up looking for work because they believe they cannot find jobs. . . .

THE COMPOSITION OF CYCLICAL AND STRUCTURAL UNEMPLOYMENT

The unemployment problem can be divided into two components, cyclical and structural unemployment. The term *cyclical unemployment* is used to refer to the unemployment associated with cyclical downturns in aggregate economic activity. The incremental unemployment associated with the recent recession would fall into this category. The term *structural unemployment* is used to refer to the unemployment that remains even after cyclical recoveries in aggregate economic activity.

In large part, structural unemployment is a natural concomitant of a dynamic economy with constantly changing patterns of demand. Labor markets are in constant flux, with people entering and leaving the labor force, losing or quitting old jobs, and looking for and acquiring new jobs. Some amount of structural unemployment is an inevitable aspect of a large modern industrial economy such as ours. It is important to realize that although expansionary macroeconomic policies cannot reduce structual unemployment permanently, certain microeconomic policy interventions can affect the ease and speed of the process that matches workers with jobs. . . .

COMBATING CYCLICAL UNEMPLOYMENT

High rates of cyclical unemployment, which the American economy is now experiencing, are largely a consequence of fluctuations in aggregate demand caused by macroeconomic policies and shocks to the economy. . . . [T]he historical experience of the United States and other countries suggests that disinflation is generally associated with lost output and increased unemployment. During periods of disinflation and recession, the measures available to reduce the pain of the transition from accelerating inflation to price stability are limited. Greater fiscal or monetary stimulus might increase employment, but only at the risk of igniting inflation. . . .

The Limits of Macroeconomic Policy

The only way to reduce current high levels of cyclical unemployment is for the United States to achieve a sound recovery from the recent recession. Avoiding future recurrences of high cyclical unemployment requires avoiding an expansion so rapid as to lead to rapidly increasing inflation. Historical experience suggests that the change in the rate of inflation depends both on the rate at which economic activity is expanding

132

and on the level of economic slack. If the slack in the economy declines too rapidly, or capacity utilization is held at too high a level, inflation will tend to increase. The lower limit on unemployment below which inflation will tend to increase is referred to as the *inflation threshold* unemployment rate. . . .

COMBATING STRUCTURAL UNEMPLOYMENT

The preceding analysis suggests that it would be imprudent to use macroeconomic policies to reduce the unemployment rate below its inflation threshold level of 6 to 7 percent. Such an effort would increase inflation, and ultimately prove counterproductive as increased inflation was followed by recession. This does not mean that unemployment rates in the 6 to 7 percent range are either inevitable or desirable. The inflation threshold level of unemployment can be reduced by policies that consider the special problems of two groups of workers: (1) young people, and (2) adults experiencing long-term unemployment. It can also be reduced by reforms of the unemployment insurance system, which, while providing valuable insurance, may increase the incidence of unemployment.

The Problem of Youth Unemployment

At times of low cyclical unemployment, about half the unemployed are young people between the ages of 16 and 24. Close to one-fourth of all the unemployed are teenagers aged 16 to 19. While unemployment clearly imposes hardships on youths, it has very different economic impacts than it does for adults. Many unemployed youths are in school and looking for part-time work. Most of this group, and many other young people who have left school, are not economically independent, but rather live at home and rely on their parents for financial support. Many other young people experience only brief periods of unemployment as they move from one job to the next. . . .

The United States in the World Economy: Strains on the System

During the 1970s the world's market economies became more integrated with each other than ever before. Exports and imports as a share of gross national product (GNP) reached record levels for most industrial countries, while international lending and direct foreign investment grew even faster than world trade. This closer linkage of economies was mutually beneficial. It allowed producers in each country to take greater advantage of their country's special resources and knowledge, and to take advantage of economies of scale. At the same time, it allowed each country to consume a wider variety of products, at lower costs, than it could produce itself.

Underlying the growth in world trade and investment was a progressive reduction of barriers to trade. The postwar period was marked by a series of agreements to liberalize trade: both multilateral, like the Kennedy Round, and bilateral, like the Canada-U.S. auto pact.

In spite of its huge benefits, however, this liberalized trading system is now in serious danger. Within the United States, demands for protection against imports and for export subsidies have grown as a combination of structural changes, sectoral problems, and short-run macroeconomic developments has led to a perception that we are becoming uncompetitive in world markets. In Europe, a growing structural unemployment problem, aggravated by the recession, has increased protectionist pressures. In the developing countries a financial crisis threatens the integration of capital markets and is pushing many countries back toward the exchange controls and import restrictions they had begun to dismantle.

These problems must not be allowed to disrupt world trade. If the system comes apart — if the world's nations allow themselves to be caught up in a spiral of retaliatory trade restrictions — a long time may pass before the pieces are put back together....

LONG-RUN TRENDS IN U.S. COMPETITIVENESS: PERCEPTIONS AND REALITIES

Concern over the international competitiveness of the United States is as high as it has ever been. It is argued with increasing frequency that U.S. business has steadily lost ground in the international marketplace. This alleged poor performance is often attributed both to failures of management in the United States and to the support given to foreign businesses by their home governments. Feeding the perception of declining competitiveness is the persistent U.S. deficit in merchandise trade, especially the imbalance in trade with Japan.

Changes in U.S. trade performance must, however, be put into the context of changes in the U.S. role in the world economy. This wider approach reveals that much of the concern about long-run competitiveness is based on misperceptions. Although the recent appreciation of the dollar has created a temporary loss of competitiveness, the United States has not experienced a persistent loss of ability to sell its products on international markets; in fact, in the 1970s the United States held its own in terms of output, exports, and unemployment. Changes in the relationship of the United States to the world economy, however, have made the United States look less competitive by some traditional measures....

The Issue of U.S. Trade with Japan

The perception of diminished U.S. competitiveness stems not only from the U.S. trade deficit but from an impression that U.S. trade performance compares poorly with that of other countries, especially that of Japan. Japan runs a huge surplus in its manufactures trade, while the United

States runs only a small one, and Japan also has a large surplus in its bilateral trade with the United States. These facts are often attributed to Japanese trade restrictions. Japan does maintain restrictions which seriously hurt U.S. businesses. Trade restrictions, however, do not in the long run improve the Japanese trade balance; as discussed more fully below, they lead to offsetting increases in other imports or declines in exports. The main explanation of Japan's surplus in manufactures trade and in trade with the United States is that Japan, with few natural resources, incurs huge deficits in its trade in primary products, especially oil, and with primary producers, especially the Organization of Petroleum Exporting Countries (OPEC). The surpluses in the rest of Japan's trade offset these deficits. . . .

Although Japanese trade policy does not play a central role in causing the bilateral trade imbalance with the United States, Japanese import restrictions remain a major source of friction. Japan maintains a variety of nontariff barriers against imports. . . . As the fastest growing and second largest market economy, Japan has a responsibility to help sustain the open trading system. A major trade liberalization by Japan would do much to relieve the political strains on that system, while the failure of Japan to make more than token concessions would intensify them. . . .

EXCHANGE RATES AND THE BALANCE OF PAYMENTS

During 1982 the dollar rose against other major currencies to its highest level since the beginning of floating exchange rates in 1973. The strength of the dollar provided some benefits to the U.S. economy by reducing import prices and thus accelerating progress against inflation. On the other hand, the strong dollar caused severe problems by decreasing the cost competitiveness of exported U.S. goods.

Causes of the Dollar's Strength

Exchange-rate movements are not well understood. Econometric models of exchange-rate determination proposed in the past decade have not shown any consistent ability to track past exchange-rate movements, let alone predict future changes. Nevertheless, careful analysis can narrow the range of plausible explanations of the dollar's rise.

The recent appreciation of the dollar, unlike many earlier exchange-rate movements, did not simply reflect contemporaneous changes in relative price levels. The well-known theory of purchasing power parity suggests that the rate of change in the exchange rate should equal the difference between the foreign and domestic inflation rates. Over the very long run, or in situations of very large differences in inflation rates, the purchasing power parity theory has proved to be a useful guide. But the theory has little or no power to explain the recent rise of the dollar. Price increases over the past 2 years in Germany and Japan, for instance, were lower than in the United States. Yet the dollar appreciated dramatically during that period against both the mark and yen....

An Undervalued Yen?

The explanations of the strong dollar discussed so far leave out a view which has received considerable attention — that the strength of the dollar reflects deliberate undervaluation of their currencies by our competitors, especially Japan. This view is important enough in its implications for U.S. international economic policy to deserve separate treatment.

Arguments that the yen is undervalued are of two types, which are basically independent of one another. One argument is that the Japanese government has persistently kept the yen undervalued. The other is that the Japanese have only recently engineered a decline in the yen to gain competitive advantage. Neither of these views appears correct in light of the actual behavior of Japan's balance of payments and exchange rate....

To show that there is no special yen issue is not to deny that a substantial deterioration has occurred in the relative cost position of U.S. firms. This deterioration was actually larger relative to other industrial countries, but since Japan is the United States' most important competitor, the depreciation of the yen worries U.S. firms more. There is no special yen issue, but the strong dollar does pose genuine problems.

Effects of a Strong Dollar on U.S. Trade

The rise of the dollar was associated with a large rise in the production costs of U.S. firms relative to those of foreign competitors. To take one measure, unit labor costs in U.S. manufacturing rose 32 percent relative to those of a weighted average of other industrial countries from their low point in the third quarter of 1980 to the second quarter of 1982. This rise in relative costs has at least temporarily reduced the international competitiveness of U.S. industry dramatically. Other U.S. exporting and import-competing sectors, especially agriculture, have also been squeezed.

Despite this deterioration in competitive position, it was only in the third quarter of 1982 that the U.S. trade deficit began to show a significant increase. This delay was in line with previous experience of the effect of exchange rates on trade. The full effect of changes in exchange rates on the volume of exports and imports is felt only after some time has passed, because some trade takes place under contracts signed in advance and because customers do not always change suppliers immediately when relative prices change. The short-term effect of a rise in the dollar is to reduce import prices, which actually tends to *improve* the trade balance. Although the negative effects eventually dominate, some econometric estimates suggest that the full negative effect is not felt for more than 2 years.

As the effects of the strong dollar are increasingly reflected in U.S. trade, the trade deficit will widen. Economic developments elsewhere in the world will also contribute to a widening trade deficit. The recession in other industrial countries will depress the demand for U.S. exports, and financial constraints in developing countries will lead them to import less. Both developments will have negative consequences for U.S. exports. Record trade and current account deficits in 1983 will almost surely result.

Whether the trade and current account deficits persist will largely depend on U.S. macroeconomic policies, particularly on the fiscal side. If large budget deficits are allowed to continue to depress the U.S. national saving rate, real interest rates may rise again, sustaining or even increasing the high real exchange rate of the dollar. In this case the trade deficit could remain high for several years. . . .

Protection and Export Promotion

The negative effect of the strong dollar on the competitiveness of many U.S. firms has fueled pressures for an interventionist trade policy. These pressures must be resisted. Protecting import-competing industries or subsidizing exports is not just a harmful long-run policy. With a floating exchange rate, such policies would fail to improve the trade balance or create employment even in the short run. . . .

The strength of the dollar has put considerable strain on the resolve of the United States to remain committed to free trade. This strain is not unique to the international sector. The recession and high interest rates have also put a strain on the resolve to let other types of markets, from housing to labor markets, operate freely. If there is special reason for concern about the international side, it is because of the danger that mistakes in U.S. policy could set off a spiral of retaliation among all the major trading nations.

The competitiveness of U.S. business as a whole — as opposed to that of particular sectors — and the balance of payments are macroeconomic phenomena. Microeconomic interventions cannot cure macroeconomic problems; they can only make one sector better off by hurting other sectors even more. The most effective strategy the United States can pursue for its exporting and import-competing sectors is to get its overall economic house in order — above all, by bringing budget deficits and real interest rates under control. . . .

THE INTERNATIONAL DEBT PROBLEM

Different problems from those facing the United States and Europe afflict the economies of the developing nations. The problems of these economies have accumulated over the last several years and are products of both domestic policy mistakes and external developments, such as oil price increases, the recession in industrial countries, and high real interest rates. In the summer and fall of 1982 the problems came to a head in the form of a sharp reduction in international lending to the developing countries.

Debt-Financed Growth in the 1970s

Until recently, the growth of such middle income developing countries as Brazil, South Korea, and Taiwan was widely viewed as one of the great success stories of the 1970s. Particularly notable was their success in expanding exports of manufactured goods. While the growth of these exports did give rise to some adjustment problems in industrial countries, the successes of some middle income countries were undoubtedly a highly favorable development for the United States. Such success provided a dramatic demonstration to other countries of the potential of market-oriented economic policies.

An important aspect of growth in the developing world, however, was heavy borrowing from foreign sources. There is nothing inherently wrong in external borrowing to finance growth. Some of the developed countries, including the United States, relied heavily on foreign capital during earlier periods of industrialization. But some developing nations borrowed too much, investing in projects of doubtful productivity. When overly optimistic expectations about export earnings and interest rates turned out to have been wrong, these countries found themselves in serious financial difficulty.

From 1973 to 1981 the medium- and long-term external debt of non-oil developing countries rose at an annual rate of more than 20 percent. . . .

Causes of the Liquidity Problem

Excessive borrowing by some developing countries made an eventual financial problem inevitable. The proximate factor which brought the era of debt-financed growth to a halt was, however, a sharp deterioration in the world economy. The rise in oil prices in 1979 was a blow to many debtor countries, and further strains resulted from disinflation in the United States and other industrial countries. . . .

The result of these developments was that banks, which had been willing to lend large amounts to developing countries throughout the 1970s, lost confidence that the loans would be promptly repaid. . . .

Implications of the Debt Problem

The debt situation of the developing countries poses two problems for the world economy. Although quite unlikely, failure to resolve the debt situation in an orderly way could lead to major financial market disruptions. More likely — indeed, it has already happened to a considerable extent — is a situation of forced austerity in debtor countries, with adverse effects on world trade and output. . . .

The Outlook for Debtor Nations

The problems of the developing countries are not insoluble. If growth in the world economy resumes and real interest rates fall to historical levels, the debt burden of even the most heavily indebted countries will become much more manageable. Mexico and Brazil, among the most heavily indebted countries, both have debts well below half their GNPs. At a historically typical real interest rate of 2 percent, the real burden of debt service would fall to less than 1 percent of GNP — a fully manageable level in a growing economy.

The key to recovery from the debt problem, however, lies in increased exports from the debtor countries. Import restrictions by the developing countries can only accomplish so much in improving their trade balances. Imports have already fallen considerably in high debt countries in the last year, leaving limited room for further cuts. As growth resumes among the debtor countries, they will tend to import more, and will need to export more to pay for the imports. They will not be able to do this if the industrial countries, including the United States, institute new protectionist measures. . . .

Review of 1982 and the Economic Outlook

For the U.S. economy, 1982 was a year of painful transition toward price stability. The momentum of high inflation, built up over the last 15 years, was broken and inflation was reduced to its lowest rate in a decade. Success in reducing inflation, however, was accompanied by a recession that began in mid-1981 and lingered through 1982. A drop in real exports, along with inventory adjustments, accounted for the decline in U.S. production. Despite the recession, final sales to domestic purchasers increased. Expenditures for some interest-sensitive goods, such as housing and consumer durable goods, registered their first rise in recent years.

Economic developments in 1982 clearly set the stage for a recovery in 1983. The sizable slowdown in inflation contributed to the sharp drop in interest rates in the summer of 1982. The inventory cycle that held down production in 1982 is expected to turn around sometime in 1983. This development, combined with recovery in housing and durable consumer goods and continuing gains in defense spending, is expected to bring moderate sustainable economic recovery. Prospects are good that this recovery can be maintained through the 1980s without reigniting inflationary pressures. . . .

PROSPECTS FOR 1983

Assuming that the Administration's 1984 budget proposals are enacted and that the monetary aggregates grow within the Federal Reserve's target ranges, the prospects for a moderate, sustainable economic recovery beginning early in 1983 are good. As was true in the early stages of previous recoveries, the unemployment rate is likely to stabilize for several months before a downward trend becomes evident. A pattern of reduced inflation in 1982 is expected to continue in 1983. The sharp rise in the Federal budget deficit reflects reduced receipts because of lower inflation, as well as the effects of the 1981-82 recession.

The expectation of economic recovery is based on the view that continuing strength in household and defense spending will bring a turnaround in the inventory cycle. Cuts in production and increases in sales brought business inventories more in line with sales by the end of 1982. Future sales gains are thus likely to be met by increases in production, income, and employment, enhancing sales further. Once even a moderate but sustained increase in sales is underway, this sequence of events may lead to a temporary surge of above-average economic growth.

Increases in sales will come primarily from households whose income will be bolstered by the third stage of the personal income tax cut, whose debt burden has declined sharply relative to income and assets, and whose financial assets, in many cases, appreciated in rallies in the stock and bond markets. With continued moderate increases in food and oil prices, more income will become available for other consumer purchases. Because outlays on durable consumer goods and houses have been depressed for the last 4 years, consumers are expected to devote increases in their income, and perhaps some of the recent gains in their financial wealth, to replenishing their holdings of durable goods. The sharp easing of credit terms and lower house price increases have already encouraged more households to consider buying houses. This uptrend is expected to intensify in 1983. New house purchases are invariably followed by a pickup in expenditures for furniture, appliances, and other housing-related goods.

The pace of the recovery in 1983 will probably be moderate by historical standards. Low capacity utilization rates and the need to rebuild corporate liquidity will restrain capital spending. The worldwide recession and the lagged effect of the appreciation of the dollar will curtail the growth of exports. Continued reductions in the nondefense public sector will limit it as a source of increased aggregate demand.

PROSPECTS AND POLICIES BEYOND 1983

Economic prospects for the rest of the 1980s depend greatly on the economic policies that are followed. The Administration believes that the four-point program it has pursued — reducing the growth of Federal outlays, taxes, regulation, and the money supply — constitutes the best approach for attaining and maintaining the economic goals set forth in the Full Employment and Balanced Growth Act of 1978.

The Full Employment and Balanced Growth Act calls for annual numerical goals for several key economic indicators over a 5-year period. The projections ... show gradual, steady progress toward our economic goals. These figures illustrate the Administration's belief, explained in Chapter 1, that policies based on consistent, long-term objectives can simultaneously achieve full employment, price stability, and sustained growth in real income. A major cause of our present economic ills was the inclination in the past to pursue one economic goal single-mindedly, without adequate attention to the longer run consequences for other economic objectives. This Administration remains determined to avoid the errors of past policies.

A major prerequisite for achieving our economic goals is control of inflation. Marked progress toward this end has been made in the last 2 years. With continued moderate growth in the monetary aggregates, increased reliance on the private sector, and increased domestic and international economic competition, the prospects for sustaining and extending the progress against inflation are now quite favorable.

An important factor in achieving and sustaining high real economic growth is a high level of capital formation. . . . Controlling the Federal deficit is now the single most important method of encouraging more capital formation.

A critical element in achieving healthy economic growth is maintaining a liberal worldwide trading system. . . .

Just as an open worldwide trading system is crucial for the free world economies, a competitive free market system unfettered by unnecessary government regulation is essential for a strong domestic economy. . . .

The year 1983 is expected to be the first of many years of sustained economic growth. Continued economic growth is the only way to sustain progress in reducing unemployment. But macroeconomic policies alone cannot reduce structural unemployment and achieve an acceptable level of employment. . . .

One major remaining threat to a sustainable, balanced recovery is the danger that large Federal budget deficits would preclude the continuing declines in real interest rates that are necessary for healthy growth in all sectors of the economy. The Administration's 1984 budget provides a plan which can lead to a steady decline in budget deficits and thus, ultimately, to a balanced Federal budget.

REPORT ON ROLE OF U. S. JEWS IN THE HOLOCAUST

February 8, 1983

The 35 members of the American Jewish Commission on the Holocaust, chaired by former Supreme Court Associate Justice Arthur J. Goldberg, concluded in their February 8 interim report that American Jews were slow to react to the danger Nazi Germany posed to European Jews from 1939 to 1945, when the Nazis systematically killed six million Jewish people. American Jews, the report said, never mounted a sustained, all-out mobilization to save the millions of Jews threatened with extinction in World War II. The privately funded commission, established in September 1981, was composed of rabbis, jurists and political leaders. It was expected that the final report would be issued in 1984.

"Did American Jews do everything they might have done?" was the central question posed in the report. The commission's answer: "In hindsight, probably not. They were so benumbed by the magnitude of this unprecedented catastrophe — as were the European Jews — that they were slow in moving from knowledge to belief to action. . . .

"Even if American Jews had been united and organized and had taken more action on behalf of European Jews, would it have had a major impact on rescue? We doubt it. The number who could have been saved once the Holocaust started was extremely limited by Hitler's determined, systematic plan of complete extermination, by the acquiescence or indifference of the United States, British and Soviet and almost all other governments. . . . American Jewry lacked the numbers, the resources, the power and the organization to have a major impact in overcoming these obstacles and limitations."

143

Allied Governments Faulted

The commission faulted major American Jewish organizations for what it saw as a host of mistakes, including timidity, internal squabbling and wishful thinking about Nazi intentions. But it avoided any condemnations of Jewish organizations in the United States. "It should be recognized," the report said, "that the American Jewish community of 1939-45 . . . had little power or influence. Most Jews were first or second generation Americans, still trying to pull themselves up by their bootstraps."

The report placed major responsibility for failing to act on the Allied countries, rather than on the Jewish organizations. "The Allied governments," the report maintained, "developed the power necessary to defeat Hitler, but survival, national interest and victory were their top priorities, not the rescue of Jews. And the American Jews could do little without the cooperation of the United States and British governments."

Until the Japanese attacked Pearl Harbor in 1941, the United States, in the throes of the Great Depression, followed an isolationist foreign policy. The Depression had given rise to tight immigration restrictions because Americans did not want foreigners coming in to compete for scarce jobs. But even when a labor shortage developed during the war, there was no substantial move to loosen the restrictions on immigration that would allow European Jews to enter the country. According to the report, neo-Nazi groups stimulated anti-Jewish sentiment.

The British considered Jews "enemy aliens" and generally barred them from entering territories of the British Empire, the report said. Among actions damaging to the fate of the European Jews, the report listed British efforts to curtail Jewish emigration to Palestine in 1939. Those efforts "cut off all but a relative handful of Jews from their most likely avenue of escape. This policy — to which the United States made no strong objections — was to become a major stumbling block to the rescue of Jews from the Holocaust, and hence a contributing cause to countless deaths," the report said.

Limitations of Jewish Organizations

The report described the varied efforts of different Jewish organizations as they reacted to the Holocaust. The American Jewish Congress in the United States and the Zionist Agency in Palestine smuggled food parcels and medical supplies to Jews trapped in Axis territories and "were able to smuggle a limited number of Jews out." But American Jews "neither affluent nor influential . . . were preoccupied with Jewish problems, such as the depression and World War II . . . Jewish organizations were generally small, understaffed and underfinanced."

Jews were limited, too, the report pointed out, not only by small numbers and internal divisions but by "tragic misconceptions" about the situation that confronted them. Among them was an assumption that Nazi policy was only a particularly virulent form of traditional European anti-Semitism.

While the report might undergo revisions before final adoption, probably in 1984, commission members, who were prominent rabbis, jurists and political leaders, said they expected no major changes in its main conclusions. The tone of the interim report, particularly its charges of the American Jewish community's ineffectiveness, was considerably more moderate than an earlier draft issued in 1982. Several Jewish groups, among them the American Jewish Committee, the American Jewish Congress and the World Jewish Congress, had condemned its assertion that "in the face of Hitler's total war of extermination against the Jews of Europe, the Jewish leadership in America at no stage decided to proclaim total mobilization for rescue."

The first draft led to a dispute that caused Goldberg, the commission's founder, initially to withdraw his financial support for the study. However, Goldberg said in January 1983 that he would provide the necessary funds so the commission could complete its work. A month later the panel issued its interim report.

Following are excerpts from the Interim Report of the American Jewish Commission on the Holocaust, issued February 8, 1983:

Preface

The American Jewish Commission on the Holocaust was formed in 1981 on the initiative of a number of American Jewish leaders. It was created with a view to conducting an objective inquiry into the actions and attitudes of American Jewish leaders and organization[s] concerning the Holocaust during those years of World War II when that great tragedy was impending and in progress. The underlying aim of the initiators of the project was not to make moral judgments but rather to enable later generations to learn from this experience whatever might help prevent a similar tragedy from ever again befalling the Jews or any other people.

Former U.S. Supreme Court Justice Arthur J. Goldberg accepted the Chairmanship of the Commission. On his invitation, 35 distinguished Jewish leaders from many walks of American life consented to serve as officers and members. The Report that follows is the result of their joint deliberations and of the scholarly work done under their direction.

The Commission's membership of 35 is larger than originally intended. While the Commission was being established, it was suggested that additional members, identified with American Jewish organizations should be named; thus the actions of those who had led these organizations during the years under consideration would not be left exclusively to the evaluation of scholars who might not be sufficiently aware of the terrible dilemmas the Jewish leadership faced in that period. The organizers of the Commission viewed this concern with sympathy and considered it legitimate; hence, members were added. Though the members are in many cases officials of Jewish organizations, each served the Commission in an individual capacity and not as a representative of an organization.

WHY THIS STUDY?

It is a striking fact that in the voluminous published material on the Holocaust, not a single book deals primarily with the role of one of the most important groups involved; namely, the leaders of the major American Jewish organizations. The role of every other key group and leader has been thoroughly studied: Franklin D. Roosevelt and the State Department; Winston Churchill and the British Foreign and Colonial Offices; the Vatican and other Christian church authorities; the International Committee of the Red Cross — and, of course, Hitler, the Nazi hierarchy, and the rulers of other Axis powers and of the Nazis' satellite and conquered countries. No comparable study of the role of American Jewry exists.

To be sure, the role of American Jewish leaders has not been touched upon in histories of the Holocaust, but references to them appear only as part of a larger tableau. There are also studies of individual American Jewish organizations, notably Yehuda Bauer's recent book on the American Jewish Joint Distribution Committee 1939-1945 and Naomi Cohen's on the American Jewish Committee. Still, these do not add up to what, in our view, is needed — an objective study of the American Jewish leadership as a whole, including interactions among them, with the mass of American Jewry and with the more powerful actors in the tragedy, the Nazi, American and British governments.

In dealing with the Holocaust it warrants emphasis that the Nazis were the murderers and the Jews were the victims of this unprecedented crime against humanity — the murder of six million European Jews.

Jews everywhere, Americans included, were in a true sense the victims of Hitler's bestiality. In the history of the Jewish people, victims of many persecutions, the lives of Jews anywhere have been of deep concern to Jews everywhere. And the destruction of European Jewry was a double tragedy of horrendous proportions — the loss of precious lives and the loss of a great part of the Jewish heritage. All Jews suffered and continue to suffer from the Holocaust.

Why, then, have we undertaken this study? It is certainly not to condemn or pass judgment on the American Jewish leadership. We do not pretend that we would have been wiser or more effective, given the atmosphere of the time and the overwhelming obstacles they faced. But we feel that, given the advantage of hindsight, we can learn from their experience so that Jews may face future crises with better understanding and organization.

We are aware of the limitations on the power and influence of the American Jewish leadership. Once Hitler had decided to exterminate the Jews and had spread his hegemony over Eastern Europe and much of the Soviet Union, the masses of European Jewry were at his mercy. The Allied governments developed the power necessary to defeat Hitler, but survival, national interest and victory were their top priorities, not the rescue of Jews. And the American Jews could do little without the cooperation of the United States and British governments.

Even within these limitations, the American Jewish leaders of that time faced formidable obstacles. Their organizations were small and weakly financed. The special interest groups aligned against them, particularly on the vital question of reducing immigration barriers, were far more powerful. There was no organized Jewish lobby. The Jewish organizations had not yet developed the techniques which various ethnic groups have now learned to use in bringing home to government leaders and the general press the crux of urgent issues. The general American press gave relatively little attention to the Holocaust. The Yiddish press was far more informative and penetrating, but their audience was limited to the Yiddish-reading segments of the five million Jews, who in total represented only a small fraction of the American population. And the very enormity of what was happening to the Jews of Europe complicated the task of making it comprehensible and believable.

Certainly the vast majority of European Jews were doomed by the end of 1941, regardless of what American Jewry did. A remnant survived. In most cases their survival was an incidental result of Allied war aims rather than a deliberate campaign of rescue. In many cases they were rescued with the help of American Jewish organizations. How extensive were the rescue efforts of American Jewry? Could more have been done to save hundreds, thousands, or even tens of thousands more of the six million who died? Were all opportunities explored promptly and fully? Did the American Jewish leadership give adequate priority to rescue? How effective were their efforts? Were their plans and actions coordinated? Were their errors of omission or commission? These are some of the questions we intend to explore.

THE PROCESS

The process of preparing the Report, as well as the background papers and documents on which it rests, went through three phases.

1. A Research Group collected the documentary and background material and prepared first drafts.

2. The Research Group's drafts were evaluated by a Review Committee composed of scholars and specialists in the field. The Committee's criticisms and suggestions were taken into account, and in many cases incorporated, in revised drafts.

3. The Commission evaluated the drafts submitted to it, made decisions and issued instructions to the Research Group. On that basis the present Report was prepared and submitted to the Commission, which gave its approval.

The analysis, findings and conclusions in this Report reflect the general consensus of the Commission. Undoubtedly, no two Commission members would have written this Report in exactly the same way; differences of emphasis and nuance are inevitable. Where members wished to enter individual reservations on specific points, these are duly recorded. . . .

We have not presumed to sit in judgment, nor to render a verdict, on the actions discussed in this Report. Our objective has been more modest: to record and publish the truth, as nearly as we would determine it, as to what American Jewish leaders did, and what indeed they might have been able to do in all the circumstances, to mitigate the massive evils of the Holocaust. We have sought thus to add to the historical record of these terrible events — a record to which future decision-makers may turn for guidance.

The Drama and the Actors

To gain a clear perspective on our subject it is necessary to recall its historical setting. The Holocaust was a uniquely horrible chapter in the global tragedy that culminated in the Second World War. The perpetrators of the Holocaust, its 6 million victims, the Allied governments and Jewish communities who responded, or failed to respond, to it — all these were the actors in that larger global drama.

NAZI AGGRESSION AND THE FLIGHT FROM REALITY

The international political circumstances and attitudes which led to World War II also, to a great extent, paved the way for the Holocaust. These circumstances can be briefly summarized:

• Germany, defeated, disarmed and punished for its war guilt in World War I, and wracked with economic distress — yet still, in its underlying strength, the chief power of Europe — sought a leader out of its troubles. In 1933 it embraced the demagogue Adolph Hitler with his virulent antisemitism, contempt for democracy, and advocacy of world domination by a German master race.

• France and Britain, exhausted and demoralized by the heavy cost of their 1918 victory, based their policy toward Hitler on wishful thinking. They discounted frank declarations of his aims and did nothing effective to stop his treaty-breaking rearmament program and his bloodless, step-by-step territorial advances in 1936-39. As Winston Churchill later wrote, these two powers, while Hitler's armies were still much weaker than theirs, engaged in a "five or six years' policy of easy-going placatory appeasement" — only to take their stand at long last on Poland, when Nazi military might was fully marshaled — thus precipitating "an obviously imminent war on far worse conditions and on the greatest scale." [Winston Churchill]

• Stalin, the Soviet dictator, signed in August 1939 his cynical pact with

Hitler, partitioning Poland between them.

• The United States, in the throes of the Great Depression, followed an isolationist foreign policy. Most Americans were unwilling to be drawn into European power struggles or to take sides between Hitler and his intended victims. Not until the Japanese attack on Pearl Harbor in December 1941 was this attitude largely dissipated.

This long and feckless flight from reality by the Western powers, during the years when Hitler's Germany was openly preparing its onslaught, placed the Allies in a position of grave weakness when the worldwide battle was finally seen to be inevitable. The weakness was political as well as military, and led Britain in particular to resort to diplomatic maneuvers which might not even have been considered had London been leading from strength. An instance, especially pertinent to our story, is Britain's White Paper of May 17, 1939, cutting back sharply on, and promising to end entirely within five years, Jewish immigration into the Palestine Mandate. It was clearly an attempt to compete for the favor of the Arabs, then under increasing influence from Germany. Thus the appeasement of Hitler, which had already put millions of European Jews in peril of their lives, was further compounded by a step which cut off all but a relative handful of those same Jews from their most likely avenue of escape. This policy — to which the United States made no strong objections — was to become a major stumbling block to the rescue of Jews from the Holocaust, and hence a contributing cause to countless deaths.

Up to 1941 Hitler's policy was to rid Europe of the Jews rather than to kill them. Why, then, did so many Jews remain in Germany and Austria, only to be slaughtered later? There were several factors at work. Many older Jews were reluctant to leave friends, family and familiar surroundings, and were inclined to clutch at straws of hope that the madness would pass. Moreover, to leave Germany a Jew initially had to give up 80 percent of his property and savings — and later all except 10 Reichsmarks. Finally, most potential countries of refuge were in the throes of the Depression and put up formidable barriers to immigration or even temporary haven. As became clear in July 1938 at the 32-nation conference on refugees at Evian, France, the numbers of Jewish refugees governments would admit were pitifully small compared with the numbers who needed rescue. These restrictive policies, which were exploited in Nazi propaganda, encountered little dissent from Roosevelt's Jewish advisers, who were keenly aware of widespread opposition to the influx of multitudes of new immigrants at a time of massive unemployment.

All these circumstances combined to hold down the prewar flight of Jews from Nazi control. Only 37 thousand (among them Albert Einstein) fled Germany in 1933 after Hitler came to power. By 1938 only about 150,000 had left. Some 350,000 then remained — about half of them over 45, since usually it was the younger generation who emigrated at the urging of their elders. In 1938 — especially after the brutal *Kristallnacht* rampage in November of that year — and the prewar months of 1939, about 200,000 additional German Jews left, while approximately the same number of

Austrian Jews came under German rule as a result of the March 1938 Anschluss.

Then, with the outbreak of war in September 1939, an already alarming picture changed drastically for the worse. Hitler's empire expanded dramatically, absorbing additional millions of Jews in Poland immediately, and soon afterward in other parts of Europe. Simultaneously, the doors of escape were locked from the inside as the Nazis closed their frontiers, which thereafter could only be passed with help from the outside. Although Western governments at last somewhat relaxed their barriers against immigrants and refugees, no country even then would go as far as to open its borders to large-scale resettlement of European Jews — their only hope, as it turned out, of escaping virtually total destruction. Hitler's formal decision in 1941 to slaughter all Jews coming under Nazi control — the "Final Solution" — was taken only after it had become evident that other countries were not prepared to accept them in sufficient numbers to accommodate his fiendish goal of ridding Europe of all Jews by terror, extortion and expulsion.

THE ALLIED GOVERNMENTS, 1939-45

The record shows that all Allied governments were well aware of Hitler's extermination policy but, for a variety of reasons, were generally reticent and evasive about calling attention to the fact that his target for genocide was the Jews. Finally, in December 1942, the United Nations, as they then began to call themselves, issued a brief but eloquent statement on the mass slaughter of Jews; this was a full 18 months after it had begun. They made little or no attempt until very late in the war to rescue Jews from the Holocaust, and in some cases actually obstructed such attempts by others. There was great concern about where they could put any massive number of Jewish refugess. Their attitude on the subject was construed by the Nazi authorities as tantamount to acquiesence. . . .

In 1942 and thereafter, when the plight of Europe's Jews had become truly desperate, the British and American official attitudes remained much the same. The two governments had first-hand intelligence on the Jewish condition in Nazi-occupied lands and were currently informed on steps to carry out the "Final Solution." . . . Yet at no time did they acknowledge this monstrous policy as an official Nazi war aim or declare their intention to thwart it. On December 17, 1942, the date of the one and only Allied statement of protest mentioned, above, Nazi propaganda minister Josef Paul Goebbels wrote in his diary. "At bottom . . . I believe both the English and the Americans are happy that we are exterminating the Jewish riffraff." Throughout the war, there is abundant documentary evidence of a determination on the part of the British and American governments to avoid this issue. . . .

Some rescue-minded Jews expressed open opposition to bombing the death camps on the grounds that this would kill even more Jews. A. Leon Kubowitzki, for example, proposed rather that paratroopers be used for rescue. From today's perspective, this fear appears ill-founded. Unfortunately, this division of opinion among Jewish leaders made it easier for Allied leaders to pursue their policy of not bombing camps.

The attitude which such actions revealed, especially in the case of the U.S. State Department, was aptly characterized in the title of a memorandum dated January 18, 1944 entitled *On the Acquiescence of This Government in the Murder of European Jews.* The memorandum was written by Josiah E. Bubois, then assistant general counsel of the U.S. Treasury Department, and addressed to Secretary of the Treasury Henry Morgenthau, Jr. To substantiate the charge of acquiescence — in contrast to mere inattention or indifference — the memorandum gave specific facts about State Department actions and summarized them as follows:

> (1) They have not only failed to use the Governmental *machinery* at their disposal to rescue Jews from Hitler, but have even gone so far as to use this Government machinery to prevent the rescue of these Jews.
>
> (2) They have not only failed to cooperate with *private organizations* in the efforts of these organizations to work out individual programs of their own, but have taken steps designed to prevent these programs from being put into effect.
>
> (3) They not only have failed to facilitate the obtaining of information concerning Hitler's plans to exterminate the Jews of Europe but in their official capacity have gone so far as to surreptitiously attempt to stop the obtaining of information concerning the murder of the Jewish population in Europe.
>
> (4) They have tried to cover up their guilt by:
>
>> (a) concealment and misrepresentation;
>>
>> (b) the giving of false and misleading explanations for their failures to act and their attempts to prevent action; and
>>
>> (c) the issuance of false and misleading statements concerning the "action" which they have taken to date.

In justice it should be recalled that U.S. policy on this question was not completely static throughout the war. An important development was the creation of the War Refugee Board by Executive Order 9417, January 22, 1944. . . . [T]his body succeeded in relaxing the application of curbs on the sending of money abroad, and on contacts with enemy authorities, in such a way as to facilitate rescue efforts by the American Joint Distribution Committee and other Jewish organizations. In January 1944 President Roosevelt's executive order creating the WRB was sent by the State Department to U.S. diplomatic posts abroad with accompanying instructions to help in the rescue of the Jews. . . .

The tragic fact, however, is that this improvement in policy came too late to do very much good. By mid-1943, Polish Jewry had been nearly wiped out, and by November of that year the "Greater German Reich" (embracing prewar Germany, Austria, Luxembourg, and parts of Poland, France and Belgium) had been officially declared *Judenrein,* or purged of Jews; and the slaughter of Jews in occupied areas of the Soviet Union had been enormous.

The Western Allies were not alone in displaying such attitudes. Neutral

Switzerland, for example, forced Jews arriving at its border to turn back to certain death — even though, as Swiss authorities have since acknowledged, they could have admitted these people without jeopardizing Swiss security. As for the Soviet Union, its attitude seemed one of total indifference and acquiescence. Well informed by his underground in Germany, Poland and elsewhere in Eastern Europe, Stalin did nothing to save or help the Jews, either during the period of the Nazi-Soviet pact or later during the Red Army's victorious war against Germany, except as an incidental by-product of his own war aims. For all of the Allies, national interest and winning the war were the paramount, all-absorbing goals.

The Soviets did, however, evacuate large numbers of Jews along with other civilians as they retreated before the Nazi invasion in 1941. And, like the Western Allies, liberated Jews and other inmates from concentration camps as they pushed Nazi troops back again in the campaigns to defeat Nazi Germany. But again like the Western Allies, the Soviets were reluctant to acknowledge a special Jewish problem. Even today they suppress references to the fact that the people slaughtered at Babi Yar were Jewish. . . .

The American Jewish Community

To understand how American Jewry responded to the Holocaust and to the policies of the United States government, we must first review the nature of Jewish organizational life in the United States from the days of the *Landsmannschaften* (mutual aid societies of Jews from particular European towns or districts) to the present. Jewish organizational life in America has never been monolithic, and certainly was not so in the period under study. Not only between Jewish organizations but also within them vigorous debate, tensions and rivalries were common. Attempts to unify the Jewish community to meet the challenge of catastrophe in Europe were short-lived. Nevertheless, as will be seen below, it is possible to discern common tendencies in the ideas and attitudes of leading Jews and Jewish organizations in America. . . .

In considering the activities of the Jewish organizations, it should be recognized that the American Jewish Community of 1939-45 was not the community as we know it today. It had little power or influence. Most Jews were first or second generation Americans, still trying to pull themselves up by their bootstraps. In general, they were neither affluent nor influential.

The Jewish organizations were, for the most part, small, understaffed and underfinanced. Most proceedings were conducted in Yiddish.

Most assimilated Jews were preoccupied with American problems, such as the depression and World War II. Most of those of combat age served in the armed forces, while others were in official positions or defense work. Few of them had much time or energy left from these tasks.

Orthodox Jews were generally those with the closest emotional ties to

the Jews of Europe, but their activities were centered largely in Syna-
gogues and religious services. They were not prominent on the national
scene, where they were much less influential than the American Jewish
Committee, the American Jewish Congress or the B'nai B'rith, but they
gave a very high priority to the rescue of their European brethren.

The Zionist groups identified with the Yishuv in Palestine. Their
primary goal was the survival of the Yishuv and the establishment of a
Jewish state. Despite their relatively small numbers, they took the
leadership at the two major wartime gatherings of American Jewish
organizations, the Biltmore Conference and the American Jewish Conference in 1943. After the war, the establishment of Israel gave survivors one
country where the doors were opened wide, a matter of great significance.
Even during the war, despite their own tenuous situation, the Yishuv in
Palestine made notable efforts at rescue through the Jewish Agency.
Indeed, their rescue actions, often involving parachuting and infiltration in
extreme danger, were the most heroic.

There were prominent Jews close to President Roosevelt, notably
Benjamin Cohen, Samuel Rosenman, David Niles, Felix Frankfurter,
Herbert Lehman and Sidney Hillman. In general, however, they saw their
role principally as patriotic Americans bolstering a president carrying the
heavy burdens of overcoming a great depression and fighting World War
II. They did not speak out strongly for special action on behalf of the Jews
of Europe.

It should also be borne in mind that most Jewish organizations in the
country were not independent bodies but branches of world bodies.
Moreover, some key leaders on the American Jewish scene were not
Americans. . . .

Given these circumstances, the historian often finds it difficult to
distinguish between the American Jewish leadership and the leadership of
international Jewish organizations. For the same reason it is difficult to
locate responsibility, as between the world bodies and the American
institutions, for the success or failure of relief and rescue efforts on behalf
of the Jews of Europe. . . .

In 1939 there were four major defense organizations operating in the
United States. There was the prestigious and wealthy American Jewish
Committee, founded in 1906; the American Jewish Congress, and its
affiliate the World Jewish Congress (1936), first organized in 1915 and
reorganized by Stephen Wise in 1922; the B'nai B'rith, founded in 1843,
and its affiliate the Anti-Defamation League (1913) which served as
"America's principal watchdog against anti-Semitism"; and the Jewish
Labor Committee, established in 1934, representing 756 different Jewish
labor groups in the United States.

Joining these four defense organizations was also one relief organization
which was to play a leading role in the rescue effort. This organization was
the American Joint Distribution Committee, hereafter referred to as the
JDC or the "Joint." Founded in 1914, the JDC was originally dedicated to

providing aid to Jews where they lived but eventually changed its policy and actively participated in the rescue of European Jewry. Therefore, it is the one relief organization which must be included in any investigation of Jewish organizations involved in concerted rescue activities.

Postwar planning was an important activity of most of these groups. The strongest concentration on postwar planning was carried out by two leading American Jewish organizations, the American Jewish Committee (AJC) and the Zionist groups, notably the American Jewish Congress and the Zionist Organization of America. In the case of the Zionists this meant planning for the creation of the Jewish National Home in Palestine. . . .

In retrospect the AJC leadership may be seen to have been overly cautious and to have carried on in a business-as-usual manner during a disaster of monumental proportions. At the time they were bitterly attacked by rival Zionists for their "cowardly" attitude. . . .

Yet the AJC leaders were not indifferent to the fate of the European Jews. . . .

Still, even after Hitler invaded the Soviet Union and news of the mass slaughter of Jews became known, the AJC continued to have serious differences of principle and tactics with its Zionist rivals. It chose to focus on "the real issue, namely, the defense of civilizations against totalitarianism." It mounted a campaign to counteract anti-semitism by providing accounts of Jewish heroism and warning against the "divide and conquer tactics of the Nazis." After news of Hitler's plan to slaughter the Jews of Europe was officially acknowledged in December 1942, the AJC leaders did join leaders of the other major Jewish organizations in an approach to President Roosevelt asking that he "warn the Nazis that they will be held to strict accountability for their crimes," a request to which the President readily agreed. But after the American Jewish Conference of August-September 1943, where the Zionists dominated the decisions, the AJC again went its own way. Given the financial and numerical weakness of the American Jewish organizations as a whole and the enormity of the problem, it is regrettable that even part of these resources were dissipated by differences among them. . . .

. . . B'nai B'rith was little different from the AJC in defense activities. Through the first few years of the Nazi crisis beginning with Hitler's take-over in 1933, the B'nai B'rith could be relied upon to side with the AJC in its war with the Zionists of the AJ Congress. B'nai B'rith joined the AJC in opposing the boycott of German goods because it feared that such a protest would adversely affect the 14,000 B'nai B'rith members living in Germany, and limited its activities to the type of quiet backdoor diplomacy practiced by the AJC. . . .

THE WORLD JEWISH CONGRESS AND THE AMERICAN JEWISH CONGRESS

Although limited in funds and personnel, the World Jewish Congress (WJC), with the active collaboration of the larger and wealthier American

Jewish Congress in the United States, and the Zionist Jewish Agency in Palestine, did play a significant role in the rescue effort....

Using its overseas agents, the WJC found ways to smuggle food parcels and medical supplies to Jews trapped in Axis territories and was able to smuggle a limited number of Jews out. The WJC offices in neutral countries were also used as receiving points for information about conditions behind Axis lines. The WCJ's most notable achievement during the Holocaust years was the early discovery of the Nazi "Final Solution" plan by the director of its Swiss office, Gerhart Riegner, in 1942.

The WJC also claimed credit for obtaining an abatement of the total blockade of Axis Europe, allowing some relief aid to reach the Jews behind enemy lines; for inducing the Allies to include retribution for anti-Jewish crimes among the major purposes of the war; for helping to prevent the deportation of Bulgarian Jews to Poland; for aiding in the rescue of the Danish Jews; for helping to keep alive the imperiled Turkish Jews living in France; and for having a hand in many other successful "special projects" in the overall rescue movement.

The ACJ and the WJC expended much of their time and energy on what they referred to as "breaking the wall of silence" surrounding the treatment of the Jews....

THE JEWISH LABOR COMMITTEE

The Jewish Labor Committee (JLC) was born in 1934 out of the urge to battle the twin dangers of Fascism and antisemitism. It was originally an outgrowth of the AFL's Labor Chest, whose purpose was to help victims of Fascism, and it retained close ties with AFL throughout the war in various rescue schemes to help labor leaders and "progressive" elements both Jews and non-Jews in Nazi-occupied Europe.

The JLC represented primarily the approximately half million members of the "Jewish" trade unions of New York, the majority of whom held socialist and Bundist views, which were anti or at least non-Zionist....

... Unfortunately, it was not too effective in rousing American Jewry.

THE ORTHODOX AMERICAN JEWS

The term Orthodox, in this context, refers actually to two small organizations, Agudath Israel and Vaad Hatzalah, who cooperated closely to rescue thousands of Jews during the Holocaust. With the help of the President's Advisory Committee on Political Refugees, the Orthodox were able to rescue hundreds of the intellectual elite of Polish Orthodox Jewry — talmudic scholars who had fled to Lithuania in 1939. Most of these were taken to Shanghai in 1941, via Japan, while a smaller number of the foremost scholars were allowed entry into the U.S. on emergency visitors visas.

Originally the Orthodox organizations were insignificant in number and powerless politically. But within several years they developed a sophisticated and efficient rescue apparatus with a small but highly dedicated international network that frequently outdid the large Jewish establishment organizations (in relative and at times even in absolute terms).

The secret of their success lay in the fact that most of the personnel consisted of highly motivated Jewish scholars and laymen whose dedication to the saving of lives was paramount. The Orthodox were flexible in their approach and were ready to disregard American laws when the rescue of Jews demanded it. . . .

There were many other Jewish organizations, both large and small, that participated in the rescue effort. For example, there were the important relief agencies such as the Hebrew Sheltering and Immigration Aid Society (HIAS) and the American ORT Federation, which contributed valuable service to the rescue movement. These organizations, however, concerned themselves almost exclusively with economic aid and relief for the European refugees once they managed to escape Nazi control. The actual rescue of European Jews was left to the more politically active defense organizations. There were also several Jewish leftist organizations, such as the Jewish People's Fraternal Order, that could be counted on to support the official Stalinist position of the moment. These organizations are not considered to be part of the Jewish rescue movement.

Viewed as a whole, the record of the work of all these groups leaves no doubt that many American Jewish leaders were profoundly affected by the catastrophe facing the Jews in Europe, and made significant efforts to deal with it. What they achieved must not be dismissed as insignificant, particularly in view of their limited power and influence. As the Talmud declares, every Jew saved counts as if a whole world was redeemed. Unfortunately, there was at no time a united sustained campaign for all-out mobilization of American Jews and their organizations on behalf of massive rescue, nor an all-out organized campaign to enlist non-Jewish American support.

The fact that there was no all-out mobilization must be considered in the context of the time. As indicated above, American Jews in that period did not have substantial influence or power. Their organizations were generally small, understaffed and underfinanced. . . .

The fact must be faced that what the millions of Jews of Europe needed, and only a small proportion of them got, was rescue. Until late in the war, when Zionism began to dominate Jewish efforts . . . without achieving its hoped-for major impact on the rescue problem — Jewish efforts were predominantly aimed at traditional refugee relief. Indeed, the distinction between refugee relief and rescue was often blurred, both by the Allied governments and the Jewish organizations.

The typical beneficiary of the American Jewish organizations then operating in Europe was a person who had escaped from Nazi-dominated parts of Europe, was living in a less than legal status in a strange country, and needed food, clothing and shelter. But the problem facing millions of European Jews at that time was precisely how to *become* refugees — that is, how to escape from Nazi areas where they were in daily peril of physical attack, deportation and death. . . .

What the Jewish Leadership Knew, and When: Tragic Misconceptions

THE RECORD: NO DEARTH OF INFORMATION

It would be redundant to enter lists as to what the Allied governments and the American Jewish leadership knew about the Holocaust and when. The whole subject is an open record — those who wanted to know, knew approximately almost day by day what went on under Hitler's domination. This was especially true of government leaders and those Jews who read the Jewish press. The general American media gave surprisingly, little attention to this tragedy of unprecedented dimensions. . . .

What Hitler intended to do with the Jews — or rather, his two alternatives — either to get rid of them by forced emigration and expulsion, or by extermination — was known from the very beginning of his career. . . .

Informed American Jewish leaders knew about the concentration camps virtually from the beginning — and they knew about the Wannsee Conference of January 20, 1942, where the decision to annihilate the Jews of Europe was formalized. . . .

In the archives of most of the major Jewish organizations there are large scrapbooks and files with thousands of clippings, and many reports from Switzerland, London and Palestine with details of the extermination process. . . .

For the American public at large, the very enormity of Hitler's crimes, exceeding normal human comprehension, may have diminished the reaction. People react, selectively, to man-sized threats. It is not giant tragedies that plumb our emotional depths; it is, rather, the plight of single human beings. In a week when 3,000 people were killed in an earthquake in Iran, a lone boy falls down a well-shaft in Italy and the whole world grieves. Six million Jews are put to death, and it is Anne Frank, trembling in her garret, who remains stamped in our memory.

Even as late as December 1944, 12 percent of Americans believed that the mass murder accounts were untrue, 27 percent believed only about 100,000 people were involved and only 4 percent believed the truth — that over 5 million Jews had already been put to death.

As for the American media, they were hampered by wartime limitations on communications and the fact that they could have no reporters in Nazi-occupied territory where the criminal slaughter of the Jews was taking place. Moreover, there was a certain skepticism about atrocity reports in wartime, given the experience in World War I with false stories about alleged German atrocities in Belgium. This time the atrocities were even worse than the reports, but the media were still reacting to their earlier experience. This was not the finest hour of the general American press. . . .

Perhaps the most telling indication that rescue activities were not handicapped by lack of knowledge by the Jewish leadership is the vehement criticism leveled by some outstanding personalities within the establishment against their colleagues. . . .

One further fact should be noted in reviewing the actions of American Jews during the Holocaust. While such efforts may have been inadequate, the actions of American Christians toward Christian victims of the Nazis — except for certain compassionate Christian leaders and the Quakers — appears indifferent and callous by comparison. In fact, because of large-scale Christian indifference, Jewish funds and Jewish organizations contributed substantially to the relief of *Christian* refugees from Nazi Germany.

THREE SERIOUS MISCONCEPTIONS

Quite commonly, after some great disaster, those who look back on the event find it hard to imagine how people could have been so lacking in foresight, perception and preparation.

Hindsight, however, is a poor guide to understanding. We can better grasp why the American Jewish community dealt with the Holocaust as it did if we examine the conceptions which dominated their thinking in different phases of the tragedy.

At the outset, it was supposed that Nazism was not essentially different from the many forms of antisemitism of the past. Then, after this belief was disproved, it was widely believed that Hitler's program to exterminate the Jews was fully supported by his allies and satellites in Europe, who therefore could not be looked to for any cooperation. Finally, American Jews clung to the mistaken belief (or hope?) that the American and British governments, involved in a war for survival, would give the rescue of Jews a serious priority. . . .

. . . Despite mounting evidence of the Nazis' unique savagery, most Jews continued — at all events until the invasion of Poland — to think of these persecutions as being in the classic tradition of antisemitism — perhaps more calamitous than in the past, but nevertheless survivable.

Even as the war went on and word of the mass slaughters began to spread, this deeply inculcated perception of antisemitism obscured the vision of Jews in Europe and America. . . .

Next among the misconceptions that afflicted American Jewish leaders was the notion that Hitler's allies and satellites in Europe agreed and cooperated fully with him in his program to exterminate the Jews. This was not quite true. This misconception undoubtedly inhibited rescue efforts that would have depended on the cooperation or tacit acquiescence of authorities within the Nazi empire.

In reality, when it came to backing for their Final Solution, the Nazis had almost no allies outside of Germany itself. Each of the countries overrun by the Nazis had its own culture and personality, and attitudes toward Jews varied widely; but all had this in common: they differed with Hitler on what to do with the Jews. . . .

The old saying that "the enemy of my enemy is my friend" has often proved true in war and politics, at least in a limited tactical sense. Even those who share few other common interests often cooperate to defend themselves — and each other — against a common enemy. During World War II the Jewish leaders of the Western world, including the United States, assumed that their relationship with the governments allied against Nazi Germany was of this character. They were tragically mistaken. The United States, Britain and the Soviet Union, like nations throughout history, fought for their own national interests, not for Jewish interests. Yet American Jewish leaders, despite individual differences, accepted Roosevelt's assurances that the cause of Jewish survival was identical with the cause of Allied victory. Perhaps they saw no alternative and, in any case, there was a degree of truth in those assurances. Their loyalty to the Allied cause was exemplary. . . .

It is true that Jewish leaders were frequently in contact with U.S. officials and made representations on behalf of European Jewry as effectively as they felt they could in the circumstances. But they quickly became aware of the limits of official willingness to act, and adjusted to those limits. Indeed, many American Jews, like their government, shied away from the overwhelming fact of the Holocaust. Hollywood, an industry dominated by Jews, did not produce a single film on the subject during World War II. To some extent this avoidance was also practiced by the most prestigious Jewish-owned newspapers, *The New York Times* and *The Washington Post.* . . .

Why did Jewish leaders act in such a reticent fashion at that crucial moment in their people's history? Why did they allow themselves to be persuaded that the Allied governments had their cause at heart?

A part of the answer may lie in response patterns built up during centuries of the Diaspora. Lacking a national power base of their own, Jews were still restrained by a history which had taught them not to draw attention to themselves and to seek accommodation with the ruling powers. When they entered the political arena, they usually did so not as Jews pursuing legitimate Jewish interests, but either as mainstream politicians, assimilated to the dominant culture, or else as idealists fighting for the rights of all men.

Moreover, the American Jews had legitimate reasons for both gratitude and loyalty to the United States and Roosevelt. . . .

Concluding Observations

. . . Now, using the benefit of hindsight, we should like to make some concluding observations of our own. In doing so we do not pretend that we would have been wiser or acted more effectively if we had had the responsibility at the time. Our purpose throughout has not been to judge but to learn.

On the basis of the research done for the Commission, we make the following observations:

1. The Holocaust — the planned, deliberate murder of 6 million European Jews by Adolf Hitler and his minions — was an unprecedented crime against humanity. Nothing comparable must ever be allowed to happen again.

2. American Jews were also victims of the Nazi crimes. Many lost mothers, fathers, grandparents, brothers, sisters, cousins and other relatives. And all Jews suffered from the destruction of European Jewry; its culture, its learning, and its traditions were a vital part of the Jewish heritage, destroyed by Hitler.

3. Did American Jews do everything they might have done? In hindsight, probably not. They were so benumbed by the magnitude of this unprecedented catastrophe — as were the European Jews — that they were slow in moving from knowledge to belief to action. At no time did they mount an all-out, unified, sustained mobilization for rescue.

Had we been in their situation, would we have done better? Not likely. In fact our inquiry showed that they did more than was generally realized, even though it falls short by contemporary standards. Moreover, they did much more than other ethnic groups and even helped significantly to rescue non-Jews. And, in proportion to resources, they did far more than governments, which frequently posed obstacles to the rescue of Jews and rarely took action to help them.

4. During the Holocaust the American Jewish community was weak and disorganized. Its effectiveness was further handicapped by rivalries and disunity and by the devotion of the overwhelming majority of Jews to President Roosevelt. Their devotion was such that they gave him complete loyalty and did not use leverage to prompt action by him on behalf of the millions of Hitler's Jewish victims. Moreover, most activist Jews were serving in the U.S. armed forces and, consequently, not available for activity in the U.S. on behalf of rescue.

5. Even if American Jews had been united and organized and had taken more action on behalf of European Jews, would it have had a major impact on rescue? We doubt it. The number who could have been saved once the Holocaust started was extremely limited — by Hitler's determined, systematic plan of complete extermination and his physical control over almost the entire European Jewish population; by the acquiescence or indifference of the United States, British, Soviet and almost all other governments; and by the lack of concern and human solidarity on the part of the overwhelming majority of non-Jews. American Jewry lacked the numbers, the resources, the power and the organization to have a major impact in overcoming these obstacles and limitations. Yet even though American Jewry could not have saved more than a small fraction of Hitler's victims, every life is precious and it was crucially important to try.

Nothing we say or do can bring back even one of the 6 million dead and nothing can make up for their loss. Yet at least we should learn from the experience, and we believe that there are profound lessons to be derived from it.

1. *Jewish causes must be championed strongly, persistently and effectively by Jews.* Non-Jewish allies can be won over — indeed, given the fact that Jews constitute such a tiny fraction of the American population and an even tinier fraction of world population and power, allies are usually essential — but the genuine concern of non-Jews for Jewish causes can not be taken for granted. Callousness, anti-semitism, self-interest and national interest are prevalent everywhere. Jewish leaders must take all those factors into account in planning their strategy and tactics.

2. *Consequently, American Jews need strong organizations and effective lobbying.*

3. *On critical issues the American Jewish community will be more effective when it is united.*

4. *Techniques must be developed for bringing home to the media the importance of issues critical to the Jewish community.* It can never be taken for granted that the media will give adequate attention to and understanding of such issues.

5. *There should be increased emphasis on education about the Holocaust, both in schools and the media.* Such education can help to build resistance against the deadly viruses of racism, hatred and inhumanity.

6. *A threat to the safety and rights of any Jewish community is a threat not only to other Jewish communities but also to the safety and rights of all, Jews and non-Jews.* As the Nazi experience demonstrates, Jews are usually the first target of a despot but the repression and cruelty invariably widens to include other victims. Jews and non-Jews must be alert and vigilant to combat neo-Nazism and other movements that trample on human rights and dignity.

7. *American Jews must never again fear to raise their voices and use their influence when Jewish lives are threatened.*

PALESTINIAN MASSACRE REPORT

February 8, 1983

In its final report, issued February 8, the Israeli Commission of Inquiry into the Events at the Refugee Camps in Beirut placed indirect responsiblity for the September 1982 massacre of Lebanese and Palestinian civilians in the Shatilla and Sabra refugee camps squarely on the shoulders of Israel and recommended the firing of several top Israeli officials. Prime Minister Menachem Begin had established the commission of inquiry on September 28, 1982, and named Yitzhak Kahan, president of the Israeli Supreme Court, as its chairman. Aharon Barak, a Supreme Court justice, and Yona Efrat, a retired major general, served on the panel as well. The commission had power to subpoena witnesses to testify before it, but its recommendations were not legally binding on the government.

Background

On September 14, 1982, Lebanese president-elect Bashir Gemayel was killed when a bomb exploded in the headquarters of his Christian Phalangist Party in east Beirut. No one claimed responsibility for the bombing, which many feared would trigger a new outbreak of violence between Gemayel's forces and Moslem militiamen. Gemayel's assassination and the subsequent fears of new civil strife prompted Israeli forces to move into west Beirut on September 15.

Israeli arms surrounded the Palestinian camps of Sabra and Shatilla, Beirut, on September 15. Palestinian guerrillas who had escaped evacua-

tion were thought to be hiding in the camps. Israeli troops permitted the Phalangist militiamen to enter the camps September 16 to root out the terrorists. Inside the camps, however, the Phalangists began mass killings of civilians. By the time the massacre had ended two days later, more than 300 people were believed dead, and 900 were reported missing.

As details of the massacre emerged, attention focused on Israel's role in the attack. Demands for an investigation came from American groups, international organizations and the Israeli public. Begin initially rejected any inquiry because it would be seen as an admission of guilt. Israel, he maintained, was blameless, and allegations of Israeli involvement were a "blood libel." But Israeli citizens, shocked and shaken by the massacre, September 25 staged the largest rally in Israel's history. Hundreds of thousands of Israelis gathered in Tel Aviv to protest Begin's action. The prime minister bowed to the mounting pressure and formally requested an independent investigation.

The Commission's Report

The commission placed direct responsibility for the massacre with the Phalangists. "All evidence indicates that the massacre was perpetrated by the Phalangists between the time they entered the camps on Thursday [September 16]... and their departure from the camps on Saturday [September 18]... The victims were found in those areas where the Phalangists were in military control.... No other military force aside from the Phalangists was seen by any one of the witnesses in the area of the camps where the massacre was carried out or at the time of the entrance into or exit from this area." The report concluded that no Israeli soldiers had taken part in the killings and that there had been no conspiracy between Israeli forces and the Phalangist militia to commit a massacre.

Although the commission absolved Israel of any direct blame for the massacre, it held the Begin government indirectly responsible. The panel based its doctrine of "indirect responsibility" on "the obligations applying to every civilized nation and the ethical rules accepted by civilized peoples." With particular regard to Jewish history, the report stated "The Jewish public's stand has always been that the responsibility for such deeds falls not only on those who rioted and committed atrocities, but also on those who were responsible for safety and public order, who could have prevented the disturbances and did not fulfill their obligations in this respect."

The commission held the Israeli government indirectly responsible in two major areas. First, given the assassination of Phalangist leader Bashir Gemayel and the subsequent heightening of historic tensions between Moslem and Christian factions, Israeli officials should have realized the probability of a massacre and taken steps to supervise the militiamen.

Second, Israel should have acted immediately and decisively to stop the Phalangists. Testimony heard by the commission indicated that reports of the killings reached Israeli military commanders as early as Thursday night, September 16. Yet the Phalangists were not ordered out of the camps until Saturday morning, September 18. ". . . [I]t is clear from the course of events that when the reports began to arrive about the actions of the Phalangists in the camps, no proper heed was taken of these reports, the correct conclusions were not drawn from them, and no energetic and immediate actions were taken to restrain the Phalangists and put a stop to their actions. This both reflects and exhausts Israel's direct responsibility for what occurred in the refugee camps," the commission concluded.

Implications for Israeli Leadership

The commission's recommendations resulted in the dismissal of several key Israeli government officials and criticism or censure of others. The report criticized Begin for his lack of interest in the actions of the Phalangist militiamen. The Israeli prime minister did not know in advance that the Phalangists had been allowed into the camps and first heard reports of the killings on a British Broadcasting Corp. radio broadcast. The panel noted that Begin had been informed at a Thursday afternoon Cabinet meeting of the military decision to allow the Phalangists into the camps, yet showed "absolutely no interest in their actions." Had the prime minister indicated interest in those actions, the panel stated, the defense minister and chief of staff of the Israeli Defense Forces (IDF) would have taken appropriate measures to ensure the safety of the civilian population. Although the commission condemned Begin's indifference, it found that his conduct did not warrant a call for his resignation.

Begin's foreign minister, Yitzhak Shamir, was censured for not passing along early information he had received from another minister about the massacre, but the commission found that his actions did not warrant asking for his resignation. The commission also criticized the head of Israel's intelligence agency, the Mossad, whose identity is kept secret, for remaining silent on the dangers inherent in the Phalangist operation, but it recommended no further action against him.

The panel was much more critical of Defense Minister Ariel Sharon and several top Israeli army officers. Sharon, accused of "blunders" tantamount to "non-fulfillment of a duty," made the military decision authorizing the entry of the Phalangist militiamen into the camps. The panel found that Sharon should have foreseen the probability of a massacre and taken steps to ensure Israeli control over Phalangist actions. In its final report, the commission recommended that Sharon resign immediately or be dismissed. Sharon quit his post in the Israeli Cabinet on February 11.

The commission's findings on Lt. Gen. Rafael Eitan, the IDF chief of staff, and Maj. Gen. Yehoshua Saguy, director of military intelligence, were similar to those regarding Sharon. During the inquiry, Eitan testified that the Phalangist militiamen were a disciplined army interested in promoting good relations with the Moslems for their mutual political benefit. The panel rejected this claim, saying that Eitan "was well aware that the Phalangists were full of feelings of hatred toward the Palestinians." Eitan was due to retire in April 1983, so it was pointless to ask for his resignation. The commission recommended that Saguy, accused of indifference, inattention and negligence, be dismissed.

The report charged Brig. Gen. Amos Yaron, Israeli division commander for the Beirut area, with failure to act when informed of the massacre, thereby allowing the militiamen to send reinforcements into the camps. The report recommmended that Yaron be relieved of his field command for at least three years. The head of Israel's Northern Command, Maj. Gen. Amir Drori, was credited with trying to stop the massacre but faulted for his failure to follow through. The report did not recommend punitive action.

Following are excerpts from the final report of the Israeli Commission of Inquiry into the Events at the Refugee Camps in Beirut, made available February 8, 1983. (Boldface headings in brackets have been added by Congressional Quarterly to highlight the organization of the text.):

The Direct Responsibility

. . . [A]ll the evidence indicates that the massacre was perpetrated by the Phalangists between the time they entered the camps on Thursday, 16.9.82, at 18.00 hours, and their departure from the camps on Saturday, 18.9.82, at approximately 8 A.M. The victims were found in those areas where the Phalangists were in military control during the aforementioned time period. No other military force aside from the Phalangists was seen by any one of the witnesses in the area of the camps where the massacre was carried out or at the time of the entrance into or exit from this area. The camps were surrounded on all sides: on three sides by I.D.F. forces and on the fourth side was a city line (that divided between East and West Beirut) that was under Phalangist control. . . .

. . . [W]e heard testimony from two doctors and a nurse who worked in the Gaza hospital, which was run by and for Palestinians. There is no cause to suspect that any of these witnesses have any special sympathy for Israel, and it is clear to us — both from their choosing that place of employment and from our impression of their appearance before us — that they sympathize with the Palestinians and desired to render service to Palestinians in need. From these witnesses' testimony, it is clear that the armed military unit that took them out of the hospital on Saturday morning and brought them to the building that formerly belonged to the U.N. was a Phalangist unit. The witness Ms. Siegel did indeed tell of a visit to the hospital at 7 P.M. on Friday evening of two men dressed in civilian clothes who spoke to the staff in German, and she hinted at the possibility that perhaps they were Sephardic Jews; but this assumption has no basis in fact, and it can be explained by her tendentiousness. Ms. Siegel even said that these men looked like Arabs. It is clear that these men did not belong to an armed force that penetrated the camps at the time. The two doctors Ang and Morris did not see any other military force aside from the Phalangists, who presented themselves as soldiers of a Lebanese force. . . . The testimony of these three witnesses also indicates that the only military force seen in the area was a Phalangist one. A similar conclusion can be drawn from the statement of Norwegian journalist John Habo.

[Personnel of Major Haddad]

In the course of the events and also thereafter, rumors spread that personnel of Major [Saad] Haddad were perpetrating a massacre or participating in a massacre. No basis was found for these rumors. The I.D.F. liaison officer with Major Haddad's forces testified that no unit of that force had crossed the Awali River that week. We have no reason to doubt that testimony. As we have already noted, the relations between the Phalangists and the forces of Major Haddad were poor, and friction existed between those two forces. For this reason, too, it is inconceivable that a force from Major Haddad's army took part in military operations of the Phalangists in the camps, nor was there any hint of such cooperation. Although three persons from southern Lebanon — two of them from the Civil Guard in southern Lebanon — were in West Beirut on Friday afternoon, and got caught in the exchanges of fire between an I.D.F. unit and [Walid] Jumblat's militia, with one of them being killed in those exchanges, this did not take place in the area of the camps; and the investigation that was carried out showed that the three of them had come to Beirut on a private visit. There is no indication in this event that Haddad's men were at the site where the massacre was perpetrated. . . .

It cannot be ruled out that the rumors about the participation of Haddad's men in the massacre also had their origin in the fact that Major Haddad arrived at Beirut airport on Friday, 17.9.82. From the testimony of the I.D.F. liaison officer with Major Haddad's force, and from Major Haddad's testimony, it is clear that this visit by Major Haddad to the suburbs of Beirut and the vicinity had no connection with the events that took place in the camps. Major Haddad arrived at Beirut airport in an air force helicopter at 8:30 A.M. on 17.9.82. The purpose of his visit was to pay a condolence call on the Gemayel family at Bikfeiya. . . .

We cannot rule out the possibility — although no evidence to this effect was found either — that one of the men from Major Haddad's forces who was visiting in Beirut during this period infiltrated into the camps, particularly in the interim period between the departure of the Phalangists and the entry of the Lebanese Army, and committed illegal acts there; but if this did happen, no responsibility, either direct or indirect, is to be inputed to the commanders of Major Haddad's forces.

[Accusations Against Israelis]

Here and there, hints, and even accusations, were thrown out to the effect that I.D.F. soldiers were in the camps at the time the massacre was perpetrated. We have no doubt that these notions are completely groundless and constitute a baseless libel. One witness, Mr. Franklin Pierce Lamb, of the United States, informed us of the fact that on 22.9.82 a civilian ID card and a military dogtag belonging to a soldier named Benny Haim Ben Yosef, born on 9.7.61, were found in the Sabra camp. Following that testimony, these details were investigated and it was found that a soldier bearing that name was in a hospital after having undergone operations for wounds he sustained during the entry into West Beirut. . . . The discovery of these documents belonging to an I.D.F. soldier in the camp does not indicate that any I.D.F. soldiers were in the camp while the massacre was being perpetrated.

Mr. Lamb also testified — not from personal knowledge but based on what he had heard from others — that cluster bombs were piled under bodies found in the camps, apparently as booby-traps. . . . He raised the question whether the Phalangists, or the forces of Major Haddad — if any of them were in the camps — possessed the requisite technical skills to make use of these bombs as booby-traps. This question implies that the bombs were placed beneath the bodies by I.D.F. personnel. That implication is totally without foundation. . . .

[Denials by Phalangists]

Following the massacre, the Phalangist commanders denied, in various interviews in the media, that they had perpetrated the massacre. On Sunday, 19.9.82. the Chief of Staff and Major General Drori met with the Phalangist commanders. Notes of that meeting were taken by a representative of the Mossad [Israeli civilian intelligence service] who was present. The Chief of Staff told the Phalangist commanders that he had come from the camps; it was said that a massacre had taken place there and that for the sake of their future they must admit to having perpetrated the acts and explain the matter, otherwise they would have no future in Lebanon. Their reaction was that if the Chief of Staff says they must do so, they would. The Chief of Staff formed the impression that they were bewildered, that it was possible that they did not know what had happened in the camps and had no control over their people there. Even after that meeting the Phalangist heads continued in their public appearances to deny any connection with the massacre. That denial is patently incorrect.

Contentions and accusations were advanced that even if I.D.F. personnel had not shed the blood of the massacred, the entry of the Phalangists into the camps had been carried out with the prior knowledge that a massacre would be perpetrated there and with the intention that this should indeed take place; and therefore all those who had enabled the entry of the Phalangists into the camps should be regarded as accomplices to the acts of slaughter and sharing in direct responsibility. These accusations, too, are unfounded. We have no doubt that no conspiracy or plot was entered into between anyone from the Israeli political echelon or from the military echelon in the I.D.F. and the Phalangists, with the aim of perpetrating atrocities in the camps. The decision to have the Phalangists enter the camps was taken with the aim of preventing further losses in the war in Lebanon; to accede to the pressure of public opinion in Israel, which was angry that the Phalangists, who were reaping the fruits of the war, were taking no part in it, and to take advantage of the Phalangists' professional service and their skills in identifying terrorists and in discovering arms caches. No intention existed on the part of any Israeli element to harm the non-combatant population in the camps. It is true that in the war in Lebanon, and particularly during the siege of West Beirut, the civilian population sustained losses, with old people, women and children among the casualties, but this was the result of belligerent actions which claim victims even among those who do not fight.... We assert that in having the Phalangists enter the camps, no intention existed on the part of anyone who acted on behalf of Israel to harm the non-combatant population, and that the events that followed did not have the concurrence or assent of anyone from the political or civilian echelon who was active regarding the Phalangists' entry into the camps.

It was alleged that the atrocities being perpetrated in the camps were visible from the roof of the forward command post, that the fact that they were being committed was also discernible from the sounds emanating from the camps, and that the senior I.D.F. commanders who were on the roof of the forward command post for two days certainly saw or heard what was going on in the camps. We have already determined above that events in the camps, in the area where the Phalangists entered, were not visible from the roof of the forward command post. It has also been made clear that no sounds from which it could be inferred that a massacre was being perpetrated in the camps reached that place....

[Doctors and Nurses]

Here we must add that when the group of doctors and nurses met I.D.F. officers on Saturday morning, at a time when it was already clear to them that they were out of danger, they made no complaint that a massacre had been perpetrated in the camps. When we asked the witnesses from this group why they had not informed the I.D.F. officers about the massacre, they replied that they had not known about it. The fact that the doctors and nurses who were in the Gaza Hospital — which is proximate to the site of the event and where persons wounded in combative action and frightened persons from the camps arrived — did not know about the massacre but only about isolated instances of injury which they had seen for themselves, also shows that those who were nearby but not actually inside the camps did not form the impression from what they saw and heard that a massacre of hundreds of people was taking place. Nor did members of a unit of the Lebanese Army who were stationed near the places of entry into the camps know anything about the massacre until after the Phalangists had departed.

Our conclusion is therefore that the direct responsibility for the perpetration of the acts of slaughter rests on the Phalangist forces. No evidence was brought before us that Phalangist personnel received explicit orders from their command to perpetrate acts of slaughter, but it is evident that the forces who entered the area were steeped in hatred for the Palestinians, in the wake of the atrocities and severe injuries done to the Christians during the civil war in Lebanon by the Palestinians and those who fought alongside them; and these feelings of hatred were compounded by a longing for revenge in the wake of the assassination of the Phalangists' admired leader Bashir and the killing of several dozen Phalangists two days before their entry into the camps. . . .

The Indirect Responsibility

Before we discuss the essence of the problem of the indirect responsibility of Israel, or of those who operated at its behest, we perceive it to be necessary to deal with objections that have been voiced on various occasions, according to which if Israel's direct responsibility for the atrocities is negated — i.e., if it is determined that the blood of those killed was not shed by I.D.F. soldiers and I.D.F. forces, or that others operating at the behest of the state were not parties to the atrocities, then there is no place for further discussion of the problem of indirect responsibility. The argument is that no responsibility should be laid on Israel for deeds perpetrated outside of its borders by members of the Christian community against Palestinians in that same country or against Moslems located within the area of the camps. A certain echo of this approach may be found in statements made in the cabinet meeting of 19.9.82 and in statements released to the public by various sources.

We cannot accept this position. If it indeed becomes clear that those who decided on the entry of the Phalangists into the camps should have foreseen — from the information at their disposal and from things which were common knowledge — that there was danger of a massacre, and no steps were taken which might have been taken to prevent this danger or at least to greatly reduce the possibility that deeds of this type might be done, then those who made the decisions and those who implemented them are indirectly responsible for what ultimately occurred, even if they did not intend this to happen and merely disregarded the anticipated danger. A similar indirect responsibility also falls on those who knew of the decision: it was their duty, by virtue of their position and their office, to warn of the danger, and they did not fulfill this duty. It is also not possible to absolve of such indirect responsibility those persons who, when they received the first reports of what was happening in the camps, did not rush to prevent the continuation of the Phalangists' actions and did not do everything within their power to stop them. It is not our function as a commission of inquiry to lay a precise legal foundation for such indirect responsibility. It may be that from a legal perspective, the issue of responsibility is not unequivocal, in view of the lack of clarity regarding the status of the State of Israel and its forces in Lebanese territory. If the territory of West Beirut may be viewed at the time of the events as occupied territory — and we do not determine that such indeed is the case from a legal perspective — then it is the duty of the occupier, according to the rules of usual and customary international law, to do all it can to insure the public's well-being and security. Even if these legal norms are invalid regarding the situation which the Israeli government and the forces operating at its instructions found themselves in at the time of the events, still, as far as the obligations applying to every civilized nation and the ethical rules accepted by civilized peoples go, the problem of indirect responsibility cannot be disregarded.... When we are dealing with the issue of indirect responsibility, it should also not be forgotten that the Jews in various lands of exile and also in the land of Israel when it was under foreign rule suffered greatly from pogroms perpetrated by various hooligans; and the danger of disturbances against Jews in various lands, it seems evident, has not yet passed. The Jewish public's stand has always been that the responsibility for such deeds falls not only on those who rioted and committed the atrocities but also on those who were responsible for safety and public order, who could have prevented the disturbances and did not fulfill their obligations in this respect....

The heads of Government in Israel and the heads of the I.D.F. who testified before us were for the most part firm in their view that what happened in the camps was an unexpected occurrence, in the nature of a disaster which no one had imagined and which could not have been — or, at all events, need not have been — foreseen....

[Reason for Apprehension]

In our view, everyone who had anything to do with events in Lebanon should have felt apprehension about a massacre in the camps if armed Phalangist forces were to be moved into them without the I.D.F. exercising concrete and effective supervision and scrutiny of them. All those concerned were well aware that combat morality among the various combatant groups in Lebanon differs from the norm in the I.D.F., that the combatants in Lebanon belittle the value of human life far beyond what is necessary and accepted in wars between civilized peoples, and that various atrocities against the non-combatant population had been widespread in Lebanon since 1975. It was well known that the Phalangists harbor deep enmity for the Palestinians, viewing them as the source of all the troubles that afflicted Lebanon during the years of the civil war.... To this backdrop of the Palestinians were added the profound shock in the wake of Bashir's death along with a group of Phalangists in the explosion at Ashrafiya, and the feeling of revenge that event must arouse, even without the identity of the assailant being known.

[Weighing Experts' Testimony]

The written and oral summations presented to us stressed that most of the experts whose remarks were brought before the commission — both Military Intelligence personnel and Mossad personnel — had expressed the view that given the state of affairs existing when the decision was taken to have the Phalangists enter the camps, it could not be foreseen that the Phalangists would perpetrate a massacre, or at all events the probability of that occurring was low; and had they been asked for their opinion at the time, they would have raised no objections to the decision. We are not prepared to attach any importance to these statements, and not necessarily due to the fact that this evaluation was refuted by reality. It is our impression that the remarks of the experts on this matter were influenced to a certain extent by the desire of each of them to justify his action or lack thereof, the experts having failed to raise any objection to the entry of the Phalangists into the camp when they learned of it. In contrast to the approach of these experts, there were cases in which other personnel, both from military intelligence, from other I.D.F. branches and from outside the governmental framework, warned — as soon as they learned of the Phalangists' entry into the camps, and on earlier occasions when the Phalangists' role in the war was discussed — that the danger of a massacre was great and that the Phalangists would take advantage of every opportunity offered them to wreak vengeance on the Palestinians. . . .

[Reasons for Phalangist Role]

We do not say that the decision to have the Phalangists enter the camps should under no circumstances have been made and was totally unwarranted. Serious considerations existed in favor of such a decision; and on this matter we shall repeat what has already been mentioned, that an understandable desire existed to prevent I.D.F. losses in hazardous combat in a built-up area, that it was justified to demand of the Phalangists to take part in combat which they regarded as a broad opening to assume power and for the restoration of Lebanese independence, and that the Phalangists were more expert than the I.D.F. in uncovering and identifying terrorists. These are weighty considerations; and had the decision makers and executors been aware of the danger of harm to the civilian population on the part of the Phalangists but had nevertheless, having considered all the circumstances, decided to have the Phalangists enter the camps while taking all possible steps to prevent harm coming to the civilian population, it is possible that there would be no place to be critical of them, even if ultimately it had emerged that the decision had caused undesirable results and had caused damage. However, as it transpired, no examination was made of all the considerations and their ramifications; hence, the appropriate orders were not issued to the executors of the decisions and insufficient heed was taken to adopt the required measures. Herein lies the basis for imputing indirect responsibility to those persons who in our view did not fulfill the obligations placed on them.

To sum up this chapter, we assert that the atrocities in the refugee camps were perpetrated by members of the Phalangists and that absolutely no direct responsibility devolves upon Israel or upon those who acted in its behalf. At the same time, it is clear from what we have said above that the decision on the entry of the Phalangists into the refugee camps was taken without consideration of the danger — which the makers and executors of the decision were obligated to foresee as probable — that the Phalangists would commit massacres and pogroms against the inhabitants of the camps and without an examination of the means for preventing this danger. Similarly, it is clear from the course of events that when the reports began to arrive about the actions of the Phalangists in the camps, no proper heed was taken of these reports, the correct conclusions were not drawn from them and no energetic and immediate actions were taken to restrain the Phalangists and put a stop to their actions. This both reflects and exhausts Israel's indirect responsibility for what occurred in the refugee camps. We shall discuss the responsibility of those who acted in Israel's behalf and in its name in the following chapter.

Personal Responsibility

In accordance with a resolution adopted by the Commission on 24.1.82, notices were sent ... to nine persons regarding the harm liable to be done to them by the inquiry and its results. . . .

THE PRIME MINISTER, MR. MENACHEM BEGIN

The notice sent to the Prime Minister, Mr. Menachem Begin, stated that he was liable to be harmed if the commission were to determine "that the Prime Minister did not properly weigh the part to be played by the Lebanese Forces during and in the wake of the I.D.F.'s entry into West Beirut and disregarded the danger of acts of revenge and bloodshed by these forces vis-à-vis the population in the refugee camps."

The Prime Minister's response to the notice stated that in the conversations between him and the Defense Minister in which the decision was taken to have I.D.F. units enter West Beirut, and in the conversations he had held with the Chief of Staff during the night between 14.9.82 and 15.9.82, nothing at all was said about a possible operation by the Lebanese Forces.

The Prime Minister testified that only in the Cabinet session of 16.9.82 did he hear about the agreement with the Phalangists that they would operate in the camps, and that until then, in all the conversations he had held with the Defense Minister and with the Chief of Staff, nothing had been said about the role of the Phalangists or their participation in the operations in West Beirut. He added that since this matter had not come up in the reports he received from the Defense Minister and the Chief of Staff, he had raised no questions about it. The Prime Minister's remarks in this regard are consistent with the testimony of the Defense Minister and the Chief of Staff and with the existing documents concerning the content of the conversations with the Prime Minister. . . .

. . . The tasks of the Prime Minister are many and diverse, and he was entitled to rely on the optimistic and calming report of the Defense Minister that the entire operation was proceeding without any hitches and in the most satisfactory manner. . . .

We have already said above, when we discussed the question of indirect responsibility, that in our view, because of things that were well known to all, it should have been foreseen that the danger of a massacre existed if the Phalangists were to enter the camps without measures being taken to prevent them from committing acts such as these. We are unable to accept the Prime Minister's remarks that he was absolutely unaware of such a danger. . . .

. . . [T]he Prime Minister first heard about the Phalangists' entry into camps about 36 hours after the decision to that effect was taken and did not learn of the decision until the Cabinet session. When he heard about the Phalangists' entry into the camps, it had already taken place. According to the "rosy" reports the Prime Minister received from the Defense Minister and the Chief of Staff, the Prime Minister was entitled to assume at that time that all the operations in West Beirut had been performed in the best possible manner and had nearly been concluded. We believe that in these circumstances it was not incumbent upon the Prime Minister to object to the Phalangists' entry into the camps or to order their removal. On the other hand, we find no reason to exempt the Prime Minister from responsibility for not having evinced, during or after the Cabinet session, any interest in the Phalangists' actions in the camps. It has already been noted above that no report about the Phalangists' operations reached the Prime Minister, except perhaps for the complaint regarding the Gaza Hospital, until he heard a BBC broadcast toward evening on Saturday. For two days after the Prime Minister heard about the Phalangists' entry, he showed absolutely no interest in their actions in the camps. This indifference would have been justifiable if we were to accept the Prime Minister's position that it was impossible and unnecessary to foresee the possibility that the Phalangists would commit acts of revenge; but we have already explained above that according to what the Prime Minister knew, according to what he heard in the Thursday cabinet session, and according to what he said about the purpose of the move into Beirut, such a possibility was not unknown to him. It may be assumed that a manifestation of interest by him in this matter, after he had learned of the Phalangists' entry, would have increased the alertness of the Defense Minister and the Chief of Staff to the need to take appropriate measures to meet the expected danger. The Prime Minister's lack of involvement in the entire matter casts on him a certain degree of responsibility.

THE MINISTER OF DEFENSE, MR. ARIEL SHARON

The notice sent to the Minister of Defense . . . stated that the Minister of Defense might be harmed if the commission determined that he ignored or disregarded the danger of acts of revenge or bloodshed perpetrated by Lebanese forces against the population of the refugee camps in Beirut and did not order the adoption of the appropriate steps to avoid this risk and that he did not order the withdrawal of the Lebanese forces from the refugee camps as quickly as possible and the adoption of measures to protect the population in the camps when information reached him about the acts of killing or excesses that were perpetrated by the Lebanese forces.

In his testimony before us, and in statements he issued beforehand, the Minister of Defense also adopted the position that no one had imagined the Phalangists would carry out a massacre in the camps and that it was a tragedy that could not be foreseen. . . .

It is true that no clear warning was provided by military intelligence or the Mossad about what might happen if the Phalangist forces entered the camps, and we will relate to this matter when we discuss the responsibility of the director of Military Intelligence and the head of the Mossad. But in our view, even without such warning, it is impossible to justify the Minister of Defense's disregard of the danger of a massacre. . . . In the circumstances that prevailed after Bashir's assassination, no prophetic powers were required to know that concrete danger of acts of slaughter existed when the Phalangists were moved into the camps without the I.D.F.'s being with them in that operation and without the I.D.F. being able to maintain effective and ongoing supervision of their actions there. The sense of such a danger should have been in the consciousness of every knowledgeable person who was close to this subject, and certainly in the consciousness of the Defense Minister, who took an active part in everything relating to the war. His involvement in the war was deep, and the connection with the Phalangists was under his constant care. . . . As a politician responsible for Israel's security affairs and as the minister who took an active part in directing the political and military moves in the war in Lebanon, it was the duty of the Defense Minister to take into account all the reasonable considerations for and against having the Phalangists enter the camps and not to disregard entirely the serious consideration mitigating against such an action, namely that the Phalangists were liable to commit atrocities and that it was necessary to forestall this possibility as a humanitarian obligation and also to prevent the political damage it would entail. From the Defense Minister himself we know that this consideration did not concern him in the least, and that this matter, with all its ramifications, was neither discussed nor examined in the meetings and discussions held by the Defense Minister. In our view, the Minister of Defense made a grave mistake when he ignored the danger of acts of revenge and bloodshed by the Phalangists against the population in the refugee camps. . . .

... [I]n his meetings with the Phalangist commanders, the Defense Minister made no attempt to point out to them the gravity of the danger that their men would commit acts of slaughter. ...

Had it become clear to the Defense Minister that no real supervision could be exercised over the Phalangist force that entered the camps with the I.D.F.'s assent, his duty would have been to prevent their entry. The usefulness of the Phalangists' entry into the camps was wholly disproportionate to the damage their entry could cause if it were uncontrolled. A good many people who heard about the Phalangists' entry into the camps were aware of this even before the first reports arrived about the massacre. ...

We do not accept the contention that the Defense Minister did not need to hear that the Phalangists would commit acts of killing because in all outward aspects they looked like a disciplined and organized army. It could not be inferred from the Phalangists' orderly military organization that their attitude toward human life and to the noncombatant population had basically changed. ...

It is our view that responsibility is to be imputed to the Minister of Defense for having disregarded the danger of acts of vengeance and bloodshed by the Phalangists against the population of the refugee camps and having failed to take this danger into account when he decided to have the Phalangists enter the camps. In addition, responsibility is to be imputed to the Minister of Defense for not ordering appropriate measures for preventing or reducing the danger of massacre as a condition for the Phalangists' entry into the camps. These blunders constitute the non-fulfillment of a duty with which the Defense Minister was charged.

We do not believe that responsibility is to be imputed to the Defense Minister for not ordering the removal of the Phalangists from the camps when the first reports reached him about the acts of killing being committed there. As was detailed above, such reports initially reached the Defense Minister on Friday evening; but at the same time, he had heard from the Chief of Staff that the Phalangists' operation had been halted, that they had been ordered to leave the camps and that their departure would be effected by 5 A.M. Saturday. These preventive steps might well have seemed sufficient to the Defense Minister at that time, and it was not his duty to order additional steps to be taken or to have the departure time moved up, a step which was of doubtful feasibility.

THE FOREIGN MINISTER, MR. YITZHAK SHAMIR

The Foreign Minister, Mr. Yitzhak Shamir, was sent a notice ... that he might be harmed if the commission determined that, after he heard from Minister [Mordechai] Zipori on 17.9.82 of the report regarding the Phalangists' actions in the refugee camps, he did not take the appropriate steps to clarify whether this information was based in fact and did not bring the information to the knowledge of the Prime Minister or the Minister of Defense.

In the memorandum that the Foreign Minister submitted to us in response to the aforementioned notice, he explained that what he had heard from Minister Zipori about the "unruliness" of the Phalangists did not lead him to understand that it was a matter of a massacre; he thought, rather, that it was a matter of fighting against terrorists. . . .

It is not easy to decide between the conflicting versions of what Minister Zipori said to the Foreign Minister. We tend to the opinion that in the telephone conversation Minister Zipori spoke of a "slaughter" being perpetrated by the Phalangists, and it is possible that he also spoke of "unruliness." Nevertheless, we are unable to rule out the possibility that the Foreign Minister did not catch or did not properly understand the significance of what he heard from Minister Zipori. The Foreign Minister likewise did not conceal that in relating to what Minister Zipori had told him, he was influenced by his knowledge that Minister Zipori was opposed to the policy of the Minister of Defense and the Chief of Staff regarding the war in Lebanon, and particularly to cooperation with the Phalangists.

The phenomenon that came to light in this case — namely, that the statement of one minister to another did not receive the attention it deserved because of faulty relations between members of the Cabinet — is regrettable and worrisome. The impression we got is that the Foreign Minister did not make any real attempt to check whether there was anything in what he had heard from Minister Zipori on the Phalangists' operation in the camps because he had an *a priori* skeptical attitude toward the statement of the minister who reported this information to him. It is difficult to find a justification for such disdain for information that came from a member of the Cabinet, especially under the circumstances in which the information was reported. . . . The Foreign Minister should at least have called the Defense Minister's attention to the information he had received and not contented himself with asking someone in his office whether any new information had come in from Beirut and with the expectation that those people coming to his office would know what was going on and would tell him if anything out of the ordinary had happened. In our view, the Foreign Minister erred in not taking any measures after the conversation with Minister Zipori in regard to what he had heard from Zipori about the Phalangist actions in the camps. . . .

Recommendations

With regard to the following recommendations concerning a group of men who hold senior positions in the Government and the Israeli Defense Forces, we have taken into account the fact that each one of these men has to his credit the performance of many public or military services rendered with sacrifice and devotion on behalf of the state of Israel. If nevertheless we have reached the conclusion that it is incumbent upon us to recommend certain measures against some of these men, it is out of the recognition that the gravity of the matter and its implications for the underpinnings of public morality in the state of Israel call for such measures.

THE PRIME MINISTER, THE FOREIGN MINISTER/ AND THE HEAD OF THE MOSSAD

We have heretofore established the facts and conclusion with regard to the responsibility of the Prime Minister, the Foreign Minister and the head of the Mossad. In view of what we have determined with regard to the extent of the responsibility of each of them, we are of the opinion that it is sufficient to determine responsibility, and there is no need for any further recommendations.

G.O.C. NORTHERN COMMAND, MAJ. GEN. AMIR DRORI

... Major General Drori was charged with many difficult and complicated tasks during the week the I.D.F. entered West Beirut, missions which he had to accomplish after a long period of difficult warfare. He took certain measures for terminating the Phalangists' actions, and his guilt lies in that he did not continue with these actions. Taking into account these circumstances, it appears to us that it is sufficient to determine the responsibility of Major General Drori without recourse to any further recommendation.

THE MINISTER OF DEFENSE, MR. ARIEL SHARON

We have found, as has been detailed in this report, that the Minister of Defense bears personal responsibility. In our opinion, it is fitting that the Minister of Defense draw the appropriate personal conclusions arising out of the defects revealed with regard to the manner in which he discharged the duties of his office — and if necessary, that the Prime Minister consider whether he should exercise his authority under Section 21-A (a) of the Basic Law: the Government, according to which "the Prime Minister may, after informing the Cabinet of his intention to do so, remove a minister from office."

THE CHIEF OF STAFF, LT.-GEN. RAFAEL EITAN

We have arrived at grave conclusions with regard to the acts and omissions of the Chief of Staff, Lt.-Gen. Rafael Eitan. The Chief of Staff is about to complete his term of service in April, 1983. Taking into account the fact that an extension of his term is not under consideration, there is no [practical] significance to a recommendation with regard to his continuing in office as Chief of Staff, and therefore we have resolved that it is sufficient to determine responsibility without making any further recommendation.

THE DIRECTOR OF MILITARY INTELLIGENCE, MAJOR GENERAL YEHOSHUA SAGUY

We have detailed the various extremely serious omissions of the director of Military Intelligence, Major General Yehoshua Saguy, in discharging the duties of his office. We recommend that Major General Yehoshua Saguy not continue as director of Military Intelligence.

DIVISION COMMANDER BRIGADIER GENERAL AMOS YARON

... [W]e recommend that Brigadier General Amos Yaron not serve in the capacity of a field commander in the Israel Defense Forces, and that this recommendation not be reconsidered before three years have passed.

In the course of this inquiry, shortcomings in the functioning of [several] establishments have been revealed.... One must learn the appropriate lessons from these shortcomings, and we recommend that, in addition to internal control in this matter, an investigation into the shortcomings and the manner of correcting them be undertaken by an expert or experts to be appointed by a Ministerial Defense Committee. If in the course of this investigation it be found that certain persons bear responsibility for these shortcomings, it is fitting that the appropriate conclusions be drawn in their regard, whether in accordance with the appropriate provisions of the military legal code, or in some other manner.

Closing Remarks

In the witnesses' testimony and in various documents, stress is laid on the difference between the usual battle ethics of the I.D.F. and the battle ethics of the bloody clashes and combat actions among various ethnic groups, militias, and fighting forces in Lebanon. The difference is considerable. In the war the I.D.F. waged in Lebanon, many civilians were injured and much loss of life was caused, despite the effort the I.D.F. and its soldiers made not to harm civilians. On more than one occasion, this effort caused the I.D.F. troops additional casualties. During the months of the war, I.D.F. soldiers witnessed many sights of killing, destruction, and ruin. From their reactions (about which we have heard) to acts of brutality against civilians, it would appear that despite the terrible sights and experiences of the war and despite the soldier's obligation to behave as a fighter with a certain degree of callousness, I.D.F. soldiers did not lose their sensitivity to atrocities that were perpetrated on non-combatants either out of cruelty or to give vent to vengeful feelings. It is regrettable that the reaction by I.D.F. soldiers to such deeds was not always forceful enough to bring a halt to the despicable acts. It seems to us that the I.D.F. should continue to foster the [consciousness of] basic moral obligations which must be kept even in war conditions, without prejudicing the I.D.F.'s combat ability. The circumstances of combat require the combatants to be tough — which means to give priority to sticking to the objective and being willing to make sacrifices — in order to attain the objectives assigned to them even under the most difficult conditions. But the end never justifies the means, and basic ethical and human values must be maintained in the use of arms.

Among the responses to the commission from the public, there were those who expressed dissatisfaction with the holding of an inquiry on a subject not directly related to Israel's responsibility. The argument was advanced that in previous instances of massacre in Lebanon, when the lives of many more people were taken than those of the victims who fell in Sabra and Shatilla, world opinion was not shocked and no inquiry commissions were established. We cannot justify this approach to the issue of holding an inquiry, and not only for the formal reason that it was not we who decided to hold the inquiry, but rather the Israeli Government resolved thereon. The main purpose of the inquiry was to bring to light all the important facts relating to the perpetration of the atrocities; it therefore has importance from the perspective of Israel's moral fortitude and its functioning as a democratic state that scrupulously maintains the fundamental principles of the civilized world. . . .

STATE DEPARTMENT REPORT
ON HUMAN RIGHTS
February 8, 1983

The Reagan administration, identifying human rights as the "core of American foreign policy," issued its annual human rights report to Congress February 8. The conclusion of the 1,300-page study was that little progress had been made throughout the world and that serious human rights violations continued in 1982. Prepared for the Senate Foreign Relations Committee and the House Foreign Affairs Committee, the report was highly critical, as usual, of the Soviet Union's repressive policies and those of its allies. (Human rights report, Historic Documents of 1982, p. 118)

The 1982 report included lengthy descriptions of human rights infractions in Middle Eastern and Asian countries, as well as nations where the administration had tried to strengthen U.S. relations, particularly El Salvador. The most accusatory section of the report was the section on Vietnam. Elliot Abrams, assistant secretary of state for human rights, said at a press conference that Vietnam "... seemed to me the worst country to live in."

For its analysis, the Country Report On Human Rights Practices for 1982 *defined human rights within two broad categories. First to be considered was the "right to be free from governmental violations of the integrity of the person—violations such as killings, torture, cruel, inhuman, or degrading treatment or punishment; arbitrary arrest or imprisonment; denial of fair public trial; and invasion of the home." Second, the report measured human rights as the "right to enjoy civil and political liberties, including freedom of speech, press, religion, and assembly; the right of citizens to participate in governing themselves; the right to travel freely within and outside one's own country; the right to be free from discrimination based on race or sex." The document examined the status of human rights along these guidelines in 162 countries in 1982.*

A lengthy introduction further outlined the areas given serious consideration in the 1982 report. These more refined definitions of human rights included an emphasis on labor unions and the right to organize and assemble. A closer look at each country's political process and the right to participate also was given high priority. The document noted, "Political participation is not only an important right in itself, but also the best guarantee that other rights will be observed." An evaluation of this right meant a realistic look at a country's election process and the existence of opposing candidates. The report also recognized the violation of human rights by opposition and insurgent groups, and not only the actions and policies of a current government. "Such pressures on a government or society do not excuse human rights violations, but an awareness of them is vital to a full understanding of the human rights situation," said the report.

Originally mandated by the Foreign Assistance Act of 1961, the State Department was required to review annually human rights activities in nations receiving aid from the United States and, since 1979, each country belonging to the United Nations. The government assessment, largely used to determine the level of foreign assistance allotted to many of these countries, was based on information furnished by U.S. missions abroad, congressional studies, non-governmental groups and international human rights organizations.

The 1982 report was not endorsed overwhelmingly by the participating human rights organizations. Reviews issued by Americas Watch, Helsinki Watch and Lawyers Committee for International Human Rights were highly critical of much of the administration's findings. After reviewing the individual reports of 22 countries, the groups accused the administration of "serious distortions or inaccuracies" in recording violations in countries such as El Salvador, Argentina and Chile. They regarded some of the reports as unrealistic and favorably biased to offending nations considered necessary allies of the United States. The monitoring groups, however, conceded that the administration had made some improvements in accurately reporting conditions.

In defense of an administration that had been criticized for a relaxed human rights position, especially toward politically friendly regimes, the report commended Reagan's tactic of promoting the development of "long-term democracy" throughout the world. Outlining the administration's policies, the State Department document said, ". . . with friendly countries, we prefer to use diplomacy, not public pronouncements. We seek not to isolate them for their injustices and thereby render ourselves ineffective, but to use our influence to effect desirable change. Our aim is to achieve results, not to make self-satisfying but ineffective gestures."

Following are excerpts from the State Department's Country Reports on Human Rights Practices for 1982, *released February 8, 1983:*

Afghanistan

... Soviet advisors have moved into controlling positions in the Afghan government ministries, in the army, and in the organs of the security apparatus and are involved in all significant decisions. The Sovietization of important institutions such as industries, the media, and the educational system, is now complete. The Soviets control the central Government of Afghanistan. They appear to have no intention of withdrawing their soldiers nor their influence.

The most pervasive and systematic violator of Afghan human rights is the Kabul regime's 20,000-strong secret police organization, known officially as the State Information Services and unofficially by its Persian acronym, KHAD. KHAD's chief, Dr. Najibullah, is a Party politburo member and a Parcham faction leader. Najibullah presides over a multi-faceted organization which is modeled upon the Soviet KGB and is responsible for foreign and domestic intelligence collection and clandestine operations; for maintaining public order through surveillance, arrest, imprisonment, interrogation, torture, trial, and sentencing; and even, via its military wing, for the conduct of the Soviet-sponsored war. In a closed society, and with no rival institution capable of checking its influence, KHAD is the law in Kabul and other cities and towns controlled by the regime. KGB officers are assigned to every major department of KHAD, from the director's office down, and all major KHAD operations require Soviet approval before implementation. In effect, KHAD has become an increasingly efficient agent of terror and repression and a prime tool for Soviet control of the Afghan population.

Violations of human rights in Afghanistan take place in the context of a bitter war between a martial and highly independent people and a powerful and determined invader. The Soviet Union seeks not only to dominate Afghanistan militarily, but to convert that traditional and highly uncentralized Muslim society into a modern communist state. To achieve this, the Soviets are using not only military force, Soviet decision-makers in all major Afghan government offices, and an all-pervasive secret police apparatus, but also a large-scale, long-term program of training and indoctrinating Afghan young people and children in the Soviet Union and Eastern Bloc countries. This multi-faceted effort is supported by the small corps of communists who make up the party. Party leaders claim approximately 60,000 members, which would constitute only .4 percent of the Afghan population, estimated to have been 15 million before the Soviet invasion. The overwhelming majority of Afghans has chosen to resist the

Soviets and their puppet regime. The result of this conflict is the tearing apart of Afghanistan and above all, the inflicting of great hardship on the general population.

The scope and efficiency of the secret police are increasing in areas of the country under regime control. The result is the creation of a pervasive atmosphere of mutual suspicion and fear in the cities and towns controlled by the regime. Tensions in urban areas are heightened by the systematic violation of the sanctity of the home by military and secret police forces searching for arms, new recruits, loot, and political opponents. In the countryside, where the regime's control is generally minimal or non-existent, a different order of human rights is being violated. The population in war zones suffers loss of property and life from increasingly frequent bombardments by regime and Soviet forces....

... [T]he [Babrak] Karmal regime has grown more repressive with time and this trend appears to be accelerating. With the Soviet military offensives of 1982 the civilian population throughout Afghanistan suffered greater devastation than ever before. As KHAD's power and efficiency increase, so does its control over the population; as the Afghan army's need for recruits continues to be a major problem, so sweeps for draft-age men will continue. Thus the situation for human rights in Afghanistan is likely to deteriorate still further as the struggle continues between the Soviet and Babrak regime forces on one hand and the mujahidin on the other....

Summary execution is not uncommon on the battlefield and in Afghan prisons. After interrogation, captured mujahidin are often killed out of hand, as are Afghan soldiers attempting to defect to the resistance. In mid-1982, over a dozen imprisoned members of an extreme leftist group opposed to the regime were taken from their cells and machine-gunned by prison officials in retaliation for a series of assassinations reportedly carried out by other members of the organization.

The mujahidin have responded in kind. At the beginning of the conflict resistance fighters usually killed captured Soviet prisoners. More recently, however, some resistance leaders have kept Soviet prisoners in their custody....

Conditions at the Pol-e-Charkhi prison near Kabul, the largest in the country, vary from acceptable, by traditional Afghan norms, to conditions constituting extreme violations of human rights. The food is inadequate, cells overcrowded, and sanitary facilities virtually non-existent, but the majority of prisoners are allowed the freedom of the central courtyard during the day and may receive food, laundry, and money sent by relatives. A smaller number of prisoners, primarily foreigners or relatives of officials of previous communist governments, are accorded better quarters, food, and other privileges. Other prisoners, however, according to reliable reports, are kept in darkness and solitary confinement. According to an eyewitness account, prisoners are sometimes bound so tightly and for so long that they are unable to feed themselves when freed from their bonds. Bad as they are at the Pol-e-Charki prison, conditions at the Kabul city jail, the detention cells at the Prime Ministry, and various KHAD installations in Kabul appear to be considerably worse, leading some prisoners to bribe officials in order to be transferred to Pol-e-Charki prison. One man who was held and then released from the Prime Ministry detention center spoke of huge cells, holding three to four hundred prisoners, with no room for the inmates to sit or lie down. Similar cells held equal numbers of women. Information about conditions inside provincial prisons, which are often the targets of resistance attacks, is limited, but they appear to be very grim. . . .

Argentina

The Argentine armed forces have held power since 1976. The military government instituted major changes, however, in 1982, easing restraints on political and civil liberties and committing itself to elections by not later than November 1983, with the restoration of a constitutional Government set for not later than March 1984. These changes occurred in the wake of severe and growing economic problems and Argentina's defeat in the Falklands/Malvinas conflict. They followed six years of military rule, characterized by the use of harsh measures to end terrorism and curb political dissent, severe limitations on political activity, and the frequent lack of protection of individual rights. During that time, the Government was unable to establish a solid basis for economic growth or a basic political restructuring.

In June 1982, President [Leopóldo] Galtieri was replaced by General (Ret.) Reynaldo Bignone. The new administration lifted the formal ban on political activity on July 1 and in August promulgated a political parties law which required new registration of party members to be followed by internal party elections in preparation for the national elections. Trade unions, while circumscribed by government intervention dating from 1976, have been free to function in many cases as though there were no controls. Late 1982 witnessed an upsurge in political and labor activity. Political parties (including the communists) staged large rallies, human rights groups held demonstrations, and labor organized a successful national strike. At least 100,000 people, organized by political, union, and human rights groups, took part in a "March for Democracy" in downtown Buenos Aires in mid-December. The overall result has been a major change in the exercise of political rights during the second half of 1982.

The press also has been less inhibited in 1982 than at any time since the early 1970s. Criticism of government policies and programs became a matter of course. Four small publications were closed briefly late in the year, but overall freedom to discuss sensitive political and social questions expanded markedly. In the electronic media, sensitive subjects have been openly treated on radio, but less so on state-owned television.

The judicial system displayed greater independence in 1982. The Supreme Court overturned a military court ruling for the first time. Lower courts have been increasingly receptive to habeas corpus petitions filed on behalf of prisoners held under state of siege powers. The courts ruled in favor of three of the periodicals closed by the authorities. . . .

Despite the significant expansion of civil and political liberties, incidents of violence occurred in 1982 which many believed to have been provoked by elements linked to the state security organizations but operating without the sanction of the Government. . . .

There were no reported disappearances in 1982. Human rights groups and some political parties have concentrated on efforts to force an accounting for past disappearances which numbered in the thousands, including appropriate punishment of those responsible. These efforts gained impetus when the press reported that unmarked gravesites contained the bodies of persons who disappeared during the mid-to-late 1970s. Given the widespread belief that many of the disappeared were killed with the complicity of official security personnel, this issue is a highly sensitive and important one for the return to democratic government. The Government initiated efforts to try to reach an understanding with future civilian leaders on this issue prior to the departure of the military Government. By late 1982, the Government is believed privately to have provided information to family members regarding deaths and burial sites in approximately one fifth of the cases of persons whose disappearance was reported to the Government between 1974 and 1982. . . .

Demands that the authorities account for the large number of people who disappeared in the past became a major national issue in 1982. Considerable disagreement remains as to how many persons disappeared. The most carefully documented list, compiled by the Argentine Permanent Assembly for Human Rights, contains approximately 6,000 names. Other estimates are much higher. It is generally believed that most of those who disappeared over the years are dead, many as a result of actions by security forces but also some at the hands of terrorist groups.

In late 1982, the press, political parties, and human rights organizations joined in demanding investigations of unmarked graves recently identified and thought to contain the bodies of some of the disappeared and calling for legal action against those responsible. . . .

Human rights organizations operated with increased effectiveness in 1982 despite minor incidents of harassment and surveillance. With the general trend toward political liberalization, a number of prominent organizations and individuals began to pursue themes formerly espoused almost exclusively by human rights groups. Political parties, labor unions, professional organizations, and the hierarchy of the Catholic church have adopted some of the objectives pioneered since the mid-1970s by the Mothers of the Plaza de Mayo, the Permanent Assembly for Human Rights, and similar organizations. In the meantime, human rights groups have stepped up their activities and expanded the scope of their efforts. The Mothers' weekly vigils in the Plaza de Mayo are being broadened into marches to other centers of Buenos Aires, giving them an expanded public profile. Human rights groups have also taken an increasingly active role at political conventions and meetings. Associated organizations are increasing their activities in the capital and the provinces, providing legal and social assistance services without official hindrance. . . .

Amnesty International's 1982 report, covering 1981, stated that that organization's main concerns in Argentina "continued to be the unresolved question of the 'disappeared' prisoners, and arbitrary detention without trial." The Freedom House report for 1982 classified Argentina as "not free," The Washington Office on Latin America's 1982 report also cited continuing human rights problems. . . .

Chile

. . . A continuing "state of emergency" has been extended regularly every three months since 1973. It gives the Government extraordinary authority to deal with an extremist threat, although the same powers are often used against non-violent dissenters as well. Government actions taken under these emergency powers are not subject to judicial modification. In several instances, however, the courts and press have taken positions defending human rights. Police detentions are authorized prior to public notification of the arrest, but in most cases such detentions are limited to an investigatory period of five days. In general it appears that both police and judicial procedures for avoiding infringements of constitutionally-guaranteed rights have improved recently.

There are, on the other hand, continued credible reports of torture and abuse by the police and security forces. According to the Inter-American Human Rights Commission, a large part of the rights and liberties guaranteed by the Inter-American Declaration of the Rights and Duties of Man is severely restricted in Chile. In addition, both administratively authorized internal exile and expulsion from the country are permitted under the transitional articles of the Constitution and have been used by the Government.

In October 1982, President [Augusto] Pinochet established a commission to review the cases of those currently exiled. The commission completed its report in mid-December and on December 24, 1982, the Government announced that 125 exiles would be re-admitted to Chile. The commission was then disbanded, but it is understood that others from the large exile community abroad will be readmitted subsequently. Nevertheless, there were several new expulsions during the existence of the commission.

Political parties remain formally dissolved and freedom of speech and assembly are restricted, although some political activity and considerable criticism and press discussion are tolerated. Labor union activity is restrained but collective bargaining and a limited right to strike were restored in 1979 under a new labor law.

. . . The year 1982 was characterized by growing economic problems and high unemployment. The recession has affected all strata of society but lower income groups have been the most seriously affected by the loss of jobs. New public works projects are being initiated and old ones augmented to help provide jobs. In addition, social spending has grown to about 59 percent of the government budget and is now more carefully focused on poorer segments of the population. Important efforts in health and nutrition programs have substantially cut infant mortality over the past decade. . . .

There has been a continued decline in politically motivated deaths when compared to the 1973-77 post-coup period. Five killings occurred in 1982 which very probably were politically motivated. Two persons were killed in January, when Government security forces shot two members of the Movement of the Revolutionary Left in armed clashes resulting from investigations into the November 1981 assassination of three police detectives. In February, Chilean labor leader Tucapel Jimenez was murdered. Continuing official efforts to find his killers have not been successful. Allegations have been made that the Government was responsible. In March, a former communist youth leader, Rene Basoa, was killed, allegedly by former comrades because of information he had given Government security forces. His killers have not been found. . . .

According to human rights sources, in 1982, 57 persons filed complaints of torture or cruel and unusual punishment before the courts, compared with a 1981 total of 68. Most individuals alleged that they were subjected to beatings, electric shocks, or threats, particularly during the first days of their detention prior to arraignment. The 1981 Constitution prohibits "use of all illegal pressure" and "guarantees to all persons the right to life and to the physical and psychic integrity of the individual," and high-level Government officials publicly and privately deny that the use of torture is authorized. While the courts have required investigations of some complaints, to date none has been officially substantiated. Most charges of torture were against the National Center for Information, which is the successor security agency to the National Intelligence Directorate, known widely as the "DINA." Torture was generally alleged to have taken place at secret detention centers. Amnesty International lists numerous cases of torture in its 1982 report. Some of the allegations of torture appear credible. . . .

There were 1213 security arrests in Chile in 1982, of which 312 were individual detentions and 901 mass arrests. The great majority were released within five days of their arrest without charges for lack of sufficient evidence. Sixty-six persons, including some of the above, were "internally exiled," normally for periods of three months, by administrative order not subject to judicial review. Most were sent to distant villages as punishment for illegal political activities. The Inter-American Human Rights Commission has stated that the Government has returned to its previous practice of arresting dissidents without reference to due process of law. . . .

El Salvador

During 1982 El Salvador changed from a country ruled by a civilian-military junta to one in transition to a multiparty democracy. This change was brought about by the election on March 28 of a Constituent Assembly in the country's first truly free election in fifty years. . . . Constitutional democracy in El Salvador continues to be limited by the suspension of constitutional rights in a response to the present military emergency resulting from guerrilla and terrorist attacks. The armed forces remain a significant political force in the country.

All human rights conditions in El Salvador are strongly affected by the on-going civil strife. As is common during civil strife, the achievement of a public order, that would protect each person's rights, has been disrupted by military operations, partisan hatreds, acts of revenge, the satisfaction of personal grudges, pervasive fear, and a prevailing uncertainty dominated by violence. This situation contributed to, and is complicated by, the near-paralysis of the judicial system, which is caused in part by corruption and intimidation and which is most evident when crimes of a political nature are being considered.

Civil strife has led to human rights violations by all parties involved in the conflict, the guerrillas of the left, terrorist groups on the right, and the forces employed by the Government. In 1982, the armed conflict continued between the elected government supported by the armed forces, and the leftist Democratic Revolutionary Front and the Farabundo Marti National Liberation Front (FDR/FMLN), which are trying to destroy the country's economy and seize political power by force of arms. An intense guerrilla war in the countryside and both urban and rural terrorism, in accordance with the guerrillas' strategy of prolonged warfare, characterize the military security situation. The Salvadoran armed forces reportedly suffered 1,073 killed in action and 2,584 wounded in action during 1982.

Serious human rights problems continued in El Salvador in 1982, despite signs of improvement throughout the year. Incidents of political assassinations, killings of civilians, disappearances, and torture continue to be reported, although at substantially lower levels than in 1981. The judicial system has failed to function effectively in the face of a guerrilla movement and abuses committed by elements of the security forces and rightist groups. In 1982, the armed forces demonstrated an increased awareness of the need to respect human rights and took some limited steps to improve their performance. Guerrillas were taken prisoner during combat operations, and some military personnel were disciplined for human rights abuses. The new Government established an official Human Rights Commission to scrutinize instances of human rights violations. The exercise of civil liberties remains severely curtailed by the passage of state of siege Decree 507.

In December 1980, the then-ruling junta decreed a state of siege to grant the armed forces a legal basis for the exercise of extraordinary authority in combating insurgency. It has been renewed every thirty days since. State of siege Decree 507 is based on Article 177 of the 1962 Constitution, which permits the temporary suspension of constitutional guarantees of individual rights in times of civil strife or subversion. Rights suspended include free transit, inviolability of correspondence, free expression and free assembly. The armed forces have the legal right to arrest without a warrant. Individuals charged with crimes against the state (e.g., sedition, treason) or related crimes (e.g., acts of terrorism) are remanded to secret military tribunals and subject to the Military Code of Justice.

Whether the Government bears full responsibility for the crimes of certain rightist elements, and the members of the security forces associated with them, is difficult to establish for two reasons. First, the [Alvaro] Magana Government presides uneasily over a collection of quite diverse parties in the Constituent Assembly and other non-government groups, whose actions it does not or cannot fully control. Second, it is characteristic of Salvadoran society that personal loyalties to relatives or locally powerful individuals are strong and often compete with loyalties to legal superiors within the organizations of the Government or to officers within the military chain of command. Thus, it is often difficult to know whether, in taking a given action, a member of the security force is obeying orders handed down through the military or Government chain of command, carrying out the wishes of some local patron or acting on his own. . . .

Violence in El Salvador is endemic. Political polarization has exacerbated the levels of violence. Extremes of the right and the left regularly utilize assassination to eliminate and terrorize suspected opposition members and their sympathizers. Political assassination claims victims from all social classes. It is an institutionalized method in the warfare between the guerrillas of the FMLN and the far right, together with their sympathizers in the Salvadoran armed forces. Some groups associated with the military security forces identify and eliminate suspected collaborators of the FMLN and the FDR. Leftist terrorists in turn assassinate members of the armed forces, members of the paramilitary forces, civilian government authorities, and other citizens.

Attribution of killings is difficult. Groups rarely claim responsibility and witnesses are often reluctant to give testimony to an atrocity. Many victims could have been the targets of either the right or the left, or in at least some cases, victims of common violent crime. A number of political leaders, including about 26 local leaders of the Christian Democratic Party, were assassinated in 1982. Personally motivated assassination has on occasion been disguised as political assassination. At times the circumstances or the identity of victims can point to the perpetrator. For example, the assassination of the president of the International Trade Fair, Nicolas Nasser, on July 15, 1982, was likely to have been perpetrated by leftist terrorists, while many of the individuals removed from their homes after dark in urban areas and later found dead may be considered victims of armed groups of the right, including elements of the security forces.

There was a significant decrease in civilian deaths attributed to political violence in 1982. This decrease follows the downward trend identified in the latter half of 1981. The average of 445 deaths per month (as measured by press reports) in 1981 fell to an average of 219 deaths per month during 1982. While it is certain that these figures underreport the actual incidence of political violence, they do reflect trends. Supporting evidence of the decline in political violence can be derived from reports in the press of disappeared persons, some of whom undoubtedly were killed. These dropped from an average of 160 per month in 1981 to 38 in 1982. . . .

In 1982, the organized death squads of the far right virtually disappeared from the public scene. The most prominent of the death squads, the Maximiliano Hernandez Martinez Brigade, made only two public statements in 1982, both denying connection with other groups linked to extreme rightist violence. While such squads may continue to exist, their program of sowing public terror through violent elimination of suspected subversives appears to have subsided.

The leadership of the armed forces demonstrated a concern for reducing political violence in 1982. However, because of the inability of the judicial system to deal with politically-motivated crimes, a thorough administration of justice is unlikely in the near future. Nevertheless, Defense Minister General Garcia issued orders in March, based on a previously developed code of conduct, that those accused of human rights violations would be punished. A special campaign was directed at the civil defense forces, whose members have been accused of human rights abuses. General Garcia spoke to over 200 local commanders of civil defense forces on October 6, 1982. In that well-publicized meeting, he warned commanders that human rights violations were betrayals of public and armed forces trust and would be punished. . . .

Kampuchea

Claims to authority in Kampuchea are divided between the Coalition Government of Democratic Kampuchea (CGDK) and the so-called People's Republic of Kampuchea (PRK). In 1982, as in the previous three years, the United National General Assembly voted overwhelmingly to accept the credentials of the CGDK.

The Coalition Government of Democratic Kampuchea, headed by leading non-communist national politician, Prince Norodom Sikanouk as President and Chief of State, is a coalition between the communist regime which held power from 1975-79 and the non-communist resistance groups created after Vietnam's 1978 invasion of Kampuchea. The non-communist resistance groups include the Khmer People's National Liberation Front, a political body with a philosophy closer to European liberal thought under former Premier Son Sann, and the National United Front for an Independent, Peaceful, Neutral and Cooperative Cambodia under Prince Sihanouk, who earlier ruled as hereditary king. The appeal of Prince Sihanouk's organization centers on the Prince's stature and the group's espousal of Western democratic ideals. The 1975-79 communist regime, styled Democratic Kampuchea, established itself under the authority of the Communist Party of Kampuchea, a Marxist-Leninist organization and better known as the Khmer Rouge. During its rule, the Khmer Rouge dedicated itself to a thorough and brutal restructuring of Khmer society and individual personality. One of history's worst human rights violators, the Khmer Rouge, subsequent to its ouster from Phnom Penh, claimed democratic goals for Kampuchea, and has undertaken a campaign to convince the Khmer that it has given up many of its egregious human rights practices. These moves, however, have not eased the profound alienation between the Khmer Rouge regime and most of the population.

The so-called People's Republic of Kampuchea, installed by the Vietnamese army in the wake of its December 1978 invasion of Kampuchea, claims Marxism-Leninism as its political ideology. Only one political group is permitted — the People's Revolutionary Party of Kampuchea, a communist party whose leadership publicly emerged in May 1981. The regime seeks legitimacy among the Khmer people by promising a return to traditional cultural values, but in the framework of its communist party. Vietnam continues to dominate and control the regime and prevent the Khmer people from exercising their right of self-determination. . . .

In 1982 human rights violations in PRK areas continued with extensive limitations on civil and political rights. Vietnamese occupation and the lack of self-determination are the fundamental human rights issues. The food situation improved and the material needs of the population promised to ease if conditions of climate proved normal. About 180,000 Vietnamese troops continue to occupy Kampuchea, and an extensive Vietnamese apparatus of advisors supervises the activities of all party, government, and military entities of the PRK. No political parties exist other than the official one, the People's Revolutionary Party of Kampuchea, and the increasing activities of the PRK internal security forces as well as the Vietnamese troops continue to cause anxiety within Kampuchea. Within the PRK areas of Kampuchea and among resistance groups the right to trial does not exist. In Kampuchea political prisons exist in Phnom Penh and in the provinces. Execution without trial has been convincingly alleged by sources in Phnom Penh. Summary execution of "spies and traitors" have reportedly taken place in resistance camps, most notably those of the former DK regime, despite its promulgation of various laws prohibiting this in late 1981.

Since September 1981 new evidence in the form of organic samples has been found in Southeast Asia and lends weight to charges that the Vietnamese allies of the PRK regime are employing lethal chemical/biological agents against DK and non-communist Khmer resistance groups along the Thai-Kampuchean border. . . .

No major changes have taken place in the human rights situation in Kampuchea over the past year. Nor is it possible to see any trends toward an improvement in the state of human rights as long as the country remains occupied by Vietnamese troops and war continues between the Vietnamese and their Khmer allies against the Khmer resistance. . . .

Political murder still exists in Kampuchea. The most grievous offender of modern times, the Khmer Rouge, promulgated a law against killing in July 1981 that ostensibly imposes harsher penalties on officials than on other murderers. No official is known to have been tried to date. . . .

Reports from Phnom Penh assert Heng Samrin security officials are responsible for regular disappearances. Most of those who disappear are thought to be imprisoned. The treatment of such individuals is harsh. Information is inadequate to say how long they are held. Some newly returned refugees from the Thai-Khmer border are said to be called by the authorities to resettle in new areas on government-prepared land. These people are not heard from again by family, friends, or neighbors. While a problem in the past, there have been very few reports of disappearances during 1982 in Khmer Rouge-controlled areas. . . .

The Khmer Rouge dismantled the previous state religion, Buddhism, defrocking some 70,000 monks, forcing many to marry and all to labor, and turning pagodas into warehouses. Since 1979, they have tried to give the impression of reform. They have built pagodas in their zone at Phnom Melai, and in January 1982 welcomed one old and senior monk visiting from abroad. Christianity and Islam were even more ruthlessly suppressed and are not known to have received Khmer Rouge-sponsored revivals in recent years.

In the PRK, the regime has permitted the return of religious practices, but has not reinstituted Buddhism as the state religion. In 1981 the supreme patriarch told journalists that 3,000 monks have been re-robed and 700 pagodas are open. Only men over 50 may officially re-robe or become novices, but a number of younger men have been quietly ordained with the tacit acceptance of local PRK authorities. The supreme patriarch himself is a member of the PRK National Front for Construction and Defense and is vice-president of the National Assembly, elected in May 1981.

Christian groups in the PRK are harassed. The Protestant community of about 2,200 people in 400 families is not authorized to meet, but does so clandestinely. Roman Catholics in Phnom Penh are said to be prohibited from meeting, but one small community in a major rural center is said to have received authorization to meet on Sundays. Non-communist resistance camps afford full freedom of religion. . . .

Vietnam

. . . The . . . historical event of significance for human rights in Vietnam since 1975 was the Vietnamese invasion of Kampuchea in late 1978. By engaging in this invasion, Vietnam has been unable to devote resources to reconstruction from the wounds of its earlier struggle to conquer the

South. Instead, it has poured resources and manpower into Kampuchea on a vast scale.

Vietnam has engaged in human rights violations toward the Kampuchean people as a result of its occupation and control of its neighbor. Reported violations have included forced labor, denial of legal process, and forced relocations. Vietnam continues to control all policies and actions of the Kampuchean Government, and thus must bear a heavy responsibility for any violations occurring under its rule.

Vietnamese forces have used lethal trichothecene toxins (commonly known as "yellow rain") and other combinations of chemical agents in Laos and Kampuchea, frequently against civilian populations. . . .

The Vietnamese citizen today is potentially the victim of arbitrary arrest either for past association with the former regime or for espousal of political ideas contrary to communist ideology. He has the obligation to vote, but all candidates are approved by the Communist Party. Despite legally guaranteed freedom of religion, many religious leaders have been imprisoned. No press exists other that that controlled by the regime.

There was very little improvement in the state of human rights in Vietnam in 1982. There have been some releases from reeducation camps, but not large numbers and over 60,000 remain incarcerated after seven years without trial. The most encouraging event was increased cooperation by government authorities in permitting the Amerasian children of US citizens formerly resident in southern Vietnam to leave for the US, and the expansion of a program of family reunification as relatives of Vietnamese residents of other countries legally emigrate from Vietnam.

Economically, most citizens are not appreciably above the subsistance level. Vietnam still is not self-sufficient in food production — largely a result of arbitrary and incompetent economic politics. Packages from relatives abroad enable many to survive. Food is insufficient for most Vietnamese and what is available is rationed or highly priced on the free market. Inflation is high and corruption rampant while wages are stagnant. Hanoi has often denied working papers and ration coupons to many of its citizens deemed politically unacceptable. Many reeducation camp return-ees among others are thus forced to exist on their own in an underground economy, as the only legal option left open to them is moving to the "New Economic Zones." These actions by the Vietamese Government deny many of its citizens the most basic of all human rights; that of survival. The potential for human rights abuse in Vietnam's export of workers to the USSR and Eastern Europe, apparently to help pay Vietnam's debts, is a source of concern.

The forecast, both for the long and short term, remains bleak. For ideological reasons, as well as out of concern for their power and survival, the leadership will continue to maintain tight control and limit freedom. As long as Vietnam remains mired in Kampuchea, it will lack the resources to invest in reconstruction of its devastated economy. Any improvement in Vietnam's economy is likely to be marginal. Slight liberalization in economic policy is not likely to result in liberalization of cultural or human rights policies. . . .

Economic development continues to be thwarted by the impact of attempts to socialize Southern agriculture, output loss from the flight of skilled and entrepreneurial workers, and the high cost of maintaining defenses against China. Of particular importance is the cost of the war effort in Kampuchea, which diverts badly needed resources and personnel. The regime has exported scarce domestically produced agricultural and consumer goods for political purposes and in order to repay a portion of the massive assistance received from the USSR.

About 45,000 Vietnamese workers have been sent under contract to work in various occupations in the USSR as well as Eastern Europe. There is little doubt that a significant portion of their wages is deducted to help pay for Vietnam's debts to these countries. Complaints about working conditions, including inadequate winter clothing, have been reported. It appears that many of the workers enter this work program in order to escape the poverty and unemployment of present day Vietnam. The potential for human rights abuse, however, remains a source of concern. . . .

U.S.-CANADIAN STUDY, ACID RAIN REPORT

February 21, June 8, 1983

The causes, effects and treatment of acid rain were the topics of several reports published in 1983, beginning with a joint government-sponsored U.S.-Canadian study released February 21. The report was the result of a Memorandum of Intent on Transboundary Air Pollution, a bilateral agreement signed by Canada and the United States in 1980 during the Jimmy Carter administration.

The issue of acid deposition had become a persistent irritant between the two countries because most of the acid rain falling on Canadian soil allegedly came from emission sources in the United States. Government officials, scientists and environmentalists hoped the study would bring about a mutual agreement on the treatment of the issue. However, the findings only deepened the diplomatic debate because U.S. and Canadian scientists failed to reach a consensus on the effects of acid rain and the need for increased emission controls.

Causes and Effects of Acid Rain

The scientists who participated in the study agreed that acid rain was the result of sulphur dioxide and nitrogen oxide emissions from the burning of fossil fuels, notably coal, in both the United States and Canada. The primary sources of these pollutants were utility power plants, factories and automobiles. Utility and industrial plants in the Ohio River Valley and Ontario were particularly suspect. Carried by prevailing winds, often far from the emission source, the pollutants experienced a chemical change in the Earth's atmosphere. Depending on

197

meteorological conditions, the altered compounds returned to Earth as sulphuric and nitric acids in rain, snow and dry particles. Sulphuric acid had the more damaging effect on ecological systems, according to test results.

Although numerous scientific studies substantiated the effects of acid rain on forests, vegetation and buildings in the United States, the destructive process was more readily apparent in aquatic systems. Lakes and streams were able to neutralize moderate levels of acid rain, but continuous deposition and sudden onslaughts after snowmelts were disastrous. The deaths of large numbers of fish because of the buildup of acid concentration trapped in snow and released in the spring were common. The highly acidic condition of temporary pools formed by snowmelts and spring rains, breeding grounds for many species of frogs and salamanders, was responsible for embryonic deformities and deaths. Another bi-product of acidification was the leaching of toxic metals (such as aluminum) from the soil. Those metals were dangerous to fish and other aquatic life and also could be lethal to predators, including man, who ingested contaminated plants and animals.

U.S.-Canadian Disagreements

The U.S. scientists on the panel concluded that there needed to be further research on the cause-and-effect relationship of acid rain, and, therefore, they did not recommend immediate action to tighten emission-control regulations. That view was shared by Ronald Reagan's administration as well as spokesmen for utility and coal industries. But the U.S. scientists' cautious findings, contrary to those of their Canadian peers, were a disappointment to the Canadian government. Formal negotiations between the two countries on the acid rain issue had begun in June 1981 but became stalled a year later when the United States refused to accept Canada's proposal for a bilateral 50 percent reduction of acid-rain-causing emissions.

The U.S. and Canadian scientists disagreed on critical issues involving the environmental effects of acid rain and whether, therefore, there was a need to reduce emissions. The U.S. team concluded in the report that although "biological changes have occurred in areas receiving acidic deposition," it was not certain that man-made pollutants were primarily responsible, because "cause and effects relationships have often not been clearly established." In contrast, the Canadian scientists identified acid deposition as having caused "long-term and short-term acidification of ... surface waters in Canada and the U.S."

In recommending a 50 percent decrease of sulphuric emissions, they concluded that a reduction of acidic deposition would "reduce further damage ... and would lead to eventual recovery of those waters that have already been altered chemically and biologically. Loss of genetic stock [fish] would not be reversible."

Canadian government officials critical of the divided report charged the Reagan administration with undermining the joint project. Reagan had replaced a number of Carter appointees on the team and reportedly had failed to support two additional working groups that originally were called for in the memorandum creating the project. In the storm of protest that followed the study's release, John Roberts, the Canadian minister of the environment, submitted the joint findings to the Royal Society of Canada for review. The White House appointed a group to do the same. The review panels announced their conclusions in July 1983. The Royal Society of Canada group, headed by Kenneth Hare, and the U.S. review panel, chaired by William A. Nirenberg, agreed that sufficient scientific evidence existed to warrant the immediate revision and strengthening of emission controls. Both chairmen wrote to Secretary of State George P. Shultz and the Canadian Minister of External Affairs recommending a sulphur dioxide control program for the United States and Canada.

Other Studies, Administration Actions

The issue continued to be controversial throughout 1983, with the release of other scientific studies supporting the causal relationship between emissions and acid rain. In a highly publicized June 8 report, a U.S. government Interagency Task Force on Acid Precipitation, composed of officials from 12 federal agencies, concluded that man-made pollutants were the major source of acid precipitation and were responsible for the acidification of fresh water and the destruction of aquatic life in the Northeast. The report, however, did not recommend measures to combat the danger. The first annual report of the task force, which was authorized to conduct its study over a 10-year period, stated that not enough was known about the extent and rate of damage caused by man-made pollutants. But Chris Bernabo, director of the task force, said the report did not imply that Congress or the administration should wait until the group completed its 10-year program before acting. Bernabo pointed out that there was a consensus within the scientific community on the source of acid precipitation and the report merely was a state-of-the-science study.

The release of the task force's report was prompted by the imminent release of the National Academy of Sciences report, Acid Deposition: Atmospheric Processes in Eastern North America. *That report, prepared by the National Research Council and released June 29, 1981, said the amount of acid rain, snow and dry particles was in proportion to the amount of sulphur dioxide and nitrogen oxides emitted from man-made sources. It concluded that a 50 percent reduction in sulphur dioxide emissions would result in an equal reduction of acid precipitation.*

The academy report added weight to demands for an immediate emissions-control policy, but it stopped short of offering specific proposals. Jack Calvert, chairman of the project, said that although a decrease of emissions would result in a similar decrease in acid rain, the study did not advocate a policy of uniform reductions. Calvert went on to say that any emission-control policy should be based on an analysis of "alternative control strategies."

Responding to the reports citing the cause-and-effect relationship of industrial emissions and acid rain, William D. Ruckelshaus, director of the Environmental Protection Agency, ordered a reassessment of EPA policy. (His predecessor, Anne Burford, had maintained that no emission-control program should be adopted until more was known on the subject.) Ruckelshaus reportedly had planned to present an acid rain reduction program for presidential approval by the end of September but put off acting because of opposition within the administration.

Following are excerpts from the executive summaries of U.S.-Canadian work group reports on acid rain, submitted to the U.S.-Canadian Coordinating Committee February 21, 1983, and from the executive summary of the annual report of the Interagency Task Force on Acid Precipitation, submitted June 8, 1983:

WORK GROUP REPORTS

INTRODUCTION

Wet and dry deposition of acidic substances and other pollutants are currently being observed over most of eastern North America. The Impact Assessment Work Group was charged with identifying and making an assessment of the key physical and biological consequences possibly related to these transboundary air pollutants.

During the Work Group's assessment of these effects it has been necessary to conduct the work along strictly disciplinary lines. Thus the presentation of our findings follows a sectoral approach (i.e., aquatic, terrestrial). While this approach has been useful for organizing and presenting our findings, it has also limited our consideration of the interactions which exist among these sectors. These effects do not occur in isolation. . . .

AQUATIC ECOSYSTEM EFFECTS - CANADA

The potential effects from the deposition of acid and associated ions and compounds (sulphur dioxide, sulphate, nitrate, ammonia, and others) on water quality, and on the aquatic ecosystem, appear to be more fully quantified and understood than for terrestrial ecosystems. Data have been drawn from a number of study areas in eastern North America including Labrador, Newfoundland, Nova Scotia, New Brunswick, the southern part of the Canadian Shield in Quebec, and Ontario. Primary study areas in the U.S. are found in New Hampshire and southern Maine, Adirondack Park in New York, the Boundary Waters Canoe Area of Minnesota, and numerous lakes in north-central Wisconsin.

The findings and conclusions of the Work Group with respect to acidification effects are contained in the following statements:

> Sulphuric acid has been identified as the dominant compound contributing to the long-term surface water acidification process. Nitric acid contributes to the acidity of precipitation, but is less important in eastern North America than sulphuric acid in long-term acidification of surface waters. Nitric acid contributes to pH depression of surface waters during periods of snowmelt and heavy rain runoff in some areas. . . .

Short-term pH Depressions

While the rate of change of water quality of lakes (i.e., the time required for a lake to become acidified) is one of the least well-defined aspects of the acidification process, there is evidence that current acid loadings are damaging to fish populations and other biota due to short-term pH depressions following snowmelt and storm runoff. Both sulphate and nitrate are associated with short-term changes in water chemistry but in the majority of surveyed cases sulphate appears to be the larger contributor to the total acidity.

Short-term pH depressions, and elevated concentrations of metals, particularly aluminum, have been observed during periods of high infiltration or runoff. Metal accumulation in surface waters (Al, Mn, Fe, Zn, Cd, Cu, Pb, and Ni), first noted in streams and lakes of Scandinavia, also has been reported from such places as Hubbard Brook, the Adirondacks, and the Great Smoky Mountains of the U.S., and the southern Precambrian Shield area of Ontario, Canada. Artificial acidification of a lake in the Experimental Lakes Area of Ontario has also shown rapid mobilization of metals from lake sediments to the water column. . . .

A very large number of surface waters are being affected by acidic deposition, even though the total number of lakes and rivers in eastern North America which are *known* to have been acidified (alkalinity less than 0) by atmospheric acidic deposition is a relatively small percentage of the total aquatic resource.

Biological Effects

Detailed studies of watersheds have been carried out in sensitive regions of North America and Scandinavia under a range of sulphate deposition rates. The results of the studies conducted in North America are described below.

Observed changes in aquatic life have been both correlated with measured changes in the pH of water and compared for waters of different pH values. Differences have been documented in species composition and dominance and size of plankton communities in lakes of varying pH. Study results show that the number of species is lower in low pH lakes compared to lakes of higher pH. These alterations may have important implications for organisms higher in the food chain. Individual lakes often experience several symptoms of acidification at the same time. For example, on Ontario, Plastic Lake inlet streams have low pH and high aluminum concentrations during spring runoff and extensive growth of filamentous green algae, and fish kills have been observed in Plastic Lake.

For those regions currently receiving loadings of sulphate in precipitation of less than 17 kg/ha.yr (Wisconsin, Minnesota and northwestern Ontario), there have been no observed detrimental chemical or biological effects.

For regions currently receiving between 20 and 30 kg/ha.yr sulphate in precipitation there is evidence of chemical alteration and acidification. In Nova Scotia rivers which currently have pH less than 5 there have been salmon population reductions as documented by 40 years of catch records. Fish stocks have remained viable in adjacent rivers with pH values presently greater than 5. Water chemistry records (1954-55 to 1980-81) have indicated a decine in pH to values presently less than 5 for other rivers in the same area. In Maine there is evidence of pH declines over time and loss of alkalinity from surface waters. In Muskoka-Haliburton there is historical evidence of loss of alkalinity for one study lake and there is documentation of pH depressions in all study lakes and streams with low alkalinity. Fish kills were observed in the shore zone of a study lake during spring melt. In the Algoma region there are elevated sulphate and aluminum levels in some headwater lakes. . . .

In the Adirondack Mountains of New York, comparison of data from the 1930s with recent surveys has shown that some more lakes have been acidified. Fish populations have been lost from 180 lakes. Elevated aluminum concentrations in surface waters have been associated with low pH and survival of stocked trout is reduced by the aluminum.

In the Hubbard Brook study area in New Hampshire where the influx of chemicals is limited principally to precipitation and dry deposition there are pH depressions in streams during snowmelt of 1 to 2 units. Elevated levels of aluminum were observed in headwater streams.

Many species of frogs, toads and salamanders breed in temporary pools formed by the mixture of spring rains and snowmelt. Such pools are subjected to pH depression. Embryonic deformities and mortalities in the yellow spotted salamander which breeds in temporary meltwater pools have been observed in New York State where the acidity of the meltwater pools was 1.5 pH units lower than that of nearby permanent ponds. Population densities of the bullfrog and woodfrog were reduced in acidic streams and ponds in Ontario.

A lake acidification experiment in northwestern Ontario clearly shows that alterations to aquatic food chains begin at pH values slightly below 6.0. The remarkable agreement between these whole-lake experiments and observational studies in Scandinavia and eastern North America provides strong evidence that the observed declines in fisheries are caused by acidification and not by other ecological stresses.

Extent of Effects

The terrestrial mapping analysis for eastern Canada supported by surface water chemistry has demonstrated that the watersheds of sensitive (low alkalinity) aquatic ecosystems where effects have been observed have a low potential to reduce acidity and are representative, in terms of soil and geological characteristics, of much larger areas of eastern Canada.

Similarly, using related but different criteria, maps have been developed which characterize considerable areas of the northeastern United States as having low potential to reduce acidity. Therefore, there is reason to expect that there are sensitive surface waters in these other areas which would experience similar effects if subjected to deposition rates comparable to those in the study areas. However, quantification of the number of lakes and rivers susceptible to acidification in both countries will require validation of the terrestrial mapping methodologies and increased information on the chemistry of lakes and streams.

The present empirical evidence covers a broad spectrum of physical and climatological conditions across northeastern North America and therefore provides a reasonable basis on which to make judgements on potential loading effect relationships. However the data do have some deficiencies. More data on historical trends of deposition and associated chemical and biological characteristics would improve our understanding of long-term rates and effects of acidification. In addition, a better understanding of all the mechanisms involved in the acidification process will enhance our ability to estimate loading/response relationships precisely. Therefore any estimates of loading/response relationships should be strengthened in the light of new scientific information as it becomes available.

Target Loadings

. . . Based on the results of the empirical studies, interpretation of long-term water quality data, studies of sediment cores and models that have been reviewed, we conclude that acidic deposition has caused long-term and short-term acidification of sensitive (low alkalinity) surface waters in Canada and the U.S. The Work Group concludes on the basis of our understanding of the acidification process that reductions from present levels of total sulphur deposition in some areas would reduce further damage to sensitive (low alkalinity) surface waters and would lead to eventual recovery of those waters that have already been altered chemically or biologically. Loss of genetic stock would not be reversible.

The Canadian members of the Work Group propose that present deposition of sulphate in precipitation be reduced to less than 20 kg/ha.yr in order to protect all but the most sensitive aquatic ecosystems in Canada. In those areas where there is a high potential to reduce acidity and surface alkalinity is generally greater than 200 μeq/L, the Canadian members recognize that a higher loading rate is acceptable.

As loading reductions take place and additional information is gathered on precipitation, surface water chemistry and watershed response, it may be possible to refine regional loading requirements.

AQUATIC ECOSYSTEM EFFECTS - UNITED STATES

Acidic deposition has been reported in the literature as a cause of both long-term and short-term episodic depressions in pH and loss in alkalinity in some lakes and streams in the U.S. and Canada.

Elevated concentrations of toxic elements, such as aluminum, and biological effects including losses in fish populations have been reported to accompany some of these pH depressions. In most of the reported cases, clear relationships were not established between acidic deposition and observed effects. Conclusions are based on an understanding of the acidification process although mechanisms which control this process are often not completely understood.

The following summary statements are observations reported to be occurring in areas receiving acidic deposition.

Both sulphuric and nitric acid contribute to the acidity of precipitation. It appears, however, that sulphuric acid contributes more to long-term acidification of surface waters than does nitric acid. Nitric acid can contribute to pH depression of surface waters during periods of snowmelt and heavy rain runoff in some areas. Studies of lakes in eastern North America indicate that atmospheric deposition accounts for sulphate levels in some waters in excess of those expected from natural processes. Lake study areas are located in Labrador, Newfoundland, Nova Scotia, New Brunswick, the southern part of the Canadian Shield in Quebec, and in eight regions of Ontario. Primary study areas in the U.S. are found in New Hampshire and southern Maine, Adirondack Park in New York, the Boundary Waters Canoe Area of Minnesota, and numerous lakes in north-central Wisconsin.

There is evidence of long-term reductions of pH and alkalinity and other water quality changes for some low alkalinity surface waters. The rate of change of pH and alkalinity in lakes is one of the least well defined aspects of the acidification process. However, there is evidence of short-term pH depressions in some waters following high runoff from snowmelt and storm activity. Both sulphate and nitrate are associated with short-term changes in water chemistry but, in the majority of surveyed cases, sulphate appears to be the larger contributor to total acidity.

Short-term pH depressions and elevated concentrations of metals, particularly aluminum, iron, zinc, and manganese have been observed during periods of high runoff. Metal mobilization from some watersheds, first noted in streams and lakes of Scandinavia, also has been reported from such places as Hubbard Brook, the Adirondacks, and the Great Smoky Mountains of the U.S., and Sudbury, Muskoka, and Plastic Lake in Ontario, Canada. Artificial acidification of a lake in the Experimental Lakes Area of Ontario has shown mobilization of metals from lake sediments to the water column.

Sediments from lakes in Maine, Vermont, and New Hampshire suggest increased acidity in aquatic ecosystems. It has been inferred from declines in metals (zinc, copper, iron, calcium, magnesium and manganese) in the sediments that the acidity of the water increased since the late 1800s. Low pH maintains metals in the water column, where they can be flushed out of the system before being deposited in the sediments. Diatom data are less complete, but they also indicate a pH decline since the early 1900s. . . .

The total number of lakes and rivers in eastern North America that are thought to have been acidified by acidic deposition is a very small percentage of the total aquatic resource. In the absence of effects from mine drainage and industrial waste water, the symptoms of acidification (e.g., long-term pH declines and/or short-term pH depressions of surface waters with loss of fish populations) have been observed only in clearwater lakes and streams with accompanying elevated concentrations of sulphate and/or nitrate. Natural acidification processes do occur but their effects appear greatest in coloured surface waters. Land use changes, such as fires, logging, and housing developments, have taken place in many areas with low alkalinity surface waters. However, the symptoms of acidification have not been observed in clearwater lakes and streams except in areas receiving high levels of acidic deposition. . . .

Observed changes in aquatic life have both been correlated with measured changes in the pH of water and inferred by comparisons of waters of different pH values. Differences have been documented in species composition and dominance and size of plankton communities in lakes of varying pH. Study results show that the number of species is lower in low pH lakes compared to lakes of higher pH. These differences may have important implications for organisms higher in the food chain, but studies to date have not been done that might establish this connection. . . .

Atlantic salmon populations have disappeared from nine rivers in Nova Scotia but remain in rivers in the same area having higher pH due to greater alkalinity. Decreases in alkalinity and the pH of water over time have been observed in some low pH rivers in Nova Scotia. However, historical chemical data do not exist for the period of major decline in angling success nor do they exist for rivers in which fish declined.

Detailed studies of watersheds and clusters of lakes have been carried out in regions of North America and Scandinavia containing low alkalinity lakes and streams under a range of sulphate deposition rates. The results of those studies conducted in North America are summarized below.

There have been no reported chemical or biological effects for regions currently receiving loadings of sulphate in precipitation at rates less than about 20 kg/ha.yr.

Evidence of chemical change exists for some waters in regions currently estimated or measured to be receiving between about 20-30 kg/ha.yr sulphate in precipitation. In Nova Scotia rivers, 40 years of historical records document reductions in angling success for Atlantic salmon in nine rivers of low pH. Records over later periods for other nearby rivers document decreases in alkalinity and pH. In Maine there is evidence of pH declines over time and loss of alkalinity from some surface waters. In Muskoka-Haliburton historical evidence documents loss of alkalinity for one lake and pH depressions in the number of lakes and streams. Fish confined to the inlet of one lake died during spring melt. In the Algoma region there are elevated sulphate and aluminum levels in some headwater lakes.

Long-term chemical and/or biological effects and short-term chemical effects have been observed in some low alkalinity surface waters experiencing loadings greater than about 30 kg/ha.yr. In Quebec, sulphate concentrations in surface waters decrease towards the east and north in parallel with the deposition pattern of sulphate. Sulphate concentrations are equal to or greater than the bicarbonate concentration in some lakes in the southwest part of the province. In the Adirondack Mountains of New York comparison of data from the 1930s with recent surveys has shown that more lakes are now in low pH categories. The relative contribution of natural and anthropogenic sources to acidification of these lakes is not known. The New York Department of Environmental Conservation has concluded that at least 180 former brook trout ponds are acidic and no longer support brook trout, although a direct association with acidic deposition has not been established. In the Hubbard Brook study area in New Hampshire there are pH depressions in some streams during snowmelt of 1 to 2 units.

In the watershed studies summarized above, sulphate in precipitation was used as a surrogate for total acid loading. Sulphate in precipitation can be reliably measured. It is recognized that dry deposition of sulphate and sulphur dioxide, and the wet and dry deposition of nitrogen oxides, nitric acid, particulate nitrate and ammonia, as well as other compounds, also contribute to acidic deposition. The use of a single substance as a surrogate for acidic loadings adds unknown error owing to site-to-site variability in: (1) composition of deposition, and (2) ability of watersheds to neutralize incoming acidity. Wet and dry deposition of sulphur compounds appeared to predominate in long-term acidification.

Insufficient data are available to relate nitrate deposition to short-term water quality effects. Therefore, we are unable to develop nitrate loading/response relationships.

The terrestrial mapping analysis for eastern Canada has demonstrated that the watersheds in which some surface waters have been observed to experience effects are representative, in terms of soil and geological characteristics, of larger areas of eastern Canada. The level of variability within terrain classes is not known.

An alkalinity map of the U.S. shows the location of regions where the mean alkalinity of most of the sampled surface waters is less than 200 μeg/L. There is reason to believe that some of these low alkalinity surface waters could experience effects similar to those noted in detailed study sites receiving similar total acidic deposition loadings. However, quantification of the number of lakes and rivers in both countries susceptible to acidification at specific loading rates would require validation of mapping methodologies and increased information on loading rates and the chemistry of lakes and streams. The present empirical evidence covers a broad spectrum of physical and climatological conditions across northeastern North America and therefore provides a basis on which to make only qualitative judgements regarding relationships between acidic loading rates and effects.

Based on the results of the empirical studies, interpretation of long-term water quality data and studies of sediment cores that have been reviewed, we conclude that acidic deposition has caused long- and short-term acidification of some low alkalinity surface waters in Canada and the U.S. Based on our understanding of the acidification process the Work Group concludes that reductions from present levels of total sulphur deposition would reduce further chemical and biological alterations to low alkalinity surface waters currently experiencing effects and would lead to eventual recovery of those waters that have been altered by deposition.

The U.S. members conclude that reductions in pH, loss of alkalinity, and associated biological changes have occurred in areas receiving acidic deposition, but cause and effects relationships have often not been clearly established. The relative contributions of acidic inputs from the atmosphere, land use changes, and natural terrestrial processes are not known. The key terrestrial processes which provide acidity to the aquatic processes which provide acidity to the aquatic systems and/or ameliorate atmospheric acidic inputs are neither known or quantified. The key chemical and biological processes which interact in aquatic ecosystems to determine the chemical environment are not known or quantified. Based on this status of the scientific knowledge, the U.S. Work Group concludes that it is not now possible to derive quantitative loading/effects relationships.

INTERAGENCY TASK FORCE SUMMARY

This statutory Annual Report to the President and the Congress by the Interagency Task Force on Acid Precipitation marks the end of the first full year of an integrated research effort by the Federal agencies. The National Acid Precipitation Assessment Program is coordinated by the Task Force and focuses federally-funded research on the timely development of a firmer scientific basis for policy decisions.

This report summarizes the major research findings and accomplishments of the National Program's first year, with particular emphasis on their bearing on acid precipitation policy questions. It provides a brief overview of the available scientific information relevant to policy formulation. As the National Program progresses, future annual reports will provide updates and increasingly better information to assist decisionmakers and the public in continuing to resolve the "acid rain" issue. The program will integrate findings from diverse research areas in order to arrive at successively better answers to key questions, such as:

• What are the current and potential effects of acid deposition within each region, and to what extent could these be ameliorated by lower deposition levels or other mitigation methods?

• What is the quantitative relationship between the release of certain pollutants into the atmosphere and the amount of acidic materials that are deposited?

• What are the costs and environmental impacts of these effects, as well as the costs and benefits of controlling pollutant releases?

In accordance with the Acid Precipitation Act of 1980 (P.L. 96-294), the Task Force is vigorously implementing a comprehensive research program. Federally-funded acid deposition research has doubled, from about $11 million in FY 1980 to $22.3 million for FY 1983. The National Program is producing results at an increasing rate, disseminating them as soon as they become available. However, as recognized in the Act, it will take a systematic effort over a number of years to adequately address all the major uncertainties about the causes, effects, and management of acid deposition.

This overview on the current state of the science is based on information from all available sources, including research supported by Federal agencies, States, environmental organizations, private sector groups, and other nations.

CAUSES

Man-made atmospheric pollutants are probably the major contributors to acid deposition in northeastern North America. The approximate coincidence of the region of highest precipitation acidity with the areas of greatest sulfur dioxide and nitrogen oxides emissions provides circumstantial evidence to support this assertion. This conclusion is also supported by preliminary meteorological studies tracking the physical movement of one pollutant (sulfur dioxide) from sources of emission to suspected areas of deposition.

The National Program is also studying another contributory pollutant (oxides of nitrogen) and chemical substances suspected of being factors in controlling acid deposition. Current data and available methods, however, are not sufficient to quantify relationships between pollutant emissions and acid deposition on a regional scale, or under varying conditions. Nor is it yet possible to identify the specific change in acid deposition patterns that would result from a given change in precursor emissions.

In addition to man-made sources, natural sources of acid precursors are known to exist. On a global scale, it is roughly estimated that half the sulfur in the atmosphere is from natural emissions. Regionally, preliminary findings suggest that natural sources might contribute significantly to the acidity of precipitation in some areas, such as the southeastern United States. In the northestern United States natural sources are believed to be minor contributors to acid deposition. The National Program includes research to increase our meager knowledge of the strengths, character, and distibution of natural sources of sulfur and nitrogen that can contribute to acidity as well as alkaline dusts that neutralize acids in precipitation. This information will be used to assess the potential significance of these sources in contributing to acid deposition in sensitive areas.

SOURCE/RECEPTOR RELATIONSHIP

To formulate scientifically based control strategies, the relationship between emission of precursor pollutants and deposition of acidic material at sensitive receptors should be reliably established.

The ability of current generation models to predict source/receptor relationships with adequate resolution and accuracy is an unresolved issue. A study on the ability of eight models to predict the deposition of sulfur emissions in eastern North America found only a few suitable monitoring data points. While a method is now available to properly evaluate model performance, more data (quality assured and available as a time series) is needed to quantify the uncertainties in model predictions. In addition there are widely differing views of the relative importance of local sources (acid deposition from nearby sources of pollution) and long-range trans-port (acid deposition from far-removed sources of pollution) on the receptors in the local region.

Because of the urgent need to improve our ability to make predictions that reasonably estimate the change in amounts of acid deposition expected from decreases in pollution levels, the National Program includes several simultaneous approaches:

1. For near-term assessments, modifying current-generation models to refine their accommodation of chemical and physical factors over shorter periods of time;

2. Constructing a new generation of models to more effectively treat the physical movement of pollutants in the atmosphere, as well as the mechanisms for their conversion to acids and deposition;

3. Designing a series of field experiments to provide empirical, quantitative evidence of the relationship of pollution source to acid deposition; and

4. Upgrading and evaluating a suitable local/mesoscale model to quantify the relative contribution of local versus long-range transport on receptors.

Intensive efforts underway ... should enhance our ability to project the consequences of changes in emission patterns.

IMPACTS

Among the possible effects of acid deposition, aquatic impacts are currently of greatest concern because of the sensitivity of certain surface waters to acidification and the known potential for damage to fish and other organisms. Initial surveys indicate that a small number of lakes concentrated in the sensitive regions of northeastern North America have been acidified, and their biota have changed.

In the Adirondacks, one of the most sensitive regions in North America, the State of New York has classified 3.6 percent of lake area as in "critical" condition (7,466 acres of 246,388 acres total) and 14 percent endangered; 84 percent were surveyed. Acid deposition is probably the major contributor to this acidification, but the rates of change and the factors controlling it are still poorly understood.

Many of the reported cases that suggest acid deposition is the cause of some observed change in an aquatic ecosystem are based on circumstantial evidence and lack documentation of the mechanisms linking cause and effect. At present, the extent of actual aquatic damages is not well established. The question of long-term trends in freshwater acidification also remains uncertain.

The National Program produced maps in FY 1982 depicting the regions where surface waters could be most susceptible to acidification, and improved regional monitoring and testing programs will produce more detailed and reliable inventories of the extent of damages and the location and value of resources at risk.

Beyond the alteration of the chemistry and biology of certain sensitive surface waters, the other effects of acid deposition in North America are undetermined. There is concern about possible effects on crops, forests, wetlands, soils, building materials, and indirect effects on human health (through drinking water or food). Although mechanisms for such effects are known, evidence has not yet demonstrated that they are widely occurring under ambient acid deposition in North America. For instance, although experimental studies with simulated acid rain have shown both positive and negative effects on crop species, effects on crops growing under actual field conditions have not been determined.

Similarly, although a dieback of spruce trees on mountain sites in New England is observable, the relative contribution of potential causes — acid deposition, drought, disease, and other pollutants — is still undetermined. In contrast to acid deposition, the effects of ozone and other air pollutants on crops and forests are well documented. The National Program is speeding up investigations and analyses to determine the actual effects of acid deposition. . . .

REPORT ON INTERNMENT
OF JAPANESE-AMERICANS
February 24, 1983

Thirty-eight years after Executive Order 9066 authorizing the internment of Americans of Japanese descent was signed by President Franklin D. Roosevelt, the Commission on Wartime Relocation and Internment of Civilians, established by Congress in 1980, concluded in February 1983 that a "grave injustice" had been done to the Japanese-Americans. In its 467-page report, entitled "Personal Justice Denied," the panel decried the government's actions in relocating approximately 120,000 American citizens living on the West Coast to internment camps in the spring of 1942.

Executive Order 9066, issued February 19, 1942, gave the secretary of war authority to "exclude any and all persons, citizens and aliens, from designated areas in order to provide security against sabotage, espionage and fifth column activity." The order was prompted by the Japanese attack on Pearl Harbor, December 7, 1941, and the United States' subsequent declaration of war against Japan.

Soon after the order was issued, all Americans of Japanese descent were prohibited from working or traveling on the West Coast. When Japanese-Americans failed to comply with that "voluntary" order, they were transferred by the Army to "assembly centers" and later to permanent "relocation centers" in six western states and Arkansas. By the end of 1942, 106,770 people had been transported to relocation centers.

Release from the camps was based upon a "loyalty review" conducted by the the civilian agency in charge of the camps. Although many of those interned eventually left to join the Army, attend college outside of the West Coast or find private employment, a large number remained in the camps until the prohibition against returning to their homes was lifted in December 1944.

In addition to transporting Americans of Japanese descent, the government in 1942 relocated approximately 878 Alaskan native Aleutian Islanders to detention centers housed in abandoned gold mines or fish cannery buildings in southeastern Alaska. The Aleuts were held, in what were generally considered to be deplorable conditions, until 1944 and 1945.

The Aleutian Islands were strategically important to both the United States and Japan. In June 1942 the Japanese captured the two westernmost islands. During the Japanese offensive, military commanders in Alaska had ordered the Aleut evacuation for safety reasons. An estimated 10 percent of the evacuated Aleuts died during their two- or three-year stay in the camps.

Commission's Report and Compensation

The commission's report said, "In sum, the record does not permit the conclusion that military necessity warranted the exclusion of ethnic Japanese from the West Coast." It placed the burden of guilt largely upon President Roosevelt, although it noted that Congress sanctioned the action and the Supreme Court "held the exclusion constitutionally permissible in the context of war." No documented acts of espionage were committed by Americans of Japanese descent during the war, or by Japanese aliens living on the West coast, according to the report.

In 1948 Congress appropriated $132 million for 23,000 property claims made by the displaced Japanese-Americans. But Congress did not investigate whether or not the internment was justified.

The congressionally appointed commission followed its February report on June 16 by issuing a more specific recommendation that the government should pay $20,000 each to the 60,000 internees who were still alive. The payments, totaling $1.5 billion, were to be awarded as "an act of national apology." The panel also proposed granting pardons to Japanese-Americans convicted on criminal charges in connection with resisting the evacuation from their homes to the camps.

The commission also found the Aleutian evacuation reprehensible. "In sum, despite the fact that the Aleutians were a theatre of war from which evacuation was a sound policy, there was no justification for the manner in which the Aleuts were treated in the camps in southeastern Alaska, nor for failing to compensate them fully for their material losses."

Only one member of the panel, and the only congressional delegate,

Rep. Dan. Lundgren, R-Calif., opposed the proposal for reparations to individual citizens. Although he acknowledged that Japanese-Americans had suffered grave injustices, Lundgren said they were no more entitled to payments than blacks or American Indians.

Meanwhile in Congress, bills were introduced that incorporated the commission's recommendations for compensation of Japanese-Americans and Aleuts. And three Supreme Court decisions that affirmed the legality of the Japanese-American internment program were under challenge in federal courts in late 1983.

Following are excerpts from the February 24, 1983, report of the Commission on Wartime Relocation and Internment of Civilians:

The Commission on Wartime Relocation and Internment of Civilians was established by act of Congress in 1980 and directed to

1. review the facts and circumstances surrounding Executive Order Numbered 9066, issued February 19, 1942, and the impact of such Executive Order on American citizens and permanent resident aliens;
2. review directives of United States military forces requiring the relocation and, in some cases, detention in internment camps of American citizens, including Aleut civilians, and permanent resident aliens of the Aleutian and Pribilof Islands; and
3. recommend appropriate remedies.

In fulfilling this mandate, the Commission held 20 days of hearings in cities across the country, particularly on the West Coast, hearing testimony from more than 750 witnesses: evacuees, former government officials, public figures, interested citizens, and historians and other professionals who have studied the subjects of Commission inquiry. An extensive effort was made to locate and to review the records of government action and to analyze other sources of information including contemporary writings, personal accounts and historical analyses.

By presenting this report to Congress, the Commission fulfills the instruction to submit a written report of its findings. Like the body of the report, this summary is divided into two parts. The first describes actions taken pursuant to Executive Order 9066, particularly the treatment of American citizens of Japanese descent and resident aliens of Japanese nationality. The second covers the treatment of Aleuts from the Aleutian and Pribilof Islands.

Part I: Nisei and Issei*

On February 19, 1942, ten weeks after the Pearl Harbor attack, President Franklin D. Roosevelt signed Executive Order 9066, which gave to the Secretary of War and the military commanders to whom he delegated authority, the power to exclude any and all persons, citizens and aliens, from designated areas in order to provide security against sabotage, espionage and fifth column activity. Shortly thereafter, all American citizens of Japanese descent were prohibited from living, working or traveling on the West Coast of the United States. The same prohibition applied to the generation of Japanese immigrants who, pursuant to federal law and despite long residence in the United States, were not permitted to become American citizens. Initially, this exclusion was to be carried out by "voluntary" relocation. That policy inevitably failed, and these American citizens and their alien parents were removed by the Army, first to "assembly centers" — temporary quarters at racetracks and fairgrounds — and then to "relocation centers" — bleak barrack camps mostly in desolate areas of the West. The camps were surrounded by barbed wire and guarded by military police. Departure was permitted only after a loyalty review on terms set, in consultation with the military, by the War Relocation Authority, the civilian agency that ran the camps. Many of those removed from the West Coast were eventually allowed to leave the camps to join the Army, go to college outside the West Coast or to whatever private employment was available. For a larger number, however, the war years were spent behind barbed wire; and for those who were released, the prohibition against returning to their homes and occupations on the West Coast was not lifted until December 1944.

This policy of exclusion, removal and detention was executed against 120,000 people without individual review, and exclusion was continued virtually without regard for their demonstrated loyalty to the United States. Congress was fully aware of and supported the policy of removal and detention; it sanctioned the exclusion by enacting a statute which made criminal the violation of orders issued pursuant to Executive Order 9066. The United States Supreme Court held the exclusion constitutionally permissible in the context of war, but struck down the incarceration of admittedly loyal American citizens on the ground that it was not based on statutory authority.

All this was done despite the fact that not a single documented act of espionage, sabotage or fifth column activity was committed by an American citizen of Japanese ancestry or by a resident Japanese alien on the West Coast.

No mass exclusion or detention, in any part of the country, was ordered against American citizens of German or Italian descent. Official actions against enemy aliens of other nationalities were much more individualized and selective than those imposed on the ethnic Japanese.

The exclusion, removal and detention inflicted tremendous human cost. There was the obvious cost of homes and businesses sold or abandoned under circumstances of great distress, as well as injury to careers and

---

* The first generation of ethnic Japanese born in the United States are *Nisei;* the *Issei* are the immigrant generation from Japan; and those who returned to Japan as children for education are *Kibei.*

professional advancement. But, most important, there was the loss of liberty and the personal stigma of suspected disloyalty for thousands of people who knew themselves to be devoted to their country's cause and to its ideals but whose repeated protestations of loyalty were discounted — only to be demonstrated beyond any doubt by the record of Nisei solders, who returned from the battlefields of Europe as the most decorated and distinguished combat unit of World War II, and by the thousands of other Nisei who served against the enemy in the Pacific, mostly in military intelligence. The wounds of the exclusion and detention have healed in some respects, but the scars of that experience remain, painfully real in the minds of those who lived through the suffering and deprivation of the camps.

The personal injustice of excluding, removing and detaining loyal American citizens is manifest. Such events are extraordinary and unique in American history. For every citizen and for American public life, they pose haunting questions about our country and its past. It has been the Commission's task to examine the central decisions of this history — the decision to exclude, the decision to detain, the decision to release from detention and the decision to end exclusion. The Commission has analyzed both how and why those decisions were made, and what their consequences were. And in order to illuminate those events, the mainland experience was compared to the treatment of Japanese Americans in Hawaii and to the experience of other Americans of enemy alien descent, particularly German Americans.

THE DECISION TO EXCLUDE

The Context of the Decision

First, the exclusion and removal were attacks on the ethnic Japanese which followed a long and ugly history of West Coast anti-Japanese agitation and legislation. Antipathy and hostility toward the ethnic Japanese was a major factor of the public life of the West Coast states for more than forty years before Pearl Harbor. Under pressure from California, immigration from Japan had been severely restricted in 1908 and entirely prohibited in 1924. Japanese immigrants were barred from American citizenship, although their children born here were citizens by birth. California and the other western states prohibited Japanese immigrants from owning land. In part the hostility was economic, emerging in various white American groups who began to feel competition, particularly in agriculture, the principal occupation of the immigrants. The anti-Japanese agitation also fed on racial stereotypes and fears: the "yellow peril" of an unknown Asian culture achieving substantial influence on the Pacific Coast or of a Japanese population alleged to be growing far faster than the white population. This agitation and hostility persisted, even though the ethnic Japanese never exceeded three percent of the population of California, the state of greatest concentration.

The ethnic Japanese, small in number and with no political voice — the citizen generation was just reaching voting age in 1940 — had become a convenient target for political demagogues, and over the years all the major parties indulged in anti-Japanese rhetoric and programs. Political bullying was supported by organized interest groups who adopted anti-Japanese agitation as a consistent part of their program: the Native Sons and Daughters of the Golden West, the Joint Immigration Committee, the American Legion, the California State Federation of Labor and the California State Grange.

This agitation attacked a number of ethnic Japanese cultural traits or patterns which were woven into a bogus theory that the ethnic Japanese could not or would not assimilate or become "American." Dual citizenship, Shinto, Japanese language schools, and the education of many ethnic Japanese children in Japan were all used as evidence. But as a matter of fact, Japan's law on dual citizenship went no further than those of many European countries in claiming the allegiance of the children of its nationals born abroad. Only a small number of ethnic Japanese subscribed to Shinto, which in some forms included veneration of the Emperor. The language schools were not unlike those of other first-generation immigrants, and the return of some children to Japan for education was as much a reaction to hostile discrimination and an uncertain future as it was a commitment to the mores, much less the political doctrines, of Japan. Nevertheless, in 1942 these popular misconceptions infected the views of a great many West Coast people....

Second, Japanese armies in the Pacific won a rapid, startling string of victories against the United States and its allies in the first months of World War II. On the same day as the attack on Pearl Harbor, the Japanese struck the Malay Peninsula, Hong Kong, Wake and Midway Islands and attacked the Philippines. The next day the Japanese Army invaded Thailand. On December 13 Guam fell; on December 24 and 25 the Japanese captured Wake Island and occupied Hong Kong. Manila was evacuated on December 27, and the American army retreated to the Bataan Peninsula. After three months the troops isolated in the Philippines were forced to surrender unconditionally — the worst American defeat since the Civil War. In January and February 1942, the military position of the United States in the Pacific was perilous. There was fear of Japanese attacks on the West Coast.

Next, contrary to the facts, there was a widespread belief, supported by a statement by Frank Knox, Secretary of the Navy, that the Pearl Harbor attack had been aided by sabotage and fifth column activity by ethnic Japanese in Hawaii. Shortly after Pearl Harbor the government knew that this was not true, but took no effective measures to disabuse public belief that disloyalty had contributed to massive American losses on December 7, 1941. Thus the country was unfairly led to believe that both American citizens of Japanese descent and resident Japanese aliens threatened American security.

Fourth, as anti-Japanese organizations began to speak out and rumors from Hawaii spread, West Coast politicians quickly took up the familiar anti-Japanese cry. The Congressional delegations in Washington organized themselves and pressed the War and Justice Departments and the President for stern measures to control the ethnic Japanese — moving quickly from control of aliens to evacuation and removal of citizens. In California, Governor [Culbert] Olson, Attorney General [Earl] Warren, Mayor [Fletcher] Bowron of Los Angeles and many local authorities joined the clamor. These opinions were not informed by any knowledge of actual military risks, rather they were stoked by virulent agitation which encountered little opposition. Only a few churchmen and academicians were prepared to defend the ethnic Japanese. There was little or no political risk in claiming that it was "better to be safe than sorry" and, as many did, that the best way for ethnic Japanese to prove their loyalty was to volunteer to enter detention. The press amplified the unreflective emotional excitement of the hour. Through late January and early February 1942, the rising clamor from the West Coast was heard within the federal government as its demands became more draconian.

Making and Justifying the Decision

The exclusion of the ethnic Japanese from the West Coast was recommended to the Secretary of War, Henry L. Stimson, by Lieutenant General John L. DeWitt, Commanding General of the Western Defense Command with responsibility for West Coast security. President Roosevelt relied on Secretary Stimson's recommendations in issuing Executive Order 9066.

The justification given for the measure was military necessity. The claim of military necessity is most clearly set out in three places: General DeWitt's February 14, 1942, recommendation to Secretary Stimson for exclusion; General DeWitt's *Final Report: Japanese Evacuation from the West Coast, 1942;* and the government's brief in the Supreme Court defending the Executive Order in *Hirabayashi* v. *United States* [1943]. General DeWitt's February 1942 recommendation presented the following rationale for the exclusion:

> In the war in which we are now engaged racial affinities are not severed by migration. The Japanese race is an enemy race and while many second and third generation Japanese born on United States soil, possessed of United States citizenship, have become "Americanized," the racial strains are undiluted. To conclude otherwise is to expect that children born of white parents on Japanese soil sever all racial affinity and become loyal Japanese subjects, ready to fight and, if necessary, to die for Japan in a war against the nation of their parents. That Japan is allied with Germany and Italy in this struggle is no ground for assuming that any Japanese, barred from assimilation by convention as he is, though born and raised in the United States, will not turn against this nation when the final test of loyalty comes. It, therefore, follows that along the vital Pacific Coast over 112,000 potential enemies, of Japanese extraction, are at large today. There are indications that these were organized and ready for concerted action at a favorable opportunity. The very fact that

no sabotage has taken place to date is a disturbing and confirming indication that such action will be taken.

There are two unfounded justifications for exclusion expressed here: first, that ethnicity ultimately determines loyalty; second, that "indications" suggest that ethnic Japanese "are organized and ready for concerted action" — the best argument for this being the fact that it hadn't happened.

The first evaluation is not a military one but one for sociologists or historians. It runs counter to a basic premise on which the American nation of immigrants is built — that loyalty to the United States is a matter of individual choice and not determined by ties to an ancestral country. In the case of German Americans, the First World War demonstrated that race did not determine loyalty, and no negative assumption was made with regard to citizens of German or Italian descent during the Second World War. The second judgment was, by the General's own admission, unsupported by any evidence. General DeWitt's recommendation clearly does not provide a credible rationale, based on military expertise, for the necessity of exclusion.

In his 1943 *Final Report,* General DeWitt cited a number of factors in support of the exclusion decision: signaling from shore to enemy submarines; arms and contraband found by the FBI during raids on ethnic Japanese homes and businesses; dangers to the ethnic Japanese from vigilantes; concentration of ethnic Japanese around or near military sensitive areas; the number of Japanese ethnic organizations on the coast which might shelter pro-Japanese attitudes or activities such as Emperor-worshipping Shinto; and the presence of the Kibei, who had spent some time in Japan.

The first two items point to demonstrable military danger. But the reports of shore-to-ship signaling were investigated by the Federal Communications Commission, the agency with relevant expertise, and no identifiable cases of such signaling were substantiated. The FBI did confiscate arms and contraband from some ethnic Japanese, but most were items normally in the possession of any law-abiding civilian, and the FBI concluded that these searches had uncovered no dangerous persons that "we could not otherwise know about." Thus neither of these "facts" militarily justified exclusion.

There had been some acts of violence against ethnic Japanese on the West Coast and feeling against them ran high, but "protective custody" is not an acceptable rationale for exclusion. Protection against vigilantes is a civilian matter that would involve the military only in extreme cases. But there is no evidence that such extremity had been reached on the West Coast in early 1942. Moreover, "protective custody" could never justify exclusion and detention for months and years.

General DeWitt's remaining points are repeated in the *Hirabayashi* brief, which also emphasizes dual nationality, Japanese language schools and the high percentage of aliens (who, by law, had been barred from acquiring American citizenship) in the ethnic population. These facts represent broad social judgments of little or no military significance in themselves. None supports the claim of disloyalty to the United States and all were entirely legal. If the same standards were applied to other ethnic groups, as Morton Grodzins, an early analyst of the exclusion decision, applied it to ethnic Italians on the West Coast, an equally compelling and meaningless case for "disloyalty" could be made. In short, these social and cultural patterns were not evidence of any threat to West Coast military security.

In sum, the record does not permit the conclusion that military necessity warranted the exclusion of ethnic Japanese from the West Coast.

The Conditions Which Permitted the Decision

Having concluded that no military necessity supported the exclusion, the Commission has attempted to determine how the decision came to be made.

First, General DeWitt apparently believed what he told Secretary Stimson: ethnicity determined loyalty. Moreover, he believed that the ethnic Japanese were so alien to the thought processes of white Americans that it was impossible to distinguish the loyal from the disloyal. On this basis he believed them to be potential enemies among whom loyalty could not be determined.

Second, the FBI and members of Naval Intelligence who had relevant intelligence responsibility were ignored when they stated that nothing more than careful watching of suspicious individuals or individual reviews of loyalty were called for by existing circumstances. In addition, the opinions of the Army General Staff that no sustained Japanese attack on the West Coast was possible were ignored.

Third, General DeWitt relied heavily on civilian politicians rather than informed military judgments in reaching his conclusions as to what actions were necessary, and civilian politicians largely repeated the prejudiced, unfounded themes of anti-Japanese factions and interest groups on the West Coast.

Fourth, no effective measures were taken by President Roosevelt to calm the West Coast public and refute the rumors of sabotage and fifth column activity at Pearl Harbor.

Fifth, General DeWitt was temperamentally disposed to exaggerate the measures necessary to maintain security and placed security far ahead of any concern for the liberty of citizens.

Sixth, Secretary Stimson and John J. McCloy, Assistant Secretary of War, both of whose views on race differed from those of General DeWitt, failed to insist on a clear military justification for the measures General DeWitt wished to undertake.

Seventh, Attorney General Francis Biddle, while contending that exclusion was unnecessary, did not argue to the President that failure to make out a case of military necessity on the facts would render the exclusion constitutionally impermissible or that the Constitution prohibited exclusion on the basis of ethnicity given the facts on the West Coast.

Eighth, those representing the interests of civil rights and civil liberties in Congress, the press and other public forums were silent or indeed supported exclusion. Thus there was no effective opposition to the measures vociferously sought by numerous West Coast interest groups, politicians and journalists.

Finally, President Roosevelt, without raising the question to the level of Cabinet discussion or requiring any careful or thorough review of the situation, and despite the Attorney General's arguments and other information before him, agreed with Secretary Stimson. . . .

THE DECISION TO DETAIN

With the signing of Executive Order 9066, the course of the President and the War Department was set: American citizens and alien residents of Japanese ancestry would be compelled to leave the West Coast on the basis of wartime military necessity. For the War Department and the Western Defense Command, the problem became primarily one of method and operation, not basic policy. General DeWitt first tried "voluntary" resettlement: the ethnic Japanese were to move outside restricted military zones of the West Coast but otherwise were free to go wherever they chose. From a military standpoint this policy was bizarre, and it was utterly impractical. If the ethnic Japanese had been excluded because they were potential saboteurs and spies, any such danger was not extinguished by leaving them at large in the interior where there were, of course, innumerable dams, power lines, bridges and war industries to be disrupted or spied upon. Conceivably sabotage in the interior could be synchronized with a Japanese raid or invasion for a powerful fifth column effect. This raises serious doubts as to how grave the War Department believed the supposed threat to be. Indeed, the implications were not lost on the citizens and politicians of the interior western states, who objected in the belief that people who threatened wartime security in California were equally dangerous in Wyoming and Idaho.

The War Relocation Authority (WRA), the civilian agency created by the President to supervise the relocation and initially directed by Milton Eisenhower, proceeded on the premise that the vast majority of evacuees were law-abiding and loyal, and that, once off the West Coast, they should be returned quickly to conditions approximating normal life. This view was strenuously opposed by the people and politicians of the mountain states. In April 1942, Milton Eisenhower met with the governors and officials of the mountain states. They objected to California using the interior states as a "dumping ground" for a California "problem." They argued that people in their states were so bitter over the voluntary evacuation that unguarded evacuees would face physical danger. They wanted guarantees that the government would forbid evacuees to acquire land and that it would remove them at the end of the war. Again and again, detention camps for evacuees were urged. The consensus was that a plan for reception centers was acceptable so long as the evacuees remained under guard within the centers.

In the circumstances, Milton Eisenhower decided that the plan to move the evacuees into private employment would be abandoned, at least temporarily. The War Relocation Authority dropped resettlement and adopted confinement. Notwithstanding WRA's belief that evacuees should be returned to normal productive life, it had, in effect, become their jailer. The politicians of the interior states had achieved the program of detention.

The evacuees were to be held in camps behind barbed wire and released only with government approval. For this course of action no military justification was proffered. Instead, the WRA contended that these steps were necessary for the benefit of evacuees and that controls on their departure were designed to assure they would not be mistreated by other Americans on leaving the camps.

It follows from the conclusion that there was no justification in military necessity for the exclusion, that there was no basis for the detention.

THE EFFECT OF THE EXCLUSION AND DETENTION

The history of the relocation camps and the assembly centers that preceded them is one of suffering and deprivation visited on people against whom no charges were, or could have been, brought. The Commission hearing record is full of poignant, searing testimony that recounts the economic and personal losses and injury caused by the exclusion and deprivation of detention. No summary can do this testimony justice.

Families could take to the assembly centers and the camps only what they could carry. Camp living conditions were Spartan. People were housed in tar-papered barrack rooms of no more than 20 by 24 feet. Each room housed a family, regardless of family size. Construction was often shoddy. Privacy was practically impossible and furnishings were minimal. Eating and bathing were in mass facilities. Under continuing pressure from those who blindly held to the belief that evacuees harbored disloyal intentions, the wages paid for work at the camps were kept to the minimal level of $12 a month for unskilled labor, rising to $19 a month for professional employees. Mass living prevented normal family communication and activities. Heads of families, no longer providing food and shelter, found their authority to lead and to discipline diminished.

The normal functions of community life continued but almost always under a handicap — doctors were in short supply; schools which taught typing had no typewriters and worked from hand-me-down school books; there were not enough jobs.

The camp experience carried a stigma that no other Americans suffered.

The evacuees themselves expressed the indignity of their conditions with particular power:

> On May 16, 1942, my mother, two sisters, niece, nephew, and I left ... by train. Father joined us later. Brother left earlier by bus. We took whatever we could carry. So much we left behind, but the most valuable thing I lost was freedom.

> Henry went to the Control Station to register the family. He came home with twenty tags, all numbered 10710, tags to be attached to each piece of baggage, and one to hang from our coat lapels. From then on, we were known as Family #10710.

The government's efforts to "Americanize" the children in the camps were bitterly ironic:

> An oft-repeated ritual in relocation camp schools ... was the salute to the flag followed by the singing of "My country, 'tis of thee, sweet land of liberty" — a ceremony Caucasian teachers found embarassingly awkward if not cruelly poignant in the austere prison-camp setting.

> In some ways, I suppose, my life was not too different from a lot of kids in America between the years 1942 and 1945. I spent a good part of my time playing with my brothers and sisters, learned to shoot marbles, watched sandlot baseball and envied the older kids who wore Boy Scout uniforms. We shared with the rest of America the same movies, screen heroes and listened to the same heart-rending songs of the forties. We imported much of America into the camps because, after all, we were Americans. Through imitation of my brothers, who attended grade school within the camp, I learned the salute to the flag by the time I was five years old. I was learning, as best one could learn in Manzanar, what it meant to live in America. But, I was also learning the sometimes bitter price one has to pay for it.

After the war, through the Japanese American Evacuation Claims Act, the government attempted to compensate for the losses of real and personal property; inevitably that effort did not secure full or fair compensation. There were many kinds of injury the Evacuation Claims Act made no attempt to compensate: the stigma placed on people who fell under the exclusion and relocation orders; the deprivation of liberty suffered during detention; the psychological impact of exclusion and relocation; the breakdown of family structure; the loss of earnings or profits; physical injury or illness during detention.

THE DECISION TO END DETENTION

By October 1942, the government held over 100,000 evacuees in relocation camps. After the tide of war turned with the American victory at Midway in June 1942, the possibility of serious Japanese attack was no longer credible; detention and exclusion became increasingly difficult to defend. Nevertheless, other than an ineffective leave program run by the War Relocation Authority, the government had no plans to remedy the situation and no means of distinguishing the loyal from the disloyal. Total control of these civilians in the presumed interest of state security was rapidly becoming the accepted norm.

Determining the basis on which detention would be ended required the government to focus on the justification for controlling the ethnic Japanese. If the government took the position that race determined loyalty or that it was impossible to distinguish the loyal from the disloyal because "Japanese" patterns of thought and behavior were too alien to white Americans, there would be little incentive to end detention. If the government maintained the position that distinguishing the loyal from the disloyal was possible and that exclusion and detention were required only by the necessity of acting quickly under the threat of Japanese attack in early 1942, then a program to release those considered loyal should have been instituted in the spring of 1942 when people were confined in the assembly centers.

Neither position totally prevailed. General DeWitt and the Western Defense Command took the first position and opposed any review that would determine loyalty or threaten continued exclusion from the West Coast. Thus, there was no loyalty review during the assembly center period. Secretary Stimson and Assistant Secretary McCloy took the second view, but did not act on it until the end of 1942 and then only in a limited manner. At the end of 1942, over General DeWitt's opposition, Secretary Stimson, Assistant Secretary McCloy and General George C. Marshall, Chief of Staff, decided to establish a volunteer combat team of Nisei soldiers. The volunteers were to come from those who had passed a loyalty review. To avoid the obvious unfairness of allowing only those joining the military to establish their loyalty and leave the camps, the War Department joined WRA in expanding the loyalty review program to all adult evacuees.

This program was significant, but remained a compromise. It provided an opportunity to demonstrate loyalty to the United States on the battlefields; despite the human sacrifice involved, this was of immense practical importance in obtaining postwar acceptance for the ethnic Japanese. It opened the gates of the camps for some and began some reestablishment of normal life. But, with no apparent rationale or justification, it did not end exclusion of the loyal from the West Coast. The review program did not extend the presumption of loyalty to American citizens of Japanese descent, who were subject to an investigation and review not applied to other ethnic groups.

Equally important, although the loyalty review program was the first major government decision in which the interests of evacuees prevailed, the program was conducted so insensitively, with such lack of understanding of the evacuees' circumstances, that it became one of the most divisive and wrenching episodes of the camp detention.

After almost a year of what the evacuees considered utterly unjust treatment at the hands of the government, the loyalty review program began with filling out a questionnaire which posed two questions requiring declarations of complete loyalty to the United States. Thus, the questionnaire demanded a personal expression of position from each evacuee — a choice between faith in one's future in America and outrage at present injustice. Understandably most evacuees probably had deeply ambiguous feelings about a government whose rhetorical values of liberty and equality they wished to believe, but who found their present treatment in painful contradiction to those values. The loyalty questionnaire left little room to express that ambiguity. Indeed, it provided an effective point of protest and organization against the government, from which more and more evacuees felt alienated. The questionnaire finally addressed the central questions of loyalty that underlay the exclusion policy, a question which had been the predominant political and personal issue for the ethnic Japanese over the past year; answering it required confronting the conflicting emotions aroused by their relation to the government. Evacuee testimony shows the intensity of conflicting emotions:

> I answered both questions number 27 and 28 [the loyalty questions] in the negative, not because of disloyalty but due to the disgusting and shabby treatment given us. A few months after completing the questionnaire, U.S. Army officers appeared at our camp and gave us an interview to confirm our answers to the questions 27 and 28, and followed up with a question that in essence asked: "Are you going to give up or renounce your U.S. citizenship?" to which I promptly replied in the affirmative as a rebellious move. Sometime after the interview, a form letter from the Immigration and Naturalization Service arrived saying if I wanted to renounce my U.S. citizenship, sign the form letter and return. Well, I kept the Immigration and Naturalization Service waiting.

> Well, I am one of those that said "no, no" on it, one of the "no, no" boys, and it is not that I was proud about it, it was just that our legal rights were violated and I wanted to fight back. However, I didn't want to take this sitting down. I was really angry. It just got me so damned mad. Whatever we do, there was no help from outside, and it seems to me that we are a race that doesn't count. So therefore, this was one of the reasons for the "no, no" answer.

Personal responses to the questionnaire inescapably became public acts open to community debate and scrutiny within the closed world of the camps. This made difficult choices excruciating:

> After I volunteered for the [military] service, some people that I knew refused to speak to me. Some older people later questioned my father for letting me volunteer, but he told them that I was old enough to make up my own mind.

> The resulting infighting, beatings, and verbal abuses left families torn apart, parents against children, brothers against sisters, relatives against relatives, and friends against friends. So bitter was all this that even to this day, there are many amongst us who do not speak about that period for fear that the same harsh feelings might arise up again to the surface.

The loyalty review program was a point of decision and division for those in the camps. The avowedly loyal were eligible for release; those who were unwilling to profess loyalty or whom the government distrusted were segregated from the main body of evacuees into the Tule Lake camp, which rapidly became a center of disaffection and protest against the government and its policies. . . .

THE DECISION TO END EXCLUSION

The loyalty review should logically have led to the conclusion that no justification existed for excluding loyal American citizens from the West Coast. Secretary Stimson, Assistant Secretary McCloy and General Marshall reached this position in the spring of 1943. Nevertheless, the exclusion was not ended until December 1944. No plausible reason connected to any wartime security has been offered for this eighteen to twenty month delay in allowing the ethnic Japanese to return to their homes, jobs and businesses on the West Coast, despite the fact that the delay meant, as a practical matter, that confinement in the relocation camps continued for the great majority of evacuees for another year and a half.

Between May 1943 and May 1944, War Department officials did not make public their opinion that exclusion of loyal ethnic Japanese from the West Coast no longer had any military justification. If the President was unaware of this view, the plausible explanation is that Secretary Stimson and Assistant Secretary McCloy were unwilling, or believed themselves unable, to face down political opposition on the West Coast. General DeWitt repeatedly expressed opposition until he left the Western Defense Command in the fall of 1943, as did West Coast anti-Japanese factions and politicans.

In May 1944 Secretary Stimson put before President Roosevelt and the Cabinet his position that the exclusion no longer had a military justification. But the President was unwilling to act to end the exclusion until the first Cabinet meeting following the Presidential election of November 1944. The inescapable conclusion from this factual pattern is that the delay was motivated by political considerations.

By the participants' own accounts, there is no rational explanation for maintaining the exclusion of loyal ethnic Japanese from the West Coast for the eighteen months after May 1943 — except political pressure and fear. Certainly there was no justification arising out of military necessity.

THE COMPARISONS

To either side of the Commission's account of the exclusion, removal and detention, there is a version argued by various witnesses that makes a radically different analysis of the events. Some contend that, forty years later, we cannot recreate the atmosphere and events of 1942 and that the extreme measures taken then were solely to protect the nation's safety when there was no reasonable alternative. Others see in these events only the animus of racial hatred directed toward people whose skin was not white. Events in Hawaii in World War II and the historical treatment of Germans and German Americans shows that neither analysis is satisfactory.

When Japan attacked Pearl Harbor, nearly 158,000 persons of Japanese ancestry lived in Hawaii — more than 35 percent of the population. Surely, if there were dangers from espionage, sabotage and fifth column activity by

American citizens and resident aliens of Japanese ancestry, danger would be greatest in Hawaii, and one would anticipate that the most swift and severe measures would be taken there. But nothing of the sort happened. Less than 2,000 ethnic Japanese in Hawaii were taken into custody during the war — barely one percent of the population of Japanese descent. Many factors contributed to this reaction.

Hawaii was more ethnically mixed and racially tolerant than the West Coast. Race relations in Hawaii before the war were not infected with the same virulent antagonism of 75 years of agitation. While anti-Asian feeling existed in the territory, it did not represent the longtime views of well-organized groups as it did on the West Coast and, without statehood, xenophobia had no effective voice in the Congress.

The larger population of ethnic Japanese in Hawaii was also a factor. It is one thing to vent frustration and historical prejudice on a scant two percent of the population; it is very different to disrupt a local economy and tear a social fabric by locking up more than one-third of a territory's people. And in Hawaii the half-measure of exclusion from military areas would have been meaningless.

In large social terms, the Army had much greater control of day-to-day events in Hawaii. Martial law was declared in December 1941, suspending the writ of habeas corpus, so that through the critical first months of the war, the military's recognized power to deal with any emergency was far greater than on the West Coast.

Individuals were also significant in the Hawaiian equation. The War Department gave great discretion to the commanding general of each defense area and this brought to bear very different attitudes toward persons of Japanese ancestry in Hawaii and on the West Coast. The commanding general in Hawaii, Delos Emmons, restrained plans to take radical measures, raising practical problems of labor shortages and transportation until the pressure to evacuate the Hawaiian Islands subsided. General Emmons does not appear to have been a man of dogmatic racial views; he appears to have argued quietly but consistently for treating the ethnic Japanese as loyal to the United States, absent evidence to the contrary.

This policy was clearly much more congruent with basic American law and values. It was also a much sounder policy in practice. The remarkably high rate of enlistment in the Army in Hawaii is in sharp contrast to the doubt and alienation that marred the recruitment of Army volunteers in the relocation camps. The wartime experience in Hawaii left behind neither the extensive economic losses and injury suffered on the mainland nor the psychological burden of the direct experience of unjust exclusion and detention.

The German American experience in the First World War was far less traumatic and damaging than that of the ethnic Japanese in the Second World War, but it underscores the power of war fears and war hysteria to produce irrational but emotionally powerful reactions to people whose ethnicity links them to the enemy.

There were obvious differences between the position of people of German descent in the United States in 1917 and the ethnic Japanese at the start of the Second World War. In 1917, more than 8,000,000 people in the United States had been born in Germany or had one or both parents born there. Although German Americans were not massively represented politically, their numbers gave them notable political strength and support from political spokesmen outside the ethnic group.

The history of the First World War bears a suggestive resemblance to the events of 1942: rumors in the press of sabotage and espionage, use of a stereotype of the German as an unassimilable and rapacious Hun, followed by an effort to suppress those institutions — the language, the press and the churches — that were most palpably foreign and perceived as the seedbed of Kaiserism. There were numerous examples of official and quasi-governmental harassment and fruitless investigation of German Americans and resident German aliens. This history is made even more disturbing by the absence of an extensive history of anti-German agitation before the war.

The promulgation of Executive Order 9066 was not justified by military necessity, and the decisions which followed from it — detention, ending detention and ending exclusion — were not driven by analysis of military conditions. The broad historical causes which shaped these decisions were race prejudice, war hysteria and a failure of political leadership. Widespread ignorance of Japanese Americans contributed to a policy conceived in haste and executed in an atmosphere of fear and anger at Japan. A grave injustice was done to American citizens and resident aliens of Japanese ancestry who, without individual review or any probative evidence against them, were excluded, removed and detained by the United States during World War II.

In memoirs and other statements after the war, many of those involved in the exclusion, removal and detention passed judgment on those events. While believing in the context of the time that evacuation was a legitimate exercise of the war powers, Henry L. Stimson recognized that "to loyal citizens this forced evacuation was a personal injustice." In his autobiography, Francis Biddle reiterated his beliefs at the time: "the program was ill-advised, unnecessary and unnecessarily cruel." Justice William O. Douglas, who joined the majority opinion in *Korematsu* which held the evacuation constitutionally permissible, found that the evacuation case "was ever on my conscience." Milton Eisenhower described the evacuation to the relocation camps as "an inhuman mistake." Chief Justice Earl Warren, who had urged evacuation as Attorney General of California, stated, "I have since deeply regretted the removal order and my own testimony advocating it, because it was not in keeping with our American concept of freedom and the rights of citizens." Justice Tom C. Clark, who had been liaison between the Justice Department and the Western Defense Command, concluded, "Looking back on it today [the evacuation] was, of course, a mistake."

During the struggle for naval supremacy in the Pacific in World War II, the Aleutian Islands were strategically valuable to both the United States and Japan. Beginning in March 1942, United States military intelligence repeatedly warned Alaska defense commanders that Japanese aggression into the Aleutian Islands was imminent. In June 1942, the Japanese attacked and held the two westernmost Aleutians, Kiska and Attu. These islands remained in Japanese hands until July and August 1943. During the Japanese offensive in June 1942, American military commanders in Alaska ordered the evacuation of the Aleuts from many islands to places of relative safety. The government placed the evacuees in camps in southeast Alaska where they remained in deplorable conditions until being allowed to return to their islands in 1944 and 1945....

March

COURT ON AGE DISCRIMINATION
March 2, 1983

In a 5-4 vote the Supreme Court ruled March 2 that Congress has the power to protect state and local government employees from age discrimination. The effect of the case — Equal Employment Opportunity Commission v. Wyoming — was to overrule a 1976 Court decision that had given new constitutional support to the principle of states' rights.

The state of Wyoming had used the 1976 case, National League of Cities v. Usery, *as part of its argument that the Constitution barred federal interference in state employment decisions, such as mandatory retirement. But in ruling against the state the Court concluded that the degree of federal intrusion in the Wyoming case was "sufficiently less serious than it was in* National League of Cities *so as to make it unnecessary for us to override Congress' express choice to extend its regulatory authority to the states." (Historic Documents of 1976, p. 377)*

Background

In National League of Cities *the Court held that federal minimum wage and hour standards had been extended unconstitutionally to state and local government employees by a 1974 amendment to the Fair Labor Standards Act. Writing for the majority, Justice William H. Rehnquist stated that the 10th Amendment, which requires that all constitutional power not specifically granted to the federal government or denied to the states be reserved to the states and the people, protected states against such federal interference.*

Until then the 10th Amendment had been thought by judges and constitutional scholars to have little meaning. After the National League of Cities *decision, many lower courts began invalidating federal laws on the grounds that they violated the 10th Amendment.*

The Wyoming case began in 1974 when Congress amended the 1967 Age Discrimination in Employment Act to include state and local government employees. The act prohibited mandatory retirement before age 70. When Bill Crump was forced to retire at age 55 from his job as supervisor for the Wyoming Game and Fish Department, he complained to the Equal Employment Opportunity Commission, claiming that the state had violated the federal act. The commission sued the state, and the state responded by challenging the constitutionality of the 1974 amendments to the discrimination law.

Federal District Court Reversed

In 1981 a federal district judge ruled in favor of Wyoming. It was this decision that the Supreme Court reversed. Citing passages from the National League of Cities *decision, Justice William J. Brennan Jr. concluded that the age discrimination ban did not " 'directly impair' the State's ability to 'structure integral operations in the areas of traditional governmental function.' "*

The age law still permitted Wyoming to review the fitness of its game wardens and dismiss those it found to be unfit. It even allowed the state to continue forcing all game wardens to retire at age 55, if it could demonstrate that age was a "bona fide occupational qualification" for a game warden, Brennan wrote.

Brennan was joined in his decision by Justices Byron R. White, Thurgood Marshall, John Paul Stevens and Harry A. Blackmun, who cast a key vote. Blackmun had voted with the majority, against Brennan, in the National League of Cities *decision. In a concurring opinion, Stevens stated his belief that the* National League of Cities *decision should be overturned.*

Chief Justice Warren E. Burger was joined in dissent by Justices Rehnquist, Sandra Day O'Connor, and Lewis F. Powell Jr. Burger criticized the majority for allowing Congress to "dictate to the states . . . detailed standards governing the selection of state employees, including those charged with protecting people and homes from crimes and fires."

> *Following are excerpts from the Supreme Court's March 2, 1983, decision in* Equal Employment Opportunity Commission v. Wyoming, *from the concurring opinion of Associate Justice John Paul Stevens and from the dissent by Chief Justice Warren E. Burger:*

No. 81-554

| Equal Employment Opportunity Commission, Appellant *v.* Wyoming et al. | Appeal from the United States District Court, District of Wyoming |

[March 2, 1983]

JUSTICE BRENNAN delivered the opinion of the Court.

Under the Age Discrimination in Employment Act of 1967, as amended, (ADEA or Act), it is unlawful for an employer to discriminate against any employee or potential employee on the basis of age, except "where age is a bona fide occupational qualification reasonably necessary to the normal operation of the particular business, or where the differentiation is based on reasonable factors other than age." The question presented in this case is whether Congress acted constitutionally when, in 1974, it extended the definition "employer" under § 11 (b) of the Act to include state and local governments. The United States District Court for the District of Wyoming, in an enforcement action brought by the Equal Employment Opportunity Commission (EEOC or Commission), held that, at least as applied to certain classes of state workers, the extension was unconstitutional. The Commission filed a direct appeal under 28 U.S.C. § 1252, and we noted probable jurisdiction. We now reverse.

I

Efforts in Congress to prohibit arbitrary age discrimination date back at least to the 1950s. During floor debate over what was to become Title VII of the Civil Rights Act of 1964, amendments were offered in both the House and the Senate to ban discrimination on the basis of age as well as race, color, religion, sex, and national origin. These amendments were opposed at least in part on the basis that Congress did not yet have enough information to make a considered judgment about the nature of age discrimination, and each was ultimately defeated. Title VII did, however, include a provision which directed the Secretary of Labor to "make a full and complete study of the factors which might tend to result in discrimination in employment because of age and of the consequences of such discrimination on the economy and individuals affected," and to report the results of that study to Congress. That report was transmitted approximately one year later.

In 1966, Congress directed the Secretary of Labor to submit specific legislative proposals for prohibiting age discrimination. The Secretary transmitted a draft bill in early 1967, and the President, in a message to Congress on older Americans, recommended its enactment and expressed serious concern about the problem of age discrimination. Congress undertook further study of its own, and Committees in both the House and the Senate conducted detailed hearings on the proposed legislation.

The Report of the Secretary of Labor, whose findings were confirmed throughout the extensive fact-finding undertaken by the Executive Branch and Congress, came to the following basic conclusions: (1) Many employers adopted specific age limitations in those States that had not prohibited them by their own anti-discrimination laws, although many other employers were able to operate successfully without them. (2) In the aggregate, these age limitations had a marked effect upon the employment of older workers. (3) Although age discrimination rarely was based on the sort of animus motivating some other forms of discrimination, it was based in large part on stereotypes unsupported by objective fact, and was often defended on grounds different from its actual causes. (4) Moreover, the available empirical evidence demonstrated that arbitrary age lines were in fact generally unfounded and that, as an overall matter, the performance of older workers was at least as good as that of younger workers. (5) Finally, arbitrary age discrimination was profoundly harmful in at least two ways. First, it deprived the national economy of the productive labor of millions of individuals and imposed on the governmental treasury substantially increased costs in unemployment insurance and federal Social Security benefits. Second, it inflicted on individual workers the economic and psychological injury accompanying the loss of the opportunity to engage in productive and satisfying occupations.

The product of the process of fact-finding and deliberation formally begun in 1964 was the Age Discrimination in Employment Act of 1967. The preamble to the Act emphasized both the individual and social costs of age discrimination. The provisions of the Act as relevant here prohibited various forms of age discrimination in employment, including the discharge of workers on the basis of their age. The protection of the Act was limited, however, to workers between the ages of 40 and 65, raised to age 70 in 1978. Moreover, in order to insure that employers were permitted to use neutral criteria not directly dependent on age, and in recognition of the fact that even criteria that are based on age are occasionally justified, the Act provided that certain otherwise prohibited employment practices would not be unlawful "where age is a bona fide occupational qualification reasonably necessary to the normal operation of the particular business, or where the differentiation is based on reasonable factors other than age."

The ADEA, as originally passed in 1967, did not apply to the Federal Government, to the States or their political subdivisions, or to employers with fewer than 25 employees. In a report issued in 1973, a Senate committee found this gap in coverage to be serious, and commented that "[t]here is. . . evidence that, like the corporate world, government managers also create an environment where young is sometimes better than old." In 1947, Congress extended the substantive prohibitions of the Act to employers having at least 20 workers, and to the Federal and State Governments.

II

Prior to the district court decision in this case, every federal court that considered the question upheld the constitutionality of the 1974 extension of the Age Discrimination in Employment Act to state and local workers as an exercise of Congress's power under either the Commerce Clause or § 5 of the Fourteenth Amendment.

This case arose out of the involuntary retirement at age 55 of Bill Crump, a District Game Division supervisor for the Wyoming Game and Fish Department. Crump's dismissal was based on a Wyoming statute that conditions further employment for Game and Fish Wardens who reach the age of 55 on "the approval of [their] employer." Crump filed a complaint with the EEOC, alleging that the Game and Fish Department had violated the Age Discrimination in Employment Act. After conciliation efforts between the Commission and the Game and Fish Department failed, the Commission filed suit in the District Court for the District of Wyoming against the State and various of its officials seeking declaratory and injunctive relief, back pay, and liquidated damages on behalf of Mr. Crump and others similarly situated.

The District Court, upon a motion by the defendants, dismissed the suit. It held that the Age Discrimination in Employment Act violated the doctrine of Tenth Amendment immunity articulated in *National League of Cities* v. *Usery* (1976), at least insofar as it regulated Wyoming's employment relationship with its game wardens and other law enforcement officials. The District Court also held, citing *Pennhurst State School* v. *Halderman* (1981), that the application of the ADEA to the States could not be justified as an exercise of Congress's power under § 5 of the Fourteenth Amendment because Congress did not explicitly state that it invoked that power in passing the 1974 amendments.

III

The appellees have not claimed either in the District Court or in this Court that Congress exceeded the scope of its affirmative grant of power under the Commerce Clause in enacting the ADEA. See generally *National League of Cities* v. *Usery; Heart of Atlanta Motel* v. *United States* (1964). Rather, the District Court held and appellees argue that, at least with respect to state game wardens, application of the ADEA to the States is precluded by virtue of external constraints imposed on Congress's commerce powers by the Tenth Amendment.

A

National League of Cities v. *Usery* struck down Congress's attempt to extend the wage and hour provisions of the Fair Labor Standards Act to state and local governments. *National League of Cities* was grounded on a concern that the imposition of certain federal regulations on state governments might, if left unchecked, "allow 'the National Government [to] devour the essentials of state sovereignty,'" (quoting *Maryland* v. *Wirtz* (1968) (Douglas, J., dissenting)). It therefore drew from the Tenth Amendment an "affirmative limitation on the exercise of [congressional power under the Commerce Clause] akin to other commerce power affirmative limitations contained in the Constitution." The principle of immunity articulated in *National League of Cities* is a functional doctrine, however, whose ultimate purpose is not to create a sacred province of state autonomy, but to ensure that the unique benefits of a federal system in which the States enjoy a "separate and independent existence" ... not be lost through undue federal interference in certain core state functions. See *FERC* v. *Mississippi* (1982); *United Transportation Union* v. *Long Island R. Co.* (1982); *Hodel* v. *Virginia Surface Mining & Reclamation Assn., Inc.* (1981).

Hodel v. *Virginia Surface Mining & Reclamation Assn., Inc.* summarized the hurdles that confront any claim that a state or local governmental unit should be immune from an otherwise legitimate exercise of the federal power to regulate commerce:

> "[I]n order to succeed, a claim that congressional commerce power legislation is invalid under the reasoning of *National League of Cities* must satisfy *each* of three requirements. First, there must be a showing that the challenged statute regulates the 'States as States.' Second, the federal regulation must address matters that are indisputably 'attribute[s] of state sovereignty.' And third, it must be apparent that the States' compliance with the federal law would directly impair their ability 'to structure integral operations in areas of traditional governmental functions.'"

Moreover,

> "Demonstrating that these three requirements are met does not ... guarantee that a Tenth Amendment challenge to congressional commerce power action will succeed. There are situations in which the nature of the federal interest advanced may be such that it justifies state submission."

See also *United Transportation Union* v. *Long Island R. Co.* The first requirement — that the challenged federal statute regulate the "States" — is plainly met in this case. The second requirement — that the federal statute address an "undoubted attribute of state sovereignty" — poses significantly more difficulties. We need not definitively resolve this issue, however, nor do we have any occasion to reach the final balancing step of the inquiry described in *Hodel,* for we are convinced that, even if Wyoming's decision to impose forced retirement on its game wardens does involve the exercise of an attribute of state sovereignty, the Age Discrimination in Employment Act does not "directly impair" the State's ability to "structure integral operations in areas of traditional governmental functions."

B

The management of state parks is clearly a traditional state function.

National League of Cities. As we have already emphasized, however, the purpose of the doctrine of immunity articulated in *National League of Cities* was to protect States from federal intrusions that might threaten their "separate and independent existence." Our decision as to whether the federal law at issue here directly impairs the States' ability to structure their integral operations must therefore depend, as it did in *National League of Cities* itself, on considerations of degree.... We conclude that the degree of federal intrusion in this case is sufficiently less serious than it was in *National League of Cities* so as to make it unnecessary for us to override Congress's express choice to extend its regulatory authority to the States.

In this case, appellees claim no substantial stake in their retirement policy other than "assur[ing] the physical preparedness of Wyoming game wardens to perform their duties." Under the ADEA, however, the State may still, at the very least, assess the fitness of its game wardens and dismiss those wardens whom it reasonably finds to be unfit. Put another way, the Act requires the State to achieve its goals in a more individualized and careful manner than would otherwise be the case, but it does not require the State to abandon those goals, or to abandon the public policy decisions underlying them. *FERC* v. *Mississippi.*

Perhaps more important, appellees remain free under the ADEA to continue to do *precisely what they are doing now,* if they can demonstrate that age is a "bona fide occupational qualification" for the job of game warden. Thus, in distinct contrast to the situation in *National League of Cities,* even the State's discretion to achieve its goals *in the way it thinks best* is not being overridden entirely, but is merely being tested against a reasonable federal standard.

Finally, the Court's concern in *National League of Cities* was not only with the effect of the federal regulatory scheme on the particular decisions it was purporting to regulate, but also with the potential impact of that scheme on the States' ability to structure operations and set priorities over a wide range of decisions. Indeed, *National League of Cities* spelled out in some detail how application of the federal wage and hour statute to the States threatened a virtual chain reaction of substantial and almost certainly unintended consequential effects on state decisionmaking. Nothing in this case, however, portends anything like the same wide-ranging and profound threat to the structure of State governance.

The most tangible consequential effect identified in *National League of Cities* was financial: forcing the States to pay their workers a minimum wage and an overtime rate would leave them with less money for other vital state programs. The test of such financial effect as drawn in *National League of Cities* does not depend, however, on "particularized assessments of actual impact," which may vary from State to State and time to time, but on a more generalized inquiry, essentially legal rather than factual, into the direct and obvious effect of the federal legislation on the ability of the States to allocate their resources. In this case, we cannot conclude from the nature of the ADEA that it will have either a direct or an obvious negative effect on state finances. Older workers with seniority may tend to get paid more than younger workers without seniority, and may by their continued employment accrue increased benefits when they do retire. But these increased costs, even if they were not largely speculative in their own right, might very well be outweighed by a number of other factors: Those same older workers, as long as they remain employed, will not have to be paid any pension benefits at all, and will continue to contribute to the pension fund. And, when they do retire, they will likely, as an actuarial matter, receive benefits for fewer years than workers who retire early. Admittedly, as some of the *amici* point out, the costs of certain state health and other benefit plans would increase if they were automatically extended to older workers now forced to retire at an early age. But Congress, in passing the ADEA, included a provision specifically disclaiming a construction of the Act which would require that the health and similar benefits received by older worker be in all respects identical to those received by younger workers.

The second consequential effect identified in *National League of Cities* was on the States' ability to use their employment relationship with their citizens as a tool for pursuing social and economic policies beyond their immediate managerial goals. . . . Appellees, however, have claimed no such purposes for Wyoming's involuntary retirement statute. Moreover, whatever broader social or economic purposes could be imagined for this particular Wyoming statute would not, we are convinced, bring with them either the breadth or the importance of the state policies identified in *National League of Cities*.

IV

The extension of the ADEA to cover state and local governments, both on its face and as applied in this case, was a valid exercise of Congress's powers under the Commerce Clause. We need not decide whether it could also be upheld as an exercise of Congress's powers under § 5 of the Fourteenth Amendment. The judgment of the District Court is reversed, and the case is remanded for further proceedings consistent with this opinion.

So ordered.

JUSTICE STEVENS, concurring.

. . . There have been occasions when the Court has given a miserly construction to the Commerce Clause. But as the needs of a dynamic and constantly expanding national economy have changed, this Court has construed the Commerce Clause to reflect the intent of the Framers of the Constitution — to confer a power on the national government adequate to discharge its central mission. In this process the Court has repeatedly repudiated cases that had narrowly construed the clause. The development of judicial doctrine has accommodated the transition from a purely local, to a regional, and ultimately to a national economy. . . .

In the statutes challenged in this case and in *National League of Cities v. Usery* (1974), Congress exercised its power to regulate the American labor market. There was a time when this Court would have denied that Congress had any such power, but that chapter in our judicial history has long been closed. Today, there should be universal agreement on the proposition that Congress has ample power to regulate the terms and conditions of employment throughout the economy. Because of the interdependence of the segments of the economy and the importance and magnitude of government employment, a comprehensive Congressional policy to regulate the labor market may require coverage of both public and private sectors to be effective. . . .

CHIEF JUSTICE BURGER, with whom JUSTICE POWELL, JUSTICE REHNQUIST, and JUSTICE O'CONNOR join, dissenting.

The Court decides today that Congress may dictate to the states, and their political subdivisions, detailed standards governing the selection of state employees, including those charged with protecting people and homes from crimes and fires. Although the opinion reads the Constitution to allow Congress to usurp this fundamental state function, I have reexamined that document and I fail to see where it grants to the national government the power to impose such strictures on the states either expressly or by implication. Those strictures are not required by any holding of this Court, and it is not wholly without significance that Congress has not placed similar limits on itself in the exercise of its own sovereign powers. Accordingly, I would hold the Age Discrimination in Employment Act (Age Act) unconstitutional as applied to the states, and affirm the judgment of the District Court.

I

I begin by analyzing the Commerce Clause rationale, for it was upon this power that Congress expressly relied when it originally enacted the Age Act in 1967 and when it extended its protections to state and local government employees.

We have had several occasions in recent years to investigate the scope of congressional authority to legislate under the Commerce Clause, see, e. g., *National League of Cities* v. *Usery* (1976); *Hodel* v. *Virginia Surface and Mining Reclamation Association, Inc.* (1981); *United Transportation Union* v. *Long Island R.R.* (1982). The wisdom to be drawn from these cases is that Congress' authority under the Commerce Clause is restricted by the protections afforded the states by Tenth Amendment. . . .

It is beyond dispute that the statute can give rise to increased employment costs caused by forced employment of older individuals. Since these employees tend to be at the upper end of the pay scale, the cost of their wages while they are still in the work force is greater. And since most pension plans calculate retirement benefits on the basis of maximum salary or number of years of service, pension costs are greater when an older employee retires. The employer is also forced to pay more for insuring the health of older employees because, as a group, they inevitably carry a higher-than-average risk of illness. . . . Since they are — especially in law enforcement — also more prone to on-the-job injuries, it is reasonable to conclude that the employer's disability costs are increased. . . .

Non-economic hardships are equally severe. Employers are prevented from hiring those physically best able to do the job. Since older workers occupy a disproportionate share of the upper-level and supervisory positions, a bar on mandatory retirement also impedes promotion opportunities. Lack of such opportunities tends to undermine younger employees' incentive to strive for excellence, and impedes the state from fulfilling affirmative action objectives.

The Federal Government can hardly claim that the objectives of decreasing costs and increasing promotional opportunities are impermissible: many of the same goals are cited repeatedly to justify the "enclaves" of federal exceptions to the Age Act. For example, mandatory retirement is still the rule in the Armed Services and the Foreign Service despite passage of the Age Act. The House Committee on Armed Services continues, apparently, to think it essential to have a mechanism to assure that officers from positions of command are vigorous and free from infirmities generally associated with age. Similarly, the House Committee on Post Office and Civil Service, while acknowledging the "unfairness of a mandatory retirement age," concluded that it remains necessary in the Foreign Service. . . . It is difficult to grasp just how Congress reconciles that view with its legislation forcing the states to comply with rigid standards. . . .

It is simply not accurate to state that Wyoming is resting its challenge to the Age Act on a "sovereign" right to discriminate; as I read it, Wyoming is asserting a right to set standards to meet local needs. Nor do I believe that these largely theoretical benefits to the Federal Government outweigh the very real danger that a fire may burn out of control because the firefighters are not physically able to cope; or that a criminal may escape because a law-enforcement officer's reflexes are too slow to react swiftly enough to apprehend an offender; or that an officer may be injured or killed for want of capacity to defend himself. These factors may not be real to Congress but it is not Congress' responsibility to prevent them; they are nonetheless real to the states. I would hold that Commerce Clause powers are wholly insufficient to bar the states from dealing with or preventing these dangers in a rational manner. Wyoming's solution is plainly a rational means. . . .

POPE'S JOURNEY
TO CENTRAL AMERICA
March 2-9, 1983

Pope John Paul II traveled to eight Central American and Caribbean nations March 2-9. It was his seventeenth trip abroad and one that took him to a region that was as bitterly divided over religion as it was over politics. In Central America he visited countries ruled by elected civilians, leftist revolutionaries and rightist generals. In Haiti he met with the country's 33-year-old self-proclaimed President-for-Life. In each country the pope addressed messages to specific audiences, including youth, Indians and the Catholic laity clergy. Millions of the region's 20 million Roman Catholics saw the 62-year-old pope.

Costa Rica, which has a democratic government with no church-state conflict, was the pope's first stop. In his address to an audience of young people he said that "a great part of Central America is tasting the bitter fruits of the seed sown by injustice, by hatred and by violence." He said the young had "the grave responsibility to break the chain of hatred producing hatred, and violence begetting violence .... You are called to replace hatred with the civilization of love."

On March 4 the pope traveled to Nicaragua where political conflicts had divided sharply the Roman Catholic Church after the leftist Sandinist government came to power in 1979. Nicaragua's Roman Catholic Church initially had supported the 1979 insurrection against the Somoza regime. Subsequently, however, the church was divided between supporters of the Sandinist government, who had formed left-leaning "people's churches," and critics of the government, led by Archbishop Miguel Obando Bravo. There also was controversy over five Roman

241

Catholic priests who held government positions in defiance of the Vatican's orders to resign.

In Managua, the capital of Nicaragua, the pope called for unity among all members of the church. Frequently Sandinista youths interrupted him. The pope told his half a million listeners, "The church's unity signifies and demands from us a radical overcoming of all tendencies toward disassociation."

In Panama March 5 and Honduras March 8 the pontiff spoke out against divorce, contraception and abortion and warned lay preachers against becoming tools of radical political movements.

Pope in El Salvador and Guatemala

The pope's 20-minute homily March 6 in San Salvador, capital of El Salvador, focused on a plea for peace and reconciliation. All people in Central America, he charged, had the "obligation to be artisans of peace." The Roman Catholic Church in El Salvador was deeply divided in its response to the country's three-year-old civil war.

In San Salvador the pope visited the tomb of Archbishop Oscar Romero who had devoted considerable efforts to ending the violence in the country. A sniper assassinated him as he offered mass in 1980. Also in San Salvador the pope addressed a speech to priests. The priest, he said, "must be the man of dialogue. He must take on boldly the risky task of being a mediator and making himself a bridge between opposed tendencies."

In his March 7 homilies in Guatemala the pope repeatedly condemned violence and the persecution of Indians there, emphasizing the themes of human rights and the sanctity of human life. These were matters of high sensitivity in Guatemala where the government of born-again Christian General Effrain Rios Montt executed six men a few days before the pope's visit, despite pleas by the Holy See that they be spared. The six prisoners, five Guatemalans and a Honduran, were found guilty of kidnapping and "terrorist crimes" and sentenced to death February 2 by secret tribunals. They received last-minute stays of execution, but on March 2 a court rejected their appeal.

The pope commented that "... man is endowed with immense dignity and that when man is trampled, when his rights are violated, when flagrant injustices are committed against him, when he undergoes tortures, when he is violated by kidnapping or his right to life is violated, a crime and a very grave offense against God is committed."

During a two-hour visit to Belize, a former British colony, the pope asked again for unity among Christians, speaking at that English-speaking country's largest gathering ever.

The pope ended his tour in Haiti, the poorest and most densely populated nation in the Western Hemisphere. Although he stressed the need for social change and respect for human rights in every country he visited, the pope's message in Haiti was more explicit. "There should be," he said, "the possibility to eat one's full, to satisfy one's hunger, to be well kept, to have housing, schooling, victory over illiteracy ... everything which ensures that men and women, children and the aged can live truly human lives."

Following are excerpts from Pope John Paul II's address at San José, Costa Rica, March 3, 1983; the pope's homily during a mass March 4 in Managua, Nicaragua; a homily delivered during mass in San Salvador, El Salvador, March 6; a speech delivered March 6 to priests in San Salvador; a homily delivered during celebration of the eucharist March 7 in Guatemala City; a homily delivered March 7 during mass in Quezeltenango, Guatemala; and a homily delivered during mass March 9 in Port-au-Prince, Haiti:

ADDRESS AT SAN JOSÉ

... Christ calls you to commit yourselves in favor of the good, in favor of doing away with egoism and sin in all its forms. He wants you to build up a society where moral values are cultivated, those which God desires to see in the hearts and lives of men and women. Christ invites you to be faithful children of God: doers of good and of justice, practicing fraternity, love, honesty and concord. Christ encourages you to bear the spirit of the gospel ever in your minds and in your actions: love for man (cf. Mt. 22:40).

For only in this manner, with such an understanding of man's depths in the light of God, will you be able to work efficaciously that "this society that you are going to build up should respect the dignity, the liberty and the rights of individuals. These individuals are you" (Vatican Council II, ["Message to Youth"], 3) They are you and all those who — never forget this — are children of God, and so bear the demanding title of being your brothers.

3. This commitment in favor of man is not easy. It is a very demanding task to work for his elevation and to see that his dignity is always acknowledged and respected. A profound motivation is needed for participating in this task, one capable of defeating fatigue and skepticism, doubt, even the smile of those who remain away, suiting their own convenience and regarding anyone capable of altruism as ingenuous.

For you young Christians the deep motive capable of transforming your actions is your faith in Christ. It shows you that it is worth while making an effort to be better, that it is worth the trouble to work for a more just society, that it is worth the effort to defend the innocent, the oppressed, the poor; that it is worth the trouble of suffering in order to relieve the

243

sufferings of others; that it is worth the trouble to dignify one's fellow man ever more and more. . . .

4. The church trusts that you will be able to be strong and valiant, lucid and persevering along that path and that, with your gaze fixed on the good and animated by your faith, you will be capable of resisting the philosophies of egoism, of hedonism, of despair, of annihilation, of hatred, of violence. You know the bitter fruits which they produce. How many tears, how much blood has been shed because of violence, the fruit of hatred and egoism!

A young person letting himself or herself be dominated by egoism impoverishes his outlook, lowers his vital energies, ruins his own youth and impedes adequate growth of his personality. On the contrary, an authentic person, far from shutting himself up in himself, is open to everything around him. He grows, matures and develops according to the way he serves and generously commits himself.

Behind egoism lies the philosophy of pleasure. How many young people unfortunately are borne off by the stream of hedonism, which is presented as a supreme value. It leads them to sexual license, to alcoholism, to drugs and to other vices which destroy their ardent strength and weaken their capacity for facing up to indispensable social reforms.

A natural consequence of egoism and absolutized pleasure is despair leading to the philosophy of the void, of nothingness. An authentic young person believes in life and brims with hope. He is convinced that God is calling him in Christ to realize himself in an integral manner, up to the stature of the perfect man and the fullness of maturity (cf. Eph 4:13).

5. And what shall I say to you, dear young people, of the horrors of hatred and violence? It is a sad reality that at this very moment a great part of Central America is tasting the bitter fruits of the seed sown by injustice, by hatred and by violence.

In the face of this situation of death and confrontation, the pope feels the urgent need to repeat to you young people Christ's word: "I give you a new commandment: Love one another" (Jn. 13:34), and also the phrase solemnly uttered by my predecessor Paul VI at Bogota: "Violence is neither Christian nor evangelical" (Discourse of Aug. 23, 1968).

Yes, most beloved young people, you have the grave responsibility to break the chain of hatred producing hatred, and violence begetting violence. You have to create a world better than that of your ancestors. Unless you do so, the blood will continue flowing and tomorrow tears will attest to the pain of your own children. I ask you then, as a brother and friend, to fight with all the energy of your youth against hatred and violence, until love and peace are reestablished in your nations.

You are called to teach others the lesson of love, of Christian love, which is human and divine at the same time.

You are called to replace hatred with the civilization of love.

You will be able to do this by going along the path of authentic friendship, of that which always leads to the loftiest and noble things. The path of friendship you learn from Christ, who must always be your model and great friend. You should reject civilly all who resort to hatred and its expressions as a means of forging a new society....

HOMILY AT MANAGUA

2. ... It is a matter above all of the unity of the church, of the people of God, of the flock of the one shepherd but also, as the Second Vatican Council teaches, of the "unity of the whole of mankind" of which the one church is "a sacrament or sign" (cf. *Lumen Gentium*, 1), as she is of every man's "intimate union with God."

The sad inheritance of division among mankind, provoked by the sin of pride (cf. Gn. 1:49), endures over the centuries; its consequences are wars, oppressions, persecutions of some by others, hatreds, conflicts of every kind.

But Jesus Christ came to re-establish the lost unity, so that there should be "one flock" and "one shepherd" (Jn. 10:16), a shepherd whose voice the sheep "know," whereas they do not know the voice of strange shepherds *(ibid.* 4-5). He is the unique "gate" through which to enter *(ibid,* 1)....

4. The unity of the church is actually brought into question when before the powerful factors constituting and maintaining it — the faith itself, the revealed word, the sacraments, obedience to the bishops and the pope, the sense of a common vocation and responsibility in Christ's task in the word — are put earthly considerations, unacceptable ideological compromises, temporal options including conceptions of the church which take the place of the true one.

Yes, my beloved Central American and Nicaraguan brothers: When the Christian, whatever his condition may be, prefers any other doctrine or ideology to the teachings of the apostles and the church, when he makes these doctrines the criterion of our vocation, when he decides to reinterpret catechesis, religious teaching, preaching, according to his own categories, when "parallel magisteriums" are installed, ... then is the church's unity weakened and the exercise of her mission to be "the sacrament of unity" to all men made more difficult. The church's unity signifies and demands from us a radical over-coming of all tendencies toward disassociation. It means and demands a revision of our scale of values. It means and demands that we submit our doctrinal conceptions and our pastoral projects to the magisterium of the church, represented by the pope and the bishops. This applies in the field of the church's social teaching as well, as developed by my predecessors and by myself.

No Christian, especially those with titles signifying a special consecration in the church, should become responsible for breaking this unity, acting outside of or against the will of the bishops "whom the Holy Spirit has set to guide the church of God" (Acts 20:28). This holds good in every situation and country; no process of development or social elevation which may be undertaken can legitimately compromise the identity and religious liberty of a people, the transcendent dimension of the human person and the sacred character of the church and her ministers.

5. The unity of the church is the work and gift of Jesus Christ. It is built up in reference to him and around him. But Christ entrusted to bishops the most important ministry of unity in his local churches (cf. *Lumen Gentium*, 26). It is for them, in communion with the pope, and never without him, *(ibid,* 22) to promote the unity of the church, and in that way to build up in that unity the communities, groups, diverse tendencies and categories of persons existing in a local church and in the great community of the universal church.... A proof of the unity of the church in a particular place is respect for the pastoral orientations given by the bishops to their clergy and faithful. This organic pastoral action is a powerful guarantee of ecclesial unity. It is a duty especially incumbent on priests, religious and other pastoral workers.

But the duty to build and maintain unity is also a responsibility of all members of the church, linked by a single baptism, in the same profession of faith, in obedience to their proper bishop and faithful to the successor of Peter.

Dear brothers: Bear well in mind that there are cases where unity is preserved only when everyone is capable of giving up his own ideas, plans and commitments, including good ones — but how much more when they lack the necessary ecclesial reference! — and of doing so for the higher good of communion with the bishop, with the pope, with the whole church.

A divided church ... will not be able to accomplish its mission "of sacrament, that is to say, as sign and instrument of unity in the country." I therefore alerted you then about how "absurd and dangerous it is to imagine oneself thus as another church, conceived solely as 'charismatic' and not institutional, 'new' and not traditional, alternative and, as has been said lately, a people's church." I want to reaffirm these words here before you. The church must keep herself united in order to counter and arrest the various direct or indirect forms of materialism which her mission encounters in the world.

There must be unity to announce the true message of the Gospel — according to the norms of tradition and the magisterium — and a unity free of distortions caused by whatever human ideology or political program.

The Gospel thus understood leads to the spirit of truth and the liberty of the children of God, "so that they do not let themselves be confused by anti-educational and contingent propaganda." And at the same time it educates man for eternal life. . . .

HOMILY AT SAN SALVADOR

... 3. If God had abandoned us to our own resources, which are so limited and faltering, we would have no reason to expect humanity to live as a family, as children of the same Father. But God came to us definitively in Jesus. In his cross we experience the victory of life over death, of love over hatred. The cross, once the symbol of insult and bitter defeat, becomes the font of life.

From the cross flow torrents of the love of God which pardons and reconciles. With the blood of Christ we can overcome evil with good: the evil which penetrates hearts and social structures; the evil of divisions among peoples which has sown the world with graves, with wars, with that terrible spiral of hatred which destroys and annihilates in a dark and senseless manner.

How many homes destroyed, how many refugees, exiles and displaced persons, how many orphans, how many noble, innocent lives cruelly and brutally bludgeoned — priests, and men and women religious as well, faithful servants of the church; and even the zealous and venerated pastor who was archbishop of this flock, Archbishop Oscar Arnulfo Romero, who, like his brothers in the episcopate, sought to end violence and re-establish peace. In commemorating him, I ask that his memory be ever respected and that no ideological interest try to use for their own purposes his sacrifice, that of a shepherd committed to his flock.

The cross destroys the wall of separation: hatred. Man frequently seeks arguments for tranquilizing his conscience, which accuses him if he does evil. And he comes sometimes to raise hatred to such a level that it is confused with the nobility of a cause, even to the point of identifying it with an act capable of restoring love. Christ heals man's heart at the root. His love purifies us and opens our eyes to distinguish between what comes from God and what comes from our passions.

4. Christ's pardon shines like a new dawn, like a new morning. It is the new land, "good and spacious," toward which God calls us, as we have just read in the book of Exodus (Ex.3:8). This is the land where the oppression of hatred ought to disappear and give place to Christian sentiments: "Because you are God's chosen ones, holy and beloved, clothe yourselves with heartfelt mercy, with kindness, humility, meekness and patience. Bear with one another, forgive whatever grievances you have against one another. Forgive as the Lord has forgiven you" (Col. 3:12-24).

Christ's redeeming love does not allow us to close ourselves up in the prison of egoism, which refuses authentic dialogue, denies the rights of others and puts them in the category of enemies to be combated.

I made a call in my last message for the World Day of Peace for overcoming the obstacles in the way of dialogue. I pointed out that: "For all the more reason one must mention the tactical and deliberate lie, which misuses language, which has recourse to the most sophisticated techniques of propaganda, which deceives and distorts dialogue and incites to aggression. Finally, dialogue is fixed and sterile when certain parties are fostered by ideologies which, in spite of their declarations, are opposed to the dignity of the human person, to his or her just aspirations according to the healthy principles of reason, of the natural and eternal law, ideologies which see the motive force of history in struggle, which see the source of rights in force, that see in the discernment of the enemy the ABC of politics. . . ."

The dialogue asked for by the church is not a tactical truce to fortify positions as part of a plan to continue the fighting. Instead it is a sincere effort to answer, with the search for agreements, the anguish, the pain, the weariness, the fatigue of so many who long for peace, of so very many who desire to live, to rise again from the ashes, to seek the warmth of the smiles of children, far from terror and in a climate of democratic coexistence. . . .

6. . . . I do not argue for an artificial peace which conceals problems and disregards worn-out mechanisms which ought to be repaired. It is a question of peace in truth, in justice, in the integral acknowledgment of the rights of the human person. It is a peace for all, all ages, conditions, groups, origins, political options. No one must be excluded from the effort for peace. Each and every person in Central America, in this noble nation which proudly bears the name of El Salvador, each and every person in Guatemala and Nicaragua, Honduras, Costa Rica, Panama, Belize and Haiti, each and every person, governors and the governed, city dwellers and rural people; each and every one, businessmen and workers, teachers and pupils — all have the obligation to be artisans of peace. Let there be peace among your people. Let the frontiers not the zones of tension, but arms open in reconciliation.

7. It is urgent to bury the violence which has cost so many victims in this and other nations. How? With true conversion to Jesus Christ; with reconciliation capable of bringing together as brothers and sisters those who are today separated by political, social, economic and ideological walls; with mechanisms and instruments of authentic participation in economic and social affairs; with access to the goods of the earth for all, with the possibility of self-realization through labor; in a word, through the application of the church's social doctrine. In this regard there must be inserted a valiant and generous effort in favor of justice, which may never be dispensed with.

This is an atmosphere of renunciation of violence. The Sermon on the Mount is the Christian's Magna Carta: "Blessed are the peacemakers, for they shall be called children of God" (Mt. 5:9). This is what all of you must be: artisans of peace and reconciliation, asking it from God and working for it. . . .

SPEECH AT SAN SALVADOR

. . . 3. In recalling fidelity to Christ, our sole master and teacher, and his Gospel, I want to exhort you to keep the doctrine of the church's faith alive and intense. It is worthwhile committing oneself even to the offering up of your life for that cause. It is worthless to give your life for an ideology, for a Gospel that has been mutilated and instrumentalized for a partisan option. The priest to whom the Gospel and the wealth of the deposit of faith are entrusted must first identify himself with this doctrinal integrity, so as to be a faithful transmitter at the same time of the church's doctrine, in communion with the magisterium — a transmission of the faith which is not limited to one's own diocese or country, but which has to open itself up to the church's missionary dimension.

Therefore in order to be an educator in the faith of the people, the priest must drink in the Gospel at the feet of the Master during hours of personal prayer, meditation on scripture and praise to the Lord in the Liturgy of the Hours. He must deepen his own understanding of the church's comprehension of the message and bring it to light in assiduous study calling for commitment to permanent instruction, a commitment which is so necessary today for deepening, detailing and actualizing knowledge of theology in its various dimensions: dogma, moral, liturgy, pastoral ministry, spirituality. All this is supported by an authentic biblical theology.

4. Your people are sincere and intelligent. They expect from you such integral preaching of the Catholic faith, which is sown from full hands on the fertile soil of a traditional and receptive faith, of a popular piety which, even if it is always in need of being evangelized, is yet a field which the Spirit has plowed so as to make it ready for evangelization and catechesis.

Are not the painful events through which this country is passing a sign of the need for an intensification of such sowing? Don't your people ask for reasons for believing and hoping, motivations for loving and building, such as can come only from Christ and his church?

So do not defraud the Lord's poor who ask you for the bread of the Gospel, the solid food of the secure and integral Catholic faith, so that they may know how to choose in the face of other preachings and ideologies which are not the message of Jesus Christ and of his church. Your ecclesial task lies in this, your commitment of priority. Remember, my dear brothers, that — as I told the priests and religious of Mexico — "You are not social directors, political leaders or officials of a temporal power" (Jan. 27, 1979).

Generous young people expect your faithful and authorized word. Already they no longer believe in the facile promises of a capitalist society, and they sometimes succumb to the mirage of a revolutionary commitment which wishes to change things and structures and often resorts to violence. Aren't many young people also waiting for that preaching of a saving and liberating Christ, who changes the heart and stimulates a peaceful yet decisive revolution, the fruit of Christian love? And if they are fascinated by other leaders, wouldn't that be because Christ has not been presented to them adequately, without distortions?

5. You are priests with a grave responsibility at this hour for the church and for your nation. I deposit into your hands the necessary task of communion and dialogue.

The priest is actually the servant of the ecclesial communion. It is for him to gather the Christian community in order that it may live the eucharist in such a way as to celebrate the mystery of Jesus, the font and school of the life of communities. Hence his place is above all at the altar;

to preach the word and celebrate the sacraments, to offer the sacrifice and distribute the bread of life.

The faithful in need of a word of counsel or consolation want to find the priest ready and easily identifiable, even through his manner of dress. All those who need the grace of forgiveness and reconciliation expect that it will be easy for them to find a priest exercising this indispensable ministry of salvation, where personal contact facilitates the growth and maturation of Christians.

Today more than ever, in view of the shortage of priests and the great needs of the church community, the priest is called to an intelligent mission of promoting lay service, of inspiration of the community, of the faithful's taking responsibility for those ministries within their competence by reason of their baptism. . . .

6. The priest must be the man of dialogue. He must take on boldly the risky task of being a mediator and making himself a bridge between opposed tendencies, to nourish concord, to seek just solutions to difficult situations. The option of the Christian, and even more of the priest, becomes dramatic at times. Although he remains firmly against error, he cannot be against anybody since we are all brothers or, at most, enemies who ought to love in accordance with the Gospel. The priest must embrace all, since all are God's children, and he has to give his life for all his brothers if necessary. It is here that the priest's drama is often rooted, for he is driven by opposing tendencies and harassed by partisan options.

He is called to make a preferential option for the poor, but he cannot disregard the fact that there is radical poverty wherever God is not alive and in the hearts of people who are slaves to power, to pleasure, to money, to violence. He must extend his mission to these poor too.

The priest is therefore the prisoner of God's mercy and not only a preacher of justice. He has to make the message of conversion resound for all, and he has to announce reconciliation in Christ Jesus, who is our peace, and break down every wall of division among persons (cf. Eph. 2:14). . . .

7. The priest's life, like Christ's, is a service of love. The best testimony of a radical option for Christ and the Gospel consists in being able to say these words of the church's prayer truly: "Let us live no longer for ourselves but for him who died and was raised up again" (Fourth Eucharistic Prayer). To live for him is to live as he did, and his word in this regard is a decisive one: "Anyone among you who wants to rank first of all must serve the needs of all. Such is the case with the Son of Man, who comes, not to be served by others, but to serve; to give his own life as ransom for many" (Mt. 20:27-28).

Your simplicity and sincerity, your poverty and friendliness will be a clear sign of your consecration to the gospel. With your readiness to listen, to receive, to help the brethren materially and spiritually, you will be witnesses to him who did not come to be served but to serve. In the purity of intention of your service and in detachment from material things you will find freedom to be witnesses to him who came to us as the servant of the Lord and gave himself wholly to us, since he gave his life for us. . . .

HOMILY AT GUATEMALA CITY

4. . . . You ought to love this church always. With the efforts of her best children, she did very much to help forge your personality and liberty. She has been present in the most glorious events of your history. She has been and still is by your side when fortune smiles or sorrow overcomes you. She has tried to dissipate ignorance by throwing the light of education on the minds and hearts of her children in her schools, colleges and universities. She has raised and continues to raise her voice to condemn injustices, to denounce outrages, above all those against the poor and humble, not in the name of ideologies of whatever sort they be, but in the name of Jesus Christ, of his Gospel, of his message of love and peace, justice, truth and liberty.

Love the church, for she constantly calls upon you to do good and detest sin; to give up all vice and corruption; to live in holiness; to make Christ, the way, truth and life, the perfect model of your personal and social conduct; to follow paths of greater justice and respect for the rights of man; to live more as brothers than as adversaries.

5. This faith and love for the church have to show their fruitfulness in life, they have to be shown by works. This is Jesus' teaching: "None of those who cry out 'Lord, Lord,' will enter the kingdom of God, but only the one who does the will of my Father in heaven" (Mt. 7:21). We have just heard from the apostle St. James that faith without works is dead. What is the use of someone saying, "I have faith," unless he has works? Man is justified by works and not by faith alone (cf. Jas. 2:14f.)

Faith teaches us that man is the image and likeness of God (cf. Gn. 1:27). This means that man is endowed with immense dignity and that when man is trampled, when his rights are violated, when flagrant injustices are committed against him, when he undergoes tortures, when he is violated by kidnapping or his right to life is violated, a crime and a very grave offense against God is committed. It is then that Christ returns to walk again the way of the cross and suffers the horrors of the crucifixion in the person who is destitute, oppressed.

Men of all positions and ideologies who hear me: Give heed to the supplication I address to you. Heed it. Because I make it from the depths of my faith, of my confidence in and love for suffering man. Heed it, for I make it in Christ's name. Remember that every man is your brother and be converted into respectful defenders of his dignity. And beyond any social, political, ideological, racial and religious difference, the life of your brother, of each man, must always be assured above all.

6. Let us remember, however, that one can make one's brother die little by little, day by day, when he is deprived of access to the goods which God created for the benefit of all, not just the profit of a few. This human promotion is an integral part of evangelization and the faith. . . .

I exhort you likewise to share your own faith clearly and boldly, so as to practice charity, especially with those most in need or not able to get on alone, such as the aged, the infirm, the subnormal, and those who are victims from time to time of the elements of nature. And always keep up relationships of respect and justice with those who can look after themselves.

I call upon those responsible for the peoples, above all those feeling the interior call of the Christian faith, with affection I call upon them to commit themselves fully and decisively to effective and urgent means to bring the recourses of justice to the most unprotected sectors of society. Let those be the prime beneficiaries of appropriate legal safeguards.

In order to avoid any extremism and consolidate an authentic peace, nothing is better than restoring dignity to those suffering from injustice, contempt and poverty. . . .

HOMILY AT QUEZALTENANGO

2. . . . Christ ensures that all shall accept that you are a race blessed by God, that all men and women have the same dignity and value before him; that we are all children of the Father who is in heaven; that no one must despise or mistreat another human being, for God will punish him; that we must all aid each other, the most abandoned above all.

3. The church brings you the saving message of Christ in an attitude of profound respect and love. She is very conscious that when she announces the Gospel she must incarnate herself in peoples who accept the faith and take on their cultures.

Your indigenous cultures are the wealth of the peoples, they are effective means for transmitting the faith, they are ways of living your relationship with God, with men and with the world. They therefore deserve the utmost respect, esteem, sympathy and support on the part of all humanity. These cultures have actually left impressive monuments — those of the Mayas, the Aztecs, the Incas and many others — which we still contemplate with astonishment today.

As I think of so many missionaries, evangelizers, catechists, apostles who have announced Jesus Christ to you — all of them animated by generous zeal and great love for you — I admire and bless their exemplary commitment, rewarded with abundant fruits for the Gospel. The work of evangelization does not destroy but incarnates itself in your values; it consolidates and reinforces them. It causes the seed to grow which was cast by the "word of God, who, before he became flesh in order to save all things and to sum them up in himself, was in the world already as the true light that enlightens every man," as the last council, Vatican II, has taught (*Gaudium et Spes*, 57).

However, this does not impede the church, which is faithful to the universality of its mission, from announcing Jesus Christ and inviting all races and all peoples to accept her message. With evangelization, the church renews cultures, combats errors, fertilizes traditions, consolidates them and restores them in Christ (cf. *Gaudium et Spes*, 58).

Your bishops have said with clarity along that line and together with the episcopate of Latin America: "The church's mission is to bear witness to 'the true God and one Lord.' Hence there is nothing insulting in the fact that evangelization invites peoples to abandon false concepts of God, anti-natural conduct and aberrant manipulation of some people by others" (Puebla, 406).

4. But the church not only respects and evangelizes peoples and cultures; she has also been the defender of the authentic cultural values of each ethnic group.

At this moment also, dear sons and daughters, the church knows the emarginization which you suffer, the injustices which you have to contend with, the serious difficulties you meet in defending your lands and your rights, the frequent lack of respect for your customs and traditions.

Therefore, as she carries through her evangelizing task, she seeks to be near you and raise her voice in condemnation when your dignity as human beings and children of God is violated. She wants to be together with you peacefully, as the Gospel demands, but with decision and energy in obtaining acknowledgment and promotion of your dignity and your rights as persons.

For this reason, from this place and in solemn form, I call upon rulers, in the name of the church, for ever more adequate legislation to shield you effectively from abuses and to assure you of the environment and means adequate for your normal development.

I ask with insistence that the free practice of your Christian faith not be made difficult, that no one claim ever again to confuse authentic evangelization with subversion and that ministers of religion may exercise their mission in security and without hindrances. And do not let yourselves be made use of by ideologies inciting you to violence and death.

I ask that your reservations be respected, above all that the sacred character of your life be safeguarded. Let no one on any account despise your existence, since God forbids us to kill and commands us to love each other as brothers.

Finally, I exhort those with responsibility to see to your human and cultural elevation. Let schools be provided for this purpose, medical means too, without any kind of discrimination.

With profound love for all, I exhort you to follow the ways of concrete solutions traced out by the church in her social teaching, so as to arrive in this way at necessary reforms, while avoiding all recourse to violence. . . .

SPEECH AT PORT-AU-PRINCE

1. . . . For the first time in my visits to Latin America I am present in a country where the majority of the population consists of colored people, particularly blacks. I see this as a sign of great importance, for it is thus given to me to enter directly into relation with the third component of the culture and civilization of these peoples of Latin and Central America:

people coming from Africa, profoundly integrated with the other civilizations originating in America itself or coming from Europe, so as to form a typical reality from all that wealth of culture.

This country was the first in Latin America to proclaim itself independent. It is therefore called in a special fashion to develop on its own soil, in an atmospehre of liberty, to the extent of its means and with effort by all, a work of true human and social advance, so that all its sons and daughters may work there at their ease without feeling constrained to go somewhere else to seek — often in painful conditions — what they ought to be able to find at home. . . .

4. . . . Whoever partakes of the eucharist is called to follow the example of Jesus, whom he has received in himself or herself. He is called to imitate his love and serve his neighbor, even to the point of washing his feet. And, like you, it is the church, the church as a whole, the church in Haiti, which has to commit itself thoroughly to the good of the brethren, of all but above all of the poorest, precisely because it has been celebrating a eucharistic congress. Does she not really celebrate the eucharist always? The eucharist is the sacrament of love and service.

As the slogan for your congress you chose "Something has to change here." Well, in the eucharist you find the inspiration, the strength and the perseverance to commit yourselves in this process of change.

It really is necessary for things to change. In preparing the congress the church had the courage to look the dire realities of the present in the face, and I am sure that it is the same for all people of good will, for all those who love their country deeply. You certainly have a beautiful country with numerous human resources. And we may speak of an innate and generous religious sentiment in you and of the vitality and popular character of the church. But Christians have also observed division, injustice, excessive inequality, degradation of the quality of life, poverty, hunger, fear in a great number of people. Christians have thought of the peasants unable to make a living from their land, of people crowded without work in the cities, families broken up and displaced, the victims of various other frustrations. And yet, they are convinced that solutions exist in solidarity. It is necessary for the "poor" of all kinds to begin to hope again. The church retains a prophetic mission in this field which is inseparable from her religious mission and it calls for liberty to carry it through: not to accuse, not just to arouse consciousness of the evil, but to contribute positively to recovery by mustering all consciences, more particularly the consciences of all those with responsibility in the villages, in the cities and at the national level, to arouse them to act in conformity with the Gospel and the church's social teaching.

There is really a profound need of justice, of a better distribution of goods, of more equitable organization of society, with more participation, a more distinterested concept of service to all on the part of those who have responsibilities. There is a rightful desire for free expression through the media and in politics, with respect for the opinions of others and the common good; there is a need for more open and easier access to goods and services. These may not remain the privilege of a few. For example, there should be the possibility to eat one's full, to satisfy one's hunger, to be well kept, to have housing, schooling, victory over illiteracy, honest and dignified work, social security, respect for family responsibilities and for the basic rights of man: in a few words, everything which ensures that men and women, children and the aged can live truly human lives.

It is not a question of dreaming of riches or of the consumer society, but it is a question for all of a level of living worthy of the human person, the sons and daughters of God. And this is not impossible if all vital forces in the country unite in one same effort and count also on that international solidarity which is always desirable. Christians wish to be people of hope, of love and of responsible action.

Yes, the fact of being members of the body of Christ and of taking part in his eucharistic banquet commits you to promoting such change. It is your way of washing each other's feet, after Christ's example. You will do this without violence, without murders, without fratricidal struggles, which often only engender further oppressions. You will do it in respect for love and liberty.

I congratulate all those who are working at this, who are defending the rights of the poor often with inadequate means, I would say "with their bare hands." I appeal to all who have control over power, wealth and culture to grasp their grave and urgent responsibility toward all their brothers and sisters. That is the honor in their position. I tell them too that I have confidence in them and I pray for them. . . .

NEW FBI GUIDELINES
ON DOMESTIC SECURITY
March 7, 1983

Attorney General William French Smith announced new guidelines for the Federal Bureau of Investigation (FBI) that gave the agency greater latitude in its domestic security/terrorism investigations. The new guidelines, made public March 7, governed FBI investigations of politically motivated crimes by individuals or groups not acting on behalf of a foreign power.

In 1976 Ford administration Attorney General Edward H. Levi issued the first set of regulations governing FBI domestic security surveillance. The Levi rules followed disclosures of widespread FBI monitoring of domestic groups during the 1960s and 1970s. Various civil rights, antiwar, feminist, socialist and communist organizations were targets of FBI investigations in that period. The Levi guidelines curtailed some of the FBI's intelligence activities and provided tighter rules for agency investigations.

New guidelines were needed, Smith explained, to provide better protection for the public from violence-prone groups. Those groups had become more fluid and their techniques had increased in sophistication in the seven years after the first guidelines were formulated. "The time has ... come to eliminate separate regulations for domestic security/terrorism investigations and treat these matters as an integral part of FBI's general law enforcement responsibilities," Smith said. Therefore, to simplify the job of FBI field agents, the new guidelines for domestic security/terrorism investigations were combined for the first time with those for general crimes and racketeering enterprises.

Broader Authority for the FBI

The new rules stated that "a domestic security/terrorism investigation may be initiated when the facts or circumstances reasonably indicate that two or more persons are engaged in an enterprise for the purpose of furthering political or social goals wholly or in part through activities that involve force or violence and a violation of the criminal laws of the United States." The new standard of "reasonable indication" was substantially broader than that of "probable cause" used in the 1976 guidelines.

The new rules also stated that FBI agents could investigate groups that "advocate criminal activity or indicate an apparent intent to engage in crime, particularly crimes of violence." Investigations of such "advocacy" cases, in which groups had taken no concrete actions, had long been a sensitive area for law enforcement officials. Justice Department officials admitted that "there can be special First Amendment concerns in these investigations."

Under the new guidelines, the FBI could send an infiltrator or informer into a group in the preliminary stages of an investigation. The previous guidelines had explicitly prohibited such infiltration in preliminary investigations.

A further change resulting from the new guidelines was the introduction of the "criminal enterprise" concept in domestic security cases. That procedure, which allowed agents to investigate factions or related groups as part of a single "criminal enterprise" had been used successfully in organized crime cases. For example, according to the Justice Department, "[I]f . . . members of a group are providing safehouses, money, or weapons supporting the criminal activities of a terrorist group, they would be investigated as part of the same criminal enterprise. This avoids the necessity of opening a separate investigation." . . .

Reaction to the Guidelines

Reaction to the new guidelines was mixed. On Capitol Hill, Sen. Jeremiah Denton, R-Ala., chairman of the Senate Judiciary Security and Terrorism Subcommittee, called the rules "a step in the right direction." However, Rep. Don Edwards, D-Calif., chairman of the House Judiciary Civil and Constitutional Rights Subcommittee, warned that some of the broadened power given to FBI investigators under the new rules might "chill legitimate First Amendment activity." The American Civil Liberties Union (ACLU) also expressed concern over possible threats to the constitutionally protected right of free speech. The ACLU called on Congress to scrutinize the guidelines and "to ask the FBI to clarify the scope" of the new rules.

In a series of letters to legislators and in congressional testimony, the FBI attempted to alleviate these concerns. John Hotis, a special assistant to FBI Director William H. Webster, stated, "We changed the guidelines not to unleash the bureau, but to integrate the rules." He said, "The new guidelines don't really allow us to do things we couldn't do before anyway."

> *Following are excerpts from the attorney general's guide-lines on general crimes, racketeering enterprise and domestic security/terrorism investigations, released March 7, 1983:*

B. DOMESTIC SECURITY/TERRORISM INVESTIGATIONS

This section focuses on investigations of enterprises, other than those involved in international terrorism, whose goals are to achieve political or social change through activities that involve force or violence. Like racketeering enterprise investigations, it is concerned with the investigation of entire enterprises, rather than individual participants and specific criminal acts, and authorizes investigations to determine the structure and scope of the enterprise as well as the relationship of the members.

1. General Authority

a. A domestic security/terrorism investigation may be initiated when the facts or circumstances reasonably indicate that two or more persons are engaged in an enterprise for the purpose of furthering political or social goals wholly or in part through activities that involve force or violence and a violation of the criminal laws of the United States. The standard of "reasonable indication" is identical to that governing the initiation of a general crimes investigation under Part II. In determining whether an investigation should be conducted, the FBI shall consider all of the circumstances including: (1) the magnitude of the threatened harm; (2) the likelihood it will occur; (3) the immediacy of the threat; and (4) the danger to privacy and free expression posed by an investigation.

b. Authority to conduct domestic security/terrorism investigations is separate from and in addition to general crimes investigative authority under Part II, racketeering enterprise investigations under Part III A and international terrorism investigations under the Attorney General's Guidelines for Foreign Intelligence Collection and Foreign Counterintelligence Investigations. Information warranting initiation of an investigation under this section may be obtained through the course of a general crimes inquiry or investigation, a racketeering enterprise investigation, or an investigation of international terrorism. Conversely, a domestic security/terrorism investigation may yield information warranting a general crimes inquiry or investigation, a racketeering enterprise investigation, or an investigation of international terrorism.

c. In the absence of any information indicating planned violence by a group or enterprise, mere speculation that force or violence might occur during the course of an otherwise peaceable demonstration is not sufficient grounds for initiation of an investigation under this section. For alternative authorities see Part II relating to General Crimes Investigations and the Attorney General's Guidelines on "Reporting on Civil Disorders and Demonstrations Involving a Federal Interest." This does not preclude the collection of information about public demonstrations by enterprises that are under active investigation pursuant to paragraph B 1(a) above.

2. Purpose

The immediate purpose of a domestic security/terrorism investigation is to obtain information concerning the nature and structure of the enterprise as specifically delineated in paragraph (3) below, with a view to the longer range objectives of detection, prevention, and prosecution of the criminal activities of the enterprise.

3. Scope

a. A domestic security/terrorism investigation initiated under these guidelines may collect such information as:

(i) the members of the enterprise and other persons likely to be knowingly acting in furtherance of its criminal objectives, provided that the information concerns such persons' activities on behalf or in furtherance of the enterprise;
(ii) the finances of the enterprise;
(iii) the geographical dimensions of the enterprise; and
(iv) past and future activities and goals of the enterprise.

b. In obtaining the foregoing information, any lawful investigative technique may be used in accordance with requirements of Part IV.

4. Authorization and Renewal

a. A domestic security/terrorism investigation may be authorized by the Director or designated Assistant Director upon a written recommendation setting forth the facts or circumstances reasonably indicating the existence of an enterprise as described in this subsection. In such cases, the FBI shall notify the Office of Intelligence Policy and Review of the opening of the investigation. In all investigations the Attorney General may, as he deems necessary, request the FBI to provide a report on the status of the investigation.

b. A domestic security/terrorism investigation may be initially authorized for a period of up to 180 days. An investigation may be continued upon renewed authorization for additional periods each not to exceed 180 days. Renewal authorization shall be obtained from the Director or designated Assistant Director.

c. Investigations shall be reviewed by the Director or designated Senior Headquarters official on or before the expiration period for which the investigation and each renewal thereof is authorized.

d. Each investigation should be reviewed at least annually to insure that the threshold standard is satisfied and that continued allocation of investigative resources is warranted. In some cases, the enterprise may meet the threshold standard but be temporarily inactive in the sense that it has not engaged in recent acts of violence, nor is there any immediate threat of harm — yet the composition, goals and prior history of the group suggests the need for continuing federal interest. Under those circumstances, the investigation may be continued but reasonable efforts should be made to limit the coverage to information which might indicate a change in the status or criminal objectives of the enterprise.

e. An investigation which has been terminated may be reopened upon a showing of the same standard and pursuant to the same procedures as required for initiation of an investigation.

f. The FBI shall report the progress of a domestic security/terrorism investigation to the Office of Intelligence Policy and Review not later than 180 days after the initiation thereof, and the results at the end of each year the investigation continues. The Office of Intelligence Policy and Review shall review the results of each investigation at least annually. . . .

GANDHI ADDRESS
TO NON-ALIGNED PARLEY
March 7, 1983

Focusing on the troubled world economy and on political and disarmament issues, the 101 non-aligned nations held their seventh summit in New Delhi, India, March 7-12. Most of the participants were from Third World countries, representing close to a billion people. The non-aligned group had held its first meeting in Belgrade, Yugoslavia, in 1961, with 25 nations represented.

The 1983 conference produced a moderate final resolution that moved away from the pro-Soviet stance adopted by the previous meeting, held in Cuba in 1979, during which Cuban Premier Fidel Castro vigorously attacked the United States. In 1983 there were only 11 direct criticisms of United States' policies and actions, far fewer than in earlier non-aligned conference statements, and the report referred to the Soviet Union only once. The group scheduled an eighth summit for 1986. (Meeting in Cuba, Historic Documents of 1979, p. 681)

The 1983 meeting took place during a worldwide recession that had a particularly severe impact on Third World countries, although many had overborrowed and overspent even before the recession began in 1980. Many Third World governments by 1983 were grappling with bankruptcies, rising unemployment and potentially explosive social and economic pressures, further aggravated by low prices for their traditional exports of raw materials.

In her keynote address, India's Prime Minister Indira Gandhi outlined the subjects members would focus on during the conference: the worsening state of many Third World economies, those nations' international

*trade problems with the industrialized West and the global threat of
nuclear war.*

*Gandhi blamed developed countries for the Third World's economic
plight and called for the adoption of several measures to improve
international economic relations. "Developing countries get less for what
we produce, while we pay more for the industrial goods we import," she
said. "[W]e ask not for charity or philanthropy but sound economic
sense." The prime minister proposed convening a United Nations conference on money and finance for development to reform the world monetary system. She also suggested that industrialized and developing
countries meet to discuss debt restructuring for the Third World, whose
debt had reached a staggering $600 billion to $700 billion in 1983.
Servicing the debt absorbed more than a quarter of the export earnings of
these countries, Gandhi noted.*

*The speech touched on a number of regional political issues, including
the Indian government's support for the Palestinian cause. "We are of
one mind in our support for the brave, homeless and much harassed
Palestinian people," Gandhi said. "Israel feels free to commit any
outrage, unabashed in its aggression, unrepentant about its transgressions of international law and order." Gandhi attacked another American
ally, South Africa, terming that nation a "notorious outlaw" that "defies
the international family with impunity."*

*The prime minister was particularly critical of huge global military
expenditures, saying that the nuclear arms race had produced an
"untenable strategy of deterrence." She pointed to what she called "the
paradox of our age" — increasingly sophisticated weapons and unsophis-
ticated minds.*

> *Following are excerpts from Indian prime minister Indira
> Gandhi's keynote address to the non-aligned nations meet-
> ing in New Delhi March 7, 1983. (Boldface headings in
> brackets have been added by Congressional Quarterly to
> highlight the organization of the text.):*

... Humankind is balancing on the brink of the collapse of the world
economic system and annihilation through nuclear war. Should these
tragedies occur, can anyone of us, large, small, rich or poor, from North or
South, West or East, hope to escape? Let us analyse the economic crisis.
We of the developing world have no margin of safety. We shall be the first
and worst sufferers in any economic breakdown. In this interdependent
world, where you cannot 'stir a flower without troubling a star', even the
most affluent are not immune to such disturbances.

Since Havana, there have been four consecutive years of stagnation or
decline in the world economy. World production regressed by 1.2 per cent
in 1981 and trade stagnated last year. Unemployment in developed

countries now exceeds 30 million, or 10 per cent of the labour force on the average, the highest level since the Great Depression. In poorer countries, where unemployment is chronic, the situation is particularly harrowing. Human problems have grown enormously in oil-importing developing countries, especially the low-income ones.

Since 1979, the current balance of payments deficits of the developing countries and their debt burdens have doubled to $US 100 billion and $US 600 billion respectively. Medium and long-term lending to them fell by over $US 10 billion. Concessional assistance has rapidly declined. The reduction in contributions by a major donor to the International Development Association has considerably limited the capacity of the World Bank to assist low-income countries. The export earnings of developing countries have gone down by $US 40 billion over the last two years. Commodity prices, which were declining, have collapsed. The levels now are the lowest in the last 50 years. Developing countries get less for what we produce, while we pay more for the industrial goods we import. Interest rates are at an all-time high.

In spite of Ottawa, Cancun and Versailles, the dialogue between the developed and developing has not even begun. Only a few in the North realize that the sustained social and economic development of the South is in its own interest. Thus we ask not for charity or philanthropy but sound economic sense. Such co-operation between North and South will be of mutual benefit.

[International Economic Problems]

The Non-Aligned Movement has stood firmly for a thorough-going restructuring of international economic relations. We are against exploitation. We are for each nation's right to its resources and policies. We want an equal voice in the operation of international institutions. We reiterate our commitment to the establishment of a New International Economic Order based on justice and equality. At this meeting, we should also devise a coherent programme of measures to be taken immediately to help developing countries in areas of critical importance. We should outline a strategy for follow-up action at the forthcoming Sixth Session of the United Nations Conference on Trade and Development and other major international conferences. An International Conference on Money and Finance for Development which is not weighted in favour of the North is an urgent need. Problems of money and finance also burden the countries of the North and have to be solved in a mutually beneficial manner. Such a conference should suggest comprehensive reforms of the international monetary and financial system, which is now recognized as out-of-date, inequitable and inadequate. It should facilitate the mobilization of developmental finance for investment in vital areas such as food, energy and industrial development. A major debt restructuring exercise must be undertaken. The debt problem of developing countries has assumed an unprecedented dimension. Its servicing alone absorbs over a quarter of their total export earnings.

Long-range solutions need time and preparation. Immediate problems brook no delay. Some countries are more critically affected than others. Some are in desperate straits. They cannot wait for action by the world community as a whole. Our Movement has an obligation to them and this is not beyond the human resources, technological skills, industrial capacities, even the finances that we now possess. Self-reliance should start with the weakest amongst us, and assistance be aimed at self-development.

Meanwhile technological change rushes on, giving further advantage to the already affluent. No one has the time to think whether its consequences are benign or malign. To keep up, even societies which can ill afford some of these technical products feel they must acquire them. Non-alignment may shield us from war, but science is important for us to eradicate poverty. However, at present 97 per cent of the world's research is not relevant to us because it is earmarked for the priorities and the induced appetites of technological leaders. Science will work for our basic needs only if we direct our own scientific policies towards these problems, especially those of the smallest and poorest amongst us. Each of our countries must strengthen its domestic base of science and technology and collectively we should devise more effective mechanisms for the pooling of our experiences. Earlier non-aligned gatherings have considered this subject. At this Summit can we move forward to make collective self-reliance a reality?

In the last few years some areas of co-operation have been identified. Effective co-operation in agriculture, irrigation, research in plant varieties, public health, technical training and small industries will reduce our dependence on the high-cost economies of the affluent and on business corporations which profit from us. Lack of communication is a major constriction. We just do not know enough about one another, or what we are capable of giving and receiving. Information is a vital input for development. Our economists and scientists should study and take a holistic view of problems relating to co-operation amongst ourselves in planning, development and economic exchanges. The economic experience and theories of industrialized countries are not necessarily valid in our circumstances.

Some people still consider concern for the environment an expensive and perhaps unnecessary luxury. But the preservation of the environment is an economic consideration since it is closely related to the depletion, restoration and increase of resources. In any policy decision and its implementation we must balance present gains with likely damage in the not too distant future. Human ecology needs a more total and comprehensive approach. . .

[World Peace and Disarmament]

Development, independence, disarmament and peace are closely related.

Can there be peace alongside nuclear weapons? . . . It has been pointed out that global military expenditure is twenty times the total official development assistance. Each day, each hour, the size and lethality of nuclear weapons increase. A nuclear aircraft carrier costs $US 4 billion, which is more than the GNP of 53 countries. The hood of the cobra is spread. Humankind watches in frozen fear, hoping against hope that it will not strike. Never before has our earth faced so much death and danger. The destructive power contained in nuclear stockpiles can kill human life, indeed all life, many times over and might well prevent its reappearance for ages to come. Terrifying is the vividness of such descriptions by scientists. Yet some statesmen and strategists act as though there is not much difference between these and earlier artillery pieces. The arms race continues, because of the pursuit of power and desire for one-upmanship, and also because many industries and interests flourish on it. More recently the notion has been propagated that tactical nuclear weapons are usable in "limited wars". Powerful States propagate the untenable doctrine of deterrence. New areas are being brought into the scope of strategic groupings, military blocks and alliances. New bases and facilities are being established. That is why our responses must be surer, swifter and sharper.

The desire for peace is universal even within countries which themselves produce nuclear weapons and in those where they are deployed. The Non-Aligned Movement is history's biggest peace movement. It welcomes these spontaneous upsurges of peoples. But governments persist in propounding, practising and pursuing the self-same strategic interests, spheres of influence, balance of power and tutelary relations reminiscent of the earlier theory of divine right.

The paradox of our age is that while weapons become increasingly sophisticated, minds remain imprisoned in ideas of simpler times. Technically, the colonial age has ended. But the wish to dominate persists. Neo-colonialism comes wrapped in all types of packages — in technology and communications, commerce and culture. It takes boldness and integrity to resist it. There are intense political and economic pressures. The limited economic viability, indeed the very survival of many of the non-aligned, especially those with small populations, is threatened through artificial barriers in trade, technology transfer and access to resources. It should be within our ability to devise measures to help these small nations to maintain their independence and non-alignment.

Only with co-existence can there be any existence. We regard non-interference and non-intervention as basic laws of international behaviour. Yet different types of interventions, open or covert, do take place in Asia, in Africa, in Latin America. They are all intolerable and unacceptable. Interference leads to intervention and one intervention often attracts another. No single power or group of powers has the justification or moral authority to so interfere or intervene. You cannot condemn one instance but condone another. Each situation has its own origins. Whatever they be, solutions must be political and peaceful. All States must abide by the principle that force or the threat of force will not be used against the territorial integrity or political independence of another State.

What makes interference possible? Our economic weakness, yes, but also our differences, and the discords within our Movement. At our meetings it is a tradition to avoid discussion on conflicts between member countries. We try to concentrate on matters which unite, and to enlarge such unity rather than get caught in acrimonious internecine conflicts. But so many have approached me and so sincere is our friendship for Iran and Iraq, so strong our desire, that I appeal to Iran and Iraq to end their tragic war. I believe that this is the unanimous view of all their friends, who wish them well. We hope also for early normalcy in Afghanistan.

We are of one mind in our support for the brave, homeless and much harassed Palestinian people. Israel feels free to commit any outrage, unabashed in its aggression, unrepentant about its transgressions of international law and behaviour. But can it forever obstruct the legitimate rights of Palestinians? The other notorious outlaw is the South African regime which defies the international family with impunity. It has been rightly observed that the very existence of the Government of Pretoria, which institutionalizes racism, negates the oneness of the human race. Aggression against its own people, and those of Namibia and other neighbours, is an affront. A third issue on which we stand as one is in opposing the intensive militarization of the Indian Ocean and the nuclearization of the Diego Garcia base. We should redouble our efforts to ensure that the United Nations Conference on the Indian Ocean is convened as earlier decided. The littoral States, the Non-Aligned Movement and the United Nations have declared time and again that the Indian Ocean should be a zone of peace. Can we develop the strength to make this reality?

How do we gain strength? By all of us striving to become economically and technologically self-reliant. By settling through peaceful discussions whatever differences we have with one another. By resisting the intervention of others in our internal affairs. And by strengthening the United Nations Organization....

Our plans for a better life for each of our peoples depend on world peace and the reversal of the arms race. Only general and complete disarmament can provide credible security. Negotiations confined to a closed circle of nuclear-weapon powers have made little progress. We are non-nuclear States, who want nuclear energy used only for peace. But we too have a right to live and be heard. In the name of humanity and on behalf of us all, I call upon nuclear-weapon powers to give up the use or threat of use of nuclear weapons in any circumstances; suspend all nuclear weapon tests and the production and deployment of nuclear weapons; and resume disarmament negotiations with determination to reach agreement....

REAGAN SPEECH
TO EVANGELICALS
March 8, 1983

Addressing the National Association of Evangelicals March 8, President Ronald Reagan presented his domestic and foreign policies in strongly moralistic and religious terms. The speech outlined Reagan's conservative stand on several controversial issues and was seen by some as an attempt to mend fences with the religious right that had backed him in his 1980 election.

The president defended his administration's decision to have federally funded clinics notify parents when their teen-age daughters were given birth control drugs or devices. This decision, popularly dubbed the "squeal rule," had stirred up controversy earlier in the year. Opponents argued that the rule violated the girls' privacy, that teens no longer would use the clinics and that the number of illegitimate births and abortions would increase. Reagan argued that the issue of morality should be part of sexual activity and he maintained, "The right of parents and the rights of family take precedence over those of Washington-based bureaucrats and social engineers."

In short order the president addressed several other social issues. He called on Congress to act speedily to pass his constitutional amendment "to restore prayer to public schools." He promised a renewed fight to end "abortion on demand." He said, "Human life legislation ending this tragedy will some day pass the Congress, and you and I must never rest until it does." The president urged Congress to hold hearings and pass legislation to protect handicapped and disabled children from "infanticide or mercy killing." Wrapping up his discussion of domestic issues,

Reagan stated his belief that "America is in the midst of a spiritual awakening and a moral renewal," and he urged a continuation of the fight against racism and other forms of bigotry.

Focus of Evil

Reagan portrayed America as a God-fearing nation and the Soviet Union as a godless one. He called Soviet communism "the focus of evil in the modern world," and he warned of the Soviets' "aggressive impulses" and "global desires." An arms freeze, the president contended, "would place the United States in a position of military and moral inferiority." He exhorted his audience to beware of the temptation to label both sides in the arms race equally at fault and thereby remove themselves from the struggle between right and wrong.

This language expressed Reagan's irritation at the National Conference of Catholic Bishops, which planned a well-publicized May vote on the final version of their pastoral letter endorsing a nuclear freeze. Many Protestant denominations and three branches of U.S. Judaism had taken similar stands against nuclear arms. (Pastoral letter, Historic Documents of 1982, p. 885)

Observers also saw the president's strong anti-Soviet language and anti-freeze remarks as an attempt to induce Congress to approve a large rise in military spending, thereby enabling Reagan's arms negotiators to bargain with the Soviets from a position of strength.

Reactions

The Soviets, predictably, criticized Reagan's speech. The Soviet government press agency Tass March 9 called Reagan's remarks "provocative" and said they demonstrated that his administration "can think only in terms of confrontation and bellicose, lunatic anticommunism."

The president's speech came under attack from some domestic sources as well. Historian Henry Steele Commager termed Reagan's address "the worst presidential speech in American history." Commager stated, "No other presidential speech has so flagrantly allied the government with religion. It was a gross appeal to religious prejudice."

On Capitol Hill some Democrats criticized the speech as harmful to arms control negotiations and likely to polarize the national debate on arms issues. But the forceful address received praise from conservatives. Paul Weyrich, who headed the conservative Committee for the Survival of a Free Congress, said the speech "might as well have been a declaration of candidacy." He added, "If Ronald Reagan had sounded like that in 1982, the Republicans wouldn't have lost as many seats as they did."

Following are excerpts from a speech by President Ronald Reagan to the National Association of Evangelicals, delivered March 8, 1983, in Orlando, Fla. (Boldface headings in brackets have been added by Congressional Quarterly to highlight the organization of the text.):

... I'm pleased to be here with you who are keeping America great by keeping her good. ...

... I want you to know that this administration is motivated by a political philosophy that sees the greatness of America in you, her people, and in your families, churches, neighborhoods, communities — the institutions that foster and nourish values like concern for others and respect for the rule of law under God.

Now, I don't have to tell you that this puts us in opposition to, or at least out of step with, a prevailing attitude of many who have turned to a modern-day secularism, discarding the tried and time-tested values upon which our very civilization is based. No matter how well intentioned, their value system is radically different from that of most Americans. And while they proclaim that they're freeing us from superstitions of the past, they've taken upon themselves the job of superintending us by government rule and regulation. Sometimes their voices are louder than ours, but they are not yet a majority.

An example of that vocal superiority is evident in a controversy now going on in Washington. And since I'm involved, I've been waiting to hear from the parents of young America. How far are they willing to go in giving to government their prerogatives as parents?

Let me state the case as briefly and simply as I can. An organization of citizens, sincerely motivated and deeply concerned about the increase in illegitimate births and abortions involving girls well below the age of consent, sometime ago established a nationwide network of clinics to offer help to these girls and, hopefully, alleviate this situation. Now, again, let me say, I do not fault their intent. However, in their well-intentioned effort, these clinics have decided to provide advice and birth control drugs and devices to underage girls without the knowledge of their parents.

For some years now, the Federal Government has helped with funds to subsidize these clinics. In providing for this, the Congress decreed that every effort would be made to maximize parental participation. Nevertheless, the drugs and devices are prescribed without getting parental consent or giving notification after they've done so. Girls termed "sexually active" — and that has replaced the word "promiscuous" — are given this help in order to prevent illegitimate birth or abortion.

['Squeal Rule' and School Prayer]

Well, we have ordered clinics receiving Federal funds to notify the parents such help has been given. One of the Nation's leading newspapers has created the term "squeal rule" in editorializing against us for doing this, and we're being criticized for violating the privacy of young people. A judge has recently granted an injunction against an enforcement of our rule. I've watched TV panel shows discuss this issue, seen columnists pontificating on our error, but no one seems to mention morality as playing a part in the subject of sex.

Is all of Judeo-Christian tradition wrong? Are we to believe that something so sacred can be looked upon as a purely physical thing with no potential for emotional and psychological harm? And isn't it the parents' right to give counsel and advice to keep their children from making mistakes that may affect their entire lives?

Many of us in government would like to know what parents think about this intrusion in their family by government. We're going to fight in the courts. The right of parents and the rights of family take precedence over those of Washington-based bureaucrats and social engineers.

But the fight against parental notification is really only one example of many attempts to water down traditional values and even abrogate the original terms of American democracy. Freedom prospers when religion is vibrant and the rule of law under God is acknowledged. When our Founding Fathers passed the first amendment, they sought to protect churches from government interference. They never intended to construct a wall of hostility between government and the concept of religious belief itself.

The evidence of this permeates our history and our government. The Declaration of Independence mentions the Supreme Being no less than four times. "In God We Trust" is engraved on our coinage. The Supreme Court opens its proceedings with a religious invocation. And the Members of Congress open their sessions with a prayer. I just happen to believe the schoolchildren of the United States are entitled to the same privileges as Supreme Court Justices and Congressmen.

Last year, I sent the Congress a constitutional amendment to restore prayer to public schools. Already this session, there's growing bipartisan support for the amendment, and I am calling on the Congress to act speedily to pass it and to let our children pray.

Perhaps some of you read recently about the Lubbock school case, where a judge actually ruled that it was unconstitutional for a school district to give equal treatment to religious and nonreligious student groups, even when the group meetings were being held during the students' own time. The first amendment never intended to require government to discriminate against religious speech.

Senators [Jeremiah] Denton [R-Ala.] and [Mark] Hatfield [R-Ore.] have proposed legislation in the Congress on the whole question of prohibiting discrimination against religious forms of student speech. Such legislation could go far to restore freedom of religious speech for public school students. And I hope the Congress considers these bills quickly. And with your help, I think it's possible we could also get the constitutional amendment through the Congress this year.

[Abortion and Rights of Handicapped]

More than a decade ago, a Supreme Court decision literally wiped off the books of 50 States statutes protecting the rights of unborn children. Abortion on demand now takes the lives of up to 1 1/2 million unborn children a year. Human life legislation ending this tragedy will some day pass the Congress, and you and I must never rest until it does. Unless and until it can be proven that the unborn child is not a living entity, then its right to life, liberty, and the pursuit of happiness must be protected.

You may remember that when abortion on demand began, many, and, indeed, I'm sure many of you, warned that the practice would lead to a decline in respect for human life, that the philosophical premises used to justify abortion on demand would ultimately be used to justify other attacks on the sacredness of human life — infanticide or mercy killing. Tragically enough, those warnings proved all too true. Only last year a court permitted the death by starvation of a handicapped infant.

I have directed the Health and Human Services Department to make clear to every health care facility in the United States that the Rehabilitation Act of 1973 protects all handicapped persons against discrimination based on handicaps, including infants. And we have taken the further step of requiring that each and every recipient of Federal funds who provides health care services to infants must post and keep posted in a conspicuous place a notice stating that "discriminatory failure to feed and care for handicapped infants in this facility is prohibited by Federal law." It also lists a 24-hour, toll-free number so that nurses and other may report violations in time to save the infant's life.

In addition, recent legislation introduced in the Congress by Representative Henry Hyde of Illinois not only increases restrictions on publicly financed abortions, it also addresses this whole problem of infanticide. I urge the Congress to begin hearings and to adopt legislation that will protect the right of life to all children, including the disabled or handicapped.

[Spiritual Awakening in America]

Now, I'm sure that you must get discouraged at times, but you've done better than you know, perhaps. There's a great spiritual awakening in America, a renewal of the traditional values that have been the bedrock of America's goodness and greatness.

One recent survey by a Washington-based research council concluded that Americans were far more religious than the people of other nations; 95 percent of those surveyed expressed a belief in God and a huge majority believed the Ten Commandments had real meaning in their lives. And another study has found that an overwhelming majority of Americans disapprove of adultery, teenage sex, pornography, abortion, and hard drugs. And this same study showed a deep reverence for the importance of family ties and religious belief.

I think the items that we've discussed here today must be a key part of the Nation's political agenda. For the first time the Congress is openly and seriously debating and dealing with the prayer and abortion issues — and that's enormous progress right there. I repeat: America is in the midst of a spiritual awakening and a moral renewal. And with your Biblical keynote, I say today, "Yes, let justice roll on like a river, righteousness like a never-failing stream."

Now, obviously, much of this new political and social consensus I've talked about is based on a positive view of American history, one that takes pride in our country's accomplishments and record. But we must never forget that no government schemes are going to perfect man. We know that living in this world means dealing with what philosophers would call the phenomenology of evil or, as theologians would put it, the doctrine of sin.

There is sin and evil in the world, and we're enjoined by Scripture and the Lord Jesus to oppose it with all our might. Our nation, too, has a legacy of evil with which it must deal. The glory of this land has been its capacity for transcending the moral evils of our past. For example, the long struggle of minority citizens for equal rights, once a source of disunity and civil war, is now a point of pride for all Americans. We must never go back. There is no room for racism, anti-Semitism, or other forms of ethnic and racial hatred in this country.

I know that you've been horrified, as have I, by the resurgence of some hate groups preaching bigotry and prejudice. Use the mighty voice of your pulpits and the powerful standing of your churches to denounce and isolate these hate groups in our midst. The commandment given us is clear and simple: "Thou shalt love thy neighbor as thyself."

But whatever sad episodes exist in our past, any objective observer must hold a positive view of American history, a history that has been the story of hopes fulfilled and dreams made into reality. Especially in this century, America has kept alight the torch of freedom, but not just for ourselves but for millions of others around the world.

And this brings me to my final point today. During my first press conference as President, in answer to a direct question, I pointed out that, as good Marxist-Leninists, the Soviet leaders have openly and publicly declared that the only morality they recognize is that which will further their cause, which is world revolution. I think I should point out I was only quoting Lenin, their guiding spirit, who said in 1920 that they repudiate all morality that proceeds from supernatural ideas — that's their name for religion — or ideas that are outside class conceptions. Morality is entirely subordinate to the interests of class war. And everything is moral that is necessary for the annihilation of the old, exploiting social order and for uniting the proletariat.

Well, I think the refusal of many influential people to accept this elementary fact of Soviet doctrine illustrates an historical reluctance to see totalitarian powers for what they are. We saw this phenomenon in the 1930s. We see it too often today.

This doesn't mean we should isolate ourselves and refuse to seek an understanding with them. I intend to do everything I can to persuade them of our peaceful intent, to remind them that it was the West that refused to use its nuclear monopoly in the forties and fifties for territorial gain and which now proposes 50 percent cut in strategic ballistic missiles and the elimination of an entire class of land-based, intermediate-range nuclear missiles.

[Danger of Nuclear Freeze]

At the same time, however, they must be made to understand we will never compromise our principles and standards. We will never give away our freedom. We will never abandon our belief in God. And we will never stop searching for a genuine peace. But we can assure none of these things America stands for through the so-called nuclear freeze solutions proposed by some.

The truth is that a freeze now would be a very dangerous fraud, for that is merely the illusion of peace. The reality is that we must find peace through strength.

I would agree to a freeze if only we could freeze the Soviets' global desires. A freeze at current levels of weapons would remove any incentive for the Soviets to negotiate seriously in Geneva and virtually end our chances to achieve the major arms reductions which we have proposed. Instead, they would achieve their objectives through the freeze.

A freeze would reward the Soviet Union for its enormous and unparalleled military buildup. It would prevent the essential and long overdue modernization of United States and allied defenses and would leave our aging forces increasingly vulnerable. And an honest freeze would require extensive prior negotiations on the systems and numbers to be limited and on the measures to ensure effective verification and compliance. And the kind of a freeze that has been suggested would be virtually impossible to verify. Such a major effort would divert us completely from our current negotiations on achieving substantial reductions.

A number of years ago, I heard a young father, a very prominent young man in the entertainment world, addressing a tremendous gathering in California. It was during the time of the cold war, and communism and our own way of life were very much on people's minds. And he was speaking to that subject. And suddenly, though, I heard him saying, "I love my little girls more than anything —" And I said to myself, "Oh, no, don't. You can't — don't say that." But I had underestimated him. He went on: "I would rather see my little girls die now, still believing in God, than have them grow up under communism and one day die no longer believing in God."

There were thousands of young people in that audience. They came to their feet with shouts of joy. They had instantly recognized the profound truth in what he had said, with regard to the physical and the soul and what was truly important.

Yes, let us pray for the salvation of all of those who live in that totalitarian darkness — pray they will discover the joy of knowing God. But until they do, let us be aware that while they preach the supremacy of the state, declare its omnipotence over individual man, and predict its eventual domination of all peoples on the Earth, they are the focus of evil in the modern world.

It was C. S. Lewis who, in his unforgettable "Screwtape Letters," wrote: "The greatest evil is not done now in those sordid 'dens of crime' that Dickens loved to paint. It is not even done in concentration camps and labor camps. In those we see its final result. But it is conceived and ordered (moved, seconded, carried and minuted) in clear, carpeted, warmed, and well-lighted offices, by quiet men with white collars and cut fingernails and smooth-shaven cheeks who do not need to raise their voice."

Well, because these "quiet men" do not "raise their voices," because they sometimes speak in soothing tones of brotherhood and peace, because, like other dictators before them, they're always making "their final territorial demand," some would have us accept them at their word and accommodate ourselves to their aggressive impulses. But if history teaches anything, it teaches that simple-minded appeasement or wishful thinking about our adversaries is folly. It means the betrayal of our past, the squandering of our freedom.

So, I urge you to speak out against those who would place the United States in a position of military and moral inferiority. You know, I've always believed that old Screwtape reserved his best efforts for those of you in the church. So, in your discussions of the nuclear freeze proposals, I urge you to beware the temptation of pride — the temptation of blithely declaring yourselves above it all and label both sides equally at fault, to ignore the facts of history and the aggressive impulses of an evil empire, to simply call the arms race a giant misunderstanding and thereby remove yourself from the struggle between right and wrong and good and evil.

I ask you to resist the attempts of those who would have you withhold your support for our efforts, this administration's efforts, to keep America strong and free, while we negotiate real and verifiable reductions in the world's nuclear arsenals and one day, with God's help, their total elimination.

[Importance of Spiritual Strength]

While America's military strength is important, let me add here that I've always maintained that the struggle now going on for the world will never be decided by bombs or rockets, by armies or military might. The real crisis we face today is a spiritual one; at root, it is a test of moral will and faith.

Whittaker Chambers, the man whose own religious conversion made him a witness to one of the terrible traumas of our time, the Hiss-Chambers case, wrote that the crisis of the Western World exists to the degree in which the West is indifferent to God, the degree to which it collaborates in communism's attempt to make man stand alone without God. And then he said, for Marxism-Leninism is actually the second oldest faith, first proclaimed in the Garden of Eden with the words of temptation, "Ye shall be as gods."

The Western World can answer this challenge, he wrote, "but only provided that its faith in God and the freedom He enjoins is as great as Communism's faith in Man."

I believe we shall rise to the challenge. I believe that communism is another sad, bizarre chapter in human history whose last pages even now are being written. I believe this because the source of our strength in the quest for human freedom is not material, but spiritual. And because it knows no limitation, it must terrify and ultimately triumph over those who would enslave their fellow man. For in the words of Isaiah: "He giveth power to the faint; and to them that have no might He increased strength. . . . But they that wait upon the Lord shall renew their strength; they shall mount up with wings as eagles; they shall run, and not be weary. . . ."

Yes, change your world. One of our Founding Fathers, Thomas Paine, said, "We have it within our power to begin the world over again." We can do it, doing together what no one church could do by itself.

God bless you, and thank you very much.

MEDICAL COMMISSION REPORT ON LIFE-SUSTAINING MEASURES

March 21, 1983

A presidential commission established to study medical ethical issues March 21 released a report, "Deciding to Forego Life-Sustaining Treatment," that attempted to set forth some guidelines on a complex and controversial subject. Established by Congress in 1978, the President's Commission for the Study of Ethical Problems in Medicine and Biomedical and Behavioral Research began work in 1980 during the last year of Jimmy Carter's presidency. The panel produced 11 substantive reports, including a widely circulated study on determining the occurrence of death and a report on the use of genetic screening and engineering research.

As commission Chairman Morris B. Abram, a New York lawyer and former president of Brandeis University, explained in his cover letter to President Ronald Reagan, the question of a patient's choice to die "was not part of our original legislative mandate but was added as a natural outgrowth of our studies on informed consent, the 'definition' of death, and access to health care and because it seemed to us to involve some of the most important and troubling ethical and legal questions in modern medicine." (Access to health care, p. 317)

In the introduction to its report, the 11-member panel (made up of doctors, lawyers, theologians and public policy experts) noted that new breakthroughs in medicine — such as cardiopulmonary resuscitation (CPR), chemotherapy in cancer treatment and organ transplantation — "have made it possible to retard and even to reverse many conditions that were until recently regarded as fatal. Matters once the province of fate have now become a matter of human choice, a development that has profound ethical and legal implications."

Whereas in 1949 only 50 percent of Americans died in hospitals and long-term care institutions such as nursing homes, by 1983 about 80 percent of U.S. deaths occurred in institutions. "The change in where very ill patients are treated permits health care professionals to marshal the instruments of scientific medicine more effectively. But people who are dying may well find such a setting alienating and unsupportive," the commission noted.

Treatment Decision Making

The legal rights of terminally ill patients to end their treatment had been a subject of growing concern in recent years. Courts in some states had held that a mentally competent patient could make such choices, regardless of the doctor's opinion, but there was no uniform standard. In the commission's view, Abram wrote, "the authority of competent, informed patients to decide about their health care encompasses the decision to forego treatment and allow death to occur. We note, however, that all patients, including those who reject various forms of life-support, should receive other appropriate medical care to preserve their dignity and minimize suffering to the greatest extent possible."

"Physician attitudes toward communication with terminally ill patients have changed dramatically in recent years," the commission said. According to a 1978 study, 97 percent of physicians surveyed said they preferred to tell cancer patients of their diagnosis, compared with only 10 percent of those polled in 1961. Nonetheless, many health care providers continued to exercise "misguided paternalism" in neglecting to inform patients about their condition, said Dr. Joanne Lynn, assistant director of the commission.

Addressing the issue of "withholding versus withdrawing treatment," the panel noted that many health care providers were "uncomfortable about stopping a treatment that has already been started because doing so seems to them to constitute killing the patient. By contrast, not starting a therapy seems acceptable, supposedly because it involves an omission rather than an action. . . . Adopting the opposite view — that treatment, once started, cannot be stopped, or that stopping requires much greater justification than not starting — is likely to have serious adverse consequences. Treatment might be continued for longer than is optimal for the patient, even to the point where it is causing positive harm with little or no compensating benefit. An even more troubling wrong occurs when a treatment that might save life or improve health is not started because the health care personnel are afraid that they will find it very difficult to stop the treatment if, as is fairly likely, it proves to be of little benefit and greatly burdens the patient."

The commission endorsed the use of pain-relieving drugs and proce-dures "known to risk death in order to relieve suffering as well as to pursue a return to health." (An example is the use of morphine to relieve pain, although one of its side effects is to cause respiratory depression.) "Medicine's role in relieving suffering is especially important when a patient is going to die soon, since the suffering of such a patient is not an unavoidable aspect of treatment that might restore health, as it might be for a patient with a curable condition," the panel wrote.

Comatose Patients

When patients were not competent to make judgments related to their own treatment — for example, when they were suffering from permanent loss of consciousness — the panel suggested that existing legal proce-dures such as advance directives could be adopted to allow persons while competent to designate someone to act on their behalf and to express their wishes about treatment. "When it is not possible to know what a particular patient would have chosen — as, for example, with seriously ill infants — those who make the choices should attempt to serve the patient's best interests, judged from the patient's vantage point," Abram wrote. A decision to remove a patient from a respirator could, for example, be made by family members or others acting on the patient's behalf, because "the law does not and should not require any particular therapies to be applied or continued."

The problems involved in dealing with unconscious patients had come to public attention in 1975 in the case of Karen Ann Quinlan, then 21 years old. Quinlan lapsed into a coma, and her father sought court appointment as her guardian for the express purpose of authorizing the removal of her respirator, whether or not she died as a consequence. Although her physicians opposed the move, the New Jersey Supreme Court granted the request. Quinlan's doctors gradually discontinued the respirator during May of 1976, and she was able to breathe on her own. As of the end of 1983, she was alive and being cared for in a New Jersey nursing home. (Background, Historic Documents of 1975, pp. 805-824; Historic Documents of 1976, pp. 198-219)

The commission had addressed the issue of defining death in a previous report of that title, released in July 1981. Because physicians were able to keep patients alive even when they were unable to breathe spontaneously, the panel recommended that, in addition to the tradi-tional standard of heart and lung functions, death be defined as the irreversible loss of all functions of the entire brain. According to this standard, Quinlan would be declared alive, because she never experi-enced irreversible cessation of all brain functions but rather retained function of the brain stem and was diagnosed as being in a "persistent vegetative state."

Although some states already had brain-death statutes, the commission worked with the American Bar Association, the American Medical Association and the National Conference of Commissioners on Uniform State Laws to draw up a model code, the Uniform Determination of Death Act, which was subsequently adopted by a number of states.

Newborn Infant Care

On a subject that had become increasingly controversial, the report contained a chapter on seriously ill newborns, cautioning that "a very strict standard" should be used in making treatment decisions for infants born with serious defects. The debate had been sparked by the April 1982 death of an infant boy, known as "Baby Doe," in Bloomington, Ind. The infant had been born with Down's syndrome (a disease characterized by mental retardation) and other complications requiring surgery. The baby died after the parents, doctors and a state court had approved a complete cutoff of food and medical care. The case was one of a number that had surfaced in which parents of infants born with Down's syndrome and a blockage of the esophagus that prevented food from reaching the stomach had refused to allow surgery to remove the obstruction.

In response to the debate sparked by these occurrences, the Reagan administration March 22 issued regulations that would deny federal aid to hospitals that prevented seriously ill newborns from receiving food or medical care. The rules, issued by the president as an executive order, would have required all hospitals receiving federal funds to post notices in delivery wards and intensive care and pediatric nurseries stating that "Discriminatory failure to feed and care for handicapped infants in this facility is prohibited by federal law." The rules also proposed to establish a 24-hour toll-free "hotline" to allow anyone aware of a violation to report it to federal authorities.

The regulations had been supported by right-to-life and other conservative groups and opposed by the American Academy of Pediatrics and the National Association of Children's Hospitals. Opponents argued that the regulations represented an unwarranted federal intrusion into decisions that should be left to parents and doctors.

"Within constraints of equity and availability, infants should receive all therapies that are clearly beneficial to them," the presidential commission concluded in its report. "For example, an otherwise healthy Down's syndrome child whose life is threatened by a surgically correctable complication should receive the surgery because he or she benefit from it," regardless of the parents' wishes. But the commission took issue with the Reagan administration's regulations, noting that "using financial sanctions against institutions to punish an 'incorrect' decision in a particular case is likely to be ineffective and to lead to excessively detailed regulations that would involve government re-

imbursement officials in bedside decisionmaking."

On April 14 a federal judge in Washington, D.C., struck down the controversial "Baby Doe" rule, calling it a "hasty and ill-considered" response to one of the "most difficult medical and ethical problems facing our society." U.S. District Court Judge Gerhard A. Gesell voided the regulation on procedural grounds, finding that it violated administrative procedure laws requiring time for public comment. Health and Human Services (HHS) Secretary Margaret M. Heckler said the government would appeal and would revise the regulation.

The American Academy of Pediatrics said it was "very gratified with the court's decision," adding, "we look forward now to cooperating with the HHS secretary ... to find a better way to solve this very sensitive problem."

The controversy continued, however, this time concerning the case of a female infant, "Baby Jane Doe," who was born October 11 in Port Jefferson, N. Y., with an opening in the spinal cord, water on the brain and an abnormally small head. The parents were advised that surgery might permit their daughter to live into her twenties but that she would be severely retarded and partially paralyzed. Without surgery, she might live two years. They chose not to have surgery performed. A pro-life lawyer challenged their decision and the Justice Department entered the case to obtain medical records to determine if the decision violated the infant's civil rights. When a federal district judge refused the request in December, the department said it would appeal the ruling.

Meanwhile, Congress was considering revising the 1974 Child Abuse Prevention and Treatment Act to add protections to handicapped newborns in hospitals. A bill introduced in 1982 by Rep. Austin J. Murphy, D-Pa., would expand the definition of child abuse to include the withholding of food or medical treatment from handicapped infants. It also would require states to ensure that nutrition, medical and general care and social services were provided those with life-threatening congenital defects.

Following are excerpts from the March 21, 1983, report, "Deciding to Forego Life-Sustaining Treatment," issued by the President's Commission for the Study of Ethical Problems in Medicine and Biomedical and Behavioral Research. (Boldface headings in brackets have been added by Congressional Quarterly to highlight the organization of the text.):

Introduction and Summary

Americans seem to be increasingly concerned with decisions about death and dying. Why is a subject once thought taboo now so frequently aired by the popular media, debated in academic forums and professional societies, and litigated in well-publicized court cases?

Perhaps it is because death is less of a private matter than it once was. Today, dying more often than not occurs under medical supervision, usually in a hospital or nursing home. Actions that take place in such settings involve more people, and the resolution of disagreements among them is more likely to require formal rules and means of adjudication. Moreover, patients dying in health care institutions today typically have fewer of the sources of nonmedical support, such as family and church, that once helped people in their final days.

Also important, no doubt, are the biomedical developments of the past several decades. Without removing the sense of loss, finality, and mystery that have always accompanied death, these new developments have made death more a matter of deliberate decision. For almost any life-threatening condition, some intervention can now delay the moment of death. Frequent dramatic breakthroughs — insulin, antibiotics, resuscitation, chemotherapy, kidney dialysis, and organ transplantation, to name but a few — have made it possible to retard and even to reverse many conditions that were until recently regarded as fatal. Matters once the province of fate have now become a matter of human choice, a development that has profound ethical and legal implications.

Moreover, medical technology often renders patients less able to communicate or to direct the course of treatment. Even for mentally competent patients, other people must usually assist in making treatment decisions or at least acquiesce in carrying them out. Consequently, in recent years there has been a continuing clarification of the rights, duties, and liabilities of all concerned, a process in which professionals, ethical and legal commentators, and — with increasing frequency — the courts and legislatures have been involved.

Thus, the Commission found this an appropriate time to reexamine the way decisions are and ought to be made about whether or not to forego life-sustaining treatment. For example, may a patient's withdrawal from treatment ever be forbidden? Should physicians acquiesce in patients' wishes regarding therapy? Should they offer patients the option to forego life-sustaining therapy? Does it make any difference if the treatment has already been started, or involves mechanical systems of life support, or is very costly?

SUMMARY OF CONCLUSIONS

Building on a central conclusion of its report on informed consent — that decisions about health care ultimately rest with competent patients — the Commission in this Report examines the situations in which a patient's choice to forego life-sustaining therapy may be limited on moral or legal grounds. In addition to providing clarification of the issues, the Report suggests appropriate procedures for decisions regarding both competent and incompetent patients and scrutinizes the role of various public and private bodies in shaping and regulating the process.

These aims are the only ones that this Commission believes to be within the scope of its role. The Report does not judge any particular future case nor provide a guidebook of the morally correct choice for patients and health care providers who are facing such a decision. Rather, the Commission intends to illuminate the strengths and weaknesses of various considerations and various instruments of social policy. Clarifying the relevant considerations and prohibitions may help decisionmakers, but it may also force them to confront painful realities more directly. The Commission hopes that this Report will help improve the process, but recognizes that an improved process will not necessarily make decisions easier.

The Report addresses a broad range of problems and patient situations. Serious questions about whether life should be sustained through a particular treatment usually arise when a patient is suffering from a known disease likely to prove fatal in the near future rather than in an unanticipated emergency (where any decisionmaking would necessarily have to be truncated). Life-sustaining treatment, as used here, encompasses all health care interventions that have the effect of increasing the life span of the patient. Although the term includes respirators, kidney machines, and all the paraphernalia of modern medicine, it also includes home physical therapy, nursing support for activities of daily living, and special feeding procedures, provided that one of the effects of the treatment is to prolong a patient's life.

The issues addressed in this Report are complex and their resolution depends not only on the context of particular decisions but also on their relationship to other values and principles. Thus, it is exceptionally difficult to summarize the Commission's conclusions on this subject. The synopsis provided here should be read in the context of the reasoning, elaboration, and qualifications provided in the chapters that follow.

(1) The voluntary choice of a competent and informed patient should determine whether or not life-sustaining therapy will be undertaken, just as such choices provide the basis for other decisions about medical treatment. Health care institutions and professionals should try to enhance patients' abilities to make decisions on their own behalf and to promote understanding of the available treatment options.

(2) Health care professionals serve patients best by maintaining a presumption in favor of sustaining life, while recognizing that competent patients are entitled to choose to forego any treatments, including those that sustain life.

(3) As in medical decisionmaking generally, some constraints on patients' decisions are justified.

- Health care professionals or institutions may decline to provide a particular option because that choice would violate their conscience or professional judgment, though in doing so they may not abandon a patient.
- Health care institutions may justifiably restrict the availability of certain options in order to use limited resources more effectively or

285

to enhance equity in allocating them.

● Society may decide to limit the availability of certain options for care in order to advance equity or the general welfare, but such policies should not be applied initially nor especially forcefully to medical options that could sustain life.

● Information about the existence and justification of any of these constraints must be available to patients or their surrogates.

(4) Governmental agencies, institutional providers of care, individual practitioners, and the general public should try to improve the medically beneficial options that are available to dying patients. Specific attention should be paid to making respectful, responsive, and competent care available for people who choose to forego life-sustaining therapy or for whom no such therapies are available.

(5) Several distinctions are employed by health care professionals and others in deliberating about whether a choice that leads to an earlier death would be acceptable or unacceptable in a particular case. Unfortunately, people often treat these distinctions — between acts and omissions that cause death, between withholding and withdrawing care, between an intended death and one that is merely foreseeable, and between ordinary and extraordinary treatment — as though applying them decided the issue, which it does not. Although there is a danger that relying on such labels will take the place of analysis, these distinctions can still be helpful if attention is directed to the reasoning behind them. . . .

(6) Achieving medically and morally appropriate decisions does not require changes in statutes concerning homicide or wrongful death, given appropriate prosecutorial discretion and judicial interpretation.

(7) Primary responsibility for ensuring that morally justified processes of decisionmaking are followed lies with physicians. Health care institutions also have a responsibility to ensure that there are appropriate procedures to enhance patients' competence, to provide for designation of surrogates, to guarantee that patients are adequately informed, to overcome the influence of dominant institutional biases, to provide review of decisionmaking, and to refer cases to the courts appropriately. The Commission is not recommending that hospitals and other institutions take over decisions about patient care; there is no substitute for the dedication, compassion, and professional judgment of physicians. Nevertheless, institutions need to develop policies because their decisions have profound effects on patient outcomes, because society looks to these institutions to ensure the means necessary to preserve both health and the value of self-determination, and because they are conveniently situated to provide efficient, confidential, and rapid supervision and review. . . .

Incompetent Patients Generally

(8) Physicians who make initial assessments of patients' competence and others who review these assessments should be responsible for judging

whether a particular patient's decisionmaking abilities are sufficient to meet the demands of the specific decision at hand.

(9) To protect the interests of patients who have insufficient capacity to make particular decisions and to ensure their well-being and self-determination:

- An appropriate surrogate, ordinarily a family member, should be named to make decisions for such patients. The decisions of surrogates should, when possible, attempt to replicate the ones that the patient would make if capable of doing so. When lack of evidence about the patient's wishes precludes this, decisions by surrogates should seek to protect the patient's best interests. Because such decisions are not instances of self-choice by the patient, the range of acceptable decisions by surrogates is sometimes not as broad as it would be for patients making decisions for themselves.

- The medical staff, along with the trustees and administrators of health care institutions, should explore and evaluate various formal and informal administrative arrangements for review and consultation, such as "ethics committees," particularly for decisions that have life-or-death consequences for incompetent patients.

- State courts and legislatures should consider making provision for advance directives through which people designate others to make health care decisions on their behalf and/or give instructions about their care. Such advance directives provide a means of preserving some self-determination for patients who may lose their decisionmaking capacity. Durable powers of attorney are preferable to "living wills" since they are more generally applicable and provide a better vehicle for patients to exercise self-determination, though experience with both is limited.

- Health care professionals and institutions should adopt clear, explicit, and publicly available policies regarding how and by whom decisions are to be made for patients who lack adequate decisionmaking capacity.

- Families, health care institutions, and professionals should work together to make decisions for patients who lack decisionmaking capacity. Recourse to the courts should be reserved for the occasions when adjudication is clearly required by state law or when concerned parties have disagreements that they cannot resolve over matters of substantial import. Courts and legislatures should be cautious about requiring judicial review of routine health care decisons for patients with inadequate decisionmaking capacity.

Patients with Permanent Loss of Consciousness

(10) Current understanding of brain functions allows a reliable diagnosis of permanent loss of consciousness for some patients. Whether or not life-sustaining treatment is given is of much less importance to such patients than to others.

(11) The decisions of patients' families should determine what sort of medical care permanently unconscious patients receive. Other than requiring appropriate decisionmaking procedures for these patients, the law does not and should not require any particular therapies to be applied or continued, with the exception of basic nursing care that is needed to ensure dignified and respectful treatment of the patient.

(12) Access to costly care for patients who have permanently lost consciousness may justifiably be restricted on the basis of resource use in two ways: by a physician or institution that otherwise would have to deny significantly beneficial care to another specific patient, or by legitimate mechanisms of policy formulation and application if and only if the provision of certain kinds of care to these patients were clearly causing serious inequities in the use of community resources.

Seriously Ill Newborns

(13) Parents should be the surrogates for a seriously ill newborn unless they are unqualified by decisionmaking incapacity, an unresolvable disagreement between them, or their choice of a course of action that is clearly against the infant's best interests.

(14) Therapies expected to be futile for a seriously ill newborn need not be provided; parents, health care professionals and institutions, and reimbursement sources, however, should ensure the infant's comfort.

(15) Within constraints of equity and availability, infants should receive all therapies that are clearly beneficial to them. For example, an otherwise healthy Down Syndrome child whose life is threatened by a surgically correctable complication should receive the surgery because he or she would clearly benefit from it.

- The concept of benefit necessarily makes reference to the context of the infant's present and future treatment, taking into account such matters as the level of biomedical knowledge and technology and the availability of services necessary for the child's treatment.
- The dependence of benefit upon context underlines society's special obligation to provide necessary services for handicapped children and their families, which rests on the special ethical duties owed to newborns with undeserved disadvantages and on the general ethical duty of the community to ensure equitable access for all persons to an adequate level of health care.

(16) Decisionmakers should have access to the most accurate and up-to-date information as they consider individual cases.

- Physicians should obtain appropriate consultations and referrals.
- The significance of the diagnoses and the prognoses under each treatment option must be conveyed to the parents (or other surrogates).

(17) The medical staff, administrators, and trustees of each institution that provides care to seriously ill newborns should take the responsibility for ensuring good decisionmaking practices. Accrediting bodies may want

to require that institutions have appropriate policies in this area.

- An institution should have clear and explicit policies that require prospective or retrospective review of decisions when life-sustaining treatment for an infant might be foregone or when parents and providers disagree about the correct decision for an infant. Certain categories of clearly futile therapies could be explicitly excluded from review.
- The best interests of an infant should be pursued when those interests are clear.
- The policies should allow for the exercise of parental discretion when a child's interests are ambiguous.
- Decisions should be referred to public agencies (including courts) for review when necessary to determine whether parents should be disqualified as decisionmakers and, if so, who should decide the course of treatment that would be in the best interests of their child.

(18) The legal system has various — though limited — roles in ensuring that seriously ill infants receive the correct care.

- Civil courts are ultimately the appropriate decisionmakers concerning the disqualification of parents as surrogates and the designation of surrogates to serve in their stead.
- Special statutes requiring providers to bring such cases to the attention of civil authorities do not seem warranted, since state laws already require providers to report cases of child abuse or neglect to social service agencies; nevertheless, educating providers about their responsibilities is important.
- Although criminal penalties should be available to punish serious errors, the ability of the criminal law to ensure good decisionmaking in individual cases is limited.
- Governmental agencies that reimburse for health care may insist that institutions have policies and procedures regarding decisionmaking, but using financial sanctions against institutions to punish an "incorrect" decision in a particular case is likely to be ineffective and to lead to excessively detailed regulations that would involve government reimbursement officials in bedside decisionmaking. Furthermore, such sanctions could actually penalize other patients and providers in an unjust way.

Cardiopulmonary Resuscitation

(19) A presumption favoring resuscitation of hospitalized patients in the event of unexpected cardiac arrest is justified.

(20) A competent and informed patient or an incompetent patient's surrogate is entitled to decide with the attending physician that an order against resuscitation should be written in the chart. When cardiac arrest is likely, a patient (or a surrogate) should usually be informed and offered the chance specifically to decide for or against resuscitation.

(21) Physicians have a duty to assess for each hospitalized patient

whether resuscitation is likely, on balance, to benefit the patient, to fail to benefit, or to have uncertain effect.

- When a patient will not benefit from resuscitation, a decision not to resuscitate, with the consent of the patient or surrogate, is justified.
- When a physician's assessment conflicts with a competent patient's decision, further discussion and consultation are appropriate; ultimately the physician must follow the patient's decision or transfer responsibility for that patient to another physician.
- When a physician's assessment conflicts with that of an incompetent patient's surrogate, further discussion, consultation, review by an institutional committee, and, if necessary, judicial review should be sought.

(22) To protect the interests of patients and their families, health care institutions should have explicit policies and procedures governing orders not to resuscitate,and accrediting bodies should require such policies.

- Such policies should require that orders not to resuscitate be in written form and that they delineate who has the authority both to write such orders and to stop a resuscitation effort in progress.
- Federal agencies responsible for the direct provision of patient care (such as the Veterans Administration, the Public Health Service, and the Department of Defense) should ensure that their health care facilities adopt appropriate policies.

(23) The entry of an order not to resuscitate holds no necessary implications for any other therapeutic decisions, and the level or extent of health care that will be reimbursed under public or private insurance programs should never be linked to such orders.

(24) The education of health care professionals should ensure that they know how to help patients and family make ethically justified decisions for or against resuscitation; those responsible for professional licensure and certification may want to assess knowledge in these areas.

THE COMMISSION'S INQUIRY

When the Commission convened in January 1980, it decided to take up first its Congressional mandate to report on "the matter of defining death, including the advisability of developing a uniform definition of death." In July 1981 the Commission reported its conclusions in *Defining Death* and recommended the adoption of the Uniform Determination of Death Act (UDDA), which was developed in collaboration with the American Bar Association, the American Medical Association, and the National Conference of Commissioners on Uniform State Laws.

During hearings on this subject, the Commission learned that many people were troubled by the uncertainties about the correct care to provide for patients with serious deficits in "higher brain" functions — such as those required for thinking, communicating, and consciously responding to others or to the environment. Decisions about the care of such patients were seen to be at least as troubling as decisions about those who have permanently lost all brain functions. The most pointed example brought to the attention of the Commission is the group of patients who are so damaged as to be permanently devoid of any consciousness — the most severe brain damage compatible with life. The Commission concluded that the situation of such patients — like Karen Quinlan — merited its attention. In *Defining Death,* the Commission stated an intention to report subsequently on the treatment of patients who are dying but not dead.

The present study was undertaken not merely because of the study on the determination of death but also because of its broader relationship to work done by the Commission in several areas over the past three years. Under its mandate, the Commission is authorized to undertake investigation "of any other appropriate matter ... consistent with the purposes of [its authorizing statute] on its own initiative." Decisons about life-sustaining therapy involve the direct and concrete application of the principles of decisionmaking in medicine, which was the subject of the Commission's mandated study on informed consent. Such decisions also illustrate the ways questions of equity in the allocation of often scarce and expensive resources are resolved, a subject addressed by the Commission in another mandated study. The present Report thus represents an effort to apply the conclusions of two previous studies to a particular area of current concern, while also responding to some particularly difficult clinical and ethical problems noted in *Defining Death.*

The Commission received testimony and public comment on the subject of this Report at four public hearings in as many cities; witnesses from medicine, nursing, hospital administration, the social sciences, philosophy, theology, and law, as well as patients and family members, testified. It also deliberated on partial drafts of the Report at eight Commission meetings. On December 15, 1982, a final draft was discussed and approved unanimously, subject to editorial corrections....

The Elements of Good Decisionmaking

Patients whose medical conditions require treatment to sustain life usually want the treatment and benefit from it. Sometimes, however, a treatment is so undesirable in itself or the life it sustains is so brief and burdened that a patient — or a surrogate acting on the patient's behalf — decides that it would be better to forego the treatment....

SHARED DECISIONMAKING

In considering the issue of informed consent, the Commission recommended that patient and provider collaborate in a continuing process intended to make decisions that will advance the patient's interests both in health (and well-being generally) and in self-determination. The Commission argued that decisions about the treatments that best promote a patient's health and well-being must be based on the particular patient's values and goals; no uniform, objective determination can be adequate — whether defined by society or by health professionals.

Respect for the self-determination of competent patients is of special importance in decisions to forego life-sustaining treatment because different people will have markedly different needs and concerns during the final period of their lives; living a little longer will be of distinctly different value to them. Decisions about life-sustaining treatment, which commonly affect more than one goal of a patient (for example, prolongation of life and relief of suffering) create special tensions. Nonetheless, a process of collaborating and sharing information and responsibility between care givers and patients generally results in mutually satisfactory decisions. Even when it does not, the primacy of a patient's interests in self-determination and in honoring the patient's own view of well-being warrant leaving with the patient the final authority to decide....

In most circumstances, patients are presumed to be capable of making decisions about their own care. When a patient's capability to make final decisions is seriously limited, he or she needs to be protected against the adverse consequences of a flawed choice. Yet any mechanism that offers such protection also risks abuse; the individual's ability to direct his or her own life might be frustrated in an unwarranted manner. In its report on informed consent, the Commission recommended that a surrogate — typically a close relative or friend — be named when a patient lacks the capacity to make particular medical decisions. As much as possible, surrogates and providers of care should then make decisions as the particular patient would have....

Just as for medical treatment generally, deciding about a patient's decisionmaking abilities when the patient is facing a complex and confusing situation or making a decision of great consequence requires both the wise judgment of others and procedures that regularly yield morally and legally acceptable decisions. The Commission has found no reason for decisions about life-sustaining therapy to be considered differently from other treatment decisions. A decision to forego such treatment is awesome because it hastens death, but that does not change the elements of decisionmaking capacity and need not require greater abilities on the part of a patient. Decisions about the length of life are not necessarily more demanding of a patient's capabilities than other important decisions. And decisions that might shorten life are not always regarded by patients as difficult ones: a patient who even with treatment has a very short time to live may find a few additional hours rather unimportant, especially if the person has had a chance to take leave of loved ones and is reconciled to his or her situation.

Thus, determining whether or not a patient lacks the capacity to make a decision to forego life-sustaining treatment will rest on generally applicable principles for making assessments of decisional incapacity in medical care. Of course, when a patient who could have a substantial time to live rejects life-sustaining treatment, close inquiry into the components of that person's decisionmaking capacity is warranted in order to protect the individual from harms that arise from incapacities that themselves diminish the value of self-determination. . . .

Shaping the Patient's Deliberations

How information is communicated and continuing care is provided can forcefully induce a patient to make certain choices. In many medical care situations patients are dependent and professionals are relatively powerful. This disparity creates an obligation for professionals to reduce the understandable tendency of some patients to receive and act upon either a distorted understanding of their medical situation or a feeling of powerlessness, so that individuals can truly decide in accord with their own values and goals.

Helping to shape the deliberations of a patient who must decide about the course and duration of his or her life is a complex and weighty obligation. For example, letting a patient know that his or her death is now seen by others to be appropriate — or at least not unexpected — may be "giving permission to die" to a patient who no longer wishes to struggle against overwhelming odds. On the other hand, it may encourage overly rapid acceptance of death by a patient who feels rejected and unimportant.

Deciding on the best response and role is especially difficult for families and often inescapably uncertain. Clearly, family members do best by sustaining the patient's courage and hope, and by advancing the person's interests (and limiting self-serving actions) as much as possible. But family members usually cannot be dispassionate and emotionally uninvolved, nor should they try to be. In addition to any practical effects of the illness, they suffer from fear, anxiety, and grief — often as much or more than the patient. Thus, their ability to respond to the patient's needs is determined by their own capabilities under the circumstances. . . .

The individual health care provider is likely to help dying patients most by maintaining a predisposition for sustaining life (while accepting that a prolongation of dying may serve no worthwhile purpose for a particular patient). Indeed, this favoring of life is part of society's expectation regarding health care professionals. Commonly, it is supported by a personal belief or value commitment and by a recognition of the needs of dying patients for reassurance about the worth of their own lives. Until it is quite clear that a patient is making an informed, deliberate, and voluntary decision to forego specific life-sustaining interventions, health care providers should look for and enhance any feelings the patient has about not yet acquiescing in death. As death comes closer, such sentiments generally recede; until then, there need be no haste to encourage a patient's acceptance of death. . . .

Lawyers, health care professionals, and policymakers today are in general accord that treatment refusals by dying patients should be honored. Physicians commonly acquiesce in the wishes of competent patients not to receive specified treatments, even when failure to provide those treatments will increase the chance — or make certain — that the patient will die soon. When some patients are dying of a disease process that cannot be arrested, physicians may, for example, write orders not to provide resuscitation if the heart should stop, forego antibiotic treatment of pneumonia and other infections, cease use of respirators, or withhold aggressive therapy from overwhelmingly burned patients. Courts have sanctioned such decisions by guardians for incompetent patients, as well as by competent patients who might have lived for an indefinite period if treated. Although declining to start or continue life-sustaining treatment is often acceptable, health care providers properly refuse to honor a patient's request to be directly killed. Not only would killing, as by violence or strychnine, be outside the bounds of accepted medical practice, but as murder it would be subject to a range of criminal sanctions, regardless of the provider's motives. . . .

One serious consequence of maintaining the legal prohibition against direct killing of terminally ill patients could be the prolongation of suffering. In the final stages of some diseases, such as cancer, patients may undergo unbearable suffering that only ends in death. Some have claimed that sometimes the only way to improve such patients' lot is to actively and intentionally end their lives. If such steps are forbidden, physicians and family might be forced to deny these patients the relief they seek and to prolong their agony pointlessly.

If this were a common consequence of a policy prohibiting all active termination of human life, it should force a reevaluation of maintaining the prohibition. Rarely, however, does such suffering persist when there is adequate use of pain-relieving drugs and procedures. Health care professionals ought to realize that they are already authorized and obligated to use such means with a patient's or surrogate's consent, even if an earlier death is likely to result. The Commission endorses allowing physicians and patients to select treatments known to risk death in order to relieve suffering as well as to pursue a return to health. . . .

Discussions between a physician and competent patient . . . allow redefinition of their relationship and alteration of their expectations and thus of any resulting obligations. For example, a physician and patient could agree to a time-limited trial of a particular intervention, with an understanding that unless the therapy achieved certain goals it should be stopped. Moreover, these relationships and expectations, with their resultant obligations, need not be treated as fixed when public policy is being made but can be redefined where appropriate. Of course, most withdrawals of treatment involve explicit decisions while withholdings are commonly implicit and not clearly discussed (although, in conformity with the Commission's recommendations, they should be discussed, except in emergency situations). Although this may make the withdrawal of treatment more anguishing, or even more likely to precipitate external review, it does not make it morally different.

Adopting the opposite view — that treatment, once started, cannot be stopped, or that stopping requires much greater justification than not starting — is likely to have serious adverse consequences. Treatment might be continued for longer than is optimal for the patient, even to the point where it is causing positive harm with little or no compensating benefit. An even more troubling wrong occurs when a treatment that might save life or improve health is not started because the health care personnel are afraid that they will find it very difficult to stop the treatment if, as is fairly likely, it proves to be of little benefit and greatly burdens the patient. . . .

Ironically, if there is any call to draw a moral distinction between withholding and withdrawing, it generally cuts the opposite way from the usual formulation: greater justification ought to be required to withhold than to withdraw treatment. Whether a particular treatment will have positive effects is often highly uncertain before the therapy has been tried. If a trial of therapy makes clear that it is not helpful to the patient, this is actual evidence (rather than mere surmise) to support stopping because the therapeutic benefit that earlier was a possibility has been found to be clearly unobtainable. . . .

[Constraints on a Patient's Decision]

. . . Most patients' decisions about life-sustaining therapy involve the use of societal resources and thus have consequences for many other people. How and to what extent should the decisionmaking process take this into account?

Life-sustaining therapies can be very expensive. Even when a therapy itself is not expensive (such as antibiotic therapy for an infection or temporary intravenous feeding), the total expense of maintaining a patient who would not survive without the therapy can be substantial. Very few patients pay directly for health care. Instead, costs are routinely spread over large groups of people through public and private mechanisms, including private health insurance, government financing programs such as Medicare and Medicaid, and the provision of free care by governmental and charitable institutions. . . .

Undeniably, the role that health care plays in sustaining life is very important, but the fact that a therapy is life-sustaining does not automatically create an obligation to provide it. Rather, the therapy must offer benefits proportionate to the costs — financial and otherwise — and the benefit provided must be comparable to that provided other patients in similar circumstances. For example, care for chronic conditions that interfere with the enjoyment of life (for example, arthritis) might be given greater importance than care that merely sustains a very limited existence (such as artificial support of major organ systems for patients who are already bedridden and in pain).

Though it is acceptable in principle — and probably unavoidable in practice — to consider cost in deciding about health care, explicitly restricting treatment decisions on financial grounds poses significant dangers. Because people vary greatly in the value they attach to particular forms of life-extension, uniform rules based on objective measures of disease would create unacceptable consequences in some cases. For example, people differ in their attitudes about life on a respirator — some treasure each additional minute of life, whereas others find the treatment intolerable. And individual views change with time and circumstances; a patient may want very vigorous treatment until a family member who lives far away arrives or a grandchild is born, while finding the same treatment unwarranted thereafter. . . .

Although society might be justified in limiting access for some very costly forms of life-sustaining treatment, the Commission does not believe that it would now be wise to focus decisions about such therapy on the issue of cost-containment. Nor should discussions of cost-containment begin with consideration of life-sustaining treatments. If potential benefits must be foregone, they should first be in areas that allow more dispassionate reflection and opportunity to rectify errors. Where resource allocation policies do limit the availability of life-sustaining therapies, steps should be taken to help patients understand these policies and the reasons they were enacted. This will help patients accept the policies or see the need to seek alternative ways to obtain the desired care. More stringent constraints on the availability of life-sustaining therapies should not be imposed on those who are dependent on public programs than would be found acceptable by Americans who pay for their health care through private insurance coverage. . . .

[Inadequate Decisionmaking Capacity]

[SURROGATE DECISIONMAKING]

. . . When a patient lacks the capacity to make a decision, a surrogate decisionmaker should be designated. Ordinarily this will be the patient's next of kin, although it may be a close friend or another relative if the responsible health care professional judges that this other person is in fact the best advocate for the patient's interests.

The Commission's broad use of the term "family" reflects a recognition of the fact that often those with most knowledge and concern for a patient are not relatives by blood or marriage. Although more than one person may fall within this category, it will be necessary to designate one person as the principal decisionmaker for the incapacitated patient. One possibility is to define presumptive priority — for example, that a person living with his or her spouse will speak for that spouse, that adult children will speak for the elderly, widowed parents, etc. Although such presumptions may be helpful in some cases, the Commission believes that the health care practitioner is responsible for determining who should act as the patient's surrogate. No neat formulas will capture the complexities involved in determining who among a patient's friends and relatives knows the patient best and is most capable of making decisions in the patient's place. The responsibility is therefore on the practitioner either to assign this role of spokesperson (subject to appropriate institutional review) or to seek judicial appointment of a guardian.

The Commission believes that, for several reasons, a family member ought usually to be designated as surrogate to make health care decisions for an incapacitated patient in consultation with the physician and other health care professionals....

ADVANCE DIRECTIVES

An "advance directive" lets people anticipate that they may be unable to participate in future decisions about their own health care — an "instruction directive" specifies the types of care a person wants (or does not want) to receive; a "proxy directive" specifies the surrogate a person wants to make such decisions if the person is ever unable to do so; and the two forms may be combined. Honoring such a directive shows respect for self-determination in that it fulfills two of the three values that underlie self-determination. First, following a directive, particularly one that gives specific instructions about types of acceptable and unacceptable interventions, fulfills the instrumental role of self-determination by promoting the patient's subjective, individual evaluation of well-being. Second, honoring the directive shows respect for the patient as a person....

... The Commission commends the use of advance directives. Health care professionals should be familiar with their state's legal mechanisms for implementing advance directives on life-sustaining treatment and encourage patients to use these resources. In particular, practitioners can alert patients to the existence of durable power of attorney devices (in states where they exist) and urge them to discuss their desires about treatment with a proxy decisionmaker. In states without applicable legislation, practitioners can still inform their patients of the value of making their wishes known, whether through a living will or more individual instructions regarding the use of life-sustaining procedures under various circumstances.

Institutions concerned with patient and practitioner education have an important role to play in encouraging patients to become familiar with and use advance directives, and in familiarizing practitioners with the ethical and practical desirability of their patients using these mechanisms. Finally, legislators should be encouraged to draft flexible and clear statutes that give appropriate legal authority to those who write and rely upon advance directives. Such legislation needs to balance the provisions aimed at restricting likely abuses and those intended to allow flexibility and individuality for patients and proxies....

[Permanent Loss of Consciousness]

... Physicians arrive at prognoses of permanent unconsciousness only after patients have received vigorous medical attention, careful observation, and complete diagnostic studies, usually over a prolonged period.

During this time when improvement is thought to be possible, it is appropriate for therapies to be intensive and aggressive, both to reverse unconsciousness and to overcome any other problems. Once it is clear that the loss of consciousness is permanent, however, the goals of continued therapy need to be examined.

... The primary basis for medical treatment of patients is the prospect that each individual's interests (specifically, the interest in well-being) will be promoted. Thus, treatment ordinarily aims to benefit a patient through preserving life, relieving pain and suffering, protecting against disability, and returning maximally effective functioning. If a prognosis of permanent unconsciousness is correct, however, continued treatment cannot confer such benefits. Pain and suffering are absent, as are joy, satisfaction, and pleasure. Disability is total and no return to an even minimal level of social or human functioning is possible.

Any value to the patient from continued care and maintenance under such circumstances would seem to reside in the very small probability that the prognosis of permanence is incorrect. Although therapy might appear to be in the patient's interest because it preserves the remote chance of recovery of consciousness, there are two substantial objections to providing vigorous therapy for permanently unconscious patients.

First, the few patients who have recovered consciousness after a prolonged period of unconsciousness were severely disabled. The degree of permanent damage varied but commonly included inability to speak or see, permanent distortion of the limbs, and paralysis. Being returned to such a state would be regarded as of very limited benefit by most patients; it may even be considered harmful if a particular patient would have refused treatments expected to produce this outcome. Thus, even the extremely small likelihood of "recovery" cannot be equated with returning to a normal or relatively well functioning state. Second, long-term treatment commonly imposes severe financial and emotional burdens on a patient's family, people whose welfare most patients, before they lost consciousness, placed a high value on. For both these reasons, then, continued treatment beyond a minimal level will often not serve the interests of permanently unconscious patients optimally. ...

When there are several treatment options that are acceptable to all interested parties and there is no advance directive from the patient, the option actually followed should generally be the one selected by the family. When no alternative is acceptable to all concerned, an attempt to reach an acceptable compromise is preferable to forcing a confrontation. If substitution of another provider, institution, or funding would achieve accord and is possible, such a course should be followed. Where institutional ethics committees exist, their assistance should be sought since the advice of a group of concerned but disinterested people may foster understanding and agreement.

If disagreement between at least two of these parties — the health care professionals, the family members, and the institution — persists after institutional review, recourse to the courts for the appointment of a guardian may be both appropriate and unavoidable. Any physician involved in such a proceeding is under a strong moral obligation to assist in educating the lawyers and the court about the complexities of the situation. Courts ought to avoid deciding among treatment options, however, because explicit judicial decisions may prematurely rigidify the options available and paralyze the exercise of judgment by the parties directly involved. Rather, the court should appoint a responsible surrogate who is charged with collecting and considering the relevant information and making a decision, which might then be reported to the court. . . .

In sum, the Commission finds good decisionmaking regarding patients who have permanently lost consciousness to be possible without changes in law or other public policy. The medical profession should continue to carry its weighty obligation to establish diagnoses well and to help families understand these tragic situations. Health care institutions need to provide good policies to govern decisionmaking, including appropriate sources of consultation and advice. Family and friends of the permanently unconscious patient bear not only the protracted tragedy of their loss but also the substantial responsibility of collaborating in decisionmaking. When families can direct the care of an unconscious family member, practices and policies should encourage them to do so and should restrict the degree to which outsiders may intervene in these matters. Courts and legislatures should not encourage routine resort to the judicial system for the actual decisionmaking. Instead, courts ought to ensure that appropriate surrogates are designated and that surrogates are allowed an appropriate range of discretion.

Seriously Ill Newborns

. . . Remarkable advances in neonatal care now make it possible to sustain the lives of many newborn infants who only one or two decades ago would have died in the first days or weeks after birth. Between 1970 and 1980, the death rate in the first 28 days of life (the neonatal period) was almost halved, the greatest proportional decrease in any decade since national birth statistics were first gathered in 1915. Improvement among the smallest infants — those at greatest risk of death and illness — has been especially dramatic: for newborns weighing 1000-1500 grams, the mortality rate has dropped from 50% to 20% since 1961; fully half the live-born infants weighing less than 1000 grams (2.2 pounds) now survive, compared with less than 10% just 20 years ago. And marked improvements have also been reported in the survival rate of infants with certain congenital defects.

Not all seriously ill newborns fare well, however. Some infants with low birth weight or severe defects cannot survive for long, despite the most aggressive efforts to save them; others suffer severe impairments either as a component of their conditions or as a result of treatments. Thus medicine's increased ability to forestall death in seriously ill newborns has magnified the already difficult task of physicians and parents who must attempt to assess which infants will benefit from various medical interventions, and which will not. Not only does this test the limits of medical certainty in diagnosis and prognosis, it also raises profound ethical issues. . . .

Two types of congenital abnormalities have been especially prominent in discussions of the ethics of neonatal care: neural tube defects (NTDs), and permanent handicaps combined with surgically correctable, life-threatening lesions. Defects involving the neural tube, which is the embryonic precursor of the brain and spinal cord, are among the most common serious birth defects of unknown etiology, affecting approximately two of every 1000 babies born in the United States. One type of NTD is anencephaly, a condition in which the brain is entirely or substantially absent. Anencephalic infants usually die within a few hours or days. Another type of NTD, meningomyelocele (spina bifida) involves abnormal development of the brain or spinal cord. Spina bifida causes physical and/or mental impairments that range widely in severity and frequently involve many organ systems. Vigorous surgical, medical and rehabilitative therapies have improved the prognosis for many children with spina bifida. Some individuals with this condition have normal intelligence and can lead independent lives.

Public attention has recently been focused on the second group of cases — infants who have both a correctable life-threatening defect *and* a permanent, irremediable handicap that is not life-threatening, such as mental retardation. One well-known example is Down Syndrome, which occurs once in about every 700 live births. Individuals with Down Syndrome are mentally retarded, although the precise extent of retardation cannot be determined in early infancy. Babies with this syndrome often have other congenital defects, particularly cardiac abnormalities. Most Down Syndrome infants do not require any unusual medical care at birth, but a minority have a complication that would be fatal unless surgically corrected during the first year of life. The two most common problems are gastrointestinal blockage and congenital heart defects. Children with an obstruction at the outlet of the stomach, for example, cannot be fed; untreated, they would develop a fatal pneumonia or starve to death. Surgical repair of this defect, however, is typically successful. . . .

CURRENT DECISIONMAKING PRACTICES

. . . A major stimulus to the ethical and legal debate on foregoing life-sustaining treatment for newborns was provided by a 1973 medical journal article that described how and why nontreatment had been chosen for 43 of the 299 babies who died in a 30-month period in the intensive care nursery of Yale-New Haven Hospital. The decision against treatment followed deliberations in which "parents and physicians . . . concluded that prognosis for meaningful life was extremely poor or hopeless." The authors argued strongly for leaving such decisions to parents and physicians.

Other physicians confirmed that decisions to forego therapy are part of everyday life in the neonatal intensive care unit; with rare exceptions, these choices have been made by parents and physicians without review by courts or any other body. This approach has been endorsed by the American Medical Association, whose Judicial Council holds that "the decision whether to exert maximal efforts to sustain life [of seriously deformed newborns] should be the choice of the parents.". . .

AN ETHICAL BASIS FOR DECISIONMAKING

Since newborns are unable to make decisions, they will always need a surrogate to decide for them. In nearly all cases, parents are best situated to collaborate with practitioners in making decisions about an infant's care, and the range of choices practitioners offer should normally reflect the parents' preferences regarding treatment. . . . Parents are usually present, concerned, willing to become informed, and cognizant of the values of the culture in which the child will be raised. They can be expected to try to make decisions that advance the newborn's best interests. Health care professionals and institutions, and society generally, bear responsibility to ensure that decisionmaking practices are adequate. . . .

When parental decisionmaking seems not to take account of a child's best interest, however, the stage is set for public intervention. This issue has usually arisen in cases in which the parent's values differ from those

Treatment Options for Seriously Ill Newborns—Physician's Assessment in Relation to Parent's Preference

Physician's Assessment of Treatment Options*	Parents Prefer to Accept Treatment**	Parents Prefer to Forego Treatment**
Clearly beneficial	Provide treatment	Provide treatment during review process
Ambiguous or uncertain	Provide treatment	Forego treatment
Futile	Provide treatment	Forego treatment unless provider declines to do so

* The assessment of the value to the infant of the treatments available will initially be by the attending physician. Both when this assessment is unclear and when the joint decision between parents and physician is to forego treatment, this assessment would be reviewed by intra-institutional mechanisms and possibly thereafter by court.
** The choice made by the infant's parents or other duly authorized surrogate who has adequate decisionmaking capacity and has been adequately informed, based on their assessment of the infant's best interests.

common in society. For example, parents are free to inculcate in their children a religious belief that precludes the acceptance of transfused blood. But when a transfusion is necessary for the success of surgery that would be life-saving or without which a child would suffer substantial, irreversible harm, parents' prerogatives must yield to the child's interest in life or in leading a reasonably healthy life. Parents are not, as the Supreme court has stated, entitled to make martyrs of their children. . . .

Many therapies undertaken to save the lives of seriously ill newborns will leave the survivors with permanent handicaps, either from the underlying defect (such as heart surgery not affecting the retardation of a Down Syndrome infant) or from the therapy itself (as when mechanical ventilation for a premature baby results in blindness or a scarred trachea). One of the most troubling and persistent issues in this entire area is whether, or to what extent, the expectation of such handicaps should be considered in deciding to treat or not to treat a seriously ill newborn. The Commission has concluded that a very restrictive standard is appropriate: such permanent handicaps justify a decision not to provide life-sustaining treatment only when they are so severe that continued existence would not be a net benefit to the infant. Though inevitably somewhat subjective and imprecise in actual application, the concept of "benefit" excludes honoring idiosyncratic views that might be allowed if a person were deciding about his or her own treatment. Rather, net benefit is absent only if the burdens imposed on the patient by the disability or its treatment would lead a competent decisionmaker to choose to forego the treatment. As in all surrogate decisionmaking, the surrogate is obligated to try to evaluate benefits and burdens from the infant's own perspective. The Commission believes that the handicaps of Down Syndrome, for example, are not in themselves of this magnitude and do not justify failing to provide medically proven treatment, such as surgical correction of a blocked intestinal tract.

This is a very strict standard in that it excludes consideration of the negative effects of an impaired child's life on other persons, including parents, siblings, and society. Although abiding by this standard may be difficult in specific cases, it is all too easy to undervalue the lives of handicapped infants; the Commission finds it imperative to counteract this by treating them no less vigorously than their healthy peers or than older children with similar handicaps would be treated.

. . . When there is no therapy that can benefit an infant, as in anencephaly or certain severe cardiac deformities, a decision by surrogates and providers not to try predictably futile endeavors is ethically and legally justifiable. Such therapies do not help the child, are sometimes painful for the infant (and probably distressing to the parents), and offer no reasonable probability of saving life for a substantial period. The moment of death for these infants might be delayed for a short time — perhaps as long as a few weeks — by vigorous therapy. Of course, the prolongation of life — and hope against hope — may be enough to lead some parents to want to try a therapy believed by physicians to be futile.

As long as this choice does not cause substantial suffering for the child, providers should accept it, although individual health care professionals who find it personally offensive to engage in futile treatment may arrange to withdraw from the case.

Just as with older patients, even when cure or saving of life are out of reach, obligations to comfort and respect a dying person remain. Thus infants whose lives are destined to be brief are owed whatever relief from suffering and enhancement of life can be provided, including feeding, medication for pain, and sedation, as appropriate. Moreover, it may be possible for parents to hold and comfort the child once the elaborate means of life support are withdrawn, which can be very important to all concerned in symbolic and existential as well as physical terms. . . .

The Commission concludes that hospitals that care for seriously ill newborns should have explicit policies on decisionmaking procedures in cases involving life-sustaining treatment for these infants; accrediting bodies could appropriately require this. Such policies should provide for internal review whenever parents and the attending physician decide that life-sustaining therapy should be foregone. Other cases, such as when the physician and parents disagree, might well also be reviewed. The policy should allow for different types of review and be flexible enough to deal appropriately with the range of cases that could arise. Some cases may require only a medical consultation to confirm a diagnosis of an inevitably fatal condition, for example. In other cases, when the benefits of therapy are less clear, an "ethics committee" or similar body might be designated to review the decisionmaking process. This approach would ensure that an individual or group whose function is to promote good decisionmaking reviews the most difficult cases. Cases included in this category should certainly encompass those in which a decision to forego life-sustaining therapy has been proposed because of a physical or mental handicap, as well as cases where a dispute has arisen among care givers and surrogates over the proper course of treatment. . . .

REAGAN ON DEFENSE IN SPACE

March 23, 1983

In a nationally televised address billed as the first in a series of statements intended to dramatize the magnitude of the Soviet strategic threat and to win support for deploying new missile systems, President Ronald Reagan March 23 held out the possibility of a radical break with post-World War II strategic defense concepts.

Instead of the current policy of deterrence — threatening massive nuclear retaliation to forestall a Soviet attack on the United States — Reagan proposed developing weapons that could destroy missiles launched by the U.S.S.R. before they hit the United States. According to Reagan, such a shift in policy held out "the promise of changing the course of human history."

Reagan gave no details about the plan in calling on the scientific community to undertake "a long-term research and development program to begin to achieve our ultimate goal of eliminating the threat posed by strategic nuclear missiles." On March 23 he issued an executive order calling for an "intensive effort" to "define a long-term development program" for missile defense. Administration officials acknowledged that the project would take decades to reach fruition, with no guarantee of success.

As of 1983, approximately $1 billion annually was being spent on developing laser and particle beam projects in the United States. The administration planned to increase spending for space military projects, amounting to about $8.5 billion in 1983, by 10 percent each year over a five-year period.

Mixed Reaction to Proposal

The president's futuristic proposal encountered a mixed reception. The feasibility of such a system was questioned, and many members of Congress expressed concern about the potentially destabilizing impact it would have on the arms race. Sen. Edward M. Kennedy, D-Mass., called the proposal a "reckless Star Wars scheme." Possession by one side of a system thought to be a foolproof missile defense might lead an aggressor to feel it could launch a nuclear surprise attack against the other side while being confident that a retaliatory blow could be stopped or deterred with its own defensive missiles.

A number of European commentators maintained that emphasizing a U.S. missile defense system aimed primarily at Soviet intercontinental ballistic missiles (ICBMs) would "decouple" Western Europe from the U.S. security umbrella.

Denouncing the proposal as "irresponsible," Soviet leader Yuri Andropov said it would "open the floodgates to a runaway race for all types of strategic arms, both defensive and offensive." Andropov added that in embarking on arms control negotiations the two superpowers had "agreed that there is an inseverable interrelationship between strategic offensive and defensive weapons." He said it was "not by chance" that the 1972 Anti-Ballistic Missile (ABM) Treaty was signed simultaneously with the treaty limiting strategic arms (SALT I). He warned that "the Soviet Union will never allow" the development of ABM systems that could render its ICBMs impotent.

Some American observers contended that Reagan's proposal would violate the terms of the 1972 ABM treaty, under which each party agreed "not to deploy ABM systems for a defense of the territory of its country." (Each side originally was allowed to construct two ABM systems; this subsequently was reduced to one.) According to Gerard C. Smith, who was the chief U.S. negotiator to the SALT I negotiations, the only objective interpretation of the treaty was that "any exotic system is banned."

Reagan acknowledged the problems associated with an ABM system. "I clearly recognize that defensive systems have limitations and raise certain problems and ambiguities," he said in his speech. "If paired with offensive systems, they can be viewed as fostering an aggressive policy and no one wants that."

The president's emphasis on a defense system echoed the call sounded for a number of years by a small but energetic band of military experts, scientists and conservatives. Its leading spokesman in Congress was Sen. Malcolm Wallop, R-Wyo., who claimed that new breakthroughs in anti-missile technology made Reagan's proposal feasible. "As a practical matter, in order to minimize the number of Soviet warheads reaching the U.S., we are going to have to build systems to destroy Soviet missiles in flight," Wallop wrote in The Washington Post *February 6, 1983. "I believe a variety of good defenses against ballistic missiles is possible. . . . The technology of space-based lasers gives substantial hope that attacking Soviet missiles could be defeated, or at the very least severely thinned, just after they rose out of the atmosphere."*

Wallop's view was supported by a blue-ribbon panel of scientists chaired by the former director of the National Aeronautics and Space Administration, James C. Fletcher. The panel, established after Reagan's March speech, explored the technical feasibility of various defense systems and recommended that spending for research in the area be increased to as much as $27 billion for the fiscal 1985-89 period.

Testifying before the House Armed Services Committee November 10, Pentagon research chief Richard D. DeLauer cautioned that it would take two decades to develop a nationwide shield against Soviet nuclear missiles, and he warned the panel it would be "staggered by the cost" of deploying such a defense.

Budget Battle, Soviet Threat

In other aspects of his address, Reagan broke no dramatic new ground in his running battle with Congress over his $280.5 billion fiscal 1984 defense budget request. The president had begun his public battle against defense cuts March 18, as part of a broadside against a budget resolution drafted by House Democrats that would trim the defense request. "Nothing could bring greater joy to the Kremlin than to see the United States abandon its defense rebuilding program after barely one year," Reagan warned.

Reagan spent much of his 30-minute March 23 speech detailing the Soviet buildup since 1974 of "what can only be considered an offensive force. . . . They didn't stop when their forces exceeded any requirements of a legitimate defensive capability." The president illustrated his remarks with a number of photographs taken by U.S. reconnaissance planes of Soviet-manufactured equipment in Cuba and Nicaragua and military installations built with Cuban assistance on the Caribbean island of Grenada. (The airfield in Grenada, built with Soviet and Cuban assistance, became the object of a U.S. invasion in late October. See p. 847.)

These military installations illustrated the extent to which Moscow had become emboldened in the use of its power, Reagan argued. His own defense budget, aimed at countering that Soviet buildup, already had been "trimmed to the limits of safety," Reagan said. "There is no logical way that you can say, let's spend x billion dollars less," he insisted. "You can only say, which part of our defense measures do we believe we can do without and still have security against all contingencies?"

In a televised response taped on behalf of congressional Democrats,

Sen. Daniel K. Inouye, D-Hawaii, said that Reagan understated U.S. military strengths: "You have failed to present an honest picture," Inouye charged.

> *Following is the text of President Reagan's televised address on defense policy, delivered March 23, 1983.* (Boldface headings in brackets have been added by Congressional Quarterly to highlight the organization of the text.)

My fellow Americans, thank you for sharing your time with me tonight.

The subject I want to discuss with you, peace and national security, is both timely and important. Timely, because I've reached a decision which offers a new hope for our children in the 21st century, a decision I'll tell you about in a few minutes. And important because there's a very big decision that you must make for yourselves. This subject involves the most basic duty that any President and any people share, the duty to protect and strengthen the peace.

At the beginning of this year, I submitted to the Congress a defense budget which reflects my best judgment of the best understanding of the experts and specialists who advise me about what we and our allies must do to protect our people in the years ahead. That budget is much more than a long list of numbers, for behind all the numbers lies America's ability to prevent the greatest of human tragedies and preserve our free way of life in a sometimes dangerous world. It is part of a careful, long-term plan to make America strong again after too many years of neglect and mistakes.

Our efforts to rebuild America's defenses and strengthen the peace began 2 years ago when we requested a major increase in the defense program. Since then, the amount of those increases we first proposed has been reduced by half, through improvements in management and procurement and other savings.

The budget request that is now before the Congress has been trimmed to the limits of safety. Further deep cuts cannot be made without seriously endangering the security of the Nation. The choice is up to the men and women you have elected to the Congress, and that means the choice is up to you.

Tonight, I want to explain to you what this defense debate is all about and why I'm convinced that the budget now before the Congress is necessary, responsible, and deserving of your support. And I want to offer hope for the future.

But first, let me say what the defense debate is not about. It is not about spending arithmetic. I know that in the last few weeks you've been bombarded with numbers and percentages. Some say we need only a 5-percent increase in defense spending. The so-called alternate budget backed by liberals in the House of Representatives would lower the figure to 2 to 3 percent, cutting our defense spending by $163 billion over the next 5 years. The trouble with all these numbers is that they tell us little about the kind of defense program America needs or the benefits in security and freedom that our defense effort buys for us.

What seems to have been lost in all this debate is the simple truth of how a defense budget is arrived at. It isn't done by deciding to spend a certain number of dollars. Those loud voices that are occasionally heard charging that the Government is trying to solve a security problem by throwing money at it are nothing more than noise based on ignorance. We start by considering what must be done to maintain peace and review all the possible threats against our security. Then a strategy for strengthening peace and defending against those threats must be agreed upon. And, finally, our defense establishment must be evaluated to see what is necessary to protect against any or all of the potential threats. The cost of achieving these ends is totaled up and the result is the budget for national defense.

There is no logical way that you can say, let's spend x billion dollars less. You can only say, which part of our defense measures do we believe we can do without and still have security against all contingencies? Anyone in the Congress who advocates a percentage or a specific dollar cut in defense spending should be made to say what part of our defenses he would eliminate, and he should be candid enough to acknowledge that his cuts mean cutting our commitments to allies or inviting greater risk or both.

The defense policy of the United States is based on a simple premise: The United States does not start fights. We will never be an aggressor. We maintain our strength in order to deter and defend against aggression — to preserve freedom and peace.

Since the dawn of the atomic age, we've sought to reduce the risk of war by maintaining a strong deterrent and by seeking genuine arms control. "Deterrence" means simply this: making sure any adversary who thinks about attacking the United States, or our allies, or our vital interests, concludes that the risks to him outweigh any potential gains. Once he understands that, he won't attack. We maintain the peace through our strength; weakness only invites aggression.

This strategy of deterrence has not changed. It still works. But what it takes to maintain deterrence has changed. It took one kind of military force to deter an attack when we had far more nuclear weapons than any other power; it takes another kind now that the Soviets, for example, have enough accurate and powerful nuclear weapons to destroy virtually all of our missiles on the ground. Now, this is not to say that the Soviet Union is planning to make war on us. Nor do I believe a war is inevitable — quite the contrary. But what must be recognized is that our security is based on being prepared to meet all threats.

There was a time when we depended on coastal forts and artillery batteries, because, with the weaponry of that day, any attack would have had to come by sea. Well, this is a different world, and our defenses must be based on recognition and awareness of the weaponry possessed by other nations in the nuclear age.

We can't afford to believe that we will never be threatened. There have been two world wars in my lifetime. We didn't start them and, indeed, did everything we could to avoid being drawn into them. But we were ill-prepared for both — had we been better prepared, peace might have been preserved.

[Soviet Military Buildup]

For 20 years, the Soviet Union has been accumulating enormous military might. They didn't stop when their forces exceeded all requirements of a legitimate defensive capability. And they haven't stopped now. During the past decade and a half, the Soviets have built up a massive arsenal of new strategic nuclear weapons — weapons that can strike directly at the United States.

As an example, the United States introduced its last new intercontinental ballistic missile, the Minute Man III, in 1969, and we're now dismantling our even older Titan missiles. But what has the Soviet Union done in these intervening years? Well, since 1969 the Soviet Union has built five new classes of ICBM's, and upgraded these eight times. As a result, their missiles are much more powerful and accurate than they were several years ago, and they continue to develop more, while ours are increasingly obsolete.

The same thing has happened in other areas. Over the same period, the Soviet Union built 4 new classes of submarine-launched ballistic missiles and over 60 new missile submarines. We built 2 new types of submarine missiles and actually withdrew 10 submarines from strategic missions. The Soviet Union built over 200 new Backfire bombers, and their brand new Blackjack bomber is now under development. We haven't built a new long-range bomber since our B-52's were deployed about a quarter of a century ago, and we've already retired several hundred of those because of old age. Indeed, despite what many people think, our strategic forces only cost about 15 percent of the defense budget.

Another example of what's happened: In 1978 the Soviets had 600 intermediate-range nuclear missiles based on land and were beginning to add the SS-20 — a new, highly accurate, mobile missile, with 3 warheads. We had none. Since then the Soviets have strengthened their lead. By the end of 1979, when Soviet leader Brezhnev declared "a balance now exists," the Soviets had over 800 warheads. We still had none. A year ago this month, Mr. Brezhnev pledged a moratorium, or freeze, on SS-20 deployment. But by last August, their 800 warheads had become more than 1,200. We still had none. Some freeze. At this time Soviet Defense Minister Ustinov announced "approximate parity of forces continues to exist." But the Soviets are still adding an average of 3 new warheads a week, and now have 1,300. These warheads can reach their targets in a matter of a few minutes. We still have none. So far, it seems that the Soviet definition of parity is a box score of 1,300 to nothing, in their favor.

So, together with our NATO allies, we decided in 1979 to deploy new weapons, beginning this year, as a deterrent to their SS-20's and as an incentive to the Soviet Union to meet us in serious arms control negotiations. We will begin that deployment late this year. At the same time, however, we're willing to cancel our program if the Soviets will dismantle theirs. This is what we've called a zero-zero plan. The Soviets are now at the negotiating table — and I think it's fair to say that without our planned deployments, they wouldn't be there.

Now, let's consider conventional forces. Since 1974 the United States has produced 3,050 tactical combat aircraft. By contrast, the Soviet Union has produced twice as many. When we look at attack submarines, the United States has produced 27 while the Soviet Union has produced 61. For armored vehicles, including tanks, we have produced 1,200. The Soviet Union has produced 54,000 — nearly 5 to 1 in their favor. Finally, with artillery, we have produced 950 artillery and rocket launchers while the Soviets have produced more than 13,000 — a staggering 14 to 1 ratio.

There was a time when we were able to offset superior Soviet numbers with higher quality, but today they are building weapons as sophisticated and modern as our own.

[Threat of Soviet Expansionism]

As the Soviets have increased their military power, they have been emboldened to extend that power. They're spreading their military influence in ways that can directly challenge our vital interests and those of our allies.

The following aerial photographs, most of them secret until now, illustrate this point in a crucial area very close to home: Central America and the Caribbean Basin. They're not dramatic photographs. But I think they help give you a better understanding of what I'm talking about.

This Soviet intelligence collection facility, less than a hundred miles from our coast, is the largest of its kind in the world. The acres and acres of antennae fields and intelligence monitors are targeted on key U.S. military installations and sensitive activities. The installation in Lourdes, Cuba, is manned by 1,500 Soviet technicians. And the satellite ground station allows instant communications with Moscow. This 28-square-mile facility has grown by more than 60 percent in size and capability during the past decade.

In western Cuba, we see this military airfield and it [sic] complement of modern, Soviet-built Mig-23 aircraft. The Soviet Union uses this Cuban airfield for its own long-range reconnaissance missions. And earlier this month, two modern Soviet antisubmarine warfare aircraft began operating from it. During the past 2 years, the level of Soviet arms exports to Cuba can only be compared to the levels reached during the Cuban missile crisis 20 years ago.

This third photo, which is the only one in this series that has been previously made public, shows Soviet military hardware that has made its way to Central America. This airfield with its MI-8 helicopters, anti-aircraft guns, and protected fighter sites is one of a number of military facilities in Nicaragua which has received Soviet equipment funneled through Cuba, and reflects the massive military buildup going on in that country.

On the small island of Grenada, at the southern end of the Caribbean chain, the Cubans, with Soviet financing and backing, are in the process of building an airfield with a 10,000-foot runway. Grenada doesn't even have an air force. Who is it intended for? The Caribbean is a very important passageway for our international commerce and military lines of communication. More than half of all American oil imports now pass through the Caribbean. The rapid buildup of Grenada's military potential is unrelated to any conceivable threat to this island country of under 110,000 people and totally at odds with the pattern of other eastern Caribbean States, most of which are unarmed.

The Soviet-Cuban militarization of Grenada, in short, can only be seen as power projection into the region. And it is in this important economic and strategic area that we're trying to help the governments of El Salvador, Costa Rica, Honduras, and others in their struggles for democracy against guerrillas supported through Cuba and Nicaragua.

These pictures only tell a small part of the story. I wish I could show you more without compromising our most sensitive intelligence sources and methods. But the Soviet Union is also supporting Cuban military forces in Angola and Ethiopia. They have bases in Ethiopia and South Yemen, near the Persian Gulf oil fields. They've taken over the port that we built at Cam Ranh Bay in Vietnam. And now for the first time in history, the Soviet Navy is a force to be reckoned with in the South Pacific.

Some people may still ask: Would the Soviets ever use their formidable military power? Well, again, can we afford to believe they won't? There is Afghanistan. And in Poland, the Soviets denied the will of the people and in so doing demonstrated to the world how their military power could also be used to intimidate.

The final fact is that the Soviet Union is acquiring what can only be considered an offensive military force. They have continued to build far more intercontinental ballistic missiles than they could possibly need simply to deter an attack. Their conventional forces are trained and equipped not so much to defend against an attack as they are to permit sudden, surprise offensives of their own.

Our NATO allies have assumed a great defense burden, including the military draft in most countries. We're working with them and our other friends around the world to do more. Our defensive strategy means we need military forces that can move very quickly, forces that are trained and ready to respond to any emergency.

Every item in our defense program — our ships, our tanks, our planes, our funds for training and spare parts — is intended for one all-important purpose: to keep the peace. Unfortunately, a decade of neglecting our military forces had called into question our ability to do that.

When I took office in January 1981, I was appalled by what I found: American planes that couldn't fly and American ships that couldn't sail for lack of spare parts and trained personnel and insufficient fuel and ammunition for essential training. The inevitable result of all this was poor morale in our Armed Forces, difficulty in recruiting the brightest young Americans to wear the uniform, and difficulty in convincing our most experienced military personnel to stay on.

There was a real question then about how well we could meet a crisis. And it was obvious that we had to begin a major modernization program to ensure we could deter aggression and preserve the peace in the years ahead.

We had to move immediately to improve the basic readiness and staying power of our conventional forces, so they could meet — and therefore help deter — a crisis. We had to make up for lost years of investment by moving forward with a long-term plan to prepare our forces to counter the military capabilities our adversaries were developing for the future.

I know that all of you want peace, and so do I. I know too that many of you seriously believe that a nuclear freeze would further the cause of peace. But a freeze now would make us less, not more, secure and would raise, not reduce, the risks of war. It would be largely unverifiable and would seriously undercut our negotiations on arms reduction. It would reward the Soviets for their massive military buildup while preventing us from modernizing our aging and increasingly vulnerable forces. With their present margin of superiority, why should they agree to arms reductions knowing that we were prohibited from catching up?

Believe me, it wasn't pleasant for someone who had come to Washington determined to reduce government spending, but we had to move forward with the task of repairing our defenses or we would lose our ability to deter conflict now and in the future. We had to demonstrate to any adversary that aggression could not succeed, and that the only real solution was substantial, equitable, and effectively verifiable arms reduction — the kind we're working for right now in Geneva.

[Rebuilding American Military]

Thanks to your strong support, and bipartisan support from the Congress, we began to turn things around. Already, we're seeing some very encouraging results. Quality recruitment and retention are up dramatically — more high school graduates are choosing military careers, and more experienced career personnel are choosing to stay. Our men and women in uniform at last are getting the tools and training they need to do their jobs.

Ask around today, especially among our young people, and I think you will find a whole new attitude toward serving their country. This reflects more than just better pay, equipment, and leadership. You the American people have sent a signal to these young people that it is once again an honor to wear the uniform. That's not something you measure in a budget, but it's a very real part of our nation's strength.

It'll take us longer to build the kind of equipment we need to keep peace in the future, but we've made a good start.

We haven't built a new long-range bomber for 21 years. Now we're building the B-1. We hadn't launched one new strategic submarine for 17 years. Now we're building one Trident submarine a year. Our land-based missiles are increasingly threatened by the many huge, new Soviet ICBM's. We're determining how to solve that problem. At the same time, we're working in the START [Strategic Arms Reduction Talks] and INF [Intermediate Nuclear Force] negotiations with the goal of achieving deep reductions in the strategic and intermediate nuclear arsenals of both sides.

We have also begun the long-needed modernization of our conventional forces. The Army is getting its first new tank in 20 years. The Air Force is modernizing. We're rebuilding our Navy, which shrank from about a thousand ships in the late 1960's to 453 during the 1970's. Our nation needs a superior navy to support our military forces and vital interests overseas. We're now on the road to achieving a 600-ship navy and increasing the amphibious capabilities of our marines, who are now serving the cause of peace in Lebanon. And we're building a real capability to assist our friends in the vitally important Indian Ocean and Persian Gulf region.

This adds up to a major effort, and it isn't cheap. It comes at a time when there are many other pressures on our budget and when the American people have already had to make major sacrifices during the recession. But we must not be misled by those who would make defense once again the scapegoat of the Federal budget.

The fact is that in the past few decades we have seen a dramatic shift in how we spend the taxpayer's dollar. Back in 1955, payments to individuals took up only about 20 percent of the Federal budget. For nearly three decades, these payments steadily increased and this year will account for 49 percent of the budget. By contrast, in 1955 defense took up more than half of the Federal budget. By 1980 this spending had fallen to a low of 23 percent. Even with the increase that I am requesting this year, defense will still amount to only 28 percent of the budget.

The calls for cutting back the defense budget come in nice, simple arithmetic. They're the same kind of talk that led the democracies to neglect their defenses in the 1930's and invited the tragedy of World War II. We must not let that grim chapter of history repeat itself through apathy or neglect.

This is why I'm speaking to you tonight — to urge you to tell your Senators and Congressmen that you know we must continue to restore our military strength. If we stop in midstream, we will send a signal of decline, of lessened will, to friends and adversaries alike. Free people must voluntarily, through open debate and democratic means, meet the challenge that totalitarians pose by compulsion. It's up to us, in our time, to choose and choose wisely between the hard but necessary task of preserving peace and freedom and the temptation to ignore our duty and blindly hope for the best while the enemies of freedom grow stronger day by day.

The solution is well within our grasp. But to reach it, there is simply no alternative but to continue this year, in this budget, to provide the resources we need to preserve the peace and guarantee our freedom.

Now, thus far tonight I've shared with you my thoughts on the problems of national security we must face together. My predecessors in the Oval Office have appeared before you on other occasions to describe the threat posed by Soviet power and have proposed steps to address that threat. But since the advent of nuclear weapons, those steps have been increasingly directed toward deterrence of aggression through the promise of retaliation.

This approach to stability through offensive threat has worked. We and our allies have succeeded in preventing nuclear war for more than three decades. In recent months, however, my advisers, including in particular the Joint Chiefs of Staff, have underscored the necessity to break out of a future that relies solely on offensive retaliation for our security.

Over the course of these discussions, I have become more and more deeply convinced that the human spirit must be capable of rising above dealing with other nations and human beings by threatening their existence. Feeling this way, I believe we must thoroughly examine every opportunity for reducing tensions and for introducing greater stability into the strategic calculus on both sides.

One of the most important contributions we can make is, of course, to lower the level of all arms, and particularly nuclear arms. We're engaged right now in several negotiations with the Soviet Union to bring about a mutual reduction of weapons. I will report to you a week from tomorrow my thoughts on that score. But let me just say, I'm totally committed to this course.

If the Soviet Union will join with us in our effort to achieve major reduction, we will have succeeded in stabilizing the nuclear balance. Nevertheless, it will still be necessary to rely on the specter of retaliation, on mutual threat. And that's a sad commentary on the human condition. Wouldn't it be better to save lives than to avenge them? Are we not capable of demonstrating our peaceful intentions by applying all our abilities and our ingenuity to achieving a truly lasting stability? I think we are. Indeed, we must.

After careful consultation with my advisers, including the Joint Chiefs of Staff, I believe there is a way. Let me share with you a vision of the future which offers hope. It is that we embark on a program to counter the awesome Soviet missile threat with measures that are defensive. Let us turn to the very strengths in technology that spawned our great industrial base and that have given us the quality of life we enjoy today.

What if free people could live secure in the knowledge that their security did not rest upon the threat of instant U.S. retaliation to deter a Soviet attack, that we could intercept and destroy strategic ballistic missiles before they reached our own soil or that of our allies?

I know this is a formidable, technical task, one that may not be accomplished before the end of this century. Yet, current technology has attained a level of sophistication where it's reasonable for us to begin this effort. It will take years, probably decades of effort on many fronts. There will be failures and setbacks, just as there will be successes and break-throughs. And as we proceed, we must remain constant in preserving the nuclear deterrent and maintaining a solid capability for flexible response. But isn't it worth every investment necessary to free the world from the threat of nuclear war? We know it is.

In the meantime, we will continue to pursue real reductions in nuclear arms, negotiating from a position of strength that can be ensured only by modernizing our strategic forces. At the same time, we must take steps to reduce the risk of a conventional military conflict escalating to nuclear war by improving our non-nuclear capabilities.

America does possess — now — the technologies to attain very signifi-cant improvements in the effectiveness of our conventional, non-nuclear forces. Proceeding boldly with these new technologies, we can significantly reduce any incentive that the Soviet Union may have to threaten attack against the United States or its allies.

As we pursue our goal of defensive technologies, we recognize that our allies rely upon our strategic offensive power to deter attacks against them. Their vital interests and ours are inextricably linked. Their safety and ours are one. And no change in technology can or will alter that reality. We must and shall continue to honor our commitments.

I clearly recognize that defensive systems have limitations and raise certain problems and ambiguities. If paired with offensive systems, they can be viewed as fostering an aggressive policy, and no one wants that. But with these considerations firmly in mind, I call upon the scientific community in our country, those who gave us nuclear weapons, to turn their great talents now to the cause of mankind and world peace, to give us the means of rendering these nuclear weapons impotent and obsolete.

Tonight, consistent with our obligations of the ABM treaty and rec-ognizing the need for closer consultation with our allies, I'm taking an important first step. I am directing a comprehensive and intensive effort to define a long-term research and development program to begin to achieve our ultimate goal of eliminating the threat posed by strategic nuclear missiles. This could pave the way for arms control measures to eliminate the weapons themselves. We seek neither military superiority nor political advantage. Our only purpose — one all people share — is to search for ways to reduce the danger of nuclear war.

My fellow Americans, tonight we're launching an effort which holds the promise of changing the course of human history. There will be risks, and results take time. But I believe we can do it. As we cross this threshold, I ask for you prayers and your support.

Thank you, good night, and God bless you.

COMMISSION REPORT ON ACCESS TO HEALTH CARE

March 28, 1983

In its final report in a series of studies on ethical issues in medicine, an 11-member presidential commission concluded March 28 that all Americans should be entitled to an "adequate level" of health care, "without being subject to excessive burdens." Although it made no concrete legislative recommendations, the commission cautioned that efforts to cut soaring health costs should not jeopardize equally important measures to make certain that all Americans received necessary medical treatment.

The panel, which had reported on the ethical implications of a number of controversial medical subjects — including the definition of death and the problems involved in deciding to terminate life-sustaining treatment — was careful to distinguish equitable access to health care for all persons — a desirable goal — from receipt of an equal level of health care (that is, an equal quantity of health care dollars) or provision of all health care that would be beneficial to an individual. Given the rising costs of health care — projected to total $362.3 billion for the nation in 1983 — the commission noted that the last two goals were unrealistic and that choices would have to be made in the selection of equitable treatment "in comparison with other goods and services to which those resources might be allocated."

The report endorsed the existing U.S. health care system, characterized by a mix of private and public efforts. Although it was critical of administration and congressional moves to cut back on a number of public programs, including the Medicaid state-federal program for the poor and disabled, the federal Medicare program for the elderly and Social Security disability insurance, the panel did not advocate greater direct participation by the government in medical care. (Commission background and report on foregoing life-sustaining treatment, p. 279)

"The obligation we have described is one of all to all, not a special standard that applies only to the poor," wrote commission Chairman Morris B. Abram in submitting the report to President Ronald Reagan and Congress. "This does not mean, however, that the Federal government need be involved in the health care of all Americans...."

Noting that from 18 million to 25 million Americans had no health insurance, the commission concluded that "leaving health care solely to market forces" was not acceptable. An adequate level of health care, according to the commission, should be viewed "as a floor below which no one ought to fall, not a ceiling above which no one may rise." What was "adequate" was subject to revisions according to society's changing values.

Health Care Costs vs. Adequate Access

Rising hospital and physicians' charges were reflected in the rapidly growing cost of Medicare, Medicaid and other public health programs, which were projected to cost $75 billion, or 9.5 percent of the federal budget in fiscal 1983. The commission noted that medical expenditures were rising in part because payment to a great extent had been shifted to third parties. Patients paid only 29 percent of the nation's health care bill; public funds, including Medicare and Medicaid, paid 43 percent, and private insurance companies covered the remainder. Both private and public insurance plans reimbursed health care providers on a fee-for-service basis for "reasonable" treatment costs, a system that many believed offered neither physicians nor hospital administrators any incentive to control costs. Essentially, the more they charged, the more they made.

Another factor behind rising health care costs noted by the commission was related to advances in medical technology that entailed expensive equipment, such as the sophisticated X-ray device called a computerized axial tomography (CAT) scanner, or complicated surgical procedures such as coronary bypass operations and organ transplants. Other innovative hospital services, such as intensive care units and kidney dialysis machines, also entailed high per-patient charges. The suggestion that such services be used with greater discretion had stirred intense debate over the moral implications of applying "cost-benefit" analysis to decisions regarding human life.

The economic recession also had a significant impact on access to health care, the commission pointed out. When workers were laid off or fired, they frequently lost company-provided health insurance benefits.

Reagan Cost-Control Proposals

In his January 1983 budget message, President Reagan described the rate of health care cost increases as "excessive," undermining "people's ability to purchase needed health care." The administration proposed a series of reform measures reflecting the president's often-stated goal of reducing government influence and restoring public services to the private sector. One of its proposals, to set up a new system to reimburse hospitals for treating Medicare patients, was approved by Congress in March as part of the Social Security rescue bill. By setting fixed payment rates in advance, the new system was intended to end the existing policy of paying hospitals whatever it cost them to treat beneficiaries. Critics noted, however, that the plan would not prohibit hospitals from shifting extra Medicare costs to private insurance companies, which then would pass them on to their clients through higher premiums. (Social Security bill, p. 57)

The commission criticized proposals to charge Medicaid recipients a nominal fee for each day in the hospital or each visit to a doctor's office. "Even a small out-of-pocket charge can constitute a substantial burden for some Medicaid participants," the panel said. Although such proposals were intended to eliminate wasteful use of health services, "for Medicaid recipients [they are] more likely to discourage the use of valuable care."

While it found fault with efforts to curtail some federal programs, the commission labeled as "acceptable" measures to eliminate tax exemptions for employer-sponsored health insurance plans and medical expense income tax deductions that cost the Treasury $36.8 billion in foregone revenues in 1980. The panel concluded that tightening the exemptions as proposed by Reagan (and strongly opposed by labor unions) would not adversely affect access to health care because the deductions primarily benefited middle- and upper-income persons.

Following are excerpts from the report of the President's Commission for the Study of Ethical Problems in Medicine and Biomedical Research, "Securing Access to Health Care," released March 28, 1983. (Boldface headings in brackets have been added by Congressional Quarterly to highlight the organization of the text.):

Introduction

The prevention of death and disability, the relief of pain and suffering, the restoration of functioning: these are the aims of health care. Beyond its tangible benefits, health care touches on countless important and in some ways mysterious aspects of personal life that invest it with significant value as a thing in itself. In recognition of these special features, the President's Commission was mandated to study the ethical and legal implications of differences in the availability of health services. In this Report to the President and Congress, the Commission sets forth an ethical standard: access for all to an adequate level of care without the imposition of excessive burdens. It believes that this is the standard against which proposals for legislation and regulation in this field ought to be measured.

In fulfilling its mandate from Congress, the Commission discusses an ethical response to differences in people's access to health care. To do so, it is necessary both to examine the extent of those differences and to try to understand how they arise. . . .

Health care is a field in which two important American traditions are manifested: the responsibility of each individual for his or her own welfare and the obligations of the community to its members. These two values are complementary rather than conflicting. . . .

Since the nineteenth century, the United States has acted — through the founding of the Public Health Service and of hospitals for seamen, veterans, and native Americans, and through special health programs for mothers and infants, children, the elderly, the disabled, and the poor — to reaffirm the special place of health care in American society. With the greatly increased powers of biomedical science to cure as well as to relieve suffering, these traditional concerns about the special importance of health care have been magnified.

In both their means and their particular objectives, public programs in health care have varied over the years. Some have been aimed at assuring the productivity of the work force, others at protecting particularly vulnerable or deserving groups, still others at manifesting the country's commitment to equality of opportunity. Nonetheless, most programs have rested on a common rationale: to ensure that care be made accessible to a group whose health needs would otherwise not be adequately met.

The consequence of leaving health care solely to market forces — the mechanism by which most things are allocated in American society — is not viewed as acceptable when a significant portion of the population lacks access to health services. Of course, government financing programs, such as Medicare and Medicaid as well as public programs that provide care directly to veterans and the military and through local public hospitals, have greatly improved access to health care. These efforts, coupled with the expanded availability of private health insurance, have resulted in almost 90% of Americans having some form of health insurance coverage. Yet the patchwork of government programs and the uneven availability of private health insurance through the workplace have excluded millions of people. The Surgeon General has stated that "with rising unemployment, the numbers are shifting rapidly. We estimate that from 18 to 25 million Americans — 8 to 11 percent of the population — have no health-insurance coverage at all." Many of these people lack effective access to health care, and many more who have some form of insurance are unprotected from the severe financial burdens of sickness.

Nor is this a problem only for the moment. The Secretary of Health and

Human Services recently observed that despite the excellence of American medical care, "we do have this perennial problem of about 10% of the population falling through the cracks." What is needed now are ethical principles that offer practical guidance so that health policymakers in Federal, state, and local governments can act responsibly in an era of fiscal belt tightening without abandoning society's commitment to fair and adequate health care.

SUMMARY OF CONCLUSIONS

In this Report, the President's Commission does not propose any new policy initiatives, for its mandate lies in ethics not in health policy development. But it has tried to provide a framework within which debates about health policy might take place, and on the basis of which policymakers can ascertain whether some proposals do a better job than others of securing health care on an equitable basis.

In 1952, the President's Commission on the Health Needs of the Nation concluded that "access to the means for the attainment and preservation of health is a basic human right." Instead of speaking in terms of "rights," however, the current Commission believes its conclusions are better expressed in terms of "ethical obligations."

The Commission concludes that society has an ethical obligation to ensure equitable access to health care for all. This obligation rests on the special importance of health care: its role in relieving suffering, preventing premature death, restoring functioning, increasing opportunity, providing information about an individual's condition, and giving evidence of mutual empathy and compassion. Furthermore, although life-style and the environment can affect health status, differences in the need for health care are for the most part undeserved and not within an individual's control. . . .

The social obligation is balanced by individual obligations. Individuals ought to pay a fair share of the cost of their own health care and take reasonable steps to provide for such care when they can do so without excessive burdens. Nevertheless, the origins of health needs are too complex, and their manifestation too acute and severe, to permit care to be regularly denied on the grounds that individuals are solely responsible for their own health.

Equitable access to health care requires that all citizens be able to secure an adequate level of care without excessive burdens. Discussions of a right to health care have frequently been premised on offering patients access to all beneficial care, to all care that others are receiving, or to all that they need — or want. By creating impossible demands on society's resources for health care, such formulations have risked negating the entire notion of a moral obligation to secure care for those who lack it. In their place, the Commission proposes a standard of "an adequate level of care," which should be thought of as a floor below which no one ought to fall, not a ceiling above which no one may rise.

A determination of this level will take into account the value of various types of health care in relation to each other as well as the value of health care in relation to other important goods for which societal resources are needed. Consequently, changes in the availability of resources, in the effectiveness of different forms of health care, or in society's priorities may result in a revision of what is considered "adequate."

Equitable access also means that the burdens borne by individuals in obtaining adequate care (the financial impact of the cost of care, travel to the health care provider, and so forth) ought not to be excessive or to fall disproportionately on particular individuals.

When equity occurs through the operation of private forces, there is no need for government involvement, but the ultimate responsibility for ensuring that society's obligation is met, through a combination of public and private sector arrangements, rests with the Federal government. Private health care providers and insurers, charitable bodies, and local and state governments all have roles to play in the health care system in the United States. Yet the Federal government has the ultimate responsibility for seeing that health care is available to all when the market, private charity, and government efforts at the state and local level are insufficient in achieving equity.

The cost of achieving equitable access to health care ought to be shared fairly. The cost of securing health care for those unable to pay ought to be spread equitably at the national level and not allowed to fall more heavily on the shoulders of particular practitioners, institutions, or residents of different localities. In generating the resources needed to achieve equity of access, those with greater financial resources should shoulder a greater proportion of the costs. Also, priority in the use of public subsidies should be given to achieving equitable access for all before government resources are devoted to securing more care for people who already receive an adequate level.

Efforts to contain rising health care costs are important but should not focus on limiting the attainment of equitable access for the least well served portion of the public. The achievement of equitable access is an obligation of sufficient moral urgency to warrant devoting the necessary resources to it. However, the nature of the task means that it will not be achieved immediately. While striving to meet this ethical obligation, society may also engage in efforts to contain total health costs — efforts that themselve are likely to be difficult and time-consuming. Indeed, the Commission recognizes that efforts to rein in currently escalating health care costs have an ethical aspect because the call for adequate health care for all may not be heeded until such efforts are undertaken. If the nation concludes that too much is being spent on health care, it is appropriate to eliminate expenditures that are wasteful or that do not produce benefits comparable to those that would flow from alternate uses of these funds. But measures designed to contain health care costs that exacerbate existing inequities or impede the achievment of equity are unacceptable from a moral standpoint. Moreover, they are unlikely by themselves to be successful since they will probably lead to a shifting of costs to other entities, rather than to a reduction of total expenditures. . . .

An Ethical Framework

THE CONCEPT OF EQUITABLE ACCESS TO HEALTH CARE

The special nature of health care helps to explain why it ought to be accessible, in a fair fashion, to all. But if this ethical conclusion is to provide a basis for evaluating current patterns of access to health care and proposed health policies, the meaning of fairness or equity in this context must be clarified. The concept of equitable access needs definition in its two main aspects: the level of care that ought to be available to all and the extent to which burdens can be imposed on those who obtain these services.

Access to What? "Equitable access" could be interpreted in a number of ways: equality of access, access to whatever an individual needs or would benefit from, or access to an adequate level of care.

Equity as equality. It has been suggested that equity is achieved either when everyone is assured of receiving an equal quantity of health care dollars or when people enjoy equal health. The most common characterization of equity as equality, however, is as providing everyone with the same level of health care. In this view, it follows that if a given level of care is available to one individual it must be available to all. . . .

As long as significant inequalities in income and wealth persist, inequalities in the use of health care can be expected beyond those created by differences in need. Given people with the same pattern of preferences and equal health care needs, those with greater financial resources will purchase more health care. Conversely, given equal financial resources, the different patterns of health care preferences that typically exist in any population will result in a different use of health services by people with equal health care needs. Trying to prevent such inequalities would require interfering with people's liberty to use their income to purchase an important good like health care while leaving them free to use it for frivolous or inessential ends. Prohibiting people with higher incomes or stronger preferences for health care from purchasing more care than everyone else gets would not be feasible, and would probably result in a black market for health care.

Equity as access solely according to benefit or need. Interpreting equitable access to mean that everyone must receive all health care that is of any benefit to them also has unacceptable implications. Unless health is the only good or resources are unlimited, it would be irrational for a society — as for an individual — to make a commitment to provide whatever health care might be beneficial regardless of cost. Although health care is of special importance, it is surely not all that is important to people. Pushed to an extreme, this criterion might swallow up all of society's resources, since there is virtually no end to the funds that could be devoted to possibly beneficial care for diseases and disabilities and to their prevention. . . .

Equity as an adequate level of health care. Although neither "everything needed" nor "everything beneficial" nor "everything that anyone else is getting" are defensible ways of understanding equitable access, the special nature of health care dictates that everyone have access to *some* level of care: enough care to achieve sufficient welfare, opportunity, information, and evidence of interpersonal concern to facilitate a reasonably full and satisfying life. That level can be termed "an adequate level of health care." The difficulty of sharpening this amorphous notion into a workable foundation for health policy is a major problem in the United States today. . . .

Understanding equitable access to health care to mean that everyone should be able to secure an adequate level of care has several strengths. Because an adequate level of care may be less than "all beneficial care" and because it does not require that all needs be satisfied, it acknowledges the need for setting priorities within health care and signals a clear recognition that society's resources are limited and that there are other goods besides health. Thus, interpreting equity as access to adequate care does not generate an open-ended obligation. . . .

In addition, since providing an adequate level of care is a limited moral requirement, this definition also avoids the unacceptable restriction on individual liberty entailed by the view that equity requires equality. Provided that an adequate level is available to all, those who prefer to use their resources to obtain care that exceeds that level do not offend any ethical principle in doing so. Finally, the concept of adequacy, as the Commission understands it, is society-relative. The content of adequate care will depend upon the overall resources available in a given society, and can take into account a consensus of expectations about what is adequate in a particular society at a particular time in its historical development. This permits the definition of adequacy to be altered as societal resources and expectations change. . . .

WHO SHOULD ENSURE THAT SOCIETY'S OBLIGATION IS MET?

In this country, the chief mechanism by which the cost of health care is spread among individuals is through the purchase of insurance. Another method of distributing health care costs is to rely on acts of charity in which individuals, such as relatives and care givers, and institutions assume responsibility for absorbing some or all of a person's health care expenses. These private forces cannot be expected to achieve equitable access for all, however. States and localities have also played important roles in attempting to secure health care for those in need. To the extent that actions of the market, private charity, and lower levels of government are insufficient in achieving equity, the responsibility rests with Federal government. The actual provision of care may be through arrangements in the private section as well as through public institutions, such as local hospitals.

Market Mechanisms in Health Care. One means societies employ for meeting needs for goods and services that individuals cannot produce by themselves is the complex legal and economic mechanism known as a market. When health care is distributed through markets, however, an acceptable distribution is not achieved; indeed, given limitations in the way markets work, this result is practically inevitable. . . .

[I]f the distribution of health care were left solely to the market, some people would not get an adequate amount and others would get too much — not just more than an adequate level but more than they themselves really want given the costs they bear directly and through insurance premiums. The first is an ethical issue; the second, though not a moral problem, makes the solution of the first more difficult. . . .

The private market does not adjust the financial burden of care to differences in income. Yet poverty and ill health are correlated — with the causal factors working in both directions. Therefore, the poor are in a double bind: they need more medical care but they have less money to purchase it or less insurance protection to secure it. . . .

Although it is appropriate that all levels of government be involved in seeing that equitable access to health care is achieved, the *ultimate* responsibility for ensuring that this obligation is met rests with the Federal government. The Commission believes it is extremely important to distinguish between the view that the Federal government ought to provide care and the view that the Federal governemnt is ultimately responsible for seeing that there is equitable access to care. It is the latter view that the Commission endorses. . . .

Although the Commission recognizes the necessity of government involvement in ensuring equity of access, it believes that such activity must be carefully crafted and implemented in order to achieve its intended purpose. Public concern about the inability of the market and of private charity to secure access to health care for all has led to extensive government involvement in the financing and delivery of health care. This involvement has come about largely as a result of ad hoc responses to specific problems; the result has been a patchwork of public initiatives at the local, state, and Federal level. These efforts have done much to make health care more widely available to all citizens, but, as discussed . . . , they have not achieved equity of access.

To a large extent, this is the result of a lack of consensus about the nature of the goal and the proper role of government in pursuing it. But to some degree, it may also be the product of the nature of government activity. In some instances, government programs . . . have not been designed well enough to achieve the purposes intended or have been subverted to serve purposes explicitly not intended.

In the case of health care, it is extremely difficult to devise public strategies that, on the one hand, do not encourage the misuse of health services and, on the other hand, are not so restrictive as to unnecessarily or arbitrarily limit available care. There is a growing concern, for example, that government assistance in the form of tax exemptions for the purchase of employment-related health insurance has led to the overuse of many services of only very marginal benefit. Similarly, government programs that pay for health care directly (such as Medicaid) have been subject to fraud and abuse by both beneficiaries and providers. Alternatively, efforts to avoid misuse and abuse have at times caused local, state, and Federal programs to suffer from excessive bureaucracy, red tape, inflexibility, and unreasonable interference in individual choice. Also, as with private charity, government programs have not always avoided the unfortunate effects on the human spirit of "discretionary benevolence," especially in those programs requiring income or means tests.

It is also possible that as the government role in health care increases, the private sector's role will decrease in unforeseen and undesired ways. For example, government efforts to ensure access to nursing home care might lead to a lessening of support from family, friends, and other private sources for people who could be cared for in their homes. Although these kinds of problems do not inevitably accompany governmental involvement, they do occur and their presence provides evidence of the need for thoughtful and careful structuring of any government enterprise....

... Equity not only requires that no one bear an excessive burden to obtain care; it also requires fairness in the distribution of the cost to achieve this situation....

A fundamental conclusion ... is that the healthy should share in the cost of adequate care for those who are less healthy. In light of the importance of health care and the fact that differences in the need for care are largely undeserved, the cost of illness should be spread broadly without regard to people's actual or probable use of care. In practical terms, this means out-of-pocket payments for health care should be minimized and insurance premiums or health care taxes should be independent of a person's state of health....

Patterns of Access to Health Care

... This chapter has focused on identifying disparities in people's access to care that are based on considerations other than their need for health and medical services, particularly disparities associated with income, race, and place of residence. The Commission concludes that many differences in access to care do exist that cannot be explained by differences in need or health condition. These disparities take many forms: variations in the level of financial protection against health care costs, in the financial impact of health care expenses, in the use of services, in the availability of health resources, and in the use of different settings offering varying levels of quality of care.

In evaluating the ethical implications of these patterns of access, the

Commission believes it appropriate to rely on two principles: differences among groups should be considered inequitable when they preclude the receipt of an adequate level of health care or when they place an excessive burden on people who do obtain care. The absence of accepted standards of either measure complicate this evaluation and, as a result, the Commission has relied in part on relative comparisions as indicators of inequitable patterns of access to health care. Clearly, not all *differences* are *inequities*. In some cases, the Commission's conclusions about whether differences in access meet the requirements of equity are explicit; in others, the findings are less definite.

Specifically, the Commission finds that a substantial number of people — from 22 to 25 million at any one point in time — lack insurance coverage.... Another 19 million with very limited coverage are considered seriously underprotected against medical expenses. In the Commission's view, the inability to pay appears to be a critical factor affecting entry into the health care system and an important determinant of the use of services. The current pattern of insurance coverage resembles a patchwork quilt — with coverage depending in large part on where and whether a person is employed and on whether someone meets specific requirements to qualify for coverage under a public program. Lack of insurance is most pronounced among the very poor, the near-poor, racial and ethnic minorities, and residents of rural areas, but it is a problem that affects the entire population. The absence of health insurance — either public or private — fails both "ethical tests": it denies equitable access to an adequate level of care and it places the uninsured at risk of undue financial hardship.

The Commission finds that wide variations exist in the impact of medical expenses on people at various income levels. The financial burden of health care costs can fall heavily upon any family without comprehensive insurance that experiences very high medical expenses. Families of modest income, who are least able to absorb these costs without hardship, devote a greater share of their budgets to medical care than more affluent families do.

Obviously, when the proportion of personal financial resources required to obtain health care jeopardizes people's ability to acquire such essentials as food, housing, and basic utilities, the sacrifice is too great to meet the requirements of equity. At what point the financial burden of securing health care becomes inequitable when less compelling choices are at stake is less clear. Although the Commission does not presume to identify when the financial burdens of health care costs become ethically unacceptable, it does recognize that the current disparities raise questions of equity. Thus, the Commission proposes that differences in the proportion of income devoted to health care expenses be consistent with an adequate level of care being within the reach of all Americans.

Substantial improvements have occurred in the geographic distribution of health professionals and facilities. Yet people in some rural and inner-city communities still find it difficult to secure health services because of insufficient health care resources....

The Commission believes that the distribution of health personnel and facilities should be sufficient to ensure reasonable geographic access to an adequate level of care....

... Although the Commission recognizes the difficulty inherent in assessing the quality of care, it feels that some unrefined assumptions can be made about the services available in various settings, especially with regard to the continuity, comprehensiveness, and coordination of services. Equity is not achieved when people receive care that fails to meet the standards of adequacy — in either content or quality.

The Commission recognizes that disparities persist in the amounts of services used by different groups with similar health problems. Despite substantial progress in the use of health services by low-income individuals and by minorities, these groups continue to use many health services at lower rates than others with comparable health conditions. Differences also persist in the mix of services received by different groups and in when that care is initiated.

The Commission believes that great uniformity in the use of health care by individuals with similar health conditions is a precursor to equitable access. At the same time, it recognizes the problems in evaluating differences in the amounts of care received by different groups without accepted benchmarks as to what constitutes appropriate, optimal, or adequate use. It does, however, consider rate of use as a significant indicator of equitable access and feels that progress in reducing existing disparities should not await the development of agreed-upon explicit standards.

As already noted, it is difficult to distinguish how the use of health care is influenced by someone's "motivation" or propensity to seek care as against financial, geographic, social, or cultural considerations such as language barriers or lack of knowledge....

The lack of access to care can have serious health, economic, and social consequences for both society as a whole and for individuals. The most obvious of these is that people affected by lack of access may go without needed services and suffer the consequences. Or they may delay in acquiring care or may defer needed treatment. Evidence suggests that people with compromised access are more likely to be hospitalized when their illness is at a more advanced stage....

[Impact of Government Action]

In the overview of government involvement in health care provided in this chapter, the Commission finds significant accomplishments. Although private initiatives, both individual and collective, have played a major role in securing access to care, the disparities documented [previously] ... would be much greater were it not for government involvement. Nevertheless, problems have arisen that undermine the ability of government programs to achieve their goals.

At the root of these problems is a lack of consensus on the proper role of government in health care. Certain underlying and sometimes contradictory principles can be imperfectly distinguished. A strong societal preference exists for private solutions — for limiting the role of government in health care, particularly its role in the direct provision of personal health care to individuals. Thus Federal policy has emphasized temporary measures to increase the supply of services both generally and in areas of greatest need, as well as programs to provide individuals with the financial means to obtain care from the private sector. Most of these programs — the subsidies to medical education and hospital construction, for example, and medical care financing programs such as Medicaid and Medicare — have been designed to interfere as little as possible with private sector arrangements. Others — those intended to provide services more directly, such as the National Health Service Corps and community health centers — illustrate the conflicts that occur when government actions run counter to this approach.

At the same time, the very existence of a wide array of government programs is evidence of a felt obligation to ensure access to health care. The clearest indication can be found in the history of the public hospital. For many decades, locally funded hospitals have served as providers of care for people who have no other way to obtain it. Yet little progress has been made in developing methods to define and deliver the "right" level of care. Similarly, Americans clearly feel that some burdens in obtaining care are excessive, but there is uncertainty about how much individual responsibility people should be expected to take for obtaining and paying for care.

Thus, people often receive either too little or too much publicly supported care. On the one hand, care is extensively subsidized (through the Federal tax system) for people who could take more financial responsibility for their own care without an excessive burden. On the other hand, stringent limits on publicly funded services cause others to be denied adequate care, or to obtain it only at great personal cost. Public health "insurance" programs, such as Medicaid, fail to secure adequate care for many low-income people while providing care for others that is more than adequate. Often the amount of public medical assistance varies arbitrarily, based on personal characteristics irrelevant from an ethical standpoint — type of employment, for example, in the case of tax subsidies; marital status or place of residence, in the case of Medicaid....

... Both the subsidies to medical education and the Hill-Burton [hospital construction aid] program illustrate the reluctance of the government to place significant constraints on providers' freedom of action, even when large sums of public money are involved. Both programs relied on positive financial incentives to meet societal goals. Subsidized medical school graduates could avoid the service obligations of their loans by repaying the money they had received, sometimes on very favorable terms. Although the Hill-Burton Act was designed to get hospital beds to the places with greatest need, it did not provide the means to force the issue.

And projects that did not qualify for Hill-Burton money could still be built with private or other state and local funds. . . .

. . . The fact that the neighborhood health centers were designed expressly to serve the poor has generated controversy. Health care that is provided through institutions that serve only the poor is suspect in the United States. It raises the specter of "two-class care" and of unacceptable limits on the choices of the disadvantaged. Health centers might better be considered as examples of "two-track care"; available evidence suggests that the care provided may have different characteristics but that it is not inferior to that offered in mainstream medicine. In fact, since an express goal of the program was to tailor the care provided to the special needs of poor populations (who may, for example, be exposed to specific health risks in their living environment), the care offered in centers may be of higher quality because it is more appropriate to need. Overall, health centers have increased people's options, since they were placed in locations where residents' choices had been extremely limited. . . .

[PUBLIC GENERAL HOSPITALS]

The public general hospital is the major exception to the rule that governments have not directly provided personal health care. Public support for these hospitals as "providers of last resort" is evidence of a societal consensus that everyone should have access to some level of care. Yet the variations in amount, content, and quality of care provided by these hospitals in different locations point up the lack of agreement about what that level of care should be. Furthermore, public hospitals illustrate the difficulties that this lack of consensus causes for the appropriate distribution of the cost of care. The assignment to local governments of fiscal responsibility for health care for the poor has been matched by neither the willingness nor the capacity to fund an adequate level of care in local communities. . . .

The main problem with public hospitals lies in the distribution of the cost of care. Public hospitals get their revenue from patients who pay for a part of their care, from Medicare and Medicaid, from other third-party payors, and from public appropriations, overwhelmingly at the local level. Yet these revenue sources are often inadequate to maintain the high standard of care intended and no one seems willing to shoulder additional financial burdens. . . .

SUBSIDIES FOR THE PURCHASE OF MEDICAL CARE

Subsidies for the purchase of care enable government to lower financial barriers to access while leaving to the private sector the task of providing care. The best-known programs of this type are Medicare and Medicaid, which finance care for the aged, the disabled, and certain categories of the poor. These programs have greatly improved access for those covered. Nevertheless, in basic structure and in actual implementation they have problems that keep them from reaching their potential in promoting equitable access for all.

Not generally realized is the extent to which the Federal government also subsidizes the purchase of care by middle- and upper-income people through special provisions in the tax code. The estimated amount of Federal revenue lost as a result of these tax advantages is close to the total Federal and state expenditures on the poor under Medicaid. The tax subsidies weaken the incentives on consumers and providers to hold down costs and to forego low-benefit care. Moreover, they provide greater assistance to those with lesser need, contributing to inequities in the distribution of the cost of care....

... By subsidizing comprehensive insurance coverage, tax subsidies make the already weak cost-control incentives in the medical care market even weaker. Aggregate expenditures are inflated by expenditures on wasteful care. Patients are less sensitive to differences in prices among providers; both patients and providers have less incentive to choose cost-effective methods of treatment. Consumers and employers are less sensitive to differences in the cost of insurance plans; thus insurers, who could play a role in keeping down health care costs, have little incentive to do so. Many analysts believe these effects of tax subsidies are an important reason why the cost of care is higher than it would otherwise be. To the extent that this is true, the burden in out-of-pocket cost it imposes on people less comprehensively insured, and particularly on the uninsured, is magnified....

Using 1977 data from the National Medical Care Expenditure Survey, the Federal expenditures under Medicare, Medicaid, and the income tax subsidies by income group can be compared.... Medicare spends a fairly similar amount on each income group. Medicaid spends more on the poor, while the income tax subsidies mainly benefit the better off. The group that receives the least assistance from all three programs combined is the "other low-income group." On a per capita basis, expenditures under Medicaid decrease as income increases; payments under Medicare also decrease but less sharply; and the income tax subsidies increase sharply with income. Overall, middle-income people receive the least assistance on a per capita basis under all three programs combined.

This pattern of expenditure is difficult to justify from an ethical standpoint....

CONCERNS ABOUT HEALTH CARE COSTS

... The dramatic rise in health care costs during the past 15 years has recently received a great deal of attention. Concerns have been voiced about the higher total expenditures for health care generally and about the increasing share of government resources devoted to health care. In 1965, Americans spent $42 billion on health care; by 1981 total outlays amounted to $287 billion. The share of the Gross National Product (GNP) devoted to health care rose from 6.0% to 9.8% during this period. Not only has the price of health care goods and services risen at a faster rate than other consumer prices, but the growing share of national wealth devoted to health care has led to understandable concern about the limitations being placed on alternative uses of these resources.

The rise of total spending has been accompanied by a marked shift in the source of financing: government expenditures at the local, state, and Federal levels have accounted for an increasing share of total health care outlays. In 1965, 26% of all national health care expenditures were from public funds; by 1981, that figure reached almost 43% — that is, $123 billion of the $287 billion in total health expenditures that year.... [T]hese outlays take several forms, including programs that finance and deliver care for the underserved and the expansion of health care for the total population through the training of health professionals, the construction of hospitals, and research. In addition, the government provides an indirect subsidy for the purchase of employment-related health insurance (although this subsidy is not included in the $123 billion figure).

There is no magical share of the nation's resources that is obviously "correct" for health care. The important question is whether the level of spending reflects the priorities of the American people. Americans have traditionally placed great value on the ready availability of high-quality care. Most would not want to face sharp restrictions in the care available when they or their loved ones are ill. Nevertheless, there seem to be new doubts that the public is receiving sufficient benefits to justify the increased spending. The current preoccupation with rising expenditures may really reflect these doubts rather than dissatisfaction with the level of spending itself.

Eliminating Wasteful Practices. A growing body of expert opinion provides some foundation for this concern about whether Americans are getting their money's worth. Clearly, the availability of medical care has made and will continue to make a tremendous difference to health, for the population as a whole and for individuals with special health problems. Nevertheless, there is evidence that in some cases services could be produced and delivered more inexpensively, and that in other cases fewer services could be provided with little or no effect on a patient's well-being. Indeed, there may be instances when patients would actually be better off with less care. If inefficiencies could be reduced and inappropriate care discouraged, the total savings could be considerable. These savings could be used to improve the distribution of care, so that more people could enjoy the benefits of American medicine without diverting resources from other important social purposes.

Governmental bodies can . . . take steps to control health care costs in response to public concern over wasteful spending and its harmful effects on public programs and, therefore, on taxpayers. The development of certificate-of-need programs and regulation of hospital reimbursement by some states are examples of such efforts. When government does attempt to reduce health care spending, however, it is essential that it do so in an equitable manner. The burden of cost containment should not be borne mainly by those least able to afford it, who have had to rely most heavily on public funds to secure health care services....

... [A] reduction in Federal funding of Medicaid would worsen existing inequities in the distribution of the cost of care. Since some of the care will still be provided, payment will simply be shifted to another source. State-supported teaching hospitals and local public hospitals will most likely treat a large share of the former Medicaid beneficiaries; they will pass these added costs on to other patients (and their insurers) or to taxpayers or they will be forced to use funds intended for other purposes, such as teaching and research, to care for these patients. The Health Insurance Association of America estimates that during 1982 hospitals providing a great deal of care to the poor will shift on to patients with commercial insurance $4.8 billion of the costs incurred because of reductions in Medicaid and Medicare. Physicians who do not turn away those low-income patients who are no longer eligible for Medicaid or whose coverage of benefits has been restricted will be forced to absorb the cost of these "charity" patients. Cutbacks in Medicaid thus are likely to transfer a greater share of the burden of caring for these individuals from the Federal level (where it is distributed more evenly) to state and local taxpayers, health care professionals, and privately insured patients.

Paradoxically, some of these cost-control measures may lower Federal outlays in the short run but may actually increase total costs. For example, people who are no longer eligible for Medicaid are likely to seek care in public hospital emergency rooms and outpatient departments rather than in physicians' offices and clinics. Yet hospitals are more expensive settings for routine care and are less likely to provide the information, preventive measures, and follow-up services that could control the need for costly acute care....

Social Security Disability. In 1980 Congress enacted legislation to improve accountability in the Social Security Disability Program by encouraging the review of new applicants. Under this prospective review, those who failed to demonstrate disability would be denied Social Security payments as well as the Medicare benefits they are entitled to after two years in the disability program. Concern has been expressed, however, that program administrators have gone beyond the intent of the 1980 statute in order to reduce expenditures in the Social Security and Medicare programs by reviewing not only new applicants but also many current beneficiaries, by accelerating the pace of the review process, and by establishing an expectation of a significant rate of denials. In short, the process of "weeding out" ineligible enrollees appears to have become one of terminating a substantial number of beneficiaries for the purpose of budgetary savings. Over half the recent disability reviews have resulted in denial or termination of benefits, yet two-thirds of those deicsions have been reversed on appeal.

This process has significant implications for the health of those undergoing review: people removed from the disability program have few, if any, alternatives for health insurance because they are considered unattractive risks by commercial insurers. Any insurance that is offered, often at very high rates, is usually of little value because many policies exclude coverage of "preexisting conditions." Furthermore, terminated beneficiaries will find it hard to afford insurance since their disabled condition usually precludes gainful employment. In the absence of other public programs, the denial or revocation of eligibility leaves disabled persons with little assurance of securing an adequate level of health care or with the prospect of a crushing financial burden if care is obtained. The ethical obligation to secure equitable access to care would be better met if the procedures ensured Medicare coverage during the many months of any appeals process and if the review process were used as intended, rather than as a temporary cost-cutting device. . . .

Tax Subsidies. Reducing the tax exemption [for employers' payment of employees' health insurance] would have several ethical implications. First, if properly designed, it is unlikely that such measures would compromise access to adequate health care. It is anticipated that comprehensively insured individuals would be encouraged to use less care that, according to their own priorities, is less beneficial than other uses of their own funds.

Second, this approach to cost containment would not have a disproportionate impact on the most economically vulnerable people who have the greatest difficulty in securing care. Since cuts in the government tax subsidy for employees' health benefits primarily affect middle- and upper-income families, they are likely to reduce total health expenditures by encouraging the people most able to pay for health care to be more selective in their use of services. From an ethical standpoint cost containment should not be aimed chiefly at those for whom access to care is most tenuous.

Third, reductions in the tax exemption would limit the use of public monies to support the purchase of care that is less essential to well-being and opportunity. A fair distribution of cost requires that government funds not finance the receipt of "higher-than-adequate" care for some individuals until access to adequate care for all is ensured. . . .

OTA REPORT
ON ALCOHOLISM TREATMENT
March 31, 1983

The cost of alcoholism to U.S. society might be as great as $120 billion a year, according to a study released March 31 by the Office of Technology Assessment (OTA).

The study, The Effectiveness and Costs of Alcoholism Treatment, *estimated that 10 million to 15 million Americans were alcoholics and as many as 35 million more might be affected indirectly, mostly as family members of alcoholics.*

While the monetary repercussions of alcoholism were enormous, the human toll was even greater. Alcohol and alcoholism were thought to be involved in half of all automobile accidents, half of all murders and one-fourth of all suicides, although precise statistics were not available. Alcoholism was one of the major causes of divorce and accounted for nearly half of all the problems brought to family courts, according to the OTA study.

But even though the disease affected one in three American families, according to a November 1982 Gallup poll, approximately 85 percent of all alcoholics received no treatment. In fact, although various cures had been developed, the OTA assessment found that researchers still did not know if certain treatments were more effective than others.

OTA, a non-partisan arm of Congress, commissioned the study as part of its continuing evaluation of medical care and treatment costs. In 1982 Medicare alone spent approximately $150 million to treat alcoholism directly. That figure was far higher when hospital admissions for illnesses *aggravated by alcohol, such as liver disease, were taken into account.*

Costs and Effectiveness of Treatment

As the federal government searched for ways to reduce the costs of treating alcoholism, members of Congress and others questioned the treatment's effectiveness and whether substitute measures could be taken at lower cost.

In the past Medicare and Medicaid, through their reimbursement regulations, paid primarily for treatment in hospitals. However, in September 1982 new Medicare regulations reversed the trend to hospitalization by promoting the use of outpatient treatment.

The OTA researchers found that existing studies did not indicate whether hospitalization was more effective than outpatient treatment. The new study concluded, however, that any medically accepted treatment was better and more cost effective than not providing any treatment. Additional research would have to be done, the report said, to find out if relatively low-cost treatments, such as peer groups (primary among them Alcoholics Anonymous) and outpatient counseling, such as mental health centers, were as effective as hospitalization.

Studies on Causes of Alcoholism

The National Institute of Alcohol Abuse and Alcoholism (NIAAA) in 1983 began a long-term study of the lasting effects of alcohol abuse and its causes. The study was being conducted at the National Institutes of Health in Bethesda, Md.

According to an August 26, 1983, Washington Post *article, NIAAA researchers believed there might be a psychobiological link that either triggered alcoholism or created a genetic predisposition to it. The researchers' work led them to the neurotransmitter serotonin, one of the chemicals in the brain that affect mood and behavior. Serotonin secretions apparently trigger feelings of cheerfulness and good will. Research found that alcoholics and depressed (but non-drinking) relatives of alcoholics had lower-than-normal concentrations of a chemical produced when serotonin was metabolized.*

Dr. Markku Linnoila, an NIAAA psychiatrist and clinical pharmacologist who conducted the study, found that alcohol tended to release serotonin. Linnoila theorized that, as a consequence, alcoholics might drink to achieve a feeling of well-being.

Other researchers believed that there might be a second explanation for alcoholism — the addictive personality. According to a June 30, 1982, article in The Washington Post, *a person sharing certain personality traits with other addicts, including drug addicts and compulsive gam-blers, was found to be far more prone to alcoholism than persons not having those traits. Some of the traits that seemed to be indicators of addictive behavior were impulsiveness, sociability, feelings that life was meaningless and low self-esteem.*

Researchers developed a test known as the MacAndrew Scale that was able to pick, with 75 percent accuracy, persons in a group with a predeliction to addiction. Gloria Leon, a clinical psychologist at the University of Minnesota, said that 13 years after the MacAndrew test was given to incoming freshmen, interviewers found that 85 percent of those who had scored high on the scale were alcoholics. None of the students had an alcohol problem when they took the test, Leon said.

Despite the findings of those two studies, the OTA report found that society still had more questions about alcoholism, its causes and treat-ment, than it had answers.

The researchers concluded by applauding the changes in Medicare and Medicaid regulations regarding the hospitalization of alcoholics, noting that the measures probably would result in more cost-effective treatment. However, the OTA study recommended that the 1982 regulations be studied carefully before the government implemented additional cost-cutting measures. Additional revisions might make it difficult for alcohol-ics to receive needed hospitalization and might not save money, the report warned.

Following are excerpts from the March 31, 1983, congres-sional Office of Technology Assessment report, The Effec-tiveness and Costs of Alcoholism Treatment:

The Alcoholism Problem

Alcoholism constitutes a vast syndrome of medical, economic, psycho-logical, and social problems related to the consumption of alcohol (etha-nol). The social and economic costs to society of alcoholism, particularly to the health care system, are staggering. From 10 million to 15 million Americans have serious problems directly related to the use of alcohol, and up to 35 million more individuals are estimated to be affected indirectly. Although estimates are imprecise, alcoholism and alcohol abuse have been implicated in half of all automobile accidents, half of all homicides, and one-quarter of all suicides.

Alcoholism may be responsible for up to 15 percent of the Nation's health care costs and for significantly lowering the productivity of workers at all strata of the economic system.... But the primary costs of alcoholism to society are more than economic. Alcoholism and alcohol abuse also adversely affect the health, social relations, psychological well-being, and economic status of a large number of individuals. The extent of these effects is difficult to determine, because an alcoholic may create problems for many others, including family, friends, and coworkers.

OVERVIEW OF ALCOHOLISM

Use of Alcohol

A substantial percentage of the American population uses alcoholic beverages, at least occasionally. The Gallup poll, which began collecting data about alcohol use in 1939, has reported relatively stable patterns in alcohol use over the past few decades. Consistently, about two-thirds of the adult population (66 percent of women and 77 percent of men) report at least occasional use of alcoholic beverages. In recent years, the range in use has been from 60 to 70 percent. Per capita consumption has also remained stable at about 2.6 gallons per year. In the United States, however, about 10 percent of the population accounts for more than half the alcohol consumed; less than half is consumed by a large group of infrequent drinkers and a small group of regular moderate drinkers.

Most users of alcohol are not considered alcoholics, "problem drinkers," or even "heavy drinkers." A National Academy of Sciences panel has estimated that among adults, only 9 percent are problem drinkers (in some cases, this includes individuals who drink 1 ounce per day of pure alcohol). Less than half of those considered heavy drinkers — 10 percent of those who regularly drink alcohol — would be considered alcoholic.

Effects of Alcoholism

Reliable data on the effects of alcoholism and alcohol abuse are difficult to obtain, in part because of the many individuals affected and the complexity of effects, but also because alcohol use is widespread, and for most individuals, a normal social custom. Moreover, the absence of information about individuals with alcohol-use problems who are not in formal treatment programs makes it difficult both to assess the pervasiveness of the alcohol abuse problem and to document the impact of current alcoholism treatment efforts.

Alcohol (ethanol) — especially when consumed in large quantities or habitually — is related to various health problems such as organ damage (particularly, the liver), brain dysfunction, cardiovascular disease, and mental disorders. It has a significant effect on mortality rates; in general, the life expectancy of alcoholics is 10 to 12 years shorter than average. Cirrhosis of the liver, a direct result of long-term alcohol consumption, is currently the fourth leading fatal disease in the United States. When other effects of alcohol abuse are counted, alcoholism is an even more significant mortality factor. In addition, alcoholics have significantly higher suicide rates than do nonalcoholics (up to 58 times greater in some groups of alcoholics) and accident rates that are significantly greater than normal.

Each of these factors results in a significant number of deaths for individuals who abuse alcohol at all age levels. In terms of morbidity, it has been estimated that alcoholic patients comprise from 30 to 50 percent of all hospital admissions, excluding obstetrics. While these admissions are most often for other disorders, alcoholism complicates ... recovery.

Estimated to be a significant factor in up to 40 percent of all problems brought to family courts, alcohol use is known to be a major factor in divorce and has been associated with destabilization of families. In addition, automobile, home, and industrial accidents and crimes such as assault, rape, and wife battering have also been associated with alcohol use. In recent years, public recognition of the problems involved in alcohol use has increased. For example, only 12 percent of families surveyed in a Gallup poll in 1966 agreed that liquor adversely affected their family lives. In 1981, this figure rose to 22 percent, and a recent Gallup poll indicated that 33 percent of families surveyed indicate that alcohol use has caused serious family problems.

Government recognition of the problem resulted in the establishment, just over 10 years ago, of the National Institute on Alcohol Abuse and Alcoholism (NIAAA) and the requirement of periodic reports to Congress on progress in combating alcoholism. Health professionals and researchers are becoming more knowledgeable about alcoholism as more data about the problems posed by the effects of alcoholism become known.

Treatment

Despite the range of problems caused by alcoholism and alcohol abuse, an estimated 85 percent of alcoholics and problem drinkers receive no treatment for their condition. In 1977, although approximately 1.6 million alcoholics and problem drinkers received treatment from private and public sources and over 600,000 alcoholics participated in meetings of Alcoholics Anonymous (AA) groups, at least 8 million to 10 million other alcoholics and problem drinkers did not receive any treatment. In considering the effectiveness of current treatments, it should be recognized that the majority of alcoholics and problem drinkers do not receive treatment.

PERSPECTIVES ON ALCOHOLISM

Although alcoholism and alcohol abuse are today acknowledged to be multifaceted medical, psychological, and social problems, they have not always been viewed this way. Alcohol abuse was, historically, either accepted as normal behavior or, in some caes, viewed as a moral problem and treated as criminal behavior. In the 1950s, though, both the World Health Organization (WHO) and the American Medical Association gave formal recognition to alcoholism as a medical disease. The most prominent advocator of a medically based concept of alcoholism is a physician, [E. M.] Jellinek, whose work has been the basis of most currently used definition.

Despite increasing emphasis on alcoholism as a medical rather than a criminal or moral problem, experts continue to disagree about what constitutes alcoholism, and there is probably no single best definition. Some definitions of alcoholism consider merely the quantity of alcohol consumed or the frequency of drunkenness. More recent definitions consider the degree to which serious medical or social dysfunctions result from alcohol use and the degree of psychological dependence or physical addiction to alcohol. Whatever definition is employed, however, it is often difficult to obtain reliable diagnostic data. This compounds definitional problems and influences diagnostic decisions and treatment of alcohol abusers.

The most recent *Diagnostic and Statistical Manual* distinguishes between "alcohol abuse" and "alcohol dependence." Diagnostic criteria for "alcohol abuse" include: drinking nonbeverage alcohol; going on binges (remaining intoxicated throughout the day for at least 2 days); occasionally drinking a fifth of spirits (or its equivalent in wine or beer); and having had two or more blackouts, as well as impaired social or occupational functioning due to alcohol. In addition, problems must have existed for a month or more. The diagnostic criteria for alcohol dependence, traditionally referred to as alcoholism, include the criteria for alcohol abuse and two additional criteria: tolerance and withdrawal. Tolerance is defined as "the need for markedly increased amounts of alcohol to achieve the desired effect, or diminished effect with regular use of [the] same amount." Withdrawal includes "morning 'shakes' and malaise relieved by drinking."

The determination of the underlying causes of alcoholism has been even more intensely debated than the definition of alcoholism. At least three major views of the etiology of alcoholism can be identified: 1) medical, 2) psychological, and 3) sociocultural. Each of these perspectives is associated with a particular set of treatment approaches. As described below, however, treatment is often based on several etiological perspectives, and practitioners often accept the view that alcoholism is based on multiple factors.

Medical Perspective

The medical perspective focuses on biological, chemical, and genetic etiological factors. From the medical perspective, alcoholism is considered a disease caused by physiological malfunctioning and requires treatment by a physician. Jellinek posited that alcoholism represents a multifaceted syndrome. In many cases, the alcoholism syndrome follows a particular course of progressive deterioration unless the problem is treated. Jellinek believed that the only effective form of treatment is that whose goal is of total abstinence from alcoholic beverages.

Alcoholism may be conceptualized as the "last stage in a continuum of drinking that extends from social drinking to heavy drinking to problem drinking to alcoholism, where each population [of drinkers] represents a subcategory of the one preceding it." For present purposes, however, the terms alcoholic, alcohol abuser, and problem drinker will often be used interchangeably. This usage reflects that fact that problems associated with alcohol use and abuse may be progressive, but that drinkers may seek treatment at any point in the continuum and for various reasons. The treatment literature does not always distinguish appropriateness of treatments for patients at different points in the continuum. . . .

Use of the disease concept became prevalent and was used to refer to various alcohol-related problems. Jellinek later encouraged the wider use of the disease concept in order to get hospitals and physicians involved so that alcoholics could receive some treatment. Through these highly successful efforts, a medically based alcoholism treatment system has evolved that incorporates a range of approaches, including those that are medically, as well as nonmedically, based.

A number of biochemical and physiological mechanisms have been offered to explain the cause of alcoholism. One theory postulates that alcoholism evolves from an inherited metabolic defect that creates a need for certain substances and that alcohol alleviates the symptoms of the deficiency. A second hypothesis is that alcoholism is the result of an endocrime dysfunction. There is no strong empirical evidence for either of these theories.

Genetic theories of the etiology of alcoholism have been proposed at a number of points. Metabolic research with alcoholic populations, however, has been unable to distinguish between effects caused by genetic factors and those produced by chronic ethanol ingestion. Nonetheless, evidence suggests that genetic factors may be an important predisposing factor in the onset of alcoholism. Support for a genetic view is provided by carefully controlled family, half-sibling, adoptee, and twin studies. These studies have found that among children separated from their biological parents at birth, the presence of alcoholism in the biological parents was a much better predictor of alcoholism in the child than was the presence of alcoholism in an adoptive parent. . . .

Psychological Perspective

The psychological perspective views alcoholism as arising from motivational and emotional dysfunctions in individuals. When dysfunction is preceded by, or occurs in the absence of, problem drinking, alcoholism is considered to be a secondary diagnosis. When there are no major preexisting psychiatric problems, alcoholism is the primary diagnosis. There are actually several psychological perspectives, representing different theoretical approaches to alcoholism. These perspectives include: 1) behavioral, 2) psychodynamic, and 3) systems approaches.

Behavior theorists view alcoholism as a learned response. In their view, the drinking of alcohol becomes "reinforcing"; i.e., the drinking of alcohol is associated with positive, rewarding experiences. Positive reinforcers for alcohol use include tension reduction, release of inhibitions, and facilitation of social interaction. Learning particular alcohol responses can occur through classical conditioning (Pavlovian), operant conditioning (Skinnerian), or modeling processes. Each of these conditioning processes indicates a separate mechanism through which alcoholism develops. . . .

From the traditional psychoanalytic perspective, alcoholism is seen as a symptom of underlying pathology resulting from unconscious conflicts. These conflicts are assumed to be the result of early childhood experiences and an outgrowth of interactions and fantasies about relationships within the nuclear family. According to this application of psychoanalytic theory, once the conflict is recognized and the patient is helped to gain insight into the problem, dysfunctional drinking behavior will stop naturally. . . .

Psychoanalytic theory, while historically very important and influential, is no longer theoretically dominant. More important today is the psycho-dynamic position that builds on some of the basic assumptions of original psychoanalytic theory, but has modified and adapted its components. From this perspective, all behavior, including alcoholism, is seen as being heavily shaped by early experiences, but maintained by current events.

The belief that alcoholism is sustained by a pathological environment underlies the systems theory approach to alcoholism. In this view, alco-holic behavior in an individual is seen as only the tip of an iceberg, the ice-berg being a continuing and immediate pathological interpersonal system. This system is usually the family, but it can also be significant other interpersonal networks in which the alcoholic participates. Although the systems approach is considered here a psychological perspective, in that the source of the problem is seen as the individual, the systems view shares much in common with the sociocultural perspective on alcoholism.

Sociocultural Perspective

From the sociocultural perspective, alcohol abuse is seen as the product of living in a particular social and cultural milieu. Drinking behaviors may be regarded as learned, but the sociocultural interpretation (unlike the behavioral theory interpretation) is that these behaviors are the result of a lifelong socialization and acculturation process. Ethnicity, age, socioeco-nomic class, religion, and gender are seen as important factors that shape an individual's behavior. Children are socialized in the culturally pre-scribed beliefs, attitudes, and behaviors toward alcohol. The variance in the occurrence of alcoholism among different groups is cited as evidence to support this theory. Consistent reports of high rates of alcoholism among the Irish, American Indians, and Swedes, compared to lower rates among Jews, Mormons, and Chinese are frequently cited. . . .

POPULATIONS: INCIDENCE AND TREATMENT

Although alcoholism is widespread among various demographic and social groups, problems with alcoholism may have different bases across groups and may manifest themselves differently. [S. D.] Solomon articu-lates the need to develop alcoholism treatments tailored to the diverse needs of subpopulations. Like [E. M] Pattison, Solomon argues that demographic characteristics such as gender, race, ethnicity, social class, and age, as well as the life situations of alcoholics, critically influence both treatment selection and treatment effectiveness.

Having a job, a stable income, and a reliable set of social and personal supports correlate positively with treatment outcomes. Men and women from lower socioeconomic classes — those most dependent on public resources, such as Medicaid and Medicare, for health service — appear to suffer more extensive drinking problems and respond less well to traditional treatment services than do middle- and upper-class adults. Being working class or poor in the United States often involves unstable unemployment prospects and related disruptions of stable family relationships. Such multiplicity of problems undermines simple or inexpensive interventions designed to reduce alcohol problems.

It has been consistently documented that men across all social classes receive more alcoholism services than do women.... [M]ale alcoholics in treatment tended to be unemployed, unmarried, southern, of lower socioeconomic status, and Protestant....

Many surveys indicate an overall decline in alcohol use with age, indicating, perhaps, less need for treatment services among elderly populations. Among elderly people who drink, however, a significant number have alcohol problems....

Youth and Adolescents

Surveys of alcohol use have indicated that a substantial proportion of youths drink excessively. In 1978, youths 18 and under comprised 4.5 percent, and individuals between the ages of 19 and 24 comprised 14 percent, of those served by NIAAA-funded alcoholism treatment projects. [S. E.] Donovan and [R.] Jessor report that approximately 5 percent of both girls and boys in the seventh grade are problem drinkers; the proportion of problem drinkers increases steadily in each grade, until by grade 12 almost 40 percent of males and 20.6 percent of females are problem drinkers. NIAAA reports that a national survey of men aged 21 to 59 showed that the highest proportion of drinking problems are in the group aged 21 to 24.

Donovan and Jessor define problem drinking for youth and adolescents as having been drunk five or more times and/or having two or more life areas in which negative consequences occurred in the past year. Although this is a liberal standard, compared to those used to identify alcoholics, it highlights the seriousness of adolescent alcohol use. Probably the most alarming consequence of adolescent and young adult drinking is its relationship to fatal driving accidents. Recently, the Secretary of Transportation called for a uniform requirement that the minimum age for those purchasing alcoholic beverages be 21 years.

The most reliable predicator of drinking among youths is the drinking behavior of their parents, although peers have an important influence. In

343

81 percent of families in which both parents drink, children also drink; in 72 percent of families with two abstaining parents, children do not drink. A number of sociocultural influences predisposes young people toward drinking. These include residence in an urban area, divorced or separated parents, a poor parent-child relationship, and high socioeconomic status.

Women

Women comprise only 20 to 40 percent of those served in alcohol treatment facilities, but the question of whether women are less prone to alcoholism or are an underserved population has not yet been answered.

There is evidence that women tolerate alcohol less well than men. They reach a higher blood-alcohol level faster and are more at risk for the development of biomedical consequences. About 16 percent of women alcoholics develop liver disease compared to 8 percent of men, and women appear to be at higher risk of death from alcoholism than are their male counterparts. Although alcoholism typically has a later onset in women than in men, there is evidence of "telescoping" in women, whereby medical problems develop faster than in men.

One explanation for their relatively low rate of treatment is that women may be less "visible" in their need for services (e.g., the homemaker who drinks during the day), and family members and coworkers may be more reluctant to intervene with women drinkers. Furthermore, epidemiological surveys may be insensitive to characteristics of female alcoholics, in part because alcoholism is more of a stigma for women than for men. It is also possible that because women are more likely to be multiple drug abusers, their alcohol addiction is camouflaged.

The proportion of women who drink has risen from one-third prior to World War II to two-thirds at the present time. As to which women are more likely to become alcoholics, efforts to delineate a female alcoholic syndrome have been disappointing. . . .

It is believed that additional attention must be paid to the needs of women alcoholics. This attention seems warranted, both because of increased recognition of the problem of women drinkers and, also, because women are childbearers primarily responsible for child care. The fetal alcohol syndrome, which encompasses a broad range of brain dysfunctions, growth deficiencies, and malformations among children born of alcoholic mothers, is believed to represent a significant health risk.

Blacks

Although blacks are overrepresented in the population seeking alcoholism treatment in NIAAA-funded programs, there is evidence that the vast majority of black alcoholics either do not receive any treatment at all or receive treatment less often than members of other groups. It has been hypothesized that blacks may not seek treatment because of pressures in the black community to deny that alcoholism is a problem. If it is acknowledged as a problem, there are pressures to treat it as a moral issue rather than a medical one. It may also be, as one study found, that black alcoholics are referred for treatment less often despite greater prevalence because higher levels of drinking are assumed to be normal.

Current social conditions, such as the high rate of unemployment among blacks and the low level of jobs among those who are employed, are believed to be important factors leading to the high incidence of alcoholism. . . .

Hispanics

Despite the research showing that problem drinking is relatively widespread among the Spanish-speaking population, both here and in their native countries, systematic data on alcohol use and abuse among Hispanics are sparse. Interpretation of existing data is complicated further by the number of different ethnic groups included as Hispanic and by the heterogeneity of subgroups. Most research on problem drinking among Hispanics has focused on Mexican Americans, with less research attention being given to the alcohol problems of Puerto Rican, Cuban, Central American, and South American Hispanics.

Problem drinking among Hispanics has been hypothesized to be a result of acculturation stress, the Latin idea of "machismo," cultural acceptance, and economic deprivation. Machismo, in particular, contributes to denial of the alcohol problem and, thus, creates a barrier to seeking treatment. This also affects alcoholic Hispanic women, whose husbands restrict their access to such treatment. . . .

American Indians

The prevalence of American Indians in NIAAA-funded alcoholism treatment programs is more than 10 times what would be expected on the basis of census figures. A high incidence of alcohol-related problems among Indians has been documented, including arrests for public drunkenness and crimes associated with alcohol; high death rates from cirrhosis of the liver; accidents, suicide, and homicide; and fetal alcohol syndrome. These findings may be a function of the attention given by the Federal Government to the American Indian population and special programs established to aid the Indians. The absence of definitive studies precludes accurate estimation of the prevalence of alcohol-related problems in American Indians. . . .

Individual Difference Factors

In addition to varying with respect to sociodemographic factors, alcoholics vary in patterns of drinking, treatment, and severity of psychological and medical history symptoms. Although there are few reliable indicators of the factors that lead clients into treatment, psychological factors of dependency/passivity, intellectual and emotional functioning, self-esteem, hostility, and motivation have been found to relate to successful outcomes in a variety of studies. These factors are of weaker predictive ability than are demographic factors. Somewhat paradoxically, good indicators of treatment success include having had one's first intoxication and first alcohol-related problems at a later age, having had a longer history of heavy drinking, and having had a history of AA contact prior to treatment. While a longer history of heavy drinking is a good predictor, severe symptoms at intake are not. Symptoms of a periodic rather than a daily drinking pattern, abstinence prior to treatment, and absence of delirium tremens, are particularly predictive of good outcomes. These drinking behavior variables may be more predictive of successful outcomes than are social and psychological factors. . . .

Approaches to Alcoholism Treatment

Given the diversity of etiological understandings of alcoholism and the populations affected, it is not surprising that there are diverse treatments. Described below are the treatment modalities, settings, and providers that comprise the present health care system for alcoholism. It is important to recognize that each of the system components to be described affects the others, that specific modes of treatment can be offered in multiple settings, and that treatment providers often use several modalities and settings as part of a treatment program.

TREATMENT MODALITIES

The major treatments for alcoholism can be organized into three major approaches, which parallel etiological perspectives: 1) medical, 2) psychological, and 3) sociocultural. In practice, treatments often overlap, with psychologically oriented treatments using medications as adjuncts and drug treatments being combined with psychological techniques. In fact, the approach used with alcoholics in most treatment settings is eclectic and multivariant, with several approaches being utilized at the same time.

Medical Approaches

The difficulty of delineating the basis of alcoholism treatments is clear in any attempt to identify medical approaches. Three types of medical treatment are described here, one having to do with detoxification and the others with the use of drugs. Additional treatments that could have been included because they are often delivered by physicians, such as chemical aversion therapy and psychotherapy, are discussed as psychological approaches. The classification is less important than the nature of the treatment.

Detoxification

In the context of the present report, detoxification is not an actual alcoholism treatment, because it is not designed to treat the underlying dependence on alcohol. However, medical intervention may be necessary to manage withdrawal from alcohol and may be necessary as the first step in a treatment program. Chronic alcohol intake results in cellular alterations to which the body adapts, and withdrawal reactions may include heightened sensitivity to sensory stimuli, hyperactivity of reflexes, muscular tension and tremor, over-alertness, anxiety, insomnia, and reduced seizure threshold. The withdrawal reaction itself causes additional physical stress, and problems may be further complicated when withdrawal results from the need to recover from surgery or serious injury. The severity of symptoms depends on the intensity and duration of the patients' drinking problem.

A recommendation of hospitalization for detoxification is made for patients with severe withdrawal symptoms, medical or surgical complications, or other evidence of moderate to severe withdrawal such as a history of seizures during past withdrawals. Detoxification can also be handled on an outpatient basis or in a nonmedical setting (a detoxification center), although medical backup is required in the event of emergencies. Increasingly, efforts are being made to detoxify patients without hospitalization, although that is safe only if the patient has no implications and has available supervision.

Support services are often an important part of the treatment for withdrawal. The use of supportive services without pharmacological treatment (e.g., reassurance, reality orientation, and frequent monitoring of signs and symptoms) is known as social detoxification and has been found to be safe and effective for patients who are not experiencing severe reactions. . . .

Mood-Altering Drugs

Antidepressant medications have a long history of use in the treatment of alcoholics. The logic of their use seems persuasive, since alcoholism and depression are often inseparable. Most commonly prescribed are the tricyclic antidepressants and lithium. However, the side effects associated with these drugs and the deleterious and, at times, fatal effects of ingesting these drugs along with alcohol make their use questionable. Furthermore, these medications treat the affective disorder associated with alcohol abuse, but not alcoholism itself. . . .

Sensitizing Agents

Disulfiram (Antabuse®) is the most commonly used drug in alcoholism treatment. Antabuse® does not cure alcohol craving or dependence per se, but causes psychological effects such as respiratory difficulty, nausea, vomiting, and sweating when alcohol is ingested while the drug is active.

The intensity of reactions depends both on drug dosage and amount of alcohol subsequently ingested — with large doses of Antabuse® and alcohol combined, reactions may be fatal. After taking Antabuse®, the patient's desire to drink will be dulled by the thought of inevitably getting sick. One disadvantage is that a person can stop the Antabuse® regimen at any point and shortly thereafter (within 24 to 48 hours) be able to drink with impunity. For patients who are motivated to abstain, however, life is simplified by Antabuse®, as there is only one decision a day — either to take the pill or not to take the pill. For this reason, Antabuse®-based treatment has been described as a method of "ego-reinforcement"....

Psychological Treatments

The forms of psychological treatment vary widely and, as with medical treatment, are difficult to classify. Behavioral approaches, although based on only one of several important themes used to explain alcoholism, have been widely employed in recent years to treat alcoholics. Other psychological therapies (including nonbehavioral and the related systems approaches), while extensively employed generally, have been used less frequently to treat alcoholism specifically.

A large number of behavioral techniques to treat alcoholics have been developed over the last 30 years. Based on research that investigates how individuals learn and maintain habits, behavioral approaches are supported by an extensive basic research literature and substantial evidence of their effectiveness in treating other disorders. Often, behavioral treatments are used in conjunction with other psychological treatments as part of broad-spectrum treatment packages.

One type of behavioral technique used with alcoholics is referred to as blood-alcohol level discrimination training. Based on the assumption that alcoholics do not accurately process information about their level of intoxication, the procedure teaches alcoholics how to estimate correctly their blood-alcohol level....

A second group of behavioral techniques is used to train alcoholics to relax. These techniques are based on a tension-reduction hypothesis and an assumption that alcohol is ingested to reduce stress....

Various nonbehavioral psychotherapies are also employed with alcoholics. Nonbehavioral psychotherapy can be delivered on a one-to-one basis, in families, or in groups. The length of individual therapy varies, ranging from short term, of 12 or fewer sessions, to long term, from 2 to 7 years. The kinds of approaches vary widely enough although the approaches all have the goal of aiding the alcoholic (or family members) to understand and deal with physical or psychological dependence on alcohol....

Sociocultural Approaches

The essence of sociocultural approaches is the assumption that the successful treatment of alcoholics requires changing the social environment within which such individuals function. Such approaches share the rationale of group and family psychotherapies about the need to change the alcoholic's environment. In practice, this often means removing the alcoholic individual temporarily from his or her home and placing that individual in a new setting, such as an alcohol treatment facility. Changing the environment may also mean creating a whole new culture for the alcoholic, such as that which Alcoholics Anonymous (AA) provides.

AA is a volunteer self-help organization, which, although not a formal treatment provider, is perhaps the major resource for alcoholics in this country and elsewhere. It provides a new ideology for members by supporting abstinence from alcohol, a sense of belonging, and an involving set of activities. . . .

Combination of Treatment Modalities

Although a variety of treatment modalities have been described, it is important to note that alcoholics and alcohol abusers are rarely, if ever, treated with only one method. Thus, for example, hospitals that employ aversion conditioning may also use individual and group counseling and participation in AA as part of the treatment regimen. Psychodynamically oriented therapists may also use desensitization techniques and prescribe Antabuse® or a mood-altering drug to encourage the alcoholic to remain in treatment. Treatment providers may refer indigent alcoholics to vocational training or those with severe psychopathology for psychiatric care. The important point is that, in practice, no single treatment is considered sufficient for treatment of alcoholism.

TREATMENT SETTINGS AND PROVIDERS

A major focus of research on treatment effectiveness is often on the setting within which treatment is provided. Recently, research has begun to assess characteristics of settings in an attempt to discover effective treatment programs and appropriate patient-setting matches. Differentiating between various settings, however, is often difficult. Below, the most common treatment settings for alcoholism and the providers who deliver alcoholism services are described.

The distinguishing characteristic of inpatient care is overnight stay in a medical facility. Inpatient settings include: 1) alcoholism detoxification units and alcoholism rehabilitation units in general hospitals, 2) alcoholism treatment units in State and private psychiatric hospitals, and 3) free-standing alcoholism rehabilitation facilities. . . .

In addition to services provided on an inpatient basis, some alcoholism services are provided on an outpatient basis in nonmedically oriented residential facilities and in a variety of other settings. Like inpatient facilities, outpatient facilities vary in the extent of their medical orientation. The more medically oriented outpatient facilities include: 1) private physicians' offices, 2) community mental health centers, 3) some free-standing outpatient clinics, and 4) day care hospitalization programs. The less medically oriented include the remaining free-standing outpatient clinics. . . .

For this study, residential programs that provide primarily rehabilitation services to patients are considered here to be intermediate care facilities. Many of the patients of such programs have formerly been treated in hospitals. Such facilities include halfway houses, quarterway houses, and recovery homes. Typically, intermediate care facilities are community-based and peer group-oriented residences. They attempt to provide food, shelter, and supportive services in a nondrinking atmosphere. Residents in these programs are considered recovering alcoholics. They are ambulatory and mentally competent. Typically, they are without spouse or immediate family. The facility seems to provide psychological support and help with problems such as reentry to the work force.

Alcoholism treatment services are provided to varying degrees by correctional facilities, the military, driving while intoxicated programs, business and industry, and the so-called skid-row system of agencies. Various Federal and local government agencies support alcoholism treatment programs in correctional and military faciliites, but the contribution of these programs to alcoholism treatment, as well as the contribution of employee assistance programs, is relatively small. Most such programs serve only as referral sources to the kinds of programs discussed previously and do not provide direct treatment.

Utilization

Estimating the use of treatment settings is made difficult by the multiple sources of data and by the tendency of patients to seek and receive treatment in multiple settings, even over the course of relatively short time periods. Until recently, when authority for alcoholism treatment programs was given to States with Federal assistance through block grants, each NIAAA-funded treatment center and each project were required to collect and report data on treatment utilization.

In 1980, 460 NIAAA-funded projects reported serving almost 250,000 people. The vast majority (83 percent) of patients in NIAAA projects received outpatient treatment, sometimes in conjunction with inpatient treatment. Of the patients who received 24-hour residential care (some of these patients also receive outpatient care), 3 percent were hospital inpatients and 23 percent were in other facilities. The most common inpatient treatment was detoxification, either social (41 percent) or medical (31 percent). The most common outpatient service was individual counseling (50 percent), followed by group counseling (21 percent) and crisis intervention (11 percent). Approximately one-quarter of the patients received followup or aftercare. . . .

Another major issue in the treatment of alcoholism concerns . . . what degree of staff professionalization is required for treatment effectiveness. . . .

Conclusions

The treatments used for alcoholism are diverse, including treatments based on medical and psychotherapeutic approaches, as well as treatments based on various other approaches, such as self-help programs based on the AA model. Most treatment programs combine a variety of techniques. Adding to the complex number of treatments is the fact that the settings where treatment is delivered differ from one another on a number of key dimensions, including outpatient versus inpatient treatments, staffing patterns, and the kinds of populations who choose or are chosen for the setting. Moreover, alcohol abuse is present in various population groups, although it may manifest itself differently and require different forms of treatment. . . .

In comparing reviews and studies of alcohol treatment programs, this complexity of etiology, treatment, settings, and patients must be kept in mind. Many studies focus on a single aspect of treatment or explore a particular hypothesis, making comparisons between studies extremely difficult. General statements must be offered with great caution. . . .

Research on the Effectiveness of Alcoholism Treatment

Despite the lack of well-controlled and generalizable research on the efficacy and effectiveness of treatments for alcoholism, there is a vast literature that describes and analyzes treatment effects. The literature goes back as many years as alcoholism and alcohol abuse have been problems. In recent years, the amount of work has dramatically increased and its quality has improved. . . .

The . . . reviews [conducted by researchers] suggest a need for providing various treatments for alcoholism, although evidence on the superiority of particular treatments is lacking. The important policy issue — i.e., the extent to which alcoholism treatment should be supported — is thus only partially addressed. The question of which treatments have the best demonstrated effectiveness under particular conditions for which patients remains unanswered. . . .

Perhaps the most controversial treatment issue concerns the use of inpatient v. outpatient treatment settings. The necessity for hospitalizing alcoholics — i.e., for providing treatment over and above that necessary for detoxification or dealing with medical complications of ethanol use, is both a substantive problem (relating to treatment goals and effectiveness) and a significant policy problem (because of the high costs associated with hospitalization). Unfortunately, assessments of the effectiveness of particular settings are difficult to separate from the effectiveness of treatment modalities. The setting of treatment is only one factor influencing treatment effectiveness. . . .

There seems to be consensus across a number of literature reviews that inpatient treatment is not superior to outpatient care for alcoholism, but most of the available research is flawed because the effects of treatment variables cannot be distinguished from the effects of patient variables. Thus, more severely impaired patients and those of higher socioeconomic status are more typically assigned to, or arrange to receive, inpatient treatment. Furthermore, a distinction is not often made between hospital- and non-hospital-based inpatient (i.e., residential) treatment, although the nature of such settings may be very different. Not making this distinction results in the aggregating of results from different types of inpatient settings in literature reviews. Because alcoholism treatment takes place in a variety of hospital settings it may be important to distinguish between their effects. . . .

Research on treatment for alcoholism and alcohol abuse seems to be in transition. The 1970s saw a number of attempts to summarize conclusions of piecemeal research on treatment conducted during the last several decades. The conclusion of many of these reviews is that treatment seems better than no treatment, but that methodological problems render it difficult to conclude that any specific treatment is more effective than any other. Importantly, however, various treatments — such as aversion conditioning or AA — have been shown to be effective for some patients under some conditions. Given the diversity of alcohol problems and patients, what seem necessary are treatments tailored to specific patients.

What is also clear is that further research must be conducted to test competing claims. Although some of this research can reasonably be done without direct Government support (e.g., by proprietary organizations), a Federal role seems needed to develop such research. Ideally, both experimental and clinical trial research would be supported. Such methods, although not without their own problems, offer the best hope for providing objective and unambiguous data about treatment effectiveness.

Aside from questions of effectiveness (and, to a certain extent, of safety), efficiency issues must also be addressed. It is clear from even a cursory review of the literature, that the costs of alcoholism and alcohol abuse are very large. As the costs for treatment increase, evidence is needed about which treatments offer the greatest value for the resources required. . . .

IMPLICATIONS OF CURRENT DEVELOPMENTS

Reimbursement systems, particularly the Medicare and Medicaid programs, have emphasized inpatient, medically based treatment for alcoholism. Although there may be some patients for whom such intensive treatment is necessary and appropriate, it is also true that there are many for whom it is not appropriate. In fact, because of the stigma and time required to be treated in an acute care facility, many will not seek such treatment.

The evidence does not seem strong enough, however, to support further restricting benefits for inpatient services. Since it would not be possible to restrict acute care admissions, the likely result of not funding residential or free-standing treatment settings would probably be to increase use of acute care facilities. This situation might result if alcoholic patients were admitted under other primary diagnoses.

The best strategies would seem to be ones that encourage early outpatient treatment and continuing aftercare service on an outpatient basis. Given both research evidence that does not clearly indicate the necessity of inpatient care and the lower cost of outpatient treatment, such a strategy might lead to better use of health care resources. The recent changes in Medicare guidelines appear to be consistent with this direction. Reimbursement criteria for inpatient services are tightened, while the availability of reimbursement for outpatient treatment is increased. The new guidelines also allow for nonmedically trained personnel to be more involved in treatment.

Although it appears that the new guidelines will have positive effects in making the treatment system more efficient, it may be difficult to determine, even in a crude way, the impact of these changes. They are being introduced nationwide and at a time when the health care system and the economy are undergoing major changes. There will be no comparative data on whether and how they are effective. In addition, because the responsibility for a majority of alcoholism treatment services has been transferred from the Federal Government to the States, national data may no longer be available. It may be unclear whether the new regulations simply make possible the treatment of a larger group of alcoholics and alcohol abusers, whether their use of the benefit represents changes in the diagnostic labels given patients, and whether they achieve the intended effect of the legislation.

In light of the above, the demonstration program being carried out by HCFA/NIAAA assumes even greater importance. It is unfortunate that this study is not being done in a more experimental way and that plans for data collection are not further developed at this point. The demonstration project represents an important opportunity to collect data about the optimum treatment for alcoholism. The failure to take advantage of this opportunity may mean an even longer delay in understanding the impact of existing policy.

Conclusions

Alcoholism treatment has evolved slowly but steadily over the last 30 years in conjunction with the medical system. Although the evidence is not without methodological problems, it seems clear that alcoholism treatment has demonstrable benefits. The hypothesis that alcoholism treatment is cost beneficial seems more strongly supported than alternative hypotheses. However, the Medicare system needs adjustment in order to encourage less costly and more effective forms of treatment.

The most recent changes in Medicare guidelines seem a necessary and correct step in this process. It is possible, if inpatient treatment were further restricted, that alcoholic patients would be admitted to acute care hospitals under other primary diagnoses. The additional costs of such a development are clearly impossible to estimate. It would seem reasonable not to change eligibility standards further, however, until more information is available to indicate the effects of recent evolutionary changes in the reimbursement system. To the extent that research evidence can be developed, reimbursement decisions can be made with more confidence.

April

POLICE FOUNDATION REPORT ON DOMESTIC VIOLENCE

April 6, 1983

Evidence that could refute commonly held conceptions about preventing recurrences of domestic violence was contained in a report released April 6 by the Police Foundation, a private research organization. Based on a 16 1/2-month police experiment in Minneapolis, Minn., the study sought to determine which of three responses was most likely to prevent a recurrence of domestic violence: arrest, ordering the perpetrator to leave the premises for eight hours, or mediating the dispute and providing informal advice. The results of the study, in which about 30 police officers responded to 328 cases of domestic violence, found that recurrences were less likely if the violent individual was arrested.

Minneapolis Experiment

The experiment called for the officers to respond at random, using one of the three methods. A six-month monitoring period determined whether the violence was repeated. The results of the study, which analyzed 252 of the cases, found that violence recurred in only 10 percent of cases where an arrest had been made, compared with 17 percent for couples offered advice and 24 percent for couples temporarily separated. The study involved only simple (misdemeanor) domestic assaults where both the suspect and the victim were present when the police arrived. Cases of life-threatening or severe injury, usually labeled a felony (aggravated assault), were excluded. "The findings suggest that other things being equal, arrest may be the most effective approach, and separation may be the least effective approach" to preventing repeat offenses, the prelimi-

nary report concluded. But it cautioned, "Since other things are not usually equal ... it would probably be a mistake to conclude that arrest should be mandatory in all cases of simple domestic assault." The report found that incarceration probably was not a factor in the lower percentage of repeat offenses. Of those arrested, 43 percent were released within one day, another 43 percent were released within one week, and only 14 percent were released after one week or had not been released at the time of the follow-up interview with the victim. "This much incarceration is nowhere close to eating up 60 percent of the time at risk of the send group [persons sent out of the home for eight hours], which is what would be required to explain away the differences as an incapicitation effort," the study said.

In reaching its conclusion, the report challenged the theory held by many clinical psychologists that mediation and counseling were to be preferred to arrest as the best method of dealing with domestic violence. At the same time, the findings appeared to support the argument advanced by many women's groups that arrest was the surest way to prevent recurrence of spouse assault.

Reaction to the Study: Cautious Praise

A number of sociologists praised the report. James Q. Wilson, professor of government at Harvard University and vice chairman of the Police Foundation, said it was "a very significant study. It is almost the first time, perhaps indeed the first time ever, that anyone has attempted to assess the deterrent effect of arrest in a truly experimental way." Wilson said the findings provided "highly significant, although not conclusive," evidence that arrest could deter crime. Peter H. Rossi, professor of sociology at the University of Massachusetts and a former president of the American Sociological Association, said the report was "the first piece of evidence I know of that something can reduce the amount of violence" in domestic assault cases. Albert J. Reiss Jr., a sociology professor at Yale University and chairman of a research advisory committee at the Police Foundation, called it "a very interesting and significant experimental study" that produced "solid findings."

However, the authors of the report, Lawrence W. Sherman, director of research at the Police Foundation and professor at the University of Maryland, and Richard A. Berk of the University of California at Santa Barbara, cautioned that the study had a number of shortcomings. They noted that the way in which members of the police force interpreted "advice" varied considerably. "Some of them give threats and leave. Others sit down and talk. Others refer the couple to counseling, women's shelters, or the police chaplain. Depending on how it is done, it is still possible that some advising may be more effective than arrest. . . ."

The preliminary report did not address a number of underlying problems in dealing with domestic violence. Many cases of spouse battering have gone unreported, and police authorities often have been reluctant to get involved in such cases since spouse assault traditionally has been thought of not as a crime, but as a private marital squabble. Police indifference may have contributed to the reluctance of many battered spouses to even call the police. Police have been reluctant to get involved in domestic fights largely because they lacked training, although a growing number of police departments have formed specially trained units to deal with domestic disputes. Another reason for police reluctance was that many battered women were hesitant to prosecute their husbands. However, several states have modified their laws to make it easier to arrest wife batterers, and prosecutors in recent years have shown an increased willingness to bring domestic violence cases to trial.

Following is the text of "Police Responses to Domestic Assault: Preliminary Findings," by Lawrence W. Sherman and Richard A. Berk, prepared for the Police Foundation and released April 6, 1983:

Abstract

Does punishment deter criminals? Or does it just make their behavior worse?

Nowhere is the debate over these questions more evident than in police responses to domestic violence. Some police, like labeling theorists in sociology, argue that arresting people for minor acts of domestic violence will only increase the seriousness and frequency of the violence. Some feminist groups, like some deterrence theorists, argue that arresting suspects of domestic violence will reduce the suspects' use of violence.

With the support of the National Institute of Justice, the Police Foundation and the Minneapolis Police Department tested these hypotheses in a field experiment. Three police responses to simple assault were systematically assigned: arrest, "advice" or informal mediation, and an order to the suspect to leave for eight hours. The behavior of the suspect was tracked for six months after the police intervention, with a variety of measures. Preliminary analysis of the official recidivism measures suggests that the arrested suspects manifested significantly less violence than those who were ordered to leave, and less violence than those who were advised but not separated.

Other interpretations of the results are possible. But if this one is correct, it suggests that police should reverse their current practice of rarely making arrests and frequently separating the parties. The findings suggest that other things being equal, arrest may be the most effective approach, and separation may be the least effective approach. Since other things are not usually equal, however, it would probably be a mistake to conclude that arrest should be mandatory in *all* cases of simple domestic assault.

The Policy Problem

For many years, police have been reluctant to make arrests in response to domestic violence, one of the more common situations they face. [R.I.] Parnas' (1972) qualitative observations of the Chicago police found four categories of police action in these situations: negotiating or otherwise "talking out" the dispute, threatening the disputants and then leaving, asking one of the parties to leave the premises, or (very rarely) making an arrest. Parnas offers ten different reasons why police avoid making arrests, one of which is an explicit labeling theory formulation: the offender, angered by his arrest, may cause more serious harm to the victim upon his return to the family home.

The reluctance of police to make arrests for this offense is reported in many other cities. Surveys of battered women who tried to have their domestic assailants arrested report that arrest occurred in 10% or 3% of the cases. Surveys of police agencies in Illinois and New York found explicit policies against arrest in the majority of the agencies surveyed. Despite the fact that violence is reported to be present in one-third to two-thirds of all domestic disturbances police respond to, police department data show arrests in only 5 percent of those disturbances in Oakland, 6 percent of those disturbances in a Colorado city and 6 percent in Los Angeles County.

The best available evidence on the frequency of arrest is the observations from the [Donald] Black and Reiss study of Boston, Washington and Chicago police in 1966, reported in Black. Police responding to disputes in those cities made arrests in 27% of violent felonies and 17% of the violent misdemeanors. Among married couples, they made arrests in 26% of the cases, but tried to remove one of the parties in 38% of the cases.

The apparent preference of many police for separation rather than arrests of the suspect has been attacked from two directions over the last fifteen years. The original attack came from clinical psychologists, who agreed that police should rarely make arrests in domestic assault cases, but who wanted the police to mediate rather than separate. A highly publicized demonstration project of teaching police special counseling skills for family crisis intervention failed to show a reduction in violence, but was interpreted as a success nonetheless. By 1977, a national survey of police agencies with 100 or more officers found that over 70 percent of them reported a family crisis intervention training program in operation. While it is not clear whether these programs reduced separation and increased mediation, evaluations of some of them reported a decline in arrests, which many programs adopted as a specific goal.

By the mid-1970s, police practices were attacked from the opposite direction by feminist groups. No sooner had the psychologists succeeded in having many police agencies treat domestic violence intervention as "half social work and half police work" than feminists began to argue police put "too much emphasis on the social work aspect and not enough on the criminal." Widely publicized lawsuits in New York and Oakland sought to compel police to make arrests in every case of domestic assault, and state legislatures were lobbied successfully to reduce the evidentiary requirements needed for police to make arrests for misdemeanor domestic assaults. Some legislatures have even passed statutes *requiring* police to make arrests in these cases.

The feminist critique was bolstered by a study that suggested the seriousness of police interventions in these cases. It found that in the two years prior to the occurrence of a sample of domestic homicides, police had intervened in disputes involving 85% of the victims at least once and in 54% of the cases five or more times. But it is impossible to determine from the cross sectional data whether making more or fewer arrests would have reduced the homicide rate after police intervention.

In sum, police officers confronting a domestic assault suspect faces [*sic*] at least three conflicting options, urged on them by different groups with different theories. The officers' colleagues might recommend forced separation as a means of achieving short-term peace. The officers' trainers might recommend mediation as a means of getting to the underlying cause of the "dispute" (in which both parties are implicitly assumed to be at fault). The local women's organizations may recommend that the officer protect the victim (whose fault, if any, is legally irrelevant) and enforce the law to deter such acts in the future. If the officers take sociology courses, they will conclude that labeling theorists imply mediation would be the response least likely to provoke further violence, with separation a mild label and arrest a severe label likely to engender secondary deviance. The officers' reading of the deterrence doctrine would be exactly opposite: arrest would cause the greatest discomfort, separation the next greatest, and mediation the least discomfort, so they should deter subsequent violent acts in that descending rank order of effectiveness.

The Original Research Design

In order to shed some empirical light on these conflicting recommendations, the Police Foundation and the Minneapolis Police Department agreed to conduct a classic experiment. The design called for systematic use of arrest, separation, and some form of mediation, with a six month follow-up period to measure the frequency and seriousness of violence after each police intervention. The systematic use of these treatments, unlike a cross-sectional survey of police actions and subsequent violence, is much more effective in holding other factors constant. With sufficient numbers of cases, the social characteristics of the suspects in all three treatment groups should be very similar. The only difference between them should be due to the police actions, not to pre-existing differences in the average group tendencies to commit violence.

The design only applied to simple (misdemeanor) domestic assaults where both the suspect and the victim were present when the police arrived. The experiment included only those cases in which police were empowered (but not required) to make arrests under Minnesota state law: the police officer must have probable cause to believe that a cohabitant or spouse had assaulted the victim within the last four hours. Cases of life-threatening or severe injury, usually labeled as a felony (aggravated assault), were excluded from the design.

The predominantly minority female research staff was then supposed to contact the victims (of whom 57% were white, 23% were black, and 18% were Indian . . .) for one long inteview, and telephone followup interviews every two weeks for 24 weeks. The interviews were designed to measure the frequency and seriousness of victimizations caused by the suspect after the police interventions. We even planned to interview the offenders, although without much optimism about a high response rate. The research staff were also to gather data on offense reports or arrest reports that mentioned the suspect's names during the six month followup, as well as police cars dispatched for domestic disturbances to the victim's address. . . .

Results

This preliminary analysis examines two of the possible outcome measures. One is a "failure" of the suspect to survive the six month followup period without having police generate a written report on the suspect for domestic violence, either through an offense report, an arrest report, or a subsequent report to the project research staff of a randomized (or other) intervention by study officers. A second measure comes from the initial interviews, in which the research staff asked the victims what happened when the couple was alone again without the police present. The official recidivism or "failure" data demonstrate a strong difference between suspects arrested and suspects ordered to leave the residence for eight hours. The "sent" suspects were almost two and a half times more likely to generate a new official report of domestic violence than the arrested suspects, a difference that is statistically significant. The differences between advise and send, and between advise and arrest could have been obtained by chance. But additional analyses of these differences makes all of them close to being statistically significant.

An obvious rival hypothesis to the deterrent effect of arrest is that arrest incapacitates. If the arrested suspects spend a large portion of the next six months in jail, they would be expected to have lower recidivism rates. But the initial interview data show this is not the case: of those arrested, 43% were released within one day, another 43% were released within one week, and only 14% were released after one week or had not yet been released at the time of the initial victim interview. This much incarceration is nowhere close to eating up 60% of the time at risk of the send group, which is what would be required to explain away the differences as an incapacitation effect. We can therefore eliminate incapacitation as an explanation of the differences in six-month recidivism rates.

Discussion

How much should one make of these results? Several cautions are clearly required before reaching any policy conclusions, yet there are reasons to place some confidence in these results regardless of the cautions.

One caution is that this paper only presents two measures of recidivism. We have yet to analyze several other measures. One is the followup interviews of the victims, reporting the frequency and seriousness of the violence they suffered over six months, much of which may not have come to the attention of the police. Another measure is the record of police cars dispatched to the victims' addresses for domestics or related calls for service over the six month followup period. Since all measurement is imperfect, multiple measures pointing to the same conclusions strengthen confidence in the conclusion. If these additional measures of six month recidivism show the same differences across police actions, then we can be much more confident that the differences are real. If they do not show the same pattern, then the interpretation of the results will become less certain. But since the first cut at the followup interview data shows the same pattern as the official recidivism data, we are optimistic that the measures will not be inconsistent.

A further caution is that the "advise" category is a catchall, done in different ways by different officers. Some of them give threats and leave. Others sit down and talk. Others refer the couple to counseling, women's shelters, or the police chaplain. Depending on how it is done, it is still possible that some advising may be more effective than arrest, or even less effective than send, in reducing the risks of subsequent violence.

Despite all the cautions, it is clear that the recidivism measure is lowest when police make arrests. And in many ways, it is the most important measure in the study. It is also the measure that has been used to evaluate most programs for reducing individual criminal behavior. So it is not totally incautious to assume that we do have some reliable differences in violence in the three categories.

What of the policy implications of these findings? We should be very cautious in jumping to policy recommendations from these data. Even when the analysis is complete, it will still only be one experiment. In the physical sciences, many replications — sometimes hundreds — would be needed before reaching a policy conclusion. Moreover, it is still possible that the other measure of recidivism may be inconsistent with the police report data presented here.

Nonetheless, public policy cannot always wait for perfect information, and must rely on the best available facts, even if they turn out later to be wrong. Whether by subsequent analysis of these data, or by subsequent replications, it is possible that further study could lead to different conclusions. Hence, policy-makers should never assume studies "prove" anything; studies merely provide one more piece of information.

This preliminary analysis apparently suggests that, other things being equal, police should arrest suspects for simple domestic assault rather than sending them out of the residence, or even (perhaps) advising the couple. This implication is weakened by all the cautions we have noted. But it is strengthened by the nature of the recidivism measure. Assuming that those offenders who are more aggressive to the police are also more aggressive to their spouses, these findings probably show how to deal with that most aggressive group of tough cases. Even if the other measures show different patterns for the full range of offenders, these findings could still hold true for what are possibly the most serious cases. We can check this by analyzing the other measures while controlling for criminal records, sample size permitting.

Other things are not equal, of course. Police actions may always have different effects on different people, depending on the maze of factors that influence human behavior. Just as there is no replacement for a doctor's diagnostic judgment, there may be no replacement for a police officer's judgment. Both doctors and police can be wrong, but their use of judgment may be preferable to an automatic rule that applies to every case of lymphatic cancer or spouse assault.

No matter how reliable these findings, there may still be cases in which arrest will backfire. We will try to say more about that in subsequent reports. But the last policy implication that should be drawn from this analysis is that arrests for simple domestic assault should be made mandatory. It may be reasonable to recommend from these findings that police should make *more* arrests and fewer sends. The data do not necessarily support a recommendation of *always* making an arrest.

MX COMMISSION REPORT

April 6, 1983

An influential endorsement for developing the controversial MX inter-continental ballistic missile (ICBM) was given April 6 when a presidential commission recommended that the United States go ahead with producing 100 of the huge nuclear weapons and deploy them in existing missile silos. At the same time, the blue-ribbon panel urged the Pentagon to begin developing a new, smaller missile that could become the keystone of a radical new approach to stabilizing the nuclear balance between U.S. and Soviet nuclear forces. The report was made public April 11.

President Ronald Reagan had turned over the question of the future of the U.S. missile force to the commission January 3 after Congress in December 1982 turned down the administration's "dense pack" MX basing proposal. Similarly, the Carter administration had been unable to win congressional approval of its plan to base the MX in a "race track" configuration covering hundreds of miles in lightly populated areas of the West. (Background on MX, Historic Documents of 1982, p. 903)

Chaired by Brent Scowcroft, former national security adviser to Presidents Richard Nixon and Gerald R. Ford, the panel's 10 senior members and seven "senior consultants" included four former secretaries of defense and two former secretaries of state. Efforts were made to devise a politically acceptable plan for housing the 100-ton, multi-warhead missile, the newest in America's strategic land-based nuclear arsenal. President Reagan April 19 endorsed the plan as "absolutely essential both for maintaining an effective deterrent [to a Soviet attack] and for achieving successful arms reductions" in U.S.-Soviet strategic arms reduction (START).

Highlights of Commission Report

The presidential commission acknowledged that silo-based MXs would be as vulnerable to Soviet missiles as the existing Minuteman ICBMs housed in those silos. Thus, after nearly a decade in which the public debate over MX had been dominated by the search for a basing method that would permit the MX to survive a massive Soviet attack, the commission abandoned the argument for MX as being a more "survivable" successor to Minuteman.

Instead, it justified MX (shorthand for "missile experimental") on grounds of its military potency and political symbolism — as a counterweight to several hundred existing Soviet missiles, some of which were even more lethal than MX. With 10 warheads, more accurate and potentially more powerful than the three warheads on the existing Minuteman III missile, MX was designed to destroy armored underground targets, such as ICBM silos and command centers. By most estimates, approximately 600 Soviet ICBMs, carrying six to 10 warheads each, possessed such so-called "hard-target kill capability."

In tandem with MX, production of a small, single-warhead missile would deal with the survivability problem over the long run, the commission argued. Because the projected new missile would weigh about 30,000 pounds — compared with 192,000 pounds for MX — its launchers could be made mobile in ways that would be difficult or impossible for MX launchers, thus thwarting a Soviet attack.

As a third component of the commission's package, linked to the new small missile, the panel held out the hope of inducing Moscow to join the United States in gradually shifting their land-based missile forces to single-warhead weapons. The commission said this would restore a degree of stability to the nuclear balance that had been lost with the advent of missiles that could carry accurate MIRVs — multiple warheads.

Most defense experts agreed that accurate MIRVs made the strategic balance "unstable" because, while both superpowers had roughly similar numbers of missiles, MIRVs conferred at least a theoretical advantage to whichever side fired its missiles first in a crisis. Because each attacking missile could destroy several of the opponent's not-yet-launched missiles (using its multiple warheads), an attacker could obliterate his opponent's missile force while retaining most of his own missiles.

Arguments for Deploying the MX

Nonetheless, the commission cited four principal reasons for going ahead with deploying 100 MXs (the number Reagan had sought). Many of the panel's arguments in favor of MX production were similar to those previously advanced by the Reagan administration.

● *Impact on the START negotiations. Past experience indicated that "arms control negotiations — in particular the Soviets' willingness to enter agreements that will enhance stability — are heavily influenced by ongoing programs," the panel said. "It is illusory to believe that we could obtain a satisfactory agreement with the Soviets if we unilaterally terminated the only new U.S. ICBM program that could lead to deployment in this decade."*

● *Impact on Soviet perceptions. "Effective deterrence is in no small measure a question of the Soviets' perceptions of our national will and cohesion," the panel stated. "Cancelling the MX, when it is ready for flight testing, when over $5 billion have already been spent on it, and when its importance has been stressed by the last four Presidents, does not communicate to the Soviets that we have the will essential to effective deterrence. Quite the opposite."*

● *Impact on the strategic balance. The MX would give the United States a "credible capability for controlled, prompt, limited attack on hard targets" to counter the Soviets' existing "massive ability to destroy hardened land-based military targets."*

● *Need to retain and modernize the ICBM force. Noting that the existing ICBM fleet was "aging significantly," the panel said the MX, with its greater throw weight (total weight of warheads carried), would be better able than the Minuteman to get through Soviet missile defenses by carrying decoys and other penetration devices.*

Vulnerability Issue Downgraded

Although the panel acknowledged that "reasonable survivability of fixed targets, such as ICBM silos, may not outlast this century," it implicitly called into question the so-called "window of vulnerability" emphasized in the early days of the Reagan administration. In so doing, the commission reaffirmed the longstanding commitment to the strategic triad of forces (land-based ICBMs, submarine-launched ballistic missiles and nuclear warheads carried by long-range bombers) by noting that the Soviets would have to count on the survivability of some U.S. bombers and submarines if they launched a massive attack on American land-based ICBMs. And Moscow also would have to take into consideration the possibility that MXs would be available for use "in any circumstances other than that of a massive surprise attack on the United States."

In concluding that silo-based MX missiles would be as vulnerable to Soviet missiles as the existing Minuteman, and thus divorcing the missile from the quest for survivability, the commission opened up for future debate what long had been a key issue among defense and arms control specialists: whether deterrence required a rough symmetry in the U.S. and Soviet ICBM force; that is, whether the United States needed missiles that were militarily and symbolically equivalent to the Soviets'.

If either side's strategic forces could be made more secure "by arms control agreements which lead both sides toward more survivable modes of basing than is possible with large launchers and missiles, the increase in stability would be further enhanced," the panel predicted. U.S. initiatives in that direction might prod the Soviets to do likewise.

Congress Approves MX Funds

Scowcroft said the report was a "consensus" approach that had "the best chance" of success on Capitol Hill. Nevertheless, the report's recommendation for a return to a basing plan that had been attacked in Congress as vulnerable to Soviet attack and its emphasis on a new generation of missiles, might "confound, complicate and frustrate" efforts to go ahead with MX production and deployment, he conceded.

A number of members of Congress indicated that they would support the recommendations of the bipartisan commission. A few members, however, opposed support for any MX deployment scheme that did not promise to be invulnerable to Soviet attack.

And liberal members remained adamantly opposed to deployment of powerful, accurate missiles. In their view, deterrence resulted from the sheer destructive power of each superpower's nuclear arsenal and not from either side's detailed calculations of how particular nuclear war scenarios might be played out. From this perspective, the alleged advantages of Soviet ICBMs were inconsequential, given the thousands of U.S. warheads on bombers and missile submarines that would survive a Soviet attack on U.S. ICBMs.

Reagan's endorsement of the Scowcroft commission's recommendations led the way toward deployment of the MX. The House May 24 and the Senate May 25 approved legislation that permitted funds to be used for MX flight testing and for housing the missile in reinforced Minuteman silos. During the MX debate, several members from each chamber warned the White House that their continued support for MX would depend on the administration's good faith in pursuing arms control efforts.

The president followed up his assurances by announcing modifications in the U.S. position at the START talks. The changes, announced June 8, brought the U.S. position more in line with the commission's recommendation that U.S. policy encourage a gradual shift in both arsenals away from large MIRVed warheads to smaller, single-warhead missiles. (Further Reagan arms control proposals, p. 791)

The MX had another hurdle to clear — the House and Senate vote on production funds for the missile. Lobbying was intense, especially on the part of the White House. Opposing MX production funds were groups such as Common Cause, SANE, the Council for a Livable World and an assortment of religious and environmental organizations.

The administration and congressional MX supporters prevailed when the Democratic House July 20 voted 220-207 to approve production of the MX. The Republican-controlled Senate followed suit July 26 by a vote of 58-41, only slightly closer than the 59-39 previous vote to continue flight-testing of the missile. House-Senate conferees on the bill Aug. 4 agreed to fund 21 of the missiles ($2.1 billion) rather than the 27 ($2.4 billion) requested and approved by the Senate. The closeness of the July House vote indicated, however, that MX still might not travel a smooth path toward deployment.

The principal argument in favor of going ahead with MX production was its value as a bargaining tool in the START talks. In a letter to House members, Reagan said the MX was a "lever that is working . . . to keep the Soviets moving at the negotiation tables. . . ."

Following are excerpts from the "Report of the President's Commission on Strategic Forces," submitted April 6, 1983. (Boldface headings in brackets have been added by Congressional Quarterly to highlight the organization of the text.):

Strategic Modernization Programs
ICBM PROGRAMS

. . . The Commission has concluded that the preferred approach for modernizing our ICBM force seems to have three components: initiating engineering design of a single-warhead small ICBM, to reduce target value and permit flexibility in basing for better long-term survivability; seeking arms control agreements designed to enhance strategic stability; and deploying MX missiles in existing silos now to satisfy the immediate needs of our ICBM force and to aid that transition.

A more stable structure of ICBM deployments would exist if both sides moved toward more survivable methods of basing than is possible when there is primary dependence on large launchers and missiles. Thus from the point of view of enhancing such stability, the Commission believes that there is considerable merit in moving toward an ICBM force structure in which potential targets are of comparatively low value — missiles containing only one warhead. A single-warhead ICBM, suitably based, inherently denies an attacker the opportunity to destroy more than one warhead with one attacking warhead. The need to have basing flexibility, and particularly the need to keep open the option for different types of mobile basing, also suggests a missile of small size. If force survivability can be additionally increased by arms control agreements which lead both sides toward more survivable modes of basing than is possible with large launchers and missiles, the increase in stability would be further enhanced.

In the meantime, however, deployment of MX is essential in order to remove the Soviet advantage in ICBM capability and to help deter the threat of conventional or limited nuclear attacks on the alliance. Such deployment is also necessary to encourage the Soviets to move toward the more stable regime of deployments and arms control. . . .

The Commission stresses that these two aspects of ICBM modernization and this approach toward arms control are integrally related. They point toward the same objective — permitting the U.S. and encouraging the Soviets to move toward more stable ICBM deployments over time in a way that is consistent with arms control agreements having the objective of reducing the risk of war. The Commission is unanimous that no one part of the proposed program can accomplish this alone.

[Small, Single-Warhead ICBM]

The Commission believes that a single-warhead missile weighing about fifteen tons (rather than the nearly 100 tons of MX) may offer greater flexibility in the long-run effort to obtain an ICBM force that is highly survivable, even when viewed in isolation, and that can consequently serve as a hedge against potential threats to the submarine force.

The Commission thus recommends beginning engineering design of such an ICBM, leading to the initiation of full-scale development in 1987 and an initial operating capability in the early 1990s. The design of such a missile, hardened against nuclear effects, can be achieved with current technology. It should have sufficient accuracy and yield to put Soviet hardened military targets at risk. During that period an approach toward arms control, consistent with such deployments, should also seek to encourage the Soviets to move toward a more stable ICBM force structure at levels which would obviate the need to deploy very large numbers of such missiles. The development effort for such a missile need not and should not be burdened with the uncertainties accompanying a crash program; thus its timing can be such that competitive development is feasible.

Decisions about such a small missile and its basing will be influenced by several potential developments: the evolution of Soviet strategic programs, the path of arms control negotiations and agreements, general trends in technology, the cost of the program, operational considerations, and the results of our own research on specific basing modes. Although the small missile program should be pursued vigorously, the way these uncertainties are resolved will inevitably influence the size and nature of the program. We should keep in mind, however, that having several different modes of deployment may serve our objective of stability. The objective for the United States should be to have an overall program that will so confound, complicate, and frustrate the efforts of Soviet strategic war planners that, even in moments of stress, they could not believe that they could attack our ICBM forces effectively.

Different ICBM deployment modes by the U.S. would require different types of planned Soviet attacks. Deployment in hardened silos would require the Soviets to plan to use warheads that are large, accurate, or both. Moreover, for those silos or shelters holding a missile with only one warhead, each would present a far less attractive target than would be the case for a silo containing a large missile with many MIRVs. Mobile deployments of U.S. missiles would require the Soviets to try to barrage large areas using a number of warheads for each of our warheads at risk, to develop very sophisticated intelligence systems, or both. In this context, deployment of a small single-warhead ICBM in hardened mobile launchers is of particular interest because it could permit deployment in peacetime in limited areas such as military reservations. Land-mobile deployments without hard launchers could be threatened by a relatively small attack — in the absence of an appropriate arms control agreement — unless our own missiles were distributed widely across the country in peacetime. The key advantages of a small single-warhead missile are that it would reduce the value of each strategic target and that it is also compatible with either fixed or mobile deployments, or with combinations of the two.

As discussed below ... deployment of such small missiles would be compatible with arms control agreements reducing the number of warheads, in which case only a small number of such missiles would probably need to be deployed. If the Soviets proved unwilling to reach such agreements, however, the U.S. could deploy whatever number of small missiles were [sic] required — in whatever mix of basing modes — to maintain an adequate overall deterrent.

[Continuing Need for MX]

There are important needs on several grounds for ICBM modernization that cannot be met by the small, single-warhead ICBM.

First, arms control negotiations — in particular the Soviets' willingness to enter agreements that will enhance stability — are heavily influenced by ongoing programs. The ABM Treaty of 1972, for example, came about only because the United States maintained an ongoing ABM program and indeed made a decision to make a limited deployment. It is illusory to believe that we could obtain a satisfactory agreement with the Soviets limiting ICBM deployments if we unilaterally terminated the only new U.S. ICBM program that could lead to deployment in this decade. Such a termination would effectively communicate to the Soviets that we were unable to neutralize their advantage in multiple-warhead ICBMs. Abandoning the MX at this time in search of a substitute would jeopardize, not enhance, the likelihood of reaching a stabilizing and equitable agreement. It would also undermine the incentives to the Soviets to change the nature of their own ICBM force and thus the environment most conducive to the deployment of a small missile.

Second, effective deterrence is in no small measure a question of the Soviets' perception of our national will and cohesion. Cancelling the MX, when it is ready for flight testing, when over $5 billion have already been spent on it, and when its importance has been stressed by the last four

Presidents, does not communicate to the Soviets that we have the will essential to effective deterrence. Quite the opposite.

Third, the serious imbalance between the Soviets' massive ability to destroy hardened land-based military targets with their ballistic missile force and our lack of such a capability must be redressed promptly. Our ability to assure our allies that we have the capability and will to stand with them, with whatever forces are necessary, if the alliance is threatened by massive conventional, chemical or biological, or limited nuclear attack, is in question as long as this imbalance exists. Even before the Soviet leaders, in a grave crisis, considered using the first tank regiment or the first SS-20 missile against NATO, they must be required to face what war would mean to them. In order to augment what we would hope would be an inherent sense of conservation and caution on their part, we must have a credible capability for controlled, prompt, limited attack on hard targets ourselves. This capability casts a shadow over the calculus of Soviet risk-taking at any level of confrontation with the West. Consequently, in the interest of the alliance as a whole, we cannot safely permit a situation to continue wherein the Soviets have the capability promptly to destroy a range of hardened military targets and we do not.

Fourth, our current ICBM force is aging significantly. The Titan II force is being retired for this reason and extensive Minuteman rehabilitation programs are planned to keep those missiles operational.

. . . As Soviet ABM modernization and modern surface-to-air missile development and deployment proceed — even within the limitations of the ABM treaty — it is important to be able to match any possible Soviet breakout from that treaty with strategic forces that have the throw-weight to carry sufficient numbers of decoys and other penetration aids. . . . Having in production a missile that could effectively counter such a Soviet step should help deter them from taking it. . . .

These objectives can all be accomplished, at reasonable cost, by deploying MX missiles in current Minuteman silos.

In the judgment of the Commission, the vulnerability of such silos in the near term, viewed in isolation, is not a sufficiently dominant part of the overall problem of ICBM modernization to warrant other immediate steps being taken such as closely-spacing new silos or ABM defense of those silos. This is because of the mutual survivability shared by the ICBM force and the bomber force in view of the different types of attacks that would need to be launched at each. . . . To deter . . . surprise attacks we can reasonably rely both on our other strategic forces and on the range of operational uncertainties that the Soviets would have to consider in planning such aggression — as long as we have underway a program for long-term ICBM survivability such as that for the small, single warhead ICBM to hedge against long-term vulnerability for the rest of our forces. . . .

A program of deploying on the order of 100 MX missiles in existing Minuteman silos would . . . accomplish the objectives set forth . . . and it would do so without threatening stability. . . .

Arms Control

... Over the long run, stability would be fostered by a dual approach toward arms control and ICBM deployments which moves toward encouraging small, single-warhead ICBMs. This requires that arms control limitations and reductions be couched, not in terms of launchers, but in terms of equal levels of warheads of roughly equivalent yield. Such an approach could permit relatively simple agreements, using appropriate counting rules, that exert pressure to reduce the overall number and destructive power of nuclear weapons and at the same time give each side an incentive to move toward more stable and less vulnerable deployments.

Arms control agreements of this sort — simple and flexible enough to permit stabilizing development and modernization programs, while imposing quantitative limits and reductions — can make an important contribution to the stability of the strategic balance. An agreement that permitted modernization of forces and also provided an incentive to reduce while modernizing, in ways that would enhance stability, would be highly desirable. It would have the considerable benefit of capping both sides' strategic forces at levels that would be considerably lower than they would otherwise reach over time. It would also recognize, realistically, that each side will naturally desire to configure its own strategic forces. Simple aggregate limits of this sort are likely to be more practical, stabilizing, and lasting than elaborate, detailed limitations on force structure and modernization whose ultimate consequences cannot be confidently anticipated.

Encouraging stability by giving incentives to move toward less vulnerable deployments is more important than reducing quickly the absolute number of warheads deployed. Reductions in warhead numbers, while desirable for long-term reasons of limiting the cost of strategic systems, should not be undertaken at the expense of influencing the characteristics of strategic deployments. For example, warhead reductions, while desirable, should not be proposed or undertaken at a rate that leads us to limit the number of launching platforms to such low levels that their survivability is made more questionable.

For a variety of historical, technical, and verification reasons, both the SALT II unratified treaty and the current START proposal contain proposals to limit or reduce the number of ICBM launchers or missiles. Unfortunately this has helped produce the tendency to identify arms control with launcher or missile limits, and to lead some to identify successful arms control with low or reduced launcher or missile limits. This has, in turn, led to an incentive to build launchers and missiles as large as possible and to put as many warheads as possible into each missile. Such an incentive has been augmented by the cost savings involved in putting a given number of warheads on a few large missiles rather than on a number of smaller ones. ...

We will have for some time strategic forces in which the number of launchers on one side are outnumbered many times over by the number of warheads on the other. Under such circumstances, it is not stabilizing to use arms control to require mutual reductions in the number of launching platforms (e.g. submarines or ICBM launchers) or missiles. Such a requirement further increases the ratio of warheads to targets. It does not promote deterrence and reduce the risk of war for the Soviets to have many more times the number of accurate warheads capable of destroying hard targets than the U.S. has ICBM launchers.

In time we should try to promote an evolution toward forces in which — with an equal number of warheads — each side is encouraged to see to the survivability of its own forces in a way that does not threaten the other. But if the Soviet Union chooses to retain a large force of large missiles, each with many warheads, the U.S. must be free to match this by the sort of deployment it chooses. Any arms control agreement equating SS-18s and small single-warhead ICBMs because each is one missile or because each is on one launcher would be destabilizing in the extreme. . . .

. . . [I]t should be noted that, as a method of restricting ICBM modernization, the negotiated SALT II Treaty, which would have expired in 1985, would have prohibited testing of more than one new ICBM. The two-part ICBM modernization program suggested by the Commission would not violate that negotiated agreement because testing of a small, single-warhead ICBM could not begin before this expiration date. Of more long-term importance, however, the approach toward arms control and force modernization suggested here is fundamentally compatible with the sort of stability that SALT II sought to achieve. SALT II specifically contemplated the negotiation of extension agreements with improved terms, and there is no reason to doubt that future extension agreements would have allowed the testing and deployment of a second new ICBM missile with the stabilizing potential of a small, single-warhead ICBM. Moreover, the Soviets have tested two new ICBMs since October 1982.

The current Administration's START proposal is centered on warhead limitations and reductions, with some attention to throw-weight limitations. These are consistent with the Commission's recommended program. It also contains a proposed limit on launchers that the Commission believes should be reassessed since it is not compatible with a desirable evolution toward small, single-warhead ICBMs.

Some current arms control proposals in Congress concentrate on warhead limitations in which reductions are forced in warhead numbers as a price of modernization; others seek explicitly to encourage movement toward small, single-warhead ICBMs on both sides. These general directions are also consistent with the approach suggested in this report.

The Commission urges the continuation of vigorous pursuit of arms control; it is beyond the scope of this report, however, for the Commission to recommend specific arms control proposals, the size of numerical limits, or the pace and scope of reductions. Of course any arms control proposal must be carefully designed with a view to compliance and verification. . . .

REPORT OF INTER-AMERICAN DIALOGUE COMMISSION

April 7, 1983

A group of 48 leading private citizens from the United States, Latin America and Canada, most of whom had held high-level government positions in the recent past, participated in a five-month-long "Inter-American Dialogue" sponsored by the Woodrow Wilson International Center for Scholars. From October 1982 through March 1983 the group discussed issues of mutual concern: economic interdependence, social and political development and military security.

Issued in April 1983, the commission's report concluded that poverty, not external military pressure, was the major cause of the region's political, economic and social instability. The group recommended that meaningful solutions could come chiefly from a "many-sided dialogue" involving regional governments, opposition forces and influential outside powers, including the United States and the Soviet Union. Economic and social development was the ultimate key to Central American peace and prosperity, the report said.

The report received wide press coverage in part because of the prestige of the group's participants, who included cochairmen Sol Linowitz, former U.S. ambassador to the Organization of American States, and Galo Plaza, former president of Ecuador.

Contrast With Reagan Policies

The group's observations mirrored the feelings of many congressional leaders who opposed President Ronald Reagan's emphasis on the military situation in Central America.

Less than three weeks after the commission report was published, Reagan addressed a nationally televised joint session of Congress to urge deployment of more U.S. military equipment and advisers to assist the U.S.-supported government of El Salvador as well as guerrilla forces fighting the leftist, Cuban- and Soviet-supported Sandinista regime in Nicaragua. The president emphasized the threat posed to the entire hemisphere by the turmoil in Central America. (Reagan address, p. 439)

In contrast to the president's address, the Inter-American Dialogue participants suggested that while the United States had legitimate concerns about threats to its security arising from revolutionary conditions in Central America, many Latin Americans felt "profound change [was] inevitable in their region, and that an emphasis on immediate stability is therefore misguided." The report said the United States should recognize that "some relative loss of U.S. influence [in the region] is to be expected in a rapidly changing world, and that the risks of intervention considerably outweigh those of a more restrained role."

Economic, Social and Political Issues

The report, entitled The Americas at a Crossroads, *opened with a discussion of economic interdependence among the nations of North, Central and South America. Because Latin American governments had borrowed heavily from North American banks and were suffering particularly from the worldwide recession, which cut sharply into their export markets, the servicing and repayment of their debts was in jeopardy. Consequently, the financial stability of the entire hemisphere was seriously threatened. The forum's participants recommended a variety of steps that international lenders and borrowers should take to preserve the long-term health of the fragile system.* (International Monetary Fund meeting, p. 801)

The report also discussed methods of promoting social and political progress, emphasizing why the group felt that the major powers should adopt a "hands-off" attitude toward fledgling Central American democracies. "We want to see the incipient trend toward democratization prosper," wrote the authors, "but we fear that efforts from abroad to advance the process could produce adverse effects if they are interventionist." However, the group supported "carefully considered" multilateral action to protect human rights, calling it an "international obligation." (State Department human rights report, p. 181)

Peacekeeping Proposals

The third section of the report, dealing with security and peacekeeping

*issues, presented specific alternatives to existing U.S. policy. It recom-
mended initiating a dialogue among all of the involved parties, including
the Soviet Union and Cuba, possibly under the aegis of a proposal made
by Colombia, Mexico, Panama and Venezuela in January 1983. That
plan called for removing Latin American issues from the East-West
confrontation in which, the signatories charged, the Reagan administration had placed them. The four-nation group also offered to facilitate the
negotiations.*

*The United States could contribute greatly to peace in the region, the
Inter-American Dialogue group concluded, by making it "unequivocally
clear" that it was committed to "respect national sovereignty" and
refraining from overt and covert intervention. The participants also
urged Cuba, the Soviet Union and the United States to pledge an end to
all actions "regarded as aggressive and threatening by the other," just as
they had at the end of the 1962 Cuban missile crisis.*

*Following are excerpts from the April 7, 1983, report of the
Inter-American Dialogue Commission, entitled* The Americas at a Crossroads:

Introduction

The Americas are at a crossroads, at a juncture of unusual danger and of
special opportunity.

After three decades of sustained economic growth, Latin America now
faces severe depression. Not only has growth in the region ceased — 1982
was the first year in forty that gross income in Latin America declined —
but financial systems are faltering, bankruptcies are common, trade has
declined, and unemployment is staggering.

Last year also saw the outbreak of the Malvinas/Falklands war, the first
outright military confrontation in memory between a Latin American
nation and one from outside the Hemisphere. Recent years have also seen
intense frictions over the borders between Argentina and Chile and
between Peru and Ecuador, as well as smoldering conflicts between
Venezuela and Guyana, Guatemala and Belize, and Nicaragua and Colombia. For the first time since the 1930s, multiple border wars seem possible
in Latin America.

In Central America, scene of so much tragedy, civil wars are escalating
within several nations and armed clashes across borders are threatening.
Military involvement in the region by non-Central American nations
appears to be escalating as well, and the danger of a reigon-wide conflagra-
tion cannot be discounted.

Immigration, long a fact of life in hemispheric affairs, is increasing and
becoming more conflictive. The combination of economic downturn and
political convulsions increases the pressure to emigrate, while economic
difficulties in the receiving countries produce frictions, restrictionist

policies, and even violence.

And the inter-American system, the institutional network the countries of the Western Hemisphere have evolved to solve their common problems, is in serious disarray. The intra-hemispheric divisions displayed during the South Atlantic crisis were the most dramatic evidence to date that the Organization of American States is not able to come to grips with some of the major problems the Hemisphere faces in the 1980s.

All these problems are severe; some are critical. Constructive steps have been taken in recent months to confront the immediate financial crisis, but much remains to be done. Failure to face the region's difficulties more effectively would mean a major deterioration not only in inter-American relations but also in the daily lives of citizens throughout the Hemisphere.

But when conditions of crisis are perceived and faced imaginatively, special opportunities for progress exist. We urge greater cooperation between the United States and the countries of Latin America and the Caribbean on the basis of mutual recognition of changing realities. We are heartened by growing evidence that concerted action is possible in this Hemisphere, and that shared values — a deep commitment to democracy and human rights, for example — are being reaffirmed. We believe that Americans, North and South, can forge a more hopeful future if we work together in the years ahead.

We are citizens from many different countries of the Hemisphere — men and women of different generations, from different political perspectives and professional backgrounds. Our experiences and some of our premises are different but we also share common values, convictions, and concerns. It is in recognition of what we share that we came together, and that we now issue this report. . . .

Economic and Financial Issues

Propelled by the worst world-wide economic crisis in half a century, economic and financial questions today dominate the inter-American agenda as never before. The development prospects of all Latin American countries have been threatened by a series of unprecedented external shocks. The repercussions of Latin America's crisis, in turn, are felt in the international financial and trading systems, and in the balance sheets of United States banks, exporters, and foreign investors.

Although no two countries followed the same path to the present situation, some general patterns can be seen. For most, the very dynamism and favorable prospects of their economies during most of the 1970s encouraged ambitious economic policies that yielded rapid rates of growth — financed by increasing foreign indebtedness (and by high fiscal deficits, in some cases) and critically dependent on expanding export markets. This strategy, now confronting a much deteriorated external environment, has led to a financial crisis throughout the region. Unprecedentedly high levels of external debt service, combined with the scissors effect of climbing interest rates and falling export revenues, have brought Mexico, Brazil,

Argentina, Chile, Costa Rica, and others to dire straits. Almost overnight, debt management has acquired a central place not only in economic policy but also in the domestic politics of many countries of the region.

The financial crisis is also a problem for the United States. *The Latin American exposure of the nine largest U.S. banks now amounts, on average, to well over 100 percent of their equity.* Hundreds of regional banks across the United States are also concerned about their loans in Latin America. The entire, closely interlinked, financial system is under challenge.

At the same time, thousands of United States producers have felt the constriction of their once flourishing Latin American market. Latin America's sharp reduction of imports in 1982 hit them with particular force. This impact is significant, for the United States is responsible for more than 30 percent of all sales to the region. Latin America as a region is now the third largest purchaser of U.S. industrial exports and particularly of capital goods, and accounted in 1980 for 17.6 percent of all U.S. exports.

U.S. involvement in Latin America's current crisis dramatizes a trend that has long been underway: the enhanced interdependence that increases the stake of the United States in Latin America's economic health. . . .

Broad interests of the United States and indeed of the world economy, are thus at stake in the current debt crisis. If major Latin American borrowers were to become insolvent and unable to service their debts, the impact on the United States and the international financial system would be severe and unpredictable, and world economic activity might well be disrupted. . . .

The immediate crisis captures headlines, but the economic issues go deeper. Commercial banks, international financial institutions, and governments have already agreed on emergency measures to avoid immediate collapse. But it remains to be seen whether they will now pursue the longer-term basic reforms that are necessary to avert recurrence of the grim 1982 results that saw per capita incomes decline in virtually all the countries of the hemisphere, North and South.

The fact must be faced that today's problems are more than a passing phase. They are a sign of — and a stimulus to — a profound transition in inter-American economic relations. The responses to them are bound to influence hemispheric development strategies in the years ahead and, thereby, the character of U.S.-Latin American relations. . . .

It is also clear that these economic issues go far beyond the region. Many developed countries besides the United States have large financial and commercial interests in Latin America. Indeed, the presence of European nations and Japan in the region has expanded over the last decade. The involvement of these countries, their private sectors, and other agencies, is essential. The United States, even while it has an opportunity and obligation to lead, cannot alone sustain the recovery of the global economy.

The economic challenge facing the countries of the hemisphere is twofold: to forge a cooperative solution to manage the immediate liquidity crisis, and to help resume sustained economic growth and development.

The stakes are high. In the last analysis, hemispheric security depends upon political stability built, in turn, upon an expanding economy in which all can equitably share. . . .

If Latin American countries fail to impose more effective financial discipline and fail to honor their debts; if commercial banks stop lending; or if the U.S. and other major governments ignore the crisis, everyone will suffer. To avert a self-inflicted tragedy, a cooperative, mutually beneficial approach must be found — one that realistically balances the problems and capabilities of the leaders [sic] and borrowers, private financial institutions, international organizations, and concerned governments. We believe that time still exists for the United States and Latin America to work together to restore economic growth and financial stability. But the need is urgent, and delay could mean disaster. . . .

Managing the crisis is the urgent task of the moment, on which all future hopes now depend. But the fundamental task remains the same: Latin America's development. For decades if not generations to come, Latin America will continue to require large capital inflows to attain its full growth potential — just as the United States, Canada, and Australia all did during the nineteenth century. Side by side with their integration into global capital markets, the countries of the region must also increase their earnings from foreign trade in order to service — and eventually repay — their foreign debts. *In the long term, debt and trade are two aspects of the same problem.* In recent years, Latin America as a region has borrowed much more heavily than it has exported. That balance will have to be rectified if liquidity problems are not to become a permanent constraint on future growth.

A first requirement for restoring the balance, as well as for easing the short-term liquidity crisis, is for the industrial countries to achieve a substainable recovery from the present recession. Only then will the prices of Latin America's export commodities return to normal levels, markets for its other exports expand, and its foreign-exchange revenues increase. . . .

The need for . . . adjustments is not easy to see in a time of slow growth, especially for those most directly affected. Hard-pressed producers and their governments are all too likely to follow a vicious cycle in which protective measures only aggravate the ills they are meant to cure. In the United States, producers with excess capacity, and especially their workers, tend to resist the penetration of competing products. Developing-country imports are wrongly blamed for lost jobs when, in fact, aggregate demand and technological change have been far more influential in determining the pattern of employment. Meanwhile, investment needed to finance capacity in new sectors remains insufficient as long as corporate profits lag.

Latin American producers, for their part, when faced with a slow growth of world trade, tend to prefer internal markets and even promote tariff and other restrictive policies which prejudice expansion of exports. In this situation, the trade surplus required to service debt will derive from reduced imports, not increased exports. Conflicts will multiply over limited access of U.S. producers to Latin American markets, even while slow Latin American export growth translates into slower and less efficient growth of production within Latin America itself.

Slow growth therefore poses a real danger of protectionism and mutual recrimination rather than mutual benefits. Often the recrimination centers on grievances that are largely imaginary. *U.S. protectionism, for example, has been much criticized in Latin America, even though it has not been a significant factor in the disappointing export performance of many countries in the region.* Their declining export earnings are primarily the result of recession, not of U.S. trade policy. U.S. imports from Latin America, particularly of manufactured products, have continued to expand....

World economic recovery will make ... restrictive policies less attractive and perceptions less distorted. It will begin to ease the debt service burden weighing on Latin American countries, and encourage the flow of new capital. To achieve it is the first imperative of any strategy for Latin America's long-term development.

But the tonic of more rapid growth must be accompanied by deliberate policies to reinforce the mutual benefits of such growth. We therefore recommend ... steps to encourage and ensure an adequate flow of capital, to restructure debt, and to expand trade....

Social and Political Issues

...We are deeply concerned ... lest governments and multilateral institutions become so preoccupied with immediate economic issues that they ignore the social and political implications of their proposed solutions. Unless concerted attention is devoted to these implications, remedies for the current crisis may turn out to have side effects as serious, in their way, as the ills being addressed. Austerity programs that reinforce inequities and require repression, for instance, would exacerbate fragmentation, polarization, and violence. Equally troubling, a narrow focus on immediate economic issues might cause nations to miss broader opportunities to improve the conditions of life for the peoples of the Hemisphere. Much of Latin America has moved in the last three or four years toward more open and representative politics. That progress will be jeopardized if economic policies are formulated without taking into account their social and political consequences.

Much of Latin America is at a political crossroads. The military regimes that displaced representative democracies in the 1960s and 1970s have lost strength in recent years, their legitimacy and authority weakened by abuses of human rights and by economic reverses. The bases are being laid for a renewal of democracy in much of the Western Hemisphere, founded on a new awareness that democratization requires not just elected politicians taking office but the long-term building of civic and social institutions supportive of open and participatory policies.

If these democratic openings are to take hold, governments and political movements must enlist the participation of the great majority of Latin Americans by responding to their desire for improved conditions of life. Most Latin American countries, building on steady economic growth and sustained urbanization, have made substantial gains in such areas as health and education. Still, World Bank estimates show that one-half of Latin America's rural population and one-quarter of its city dwellers remain in "absolute poverty," meaning that they cannot afford a minimally adequate diet. At least another one-third of the region's population is poor by most contemporary standards.

The persistent poverty of two-thirds of the people of Latin America is the major cause of the Hemisphere's social unrest. Poverty, inequality, and injustice led to political protest and polarization. Polarization, in turn, frequently leads to repression, followed by cycles of violent opposition, widespread violations of human rights, and greater social injustice. In order to break this cycle, to increase the opportunities for human fulfillment, and to build more stable societies, sustained commitments to alleviate poverty are urgently needed throughout the Americas. Economic austerity programs which improve current national accounts at the expense of the poorest sectors will undermine the chances of lasting national progress. . . .

TRANSITIONS TO DEMOCRACY

Within the past few years, military regimes have given way to elected governments in Bolivia, Ecuador, Honduras and Peru. Last year the Dominican Republic managed its fifth consecutive contested Presidential election. In November, Brazil had a massive turnout for congressional and state elections, that country's most important electoral contest in 20 years; and Uruguay held party elections looking toward the restoration of constitutional democracy. Argentina's military rulers have announced procedures and a date for returning the country to democratic politics. Chile, once South America's most vital democracy, has made little progress as yet toward opening its politics, but increasingly strong demands to do so are being heard.

We recognize the difficulty of broadening and sustaining the trend toward democratization — toward the progressive achievement of social justice in a context of political freedom, broad participation, regular and free elections, and constitutional guarantees. The current economic crisis, and the austerity measures which it demands, compound the difficulty. The need for sacrifices increases the problem of governance at a time when democratization in most countries is still fragile.

The fact is, however, that authoritarian regimes which impose harsh discipline on their people lost their legitimacy and ultimately their authority. Today's severe economic crisis can be more effectively managed by governments that enjoy popular understanding and support. Such governments are also more likely to distribute the burden of dealing with the crisis fairly among their population.

Many Latin American countries have in recent years experienced wrenching internal conflicts and divisions that are not easily forgotten. These divisions can only be overcome through long-term, broad-based national commitments to greater social justice. We believe that the renewal and expansion of democratic procedures offer the best hope that such commitments will become a reality. We further recognize that for democratization to be secure; it must be based on a process of reconciliation and not on the triumph of one portion of the population over another. At the same time, democratization is itself the surest way of protecting human rights.

By its nature, democratization is a national process for which individuals and institutions within each country must be responsible. *Democracy is not an export commodity; it must be nurtured and developed within each nation. We doubt that any government (perhaps least of all that of the most powerful country in the Hemisphere) can contribute much in a very direct way to building democratic political institutions in other countries.....*

HUMAN RIGHTS

Human rights violations have plagued the Americas in recent years. Torture, political assassination, "disappearances," and other horrors have been practiced on a wide scale even in nations formerly recognized for their humane politics. These violations warrant unremitting concern by all nations of the Hemisphere.

Virtually everyone in the Americas supports human rights in the abstract. But people differ widely in what they mean by human rights and what measures they think legitimate and effective in ensuring them. They disagree on the relative importance of different kinds of rights — and also on whether, to what extent, and how human rights should be promoted across international borders. They also differ regarding the weight they assign to certain rights when these appear to be in conflict with other objectives, such as economic growth and national security. We believe it is important to recognize and confront these differences, and not to gloss over them.

Three major categories of human rights may be distinguished: (1) rights pertaining to the physical integrity of the person; (2) civil and political rights; and (3) economic and social rights. All these rights are important, but we unanimously affirm the primacy of protecting the physical integrity of the person....

We are less in agreement regarding the priority that should be accorded to political and civil rights as compared with economic and social rights. Most of us believe that the right of all citizens to take part in independent political activity, including freely contested elections, is the necessary basis for economic progress and social justice, and that political systems which guarantee this right are most likely to adopt positive social and economic policies which respond to the demands of their electorates. Some of us, on the other hand, maintain that human beings must satisfy their basic material and social needs before they can effectively participate in the civil and political arena. We all agree that human rights of either kind cannot be truly assured without the other and, therefore, that a comprehensive approach is required; but we also know this formulation may obscure the choices and trade-offs that must be made in concrete situations.

In general, if forced to choose, most of us would give priority to strengthening democratic procedures and extending them to all the people. Others would place greater stress on social and economic reforms, even at the price of delaying the achievement of political democracy. Given the widespread poverty and deep inequality in Latin America, this latter perspective is understandable. Nevertheless, most of us fear that post-ponement of civil and political rights, including the rights of free expression, would only serve to encourage tyranny and further injustice.

In each nation of the Hemisphere, the protection and advancement of human rights is primarily the domestic responsibility of the national government. But it is also a legitimate international concern. It should be reflected in the foreign policies of governments and in the programs of international organizations. *Carefully considered multilateral action to protect fundamental human rights is not intervention but an international obligation....*

MIGRATION

The flow of large numbers of people across international boundaries has always been a major fact of life in the Americas. Most of the American republics are largely nations of immigrants.

The great bulk of this migration is still, as in the past, economically motivated. It responds both to the "push" of unemployment, declining agriculture and other economic adversities in the poorer countries, and to the "pull" of employment opportunities, higher wage rates, and social services in the richer countries in recent years. Economic migrants have moved in large numbers, not only to the United States but also to Venezuela (especially from Colombia), to Argentina (especially from Bolivia), to Brazil (from other countries of the Southern Cone), to the Dominican Republic (especially from Haiti), and within Central America. This migration may be temporary or permanent (many seasonal workers go home when their jobs are done) — legal or illegal, regulated or unregulated. But it is virtually certain to continue, for it responds to underlying economic realities.

Politically motivated migration — the flight of refugees from persecution, repression, or violence — involves smaller numbers but has been on the rise. Many Chileans, Argentines, Uruguayans, Bolivians, and Brazilians fled their countries in the 1960s and early 1970s. Almost one million Cubans have left that island since Fidel Castro took over in 1959, the latest wave in the Mariel boat lift in 1980. More recently, refugees from war and political turmoil in El Salvador, Nicaragua, Honduras, and Guatemala have been leaving for neighboring countries and for the United States.

For all the countries involved, these movements of people have brought many benefits and many problems. There is need throughout the Hemisphere for a better understanding of migration's effects, both good and bad — and for cooperative efforts to regulate it, and to reduce the pressure for it, in ways that will equitably serve the interests of all.

Migration policy presents a fundamental tension between the principles of national sovereignty and interdependence. Although receiving nations have an undeniable sovereign right — and often a practical need — to regulate immigration, strong practical as well as ethical arguments can be raised against unilateral efforts merely to block migratory tides that are impelled by human necessity. By the same token, sending countries, as a matter of both self-interest and international comity, have a responsibility to alleviate the conditions that cause people to emigrate.

We believe that economic migration should be dealt with primarily at its point of origin. It is important to encourage economic policies in the sending countries which will contribute to sustained, balanced, and equitable development. Formulas of economic growth that ignore problems of unemployment, income concentration, and lack of access to basic social services and benefits will accelerate, not curb, emigration....

Security and Peacekeeping Issues

Security is at the heart of international relations and near the top of the inter-American agenda. Complex questions abound, touching on problems of sovereignty and, at times of national survival. It is, therefore, not surprising that the discussions of security within our Dialogue generated some disagreements, and that differences persisted after considerable deliberation.

On two important points, however, we all agreed: First, *the basic roots of insecurity — and the basic problems of security — in this Hemisphere are primarily economic, social, and political, not military. Second, the sources of insecurity are mainly internal to each nation, and that external influences are secondary.*

It is our firm conviction that even where there is a military dimension to conflict, as in Central America, the solutions ultimately lie in economic and social development and political dialogue, not in weapons or military advisers. Even when external support for insurrection clearly is present, as in El Salvador, the underlying problems remain domestic.

We emphasize our accord on these two points, and on the importance of the economic, social, and political issues dealt with in previous chapters of this report. To focus on security concerns without devoting requisite attention to the underlying issues is to misunderstand the dimensions of the problem and to miss the mark....

In our extensive discussions, we analyzed the nature of security interests for the United States and for Latin American nations, and explored whether and how they are compatible.

We identified three levels of security concern. The most basic is to limit those forms of Soviet and Cuban influence that pose a real danger of turning the countries of the region into instruments of hostile extra-hemispheric purpose. This means limiting the deployment of Soviet and Cuban military forces and facilities in the region, and preventing their acquisition of physical facilities that could be used to project significant hostile power against countries of this Hemisphere. Any regional security policy must squarely address this fundamental and shared concern.

At a second level, many in the United States and some in Latin America believe that any Marxist-oriented movement — even if not significantly supported by the Soviet Union or Cuba — poses a security threat because it may later offer a foothold for hostile influence. Some also fear that successful insurrections will have a ripple or "domino" effect in neighboring countries, and should therefore be countered.

The third aspect of security is more elusive, for it contains a strong psychological component. Some events, especially those that enhance the autonomy of a Latin American state, may be perceived, especially in the United States, as losses in global prestige, in the world-wide competition with the Soviet Union for influence, or in self-esteem — even though they do not affect specific U.S. interests. Although many Latin Americans believe that a diminished U.S. role in the Hemisphere need not pose a security threat or may actually enhance their own security, there is a tendency in some circles in the United States to see any loss of such influence as diminishing U.S. security.

From the Latin American perspective as we noted above, security mainly involves achieving national integration and also preventing foreign interference — whether from outside the Americas or from one of this Hemisphere's nations, including Cuba and the United States. Internal reforms or revolutionary changes that a Latin American nation or movement may regard as necessary sometimes clash with second- or third-level security concerns in the United States. Foreign policy initiatives that Latin American nations take in pursuit of their interests may also contradict concepts of security held by some in the United States. For example, development of cultural, diplomatic, and economic exchanges between countries of Latin America and the Soviet Union are sometimes deemed a reason for concern in the United States but are broadly supported in Latin America. Recurrent tension and misunderstanding over such matters are likely to continue.

The prevailing Latin American and North American concepts of security, although different at times, are, we believe, reconcilable. Both North Americans and Latin Americans stress self-determination and non-intervention as norms. Both understand that social and economic progress is vital for achieving political stability and protecting national and international security. The differences that arise are primarily matters of emphasis and of the assessment of risks.

We all favor keeping Latin America and the Caribbean out of the East-

West conflict to the greatest extent possible. It does not serve that purpose for the United States to oppose changes in the region simply because they diminish U.S. influence and hence are perceived as advantageous to Cuba and the Soviet Union, unless they are clearly related to basic security concerns. We believe that the United States can better achieve its long-term interest in regional stability, one shared by Latin Americans, by exercising measured restraint in the projection of its own power.

The inherent tension between Latin America's urge for autonomy and the U.S. concern for preserving influence can be reconciled. What is required is recognition in the United States that some relative loss of U.S. influence is to be expected in a rapidly changing world, and that the risks of intervention considerably outweigh those of a more restrained role.

All these general considerations affect our view of the Central American crisis. The human cost of the conflicts in Central America is staggering, and increases every week. One hundred thousand people have been killed by the fighting during the last five years, and a million have been displaced. Economic damage and disruption is massive, and will take many years to repair. Polarization continues to worsen, and foreign intervention escalates. This tragedy must end.

We offer no detailed blueprint for resolving Central America's problems; such a task would be too ambitious for a group such as ours. We do, however, offer a general framework for consideration by all parties, hoping that we can help to stimulate fresh thinking.

To deal with the hostilities in Central America, we favor dialogue: between the governments in El Salvador, Nicaragua, and Guatemala and the respective opposition movements in those countries; between Nicaragua and each of its neighbors; between Cuba and all the countries of Central America; and between the United States and Cuba, and the United States and Nicaragua, respectively; as well as between the United States and the Soviet Union.

The single aim of all these discussions would be to explore whether the vital interests of each of the parties can be safeguarded without continuing war in Central America — whether the elements of a settlement that satisfies the interests of each party can be fashioned. The discussions need not be publicized in their initial stages. Quiet contacts may be more fruitful as a way of building reciprocal assurances. They would be based on the principles of national sovereignty, self-determination, and non-intervention, a tradition of values avowed by all the parties.

Our approach is based on two major premises. One, as indicated above, is that most citizens and governments throughout the Hemisphere oppose an expansion of Soviet and Cuban military presence in the Americas. Even revolutionary movements now seeking power in Central America should have little desire to convert their countries into Soviet or Cuban bases. We believe they may be less tempted to do so if they feel secure from subversion or harassment. They recognize how precarious their position would be should they achieve power, and that they would incur additional

U.S. hostility by inviting a Soviet or Cuban military presence.

The second premise is that the United States could do much to foster a climate of security in the region by making unequivocally clear its commitment to respect national sovereignty. If reciprocal and mutual security is to be fashioned in a region that has often experienced overt and covert U.S. intervention, it would be useful to provide unmistakable assurances that the United States will refrain from reverting to these practices.

Procedurally, we strongly endorse the initiative taken by Colombia, Mexico, Panama, and Venezuela in the recent Contadora Declaration, offering their good offices in seeking peaceful solutions to Central America's problems. We call on the presidents of these countries to go a step further and involve themselves directly in regional negotiations. These countries are well positioned to play such a role, for they enjoy good relations with the countries of Central America and with the United States, and most of them have relations with Cuba. They have an urgent interest in ending Central America's tragedy, and they have the confidence of the relevant actors. *The United States should make it clear that it favors and encourages an active role by the Contadora group in seeking an end to the Central American conflict, and that it stands ready to join the discussions as may be appropriate.*

Beyond this, many of us believe that the U.S.-Soviet understandings of 1962, 1970, and 1979 with respect to Cuba might provide the basis for a wider accord that could enhance the collective security of the entire region. The heart of the original understanding was that each side would cease actions regarded as aggressive and threatening by the other. The Soviet Union removed strategic facilities from Cuba and pledged not to reintroduce them, and the United States pledged to end threats to invade or efforts to subvert the Cuban government. As amended in subsequent years, the understandings have been extended to assure that the Soviet Union would not use Cuba as a strategic naval base, that Soviet forces in Cuba would have only a training and not a combat function, and that those forces would not be expanded. For over 20 years, these accords have contributed to protecting major political and security interests of both the United States and the Soviet Union. The agreement has also served Cuba's interest although it has never been a party to the understandings.

The basic principle of the U.S.-Soviet understandings on Cuba could be extended to Central America and the rest of the Caribbean. The Soviet Union and Cuba could pledge not to deploy strategic or conventional combat forces to any part of the Caribbean and Central America, nor to change the character of military personnel either may have in Nicaragua or Grenada from a training to a combat function. They could also pledge not to install facilities or engage in activities that would pose a threat to other states of the Americas. The United States, the Soviet Union, Cuba, and all other governments of the region could further pledge not to intervene or interfere in the internal affairs of other nations of the area, provided others also fulfill their commitments. They could pledge not to supply assistance to revolutionary or counter-revolutionary movements that might seek to overthrow governments; to terminate any such aid currently being given; and not to allow their territories to be used for subverting other governments. States would be asked to give such commitments as a condition of receiving reciprocal assurances from other states. Revolutionary movements seeking power in the region would be encouraged to recognize these understandings, to behave accordingly, and at a minimum, to express their own determination not to accept foreign forces or bases should they gain or share power.

Such understandings need not be the result of formal negotiations or multilateral agreements. Individual parties could indicate their willingness to behave in certain ways provided that other parties abided by similar commitments. The commitments would be contingent and revocable if any party failed to adhere to its pledges. Appropriate procedures would have to be established to monitor continued adherence. Although that is no small requirement, it need not be impossible to achieve....

We believe ... that negotiations should be tried. In El Salvador, negotiations could begin at once to prepare for free, internationally supervised elections on the basis of security guarantees for all parties and participants. In the region as a whole, a major effort should be undertaken to find a way for settling the conflicts on a basis that recognizes the vital interests of each party.

We know that some will object to our recommendation because it would not assure a change in the level of Cuban and Soviet presence already achieved in the region. By U.S. estimates, there are some ten to thirteen thousand Soviet and Eastern European personnel in Cuba, including a three-thousand-man Soviet brigade. In Nicaragua, there are said to be about two thousand Cuban, Soviet and Eastern European military and security advisers, and the Cuban presence in Grenada reportedly numbers above three hundred. We share others' concern about these developments; our aim is precisely to contain and reverse this trend.

Some doubt that firm assurances could be given against the extension of Cuban and Soviet facilities, but think that this is not the main problem in any case. They focus on the possibility that revolutionary regimes in Central America and the Caribbean might exert a "domino" effect on their neighbors, perhaps eventually putting at risk security interests of the United States and other nations. We believe, however, that sharp external confrontation with revolutionary regimes is more likely eventually to breed intensified nationalist and revolutionary sentiment than the more restrained approach we recommend. Threats should be evaluated in the light of the magnitude of the risk and of the likelihood of its occurrence; policies that magnify a danger out of proportion can themselves become part of the problem.

None of this is to deny that political changes in countries of Latin America may disappoint, irritate, or disturb other countries of the Hemisphere, including the United States. No nation need hide its preferences; false honeymoons between established powers (including the United

States) and revolutionary movements really do neither any good. The aim should not be to curry favor with revolutionary movements or regimes, but rather to assure that they will respect the legitimate security interests of others.

HARVARD PRESIDENT ON LEGAL SYSTEM
April 21, 1983

Using the vehicle of the annual report to the board of overseers, Harvard University President Derek C. Bok joined a number of other legal experts in decrying what he described as "glaring problems" in the nation's legal system. Bok, a lawyer and former dean of the Harvard Law School, likened the state of the profession in 1983 to that of the health care system 20 years earlier: costly, complex and filled with delays for those Americans who were not well-to-do. "There is far too much law for those who can afford it and far too little for those who cannot," Bok said. "No one can be satisfied with this state of affairs.... The blunt, inexcusable fact is that this nation, which prides itself on efficiency and justice, has developed a legal system that is the most expensive in the world, yet cannot manage to protect the rights of most of its citizens."

Too many regulations and elaborate laws, too many lawyers and increasingly complicated litigation procedures lay at the root of the problem, according to Bok. The result was "much waste of money that could be put to better purposes." Noting that the United States had the largest per capita number of lawyers of any major industrialized nation — 20 times that of Japan — Bok said, "legal costs are primarily people costs." Law schools themselves bore a large share of the responsibility for the high costs of the system. Particularly in terms of human talent, the fact that law schools attracted "an unusually large proportion of the exceptionally gifted" meant that scarce resources were being diverted from other professions, such as engineering, that made more valuable contributions to economic growth.

*The former law school dean was especially critical of the legal educa-
tion curriculum that, he said, trained students "more for conflict than for
the gentler arts of reconciliation and accommodation." More emphasis
needed to be placed on training lawyers to deal with the poor, through
establishing legal services organizations, and on developing methods of
settling disputes less expensively. There should be more research into
methods of revising the system in general, he said. Bok had praise for
Harvard Law School, however, which he placed among the "pioneers" in
its experiments with new teaching methods and research into the
feasibility of new legal institutions, such as prepaid legal services
organizations modeled on prepaid health care plans.*

An Expensive, Complex System

*Bok was among a number of prominent lawyers, scholars and members
of the judiciary who had criticized various aspects of the nation's legal
system. In 1982 seven of the nine Supreme Court justices publicly
complained of the heavy workload of the Court and the impact of ever-in-
creasing litigation on the administration of justice throughout the federal
legal system.* (Historic Documents of 1982, p. 705)

*But there was wide disagreement on what was wrong with the system
and what should be rectified. For example, Chief Justice Warren E.
Burger May 17, 1983, warned that there was "an almost irrational focus
— virtually a mania — on litigation as a way to solve all problems." By
contrast, Bok said that "it is not clear that we are a madly litigious
society." Although the number of disputes actually taken to court did not
appear to be rising, the complexity of the legal process and time involved
in pretrial actions seemed to be increasing, he said.*

An article in the June 1, 1983, New York Times *discussed the diversity
of opinions about reforming the system, citing the dramatic rise in the
number of civil suits filed in federal courts (a 14 percent increase in 1982
over 1981), federal court appeals (a sevenfold increase since 1960) and
civil suits heard in state courts (a 22 percent increase in 1981 over 1977).
Beyond numbers alone, the nature of the lawsuits themselves had taxed
the system's resources. New kinds of cases had developed (such as the
lawsuit brought against the psychiatrist of John W. Hinckley Jr., who
attempted to assassinate President Ronald Reagan in 1981), more awards
involved $1 million or more in damages, and the complexity of cases
pitted arrays of lawyers and witnesses against one another in costly and
time-consuming procedures. The growing body of federal regulation also
contributed to the legal quagmire. Product liability and malpractice suits
had increased dramatically and in turn caused manufacturers, physicians and others to pay out more in legal expenses and insurance
premiums.*

Plight of Individuals

Some of the backlog and other problems confronting the system were due to the fact that more and more individuals were able to take civil rights discrimination, product liability, occupational injury and other cases to court as a result of what many considered to be worthwhile legislative advances in those fields. A number of courts made it easier to facilitate such suits, and observers pointed out that juries had become increasingly sympathetic to the plight of an individual who sued a large manufacturer or a wealthy physician. In addition, opening the judicial system to the less powerful or disadvantaged gave rise to a new specialty of litigation, the awarding of legal fees.

The result "of a process that concentrates so heavily on the plight of individual litigants and gives so little heed to the effects on the system as a whole," according to Bok, was a "constant stream of rules [that] leave a wake strewn with the disappointed hopes of those who find the legal system too complicated to understand, too quixotic to command respect, and too expensive to be of much practical use."

Following are excerpts, criticizing the U.S. legal system, from the 1981-1982 report presented to the board of overseers by Harvard University President Derek C. Bok April 21, 1983:

To the Members of the Board of Overseers:
Ladies and Gentlemen, I have the honor to present my report for 1981-82.

All graduate schools risk becoming captives of their professions, absorbed in preparing skilled professionals and seeking new knowledge for practitioners to employ. This preoccupation is understandable, since the acquisition and transmission of specialized knowledge are the central tasks of a professional school. But they are not its only tasks. A vigorous school should address the larger problems of its calling, serving as a conscience to its profession and a stimulus for change. In fulfilling this function, a faculty must be knowledgeable enough to speak convincingly to practitioners, detached enough to see the blemishes of their profession, skilled enough in research and analysis to explore each defect thoroughly and offer thoughtful suggestions for reform.

These responsibilities are always important, but particularly so today when the public is disenchanted with the professions and highly critical of their performance. I have therefore resolved to make this theme the subject of my report. the discussion that follows concentrates on one profession, the law, seeking first to describe the most glaring problems of the legal system and then to suggest the efforts that our Law School can make — and indeed, is already beginning to make — to address these shortcomings. . . .

A Flawed System

... Our legal system bears a strong resemblance to our health care system twenty years ago. At that time, the medical care offered to paying patients was rapidly becoming more effective, more sophisticated — and more expensive as well. But quality medicine was available only to the well-to-do or to those who happened to be covered by an adequate prepaid plan. Millions of people with modest incomes could not afford decent care; they visited doctors less often and their mortality rates were distinctly higher.

From my distant perch, our legal system seems to occupy a comparable position today. As in medicine, there is much in our law that represents a triumph of the human spirit: the steadfast defense of individual freedom and civil liberties, the constant elevation of reason over prejudice and passion, the protections afforded to minority and disadvantaged groups. But there are also similarities of a darker kind. The laws that govern affluent clients and large institutions are numerous, intricate, and applied by highly sophisticated practitioners. In this sector of society, rules proliferate, law suits abound, and the cost of legal services grows much faster than the cost of living. For the bulk of the population, however, the situation is very different. Access to the courts may be open in principle. In practice, however, most people find their legal rights severely compromised by the cost of legal services, the baffling complications of existing rules and procedures, and the long, frustrating delays involved in bringing proceedings to a conclusion. From afar, therefore, the legal system looks grossly inequitable and inefficient. There is far too much law for those who can afford it and far too little for those who cannot. No one can be satisfied with this state of affairs. ...

One half of our difficulty lies in the burdens and costs of our tangle of laws and legal procedures. Contrary to popular belief, it is not clear that we are a madly litigious society. It is true that we have experienced a rapid growth in the number of complaints filed in our courts. But filings are often only a prelude to some kind of voluntary settlement. The number of disputes *actually litigated* in the United States does not appear to be rising much faster than the population as a whole. Our courts may *seem* crowded, since we have relatively few judges compared with many industrial nations. Nevertheless, our volume of litigated cases is not demonstrably larger in relation to our total population than that of other Western nations.

At the same time, the complexity of litigation seems to be increasing. Even if a case is settled without trial, preliminary motions and discovery procedures may occupy much time of judges and attorneys. Moreover, the country has experienced a marked growth in statutes and administrative regulations. ... Paralleling these trends, the supply of lawyers has doubled since 1960 so that the United States now boasts the largest number of attorneys per thousand population of any major industrialized nation — three times as many as in Germany, ten times the number in Sweden, and a whopping twenty times the figure in Japan. In sum, though there may not be more court cases, the country has more legal work to do and many more attorneys to do it. Just what society pays for this profusion of law is hard to guess. Lloyd Cutler [a Washington, D.C., lawyer] has put the figure at $30 billion a year, but the truth is that no one has bothered to find out. Be that as it may, legal costs are primarily people costs, and if we mark the growth in the total number of lawyers and the average compensation of attorneys, it is clear that legal expenditures have been climbing more rapidly than the gross national product for many years. . . .

. . . [O]ur legal system leads to much waste of money that could be put to better purposes. But even greater costs result from the heavy use of human talent. Not only does the law absorb many more young people in America than in any other industrialized nation; it attracts an unusually large proportion of the exceptionally gifted. . . .

The net result of these trends is a massive diversion of exceptional talent into pursuits that often add little to the growth of the economy, the pursuit of culture, or the enhancement of the human spirit. I cannot press this point too strongly. . . .

. . . A nation's values and problems are mirrored in the ways in which it uses its ablest people. In Japan, a country only half our size, 30 percent more engineers graduate each year than in all the United States. But Japan boasts a total of less than 15,000 lawyers, while American universities graduate 35,000 *every year*. It would be hard to claim that these differences have no practical consequences. As the Japanese put it, "Engineers make the pie grow larger; lawyers only decide how to carve it up."

The elaborateness of our laws and the complexity of our procedures absorb the energies of this giant bar, raise the cost of legal services, and help produce the other great problem of our legal system — the lack of access for the poor and middle class. The results are embarrassing to behold. Criminal defendants are herded through the courts at a speed that precludes individual attention, leaving countless accused to the mercy of inexperienced counsel who determine their fate in hasty plea bargaining with the prosecution. On the civil side, the cost of hiring a lawyer and the mysteries of the legal process discourage most people of modest means from trying to enforce their rights. Every study of common forms of litigation, such as medical malpractice, tenant evictions, or debt collections, reveals that for each successful suit there are several others that could be won if the victims had the money and the will to secure a lawyer. . . .

. . . As many observers have testified, the costs and delays of our system force countless victims to accept inadequate settlements or to give up any attempt to vindicate their legal rights.

. . . The blunt, inexcusable fact is that this nation, which prides itself on efficiency and justice, has developed a legal system that is the most expensive in the world, yet cannot manage to protect the rights of most of its citizens.

The Roots of Our Predicament

... The roots of our predicament ... are more complex than popular impressions would allow. Many factors contribute to the volume of disputes and the intricacies of legal rules. Industrialization and technology produce new forms of conflict and injury; new knowledge extends our understanding of causation giving rise to novel theories of liability; fresh government initiatives create new interests and limit private activity in ways that lead to legal controversy. Amid these many causes, however, one thread runs particularly vividly. At bottom, ours is a society built on individualism, competition, and success. These values bring great personal freedom and mobilize powerful energies. At the same time, they arouse great temptations to shoulder aside one's competitors, to cut corners, to ignore the interests of others in the struggle to succeed. In such a world, much responsibility rests on those who umpire the contest. As society demands higher standards of fairness and decency, the rules of the game tend to multiply and the umpire's burden grows constantly heavier.

Faced with these pressures, judges and legislators have responded in a manner that reflects our distinctive legal traditions. One hallmark of that tradition is a steadfast faith in intricate procedures where evidence and arguments are presented through an adversary process to a neutral judge who renders a decision on the merits. Compared with procedures used in other advanced countries, ours are elaborate and hence relatively expensive. They also force the parties, rather than the state, to bear most of the cost of finding the facts, thus adding further to the burden of going to court. ...

This environment produces a special kind of justice. It leads officials to exaggerate the law's capacity to produce social change while underestimating the cost of establishing rules that can be enforced effectively throughout the society. Since laws seem deceptively potent and cheap, they multiply quickly. Though most of them may be plausible in isolation, they are often confusing and burdensome in the aggregate, at least to those who have to take them seriously. Contrary to the views of left-wing scholars, the results are not simply a form of exploitation to oppress poor, defenseless people; the wealthy and the powerful also chafe under the burden. For established institutions, in particular, the typical result is a stifling burden of regulations, delays, and legal uncertainties that inhibit progress and allow unscrupulous parties to misuse the law to harass and manipulate their victims. For those of modest means, however, the results are even more dispiriting. Laws and procedural safeguards may proliferate, but they are of scant use to those who cannot afford a lawyer. All too often the ultimate effect is to aggravate costs and delays that deny legal protection to large majorities of the population. ...

Devising adequate remedies for this predicament will be extremely difficult. But certain points seem clear. To begin with, there is no single solution for our problems. Individual measures will not merely be ineffective; they may actually make the situation worse. For example, Chief Justice

Burger periodically calls for massive improvements in the training of trial lawyers. At first glance, who could object to such a proposal? But it is probable that such a reform, *standing by itself,* would increase litigation, lengthen trials, and add significantly to the very burdens which the Chief Justice wishes to lighten.

An effective program will require not only multiple efforts but a mixture that involves attempts to simplify rules and procedures as well as measures that give greater access to the poor and middle class. Access without simplification will be wasteful and expensive; simplification without access will be unjust.

A program embodying these principles will include initiatives along a number of lines already described. Lawmakers will need to adopt no-fault car insurance everywhere and extend the no-fault concept to new fields of liability. Legislatures will have to take a hard look at provisions for treble damages and other artificial incentives that stimulate litigation. Agency officials will want to mount a broad review of existing laws to simplify rules and eliminate regulations that do not serve a demonstrable public purpose. These efforts at simplification must be accompanied by larger appropriations to make legal counsel available to the poor. But money alone will not suffice. In cases involving debtors and creditors, landlords and tenants, and other disputes that touch the lives of ordinary folk, judges will have to develop less costly ways of resolving disputes, since expensive adversary trials ultimately deny access, and therefore justice, to countless deserving people. Likewise, lawyers will need to devise new institutions to supply legal services more cheaply. Such changes, in turn, will undoubtedly force the organized bar to reexamine traditional attitudes toward fee-for-service and the unauthorized practice of law.

These steps will be difficult enough, but I suspect that even they will prove to be only palliatives. To make real progress, two added initiatives will be needed.

To begin with, an effective legal system will probably require greater efforts to plan and coordinate the work of our many separate courts and jurisdictions. In a system filled with different tribunals, each preoccupied with the random disputes that happen to pass before it, every judge can conscientiously perform his appointed task and still unwittingly subject many individuals to injustices and incongruous results. In some way, we need to develop mechanisms for reviewing whole bodies of law and their effects on the people they purport to serve. Only then can the appropriate officials set objectives and develop coordinated strategies to allow fields of law such as personal liability or environmental protection or employment discrimination to do a better job of meeting the needs of those whose lives they affect.

In addition, judges, lawmakers, scholars will all have to recognize that our conception of the role of law has fallen into disrepair. In its place, they will need to search for a new understanding that is no less sensitive to injustice but more realistic in accounting for the limits and costs of legal rules in ordering human affairs. Such an effort should result in fewer rules,

397

but rules that are more fundamental, better understood, and more widely enforced throughout the society. Lacking such a vision, judges and regulators will continue to drift toward a general willingness to intervene whenever they feel that one person has suffered at the hands of another. That is the logical end of a process that concentrates so heavily on the plight of individual litigants and gives so little heed to the effects on the system as a whole. What emerges from this process is a spurious form of justice. In such a world, the law may seem enlightened and humane, but its constant stream of rules will leave a wake strewn with the disappointed hopes of those who find the legal system too complicated to understand, too quixotic to command respect, and too expensive to be of much practical use.

The Role of Law Schools

The prospects for achieving such reforms are daunting, I realize. A comprehensive effort to improve our legal system will call for help from every quarter: lawyers, judges, legislators, regulatory officials. I will not try to describe the contributions that each of these parties can make. The occasion does not allow it, and my qualifications are unequal to the task. My immediate concerns lie with education, and it is there that I would concentrate my attention.

One way by which educational institutions can contribute to reform is to mobilize their capacities for generating new knowledge. The public complains about the cost of legal services, but no one has discovered how much money we spend each year on our legal system. . . . Nor has anyone done much to explore the forces that encourage or inhibit litigation so that we can better predict the rise and fall of legal activity.

Our limited knowledge seriously inhibits efforts to increase efficiency and access in the legal system. It is idle to talk of sunset provisions if lawmakers lack the methods to assess the costs and benefits of legislation. It is useless to create arbitration panels and mediation services if no one troubles to test their performance against predetermined criteria. It is reckless to offer proposals to ease congestion in the courts if even the proponents cannot tell whether such measures will achieve their goal or simply evoke more litigation (much as wider highways often succeed in merely calling forth more cars). Worst of all, it will be impossible ever to develop more sensible theories of the appropriate role of law if we do not make greater efforts to examine the effects of the laws we already have.

Although these points seem obvious enough, law schools have done surprisingly little to seek the knowledge that the legal system requires. Even the most rudimentary facts about the legal system are unknown or misunderstood. We still do not know how much money is spent on legal disputes and services in the United States. . . .

If law schools are to do their share in attacking the basic problems of our legal system, they will need to adapt their teaching as well as their research. The hallmark of the curriculum continues to be its emphasis on training students to define the issues carefully and to marshall all of the arguments and counterarguments on either side. Law schools celebrate this effort by constantly telling students that they are being taught "to think like a lawyer." But one can admire the virtues of careful analysis and still believe that the times cry out for more than these traditional skills. As I have tried to point out, the capacity to think like a lawyer has produced many triumphs, but it has also helped to produce a legal system that is among the most expensive and least efficient in the world.

One example of this problem is the familiar tilt in the law curriculum toward preparing students for legal combat. . . .

Many people have debated whether lawyers exacerbate controversy or help to prevent it from arising. Doubtless, they do some of each. But everyone must agree that law schools train their students more for conflict than for the gentler arts of reconciliation and accommodation. This emphasis is likely to serve the profession poorly. In fact, lawyers devote more time to negotiating conflicts than they spend in the library or the courtroom, and studies show that their bargaining efforts accomplish more for their clients. Over the next generation, I predict, society's greatest opportunities will lie in tapping human inclinations toward collaboration and compromise rather than stirring our proclivities for competition and rivalry. If lawyers are not leaders in marshaling cooperation and designing mechanisms which allow it to flourish, they will not be at the center of the most creative social experiments of our time.

Another glaring deficiency is the lack of attention given to the very problems of the legal system that I have been discussing. . . .

Leadership also calls for more than merely preparing leaders of the bar. Law schools will need to take the initiative in educating for a broader range of legal needs in our society. An efficient system of extending access to legal services throughout the society will demand the imaginative use of paralegal personnel. An effective system for extending legal protection to the poor must involve greater efforts to educate the disadvantaged about their rights, so that they can defend their interests without being exploited or having to go to court. A serious attempt to provide cheaper methods of resolving disputes will require skilled mediators and judges, who are trained to play a much more active part in guiding proceedings toward a fair solution. In short, a just and effective legal system will not merely call for a revised curriculum; it will entail the education of new categories of people. It is time that our law schools began to take the lead in helping devise such training.

Beyond education and research, law schools can also help to create new institutions more efficient than traditional law firms in delivering legal services to the poor and middle class. As in medicine, these organizations will benefit if they are linked to a university so that they can offer teaching opportunities and intellectual stimulation to their attorneys while drawing upon the services of second- and third-year law students. . . .

The law school that seizes these opportunities could become a more interesting place, experimenting with new methods of teaching, new forms of research, even new institutional settings for combining instruction with legal services. Fortunately, a handful of schools seem intent upon exploring these opportunities. I am pleased that Harvard Law School can be numbered among these pioneers. . . .

Conclusion

The problems I have dwelt on here are but examples of the many difficulties that have produced wide discontent with all our major professions. Doctors are assailed for failing to control health costs and for pursuing specialization and advanced technology at the expense of a humane consideration for the welfare of their patients. Business is attacked for the salaries of its executives, for its failure to prepare adequately for competition from abroad, for its inability to cooperate effectively with the government in addressing major social problems. Public servants are pilloried for their bureaucratic ways, their inefficiencies, their lack of sensitivity to the problems of those they seek to regulate.

In short, the public seems critical of all institutions and increasingly concerned that the country is no longer working well. International comparisons — industrial productivity, infant mortality, the extent of pollution, crime, poverty, and many other social ills — seem to give ample reason for this concern. Universities cannot hope to solve such problems by themselves. Progress calls for cooperation from many institutions beyond the reach of the campus. But faculties can supply knowledge that is often vital to the development of sound solutions. Universities can also prepare able people with a broad view of their profession and with skills to help address its problems. Unfortunately, most professional schools have done little to meet this challenge. They have concentrated on training practitioners for successful careers while failing to acquaint them with the larger problems that have aroused such concern within the society. At long last, our law school seems disposed to break out of this narrow mold, enlisting faculty and students in a common concern for the failings of a costly and often inaccessible legal system. We should applaud this initiative and wish them every success in their new enterprise.

WESTMORELAND/CBS CONTROVERSY
April 26, 1983

On April 26 CBS News released the text of its internal investigation into a controversial television documentary on the Vietnam War. The program, which had aired on January 23, 1982, implied that Gen. William C. Westmoreland, commander of the U.S. military in Vietnam, and others had conspired to deceive the American public regarding the strength of enemy troops in Vietnam. Westmoreland claimed he had been libeled by CBS and in September 1982 sued the network for $120 million.

Release of the report came after Judge Pierre N. Leval of the U.S. District Court in New York City ordered CBS to turn over its investigation text to Westmoreland, rejecting the network's contention that the report was an in-house document protected by First Amendment free-press guarantees. Westmoreland sought the report to bolster his claim that CBS deliberately had excluded from the documentary material that refuted the conspiracy theory.

Background

On January 23, 1982, CBS broadcast a program entitled "The Uncounted Enemy: A Vietnam Deception." The show, produced by George Crile and narrated by Mike Wallace, contended that "Americans were misinformed about the nature and the size of the enemy we were facing" in Vietnam and that there was "a conscious effort — indeed, a conspiracy at the highest levels of American military intelligence — to suppress and alter critical intelligence on the enemy in the year leading up to the

[1968] Tet offensive" launched by the North Vietnamese communist forces. A former CIA analyst, Samuel A. Adams, researched much of the show's content and worked as a paid consultant on the production.

Three days after the broadcast, Westmoreland held a news conference to challenge the show's conclusions. He was joined by five of his military and civilian associates from Vietnam.

In late May 1982 a TV Guide *article entitled "Anatomy of a Smear"* criticized the documentary on a number of counts, including inaccuracy and unfairness of presentation. However, the article did not challenge the show's conspiracy premise.

In response to the TV Guide *charges and surrounding publicity, CBS News President Van Gordon Sauter ordered an internal investigation. Burton Benjamin, a CBS News senior executive producer, directed the probe. His report, completed in July, examined point by point the charges leveled by* TV Guide. In *his summary Benjamin concluded there were 11 "principal flaws" in the preparation of the documentary, including failure to prove the existence of a conspiracy, "an imbalance in presenting the two sides of the issue," "coddling of sympathetic witnesses" and "other violations of CBS News Guidelines."*

Upon completion of the internal investigation, Sauter made public a memorandum in July. He stated that there had been flaws in the preparation of the documentary but that the network stood behind the substance of the show. The Benjamin report supported that decision, the memo implied.

Lawsuit

In September 1982 Westmoreland filed suit against CBS, alleging that he had been libeled both by the original broadcast and by Sauter's memorandum. To support his claim that the broadcast was deliberately one-sided, Westmoreland sought a copy of the CBS investigation report.

In ordering CBS to turn over a copy of the Benjamin report to Westmoreland on April 21, Judge Leval maintained that the network had no right to keep the report confidential because CBS in July had cited portions of the report to substantiate points made in the documentary.

As a public figure, Westmoreland had to prove that CBS broadcast the documentary either knowing it was false or not caring whether it was true or false. The Benjamin report, according to Leval, "may well lead to evidence of degree of care for accuracy, concern for truthfulness and possible bias, prejudgment or malice."

The court's decision to force CBS to make public the report on its investigation raised concerns among the press regarding a news organization's right to privacy. In a prepared statement, CBS contended that "it *is imperative that journalists be able to conduct post-broadcast and post-publication examinations of their work," and "confidentiality is important" if those efforts to be honest with themselves and the public were to be meaningful. News organizations also worried about the increase in the number of libel cases filed; they feared that more plaintiffs would file suit if they believed they could get hold of internal documents (such as the Benjamin report) that might support their claims.*

Those on the other side of the argument, however, maintained that news organizations, like other businesses, should openly admit their mistakes. They argued further that disclosure of internal investigations could lead to a more careful and responsible press.

> *Following are excerpts from the memorandum of investigation released April 26, 1983, by CBS concerning the CBS News Reports documentary, "The Uncounted Enemy: A Vietnam Deception," and from an article in* TV Guide *criticizing the documentary.*

Introduction

This paper is written at the direction of the management of CBS and CBS News. It began on May 24, 1982, when Van Gordon Sauter, president of CBS News, phoned the writer from San Francisco and asked if he would undertake the examination.

The *TV Guide* cover article, "Anatomy of a Smear," by Don Kowet and Sally Bedell (May 29-June 4 issue) had just appeared. The writer told Mr. Sauter he would take on the project.

The story was one of inordinate complexity. The 90-minute broadcast of January 23, 1982, had taken approximately 15 months to complete. The *TV Guide* article had taken two months to prepare.

The core of this report is a point-by-point examination of the charges leveled by *TV Guide*. But it goes beyond that. It includes an examination of the charges made in the January 26, 1982, news conference called in Washington by General William C. Westmoreland, commander, U.S. Military Assistance Command, Vietnam [MACV], from 1964 to 1968. General Westmoreland was joined by five of his military and civilian associates from Vietnam. . . .

Background

Much of the story in the CBS News documentary was not new. It was new to television as a prime-time documentary. Samuel A. Adams had been conducting his research for 15 years, first as an analyst for Central Intelligence and since 1973, when he resigned, as a civilian. In a computer search of *The New York Times* Information Bank I, we found 36 references to Adams and his work. Adams and George Crile, the producer of the broadcast, state that the infiltration figures in the broadcast were new. They also state that this is the first time MACV intelligence officers have publicly stated what they believed to be wrongdoing. . . .

The *TV Guide* Charges

The charges of Kowet and Bedell can be broken down in several ways. We will deal with them chronologically, i.e. as they were given in the piece. Looked at this way, there are 11 major charges. However, some of them contain subcharges and so the overall total is higher.

The Theme

> The evidence amassed by CBS seemed to prove the U.S. military's intelligence operation in Vietnam, led by General Westmoreland, conspired to deceive President Lyndon Johnson, the Congress and the American public. Beginning in 1967, the documentary charges, Westmoreland had systematically underreported to his superiors the size and strength of the enemy, in order to make it appear that he was indeed winning the "war of attrition."   *TV Guide, page 3*

George Crile [producer of the CBS program], in his "White Paper" . . . maintains this was the theme:

> That in 1967, American military and civilian intelligence discovered evidence indicating the existence of a dramatically larger enemy than previously reported . . . that instead of alerting the country, U.S. military intelligence under General Westmoreland commenced to suppress and alter its intelligence reports, in order to conceal this discovery from the American public, the Congress, and perhaps even the President.

It is important to note as Crile points out, "Nowhere in the article do the authors challenge the central premise of the broadcast. . . ."

CBS began the project already convinced that a conspiracy had been perpetrated and turned a deaf ear toward evidence that suggested otherwise.   *TV Guide, page 4*

A. The Blue Sheet is filled with references to conspiracy.   *TV Guide, page 5*

The so-called Blue Sheet, which producers prepare for management to outline and protect ideas they want approved, is dated November 24, 1980, and runs 16 single-spaced pages. It is much longer than most Blue Sheets, many of which run only a single page. Crile attributes this to the complexity of the subject matter. . . . *TV Guide* quotes Crile as saying "Conspiracy . . . was a characterization which we agreed to use in the script at the very end, after reviewing everything in the show." Crile in his interview with us (June 15, 1982):

> It was absolutely proper to use the word conspiracy. We went through everybody before we used the word. It was the only word that worked for me to explain the pattern of events.

The word is used once in the broadcast. . . .

However, a reading of the Blue Sheet finds the word "conspiracy" used 24 times and the word "conspirator" five times.

"Conspiracy" was used in the full-page ad for the broadcast. . . .

The use of the word "conspiracy" has engendered considerable controversy. . . .

B. The Blue Sheet scenarios would appear virtually intact in the documentary.   *TV Guide, page 6*

The Blue Sheet does closely resemble the finished broadcast. In a June, 1982, memorandum to Mike Wallace (no date), Crile wrote:

> I presented Bill Leonard, Bob Chandler, Roger Colloff, and Howard Stringer with a 16-page, single spaced Blue Sheet, spelling out in great detail what I believed I could put on film and present as a documentary for CBS REPORTS. Throughout that Blue Sheet were references to "conspiracy." Throughout that Blue Sheet were references to Adams and a careful spelling out of the unusual and awkward relationship Adams would have to the project if we decided to take him on and pay him. As Bill Leonard said: "these things either happened or they didn't; if they happened it was a very important story and we should run it." My commission was to go out *with* Adams and prove on film that these people would testify to what Adams told us they had told him. So I did. And CBS News with its eyes wide open, looked at the interviews, decided to commission the documentary, hire Adams and sent us on our way to complete the word as spelled out in the Blue Sheet. The documentary they got is the documentary they commissioned. . . .

C. CBS carefully selected from Sam Adams' list of 60 only those who would support the conspiracy theory.   *TV Guide, page 6*

The word "carefully" is loaded and I would not call it the "conspiracy theory" but rather the premise of the broadcast. The 8 people who supported Adams were all on the list, so were Westmoreland and Graham. Other than that, the charge appears to be true. . . .

CBS paid $25,000 to a consultant on the program without adequately investigating his 14-year quest to prove the program's conspiracy theory.   *TV Guide, page 6*

CBS News did pay Adams $25,000 in five installments. His expenses totalled an additional $4,904.69.... Adams worked on the broadcast for the better part of a year.

Since he was also interviewed on camera, he should have been identified in the script as a *paid* consultant. Not doing so was a violation of CBS News Guidelines....

Wallace, Colloff and Stringer never did any more to examine Adams' credibility than simply sit down and chat with him. TV Guide, page 6

Crile maintains that in 1975, he and *Harper's* editor Lewis Lapham did check Adams very carefully. He said Thomas Powers, author of *The Man Who Kept the Secrets,* a biography of Richard Helms, endorsed Adams and his research. He emphasizes that it wasn't only Adams and his research but eight former military officers and CIA men, willing to go on camera to corroborate the story, that gave the broadcast its credibility....

CBS violated its own official guidelines by rehearsing its paid consultant before he was interviewed on camera *TV Guide, page 4*

... This charge ... is open to question....

CBS screened for a sympathetic witness — in order to persuade him to re-do his on-camera interview — the statements of other witnesses already on film. But CBS never offered the targets of its conspiracy charge any opportunity, before their interviews, to hear their accusers, or to have a second chance before the cameras. *TV Guide, page 11*

One man, George Allen, formerly of Central Intelligence in Vietnam and Washington, was interviewed twice in New York on May 26 and June 29, 1981.

The interviews were shot in different locations but Allen was asked to wear the same suit.

Before the second interview, he was shown film of three other interviews (McChristian, Hawkins, Hovey), all of whom were on his side of the argument. The statement that these screenings were designed to "persuade" Allen to do the interview is inaccurate. He had already done it once. Crile says the screenings were more in the nature of reassuring him....

The questions asked in the two interviews were virtually the same. The main difference was that in the second interview, some questions were asked about statements made by Lt. Gen. Daniel Graham who was interviewed on June 3, 1981 after the first Allen interview.

The double interview and the screenings are a violation of CBS News

Guidelines quoted previously, i.e. that interviews be "spontaneous and unrehearsed."

The second part of the charge — that CBS never offered the other side a chance to hear their "accusers" — is true but the analogy is skewed. Allen was allowed to hear not his "accusers" but the people who supported his argument. . . .

CBS asked sympathetic witnesses soft questions, while grilling unfriendly witnesses with prosecutorial zeal. *TV Guide, page 4*

A reading of the full, unedited transcripts for the broadcast, some 20 hours of them, lends credence to the charge that the tone was harsher during the interviews of the so-called "unfriendly witnesses" (Westmoreland, Graham, and Rostow) than it was during the interviews of the so-called "sympathetic witnesses" (Adams, Allen, Hawkins, McChristian, McArthur, Hamscher, Cooley, Meachem and Hovey).

Westmoreland was not well prepared. The telephone calls to him about the areas to be discussed were vague. A letter spelling this out arrived the day before the interview. *TV Guide, pages 9 and 10*

The interview with General William Westmoreland took place on May 16, 1981, at a New York hotel. On May 7, Crile and Wallace spoke with Westmoreland in South Carolina by phone. Crile (interview, June 15, 1981): "It was not difficult to reach him or get him to appear. It was tough to get through to him what we talking about — intelligence under him. He has always had a good cover story. . . . We told him we were doing the documentary on the role of intelligence using Tet as a jumping off point and were we alert to enemy strength? . . ."

Westmoreland's full transcript is contradictory. At one point he demonstrates he has done some preparation. In a discussion of enemy killed, Wallace cites the number 80,000. Westmoreland says it's 55,000 adding: "And I remember that because I just read the report that Admiral Sharp and I wrote.". . . And yet, on the next page, he says: "I can't remember figures like that. You've . . . done some research. I haven't done any research. I'm just reflecting on my memory."

CBS misrepresented the accounts of events provided by some witnesses, while ignoring altogether other witnesses who might have been able to challenge CBS' assertions. *TV Guide, page 10*

A. Westmoreland was misrepresented. At least 10 times Westmoreland says the size of the enemy was overestimated at Tet. This view was never offered on the Show. *TV Guide, page 10*

Westmoreland did make this assertion — that rather than underestimating the enemy at Tet, we overestimated him. He says this eight times, not "at least ten times." None of it was used on the broadcast.

B. Infiltration figures. CBS knew in fall of 1967 MACV figures had never climbed above 8,000 a month. When asked, Westmoreland says 20,000 a month. The discrepancy with his 1967 "Meet the Press" estimate of 5500-6000. Westmoreland sends his so-called "correction" letter about this after interview which Crile never shows to his superiors at CBS or treats on the air.   TV Guide, page 10

Here we enter the arcane world of infiltration figures. What *TV Guide* never deals with is that both figures may be wrong. The Vietnam War was a non-linear conflict, unlike World War II or Korea where intelligence could measure the armies along fronts or lines of battle. It has been said that even today, seven years after the end of the Vietnam War, military historians cannot give enemy strength figures with absolute precision. One compelling reason may be that there was no flood of captured enemy documents after the conflict was over. We did not win this war.

C. Lt. Gen. Daniel Graham was a tough interview: out of 90 minutes only 20 seconds of denials aired.   TV Guide, page 11

General Graham, Westmoreland's chief of the Current Intelligence and Estimates Division J-2 MACV, was interviewed by Mike Wallace for over an hour and two sound bites totalling 21 seconds were used.

This was a judgement call on the part of the producer, and in this business there are hundreds of such calls in any documentary....

D. Walt W. Rostow was interviewed for three hours and nothing was used. He could have told what LBJ [President Lyndon Johnson] knew about the intelligence controversy.   TV Guide, pages 11 and 12

Walt W. Rostow, special assistant and security advisor to President Johnson, was interviewed by Mike Wallace in New York on July 24, 1981. It was the last interview filmed for the broadcast. None of Rostow's remarks were used....

E. CBS had not sought out a number of officials pivotal to the controversy covered by the program.

... General [Phillip] Davidson succeeded General McChristian as the J-2, MACV, Chief of Military Intelligence in Saigon, on May 27, 1967. He held that post until May 10, 1969. Tet therefore came on his watch. He was Lt. General Daniel Graham's boss.

TV Guide describes Davidson as the "most important" of the omitted interviews. The magazine claims that Crile and Wallace did not interview him because, as Wallace told Westmoreland, "General Davidson is a very, very sick man. . . . (Westmoreland interview, May 16, 1981). Instead, Davidson told the magazine that he had been treated successfully for cancer in 1974 and was now "healthy.". . .

F. The McChristian-Hawkins briefing misrepresented statements from the two men. Their comments about three separate incidents were woven together into what seemed to be one pivotal meeting.   TV Guide, page 13

From our reading of the unedited transcripts, there were clearly two meetings woven into one. . . .

G. CBS said McChristian's report was suppressed, and he was transferred out of Vietnam, implying the two were linked.   TV Guide, page 14

TV Guide here is quoting from the unedited transcript of the McChristian interview with George Crile: . . . Nowhere in his interview with Crile did McChristian say that any of his estimates were "suppressed."

On his transfer being linked to his enemy strength estimates, McChristian is pressed repeatedly in his interview with Crile but never concedes that this is so. . . .

H. CBS made it appear that Col. George Hamscher was the head of the MACV delegation to the national intelligence estimates meeting in Langley, Va.   TV Guide, page 14

. . . The juxtaposition of the lead and then Hamscher coming up on screen gives the impression that he is the head of MACV. Crile says (interview June 12, 1982) that Wallace's bridging narration line: "Col. George Hamscher was one of several members of the military delegation. . . ." takes care of this. . . .

I. The real head of the MACV delegation, General George Godding, was never identified.   TV Guide, page 14

Godding was not interviewed on camera for the broadcast. *TV Guide* quotes Sam Adams as saying the reason Godding was not identified in the script was "the same old problem . . . the mention of too many names." Adams (interview June 21, 1982) confirms that he said this. . . .

J. The 300,000 ceiling — Sam Adams' "smoking gun" proving a Westmoreland-led conspiracy — was the general's order not to go over that number for enemy strength at the national intelligence estimate meeting in Langley.   TV Guide, page 14

This charge, about which *TV Guide* makes much, is poised on this question: At the 1967 Langley meeting did someone from MACV have a piece of paper saying "Don't go over 300,000" or was the position "defend the MACV order-of-battle figure for May?" The latter position was for an enemy-strength figure of 296,000. Is this a 4000-man argument?

The broadcast script says unequivocally "... the head of MACV's delegation told us that General Westmoreland had, in fact, personally instructed him not to allow the total to go over 300,000."

Nowhere in the more than 20 hours of transcripts we have read does anyone say specifically that there was a 300,000 ceiling. *TV Guide* charges that Colonel Hawkins told Crile no fewer than four times that he had not been given a numerical ceiling. We can confirm that three times (*TV Guide's* fourth time was a reverse question) Hawkins refuses to confirm a 300,000 ceiling. What he does say a number of times is that he was ordered to defend the MACV command position (296,000). ... Crile argues (interview June 15, 1982) that the difference between a ceiling of 300,000 and defending MACV's 296,000 is no more than a "semantic trick."....

CBS took quotes out of context, in one case showing Westmoreland reacting to a meeting that took place at the Pentagon when actually he was responding to a question about another meeting that took place in Saigon.   *TV Guide, pages 14 and 15*

A reading of the unedited transcript confirms the charge. On the broadcast Wallace's narration is about an August 1967 National Intelligence Estimate meeting at the Pentagon. He interviews Colonel Hamscher about this. Then we come to General Westmoreland on the next page. He is responding to a question about another meeting — an order-of-battle meeting in Saigon in September 1967. Cut into this sequence, the General's answer is not about the same meeting the broadcast has been dealing with....

Sam Adams now doubts the broadcast's premise and Adams told the magazine that if there was a conspiracy it originated at the White House, not with Westmoreland.   *TV Guide, page 15*

This charge is denied by Sam Adams. In his interview with us (June 21, 1982) he says: "If I had a problem with the show it was that it hung the rap too much on Westmoreland and not enough White House involvement.... I wouldn't say the premise of the show is that Westmoreland is the perpetrator...."

Crile's supervisors at CBS News failed to oversee his work effectively.   *TV Guide, page 15*

TV Guide provided no supporting data to prove its charge....

TV Guide **says if this broadcast is any indication, network news departments are not doing enough to keep their own houses in order and news safeguards for fairness and accuracy need tightening, if not wholesale revision.**   *TV Guide, page 1*

This seems to us an editorial opinion, not reportage. As such, we see no point in addressing ourselves to it.

This concludes the *TV Guide* charges. . . .

CBS News Guidelines Irregularities

Throughout this paper we have listed some violations of CBS News Guidelines, such as interviewing the same man (Allen) twice. There were other violations involving a section of the Guidelines.

> If the answer to an interview question, as that answer appears in the broadcast, is derived, in part or in whole, from the answers to other questions, the broadcast will so indicate, either in lead-in narration, bridging narration lines during the interview, or appropriate audio lines.

In short, what this section says is that you cannot cut together two answers from two separate questions as a single answer to one question. . . .

Summary

Based on our examination, the broadcast had these principal flaws:

● The premise was obviously and historically controversial. There was an imbalance in presenting the two sides of the issue. For every McChristian, there was a Davidson; for every Hawkins, a Morris; for every Allen, a Carver.

● A "conspiracy," given the accepted definition of the word, was not proved.

● The double interview of George Allen.

● The screening of interviews for Allen.

● Sam Adams not being properly identified as a *paid* consultant.

● Journalistic oversight which permitted two McChristian-Hawkins meetings to appear to be one meeting.

● Journalistic oversight which permitted General Westmoreland to discuss one meeting which was then cut into a sequence about another meeting.

● Other violations of CBS News Guidelines.

● The coddling of sympathetic witnesses.

● The lack of journalistic enterprise in trying to find General Davidson or in checking out his "illness."

● Imprecisions in the handling of the Hamscher introduction and in the "Meet the Press" matter involving Westmoreland's "correction letter."

On the other hand, *TV Guide* may have been wise in not challenging the premise of the broadcast. It seems odd, to say the least, for the magazine to launch an attack of this dimension and still say of its investigation: "Its purpose was not to confirm or deny the existence of the 'conspiracy' that CBS's journalists say existed."

The reason for that may be that even today military historians cannot tell you whether or not MACV "cooked the books" as the broadcast states. The flow of definitive information is painfully slow and may never be conclusive. . . .

EDUCATION REPORT: 'A NATION AT RISK'
April 26, 1983

The quality of American education, a persistent concern of educators, parents, employers and, at times, politicans, surfaced as an urgent social and political issue in 1983 with the release of a plethora of reports detailing the system's alleged weaknesses and faults. "A Nation At Risk," the study that led the growing chorus of criticism, was the product of the National Commission on Educational Excellence, a blue-ribbon panel appointed by Education Secretary T. H. Bell. The commission's findings, released April 26, were reinforced by subsequent reports compiled under the auspices of a variety of organizations including the Twentieth Century Fund, the Carnegie Foundation, and the National Science Board.

'Unilateral Educational Disarmament'

The National Commission's report was prefaced with a stern message warning of a "tide of mediocrity [threatening] our very future as a Nation and a people" unless drastic measures were taken to revise the ailing system.

The study found that the United States not only had failed to keep abreast of most industrialized countries in educational quality, but had fallen behind so badly that "If an unfriendly foreign power had attempted to impose on America the mediocre educational performance that exists today, we might well have viewed it as an act of war. As it stands, we have allowed this to happen to ourselves .... We have, in

413

effect, been committing an act of unthinking, unilateral educational disarmament."

The commission's recommendations were far reaching, stringent and expensive. Addressing the fundamental issue of academic content, the commission outlined the need for "new basics" and recommended tightening high school graduation requirements for all students to include four years of English, three years of mathematics, science and social studies and one-half year of computer science. The study and mastery of a foreign language also was highly recommended, beginning at the elementary school level. To enable high school students to meet the more rigorous requirements called for in the report, the need for a sound curriculum in the elementary grades, particularly language development and writing skills, was emphasized.

The commission cited the need to raise academic standards at all educational levels, including stricter college admission requirements. The higher standards would require revising textbooks and other teaching tools, with special federal funds earmarked to develop texts geared to the needs of disadvantaged, disabled and gifted children.

To take full advantage of this revised curriculum, the commission suggested extending the school day to seven hours and the school year to 200 to 220 days from the existing 180, in addition to assigning "far more homework" for high school students and making more effective use of school time.

The commission's study also included proposals for improving the teaching profession by increasing salaries, providing tenure and granting promotion based on merit and not seniority. The issue of merit pay was a sensitive one among teachers, and the pros and cons of instituting such a system continued to divide those in the profession throughout 1983.

Federal, State and Local Responsibilities

The commission's final recommendations dealt with the controversial issues of fiscal and leadership responsibilities needed to implement the suggested reforms. While the panel held state and local officials primarily responsible for financing public education, as has traditionally been the case, it held the federal government accountable for identifying priorities and contributing support to the nation's educational needs. The report further called on the federal government to provide the leadership necessary to promote and provide superior education as a primary national interest.

"A Nation At Risk" was submitted to President Ronald Reagan at a time when he was calling for dismantling the Education Department, cutting the education budget and enacting tax credits for tuition paid to private schools. But it was Reagan's interpretation of the commission's

fiscal and leadership recommendations that most offended concerned educators. Attributing the reported "rising tide of mediocrity" to 20 years of increased, but ineffectively used, federal funds for education, Reagan maintained that the study supported his position calling for a weaker federal role in education.

Receiving the report at a White House ceremony, the president said, "Your call for an end to Federal intrusion is consistent with our task of redefining the Federal role in education. I believe that parents, not Government, have the primary responsibility for the education of their children. Parental authority is not a right conveyed by the state; rather, parents delegate to their elected school board representatives and State legislators the responsibility for their children's schooling."

In contrast to Reagan's view, most educators interpreted the comprehensive list of recommended reforms as requiring a deeper federal commitment to education. Commissioner Gerald Holton, professor of physics and science history at Harvard University, said he regretted that "the climate in the executive branch of government at this time is such as to not embrace the leadership responsibility that is spelled out in the report."

Other Reports

A number of reports and recommendations to improve the quality of education were released throughout 1983. Most of the studies confirmed the findings of the National Commission on Excellence in Education and suggested courses of action comparable to those outlined in its report. The Twentieth Century Fund's Task Force, for example, in a May 5 report called for increased federal funding of English language programs, especially in disadvantaged areas of the country and localities with high concentrations of immigrants. Rather than offer bilingual education, the task force said, English proficiency should be emphasized to help ensure equal educational and employment opportunities for all citizens.

A report more optimistic than the National Commission's evaluation was released September 14 by the Carnegie Foundation for the Advancement of Teaching. The foundation acknowledged slight improvements in national test scores and interpreted the revived interest in education standards as a positive trend. But the core of the foundation's recommendations was that better teachers were the key to upgrading educational standards. To achieve this, the report suggested raising salaries, improving working conditions, instituting meritorious advancement and revising teacher-training programs.

Focusing on the need to rebuild science and mathematics education, a 20-member commission appointed by the National Science Board offered its proposals September 12. The product of a 17-month study, the report strongly recommended rebuilding math and science curricula for kinder-

*garten through high school. The panel suggested that the federal govern-
ment invest approximately $4.6 billion over a six-year period to develop a
revised curriculum, assist in establishing 2,000 "exemplary" science and
math schools and retrain teachers. The suggested reforms were based on
the national goal of providing American youth with the skills necessary
to compete in an increasingly technological world, a sentiment echoed in
all the education studies.*

*Although there was widespread alarm over the state of U.S. education,
the concern expressed by educators and parents suggested a renewed
commitment on all levels to improve the quality of education. While the
measures necessary to repair the system were severe, all the reports cited
were optimistic that the new goals could be reached. As the National
Commission on Excellence in Education concluded, "We are the inheritors of a past that gives us every reason to believe that we will succeed."*

> *Following is the text of the report of the National Commis-
> sion on Excellence in Education, "A Nation At Risk,"
> released April 26, 1983:*

Our Nation is at risk. Our once unchallenged preeminence in commerce,
industry, science, and technological innovation is being overtaken by
competitors throughout the world. This report is concerned with only one
of the many causes and dimensions of the problem, but it is the one that
undergirds American prosperity, security, and civility. We report to the
American people that while we can take justifiable pride in what our
schools and colleges have historically accomplished and contributed to the
United States and the well-being of its people, the educational foundations
of our society are presently being eroded by a rising tide of mediocrity that
threatens our very future as a Nation and a people. What was unimaginable a generation ago has begun to occur — others are matching and
surpassing our educational attainments.

If an unfriendly foreign power had attempted to impose on America the
mediocre educational performance that exists today, we might well have
viewed it as an act of war. As it stands, we have allowed this to happen to
ourselves. We have even squandered the gains in student achievement
made in the wake of the Sputnik challenge. Moreover, we have dismantled
essential support systems which helped make those gains possible. We
have, in effect, been committing an act of unthinking, unilateral educational disarmament.

Our society and its educational institutions seem to have lost sight of the
basic purposes of schooling, and of the high expectations and disciplined
effort needed to attain them. This report, the result of 18 months of study,
seeks to generate reform of our educational system in fundamental ways
and to renew the Nation's commitment to schools and colleges of high
quality throughout the length and breadth of our land.

That we have compromised this commitment is, upon reflection, hardly surprising, given the multitude of often conflicting demands we have placed on our Nation's schools and colleges. They are routinely called on to provide solutions to personal, social, and political problems that the home and other institutions either will not or cannot resolve. We must understand that these demands on our schools and colleges often exact an educational cost as well as a financial one.

On the occasion of the Commission's first meeting, President Reagan noted the central importance of education in American life when he said: "Certainly there are few areas of American life as important to our society, to our people, and to our families as our schools and colleges." This report, therefore, is as much an open letter to the American people as it is a report to the Secretary of Education. We are confident that the American people, properly informed, will do what is right for their children and for the generations to come.

The Risk

History is not kind to idlers. The time is long past when America's destiny was assured simply by an abundance of natural resources and inexhaustible human enthusiasm, and by our relative isolation from the malignant problems of older civilizations. The world is indeed one global village. We live among determined, well-educated, and strongly motivated competitors. We compete with them for international standing and markets, not only with products but also with the ideas of our laboratories and neighborhood workshops. America's position in the world may once have been reasonably secure with only a few exceptionally well-trained men and women. It is no longer.

The risk is not only that the Japanese make automobiles more efficiently than Americans and have government subsidies for development and export. It is not just that the South Koreans recently built the world's most efficient steel mill, or that American machine tools, once the pride of the world, are being displaced by German products. It is also that these developments signify a redistribution of trained capability throughout the globe. Knowledge, learning, information, and skilled intelligence are the new raw materials of international commerce and are today spreading throughout the world as vigorously as miracle drugs, synthetic fertilizers, and blue jeans did earlier. If only to keep and improve on the slim competitive edge we still retain in world markets, we must dedicate ourselves to the reform of our educational system for the benefit of all — old and young alike, affluent and poor, majority and minority. Learning is the indispensable investment required for success in the "information age" we are entering.

Our concern, however, goes well beyond matters such as industry and commerce. It also includes the intellectual, moral, and spiritual strengths of our people which knit together the very fabric of our society. The people of the United States need to know that individuals in our society who do not possess the levels of skill, literacy, and training essential to this new era will be effectively disenfranchised, not simply from the material rewards that accompany competent performance, but also from the chance to participate fully in our national life. A high level of shared education is essential to a free, democratic society and to the fostering of a common culture, especially in a country that prides itself on pluralism and individual freedom.

For our country to function, citizens must be able to reach some common understandings on complex issues, often on short notice and on the basis of conflicting or incomplete evidence. Education helps form these common understandings, a point Thomas Jefferson made long ago in his justly famous dictum:

> I know no safe depository of the ultimate powers of the society but the people themselves; and if we think them not enlightened enough to exercise their control with a wholesome discretion, the remedy is not to take it from them but to inform their discretion.

Part of what is at risk is the promise first made on this continent: All, regardless of race or class or economic status, are entitled to a fair chance and to the tools for developing their individual powers of mind and spirit to the utmost. This promise means that all children by virtue of their own efforts, competently guided, can hope to attain the mature and informed judgment needed to secure gainful employment and to manage their own lives, thereby serving not only their own interests but also the progress of society itself.

Indicators of the Risk

The educational dimensions of the risk before us have been amply documented in testimony received by the Commission. For example:

- International comparisons of student achievement, completed a decade ago, reveal that on 19 academic tests American students were never first or second and, in comparison with other industrialized nations, were last seven times.

- Some 23 million American adults are functionally illiterate by the simplest tests of everyday reading, writing, and comprehension.

  About 13 percent of all 17-year-olds in the United States can be considered functionally illiterate. Functional illiteracy among minority youth may run as high as 40 percent.

- Average achievement of high school students on most standardized tests is now lower than 26 years ago when Sputnik was launched.

- Over half the population of gifted students do not match their tested ability with comparable achievement in school.

- The College Board's Scholastic Aptitude Tests (SAT) demonstrate a virtually unbroken decline from 1963 to 1980. Average verbal scores fell over 50 points and average mathematics scores dropped nearly 40 points.

- College Board achievement tests also reveal consistent declines in recent years in such subjects as physics and English.
- Both the number and proportion of students demonstrating superior achievement on the SATs (i.e., those with scores of 650 or higher) have also dramatically declined.
- Many 17-year-olds do not possess the "higher order" intellectual skills we should expect of them. Nearly 40 percent cannot draw inferences from written material; only one-fifth can write a persuasive essay; and only one-third can solve a mathematics problem requiring several steps.
- There was a steady decline in science achievement scores of U.S. 17-year-olds as measured by national assessments of science in 1969, 1973, and 1977.
- Between 1975 and 1980, remedial mathematics courses in public 4-year colleges increased by 72 percent and now constitute one-quarter of all mathematics courses taught in those institutions.
- Average tested achievement of students graduating from college is also lower.
- Business and military leaders complain that they are required to spend millions of dollars on costly remedial education and training programs in such basic skills as reading, writing, spelling, and computation. The Department of the Navy, for example, reported to the Commission that one-quarter of its recent recruits cannot read at the ninth grade level, the minimum needed simply to understand written safety instructions. Without remedial work they cannot even begin, much less complete, the sophisticated training essential in much of the modern military.

These deficiencies come at a time when the demand for highly skilled workers in new fields is accelerating rapidly. For example:

- Computers and computer-controlled equipment are penetrating every aspect of our lives — homes, factories, and offices.
- One estimate indicates that by the turn of the century millions of jobs will involve laser technology and robotics.
- Technology is radically transforming a host of other occupations. They include health care, medical science, energy production, food processing, construction, and the building, repair, and maintenance of sophisticated scientific, educational, military, and industrial equipment.

Analysts examining these indicators of student performance and the demands for new skills have made some chilling observations. Educational researcher Paul Hurd concluded at the end of a thorough national survey of student achievement that within the context of the modern scientific revolution, "We are raising a new generation of Americans that is scientifically and technologically illiterate." In a similar vein, John Slaughter, a former Director of the National Science Foundation, warned of "a growing chasm between a small scientific and technological elite and a citizenry ill-informed, indeed uninformed, on issues with a science component."

But the problem does not stop there, nor do all observers see it the same way. Some worry that schools may emphasize such rudiments as reading and computation at the expense of other essential skills such as comprehension, analysis, solving problems, and drawing conclusions. Still others are concerned that an over-emphasis on technical and occupational skills will leave little time for studying the arts and humanities that so enrich daily life, help maintain civility, and develop a sense of community. Knowledge of the humanities, they maintain, must be harnessed to science and technology if the latter are to remain creative and humane, just as the humanities need to be informed by science and technology if they are to remain relevant to the human condition. Another analyst, Paul Copperman, has drawn a sobering conclusion. Until now, he has noted:

> Each generation of Americans has outstripped its parents in education, in literacy, and in economic attainment. For the first time in the history of our country, the educational skills of one generation will not surpass, will not equal, will not even approach, those of their parents.

It is important, of course, to recognize that *the average citizen* today is better educated and more knowledgeable than the average citizen of a generation ago — more literate, and exposed to more mathematics, literature, and science. The positive impact of this fact on the well-being of our country and the lives of our people cannot be overstated. Nevertheless, *the average graduate* of our schools and colleges today is not as well-educated as the average graduate of 25 or 35 years ago, when a much smaller proportion of our population completed high school and college. The negative impact of this fact likewise cannot be overstated.

Hope and Frustration

Statistics and their interpretation by experts show only the surface dimension of the difficulties we face. Beneath them lies a tension between hope and frustration that characterizes current attitudes about education at every level.

We have heard the voices of high school and college students, school board members, and teachers; of leaders of industry, minority groups, and higher education; of parents and State officials. We could hear the hope evident in their commitment to quality education and in their descriptions of outstanding programs and schools. We could also hear the intensity of their frustration, a growing impatience with shoddiness in many walks of American life, and the complaint that this shoddiness is too often reflected in our schools and colleges. Their frustration threatens to overwhelm their hope.

What lies behind this emerging national sense of frustration can be described as both a dimming of personal expectations and the fear of losing a shared vision for America.

On the personal level the student, the parent, and the caring teacher all perceive that a basic promise is not being kept. More and more young people emerge from high school ready neither for college nor for work. This predicament becomes more acute as the knowledge base continues its rapid expansion, the number of traditional jobs shrinks, and new jobs demand greater sophistication and preparation.

On a broader scale, we sense that this undertone of frustration has significant political implications, for it cuts across ages, generations, races, and political and economic groups. We have come to understand that the public will demand that educational and political leaders act forcefully and effectively on these issues. Indeed, such demands have already appeared and could well become a unifying national preoccupation. This unity, however, can be achieved only if we avoid the unproductive tendency of some to search for scapegoats among the victims, such as the beleaguered teachers.

On the positive side is the significant movement by political and educational leaders to search for solutions — so far centering largely on the nearly desperate need for increased support for the teaching of mathematics and science. This movement is but a start on what we believe is a larger and more educationally encompassing need to improve teaching and learning in fields such as English, history, geography, economics, and foreign languages. We believe this movement must be broadened and directed toward reform and excellence throughout education.

Excellence in Education

We define "excellence" to mean several related things. At the level of the *individual learner,* it means performing on the boundary of individual ability in ways that test and push back personal limits, in school and in the workplace. Excellence characterizes a *school or college* that sets high expectations and goals for all learners, then tries in every way possible to help students reach them. Excellence characterizes a *society* that has adopted these policies, for it will then be prepared through the education and skill of its people to respond to the challenges of a rapidly changing world. Our Nation's people and its schools and colleges must be committed to achieving excellence in all these senses.

We do not believe that a public commitment to excellence and educational reform must be made at the expense of a strong public commitment to the equitable treatment of our diverse population. The twin goals of equity and high-quality schooling have profound and practical meaning for our economy and society, and we cannot permit one to yield to the other either in principle or in practice. To do so would deny young people their chance to learn and live according to their aspirations and abilities. It also would lead to a generalized accommodation to mediocrity in our society on the one hand or the creation of an undemocratic elitism on the other.

Our goal must be to develop the talents of all to their fullest. Attaining that goal requires that we expect and assist all students to work to the limits of their capabilities. We should expect schools to have genuinely high standards rather than minimum ones, and parents to support and encourage their children to make the most of their talents and abilities.

The search for solutions to our educational problems must also include a commitment to life-long learning. The task of rebuilding our system of learning is enormous and must be properly understood and taken seriously: Although a million and a half new workers enter the economy each year from our schools and colleges, the adults working today will still make up about 75 percent of the workforce in the year 2000. These workers, and new entrants into the workforce, will need further education and retraining if they — and we as a Nation — are to thrive and prosper.

The Learning Society

In a world of ever-accelerating competition and change in the conditions of the workplace, of ever-greater danger, and of ever-larger opportunities for those prepared to meet them, educational reform should focus on the goal of creating a Learning Society. At the heart of such a society is the commitment to a set of values and to a system of education that affords all members the opportunity to stretch their minds to full capacity, from early childhood through adulthood, learning more as the world itself changes. Such a society has as a basic foundation the idea that education is important not only because of what it contributes to one's career goals but also because of the value it adds to the general quality of one's life. Also at the heart of the Learning Society are educational opportunities extending far beyond the traditional institutions of learning, our schools and colleges. They extend into homes and workplaces; into libraries, art galleries, museums, and science centers; indeed, into every place where the individual can develop and mature in work and life. In our view, formal schooling in youth is the essential foundation for learning throughout one's life. But without life-long learning, one's skills will become rapidly dated.

In contrast to the ideal of the Learning Society, however, we find that for too many people education means doing the minimum work necessary for the moment, then coasting through life on what may have been learned in its first quarter. But this should not surprise us because we tend to express our educational standards and expectations largely in terms of "minimum requirements." And where there should be a coherent continuum of learning, we have none, but instead an often incoherent, outdated patchwork quilt. Many individual, sometimes heroic, examples of schools and colleges of great merit do exist. Our findings and testimony confirm the vitality of a number of notable schools and programs, but their very distinction stands out against a vast mass shaped by tensions and pressures that inhibit systematic academic and vocational achievement for the majority of students. In some metropolitan areas basic literacy has become the goal rather than the starting point. In some colleges maintaining enrollments is of greater day-to-day concern than maintaining rigorous academic standards. And the ideal of academic excellence as the primary goal of schooling seems to be fading across the board in American education.

Thus, we issue this call to all who care about America and its future: to parents and students; to teachers, administrators, and school board members; to colleges and industry; to union members and military leaders; to governors and State legislators; to the President; to members of Congress and other public officials; to members of learned and scientific societies; to the print and electronic media; to concerned citizens everywhere. America is at risk.

We are confident that America can address this risk. If the tasks we set forth are initiated now and our recommendations are fully realized over the next several years, we can expect reform of our Nation's schools, colleges, and universities. This would also reverse the current declining trend — a trend that stems more from weakness of purpose, confusion of vision, underuse of talent, and lack of leadership, than from conditions beyond our control.

The Tools at Hand

It is our conviction that the essential raw materials needed to reform our educational system are waiting to be mobilized through effective leadership:

- the natural abilities of the young that cry out to be developed and the undiminished concern of parents for the well-being of their children;
- the commitment of the Nation to high retention rates in schools and colleges and to full access to education for all;
- the persistent and authentic American dream that superior performance can raise one's state in life and shape one's own future;
- the dedication, against all odds, that keeps teachers serving in schools and colleges, even as the rewards diminish;
- our better understanding of learning and teaching and the implications of this knowledge for school practice, and the numerous examples of local success as a result of superior effort and effective dissemination;
- the ingenuity of our policymakers, scientists, State and local educators, and scholars in formulating solutions once problems are better understood;
- the traditional belief that paying for education is an investment in ever-renewable human resources that are more durable and flexible than capital plant and equipment, and the availability in this country of sufficient financial means to invest in education;

- the equally sound tradition, from the Northwest Ordinance of 1787 until today, that the Federal Government should supplement State, local, and other resources to foster key national educational goals; and

- the voluntary efforts of individuals, businesses, and parent and civic groups to cooperate in strengthening educational programs.

These raw materials, combined with the unparalleled array of educational organizations in America, offer us the possibility to create a Learning Society, in which public, private, and parochial schools; colleges and universities; vocational and technical schools and institutes; libraries; science centers, museums, and other cultural institutions; and corporate training and retraining programs offer opportunities and choices for all to learn throughout life.

The Public's Commitment

Of all the tools at hand, the public's support for education is the most powerful. In a message to a National Academy of Sciences meeting in May 1982, President Reagan commented on this fact when he said:

This public awareness — and I hope public action — is long overdue.... This country was built on American respect for education.... Our challenge now is to create a resurgence of that thirst for education that typifies our Nation's history.

The most recent (1982) Gallup Poll of the *Public's Attitudes Toward the Public Schools* strongly supported a theme heard during our hearings: People are steadfast in their belief that education is the major foundation for the future strength of this country. They even considered education more important than developing the best industrial system or the strongest military force, perhaps because they understood education as the cornerstone of both. They also held that education is "extremely important" to one's future success, and that public education should be the top priority for additional Federal funds. Education occupied first place among 12 funding categories considered in the survey — above health care, welfare, and military defense, with 55 percent selecting public education as one of their first three choices. Very clearly, the public understands the primary importance of education as the foundation for a satisfying life, an enlightened and civil society, a strong economy, and a secure Nation.

At the same time, the public has no patience with undemanding and superfluous high school offerings. In another survey, more than 75 percent of all those questioned believed every student planning to go to college should take 4 years of mathematics, English, history/U.S. government, and science, with more than 50 percent adding 2 years each of a foreign language and economics or business. The public even supports requiring much of this curriculum for students who do not plan to go to college. These standards far exceed the strictest high school graduation requirements of any State today, and they also exceed the admission standards of all but a handful of our most selective colleges and universities.

Another dimension of the public's support offers the prospect of constructive reform. The best term to characterize it may simply be the honorable word "patriotism." Citizens know intuitively what some of the best economists have shown in their research, that education is one of the chief engines of a society's material well-being. They know, too, that education is the common bond of a pluralistic society and helps tie us to other cultures around the globe. Citizens also know in their bones that the safety of the United States depends principally on the wit, skill, and spirit of a self-confident people, today and tomorrow. It is, therefore, essential — especially in a period of long-term decline in educational achievement — for government at all levels to affirm its responsibility for nurturing the Nation's intellectual capital.

And perhaps most important, citizens know and believe that the meaning of America to the rest of the world must be something better than it seems to many today. Americans like to think of this Nation as the preeminent country for generating the great ideas and material benefits for all mankind. The citizen is dismayed at a steady 15-year decline in industrial productivity, as one great American industry after another falls to world competition. The citizen wants the country to act on the belief, expressed in our hearings and by the large majority in the Gallup Poll, that education should be at the top of the Nation's agenda.

Findings

We conclude that declines in educational performance are in large part the result of disturbing inadequacies in the way the educational process itself is often conducted. The findings that follow, culled from a much more extensive list, reflect four important aspects of the educational process: content, expectations, time, and teaching.

FINDINGS REGARDING CONTENT

By content we mean the very "stuff" of education, the curriculum. Because of our concern about the curriculum, the Commission examined patterns of courses high school students took in 1964-69 compared with course patterns in 1976-81. On the basis of these analyses we conclude:

- Secondary school curricula have been homogenized, diluted, and diffused to the point that they no longer have a central purpose. In effect, we have a cafeteria-style curriculum in which the appetizers and desserts can easily be mistaken for the main courses. Students have migrated from vocational and college preparatory programs to "general track" courses in large numbers. The proportion of students taking a general program of study has increased from 12 percent in 1964 to 42 percent in 1979.

- This curricular smorgasbord, combined with extensive student choice, explains a great deal about where we find ourselves today. We offer intermediate algebra, but only 31 percent of our recent high school graduates complete it; we offer French I, but only 13 percent complete it; and we offer geography, but only 16 percent complete it. Calculus is available in schools enrolling about 60 percent of all students, but only 6 percent of all students complete it.

- Twenty-five percent of the credits earned by general track high school students are in physical and health education, work experience outside the school, remedial English and mathematics, and personal service and development courses, such as training for adulthood and marriage.

FINDINGS REGARDING EXPECTATIONS

We define expectations in terms of the level of knowledge, abilities, and skills school and college graduates should possess. They also refer to the time, hard work, behavior, self-discipline, and motivation that are essential for high student achievement. Such expectations are expressed to students in several different ways:

- by grades, which reflect the degree to which students demonstrate their mastery of subject matter;

- through high school and college graduation requirements, which tell students which subjects are most important;

- by the presence or absence of rigorous examinations requiring students to demonstrate their mastery of content and skill before receiving a diploma or a degree;

- by college admissions requirements, which reinforce high school standards; and

- by the difficulty of the subject matter students confront in their texts and assigned readings.

Our analyses in each of these areas indicate notable deficiencies:

- The amount of homework for high school seniors has decreased (two-thirds report less than 1 hour a night) and grades have risen as average student achievement has been declining.

- In many other industrialized nations, courses in mathematics (other than arithmetic or general mathematics), biology, chemistry, physics, and geography start in grade 6 and are required of *all* students. The time spent on these subjects, based on class hours, is about three times that spent by even the most science-oriented U.S. students, i.e., those who select 4 years of science and mathematics in secondary school.

- A 1980 State-by-State survey of high school diploma requirements reveals that only eight States require high schools to offer foreign language instruction, but none require students to take the courses. Thirty-five States require only 1 year of mathematics, and 36 require only 1 year of science for a diploma.

- In 13 States, 50 percent or more of the units required for high school graduation may be electives chosen by the student. Given this freedom to choose the substance of half or more of their education, many students opt for less demanding personal service courses, such as bachelor living.

- "Minimum competency" examinations (now required in 37 States) fall short of what is needed, as the "minimum" tends to become the "maximum," thus lowering educational standards for all.

- One-fifth of all 4-year public colleges in the United States must accept every high school graduate within the State regardless of program followed or grades, thereby serving notice to high school students that they can expect to attend college even if they do not follow a demanding course of study in high school or perform well.

- About 23 percent of our more selective colleges and universities reported that their general level of selectivity declined during the 1970s, and 29 percent reported reducing the number of specific high school courses required for admission (usually by dropping foreign language requirements, which are now specified as a condition for admission by only one-fifth of our institutions of higher education).

- Too few experienced teachers and scholars are involved in writing textbooks. During the past decade or so a large number of texts have been "written down" by their publishers to ever-lower reading levels in response to perceived market demands.

- A recent study by Education Products Information Exchange revealed that a majority of students were able to master 80 percent of the material in some of their subject-matter texts before they had even opened the books. Many books do not challenge the students to whom they are assigned.

- Expenditures for textbooks and other instructional materials have declined by 50 percent over the past 17 years. While some recommend a level of spending on texts of between 5 and 10 percent of the operating costs of schools, the budgets for basal texts and related materials have been dropping during the past decade and a half to only 0.7 percent today.

FINDINGS REGARDING TIME

Evidence presented to the Commission demonstrates three disturbing facts about the use that American schools and students make of time: (1) compared with other nations, American students spend much less time on school work; (2) time spent in the classroom and on homework is often used ineffectively; and (3) schools are not doing enough to help students

develop either the study skills required to use time well or the willingness
to spend more time on school work.

- In England and other industrialized countries, it is not unusual for
  academic high school students to spend 8 hours a day at school, 220
  days per year. In the United States, by contrast, the typical school
  day lasts 6 hours and the school year is 180 days.

- In many schools, the time spent learning how to cook and drive
  counts as much toward a high school diploma as the time spent
  studying mathematics, English, chemistry, U.S. history, or biology.

- A study of the school week in the United States found that some
  schools provided students only 17 hours of academic instruction
  during the week, and the average school provided about 22.

- A California study of individual classrooms found that because of
  poor management of classroom time, some elementary students
  received only one-fifth of the instruction others received in reading
  comprehension.

- In most schools, the teaching of study skills is haphazard and
  unplanned. Consequently, many students complete high school and
  enter college without disciplined and systematic study habits.

FINDINGS REGARDING TEACHING

The Commission found that not enough of the academically able
students are being attracted to teaching; that teacher preparation programs need substantial improvement; that the professional working life of
teachers is on the whole unacceptable; and that a serious shortage of
teachers exists in key fields.

- Too many teachers are being drawn from the bottom quarter of
  graduating high school and college students.

- The teacher preparation curriculum is weighted heavily with courses
  in "educational methods" at the expense of courses in subjects to be
  taught. A survey of 1,350 institutions training teachers indicated
  that 41 percent of the time of elementary school teacher candidates
  is spent in education courses, which reduces the amount of time
  available for subject matter courses.

- The average salary after 12 years of teaching is only $17,000 per
  year, and many teachers are required to supplement their income
  with part-time and summer employment. In addition, individual
  teachers have little influence in such critical professional decisions
  as, for example, textbook selection.

- Despite widespread publicity about an overpopulation of teachers,
  severe shortages of certain kinds of teachers exist: in the fields of
  mathematics, science, and foreign languages; and among specialists
  in education for gifted and talented, language minority, and handicapped students.

- The shortage of teachers in mathematics and science is particularly severe. A 1981 survey of 45 States revealed shortages of mathematics teachers in 43 States, critical shortages of earth sciences teachers in 33 States, and of physics teachers everywhere.
- Half of the newly employed mathematics, science, and English teachers are not qualified to teach these subjects; fewer than one-third of U.S. high schools offer physics taught by qualified teachers.

Recommendations

In light of the urgent need for improvement, both immediate and long term, this Commission has agreed on a set of recommendations that the American people can begin to act on now, that can be implemented over the next several years, and that promise lasting reform. The topics are familiar; there is little mystery about what we believe must be done. Many schools, districts, and States are already giving serious and constructive attention to these matters, even though their plans may differ from our recommendations in some details.

We wish to note that we refer to public, private, and parochial schools and colleges alike. All are valuable national resources. Examples of actions similar to those recommended below can be found in each of them.

We must emphasize that the variety of student aspirations, abilities, and preparation requires that appropriate content be available to satisfy diverse needs. Attention must be directed to both the nature of the content available and to the needs of particular learners. The most gifted students, for example, may need a curriculum enriched and accelerated beyond even the needs of other students of high ability. Similarly, educationally disadvantaged students may require special curriculum materials, smaller classes, or individual tutoring to help them master the material presented. Nevertheless, there remains a common expectation: We must demand the best effort and performance from all students, whether they are gifted or less able, affluent or disadvantaged, whether destined for college, the farm, or industry.

Our recommendations are based on the beliefs that everyone can learn, that everyone is born with an *urge* to learn which can be nurtured, that a solid high school education is within the reach of virtually all, and that life-long learning will equip people with the skills required for new careers and for citizenship.

Recommendation A: Content

We recommend *that State and local high school graduation requirements be strengthened and that,* at a minimum, all *students seeking a diploma be required to lay the foundations in the Five New Basics by taking the following curriculum during their 4 years of high school: (a) 4 years of English; (b) 3 years of mathematics; (c) 3 years of science; (d) 3* *years of social studies; and (e) one-half year of computer science. For the college-bound, 2 years of foreign language in high school are strongly recommended in addition to those taken earlier.*

Whatever the student's educational or work objectives, knowledge of the New Basics is the foundation of success for the after-school years and, therefore, forms the core of the modern curriculum. A high level of shared education in these Basics, together with work in the fine and performing arts and foreign languages, constitutes the mind and spirit of our culture. The following Implementing Recommendations are intended as illustrative descriptions. They are included here to clarify what we mean by the essentials of a strong curriculum.

IMPLEMENTING RECOMMENDATIONS

1. The teaching of *English* in high school should equip graduates to: (a) comprehend, interpret, evaluate, and use what they read; (b) write well-organized, effective papers; (c) listen effectively and discuss ideas intelligently; and (d) know our literary heritage and how it enhances imagination and ethical understanding, and how it relates to the customs, ideas, and values of today's life and culture.

2. The teaching of *mathematics* in high school should equip graduates to: (a) understand geometric and algebraic concepts; (b) understand elementary probability and statistics; (c) apply mathematics in everyday situations; and (d) estimate, approximate, measure, and test the accuracy of their calculations. In addition to the traditional sequence of studies available for college-bound students, new, equally demanding mathematics curricula need to be developed for those who do not plan to continue their formal education immediately.

3. The teaching of *science* in high school should provide graduates with an introduction to: (a) the concepts, laws, and processes of the physical and biological sciences; (b) the methods of scientific inquiry and reasoning; (c) the application of scientific knowledge to everyday life; and (d) the social and environmental implications of scientific and technological development. Science courses must be revised and updated for both the college-bound and those not intending to go to college. An example of such work is the American Chemical Society's "Chemistry in the Community" program.

4. The teaching of *social studies* in high school should be designed to: (a) enable students to fix their places and possibilities within the larger social and cultural structure; (b) understand the broad sweep of both ancient and contemporary ideas that have shaped our world; and (c) understand the fundamentals of how our economic system works and how our political system functions; and (d) grasp the difference between free and repressive societies. An understanding of each of these areas is requisite to the informed and committed exercise of citizenship in our free society.

5. The teaching of *computer science* in high school should equip graduates to: (a) understand the computer as an information, computation, and communication device; (b) use the computer in the study of the other Basics and for personal and work-related purposes; and (c) understand the world of computers, electronics, and related technologies.

In addition to the New Basics, other important curriculum matters must be addressed.

6. Achieving proficiency in a *foreign language* ordinarily requires from 4 to 6 years of study and should, therefore, be started in the elementary grades. We believe it is desirable that students achieve such proficiency because study of a foreign language introduces students to non-English-speaking cultures, heightens awareness and comprehension of one's native tongue, and serves the Nation's needs in commerce, diplomacy, defense, and education.

7. The high school curriculum should also provide students with programs requiring rigorous effort in subjects that advance students' personal, educational, and occupational goals, such as the fine and performing arts and vocational education. These areas complement the New Basics, and they should demand the same level of performance as the Basics.

8. The curriculum in the crucial eight grades leading to the high school years should be specifically designed to provide a sound base for study in those and later years in such areas as English language development and writing, computational and problem solving skills, science, social studies, foreign language, and the arts. These years should foster an enthusiasm for learning and the development of the individual's gifts and talents.

9. We encourage the continuation of efforts by groups such as the American Chemical Society, the American Association for the Advancement of Science, the Modern Language Association, and the National Councils of Teachers of English and Teachers of Mathematics, to revise, update, improve, and make available new and more diverse curricular materials. We applaud the consortia of educators and scientific, industrial, and scholarly societies that cooperate to improve the school curriculum.

Recommendation B: Standards and Expectations

We recommend *that schools, colleges, and universities adopt more rigorous and measurable standards, and higher expectations, for academic performance and student conduct, and that 4-year colleges and universities raise their requirements for admission. This will help students do their best educationally with challenging materials in an environment that supports learning and authentic accomplishment.*

IMPLEMENTING RECOMMENDATIONS

1. Grades should be indicators of academic achievement so they can be relied on as evidence of a student's readiness for further study.

2. Four-year colleges and universities should raise their admissions requirements and advise all potential applicants of the standards for admission in terms of specific courses required, performance in these areas, and levels of achievement on standardized achievement tests in each of the five Basics and, where applicable, foreign languages.

3. Standardized tests of achievement (not to be confused with aptitude tests) should be administered at major transition points from one level of schooling to another and particularly from high school to college or work. The purposes of these tests would be to: (a) certify the student's credentials; (b) identify the need for remedial intervention; and (c) identify the opportunity for advanced or accelerated work. The tests should be administered as part of a nationwide (but not Federal) system of State and local standardized tests. This system should include other diagnostic procedures

that assist teachers and students to evaluate student progress.

4. Textbooks and other tools of learning and teaching should be upgraded and updated to assure more rigorous content. We call upon university scientists, scholars, and members of professional societies, in collaboration with master teachers, to help in this task, as they did in the post-Sputnik era. They should assist willing publishers in developing the products or publish their own alternatives where there are persistent inadequacies.

5. In considering textbooks for adoption, States and school districts should: (a) evaluate texts and other materials on their ability to present rigorous and challenging material clearly; and (b) require publishers to furnish evaluation data on the material's effectiveness.

6. Because no textbook in any subject can be geared to the needs of all students, funds should be made available to support text development in "thin-market" areas, such as those for disadvantaged students, the learning disabled, and the gifted and talented.

7. To assure quality, all publishers should furnish evidence of the quality and appropriateness of textbooks, based on results from field trials and credible evaluations. In view of the enormous numbers and varieties of texts available, more widespread consumer information services for purchasers are badly needed.

8. New instructional materials should reflect the most current applications of technology in appropriate curriculum areas, the best scholarship in each discipline, and research in learning and teaching.

Recommendation C: Time

We recommend *that significantly more time be devoted to learning the New Basics. This will require more effective use of the existing school day, a longer school day, or a lengthened school year.*

IMPLEMENTING RECOMMENDATIONS

- 1. Students in high schools should be assigned far more homework than is now the case.

- 2. Instruction in effective study and work skills, which are essential if school and independent time is to be used efficiently, should be introduced in the early grades and continued throughout the student's schooling.

- 3. School districts and State legislatures should strongly consider 7-hour school days, as well as a 200- to 220-day school year.

- 4. The time available for learning should be expanded through better classroom management and organization of the school day. If necessary, additional time should be found to meet the special needs of slow learners, the gifted, and others who need more instructional diversity than can be accommodated during a conventional school day or school year.

- 5. The burden on teachers for maintaining discipline should be reduced through the development of firm and fair codes of student conduct that are enforced consistently, and by considering alternative classrooms, programs, and schools to meet the needs of continually disruptive students.

- 6. Attendance policies with clear incentives and sanctions should be used to reduce the amount of time lost through student absenteeism and tardiness.

- 7. Administrative burdens on the teacher and related intrusions into the school day should be reduced to add time for teaching and learning.
- 8. Placement and grouping of students, as well as promotion and graduation policies, should be guided by the academic progress of students and their instructional needs, rather than by rigid adherence to age.

Recommendation D: Teaching

This recommendation *consists of seven parts. Each is intended to improve the preparation of teachers or to make teaching a more rewarding and respected profession. Each of the seven stands on its own and should not be considered solely as an implementing recommendation.*

- 1. Persons preparing to teach should be required to meet high educational standards, to demonstrate an aptitude for teaching, and to demonstrate competence in an academic discipline. Colleges and universities offering teacher preparation programs should be judged by how well their graduates meet these criteria.
- 2. Salaries for the teaching profession should be increased and should be professionally competitive, market-sensitive, and performance-based. Salary, promotion, tenure, and retention decisions should be tied to an effective evaluation system that includes peer review so that superior teachers can be rewarded, average ones encouraged, and poor ones either improved or terminated.
- 3. School boards should adopt an 11-month contract for teachers. This would ensure time for curriculum and professional development, programs for students with special needs, and a more adequate level of teacher compensation.
- 4. School boards, administrators, and teachers should cooperate to develop career ladders for teachers that distinguish among the beginning instructor, the experienced teacher, and the master teacher.
- 5. Substantial nonschool personnel resources should be employed to help solve the immediate problem of the shortage of mathematics and science teachers. Qualified individuals including recent graduates with mathematics and science degrees, graduate students, and industrial and retired scientists could, with appropriate preparation, immediately begin teaching in these fields. A number of our leading science centers have the capacity to begin educating and retraining teachers immediately. Other areas of critical teacher need, such as English, must also be addressed.
- 6. Incentives, such as grants and loans, should be made available to attract outstanding students to the teaching profession, particularly in those areas of critical shortage.
- 7. Master teachers should be involved in designing teacher preparation programs and in supervising teachers during their probationary years.

Recommendation E:
Leadership and Fiscal Support

We recommend *that citizens across the Nation hold educators and elected officials responsible for providing the leadership necessary to achieve these reforms, and that citizens provide the fiscal support and stability required to bring about the reforms we propose.*

IMPLEMENTING RECOMMENDATIONS

● 1. Principals and superintendents must play a crucial leadership role in developing school and community support for the reforms we propose, and school boards must provide them with the professional development and other support required to carry out their leadership role effectively. The Commission stresses the distinction between leadership skills involving persuasion, setting goals and developing community consensus behind them, and managerial and supervisory skills. Although the latter are necessary, we believe that school boards must consciously develop leadership skills at the school and district levels if the reforms we propose are to be achieved.

● 2. State and local officials, including school board members, governors, and legislators, have *the primary responsibility* for financing and governing the schools, and should incorporate the reforms we propose in their educational policies and fiscal planning.

● 3. The Federal Government, in cooperation with States and localities, should help meet the needs of key groups of students such as the gifted and talented, the socioeconomically disadvantaged, minority and language minority students, and the handicapped. In combination these groups include both national resources and the Nation's youth who are most at risk.

● 4. In addition, we believe the Federal Government's role includes several functions of national consequence that States and localities alone are unlikely to be able to meet: protecting constitutional and civil rights for students and school personnel; collecting data, statistics, and information about education generally; supporting curriculum improvement and research on teaching, learning, and the management of schools; supporting teacher training in areas of critical shortage or key national needs; and providing student financial assistance and research and graduate training. We believe the assistance of the Federal Government should be provided with a minimum of administrative burden and intrusiveness.

● 5. The Federal Government has *the primary responsibility* to identify the national interest in education. It should also help fund and support efforts to protect and promote that interest. It must provide the national leadership to ensure that the Nation's public and private resources are marshaled to address the issues discussed in this report.

● 6. This Commission calls upon educators, parents, and public officials at all levels to assist in bringing about the educational reform proposed in this report. We also call upon citizens to provide the financial support necessary to accomplish these purposes. Excellence costs. But in the long run mediocrity costs far more.

America Can Do It

Despite the obstacles and difficulties that inhibit the pursuit of superior education attainment, we are confident, with history as our guide, that we can meet our goal. The American educational system has responded to previous challenges with remarkable success. In the 19th century our land-grant colleges and universities provided the research and training that developed our Nation's natural resources and the rich agricultural bounty of the American farm. From the late 1800s through mid-20th century,

American schools provided the educated workforce needed to seal the success of the Industrial Revolution and to provide the margin of victory in two world wars. In the early part of this century and continuing to this very day, our schools have absorbed vast waves of immigrants and educated them and their children to productive citizenship. Similarly, the Nation's Black colleges have provided opportunity and undergraduate education to the vast majority of college-educated Black Americans.

More recently, our institutions of higher education have provided the scientists and skilled technicians who helped us transcend the boundaries of our planet. In the last 30 years, the schools have been a major vehicle for expanded social opportunity, and now graduate 75 percent of our young people from high school. Indeed, the proportion of Americans of college age enrolled in higher education is nearly twice that of Japan and far exceeds other nations such as France, West Germany, and the Soviet Union. Moreover, when international comparisons were last made a decade ago, the top 9 percent of American students compared favorably in achievement with their peers in other countries.

In addition, many large urban areas in recent years report that average student achievement in elementary schools is improving. More and more schools are also offering advanced placement programs and programs for gifted and talented students, and more and more students are enrolling in them.

We are the inheritors of a past that gives us every reason to believe that we will succeed.

A Word to Parents and Students

The task of assuring the success of our recommendations does not fall to the schools and colleges alone. Obviously, faculty members and administrators, along with policymakers and the mass media, will play a crucial role in the reform of the educational system. But even more important is the role of parents and students, and to them we speak directly.

TO PARENTS

You know that you cannot confidently launch your children into today's world unless they are of strong character and well-educated in the use of language, science, and mathematics. They must possess a deep respect for intelligence, achievement, and learning, and the skills needed to use them; for setting goals; and for disciplined work. That respect must be accompanied by an intolerance for the shoddy and second-rate masquerading as "good enough."

You have the right to demand for your children the best our schools and colleges can provide. Your vigilance and your refusal to be satisfied with less than the best are the imperative first step. But your right to a proper education for your children carries a double responsibility. As surely as you are your child's first and most influential teacher, your child's ideas about education and its significance begin with you. You must be a *living* example of what you expect your children to honor and to emulate. Moreover, you bear a responsibility to participate actively in your child's education. You should encourage more diligent study and discourage satisfaction with mediocrity and the attitude that says "let it slide"; monitor your child's study; encourage good study habits; encourage your child to take more demanding rather than less demanding courses; nurture your child's curiosity, creativity, and confidence; and be an active participant in the work of the schools. Above all, exhibit a commitment to continued learning in your own life. Finally, help your children understand that excellence in education cannot be achieved without intellectual and moral integrity coupled with hard work and commitment. Children will look to their parents and teachers as models of such virtues.

TO STUDENTS

You forfeit your chance for life at its fullest when you withhold your best effort in learning. When you give only the minimum to learning, you receive only the minimum in return. Even with your parents' best example and your teachers' best efforts, in the end it is *your* work that determines how much and how well you learn. When you work to your full capacity, you can hope to attain the knowledge and skills that will enable you to create your future and control your destiny. If you do not, you will have your future thrust upon you by others. Take hold of your life, apply your gifts and talents, work with dedication and self-discipline. Have high expectations for yourself and convert every challenge into an opportunity.

A Final Word

This is not the first or only commission on education, and some of our findings are surely not new, but old business that now at last must be done. For no one can doubt that the United States is under challenge from many quarters.

Children born today can expect to graduate from high school in the year 2000. We dedicate our report not only to these children, but also to those now in school and others to come. We firmly believe that a movement of America's schools in the direction called for by our recommendations will prepare these children for far more effective lives in a far stronger America.

Our final word, perhaps better characterized as a plea, is that all segments of our population give attention to the implementation of our recommendations. Our present plight did not appear overnight, and the responsibility for our current situation is widespread. Reform of our educational system will take time and unwavering commitment. It will require equally widespread, energetic, and dedicated action. For example, we call upon the National Academy of Sciences, National Academy of Engineering, Institute of Medicine, Science Service, National Science Foundation, Social Science Research Council, American Council of Learned Societies, National Endowment for the Humanities, National Endowment for the Arts, and other scholarly, scientific, and learned societies for their help in this effort. Help should come from students themselves; from parents, teachers, and school boards; from colleges and universities; from local, State, and Federal officials; from teachers' and administrators' organizations; from industrial and labor councils; and from other groups with interest in and responsibility for educational reform.

It is their America, and the America of all of us, that is at risk; it is to each of us that this imperative is addressed. It is by our willingness to take up the challenge, and our resolve to see it through, that America's place in the world will be either secured or forfeited. Americans have succeeded before and so we shall again.

REAGAN ON CENTRAL AMERICA; DEMOCRATIC RESPONSE

April 27, 1983

For the Reagan administration in 1983, no foreign policy issue was more pressing than the continuing turmoil in Central America. The U.S.-supported government of El Salvador was under siege by guerrillas backed by the Soviet Union, Cuba and the leftist Sandinista government of neighboring Nicaragua. There was widespread apprehension among U.S. officials that nearby friendly nations might be drawn into the conflict.

It was in this atmosphere of heightened concern that the president made an unusual appearance before a joint session of Congress to urge passage of bills providing stepped-up military and economic aid to the El Salvador government. Reagan's nationally televised speech pointed to the urgency with which the administration viewed the situation in Central America. Traditionally, presidents have addressed joint sessions of Congress only in annual State of the Union messages or times of national emergency.

Although Reagan's address broke little new policy ground, the president, by taking his case directly to Congress and the American public, focused new attention on the region.

Policy Explanation

Reagan said the problems of Central America should be of immediate concern to the United States because they "directly affect the security and well being of our own people." He noted that two-thirds of all U.S.

foreign trade and oil shipments passed through the Panama Canal and the Caribbean Sea. The main threat to the region was communist "adventurism," promoted by the Soviet Union, Cuba and Nicaragua, Reagan said.

The president devoted much of his speech to a harsh attack on the leftist government of Nicaragua, saying it "has treated us as an enemy." In his only direct reference to U.S. activities against the Nicaraguan government, Reagan said the United States was merely trying to prevent the flow of Soviet- and Cuban-supplied arms through Nicaragua to the guerrillas in El Salvador. "We do not seek [the government's] overthrow," he said. "Our interest is to ensure that it does not infect its neighbors through the export of subversion and violence."

Reagan offered "four basic goals of U.S. policy in the region":

● The first, and most general, goal was support for "democracy, reform and human freedom." He said that goal entailed U.S. aid, persuasion and leverage "to bolster humane democratic regimes where they already exist" and to help other countries develop democracy. In his only reference to human rights issues, Reagan said that "We will work at human rights problems, not walk away from them."

● The second goal was support for economic development in Central America. Reagan asked for passage of the remaining parts of his Caribbean Basin Initiative, which would provide trade benefits for countries in the region and tax incentives for U.S. business investment there. (Congress in 1982 had enacted the first part of the initiative, providing emergency economic aid for nations in the region.) (Caribbean Basin Initiative, Historic Documents of 1982, p. 179)

● The third goal was military support for friendly governments threatened by leftist subversion. "We do not view security assistance as an end in itself, but as a shield for democratization, economic development and diplomacy," the president said.

● Fourth, Reagan said the United States would support "dialogue and negotiations — both among the countries of the region and within each country." He pledged U.S. support for "verifiable and reciprocal" agreements for the withdrawal of all foreign military advisers and troops and for the renunciation of support for insurgents.

Reagan asked for "prompt" approval by Congress of his requests for military and economic aid. In his speech he mentioned only one figure, $600 million for all of Central America in fiscal 1984, which he said was "less than one-tenth of what Americans will spend this year on coin-operated video games."

Reagan directly responded to one of the greatest concerns among members of Congress — that U.S. troops eventually might be needed to bolster the governments in El Salvador and other countries. "There is no thought of sending American combat troops to Central America," he said.

"They are not needed — indeed, they have not been requested there."

The president also used the address to announce his intention to appoint a special envoy to promote negotiations in Central America. On April 28 he named former Sen. Richard "Dick" Stone, D-Fla. (1975-81), as an ambassador-at-large. Stone had been a State Department consultant on Central American affairs, primarily lobbying Congress in favor of Reagan's policies.

Democrats' Reaction to Reagan's Address

Although the president failed to elicit an enthusiastic response from most Democrats, a number of them said the speech was less confrontational than some of Reagan's previous statements on Central America. "I was very pleased by the general thrust and tone" of the speech, said Rep. Michael D. Barnes, D-Md., chairman of the Western Hemisphere Affairs Subcommittee, who had been critical of Reagan's policies in the region. But Barnes said the president "missed an opportunity" to address "the social, economic and political problems that are the base of the problems in Central America."

Sen. Christopher J. Dodd, D-Conn., delivered a formal televised response sanctioned by the Democratic leadership. Dodd said Reagan ignored the basic cause of unrest in Central America — the fact that "a very few live in isolated splendor while the very many suffer in shantytown squalor. In country after country, dictatorship or military dominance has stifled democracy and destroyed human rights." Administration policy, he said, "is ever increasing military assistance, endless military training.... This is a formula for failure."

Congressional Action, Covert Action Issue

Reagan's speech had been timed to influence congressional decisions on a wide range of issues affecting Central America. The congressional debate over U.S. economic and military support for El Salvador had been complicated by mounting unease over U.S. covert support for antigovernment rebels in Nicaragua. Congress in December 1982 had passed a law to prohibit U.S. aid "for the purpose" of overthrowing the government. But the sponsors of that law said the administration had violated or skirted it. In response, the administration said the law had not been violated because the United States did not seek to overthrow the Nicaraguan government, even though the guerrillas who received U.S. support might have that aim.

The covert action issue was the one upon which the House Democratic leadership made its stand in opposition to Reagan's Central American policies. With Speaker Thomas P. O'Neill Jr., D-Mass., and Intelligence Committee Chairman Edward P. Boland, D-Mass., leading the way, the House voted on July 28 and again on October 20 to force Reagan to stop

*backing rightist forces that were fighting to overthrow the leftist Nicara-
guan government. The votes followed an extraordinary four-hour closed
session of the House July 19, highlighted by presentations by senior
members of the Intelligence Committee.*

*When the Senate refused to follow suit on banning the aid, the issue
was thrown into the lap of two last-minute House-Senate conference
committees. They produced a compromise that limited U.S. aid to the
rebels to $24 million — about $11 million less than Reagan had planned
to spend.*

*On the issue of aid to El Salvador, Reagan found Congress somewhat
more receptive. Under sustained administration pressure, Congress eventually approved $81.3 million in military aid for El Salvador in fiscal
1983. Reagan's various requests had totaled $136.3 million. For fiscal 1984
Congress limited El Salvador's military aid to $64.8 million; Reagan had
requested $86.3 million. The president was expected to ask for an
increase in military aid funding in 1984. Congress also passed new
restrictions aimed at encouraging progress on land reform and in the trial
of those accused of murdering four American churchwomen in December
1980.*

*Congress approved without debate Reagan's requests for economic and
development aid for El Salvador: $170 million in fiscal 1983 and $158
million in 1984. At the very end of the session Congress also approved a
bill continuing through fiscal 1984 a requirement that the president
certify twice each year that El Salvador was making sufficient progress
on human rights and other issues to warrant receiving U.S. aid.* (State
Department report on human rights, p. 181)

> *Following are the texts of President Ronald Reagan's April
> 27, 1983, televised address to a joint session of Congress on
> the administration's Central American policy, and the con-
> gressional Democratic Party leadership's response, deliv-
> ered April 27 after the president's address by Sen. Christo-
> pher J. Dodd, D-Conn.:*

REAGAN'S ADDRESS ON CENTRAL AMERICA

THE PRESIDENT. Mr. Speaker, Mr. President, distinguished Members of the Congress, honored guests and my fellow Americans:

A number of times in the past years, Members of Congress and a
President have come together in meetings like this to resolve a crisis. I
have asked for this meeting in the hope that we can prevent one.

It would be hard to find many Americans who aren't aware of our stake
in the Middle East, the Persian Gulf, or the NATO line dividing the free
world from the Communist bloc, and the same could be said for Asia.

But in spite of, or maybe because of, a flurry of stories about places like Nicaragua and El Salvador and, yes, some concerted propaganda, many of us find it hard to believe we have a stake in problems involving those countries. Too many have thought of Central America as just a place way down below Mexico that can't possibly constitute a threat to our well being. And that's why I have asked for this session. Central America's problems do directly affect the security and the well being of our own people. And Central America is much closer to the United States than many of the world trouble spots that concern us. As we work to restore our own economy, we cannot afford to lose sight of our neighbors to the south.

El Salvador is nearer to Texas than Texas is to Massachusetts. Nicaragua is just as close to Miami, San Antonio, San Diego, and Tucson as those cities are to Washington where we are gathered tonight.

But nearness on the map doesn't even begin to tell the strategic importance of Central America, bordering as it does on the Caribbean, our lifeline to the outside world. Two-thirds of all our foreign trade and petroleum pass through the Panama Canal and the Caribbean. In a European crisis at least half our supplies for NATO would go through these areas by sea. It is well to remember that in early 1942 a handful of Hitler's submarines sank more tonnage there than in all of the Atlantic Ocean. And they did this without a single naval base anywhere in the area. And today the situation is different. Cuba is host to a Soviet combat brigade, a submarine base capable of servicing Soviet submarines, and military air bases visited regularly by Soviet military aircraft.

Because of its importance, the Caribbean Basin is a magnet for adventurism. We are all aware of the Libyan cargo planes refueling in Brazil a few days ago on their way to deliver medical supplies to Nicaragua. Brazilian authorities discovered the so-called supplies were actually munitions and prevented their delivery.

You may remember that last month, speaking on national television, I showed an aerial photo of an airfield being built on the island of Grenada. Well, if that airfield had been completed those planes could have refueled there and completed their journey.

If the Nazis during World War II and the Soviets today could recognize the Caribbean and Central America as vital to our interests, shouldn't we also? For several years now, under two administrations, the United States has been increasing its defense of freedom in the Caribbean Basin. And I can tell you tonight, democracy is beginning to take root in El Salvador, which until a short time ago knew only dictatorship.

The new government is now delivering on its promises of democracy, reforms and free elections. It wasn't easy, and there was resistance to many of the attempted reforms, with assassinations of some of the reformers. Guerrilla bands and urban terrorists were portrayed in a worldwide propaganda campaign as freedom fighters representative of the people. Ten days before I came into office, the guerrillas launched what they called a "final offensive" to overthrow the government. And their radio boasted that our new Administration would be too late to prevent their victory.

Well, they learned that democracy cannot be so easily defeated. President Carter did not hesitate. He authorized arms and munitions to El Salvador. The guerrilla offensive failed, but not America's will. Every President since this country assumed global responsibilities has known that those responsibilities could only be met if we pursued a bipartisan foreign policy.

As I said a moment ago, the Government of El Salvador has been keeping its promises, like the land reform program which is making thousands of farm tenants, farm owners. In a little over 3 years, 20 percent of the arable land in El Salvador has been redistributed to more than 450,000 people. That's one in ten Salvadorans who have benefited directly from this program.

El Salvador has continued to strive toward an orderly and democratic society. The government promised free elections. On March 28th, a little more than a year ago, after months of campaigning by a variety of candidates, the suffering people of El Salvador were offered a chance to vote, to choose the kind of government they wanted. And suddenly the so-called freedom fighters in the hills were exposed for what they really are — a small minority who want power for themselves and their backers, not democracy for the people. The guerrillas threatened death to anyone who voted. They destroyed hundreds of buses and trucks to keep the people from getting to the polling places. Their slogan was brutal: "Vote today, die tonight." But on election day, an unprecedented 80 percent of the electorate braved ambush and gunfire, and trudged for miles, many of them, to vote for freedom. Now that's truly fighting for freedom. We can never turn our backs on that.

Members of this Congress who went there as observers told me of a woman who was wounded by rifle fire on the way to the polls, who refused to leave the line to have her wound treated until after she had voted. Another woman had been told by the guerrillas that she would be killed when she returned from the polls, and she told the guerrillas, "You can kill me, you can kill my family, you can kill my neighbors; you can't kill us all." The real freedom fighters of El Salvador turned out to be the people of that country — the young, the old, the in-between — more than one million of them out of a population of less than five million. The world should respect this courage and not allow it to be belittled or forgotten. And again I say, in good conscience, we can never turn our backs on that.

The democratic political parties and factions in El Salvador are coming together around the common goal of seeking a political solution to their country's problems. New national elections will be held this year, and they will be open to all political parties. The government has invited the guerrillas to participate in the election and is preparing an amnesty law. The people of El Salvador are earning their freedom and they deserve our moral and material support to protect it.

Yes, there are still major problems regarding human rights, the criminal justice system, and violence against non-combatants and, like the rest of Central America, El Salvador also faces severe economic problems. But in addition to recession-depressed prices for major agricultural exports, El Salvador's economy is being deliberately sabotaged.

Tonight in El Salvador — because of ruthless guerrilla attacks — much of the fertile land cannot be cultivated; less than half the rolling stock of the railways remains operational; bridges, water facilities, telephone and electrical systems have been destroyed and damaged. In one 22-month period there were 5,000 disruptions of electrical power. One region was without electricity for a third of a year.

I think Secretary of State Shultz put it very well the other day: "Unable to win the free loyalty of El Salvador's people, the guerrillas," he said, "are deliberately and systematically depriving them of food, water, transportation, light, sanitation, and jobs. And these are the people who claim they want to help the common people." They don't want elections because they know they would be defeated. But, as the previous election showed the Salvadoran people's desire for democracy will not be defeated.

The guerrillas are not embattled peasants armed with muskets. They're professionals, sometimes with better training and weaponry than the government soldiers. The Salvadoran battalions that have received U.S. training have been conducting themselves well in the battlefield and with the civilian population. But so far we have only provided enough money to train one Salvadoran soldier out of ten, fewer than the number of guerrillas that are trained by Nicaragua and Cuba.

And let me set the record straight on Nicaragua, a country next to El Salvador. In 1979 when the new government took over in Nicaragua, after a revolution which overthrew the authoritarian rule of Somoza, everyone hoped for the growth of democracy. We in the United States did, too. By January of 1981, our emergency relief and recovery aid to Nicaragua totaled $118 million — more than provided by any other developed country. In fact, in the first 2 years of Sandinista rule, the United States directly or indirectly sent five times more aid to Nicaragua than it had in the 2 years prior to the revolution. Can anyone doubt the generosity and the good faith of the American people?

These were hardly the actions of a nation implacably hostile to Nicaragua. Yet the government of Nicaragua has treated us as an enemy. It has rejected our repeated peace efforts. It has broken its promises to us, to the Organization of American States and, most important of all, to the people of Nicaragua.

No sooner was victory achieved than a small clique ousted others who had been part of the revolution from having any voice in the government. Humberto Ortega, the Minister of Defense, declared Marxism-Leninism would be their guide, and so it is.

The Government of Nicaragua has imposed a new dictatorship. It has refused to hold the elections it promised. It has seized control of most media and subjects all media to heavy prior censorship. It denied the bishops and priests of the Roman Catholic Church the right to say Mass on radio during Holy Week. It insulted and mocked the Pope. It has driven the Miskito Indians from their homelands, burning their villages, destroying their crops and forcing them into involuntary internment camps far from home. It has moved against the private sector and free labor unions. It condoned mob action against Nicaragua's independent human rights commission and drove the director of that commission into exile.

In short, after all of these acts of repression by the government, is it any wonder that opposition has formed? Contrary to propaganda, the opponents of the Sandinistas are not diehard supporters of the previous Somoza regime. In fact, many are anti-Somoza heroes who fought beside the Sandinistas to bring down the Somoza government. Now they've been denied any part of a new government because they truly want a democracy for Nicaragua and they still do. Others are Miskito Indians fighting for their homes, their lands, and their lives.

The Sandinista revolution in Nicaragua turned out to be just an exchange of one set of autocratic rulers for another, and the people still have no freedom, no democratic rights, and more poverty. Even worse than its predecessor, it is helping Cuba and the Soviets to destabilize our hemisphere.

Meanwhile, the Government of El Salvador, making every effort to guarantee democracy, free labor unions, freedom of religion, and a free press, is under attack by guerrillas dedicated to the same philosophy that prevails in Nicaragua, Cuba and, yes, the Soviet Union. Violence has been Nicaragua's most important export to the world. It is the ultimate in hypocrisy for the unelected Nicaraguan Government to charge that we seek their overthrow when they are doing everything they can to bring down the elected Government of El Salvador. The guerrilla attacks are directed from a headquarters in Managua, the capital of Nicaragua.

But let us be clear as to the American attitude toward the Government of Nicaragua. We do not seek its overthrow. Our interest is to ensure that it does not infect its neighbors through the export of subversion and violence. Our purpose, in conformity with American and international law, is to prevent the flow of arms to El Salvador, Honduras, Guatemala, and Costa Rica. We have attempted to have a dialogue with the Government of Nicaragua, but it persists in its efforts to spread violence.

We should not, and we will not, protect the Nicaraguan Government from the anger of its own people. But we should, through diplomacy, offer an alternative. And as Nicaragua ponders its options, we can and will — with all the resources of diplomacy — protect each country of Central America from the danger of war.

Even Costa Rica, Central America's oldest and strongest democracy, a government so peaceful it doesn't even have an army, is the object of bullying and threats from Nicaragua's dictators.

Nicaragua's neighbors know that Sandinista promises of peace, non-alliance, and non-intervention have not been kept. Some 36 new military bases have been built — there were only 13 during the Somoza years.

Nicaragua's new army numbers 25,000 men, supported by a militia of 50,000. It is the largest army in Central America, supplemented by 2,000 Cuban military and security advisers. It is equipped with the most modern weapons, dozens of Soviet-made tanks, 800 Soviet-bloc trucks, Soviet 152-MM howitzers, 100 anti-aircraft guns, plus planes and helicopters. There are additional thousands of civilian advisers from Cuba, the Soviet Union, East Germany, Libya, and the PLO [Palestine Liberation Organization]. And we're attacked because we have 55 military trainers in El Salvador.

The goal of the professional guerrilla movements in Central America is as simple as it is sinister: to destabilize the entire region from the Panama Canal to Mexico. And if you doubt beyond this point, just consider what Cayetano Carpio, the now-deceased Salvadoran guerrilla leader, said earlier this month. Carpio said that after El Salvador falls, El Salvador and Nicaragua would be "arm-in-arm and struggling for the total liberation of Central America."

Nicaragua's dictatorial junta, who themselves made war and won power operating from bases in Honduras and Costa Rica, like to pretend that they are today being attacked by forces based in Honduras. The fact is, it is Nicaragua's government that threatens Honduras, not the reverse. It is Nicaragua who has moved heavy tanks close to the border, and Nicaragua who speaks of war. It was Nicaraguan radio that announced on April 8th the creation of a new, unified revolutionary coordinating board to push forward the Marxist struggle in Honduras.

Nicaragua, supported by weapons and military resources provided by the Communist bloc, represses its own people, refuses to make peace, and sponsors a guerrilla war against El Salvador.

President Truman's words are as apt today as they were in 1947, when he, too, spoke before a Joint Session of the Congress:

> At the present moment in world history nearly every nation must choose between alternative ways of life. The choice is not too often a free one. One way of life is based upon the will of the majority, and is distinguished by free institutions, representative government, free elections, guarantees of individual liberty, freedom of speech and religion, and freedom from political oppression. The second way of life is based upon the will of a minority forcibly imposed upon the majority. It relies upon terror and oppression, a controlled press and radio, fixed elections, and the suppression of personal freedoms.
>
> I believe that it must be the policy of the United States to support free peoples who are resisting attempted subjugation by armed minorities or by outside pressures. I believe that we must assist free peoples to work out their own destinies in their own way. I believe that our help should be primarily through economic and financial aid which is essential to economic stability and orderly political processes.
>
> Collapse of free institutions and loss of independence would be disastrous not only for them but for the world. Discouragement and possibly failure would quickly be the lot of neighboring peoples striving to maintain their freedom and independence.

The countries of Central America are smaller than the nations that prompted President Truman's message. But the political and strategic stakes are the same. Will our response — economic, social, military — be as appropriate and successful as Mr. Truman's bold solutions to the problems of postwar Europe?

Some people have forgotten the successes of those years — and the decades of peace, prosperity, and freedom they secured. Some people talk as though the United States were incapable of acting effectively in international affairs without risking war or damaging those we seek to help.

Are democracies required to remain passive while threats to their security and prosperity accumulate? Must we just accept the destabilization of an entire region from the Panama Canal to Mexico on our southern border? Must we sit by while independent nations of this hemisphere are integrated into the most aggressive empire the modern world has seen? Must we wait while Central Americans are driven from their homes, like the more than four million who have sought refuge out of Afghanistan or the 1½ million who have fled Indochina or the more than one million Cubans who have fled Castro's Caribbean utopia? Must we, by default, leave the people of El Salvador no choice but to flee their homes, creating another tragic human exodus?

I don't believe there is a majority in the Congress or the country that counsels passivity, resignation, defeatism, in the face of this challenge to freedom and security in our own hemisphere. [Applause] Thank you. Thank you.

I do not believe that a majority of the Congress or the country is prepared to stand by passively while the people of Central America are delivered to totalitarianism and we ourselves are left vulnerable to new dangers.

Only last week an official of the Soviet Union reiterated Brezhnev's threat to station nuclear missiles in this hemisphere — five minutes from the United States. Like an echo, Nicaragua's Commandate, Daniel Ortega, confirmed that, if asked, his country would consider accepting those missiles. I understand that today they may be having second thoughts.

Now, before I go any further, let me say to those who invoke the memory of Vietnam: There is no thought of sending American combat troops to Central America; they are not needed. [Applause]

Thank you. And, as I say they are not needed and, indeed, they have not been requested there. All our neighbors ask of us is assistance in training and arms to protect themselves while they build a better, freer life.

We must continue to encourage peace among the nations of Central America. We must support the regional efforts now underway to promote solutions to regional problems.

We cannot be certain that the Marxist-Leninist bands who believe war is an instrument of politics will be readily discouraged. It is crucial that we not become discouraged before they do. Otherwise, the region's freedom will be lost and our security damaged in ways that can hardly be calculated.

If Central America were to fall, what would the consequences be for our position in Asia, Europe, and for alliances such as NATO? If the United States cannot respond to a threat near our own borders, why should Europeans or Asians believe that we're seriously concerned about threats to them? If the Soviets can assume that nothing short of an actual attack on the United States will provoke an American response, which ally, which friend, will trust us then?

The Congress shares both the power and the responsibility for our foreign policy. Tonight, I ask you, the Congress, to join me in a bold, generous approach to the problems of peace and poverty, democracy and dictatorship in the region. Join me in a program that prevents Communists victory in the short run but goes beyond to produce for the deprived people of the area the reality of present progress and the promise of more to come.

Let us lay the foundation for a bipartisan approach to sustain the independence and freedom of the countries of Central America. We in the administration reach out to you in this spirit.

We will pursue four basic goals in Central America:

First, in response to decades of inequity and indifference, we will support democracy, reform and human freedom. This means using our assistance, our powers of persuasion and our legitimate "leverage" to bolster humane democratic systems where they already exist and to help countries on their way to that goal complete the process as quickly as human institutions can be changed. Elections — in El Salvador and also in Nicaragua — must be open to all, fair and safe. The international community must help. We will work at human rights problems, not walk away from them.

Second, in response to the challenge of world recession and, in the case of El Salvador, to the unrelenting campaign of economic sabotage by the guerrillas, we will support economic development. By a margin of 2 to 1, our aid is economic now, not military. Seventy-seven cents out of every dollar we will spend in the area this year goes for food, fertilizers, and other essentials for economic growth and development. And our economic program goes beyond traditional aid. The Caribbean Basin Initiative introduced in the House earlier today will provide powerful trade and investment incentives to help these countries achieve self-sustaining economic growth without exporting United States jobs. Our goal must be to focus our immense and growing technology, to enhance health care, agriculture, industry, and to ensure that we who inhabit this interdependent region come to know and understand each other better, retaining our diverse identities, respecting our diverse traditions and institutions.

And, *third,* in response to the military challenge from Cuba and Nicaragua, to their deliberate use of force to spread tyranny, we will support the security of the region's threatened nations. We do not view security assistance as an end in itself, but as a shield for democratization, economic development and diplomacy. No amount of reform will bring peace so long as guerrillas believe they will win by force. No amount of economic help will suffice if guerrilla units can destroy roads and bridges and power stations and crops again and again with impunity. But with better training and material help our neighbors can hold off the guerrillas and give democratic reform time to take root.

And, *fourth*, we will support dialogue and negotiations both among the countries of the region and within each country. The terms and conditions of participation in elections are negotiable. Costa Rica is a shining example of democracy. Honduras has made the move from military rule to democratic government. Guatemala is pledged to the same course. The United States will work toward a political solution in Central America which will serve the interests of the democratic process.

To support these diplomatic goals I offer these assurances: The United States will support any agreement among Central American countries for the withdrawal, under fully verifiable and reciprocal conditions, of all foreign military and security advisors and troops. We want to help opposition groups join the political process in all countries and compete by ballots instead of bullets. We will support any verifiable reciprocal agreement among Central American countries on the renunciation of support for insurgencies on neighbors' territory. And, finally, we desire to help Central America end its costly arms race, and will support any verifiable, reciprocal agreements on the non-importation of offensive weapons.

To move us toward these goals more rapidly I am tonight announcing my intention to name an Ambassador-at-Large as my special envoy to Central America. He or she will report to me through the Secretary of State. The Ambassador's responsibilities will be to lend United States support to the efforts of regional governments to bring peace to this troubled area and to work closely with the Congress to assure the fullest possible bipartisan coordination of our policies toward the region.

What I'm asking for is prompt Congressional approval for the full reprogramming of funds for key current economic and security programs so that the people of Central America can hold the line against externally supported aggression. In addition, I am asking for prompt action on the supplemental request in these same areas to carry us through the current fiscal year and for early and favorable Congressional action on my request for fiscal year 1984.

And finally, I am asking that the bipartisan consensus which last year acted on the trade and tax provisions of the Caribbean Basin Initiatives in the House again take the lead to move this vital proposal to the floor of both chambers. And, as I said before, the greatest share of these requests is targeted toward economic and humanitarian aid, not military.

What the administration is asking for on behalf of freedom in Central America is so small, so minimal, considering what is at stake. The total amount requested for aid to all of Central America in 1984 is about $600 million. That's less than one-tenth of what Americans will spend this year on coin-operated video games.

In summation, I say to you that tonight there can be no question: The national security of all the Americas is at stake in Central America. If we cannot defend ourselves there, we cannot expect to prevail elsewhere. Our credibility would collapse, our alliances would crumble, and the safety of our homeland would be put in jeopardy.

We have a vital interest, a moral duty, and a solemn responsibility. This is not a partisan issue. It is a question of our meeting our moral responsibility to ourselves, our friends, and our posterity. It is a duty that falls on all of us — the President, the Congress, and the people. We must perform it together. Who among us would wish to bear responsibility for failing to meet our shared obligation?

Thank you, God bless you, and good night.

DEMOCRATS' RESPONSE

Good evening. I want to thank the networks for the opportunity to offer a different viewpoint. While there is no unanimity in Congress — on the other side of the aisle — on Central America, tonight I am speaking for the many Americans who are concerned about our ever-deepening involvement in the military conflict in that part of the world.

I am pleased to note that the President this evening was willing to recognize an economic and political dimension of the problems in Central America, including the possibility of negotiations. Concerned Members of Congress have been pressing this point of view since he came to office. Regrettably, however, as his statement tonight demonstrates, the fundamental view continues to emphasize military problems and the search for military solutions.

In the months and years that follow this evening, after the applause has faded and the ringing phrases are forgotten, Americans will have to live with the choices we make in this fateful time of decision.

In the past, we as a nation have learned painfully that the truth is never as simple as some would paint it. Charts and statistics can be used or misused to prove any side of a case. And speeches can sound very good without being very right.

So first of all, let me state clearly that on some very important things, all Americans stand in agreement.

We will oppose the establishment of Marxist states in Central America.

We will not accept the creation of Soviet military bases in Central America.

And, we will not tolerate the placement of Soviet offensive missiles in Central America — or anywhere in this hemisphere.

Finally, we are fully prepared to defend our security and the security of the Americas, if necessary, by military means.

All patriotic Americans share these goals. But many of us in Congress, Democrats and Republicans, respectfully disagree with the President because we believe the means he has chosen will not fulfill them.

Those of us who oppose the President's policy believe that he is mistaken in critical ways. To begin with, we believe the Administration fundamentally misunderstands the causes of the conflict in Central America. We cannot afford to found so important a policy on ignorance — and the painful truth is that many of our highest officials seem to know as little about Central America in 1983 as we knew about Indochina in 1963.

I've lived with the people in this region. Let me share some facts with you about Central America.

Most of the people there are appallingly poor. They can't afford to feed their families when they're hungry. They can't find a doctor for them when they're sick. They live in rural shacks with dirt floors or city slums without plumbing or clean water. The majority can't read or write, many of them don't even know how to count.

It takes all five Spanish-speaking countries of Central America more than a year to produce what this nation does in less than three days. Virtually none of even that meager amount ever reaches the bulk of the people. In short, a very few live in isolated splendor while the very many suffer in shantytown squalor. In country after country, dictatorship or military dominance has stifled democracy and destroyed human rights.

If Central America were not racked with poverty, there would be no revolution. If Central America were not racked with hunger, there would be no revolution. If Central America were not racked with injustices, there would be no revolution. In short, there would be nothing for the Soviets to exploit. But unless those oppressive conditions change, that region will continue to seethe with revolution — with or without the Soviets.

Instead of trying to do something about the factors which breed revolution, this Administration has turned to massive military buildups at a cost of hundreds of millions of dollars. Its policy is ever increasing military assistance, endless military training, and further military involvement. This is a formula for failure. And it is a proven prescription for picking a loser. The American people know that we have been down this road before — and that it only leads to a dark tunnel of endless intervention.

Tonight the President himself told us that things were not going well in Central America. But for this the President cannot blame Congress. We have given him what he has asked. $700 million in economic and military assistance has been delivered or is on its way to El Salvador since Ronald Reagan came to office ... all at his request and all with Congressional approval. One of every five Salvadoran soldiers fighting for its government was trained right here in the United States. American soldiers are there now training Salvadoran army units which are employing modern weapons built in American factories.

Now the President asks for an even greater commitment. His requests for El Salvador alone will bring the total aid to that country during his term to more than $1 billion.

One billion dollars to counter a rebel army that, according to all reports, does not exceed 7,000 guerrillas. That means you are paying $140,000 in hard-earned tax dollars for each one of those guerrillas we are trying to defeat.

While your tax dollars have been pouring into El Salvador, the money skimmed off by that nation's rich is leaving the country. For every dollar we've sent in, more than a dollar has gone out — to numbered accounts in

Zurich or to buy stocks on Wall Street. It raises the question of why we should invest in the future of El Salvador when the wealthiest citizens of that country are investing in Swiss banks.

What return have we achieved for all we have spent? The army in El Salvador has been reluctant to fight — and it is led by an Officer Corps working a nine to five shift with weekends off. Land reform has been abandoned. At least 30,000 civilians have been killed and the majority of them have been victims of the government's own security forces. American nuns and labor advisors have been murdered — and the judicial system is so intimidated that it cannot even bring accused murderers to trial.

For those 30,000 murders, confirmed by our own Embassy, there have been fewer than 200 convictions.

American dollars alone cannot buy military victory — that is the lesson of the painful past and of this newest conflict in Central America. If we continue down that road, if we continue to ally ourselves with repression, we will not only deny our own most basic values, we will also find ourselves once again on the losing side. It is folly, pure and simple, to pursue a course which is wrong in principle — in order to wage a confict which cannot be won.

After 30,000 deaths, after hundreds of millions of dollars, with the ante going up, with no end in sight, with no hope for any real change, the time has come for a different approach. Yes, we are fully prepared to be involved in Central America. But the question is the nature and quality of our involvement. We must offer an alternative policy that can work.

First, we should use the power and influence of the United States to achieve an immediate cessation of hostilities in both El Salvador and Nicaragua. Already in both those countries too many people have died. It is time for the killing to stop.

Second, the United States should use all its power and influence to work for negotiated political settlements in Central America.

In El Salvador, the rebels have offered to negotiate unconditionally. Let us test their sincerity. We certainly have the leverage to move the government to the bargaining table. On his recent trip to that very Catholic region, the Pope lent the moral force of his office to such a step. It is practical and realistic to expect, that if we support it, these talks can get underway. And every major ally of ours in the region — Mexico, Panama, Venezuela, and Colombia — is anxious for such a step to be taken and has offered to make the arrangements.

Those same nations have volunteered to bring Nicaragua into negotiations — and Nicaragua has agreed to talk. Instead, as we know from press accounts, this Administration is conducting a not so secret war inside that country.

No one in this Congress or this country is under the delusion that the Sandinista government is a model democracy or a force for stability. But the insurgents we have supported are the remnants of the old Somoza regime — a regime whose corruption, graft, torture, and despotism made it universally despised in Nicaragua. The Sandinistas may not be winners, but right now we are backing sure losers. We are doing for the Sandinista Marxists what they could not do for themselves. We are weakening the very groups inside Nicaragua which believe in a free and democratic society. And that is the sad irony of the Administration's policy.

Third, we must restore America's role as a source of hope and a force for progress in Central America. We must help governments only if they will help their own people. We must hear the cry for bread, schools, work, and opportunity that comes from campesinos everywhere in this hemisphere. We must make violent revolution preventable by making peaceful revolution possible.

Most important, this approach would permit the United States to move with the tide of history rather than stand against it.

For us, the stakes are diplomatic, political, and strategic. But for the people of El Salvador, life itself is on the line.

I have been to that country and I know about the morticians who travel the streets each morning to collect the bodies of those summarily dispatched the night before by Salvadoran security forces — gangland-style — the victim on bended knee, thumbs wired behind the back, a bullet through the brain.

We recoil at such an image for our association with criminals such as these is not America's tradition. In other, brighter days we have stood for the aspirations of all the people who are part of the Americas. Two centuries ago, our nation raised the light of liberty before the world — and all of this hemisphere looked to us as an example and an inspiration. In this Capitol building, from which I speak tonight, men like Daniel Webster, Henry Clay, and Abraham Lincoln once spoke of an America leading the way to human progress and human rights — and people everywhere listened with hope.

There is no greater or larger ideal than the one which was forged here in the early days of this Republic. That ideal of liberty is our greatest strength as a nation; it is a powerful and peaceful weapon against tyranny of any kind anywhere in this hemisphere.

We can take the road of military escalation. But we really don't know what the next step will be, where it will lead or how much it will cost. This much, however, we do know. It will mean greater violence. It will mean greater bloodshed. It will mean greater hostilities. And, inevitably, the day will come when it will mean a regional conflict in Central America.

When that day comes — when the "dogs of war" are loose in Central America, when the cheering has stopped — we will know where the President's appeal for more American money and a deeper American commitment has taken us.

Thank you and good night.

MILITARY JUNTA, RIGHTS GROUP ON ARGENTINA'S 'DISAPPEARED'

April 28, October 12, 1983

On April 28 the military government ruling Argentina issued a report entitled "The Final Document of the Military Junta Concerning the War Against Subversion and Terrorism — Fundamental Concepts." In the report, read over national radio and television by President Reynaldo Bigone, the military attempted to justify its role in suppressing leftist insurgency during violent civil strife in the 1970s.

The report also constituted the junta's official explanation about what happened to thousands of persons who disappeared in Argentina during those turbulent years. The disappearances were widely assumed to be the work of government security forces, which were granted special powers in 1975 and overthrew the civilian government of Isabel Martinez de Peron in 1976. Argentine human rights groups and international organizations such as Amnesty International charged that the military and police abducted, tortured and killed most of the missing, estimated to number at least 6,000, and perhaps as many as 20,000.

By 1983 concern about the fate of these persons had become one of the most divisive issues in Argentina. Families of the missing had marched weekly for years to the presidential palace demanding information, and their cause had gained widespread support in Argentine society.

The Military's Report on the Missing

The junta's report declared that the anti-leftist drive was necessary to stop kidnappings, assassinations and bombings and defended police and military deeds as "acts of service" to the nation. It admitted the security forces made errors that "at times, trespass[ed] the limits of ... fundamental human rights" but asserted the errors were made in an atmosphere of "apocalyptic" panic and should be judged by God and history.

As for the missing, the report claimed that many were alive or living in exile under assumed names. The others should be presumed dead, killed in battles with security forces or by guerrilla infighting, according to the document.

The government promised to share the information it possessed on individual cases but made no mention of the mass graves that had been discovered in recent years.

The Amnesty Law

In a further step easing Argentina toward democratic government, the junta issued a Law of National Pacification in the fall that gave amnesty to all who had participated in subversive or anti-subversive activity between May 1973 and June 1982. Discredited by its defeat in the war with Great Britain over the Falkland Islands and by domestic failures, the junta had promised that free elections would be held by 1984. (Falkland Islands war, p. 3)

Although the new law did grant amnesty to many members of guerrilla organizations, it also exempted police, soldiers and paramilitary operatives from prosecution by any civilian government that might take over after the junta relinquished power — a fear that had begun to preoccupy the military.

In an October 12 letter to Gen. Bigone, Amnesty International outlined its objections to the amnesty law: It was incompatible with United Nations resolutions on human rights; it would halt investigations into illegal actions by security forces; and it would hamper probes into the fate of the missing.

Civilian Government Elected

Neither the junta's report on the missing nor the amnesty law quieted the outcry over the missing. In Argentina the report was greeted with widespread anti-government demonstrations. Several European governments also expressed dissatisfaction. The United States government refrained from direct criticism. (In 1978 Congress had banned assistance to Argentina because of human rights violations, but the Reagan administration had persuaded Congress to lift the ban partially.) (State Department human rights report, p. 181)

The matter became a major issue in the Argentine elections, held October 30. Shortly after his election, the new president, Raul Alfonsin, co-founder of an Argentine human rights organization, ordered the court martial of all members of the three juntas that had governed Argentina since 1976. By the end of 1983, at least 800 private court claims were pending on human rights, and plaintiffs had named at least 400 military and police officers involved in repression. After Alfonsin's inauguration December 10, the commanders-in-chief of the army and navy, Gen. Cristino Nicolaides and Adm. Ruben Franco, were indicted for obstructing justice in a case concerning a missing person, and Bigone was indicted in another case for illegal arrest and false testimony.

Following are excerpts from the Argentine military government's April 28, 1983, report on the "disappeared" (translated for Congressional Quarterly), Amnesty International's October 12, 1983, letter to Gen. Bigone concerning the fate of the missing, and the relevant articles of the government's "Law of National Pacification":

ARGENTINE GOVERNMENT REPORT

I. Introduction

This historic synthesis of a painful past, still recent, is meant to be a message of faith and recognition of the fight for freedom, justice and the right to life.

It is meant first for us, the people of the nation, victims of an aggression which they never deserved and invaluable and decisive participants in the achievement of the final victory. Secondly, it is meant for the world of free men to which the republic belongs and will continue to belong faithful to its historic destiny.

An experience which the nation should never again repeat is described here for the reflection of the people of Argentina and the world — hoping that, with the same grace of God, our brothers in America and the peoples of other continents might examine it, understand it and avoid it.

II. The Facts

The republic of Argentina, .·. . in the middle of the decade of the sixties, began to suffer the aggression of terrorism . . . which aimed at modifying the concept that our community has about man and the state . . . winning power by means of violence. Thefts of arms, assaults on banks and other institutions, kidnappings, extortions and . . . assassinations caused public opinion to become aware of the felonious activities of the three most powerful terrorist groups. The action of these groups, directed at paralyzing the population, was marked by a permanent and indiscriminate violation of the most fundamental human rights: assassinations, tortures and prolonged kidnappings are unquestionable proof of their criminal acts and purposes.

Their victims belonged to all social strata: workers, intellectual priests, businessmen, journalists, public officials, military judges, policemen, political leaders, union officials and even children.

Active members and definite supporters of these terrorist organizations occupied important positions in the national cabinet, in the provincial governments, in the national congress, in the provincial legislatures and in the judiciary. Neither religious organizations nor the police force was exempt from this infiltration.

Their insidious actions misled thousands of young people, many of them still adolescents, picked up by the groups by means of whichever attractive technique or simply through fear. Many died in confrontations with the police; others committed suicide in order to avoid being captured; many others deserted, having to hide from the authorities and from their own groups.

In order to have a clear idea of the magnitude of the terrorist activity, the following figures are submitted: it is noteworthy that in 1974 there were 21 attempts to capture police units, 466 incidents with explosives and 16 robberies of considerable sums of money. One hundred seventeen people were kidnapped and 110 were assassinated. In 1976, when violence reached its peak, there were 600 kidnappings and 646 assassinations, with an average of two daily victims of terrorism. Four thousand one hundred fifty terrorist actions were registered, among them attempts at capturing certain local areas, armed activities of propaganda, intimidations by extortion and criminal activities with the use of explosives.

A perusal of the journalistic chronicle corresponding to the period 1973-1979 reveals that during this time 2,050 people were killed in 742 confrontations; these figures do not include the casualties suffered by the police.

Between 1969 and 1979, 21,642 terrorist acts were registered. This number is proportional to the ... subversive structure that reached its apex with 25,000 members ..., of which 15,000 were fighting members, i.e., individuals technically capable and ideologically fanaticized to kill.

The nature ... of this type of surprise attack, permanent and systematic, made it necessary to adopt quiet procedures in the conduct of the war. It was necessary to impose the strictest secrecy about the information regarding military activity, its achievements, developing operations and the discoveries realized.

It became absolutely necessary not to alert the enemy, not to uncover the actual goals, recouping the initiative and surprise action which up until this time were the opponent's card.

During all of these operations, it was practically impossible to establish precisely the total casualties suffered by groups of delinquent terrorists and the identity of their members — even when their bodies remained in the place of the action, since they functioned under false names and with aliases known as "War Names" and because their cellular structure, *modus operandi* and fragmentation of their actions made it impossible to completely analyze their activities.

The efforts expended by the armed forces, security and police to reestablish peace and order produced progressive results. The terrorist aggression did yield gradually and the Argentinian society started to recuperate the losses sustained.... Thus a painful and hard era was culminating in which victory — finally reached — had a content coinciding with the meaning of the defeat of the violent. It was thus, because the Argentinian society maintained itself faithful to its traditions, loyal to its conscience and firm in its decision. In each one of the social sectors, [official] subversion worked out ... diverse methodologies, all of which converged toward the common goal of destroying, paralyzing or dominating the terrorists. However, subversion also failed, since it hurt a peaceful and free people in its staunchest values.

III. Principles and Procedures

The exceptional conditions in which the country lived during the period of the terrorist aggression caused the essential elements of the state to be affected at levels that made difficult its survival.

The exercise of human rights was at the mercy of violence — selective or indiscriminate — imposed by terrorist activity, translated into assassinations, kidnappings, "Revolutionary Trials," exiles and compulsory taxation.

The capability of the government to act was seriously compromised by subversive infiltration and the political vacuum caused by the death of President [Juan] Perón.

In that crucial historic moment, the armed forces were summoned by the constitutional government in order to fight subversion. (Decree No. 261 of Feb. 5, 1975 and decree No. 2772 of Oct. 6, 1975)

The national government, in search of the common good, through this legal mandate and by means of the armed forces, imposed the goal of reestablishing the rights of all the inhabitants and the essential conditions that would guarantee the inviolability of the territory and social coexistence, thus facilitating the capability of the government to function.

The armed forces, security and police acted in defense of the national community whose essential rights were not ensured and, unlike ... the subversive factions, they did not use their power directly against innocent third parties, even though indirectly these could have suffered....

The actions thus developed were the consequence of decisions that had to be made in the middle of the fight; with a measure of passion that combat and the defense of one's own life generate; in an environment tainted daily with innocent blood and destruction and before a society where panic reigned. In this framework, almost apocalyptic, errors were committed which, as happens in all wars, would, at times, trespass the limits of the respect of fundamental human rights and which are subject to the judgment of God in each conscience and the understanding of men.

The armed forces hope that this painful experience will enlighten our people so that all may find instruments compatible with ethics and with the democratic spirit of our institutions.

IV. Sequels to the Conflict

It is necessary to indicate clearly that there are many wounds not yet healed in the Argentinian society: long years of profound insecurity; frequent moments of terror; loss of family and dear ones who were felled by attacks as unjustified as crafty; maiming; long detentions and physical disappearance of people; all of them — individual and collective, physical and spiritual — are the sequels of a war that we Argentinians must surmount.

The armed forces, faithful to the goal of healing the wounds made by the fight and desiring to clarify the doubtful situations that might exist, have made available to the public the following information in the Ministry of the Interior:

● Lists of the members of terrorist organizations actually convicted and being processed by the federal justice and war councils, and held by the national executive power by virtue of Article 23 of the national constitution.

● Requests of whereabouts (of those presumed missing) registered by the Ministry of the Interior since 1974 to the present time.

● Requests of whereabouts successfully responded to by judicial or administrative means.

● Casualties caused by terrorist actions.

The case of the missing is the one which most forcibly strikes the legitimate humanitarian sentiments, the one which is used most insidiously to surprise the good faith of those who did not know ... the facts that led us to that final situation.

The experience ... allows us to affirm that many of the disappearances are a consequence of the modus operandi of the terrorists.

They change their authenic names and surnames; they are known among themselves by "War Names" and have abundant fraudulent personal documentation. These are linked to what is known as "Passage to Clandestineness." Those who decide to become members of terrorist organizations, do it surreptitiously, abandoning their family, work and social milieu. This is the most typical case: family members report a missing person whose disappearance cannot be explained or, knowing the cause, do not want to explain it.

Thus, some of "the missing" whose disappearance had been reported later appeared performing terrorist actions. In other cases, the terrorists abandoned the country clandestinely and lived outside with false identities. Others, after going into exile, returned to the country with fraudulent identities. There also exist outlawed terrorists — some within the republic, others outside.

There are cases of deserters from different organizations who live today with false identities in order to protect their own lives, either within the country or outside.

Many of the fallen during confrontations with the police did not have any type of document or had false documents and, in many cases, they had worn off finger prints. Other terrorists, when capture was imminent, committed suicide, generally by ingesting cyanide. In these cases the corpses were not claimed and, since it was impossible to identify them, they were legally buried as "NN" [not known].

Whenever it was possible, the terrorists would recover the bodies of their dead from the place of conflict. The corpses, as well as the wounded who died as a consequence of the confrontation, were destroyed or clandestinely buried by the terrorists.

[In] the fight for the supremacy of terror ... assassinations and kidnappings among the various organizations [occurred]. Terrorism, hiding under a pseudo-revolutionary code, made mockery of trials and assassinated ... members who defected or who failed on assigned missions. These were buried with false identities or in unknown places and circumstances.

The armed forces, during the development of the fight, infiltrated men in terrorist organizations. When discovered, they were killed, their burial places remaining unknown.

In much the same way, there have been cases of persons reported as missing, who later did appear and led normal lives without the knowledge of the judicial or administrative authorities.

Finally, the list of missing could be artificially increased if cases that are normally reported in all large urban centers, but not attributable to the terrorist phenomenon, were included.

It must be noted that since the circumstances under which a kidnapping is reported are subject to judicial investigation, a great number of cases for presumed crimes of illegitimate deprivation of freedom have been initiated by the office of concerned judges.

The possibility that persons considered missing could be found buried as unidentified has always been one of the principal hypotheses accepted by the government. Coinciding with this belief is the report prepared by the Inter-American Commission for Human Rights that visited the country in 1979, when it expressed that, in different cemeteries, the burial of unidentified people who had died violent deaths, principally in confrontation with the police, could be verified.

In the same vein, one hears of "missing" persons who might be found detained by the Argentinian government in unknown places in the country. All this is nothing but falsehoods utilized for political aims, since in the republic there are no secret places of detention, neither are there in the jails people who are secretly detained.

It must remain definitely clear that those who appear in lists as missing and who are not in exile or living clandestinely for legal and administrative purposes are considered as dead — even when it is impossible at present to ascertain the causes and circumstances of their deaths or their places of burial.

V. Final Considerations

The victory obtained at such great price had the support of the citizens who understood the complex phenomenon of subversion, and expressed, through their leaders, their repudiation of violence.

From this attitude of the population [it] comes clearly through that the desire of the whole nation is to put an end to a painful period of our history in order to begin, in union and liberty, the definite constitutional institutionalization of the republic.

In order to succeed in this effort, it is absolutely necessary that we have sufficient equilibrium to understand what did happen, without forgetting the circumstances that led us to the brink of disintegration as well as the responsibilities that, through action or omission, belonged to the different parts of the community, so as not to travel again over this painful road. . . .

Those who gave their life to combat the terrorist scourge deserve eternal, respectful homage and gratitude.

Those political leaders, priests, business men, union officials, magistrates or simple citizens who knew how to uphold the principles of a life style nurtured by the respect of fundamental rights of people and by the value of liberty, peace and democracy, risking their personal security and that of their families, deserve the recognition of the community.

Those who have placed their intelligence, good faith, solidarity, and piety in exercising the whole weight of their commitment to the reconciliation of the Argentinian family, are worthy of recognition and respect.

Transcending ideological differences and united as children of God, may those who lost their lives as members of terrorist organizations that assaulted the very society that had nurtured them receive their pardon.

Those who have recognized their error and have been purged from their guilt, deserve to be helped. The Argentinian society, in its generosity, is willing to receive them into its fold.

Reconciliation is the difficult beginning of an era of maturity and of responsibility assumed realistically by all. The scars are a painful memory, but also the cement of a strong democracy, of a unified and free people — a people who learned that subversion and terrorism are the inexorable death blow of freedom.

The armed forces hand over to their fellow citizens this information so that they may judge in community this mournful stage of our history which, as such, is a problem that concerns all Argentinians and that all Argentinians must solve in common, if we wish to assure the survival of the republic.

Regarding the Above, The Military Junta Declares:

1. That the information and explanations furnished in this document is all that the armed forces have available to reveal to the nation about the results and consequences of the war against subversion and terrorism.

2. That in this frame of reference, . . . only the judgment of history will be able to determine exactly who is directly responsible for unjust procedures or innocent deaths.

3. That the actions of those who belonged to the armed forces during the operations carried on during the war of liberation constituted acts of service.

4. That the armed forces acted and will act whenever necessary in fulfillment of an emerging mandate of the national government, taking advantage of all the experience gained in this painful circumstance. . . .

5. That the armed forces submit to the people and to the judgment of history these decisions that had as their goal to defend the common good, identified in this instance as the survival of the community and whose content is assumed with the authentic pain of Christians who recognize the errors that might have been committed in the fulfillment of the assigned mission.

AMNESTY INTERNATIONAL LETTER

Your Excellency,

For the past ten years Amnesty International has made frequent representations to successive Argentine governments about violations of human rights, and in particular, the practice of enforced or involuntary "disappearances." This practice has claimed thousands of victims whose cases have been meticulously documented by Amnesty International and other organizations. Evidence of official responsibility for these acts, which has been carefully compiled by Amnesty International, has been regularly transmitted to the Argentine government. Amnesty International has the honour of addressing Your Excellency on this occasion about the implications of the recently enacted Law of National Pacification on the question of "disappeared-detainees."

During the period covered by the Law, 25 May 1973-17 June 1982, Amnesty International has repeatedly called upon the Argentine authorities to take two measures: to end the policy of "disappearances" and to give a full account of the fate of those registered as "disappeared." In the case of the former, some progress has been made. Since 1980 the scale of "disappearances" has been greatly reduced, although the practice has apparently still not been eradicated. But with regard to the latter the Argentine authorities have not taken any steps to clarify the situation of "disappeared-detainees." The document published by the Argentine Junta in April 1983, which asserted that the "disappeared" should be regarded as dead, only deepened the concern about these cases among the victims' families and the international community.

The Law of National Pacification would appear to shut off the possibility of establishing the truth about the following key questions: Why were individuals abducted and on whose authority? What treatment were they subjected to? What has happened to them since?

Under international law the Argentine government itself, notwithstanding the amnesty, retains full responsibility for any human rights violations committed by its agents in enforced or involuntary "disappearances." The new Law of National Pacification is incompatible with Resolution 33/173 of the General Assembly of the United Nations, adopted in December 1978, calling upon governments "to ensure that law enforcement and security authorities or organizations are fully accountable, especially in law, in the discharge of their duties, such accountability to include legal responsibility for unjustifiable excesses which might lead to enforced or involuntary disappearances and to other violations of human rights." Furthermore Resolution XXXIV of the United Nations Sub-Commission on Prevention of Discrimination and Protection of Minorities, adopted on 10 September 1981, urged that "States in which persons have been reported to have disappeared should repeal or refrain from adopting laws which could impede inquiries concerning such disappearances."

In addition to Resolution 1983/23, adopted on 5 September 1983, the Sub-Commission also stressed the right of families to know the fate of their relatives by calling upon governments "in the event of reports of enforced or involuntary disappearances, to devote appropriate resources to searching for such persons and to undertake speedy and impartial investigations." Amnesty International believes that in three important respects the new law prevents the implementation of human rights standards: it makes it practically impossible to determine what has happened to the "disappeared" prisoners, it could encourage further human rights violations by giving the perpetrators of past crimes a sense of impunity and it prevents the perpetrators of the "disappearances" from being brought to justice.

The Law of National Pacification has been presented as an amnesty for crimes committed over the past ten years connected to subversion. Yet specific provisions of this law are particularly disquieting. Article 1 apparently gives a complete amnesty for all crimes committed by both subversives and anti-subversive groups. This would seem to represent an alteration of the military's previous position, which was that the terrorists committed crimes but those who opposed them did not. Yet on reading the subsequent articles the law appears designed to grant complete immunity from prosecution to all members of the military, police and security forces. For example, final convictions for crimes and deeds of a penal nature referred to in Article 1 will not benefit under the Law (see Article 3). But current criminal proceedings related to such offences will be submitted automatically to the appropriate Court of Appeal. Complaints or suits filed for alleged crimes and deeds included in Article 1 will be immediately dismissed (see Articles 8 and 12). Since the persons already convicted are almost exclusively "subversives" but current cases might well concern military officials, the effect of these provisions appears likely to leave imprisoned those convicted for opposition activities while giving immunity to those who have committed serious crimes against alleged subversives such as abduction, torture and murder.

Amnesty International is concerned with the latitude of interpretation that this Law allows to the Armed Forces. The stipulation in Article 5 that "no-one can be questioned, investigated or arraigned, or called upon in any manner whatsoever by dint of allegations or suspicion of having committed crimes or having participated in activities referred to in Article 1," clearly flouts numerous recommendations related to "disappearances" of both the United Nations Commission of Human Rights and the Inter-American Commission on Human Rights of the Organisation of American States. Amnesty International believes that the attempt to block all further investigations into this problem is utterly indefensible. Furthermore, if neither questioning nor investigation is permitted, how will it be possible to determine that the alleged offences do indeed fall under Article 1. According to Article 7 the law can be fully enforced "upon request by a party," which would mean that a member of the police, military or security forces, who has committed a crime covered by Article 1, can himself define the nature of the charges against him and then simply apply to the appropriate court for an amnesty. Amnesty International believes that this comes uncomfortably close to a defendant being the judge in his own case.

Amnesty International is also concerned about the provisions of the Law as they apply to Argentine citizens who are not "legally and openly resident in the country, or in Argentine territory or places under Argentine jurisdiction who, by their conduct have shown their intention of maintaining their connection with these [subversive] associations." Article 2 does not make it clear whether the Amnesty Law excludes all Argentines living abroad or whether there must also be evidence that they have continued to be associated with subversive groups. If such evidence is required it is not clear how it will be gathered and assessed.

In conclusion, given the gravity of the "disappearance" problem in Argentina, and given the obligations placed on the Argentine government under international law to:

a) investigate the circumstances of the "disappearance" of each individual, registered by Amnesty International and other human rights organizations, following his abduction by members of the police, military, or security forces;
b) explain to the family of each victim what has happened to the "disappeared" person;
c) pay appropriate compensation to the victims and/or their families for any damages suffered as a result of the "disappearance,"

Amnesty International is concerned that such measures may in practice be incompatible with the recent Law. Amnesty International therefore respectfully urges the Argentine government to annul the Law of National Pacification to allow for an appropriate solution of the problem of the "disappeared" persons.

Relevant Articles of the Law of National Pacification Mentioned in Amnesty International's Statement

ARTICLE 1

Penal actions and sentences imposed for crimes committed for terrorist or subversive purposes from 25 May 1973 to 17 June 1982 are null and void. The benefits of this Law are extended to all deeds that are actionable under penal laws, carried out with the intention of preventing, barring or ending such terrorist or subversive activities, regardless of their nature and the judicially protected right violated or property damaged. The effects of this Law apply to perpetrators, instigators, accomplices or accessories after the fact, as well as to common and military crimes that may have been committed in connection with such terrorist or subversive activities.

ARTICLE 2

The benefits included in the preceding article do not apply to members of illicit terrorist or subversive associations from the time at which the benefits of this law take effect, who are not legally and openly resident in the country or in Argentine territory or in places under Argentine jurisdiction or who, by their conduct, have shown their intention of maintaining their connection with these associations.

ARTICLE 3

Neither does this law apply to those who have been convicted for crimes and deeds of a penal nature referred to in Article 1 without prejudice to the faculties conferred on the Executive Power by Paragraph 6 of Article 86 of the Argentine Constitution to grant a pardon or to commute sentences imposed for such convictions as a means of fulfilling the conciliatory aims of this law.

ARTICLE 5

No one can be questioned, investigated or arraigned, or called upon in any manner whatsoever by dint of allegations or suspicion of having committed crimes or having participated in activities referred to in Article 1 of this law or upon supposition that one might have knowledge of such crimes or actions, or their circumstances, perpetrators, participants, instigators, accomplices or accessories after the fact.

ARTICLE 6

The present law also renders null and void civil actions related to crimes or actions described in Article 1 of this Law. A special law will set out rules for indemnification by the state.

ARTICLE 7

The present law will be fully in force from the date of its promulgation and it will be enforced ex officio or upon request by a party.

ARTICLE 8

The ordinary federal or military court, or any military agency in which cases falling prima facie under provisions of this law, are being heard or in which sentence has been passed will cease proceedings and submit such cases within forty-eight hours to the appropriate court of appeal or to the Armed Forces Supreme council, whichever is appropriate. The provisions of this law also apply to cases that are being prosecuted or have been temporarily dismissed, involving investigation of actions, the perpetrators of which have not yet been identified but are believed to be members of terrorist or subversive organizations or members of the armed forces, security agencies or the police, or are said to have invoked in the commission of the actions, such membership. All cases related to the same actions which have not yet been compiled, will be compiled by the appropriate court superintendence.

ARTICLE 12

Federal or military judges or military agencies will immediately dismiss complaints or suits filed with them for alleged crimes and acts referred to in Article 1.

May

ISRAELI-LEBANESE
SECURITY AGREEMENT
May 17, 1983

Israeli and Lebanese negotiators May 17 signed an agreement outlining the procedures for withdrawal of foreign troops from Lebanon and detailing future security arrangements between the two countries. The signing capped more than four months of talks, the first face-to-face negotiations between Lebanon and Israel since 1949. In theory, the withdrawal agreement paved the way for a new era of cooperation between Israel and Lebanon. But in reality, the accord was purely a paper pact. Israel refused to withdraw its troops from Lebanon until Syrian and Palestinian forces also left, and at the year's end troops from all three groups remained in Lebanon. In February 1984 Lebanese President Amin Gemayel said he would abrogate the pact.

The agreement came almost a year after Israel invaded Lebanon on June 6, 1982. The invasion was an attempt to lessen Syrian influence in Lebanon, oust Palestinian guerrillas from their bases and help establish a Lebanese government acceptable to Israel. (Historic Documents of 1982, p. 741)

Israeli and Lebanese officials began negotiations December 28, 1982, in the battered seaside town of Khalde, five miles south of Beirut. The talks alternated between Khalde, the target of Israeli shelling in 1982, and the northern Israeli border settlement of Qiryat Shemona, which bore its own battle scars from 1982 attacks by Palestinian guerrillas based in Lebanon.

Lebanon's chief negotiator was Antoine Fattal, a jurist, former diplomat and acting director of Lebanon's foreign ministry. Fattal's Israeli counterpart was David Kimche, director general of Israel's foreign ministry. A U.S. delegation, headed by special envoy Morris Draper, also participated.

From the outset of the talks, Lebanese and Israeli goals differed. Lebanon's primary objective was to secure the earliest possible withdrawal of foreign troops from its lands. Israel, on the other hand, sought a broader normalization of relations with Lebanon before committing itself to any troop withdrawal. That difference and others stalled the talks time and again. Through the efforts of U.S. mediators, however, the negotiating teams arrived at the compromise agreement. Secretary of State George P. Shultz shuttled between Jerusalem and Beirut April 27-May 6 in an attempt to come up with a final draft acceptable to both countries. On May 16 the Lebanese and Israeli parliaments approved the agreement. The Lebanese vote was unanimous; the Knesset vote was 57-6, with 45 members of the opposition Labor Party abstaining.

Major Provisions

Although Fattal made clear that Lebanon did not regard the security accord as a peace agreement, the document stated: "The parties confirm that the state of war between Lebanon and Israel has been terminated and no longer exists." (A full peace agreement with Israel would have been unacceptable to Lebanon's Moslem population and to other Arab states.) The agreement called for the withdrawal of Israeli troops from Lebanon within eight to 12 weeks after the accord went into effect. That event, however, was contingent upon the corresponding withdrawal of the 40,000 Syrian and 8,000 Palestinian troops also in Lebanon. Once the accord did go into effect, a Joint Liaison Committee, with the United States as a participant, would be established to supervise implementation of its terms.

Following Israeli troop withdrawal, negotiations between Lebanon and Israel regarding "movement of goods, products and persons" across the border would take place. "Liaison offices" in both countries would permit a start toward diplomatic relations.

The agreement mapped out a security region in southern Lebanon, extending northward from the Israeli border 20 to 37 miles into Lebanon, that would be patrolled by joint Israeli-Lebanese security teams. The Lebanese government, however, would have ultimate responsibility for security and police operations in the region. Detailed restrictions on forces, weapons and equipment allowed in the security region also were spelled out. The agreement called for close cooperation between the armies of the two countries and could serve as the foundation for a close military and intelligence partnership.

Several Arab nations expressed support for the agreement. Egypt and Jordan issued strong public statements backing the pact; Algeria and

Saudi Arabia offered more muted support. Opposing the agreement were Syria, Libya and South Yemen.

Syrian Opposition

From the beginning of the talks, Syria voiced opposition to any agreement between Lebanon and Israel and reminded negotiators that Syrian approval would be necessary for any settlement. In fact, the Syrian government made several attempts to thwart the negotiations. In January, shortly after the talks began, Syria announced that it planned to acquire advanced Soviet missiles capable of hitting aircraft over much of Israel. In early May Syria organized an opposition group within Lebanon in an unsuccessful attempt to block the impending accord.

Syria reacted to the signing of the agreement by immediately blocking roads linking Beirut with Syrian-controlled territory in northern and central Lebanon; this move effectively closed Beirut's overland routes to the rest of the Arab world. Telex and telephone links between Beirut and other portions of the country also were cut.

Agreement on Hold

Throughout 1983 Syria steadfastly refused to withdraw its troops from Lebanon, continued an arms buildup and demonstrated increased hostility toward Israel and the United States. Although Yasir Arafat and 4,000 of his Palestine Liberation Organization (PLO) followers were forced out of Lebanon in December, other Palestinian guerrillas remained. A number of events led to the scrapping of the agreement in early 1984, among them the collapse of the Gemayel government and defeats of the Lebanese Army by the Syrian-backed Druze militia, coupled with the September bombing of U.S. Marine headquarters, which led the Reagan administration to order a redeployment of most of the Marine peacekeeping force to ships offshore. Bowing to his opponents, Gemayel said he would abrogate the pact. (Marines bombing, p. 933)

> *Following are excerpts from the Israeli-Lebanese agreement, signed May 17, 1983, outlining the procedures for withdrawal of foreign troops from Lebanon and detailing future security arrangements between the two countries:*

The Government of the State of Israel and the Government of the Republic of Lebanon:

Bearing in mind the importance of maintaining and strengthening international peace based on freedom, equality, justice, and respect for fundamental human rights;

Reaffirming their faith in the aims and principles of the Charter of the United Nations and recognizing their right and obligation to live in peace with each other as well as with all states, within secure and recognized boundaries;

Having agreed to declare the termination of the state of war between them;

Desiring to ensure lasting security for both their states and to avoid threats and the use of force between them;

Desiring to establish their mutual relations in the manner provided for in this agreement;

Having delegated their undersigned representative plenipotentiaries, provided with full powers, in order to sign, in the presence of the representative of the United States of America, this agreement;

Have agreed to the following provisions:

ARTICLE 1

1. The parties agree and undertake to respect the sovereignty, political independence and territorial integrity of each other. They consider the existing international boundary between Israel and Lebanon inviolable.

2. The parties confirm that the state of war between Israel and Lebanon has been terminated and no longer exists.

3. Taking into account the provisions of paragraph 1 and 2, Israel undertakes to withdraw all its armed forces from Lebanon in accordance with the annex of the present agreement.

ARTICLE 2

The parties, being guided by the principles of the Charter of the United Nations and of international law, undertake to settle their disputes by peaceful means in such a manner as to promote international peace and security, and justice.

ARTICLE 3

In order to provide maximum security for Israel and Lebanon, the parties agree to establish and implement security arrangements, including the creation of a Security Region, as provided for in the annex of the present agreement.

ARTICLE 4

1. The territory of each party will not be used as a base for hostile or terrorist activity against the other party, its territory, or its people.

2. Each party will prevent the existence or organization of irregular forces, armed bands, organizations, bases, offices or infrastructure, the

aims and purposes of which include incursions or any act of terrorism into the territory of the other party, or any other activity aimed at threatening or endangering the security of the other party and safety of its people. To this end all agreements and arrangements enabling the presence and functioning on the territory of either party of elements hostile to the other party are null and void.

3. Without prejudice to the inherent right of self-defence in accordance with international law, each party will refrain:

a. From organizing, instigating, assisting, or participating in threats or acts of belligerency, subversion, or incitement or any aggression directed against the other party, its population or property, both within its territory and originating therefrom, or in the territory of the other party.

b. from using the territory of the other party for conducting a military attack against the territory of a third state.

c. from intervening in the internal or external affairs of the other party.

4. Each party undertakes to ensure that preventive action and due proceedings will be taken against persons or organizations perpetrating acts in violation of this article.

ARTICLE 5

Consistent with the termination of the state of war and within the framework of their constitutional provisions, the parties will abstain from any form of hostile propaganda against each other.

ARTICLE 6

Each party will prevent entry into, deployment in, or passage through its territory, its air space and, subject to the right of innocent passage in accordance with international law, its territorial sea, by military forces, armament, or military equipment of any state hostile to the other party.

ARTICLE 7

Except as provided in the present agreement, nothing will preclude the deployment on Lebanese territory of international forces requested and accepted by the Government of Lebanon to assist in maintaining its authority. New contributors to such forces shall be selected from among states having diplomatic relations with both parties to the present agreement.

ARTICLE 8

1. a. Upon entry into force of the present agreement, a Joint Liaison Committee will be established by the parties, in which the United States of America will be a participant, and will commence its functions. This

committee will be entrusted with the supervision of the implementation of all areas covered by the present agreement. In matters involving security arrangements, it will deal with unresolved problems referred to it by the Security Arrangements Committee established in subparagraph c. below. Decisions of this committee will be taken unanimously.

b. The Joint Liaison Committee will address itself on a continuing basis to the development of mutual relations between Israel and Lebanon, *inter alia* the regulation of the movement of goods, products and persons, communications, etc.

c. Within the framework of the Joint Liaison Committee, there will be a Security Arrangements Committee whose composition and functions are defined in the annex of the present agreement.

d. Subcommittees of the Joint Liaison Committee may be established as the need arises.

e. The Joint Liaison Committee will meet in Israel and Lebanon, alternately.

f. Each party, if it so desires and unless there is an agreed change of status, may maintain a liaison office on the territory of the other party in order to carry out the above-mentioned functions within the framework of the Joint Liaison Committee and to assist in the implementation of the present agreement.

g. The members of the Joint Liaison Committee from each of the parties will be headed by a senior government official.

h. All other matters relating to these liaison offices, their personnel, and the personnel of each party present in the territory of the other party in connection with the implementation of the present agreement will be the subject of a protocol to be concluded between the parties in the Joint Liaison Committee. Pending the conclusions of this protocol, the liaison offices and the above-mentioned personnel will be treated in accordance with the pertinent provisions of the Convention on Special Missions of December 8, 1969, including those provisions concerning privileges and immunities. The foregoing is without prejudice to the positions of the parties concerning that convention.

2. During the six-month period after the withdrawal of all Israeli armed forces from Lebanon in accordance with Article 1 of the present agreement and the simultaneous restoration of Lebanese governmental authority along the international boundary between Israel and Lebanon, and in the light of the termination of the state of war, the parties shall initiate, within the Joint Liaison Committee, *bona fide* negotiations in order to conclude agreements on the movement of goods, products and persons and their implementation on a non-discriminatory basis.

ARTICLE 9

1. Each of the two parties will take, within a time limit of one year of entry into force of the present agreement, all measures necessary for the

abrogation of treaties, laws and regulations deemed in conflict with the present agreement, subject to and in conformity with its constitutional procedures.

2. The parties undertake not to apply existing obligations, enter into any obligations, or adopt laws or regulations in conflict with the present agreement.

ARTICLE 10

1. The present agreement shall be ratified by both parties in conformity with their respective constitutional procedures. It shall enter into force on the exchange of the instruments of ratification and shall supercede the previous agreements between Israel and Lebanon. . . .

3. The present agreement may be modified, amended, or superseded by mutual agreement of the parties.

ARTICLE 11

1. Disputes between the parties arising out of the interpretation or application of the present agreement will be settled by negotiation in the Joint Liaison Committee. Any dispute of this character not so resolved shall be submitted to conciliation and, if unresolved, thereafter to an agreed procedure for a definitive resolution.

2. Notwithstanding the provisions of paragraph 1, disputes arising out of the interpretation or application of the annex shall be resolved in the framework of the Security Arrangements Committee and, if unresolved, shall thereafter, at the request of either party, be referred to the Joint Liaison Committee for resolution through negotiation.

ARTICLE 12

The present agreement shall be communicated to the Secretariat of the United Nations for registration in conformity with the provisions of Article 102 of the Charter of the United Nations.

Done at Kiryat Shmona and Khaldeh this seventeenth day of May, 1983, in triplicate in four authentic texts in the Hebrew, Arabic, English and French languages. In case of any divergence of interpretation, the English and French texts will be equally authoritative. . . .

LOVE CANAL REPORT

May 17, 1983

A federal report released May 17 found "no evidence directly establish-ing" links between chromosome damage and exposure to chemical agents in persons living near Love Canal, a neighborhood of Niagara Falls, N.Y. The results of the investigation, conducted by the Centers for Disease Control in Atlanta and two major national laboratories, challenged a controversial 1980 biomedical report commissioned by the Environmental Protection Agency (EPA) showing that 11 of 36 Love Canal residents studied had suffered chromosome aberrations as a result of exposure to hazardous chemicals dumped in the canal 30 years earlier. (Chromosomes are microscopic, rod-shaped particles carrying the genes that convey hereditary characteristics.) The 1980 study, which was instrumental in the relocation of Love Canal-area residents and used as evidence by the government in its suit against the Hooker Chemical and Plastics Corp. (which had dumped most of the waste at the canal site), had been criticized for its failure to compare the Love Canal group with persons living elsewhere. (Historic Documents of 1980, p. 445)

More than 200 families had been evacuated at government expense after 82 chemicals seeped from an underground abandoned dump into basements, yards and even into the land on which a school was built. President Jimmy Carter declared the area an environmental disaster after residents complained of illnesses, miscarriages and birth defects. Public sentiment was aroused by Love Canal, putting Congress under increased pressure from constituents for a federal program to deal with toxic wastes. The result was passage in 1980 of the Hazardous Substances

*and Hazardous Waste Response Liability and Compensation Act creating
a $1.6 billion"superfund" designed to protect the environment from
disasters similar to the one at Love Canal.*

Results of Study

*The 1983 study found "no increase in abnormalities" among 46
residents of the area adjacent to the canal and a control group of 50
persons living about a mile away. "This suggests that no specific
relationship existed between exposure to chemical agents in the Love
Canal area and increased frequency of chromosome damage," the study
concluded. The research took into account several other factors, including
sex, cigarette smoking, history of playing on the canal site and history of
attending elementary school at the school adjoining the site.*

*The two-year investigation focused primarily on possible chromosome
damage and compared two groups of residents who might have been
exposed to the Love Canal toxins. The first group consisted of 29 people
who had been living in 1978 in an area where tests of air, water and soil
had shown elevated levels of chemicals from the canal. The second group
included 17 people who had participated in the controversial 1980 study.
A third group was comprised of residents of another section of the city
deemed free of the chemicals leaking from the canal.*

*The May report cautioned, however, that "Any interpretation of the
findings of this study must take into account the limitations imposed
upon it by imprecision in assessing chemical exposure and dose, by the
nature of cytogenetic analysis, and by the design and sample size
constraints of the study itself." Moreover, the researchers said, "it must
be stressed that, had evidence of increased chromosome damage been
found in this study, it would still have been impossible to know whether
those findings might correlate with or predict later occurrence of clinical
illness."*

Congressional Research

*Shortly after their release, the results of the study were called into
question by the Office of Technology Assessment (OTA), a well-respected
congressional research agency. The OTA study, prepared by a group of
staff members headed by Joel S. Hirsch, a hazardous-waste expert for the
agency, was released June 21. The OTA report warned against resettling
the area adjacent to the canal and said that there was "limited, but not
conclusive" evidence that some toxic chemicals from the canal might still
be contaminating the neighborhood, despite government assurances to
the contrary. "With available information, it is not possible to demonstrate with certainty either that unsafe levels of toxic contamination do
or do not exist," the OTA study concluded.*

Several members of Congress, including Democratic Rep. John J. LaFalce, whose district included Love Canal, praised the OTA report for its objectivity and thoroughness. According to LaFalce, 182 families still lived in the Love Canal neighborhood, and 270 other families were on a waiting list to purchase homes there. LaFalce said he would suggest that people "not buy houses there at this juncture," but "would not say to those families who presently live there that they ought to move out."

Following are excerpts from "A Study of Cytogenetic Patterns in Persons Living Near the Love Canal," undertaken by researchers at the Centers for Disease Control, the Brookhaven National Laboratory and the Oak Ridge National Laboratory, released May 17, 1983. (Boldface headings in brackets have been added by Congressional Quarterly to highlight the organization of the text.):

Summary

Cytogenetic analyses (measurement of frequency of chromosomal aberrations and/or sister chromatid exchange (SCE)) were performed on specimens of peripheral blood from 46 residents or former residents of the residential area surrounding the Love Canal, a former dump site for chemical wastes in Niagara Falls, New York. Analyses were performed blindly with 44 matched control specimens drawn from persons living in another part of Niagara Falls.

Two sets of Love Canal participants were included. The first group consisted of 29 persons who had been living in 1978 in seven of 12 homes which directly adjoined the canal and in which testing of air, water, and soil showed elevated levels of chemicals spreading from the canal. The second group included 17 persons in whom cytogenetic analyses had been performed in 1980.

In neither group did frequencies of chromosomal aberrations (gaps, breaks, fragments, supernumerary acentrics, etc.) or of SCE differ significantly from the control levels. Karyotypes were normal in all specimens. These measures of chromosome damage took into account several possible causes of variation, including sex, cigarette smoking, history of playing on the canal site, or history of attending elementary school at a school adjoining the site. Cigarette smoking seemed to cause an increase in SCE frequency, a result observed elsewhere. Other factors, alone or in combination, were not associated with an increase in chromosome damage.

Introduction

Although improper disposal of toxic chemical wastes poses a clear risk for human health, the risk is not easily measured. Extensive studies at the Love Canal dump site in Niagara Falls, New York, giving particular attention to reproductive abnormalities and to cancer, have thus far defined no firm evidence of increased disease incidence or mortality. In the spring of 1980, results from an exploratory study of cytogenetic patterns raised questions regarding abnormal findings among residents of the Love Canal area. The present investigation was undertaken as a further, more complete test of the idea that exposure to toxic chemicals from the Love Canal dump might be associated with increased frequencies of chromosomal aberrations....

Methods

Selection of Participants

Participants in the study included two groups of residents or former residents of the Love Canal area with comparison groups selected from another section of Niagara Falls. One group of Love Canal participants (Group I) consisted of persons who in June 1978 had been living directly adjacent to the canal and in whose homes tests of basement air conducted by NYSDH [New York State Department of Health] in 1978 showed particularly high indices of chemical contamination potentially related to the canal. All 240 homes on the first two rings of homes surrounding the canal had been tested at that time, 97 on the first ring and 143 on the second. Each home was given a point rating based on three chemical determinations: the level of organic chemicals (chloroform, trichloroethylene, tetrachloroethylene, benzene, toluene, xylene, chlorobenzene, and chlorotoluene), the level of chlorotoluene alone, and the level of chlorobenzene alone. Chlorotoluene and chlorobenzene were chosen for special consideration since they are not usually found in consumer products and were therefore likely to represent migration of chemicals from the canal. A total of 43 homes (37 on the first ring and six on the second) received one or more points on a rating scale of zero to nine. The families who had been living as of June 1978 in 12 first ring homes which had a rating of three or greater were contacted for participation in the study. Each family who agreed to participate was matched to a family in a control census tract. For each family entering the study, the participation of all household members was sought. Partial family participation was accepted for inclusion in the study.

The control census tract was selected on the basis of socioeconomic similarity to the census tract containing the Love Canal.... The distance between the edge of the Love Canal census tract and the control census tract is 0.85 miles. Center to center, the inter-tract distance is 1.7 miles. Because of this distance, it is considered unlikely that persons in the control area would be exposed to airborne contaminants from Love Canal. No leaching from the Love Canal site into the control census tract seems possible given the distance involved and given the general results of environmental testing within the canal area. No dump sites have been identified in the control tract. . . .

The second group of Love Canal residents (Group II) consisted of all 36 persons originally tested in the EPA-supported cytogenetic study. Each person who agreed to participate was matched to a control participant selected from the control census tract described above, but from families other than those selected as controls for Group I. . . .

For Group I, 42 individuals were identified who had been living in the 12 selected canal area homes in June 1978. Of these, 30 persons from seven homes agreed to participate in the study. . . . The seven households containing 30 participants were matched to seven control households containing 26 individuals. Thus, 56 individuals entered the study in Group I and filled out questionnaires. Blood specimens were drawn from 55 of these persons (one canal participant chose to withdraw before blood was drawn). Cultures satisfactory for both aberration and sister chromatid exchange (SCE) analysis were prepared from 53 of the 55 participants. No cells analyzable for either aberration or SCE frequency were present in one control specimen and only for aberration frequency in another.

For Group II, 20 of the 36 eligible persons agreed to participate. (There were six couples among the group of 16 not participating.) These 20 were matched to 20 control participants, and these 40 individuals filled out questionnaires and had blood specimens drawn. Cultures satisfactory for both aberration and SEC analysis were prepared from 34 of the 40. . . .

[Results]

FREQUENCY OF BIRTH DEFECTS

Both Group I and Group II participants reported an increased frequency of a family history of birth defects when compared to their corresponding controls (eight of 29 Group I and zero of 25 Group I-controls; 13 of 17 Group II and five of 19 Group II-controls). This observation is confounded by residence of the child's mother during that pregnancy, by inclusion of disorders not generally classed as birth defects, and by multiple reporting of the same defect by different family members. In addition, medical confirmation of questionnaire responses was not performed. We rated each child born in all families since January 1, 1953, as "exposed" or "unexposed" according to the place of residence of the child's mother during that pregnancy. We then excluded as birth defects children reported to have "newborn jaundice", "pigeon toe", collapsed lungs, eczema, umbilical or other hernias, "cross-eyed", and cerebral palsy. After these adjustments, no presumed birth defects remained in Group I and only one in Group I-controls, a child with a hemangioma. . . . Eight children with presumed birth defects remained in Group II (two with deformed ears; two with phloric stenosis; and one each with three ears, a defective kidney, a collapsed mitral valve, and a "growth on the toe"), and five in Group II-controls (two with scoliosis, and one each with extra ribs, an overgrowth of bone, and a hearing loss). This apparent but not statistically significant increase in birth defect frequency in Group II ... must be viewed with caution in light of possible pre-existing selection bias.

REPRODUCIBILITY OF LABORATORY RESULTS

One laboratory scored 50% of all specimens for aberrations and 50.5% for SCE. This laboratory scored 27 of 64 (42%) Group I specimens and 24 of 38 (64%) Group II specimens for aberrations and similar percentages of specimens for SCE. This represents 43% of aberration specimens and 44% of SCE specimens from canal residents. These slight imbalances are chance occurrences because neither laboratory knew the origin of specimens. Within each group, the percentage of specimens from canal residents examined by one laboratory did not differ from that of controls examined by the same laboratory....

Chromosomal Aberrations

... The only statistically significant differences observed were the presence of fewer chromatid deletions and fewer chromatid lesions A in Group II than in matched controls. All other comparisons for Group II and all comparisons for Group I showed no significant differences between study participants and controls. Supernumerary acentric fragments were observed in small numbers in both Love Canal groups (nine specimens) and in both control groups (14 specimens). For neither Love Canal group did the frequency of such fragments differ significantly from the frequency in corresponding controls. In slides stained for chromosome differentiation, it was found that supernumerary acentrics occurred in both first and second division cells. Single metaphases containing shattered or pulverized chromosomes were recorded in a total of 11 specimens (three Group I and two Group II Love Canal participants and four controls).

Combining Groups I and II and their respective controls to achieve greater sample size and thus enhance sensitivity to detect group differences did not change these overall results. Such analysis necessarily combines participants who were selected for study by fundamentally different procedures, and it requires that statistical comparisons be made without regard to the matched selection of Group II controls.

Since no significant differences were seen between Group I and II participants and controls, all groups were combined to compare aberration frequencies by selected participant characteristics (history of play in the Love Canal area, sex, and current smoking status). No significant differences were seen with regard to history of play in the Love Canal area. Males had significantly more symmetrical translocations and proportion of rings and dicentrics with associated fragments than females. Females had significantly more non-supernumerary acentrics. Smokers had a significantly lower proportion of rings and dicentrics with associated fragments than non-smokers.

[Sister Chromatid Exchange]

Data comparing SCE frequencies by differing statistical approaches . . . [indicate that no] significant differences were found when Groups I and II were compared with their respective controls, separately or in combination. Combined comparison with respect to history of play in the Love Canal area showed a significant association between absence of such history and higher SCE frequencies for all statistical approaches used. No association was seen between SCE frequency and sex. A strong and highly significant association was present between current smoking and SCE frequency. Within each laboratory, scorers reporting higher mean SCE frequencies did not score a significantly greater percentage of controls than their counterparts reporting lower mean SCE frequencies. Scorer differences, therefore, do not account for the lack of association between mean SCE frequency and residence in the Love Canal area.

Current smoking, directly and strongly associated with SCE frequency, did not confound the significant inverse association between history of play in the Love Canal area and SCE frequency. . . . Nonsmokers who had played in the Love Canal area had a mean SCE frequency of 7.66; nonsmokers who had not played there had a mean SCE frequency of 8.42. Adjustment for current smoking status also did not reveal any association between SCE frequency, sex, and Love Canal residence (Groups I and II separately or combined). . . .

Comment

Any interpretation of the findings of this study must take into account the limitations imposed upon by imprecision in assessing chemical exposure and dose, by the nature of cytogenetic analysis, and by the design and sample size constraints of the study itself. No increase in abnormalities was found, with the methods used. This suggests that no specific relationship existed between exposure to chemical agents in the Love Canal area and increased frequency of chromosomal damage. In particular, no increased frequency of chromosomal aberrations was seen, including the category of supernumerary acentric fragments. There was no difference in the frequency of SCE between different study groups, although the previously reported elevation in SCE frequency among smokers was clearly demonstrated. . . .

The interpretation of these findings needs to be carefully considered. A fundamental problem is the fact that we have only general and indirect measures of exposure to canal chemicals, i.e., whether or not participants in the study had lived, played, or gone to school near the canal. It is not possible to assess exposure through tissue measurements of chemicals since the major chemicals in question are non-persistent in biologic systems and since exposure, in any case, occurred some time in the past. Lacking precise and objective measurement of individual exposure, the study has relied on histories of past residence and personal recollection of activities for groups of participants, many of whom had moved away from the exposure area over two years before. Objective laboratory evidence of exposure in the area is limited to environmental testing. The results of such testing do not suggest increased chemical levels in soil, air, or water except in the first two rings of homes surrounding the canal. By focusing on persons who had been living in homes on the first ring where environmental tests gave relatively high results, we have directed the study towards a high-risk population in which exposure to some extent could be objectively defined.

Against this background of imprecision in defining exposure are considerations of the way cytogenetic observations are made. Most important is the issue of reproducibility, the degree to which different microscopists duplicate each others' observations. Differences are to be expected, given the nature of microscopy. We have measured degree of observer variation in this study both between technologists in a given laboratory and between the two laboratories themselves. Although the amount of variation seen does not seem unusual for this kind of work, we have tried to minimize the effect of observer differences by giving equal weight to the results of different scorers for particular specimens. Any subjective observer bias, of course, was presumably eliminated from the study by use of blinding procedures. In order to establish a uniform interpretation of each cell recorded as abnormal by different observers, one individual in each laboratory confirmed all suspected abnormalities.

Limitations imposed by study design include issues of sample size and self-selection. The cost and time requirements of cytogenetic analysis dictated a relatively small sample size. We sought to counteract the small size by focusing on maximally exposed residents of the Love Canal area, and yet including as participants those persons who had been previously studied in 1980. Agreement to participate in the study seemed satisfactory given the delayed nature of the study (30 of 40 persons [75%] in Group I, and 20 of 36 [56%] in Group II). Participants in Group II, of course, had originally been studied as volunteers and therefore introduced an obvious element of self-selection into the study. One possible effect of this self-selection is illustrated by the greater frequency with which these particular participants reported occurrence of birth defects in their families. It is not unreasonable to suppose that these persons originally agreed to take part in the EPA-sponsored study because of particular health problems which they or their families had experienced, especially ones related to congenital abnormalities. Whatever may have governed their selection, however, does not appear to be linked to any increase in chromosomal damage as measured in the present study.

In addition to issues of exposure assessment, laboratory procedure, and study design, one must also consider the sensitivity of chemical assays for detecting relatively low exposures occurring over a period of time and perhaps ending some time prior to cytogenetic analysis. Investigations of chromosome damage, and of other subclinical biologic events, are undertaken in environmental exposure settings such as the Love Canal with the assumptions that environmental exposure causes chromosome damage and that damage persists and is detectable despite passage of time. Neither of these assumptions can be taken for granted. Although many kinds of chemicals do cause chromosome damage and some of these chemicals are present in the Love Canal, their action is clearly dose-dependent. It is not at all clear if the doses experienced by persons living near the canal can be considered great enough to have caused detectable chromosome effects. It is also uncertain whether damage leading to chromosome alterations, if it occurred, would have been of the sort which could persist in latent, non-stimulated peripheral blood lymphocytes. Chromosome alterations do persist over many years in lymphocytes following exposure to ionizing radiation. The same persistence, however, is not expected when exposure is to chemicals because of the mechanism of induction of alterations following exposure to most chemicals. Although the presence of an increase in chromosome alterations could indicate current exposure to chemical agents which cause chromosome damage, the absence of an increase does not indicate an absence of such exposure.

Finally, it must be stressed that, had evidence of increased chromosome damage been found in this study, it would still have been impossible to know whether those findings might correlate with or predict later occurrence of clinical illness. Although there are indirect reasons for thinking that chromosomal damage in lymphocytes may indicate a higher probability for an exposed group showing an increase in disorders like cancer and birth defects, no evidence directly establishing such links has yet been found for exposure to chemical agents, especially at the level of the individual. Further fundamental studies regarding the actions of chemicals in tissue may be needed before subclinical markers such as chromosome aberrations can be useful in making clinical predictions.

COURT ON TAX EXEMPTIONS
FOR DISCRIMINATORY SCHOOLS
May 24, 1983

By an 8-1 margin the Supreme Court ruled May 24 that private schools with racially discriminatory policies cannot qualify as tax-exempt organizations under the Internal Revenue Code. The decision involved two cases — Bob Jones University v. United States and Goldsboro Christian Schools, Inc. v. United States — and focused on a debate that began in 1970. At that time the Internal Revenue Service decided it no longer could justify the granting of tax-exempt status to private schools that racially discriminated. Such discrimination, the IRS reasoned, did not reflect the "charitable" concepts described by the code.

Writing for the Court, Chief Justice Warren E. Burger argued that "It would be wholly incompatible with the concepts underlying tax exemption to grant the benefit of tax-exempt status to racially discriminatory educational entities. . . . Whatever may be the rationale for such private schools' policies, and however sincere the rationale may be, racial discrimination in education is contrary to public policy."

Bob Jones University, a Christian fundamentalist school located in Greenville, S.C., admitted blacks but banned interracial dating or interracial marriage among students. Until 1975 it had refused admittance to all blacks.

Like Bob Jones University, Goldsboro Christian Schools in Goldsboro, N.C., said it believed the Bible prohibited cultural or biological mixing of races. As a rule it admitted only whites, although some children from mixed marriages had been accepted. Both Bob Jones and Goldsboro argued that the government was infringing upon their constitutional right to free exercise of religion in denying them tax-exempt status.

Tax Law and Public Policy

The cases centered on two other questions concerning the denial of tax exemptions: whether the IRS was interpreting federal tax law correctly and whether additional legislation was needed to deny the status. The Reagan administration, which had been expected to defend the IRS position, changed sides in January 1982 and sought new legislation.

Specifically, Section 501 (c) (3) of the Internal Revenue Code grants tax-exempt status to "corporations ... organized and operated exclusively for religious, charitable ... or educational purposes." Nowhere does it explicitly require that such corporations be non-discriminatory or in accord with established public policy.

According to the Supreme Court's ruling, however, there was "unmistakable evidence that, underlying all relevant parts of the Code, is the intent that entitlement to tax exemption depends on meeting certain common law standards of charity...."

"On the record before us, there can be no doubt as to the national policy ..." wrote Burger. "Indeed, it would be anomalous for the executive, legislative, and judicial branches to reach conclusions that add up to a firm public policy on racial discrimination, and at the same time have the IRS blissfully ignore what all three branches of the federal government had declared."

The Reagan administration argued that Congress had not authorized IRS to deny tax-exempt status to discriminatory schools. But members insisted that the new legislation sought by the White House was unnecessary. The Court cited congressional "non-action" on such bills as evidence that Congress agreed with the IRS policy. "In view of its prolonged and acute awareness of so important an issue, Congress' failure to act on the bills proposed on this subject provides added support for concluding that Congress acquiesced" in the IRS ruling, Burger wrote.

Rehnquist, Powell Views

Justice William H. Rehnquist, the lone dissenter, argued that the Court "should not legislate for Congress." He wrote, "Unlike the Court, I am convinced that Congress simply has failed to take this action and ... regardless of our view on the propriety of Congress' failure to legislate we are not constitutionally empowered to act for them."

Justice Lewis F. Powell Jr., although concurring with the majority, wrote that he was troubled by the extent to which the decision stressed the need for tax-exempt organizations to benefit the public interest. Such a viewpoint, he argued, "ignores the important role played by tax exemptions in encouraging diverse, indeed often sharply conflicting, activities and viewpoints." The authority to determine tax-exempt status was a power of Congress, Powell stressed, not the IRS or the judges.

Reactions to Decision

When asked about the Court decision, President Ronald Reagan stated simply, "We will obey the law." But at Bob Jones University, where flags flew at half-staff, reaction was more hostile. In a sermon in the school chapel, Rev. Bob Jones III, president of the university, said: "We're in a bad fix in America when eight evil old men and one vain and foolish woman can speak a verdict on American liberties." Civil rights groups, on the other hand, hailed the decision. Richard Larson of the American Civil Liberties Union said the decision was "so resounding that it provides a major embarrassment to . . . the Reagan administration."

Following are excerpts from the Supreme Court's May 24, 1983, decision in Bob Jones University v. United States and Goldsboro Christian Schools, Inc. v. United States, from the concurring opinion of Justice Lewis F. Powell Jr. and from the dissent by Justice William H. Rehnquist:

Nos. 81-3 and 81-1

In the Matter of Bob Jones University, Petitioner *v* United States Goldsboro Christian Schools, Inc., Petitioner *v* United States	On writs of certiorari to the United States Court of Appeals for the Fourth Circuit

[May 24, 1983]*

CHIEF JUSTICE BURGER delivered the opinion of the Court.

We granted certiorari to decide whether petitioners, nonprofit private schools that prescribe and enforce racially discriminatory admissions standards on the basis of religious doctrine, qualify as tax-exempt organizations under § 501 (c) (3) of the Internal Revenue Code of 1954.

---

* Together with No. 81-1, *Goldsboro Christian Schools, Inc.* v. *United States*, also on certiorari to the same court.

I

A

Until 1970, the Internal Revenue Service granted tax-exempt status to private schools, without regard to their racial admissions policies, under § 501 (c) (3) of the Internal Revenue Code, 26 U.S.C. § 501 (c) (3), and granted charitable deductions for contributions to such schools under § 170 of the Code, 26 U.S.C. § 170.

On January 12, 1970, a three-judge District Court for the District of Columbia issued a preliminary injunction prohibiting the IRS from according tax-exempt status to private schools in Mississippi that discriminated as to admissions on the basis of race. *Green* v. *Kennedy*, (D.D.C.), *app. dismissed sub nom. Cannon* v. *Green* (1970). Thereafter, in July 1970, the IRS concluded that it could "no longer legally justify allowing tax-exempt status [under § 501 (c) (3)] to private schools which practice racial discrimination." At the same time the IRS announced that it could not "treat gifts to such schools as charitable deductions for income tax purposes [under § 170]." By letter dated November 30, 1970, the IRS formally notified private schools, including those involved in this case, of this change in policy, "applicable to all private schools in the United States at all levels of education."

On June 30, 1971, the three-judge District Court issued its opinion on the merits of the Mississippi challenge. *Green* v. *Connally* (D.D.C.), *aff'd sub nom. Coit* v. *Green* (1971) *(per curiam)*. That court approved the IRS' amended construction of the Tax Code. The court also held that racially discriminatory private schools were not entitled to exemption under § 501 (c) (3) and that donors were not entitled to deductions for contributions to such schools under § 170. The court permanently enjoined the Commissioner of Internal Revenue from approving tax-exempt status for any school in Mississippi that did not publicly maintain a policy of nondiscrimination.

The revised policy on discrimination was formalized in Revenue Ruling 71-447, 1971-2 Cum. Bull. 230:

> "Both the courts and the Internal Revenue Service have long recognized that the statutory requirement of being 'organized and operated exclusively for religious, charitable, ... or educational purposes' was intended to express the basic common law concept [of 'charity']. . . . All charitable trusts, educational or otherwise, are subject to the requirement that the purpose of the trust may not be illegal or contrary to public policy."

Based on the "national policy to discourage racial discrimination in education," the IRS ruled that "a private school not having a racially nondiscriminatory policy as to students is not 'charitable' within the common law concepts. . . ."

The application of the IRS construction of these provisions to petitioners, two private schools with racially discriminatory admissions policies, is now before us.

B

No. 81-3, Bob Jones University v. United States

Bob Jones University is a nonprofit corporation located in Greenville, South Carolina. Its purpose is "to conduct an institution of learning . . . , giving special emphasis to the Christian religion and the ethics revealed in the Holy Scriptures." The corporation operates a school with an enrollment of approximately 5,000 students, from kindergarten through college and graduate school. Bob Jones University is not affiliated with any religious denomination, but is dedicated to the teaching and propagation of its fundamentalist Christian religious beliefs. It is both a religious and educational institution. Its teachers are required to be devout Christians, and all courses at the University are taught according to the Bible. Entering students are screened as to their religious beliefs, and their public and private conduct is strictly regulated by standards promulgated by University authorities.

The sponsors of the University genuinely believe that the Bible forbids interracial dating and marriage. To effectuate these views, Negroes were completely excluded until 1971. From 1971 to May 1975, the University accepted no applications for unmarried Negroes, but did accept applications from Negroes married within their race.

Following the decision of the United States Court of Appeals for the Fourth Circuit in *McCrary* v. *Runyon* (1976), prohibiting racial exclusion from private schools, the University revised its policy. Since May 29, 1975, the University has permitted unmarried Negroes to enroll; but a disciplinary rule prohibits interracial dating and marriage. That rule reads:

> *There is to be no interracial dating*
> 1. Students who are partners in an interracial marriage will be expelled.
> 2. Students who are members of or affiliated with any group or organization which holds as one of its goals or advocates interracial marriage will be expelled.
> 3. Students who date outside their own race will be expelled.
> 4. Students who espouse, promote, or encourage others to violate the University's dating rules and regulations will be expelled.

The University continues to deny admission to applicants engaged in an interracial marriage or known to advocate interracial marriage or dating.

Until 1970, the IRS extended tax-exempt status to Bob Jones University under § 501 (c) (3). By the letter of November 30, 1970, that followed the injunction issued in *Green* v. *Kennedy*, the IRS formally notified the University of the change in IRS policy, and announced its intention to challenge the tax-exempt status of private schools practicing racial discrimination in their admissions policies.

After failing to obtain an assurance of tax exemption through administrative means, the University instituted an action in 1971 seeking to enjoin the IRS from revoking the school's tax-exempt status. That suit culminated in *Bob Jones University* v. *Simon* (1974), in which this Court held that the Anti-Injunction Act of the Internal Revenue Code, 26 U.S.C. § 7421 (a), prohibited the University from obtaining judicial review by way of injunctive action before the assessment or collection of any tax.

Thereafter, on April 16, 1975, the IRS notified the University of the proposed revocation of its tax-exempt status. On January 19, 1976, the IRS officially revoked the University's tax-exempt status, effective as of December 1, 1970, the day after the University was formally notified of the change in IRS policy. The University subsequently filed returns under the Federal Unemployment Tax Act for the period from December 1, 1970, to December 31, 1975, and paid a tax totalling $21.00 on one employee for the calendar year of 1975. After its request for a refund was denied, the University instituted the present action, seeking to recover the $21.00 it had paid to the IRS. The Government counterclaimed for unpaid federal unemployment taxes for the taxable years 1971 through 1975, in the amount of $489,675.59, plus interest.

The United States District Court for the District of South Carolina held that revocation of the University's tax-exempt status exceeded the delegated powers of the IRS, was improper under the IRS rulings and procedures, and violated the University's rights under the Religion Clauses of the First Amendment. The court accordingly ordered the IRS to pay the University the $21.00 refund it claimed and rejected the IRS counterclaim.

The Court of Appeals for the Fourth Circuit, in a divided opinion, reversed. Citing *Green* v. *Connally*, with approval, the Court of Appeals concluded that § 501 (c) (3) must be read against the background of charitable trust law. To be eligible for an exemption under that section, an institution must be "charitable" in the common law sense, and therefore must not be contrary to public policy. In the court's view, Bob Jones University did not meet this requirement, since its "racial policies violated the clearly defined public policy, rooted in our Constitution, condemning racial discrimination and, more specifically, the government policy against subsidizing racial discrimination in education, public or private." The court held that the IRS acted within its statutory authority in revoking the University's tax-exempt status. Finally, the Court of Appeals rejected petitioner's arguments that the revocation of the tax exemption violated the Free Exercise and Establishment Clauses of the First Amendment. The case was remanded to the District Court with instructions to dismiss the University's claim for a refund and to reinstate the Government's counterclaim.

C

No. 81-1, Goldsboro Christian Schools, Inc. v. United States

Goldsboro Christian Schools is a nonprofit corporation located in Goldsboro, North Carolina. Like Bob Jones University, it was established "to conduct an institution of learning . . . , giving special emphasis to the Christian religion and the ethics revealed in the Holy scriptures." The school offers classes from kindergarten through high school, and since at least 1969 has satisfied the State of North Carolina's requirements for secular education in private schools. The school requires its high school students to take Bible-related courses, and begins each class with prayer.

Since its incorporation in 1963, Goldsboro Christian Schools has maintained a racially discriminatory admissions policy based upon its interpretation of the Bible. Goldsboro has for the most part accepted only Caucasians. On occasion, however, the school has accepted children from racially mixed marriages in which one of the parents is Caucasian.

Goldsboro never received a determination by the IRS that it was an organization entitled to tax exemption under § 501 (c) (3). Upon audit of Goldsboro's records for the years 1969 through 1972, the IRS determined that Goldsboro was not an organization described in § 501 (c) (3), and therefore was required to pay taxes under the Federal Insurance Contribution Act and the Federal Unemployment Tax Act.

Goldsboro paid the IRS $3,459.93 in withholding, social security, and unemployment taxes with respect to one employee for the years 1969 through 1972. Thereafter, Goldsboro filed a suit seeking refund of that payment, claiming that the school had been improperly denied § 501 (c) (3) exempt status. The IRS counterclaimed for $160,073.96 in unpaid social security and unemployment taxes for the years 1969 through 1972, including interest and penalties.

The District Court for the Eastern District of North Carolina decided the action on cross-motions for summary judgment. (E.D.N.C. 1977). In addressing the motions for summary judgment, the court assumed that Goldsboro's racially discriminatory admissions policy was based upon a sincerely held religious belief. The court nevertheless rejected Goldsboro's claim to tax-exempt status under § 501 (c) (3), finding that "private schools maintaining racially discriminatory admissions policies violate clearly declared federal policy and, therefore, must be denied the federal tax benefits flowing from qualification under Section 501 (c) (3)." The court also rejected Goldsboro's arguments that denial of tax-exempt status violated the Free Exercise and Establishment Clauses of the First Amendment. Accordingly, the court entered summary judgment for the Government on its counterclaim.

The Court of Appeals for the Fourth Circuit affirmed (CA4 Feb. 24, 1981). That court found an "identity for present purposes" between the *Goldsboro* case and the *Bob Jones University* case . . . and affirmed for the reasons set forth in *Bob Jones University.*

We granted certiorari in both cases (1981) and we affirm in each.

II

A

In Revenue Ruling 71-447, the IRS formalized the policy first announced in 1970, that § 170 and § 501 (c) (3) embrace the common law "charity" concept. Under that view, to qualify for a tax exemption pursuant to § 501 (c) (3), an institution must show, first, that it falls within one of the eight categories expressly set forth in that section, and second, that its activity is not contrary to settled public policy.

Section 501 (c) (3) provides that "[c]orporations ... organized and operated exclusively for religious, charitable ... or education purposes" are entitled to tax exemption. Petitioners argue that the plain language of the statute guarantees them tax-exempt status. They emphasize the absence of any language in the statute expressly requiring all exempt organizations to be "charitable" in the common law sense, and they contend that the disjunctive "or" separating the categories in § 501 (c) (3) precludes such a reading. Instead, they argue that if an institution falls within one or more of the specified categories it is automatically entitled to exemption, without regard to whether it also qualifies as "charitable." The Court of Appeals rejected that contention and concluded that petitioners' interpretation of the statute "tears section 501 (c) (3) from its roots." *United States* v. *Bob Jones University.*

It is a well-established canon of statutory construction that a court should go beyond the literal language of a statute if reliance on that language would defeat the plain purpose of the statute....

Section 501 (c) (3) therefore must be analyzed and construed within the framework of the Internal Revenue Code and against the background of the Congressional purposes. Such an examination reveals unmistakable evidence that, underlying all relevant parts of the Code, is the intent that entitlement to tax exemption depends on meeting certain common law standards of charity — namely, that an institution seeking tax-exempt status must serve a public purpose and not be contrary to established public policy.

This "charitable" concept appears explicitly in § 170 of the Code. That section contains a list of organizations virtually identical to that contained in § 501 (c) (3). It is apparent that Congress intended that list to have the same meaning in both sections. In § 170, Congress used the list of organizations in defining the term "charitable contributions." On its face, therefore, § 170 reveals that Congress' intention was to provide tax benefits to organizations serving charitable purposes. The form of § 170 simply makes plain what common sense and history tell us: in enacting both § 170 and § 501 (c) (3), Congress sought to provide tax benefits to charitable organizations, to encourage the development of private institutions that serve a useful public purpose or supplement or take the place of public institutions of the same kind.

Tax exemptions for certain institutions thought beneficial to the social order of the country as a whole, or to a particular community, are deeply rooted in our history, as in that of England. The origins of such exemptions lie in the special privileges that have long been extended to charitable trusts.

More than a century ago, this Court announced the caveat that is critical in this case:

"[I]t has now become an established principle of American law, that courts of chancery will sustain and protect ... a gift ... to public charitable uses, *provided the same is consistent with local laws and public policy....*" *Perin* v. *Carey* (1861) (emphasis added).

Soon after that, in 1878, the Court commented:

"A charitable use, *where neither law nor public policy forbids,* may be applied to almost any thing *that tends to promote the well-doing and well-being of social man.*" *Ould* v. *Washington Hospital for Foundlings* (1878) (emphasis added)....

In 1891, in a restatement of the English law of charity which has long been recognized as a leading authority in this country, Lord MacNaghten stated:

" 'Charity' in its legal sense comprises four principal divisions: trusts for the relief of poverty; *trusts for the advancement of education;* trusts for the advancement of religion; and trusts for *other purposes beneficial to the community,* not falling under any of the preceding heads." *Commissioners* v. *Pensel,* [1891] (emphasis added)....

These statements clearly reveal the legal background against which Congress enacted the first charitable exemption statute in 1894: charities were to be given preferential treatment because they provide a benefit to society.

What little floor debate occurred on the charitable exemption provisions of the 1894 Act and similar sections of later statutes leaves no doubt that Congress deemed the specified organizations entitled to tax benefits because they served desirable public purposes.... In floor debate on a similar provision in 1917, for example, Senator Hollis articulated the rationale:

"For every dollar that a man contributes to these public charities, educational, scientific, or otherwise, the public gets 100 percent."...

In enacting the Revenue Act of 1938, Congress expressly reconfirmed this view with respect to the charitable deduction provision:

"The exemption from taxation of money and property devoted to charitable and other purposes is based on the theory that the Government is compensated for the loss of revenue by its relief from financial burdens which would otherwise have to be met by appropriations from other public funds, and by the benefits resulting from the promotion of the general welfare."

A corollary to the public benefit principle is the requirement, long recognized in the law of trusts, that the purpose of a charitable trust may not be illegal or violate established public policy. In 1861, this Court stated that a public charitable use must be "consistent with local laws and public policy," *Perin* v. *Carey*. Modern commentators and courts have echoed that view....

When the Government grants exemptions or allows deductions all taxpayers are affected; the very fact of the exemption or deduction for the donor means that other taxpayers can be said to be indirect and vicarious "donors." Charitable exemptions are justified on the basis that the exempt entity confers a public benefit — a benefit which the society or the community may not itself choose or be able to provide, or which supplements and advances the work of public institutions already supported by tax revenues. History buttresses logic to make clear that, to warrant exemption under § 501 (c) (3), an institution must fall within a category specified in that section and must demonstrably serve and be in harmony with the public interest. The institution's purpose must not be so at odds with the common community conscience as to undermine any public benefit that might otherwise be conferred.

B

We are bound to approach these questions with full awareness that determinations of public benefit and public policy are sensitive matters with serious implications for the institutions affected; a declaration that a given institution is not "charitable" should be made only where there can be no doubt that the activity involved is contrary to a fundamental public policy. But there can no longer be any doubt that racial discrimination in education violates deeply and widely accepted views of elementary justice. Prior to 1954, public education in many places still was conducted under the pall of *Plessy* v. *Ferguson* (1896); racial segregation in primary and secondary education prevailed in many parts of the country.... This Court's decision in *Brown* v. *Board of Education* (1954), signalled an end to that era. Over the past quarter of a century, every pronouncement of this Court and myriad Acts of Congress and Executive Orders attest a firm national policy to prohibit racial segregation and discrimination in public education.

An unbroken line of cases following *Brown* v. *Board of Education* establishes beyond doubt this Court's view that racial discrimination in education violates a most fundamental national public policy, as well as rights of individuals.

> "The right of a student not to be segregated on racial grounds in schools ... is indeed so fundamental and pervasive that it is embraced in the concept of due process of law." *Cooper* v. *Aaron* (1958).

In *Norwood* v. *Harrison* (1973), we dealt with a non-public institution:

> "[A] private school — even one that discriminates — fulfills an important education function; *however, ... [that] legitimate educational function cannot be isolated from discriminatory practices ... [D]iscriminatory treatment exerts a pervasive influence on the entire educational process."* (Emphasis added)....

Congress in Titles IV and VI of the Civil Rights Act of 1964, clearly expressed its agreement that racial discrimination in education violates a fundamental public policy. Other sections of that Act, and numerous enactments since then, testify to the public policy against racial discrimination....

The Executive Branch has consistently placed its support behind eradication of racial discrimination. Several years before this Court's decision in *Brown* v. *Board of Education*, President Truman issued Executive Orders prohibiting racial discrimination in federal employment decisions and in classifications for the Selective Service. In 1957, President Eisenhower employed military forces to ensure compliance with federal standards in school desegregation programs. And in 1962, President Kennedy announced:

> "[T]he granting of federal assistance for . . . housing and related facilities from which Americans are excluded because of their race, color, creed, or national origin is unfair, unjust, and inconsistent with the public policy of the United States as manifested in its Constitution and laws." . . .

Few social or political issues in our history have been more vigorously debated and more extensively ventilated than the issue of racial discrimination, particularly in education. Given the stress and anguish of the history of efforts to escape from the shackles of the "separate but equal" doctrine of *Plessy* v. *Ferguson*, it cannot be said that educational institutions that, for whatever reasons, practice racial discrimination, are institutions exercising "beneficial and stabilizing influences in community life." *Walz* v. *Tax Comm'n* (1970), or should be encouraged by having all taxpayers share in their support by way of special tax status.

There can thus be no question that the interpretation of § 170 and § 501 (c) (3) announced by the IRS in 1970 was correct. That it may be seen as belated does not undermine its soundness. It would be wholly incompatible with the concepts underlying tax exemption to grant the benefit of tax-exempt status to racially discriminatory educational entities, which "exer[t] a pervasive influence on the entire educational process." *Norwood* v. *Harrison*. Whatever may be the rationale for such private schools' policies, and however sincere the rationale may be, racial discrimination in education is contrary to public policy. Racially discriminatory educational institutions cannot be viewed as conferring a public benefit within the "charitable" concept discussed earlier, or within the Congressional intent underlying § 170 and § 50 1(c) (3).

C

Petitioners contend that, regardless of whether the IRS properly concluded that racially discriminatory private schools violate public policy, only Congress can alter the scope of § 170 and § 501 (c) (3). Petitioners accordingly argue that the IRS overstepped its lawful bounds in issuing its 1970 and 1971 rulings.

Yet ever since the inception of the tax code, Congress has seen fit to vest in those administering the tax laws very broad authority to interpret those laws. In an area as complex as the tax system, the agency Congress vests with administrative responsibility must be able to exercise its authority to meet changing conditions and new problems. Indeed as early as 1918,

Congress expressly authorized the Commissioner "to make all needful rules and regulations for the enforcement" of the tax laws. The same provision, so essential to efficient and fair administration of the tax laws, has appeared in tax codes every since ... and this Court has long recognized the primary authority of the IRS and its predecessors in construing the Internal Revenue Code, see, *e.g., Commissioner* v. *Portland Cement Co.* (1981); *United States* v. *Correll* (1967); *Boske* v. *Comingore* (1900)....

In § 170 and § 501 (c) (3), Congress has identified categories of traditionally exempt institutions and has specified certain additional requirements for tax exemption. Yet the need for continuing interpretation of those statutes is unavoidable. For more than 60 years, the IRS and its predecessors have constantly been called upon to interpret these and comparable provisions, and in doing so have referred consistently to principles of charitable trust law. In Treas. Reg. 45, art. 517 (1) (1921), for example, the IRS denied charitable exemptions on the basis of proscribed political activity before the Congress itself added such conduct as a disqualifying element. In other instances, the IRS has denied charitable exemptions to otherwise qualified entities because they served too limited a class of people and thus did not provide a truly "public" benefit under the common law test.... Some years before the issuance of the rulings challenged in these cases, the IRS also ruled that contributions to community recreational facilities would not be deductible and that the facilities themselves would not be entitled to tax-exempt status, unless those facilities were open to all on a racially nondiscriminatory basis.... These rulings reflect the Commissioner's continuing duty to interpret and apply the Internal Revenue Code. See also *Textile Mills Securities Corp.* v. *Commissioner* (1941).

Guided, of course, by the Code, the IRS has the responsibility, in the first instance, to determine whether a particular entity is "charitable" for purposes of § 170 and § 501 (c) (3). This in turn may necessitate later determinations of whether given activities so violate public policy that the entities involved cannot be deemed to provide a public benefit worthy of "charitable" status. We emphasize, however, that these sensitive determinations should be made only where there is no doubt that the organization's activities violate fundamental public policy.

On the record before us, there can be no doubt as to the national policy. In 1970, when the IRS first issued the ruling challenged here, the position of all three branches of the Federal Government was unmistakably clear. The correctness of the Commissioner's conclusion that a racially discriminatory private school "is not 'charitable' within the common law concepts reflected in ... the Code" is wholly consistent with what Congress, the Executive and the courts had repeatedly declared before 1970. Indeed, it would be anomalous for the Executive, Legislative and Judicial Branches to reach conclusions that add up to a firm public policy on racial discrimination, and at the same time have the IRS blissfully ignore what all three branches of the Federal Government had declared. Clearly an educational institution engaging in practices affirmatively at odds with this declared position of the whole government cannot be seen as exercising a "beneficial and stabilizing influenc[e] in community life," *Walz* v. *Tax Comm'n*, and is not "charitable," within the meaning of § 170 and § 501 (c) (3). We therefore hold that the IRS did not exceed its authority when it announced its interpretation of § 170 and § 501 (c) (3) in 1970 and 1971.

[Section D Omitted]

III

Petitioners contend that, even if the Commissioner's policy is valid as to nonreligious private schools, that policy cannot constitutionally be applied to schools that engage in racial discrimination on the basis of sincerely held religious beliefs. As to such schools, it is argued that the IRS construction of § 170 and § 501 (c)(3) violates their free exercise rights under the Religion Clauses of the First Amendment. This contention presents claims not heretofore considered by this Court in precisely this context.

This Court has long held the Free Exercise Clause of the First Amendment an absolute prohibition against governmental regulation of religious beliefs, *Wisconsin* v. *Yoder* (1972); *Sherbert* v. *Verner* (1963); *Cantwell* v. *Connecticut* (1940). As interpreted by this Court, moreover, the Free Exercise Clause provides substantial protection for lawful conduct grounded in religious belief, see *Wisconsin* v. *Yoder*; *Thomas* v. *Review Board of the Indiana Emp. Security Div.* (1981); *Sherbert* v. *Verner*. However, "[n]ot all burdens on religion are unconstitutional. . . . The state may justify a limitation on religious liberty by showing that it is essential to accomplish an overriding governmental interest." *United States* v. *Lee* (1982). See, *e.g.*, *McDaniel* v. *Paty* (1978); *Wisconsin* v. *Yoder*; *Gillette* v. *United States* (1971).

On occasion this Court has found certain governmental interests so compelling as to allow even regulations prohibiting religiously based conduct. In *Prince* v. *Massachusetts* (1944), for example, the Court held that neutrally cast child labor laws prohibiting sale of printed materials on public streets could be applied to prohibit children from dispensing religious literature. The Court found no constitutional infirmity in "excluding [Jehovah's Witness children] from doing there what no other children may do." . . . Denial of tax benefits will inevitably have a substantial impact on the operation of private religious schools, but will not prevent those schools from observing their religious tenets.

The governmental interest at stake here is compelling. As discussed in Part II (B), the Government has a fundamental, overriding interest in eradicating racial discrimination in education — discrimination that prevailed, with official approval, for the first 165 years of this Nation's history. That governmental interest substantially outweighs whatever burden denial of tax benefits places on petitioners' exercise of their religious beliefs. The interests asserted by petitioners cannot be accommodated with that compelling governmental interest . . . and no "less restrictive means" . . . are available to achieve the governmental interest.

IV

The remaining issue is whether the IRS properly applied its policy to these petitioners. Petitioner Goldsboro Christian Schools admits that it "maintain[s] racially discriminatory policies," but seeks to justify those policies on grounds we have fully discussed. The IRS properly denied tax-exempt status to Goldsboro Christian Schools.

Petitioner Bob Jones University, however, contends that it is not racially discriminatory. It emphasizes that it now allows all races to enroll, subject only to its restrictions on the conduct of all students, including its prohibitions of association between men and women of different races, and of interracial marriage. Although a ban on intermarriage or interracial dating applies to all races, decisions of this Court firmly establish that discrimination on the basis of racial affiliation and association is a form of racial discrimination, see, *e.g., Loving* v. *Virginia* (1967); *McLaughlin* v. *Florida* (1964); *Tillman* v. *Wheaton-Haven Recreation Ass'n* (1973). We therefore find that the IRS properly applied Revenue Ruling 71-447 to Bob Jones University.

The judgments of the Court of Appeals are, accordingly,

Affirmed.

JUSTICE POWELL, concurring in part and concurring in the judgment.

. . . With all respect, I am unconvinced that the critical question in determining tax-exempt status is whether an individual organization provides a clear "public benefit" as defined by the Court. Over 106,000 organizations filed § 501 (c) (3) returns in 1981. I find it impossible to believe that all or even most of those organizations could prove that they "demonstrably serve and [are] in harmony with the public interest" or that they are "beneficial and stabilizing influences in community life." Nor I am prepared to say that petitioners, because of their racially discriminatory policies, necessarily contribute nothing of benefit to the community. It is clear from the substantially secular character of the curricula and degrees offered that petitioners provide educational benefits.

Even more troubling to me is the element of conformity that appears to inform the Court's analysis. The Court asserts that an exempt organization must "demonstrably serve and be in harmony with the public interest," must have a purpose that comports with "the common community conscience," and must not act in a manner "affirmatively at odds with [the] declared position of the whole government." Taken together, these passages suggest that the primary function of a tax-exempt organization is to act on behalf of the Government in carrying out governmentally approved policies. In my opinion, such a view of § 501 (c) (3) ignores the important role played by tax exemptions in encouraging diverse, indeed often sharply conflicting, activities and viewpoints. As JUSTICE BRENNAN has observed, private, nonprofit groups receive tax exemptions because "each group contributes to the diversity of association, viewpoint, and enterprise essential to a vigorous, pluralistic society." *Walz* [v. *Tax Comm'n* (1970)] (BRENNAN, J., concurring). Far from representing an effort to reinforce any perceived "common community conscience," the provision of tax exemptions to nonprofit groups is one indispensable means of limiting the influence of governmental orthodoxy on important areas of community life. Given the importance of our tradition of pluralism, "[t]he interest in preserving an area of untrammeled choice for private philanthropy is very great." *Jackson* v. *Statler Foundation* (CA2 1974) (Friendly, J., dissenting from denial of reconsideration en banc).

I do not suggest that these considerations always are or should be dispositive. Congress, of course, may find that some organizations do not warrant tax-exempt status. In this case I agree with the Court that Congress has determined that the policy against racial discrimination in education should override the countervailing interest in permitting unorthodox private behavior.

I would emphasize, however, that the balancing of these substantial interests is for *Congress* to perform. I am unwilling to join any suggestion that the Internal Revenue Service is invested with authority to decide which public policies are sufficiently "fundamental" to require denial of tax exemptions. Its business is to administer laws designed to produce revenue for the Government, not to promote "public policy." . . .

JUSTICE REHNQUIST, dissenting.

The Court points out that there is a strong national policy in this country against racial discrimination. To the extent that the Court states that Congress in furtherance of this policy could deny tax-exempt status to educational institutions that promote racial discrimination, I readily agree. But, unlike the Court, I am convinced that Congress simply has failed to take this action, and as this Court has said over and over again, regardless of our view on the propriety of Congress' failure to legislate we are not constitutionally empowered to act for them.

In approaching this statutory construction question the Court quite adeptly avoids the statute it is construing. This I am sure is no accident, for there is nothing in the language of § 501 (c) (3) that supports the result obtained by the Court. Section 501 (c) (3) provides tax-exempt status for:

> "Corporations, and any community chest, fund, or foundation, organized and operated exclusively for religious, charitable, scientific, testing for public safety, literary, or educational purposes, or to foster national or international amateur sports competition (but only if no part of its activities involve the provision of athletic facilities or equipment), or for the prevention of cruelty to children or animals, no part of the net earnings of which inures to the benefit of any private shareholder or individual, no substantial part of the activities of

> which is carrying on propaganda, or otherwise attempting, to influence legislation (except as otherwise provided in subsection (h)), and which does not participate in, or intervene in (including the publishing or distributing of statements), any political campaign on behalf of any candidate for public office."

With undeniable clarity, Congress has explicitly defined the requirements for § 501 (c) (3) status. An entity must be (1) a corporation, or community chest, fund, or foundation, (2) organized for one of the eight enumerated purposes, (3) operated on a nonprofit basis, and (4) free from involvement in lobbying activities and political campaigns. Nowhere is there to be found some additional, undefined public policy requirement.

The Court first seeks refuge from the obvious reading of § 501 (c) (3) by turning to § 170 of the Internal Revenue Code which provides a tax deduction for contributions made to § 501 (c) (3) organizations. In setting forth the general rule, § 170 states:

> "There shall be allowed as a deduction any charitable contribution (as defined in subsection (c)) payment of which is made without the taxable year. A charitable contribution shall be allowable as a deduction only if verified under regulations prescribed by the Secretary."

The Court seizes the words "charitable contribution" and with little discussion concludes that "[o]n its face, therefore, § 170 reveals that Congress' intention was to provide tax benefits to organizations serving charitable purposes," intimating that this implies some unspecified common law charitable trust requirement.

The Court would have been well advised to look to subsection (c) where, as § 170 (a) (1) indicates, Congress has defined a "charitable contribution":

> "For purposes of this section, the term 'charitable contribution' means a contribution or gift to or for the use of . . . [a] corporation, trust, or community chest, fund, or foundation . . . organized and operated exclusively for religious, charitable, scientific, literary, or educational purposes, or to foster national or international amateur sports competition (but only if no part of its activities involve the provision of athletic facilities or equipment), or for the prevention of cruelty to children or animals; . . . no part of the net earnings of which inures to the benefit of any private shareholder or individual; and . . . which is not disqualified for tax exemption under section 501 (c) (3) by reason of attempting to influence legislation, and which does not participate in, or intervene in (including the publishing or distributing of statements), any political campaign on behalf of any candidate for public office."

Plainly, § 170 (c) simply tracks the requirements set forth in § 501 (c) (3). Since § 170 is no more than a mirror of § 501 (c) (3) and, as the Court points out, § 170 followed § 501 (c) (3) by more than two decades, it is at best of little usefulness in finding the meaning of § 501 (c) (3).

Making a more fruitful inquiry, the Court next turns to the legislative history of § 501 (c) (3) and finds that Congress intended in that statute to offer a tax benefit to organizations that Congress believed were providing a public benefit. I certainly agree. But then the Court leaps to the conclusion that this history is proof Congress intended that an organization seeking § 501(c)(3) status "must fall within a category specified in that section *and*

must demonstrably serve and be in harmony with the public interest."
([E]mphasis added.) To the contrary, I think that the legislative history of
§ 501 (c)(3) unmistakably makes clear that *Congress has decided* what
organizations are serving a public purpose and providing a public benefit
within the meaning of § 501 (c)(3) and has clearly set forth in § 501 (c)(3)
the characteristics of such organizations. . . .

. . . Almost a century of statutory history proves that Congress itself
intended to decide what § 501 (c)(3) requires. . . . The IRS certainly is
empowered to adopt regulations for the enforcement of these specified
requirements, and the courts have authority to resolve challenges to the
IRS's exercise of this power, but Congress has left it to neither the IRS nor
the courts to select or add to the requirements of § 501 (c)(3).

The Court suggests that unless its new requirement be added to
§ 501 (c)(3), nonprofit organizations formed to teach pickpockets and
terrorists would necessarily acquire tax exempt status. Since the Court
does not challenge the characterization of *petitioners* as "educational"
institutions within the meaning of § 501 (c)(3), and in fact states several
times in the course of its opinion that petitioners *are* educational institutions, it is difficult to see how this argument advances the Court's
reasoning for disposing of petitioners' cases.

But simply because I reject the Court's heavy-handed creation of the
requirement that an organization, seeking § 501 (c)(3) status must "serve
and be in harmony with the public interest" does not mean that I would
deny to the IRS the usual authority to adopt regulations further explaining
what Congress meant by the term "educational." The IRS has fully
exercised that authority. . . . I have little doubt that neither the "Fagin
School for Pickpockets" nor a school training students for guerrilla warfare
and terrorism in other countries would meet the definitions contained in
the regulations. . . .

▼ ▼ ▼

WILLIAMSBURG ECONOMIC SUMMIT MEETING
May 29, 30, 1983

A *"demonstration of unity" was the phrase Reagan administration aides used to describe the ninth annual economic summit meeting of government leaders of the major Western industrialized nations, held at Colonial Williamsburg, Va., May 28-30. The leaders from Britain, Canada, France, Italy, Japan, the United States and West Germany agreed to pursue non-inflationary economic growth and seek improvements in the international trading and financial systems. An equally important item on the agenda was the issue of military security.*

Unlike the previous conference, held in France at Versailles in June 1982, the group was successful in avoiding open policy rifts and political discord. (Versailles summit, Historic Documents of 1982, p. 469)

National Security: Common Front

A joint statement on security issues, read by Secretary of State George P. Shultz, was viewed as a major achievement for the U.S. delegation. The statement was a show of Western political unity toward the U.S.S.R. in light of the arms control negotiation talks under way in Geneva. The statement reaffirmed the U.S.-West European commitment to proceed with deployment of intermediate-range nuclear missiles in Europe by the end of 1983 if the U.S.-Soviet negotiations on intermediate-range nuclear missile forces (INF) failed to secure an accord. The statement called upon ". . . the Soviet Union to contribute constructively to the success of the negotiations." It also warned Moscow not to try to divide the West

". . . by proposing inclusion of the deterrent forces of third countries. . . ."
This referred to the French and British weapons systems, which the
North Atlantic Treaty Organization (NATO) allies maintained were
outside NATO's direct control and therefore not to be counted in the INF
talks. The statement also said security issues "must be approached on a
global basis," a phrase sought by Prime Minister Yasuhiro Nakasone of
Japan, which was not a member of the NATO security alliance.

Difficult Economic Problems

The declaration on economic recovery was written by the leaders and
their ministers of state and finance during the three-day meeting and did
not give the Reagan administration the same clear endorsement on
economic strategy that it received on nuclear policy. President Ronald
Reagan announced the declaration May 30.

Foreign officials felt that Reagan held an overly optimistic view that
the world economy was on the road to recovery. They also rejected the
theory that an American economic upturn alone was sufficient to spur
international recovery. But all six foreign leaders agreed with Reagan
that maintaining growth without re-igniting inflation was a major
priority.

In general terms the nations agreed to ". . . pursue appropriate
monetary and budgetary policies that will be conducive to low inflation,
reduced interest rates, higher productive investment and greater employ-
ment opportunities, particularly for the young." Few specific proposals
were presented, however, because the leaders disagreed on the means to
achieve these goals.

In the view of America's allies, U.S. budget deficits absorbed almost all
of the personal savings in the United States and represented an enor-
mous drain on the world's supply of money and credit. If the Federal
Reserve accommodated the government's demand for credit by creating
more money, inflation resulted. But if the Fed refused to accommodate,
the increased demand drove up the price of money — interest rates.

It was this phenomenon, the foreign leaders argued, that had kept U.S.
"real" interest rates — the interest rate minus the inflation rate —
nearly twice as high as real interest rates overseas. So long as the
economy still was deep in recession, the demand for money and credit
remained relatively low. But anticipating a credit squeeze as the economy
recovered, lenders continued to demand high returns.

High U.S. interest rates had a serious effect on foreign nations. A
promise of bigger returns drew huge amounts of money out of those
countries and into the United States, draining funds needed by foreign
nations for investment. The demand for dollars rose while the demand for
other currencies fell, strengthening the dollar's exchange rate and weak-

ening foreign currencies. With many of their imports — particularly oil — denominated in dollars, the increase in the dollar's value fueled inflation in foreign nations.

High U.S. interest rates also exacerbated the debt problem of developing nations such as Brazil and Argentina, drastically raising the cost of their debt and decreasing their ability to pay it back. That, in turn, threatened world recovery.

The Reagan administration reluctantly conceded that U.S. interest rates were a problem but insisted that budget deficits were not to blame.

Foreign Exchange Rates, Other Issues

The spirit of compromise also affected another issue — foreign exchange rates. French President Francois Mitterand had called for a new Bretton Woods conference like the one establishing the exchange rate regime that prevailed from 1944-1971. The other nations interpreted the French president's comments as a plea for returning to fixed exchange rates, a prospect that, whatever its nostalgic appeal, was viewed as impractical by most of the summit leaders. But soon after arriving in Williamsburg May 28, Mitterand told President Reagan that the foreign press had misinterpreted his position. He was not calling for a return to fixed exchange rates; he merely was expressing a desire that the nations renew the spirit of the Bretton Woods accord in their attempts to sort out the world's monetary problems. The French president acquiesced to a watered-down commitment in the final statement to "consider the part which might, in due course, be played in [exchange rate stabilization efforts] by a high-level monetary conference."

In addition to addressing deficits and interest and exchange rates, the statement called for a "halt to protectionism" and, as recovery proceeded, the "dismantling [of] trade barriers."

The declaration also called for "intervention in exchange markets in instances where it is agreed that such intervention would be helpful" in stabilizing exchange rates, although it reaffirmed each nation's "freedom to operate independently."

In an annex to the declaration, the leaders agreed to strengthen the mechanism established at the Versailles summit in 1982 for the surveillance of the economic politics of five of the summit nations — the United States, Japan, France, West Germany and the United Kingdom — in an effort to encourage greater "convergence," or consistency, in their economic policies and performance.

Following are the texts of the Joint Statement on Security Issues, read by Secretary of State George P. Shultz May 29, 1983, and the Declaration on Economic Recovery, an-

nounced by President Ronald Reagan May 30, 1983, follow-
ing the Williamsburg, Va., summit meeting of the leaders of
Britain, Canada, France, Italy, Japan, the United States
and West Germany:

JOINT STATEMENT ON SECURITY ISSUES

1. As leaders of our seven countries, it is our first duty to defend the freedom and justice on which our democracies are based. To this end, we shall maintain sufficient military strength to deter any attack, to counter any threat, and to ensure the peace. Our arms will never be used except in response to aggression.

2. We wish to achieve lower levels of arms through serious arms control negotiations. With this statement, we reaffirm our dedication to the search for peace and meaningful arms reductions. We are ready to work with the Soviet Union to this purpose and call upon the Soviet Union to work with us.

3. Effective arms control agreements must be based on the principle of equality and must be verifiable. Proposals have been put forward from the Western side to achieve positive results in various international negotia-tions: on strategic weapons (START), on intermediate-range nuclear missiles (INF), on chemical weapons, on reduction of forces in Central Europe (MBFR), and a Conference on Disarmament in Europe (CDE).

4. We believe that we must continue to pursue these negotiations with impetus and urgency. In the area of INF, in particular, we call upon the Soviet Union to contribute constructively to the success of the negotia-tions. Attempts to divide the West by proposing inclusion of the deterrent forces of third countries, such as those of France and the United Kingdom, will fail. Consideration of these systems has no place in the INF negotiations.

5. Our nations express the strong wish that a balanced INF agreement be reached shortly. Should this occur, the negotiations will determine the level of deployment. It is well known that should this not occur, the countries concerned will proceed with the planned deployment of the U.S. systems in Europe at the end of 1983.

6. Our nations are united in efforts for arms reductions and will continue to carry out thorough and intensive consultations. The security of our countries is indivisible and must be approached on a global basis. Attempts to avoid serious negotiation by seeking to influence public opinion in our countries will fail.

7. We commit ourselves to devote our full political resources to reducing the threat of war. We have a vision of a world in which the shadow of war has been lifted from all mankind, and we are determined to pursue that vision.

DECLARATION ON ECONOMIC RECOVERY

Our nations are united in their dedication to democracy, individual freedom, creativity, moral purpose, human dignity, and personal and cultural development. It is to preserve, sustain, and extend these shared values that our prosperity is important.

The recession has put our societies through a severe test, but they have proved resilient. Significant success has been achieved in reducing inflation and interest rates; there have been improvements in productivity; and we now clearly see signs of recovery.

Nevertheless, the industrialized democracies continue to face the challenge of ensuring that the recovery materializes and endures, in order to reverse a decade of cumulative inflation and reduce unemployment. We must all focus on achieving and maintaining low inflations, and reducing interest rates from their present too-high levels. We renew our commitment to reduce structural budget deficits, in particular, by limiting the growth of expenditures.

We recognize that we must act together and that we must pursue a balanced set of policies that take into account and exploit relationships between growth, trade, and finance, in order that recovery may spread to all countries, developed and developing alike.

In pursuance of these objectives, we have agreed as follows:

(1) Our governments will pursue appropriate monetary and budgetary policies that will be conducive to low inflation, reduced interest rates, higher productive investment and greater employment opportunities, particularly for the young.

(2) The consultation process initiated at Versailles will be enhanced to promote convergence of economic performance in our economies and greater stability of exchange rates, on the lines indicated in an annex to this Declaration. We agree to pursue closer consultations on policies affecting exchange markets and on market conditions. While retaining our freedom to operate independently, we are willing to undertake coordinated intervention in exchange markets in instances where it is agreed that such intervention would be helpful.

(3) We commit ourselves to halt protectionism, and as recovery proceeds to reverse it by dismantling trade barriers. We intend to consult within appropriate existing fora on ways to implement and monitor this commitment. We shall give impetus to resolving current trade problems. We will actively pursue the current work programs in the General Agreement on Tariffs and Trade (GATT) and Organization for Economic Cooperation and Development, including trade in services and in high technology products. We should work to achieve further trade liberalization negotiations in the GATT, with particular emphasis on expanding trade with and among developing countries. We have agreed to continue consultations on proposals for a new negotiating round in the GATT.

(4) We view with concern the international financial situation, and especially the debt burdens of many developing nations. We agree to a

511

strategy based on: effective adjustment and development policies by debtor nations; adequate private and official financing; more open markets; and worldwide economic recovery. We will seek early ratification of the increases in resources for the International Monetary Fund and the General Arrangements to Borrow. We encourage closer cooperation and timely sharing of information among countries and the international institutions, in particular between the International Monetary Fund (IMF), the International Bank for Reconstruction and Development (BRD), and the GATT.

(5) We have invited Ministers of Finance, in consultation with the Managing Director of the IMF, to define the conditions for improving the international monetary system and to consider the part which might, in due course, be played in this process by a high-level international monetary conference.

(6) The weight of the recession has fallen very heavily on developing countries and we are deeply concerned about their recovery. Restoring sound economic growth while keeping our markets open is crucial. Special attention will be given to the flow of resources, in particular official development assistance, to poorer countries, and for food and energy production, both bilaterally and through appropriate international institutions. We reaffirm our commitments to provide agreed funding levels for the International Development Association. We welcome the openness to dialogue which the developing countries evinced at the recent conferences of the Non-Aligned Movement in New Delhi and the Group of 77 in Buenos Aires, and we share their commitment to engage with understanding and cooperation in the forthcoming meeting of the United Nations Conference on Trade and Development in Belgrade.

(7) We are agreed upon the need to encourage both the development of advanced technology and the public acceptance of its role in promoting growth, employment and trade. We have noted with approval the report of the Working Group on Technology, Growth and Employment which was set up at Versailles last year, and commend the progress made in the 18 cooperative projects discussed in that report. We will follow the implementation and coordination of work on these projects, and look forward to receiving a further report at our next meeting.

(8) We all share the view that more predictability and less volatility in oil prices would be helpful to world economic prospects. We agree that the fall in oil prices in no way diminishes the importance and urgency of efforts to conserve energy, to develop economic alternative energy sources, to maintain and, where possible, improve contacts between oil-exporting and importing countries, and to encourage the growth of indigenous energy production in developing countries which at present lack it.

(9) East-West economic relations should be compatible with our security interests. We take note with approval of the work of the multilateral organizations which have in recent months analyzed and drawn conclusions regarding the key aspects of East-West economic relations. We encourage continuing work by these organizations, as appropriate.

(10) We have agreed to strengthen cooperation in protection of the environment, in better use of natural resources, and in health research.

Our discussions here at Williamsburg give us new confidence in the prospects for a recovery. We have strengthened our resolve to deal cooperatively with continuing problems so as to promote a sound and sustainable recovery, bringing new jobs and a better life for the people of our own countries and of the world.

We have agreed to meet again next year, and have accepted the British Prime Minister's invitation to meet in the United Kingdom.

Annex

Strengthening Economic Cooperation for Growth and Stability

I. We have examined in the light of our experience the procedures outlined in the undertakings agreed at Versailles last year which seek to ensure greater monetary stability in the interest of balanced growth and progress of the world economy.

II. We reaffirm the objectives of achieving non-inflationary growth of income and employment, and promoting exchange market stability through policies designed to bring about greater convergence of economic performance in this direction.

III. We are reinforcing our multilateral cooperation with the International Monetary Fund in its surveillance activities, according to the procedures agreed at Versailles, through the following approach:

A. We are focusing on near-term policy actions leading to convergence of economic conditions in the medium term. The overall medium-term perspective remains essential, both to ensure that short-term policy innovations do not lead to divergence and to reassure business and financial markets.

B. In accordance with the agreement reached at Versailles, we are focusing our attention on issues in the monetary and financial fields including interaction with policies in other areas. We shall take fully into account the international implications of our own policy decisions. Policies and objectives that will be kept under review include:

(1) Monetary Policy. Disciplined non-inflationary growth of monetary aggregates, and appropriate interest rates, to avoid subsequent resurgence of inflation and rebound in interest rates, thus allowing room for sustainable growth.

(2) Fiscal Policy. We will aim, preferably through discipline over government expenditures, to reduce structural budget deficits and bear in mind the consequences of fiscal policy for interest rates and growth.

(3) Exchange Rate Policy. We will improve consultations, policy convergence and international cooperation to help stabilize exchange markets, bearing in mind our conclusions on the Exchange Market Intervention Study.

(4) Policies Toward Productivity and Employment. While relying on market signals as a guide to efficient economic decisions, we will take

513

measures to improve training and mobility of our labor forces, with particular concern for the problems of youth unemployment, and promote continued structural adjustment, especially by:

— Enhancing flexibility and openness of economies and financial markets.

— Encouraging research and development as well as profitability and productive investment.

— Continued efforts in each country, and improved international cooperation, where appropriate, on structural adjustment measures (e.g., regional, sectoral, energy policies).

IV. We shall continue to assess together regularly in this framework the progress we are making, consider any corrective action which may be necessary from time-to-time, and react promptly to significant changes.

June

COURT ON WINDFALL PROFITS

June 6, 1983

The Supreme Court June 6 removed a constitutional cloud from the 1980 windfall profits tax on oil, to the considerable relief of Congress and the administration of Ronald Reagan. In the case of United States v. Ptasnyski, the Court unanimously upheld the constitutionality of the tax, which already had brought some $26 billion into the deficit-plagued federal Treasury and was expected to yield billions more in the years ahead.

The largest tax ever levied on an American industry, the 1980 windfall profits tax was enacted by Congress at President Jimmy Carter's request. It was designed to recoup from oil producers some of the "windfall" profits expected as price controls on oil were lifted in an effort to stimulate new production. Its rate varied between 30 percent and 70 percent of the difference between the old, controlled price of crude oil at the wellhead and the current market price.

In November 1982 a federal district court judge in Wyoming ruled the tax unconstitutional because it did not apply to new oil produced on Alaska's North Slope. The judge said this exemption violated the Constitution's requirement that federal taxes be uniform throughout the United States. It was the first time a federal tax had been barred on the basis of the "uniformity clause." The state of Alaska joined the federal government in appealing the ruling. The state argued that many oil fields already had become "marginal" because of falling oil prices and that additional taxes would discourage further development.

The Supreme Court disagreed with the lower court ruling. Writing for the Court, Justice Lewis F. Powell Jr. said that a tax did not always violate the uniformity clause simply because it was framed in geographic terms. "The Uniformity Clause gives Congress wide latitude in deciding what to tax and does not prohibit it from considering geographically isolated problems," he wrote.

Powell explained that Congress considered the windfall profits tax a necessary part of its program to encourage the exploration and production of oil. Because, in certain circumstances, profits essentially unrelated to the objective of the program would be earned, Congress concluded that these profits should be taxed. But Congress devised a new "exempt" classification for some Alaskan oil and oil produced in certain offshore territorial waters. In the Court's view, Congress correctly determined that the difficulty associated with extracting this oil warranted special treatment for the producers.

The Court noted that only about 20 percent of the oil currently produced in Alaska was exempt from the tax; most was subject to the tax because it came from fields south of the Arctic Circle, which were already in production when the tax was enacted. "Nothing in the act's legislative history suggests that Congress intended to grant Alaska an undue preference at the expense of other oil-producing states," Powell said.

The decision was criticized by the Independent Petroleum Association, which represented 5,700 oil producers and owners of drilling rights, who, along with the states of Texas and Louisiana, had sued to block the tax. They contended that "the continuation of this tax will only make it that much more difficult for domestic producers to find oil; it means we'll continue our dependence on imported oil for a longer period into the future."

Following are excerpts from the unanimous June 6, 1983, Supreme Court decision in United States v. Ptasynski *upholding the constitutionality of the windfall profits tax on oil:*

<u>No. 82-1066</u>

United States, Appellant *v.* Harry Ptasynski et al.	On appeal from the United States District Court for the District of Wyoming

[June 6, 1983]

JUSTICE POWELL delivered the opinion of the Court.

The issue is whether excluding a geographically defined class of oil from the coverage of the Crude Oil Windfall Profit Tax Act violates the Uniformity Clause.

I

During the 1970s the Executive Branch regulated the price of domestic crude oil. Depending on its vintage and type, oil was divided into differing classes or tiers and assigned a corresponding ceiling price. Initially, there were only two tiers, a lower tier for "old oil" and an upper tier for new production. As the regulatory framework developed, new classes of oil were recognized.

In 1979, President Carter announced a program to remove price controls from domestic oil by September 30, 1981. By eliminating price controls, the President sought to encourage exploration for new oil and to increase production of old oil from marginally economic operations. He recognized, however, that deregulating the price of oil already in production would allow domestic producers to receive prices far in excess of their initial estimates. Accordingly, the President proposed that Congress place an excise tax on the additional revenue resulting from decontrol.

Congress responded by enacting the Crude Oil Windfall Profit Tax Act of 1980, 94 Stat. 229, 26 U.S.C. § 4986 *et seq.* The Act divides domestic crude oil into three tiers and established an adjusted base price and a tax rate for each tier. The base prices generally reflect the selling price of particular categories of oil under price controls, and the tax rates vary according to the vintages and types of oil included within each tier. The House Report explained that the Act is "designed to impose relatively high tax rates where production cannot be expected to respond very much to further increases in price and relatively low tax rates on oil whose production is likely to be responsive to price."

The Act exempts certain classes of oil from the tax, one of which is "exempt Alaskan oil." It is defined as:

"any crude oil (other than Sadlerochit oil) which is produced—

(1) from a reservoir from which oil has been produced in commercial quantities through a well located north of the Arctic Circle, or

(2) from a well located on the northerly side of the divide of the Alaska-Aleutian Range and at least 75 miles from the nearest point on the Trans-Alaska Pipeline System."

Although the Act refers to this class of oil as "exempt Alaskan oil," the reference is not entirely accurate. The Act exempts only certain oil produced in Alaska from the windfall profit tax. Indeed, less than 20% of current Alaskan production is exempt. Nor is the exemption limited to the State of Alaska. Oil produced in certain offshore territorial waters — beyond the limits of any State — is included within the exemption.

The exemption thus is not drawn on state political lines. Rather it reflects Congress' considered judgment that unique climactic and geographic conditions require that oil produced from this exempt area be treated as a separate class of oil. As Senator Gravel explained, the development and production of oil in arctic and subarctic regions is hampered by "severe weather conditions, remoteness, sensitive environmental and geological characteristics, and a lack of normal social and industrial infrastructure." ... These factors combine to make the average cost of drilling a well in Alaska as much as 15 times greater than that of drilling a well elsewhere in the United States. Accordingly, Congress chose to exempt oil produced in the defined region from the windfall profit tax. It determined that imposing such a tax "would discourage exploration and development of reservoirs in areas of extreme climatic conditions."

Six months after the Act was passed independent oil producers and royalty owners filed suit in the District Court for the District of Wyoming, seeking a refund for taxes paid under the Act. On motion for summary judgment, the District Court held that the Act violated the Uniformity Clause, Art. I, § 8, cl. 1. It recognized that Congress' power to tax is virtually without limitation, but noted that the Clause in question places one specific limit on Congress' power to impose indirect taxes. Such taxes must be uniform ... and uniformity is achieved only when the tax "operates with the same force and effect in every place where ... it is found.'"

Because the Act exempts oil from certain areas within one State, the court found that the Act does not apply uniformly throughout the United States. It recognized that Congress could have "a rational justification for the exemption," but concluded that "[d]istinctions based on geography are simply not allowed." ... It therefore held the entire windfall profit tax invalid.

We noted probable jurisdiction (1983) and now reverse.

II

Appellees advance two arguments in support of the District Court's judgment. First, they contend that the constitutional requirement that taxes be "uniform throughout the United States" prohibits Congress from exempting a specific geographic region from taxation. They concede that Congress may take geographic considerations into account in deciding what oil to tax. But they argue that the Uniformity Clause prevents Congress from framing, as it did here, the resulting tax in terms of geographic boundaries. Second, they argue that the Alaskan oil exemption was an integral part of a compromise struck by Congress. Thus, it would be inappropriate to invalidate the exemption but leave the remainder of the tax in effect. Because we find the Alaskan exemption constitutional, we do not consider whether it is severable.

A

The Uniformity Clause conditions Congress' power to impose indirect taxes. It provides that "all Duties, Imposts and Excises shall be uniform throughout the United States." The debates in the Constitutional Convention provide little evidence of the Framers' intent, but the concerns giving rise to the Clause identify its purpose more clearly. The Committee of Detail proposed as a remedy for interstate trade barriers that the power to regulate commerce among the States be vested in the national government, and the Convention agreed. Some States, however, remained apprehensive that the regionalism that had marked the Confederation would persist. There was concern that the national government would use its power over commerce to the disadvantage of particular States. The Uniformity Clause was proposed as one of several measures designed to limit the exercise of that power. . . .

This general purpose, however, does not define the precise scope of the Clause. The one issue that has been raised repeatedly is whether the requirement of uniformity encompasses some notion of equality. It was settled fairly early that the Clause does not require Congress to devise a tax that falls equally or proportionately on each State. Rather, as the Court stated in the *Head Money Cases*, (1884), a "tax is uniform when it operates with the same force and effect in every place where the subject of it is found."

Nor does the Clause prevent Congress from defining the subject of a tax by drawing distinctions between similar classes. In the *Head Money Cases*, the Court recognized that in imposing a head tax on persons coming into this country, Congress could choose to tax those persons who immigrated through the ports, but not those who immigrated at inland cities. As the Court explained, "the evil to be remedied by this legislation has no existence on our inland borders, and immigration in that quarter needed no such regulation." The tax applied to all ports alike, and the Court concluded that "there is substantial uniformity within the meaning and purpose of the Constitution." Subsequent cases have confirmed that the Framers did not intend to restrict Congress' ability to define the class of objects to be taxed. They intended only that the tax apply wherever the classification is found.

The question that remains, however, is whether the Uniformity Clause prohibits Congress from defining the class of objects to be taxed in geographic terms. The Court has not addressed this issue squarely. We recently held, however, that the uniformity provision of the Bankruptcy Clause did not require invalidation of a geographically defined class of debtors. See *Regional Rail Reorganization Act Cases*, (1974). In that litigation, creditors of bankrupt railroads challenged a statute that was passed to reorganize eight major railroads in the northeast and midwest regions of the country. They argued that the statute violated the uniformity provision of the Bankruptcy Clause because it operated only in a single statutorily defined region. The Court found that "[t]he uniformity provision does not deny Congress power to take into account differences that exist between different parts of the country, and to fashion legislation to resolve geographically isolated problems." The fact that the Act applied to a geographically defined class did not render it unconstitutional. We noted that the Act in fact had operated uniformly throughout the United States. During the period in which the Act was effective, no railroad reorganization proceeding had been pending outside the statutorily defined region.

In concluding that the uniformity provision had not been violated, we relied in large part on the *Head Money Cases,* where the effect of the statute had been to distinguish between geographic regions. We rejected the argument that "the Rail Act differs from the head tax statute because *by its own terms* the Rail Act applies only to one designated region.... The definition of the region does not obscure the reality that the legislation applies to all railroads under reorganization pursuant to § 77 during the time the Act applies."

B

With these principles in mind, we now consider whether Congress' decision to treat Alaskan oil as a separate class of oil violates the Uniformity Clause. We do not think that the language of the Clause or this Court's decisions prohibit all geographically defined classifications. As construed in the *Head Money Cases,* the Uniformity Clause requires that an excise tax apply, at the same rate, in all portions of the United States where the subject of the tax is found. Where Congress defines the subject of a tax in nongeographic terms, the Uniformity Clause is satisfied. See *Knowlton* v. *Moore.* We cannot say that when Congress uses geographic terms to identify the same subject, the classification is invalidated. The Uniformity Clause gives Congress wide latitude in deciding what to tax and does not prohibit it from considering geographically isolated problems.... But where Congress does choose to frame a tax in geographic terms, we will examine the classification closely to see if there is actual geographic discrimination.

In this case, we hold that the classification is constitutional. As discussed above, Congress considered the windfall profit tax a necessary component of its program to encourage the exploration and production of oil. It perceived that the decontrol legislation would result — in certain circumstances — in profits essentially unrelated to the objective of the program, and concluded that these profits should be taxed. Accordingly, Congress divided oil into various classes and gave more favorable treatment to those classes that would be responsive to increased prices.

Congress clearly viewed "exempt Alaskan oil" as a unique class of oil that, consistent with the scheme of the Act, merited favorable treatment. It had before it ample evidence of the disproportionate costs and difficulties — the fragile ecology, the harsh environment, and the remote location — associated with extracting oil from this region. We cannot fault its determination, based on neutral factors, that this oil required separate treatment. Nor is there any indication that Congress sought to benefit Alaska for reasons that would offend the purpose of the Clause. Nothing in the Act's legislative history suggests that Congress intended to grant

Alaska an undue preference at the expense of other oil-producing States. This is especially clear because the windfall profit tax itself falls heavily on the State of Alaska.

III

Had Congress described this class of oil in nongeographic terms, there would be no question as to the Act's constitutionality. We cannot say that identifying the class in terms of its geographic boundaries renders the exemption invalid. Where, as here, Congress has exercised its considered judgment with respect to an enormously complex problem, we are reluctant to disturb its determination. Accordingly, the judgment of the District Court is

Reversed.

RESOLUTION ON HUMAN GENETIC ENGINEERING
June 8, 1983

In a resolution made public June 8, a group of religious leaders and scientists declared their opposition to human genetic engineering and urged a ban on any attempts to engineer specific inheritable traits into human genes. The resolution, designed to draw attention to the issue of genetic engineering on human cells, captured public interest and stirred debate over the moral and scientific considerations raised by the new technology.

Jeremy Rifkin, author of a book on genetic engineering, drafted the resolution and a 10-page accompanying statement entitled "The Theological Letter Concerning the Moral Arguments Against Genetic Engineering of the Human Germline Cells." The 63 signers of Rifkin's resolution included a diverse group of Protestant and Jewish leaders, Catholic bishops, religion professors and scientists.

Technology Sparks Debate

In recent years scientists made gigantic strides in genetic engineering research, and many large universities and major biological centers were involved in such research. In one of the most notable experiments, Ohio University scientist Thomas Wagner successfully transferred a gene trait from one mammalian species to the embryos of other mammalian species. Such experiments brought the technology closer to human application, although scientists agreed that techniques to alter human genes still were some years away.

As the possibility of human genetic engineering increased, the issue stirred controversy and elicited forceful arguments over whether and how that scientific knowledge should be applied. The signers of the resolution and other opponents of human genetic engineering argued that the new science would subject the human species to "technological manipulation" and would irreversibly alter, perhaps with devastating effect, "the composition of the gene pool for all future generations of human life." The resolution signers also maintained that "no individual, group of individuals, or institutions can legitimately claim the right or authority" to decide what human traits should be kept, eliminated or changed. In the letter accompanying the resolution, Rifkin concluded, "Genetic engineering of the human germline cells represents a fundamental threat to the preservation of the human species as we know it, and should be opposed with the same courage and conviction as we now oppose the threat of nuclear extinction."

Most of the arguments supporting human genetic engineering focused on the possibility of eliminating genetically determined diseases, such as sickle-cell anemia or Down's syndrome. According to Joe Buonomo, president of the Association for Retarded Citizens of the United States, genetic research had led to early diagnosis of some mental disorders. It was possible, he said, to alter the damaged chromosome that caused Down's syndrome, the most frequent cause of mental retardation, although practical use of the technology was still some years off.

Those looking to the new science for such cures opposed the position taken by Rifkin and the other resolution signers, who advocated an outright ban on human genetic engineering research. Research should continue, some experts argued, particularly in areas that might yield cures for genetic disorders. In some cases, such as sickle-cell anemia, the disease might be cured by altering gene cells without passing those changes on to future generations.

Proposals to Establish a Federal Commission

One suggestion that received widespread support called for the formation of a federal commission to monitor the development of the new technology and make recommendations on how scientists should proceed with their research. They pointed as an example to the President's Commission on Bioethics, which existed until March 1983. The commission monitored biomedical research and made suggestions on its application. Rep. Albert Gore Jr., D-Tenn., in May 1983 introduced a measure to create a Presidential Commission on Human Genetic Engineering. The panel would be made up of scientists and religious leaders who would watch over and make recommendations on the development of human genetic engineering. Gore acknowledged the "very real and legitimate concerns" of those who want controls on the new science, but he said "some forms of genetic engineering may be desirable."

Following are the texts of the resolution and letter on the moral implications of human genetic engineering, issued June 8, 1983, by a group of theologians and scientists. (Boldface headings in brackets have been added by Congressional Quarterly to highlight the organization of the texts.):

RESOLUTION

To express the conviction that engineering specific genetic traits into the human germline not be attempted.

Whereas molecular biologists have recently succeeded in altering the sex cells of a mammalian species through genetic engineering technology;

Whereas the new advances in genetic engineering technology now raise the possibility of altering the human species;

Whereas the ability to design and program specific physiological characteristics by engineering specific genetic traits into the sperm, egg, or embryo of a human being represents a fundamental alteration in the way a human being may be formed;

Whereas programming genetic traits directly into human sex cells subjects the human species to the art of technological manipulation and architectural design;

Whereas the redesign of the human species by genetic engineering technology irreversibly alters the composition of the gene pool for all future generations of human life;

Whereas engineering fundamental changes of human sex cells necessitates that decisions be made as to which genetic traits should be programmed into the human gene pool and which should be eliminated; and

Whereas no individual, group of individuals, or institutions can legitimately claim the right or authority to make such decisions on behalf of the rest of the species alive today or for future generations: Now, therefore, be it

Resolved, That efforts to engineer specific genetic traits into the germline of the human species should not be attempted.

While the nation has begun to turn its attention to the dangers of nuclear war, little or no debate has taken place over the emergence of an entirely new technology which in time could very well pose as serious a threat to the existence of the human species as the bomb itself. We are referring to human genetic engineering. On July 22, 1982 the *New York Times* published a major editorial entitled "Whether to Make Perfect Humans." It will soon be possible, says the *Times*, to fundamentally alter the human species by engineering the genetic traits of the sex cells — the sperm and egg. Humanity's new found ability to engineer genetic traits could well lead to the creation of a new species, as different from homo-sapiens as we are to the higher apes. So grave is the threat of human genetic engineering that the *Times* suggests that we consider "the question of

527

whether the human germline should be declared inviolable."

Programming genetic traits into human sex cells subjects the human species to the art of technological manipulation and architectural design.

With the arrival of human genetic engineering, humanity approaches a crossroads in its own technological history. It will soon be possible to engineer and produce human beings by the same technological design principles as we now employ in our industrial processes.

The wholesale design of human life, in accordance with technological prerequisites, design specifications, and quality controls, raises a fundamental question. Nobel laureate biologist Dr. Salvador Lauria puts the question in its most succinct context when he asks "When does a repaired or manufactured man stop being a man . . . and become a robot, an object, an industrial product?"

The debate over genetic engineering is similar to the debate over nuclear power. For years the nuclear proponents argued that the potential benefits of nuclear power outweighed the potential harm. Today an increasingly skeptical public has begun to seriously question this basic presumption.

In a similar vein, proponents of human genetic engineering argue that the benefits outweigh the risks and that it would be irresponsible not to use this powerful new technology to eliminate serious "genetic disorders." The *New York Times* editorial board correctly addressed this conventional scientific argument by concluding in its editorial that once the scientists are able to repair genetic defects "it will become much harder to argue against adding genes that confer desired qualities, like better health, looks or brains." According to the *Times,* "There is no discernible line to be drawn between making inheritable repairs of genetic defects, and improving the species."

Once we decide to begin the process of human genetic engineering, there is really no logical place to stop. If diabetes, sickle cell anemia, and cancer are to be cured by altering the genetic make-up of an individual, why not proceed to other "disorders": myopia, color blindness, left handedness. Indeed, what is to preclude a society from deciding that a certain skin color is a disorder?

As knowledge about the genes increases, the bio-engineers will inevitably gain new insights into the functioning of more complex characteristics, such as those associated with behavior and thoughts. Many scientists are already contending that schizophrenia and other "abnormal" psychological states result from genetic disorders or defects. Others now argue that "antisocial" behavior, such as criminality and social protest, are also examples of malfunctioning genetic information. One prominent neurophysiologist has gone so far as to say "there can be no twisted thought without a twisted molecule." Many sociobiologists contend that virtually all human activity is in some way determined by our genetic make-up and that if we wish to change this situation, we must change our genes.

Whenever we begin to discuss the idea of genetic defects there is no way to limit the discussion to one or two or even a dozen so called disorders because of a hidden assumption that lies behind the very notion of "defective." Ethicist Daniel Callahan penetrates to the core of the problem when he observes that "behind the human horror at genetic defectiveness lurks ... an image of the perfect human being. The very language of 'defect,' 'abnormality,' 'disease,' and 'risk,' presupposes such an image, a kind of proto-type of perfection."

The question, then, is whether or not humanity should "begin" the process of engineering future generation of human beings by technological design in the laboratory.

What is the price we pay for embarking on a course whose final goal is the "perfection" of the human species?

First there is the ecological price to consider. It is very likely that in attempting to "perfect" the human species we will succeed in engineering our own extinction. Eliminating so called "bad genes" will lead to a dangerous narrowing of diversity in the gene pool. Since part of the strength of our gene pool consists in its very diversity, including defective genes, tampering with it might ultimately lead to extinction of the human race. It should be recalled that in the 1950's genetic modifications were made in wheat strains to create bumper crops of "super wheat." When a new strain of disease hit the fields, farmers found that their wheat was too delicate to resist. Within two years, virtually the entire crop was destroyed.

We have no doubt that a similar effort to "perfect" the human species by eliminating the so called bad genes would prove equally destructive. This simple biological fact is so patently obvious that one begins to wonder why it is so conveniently ignored by so many of the "experts" in the scientific community. Even Dr. Thomas Wagner, the scientist at Ohio University who is responsible for the first successful transfer of a gene trait from one mammalian species to the embryo of another mammalian species, has gone on record as being opposed to genetic engineering of the human germline cells because of the potentially devastating effect that such narrowing of genetic diversity might have on the ability of the human species to survive in the future. Dr. Wagner says,

> It is a terrible mistake to make a permanent, heritable change, even if it appears to be for the better, in a human being's genetic make-up. We don't know what the future brings, and we don't understand fully the process of evolution. Any species of animal needs a certain degree of diversity, some of which appears negative, in order for it to survive into the future. I don't think we should be manipulating the genetic material beyond the individual generation of the human involved.

[Past Interest in Genetics]

Then there is the question of eugenics to carefully consider. Eugenics is the inseparable ethical wing of the Age of Biotechnology. First coined by Charles Darwin's cousin, Sir Francis Galton, eugenics is generally categorized into two types, negative and positive. Negative eugenics involves the systematic elimination of so-called biologically undesirable characteristics. Positive eugenics is concerned with the use of genetic manipulation to "improve" the characteristics of an organism or species.

Eugenics is not a new phenomenon. At the turn of the century the U.S. sported a massive eugenics movement. Politicians, celebrities, academicians and prominent business leaders joined together in support of a eugenics program for the country. The frenzy over eugenics reached a fever pitch with many states passing sterilization statutes and the U.S. Congress passing a new emigration law in the 1920's based on eugenics considerations. As a consequence of the new legislation, thousands of American citizens were sterilized so they could not pass on their "inferior" traits and the federal government locked its doors to certain emigrant groups deemed biologically unfit by then existing eugenics standards.

While the Americans flirted with eugenics for the first thirty years of the twentieth century, their escapades were of minor historical account when compared with the eugenics program orchestrated by the Nazis in the 1930's and 40's. Million of Jews and other religious and ethnic groups were gassed in the German crematoriums to advance the Third Reich's dream of eliminating all but the "Aryan" race from the globe. The Nazis also embarked on a "positive" eugenics program in which thousands of S.S. officers and German women were carefully selected for their "superior" genes and mated under the auspices of the state. Impregnated women were cared for in state facilities and their offspring were donated to the Third Reich as the vanguard for the new super race that would rule the world for the next millenium.

Eugenics lay dormant for nearly a quarter of a century after World War II. Then the spectacular breakthroughs in molecular biology in the 1960's raised the spectre of a eugenics revival once again. By the mid 1970's, many scientists were beginning to worry out loud that the potential for genetic engineering might lead to a return to the kind of eugenics hysteria that swept over America and Europe earlier in the century. Speaking at a National Academy of Science forum on recombinant DNA, Ethan Signer, a biologist at MIT, warned his colleagues that

> this research is going to bring us one more step closer to genetic engineering of people. That's where they figure out how to have us produce children with ideal characteristics ... Last time around, the ideal children had blonde hair, blue eyes and Aryan genes.

The concern over a re-emergence of eugenics is well founded but misplaced. While professional ethicists watch out the front door for tell tale signs of a resurrection of the Nazi nightmare, eugenics doctrine has quietly slipped in the back door. The new eugenics is commercial not social. In place of the shrill eugenic cries for racial purity, the new commercial eugenics talks in pragmatic terms of medical benefits and improvement in the quality of life. The old eugenics was steeped in political ideology and motivated by fear and hate. The new eugenics is grounded in medical advance and the spectre of extending the human life span.

[Dangers of a 'Brave New World']

Genetic engineering, then, is coming to us not as a threat, but as a promise; not as a punishment but as a gift. And here is where the true danger lies. If the Brave New World comes, it will not be forced on us by an evil cabal of self-serving scientists and Machiavellian politicians. On the contrary, what makes opposition to the Brave New World so difficult is the seductive path that leads to it. Every new advance in human genetic engineering is likely to be heralded as a great stride forward, a boon for humankind. Every one of the breakthroughs in genetic engineering will be of benefit to someone, under some circumstance, somewhere in society. And step by step, advance by advance, we human beings might well choose to trade away the spontaneity of natural life for the predictability of technological design until the human species as we know it is transformed into a product of our own creation; a product that bears only a faint resemblance to the original.

How important is it that we eliminate all the imperfections, all the defects? What price are we willing to pay to extend our lives, to insure our own health, to do away with all of the inconveniences, the irritations, the nuisances, the infirmities, the suffering, that are so much a part of the human experience? Are we so enamored with the idea of physical perpetuation at all costs that we are even willing to subject the human species to rigid architectural design? Is guaranteeing our health worth trading away our humanity?

What is the price we pay for medical advance, for securing our own physical well being? If it means accepting the idea of reducing the human species to a technologically designed product, then it is too dear a price.

Ultimately, there is no security to be found in engineering the human species, just as we have now learned that there is no security to be found in building bigger, more sophisticated nuclear bombs.

Perhaps, if we had taken the time to look at the long range implications of our work in nuclear physics forty years ago, we might well have decided to restrict or prohibit the research and development of nuclear weaponry. Today we have the opportunity to look ahead and envision the final logical consequences of our work in genetic engineering. The question is whether we will choose to do so.

It is our hope that this resolution will represent a watershed in our thinking concerning science and technology. For the first time, it affirms the right of humanity to say no to the application of its own scientific knowledge. Just because something can be done is no longer an adequate justification for assuming it should be done or that it can't be stopped from being done. We believe we have a sacred obligation to say no when the pursuit of a specific technological path threatens the very existence of life itself.

It is with this thought in mind that we now turn to you for support of this resolution.

In deciding whether to go ahead or not with human genetic engineering we must all ask ourselves the following question. Who should we entrust with the authority to design the blueprints for the future of the human species? In the words of the Nobel laureate biologist George Wald, "Who is going to set those specifications?"

Human genetic engineering presents the human race with the most important political question it has ever had to contend with. Who do we entrust with the ultimate authority to decide which are the good genes that should be engineered into the human gene pool and which are the bad genes that should be eliminated?

Today the ultimate exercise of political power is within our grasp; the ability to control the future lives of human beings by engineering their characteristics in advance; making them a hostage of their own architecturally designed blueprints. Genetic engineering represents the power of authorship. Never before in history has such complete power over life been a possibility. The idea of imprisoning the life span of a human being by simply engineering its genetic blueprint at conception is truly awesome.

Aldous Huxley's spectre of a biologically designed caste system with its alphas, betas, gammas and deltas looms on the horizon. Our society must now ponder whether to give sanction to this fundamental departure in how human life is formed. In examining this issue, we would ask everyone to consider one simple question. Would we trust the Congress of the U.S. with the ultimate authority to decide which genes should be engineered into the human gene pool and which should be eliminated? Would we entrust the executive or judicial branch with such authority? Or the corporations and the marketplace? Or the scientists and the medical community?

Who do we designate to play God? The fact is, no individual, group, or set of institutions can legitimately claim the right or authority to make such decisions on behalf of the rest of the species alive today or for future generations.

Genetic engineering of the human germline cells represents a fundamental threat to the preservation of the human species as we know it, and should be opposed with the same courage and conviction as we now oppose the threat of nuclear extinction.

We would like your support for this proposed resolution to prohibit the engineering of genetic traits into the germline of the human species.

HHS SECRETARY ON AIDS
June 14, 1983

Health and Human Services Secretary Margaret M. Heckler described the deadly acquired immune deficiency syndrome disease, or AIDS, as the nation's number one health priority in a June 14 speech at the 51st annual convention of the U.S. Conference of Mayors in Denver. AIDS, a disease of unknown origin with no known cure, destroyed the body's infection-fighting immune system. Heckler said the fear that the disease was spreading among the general population was unfounded. She warned, however, that the number of victims might double every six months.

Total 1983 government spending on research to combat AIDS, which killed 759 of its 1,972 victims, was $26.5 million, Heckler said. That represented three times the 1982 amount. AIDS killed 80 percent of its victims within two years of diagnosis, Heckler reported. The country's first reported case of AIDS was in June 1981.

Heckler stressed several times in her speech that the general public was not in danger from AIDS. "The overwhelming majority of Americans," she said, "are not at risk in their day-to-day activities, even in dealing with AIDS victims. An important indicator of this fact is that no health personnel who have been dealing with the disease have contracted it."

Ninety-four percent of those contracting the disease, she said, belonged to four groups: homosexual or bisexual men with multiple sex partners (about 70 percent of AIDS victims were homosexual men); intravenous drug abusers; recent Haitian immigrants (5.3 percent of the total number of cases in the United States); and people with hemophilia.

"The disease is spread almost entirely through sexual contact — through the sharing of needles by drug abusers — and, less commonly, through blood or blood products," Heckler said.

At the 1983 rate of infection, five to seven new cases a day, AIDS could claim more than 100,000 victims in three years and 1.6 million in five years, the Centers for Disease Control in Atlanta reported. Fourteen countries reported having cases of AIDS. Active transmission among the high-risk groups occurred only in Canada, Haiti and the United States.

Heckler outlined three steps that people could take to prevent the further spread of AIDS: "Sexual contact should be avoided with persons known or suspected of having AIDS; members of groups at increased risk for AIDS should refrain from donating plasma and/or blood products; physicians should adhere strictly to medical indications for blood transfusions, and autologous blood transfusions are encouraged."

Physical and Psychological Effects of AIDS

AIDS destroys the body's immune defense system, leaving the victim vulnerable to a multitude of diseases, including a rare malignancy called Kaposi's sarcoma and an invidious form of pneumonia, pheumocystitis. An AIDS patient said, "There is always the overriding uncertainty that on any day you'll come down with something new that your suppressed system can't repel."

When people learned they had AIDS they often experienced a feeling of being punished for being gay. "For some the experience is a sort of second 'coming out,'" said a social worker. "They have to come to terms with their gayness all over again."

Some AIDS victims experienced considerable anger. A psychiatrist said, "They become angry at God, at society, at government, at government research funding levels and at doctors. Some of them believe that society is only interested in AIDS now that straight people may be at risk."

A number of AIDS victims as well as researchers and some politicians had accused the Reagan administration of failing to acknowledge the critical health emergency posed by the disorder.

Impact on Gay Movement

Many of the country's estimated 17 million gays — one in 10 of Americans — feared that the public's anxiety about AIDS would revive discrimination and erode the civil rights they had gained. Fourteen years earlier, a Greenwich Village riot spurred a "Gay Pride" movement. Since then gays had been given more freedom to pursue their life style openly as the nation experienced a broadened awareness of homosexuality. Some politicians admitted to being gay. Even Broadway gave its highest award to a play about homosexuality. Torch Song Trilogy, *about a drag queen's search for the meaning of family life, won two Tony Awards in 1983.*

AIDS promoted a sense of unity in the homosexual community. "I have not seen anything that has coalesced the gay community like AIDS," commented the director of a facility specializing in sexually transmitted diseases. Because of the fear of contracting AIDS, many homosexuals retreated from casual and multiple sex.

A number of gay advocates complained that society treated some AIDS victims like lepers. A gay publisher of a newspaper for homosexuals said friends of years' standing had abandoned him because of the AIDS scare. Some ambulance services refused to pick up gays. While a San Francisco television station tried to allay fears with a a program entitled, "Demystifying AIDS," two AIDS sufferers had to be interviewed by telephone because technicians refused to be in the same room with them. In hospitals, nurses balked at treating AIDS patients. Faced with shortages in blood supplies, the Red Cross issued pleas for healthy donors. Some potential donors feared they might contract AIDS while giving blood. (Since 1980 only two dozen out of 10 million blood tranfusions were linked to AIDS.)

> *Following are excerpts from a speech delivered by Health and Human Services Secretary Margaret M. Heckler June 14, 1983, before the annual U.S. Conference of Mayors in Denver.* (Boldface headings in brackets have been added by Congressional Quarterly to highlight the organization of the text.):

... Today ... I want to talk with you about an unusual and urgent situation. My subject is a disease — a disease with two names.

One name is "AIDS": Acquired Immune Deficiency Syndrome.

The other name is "fear." Not "concern." Not "caution." But unreasoned and unsubstantiated fear.

Many of you who represent some of our larger cities, and especially with large gay populations, have already been confronted with the problems of AIDS itself.

I am concerned that all of us might also be confronted with an unnecessary and unjustified level of fear, if misunderstanding of AIDS is allowed to grow. Such a level of fear could actually impede us in our real tasks — to understand and conquer this disease, and to care for its victims.

I am here to report on the *facts* about AIDS. The facts alone are an antidote to fear. And the facts are telling us, more and more clearly — *not* that AIDS is spreading throughout our population — but, to the contrary, that the risk of AIDS is confined to identifiable factors. For the overwhelming majority of Americans, there appears to be little or no risk of falling victim to this disease — in particular, through normal, daily social contacts.

Today, I would like to share with you the research into AIDS that our department is performing; to correct false information about AIDS that may have reached the public; and to assure you of my absolute commitment to finding a cure for this cruel disease.

But nothing I will say is more important than this: that the Department of Health and Human Services considers AIDS its number one health priority. Your fight against AIDS is not a solitary one. We are in the fight with you. And I am confident that we will find the answer.

As we know, AIDS is a scientifically complex, extremely puzzling disorder. But if there is one thing that is *not* mysterious about AIDS, it is *why* the disease is so frightening.

From its unknown origins to its devastating effects, AIDS is indeed a terrifying ailment.

It attacks young, productive people — and it kills 80 percent of its victims within two years of diagnosis.

It destroys the body's ability to fight infection. And there is no known path of recovery once the immune system has been attacked.

[High-Risk Groups]

For this reason, our battle will not be short or easy. To date, 595 victims have died, out of 1,552 cases reported in 35 states and the District of Columbia. Ninety-four percent of these cases have occurred in people belonging to four groups: homosexual or bisexual males with multiple sex partners; intravenous drug abusers; recent entrants from Haiti; and persons with hemophilia.

Every day, four or five new cases of AIDS are reported — perhaps doubling the number of victims every six months. At present, we do not know how to restore the immune system that has been destroyed in AIDS patients, leaving them vulnerable to a multitude of diseases. We are concerned principally because of the suffering of AIDS victims and fatality of the disease, but also from the standpoint of this nation's preparedness to cope with a long-term debilitating illness requiring intensive use of hospital facilities and personnel.

Thus, we feel that AIDS is a most urgent medical dilemma; and we recognize that AIDS presents a serious problem in our cities.

However, we *are* learning how the disease is spread — *and we are finding that there is no indication that AIDS can be transmitted through casual, everyday contacts.* Apparently, only the most intimate contact can transmit AIDS.

There have been *some* occurrences in people who do not actually belong to one of the high risk groups. But many of these cases are women who are sexual partners of men with AIDS, or at high risk for AIDS. Others, tragically, have been babies born to those women, or to women who are abusers of intravenous drugs.

Still — we can state that the disease is spread almost entirely through sexual contact — through the sharing of needles by drug abusers — and, less commonly, through blood or blood products, including transmission in-utero. There should be no cause for fear among the public that they may develop AIDS through casual contact with an AIDS patient or through blood transfusions.

These findings are crucial. They are also reassuring. Because even while AIDS is frightening for those at risk, we can say with confidence — and I repeat — that the overwhelming majority of Americans are *not* at risk in their day-to-day activities, even in dealing with AIDS victims.

An important indicator of this fact is that *no* health personnel who have been dealing with the disease have contracted it. Let me repeat that simple but all important fact. In all the years we have treated this disease, not one single doctor or nurse or other health provider has contracted AIDS. If it *were* an easily-transmitted disease, like flu, we would certainly expect some cases among health workers.

It is very important that Americans understand these facts.

As isolated research results have started coming in, and as the number of reported cases has grown, a misapprehension has taken hold. People seem to believe that the disease is growing in a way that is not actually the case. In particular, there is the misapprehension that AIDS may be "breaking out" into the general population.

But the truth is exactly the opposite.

The growing number of reported cases does *not* show a breakout from the high-risk categories. On the contrary — as more cases are reported, and as they are repeatedly and consistently traced to the high-risk groups, we can say with increasing confidence that AIDS does not threaten the population at large as a result of casual personal contact.

Nonetheless, AIDS can occur in virtually every city in the United States, and it is important for all of us to be familiar with the disease, and to be vigilant.

[Research Progress]

For this reason, I would like to outline the progress of our research.

Two years ago, in June of 1981, the Centers for Disease Control (CDC) in Atlanta, the medical detective agency of the world, first reported cases of AIDS.

Since then, CDC has mobilized its personnel and laboratories to establish a surveillance system for the disease, to identify risk factors for AIDS, and to attempt identification of a possible infectious agent. These early efforts have allowed us to identify high risk groups, to better understand the spread of the syndrome, and to make recommendations to reduce the risk of the spread of AIDS.

At the National Institutes of Health (NIH), action to combat AIDS was immediate. Within a few weeks of CDC's reporting of the disease, the research hospital at NIH began admitting AIDS patients.

Our research has been conducted in two areas: identification of the agent; and therapy. We have not yet been able to identify the causative agent, although we have been able to rule out certain suspected agents, such as nitrate inhalants. It is possible that the agent may be in an unrecognizable form, or may occur early on in the disease and then disappear, either of which would render the agent difficult to identify.

Our research into therapy has centered on the use of interferon, a chemical that occurs during the T-cell maturation process that is blocked in AIDS victims. However, to date we have not developed a satisfactory treatment.

Public Health Services researchers, as well as those in the major medical institutions of this country, are engaged in a non-stop pursuit to identify the cause of AIDS so that effective treatment and prevention measures can be developed. Seventy percent of this research is funded by grants from the National Institutes of Health.

In addition, there has been a virtual explosion of information about AIDS, thanks in large measure to Public Health Service support. The research community has been mobilized, and we are now beginning to see the results of our initial research investments. Most major medical journals now contain at least one, and frequently several, reports on new AIDS research findings. We have begun to focus and target our laboratory research on a causative agent, and the recent finding of the possible association of human T-cell leukemia virus with AIDS, has opened entire new areas of research.

[Measures to Prevent AIDS Spread]

Because of our steady work, we have learned much about the prevention of AIDS. On March 4, 1983, Dr. Edward N. Brandt Jr., assistant secretary for health, outlined steps that can be taken to prevent further spread of this disease.

1. Sexual contact should be avoided with persons known or suspected of having AIDS.

2. Members of groups at increased risk for AIDS should refrain from donating plasma and/or blood products.

3. Physicians should adhere strictly to medical indications for blood transfusions, and autologous blood transfusions are encouraged.

For several weeks, I have been in continuous briefings on AIDS: earlier at the CDC in Atlanta; most recently, at the National Institutes of Health. Last week I spent a day with scientists from CDC and NIH and the other PHS agencies involved in AIDS work. I can assure you that these are superb and dedicated scientists who are committed to solving the problem.

At the NIH research hospital, I visited with two AIDS patients and their physicians. The physicians and nurses take no unusual precautions in examining or caring for these patients, except those steps necessary to protect the patients from infection. I took no precautions myself.

In my conversations with the patients, I promised them that I would use this forum to correct the misinformation, and to squash the vicious rumors that have circulated about AIDS. I feel strongly that the American people must be given timely, accurate information to they will be neither unduly frightened nor overly complacent. I know you share my concern.

Recently, reports have alleged that AIDS can spread through routine social contact. As Mayor Koch said: "Rumors spread easier than AIDS."

First, no cases of AIDS have been transmitted from a patient to a health care provider, nor have any cases of AIDS been transmitted from laboratory specimens to laboratory workers. No evidence indicates that AIDS is spread by casual contact. On the contrary, our findings indicate that AIDS is spread almost entirely through social contact, through the sharing of needles by drug abusers, and, less commonly, through blood and/or blood products.

Second, fears that AIDS can be transmitted in the workplace or home are completely irrational. Let me emphasize this point: AIDS is extremely difficult to contract; it absolutely cannot be transmitted through casual contact with AIDS victims, with gay males, or with members of high-risk groups.

For infant cases, it is important to note that virtually all of such cases occurred to mothers who were at risk of AIDS, and are believed to represent transmission of infection during pregnancy and delivery rather than transmission through household contact.

Third, our scientists estimate that the chance of contracting AIDS through a blood transfusion is much lower than many of the other risks of blood transfusions, such as hepatitis and the risk of transfusion reactions. As the high-risk population becomes aware of the danger, and refrains from donating blood, the minimal risk existing now will diminish.

I urge you to do everything you can to be sure this information reaches all segments of our cities' populations. It is our responsibility to guarantee that the victims of AIDS do not suffer from unreasonable and unrealistic fear among the public. Their personal suffering is already great.

We know that AIDS has been especially the problem of a few large cities. But it concerns all of us. It has struck in Nashville as well as Miami. In San Diego and St. Louis, as well as San Francisco. Statistically we can expect AIDS to claim victims in virtually every city in the United States....

[Assistance to Cities]

At the federal level, our Public Health Service is currently helping the cities directly. A public health advisor on AIDS has been working in New York City for over a year. Advisors will also be assigned to San Francisco,

Los Angeles, and Miami.

In several large cities, CDC Epidemic Intelligence Service physicians previously assigned to a wide variety of public health matters are now working full-time on AIDS. New York State, which has the highest number of AIDS cases in the country, has three of these physicians; Los Angeles also has this special assistance.

We also are supporting or working on cooperative agreements on AIDS with city health departments or other city organizations. PHS has an agreement with the New York City Health Department, and is working on agreements with San Francisco. Two other agreements concern the AIDS incidence in Haitians. Most AIDS cases among Haitians in the United States are reported in either Miami or New York. In Miami a Creole-speaking public health advisor will work on an AIDS study with the University of Miami. A State University of New York study will focus on AIDS in Haitians. Both these studies will begin this summer.

We intend to direct our efforts toward every possible avenue. The Food and Drug Administration has approved a new heat treatment to reduce infectious agents in the blood factor required by hemophilia sufferers. We believe that this new process will provide hemophiliacs with protection against AIDS.

We have enabled AIDS victims to become eligible for Social Security disability benefits.

As secretary of health and human services, I have also ordered the establishment of a new AIDS Information Hotline. This will be a central source for AIDS information that will help us disseminate accurate, timely information to the public. I will announce the details for this service as soon as the telephone lines are installed.

In addition, the Public Health Service has established an AIDS Informational Bulletin, updated every two weeks, which provides the latest scientific information on AIDS. The bulletin will be available to the public, to the appropriate medical personnel, and to state and local health officials across the country.

Any reference to sharing information would not be complete without acknowledging the excellent work done by gay networks around the nation. They have responded to the crisis by offering comprehensive support to AIDS victims, and by working to inform the gay communities of the risks of AIDS, and how to minimize them. I know many of you in this audience have worked extensively with these groups, and I applaud their compassion.

[Federal Research Expenditures]

As for my department, I can assure you that we intend to aggressively pursue our efforts to discover the cause, the most effective treatment, and the prevention of AIDS.

This year, the Department of Health and Human Services will spend

$14.5 million on AIDS. The National Institutes of Health will spend $10 million on direct AIDS research. In addition, the president has asked the Congress to grant me broad authority to transfer $12 million into additional AIDS research, which will bring total spending to $26.5 million for this year. This amount far exceeds the amount we spent on toxic shock syndrome and legionnaires disease *combined* over an eight year period.

Through our grants, we have supported projects that preserve the integrity of the scientific research process. The process relies on projects to yield *accurate* medical and scientific data. No cause would be served by devoting money to hastily conceived research that might yield *in*accurate data. This is particularly critical in a disease as new and puzzling as AIDS.

On May 1st, we awarded six new research grants totalling more than $2 million for the *first year* to medial centers around the country: Harvard University, Cornell Medical Center, Mount Sinai Medical Center in New York, the University of California at San Francisco, Yeshiva University in New York, and the University of California at Los Angeles.

Today, I am very pleased to announce that the National Cancer Institute has awarded two new grants for AIDS research, effective June 1st, to two distinguished scientists:

- Dr. Bijan Safai, of Memorial Sloan-Kettering Cancer Center in New York City, a 3-year grant with $250,000 first year cost; and
- Dr. Fred Valentine, of New York University, a 3-year grant with $166,822 first year cost.

These and other worthwhile research endeavors will help to further our knowledge about AIDS in the next two years.

We have been working with you, and we will continue to work with you, and with the medical profession, and the gay communities around the country. AIDS will continue to be the number one health priority of my department until we have discovered the cause and developed the cure.

I congratulate you on forming the Conference Task Force on AIDS, which is now beginning its work, and I pledge my full cooperation.

Let us keep the vital information flowing. Be sure that all cases of AIDS are being promptly reported to the Centers for Disease Control. Be sure that the real facts about AIDS are reaching the public. Both kinds of informtion are needed as we carry out the attack on this disease.

Let us also reach out to the total community. The gay community has been affected by the AIDS epidemic in an unprecedented way. We should make special efforts to understand the needs and concerns of all the affected groups. They should be included in planning and executing AIDS programs. We should enable them to make the maximum constructive contribution as we care for victims. . . .

I can report to you that the scientific effort is underway non-stop. The commitment and the sense of urgency are impressive. In the presence of a grave medical mystery, there is a sense of resolve — and, always, a sense of hope. We are doing all that is humanly possible to stop this killer. . . .

COURT ON ABORTION

June 15, 1983

By a 6-3 vote, the Supreme Court June 15 strongly reaffirmed its landmark 1973 Roe v. Wade *ruling that the Constitution guaranteed a woman's right to have an abortion. The Court's action reversed an array of local restrictions on access to abortions that had been promulgated in the aftermath of the 1973 decision.*

The Court rulings involved cases from Missouri, Virginia and Ohio testing the validity of state and local government efforts to regulate abortion. The justices held unconstitutional provisions of a 1978 Akron, Ohio, ordinance that was considered a national model for abortion regulation. In Akron v. Akron Center for Reproductive Health, *the Court struck down legislation requiring that all abortions after the first three months of pregnancy be performed in a hospital; that physicians obtain the consent of a parent or legal guardian before performing an abortion on a minor under the age of 15; that physicians recite to women seeking abortions a litany of information about the stage of fetal development, possible abortion complications and birth-giving alternatives; that the attending physician, and no one else, inform a patient of the particular risks associated with her own pregnancy or abortion; that a waiting period of at least 24 hours be observed between the time a woman signed an "informed consent" form authorizing an abortion and the time one was performed; and that fetal remains be given some sort of "humane" disposal.*

Respect for settled precedent required the majority to reaffirm Roe v. Wade, *wrote Justice Lewis F. Powell Jr. for the majority in the* Akron case. "Legislative responses to the Court's decision have required us on several occasions, and again today, to define the limits of a State's authority to regulate the performance of abortion. And arguments continue to be made, in these cases as well, that we erred in interpreting the Constitution. Nonetheless, the doctrine of stare decisis ["Let the decision stand."] ... is a doctrine that demands respect in a society governed by the rule of law. We respect it today, and reaffirm Roe v. Wade." Powell was joined by Chief Justice Warren E. Burger and Justices William J. Brennan Jr., Thurgood Marshall, Harry A. Blackmun and John Paul Stevens.

In a lengthy footnote, Powell said there were "especially compelling reasons" for adhering to precedent in applying the principles of Roe v. Wade. "That case was considered with special care," wrote Powell, and in the decade after the decision the Court "repeatedly and consistently has accepted and applied the basic principle that a woman has a fundamental right to make the highly personal choice whether or not to terminate her pregnancy."

O'Connor's Dissent

Justice Sandra Day O'Connor, President Ronald Reagan's only appointee on the Court, wrote the key dissent. O'Connor made clear that she felt Roe v. Wade should be drastically modified, if not reversed altogether. Criticized during her 1981 confirmation hearings for refusing to condemn abortion, O'Connor spoke officially on the issue in her June 15 dissent for the first time since joining the Court. Her decision and that of the two other dissenters — Byron R. White and William H. Rehnquist — also served warning that the Court might yet overturn Roe v. Wade. White and Rehnquist were among the youngest justices on the Court. The possibility that Reagan could appoint more justices, should he serve a second term, led some observers to speculate on how long the Court's abortion stand would endure.

In her opinion, O'Connor criticized the trimester approach the Court had adopted in Roe for testing state regulations. That rationale, she warned, was "on a collision course with itself." Under Roe, a state could regulate second-trimester abortions to protect maternal health. Yet the Court in the Akron case struck down a requirement that all abortions after the first trimester be performed in hospitals, citing new medical evidence that abortion early in the second trimester could safely be performed in an outpatient clinic. She pointed out that as medical advances continued to make abortion procedures safer, "the point at which the state may regulate for reasons of maternal health is moved forward" to actual childbirth. But at the same time, she continued, "as medical science becomes better able to provide for the separate existence of the fetus, the point of viability [at which, under Roe, the state may ban *abortion unless necessary to save the life or health of the mother] is moved further back toward conception."*

O'Connor, along with White and Rehnquist, endorsed an approach suggested by the Reagan administration to uphold restrictions on abortion at any stage of pregnancy so long as the particular regulation did not unduly burden the woman's right to choose to have an abortion and was rationally related to some legitimate state purpose.

Related Cases

In a companion case, however, the Court divided 5-4 to uphold several provisions of a challenged Missouri law. Most significant was one that required "unemancipated" minors to obtain parental or judicial consent for an abortion. Powell and Chief Justice Burger joined the Akron *dissenters to uphold this requirement in the case of* Planned Parenthood Association of Kansas City, Missouri, Inc. v. Ashcroft, Ashcroft v. Planned Parenthood Association of Kansas City, Missouri.

Also upheld were Missouri's requirements that abortion tissue, like that from all other surgical procedures, be submitted to a pathologist for examination and that a second physician be present at abortions performed late in pregnancy.

Akron's ordinance required an unmarried minor under 15 years of age to obtain the written consent of one of her parents or an order approving an abortion from a court "having jurisdiction over her." Missouri's law, a revised version of one the Court struck down in 1976, required parental or judicial consent to an abortion for all unemancipated minors under 18. That law spelled out in some detail, however, the procedure through which a court might decide that a minor was mature enough to make the decision for herself.

The critical difference between the two parental consent requirements was the fact that Missouri spelled out an alternative means of obtaining the necessary consent for a minor who could not or would not obtain that consent from her parents. Although the Akron ordinance mentioned such an alternative, the justices found that it provided an insufficient opportunity for a court, on a case-by-case basis, to decide whether or not a pregnant minor was in fact mature enough to make her own decision to have an abortion.

In a third decision handed down June 15, the Court in Simopoulos v. Virginia *upheld 8-1 a Virginia law requiring second-trimester abortions to be performed in licensed hospitals. It did so because that law, unlike the invalidated Akron ordinance, permitted outpatient surgical clinics to be licensed as "hospitals." Justice John Paul Stevens was the lone dissenter in this opinion.*

Reaction

The Court's decisive stand on abortion rights drew strong reaction from groups and individuals active in the abortion issue. The decision was hailed by groups advocating freedom of choice, but anti-abortion organizations vowed to renew their efforts to amend the Constitution to ban abortion.

Sen. Robert W. Packwood, R-Ore., said he was "delighted by the decisions because they affirmed "a constitutional right that state legislatures cannot nibble away at." But Sen. Orrin G. Hatch, R-Utah, sponsor of an anti-abortion constitutional amendment, called the decisions an "abomination."

The Reagan administration, in a brief filed by Solicitor General Rex E. Lee, had urged the Court to bow out of the constitutional controversy and "accord heavy deference" to the wisdom of legislative bodies or to bear the task of endless litigation.

In a rare statement on a Supreme Court decision, President Reagan expressed "profound disappointment" and called on Congress to "make its voice heard against abortion on demand and to restore legal protections for the unborn whether by statute or constitutional amendment." Agreeing with O'Connor, Reagan said that "the legislature is the appropriate forum for resolving these issues."

> Following are excerpts from the Supreme Court's June 15, 1983, decision in Akron v. Akron Center for Reproductive Health *striking down several state laws regulating abortion and from the dissenting opinion of Sandra Day O'Connor; from the Court's decisions in* Planned Parenthood Association of Kansas City, Missouri, Inc. v. Ashcroft, *upholding several provisions of a Missouri abortion law; and from the decisions in* Simopoulos v. Virginia *upholding a Virginia law requiring second-trimester abortions to be performed in licensed hospitals:*

Nos. 81-746 and 81-1172

City of Akron, Petitioner
v.
Akron Center for Reproductive
Health, Inc., et al.

On writs of Certiorari to the United States Court of Appeals for the Sixth Circuit

Akron Center for Reproductive
Health, Inc., et al., Petitioners
v.
City of Akron et al.

JUSTICE POWELL delivered the opinion of the Court.

In this litigation we must decide the constitutionality of several provisions of an ordinance enacted by the city of Akron, Ohio, to regulate the performance of abortions. Today we also review abortion regulations enacted by the State of Missouri, see *Planned Parenthood Ass'n of Kansas City, Mo., Inc.* v. *Ashcroft*, and by the State of Virginia, see *Simopoulos* v. *Virginia.*

These cases come to us a decade after we held in *Roe* v. *Wade* (1973) that the right of privacy, grounded in the concept of personal liberty guaranteed by the Constitution, encompasses a woman's right to decide whether to terminate her pregnancy. Legislative responses to the Court's decision have required us on several occasions, and again today, to define the limits of a State's authority to regulate the performance of abortions. And arguments continue to be made, in these cases as well, that we erred in interpreting the Constitution. Nonetheless, the doctrine of *stare decisis,* while perhaps never entirely persuasive on a constitutional question, is a doctrine that demands respect in a society governed by the rule of law. We respect it today, and reaffirm *Roe* v. *Wade.*

I

In February 1978 the city council of Akron enacted Ordinance No. 160-1978, entitled "Regulation of Abortions." The ordinance sets forth 17 provisions that regulate the performance of abortions, . . . five of which are at issue in this case:

(i) Section 1870.03 requires that all abortions performed after the first trimester of pregnancy be performed in a hospital.

(ii) Section 1870.05 sets forth requirements for notification of and consent by parents before abortions may be performed on unmarried minors.

(iii) Section 1870.06 requires that the attending physician make certain specified statements to the patient "to insure that the consent for an abortion is truly informed consent."

(iv) Section 1870.07 requires a 24-hour waiting period between the time the woman signs a consent form and the time the abortion is performed.

(v) Section 1870.16 requires that fetal remains be "disposed of in a humane and sanitary manner."

A violation of any section of the ordinance is punishable as a criminal misdemeanor. If any provision is invalidated, it is to be severed from the remainder of the ordinance. The ordinance became effective on May 1, 1978.

On April 19, 1978, a lawsuit challenging virtually all of the ordinance's provisions was filed in the District Court for the Northern District of Ohio. The plaintiffs, respondents and cross-petitioners in this Court, were three corporations that operate abortion clinics in Akron and a physician who has performed abortions at one of the clinics. The defendants, petitioners and cross-respondents here, were the city of Akron and three city officials

("Akron"). Two individuals ("intervenors") were permitted to intervene as co-defendants "in their individual capacity as parents of unmarried daughters of child-bearing age." On April 27, 1978, the District Court preliminarily enjoined enforcement of the ordinance.

In August 1979, after hearing evidence, the District Court ruled on the merits. It found that plaintiffs lacked standing to challenge seven provisions of the ordinance, none of which is before this Court. The District Court invalidated four provisions, including § 1870.05 (parental notice and consent), § 1870.06(B) (requiring disclosure of facts concerning the woman's pregnancy, fetal development, the complications of abortion, and agencies available to assist the woman), and § 1870.16 (disposal of fetal remains). The court upheld the constitutionality of the remainder of the ordinance, including § 1870.03 (hospitalization for abortions after the first trimester), § 1870.06(C) (requiring disclosure of the particular risks of the woman's pregnancy and the abortion technique to be employed), and § 1870.07 (24-hour waiting period).

All parties appealed some portion of the District Court's judgment. The Court of Appeals for the Sixth Circuit affirmed in part and reversed in part. It affirmed the District Court's decision that § 1870.03's hospitalization requirement is constitutional. It also affirmed the ruling that §§ 1870.05, 1870.06(B), and 1870.16 are unconstitutional. The Court of Appeals reversed the District Court's decision on §§ 1870.06(C) and 1870.07, finding these provisions to be unconstitutional.

Three separate petitions for certiorari were filed. In light of the importance of the issues presented, and in particular the conflicting decisions as to whether a State may require that all second-trimester abortions be performed in a hospital, we granted both Akron's and the plaintiffs' petitions. We denied the intervenors' petition, *Seguin* v. *Akron Center for Reproductive Health, Inc.* . . . We now reverse the judgment of the Court of Appeals upholding Akron's hospitalization requirement, but affirm the remainder of the decision invalidating the provisions on parental consent, informed consent, waiting period, and disposal of fetal remains.

II

In *Roe* v. *Wade,* the Court held that the "right of privacy, . . . founded in the Fourteenth Amendment's concept of personal liberty and restrictions upon state action, . . . is broad enough to encompass a woman's decision whether or not to terminate her pregnancy." Although the Constitution does not specifically identify this right, the history of this Court's constitutional adjudication leaves no doubt that "the full scope of the liberty guaranteed by the Due Process Clause cannot be found in or limited by the precise terms of the specific guarantees elsewhere provided in the Constitution." *Poe* v. *Ullman* (1961). Central among these protected liberties is an individual's "freedom of personal choice in matters of marriage and family life." . . . The decision in *Roe* was based firmly on this long-recognized and essential element of personal liberty.

The Court also has recognized, because abortion is a medical procedure, that the full vindication of the woman's fundamental right necessarily requires that her physician be given "the room he needs to make his best medical judgment." *Doe* v. *Bolton* (1973). . . . The physician's exercise of this medical judgment encompasses both assisting the woman in the decisionmaking process and implementing her decision should she choose abortion. . . .

At the same time, the Court in *Roe* acknowledged that the woman's fundamental right "is not unqualified and must be considered against important state interests in abortion." But restrictive state regulation of the right to choose abortion, as with other fundamental rights subject to searching judicial examination, must be supported by a compelling state interest. We have recognized two such interests that may justify state regulation of abortions.

First, a State has an "important and legitimate interest in protecting the potentiality of human life." Although this interest exists "throughout the course of the woman's pregnancy," *Beal* v. *Doe* (1977), it becomes compelling only at viability, the point at which the fetus "has the capability of meaningful life outside the mother's womb". . . . See *Planned Parenthood of Central Mo.* v. *Danforth* (1976). At viability this interest in protecting the potential life of the unborn child is so important that the State may proscribe abortions altogether, "except when it is necessary to preserve the life or health of the mother."

Second, because a State has a legitimate concern with the health of women who undergo abortions, "a State may properly assert important interests in safeguarding health [and] in maintaining medical standards." We held in *Roe,* however, that this health interest does not become compelling until "approximately the end of the first trimester" of pregnancy. Until that time, a pregnant woman must be permitted, in consultation with her physician, to decide to have an abortion and to effectuate that decision "free of interference by the State."

This does not mean that a State never may enact a regulation touching on the woman's abortion right during the first weeks of pregnancy. Certain regulations that have no significant impact on the woman's exercise of her right may be permissible where justified by important state health objectives. In *Danforth,* we unanimously upheld two Missouri statutory provisions, applicable to the first trimester, requiring the woman to provide her informed written consent to the abortion and the physician to keep certain records, even though comparable requirements were not imposed on most other medical procedures. . . . The decisive factor was that the State met its burden of demonstrating that these regulations furthered important health-related State concerns. But even these minor regulations on the abortion procedure during the first trimester may not interfere with physician-patient consultation or with the woman's choice between abortion and childbirth. . . .

From approximately the end of the first trimester of pregnancy, the State "may regulate the abortion procedure to the extent that the regulation reasonably relates to the preservation and protection of maternal health." The State's discretion to regulate on this basis does not, however, permit it to adopt abortion regulations that depart from accepted medical practice. We have rejected a State's attempt to ban a particular second-trimester abortion procedure, where the ban would have increased the costs and limited the availability of abortions without promoting important health benefits. . . . If a State requires licensing or undertakes to regulate the performance of abortions during this period, the health standards adopted must be "legitimately related to the objective the State seeks to accomplish."

III

Section 1870.03 of the Akron ordinance requires that any abortion performed "upon a pregnant woman subsequent to the end of the first trimester of her pregnancy" must be "performed in a hospital." A "hospital" is "a general hospital or special hospital devoted to gynecology or obstetrics which is accredited by the Joint Commission on Accreditation of Hospitals or by the American Osteopathic Association." § 1870.1(B). Accreditation by these organizations requires compliance with comprehensive standards governing a wide variety of health and surgical services. The ordinance thus prevents the performance of abortions in outpatient facilities that are not part of an acute-care, full-service hospital.

In the District Court plaintiffs sought to demonstrate that this hospitalization requirement has a serious detrimental impact on a woman's ability to obtain a second-trimester abortion in Akron and that it is not reasonably related to the State's interest in the health of the pregnant woman. The District Court did not reject this argument, but rather found the evidence "not . . . so convincing that it is willing to discard the Supreme Court's formulation in *Roe*" of a line between impermissible first-trimester regulation and permissible second-trimester regulation. The Court of Appeals affirmed on a similar basis. It accepted plaintiffs' argument that Akron's hospitalization requirement did not have a reasonable health justification during at least part of the second trimester, but declined to "retreat from the 'bright line' in *Roe* v. *Wade*." We believe that the courts below misinterpreted this Court's prior decisions, and we now hold that § 1870.03 is unconstitutional.

A

In *Roe* v. *Wade* the Court held that after the end of the first trimester of pregnancy the State's interest becomes compelling, and it may "regulate the abortion procedure to the extent that the regulation reasonably relates to the preservation and protection of maternal health." We noted, for example, that States could establish requirements relating "to the facility in which the procedure is to be performed, that is, whether it must be in a hospital or may be a clinic or some other place of less-than-hospital status." In the companion case of *Doe* v. *Bolton* the Court invalidated a Georgia requirement that all abortions be performed in a hospital licensed by the State Board of Health and accredited by the Joint Commission on Accreditation of Hospitals. . . . We recognized the State's legitimate health interests in establishing, for second-trimester abortions, "standards for licensing all facilities where abortions may be performed." We found, however, that "the State must show more than [was shown in *Doe*] in order to prove that only the full resources of a licensed hospital, rather than those of some other appropriately licensed institution, satisfy these health interests."

We reaffirm today . . . that a State's interest in health regulation becomes compelling at approximately the end of the first trimester. The existence of a compelling state interest in health, however, is only the beginning of the inquiry. The State's regulation may be upheld only if it is reasonably designed to further that state interest. . . . And the Court in *Roe* did not hold that it always is reasonable for a State to adopt an abortion regulation that applies to the entire second trimester. A State necessarily must have latitude in adopting regulations of general applicability in this sensitive area. But if it appears that during a substantial portion of the second trimester the State's regulation "depart[s] from accepted medical practice," the regulation may not be upheld simply because it may be reasonable for the remaining portion of the trimester. Rather, the State is obligated to make a reasonable effort to limit the effect of its regulations to the period in the trimester during which its health interest will be furthered.

B

There can be no doubt that § 1870.03's second-trimester hospitalization requirement places a significant obstacle in the path of women seeking an abortion. A primary burden created by the requirement is additional cost to the woman. The Court of Appeals noted that there was testimony that a second-trimester abortion costs more than twice as much in a hospital as in a clinic. . . . (in-hospital abortion costs $850-$900, whereas a dilation-and-evacuation (D&E) abortion performed in a clinic costs $350-$400). Moreover, the court indicated that second-trimester abortions were rarely performed in Akron hospitals. . . . Thus, a second-trimester hospitalization requirement may force women to travel to find available facilities, resulting in both financial expense and additional health risk. It therefore is apparent that a second-trimester hospitalization requirement may significantly limit a woman's ability to obtain an abortion.

Akron does not contend that § 1870.03 imposes only an insignificant burden on women's access to abortion, but rather defends it as a reasonable health regulation. This position had strong support at the time of *Roe* v. *Wade,* as hospitalization for second-trimester abortions was recommended by the American Public Health Association (APHA) . . . and the American College of Obstetricians and Gynecologists (ACOG). . . . Since then, however, the safety of second-trimester abortions has increased dramatically. The principal reason is that the D&E procedure is now widely and successfully used for second-trimester abortions. The Court of Appeals found that there was "an abundance of evidence that D&E is the safest method of performing post-first trimester abortions today." The availability of the D&E procedure during the interval between approximately 12 and 16 weeks of pregnancy, a period during which other second-trimester abortion techniques generally cannot be used, has meant that women desiring an early second-trimester abortion no longer are forced to incur the health risks of waiting until at least the sixteenth week of pregnancy.

For our purposes, an even more significant factor is that experience indicates that D&E may be performed safely on an outpatient basis in appropriate nonhospital facilities. The evidence is strong enough to have convinced the APHA to abandon its prior recommendation of hospitalization for all second-trimester abortions. . . . Similarly, the ACOG no longer suggests that all second-trimester abortions be performed in a hospital. It recommends that abortions performed in a physician's office or outpatient clinic be limited to 14 weeks of pregnancy, but it indicates that abortions may be performed safely in "a hospital-based or in a free-standing ambulatory surgical facility, or in an outpatient clinic meeting the criteria requiring for a free-standing surgical facility," until 18 weeks of pregnancy.

These developments, and the professional commentary supporting them, constitute impressive evidence that — at least during the early weeks of the second trimester — D&E abortions may be performed as safely in an outpatient clinic as in a full-service hospital. We conclude, therefore, that "present medical knowledge," *Roe,* convincingly undercuts Akron's justification for requiring that *all* second-trimester abortions be performed in a hospital. . . .

IV

We turn next to § 1870.05(B), the provision prohibiting a physician from performing an abortion on a minor pregnant woman under the age of 15 unless he obtains "the informed written consent of one of her parents or her legal guardian" or unless the minor obtains "an order from a court having jurisdiction over her that the abortion be performed or induced." The District Court invalidated this provision because "[i]t does not establish a procedure by which a minor can avoid a parental veto of her abortion decision by demonstrating that her decision is, in fact, informed. Rather, it requires, in all cases, both the minor's informed consent and either parental consent or a court order." The Court of Appeals affirmed on the same basis.

The relevant legal standards are not in dispute. The Court has held that "the State may not impose a blanket provision . . . requiring the consent of a parent or person *in loco parentis* as a condition for abortion of an unmarried minor." *Danforth*. In *Bellotti* v. *Baird* (1979) (*Bellotti II*), a majority of the Court indicated that a State's interest in protecting immature minors will sustain a requirement of a consent substitute, either parental or judicial. . . . The *Bellotti II* plurality cautioned, however, that the State must provide an alternative procedure whereby a pregnant minor may demonstrate that she is sufficiently mature to make the abortion decision herself or that, despite her immaturity, an abortion would be in her best interests. Under these decisions, it is clear that Akron may not make a blanket determination that *all* minors under the age of 15 are too immature to make this decision or that an abortion never may be in the minor's best interests without parental approval. . . .

. . . [W]e do not think that the Akron ordinance, as applied in Ohio juvenile proceedings, is reasonably susceptible of being construed to create an "opportunity for case-by-case evaluations of the maturity of pregnant minors." We therefore affirm the Court of Appeals' judgment that § 1870.05(B) is unconstitutional.

V

The Akron ordinance provides that no abortion shall be performed except "with the informed written consent of the pregnant woman . . . given freely and without coercion." § 1870.06(A). Furthermore, "in order to insure that the consent for an abortion is truly informed consent," the woman must be "orally informed by her attending physician" of the status of her pregnancy, the development of her fetus, the date of possible viability, the physical and emotional complications that may result from an abortion, and the availability of agencies to provide her with assistance and information with respect to birth control, adoption, and childbirth. § 1870.06(B). In addition, the attending physician must inform her "of the particular risks associated with her own pregnancy and the abortion technique to be employed . . . [and] other information which in his own medical judgment is relevant to her decision as to whether to have an abortion or carry her pregnancy to term." § 1870.06(C).

The District Court found that § 1870.06(B) was unconstitutional, but that § 1870.06(C) was related to a valid state interest in maternal health. . . . The Court of Appeals concluded that both provisions were unconstitutional. . . . We affirm.

A

In *Danforth*, we upheld a Missouri law requiring a pregnant woman to "certif[y] in writing her consent to the abortion and that her consent is informed and freely given and is not the result of coercion.". . . We rejected the view that "informed consent" was too vague a term, construing it to mean "the giving of information to the patient as to just what would be done and as to its consequences. To ascribe more meaning than this might well confine the attending physician in an undesired and uncomfortable straitjacket in the practice of his profession."

The validity of an informed consent requirement thus rests on the State's interest in protecting the health of the pregnant woman. The decision to have an abortion has "implications far broader than those associated with most other kinds of medical treatment," *Bellotti II,* and thus the State legitimately may seek to ensure that it has been made "in the light of all attendant circumstances — psychological and emotional as well as physical — that might be relevant to the well-being of the patient." *Colautti* v. *Franklin* (1979). This does not mean, however, that a State has unreviewable authority to decide what information a woman must be given before she chooses to have an abortion. It remains primarily the responsibility of the physician to ensure that appropriate information is conveyed to his patient, depending on her particular circumstances. *Danforth's* recognition of the State's interest in ensuring that this information be given will not justify abortion regulations designed to influence the woman's informed choice between abortion or childbirth.

B

Viewing the city's regulations in this light, we believe that § 1870.06(B) attempts to extend the State's interest in ensuring "informed consent" beyond permissible limits. First, it is fair to say that much of the information required is designed not to inform the woman's consent but rather to persuade her to withhold it altogether. Subsection (3) requires the physician to inform his patient that "the unborn child is a human life from the moment of conception," a requirement inconsistent with the Court's holding in *Roe* v. *Wade* that a State may not adopt one theory of when life begins to justify its regulation of abortions. . . . Moreover, much of the detailed description of "the anatomical and physiological characteristics of the particular unborn child" required by subsection (3) would involve at best speculation by the physician. And subsection (5), that begins with the dubious statement that "abortion is a major surgical procedure" and proceeds to describe numerous possible physical and psychological complications of abortion, is a "parade of horribles" intended to suggest that abortion is a particularly dangerous procedure.

An additional, and equally decisive, objection to § 1870.06(B) is its intrusion upon the discretion of the pregnant woman's physician. This provision specifies a litany of information that the physician must recite to each woman regardless of whether in his judgment the information is relevant to her personal decision. For example, even if the physician believes that some of the risks outlined in subsection (5) are nonexistent for a particular patient, he remains obligated to describe them to her. In *Danforth* the Court warned against placing the physician in just such an "undesired and uncomfortable straitjacket." Consistent with its interest in ensuring informed consent, a State may require that a physician make certain that his patient understands the physical and emotional implications of having an abortion. But Akron has gone far beyond merely describing the general subject matter relevant to informed consent. By insisting upon recitation of a lengthy and inflexible list of information, Akron unreasonably has placed "obstacles in the path of the doctor upon whom [the woman is] entitled to rely for advice in connection with her decision." *Whalen* v. *Roe* (1977).

C

Section 1870.06(C) presents a different question. Under this provision, the "attending physician" must inform the woman

> "of the particular risks associated with her own pregnancy and the abortion technique to be employed including providing her with at least a general description of the medical instructions to be followed subsequent to the abortion in order to insure her safe recovery, and shall in addition provide her with such other information which in his own medical judgment is relevant to her decision as to whether to have an abortion or carry her pregnancy to term."

The information required clearly is related to maternal health and to the State's legitimate purpose in requiring informed consent. Nonetheless, the Court of Appeals determined that it interfered with the physician's medical judgment "in exactly the same way as section 1870.06(B). It requires the doctor to make certain disclosures in all cases, regardless of his own professional judgment as to the desirability of doing so." This was a misapplication of *Danforth*. There we construed "informed consent" to mean "the giving of information to the patient as to just what would be done and as to its consequences." We see no significant difference in Akron's requirement that the woman be told of the particular risks of her pregnancy and the abortion technique to be used, and be given general instructions on proper post-abortion care. Moreover, in contrast to subsection (B), § 1870.06(C) merely describes in general terms the information to be disclosed. It properly leaves the precise nature and amount of this disclosure to the physician's discretion and "medical judgment."

The Court of Appeals also held, however, that § 1870.66(C) was invalid because it required that the disclosure be made by the "attending physician." The court found that "the practice of all three plaintiff clinics has been for the counseling to be conducted by persons other than the doctor who performs the abortion," and determined that Akron had not justified requiring the physician personally to describe the health risks. Akron challenges this holding as contrary to our cases that emphasize the importance of the physician-patient relationship. In Akron's view, as in the view of the dissenting judge below, the "attending physician" requirement "does no more than seek to ensure that there is in fact a true physician-patient relationship even for the woman who goes to an abortion clinic."

Requiring physicians personally to discuss the abortion decision, its health risks, and consequences with each patient may in some cases add to the cost of providing abortions, though the record here does not suggest that ethical physicians will charge more for adhering to this typical element of the physician-patient relationship. Yet in *Roe* and subsequent cases we have "stressed repeatedly the central role of the physician, both in consulting with the woman about whether or not to have an abortion, and in determining how any abortion was to be carried out." *Colautti* v. *Franklin* (1979). Moreover, we have left no doubt that, to ensure the safety of the abortion procedure, the States may mandate that only physicians perform abortions. . . .

We are not convinced, however, that there is as vital a state need for insisting that the physician performing the abortion, or for that matter any physician, personally counsel the patient in the absence of a request. The State's interest is in ensuring that the woman's consent is informed and unpressured; the critical factor is whether she obtains the necessary information and counseling from a qualified person, not the identity of the person from whom she obtains it. Akron and intervenors strongly urge that the nonphysician counselors at the plaintiff abortion clinics are not trained or qualified to perform this important function. The courts below made no such findings, however, and on the record before us we cannot say that the woman's consent to the abortion will not be informed if a physician delegates the counseling task to another qualified individual.

In so holding, we do not suggest that the State is powerless to vindicate its interest in making certain the "important" and "stressful" decision to abort "is made with full knowledge of its nature and consequences." Nor do we imply that a physician may abdicate his essential role as the person ultimately responsible for the medical aspects of the decision to perform the abortion. A State may define the physician's responsibility to include verification that adequate counseling has been provided and that the woman's consent is informed. In addition, the State may establish reasonable minimum qualifications for those people who perform the primary counseling function. . . . In light of these alternatives, we believe that it is unreasonable for a State to insist that only a physician is competent to provide the information and counseling relevant to informed consent. We affirm the judgment of the Court of Appeals that § 1870.06(C) is invalid.

VI

The Akron ordinance prohibits a physician from performing an abortion until 24 hours after the pregnant woman signs a consent form. The District Court upheld this provision on the ground that it furthered Akron's interest in ensuring "that a woman's abortion decision is made after careful consideration of all the facts applicable to her particular situation." The Court of Appeals reversed, finding that the inflexible waiting period had "no medical basis," and that careful consideration of the abortion decision by the woman "is beyond the state's power to require." We affirm the Court of Appeals' judgment. . . .

We find that Akron has failed to demonstrate that any legitimate state interest is furthered by an arbitrary and inflexible waiting period. There is no evidence suggesting that the abortion procedure will be performed more safely. Nor are we convinced that the State's legitimate concern that the woman's decision be informed is reasonably served by requiring a 24-hour delay as a matter of course. The decision whether to proceed with an abortion is one as to which it is important to "affor[d] the physician adequate discretion in the exercise of his medical judgment." *Colautti* v. *Franklin* (1979). In accordance with the ethical standards of the profession, a physician will advise the patient to defer the abortion when he thinks this will be beneficial to her. But if a woman, after appropriate counseling, is prepared to give her written informed consent and proceed with the abortion, a State may not demand that she delay the effectuation of that decision.

VII

Section 1870.16 of the Akron ordinance requires physicians performing abortions to "insure that the remains of the unborn child are disposed of in a humane and sanitary manner." The Court of Appeals found that the word "humane" was impermissibly vague as a definition of conduct subject to criminal prosecution. The court invalidated the entire provision, declining to sever the word "humane" in order to uphold the requirement that disposal be "sanitary.". . . We confirm this judgment.

Akron contends that the purpose of § 1870.16 is simply " 'to preclude the mindless dumping of aborted fetuses on garbage piles.' " It is far from clear, however, that this provision has such a limited intent. The phrase "humane and sanitary" does, as the Court of Appeals noted, suggest a possible intent to "mandate some sort of 'decent burial' of an embryo at the earliest stages of formation." This level of uncertainty is fatal where criminal liability is imposed. . . . Because § 1870.16 fails to give a physician "fair notice that his contemplated conduct is forbidden," *United States* v. *Harriss* (1954), we agree that it violates the Due Process Clause.

VIII

We affirm the judgment of the Court of Appeals invalidating those sections of Akron's "Regulations of Abortions" ordinance that deal with parental consent, informed consent, a 24-hour waiting period, and the disposal of fetal remains. The remaining portion of the judgment, sustaining Akron's requirement that all second-trimester abortions be performed in a hospital, is reversed.

It is so ordered.

JUSTICE O'CONNOR, with whom JUSTICE WHITE and JUSTICE REHNQUIST join, dissenting.

In *Roe* v. *Wade* (1973), the Court held that the "right of privacy . . . founded in the Fourteenth Amendment's concept of personal liberty and restrictions upon state action ... is broad enough to encompass a woman's decision whether or not to terminate her pregnancy." The parties in these cases have not asked the Court to reexamine the validity of that holding and the court below did not address it. Accordingly, the Court does not reexamine its previous holding. Nonetheless, it is apparent from the Court's opinion that neither sound constitutional theory nor our need to decide cases based on the application of neutral principles can accommodate an analytical framework that varies according to the "stages" of pregnancy, where those stages, and their concomitant standards of review, differ according to the level of medical technology available when a particular challenge to state regulation occurs. The Court's analysis of the Akron regulations is inconsistent both with the methods of analysis employed in previous cases dealing with abortion, and with the Court's approach to fundamental rights in other cases.

Our recent cases indicate that a regulation imposed on "a lawful abortion 'is not unconstitutional unless it unduly burdens the right to seek an abortion.'" *Maher* v. *Roe* (1977) (quoting *Bellotti* v. *Baird* (1977) (*Bellotti I*). ... In my view, this "unduly burdensome" standard should be applied to the challenged regulations throughout the entire pregnancy without reference to the particular "stage" of pregnancy involved. If the particular regulation does not "unduly burden" the fundamental right, *Maher,* then our evaluation of that regulation is limited to our determination that the regulation irrationally relates to a legitimate state purpose. Irrespective of what we may believe is wise or prudent policy in this difficult area, "the Constitution does not constitute us as 'Platonic Guardians' nor does it vest in this Court the authority to strike down laws because they do not meet our standards of desirable social policy, 'wisdom,' or 'common sense.'" *Plyler* v. *Due* (1982).

I

The trimester or "three-stage" approach adopted by the Court in *Roe,* and, in a modified form, employed by the Court to analyze the state regulations in these cases, cannot be supported as a legitimate or useful framework for accommodating the woman's right and the State's interests. The decision of the Court today graphically illustrates why the trimester approach is a completely unworkable method of accommodating the conflicting personal rights and compelling state interests that are involved in the abortion context.

As the Court indicates today, the State's compelling interest in maternal health changes as medical technology changes, and any health regulation must not "depart from accepted medical practice." In applying this standard, the Court holds that "the safety of second-trimester abortions has increased dramatically" since 1973, when *Roe* was decided. Although a regulation such as one requiring that all second-trimester abortions be performed in hospitals "had strong support" in 1973 "as a reasonable health regulation," this regulation can no longer stand because, according to the Court's diligent research into medical and scientific literature, the dilation and evacuation procedure (D&E), used in 1973 only for first-trimester abortions, "is now widely and successfully used for second trimester abortions." Further, the medical literature relied on by the Court indicates that the D&E procedure may be performed in an appropriate non-hospital setting for "at least ... the early weeks of the second trimester...." The Court then chooses the period of 16 weeks of gestation as that point at which D&E procedures may be performed safely in a non-hospital setting, and thereby invalidates the Akron hospitalization regulation.

It is not difficult to see that despite the Court's purported adherence to the trimester approach adopted in *Roe,* the lines drawn in that decision have now been "blurred" because of what the Court accepts as technological advancement in the safety of abortion procedure. The State may no longer rely on a "bright line" that separates permissible from impermissible regulation, and it is no longer free to consider the second trimester as a unit and weigh the risks posed by all abortion procedures throughout that trimester. Rather, the State must continuously and conscientiously study contemporary medical and scientific literature in order to determine whether the effect of a particular regulation is to "depart from accepted medical practice" insofar as particular procedures and particular periods within the trimester are concerned. Assuming that legislative bodies are able to engage in this exacting task, it is difficult to believe that our Constitution *requires* that they do it as a prelude to protecting the health of their citizens. It is even more difficult to believe that this Court, without the resources available to those bodies entrusted with making legislative choices, believes itself competent to make these inquiries and to revise these standards every time the American College of Obstetricians and Gynecologists (ACOG) or similar group revises its views about what is and what is not appropriate medical procedure in this area....

Just as improvements in medical technology inevitably will move *forward* the point at which the State may regulate for reasons of maternal health, different technological improvements will move *backward* the point of viability at which the State may proscribe abortions except when necessary to preserve the life and health of the mother....

The *Roe* framework, then, is clearly on a collision course with itself. As the medical risks of various abortion procedures decrease, the point at which the State may regulate for reasons of maternal health is moved further forward to actual childbirth. As medical science becomes better able to provide for the separate existence of the fetus, the point of viability is moved further back toward conception. Moveover, it is clear that the trimester approach violates the fundamental aspiration of judicial decision making through the application of neutral principles "sufficiently absolute to give them roots throughout the community and continuity over significant periods of time...." A. COX, The Role of the Supreme Court in American Government 114 (1976). The *Roe* framework is inherently tied to the state of medical technology that exists whenever particular litigation ensues. Although legislatures are better suited to make the necessary factual judgments in this area, the Court's framework forces legislatures, as a matter of constitutional law, to speculate about what constitutes "accepted medical practice" at any given time. Without the necessary expertise or ability, courts must then pretend to act as science review boards and examine those legislative judgments.

The Court adheres to the *Roe* framework because the doctrine of *stare decisis* "demands respect in a society governed by the rule of law." Although respect for *stare decisis* cannot be challenged, "this Court's considered practice [is] not to apply *stare decisis* as rigidly in constitutional as in nonconstitutional cases." *Glidden Company* v. *Zdanok* (1962). . . .

Even assuming that there is a fundamental right to terminate pregnancy in some situations, there is no justification in law or logic for the trimester framework adopted in *Roe* and employed by the Court today on the basis of *stare decisis*. For the reasons stated above, that framework is clearly an unworkable means of balancing the fundamental right and the compelling state interests that are indisputably implicated.

II

The Court in *Roe* correctly realized that the State has important interests "in the areas of health and medical standards" and that "[t]he State has a legitimate interest in seeing to it that abortion, like any other medical procedure, is performed under circumstances that insure maximum safety for the patient." The Court also recognized that the State has "*another* important and legitimate interest in protecting the potentiality of human life." I agree completely that the State has these interests, but in my view, the point at which these interests become compelling does not depend on the trimester of pregnancy. Rather, these interests are present *throughout* pregnancy. . . .

The state interest in potential human life is . . . extant throughout pregnancy. In *Roe,* the Court held that although the State had an important and legitimate interest in protecting potential life, that interest could not become compelling until the point at which the fetus was viable. The difficulty with this analysis is clear: *potential* life is no less potential in the first weeks of pregnancy than it is at viability or afterward. At any stage in pregnancy, there is the *potential* for human life. Although the Court refused to "resolve the difficult question of when life begins," the Court chose the point of viability — when the fetus is *capable* of life independent of its mother — to permit the complete proscription of abortion. The choice of viability as the point at which the state interest in *potential* life becomes compelling is no less arbitrary than choosing any point before viability or any point afterward. Accordingly, I believe that the State's interest in protecting potential human life exists throughout the pregnancy.

III

Although the State possesses compelling interests in the protection of potential human life and in maternal health throughout pregnancy, not every regulation that the State imposes must be measured against the State's compelling interests and examined with strict scrutiny. This Court has acknowledged that "the right in *Roe* v. *Wade* can be understood only by considering both the woman's interest and the nature of the State's interference with it. *Roe* did not declare an unqualified 'constitutional right to an abortion,'.... Rather, the right protects the woman from unduly burdensome interference with her freedom to decide whether to terminate her pregnancy." The Court and its individual Justices have repeatedly utilized the "unduly burdensome" standard in abortion cases....

In determining whether the State imposes an "undue burden," we must keep in mind that when we are concerned with extremely sensitive issues, such as the one involved here, "the appropriate forum for their resolution in a democracy is the legislature. We should not forget that 'legislatures are ultimate guardians of the liberties and welfare of the people in quite as great a degree as the courts." *Missouri, K. & T. R. Co.* v. *May* (1904). This does not mean that in determining whether a regulation imposes an "undue burden" on the *Roe* right that we defer to the judgments made by state legislatures. "The point is, rather, that when we face a complex problem with many hard questions and few easy answers we do well to pay careful attention to how the other branches of Government have addressed the same problem." *Columbia Broadcasting System Inc.* v. *Democratic National Committee* (1973).

We must always be mindful that "[t]he Constitution does not compel a state to fine-tune its statutes so as to encourage or facilitate abortions. To the contrary, state action 'encouraging childbirth except in the most urgent circumstances' is 'rationally related to the legitimate government objective of protecting potential life.' "

IV

A

Section 1870.03 of the Akron ordinance requires that second-trimester abortions be performed in hospitals. The Court holds that this requirement imposes a "significant obstacle" in the form of increased cost and decreased availability of abortions, and the Court rejects the argument offered by the State that the requirement is a reasonable health regulation under *Roe*.

For the reasons stated above, I find no justification for the trimester approach used by the Court to analyze this restriction. I would apply the "unduly burdensome" test and find that the hospitalization requirement does not impose an undue burden on that decision.

The Court's reliance on increased abortion costs and decreased availability is misplaced. As the City of Akron points out, there is no evidence in this case to show that the two Akron hospitals that performed second-trimester abortions denied an abortion to any woman, or that they would not permit abortion by the D&E procedure. . . . In addition, there was no evidence presented that other hospitals in nearby areas did not provide second-trimester abortions. Further, almost *any* state regulation, including the licensing requirements that the Court *would* allow, . . . inevitably and necessarily entails increased costs for *any* abortion. In *Simopoulos* v. *Virginia,* the Court upholds the State's stringent licensing requirements that will clearly involve greater cost because the State's licensing scheme "is not an unreasonable means of furthering the State's compelling interest in" preserving maternal health. Although the Court acknowledges this indisputably correct notion in *Simopoulos,* it inexplicably refuses to apply it in this case. A health regulation, such as the hospitalization requirement, simply does not rise to the level of "official interference" with the abortion decision. . . .

Health-related factors that may legitimately be considered by the State go well beyond what various medical organizations have to say about the *physical* safety of a particular procedure. Indeed, "all factors — physical, emotional, psychological, familial, and the woman's age — [are] relevant to the well-being of the patient." *Doe* v. *Bolton* (1973). The ACOG standards, upon which the Court relies, state that "[r]egardless of advances in abortion technology, midtrimester terminations will likely remain more hazardous, expensive, and emotionally disturbing for a woman than early abortions."

The hospitalization requirement does not impose an undue burden, and it is not necessary to apply an exacting standard of review. Further, the regulation has a "rational relation" to a valid state objective of ensuring the health and welfare of its citizens. See *Williamson* v. *Lee Optical Co.* (1955).

B

Section 1870.05(B) of the Akron ordinance provides that no physician shall perform an abortion on a minor under 15 years of age unless the minor gives written consent, and the physician first obtains the informed written consent of a parent or guardian, or unless the minor first obtains "an order from a court having jurisdiction over her that the abortion be performed or induced." Despite the fact that this regulation has yet to be construed in the state courts, the Court holds that the regulation is unconstitutional because it is not "reasonably susceptible of being construed to create an 'opportunity for case-by-case evaluations of the maturity of pregnant minors.'" I believe that the Court should have abstained from declaring the ordinance unconstitutional. . . .

Assuming *arguendo* that the Court is correct in holding that a parental notification requirement would be unconstitutional as applied to mature minors, I see no reason to assume that the Akron ordinance and the state juvenile court statute compel state judges to notify the parents of a mature minor if such notification was contrary to the minor's best interests. Further, there is no reason to believe that the state courts would construe the consent requirement to impose any type of parental or judicial veto on the abortion decisions of mature minors. In light of the Court's complete lack of knowledge about how the Akron ordinance will operate, and how the Akron ordinance and the state juvenile court statute interact, our " 'scrupulous regard for the rightful independence of state governments' " counsels against "unnecessary interference by the federal courts with proper and validly administered state concerns, a course so essential to the balanced working of our federal system." *Harrison* v. *NAACP* (quoting *Mathews* v. *Rodgers* (1932)).

C

The Court invalidates the informed consent provisions of § 1870.06(B) and § 1870.06(C) of the Akron ordinance. Although it finds that subsections (1), (2), (6), and (7) of § 1870.06(B) are "certainly ... not objectionable, it refuses to sever those provisions from subsections (3), (4), and (5) because the State requires that the "acceptable" information be provided by the attending physician when "much, if not all of it, could be given by a qualified person assisting the physician." Despite the fact that the Court finds that § 1870.06(C) "properly leaves the precise nature and amount of ... disclosure to the physician's discretion and 'medical judgment,' " the Court also finds § 1870.06(C) unconstitutional because it requires that the disclosure be made by the attending physician, rather than by other "qualified persons" who work at abortion clinics.

We have approved informed consent provisions in the past even though the physician was required to deliver certain information to the patient. In *Danforth,* the Court upheld a state informed consent requirement because "[t]he decision to abort, indeed, is an important, and often a stressful one, and it is desirable and imperative that it be made with full knowledge of its nature and consequences." In *H.L.* v. *Matheson,* the Court noted that the state statute in the case required that the patient "be advised at a minimum about available adoption services, about fetal development, and about forseeable complications and risks of an abortion. See Utah Code Ann § 76-7-305 (1978). In *Planned Parenthood of Central Mo.* v. *Danforth* (1976), we rejected a constitutional attack on written consent provisions." Indeed, we have held that an informed consent provision does not "unduly burden[] the right to seek an abortion." *Bellotti I.*

The remainder of § 1870.06(B), and § 1870.06(C), impose no undue burden or drastic limitation on the abortion decision. The City of Akron is merely attempting to ensure that the decision to abort is made in light of that knowledge that the City deems relevant to informed choice. As such, these regulations do not impermissibly affect any privacy right under the Fourteenth Amendment.

D

Section 1870.07 of the Akron ordinance requires a 24-hour waiting period between the signing of a consent form and the actual performance of the abortion, except in cases of emergency.... The court below invalidated this requirement because it affected abortion decisions during the first trimester of pregnancy. The Court affirms the decision below, not on the ground that it affects early abortions, but because "Akron has failed to demonstrate that any legitimate state interest is furthered by an arbitrary and inflexible waiting period." The Court accepts the arguments made by Akron Center that the waiting period increases the costs of obtaining an abortion by requiring the pregnant woman to make two trips to the clinic, and increase the risks of abortion through delay and scheduling difficulties. The decision whether to proceed should be left to the physician's " 'discretion in the exercise of his medical judgment.' "....

Assuming *arguendo* that any additional costs are such as to impose an undue burden on the abortion decision, the State's compelling interests in maternal physical and mental health and protection of fetal life clearly justify the waiting period. As we acknowledged in *Danforth,* the decision to abort is "a stressful one," and the waiting period reasonably relates to the State's interest in ensuring that a woman does not make this serious decision in undue haste. The decision also has grave consequences for the fetus, whose life the State has a compelling interest to protect and preserve. "No other [medical] procedure involves the purposeful termination of a potential life." The waiting period is surely a small cost to impose to ensure that the woman's decision is well-considered in light of its certain and irreparable consequences on fetal life, and the possible effects on her own.

E

Finally, § 1870.16 of the Akron ordinance requires that "[a]ny physician who shall perform or induce an abortion upon a pregnant woman shall insure that the remains of the unborn child are disposed of in a humane and sanitary manner." The Court finds this provision void-for-vagueness. I disagree.

...In light of the fact that the City of Akron indicates no intent to require that physicians provide "decent burials" for fetuses, and that "humane" is no more vague than the term "sanitary," the vagueness of which Akron Center does not question, I cannot conclude that the statute is void for vagueness.

V

For the reasons set forth above, I dissent from the judgment of the Court in these cases.

No. 81-1255 and 81-1623

Planned Parenthood Association
of Kansas City, Missouri, Inc.,
et al., Petitioners
v.
John Ashcroft, Attorney General
of Missouri, et al.

John Ashcroft, Attorney General
of Missouri, et al., Petitioners
v.
Planned Parenthood Association
of Kansas City, Missouri, Inc.,
et al., Petitioners

On writs of Certiorari to the United
States Court of Appeals for the
Eighth Circuit

[June 15, 1983]

JUSTICE POWELL delivered the opinion of the Court with respect to Parts I, II, and VI, and an opinion with respect to Parts III, IV, and V, in which THE CHIEF JUSTICE joins. [JUSTICES BURGER, BRENNAN, MARSHALL, BLACKMUN and STEVENS joined in Parts I, II and VI.]

These cases, like *City of Akron* v. *Akron Center for Reproductive Health, Inc.,* and *Simopoulos* v. *Virginia,* present questions as to the validity of state statutes regulating the performance of abortions.

I

Planned Parenthood of Kansas City, Missouri, Inc., two physicians who perform abortions, and an abortion clinic ("plaintiffs") filed a complaint in the District Court for the Western District of Missouri challenging, as unconstitutional, several sections of the Missouri statutes regulating the performance of abortions. The sections relevant here include Mo. Rev. Stat. § 188.025 (Supp. 1982), requiring that abortions after 12 weeks of pregnancy be performed in a hospital; § 188.047, requiring a pathology report for each abortion performed; § 188.030, requiring the presence of a second physician during abortions performed after viability; and § 188.028, requiring minors to secure parental or judicial consent.

After hearing testimony from a number of expert witnesses, the District Court invalidated all of these sections except the pathology requirement. The Court of Appeals for the Eighth Circuit reversed the District Court's judgment with respect to § 188.028, thereby upholding the requirement that a minor secure parental or judicial consent to an abortion. It also held that the District Court erred in sustaining § 188.047, the pathology

565

requirement. The District Court's judgment with respect to the second-physician requirement was affirmed, and the case was remanded for further proceedings and findings relating to the second-trimester hospitalization requirement. On remand, the District Court affirmed its holding that the second-trimester hospitalization requirement was unconstitutional. The Court of Appeals affirmed this judgment. We granted certiorari.

The Court today in *City of Akron* has stated fully the principles that govern judicial review of state statutes regulating abortions, and these need not be repeated here. With these principles in mind, we turn to the statutes at issue.

II

In *City of Akron,* we invalidated a city ordinance requiring physicians to perform all second-trimester abortions at general or special hospitals accredited by the Joint Commission on Accreditation of Hospitals (JCAH) or by the American Osteopathic Association. Missouri's hospitalization requirements are similar to those enacted by Akron, as all second-trimester abortions must be performed in general, acute-care facilities. For the reasons stated in *City of Akron,* we held that such a requirement "unreasonably infringes upon a woman's constitutional right to obtain an abortion." For the same reasons, we affirm the Court of Appeals' judgment that § 188.025 is unconstitutional.

III

We turn now to the State's second-physician requirement. In *Roe* v. *Wade* (1973), the Court recognized that the State has a compelling interest in the life of a viable fetus: "[T]he State in promoting its interest in the potentiality of human life may, if it chooses, regulate, and even proscribe, abortion except where it is necessary, in appropriate medical judgment, for the preservation of the life or health of the mother." See *Colautti* v. *Franklin* (1979); *Beal* v. *Doe* (1977). Several of the Missouri statutes undertake such regulation. Post-viability abortions are proscribed except when necessary to preserve the life or the health of the woman. The State also forbids the use of abortion procedures fatal to the viable fetus unless alternative procedures pose a greater risk to the health of the woman.

The statutory provision at issue in this case requires the attendance of a second physician at the abortion of a viable fetus. § 188.030.3. This section requires that the second physician "take all reasonable steps in keeping with good medical practice . . . to preserve the life and health of the viable unborn child; provided that it does not pose an increased risk to the life or health of the woman." It also provides that the second physician "shall take control of and provide immediate medical care for a child born as a result of the abortion."

The lower courts invalidated § 188.030.3. The plaintiffs, respondents here on this issue, urge affirmance on the grounds that the second-physician requirement distorts the traditional doctor-patient relationship, and is both impractical and costly. They note that Missouri does not require two physicians in attendance for any other medical or surgical procedure, including childbirth or delivery of a premature infant.

The first physician's primary concern will be the life and health of the woman. Many third-trimester abortions in Missouri will be emergency operations, as the State permits these late abortions only when they are necessary to preserve the life or the health of the woman. It is not unreasonable for the State to assume that during the operation the first physician's attention and skills will be directed to preserving the woman's health, and not to protecting the actual life of those fetuses who survive the abortion procedure. Viable fetuses will be in immediate and grave danger because of their premature birth. A second physician, in situations where Missouri permits third-trimester abortions, may be of assistance to the woman's physician in preserving the health and life of the child.

By giving immediate medical attention to a fetus that is delivered alive, the second physician will assure that the State's interests are protected more fully than the first physician alone would be able to do. And given the compelling interest that the State has in preserving life, we cannot say that the Missouri requirement of a second physician in those unusual circumstances where Missouri permits a third-trimester abortion is unconstitutional. Preserving the life of a viable fetus that is aborted may not often be possible, but the State legitimately may choose to provide safeguards for the comparatively few instances of live birth that occur. We believe the second-physician requirement reasonably furthers the State's compelling interest in protecting the lives of viable fetuses, and we reverse the judgment of the Court of Appeals holding that § 188.030.3 is unconstitutional.

IV

In regulating hospital services within the State, Missouri requires that "[a]ll tissue surgically removed with the exception of such tissue as tonsils, adenoids, hernial sacs and prepuces, shall be examined by a pathologist, either on the premises or by arrangement outside of the hospital.". . . The narrow question before us is whether the State lawfully also may require the tissue removed following abortions performed in clinics as well as in hospitals to be submitted to a pathologist.

On its face and in effect, § 188.047 is reasonably related to generally accepted medical standards and "further[s] important health-related State concerns." As the Court of Appeals recognized, pathology examinations are clearly "useful and even necessary in some cases," because "abnormalities in the tissue may warn of serious, possibly fatal disorders." As a rule, it is accepted medical practice to submit *all* tissue to the examination of a pathologist. This is particularly important following abortion, because questions remain as to the long-range complications and their effect on subsequent pregnancies. . . . Recorded pathology reports, in concert with abortion complication reports, provide a statistical basis for studying those complications.

Plaintiffs argue that the physician performing the abortion is as qualified as a pathologist to make the examination. This argument disregards the fact that Missouri requires a pathologist — not the performing physician — to examine tissue after almost every type of surgery. Although this requirement is in a provision relating to surgical procedures in hospitals, many of the same procedures included within the Missouri statute customarily are performed also in outpatient clinics. No reason has been suggested why the prudence required in a hospital should not be equally appropriate in such a clinic. Indeed, there may be good reason to impose stricter standards in this respect on clinics performing abortions than on hospitals. As the testimony in the District Court indicates, medical opinion differs widely on this question. . . .

In weighing the balance between protection of a woman's health and the comparatively small additional cost of a pathologist's examination, we cannot say that the Constitution requires that a State subordinate its interest in health to minimize to this extent the cost of abortions. Even in the early weeks of pregnancy, "[c]ertain regulations that have no significant impact on the woman's exercise of her right to decide to have an abortion may be permissible where justified by important state health objectives." We think the cost of a tissue examination does not significantly burden a pregnant woman's abortion decision. The estimated cost of compliance for plaintiff Reproductive Health Services was $19.40 per abortion performed, and in light of the substantial benefits that a pathologist's examination can have, this small cost clearly is justified. . . . Accordingly, we reverse the judgment of the Court of Appeals on this issue.

V

As we noted in *City of Akron,* the relevant legal standards with respect to parental consent requirements are not in dispute. . . . A State's interest in protecting immature minors will sustain a requirement of a consent substitute, either parental or judicial. It is clear, however, that "the State must provide an alternative procedure whereby a pregnant minor may demonstrate that she is sufficiently mature to make the abortion decision herself or that, despite her immaturity, an abortion would be in her best interests." The issue here is one purely of statutory construction: whether Missouri provides a judicial alternative that is consistent with these established legal standards.

The Missouri statute, § 188.028.2, in relevant part, provides:

"(4) In the decree, the court shall for good cause:
"(a) Grant the petition for majority rights for the purpose of consenting to the abortion; or

"(b) Find the abortion to be in the best interests of the minor and give judicial consent to the abortion, setting forth the grounds for so finding; or

"(c) Deny the petition, setting forth the grounds on which the petition is denied[.]"

On its face, § 188.028.2(4) authorizes juvenile courts to choose among any of the alternatives outlined in the section. The Court of Appeals concluded that a denial of the petition permitted in subsection (c) "would initially require the court to find that the minor was not emancipated and was not mature enough to make her own decision and that an abortion was not in her best interests." Plaintiffs contend that this interpretation is unreasonable. We do not agree.

Where fairly possible, courts should construe a statute to avoid a danger of unconstitutionality. The Court of Appeals was aware, if the statute provides discretion to deny permission to a minor for *any* "good cause," that arguably it would violate the principles that this Court has set forth. It recognized, however, that before exercising any option, the juvenile court must receive evidence on "the emotional development, maturity, intellect and understanding of the minor." The court then reached the logical conclusion that "findings and the ultimate denial of the petition must be supported by a showing of 'good cause.'" The Court of Appeals reasonably found that a court could not deny a petition "for good cause" unless it first found — after having received the required evidence — that the minor was not mature enough to make her own decisions.... We conclude that the Court of Appeals correctly interpreted the statute and that § 188.028, as interpreted, avoids any constitutional infirmities.

VI

The judgment of the Court of Appeals, insofar as it invalidated Missouri's second-trimester hospitalization requirement and upheld the State's parental and judicial consent provision, is affirmed. The judgment invalidating the requirement that a second physician attend the abortion of any viable fetus is reversed....

It is so ordered.

JUSTICE BLACKMUN, with whom JUSTICE BRENNAN, JUSTICE MARSHALL, and JUSTICE STEVENS join, concurring in part and dissenting in part.

The Court's decision today in *Akron v. Akron Center for Reproductive Health, Inc.,* invalidates the city of Akron's hospitalization requirement and a host of other provisions that infringe on a woman's decision to terminate her pregnancy through abortion. I agree that Missouri's hospitalization requirement is invalid under the *Akron* analysis, and I join Parts I and II of JUSTICE POWELL's opinion in the present cases. I do not agree, however, that the remaining Missouri statutes challenged in these cases satisfy the constitutional standards set forth in *Akron* and the Court's prior decisions.

I

Missouri law provides that whenever an abortion is performed, a tissue sample must be submitted to a "board eligible or certified pathologist" for a report. This requirement applies to first trimester abortions as well as to those performed later in pregnancy. Our past decisions establish that the performance of abortions during the first trimester must be left " 'free of interference by the State.' " As we have noted in *Akron,* this does not mean that every regulation touching upon first-trimester abortions is constitutionally impermissible. But to pass constitutional muster, regulations affecting first-trimester abortions must "have no significant impact on the woman's exercise of her right" and must be "justified by important state health objectives."

Missouri's requirement of a pathologist's report is not justified by important health objectives. Although pathology examinations may be "useful and even necessary in some cases," Missouri requires more than a pathology examination and a pathology report; it demands that the examination be performed and the report prepared by a "board eligible or certified pathologist" rather than by the attending physician. Contrary to JUSTICE POWELL's assertion, this requirement of a report by a pathologist is not in accord with "generally accepted medical standards.". . .

As the Court of Appeals pointed out, there was expert testimony at trial that a nonpathologist physician is as capable of performing an adequate gross examination as is a pathologist, and that the "abnormalities which are of concern" are readily detectable by a physician. . . .

On the record before us, I must conclude that the State has not "met its burden of demonstrating that [the pathologist requirement] further[s] important health-related State concerns." There has been no showing that tissue examinations by a pathologist do more to protect health than examinations by a nonpathologist physician. Missouri does not require pathologists' reports for any other surgical procedures performed in clinics, or for minor surgery performed in hospitals. Moreover, I cannot agree with JUSTICE POWELL that Missouri's pathologist requirement has "no significant impact" on a woman's exercise of her right to an abortion. It is undisputed that this requirement may increase the cost of a first-trimester abortion by as much as $40. . . . Under these circumstances, I would hold that constitutional limits have been exceeded.

II

In Missouri, an abortion may be performed after viability only if necessary to preserve the life or health of the woman. When a post-viability abortion is performed, Missouri law provides that "there [must be] in attendance a [second] physician . . . who shall take control of and provide immediate medical care for a child born as a result of the abortion.". . .

A

The second physican requirement is upheld in this case on the basis that it "reasonably furthers the State's compelling interest in protecting the lives of viable fetuses." While I agree that a second physician indeed may aid in preserving the life of a fetus born alive, this type of aid is possible only when the abortion method used is one that may result in a live birth. Although Missouri ordinarily requires a physician performing a post-viability abortion to use the abortion method most likely to preserve fetal life, this restriction does not apply when this method "would present a greater risk to the life and health of the woman."

The District Court found that the dilation and evacuation (D&E) method of abortion entails no chance of fetal survival, and that it will nevertheless be the method of choice for some women who need post-viability abortions. In some cases, in other words, maternal health considerations will preclude the use of procedures that might result in a live birth. When a D&E abortion is performed, the second physician can do nothing to further the State's compelling interest in protecting potential life. His presence is superfluous. The second-physician requirement thus is overbroad and "imposes a burden on women in cases where the burden is not justified by any possibility of survival of the fetus."

JUSTICE POWELL apparently believes that the State's interest in preserving potential life justifies the State in requiring a second physician at all post-viability abortions because some methods other than D&E may result in live births. But this fact cannot justify requiring a second physician to attend an abortion at which the chance of a live birth is nonexistent. The choice of method presumably will be made in advance, and any need for a second physician disappears when the woman's health requires that the choice be D&E. Because the statute is not tailored to protect the State's legitimate interests, I would hold it invalid.

B

In addition, I would hold that the statute's failure to provide a clear exception for emergency situations renders it unconstitutional. As JUSTICE POWELL recognizes, an emergency may arise in which delay could be dangerous to the life or health of the woman. A second physician may not always be available in such a situation; yet the statute appears to require one. It states, in unqualified terms, that a post-viability abortion "*shall* be performed ... *only* when there is in attendance" a second physician who "*shall* take control of" any child born as a result of the abortion, and it imposes certain duties on "the physician *required* by this section to be in attendance." (Emphasis added). By requiring the attendance of a second physician even when the resulting delay may be harmful to the health of the pregnant woman, the statute impermissibly fails to make clear "that the woman's life and health must always prevail over the fetus' life and health when they conflict." *Colautti* v. *Franklin* (1979). . . .

... The statute ... remains impermissibly vague; it fails to inform the physician whether he may proceed with a post-viability abortion in an emergency, or whether he must wait for a second physician even if the woman's life or health will be further imperiled by the delay....

III

Missouri law prohibits the performance of an abortion on an uneman- cipated minor absent parental consent or a court order.

Until today, the Court has never upheld "a requirement of a consent substitute, either parental or judicial." In *Planned Parenthood of Central Mo.* v. *Danforth,* the Court invalidated a parental consent requirement on the ground that "the State does not have the constitutional authority to give a third party an absolute, and possibly arbitrary, veto over the decision of the physician and his patient, regardless of the reason for withholding the consent.". . .

Because [the Missouri statute] permits a parental or judicial veto of a minor's decision to obtain an abortion, I would hold it unconstitutional.

JUSTICE O'CONNOR, with whom JUSTICE WHITE and JUSTICE REHNQUIST join, concurring in part in the judgment and dissenting in part.

For reasons stated in my dissent in No. 81-746, *Akron* v. *Akron Center for Reproductive Health* and in No. 81-1172, *Akron Center for Reproductive Health* v. *Akron,* I believe that the second-trimester hospitalization requirement imposed by § 188.025 does not impose an undue burden on the limited right to undergo an abortion. Assuming *arguendo* that the requirement was an undue burden, it would nevertheless "reasonably relat[e] to the preservation and protection of maternal health." *Roe* v. *Wade* (1973). I therefore dissent from the Court's judgment that the requirement is unconstitutional.

I agree that second-physician requirement contained in § 188.030.3 is constitutional because the State possesses a compelling interest in protect- ing and preserving fetal life, but I believe that this state interest is extant throughout pregnancy. I therefore concur in the judgment of the Court.

I agree that pathology-report requirement imposed by § 188.047 is constitutional because it imposes no undue burden on the limited right to undergo an abortion. Because I do not believe that the validity of this requirement is contingent in any way on the trimester of pregnancy in which it is imposed, I concur in the judgment of the Court.

Assuming *arguendo* that the State cannot impose a parental veto on the decision of a minor to undergo an abortion, I agree that the parental consent provision contained in § 188.028.2 is constitutional. However, I believe that the provision is valid because it imposes no undue burden on any right that a minor may have to undergo an abortion. I concur in the judgment of the Court on this issue....

No. 81-185

Chris Simopoulos, Appellant
v.
Virginia
} On appeal from the Supreme Court
of Virginia

JUSTICE POWELL delivered the opinion of the Court.

We have considered today mandatory hospitalization requirements for second-trimester abortions in *City of Akron* v. *Akron Center for Reproductive Health, Inc.,* and *Planned Parenthood Assn. of Kansas City, Mo., Inc.* v. *Ashcroft.* The principal issue here is whether Virginia's mandatory hospitalization requirement is constitutional.

Appellant is a practicing obstetrician-gynecologist certified by the American Board of Obstetrics and Gynecology. In November, 1979, he practiced at his office in Woodbridge, Virginia, at four local hospitals, and at his clinic in Falls Church, Virginia. The Falls Church clinic has an operating room and facilities for resuscitation and emergency treatment of cardiac/respiratory arrest. Replacement and stabilization fluids are on hand. Appellant customarily performs first-trimester abortions at his clinic. During the time relevant to this case, the clinic was not licensed, nor had appellant sought any license for it.

P.M. was a 17-year old high-school student when she went to appellant's clinic on November 8, 1979. She was unmarried, and told appellant that she was approximately 22 weeks pregnant. She requested an abortion but did not want her parents to know. Examination by appellant confirmed that P.M. was five months pregnant, well into the second trimester. Appellant testified that he encouraged her to confer with her parents and discussed with her the alternative of continuing the pregnancy to term. She did return home, but never advised her parents of her decision.

Two days later, P.M. returned to the clinic with her boy friend. The abortion was performed by an injection of saline solution. P.M. told appellant that she planned to deliver the fetus in a motel, and understood him to agree to this course. Appellant gave P.M. a prescription for an analgesic and a "Post-Injection Information" sheet that stated that she had undergone "a surgical procedure" and warned of a "wide range of normal reactions." The sheet also advised that she call the physician if "heavy" bleeding began. Although P.M. did not recall being advised to go to a hospital when labor began, this was included on the instruction sheet.

P.M. went to a motel. Alone, she aborted her fetus in the motel bathroom 48 hours after the saline injection. She left the fetus, follow-up instructions, and pain medication in the wastebasket at the motel. Her boy friend took her home. Police found the fetus later that day....

Appellant was indicted for unlawfully performing an abortion during the second trimester of pregnancy outside of a licensed hospital and was convicted by the Circuit Court of Fairfax County sitting without a jury. The Supreme Court of Virginia unanimously affirmed the conviction. This appeal followed. We noted probable jurisdiction, and now affirm....

II

We consistently have recognized and reaffirm today that a State has an "important and legitimate interest in the health of the mother" that becomes " 'compelling' . . . at approximately the end of the first trimester." *Roe* v. *Wade* (1973). This interest embraces the facilities and circumstances in which abortions are performed. Appellant argues, however, that Virginia prohibits all non-hospital second-trimester abortions and that such a requirement imposes an unconstitutional burden on the right of privacy. In *City of Akron* and *Ashcroft,* we upheld such a constitutional challenge to the acute-care hospital requirements at issue there. The State of Virginia argues here that its hospitalization requirement differs significantly from the hospitalization requirements considered in *City of Akron* and *Ashcroft* and that it reasonably promotes the State's interests.

In furtherance of its compelling interest in maternal health, Virginia has enacted a hospitalization requirement for abortions performed during the second trimester. As a general proposition, physicians' offices are not regulated under Virignia law. Virginia law does not, however, permit a physician licensed in the practice of medicine and surgery to perform an abortion during the second trimester of pregnancy unless "such procedure is performed in a hospital licensed by the State Department of Health." The Virginia abortion statute itself does not define the term "hospital." This definition is found in Va. Code § 32.1-123.1, that defines "hospital" to include "outpatient . . . hospitals." Section 20.2.11 of the Department of Health's Rules and Regulations for the Licensure of Outpatient Hospitals in Virginia (1977) ("regulations") defines outpatient hospital in pertinent part as "[i]nstitutions . . . which primarily provide facilities for the performance of surgical procedures on outpatients" and provides that second-trimester abortions may be performed in these clinics. Thus, under Virginia law, a second-trimester abortion may be performed in an outpatient surgical hospital provided that facility has been licensed as a "hospital" by the State....

It is readily apparent that Virginia's second-trimester hospitalization requirement differs from those at issue in *City of Akron* and *Planned Parenthood Assn. of Kansas City, Mo., Inc.* v. *Ashcroft.* In those cases, we recognized the medical fact that, "at least during the early weeks of the second trimester[,] D&E abortions may be performed as safely in an outpatient clinic as in a full-service hospital." The requirements at issue, however, mandated that "all second-trimester abortions must be performed in general, acute-care facilities." In contrast, the Virginia statutes and regulations do not require that second-trimester abortions be performed exclusively in full-service hospitals. Under Virginia's hospitalization requirement, outpatient surgical hospitals may qualify for licensing as "hospitals" in which second-trimester abortions lawfully may be performed. Thus, our decisions in *City of Akron* and *Ashcroft* are not controlling here.

In view of its interest in protecting the health of its citizens, the State necessarily has considerable discretion in determining standards for the licensing of medical facilities. Although its discretion does not permit it to adopt abortion regulations that depart from accepted medical practice, it does have a legitimate interest in regulating second-trimester abortions and setting forth the standards for facilities in which such abortions are performed. . . .

We need not consider whether Virginia's regulations are constitutional in every particular. Despite personal knowledge of the regulations at least by the time of trial, appellant has not attacked them as being insufficiently related to the State's interest in protecting health. His challenge throughout this litigation appears to have been limited to an assertion that the State cannot require all second-trimester abortions to be performed in full-service general hospitals. In essence, appellant has argued that Virginia's hospitalization requirements are no different in substance from those reviewed in the *City of Akron* and *Ashcroft* cases. At the same time, however, appellant took the position — both before the Virginia courts and this Court — that a state licensing requirement for outpatient abortion facilities would be constitutional. We can only assume that by continuing to challenge the Virginia hospitalization requirement petitioner either views the Virginia regulations in some unspecified way as unconstitutional or challenges a hospitalization requirement that does not exist in Virginia. Yet, not until his reply brief in this Court did he elect to criticize the regulations apart from his broadside attack on the entire Virginia hospitalization requirement.

Given the plain language of the Virginia regulations and the history of their adoption, we see no reason to doubt that an adequately equipped clinic could, upon proper application, obtain an outpatient hospital license permitting the performance of second-trimester abortions. We conclude that Virginia's requirement that second-trimester abortions be performed in licensed clinics is not an unreasonable means of furthering the State's compelling interest in "protecting the woman's own health and safety." As we emphasized in *Roe*, "[t]he State has a legitimate interest in seeing to it that abortion, like any other medical procedure, is performed under circumstances that insure maximum safety for the patient." Unlike the provisions at issue in *City of Akron* and *Ashcroft*, Virginia's statute and regulations do not require that the patient be hospitalized as an inpatient or that the abortion be performed in a full-service, acute-care hospital. Rather, the State's requirement that second-trimester abortions be performed in licensed clinics appears to comport with accepted medical practice, and leaves the method and timing of the abortion precisely where they belong — with the physician and the patient.

The judgment of the Supreme Court of Virginia is

Affirmed.

JUSTICE O'CONNOR, with whom JUSTICE WHITE and JUSTICE REHNQUIST join, concurring in part and concurring in the judgment.

...I concur in the judgment of the Court insofar as it affirms the conviction. For reasons stated in my dissent in No. 81-746, *Akron* v. *Akron Center for Reproductive Health* and in No. 81-1172, *Akron Center for Reproductive Health* v. *Akron,* I do not agree that the constitutional validity of the Virginia mandatory hospitalization requirement is contingent in any way on the trimester in which it is imposed. Rather, I believe that the requirement in this case is not an undue burden on the decision to undergo an abortion.

POPE'S TRIP TO POLAND

June 16-23, 1983

Almost exactly four years after he made a dramatic and emotional visit to his native country as the first Polish pope, John Paul II returned to his beleaguered homeland for an eight-day tour June 16-23. The pope's major mission was to participate in the jubilee of Our Lady of Czestochowa, a revered icon also known as the Black Madonna. But even more significant was the impact the trip might have on the troubled Polish political situation. (Pope's trip to Poland, Historic Documents of 1979, p. 725)

The pope arrived at a time of severe economic problems and extreme, though simmering, tensions between the Communist Party government headed by Gen. Wojciech Jaruzelski and the outlawed but still-spirited independent Solidarity union movement. In light of that situation, the pope's visit had been preceded by considerable speculation about the role he might shape for the Roman Catholic Church, the strongest and oldest institution in Poland, in arranging a modus vivendi *between the communist regime and the nation's workers.*

In remarks, homilies and services delivered throughout his trip, John Paul II made it clear that the church sympathized with the formation of Solidarity in August 1980, and he decried the government's imposition of martial law in December 1981. In the aftermath of those events, the church had appeared to maintain a critical balance between strong support of workers' rights and a recognition that Poland was indeed part of the Soviet sphere of influence. (Workers' demands, Historic Documents of 1980, p. 793; imposition of martial law, Historic Documents of 1981, p. 881;

easing of martial law, Historic Documents of 1982, p. 947)

The pope had been scheduled to visit Poland a year earlier, but the Warsaw government postponed the trip, fearing widespread disturbances. As a result, the festival commemorating the 600th anniversary of Our Lady of Czestochowa had been extended. The best known of Polish shrines, venerated also as a symbol of Polish nationalism and resistance, the madonna had been revered as the protector of the nation ever since the Jasna Gora monastery in Czestochowa, where it was housed, withstood a siege of Swedish Protestants in 1665.

By 1983 many Western commentators noted that the government might view an official visit by the pope as a further legitimization of communist rule and that it was gambling on avoiding mass outbreaks of violence. On the other hand, observers speculated that the pope's presence might well embolden the Solidarity movement. A third possibility was that the church might act as a mediator between the two, obtaining government concessions to ease martial rule in return for Solidarity's agreement to mute its opposition and avoid militancy.

While the pope's visit did not have clear-cut repercussions, it did stir debate over the church's political role and it prompted apprehension by some Vatican officials that a rebirth of Solidarity might be accompanied by a crackdown on the church as well as Soviet moves into Poland.

Themes Weave Religion, Nationalism, Freedom

In addition to Warsaw, where he celebrated an outdoor mass, places visited by the pope included the Niepokalanow monastery, founded by St. Maksymillian Kolbe, a priest who volunteered to die for a fellow Pole at Auschwitz during the Nazi occupation; Czestochowa, site of the Jasna Gora monastery; the manufacturing center of Poznan; the mining center of Katowice; the industrial city of Wroclaw; the steel town of Nowa Huta, where the pope celebrated mass at a church-dedication ceremony; and Cracow, where he departed June 23. Omitted from the government-sanctioned itinerary was the port city of Gdansk, birthplace of Solidarity.

At each of his stops in the eight-city tour, huge crowds gathered to greet the pontiff and hear him celebrate mass. But, unlike the exuberance with which Polish citizens greeted the pope in 1979, the welcome in 1983 was, according to news reports, more somber and serious. There were few disturbances. The red and white banners of the outlawed Solidarity were widely apparent, along with the Polish flag, patriotic pins and symbols of the Roman Catholic Church. John Paul II repeatedly referred to the need to establish a dialogue in a spirit of mutual trust and to honor the settlement reached between workers and the government signed Aug. 30, 1980. In that agreement, which followed a wave of strikes, the communist authorities acquiesced to a number of demands; among them, they agreed to allow workers to form labor unions and to reduce government censorship. The agreement never was put into effect; labor unrest persisted, and martial law eventually was declared.

Government Defends Actions

The pope and communist leader Jaruzelski stood side by side at the official welcoming ceremonies at the Belvedere Palace in Warsaw June 17. The meeting was broadcast nationally over state television. "I come to my homeland as a pilgrim on the occasion of the jubilee of Jasna Gora," the pope said. "I come in order to be with my compatriots at a particularly difficult moment in the history of Poland. . . . And even if life in the homeland since Dec. 13, 1981, has been subjected to the severe rigors of the state of war, . . . nevertheless I do not stop hoping that social reform, announced on many occasions, . . . will gradually be put into effect."

In response, Jaruzelski defended the government's actions by saying, "The universally known course of events led us to take a decision which was dramatically difficult but necessary. We took it in extremis, as the last choice. . . . I confirm our will to abolish the state of war, as well as to apply adequate, humanitarian and legal solutions. If the situation in the country takes a good direction, that can come about in a not distant time."

After their televised remarks, the two leaders met in private for conversations described by government spokesman Jerzy Urban as "direct, long, and undoubtedly useful." The government also announced that it had agreed to a meeting between John Paul II and Lech Walesa, founder of Solidarity.

Public Statements, Private Meetings

Defying government orders to avoid politics, the pope throughout his trip invoked the spirit of Polish nationalism, indirectly linking it with the Solidarity movement, the sufferings of the Polish people under military rule and their desire to loosen the bonds of Soviet domination. He gave perhaps the strongest comments on these issues during ceremonies honoring the Black Madonna at Czestochowa June 18 and 19. Speaking to a crowd estimated at more than one million, the pope said the 1980 events that led to Solidarity's creation "touched hearts and consciences" throughout the world and marked a time "when the Polish worker stood up for himself with the Gospel in his hand and a prayer on his lips." Citing the support for free trade unions provided in his encyclical, "Laborem Exercens" ("On Human Work"), the pope said, "The experience of history teaches that organizations of this type are an indispensable element of social life, particularly in modern industrialized society." The pontiff continued, "It was in this spirit that I spoke in January 1981 during an audience granted to the delegation of Solidarity." (The delegation had been headed by Walesa, who was awarded the Nobel Peace Prize in 1983. See p. 925.)

In what many observers interpreted as a veiled admonition to the Soviet Union, the pope said in a homily delivered during mass, "The nation is truly free when it can shape itself as a community determined by unity of culture, language and history. The state is firmly sovereign when it governs society and also serves the common good of society and allows the nation to realize its own subjectivity, its own identity. . . . The nation perishes if it deforms its spirit — the nation grows when its spirit is ever more purified and no external power is able to destroy it!"

Although the pope's public statements consistently affirmed his support for Solidarity, one unscheduled event raised questions concerning the role of the church in Polish political affairs and speculation that an understanding had been reached whereby the government would lift martial law in return for Walesa's withdrawal from political activity. At John Paul II's request, Jaruzelski flew to Cracow to meet privately with the pontiff in the last hours of his visit. The two agreed that negotiations would continue and that "further contacts between the Apostolic See and the Polish People's Republic will serve the good of the state and church," according to a communiqué released after the more-than-two-hour meeting. The next morning the pope met with Walesa in an unannounced location in the Tatra Mountains. On June 24 the Vatican newspaper L'Osservatore Romano said in an editorial that Walesa "has lost his battle" to remain head of Solidarity and that "Sometimes the sacrifice of uncomfortable people is necessary so a higher good can be born for the community." The Vatican disavowed the editorial, saying that it expressed only the opinion of the writer, deputy editor Rev. Virgilio Levi, who resigned his post. The New York Times reported June 26 that Walesa told reporters, "I will not quit like a rat. I will not run away." But he said he might step down "if there was somebody else to take over the problem."

Martial Law Lifted

One month after the pope's visit, the Polish government announced it was lifting martial law. That went into effect on July 22, the anniversary of the establishment of communist rule in Poland in 1944. In practice, most elements of martial law powers were made permanent in legislative amendments to the constitution — for example, provisions making it illegal to strike, incite anti-government demonstrations and distribute literature officially considered subversive. A key amendment would permit government authorities to declare a "state of emergency" in the event of disorder and unrest, and thus assume extraordinary powers. The only major concession was the granting of amnesty for several hundred political prisoners still being detained. Most observers concluded that the lifting of martial law would make little difference in the degree of political freedom enjoyed by the people of Poland.

Following are excerpts from Pope John Paul II's and Gen. Wojciech Jaruzelski's televised remarks delivered June 17 at the Belvedere Palace in Warsaw; from the pope's homily delivered June 17 during a mass at the Dziesieciolecia Stadium in Warsaw; from a homily delivered June 19 during a mass at Czestochowa; and from remarks delivered June 20 at the Muchowiec Airport in Katowice:

POPE'S REMARKS AT BELVEDERE PALACE

1. "A prosperous and peaceful Poland is . . . in the interest of tranquillity and good cooperation among the peoples of Europe." I take the liberty of beginning my speech with the same words that I used in this same Belvedere Palace in June 1979, during my previous visit to my homeland. I repeat these words because they were said by a great friend of Poland, Pope Paul VI, to whom the church in our country owed the important work of normalization in the northern and western territories. I repeat them also because these words reflect, so to speak, the constant quintessence of what the Apostolic See thinks of Poland and what it hopes for Poland.

2. This way of thinking has an important significance against the background of our difficult historical past, beginning especially from the end of the 18th century. Precisely against the background of the partitions of Poland, the thought that "a prosperous and peaceful Poland is in the interest of tranquillity and good cooperation among the peoples of Europe" has been a postulate of international morality, as well as a healthy European reason of state. For more than 100 years this thought had to seek to establish itself amid the imperialist powers contrary to our independence; to find expression at last, at the end of World War I, in the peace treaties. The Polish nation is steadfast in its gratitude toward those who at that time were the heralds of its independent existence.

While we are here in Warsaw, Poland's capital, the memory of all these historical experiences comes to life again in a special way. Hence the words of Paul VI remain ever important, stating as they do not only that Poland has the right to sovereign existence as a state, but also that in her own place she is necessary to Europe and the world.

3. In the words quoted, Pope Paul VI underlined that "Poland . . . is in the interest of tranquillity and good co-operation among the peoples of

Europe." This affirmation has its own full eloquence against the background of World War II, which was the greatest violation of peace in this century, above all on the continent of Europe. Poland found itself at the very center of the terrible experiences of that war. For its right to sovereignty it paid with 6 million of its citizens, who sacrificed their lives on the various war fronts, in the prisons and in the extermination camps. The Polish nation has confirmed at a very high price its right to be sovereign master of the land that it inherits from its ancestors.

The memory of the terrible experience of the war lived through by Poland and by the other peoples of Europe causes one to renew once more the impassioned plea that peace should not be disturbed or endangered, and in particular that at the earliest possible moment and in an effective way, namely by frank and constructive negotiations, the arms race be remedied.

4. Coming to Poland, I have before my eyes its whole 1,000-year history and, first of all, the experiences of this century, linked with my own life.

I very much wish to thank the supreme authorities of the state for the invitation to come home, transmitted to me in a letter from the president of the Council of State. I come to my homeland as a pilgrim on the occasion of the jubilee of Jasna Gora. I come in order to be with my compatriots at a particularly difficult moment in the history of Poland after World War II. At the same time I do not lose hope that this difficult moment may become a path to social renewal, the beginning of which is established by the social agreements stipulated by the representatives of the state authorities with the representatives of the world of labor. And even if life in the homeland since Dec. 13, 1981, has been subjected to the severe rigors of the state of war, which from the beginning of the present year was suspended, nevertheless I do not stop hoping that that social reform, announced on many occasions, according to the principles so painstakingly worked out in the critical days of August 1980 and contained in the agreements, will gradually be put into effect.

This renewal is indispensable for maintaining the good name of Poland in the world, as well as in order to find a way out of the internal crisis and spare the sufferings of so many sons and daughters of the nation, my compatriots.

5. The Apostolic See devotes so many of its efforts to the cause of peace in today's world. This year is the 20th anniversary of the publication of the encyclical *Pacem in Terris* of Pope John XXIII. Pope Paul VI advanced the efforts in this field in many forms. These efforts are very numerous and at the same time generally known; it would be difficult at this moment to mention them in detail. I will mention only the initiative of the Pontifical Academy of Sciences in 1981. Eminent specialists in the scientific disciplines such as physics, biology, genetics and medicine drew up a memorandum on the foreseeable consequences of the use of atomic weapons. The memorandum was presented by the representatives of the academy to the heads of state of the Soviet Union, the United States of America, Britain and France, to the president of the assembly of the

United Nations and to the secretary general of the United Nations.

From the time of Pope Paul VI the custom was established of celebrating on New Year's Day the World Day of Peace, a custom linked with an annual message. This year the message of Jan. 1, 1983, is titled "The Dialogue for Peace, a Challenge for Our Time." I have taken the liberty of sending the text of this message also to the highest representatives of the state authority in Poland. . . .

"Dialogue for peace must be established . . . in order to resolve social conflicts, in order to seek the common good. While bearing in mind the interests of different groups, the common effort for peace must be made ceaselessly, in the exercise of fredom and duties which are democratic for all, thanks to the structures of participation and thanks to the many means of reconciliation between employers and workers, in the manner of respecting and associating the cultural, ethnic and religious groups which make up a nation. When unfortunately dialogue between government and people is absent, social peace is threatened or absent; it is like a state of war. But history and present-day observation show that many countries have succeeded or are succeeding in establishing a true working together to resolve the conflicts which arise within them or even to prevent them, by acquiring means of dialogue which are truly effective" (no. 8).

7. Distinguished gentlemen: I return once again to the words of Paul VI: "A prosperous and peaceful Poland is . . . in the interest of tranquillity and good cooperation among the peoples of Europe."

As a son of the land of Poland, I make these words in a special way my personal hope for the nation and the state. This hope I address at the same time to the representatives of authority and to the whole of society.

I ardently desire that Poland may always have her proper place among the nations of Europe, between the East and the West. I ardently desire the re-creation of conditions of "good cooperation" with all the Western nations on our continent as well as in the Americas, above all with the United States of America, where so many millions of citizens are of Polish origin. I am deeply convinced that these conditions can be created. This too is one of the tasks of dialogue — international dialogue — for peace in today's world.

I also know that the Polish episcopate constantly makes tireless efforts to ensure that the principle of dialogue proclaimed by the church may become a fruitful basis both for internal peace and for "good cooperation" between Poland and the other nations of Europe and the world.

8. I desire once more to express my gratitude for the invitation to come home. I wish also to place in the hands of the representatives of the supreme authorities of the Polish republic — both these authorities and the organs of local administration under them — my thanks for all that they have done to prepare my meeting with the nation and with the church in my homeland.

Just as I did during my previous visit, I wish finally to affirm that I will continue to consider as my own every true good of my homeland, as though I were still living in this land and perhaps even more because of the distance. With the same strength I will also continue to tell the effects of what would threaten Poland, what could do her damage, bring her dishonor, what could signify the stagnation of a depression.

In my prayer for Poland great numbers of people of good will are united with me throughout the world.

I add my expression of esteem for all the distinguished representatives of the authorities and to each one in particular, according to the office that they exercise, the dignity that is theirs, as also according to the important share of responsibility that lies upon each one of you before history and before your consciences.

I also wish to thank you for the gift offered to me, and at the same time I ask you to accept my own gift.

JARUZELSKI REMARKS, BELVEDERE PALACE

I heartily greet Your Holiness in the homeland of the Poles, into the Polish People's Republic. For the second time the pilgrim path has led the head of the Roman Catholic Church to the places of his origins; Your Holiness is upon Polish soil. We all descend from it, it is our mother. It has experienced the maledictions of history beyond human measure, often knowing malady, hunger, fire, war, for whose prevention imploring supplications were raised over the centuries. It has known the bitterness of numerous defeats and vain efforts in the destinies of the generations which went out to die "like stones thrown into trenches."

It was Your Holiness' lot to share the most tragic experiences of the 20th century, to be a member of a people condemned to extermination by the Nazi genocides. This is an unusual moral title; it confers an important particularity upon the words of the head of the Holy See.

Poland arose so as to live. It arose as an independent state, sovereign, reborn in a new, just, territorial form. Already the third generation of children is coming into the world in Polish Gdansk, Wroclaw and Szczecin. This place has not been assigned to us by a caprice of history. Forty years ago the Polish left pointed out the socialist way to the people. Precisely that historic turn has assured that the great tribute of lives and blood paid to this land by its worthier children did not go to waste. Along the way of Your Holiness' pilgrimage are to be found as an everlasting monument innumerable tombs of soldiers. Many of them conceal the ashes — as the poet said — of Russian brothers. Thousands, hundreds of thousands of those offered up their young lives as they brought us salvation. The collective memory of those cruel years is eternal: We have drawn the right conclusions from them.

The external security of the state today stands in need of real alliances. Now, as never before in our history, the frontiers of the republic are not afire. They are all frontiers of friendship. Not even a centimeter of Polish territory shall ever be the object of discussion. On this all Poles are agreed.

But, behold, once again the threat of war arises, a war far more terrible than those preceding it. Armaments have reached a dangerous, a downright critical level. War calculations have been made, limited atomic war has been programed, as if an inferno on Earth could have limits.

A great appeal against war courses through the world. Peace is today the loftiest of ends. The People's Poland has always been in the front rank of its fervent defenders. In the face of new threats it takes an active part in the peacemaking efforts of the socialist community in its constructive initiatives. The government of the People's Republic of Poland and public opinion follow with great attention the important messages coming from the Holy See in defense of the common good of all nations and of the right to live in peace.

Tension in international relations coincides with a sharpening of the internal problems of Poland. A great fire can spring from a brazier. Hence Poland's great co-responsibility in regard to peace, "ours and yours." The universally known course of events led us to take a decision which was dramatically difficult but necessary. We took it *in extremis,* as the last choice. It is said that Poland is suffering, but who will put on the balance plates the infinite sufferings of mankind, the torments and tears, which will be able to be avoided? I desire in this place to recall the memorable words of Tadeusz Kosciuszko: "It is the moment when much must be sacrificed to save all." We do not fear the judgment of posterity; it will be a just judgment. Certainly more balanced than many judgments of today.

During the preceding first pilgrimage, important and eloquent words of Your Holiness were uttered. "The state, as the expression of sovereignty, of self-determination of peoples and nations, is the regular accomplishment of order." On that rests its moral authority as well. We take up this affirmation which is in harmony with the traditional and actual comprehension of the essence of the state. We take it up with sincere acknowledgment, we welcome it. When the state grows weak or sinks in anarchy, the people pay. We in Poland know this historical truth only too well. It enlightens and clarifies our actions. Nonetheless, we do not seek facile justifications. We judge our errors in all sincerity, although power alone is not to blame; it was not it which drove the country to the brink of catastrophe. But now we wish to look above all to the future, to a better future in Poland. We have taken to the way of reforms with decision, to renewal of social life, of that of the state, of economic life. a way which shall be legal and in fact irreversible.

The moral health of the nation is very near to our hearts: to defeat vices and criminality, to take care of young, of the family, of mothers and children. The state's efforts in this field rise more and more often to the grade of acts of parliament. The present is difficult, we are struggling with contrarities. Great are our human disappointments, not few are the ills and the bitternesses. But we have gotten over the worst, the country has entered on the way leading to the better, our society knows how to elevate itself in thought above daily divisons and discords, it gives proofs every day of patriotic responsibility and generosity.

However, we are not alone in the world, we are part of universal history, we are one of so many nations. We have friends who did not abandon us at the hour of need, but inimical forces have conspired against our nation; boycotts, restrictions, represent attempts upon the material life of Polish society. Unjust accusations multiply; the picture of Poland today is deformed. . . .

Your Holiness' moral sensibility permits him — in light of all that — to judge the real dimensions of our present problems and our heritage in an equable manner. We recall the early years of reconstruction when the country, bloody and reduced to a heap of ashes, launched itself toward great goals with miserable means. Few then foresaw success. Yet Poland, the land of straw-roofed houses, the land of millions of illiterates, of months of hunger, of black misery and penury, the land of hired laborers and the unemployed, has disappeared. In the People's Poland the workers have obtained real personhood and the idea of parity and social justice is well rooted. The working class and the peasants have attained that social position for which they struggled without success for several generations. . . .

The fatherland's historical advancement is an undeniable fact. Our country has been an inseparable part of the civilization and culture of Europe for 1,000 years. The People's Poland is the heir of that patrimony. It desires to partake in its growth with equal rights. We regret the fact that our grave internal problems are made use of to our disadvantage. We will not be a pawn on someone else's chessboard. We have shed our illusions. We have to judge real intentions toward Poland not by words but by deeds. This is an old truth. Great men of our nation bore witness to it long before us. Some of them lie in the catacombs of the cathedral of Wawel.

We understand how the Polish pope is preoccupied with the lot of his native land. We consider his thoughts and appeal with great seriousness; they are marked by a spirit of mercy and patriotic disquiet. Responding twice last year to letters written to me by Your Holiness, I had the opportunity to present the point of view of the authorities, our desires and intentions.

Many things have altered since then. We have attained successive stages toward normalization. I confirm our will to abolish the state of war, as well as to apply adequate, humanitarian and legal solutions. If the situation in the country takes a good direction, that can come about in a not distant time. The future of the nation and the rank of her state will be decided above all by labor, by the creative work of scientists and technicians, by the development of teaching and culture, by the solid efforts of all peasants; but it will be decided also by the virtue of prudence, as well as by a sense of responsibility and judgment, so precious in public life.

National accord is necessary in Poland. The recent period has brought notable progress in this field. We shall go on along that path. Differences among various concepts of the world do not obstruct it. The fatherland is a home which is the work of all who have built it and go on constructing it. Fundamental differences exist today between those who build up the country and those who obstruct such building up. Our law does not condemn on the grounds of opinion. It only forbids activities directed against the state, against the constitution. Whoever carries out or supports such activity, whoever plays a dishonest game, does not deserve confidence.

The People's Poland is a good common to all Poles: members of the communities of the various confessions as well as of unbelieving citizens. However, the Catholic Church occupies a particular place in Polish society and has various links with the old and recent history of our people. Here at the Belvedere four years ago resounded the words uttered by Your Holiness: "The church does not wish any privilege for her activity, she wants only what is indispensable for performing her mission." This desire finds full compliance on the part of the authorities of our state. The church enjoys the conditions fit for carrying out her pastoral activity. Numerous proofs of this exist and are commonly known. The religious needs of the faithful are satisfied. The dialogue with the episcopal leadership goes on uninterruptedly, spaces are opened up for inducing social good and combating moral evil. Catholic laity occupy a notable place in public life. In effect, a real opportunity is taking shape for laying down good relations between state and church in the long run and in accordance with the interests of the people as a whole.

Good will will not be lacking on the part of the authorities of the Polish People's Republic for effecting this work. The visit of the head of the church is a great event. Our illustrious guest, so strongly linked with his native land, is received in Poland with enormous cordiality and with profound respect. Your Holiness' personal contribution to the work of peace, of reconciliation — so precious intellectually and morally — meets with sincere recognition. The pastoral pilgrimage of the head of the apostolic church is followed with great attention by all the world. We are confident that it will provide moral indications which will reinforce the will to mutual understanding; that it will fill a luminous page in the open book of Polish history. Your Holiness' visit solemnizes the 300th anniversary of the victory of Vienna. On this occasion I desire to offer as the gift of the authorities of the People's Republic of Poland this hussar's armor, a remembrance of the cavalry which made the work of the Polish army celebrated. I also ask you to accept this picture painted by Alexander Mroczkowski, a pupil of Jan Matejko's. May this panorama of the Tatra Mountains remind Your Holiness of the beauty of his homeland.

HOMILY DELIVERED IN WARSAW

1. Praised be Jesus Christ!
With this Christian greeting I address all the people of Warsaw, the capital of Poland, gathered here in this liturgical assembly and also all the guests who have come from outside the Archdiocese of Warsaw....

I greet the cardinal-primate of Poland as metropolitan of Warsaw, the archbishop-secretary of the episcopal conference and all the auxiliary bishops. I also greet the cardinal-metropolitan of Cracow, and all the archbishops and bishops present here. . . .

I greet the metropolitan chapter and all the clergy of Warsaw and the archdiocese, of the neighboring areas and those who have come from other regions of Poland. I greet the religious orders of men and women, the ecclesiastical seminaries and the Catholic universities represented here.

I greet you all, brothers and sisters! My fellow countrymen! . . .

3. Christ, who is "father of the future age" is at the same time "yesterday and today." When I was in Poland during the first year of my service in the See of St. Peter, I said in Warsaw, in Victory Square, that it is difficult to understand the history of our country, the "yesterday" and the "today" of our history, without Christ.

Four years later I come again as a pilgrim to Jasna Gora to take part in the national jubilee celebration of this blessed image in which for six centuries the mother of Christ has dwelt in the midst of our people. The Gospel of today's liturgy — the same one that is being read at Jasna Gora — compares this dwelling of Mary among us to her presence at Cana in Galilee. Together with her, Jesus and his disciples went there.

If we say that it is not possible to understand the "yesterday" and the "today" of our history without Christ, then the jubilee of Jasna Gora emphasizes that this presence of Christ in our history is — as at Cana in Galilee — marvelously joined to the presence of his mother. The church in Poland renders testimony to this presence, which is so dear to us, through the jubilee of Jasna Gora celebrated last year and extended through this present year. I too wish to bear witness to this same maternal presence, together with you, and for this reason I come to the homeland, with gratitude to all sectors of society for the invitation. . . .

From this city too, the capital of the nation and of the state that at the cost of the greatest sacrifices fought for the good cause during the last world war, I wish to remind everyone that Poland's right to sovereignty and also to correct development in the cultural, social and economic fields appeals to the consciences of many people and many societies in the world. As an ally, Poland maintained to the very end, indeed abundantly, the commitments she assumed in the terrible experiences of the years 1939-1945. The fate of Poland in 1983 cannot be a matter of indifference to the nations of the world, especially those of Europe and America.

Dear compatriots! Brothers and sisters! In 1944 the capital of Poland was reduced to a heap of ruins. After the war Warsaw was rebuilt as we see it today: ancient and modern at the same time. Is this not another moral victory for the nation? And so many other cities and centers in Polish territory have been rebuilt, especially in the north and west, where I shall be going in the course of this pilgrimage. . . .

"Venimus, vidimus, Deus vicit": The words of the king uttered after the victory of Vienna have been engraved on the substance of our millennium.

They also have been engraved on the substance of this jubilee of Jasna Gora, through which we express our gratitude for the 600 years of the presence of the mother of God in our history.

The yearning for victory, for a noble victory, a victory won through effort and the cross, a victory achieved even through defeats, is part of the Christian program of life, of the life of the nation likewise.

My present visit to my homeland is taking place at a difficult period: difficult for many people, difficult for the whole of society. How great these difficulties are! You yourselves, my dear compatriots, know this better than I, even if I too have lived deeply the whole experience of these years since August 1980. Moreover, that experience is important for many societies in Europe and the world; everywhere there are people who realize this. There are also those who, especially since December 1981, have been contributing aid to my nation; for this I too am grateful to everyone.

Still, the nation must live principally by its own efforts and develop by its own efforts. Alone she must achieve this victory that divine providence gives her as her task at this stage of her history. We all understand that it is not a question of a military victory, as it was 300 years ago, but rather a moral victory. Precisely this constitutes the substance of a renewal proclaimed more than once.

It is a question of the mature ordering of the life of the nation and that of the state, an order in which man's fundamental rights will be respected. Only a moral victory can draw society out of division and restore unity. Such an order can be both the victory of the governed as well as at the same time the victory of those who govern. That point must be reached by way of mutual dialogue and agreement, which is the only viable way for the nation to achieve the fullness of civil rights and the social structures which correspond to its just requirements and are capable of fostering the consensus needed by the state if it is to fulfill its role. Through this consensus the nation expresses its sovereignty concretely.

Here I quote the words of the pastoral letter of the Polish episcopate for Aug. 29, 1982:

"The Polish nation needs a true moral and social renewal so that it can rediscover faith in itself, in its future confidence in its own strength; to re-awaken moral energies and social generosity in order to be able to face the great labor of the work and necessary sacrifices that await us all. An urgent need is the rebuilding of confidence between society and power in order to construct by a shared effort the best future for the homeland and to ensure the interests of the nation and the state."

9. Dear brothers and sisters! You who are sharing in this liturgy of the pilgrim pope, your fellow countryman, in the capital of Poland! From here, from Warsaw, I am going to Jasna Gora, which the late primate of Poland, Cardinal Stefan Wyszynski, used to call "Jasna Gora of Victory" ("Bright Mountain of Victory").

I wish to take there a special gift. The gift that has been, in this jubilee year of Jasna Gora, the canonization of the Polish martyr of Auschwitz, St. Maximilian Mary. I am grateful to divine providence that I was able to perform this canonization Oct. 10, 1982.

As I leave Warsaw for Jasna Gora, I join spiritually in the procession of pilgrims that from 1711, therefore for 272 years, has traveled each year from the capital of Poland to the capital of the Queen of Poland: the pilgrimage of Warsaw. . . .

HOMILY DELIVERED AT CZESTOCHOWA

. . . Christ . . . sets before us generation after generation the great cause of freedom. Freedom is given to man by God as a measure of his dignity. At the same time, however, it is given to him as a task: "Freedom is not a relief but the toil of greatness" (L. Staff, "Behold Your Son"). In fact, people can use freedom well or badly. Through it they can build or destroy. In the evangelization of Jasna Gora there is included the call to the heritage of the children of God. The call to live in freedom. To make good use of freedom. To build up and not to destroy.

This evangelization of Jasna Gora, to live in a freedom worthy of the children of God, has its own long history, six centuries long. Mary at Cana of Galilee cooperates with her son. The same thing happens at Jasna Gora. How many pilgrims have passed through the sanctuary of Jasna Gora in six centuries? How many have been converted here, passing from the bad use to the good use of their own freedom? How many have regained the true dignity of adopted children of God? How much could the chapel of the image of Jasna Gora tell about this? How much could the confessionals of the whole basilica tell? How much could the way of the cross along the walls say? An enormous chapter in the history of souls. Perhaps this is the most fundamental dimensions of the 600th anniversary of Jasna Gora. Freedom remained and continues to remain in living people, in the sons and daughters of this land, when God sends into their hearts the spirit of his Son, so that in all interior truth they can cry out: "Abba!" ("Father!").

However, the evangelization of freedom at Jasna Gora has yet another dimension. It is the dimension of the freedom of the nation, the free homeland, restored to the dignity of a sovereign state. The nation is truly free when it can shape itself as a community determined by unity of culture, language and history. The state is firmly sovereign when it governs society and also serves the common good of society and allows the nation to realize its own subjectivity, its own identity. Among other things this involves the creation of suitable conditions of development in the fields of culture, economics and other spheres of the life of the social community. The sovereignty of the state is deeply linked to its capacity to promote the freedom of the nation, that is, to developing conditions that permit the nation to express all of its distinctive historical and cultural identity, being sovereign, that is, through the state.

These elementary truths of the moral order have manifested themselves in a dramatic way in the space of those centuries during which the image of

Jasna Gora has witnessed to the special presence of the mother of God in the history of our nation....

During my previous pilgrimage to my homeland in 1979, I said at Jasna Gora that here we have always been free. It is difficult to express in a different way what the image of the queen of Poland became for all Poles during the time when their homeland was wiped off the map of Europe as an independent state. Yes! Here at Jasna Gora there also rested the hope of the nation and the persevering effort toward the recovery of independence. "Before your altars we bring entreaties, O Lord, deign to restore to us a free homeland."

And it is here too that we have learned the fundamental truth about the freedom of the nation: The nation perishes if it deforms its spirit — the nation grows when its spirit is ever more purified and no external power is able to destroy it!

We have celebrated the millenium of the baptism when — from the year 1918 — Poland as a sovereign state reappeared on the map of Europe; we celebrated it after the horrible experience of World War II and the occupation. The jubilee of the 600th anniversary of the image of Jasna Gora is as it were an indispensable complement to that of the millenium. The complement of the great cause — a cause essential for the history of individuals and for the history of the nation.

The name of this cause is queen of Poland.

The name of this cause is mother.

We have a very difficult geopolitical situation. We have a very difficult history, especially in the course of the last few centuries. The painful experiences of history have sharpened our sensitivity in the field of the fundamental rights of man and of the nation to have freedom of conscience and religion and the right to human work respected. We also have various human weaknesses and defects and sins that we must continually keep in mind — and continually free ourselves from....

POPE'S REMARKS IN KATOWICE

... Human work really is at the heart of all social life. Through it justice and social love are formed, if the whole working sector is governed by a just moral order. But if this order is missing, injustice takes the place of justice and love is replaced by hatred.

Invoking Mary as mother of justice and social love — dear brothers and sisters, as workers of Silesia and of all Poland — you wish to express how close to your heart is that moral order that should govern the working sector.

The entire world has followed and continues to follow with emotion the events that took place in Poland before December 1981. The thing that in a special way gave public opinion cause to reflect was the fact that in these events it was a question, above all, of the moral order itself in relation to human work and not only the question of an increase in salary. Also striking was the fact that these events were free from violence, that no one was killed or wounded through them. And finally there was the fact that these events of the Polish labor world in the 1980s bore within them a religious mark too.

No one can be surprised then that here in Silesia — in this great "work basin" — the mother of Christ is venerated as mother of justice and social love.

The precise meaning of justice and social love is the fullness of the moral order, in connection with the entire social system and, in particular, the system of human work.

Work derives its fundamental value from the fact that it is performed by man. The dignity of work is based on this too, a dignity which must be respected independently of the type of work that man performs. What is essential is that man performs it. Whatever work he performs, he imprints on it the mark of his person: of his image and likeness to God himself. It is also of importance that man performs his work for someone, for others.

Work is man's obligation, both before God and before people, before his own family and before the nation, before the society to which he belongs.

Corresponding to this obligation of work are also the rights of the workers, which must be formulated within the extensive context of human rights. Social justice consists in the realization of and respect for the rights of man in relation to all the members of a given society.

Against this background, those rights that concern the work performed by man acquire a fitting eloquence. I shall not enter into details, but I shall name only the most important ones. First of all, the right to a just salary — just, which means enough for the family to live on too. Then, the right to security in case of an accident on the job. And still further, the right to a day of rest. (I remember how many times we touched the question of a work-free Sunday at Piekary.)

Joined to the area of workers' rights is also the question of trade unions. I quote what I wrote about this matter in the cycylical *Laborem Exercens:*

"The modern unions grew up from the struggle of the workers — workers in general but especially the industrial workers — to protect their just rights vis-a-vis the entrepreneurs and the owners of the means of production. Their task is to defend the existential interest of workers in all sectors in which their rights are concerned. The experience of history teaches that organizations of this type are an indispensable element of social life, especially in modern industrialized societies. Obviously this does not mean that only industrial workers can set up associations of this type. Representatives of every profession can use them to ensure their own rights. Thus there are unions of agricultural workers and of white-collar workers. . . . They are a mouthpiece for the struggle for social justice, for the just rights of working people in accordance with their individual professions. . . ."

And here in Poland, Cardinal Stefan Wyszynski said:

"It is a question of a people's right to free association; it is not a right conceded by someone, since it is a properly innate right. Hence this right is not given to us by the state. The state has the obligation only to protect and guard it so that it is not violated. This right is given by the Creator who made man as a social being. From the Creator comes the social character of human aspirations, the need to join together and to unite one with another" (Discourse, Feb. 6, 1982).

It was in this spirit that I spoke in January 1981 during an audience granted to the delegation of Solidarity, accompanied by the representative of the Polish government for permanent working contacts with the Holy See.

So then, the discussion that has been going on in Poland in recent years has a deep moral sense. It cannot be resolved in any other way than through a true dialogue between the authorities and society. The bishops of Poland many times during this period have called for such a dialogue.

Why do the workers in Poland — and, for that matter, workers all over the world — have a right to such a dialogue? Because the worker is not only an instrument of production, but also a subject who has priority over capital in the whole production process. Through his work, man is the true administrator of the work bench, of the work process, of the products of work and of their distribution. He is even ready to make sacrifices when he feels that he is truly co-responsible and can have influence on the just distribution of what has been produced overall. . . .

▼▼▼

REAPPOINTMENT OF VOLCKER
AS FEDERAL RESERVE CHAIRMAN
June 18, 1983

Ronald Reagan announced one of his most important appointments as president during his weekly five-minute noontime radio address June 18. Ending months of speculation that roiled financial markets, Reagan said he was reappointing Paul A. Volcker to a second four-year term as chairman of the Federal Reserve Board. The Senate confirmed Volcker July 27 by a vote of 84-16 to serve as head of the nation's central bank. His new term began August 6.

Financial analysts frequently referred to the Fed chairman as the second most powerful person in the United States, after the president. Members of the domestic and foreign financial communities generally had favorable reactions to the Volcker reappointment. They thought his continuation in the post was important for stability in the marketplace. Volcker said the central bank's overriding objectives included keeping inflation in check as well as assuring a prolonged expansion of the economy.

Together with his six fellow governors of the Federal Reserve Board and the presidents of the 12 regional Federal Reserve banks, the Fed chairman determined interest rates and economic growth of the domestic, and thereby international, economy. The Federal Reserve Board, a largely independent agency, sets monetary policy — the amount of money and credit available to businesses and individuals. Volcker maintained that the Fed would keep to its course, allowing moderate monetary expansion that would accommodate economic recovery.

In renaming Volcker to the Fed post, the president appointed a man who had been praised for bringing inflation under control but who had at the same time been criticized for causing the greatest economic downturn since the Depression.

When President Jimmy Carter nominated Volcker to the post in July 1979, inflation was running at nearly a 13 percent annual rate and unemployment stood at 6 percent. Despite widespread criticism, the Fed kept the money supply constricted and interest rates remained at high levels, topping at 21.5 percent in December 1980. The high cost of borrowing choked economic recovery and fostered the longest and deepest recession in post-World War II history. The unemployment rate hit a postwar high of 10.89 percent in December 1982, the mid-point of Reagan's four-year term. The recession bottomed out at the end of the year, however. Volcker's policies increased the money supply, which brought down interest rates and facilitated the beginnings of economic recovery without rekindling inflation.

In his announcement of the Fed appointment Reagan called Volcker "a man of unquestioned independence, integrity and ability." He added that Volcker was "as dedicated as I am to continuing the fight against inflation." Volcker's qualifications were beyond dispute: three tours of increasingly responsible duty at the Treasury Department, two stints as economist and long-range planner at the Chase Manhattan Bank and three Federal Reserve posts, including the presidency of the Federal Reserve Bank of New York.

Volcker issued a statement saying he was "gratified and honored by the expression of confidence by the president." He continued, "As I have said on a number of occasions, I do believe we now have a rare opportunity to achieve sustained growth on a firm foundation of stability. I am sure I can speak for the entire Federal Reserve System as to our commitment to work toward that objective." During confirmation hearings, Volcker said the Fed had taken actions to hold down the growth in the money supply in order to avert a new round of inflation.

Volcker had widespread support on Capitol Hill. Senate Majority Leader Howard H. Baker Jr., R-Tenn., strongly endorsed Volcker's reappointment during a June 5 broadcast of "Face the Nation." Baker said Volcker was a "known quantity" and his reappointment "would have a calming and tranquilizing effect on the world economy." Three chairmen of influential Senate "money" committees also backed Volcker's reappointment: Budget Chairman Pete V. Domenici, R-N.M., Finance Chairman Robert Dole, R-Kan., and Banking Chairman Jake Garn, R-Utah. It was Garn's committee that had to approve Reagan's nominee for Fed chairman before the full Senate voted on the confirmation.

Following are excerpts from President Ronald Reagan's June 18, 1983, radio address announcing the reappointment of Paul A. Volcker as chairman of the Federal Reserve Board:

My fellow Americans:

As the saying goes, we interrupt this program for a news flash. . . .

The term of the Federal Reserve Board Chairman expires August 5th. I have today asked Chairman Paul Volcker to accept reappointment for another term. He's agreed to do so, and I couldn't be more pleased. Paul Volcker is a man of unquestioned independence, integrity, and ability. He is as dedicated as I am to continuing the fight against inflation. And with him as Chairman of the Fed, I know we'll win that fight. End of news flash. . . .

▼▼▼

COURT ON REDISTRICTING

June 22, 1983

In a decision with sweeping implications for redistricting politics across the country, the Supreme Court June 22, 1983, struck down New Jersey's congressional district map as redrawn following the 1980 Census.

By a 5-4 vote the Court ruled in Karcher v. Daggett *that states must adhere as closely as possible to the "one person, one vote" standard of reapportionment — and ultimately bear the burden of proving that deviations from precise population equality were made in pursuit of a legitimate goal.*

The ruling upheld a three-judge federal panel's March 3, 1982, decision to overturn the New Jersey congressional district map. The lower court found that the 0.69 percent deviation between the state's most and least populous districts was too great, violating the "one person, one vote" principle applied to redistricting in the Supreme Court's 1964 Wesberry v. Sanders *decision.*

Dissenters argued that the decision would leave even the most minuscule population deviance open to constitutional attack.

'Good Faith Effort,' 'Unattainable Perfection'

The majority decision was written by Justice William J. Brennan Jr., a New Jersey native and the author of the landmark 1962 Baker v. Carr *decision that inaugurated the involvement of federal courts in population apportionment for political representation.*

Brennan argued that population differences between districts in the New Jersey map "could have been avoided or significantly reduced with a good-faith effort to achieve population equality." He contended that New Jersey legislators failed to prove that the deviations from population equality were made in pursuit of a nondiscriminatory goal.

Brennan gave several examples of what would constitute such a goal. "Any number of consistently applied legislative policies might justify some variance," he wrote, "including, for instance, making districts compact, respecting municipal boundaries, preserving the cores of prior districts, and avoiding contests between incumbent Representatives."

Justice Byron R. White, writing in dissent, was joined by Chief Justice Warren E. Burger and Justices Lewis F. Powell Jr. and William H. Rehnquist. Powell also filed a separate dissenting opinion.

White criticized the Court for its "unreasonable insistence on an unattainable perfection in the equalizing of congressional districts.... [U]nder the Court's rationale, even Rhode Island's plan — whose two districts have a deviation of 0.02 percent or about 95 people — would be subject to constitutional attack," White wrote.

The dissenters also expressed concern that the Court's decision would result in increased judicial intervention in legislative affairs.

National Implications of Decision

According to the National Conference of State Legislatures, 12 states had congressional maps with maximum population variances greater than that of New Jersey: Indiana (2.96 percent), Alabama (2.45 percent), Tennessee (2.40 percent), Georgia (2.0 percent), Virginia (1.81 percent), North Carolina (1.76 percent), New York (1.64 percent), Kentucky (1.39 percent), Washington (1.30 percent), Massachusetts (1.09 percent), New Mexico (0.87 percent) and Arkansas (0.78 percent). Although the Court's New Jersey decision did not invalidate congressional district lines in those states, it did leave them open to challenge.

At least two states were involved in litigation hinging on the constitutionality of population variances. In Ohio, a three-judge federal panel put off a final decision until the Supreme Court set a precedent in the New Jersey case. A population variance case against the Pennsylvania map was on appeal to the Supreme Court.

The Court sidestepped a crucial issue in redistricting politics in Karcher v. Daggett. *It did not rule on whether the New Jersey Legislature had violated the law in drawing district lines to serve Democratic interests, as alleged by Republican critics of the plan. So long as states could prove that they made a "good-faith effort" to achieve population equality, they were not prohibited from partisan gerrymandering.*

Bizarre Districts

As a partisan gerrymander, the 1982 New Jersey district map had few peers. It boasted some of the most bizarrely shaped districts in the country. One constituency stretched from the suburbs of New York City to the fringes of Trenton. Another, known as "the fishhook" by its detractors, twisted and curled through central New Jersey's industrial landscape, picking up Democratic voters along the way.

Approved by the Democratic-controlled Legislature on January 18, 1982, the map was signed into law the following day by outgoing Democratic Gov. Brendan T. Byrne, shortly before the inauguration of his Republican successor, Thomas H. Kean.

Republicans persuaded the three-judge federal panel — all Republican appointees — to overturn the Democratic map and order the Legislature to redraw congressional lines. But Brennan March 15, 1982, imposed a stay on that ruling, leaving the lines intact for the 1982 elections.

In a second decision handed down June 22, the Court divided 5-4 along different lines in upholding Wyoming's 1981 state legislative map. Although the map had a maximum population variance of .89 percent, the Court ruled in Brown v. Thomson that the state's policy of allowing every county a representative of its own was a legitimate reason for the variance in population.

Powell, joined by Justices Burger, Rehnquist, John Paul Stevens and Sandra Day O'Connor, wrote for the Court in the Wyoming case. Justices Brennan, White, Thurgood Marshall and Harry A. Blackmun dissented.

> Following are excerpts from the Supreme Court's June 22, 1983, decision in Karcher v. Daggett, holding that New Jersey's districts as redrawn by the 1980 Census violated the "one person, one vote" principle by deviating from precise population equality; from the concurring opinion of Justice Stevens; and from the dissenting opinion of Justice White:

No. 81-2057

Alan J. Karcher, Speaker, New Jersey Assembly, et al., Appellants *v.* George T. Daggett et al.	On appeal from the United States District Court for the District of New Jersey

[June 22, 1983]

JUSTICE BRENNAN delivered the opinion of the Court.

The question presented by this appeal is whether an apportionment plan for congressional districts satisfies Art. I, § 2 without need for further justification if the population of the largest district is less than one percent greater than the population of the smallest district. A three-judge District Court declared New Jersey's 1982 reapportionment plan unconstitutional on the authority of *Kirkpatrick* v. *Preisler* (1969) and *White* v. *Weiser* (1973) because the population deviations among districts, although small, were not the result of a good-faith effort to achieve population equality. We affirm.

I

After the results of the 1980 decennial census had been tabulated, the Clerk of the United States House of Representatives notified the governor of New Jersey that the number of representatives to which the State was entitled had decreased from 15 to 14. Accordingly, the New Jersey Legislature was required to reapportion the State's congressional districts. The State's 199th Legislature passed two reapportionment bills. One was vetoed by the Governor, and the second, although signed into law, occasioned significant dissatisfaction among those who felt it diluted minority voting strength in the city of Newark. In response, the 200th Legislature returned to the problem of apportioning congressional districts when it convened in January, 1982, and it swiftly passed a bill (S-711) introduced by Senator Feldman, President *pro tem* of the State Senate, which created the apportionment plan at issue in this case. The bill was signed by the Governor on January 19, 1982, becoming P.L. 1982, c. 1 (hereinafter Feldman Plan). . . .

Like every plan considered by the Legislature, the Feldman Plan contained 14 districts, with an average population per district (as determined by the 1980 census) of 526,059. Each district did not have the same population. On the average, each district differed from the "ideal" figure by 0.1384%, or about 726 people. The largest district, the Fourth District, which includes Trenton, had a population of 527,472, and the smallest, the Sixth District, embracing most of Middlesex County, a population of 523,798. The difference between them was 3,674 people, or 0.6984% of the average district. The populations of the other districts also varied. The Ninth District, including most of Bergen County, in the northeastern corner of the State, had a population of 527,349, while the population of the Third District, along the Atlantic shore, was only 524,825.

The Legislature had before it other plans with appreciably smaller population deviations between the largest and smallest districts. The one receiving the most attention in the District Court was designed by Dr. Ernest Reock, a political science professor at Rutgers University and Director of the Bureau of Government Research. A version of the Reock Plan introduced in the 200th Legislature by Assemblyman Hardwick had a maximum population difference of 2,375, or 0.4514% of the average figure.

Almost immediately after the Feldman Plan became law, a group of individuals with varying interests, including all incumbent Republican members of Congress from New Jersey, sought a declaration that the apportionment plan violated Article I. § 2 of the Constitution and an injunction against proceeding with the primary election for United States Representatives under the plan. A three-judge district court was convened pursuant to 28 U.S.C. § 2284 (a). The District Court held a hearing on Feb. 26, 1982, at which the parties submitted a number of depositions and affidavits, moved for summary judgment, and waived their right to introduce further evidence in the event the motions for summary judgment were denied.

Shortly thereafter, the District Court issued an opinion and order declaring the Feldman Plan unconstitutional. Denying the motions for summary judgment and resolving the case on the record as a whole, the District Court held that the population variances in the Feldman Plan were not "unavoidable despite a good-faith effort to achieve absolute equality," see *Kirkpatrick*. The court rejected appellants' argument that a deviation lower than the statistical imprecision of the decennial census was "the functional equivalent of mathematical equality." *Daggett* v. *Kimmelman* (NJ 1982). It also held that appellants had failed to show that the population variances were justified by the Legislature's purported goals of preserving minority voting strength and anticipating shifts in population. The District Court enjoined appellants from conducting primary or general elections under the Feldman Plan, but that order was stayed pending appeal to this Court (1982) (BRENNAN, Circuit Justice), and we noted probable jurisdiction (1982).

II

Article I. § 2 establishes a "high standard of justice and common sense" for the apportionment of congressional districts: "equal representation for equal numbers of people." *Wesberry* v. *Sanders* (1964). Precise mathematical equality, however, may be impossible to achieve in an imperfect world; therefore the "equal representation" standard is enforced only to the extent of requiring that districts be apportioned to achieve population equality "as nearly as is practicable." As we explained further in *Kirkpatrick* v. *Preisler*:

> "[T]he 'as nearly as practicable' standard requires that the State make a good-faith effort to achieve precise mathematical equality. See *Reynolds* v. *Sims* (1964). Unless population variances among congressional districts are shown to have resulted despite such effort, the State must justify each variance, no matter how small."

Article I. § 2, therefore, "permits only the limited population variances which are unavoidable despite a good-faith effort to achieve absolute equality, or for which justification is shown.". . .

Thus two basic questions shape litigation over population deviations in state legislation apportioning congressional districts. First, the court must consider whether the population differences among districts could have been reduced or eliminated altogether by a good-faith effort to draw districts of equal population. Parties challenging apportionment legislation must bear the burden of proof on this issue, and if they fail to show that the differences could have been avoided the apportionment scheme must be upheld. If, however, the plaintiffs can establish that the population differences were not the result of a good-faith effort to achieve equality, the State must bear the burden of proving that each significant variance between districts was necessary to achieve some legitimate goal. *Kirkpatrick;* cf. *Swann* v. *Adams* (1967).

III

Appellants' principal argument in this case is addressed to the first question described above. They contend that the Feldman Plan should be regarded *per se* as the product of a good-faith effort to achieve population equality because the maximum population deviation among districts is smaller than the predictable undercount in available census data.

A

Kirkpatrick squarely rejected a nearly identical argument. "The whole thrust of the 'as nearly as practicable' approach is inconsistent with adoption of fixed numerical standards which excuse population variances without regard to the circumstances of each particular case." Adopting any standard other than population equality, using the best census data available, would subtly erode the Constitution's ideal of equal representation. If state legislators knew that a certain *de minimis* level of population differences were acceptable, they would doubtless strive to achieve that level rather than equality. Furthermore, choosing a different standard would import a high degree of arbitrariness into the process of reviewing apportionment plans. In this case, appellants argue that a maximum deviation of approximately 0.7% should be considered *de minimus.* If we accept that argument, how are we to regard deviations of 0.8%, 0.95%, 1% or 1.1%?

Any standard, including absolute equality, involves a certain artificiality. As appellants point out, even the census data are not perfect, and the well-known restlessness of the American people means that population counts for particular localities are outdated long before they are completed. Yet problems with the data at hand apply equally to any population-based standard we could choose. As between two standards — equality or something-less-than equality — only the former reflects the aspirations of Art. I. § 2.

To accept the legitimacy of unjustified, though small population deviations in this case would mean to reject the basic premise of *Kirkpatrick* and *Wesberry.* We decline appellants' invitation to go that far. The unusual rigor of their standard has been noted several times. Because of that rigor, we have required that absolute population equality be the paramount objective of apportionment only in the case of congressional districts, for which the command of Art. I, § 2 as regards the national legislature outweighs the local interests that a State may deem relevant in apportioning districts for representatives to state and local legislatures, but we have not questioned the population equality standard for congressional districts. See, *e.g., White* v. *Weiser; White* v. *Regester* (1973); *Mahan* v. *Howell* (1973). The principle of population equality for congressional districts had not proved unjust or socially or economically harmful in experience.... If anything, this standard should cause less difficulty now for state legislatures than it did when we adopted it in *Wesberry*. The rapid advances in computer technology and education during the last two decades make it relatively simple to draw contiguous districts of equal population and at the same time to further whatever secondary goals the State has. Finally, to abandon unnecessarily a clear and oft-confirmed constitutional interpretation would impair our authority in other cases, *Florida Department of Health* v. *Florida Nursing Home Assn.* (1981) (STEVENS, J., concurring); *Pollock* v. *Farmers' Loan & Trust Co.* (1895) (WHITE, J., dissenting), would implicitly open the door to a plethora of requests that we reexamine other rules that some may consider burdensome and would prejudice those who have relied upon the rule of law in seeking an equipopulous congressional apportionment in New Jersey.... We thus reaffirm that there are no *de minimus* population variations, which could practically be avoided, but which nonetheless meet the standard of Art. I. § 2 without justification.

B

The sole difference between appellants' theory and the argument we rejected in *Kirkpatrick* is that appellants have proposed a *de minimis* line that gives the illusion of rationality and predictability: the "inevitable statistical imprecision of the census." They argue, "Where, as here, the deviation from ideal district size is less than the known imprecision of the census figures, that variation is the functional equivalent of zero." There are two problems with this approach. First, appellants concentrate on the extent to which the census systematically undercounts actual population — a figure which is not known precisely and which, even if it were known, would not be relevant to this case. Second, the mere existence of statistical imprecision does not make small deviations among districts the functional equivalent of equality.

In the District Court and before this Court, appellants rely exclusively on an affidavit of Dr. James Trussell, a Princeton University demographer. Dr. Trussell's carefully worded statement reviews various studies of the undercounts in the 1950, 1960, and 1970 decennial censuses, and it draws three important conclusions: (1) "the undercount in the 1980 census is likely to be above one percent"; (2) "all the evidence to date indicates that all places are not undercounted to the same extent, since the undercount rate has been shown to depend on race, sex, age, income, and education"; and (3) "[t]he distribution of the undercount in New Jersey is ...

unknown, and I see no reason to believe that it would be uniformly spread over all municipalities." Assuming for purposes of argument that each of these statements is correct, they do not support appellants' argument.

In essence, appellants' one percent benchmark is little more than an attempt to present an attractive *de minimis* line with a patina of scientific authority. Neither Dr. Trussell's statement nor any of appellants' other evidence specifies a precise level for the undercount in New Jersey, and Dr. Trussell's discussion of the census makes clear that it is impossible to develop reliable estimates of the undercount on anything but a nationwide scale. His conclusion that the 1980 undercount is "likely to be above one percent" seems to be based on the undercounts in previous censuses and a guess as to how well new procedures adopted in 1980 to reduce the undercount would work. Therefore, if we accepted appellants' theory that the national undercount level sets a limit on our ability to use census data to tell the difference between the populations of congressional districts, we might well be forced to set that level far above one percent when final analyses of the 1980 census are completed.

As Dr. Trussell admits, the existence of a one percent undercount would be irrelevant to population deviations among districts if the undercount were distributed evenly among districts. The undercount in the census affects the accuracy of the *deviations* between districts only to the extent that the undercount varies from district to district. For a one-percent undercount to explain a one-percent deviation between the census-populations of two districts, the undercount in the smaller district would have to be approximately three times as large as the undercount in the larger district. It is highly unlikely, of course, that this condition holds true, especially since appellants have utterly failed to introduce evidence showing that the districts were designed to compensate for the probable undercount. Dr. Trussell's affidavit states that the rate of undercounting may vary from municipality to municipality, but it does not discuss by how much it may vary, or to what extent those variations would be reflected at the district level, with many municipalities combined. Nor does the affidavit indicate that the factors associated with the rate of undercounting — race, sex, age, etc. — vary from district to district, or (more importantly) that the populations in the smaller districts reflect the relevant factors more than the populations in the larger districts. As Dr. Trussell admits, the distribution of the undercount in New Jersey is completely unknown. Only by bizarre coincidence could the systematic undercount in the census bear some statistical relationship to the districts drawn by the Feldman Plan.

The census may systematically undercount population, and the rate of undercounting may vary from place to place. Those facts, however, do not render meaningless the differences in population between congressional districts, as determined by uncorrected census counts. To the contrary, the census data provide the only reliable — albeit less than perfect — indication of the districts' "real" relative population levels. Even if one cannot say with certainty that one district is larger than another merely because it has a higher census count, one *can* say with certainty that the district with a larger census count is more likely to be larger than the other district than it is to be smaller or the same size. That certainty is sufficient for decisionmaking. . . . Furthermore, because the census count represents the "best population data available," see *Kirkpatrick,* it is the only basis for good-faith attempts to achieve population equality. Attempts to explain population deviations on the basis of flaws in census data must be supported with a precision not achieved here.

C

Given that the census-based population deviations in the Feldman Plan reflect real differences among the districts, it is clear that they could have been avoided or significantly reduced with a good-faith effort to achieve population equality. For that reason alone, it would be inappropriate to accept the Feldman Plan as "functionally equivalent" to a plan with districts of equal population.

The District Court found that several other plans introduced in the 200th Legislature had smaller maximum deviations than the Feldman Plan. Appellants object that the alternative plans considered by the District Court were not comparable to the Feldman Plan because their political characters differed profoundly. . . . We have never denied that apportionment is a political process, or that state legislatures could pursue legitimate secondary objectives as long as those objectives were consistent with a good-faith effort to achieve population equality at the same time. Nevertheless, the claim that political considerations require population differences among congressional districts belongs more properly to the second level of judicial inquiry in these cases, in which the State bears the burden of justifying the differences with impartiality.

In any event, it was unnecessary for the District Court to rest its finding on the existence of alternative plans with radically different political effects. As in *Kirkpatrick,* "resort to the simple device of transferring entire political subdivisions of known population between contiguous districts would have produced districts much closer to numerical equality." Starting with the Feldman Plan itself and the census data available to the Legislature at the time it was enacted, one can reduce the maximum population deviation of the plan merely by shifting a handful of municipalities from one district to another. . . . Thus the District Court did not err in finding that appellees had met their burden of showing that the Feldman Plan did not come as nearly as practicable to population equality.

IV

By itself, the foregoing discussion does not establish that the Feldman Plan is unconstitutional. Rather, appellees' success in proving that the Feldman Plan was not the product of a good-faith effort to achieve population equality means only that the burden shifted to the State to prove that the population deviations in its plan were necessary to achieve some legitimate state objective. *White* v. *Weiser* demonstrates that we are willing to defer to state legislative policies, so long as they are consistent with constitutional norms, even if they require small differences in the population of congressional districts.... Any number of consistently applied legislative policies might justify some variance, including, for instance, making districts compact, respecting municipal boundaries, preserving the cores of prior districts, and avoiding contests between incumbent Representatives. As long as the criteria are nondiscriminatory, ... these are all legitimate objectives that on a proper showing could justify minor population deviations.... The State must, however, show with some specificity that a particular objective required the specific deviations in its plan, rather than simply relying on general assertions. The showing required to justify population deviations is flexible, depending on the size of the deviations, the importance of the State's interests, the consistency with which the plan as a whole reflects those interests, and the availability of alternatives that might substantially vindicate those interests yet approximate population equality more closely. By necessity, whether deviations are justified requires case-by-case attention to these factors.

The possibility that a State could justify small variations in the census-based population of its congressional districts on the basis of some legitimate, consistently applied policy was recognized in *Kirkpatrick* itself. In that case, Missouri advanced the theory, echoed by JUSTICE WHITE in dissent ... that district-to-district differences in the number of eligible voters or projected population shifts, justified the population deviations in that case.... We rejected its arguments not because those factors were impermissible considerations in the apportionment process, but rather because of the size of the resulting deviations and because Missouri "[a]t best ... made haphazard adjustments to a scheme based on total population," made "no attempt" to account for the same factors in all districts, and generally failed to document its findings thoroughly and apply them "throughout the State in a systematic, not an *ad hoc* manner."

The District Court properly found that appellants did not justify the population deviations in this case. At argument before the District Court and on appeal in this Court, appellants emphasized only one justification for the Feldman Plan's population deviations — preserving the voting strength of racial minority groups. They submitted affidavits from mayors Kenneth Gibson of Newark and Thomas Cooke of East Orange, discussing the importance of having a large majority of black voters in Newark's Tenth District....

Under the Feldman Plan, the largest districts are the Fourth and Ninth Districts, and the smallest are the Third and Sixth. None of these districts borders on the Tenth, and only one — the Fourth — is even mentioned in appellants' discussions of preserving minority voting strength. Nowhere do appellants suggest that the large population of the Fourth District was necessary to preserve minority voting strength; in fact, the deviation between the Fourth District and other districts has the effect of diluting the votes of all residents of that district, including members of racial minorities, as compared with other districts with fewer minority voters. The record is completely silent on the relationship between preserving minority voting strength and the small populations of the Third and Sixth Districts. Therefore, the District Court's findings easily pass the "clearly erroneous" test.

V

The District Court properly applied the two-part test of *Kirkpatrick* v. *Preisler* to New Jersey's 1982 apportionment of districts for the United States House of Representatives. It correctly held that the population deviations in the plan were not functionally equal as a matter of law, and it found that the plan was not a good-faith effort to achieve population equality using the best available census data. It also correctly rejected appellants' attempt to justify the population deviations as not supported by the evidence. The judgment of the District Court, therefore, is

Affirmed.

JUSTICE STEVENS, concurring.

As an alternate ground for affirmance, the appellees contended at oral argument that the bizarre configuration of New Jersey's congressional districts, is sufficient to demonstrate that the plan was not adopted in "good faith." This argument, as I understand it, is a claim that the district boundaries are unconstitutional because they are the product of political gerrymandering. Since my vote is decisive in this case, it seems appropriate to explain how this argument influences my analysis of the question that divides the Court. As I have previously pointed out, political gerrymandering is one species of "vote dilution" that is proscribed by the Equal Protection Clause. Because an adequate judicial analysis of a gerrymandering claim raises special problems, I shall comment at some length on the legal basis for a gerrymandering claim, the standards for judging such a claim, and their relevance to the present case. . . .

Like JUSTICE WHITE, I am convinced that judicial preoccupation with the goal of perfect population equality is an inadequate method of judging the constitutionality of an apportionment plan. I would not hold that an obvious gerrymander is wholly immune from attack simply because it comes closer to perfect population equality than every competing plan. On the other hand, I do not find any virtue in the proposal to relax the standard set forth in *Wesberry* and subsequent cases, and to ignore population disparities after some arbitrarily defined threshold has been crossed. As one commentator has written, "Logic, as well as experience, tells us . . . that there can be no total sanctuaries in the political thicket, else unfairness will simply shift from one form to another." Rather, we should supplement the population equality standard with additional criteria that are no less "judicially manageable." In evaluating equal protection challenges to districting plans, just as in resolving such attacks on other forms of discriminatory action, I would consider whether the plan has a significant adverse impact on an identifiable political group, whether the plan has objective indicia of irregularity, and then, whether the State is able to produce convincing evidence that the plan nevertheless serves neutral, legitimate interests of the community as a whole.

Until two decades ago, constrained by its fear of entering a standardless political thicket, the Court simply abstained from any attempt to judge the constitutionality of legislative apportionment plans, even when the districts varied in population from 914,053 to 112,116. . . .

Even as a basis for protecting voters in their individual capacity, the "one person one vote" approach has its shortcomings. Although population disparities are easily quantified, the standard provides no measure of the significance of any numerical difference. It is easy to recognize the element of unfairness in allowing 112,116 voters to elect one congressman while another is elected by 914,053. But how significant is the difference between census counts of 527,471 and 523,798? Given the birth rate, the mortality rate, the transient character of modern society, and the acknowledged errors in the census, we all know that such differences may vanish between the date of the census and the date of the next election. Absolute population equality is impossible to achieve.

More important, mere numerical equality is not a sufficient guarantee of equal representation. Although it directly protects individuals, it protects groups only indirectly at best. . . . A voter may challenge an apportionment scheme on the ground that it gives his vote less weight than that of other voters; for that purpose it does not matter whether the plaintiff is combined with or separated from others who might share his group affiliation. It is plainly unrealistic to assume that a smaller numerical disparity will *always* produce a fairer districting plan. Indeed, as Justice Harlan correctly observed in *Wells* v. *Rockefeller* (1969), a standard "of absolute equality is perfectly compatible with 'gerrymandering' of the worst sort. A computer may grind out district lines which can totally frustrate the popular will on an overwhelming number of critical issues." Since Justice Harlan wrote, developments in computer technology have made the task of the gerrymanderer even easier. . . .

The imperfections in the numerical standard do not, of course, render it useless. It provides one neutral criterion for evaluating a districting plan. Numerical disparities may provide sufficient basis for shifting the burden of justification to the State. Moreover, if all other factors were in equipoise, it would be proper to conclude that the plan that most nearly attains the goal of complete equality would be the fairest plan. The major shortcoming of the numerical standard is its failure to take account of other relevant — indeed, more important — criteria relating to the fairness of group participation in the political process. To that extent, it may indeed be counterproductive. . . .

A glance at the map . . . shows district configurations well deserving the kind of descriptive adjectives — "uncouth" and "bizarre" — that have traditionally been used to describe acknowledged gerrymanders. I have not applied the mathematical measures of compactness to the New Jersey map, but I think it likely that the plan would not fare well. In addition, while disregarding geographical compactness, the redistricting scheme wantonly disregards county boundaries. For example, in the words of a commentator, "In a flight of cartographic fancy, the Legislature packed North Jersey Republicans into a new district many call 'the Swan.' Its long neck and twisted body stretch from the New York suburbs to the rural upper reaches of the Delaware River." That district, the Fifth, contains segments of at least seven counties. The same commentator described the Seventh District, comprised of parts of five counties, as tracing "a curving partisan path through industrial Elizabeth, liberal, academic Princeton and largely Jewish Marlboro in Monmouth County. The resulting monstrosity was called 'the Fishhook' by detractors."

Such a map prompts an inquiry into the process that led to its adoption. The plan was sponsored by the leadership in the Democratic party, which controlled both houses of the State Legislature as well as the Governor's office, and was signed into law the day before the inauguration of a Republican Governor. The legislators never formally explained the guidelines used in formulating their plan or in selecting it over other available plans. Several of the rejected plans contained districts that were more nearly equal in population, more compact, and more consistent with subdivision boundaries, including one submitted by a recognized expert, Dr. Ernest Roeck, Jr., whose impartiality and academic credentials were not challenged. The District Court found that the Roeck plan "was rejected because it did not reflect the leadership's partisan concerns." This conclusion, which arises naturally from the absence of persuasive justifications for the rejection of the Roeck plan, is buttressed by a letter written to Dr. Roeck by the Democratic Speaker of the New Jersey General Assembly. This letter frankly explained the importance to the Democrats of taking advantage of their opportunity to control redistricting after the 1980 census. The Speaker justified his own overt partisanship by describing the political considerations that had motivated the Republican majority in the adoption of district plans in New Jersey in the past — and in other states at the present. In sum, the record indicates that the decisionmaking process leading to adoption of the challenged plan was far from neutral. It was designed to increase the number of Democrats, and to decrease the number of Republicans, that New Jersey's voters would send to Congress in future years. Finally, the record does not show any legitimate justifications for the irregularities in the New Jersey plan, although concededly the case was tried on a different theory in the District Court.

Because I have not made a comparative study of other districting plans, and because the State has not had the opportunity to offer justifications specifically directed toward the additional concerns I have discussed, I cannot conclude with absolute certainty that the New Jersey plan was an unconstitutional partisan gerrymander. But I am in full agreement with the Court's holding that, because the plan embodies deviations from population equality that have not been justified by any neutral state objective, it cannot stand. Further, if population equality provides the only check on political gerrymandering, it would be virtually impossible to fashion a fair and effective remedy in a case like this. For if the shape of legislative districts is entirely unconstrained, the dominant majority could no doubt respond to an unfavorable judgment by providing an even more grotesque-appearing map that reflects acceptable numerical equality with even greater political inequality. If federal judges can prevent that consequence by taking a hard look at the shape of things to come in the remedy hearing, I believe they can also scrutinize the original map with sufficient care to determine whether distortions have any rational basis in neutral criteria. Otherwise, the promise of *Baker* v. *Carr* and *Reynolds* v. *Sims* — that judicially manageable standards can assure "full and effective participation by all citizens," ... may never be fulfilled.

JUSTICE WHITE, with whom THE CHIEF JUSTICE, JUSTICE POWELL, and JUSTICE REHNQUIST join, dissenting.

... I respectfully dissent from the Court's unreasonable insistence on an unattainable perfection in the equalizing of congressional districts. The Court's decision today is not compelled by *Kirkpatrick* v. *Preisler*, (1969) and *White* v. *Weiser* (1973). ...

I

"The achieving of fair and effective representation for all citizens is concededly the basic aim of legislative apportionment." *Reynolds* v. *Sims* (1964). One must suspend credulity to believe that the Court's draconian response to a trifling 0.6984% maximum deviation promotes "fair and effective representation" for the people of New Jersey. The requirement that "as nearly as is practicable one man's vote in a congressional election is to be worth as much as another's," *Wesberry* v. *Sanders* (1964), must be understood in light of the malapportionment in the states at the time *Wesberry* was decided. The plaintiffs in *Wesberry* were voters in a congressional district (pop. 823,680) encompassing Atlanta that was three times larger than Georgia's smallest district (272,154) and more than double the size of an average district. Because the state had not reapportioned for 30 years, the Atlanta District possessing one-fifth of Georgia's population had only one-tenth of the Congressmen. Georgia was not atypical; congressional districts throughout the country had not been redrawn for decades and deviations of over 50% were the rule. These substantial differences in district size diminished, in a real sense, the representativeness of congressional elections. The Court's invalidation of these profoundly unequal districts should not be read as a demand for precise mathematical equality between the districts. Indeed, the Court sensibly observed that "it may not be possible [for the States] to draw Congressional districts with mathematical precision." In *Reynolds* v. *Sims*,

(1964), decided the same Term, the Court disavowed a requirement of mathematical exactness for legislative districts in even more explicit terms:

> "We realize that it is a practical impossibility to arrange legislative districts so that each one has an identical number of residents, or citizens, or voters. Mathematical exactness or precision is hardly a workable constitutional requirement."

The states responded to *Wesberry* by eliminating gross disparities between congressional districts. Nevertheless, redistricting plans with far smaller variations were struck by the Court five years later in *Kirkpatrick* v. *Preisler,* and its companion, *Wells* v. *Rockefeller,* (1969). The redistricting statutes before the Court contained total percentage deviations of 5.97% and 13.1%, respectively. But *Wesberry's* "as nearly as practicable" standard was read to require "a good faith effort to achieve precise numerical equality." Over the objections of four Justices, ... *Kirkpatrick* rejected the argument that there is fixed numerical or percentage population variance small enough to be considered *de minimis* and to satisfy the "as nearly as practicable" standard. *Kirkpatrick's* rule was applied by the Court in *White* v. *Weiser,* to invalidate Texas' redistricting scheme which had a maximum population variance of 4.13%.

Just as *Wesberry* did not require *Kirkpatrick, Kirkpatrick* does not ineluctably lead to the Court's decision today. Although the Court stated that it could see "no nonarbitrary way" to pick a *de minimis* point, the maximum deviation in *Kirkpatrick,* while small, was more than eight times as large as that posed here. Moreover, the deviation in *Kirkpatrick* was not argued to fall within the officially accepted range of statistical imprecision of the census. Interestingly enough, the Missouri redistricting plan approved after *Kirkpatrick* contained a deviation of 0.629% — virtually the same deviation declared unconstitutional in this case. Accordingly, I do not view the Court's decision today as foreordained by *Kirkpatrick* and *Weiser....*

There can be little question but that the variances in the New Jersey plan are "statistically insignificant." Although the government strives to make the decennial census as accurate as humanly possible, the Census Bureau has never intimated that the results are a perfect count of the American population. The Bureau itself estimates the inexactitude in the taking of the 1970 census at 2.3%, a figure which is considerably larger than the 0.6984% maximum variance in the New Jersey plan....

Even if the 0.6984% deviation here is not encompassed within the scope of the statistical imprecision of the census, it is minuscule when compared with other variations among the districts inherent in translating census numbers into citizens' votes. First, the census "is more of an event than a process." *Gaffney* v. *Cummings,* (1973). "It measures population at only a single instant in time. District populations are constantly changing, often at different rates in either direction, up or down." As the Court admits, "the well-known restlessness of the American people means that population counts for particular localities are outdated long before they are completed." Second, far larger differences among districts are introduced because a substantial percentage of the total population is too young to register or is disqualified by alienage. Third, census figures cannot account for the proportion of all those otherwise eligible individuals who fail to register. The differences in the number of eligible voters per district for these reasons overwhelm the minimal variations attributable to the districting plan itself.

Accepting that the census, and the district plans which are based upon it, cannot be perfect represents no backsliding in our commitment to assuring fair and equal representation in the election of Congress. . . .

If today's decision simply produced an unjustified standard with little practical import, it would be bad enough. Unfortunately, I fear that the Court's insistence that "there are no *de minimis* population variations, which could practicably be avoided, but which nonetheless meet the standard of Art. I, § 2 without justification," invites further litigation of virtually every congressional redistricting plan in the nation. At least twelve states which have completed redistricting on the basis of the 1980 census have adopted plans with a higher deviation than that presented here, and four others have deviations quite similar to New Jersey's. Of course, under the Court's rationale, even Rhode Island's plan — whose two districts have a deviation of 0.02% or about 95 people — would be subject to constitutional attack.

In all such cases, state legislatures will be hard pressed to justify their preference for the selected plan. A good-faith effort to achieve population equality is not enough if the population variances are not "unavoidable." The court must consider whether the population differences could have been further "reduced or eliminated altogether." . . .

The only way a legislature or bipartisan commission can hope to avoid litigation will be to dismiss all other legitimate concerns and opt automatically for the districting plan with the smallest deviation. Yet no one can seriously contend that such an inflexible insistence upon mathematical exactness will serve to promote "fair and effective representation." The more likely result of today's extension of *Kirkpatrick* is to move closer to fulfilling Justice Fortas' prophecy that "a legislature might have to ignore the boundaries of common sense, running the congressional district line down the middle of the corridor of an apartment house or even dividing the residents of a single-family house between two districts." Such sterile and mechanistic application only brings the principle of "one man, one vote" into disrepute.

II

. . . Of course, the *principle* of population equality is not unjust; the unreasonable *application* of this principle is the rub. Leaving aside that the principle has never been applied with the vengeance witnessed today, there are many, including myself, who take issue with the Court's self-congratulatory assumption that *Kirkpatrick* has been a success. First, a decade of experience with *Kirkpatrick* has shown that "the rule of absolute equality is perfectly compatible with 'gerrymandering' of the worst sort." *Wells* v. *Rockefeller*. With ever more sophisticated computers, legislators can draw countless plans for absolute population equality, but each having its own political ramifications.... More than a decade's experience with *Kirkpatrick* demonstrates that insistence on precise numerical equality only invites those who lost in the political arena to refight their battles in federal court....

In order that legislatures have room to accommodate these legitimate non-census factors, a range of *de minimis* population deviation, like that permitted in the legislative reapportionment cases, is required. The Court's insistence that every deviation, no matter how small, be justified with specificity discourages legislatures from considering these "legitimate" factors in making their plans, lest the justification be found wanting, the plan invalidated, and a judicially drawn substitute put in its place. Moreover, the requirement of precise mathematical equality continues to invite those who would bury their political opposition to employ equipopulous gerrymanders. A *de minimis* range would not preclude such gerrymanders but would at least force the political cartographer to justify his work on its own terms.

JUSTICE POWELL, dissenting.

I

... The Court, following *Kirkpatrick*, today invalidates New Jersey's redistricting plan solely because various alternative plans, principally the one proposed by Professor Reock, had what the Court views as "appreciably smaller population deviations between the largest and smallest districts." *Ante*, at 3. Under all of the plans, the maximum population variances were under 1%. I view these differences as neither "appreciable" nor constitutionally significant. As JUSTICE WHITE demonstrates, (dissenting opinion), the Court's insistence on precise mathematical equality is self-deluding, given the inherent inaccuracies of the census data and the other difficulties in measuring the voting population of a district that will exist for a period of 10 years.... Moreover, it has become clear that *Kirkpatrick* leaves no room for proper legislative consideration of other factors, such as preservation of political and geographic boundaries, that plainly are relevant to rational reapportionment decisions....

I therefore continue to believe that the Constitution permits variations from "theoretical 'exactitude' in recognition of the impracticality of applying the *Kirkpatrick* rule as wel as in deference to legitimate state interests." *White* v. *Weiser*, (POWELL, J., concurring). Certainly when a State has adopted a districting plan with an average population deviation of 0.1384%t, and a maximum deviation of 0.6984%, it has complied with the Constitution's mandate that population be apportioned equally among districts.

II

The extraordinary map of the New Jersey congressional districts ... prompts me to comment on the separate question of gerrymandering — "the deliberate and arbitrary distortion of district boundaries and populations for partisan or personal political purposes," *Kirkpatrick*. I am in full agreement with JUSTICE WHITE's observation a decade ago that gerrymandering presents "a far greater potential threat to equality of representation" than a State's failure to achieve "precise adherence to admittedly inexact census figures." I also believe that the injuries that result from gerrymandering may rise to constitutional dimensions. As JUSTICE STEVENS observes, if a State's electoral rules "serve no purpose other than to favor one segment — whether racial, ethnic, religious, economic, or political — that may occupy a position of strength at a particular point in time, or to disadvantage a politically weak segment of the community, they violate the constitutional guarantee of equal protection." Moreover, most gerrymandering produces districts "without any regard for political subdivision or natural or historical boundary lines," *Reynolds* v. *Sims*, (1964), a result that is profoundly destructive of the apportionment goal of "fair and effective representation." A legislator cannot represent his constituents properly — nor can voters from a fragmented district exercise the ballot intelligently — when a voting district is nothing more than an artificial unit divorced from, and indeed often in conflict with, the various communities established in the State. The map attached to the Court's opinion illustrates this far better than words can describe.

I therefore am prepared to entertain constitutional challenges to partisan gerrymandering that reaches the level of discrimination described by JUSTICE STEVENS. . . . I do not suggest that the shape of a districting map itself invariably is dispositive. Some irregularity in shape is inevitable, with the degree of irregularity depending primarily on the geographic and political boundaries within the State, as well as the distribution of its population. Moreover, political considerations, even partisan ones, are inherent in a democratic system. A court, therefore, should not "attemp[t] the impossible task of extirpating politics from what are the essentially political processes of the sovereign States." . . .

In this case, one cannot rationally believe that the New Jersey Legislature considered factors other than the most partisan political goals and population equality. It hardly could be suggested, for example, that the contorted districts 3, 5, and 7 reflect any attempt to follow natural, historical, or local political boundaries. Nor do these district lines reflect any consideration of the likely effect on the quality of representation when the boundaries are so artificial that they are likely to confound the congressmen themselves. . . .

COURT ON LEGISLATIVE VETO

June 23, 1983

In a landmark decision affecting the relative powers of the legislative and executive branches of the government, the Supreme Court June 23, in a 7-2 ruling, declared the so-called "legislative veto" unconstitutional. The decision overturned a device that had been included in more than 200 laws beginning with Herbert Hoover's administration in 1932.

Historians and other experts on constitutional issues called the decision the most important constitutional ruling by the Court since its 1974 decision ordering President Richard Nixon to surrender subpoenaed White House tapes. (Historic Documents of 1974, p. 621) *Moreover, in his dissent, Justice Byron R. White wrote that the ruling "strikes down in one fell swoop provisions in more laws enacted by Congress than the Court has cumulatively invalidated in its history."*

The Court itself called attention rather dramatically to the historic significance of the decision. Although oral dissents were rare, White read aloud from the bench his long dissenting opinion. Then Chief Justice Warren E. Burger, addressing the courtroom informally and without notes, spoke of the broad constitutional issues involved. He told the Court's visitors that if the framers of the Constitution had wanted to establish a legislative veto, "they knew very well how to do it."

The broad ruling came in an obscure immigration case, Immigration and Naturalization Service v. Chadha. *The case had its beginnings in 1974 when a Kenyan who had overstayed his student visa won a decision from the Immigration and Naturalization Service (INS) suspending his deportation. The House of Representatives, exercising a legislative veto*

617

provision in the 1952 Immigration and Naturalization Act, vetoed that suspension. The student, Jagdish Rai Chadha, filed suit challenging the power of the House to take that action. Holding that the House had exceeded its constitutional powers, the 9th U.S. Circuit Court of Appeals agreed, and the Supreme Court, in its far reaching June 23 decision, upheld the ruling of the lower court.

Use of Legislative Vetoes

The legislative veto was considered a useful device by both liberals and conservatives for more than half a century. Sometimes it was included in a law with the president's acquiescence if not blessing. At other times, it was included over the president's bitter opposition. In all the laws containing the veto, Congress granted the president authority but reserved the right to block certain actions that he might take.

The first legislative veto provision was written into a law late in the Hoover administration. Seeking to reorganize the government, the president came to an agreement with the legislative branch: Congress granted Hoover the authority he wanted, provided that either the House or the Senate could veto the resulting reorganization plan.

In his dissent White pointed to the very broad range of legislation containing the veto. "The device," he wrote, "is known in every field of governmental concern: reorganization, budgets, foreign affairs, war powers, and the regulation of trade, safety, energy, the environment and the economy."

The legislative veto had become a major tool with which Congress sought to influence foreign policy. A significant example was the War Powers Resolution of 1973, which Congress enacted over President Nixon's veto. In particular, Nixon opposed a provision that allowed Congress, by passing a concurrent resolution, to force the withdrawal of U.S. troops engaged in hostilities overseas without congressional authorization.

Executive Branch: Winner or Loser?

In the wake of the Court's decision, many constitutional experts believed that, inevitably, the loss of the legislative veto would enhance the power of the president and of the executive branch generally. But others expressed the view that the ultimate loser would turn out to be the president. For example, Norman J. Ornstein, a professor of government at Catholic University, said that the veto had represented a "tacit compact" between the president and Congress that spared the latter "the hassles of ... tough political issues." After the ruling, Ornstein said, Congress "may tell the president, 'Anytime you want something, you come to us hat in hand.'"

One example of the uncertain impact of the Court's ruling involved the 1974 Budget Act's provision allowing Congress to veto presidential actions to defer, or temporarily delay (impound), the spending of previously appropriated funds. To force the spending, either chamber could adopt a resolution "vetoing" the deferral. Since deferral resolutions did not have to be signed by the president, most authorities agreed they fell within the legislative veto category struck down by the Supreme Court's decision.

Who stood to gain if congressional impoundment authority no longer existed? "It's a mixed bag," said Senate Budget Committee Chairman Pete V. Domenici, R-N.M. "Some say it will help the executive branch. . . . Some say it will help the legislative branch." One congressional aide noted that before enactment of the Budget Act the trend in court decisions on the president's authority to impound federal funds clearly had been against the executive branch. Thus, one could argue that if the issue returned to the courts, the president would lose power rather than gain. In any case, a number of observers questioned whether loss of the deferral power would seriously hamper Congress' ability to oversee the budget process because other, more important tools were not affected by the legislative veto decision.

The Court's Opinion and Dissent

Five justices joined Burger in his broad opinion. They were Justices Harry A. Blackmun, William J. Brennan Jr., Thurgood Marshall, John Paul Stevens and Sandra Day O'Connor. Justice Lewis F. Powell Jr. refused to join in the broad ruling, arguing in a concurring opinion only that the veto the House had exercised in the Chadha case was unconstitutional. In that case, he wrote, Congress had "assumed a judicial function" in violation of the principle of separation of powers."

A second dissent was by Justice William H. Rehnquist. In a brief opinion, he wrote that he did not believe that Congress intended the legislative veto provision in the 1952 Immigration and Naturalization Act to be "severable" from the rest of the law.

Writing for the majority, Burger declared that the Constitution required that all legislative actions be approved by both houses of Congress and sent to the president for his approval or disapproval. The legislative veto failed to meet that test, he said, because it excluded the president from the lawmaking process. "The president's participation in the legislative process was to protect the executive from Congress and to protect the whole people from improvident laws," Burger wrote.

The chief justice acknowledged that some of the choices made by the "framers" of the Constitution seemed to result in "clumsy, inefficient, even unworkable processes." Nevertheless, "with all the obvious flaws of *delay, untidiness and potential for abuse, we have not yet found a better way to preserve freedom than by making the exercise of power subject to the carefully crafted restraints spelled out in the Constitution," he said.*

Equalling the majority opinion in length, Justice White's dissenting opinion was one of the longest of his judicial career. By denying Congress the use of the legislative veto, he argued, the Court presented Congress with an unhappy choice: "either to refrain from delegating the necessary authority, leaving itself with a hopeless task of writing laws with the requisite specificity to cover endless special circumstances across the entire policy landscape, or in the alternative, to abdicate its lawmaking function to the executive branch and independent agencies."

White said that in his view, "neither Article I of the Constitution nor the doctrine of separation of powers" was violated by "this mechanism by which our elected representatives preserve their voice in the governance of the nation."

Following are excerpts from the Supreme Court's opinion striking down the legislative veto and from the dissenting opinion by Justice Byron R. White, June 23, 1983:

Nos. 80-1832, 80-2170 and 80-2171

Immigration and Naturalization
Service, Appellant
v.
Jagdish Rai Chadha et al.

On appeal from the United States Court of Appeals for the Ninth Circuit

United States House of
Representatives, Petitioner
v.
Immigration and Naturalization
Service et al.

United States Senate, Petitioner
v.
Immigration and Naturalization
Service et al.

On Writs of Certiorari to the United States Court of Appeals for the Ninth Circuit.

[June 23, 1983]

CHIEF JUSTICE BURGER delivered the opinion of the Court.

We granted certiorari in Nos. 80-2170 and 80-2171, and postponed consideration of the question of jurisdiction in No. 80-1832. Each presents a challenge to the constitutionality of the provision in § 244 (c) (2) of the

Immigration and Nationality Act, 8 U.S.C. § 1254 (c) (2), authorizing one House of Congress, by resolution, to invalidate the decision of the Executive Branch, pursuant to authority delegated by Congress to the Attorney General of the United States, to allow a particular deportable alien to remain in the United States.

I

Chadha is an East Indian who was born in Kenya and holds a British passport. He was lawfully admitted to the United States in 1966 on a nonimmigrant student visa. His visa expired on June 30, 1972. On October 11, 1973, the District Director of the Immigration and Naturalization Service ordered Chadha to show cause why he should not be deported for having "remained in the United States for a longer time than permitted." Pursuant to § 242 (b) of the Immigration and Nationality Act (Act), 8 U.S.C. § 1254 (b), a deportation hearing was held before an immigration judge on January 11, 1974. Chadha conceded that he was deportable for overstaying his visa and the hearing was adjourned to enable him to file an application for suspension of deportation under § 244 (a) (1) of the Act, 8 U.S.C. § 1254 (a) (1). Section 244 (a) (1) provides:

"(a) As hereinafter prescribed in this section, the Attorney General may, in his discretion, suspend deportation and adjust the status to that of an alien lawfully admitted for permanent residence, in the case of an alien who applies to the Attorney General for suspension of deportation and—

(1) is deportable under any law of the United States except the provisions specified in paragraph (2) of this subsection; has been physically present in the United States for a continuous period of not less than seven years immediately preceding the date of such application, and proves that during all of such period he was and is a person of good moral character; and is a person whose deportation would, in the opinion of the Attorney General, result in extreme hardship to the alien or to his spouse, parent, or child, who is a citizen of the United States or an alien lawfully admitted for permanent residence."

After Chadha submitted his application for suspension of deportation, the deportation hearing was resumed on February 7, 1974. On the basis of evidence adduced at the hearing, affidavits submitted with the application, and the results of a character investigation conducted by the INS, the immigration judge, on June 25, 1974, ordered that Chadha's deportation be suspended. The immigration judge found that Chadha met the requirements of § 244 (a) (1): he had resided continuously in the United States for over seven years, was of good moral character, and would suffer "extreme hardship" if deported.

Pursuant to § 244 (c) (1) of the Act, 8 U.S.C. § 1254 (c) (1), the immigration judge suspended Chadha's deportation and a report of the suspension was transmitted to Congress. Section 244 (c) (1) provides:

"Upon application by any alien who is found by the Attorney General to meet the requirements of subsection (a) of this section the Attorney General may in his discretion suspend deportation of such alien. If the deportation of any alien is suspended under the provisions of this subsection, a complete and detailed statement of the facts and pertinent provisions of law in the case shall be reported to the Congress with the reasons for such suspension. Such reports shall be submitted on the first day of each calendar month in which Congress is in session."

Once the Attorney General's recommendation for suspension of Chadha's deportation was conveyed to Congress, Congress had the power under § 244 (c) (2) of the Act, 8 U.S.C. § 1254 (c) (2), to veto the Attorney General's determination that Chadha should not be deported. Section 244 (c) (2) provides:

"(2) In the case of an alien specified in paragraph (1) of subsection (a) of this subsection—
if during the session of the Congress at which a case is reported, or prior to the close of the session of the Congress next following the session at which a case is reported, either the Senate or the House of Representatives passes a resolution stating in substance that it does not favor the suspension of such deportation, the Attorney General shall thereupon deport such alien or authorize the alien's voluntary departure at his own expense under the order of deportation in the manner provided by law. If, within the time above specified, neither the Senate nor the House of Representatives shall pass such a resolution, the Attorney General shall cancel deportation proceedings."

The June 25, 1974 order of the immigration judge suspending Chadha's deportation remained outstanding as a valid order for a year and a half. For reasons not disclosed by the record, Congress did not exercise the veto authority reserved to it under § 244 (c) (2) until the first session of the 94th Congress. This was the final session in which Congress, pursuant to § 244 (c) (2), could act to veto the Attorney General's determination that Chadha should not be deported. The session ended on December 19, 1975. Absent Congressional action, Chadha's deportation proceedings would have been cancelled after this date and his status adjusted to that of a permanent resident alien.

On December 12, 1975, Representative Eilberg, Chairman of the Judiciary Subcommittee on Immigration, Citizenship, and International Law, introduced a resolution opposing "the granting of permanent residence in the United States to [six] aliens", including Chadha. The resolution was referred to the House Committee on the Judiciary. On December 16, 1975, the resolution was discharged from further consideration by the House Committee on the Judiciary and submitted to the House of Representatives for a vote. The resolution had not been printed and was not made available to other Members of the House prior to or at the time it was voted on. So far as the record before us shows, the House consideration of the resolution was based on ... Eilberg's statement ... that

"[i]t was the feeling of the committee, after reviewing 340 cases, that the aliens contained in the resolution [Chadha and five others] did not meet these statutory requirements, particularly as it relates to hardship; and it is the opinion of the committee that their deportation should not be suspended."

The resolution was passed without debate or recorded vote. Since the House action was pursuant to § 244 (c) (2), the resolution was not treated as an Article I legislative act; it was not submitted to the Senate or presented to the President for his action.

After the House veto of the Attorney General's decision to allow Chadha to remain in the United States, the immigration judge reopened the deportation proceedings to implement the House order deporting Chadha. Chadha moved to terminate the proceedings on the ground that § 244 (c) (2) is unconstitutional. The immigration judge held that he had no authority to rule on the constitutional validity of § 244 (c) (2). On November 8, 1976, Chadha was ordered deported pursuant to the House action.

Chadha appealed the deportation order to the Board of Immigration Appeals again contending that § 244 (c) (2) is unconstitutional. The Board held that it had "no power to declare unconstitutional an act of Congress" and Chadha's appeal was dismissed.

Pursuant to § 106 (a) of the Act, 8 U.S.C. § 1105 a (a), Chadha filed a petition for review of the deportation order in the United States Court of Appeals for the Ninth Circuit. The Immigration and Naturalization Service agreed with Chadha's position before the Court of Appeals and joined him in arguing that § 244 (c) (2) is unconstitutional. In light of the importance of the question, the Court of Appeals invited both the Senate and the House of Representatives to file briefs *amici curiae.*

After full briefing and oral argument, the Court of Appeals held that the House was without constitutional authority to order Chadha's deportation; accordingly it directed the Attorney General "to cease and desist from taking any steps to deport this alien based upon the resolution enacted by the House of Representatives." *Chadha* v. *INS* (CA9 1980). The essence of its holding was that § 244 (c) (2) violates the constitutional doctrine of separation of powers.

We granted certiorari in Nos. 80-2170 and 80-2171, and postponed consideration of our jurisdiction over the appeal in No. 80-1832 . . . (1981), and we now affirm. . . .

II

[Section A Omitted]

B

Severability

Congress also contends that the provision for the one-House veto in § 244 (c) (2) cannot be severed from § 244. Congress argues that if the provision for the one-House veto is held unconstitutional, all of § 244 must fall. If § 244 in its entirety is violative of the Constitution, it follows that the Attorney General has no authority to suspend Chadha's deportation under § 244 (a) (1) and Chadha would be deported. From this, Congress argues that Chadha lacks standing to challenge the constitutionality of the one-House veto provision because he could receive no relief even if his constitutional challenge proves successful.

Only recently this Court reaffirmed that the invalid portions of a statute are to be severed "[u]nless it is evident that the Legislature would not have enacted those provisions which are within its power, independently of that which is not.' " *Buckley* v. *Valeo* (1976), quoting *Champlin Refining Co.* v. *Corporation Comm'n* (1932). Here, however, we need not embark on that elusive inquiry since Congress itself has provided the answer to the question of severability in § 406 of the Immigration and Nationality Act, 8 U.S.C. § 1101, which provides:

> "If *any* particular provision of this act, or the application thereof to *any* person or circumstance, is held invalid, *the remainder of the Act and the application of such provision to other persons or circumstances shall not be affected thereby."* (Emphasis added.)

This language is unambiguous and gives rise to a presumption that Congress did not intend the validity of the Act as a whole, or of any part of the Act, to depend upon whether the veto clause of § 244 (c) (2) was invalid. The one-House veto provision in § 244 (c) (2) is clearly a "particular provision" of the Act as that language is used in the severability clause. Congress clearly intended "the remainder of the Act" to stand if "any particular provision" were held invalid. Congress could not have more plainly authorized the presumption that the provision for a one-House veto in § 244 (c) (2) is severable from the remainder of § 244 and the Act of which it is a part. See *Electric Bond & Share Co.* v. *SEC* (1938).

The presumption as to the severability of the one-House veto provision in § 244 (c) (2) is supported by the legislative history of § 244. That section and its precursors supplanted the long established pattern of dealing with deportations like Chadha's on a case-by-case basis through private bills. Although it may be that Congress was reluctant to delegate final authority over cancellation of deportations, such reluctance is not sufficient to overcome the presumption of severability raised by § 406.

The Immigration Act of 1924, Pub. L. No. 139, § 14, 43 Stat. 153, 162, required the Secretary of Labor to deport any alien who entered or remained in the United States unlawfully. The only means by which a deportable alien could lawfully remain in the United States was to have his status altered by a private bill enacted by both Houses and presented to the President pursuant to the procedures set out in Art. I, § 7 of the Constitution. These private bills were found intolerable by Congress. . . .

Congress first authorized the Attorney General to suspend the deportation of certain aliens in the Alien Registration Act of 1940, ch. 439, § 20, 54 Stat. 671. That Act provided that an alien was to be deported, despite the Attorney General's decision to the contrary, if both Houses, by concurrent resolution, disapproved the suspension.

In 1948, Congress amended the act to broaden the category of aliens eligible for suspension of deportation. In addition, however, Congress limited the authority of the Attorney General to suspend deportations by providing that the Attorney General could not cancel a deportation unless both Houses affirmatively voted by concurrent resolution to *approve* the Attorney General's action. . . .

The proposal to permit one House of Congress to veto the Attorney General's suspension of an alien's deportation was incorporated in the Immigration and Nationality Act of 1952. . . . Plainly, Congress' desire to retain a veto in this area cannot be considered in isolation but must be viewed in the context of Congress' irritation with the burden of private immigration bills. This legislative history is not sufficient to rebut the presumption of severability raised by § 406 because there is insufficient evidence that Congress would have continued to subject itself to the onerous burdens of private bills had it known that § 244 (c) (2) would be held unconstitutional.

A provision is further presumed severable if what remains after severance "is fully operative as a law." *Champlin Refining Co.* v. *Corporation Comm'n.* There can be no doubt that § 244 is "fully operative" and workable administrative machinery without the veto provision in § 244 (c) (2). Entirely independent of the one-House veto, the administrative process enacted by Congress authorizes the Attorney General to suspend an alien's deportation under §244 (a). Congress' oversight of the exercise of this delegated authority is preserved since all such suspensions will continue to be reported to it under § 244 (c) (1). Absent the passage of a bill to the contrary, deportation proceedings will be cancelled when the period specified in § 244 (c) (2) has expired. Clearly, § 244 survives as a workable administrative mechanism without the one-House veto. . . .

[Sections C, D and E Omitted]

F

Case or Controversy

It is also contended that this is not a genuine controversy but "a friendly, non-adversary, proceeding," *Ashwander* v. *Tennessee Valley Authority* [1936] (Brandeis, J., concurring), upon which the Court should not pass. This argument rests on the fact that Chadha and the INS take the same position on the constitutionality of the one-House veto. But it would be a curious result if, in the administration of justice, a person could be denied access to the courts because the Attorney General of the United States agreed with the legal arguments asserted by the individual.

A case or controversy is presented by this case. First, from the time of Congress' formal intervention, . . . the concrete adverseness is beyond doubt. Congress is both a proper party to defend the constitutionality of § 244 (c) (2) and a proper petitioner under § 1254 (1). Second, prior to Congress' intervention, there was adequate Art. III adverseness even though the only parties were the INS and Chadha. We have already held that the INS's agreement with the Court of Appeals' decision that § 244 (c) (2) is unconstitutional does not affect that agency's "aggrieved" status for purposes of appealing that decision under 28 U.S.C. § 1252. For similar reasons, the INS's agreement with Chadha's position does not alter the fact that the INS would have deported Chadha absent the Court of Appeals' judgment. We agree with the Court of Appeals that "Chadha has asserted a concrete controversy, and our decision will have real meaning: if we rule for Chadha, he will not be deported; if we uphold § 244 (c) (2), the INS will execute its order and deport him."

Of course, there may be prudential, as opposed to Art. III, concerns about sanctioning the adjudication of this case in the absence of any participant supporting the validity of § 244 (c) (2). The Court of Appeals properly dispelled any such concerns by inviting and accepting briefs from both Houses of Congress. We have long held that Congress is the proper party to defend the validity of a statute when an agency of government, as a defendant charged with enforcing the statute, agrees with plaintiffs that the statute is inapplicable or unconstitutional. See *Cheng Fan Kwok* v. *INS* [1968]; *United States* v. *Lovett* (1946).

G

Political Question

It is also argued that this case presents a nonjusticiable political question because Chadha is merely challenging Congress' authority under the Naturalization Clause, U.S. Const. art. I, § 8, cl. 4, and the Necessary and Proper Clause, U.S. Const. art. I, § 8, cl. 18. It is argued that Congress' Article I power "To establish a uniform Rule of Naturalization", combined with the Necessary and Proper Clause, grants it unreviewable authority over the regulation of aliens. The plenary authority of Congress over aliens under Art. I, § 8, cl. 4 is not open to question, but what is challenged here is whether Congress has chosen a constitutionally permissible means of implementing that power. As we made clear in *Buckley* v. *Valeo* (1976), "Congress has plenary authority in all cases in which it has substantive legislative jurisdiction, *M'Culloch* v. *Maryland* (1819), so long as the exercise of that authority does not offend some other constitutional restriction."

A brief review of those factors which may indicate the presence of a nonjusticiable political question satisfies us that our assertion of jurisdiction over this case does no violence to the political question doctrine. As identified in *Baker* v. *Carr* (1962), a political question may arise when any one of the following circumstances is present:

> "a textually demonstrable constitutional commitment of the issue to a coordinate political department; or a lack of judicially discoverable and manageable standards for resolving it; or the impossibility of deciding without an initial policy determination of a kind clearly for nonjudicial discretion; or the impossibility of a court's undertaking independent resolution without expressing lack of the respect due coordinate branches of government; or an unusual need for unquestioning adherence to a political decision already made; or the potentiality of embarrassment from multifarious pronouncements by various departments on one question."

Congress apparently directs its assertion of nonjusticiability to the first of the *Baker* factors by asserting that Chadha's claim is "an assault on the legislative authority to enact Section 244 (c) (2)." But if this turns the question into a political question virtually every challenge to the constitutionality of a statute would be a political question. Chadha indeed argues that one House of Congress cannot constitutionally veto the Attorney General's decision to allow him to remain in this country. No policy underlying the political question doctrine suggests that Congress or the executive, or both acting in concert and in compliance with Art. I, can decide the constitutionality of a statute; that is a decision for the courts.

Other *Baker* factors are likewise inapplicable to this case. As we discuss more fully below, Art. I provides the "judicially discoverable and manageable standards" of *Baker* for resolving the question presented by this case. Those standards forestall reliance by this Court on nonjudicial "policy determinations" or any showing of disrespect for a coordinate branch. Similarly, if Chadha's arguments are accepted, § 244 (c) (2) cannot stand, and, since the constitutionality of that statute is for this Court to resolve, there is no possibility of "multifarious pronouncements" on this question.

It is correct that this controversy may, in a sense, be termed "political." But the presence of constitutional issues with significant political overtones does not automatically invoke the political question doctrine. Resolution of litigation challenging the constitutional authority of one of the three branches cannot be evaded by courts because the issues have political implications in the sense urged by Congress. *Marbury* v. *Madison* (1803), was also a "political" case, involving as it did claims under a judicial commission alleged to have been duly signed by the President but not delivered. But "courts cannot reject as 'no law suit' a bona fide controversy as to whether some action denominated 'political' exceeds constitutional authority." *Baker* v. *Carr*. . . .

III

A

We turn now to the question whether action of one House of Congress under § 244 (c) (2) violates strictures of the Constitution. We begin, of course, with the presumption that the challenged statute is valid. Its wisdom is not the concern of the courts; if a challenged action does not violate the Constitution, it must be sustained:

> "Once the meaning of an enactment is discerned and its constitutionality determined, the judicial process comes to an end. We do not sit as a committee of review, nor are we vested with the power of veto." *Tennessee Valley Authority* v. *Hill (1978)*.

By the same token, the fact that a given law or procedure is efficient, convenient, and useful in facilitating functions of government, standing alone, will not save it if it is contrary to the Constitution. Convenience and efficiency are not the primary objectives — or the hallmarks — of democratic government and our inquiry is sharpened rather than blunted by the fact that Congressional veto provisions are appearing with increasing frequency in statutes which delegate authority to executive and independent agencies. . . .

JUSTICE WHITE undertakes to make a case for the proposition that the one-House veto is a useful "political invention," and we need not challenge that assertion. We can even concede this utilitarian argument although the long range political wisdom of this "invention" is arguable. It has been vigorously debated and it is instructive to compare the views of the protagonists. . . . But policy arguments supporting even useful "political inventions" are subject to the demands of the Constitution which defines powers and, with respect to this subject, sets out just how those powers are to be exercised.

Explicit and unambiguous provisions of the Constitution prescribe and define the respective functions of the Congress and of the Executive in the legislative process. Since the precise terms of those familiar provisions are critical to the resolution of this case, we set them out verbatim. Art. I provides:

> "All legislative Powers herein granted shall be vested in a Congress of the United States, which shall consist of a Senate *and* a House of Representatives." Art. I, § 1. (Emphasis added).

> "Every Bill which shall have passed the House of Representatives *and* the Senate, *shall,* before it become a Law, be presented to the President of the United States;. . ." Art. I, § 7, cl. 2. (Emphasis added).

> "*Every* Order, Resolution, or Vote to which the Concurrence of the Senate and House of Representatives may be necessary (except on a question of Adjournment) *shall be* presented to the President of the United States; and before the Same shall take effect, *shall be* approved by him, or being disapproved by him, *shall be* repassed by two thirds of the Senate and House of Representatives, according to the Rules and Limitations prescribed in the Case of a Bill." Art. I, § 7, cl. 3. (Emphasis added).

These provisions of Art. I are integral parts of the constitutional design for the separation of powers. We have recently noted that "[t]he principle of separation of powers was not simply an abstract generalization in the minds of the Framers: it was woven into the documents that they drafted in Philadelphia in the summer of 1787." *Buckley* v. *Valeo.* Just as we relied on the textual provision of Art. II, § 2, to vindicate the principle of separation of powers in *Buckley,* we find that the purposes underlying the Presentment Clauses, Art. I, § 7, cls. 2, 3, and the bicameral requirement of Art. I, § 1 and § 7, cl. 2, guide our resolution of the important question presented in this case. The very structure of the articles delegating and separating powers under Arts. I, II, and III exemplify the concept of separation of powers and we now turn to Art. I.

B

The Presentment Clauses

The records of the Constitutional Convention reveal that the requirement that all legislation be presented to the President before becoming law was uniformly accepted by the Framers. Presentment to the President and the Presidential veto were considered so imperative that the draftsmen took special pains to assure that these requirements could not be circumvented. During the final debate on Art. I, § 7, cl. 2, James Madison expressed concern that it might easily be evaded by the simple expedient of calling a proposed law a "resolution" or "vote" rather than a "bill."

The decision to provide the President with a limited and qualified power to nullify proposed legislation by veto was based on the profound conviction of the Framers that the powers conferred on Congress were the powers to be most carefully circumscribed. It is beyond doubt that lawmaking was a power to be shared by both Houses and the President. In The Federalist No. 73, Hamilton focused on the President's role in making laws:

> "If even no propensity had ever discovered itself in the legislative body to invade the rights of the Executive, the rules of just reasoning and theoretic propriety would of themselves teach us that the one ought not to be left to the mercy of the other, but ought to possess a constitutional and effectual power of self-defense." . . .

The President's role in the lawmaking process also reflects the Framers' careful efforts to check whatever propensity a particular Congress might have to enact oppressive, improvident, or ill-considered measures. The President's veto role in the legislative process was described later during public debate on ratification:

> "It establishes a salutary check upon the legislative body, calculated to guard the community against the effects of faction, precipitancy, or of any impulse unfriendly to the public good which may happen to influence a majority of that body. . . . The primary inducement to conferring the power in question upon the Executive is to enable him to defend himself; the secondary one is to increase the chances in favor of the community against the passing of bad laws through haste, inadvertence, or design." The Federalist No. 73 (A. Hamilton).

See also *The Pocket Veto Case* (1929); *Myers* v. *United States* (1926). The Court also has observed that the Presentment Clauses serve the important purpose of assuring that a "national" perspective is grafted on the legislative process:

> "The President is a representative of the people just as the members of the Senate and of the House are, and it may be, at some times, on some subjects, that the President elected by all the people is rather more representative of them all than are the members of either body of the Legislature whose constituencies are local and not countrywide. . . ." *Myers* v. *United States.*

C

Bicameralism

The bicameral requirement of Art. I, §§ 1, 7 was of scarcely less concern to the Framers than was the Presidential veto and indeed the two concepts are interdependent. By providing that no law could take effect without the concurrence of the prescribed majority of the Members of both Houses, the

Framers reemphasized their belief, already remarked upon in connection with the Presentment Clauses, that legislation should not be enacted unless it has been carefully and fully considered by the Nation's elected officials. In the Constitutional Convention debates on the need for a bicameral legislature, James Wilson, later to become a Justice of this Court, commented:

> "Despotism comes on mankind in different shapes. Sometimes in an Executive, sometimes in a military, one. Is there danger of a Legislative despotism? Theory & practice both proclaim it. If the Legislative authority be not restrained, there can be neither liberty nor stability; and it can only be restrained by dividing it within itself, into distinct and independent branches. In a single house there is no check, but the inadequate one, of the virtue & good sense of those who compose it."

Hamilton argued that a Congress comprised of a single House was antithetical to the very purposes of the Constitution. Were the Nation to adopt a Constitution providing for only one legislative organ, he warned:

> "we shall finally accumulate, in a single body, all the most important prerogatives of sovereignty, and thus entail upon our posterity one of the most execrable forms of government that human infatuation ever contrived. Thus we should create in reality that very tyranny which the adversaries of the new Constitution either are, or affect to be, solicitous to avert." The Federalist No. 22.

This view was rooted in a general skepticism regarding the fallibility of human nature later commented on by Joseph Story:

> "Public bodies, like private persons, are occasionally under the dominion of stong passions and excitements; impatient, irritable, and impetuous. . . . If [a legislature] feels no check but its own will, it rarely has the firmness to insist upon holding a question long enough under its own view, to see and mark it in all its bearings and relations to society."

These observations are consistent with what many of the Framers expressed, none more cogently than Hamilton. . . :

> "In republican government, the legislative authority necessarily predominates. The remedy for this inconveniency is to divide the legislature into different branches; and to render them, by different modes of election and different principles of action, as little connected with each other as the nature of their common functions and their common dependence on the society will admit." The Federalist No. 51. . . .

However familiar, it is useful to recall that apart from their fear that special interests could be favored at the expense of public needs, the Framers were also concerned, although not of one mind, over the apprehensions of the smaller states. Those states feared a commonality of interest among the larger states would work to their disadvantage; representatives of the larger states, on the other hand, were skeptical of a legislature that could pass laws favoring a minority of the people. It need hardly be repeated here that the Great Compromise, under which one House was viewed as representing the people and the other the states, allayed the fears of both the large and small states.

We see therefore that the Framers were acutely conscious that the bicameral requirement and the Presentment Clauses would serve essential constitutional functions. The President's participation in the legislative process was to protect the Executive Branch from Congress and to protect the whole people from improvident laws. The division of the Congress into two distinctive bodies assures that the legislative power would be exercised only after opportunity for full study and debate in separate settings. The President's unilateral veto power, in turn, was limited by the power of two thirds of both Houses of Congress to overrule a veto thereby precluding final arbitrary action of one person. It emerges clearly that the prescription for legislative action in Art. I, §§1, 7 represents the Framers' decision that the legislative power of the Federal government be exercised in accord with a single, finely wrought and exhaustively considered, procedure.

IV

The Constitution sought to divide the delegated powers of the new federal government into three defined categories, legislative, executive and judicial, to assure, as nearly as possible, that each Branch of government would confine itself to its assigned responsibility. The hydraulic pressure inherent within each of the separate branches to exceed the outer limits of its power, even to accomplish desirable objectives, must be resisted.

Although not "hermetically" sealed from one another, *Buckley* v. *Valeo,* the power delegated to the three Branches are functionally identifiable. When any Branch acts, it is presumptively exercising the power the Constitution has delegated to it. See *Hampton & Co.* v. *United States* (1928). When the Executive acts, it presumptively acts in an executive or administrative capacity as defined in Art. II. And when, as here, one House of Congress purports to act, it is presumptively acting within its assigned sphere.

Beginning with this presumption, we must nevertheless establish that the challenged action under § 244 (c) (2) is of the kind to which the procedural requirements of Art. I, § 7 apply. Not every action taken by either House is subject to the bicameralism and presentment requirements of Art. I. Whether actions taken by either House are, in law and fact, an exercise of legislative power depends not on their form but upon "whether they contain matter which is properly to be regarded as legislative in its character and effect."

Examination of the action taken here by one House pursuant to § 244 (c) (2) reveals that it was essentially legislative in purpose and effect. In purporting to exercise power defined in Art. I, § 8, cl. 4 to "establish an uniform Rule of Naturalization," the House took action that had the purpose and effect of altering the legal rights, duties and relations of persons, including the Attorney General, Executive Branch officials and Chadha, all outside the legislative branch. Section 244 (c) (2) purports to authorize one House of Congress to require the Attorney General to deport an individual alien whose deportation otherwise would be cancelled under § 244. The one-House veto operated in this case to overrule the Attorney General and mandate Chadha's deportation; absent the House action, Chadha would remain in the United States. Congress has *acted* and its action has altered Chadha's status.

The legislative character of the one-House veto in this case is confirmed by the character of the Congressional action it supplants. Neither the House of Representatives nor the Senate contends that, absent the veto provision in § 244 (c) (2), either of them, or both of them acting together, could effectively require the Attorney General to deport an alien once the Attorney General, in the exercise of legislatively delegated authority, had determined the alien should remain in the United States. Without the challenged provision in § 244 (c) (2), this could have been achieved, if at all, only by legislation requiring deportation. Similarly, a veto by one House of Congress under § 244 (c) (2) cannot be justified as an attempt at amending the standards set out in § 244 (a) (1), or as a repeal of § 244 as applied to Chadha. Amendment and repeal of statutes, no less than enactment, must conform with Art. I.

The nature of the decision implemented by the one-House veto in this case further manifests its legislative character. After long experience with the clumsy, time consuming private bill procedure, Congress made a deliberate choice to delegate to the Executive Branch, and specifically to the Attorney General, the authority to allow deportable aliens to remain in this country in certain specified circumstances. It is not disputed that this choice to delegate authority is precisely the kind of decision that can be implemented only in accordance with the procedures set out in Art. I. Disagreement with the Attorney General's decision on Chadha's deportation — that is, Congress' decision to deport Chadha — no less than Congress' original choice to delegate to the Attorney General the authority to make that decision, involves determinations of policy that Congress can implement in only one way; bicameral passage followed by presentment to the President. Congress must abide by its delegation of authority until that delegation is legislatively altered or revoked.

Finally, we see that when the Framers intended to authorize either House of Congress to act alone and outside of its prescribed bicameral legislative role, they narrowly and precisely defined the procedure for such action. There are but four provisions in the Constitution, explicit and unambiguous, by which one House may act alone with the unreviewable force of law, not subject to the President's veto:

(a) The House of Representatives alone was given the power to initiate impeachments. Art. I, § 2, cl. 6;

(b) The Senate alone was given the power to conduct trials following impeachment on charges initiated by the House and to convict following trial. Art. I, § 3, cl. 5;

(c) The Senate alone was given final unreviewable power to approve or to disapprove presidential appointments. Art. II, § 2, cl. 2;

(d) The Senate alone was given unreviewable power to ratify treaties negotiated by the President. Art. II, § 2, cl. 2.

Clearly, when the Draftsmen sought to confer special powers on one House, independent of the other House, or of the President, they did so in explicit, unambiguous terms. These carefully defined exceptions from presentment and bicameralism underscore the difference between the legislative functions of Congress and other unilateral but important and binding one-House acts provided for in the Constitution. These exceptions are narrow, explicit, and separately justified; none of them authorize the action challenged here. On the contrary, they provide further support for the conclusion that Congressional authority is not to be implied and for the conclusion that the veto provided for in § 244 (c) (2) is not authorized by the constitutional design of the powers of the Legislative Branch.

Since it is clear that the action by the House under § 244 (c) (2) was not within any of the express constitutional exceptions authorizing one House to act alone, and equally clear that it was an exercise of legislative power, that action was subject to the standards prescribed in Article I. The bicameral requirement, the Presentment Clauses, the President's veto, and Congress' power to override a veto were intended to erect enduring checks on each Branch and to protect the people from the improvident exercise of power by mandating certain prescribed steps. To preserve those checks, and maintain the separation of powers, the carefully defined limits on the power of each Branch must not be eroded. To accomplish what has been attempted by one House of Congress in this case requires action in conformity with the express procedures of the Constitution's prescription for legislative action: passage by a majority of both Houses and present-ment to the President.

The veto authorized by § 244 (c) (2) doubtless has been in many respects a convenient shortcut; the "sharing" with the Executive by Congress of its authority over aliens in this manner is, on its face, an appealing compro-mise. In purely practical terms, it is obviously easier for action to be taken by one House without submission to the President; but it is crystal clear from the records of the Convention, contemporaneous writings and de-bates, that the Framers ranked other values higher than efficiency. The records of the Convention and debates in the States preceding ratification underscore the common desire to define and limit the exercise of the newly created federal powers affecting the states and the people. There is unmistakable expression of a determination that legislation by the na-tional Congress be a step-by-step, deliberate and deliberative process.

The choices we discern as having been made in the Constitutional Convention impose burdens on governmental processes that often seem clumsy, inefficient, even unworkable, but those hard choices were con-sciously made by men who had lived under a form of government that permitted arbitrary governmental acts to go unchecked. There is no support in the Constitution or decisions of this Court for the proposition that the cumbersomeness and delays often encountered in complying with explicit Constitutional standards may be avoided, either by the Congress or by the President. See *Youngstown Sheet & Tube Co.* v. *Sawyer* (1952).

With all the obvious flaws of delay, untidiness, and potential for abuse, we have not yet found a better way to preserve freedom than by making the exercise of power subject to the carefully crafted restraints spelled out in the Constitution.

V

We hold that the Congressional veto provision in §244 (c) 2) is severable from the Act and that it is unconstitutional. Accordingly, the judgment of the Court of Appeals is

Affirmed.

JUSTICE POWELL, concurring in the judgment.

The Court's decision, based on the Presentment Clauses, Art. I, § 7, cl. 2 and 3, apparently will invalidate every use of the legislative veto. The breadth of this holding gives one pause. Congress has included the veto in literally hundreds of statutes, dating back to the 1930s. Congress clearly views this procedure as essential to controlling the delegation of power to administrative agencies. One reasonably may disagree with Congress' assessment of the veto's utility, but the respect due its judgment as a coordinate branch of Government cautions that our holding should be no more extensive than necessary to decide this case. In my view, the case may be decided on a narrower ground. When Congress finds that a particular person does not satisfy the statutory criteria for permanent residence in this country it has assumed a judicial function in violation of the principle of separation of powers. Accordingly, I concur in the judgment. . . .

JUSTICE WHITE, dissenting.

Today the court not only invalidates § 244 (c) (2) of the Immigration and Nationality Act, but also sounds the death knell for nearly 200 other statutory provisions in which Congress has reserved a "legislative veto." For this reason, the Court's decision is of surpassing importance. And it is for this reason that the Court would have been well-advised to decide the case, if possible, on the narrower grounds of separation of powers, leaving for full consideration the constitutionality of other congressional review statutes operating on such varied matters as war powers and agency rulemaking, some of which concern the independent regulatory agencies.

The prominence of the legislative veto mechanism in our contemporary political system and its importance to Congress can hardly be overstated. It has become a central means by which Congress secures the accountability of executive and independent agencies. Without the legislative veto, Congress is faced with a Hobson's choice: either to refrain from delegating the necessary authority, leaving itself with a hopeless task of writing laws with the requisite specificity to cover endless special circumstances across the entire policy landscape, or in the alternative, to abdicate its lawmaking function to the executive branch and independent agencies. To choose the former leaves major national problems unresolved; to opt for the latter risks unaccountable policymaking by those not elected to fill that role. Accordingly, over the past five decades, the legislative veto has been placed in nearly 200 statutes. The device is known in every field of governmental concern: reorganization, budgets, foreign affairs, war powers, and regulation of trade, safety energy, the environment and the economy.

I

The legislative veto developed initially in response to the problems of reorganizing the sprawling government structure created in response to the Depression. The Reorganization Acts established the chief model for the legislative veto. When President Hoover requested authority to reorganize the government in 1929, he coupled his request that the "Congress be willing to delegate its authority over the problem (subject to defined principles) to the Executive" with a proposal for legislative review. He proposed that the Executive "should act upon approval of a joint committee of Congress or with the reservation of power of revision by Congress within some limited period adequate for its consideration." Congress followed President Hoover's suggestion and authorized reorganization subject to legislative review. Although the reorganization authority reenacted in 1933 did not contain a legislative veto provision, the provision returned during the Roosevelt Administration and has since been renewed numerous times. Over the years, the provision was used extensively. Presidents submitted 115 reorganization plans to Congress of which 23 were disapproved by Congress pursuant to legislative veto provisions.

Shortly after adoption of the Reorganization Act of 1939, Congress and the President applied the legislative veto procedure to resolve the delegation problem for national security and foreign affairs. World War II occasioned the need to transfer greater authority to the President in these areas. The legislative veto offered the means by which Congress could confer additional authority while preserving its own constitutional role. During World War II, Congress enacted over thirty statutes conferring powers on the Executive with legislative veto provisions. President Roosevelt accepted the veto as the necessary price for obtaining exceptional authority.

Over the quarter century following World War II, Presidents continued to accept legislative vetoes by one or both Houses as constitutional, while regularly denouncing provisions by which Congressional committees reviewed Executive activity. The legislative veto balanced delegations of statutory authority in new areas of governmental involvement: the space program, international agreements on nuclear energy, tariff arrangements, and adjustment of federal pay rates.

During the 1970's the legislative veto was important in resolving a series of major constitutional disputes between the President and Congress over claims of the President to broad impoundment, war, and national emergency powers. The key provision of the War Powers Resolution, 50 U.S.C. § 1544 (c), authorizes the termination by concurrent resolution of the use of armed forces in hostilities. A similar measure resolved the problem posed by Presidential claims of inherent power to impound appropriations. In conference, a compromise was achieved under which permanent impoundments, termed "rescissions," would require approval through enactment of legislation. In contrast, temporary impoundments, or "deferrals," would become effective unless disapproved by one House. This compromise provided the President with flexibility, while preserving ultimate Congressional control over the budget. Although the War Powers Resolution was enacted over President Nixon's veto, the Impoundment Control Act was enacted with the President's approval. These statutes were followed by others resolving similar problems. . . .

In the energy field, the legislative veto served to balance broad delegations in legislation emerging from the energy crisis of the 1970's. In the educational field, it was found that fragmented and narrow grant programs "inevitably lead to Executive-Legislative confrontations" because they inaptly limited the Commissioner of Education's authority. The response was to grant the Commissioner of Education rulemaking authority, subject to a legislative veto. In the trade regulation area, the veto preserved Congressional authority over the Federal Trade Commission's broad mandate to make rules to prevent businesses from engaging in "unfair or deceptive acts or practices in commerce."

Even this brief review suffices to demonstrate that the legislative veto is more than "efficient, convenient, and useful." It is an important if not indispensable political invention that allows the President and Congress to resolve major constitutional and policy differences, assures the accountability of independent regulatory agencies, and preserves Congress' control over lawmaking. Perhaps there are other means of accommodation and accountability, but the increasing reliance of Congress upon the legislative veto suggests that the alternatives to which Congress must now turn are not entirely satisfactory.

The history of the legislative veto also makes clear that it has not been a sword with which Congress has struck out to aggrandize itself at the expense of the other branches — the concerns of Madison and Hamilton. Rather, the veto has been a means of defense, a reservation of ultimate authority necessary if Congress is to fulfill its designated role under Article I as the nation's lawmaker. While the President has often objected to particular legislative vetoes, generally those left in the hands of congressional committees, the Executive has more often agreed to legislative review as the price for a broad delegation of authority. To be sure, the President may have preferred unrestricted power, but that could be precisely why Congress thought it essential to retain a check on the exercise of delegated authority.

II

For all these reasons, the apparent sweep of the Court's decision today is regrettable. The Court's Article I analysis appears to invalidate all legislative vetoes irrespective of form or subject. Because the legislative veto is commonly found as a check upon rulemaking by administrative agencies and upon broad-based policy decisions of the Executive Branch, it is particularly unfortunate that the Court reaches its decision in a case involving the exercise of a veto over deportation decisions regarding particular individuals. Courts should always be wary of striking statutes as unconstitutional; to strike an entire class of statutes based on consideration of a somewhat atypical and more-readily indictable exemplar of the class is irresponsible. It was for cases such as this one that Justice Brandeis wrote:

> "The Court has frequently called attention to the 'great gravity and delicacy' of its function in passing upon the validity of an act of Congress. . . . The Court will not 'formulate a rule of constitutional law broader than is required by the precise facts to which it is to be applied.' *Liverpool, N.Y. & P.S.S. Co. v. Emigration Commissioners, supra." Ashwander* v. *Tennessee Valley Authority* (1936) (concurring opinion).

Unfortunately, today's holding is not so limited.

If the legislative veto were as plainly unconstitutional as the Court strives to suggest, its broad ruling today would be more comprehensible. But, the constitutionality of the legislative veto is anything but clearcut. The issue divides scholars, courts, attorneys general, and the two other branches of the National Government. If the veto devices so flagrantly disregarded the requirements of Article I as the Court today suggests, I find it incomprehensible that Congress, whose members are bound by oath to uphold the Constitution, would have placed these mechanisms in nearly 200 separate laws over a period of 50 years.

The reality of the situation is that the constitutional question posed today is one of immense difficulty over which the executive and legislative branches — as well as scholars and judges — have understandably disagreed. That disagreement stems from the silence of the Constitution on the precise question: The Constitution does not directly authorize or prohibit the legislative veto. Thus, our task should be to determine whether the legislative veto is consistent with the purposes of Art. I and the principles of Separation of Powers which are reflected in that Article and throughout the Constitution. We should not find the lack of a specific constitutional authorization for the legislative veto surprising, and I would not infer disapproval of the mechanism from its absence. From the summer of 1787 to the present the government of the United States has become an endeavor far beyond the contemplation of the Framers. Only within the last half century has the complexity and size of the Federal Government's responsibilities grown so greatly that the Congress must rely on the legislative veto as the most effective if not the only means to insure their role as the nation's lawmakers. But the wisdom of the Framers was to anticipate that the nation would grow and new problems of governance would require different solutions. Accordingly, our Federal Government was intentionally chartered with the flexibility to respond to contemporary needs without losing sight of fundamental democratic principles. . . .

This is the perspective from which we should approach the novel constitutional questions presented by the legislative veto. In my view, neither Article I of the Constitution nor the doctrine of separation of powers is violated by this mechanism by which our elected representatives preserve their voice in the governance of the nation.

III

The Court holds that the disapproval of a suspension of deportation by the resolution of one House of Congress is an exercise of legislative power without compliance with the prerequisites for lawmaking set forth in Art. I of the Constitution. Specifically, the Court maintains that the provisions of § 244 (c) (2) are inconsistent with the requirement of bicameral approval, implicit in Art. I, § 1, and the requirement that all bills and resolutions that require the concurrence of both Houses be presented to the President, Art. I, § 7, cl. 2 and 3.

I do not dispute the Court's truismatic exposition of these clauses. There is no question that a bill does not become a law until it is approved by both the House and the Senate, and presented to the President. Similarly, I would not hesitate to strike an action of Congress in the form of a concurrent resolution which constituted an exercise of original lawmaking authority. I agree with the court that the President's qualified veto power is a critical element in the distribution of powers under the Constitution, widely endorsed among the Framers, and intended to serve the President as a defense against legislative encroachment and to check the "passing of bad laws through haste, inadvertence, or design." The records of the Convention reveal that it is the first purpose which figured most prominently but I acknowledge the vitality of the second. I also agree that the bicameral approval required by Art. I, §§ 1, 7 "was of scarcely less concern to the Framers than was the Presidential veto" and that the need to divide and disperse legislative power figures significantly in our scheme of Government. All of this, the Third Part of the Court's opinion, is entirely unexceptionable.

It does not, however, answer the constitutional question before us. The power to exercise a legislative veto is not the power to write new law without bicameral approval or presidential consideration. The veto must be authorized by statute and may only negative [sic] what an Executive department or independent agency has proposed. On its face, the legislative veto no more allows one House of Congress to make law than does the presidential veto confer such power upon the President. . . .

A

... When the Convention did turn its attention to the scope of Congress' lawmaking power, the Framers were expansive. The Necessary and Proper Clause, Art. I, § 8, cl. 18, vests Congress with the power "to make all laws which shall be necessary and proper for carrying into Execution the foregoing Powers [the enumerated powers of § 8], and all other Powers vested by this Constitution in the government of the United States, or in any Department or Officer thereof." It is long-settled that Congress may "exercise its best judgment in the selection of measures, to carry into execution the constitutional powers of the government," and "avail itself of experience, to exercise its reason, and to accommodate its legislation to circumstances," *McCulloch* v. *Maryland* 420 (1819).

B

The Court heeded this counsel in approving the modern administrative state. The Court's holding today that all legislative-type action must be enacted through the lawmaking process ignores that legislative authority is routinely delegated to the Executive branch, to the independent regulatory agencies, and to private individuals and groups. ...

The wisdom and the constitutionality of these broad delegations are matters that still have not been put to rest. But for present purposes, these cases establish that by virtue of congressinal delegation, legislative power can be exercised by independent agencies and Executive departments without the passage of new legislation. For some time, the sheer amount of law — the substantive rules that regulate private conduct and direct the operation of government — made by the agencies has far outnumbered the lawmaking engaged in by Congress through the traditional process. There is no question but that agency rulemaking is lawmaking in any functional or realistic sense of the term. ...

If Congress may delegate lawmaking power to independent and executive agencies, it is most difficult to understand Article I as forbidding Congress from also reserving a check on legislative power for itself. Absent the veto, the agencies receiving delegations of legislative or quasi-legislative power may issue regulations having the force of law without bicameral approval and without the President's signature. It is thus not apparent why the reservation of a veto over the exercise of that legislative power must be subject to a more exacting test. In both cases, it is enough that the initial statutory authorizations comply with the Article I requirements. ...

The Court's opinion in the present case comes closest to facing the reality of administrative lawmaking in considering the contention that the Attorney General's action in suspending deportation under § 244 is itself a legislative act. The Court posits that the Attorney General is acting in an Article II enforcement capacity under § 244. This characterization is at odds with *Mahler* v. *Eby* (1924), where the power conferred on the Executive to deport aliens was considered a delegation of legislative power. The Court suggests, however, that the Attorney General acts in an Article II capacity because "[t]he courts when a case or controversy arises, can always 'ascertain whether the will of Congress has been obeyed,' *Yakus* v. *United States* (1944), and can enforce adherence to statutory standards." This assumption is simply wrong, as the Court itself points out: "We are aware of no decision . . . where a federal court has reviewed a decision of the Attorney General suspending deportation of an alien pursuant to the standards set out in § 244 (a) (1). This is not surprising, given that no party to such action has either the motivation or the right to appeal from it." It is perhaps on the erroneous premise that judicial review may check abuses of the §244 power that the Court also submits that "The bicameral process is not necessary as a check on the Executive's administration of the laws because his administrative activity cannot reach beyond the limits of the statute that created it — a statute duly enacted pursuant to Article I."

More fundamentally, even if the Court correctly characterizes the Attorney General's authority under § 244 as an Article II Executive power, the Court concedes that certain administrative agency action, such as rulemaking, "may resemble lawmaking" and recognizes that "[t]his Court has referred to agency activity as being 'quasi-legislative' in character. *Humphrey's Executor* v. *United States* (1935)." Such rules and adjudications by the agencies meet the Court's own definition of legislative action for they "alter[] the legal rights, duties, and relations of persons . . . outside the legislative branch" and involve "determinations of policy." Under the Court's analysis, the Executive Branch and the independent agencies may make rules with the effect of law while Congress, in whom the Framers confided the legislative power, Art. I, § 1, may not exercise a veto which precludes such rules from having operative force. If the effective functioning of a complex modern government requires the delegation of vast authority which, by virtue of its breadth, is legislative or "quasi-legislative" in character, I cannot accept that Article I — which is, after all, the source of the nondelegation doctrine — should forbid Congress from qualifying that grant with a legislative veto.

C

The Court also takes no account of perhaps the most relevant consideration: However resolutions of disapproval under § 244 (c) (2) are formally characterized, in reality, a departure from the status quo occurs only upon the concurrence of opinion among the House, Senate, and President. Reservations of legislative authority to be exercised by Congress should be upheld if the exercise of such reserved authority is

consistent with the distribution of and limits upon legislative power that
Article I provides. . . .

[Section 1 Omitted]

2

The central concern of the presentation and bicameralism requirements of Article I is that when a departure from the legal status quo is
undertaken, it is done with the approval of the President and both
Houses of Congress — or, in the event of a presidential veto, a two-
thirds majority in both Houses. This interest is fully satisfied by the
operation of § 244 (c) (2). The President's approval is found in the
Attorney General's action in recommending to Congress that the deportation order for a given alien be suspended. The House and the
Senate indicate their approval of the Executive's action by not passing a
resolution of disapproval within the statutory period. Thus, a change in
the legal status quo — the deportability of the alien — is consummated
only with the approval of each of the three relevant actors. The
disagreement of any one of the three maintains the alien's pre-existing
status: the Executive may choose not to recommend suspension; the
House and Senate may each veto the recommendation. The effect on the
rights and obligations of the affected individuals and upon the legislative system is precisely the same as if a private bill were introduced but
failed to receive the necessary approval. "The President and the two
Houses enjoy exactly the same say in what the law is to be as would have
been true for each without the presence of the one-House veto, and
nothing in the law is changed absent the concurrence of the President
and a majority in each House.". . .

This very construction of the Presentment Clauses which the Executive branch now rejects was the basis upon which the Executive Branch
defended the constitutionality of the Reorganization Act, 5 U.S.C. §
906 (a) (1979), which provides that the President's proposed reorganization plans take effect only if not vetoed by either House. When the
Department of Justice advised the Senate on the constitutionality of
congressional review in reorganization legislation in 1949, it stated: "In
this procedure there is no question involved of the Congress taking
legislative action beyond its initial passage of the Reorganization Act."
This also represents the position of the Attorney General more recently.

Thus understood, § 244 (c) (2) fully effectuates the purposes of the
bicameralism and presentation requirements. I now briefly consider
possible objections to the analysis.

First, it may be asserted that Chadha's status before legislative
disapproval is one of nondeportation and that the exercise of the veto,
unlike the failure of a private bill, works a change in the status quo. This
position plainly ignores the statutory language. At no place in § 244 has
Congress delegated to the Attorney General any final power to deter-

mine which aliens shall be allowed to remain in the United States. Congress has retained the ultimate power to pass on such changes in deportable status. By its own terms, § 244 (a) states that whatever power the Attorney General has been delegated to suspend deportation and adjust status is to be exercisable only "as hereinafter prescribed in this section." Subsection (c) is part of that section. A grant of "suspension" does not cancel the alien's deportation or adjust the alien's status to that of a permanent resident alien. A suspension order is merely a "deferment of deportation," *McGrath* v. *Kristensen* (1950), which can mature into a cancellation of deportation and adjustment of status only upon the approval of Congress — by way of silence — under § 244 (c) (2). Only then does the statute authorize the Attorney General to "cancel deportation proceedings" § 244 (c) (2), and "record the alien's lawful admission for permanent residence. . . ." § 244 (d). The Immigration and Naturalization Service's action, on behalf of the Attorney General, "cannot become effective without ratification by Congress." Until that ratification occurs, the executive's action is simply a recommendation that Congress finalize the suspension — in itself, it works no legal change. . . .

IV

The Court of Appeals struck § 244 (c) (2) as violative of the constitutional principle of separation of powers. It is true that the purpose of separating the authority of government is to prevent unnecessary and dangerous concentration of power in one branch. For that reason, the Framers saw fit to divide and balance the powers of government so that each branch would be checked by the others. Virtually every part of our constitutional system bears the mark of this judgment.

But the history of the separation of powers doctrine is also a history of accommodation and practicality. Apprehensions of an overly powerful branch have not led to undue prophylactic measures that handicap the effective working of the national government as a whole. The Constitution does not contemplate total separation of the three branches of Government. *Buckley* v. *Valeo* (1976). "[A] hermetic sealing off of the three branches of Government from one another would preclude the establishment of a Nation capable of governing itself effectively."

Our decisions reflect this judgment. As already noted, the Court, recognizing that modern government must address a formidable agenda of complex policy issues, countenanced the delegation of extensive legislative authority to executive and independent agencies. *[J. W.] Hampton & Co.* v. *United States* (1928). The separation of powers doctrine has heretofore led to the invalidation of government action only when the challenged action violated some express provision in the Constitution. In *Buckley* v. *Valeo* (1976) (per curiam) and *Myers* v. *United States* (1926), congressional action compromised the appointment power of the President. See also *Springer* v. *Philippine Islands*

(1928). In *United States* v. *Klein* (1871), an Act of Congress was struck for encroaching upon judicial power, but the Court found that the Act also impinged upon the executive's exclusive pardon power. Art II, § 2. Because we must have a workable efficient government, this is as it should be.

This is the teaching of *Nixon* v. *Administrator of Gen. Servs.* (1977), which, in rejecting a separation of powers objection to a law requiring that the Administrator take custody of certain presidential papers, set forth a framework for evaluating such claims:

> "[I]n determining whether the Act disrupts the proper balance between the coordinate branches, the proper inquiry focuses on the extent to which it prevents the Executive Branch from accomplishing its constitutionally assigned functions. *United States* v. *Nixon*. Only where the potential for disruption is present must we then determine whether that impact is justified by an overriding need to promote objectives within the constitutional authority of Congress."

Section 244 (c) (2) survives this test. The legislative veto provision does not "prevent the Executive Branch from accomplishing its constitutionally assigned functions." First, it is clear that the Executive branch has no "constitutionally assigned" function of suspending the deportation of aliens. " 'Over no conceivable subject is the legislative power of Congress more complete than it is over' the admission of aliens." *Kleindiest* v. *Mandel* (1972), quoting *Oceanic Steam Navigation Co.* v. *Stranahan* (1909). Nor can it said that the inherent function of the Executive Branch in executing the law is involved. *The Steel Seizure Case* resolved that the Article II mandate for the President to execute the law is a directive to enforce the law which Congress has written. *Youngstown Sheet & Tube Co.* v. *Sawyer* (1952). "The duty of the President to see that the laws be executed is a duty that does not go beyond the laws or require him to achieve more than Congress sees fit to leave within his power." *Myers* v. *United States* (Holmes, J., dissenting); (Brandeis, J. dissenting). Here, § 244 grants the executive only a qualified suspension authority and it is only that authority which the President is constitutionally authorized to execute.

Moreover, the Court believes that the legislative veto we consider today is best characterized as an exercise of legislative or quasi-legislative authority. Under this characterization, the practice does not, even on the surface, constitute an infringement of executive or judicial prerogative. The Attorney General's suspension of deportation is equivalent to a proposal for legislation. The nature of the Attorney General's role as recommendatory is not altered because § 244 provides for congressional action through disapproval rather than by ratification. In comparison to private bills, which must be initiated in the Congress and which allow a Presidential veto to be overriden by a two-thirds majority in both Houses of Congress, § 244 augments rather than reduces the executive branch's authority. So understood, congressional review does not undermine ... the decisions of the Executive Branch.

Nor does § 244 infringe on the judicial power, as JUSTICE POWELL would hold. Section 244 makes clear that Congress has reserved its own judgment as part of the statutory process. Congressional action does not substitute for judicial review of the Attorney General's decision. The Act provides for judicial review of the refusal of the Attorney General to suspend a deportation and to transmit a recommendation to Congress. *INS* v. *Wang,* (1981) (per curiam). But the courts have not been given the authority to review whether an alien should be given permanent status; review is limited to whether the Attorney General has properly applied the statutory standards for essentially denying the alien a recommendation that his deportable status be changed by the Congress. Moreover, there is no constitutional obligation to provide any judicial review whatever for a failure to suspend deportation. "The power of Congress, therefore, to expel, like the power to exclude aliens, or any specified class of aliens, from the country, may be exercised entirely through executive officers; or Congress may call in the aid of the judiciary to ascertain any contested facts on which an alien's right to be in the country has been made by Congress to depend." *Fong Yue Ting* v. *United States* (1893). See also *Tutun* v. *United States* (1926); *Ludecke* v. *Watkins* (1948); *Harisiades* v. *Shaughnessy*(1952).

I do not suggest that all legislative vetoes are necessarily consistent with separation of powers principles. A legislative check on an inherently executive function, for example that of initiating prosecutions, poses an entirely different question. But the legislative veto device here — and in many other settings — is far from an instance of legislative tyranny over the Executive. It is a necessary check on the unavoidably expanding power of the agencies, both executive and independent, as they engage in exercising authority delegated by Congress.

V

I regret that I am in disagreement with my colleagues on the fundamental questions that this case presents. But even more I regret the destructive scope of the Court's holding. It reflects a profoundly different conception of the Constitution than that held by the courts which sanctioned the modern administrative state. Today's decision strikes down in one fell swoop provisions in more laws enacted by Congress than the court has cumulatively invalidated in its history. I fear it will now be more difficult "to insure that the fundamental policy decisions in our society will be made not by an appointed official but by the body immediately responsible to the people," *Arizona* v. *California* (1963) (Harlan, J., dissenting). I must dissent.

COURT ON UNITARY TAXATION
June 27, 1983

The Supreme Court June 27 upheld the right of states to tax U.S.-based multinational corporations on a proportion of their worldwide earnings, rather than on the earnings the corporations claimed were generated by in-state subsidiaries. The 5-3 ruling grew out of a California case involving the Container Corp. of America, a multinational incorporated in Delaware with headquarters in Illinois.

Justice William J. Brennan Jr. wrote the decision for the Court. He was joined by Justices Byron R. White, Thurgood Marshall, Harry A. Blackmun and William H. Rehnquist. Justice Lewis F. Powell Jr. wrote the dissent, joined by Chief Justice Warren E. Burger and Justice Sandra Day O'Connor. Justice John Paul Stevens took no part in the case.

At issue was the right of California's Franchise Tax Board to apply the "worldwide unitary" method for calculating a multinational corporation's taxes, a scheme pioneered in California and used by 10 other states. States using the worldwide unitary method computed a corporation's tax liability according to a "three-factor" formula that averaged the state's contribution to the company's overall sales, property and payroll. The method usually, although not inevitably, increased the corporation's state tax bill.

Had the Court decided against California, the state would have lost an estimated $500 million a year in tax revenues. About $150 million was at stake in other states that used the contested procedure. More states were expected to adopt the unitary procedure as a result of the Court's ruling.

A spokesman for the National Governors' Association expressed "delight" with the decision.

The Court's Decision

The California case arose when Container Corp. refused to compute its tax returns for 1963-1965 according to California's requirements. After paying additional assessments under protests, the company filed suit in state court for a refund. Container Corp. argued that use of California's taxing scheme violated both the due process guarantee of the 14th Amendment and the foreign commerce clause of the Constitution that regulates the states' role in international trade. Proponents of the worldwide unitary method, including the Multistate Tax Commission, contended that the procedure was essential to keep multinationals from using bookkeeping adjustments to shuffle an undue share of their profits to subsidiaries where taxes were low or nonexistant.

The Supreme Court's decision hinged on three major questions: whether Container Corp. and its California subsidiary constituted a highly integrated "unitary business" for tax purposes; whether California's tax-apportionment method was fair; and whether the state's actions intruded on areas reserved to the federal government. Brennan's majority opinion rejected Container Corp.'s arguments that the California apportionment process did not take into account cheaper production costs abroad that were not offset by lower productivity.

Although the justices conceded that California's scheme could result in double taxation for the corporation — with some earnings taxed abroad as well as in California — they did not find this argument compelling. "...[T]he three-factor formula is necessarily imperfect," Brennan noted, "... But we have seen no evidence demonstrating that the margin of error (systematic or not) inherent in the ... formula is greater than the margin of error ... inherent in the sort of separate accounting urged upon us by the appellant."

The Court's decision did not, however, extend to the states the authority to levy taxes on property or businesses owned by foreigners. The Court had, in previous cases, given states the right to apply the unitary business principle to in-state subsidiaries of corporations located in other parts of the United States. Applying the unitary business principle was more difficult in cases involving foreign governments, the opinion noted, because international relations sometimes can be affected, and state actions might provoke foreign retaliation. Attempts by states to tax foreign-owned business ventures had created serious problems with some of America's trading partners. The opinion drew attention to the fact that, because Container Corp. was owned domestically, California's action was unlikely to create international difficulties.

Political Reaction

The Court's decision could spur Congress to act on legislation that more clearly regulates state taxation of multinational business. Three bills pending in Congress would, if passed, prohibit state tax schemes such as California's.

Business was divided over the issue. Some companies sought congressional remedies, while others preferred the unitary method. Caterpillar Tractor Co., for example, had gone to court seeking to require states to use the unitary system to compute its taxes.

The Reagan administration had expressed philosophical opposition to states' use of the worldwide unitary method, largely based on fears that it might keep the federal government from speaking with one voice in international relations. The administration filed a friend-of-the-court brief that addressed these concerns in Chicago Bridge & Iron Co. *v.* Caterpillar Tractor Co., *which went before the Court in 1981 but was not decided. The administration did not intervene, however, in the California-based case.*

The majority decision took the administration's failure to file a brief as a suggestion that the foreign policy of the United States was not an issue in the California case. The dissent, however, pointed to the brief filed earlier in the still-pending Chicago Bridge *case as evidence that the federal government had serious foreign policy objections to tax schemes like the one used by California. The dissent also emphasized the danger of double taxation.*

Following are excerpts from the Supreme Court's June 27, 1983, majority opinion in Container Corporation *v.* Franchise Tax Board *upholding the worldwide unitary method for calculating state taxes, and from the dissent by Justice Lewis F. Powell Jr.:*

<u>No. 81-523</u>

Container Corporation of America, Appellant *v.* Franchise Tax Board	On appeal from the Court of Appeal of California, First Appellate District

[June 27, 1983]

[JUSTICE STEVENS took no part in the consideration or decision of this case.]

JUSTICE BRENNAN delivered the opinion of the Court.

This is another appeal claiming that the application of a State taxing scheme violates the Due Process and Commerce Clauses of the Federal Constitution. California imposes a corporate franchise tax geared to income. In common with a large number of other States, it employs the "unitary business" principle and formula apportionment in applying that tax to corporations doing business both inside and outside the State. Appellant is a Delaware corporation headquartered in Illinois and doing business in California and elsewhere. It also has a number of overseas subsidiaries incorporated in the countries in which they operate. Appellee is the California authority charged with administering the state's franchise tax. This appeal presents three questions for review: (1) Was it improper for appellee and the state courts to find that appellant and its overseas subsidiaries constituted a "unitary business" for purposes of the state tax? (2) Even if the unitary business finding was proper, do certain salient differences among national economies render the standard three-factor apportionment formula used by California so inaccurate as applied to the multinational enterprise consisting of appellant and its subsidiaries as to violate the constitutional requirement of "fair apportionment"? (3) In any event, did California have an obligation under the Foreign Commerce Clause, U.S. Const., Art. I, § 8, cl. 3, to employ the "arm's-length" analysis used by the federal government and most foreign nations in evaluating the tax consequences of inter-corporate relationships?

I

A

Various aspects of state tax systems based on the "unitary business" principle and formula apportionment have provoked repeated constitutional litigation in this Court. See, *e.g., ASARCO, Inc.* v. *Idaho State Tax Comm'n.* (1982); *F. W. Woolworth Co.* v. *Taxation and Revenue Dept.* (1982); *Exxon Corp.* v. *Wisconsin Dept. of Revenue* (1980); *Mobil Oil Corp.* v. *Commissioner of Taxes* (1980); *Moorman Mfg. Co.* v. *Bair* (1978); *General Motors Corp.* v. *Washington* (1964); *Butler Bros.* v. *McColgan* (1942); *Bass, Ratcliff & Gretton, Ltd.* v. *State Tax Comm'n.* (1924); *Underwood Typewriter Co.* v. *Chamberlain* (1920).

Under both the Due Process and the Commerce Clauses of the Constitution, a state may not, when imposing an income-based tax, "tax value earned outside its borders." *ARARCO.* In the case of a more-or-less integrated business enterprise operating in more than one State, however, arriving at precise territorial allocations of "value" is often an elusive goal, both in theory and in practice.... For this reason and others, we have long held that the Constitution imposes no single formula on the States, *Wisconsin* v. *J. C. Penney Co.* (1940), and that the taxpayer has the "distinct burden of showing by 'clear and cogent evidence' that [the state tax] results in extraterritorial values being taxed...." *Exxon Corp....*

One way of deriving locally taxable income is on the basis of formal geographical or transactional accounting. The problem with this method is that formal accounting is subject to manipulation and imprecision, and often ignores or captures inadequately the many subtle and largely unquantifiable transfers of value that take place among the components of a single enterprise.... The unitary business/formula apportionment method is a very different approach to the problem of taxing businesses operating in more than one jurisdiction. It rejects geographical or transactional accounting, and instead calculates the local tax base by first defining the scope of the "unitary business" of which the taxed enterprise's activities in the taxing jurisdiction form one part, and then apportioning the total income of that "unitary business" between the taxing jurisdiction and the rest of the world on the basis of a formula taking into account objective measures of the corporation's activities within and without the jurisdiction. This Court long ago upheld the constitutionality of the unitary business/formula apportionment method, although subject to certain constraints. See, *e.g., Hans Rees' Sons, Inc.* v. *North Carolina ex rel Maxwell* (1931); *Bass, Ratcliff & Gretton, Ltd.* v. *State Tax Comm'n.* (1924); *Underwood Typewriter Co.* v. *Chamberlain* (1920). The method has now gained wide acceptance, and is in one of its forms the basis for the Uniform Division of Income for Tax Purposes Act (Uniform Act), which has at last count been substantially adopted by 23 States, including California.

B

Two aspects of the unitary business/formula apportionment method have traditionally attracted judicial attention. These are, as one might easily guess, the notions of "unitary business" and "formula apportionment," respectively.

(1)

The Due Process and Commerce Clauses of the Constitution do not allow a State to tax income arising out of interstate activities — even on a proportional basis — unless there is a " 'minimal connection' or 'nexus' between the interstate activities and the taxing State, and 'a rational relationship between the income attributed to the State and the intrastate values of the enterprise.' " *Exxon Corporation* v. *Wisconsin Dept. of Revenue....* At the very least, this set of principles imposes the obvious and largely self-executing limitation that a State not tax a purported "unitary business" unless at least some part of it is conducted in the State.... It also requires that there be some bond of ownership or control uniting the purported "unitary business."...

In addition, the principles we have quoted require that the out-of-State activities of the purported "unitary business" be related in some concrete way to the in-State activities. The functional meaning of this requirement is that there be some sharing or exchange of value not capable of precise identification or measurement — beyond the mere flow of funds arising out of a passive investment or a distinct business operation — which renders formula apportionment a reasonable method of taxation.... In *Underwood Typewriter Co.* v. *Chamberlain* we held that a State could tax on an apportioned basis the combined income of a vertically integrated business whose various components (manufacturing, sales, etc.) operated in different States. In *Bass, Ratcliff & Gretton* we applied the same principle to a vertically integrated business operating across national boundaries. In *Butler Bros.* v. *McColgan* we recognized that the unitary business principle could apply, not only to vertically integrated enterprises, but also to a series of similar enterprises operating separately in various jurisdictions but linked by common managerial or operational resources that produced economies of scale and transfers of value. More recently, we have further refined the "unitary business" concept in *Exxon Corp.* v. *Wisconsin Dept. of Revenue* (1980), and *Mobil Oil Corp.* v. *Commissioner of Taxes* (1980), where we upheld the States' unitary business findings, and in *ASARCO, Inc.* v. *Idaho State Tax Comm'n.* (1982), and *F. W. Woolworth Co.* v. *Taxation and Revenue Dept.* (1982), in which we found such findings to have been improper.

The California statute at issue in this case, and the Uniform Act from which most of its relevant provisions are derived, tracks in large part the principles we have just discussed. In particular, the statute distinguishes between the "business income" of a multi-jurisdictional enterprise, which is apportioned by formula and its "non-business" income, which is not. Although the Statute does not explicitly require that income from distinct business enterprises be apportioned separately, this requirement antedated adoption of the Uniform Act, and has not been abandoned.

A final point that needs to be made about the unitary business concept is that it is not, so to speak, unitary: there are variations on the theme, and any number of them are logically consistent with the underlying principles motivating the approach. For example, a State might decide to respect formal corporate lines and treat the ownership of a corporate subsidiary as *per se* a passive investment. In *Mobil Oil Corp.*, however, we made clear that, as a general matter, such a *per se* rule is not constitutionally required:

> "Superficially, intercorporate division might appear to be a[n] ... attractive basis for limiting apportionability. But the form of business organization may have nothing to do with the underlying unity or diversity of business enterprise."

Thus, for example, California law provides:

> "In the case of a corporation ... owning or controlling, either directly or indirectly, another corporation, or other corporations, and in the case of a corporation ... owned or controlled, either directly or indirectly, by another corporation, the Franchise Tax Board may require a consolidated report showing the combined net income or such other facts as it deems necessary."

Even among States that take this approach, however, only some apply it in taxing American corporations with subsidiaries located in foreign countries. The difficult question we address in Part V of this opinion is whether, for reasons not implicated in *Mobil,* that particular variation on the theme is constitutionally barred.

(2)

Having determined that a certain set of activities constitute a "unitary business," a State must then apply a formula apportioning the income of that business within and without the State. Such an apportionment formula must, under both the Due Process and Commerce Clauses, be fair.... The first, and again obvious, component of fairness in an apportionment formula is what might be called internal consistency — that is the formula must be such that, if applied by every jurisdiction, it would result in no more than all of the unitary business's income being taxed. The second and more difficult requirement is what might be called external consistency — the factor or factors used in the apportionment formula must actually reflect a reasonable sense of how income is generated. The Constitution does not "invalidat[e] an apportionment formula whenever it *may* result in taxation of some income that did not have its source in the taxing State...." *Moorman Mfg. Co.* (emphasis added).... Nevertheless, we will strike down the application of an apportionment formula if the taxpayer can prove "by 'clear and cogent evidence' that the income attributed to the State is in fact 'out of all appropriate proportions to the business transacted in that State,'"... or has 'led to a grossly distorted result,'...." *Moorman Mfg. Co.*

California and the other States that have adopted the Uniform Act use a formula — commonly called the "three-factor" formula — which is based, in equal parts, on the proportion of a unitary business's total payroll, property, and sales which are located in the taxing State. We approved the three-factor formula in *Butler Bros.* v. *McCoglan.* Indeed, not only has the three-factor formula met our approval, but it has become, for reasons we discuss in more detail ... something of a benchmark against which other apportionment formulas are judged....

Besides being fair, an apportionment formula must, under the Commerce Clause, also not result in discrimination against interstate or foreign commerce.... Aside from forbidding the obvious types of discrimination against interstate or foreign commerce, this principle might have been construed to require that a state apportionment formula not differ so substantially from methods of allocation used by other jurisdictions in which the taxpayer is subject to taxation so as to produce double taxation of the same income, and a resultant tax burden higher than the taxpayer would incur if its business were limited to any one jurisdiction. At least in the interstate commerce context, however, the anti-discrimination principle has not in practice required much in addition to the requirement of fair apportionment. In *Moorman Mfg. Co.* v. *Bair,* in particular, we explained that eliminating all overlapping taxation would require this Court to establish not only a single constitutionally mandated method of taxation, but also rules regarding the application of that method in particular cases. Because that task was thought to be essentially legislative, we declined to undertake it, and held that a fairly apportioned tax would not be found invalid simply because it differed from the prevailing approach adopted by the States. . . . [H]owever, a more searching inquiry is necessary when we are confronted with the possibility of international double taxation.

[Sections II, III and IV omitted]

V

. . . [W]e conclude that California's application of the unitary business principle to appellant and its foreign subsidiaries was proper, and that its use of the standard three-factor formula to apportion the income of that unitary business was fair. This proper and fair method of taxation happens, however, to be quite different from the method employed both by the Federal Government in taxing appellant's business, and by each of the relevant foreign jurisdictions in taxing the business of appellant's subsidiaries. Each of these other taxing jurisdictions has adopted a qualified separate accounting approach — often referred to as the "arm's-length" approach — to the taxation of related corporations. Under the arm's-length approach, every corporation, even if closely tied to other corporations, is treated for most — but decidedly not all — purposes as if it were an independent entity dealing at arm's length with its affiliated corporations, and subject to taxation only by the jurisdictions in which it operates and only for the income it realizes on its own books.

If the unitary business consisting of appellant and its subsidiaries were entirely domestic, the fact that different jurisdictions applied different methods of taxation to it would probably make little constitutional difference. . . . Given that it is international, however, we must subject this case to the additional scrutiny required by the Foreign Commerce Clause. See *Mobil Oil Corp.; Japan Line, Ltd.* [1979]; *Bowman v. Chicago & N.W.R. Co.* (1888). The case most relevant to our inquiry is *Japan Line.*

A

Japan Line involved an attempt by California to impose an apparently fairly apportioned, nondiscriminatory, ad valorem property tax on cargo containers which were instrumentalities of foreign commerce and which were temporarily located in various California ports. The same cargo containers, however, were subject to an unapportioned property tax in their home port of Japan. Moreover, a convention signed by the United States and Japan made clear, at least, that neither national government could impose a tax on temporarily imported cargo containers whose home port was in the other nation. We held that "[w]hen a State seeks to tax the instrumentalities of foreign commerce, two additional considerations, beyond those articulated in [the doctrine governing the Interstate Commerce Clause], come into play." The first is the enhanced risk of multiple taxation. . . .

The second additional consideration that arises in the foreign commerce context is the possibility that a state tax will "impair federal uniformity in an area where federal uniformity is essential.". . .

On the basis of the facts in *Japan Line,* we concluded that the California tax at issue was constitutionally improper because it failed to meet either of the additional tests mandated by the Foreign Commerce Clause.

This case is similar to *Japan Line* in a number of important respects. First, the tax imposed here, like the tax imposed in *Japan Line,* has resulted in actual double taxation, in the sense that some of the income taxed without apportionment by foreign nations as attributable to appellant's foreign subsidiaries was also taxed by California as attributable to the State's share of the total income of the unitary business of which those subsidiaries are a part. Second, that double taxation stems from a serious divergence in the taxing schemes adopted by California and the foreign taxing authorities. Third, the taxing method adopted by those foreign taxing authorities is consistent with accepted international practice. Finally, our own Federal Government, to the degree it has spoken, seems to prefer the taxing method adopted by the international community to the taxing method adopted by California.

Nevertheless, there are also a number of ways in which this case is clearly distinguishable from *Japan Line.* First, it involves a tax on income rather than a tax on property. We distinguished property from income taxation in *Mobil Oil Corp.* and *Exxon Corp.,* suggesting that "[t]he reasons for allocation to a single situs that often apply in the case of property taxation carry little force" in the case of income taxation. Second, the double taxation in this case, although real, is not the "inevitabl[e]" result of the California taxing scheme. . . . In *Japan Line,* we relied strongly on the fact that one taxing jurisdiction claimed the right to tax a given value in full, and another taxing jurisdiction claimed the right to tax the same entity in part — a combination resulting necessarily in double taxation. Here, by contrast, we are faced with two distinct methods of allocating the income of a multi-national enterprise. The "arm's-length" approach divides the pie on the basis of formal accounting principles. The formula apportionment method divides the same pie on the basis of a mathematical generalization. Whether the combination of the two methods results in the same income being taxed twice or in some portion of income not being taxed at all is dependent solely on the facts of the individual case. The third difference between this case and *Japan Line* is that the tax here falls, not on the foreign owners of an instrumentality of foreign commerce, but on a corporation domiciled and headquartered in the United States. We specifically left open in *Japan Line* the application of that case to "domestically owned instrumentalities engaged in foreign commerce" and — to the extent that corporations can be analogized to cargo containers in the first place — this case falls clearly within that reservation.

In light of these considerations, our task in this case must be to determine whether the distinctions between the present tax and the tax at issue in *Japan Line* add up to a constitutionally significant difference. For the reasons we are about to explain, we conclude that they do.

B

In *Japan Line*, we said that "[e]ven a slight overlapping of tax — a problem that might be deemed *de minimis* in a domestic context — assumes importance when sensitive matters of foreign relations and national sovereignty are concerned." If we were to take that statement as an absolute prohibition on state-induced double taxation in the international context, then our analysis here would be at an end. But, in fact, such an absolute rule is no more appropriate here than it was in *Japan Line* itself, where we relied on much more than the mere fact of double taxation to strike down the state tax at issue. Although double taxation in the foreign commerce context deserves to receive close scrutiny, that scrutiny must take into account the context in which the double taxation takes place and the alternatives reasonably available to the taxing State.

In *Japan Line*, the taxing State could entirely eliminate one important source of double taxation simply by adhering to one bright-line rule: do not tax, to any extent whatsoever, cargo containers "that are owned, based, and registered abroad and that are used exclusively in international commerce. . . ." To require that the State adhere to this rule was by no means unfair, because the rule did no more than reflect consistent international practice and express federal policy. In this case, California could try to avoid double taxation simply by not taxing appellant's income at all, even though a good deal of it is plainly domestic. But no party has suggested such a rule, and its obvious unfairness requires no elaboration. Or California could try to avoid double taxation by adopting some version of the "arm's-length" approach. That course, however, would not by any means guarantee an end to double taxation.

As we have already noted, the arm's-length approach is generally based, in the first instance, on a multi-corporate enterprise's own formal accounting. But, despite that initial reliance, the arm's-length approach recognizes, as much as the formula apportionment approach, that closely related corporations can engage in a transfer of values that is not fully reflected in their formal ledgers. . . .

And, as one might expect, the United States Internal Revenue Service has developed elaborate regulations in order to give content to this general provision. Many other countries have similar provisions. A serious problem, however, is that even though most nations have adopted the arm's-length approach in its general outlines, the precise rules under which they reallocate income among affiliated corporations often differ substantially, and whenever that difference exists, the possibility of double taxation also exists. Thus, even if California were to adopt some version of the arm's-length approach, it could not eliminate the risk of double taxation of corporations subject to its franchise tax, and might in some cases end up subjecting those corporations to more serious double taxation than would occur under formula apportionment.

That California would have trouble avoiding double taxation even if it adopted the arm's-length approach is, we think, a product of the difference between a tax on income and a tax on tangible property. Allocating income among various taxing jurisdictions bears some resemblance, as we have emphasized throughout this opinion, to slicing a shadow. In the absence of a central coordinating authority, absolute consistency, even among taxing authorities whose basic approach to the task is quite similar, may just be too much to ask. If California's method of formula apportionment "inevitably" led to double taxation, that might be reason enough to render it suspect. But since it does not, it would be perverse, simply for the sake of avoiding double taxation, to require California to give up one allocation method that sometimes results in double taxation in favor of another allocation method that also sometimes results in double taxation. Cf. *Moorman Mfg. Co....*

C

We come finally to the second inquiry suggested by *Japan Line* — whether California's decision to adopt formula apportionment in the international context was impermissible because it "may impair federal uniformity in an area where federal uniformity is essential" and "prevents the Federal Government from 'speaking with one voice' in international trade," quoting *Michelin Tire Corp.* v. *Wages* (1976). In conducting this inquiry, however, we must keep in mind that if a state tax merely has foreign resonances, but does not implicate foreign affairs, we cannot infer, "[a]bsent some explicit directive from Congress, ... that treatment of foreign income at the federal level mandates identical treatment by the States." *Mobil.* ... Thus, a state tax at variance with federal policy will violate the "one voice" standard if it *either* implicates foreign policy issues which must be left to the Federal Government *or* violates a clear federal directive. The second of these considerations is, of course, essentially a species of preemption analysis.

(1)

The most obvious foreign policy implication of a state tax is the threat it might pose of offending our foreign trading partners and leading them to retaliate against the nation as a whole. In considering this issue, however, we are faced with a distinct problem. This Court has little competence in determining precisely when foreign nations will be offended by particular acts, and even less competence in deciding how to balance a particular risk of retaliation against the sovereign right of the United States as a whole to let the States tax as they please. The best that we can do, in the absence of explicit action by Congress, is to attempt to develop objective standards that reflect very general observations about the imperatives of international trade and international relations.

This case is not like *Mobil*, in which the real issue came down to a question of interstate rather than foreign commerce. Nevertheless, three distinct factors, which we have already discussed in one way or another, seem to us to weigh strongly against the conclusion that the tax imposed by California might justifiably lead to significant foreign retaliation. First, the tax here does not create an *automatic* "asymmetry," *Japan Line*, in international taxation. Second, the tax here was imposed, not on a foreign entity as was the case in *Japan Line*, but on a domestic corporation. Although, California "counts" income arguably attributable to foreign corporations in calculating the taxable income of that domestic corporation, the legal incidence of the tax falls on the domestic corporation. Third, even if foreign nations have a legitimate interest in reducing the tax burden of domestic corporations, the fact remains that appellant is without a doubt amenable to be taxed in California in one way or another, and that the amount of tax it pays is much more the function of California's tax rate than of its allocation method. Although a foreign nation might be more offended by what it considers unorthodox treatment of appellant than it would be if California simply raised its general tax rate to achieve the same economic result, we can only assume that the offense involved in either event would be attenuated at best.

A state tax may, of course, have foreign policy implications other than the threat of retaliation. We note, however, that in this case, unlike *Japan Line,* the Executive Branch has decided not to file an *amicus curiae* brief in opposition to the state tax. The lack of such a submission is by no means dispositive. Nevertheless, when combined with all the other considerations we have discussed, it does suggest that the foreign policy of the United States — whose nuances, we must emphasize again, are much more the province of the Executive Branch and Congress than of this Court — is not seriously threatened by California's decision to apply the unitary business concept and formula apportionment in calculating appellant's taxable income.

(2)

When we turn to specific indications of congressional intent, appellant's position fares no better. First, there is no claim here that the federal tax statutes themselves provide the necessary pre-emptive force. Second, although the United States is a party to a great number of tax treaties that require the Federal Government to adopt some form of arm's-length analysis in taxing the domestic income of multinational enterprises, that requirement is generally waived with respect to the taxes imposed by each of the contracting nations on its own domestic corporations. This fact, if nothing else, confirms our view that such taxation is in reality of local rather than international concern. Third, none of the tax treaties into which the United States has entered covers the taxing activities of sub-national governmental units such as States, and the Senate has on at least one occasion, in considering a proposed treaty, attached a reservation declining to give its consent to a provision in the treaty that would have extended the restriction against apportionment taxation to the States. Finally, it remains true, as we said in *Mobil,* that "Congress has long debated, but has not enacted, legislation designed to regulate state taxation of income." Thus, whether we apply the "explicit directive" standard articulated in *Mobil,* or some more relaxed standard which takes into account our residual concern about the foreign policy implications of California's tax, we cannot conclude that the California tax at issue here is preempted by federal law or fatally inconsistent with federal policy.

VI

The judgment of the California Court of Appeal is

Affirmed.

JUSTICE POWELL, with whom THE CHIEF JUSTICE and JUSTICE O'CONNOR join, dissenting.

The Court's opinion addresses the several questions presented in this case with commendable thoroughness. In my view, however, the California tax clearly violates the Foreign Commerce Clause — just as did the tax in *Japan Line, Ltd.* v. *County of Los Angeles* (1979). I therefore do not consider whether appellant and its foreign subsidiaries constitute a "unitary business" or whether the State's apportionment formula is fair.

With respect to the Foreign Commerce Clause issue, the Court candidly concedes: (i) "double taxation is a constitutionally disfavored state of affairs, particularly in the international context"; (ii) "like the tax imposed in *Japan Line,* [California's tax] has resulted in actual double taxation"; and therefore (iii) this tax "deserves to receive close scrutiny." The Court also concedes that "[t]his case is similar to *Japan Line* in a number of important respects" and that the Federal Government "seems to prefer the [arm's-length] taxing method adopted by the international community." The Court identifies several distinctions between this case and *Japan Line,* however, and sustains the validity of the California tax despite the inevitable double taxation and the incompatability with the method of taxation accepted by the international community.

In reaching its result, the Court fails to apply "close scrutiny" in a manner that meets the requirements of that exacting standard of review. Although the facts of *Japan Line* differ in some respects, they are identical on the critical questions of double taxation and federal uniformity. The principles enunciated in that case should be controlling here: a state tax is unconstitutional if it either "creates a substantial risk of international multiple taxation" or "prevents the Federal Government from 'speaking with one voice when regulating commercial relations with foreign governments.' "

I

It is undisputed that the California tax not only "creates a substantial risk of international multiple taxation," but also "has resulted in actual double taxation" in this case. . . .

. . . [T]he risk of double taxation can arise in two ways. Under the present system, it arises because California has rejected accepted international practice in favor of a tax structure that is fundamentally different in its basic assumptions. Under a uniform system, double taxation also could arise because different jurisdictions — despite their agreement on basic principles — may differ in their application of the system. But these two risks are fundamentally different. Under the former, double taxation is inevitable. It cannot be avoided without changing the system itself. Under the latter, any double taxation that exists is the result of disagreements in application. Such disagreements may be unavoidable in view of the need to make individual judgments, but problems of this kind are more likely to be resolved by international negotiation.

On its face, the present double taxation violates the Foreign Commerce Clause. I would not reject, as the Court does, the solution to this constitutional violation simply because an international system based on the principle of uniformity would not necessarily be uniform in all of the details of its operation. . . .

▼▼▼

COURT ON EXCESSIVE SENTENCES

June 28, 1983

The Supreme Court in a 5-4 decision ruled for the first time June 28 that the length of a prison sentence must bear some relationship to the severity of the crime. Citing cruel and unusual punishment in violation of the Eighth Amendment, the Court invalidated the life sentence without the possibility of parole imposed on a defendant who had seven convictions for non-violent felonies. Justice Lewis F. Powell Jr., writing for the majority in Solem v. Helm, *found the sentence "significantly disproportionate" to the crimes committed. Powell was joined by Justices William J. Brennan Jr., Thurgood Marshall, Harry A. Blackmun and John Paul Stevens.*

The Court overturned the life sentence of Jerry Helm of South Dakota, who had been convicted three times for third-degree burglary, once for grand larceny, once for obtaining money under false pretenses, once for third-offense drunk driving, and finally, in 1979, for passing a bad $100 check. Helm pleaded guilty to the 1979 offense. Ordinarily the sentence for passing a bad check would have been five years in prison and a $5,000 fine. But, because of his previous record, Helm was sentenced under South Dakota's repeat offender law, which permitted a sentence of life imprisonment without parole after three felony convictions, regardless of the seriousness of the crimes. The only relief permitted under this law was commutation by the state governor. State courts affirmed Helm's sentence, and the governor refused to commute it.

A law similar to South Dakota's could be found on the books in Nevada. Several other states had laws to contain habitual offenders, but they required at least one of the convictions to be for a violent crime.

A federal district court also stood by Helm's sentence, relying on the Supreme Court's 1980 ruling in Rummel v. Estelle. *This decision upheld a life sentence imposed on a man convicted of three relatively petty, non-violent offenses in Texas. The U.S. 8th Circuit Court of Appeals and the Supreme Court, however, found Helm's case different from Rummel's. Powell, carefully standing by the 1980 decision, explained that the Court upheld the sentence in* Rummel v. Estelle *because Rummel had the possibility of parole after 10 or 12 years. There was no such provision in Helm's sentence.*

Cruel and Unusual Punishment

While the Court had ruled frequently on a mode of punishment, usually the death penalty, and once, in 1910, on the use of shackles and hard labor, the 1983 decision marked the first time a sentence was invalidated on the basis of length. Powell wrote that the Eighth Amendment's ban on cruel and unusual punishment "prohibits not only barbaric punishments, but also sentences that are disproportionate to the crime committed." Reviewing the Eighth Amendment's history, Powell traced the modern concept of crime and punishment back to the Magna Carta and English Bill of Rights. "When the Framers of the Eighth Amendment adopted the language of the English Bill of Rights, they also adopted the English principle of proportionality," he wrote.

Powell said the courts should consider three factors when reviewing potentially excessive sentences: the gravity of the crime and the harshness of the penalty, sentences imposed upon other criminals in the same state and sentences imposed for the same crime in other states. "A state is justified in punishing a recidivist more severely than it punishes a first offender," wrote Powell, but "Helm's sentence is the most severe punishment that the state could have imposed on any criminal for any crime."

Dissenting Opinion

The dissenting opinion found fault with several points of the Court's decision. Chief Justice Warren E. Burger, writing for himself and Justices Byron R. White, William H. Rehnquist and Sandra Day O'Connor, complained that the Court "Blithely discards any concept of stare decisis *[the rule of precedent], trespasses gravely on the authority of the states, and distorts the concept of proportionality of punishment by tearing it from its moorings in capital cases."*

Pressing his support for precedent, Burger termed as "fiction" the view that Helm's crimes were petty or non-violent. Citing Helm's convictions for three burglaries and drunk driving as potentially violent, Burger considered Rummel a "... relatively 'model citizen'" in comparison. He also strongly reaffirmed a state's right to remove repeat offenders from the streets. The Court's ruling, Burger wrote, meant ". . . that a sentence is unconstitutional if it is more severe than five justices think appropriate."

Following are excerpts from the Supreme Court's June 28, 1983, decision in Solem v. Helm, *striking down excessive prison sentences, and from the dissenting opinion of Chief Justice Warren E. Burger:*

No. 82-492

Herman Solem, Warden, Petitioner *v.* Jerry Buckley Helm	On writ of certiorari to the United States Court of Appeals for the Eighth Circuit

[June 28, 1983]

JUSTICE POWELL delivered the opinion of the Court.

The issue presented is whether the Eighth Amendment proscribes a life sentence without possibility of parole for a seventh nonviolent felony.

I

By 1975 the State of South Dakota had convicted respondent Jerry Helm of six nonviolent felonies. In 1964, 1966, and 1969 Helm was convicted of third-degree burglary. In 1972 he was convicted of obtaining money under false pretenses. In 1973 he was convicted of grand larceny. And in 1975 he was convicted of third-offense driving while intoxicated. The record contains no details about the circumstances of any of these offenses, except that they were all nonviolent. . . .

In 1979 Helm was charged with uttering a "no account" check for $100. The only details we have of the crime are those given by Helm to the state trial court:

> " 'I was working in Sioux Falls, and got my check that day, was drinking and I ended up here in Rapid City with more money than I had when I started. I knew I'd done something I didn't know exactly what. If I would have known this, I would have picked the check up. I was drinking and didn't remember, stopped several places.' " *State* v. *Helm* (S.D. 1980)

After offering this explanation, Helm pleaded guilty.

Ordinarily the maximum punishment for uttering a "no account" check would have been five years imprisonment in the state penitentiary and a $5,000 fine. As a result of his criminal record, however, Helm was subject to South Dakota's recidivist statute:

> "When a defendant has been convicted of at least three prior convictions [*sic*] in addition to the principal felony, the sentence for the principal felony shall be enhanced to the sentence for a Class 1 felony." S. D. Codified Laws § 22-7-8 (1979) (amended 1981).

The maximum penalty for a "Class 1 felony" was life imprisonment in the state penitentiary and a $25,000 fine. Moreover, South Dakota law explicitly provides that parole is unavailable: "A person sentenced to life imprisonment is not eligible for parole by the board of pardons and paroles." S. D. Codified Laws § 24-15-4 (1979). The Governor is authorized to pardon prisoners, or to commute their sentences, but no other relief from sentence is available even to a rehabilitated prisoner.

Immediately after accepting Helm's guilty plea, the South Dakota Circuit Court sentenced Helm to life imprisonment under § 22-7-8. The court explained:

> " 'I think you certainly earned this sentence and certainly proven that you're an habitual criminal and the record would indicate that you're beyond rehabilitation and that the only prudent thing to do is to lock you up for the rest of your natural life, so you won't have further victims of your crimes, just be coming back before Courts. You'll have plenty of time to think this one over.' " *State* v. *Helm.*

The South Dakota Supreme Court, in a 3-2 decision, affirmed the sentence despite Helm's argument that it violated the Eighth Amendment.

After Helm had served two years in the state penitentiary, he requested the Governor to commute his sentence to a fixed term of years. Such a commutation would have had the effect of making Helm eligible to be considered for parole when he had served three-fourths of his new sentence. The Governor denied Helm's request in May 1981.

In November 1981, Helm sought habeas relief in the United States District Court for the District of South Dakota. Helm argued, among other things, that his sentence constituted cruel and unusual punishment under the Eighth and Fourteenth Amendments. Although the District Court recognized that the sentence was harsh, it concluded that this Court's recent decision in *Rummel* v. *Estelle,* (1980), was dispositive. It therefore denied the writ.

The United States Court of Appeals for the Eighth Circuit reversed. (1982). The Court of Appeals noted the *Rummel* v. *Estelle* was distinguishable. Helm's sentence of life without parole was qualitatively different from Rummel's life sentence with the prospect of parole because South Dakota has rejected rehabilitation as a goal of the criminal justice system. The Court of Appeals examined the nature of Helm's offenses, the nature of his sentence, and the sentence he could have received in other States for the same offense. It concluded, on the basis of this examination, that Helm's sentence was "grossly disproportionate to the nature of the offense." It therefore directed the District Court to issue the writ unless the State resentenced Helm.

We granted certiorari to consider the Eighth Amendment question presented by this case. (1982). We now affirm.

II

The Eighth Amendment declares: "Excessive bail shall not be required, nor excessive fines imposed, nor cruel and unusual punishments inflicted." The final clause prohibits not only barbaric punishments, but also sentences that are disproportionate to the crime committed.

A

The principle that a punishment should be proportionate to the crime is deeply rooted and frequently repeated in common-law jurisprudence. In 1215 three chapters of Magna Carta were devoted to the rule that "amercements" may not be excessive. And the principle was repeated and extended in the First Statute of Westminster, 3 Edw. I, ch. 6 (1275). These were not hollow guarantees, for the royal courts relied on them to invalidate disproportionate punishments.... When prison sentences became the normal criminal sanctions, the common law recognized that these, too, must be proportional....

The English Bill of Rights repeated the principle of proportionality in language that was later adopted in the Eighth Amendment: "excessive Baile ought not to be required nor excessive Fines imposed nor cruell and unusuall Punishments inflicted." Although the precise scope of this provision is uncertain, it at least incorporated "the longstanding principle of English law that the punishment ... should not be, by reason of its excessive length or severity, greatly disproportionate to the offense charged." ...

When the Framers of the Eighth Amendment adopted the language of the English Bill of Rights, they also adopted the English principle of proportionality. Indeed, one of the consistent themes of the era was that Americans had all the rights of English subjects.... Thus our Bill of Rights was designed in part to ensure that these rights were preserved. Although the Framers may have intended the Eighth Amendment to go beyond the scope of its English counterpart, their use of the language of the English Bill of Rights is convincing proof that they intended to provide at least the same protection — including the right to be free from excessive punishments.

B

The constitutional principle of proportionality has been recognized explicitly in this Court for almost a century. In the leading case of *Weems* v. *United States* (1910), the defendant had been convicted of falsifying a public document and sentenced to 15 years of "cadena temporal," a form of imprisonment that included hard labor in chains and permanent civil disabilities. The Court noted "that it is a precept of justice that punishment for crime should be graduated and proportioned to offense" and held that the sentence violated the Eighth Amendment. The Court endorsed the principle of proportionality as a constitutional standard and determined that the sentence before it was "cruel in its excess of imprisonment," as well as in its shackles and restrictions.

The Court next applied the principle to invalidate a criminal sentence in *Robinson* v. *California* (1962). A 90-day sentence was found to be excessive for the crime of being "addicted to the use of narcotics." The Court explained that "imprisonment for ninety days is not, in the abstract, a punishment which is either cruel or unusual." Thus there was no question of an inherently barbaric punishment. "But the question cannot be considered in the abstract. Even one day in prison would be a cruel and unusual punishment for the 'crime' of having a common cold."

Most recently, the Court has applied the principle of proportionality to hold capital punishment excessive in certain circumstances. *Enmund* v. *Florida* (1982) (death penalty excessive for felony murder when defendant did not take life, attempt to take life, or intend that a life be taken or that lethal force be used); *Coker* v. *Georgia* (1977) (plurality opinion) ("sentence of death is grossly disproportionate and excessive punishment for the crime of rape"); (POWELL, J., concurring in the judgment in part and dissenting in part) ("ordinarily death is disproportionate punishment for the crime of raping an adult woman"). And the Court has continued to recognize that the Eighth Amendment proscribes grossly disproportionate punishments, even when it has not been necessary to rely on the proscription. . . .

C

There is no basis for the State's assertion that the general principle of proportionality does not apply to felony prison sentences. The constitutional language itself suggests no exception for imprisonment. We have recognized that the Eighth Amendment imposes "parallel limitations" on bail, fines, and other punishments, *Ingraham* v. *Wright* [1977] and the text is explicit that bail and fines may not be excessive. It would be anomalous indeed if the lesser punishment of a fine and the greater punishment of death were both subject to proportionality analysis, but the intermediate punishment of imprisonment were not. There is also no historical support for such an exception. The common-law principle incorporated into the Eighth Amendment clearly applied to prison terms. . . . And our prior cases have recognized explicitly that prison sentences are subject to proportionality analysis. . . .

When we have applied the proportionality principle in capital cases, we have drawn no distinction with cases of imprisonment. . . . It is true that the "penalty of death differs from all other forms of criminal punishment, not in degree but in kind." *Furman* v. *Georgia* (1972) (Stewart, J., concurring). As a result, "our decisions [in] capital cases are of limited assistance in deciding the constitutionality of the punishment" in a noncapital case. *Rummel* v. *Estelle*. We agree, therefore, that, "[o]utside the context of capital punishment, *successful* challenges to the proportionality of particular sentences [will be] exceedingly rare." . . . This does not mean, however, that proportionality analysis is entirely inapplicable in noncapital cases.

In sum, we hold as a matter of principle that a criminal sentence must be proportionate to the crime for which the defendant has been convicted. Reviewing courts, of course, should grant substantial deference to the broad authority that legislatures necessarily possess in determining the types and limits of punishments for crimes, as well as to the discretion that trial courts possess in sentencing convicted criminals. But no penalty is *per se* constitutional. As the Court noted in *Robinson* v. *California,* a single day in prison may be unconstitutional in some circumstances.

III

A

When sentences are reviewed under the Eighth Amendment, courts should be guided by objective factors that our cases have recognized. First, we look to the gravity of the offense and the harshness of the penalty. In *Enmund,* for example, the Court examined the circumstances of the defendant's crime in great detail. In *Coker* the Court considered the seriousness of the crime of rape, and compared it to other crimes, such as murder. In *Robinson* the emphasis was placed on the nature of the "crime." And in *Weems,* the Court's opinion commented in two separate places on the pettiness of the offense. Of course, a court must consider the severity of the penalty in deciding whether it is disproportionate. . . .

Second, it may be helpful to compare the sentences imposed on other criminals in the same jurisdiction. If more serious crimes are subject to the same penalty, or to less serious penalties, that is some indication that the punishment at issue may be excessive. Thus in *Edmund* the Court noted that all of the other felony murderers on death row in Florida were more culpable than the petitioner there. The *Weems* Court identified an impressive list of more serious crimes that were subject to less serious penalties.

Third, courts may find it useful to compare the sentences imposed for commission of the same crime in other jurisdictions. In *Enmund* the Court conducted an extensive review of capital punishment statutes and determined that "only about a third of American jurisdictions would ever permit a defendant [such as Enmund] to be sentenced to die." Even in those jurisdictions, however, the dealth penalty was almost never imposed under similar circumstances. . . .

In sum, a court's proportionality analysis under the Eighth Amendment should be guided by objective criteria, including (i) the gravity of the offense and the harshness of the penalty; (ii) the sentences imposed on other criminals in the same jurisdiction; and (iii) the sentences imposed for commission of the same crime in other jurisdictions.

B

Application of these factors assumes that courts are competent to judge the gravity of an offense, at least on a relative scale. In a broad sense this assumption is justified, and courts traditionally have made these judgments — just as legislatures must make them in the first instance. Comparisons can be made in light of the harm caused or threatened to the victim or society, and the culpability of the offender. Thus in *Enmund* the Court determined that the petitioner's conduct was not as serious as his accomplices' conduct. Indeed, there are widely shared views as to the relative seriousness of crimes. For example, as the criminal laws make clear, nonviolent crimes are less serious than crimes marked by violence or the threat of violence.

There are other accepted principles that courts may apply in measuring the harm caused or threatened to the victim or society. The absolute magnitude of the crime may be relevant. Stealing a million dollars is viewed as more serious than stealing a hundred dollars — a point recognized in statutes distinguishing petty theft from grand theft. . . . Few would dispute that a lesser included offense should not be punished more severely than the greater offense. Thus a court is justified in viewing assault with intent to murder as more serious than simple assault. . . .

Turning to the culpability of the offender, there are again clear distinctions that courts may recognize and apply. In *Enmund* the Court looked at the petitioner's lack of intent to kill in determining that he was less culpable than his accomplices. Most would agree that negligent conduct is less serious than intentional conduct. South Dakota, for example, ranks criminal acts in ascending order of seriousness as follows: negligent acts, reckless acts, knowing acts, intentional acts, and malicious acts. A court, of course, is entitled to look at a defendant's motive in committing a crime. Thus a murder may be viewed as more serious when committed pursuant to a contract.

This list is by no means exhaustive. It simply illustrates that there are generally accepted criteria for comparing the severity of different crimes on a broad scale, despite the difficulties courts face in attempting to draw distinctions between similar crimes.

C

Application of the factors that we identify also assumes that courts are able to compare different sentences. This assumption, too, is justified. The easiest comparison, of course, is between capital punishment and noncapital punishments, for the death penalty is different from other punishments in kind rather than degree. For sentences of imprisonment, the problem is not so much one of ordering, but one of line-drawing. It is clear that a 25-year sentence generally is more severe than a 15-year sentence, but in most cases it would be difficult to decide that the former violates the Eighth Amendment while the latter does not. Decisions of this kind, although troubling, are not unique to this area. The courts are constantly called upon to draw similar lines in a variety of contexts. . . .

IV

It remains to apply the analytical framework established by our prior decisions to the case before us. We first consider the relevant criteria, viewing Helm's sentence as life imprisonment without possibility of parole. We then consider the State's argument that the possibility of commutation is sufficient to save an otherwise unconstitutional sentence.

A

Helm's crime was "one of the most passive felonies a person could commit." *State* v. *Helm* (Henderson, J., dissenting). It involved neither violence nor threat of violence to any person. The $100 face value of Helm's "no account" check was not trivial, but neither was it a large amount. One hundred dollars was less than half the amount South Dakota required for a felonious theft. It is easy to see why such a crime is viewed by society as among the less serious offenses.

Helm, of course, was not charged simply with uttering a "no account" check, but also with being an habitual offender. And a State is justified in punishing a recidivist more severely than it punishes a first offender. Helm's status, however, cannot be considered in the abstract. His prior offenses, although classified as felonies, were all relatively minor. All were nonviolent and none was a crime against a person. . . .

Helm's present sentence is life imprisonment without possibility of parole. Barring executive clemency, Helm will spend the rest of his life in the state penitentiary. This sentence is far more severe than the life sentence we considered in *Rummel* v. *Estelle*. Rummel was likely to have been eligible for parole within 12 years of his initial confinement, a fact on which the Court relied heavily. Helm's sentence is the most severe punishment that the State could have imposed on any criminal for any crime. Only capital punishment, a penalty not authorized in South Dakota when Helm was sentenced, exceeds it.

We next consider the sentences that could be imposed on other criminals in the same jurisdiction. . . .

Helm's habitual offender status complicates our analysis, but relevant comparisons are still possible. Under § 22-7-7, the penalty for a second or third felony is increased by one class. Thus a life sentence was mandatory when a second or third conviction was for treason, first degree manslaughter, first degree arson, or kidnapping, and a life sentence would have been authorized when a second or third conviction was for such crimes as attempted murder, placing an explosive device on an aircraft, or first degree rape. Finally, § 22-7-8, under which Helm was sentenced, authorized life imprisonment after three prior convictions, regardless of the crimes.

In sum, there were a handful of crimes that were necessarily punished by life imprisonment: murder, and, on a second or third offense, treason, first degree manslaughter, first degree arson, and kidnapping. There was a larger group for which life imprisonment was authorized in the discretion of the sentencing judge, including: treason, first degree manslaughter, first degree arson, and kidnapping; attempted murder, placing an explosive device on an aircraft, and first degree rape on a second or third offense; and any felony after three prior offenses. Finally, there was a large group of very serious offenses for which life imprisonment was not authorized, including a third offense of heroin dealing or aggravated assault.

Criminals committing any of these offenses ordinarily would be thought more deserving of punishment than one uttering a "no account" check — even when the bad-check writer had already committed six minor felonies. Moreover, there is no indication in the record that any habitual offender other than Helm has ever been given the maximum sentence on the basis of comparable crimes. It is more likely that the possibility of life imprisonment under § 22-7-8 generally is reserved for criminals such as fourth-time heroin dealers, while habitual bad-check writers receive more lenient treatment. In any event, Helm has been treated in the same manner as, or more severely than, criminals who have committed far more serious crimes.

Finally, we compare the sentences imposed for commission of the same crime in other jurisdictions. The Court of Appeals found that "Helm could have received a life sentence without parole for his offense in only one other state, Nevada," and we have no reason to doubt this finding. At the very least, therefore, it is clear that Helm could not have received such a severe sentence in 48 of the 50 States. But even under Nevada law, a life sentence without possibility of parole is merely authorized in these circumstances. We are not advised that any defendant such as Helm, whose prior offenses were so minor, actually has received the maximum penalty in Nevada. It appears that Helm was treated more severely than he would have been in any other State.

B

The State argues that the present case is essentially the same as *Rummel* v. *Estelle,* for the possibility of parole in that case is matched by the possibility of executive clemency here. The State reasons that the Governor could commute Helm's sentence to a term of years. We conclude, however, that the South Dakota commutation system is fundamentally different from the parole system that was before us in *Rummel.*

As a matter of law, parole and commutation are different concepts, despite some surface similarities. Parole is a regular part of the rehabilitative process. Assuming good behavior, it is the normal expectation in the vast majority of cases. The law generally specifies when a prisoner will be eligible to be considered for parole, and details the standards and procedures applicable at that time. See, *e.g., Greenholz* v. *Nebraska Penal Inmates* (1979) (detailing Nebraska parole procedures); *Morrissey* v. *Brewer* (1972) ("the practice of releasing prisoners on parole before the end of their sentences has become an integral part of the penological system"). Thus it is possible to predict, at least to some extent, when parole might be granted. Commutation, on the other hand, is an *ad hoc* exercise of executive clemency. A Governor may commute a sentence at any time for any reason without reference to any standards. See, *e.g., Connecticut Board of Pardons* v. *Dumschat* (1981).

We explicitly have recognized the distinction between parole and commutation in our prior cases. . . . In *Dumschat*, THE CHIEF JUSTICE . . . explained that "there is a vast difference between a denial of parole . . . and a state's refusal to commute a lawful sentence." . . .

In South Dakota commutation is more difficult to obtain than parole. For example, the board of pardons and paroles is authorized to make commutation recommendations to the Governor, but § 24-13-4 provides that "no recommendation for the commutation of . . . a life sentence, or for a pardon . . . , shall be made by less than the unanimous vote of all members of the board." In fact, no life sentence has been commuted in over eight years, while parole — where authorized — has been granted regularly during that period. Furthermore, even if Helm's sentence were commuted, he merely would be eligible to be considered for parole. Not only is there no guarantee that he would be paroled, but the South Dakota parole system is far more stringent than the one before us in *Rummel.* Helm would have to serve three-fourths of his revised sentence before he would be eligible for parole, and the provision for good-time credits is less generous.

The possibility of commutation is nothing more than a hope for "an *ad hoc* exercise of clemency." It is little different from the possibility of executive clemency that exists in every case in which a defendant challenges his sentence under the Eighth Amendment. Recognition of such a bare possibility would make judicial review under the Eighth Amendment meaningless.

V

The Constitution requires us to examine Helm's sentence to determine if it is proportionate to his crime. Applying objective criteria, we find that Helm has received the penultimate sentence for relatively minor criminal conduct. He has been treated more harshly than other criminals in the State who have committed more serious crimes. He has been treated more harshly than he would have been in any other jurisdiction, with the possible exception of a single State. We conclude that his sentence is significantly disproportionate to this crime, and is therefore prohibited by the Eighth Amendment. The judgment of the Court of Appeals is accordingly

Affirmed.

CHIEF JUSTICE BURGER, with whom JUSTICE WHITE, JUSTICE REHNQUIST, and JUSTICE O'CONNOR join, dissenting.

The controlling law governing this case is crystal clear, but today the Court blithely discards any concept of *stare decisis*, trespasses gravely on the authority of the States, and distorts the concept of proportionality of punishment by tearing it from its moorings in capital cases. Only two Terms ago, we held in *Rummel* v. *Estelle* (1980), that a life sentence imposed after only a *third* nonviolent felony conviction did not constitute cruel and unusual punishment under the Eighth Amendment. Today, the Court ignores its recent precedent and holds that a life sentence imposed after a *seventh* felony conviction constitutes cruel and unusual punishment under the Eighth Amendment. Moreover, I reject the fiction that all Helm's crimes were innocuous or nonviolent. Among his felonies were three burglaries and a third conviction for drunk driving. By comparison Rummel was a relatively "model citizen." Although today's holding cannot rationally be reconciled with *Rummel,* the Court does not purport to overrule *Rummel.* I therefore dissent.

I

A

The Court's starting premise is that the Eighth Amendment's Cruel and Unusual Punishments Clause "prohibits not only barbaric punishments, but also sentences that are disproportionate to the crime committed." What the Court means is that a sentence is unconstitutional if it is more severe than five justices think appropriate. In short, all sentences of imprisonment are subject to appellate scrutiny to ensure that they are "proportional" to the crime committed.

The Court then sets forth three assertedly "objective" factors to guide the determination of whether a given sentence of imprisonment is constitutionally excessive: (1) the "gravity of the offense and the harshness of the penalty"; (2) a comparison of the sentence imposed with "sentences imposed on other criminals in *the same* jurisdiction (emphasis added); (3) and a comparison of "the sentences imposed for commission of the same crime in *other* jurisdictions." ([E]mphasis added). In applying this analysis, the Court determines that respondent

> "has received the penultimate sentence for *relatively minor* criminal conduct. He has been treated more harshly than other criminals in the State who have committed more serious crimes. He has been treated more harshly than he would have been in any other jurisdiction, . . ." (Emphasis added).

Therefore, the Court concludes, respondent's sentence is "significantly disproportionate to his crime, and is . . . prohibited by the Eighth Amendment." This analysis is completely at odds with the reasoning of our recent holding in *Rummel,* in which, of course, JUSTICE POWELL dissented.

B

The facts in *Rummel* bear repeating. Rummel was convicted in 1964 of fraudulent use of a credit card; in 1969, he was convicted of passing a forged check; finally, in 1973 Rummel was charged with obtaining money by false pretenses, which is also a felony under Texas law. These three offenses were indeed nonviolent. Under Texas' recidivist statute, which provides for a mandatory life sentence upon conviction for a third felony, the trial judge imposed a life sentence as he was obliged to do after the jury returned a verdict of guilty of felony theft.

Rummel, in this Court, advanced precisely the same arguments that respondent advances here; we rejected those arguments notwithstanding that his case was stronger than respondent's. The test in *Rummel* which we rejected would have required us to determine on an abstract moral scale whether Rummel had received his "just deserts" for his crimes. We declined that invitation; today the Court accepts it. Will the Court now recall Rummel's case so five justices will not be parties to "disproportionate" criminal justice?

It is true, as we acknowledged in *Rummel*, that the "Court has on occasion stated that the Eighth Amendment prohibits imposition of a sentence that is grossly disproportionate to the severity of a crime." But even a cursory review of our cases shows that this type of proportionality review has been carried out only in a very limited category of cases, and never before in a case involving solely a sentence of imprisonment. In *Rummel*, we said that the proportionality concept of the capital punishment cases was inapposite because of the "unique nature of the death penalty...." "Because a sentence of death differs in kind from any sentence of imprisonment, no matter how long, our decisions applying the prohibition of cruel and unusual punishments to capital cases are of limited assistance in deciding the constitutionality of the punishment meted out to Rummel."

The *Rummel* Court also rejected the claim that *Weems* v. *United States* (1910), required it to determine whether Rummel's punishment was "disproportionate" to his crime. In *Weems*, the Court had stuck down as cruel and unusual punishment a sentence of *cadena temporal* imposed by a Philippine Court. This bizarre penalty, which was unknown to Anglo-Saxon law, entailed a minimum of 12 years' imprisonment chained day and night at the wrists and ankles, hard and painful labor while so chained, and a number of "accessories" including lifetime civil disabilities. In *Rummel* the Court carefully noted that "[*Weems'*] finding of disproportionality cannot be wrenched from the facts of that case."

The lesson the *Rummel* Court drew from *Weems* and from the capital punishment cases was that the Eighth Amendment did not authorize courts to review sentences of *imprisonment* to determine whether they were "proportional" to the crime. In language quoted incompletely by the Court, the *Rummel* Court stated:

"Given the *unique nature* of the punishments considered in *Weems* and in the death penalty cases, one could argue without fear of contradiction by any decision of this Court that for crimes concededly classified and classifiable as felonies, that is, as punishable by significant terms of imprisonment in a state penitentiary, the *length of the sentence actually imposed is purely a matter of legislative perogative.*" (Emphasis added).

Five Justices joined this clear and precise limiting language.

In context it is clear that the *Rummel* Court was not merely summarizing an argument, as the Court suggests, but was stating affirmatively the rule of law laid down. The passage from *Rummel* is followed by an explanation of why it is permissible for courts to review sentences of death or bizarre physically cruel punishments as in *Weems,* but not sentences of imprisonment. The *Rummel* Court emphasized, as has every opinion in capital causes in the past decade, that it was possible to draw a "bright line" between "the punishment of death and the various other permutations and commutations of punishment short of that ultimate sanction"; similarly, a line could be drawn between the punishment in *Weems* and "more traditional forms of imprisonment imposed under the Anglo-Saxon system." However, the *Rummel* Court emphasized that drawing lines between different sentences of imprisonment would thrust the Court inevitably "into the basic line-drawing process that is pre-eminently the province of the legislature" and produce judgments that were no more than the visceral reactions of individual Justices.

The *Rummel* Court categorically rejected the very analysis adopted by the Court today. Rummel had argued that various objective criteria existed by which the Court could determine whether his life sentence was proportional to his crimes. In rejecting Rummel's contentions, the Court explained why each was insufficient to allow it to determine in an *objective* manner whether a given sentence of imprisonment is proportionate to the crime for which it is imposed.

First, it rejected the distinctions Rummel tried to draw between violent offenses, noting that "the absence of violence does not always affect the strength of society's interest in deterring a particular crime or in punishing a particular individual." Similarly, distinctions based on the amount of money stolen are purely "subjective" matters of line drawing.

Second, the Court squarely rejected Rummel's attempt to compare his sentence with the sentence he would have received in other States — an argument that the Court today accepts. The *Rummel* Court explained that such comparisons are flawed for several reasons. For one, the recidivist laws of the various states vary widely. "It is one thing for a court to compare those States that impose capital punishment for a specific offense with those States that do not. . . . It is quite another thing for a court to attempt to evaluate the position of any particular recidivist schemes within Rummel's complex matrix." Another reason why comparison between the recidivist statutes of different States is inherently complex is that some states have comprehensive provisions for parole and others do not. Perhaps most important, such comparisons trample on fundamental concepts of federalism. Different states surely may view particular crimes as more or less severe than other states. Stealing a horse in Texas may have different consequences and warrant different punishment than stealing a horse in Rhode Island or Washington, D.C. . . .

Finally, we flatly rejected Rummel's suggestion that we measure his sentence against the sentences imposed by Texas for other crimes. . . . Rather, we held that the severity of punishment to be accorded different crimes was peculiarly a matter of legislative policy.

In short, *Rummel* held that the length of a sentence of imprisonment is a matter of legislative discretion; this is so particularly for recidivist statutes. I simply cannot understand how the Court can square *Rummel* with its holding that "a criminal sentence must be proportionate to the crime for which the defendant has been convicted." . . .

I agree with what the Court stated only days ago, that "the doctrine of *stare decisis,* while perhaps never entirely persuasive on a constitutional question, is a doctrine that demands respect in a society governed by the rule of law." *City of Akron* v. *Akron Center for Reproductive Health, Inc.* (1983). While the doctrine of *stare decisis* does not absolutely bind the Court to its prior opinions, a decent regard for the orderly development of the law and the administration of justice requires that directly controlling cases be either followed or candidly overruled. Especially is this so with respect to two key holdings only three years old. . . .

[Section II Omitted]

III

. . . It is inaccurate to say, as the Court does, that the *Rummel* holding relied on the fact that Texas had a relatively liberal parole policy. In context, it is clear that the *Rummel* Court's discussion of parole merely illustrated the difficulty of comparing sentences between different jurisdictions. However, accepting the Court's characterization of *Rummel* as accurate, the Court today misses the point. Parole was relevant to an evaluation of Rummel's life sentence because in the "real world," he was unlikely to spend his entire life behind bars. Only a fraction of "lifers" are not released within a relatively few years. In Texas, the historical evidence showed that a prisoner serving a life sentence could become eligible for parole in as little as 12 years. In South Dakota, the historical evidence shows that since, 1964, 22 life sentences have been commuted to terms of years, while requests for commutation of 25 life sentences were denied. And, of course, those requests for commutation may be renewed.

In short, there is a significant probability that respondent will experience what so many "lifers" experience. Even assuming that at the time of sentencing, respondent was likely to spend more time in prison than Rummel, that marginal difference is surely supported by respondent's greater demonstrated propensity for crime — and for more serious crime at that.

IV

It is indeed a curious business for this Court to so far intrude into the administration of criminal justice to say that a state legislature is barred by the Constitution from identifying its habitual criminals and removing them from the streets. Surely seven felony convictions warrant the conclusion that respondent is incorrigible. It is even more curious that the Court should brush aside controlling precedents that are barely in the bound volumes of United States Reports....

COURT ON TUITION TAX BREAK

June 29, 1983

As it neared the end of its 1982-83 term, the Supreme Court June 29 removed a major obstacle to President Ronald Reagan's tuition tax credit proposal by upholding the constitutionality of a somewhat similar state law.

But the Reagan plan still faced intense political and philosophical opposition from many in Congress. Some members viewed any tax break for private school parents as a threat to public education; others were more concerned about the potential costs to the federal Treasury of such a scheme.

By a 5-4 ruling in the case of **Mueller** v. **Allen,** *the justices approved a Minnesota law that gave parents a state income tax deduction for the cost of tuition, textbooks and transportation for their elementary and secondary school children. The deduction would be available regardless of whether the children attended public or private schools — a fact that was central to the Court's decision. However, because few public school students had large educational expenses, the lion's share of the benefit accrued to private school parents, most of whom sent their children to parochial schools.*

The Minnesota Case

The Court held that Minnesota's tax deduction for parents did not amount to state aid to church-related schools in violation of the First

Amendment's ban on government "establishment" of religion.

The majority found that the deduction had a secular purpose, did not have the primary effect of advancing religion and did not entangle the state in parochial school affairs. This three-part test for constitutionality had been set out by the justices in a 1971 "parochiaid" case.

Under Minnesota's law, parents could deduct up to $500 per child for elementary school expenses and up to $700 per child for secondary school costs, regardless of what kind of school the pupils attended. About 91,000 of the state's 911,000 schoolchildren attended private schools; 95 percent of them were in sectarian schools.

While acknowledging that "financial assistance provided to parents ultimately has an economic effect comparable to that of aid given directly to the schools attended by their children," the Court said "[I]t is also true ... that under Minnesota's arrangement public funds become available only as a result of numerous private choices of individual parents of school-age children."

Justice William H. Rehnquist spoke for the majority, which included Chief Justice Warren E. Burger and Justices Byron R. White, Lewis F. Powell Jr. and Sandra Day O'Connor.

The four dissenters, Thurgood Marshall, William J. Brennan Jr., Harry A. Blackmun and John Paul Stevens, took the view that the First Amendment barred states from providing "any tax benefit ... which subsidizes tuition payments to sectarian schools."

Previous Court Rulings

Beginning with its first "parochiaid" case in 1930, the Supreme Court had scrutinized many forms of state aid to church-related schools. It had ruled most of them unconstitutional.

Between 1970 and 1983 the Court struck down state laws that provided salary supplements to certain private school teachers; reimbursed private schools for teachers' salaries, textbooks and instructional materials; provided maintenance and repair grants for private schools; reimbursed non-public schools for the costs of administering certain state-required tests and keeping certain state-required records; and paid the cost of field trips taken by parochial school classes and loans for instructional materials and equipment to parochial schools or parochial school students.

In 1973 the Court in Committee for Public Education and Religious Liberty v. Nyquist *struck down a New York law under which low-income families were reimbursed for a portion of their private and parochial school tuition expenses, and higher-income parents received a comparable income tax credit. In* Nyquist, *the Court by 6-3 found that the primary beneficiaries of such aid were parochial schools. (Justice Powell, who wrote the opinion in* Nyquist, *provided a key vote in favor of the Minnesota law.)*

But the Court had not been unremittingly hostile to state efforts to aid parents in educating their children in non-public schools. In its first three parochiaid decisions — in 1930, 1947 and 1968 — the Court had upheld the challenged aid.

In the 1930 ruling the Court upheld Louisiana's program of providing secular textbooks to every schoolchild, including those attending parochial schools. Seventeen years later, it upheld a New Jersey program reimbursing parents for the cost of sending their children to school on public transportation. And in 1968 the Court endorsed New York's program of lending publicly purchased textbooks to students attending public or private secondary schools.

In each instance, the Court based its ruling in whole or in part on the theory that aid to parochial school students was permissible if it was designed to benefit all children and not just those attending parochial schools.

Meeting the Tests

The test that Minnesota's law passed was set out by the Court in the 1971 case of Lemon *v.* Kurtzman, *which involved laws in Rhode Island and Pennsylvania. To avoid violations of the First Amendment, the Court declared, a state law aiding parochial schools must have a secular purpose, must not have the primary effect of advancing or inhibiting religion and must not foster excessive government entanglement with religion.*

Minnesota's law easily passed the first and third parts of this test, according to the Court majority. By helping parents to meet the costs of education, the law "plainly serves this secular purpose of ensuring that the state's citizenry is well-educated," wrote Rehnquist.

More complex was the question of whether the law's primary effect was to advance religion. In finding that it did not have this unconstitutional effect, the majority noted that the educational expense deduction was only one of many tax deductions provided by the Legislature for Minnesota residents.

But more important, Rehnquist continued, was the fact that the deduction was available to public school parents as well. This breadth of the law was "an important index of secular effect," he wrote. On this point, the Minnesota law was "vitally different" from the tuition tax credit struck down a decade earlier in the Nyquist *case, a credit available only to parents of children in non-public schools.*

The dissenters objected to the majority's reasoning and its conclusions. "For the first time, the Court has upheld financial support for religious schools without any reason at all to assume that the support will be restricted to the secular functions of those schools and will not be used to support religious instruction," Marshall wrote. "This result is flatly at odds with the fundamental principle that a state may provide no financial support whatsoever to promote religion."

Minnesota's tax statute was unconstitutional for the same reason as the law struck down in Nyquist: *"It has a direct and immediate effect of advancing religion," he concluded.*

Impact on Pending Legislation

The effect of the Court's ruling on proposed legislation was uncertain. The Senate Finance Committee May 26, 1983, had approved Reagan's tuition tax credit proposal, which differed from the Minnesota law in several important respects.

First and foremost, the Reagan plan would benefit only parents of private and parochial school students. Second, it would provide tax credits rather than deductions. And finally, it covered only tuition outlays, not textbook costs, transportation and similar educational expenditures.

Even if the tuition tax bill was modified to conform with the Court's constitutional blueprint by making tax credits available to parents of public school students as well as those whose children attended private schools, its prospects remained clouded at best.

At a time of record federal budget deficits, any proposal entailing a major new drain on federal revenues was likely to be intensely controversial. According to the Joint Committee on Taxation, tax credits for private school tuition alone would result in losses to the Treasury of $2.8 billion in fiscal years 1984-88.

Sister Rene Oliver, associate director of Citizens for Educational Freedom, a group favoring tuition tax credits, acknowledged that the cost question could stall the legislation. But she said funding for education — both private and public — was "a matter of justice" that warranted a healthy investment of federal money, a sentiment echoed by other tax credit supporters.

The National Education Association (NEA), a longtime opponent of tuition tax credits, attacked the Court's ruling as a threat to "the growing national commitment to achieving excellence in education." The NEA added that "tuition tax credits — in whatever form they might appear — diverted badly needed tax resources away from the 90 percent of America's children who go to public schools." (Education Commission Report, p. 413)

Following are excerpts from the Supreme Court's June 29, 1983, ruling in Mueller v. Allen *upholding the constitutionality of a Minnesota law providing parents a state income tax deduction for school costs, regardless of whether their children attended public or private schools, and from the dissenting opinion of Justice Thurgood Marshall:*

No. 82-195

Van D. Mueller and June Noyes, Petitioners

v.

Clyde E. Allen, Jr., et al.

} On writ of Certiorari to the United States Court of Appeals for the Eighth Circuit

[June 29, 1983]

JUSTICE REHNQUIST delivered the opinion of the Court.

Minnesota allows taxpayers, in computing their state income tax, to deduct certain expenses incurred in providing for the education of their children. The United States Court of Appeals for the Eighth Circuit held that the Establishment Clause of the First and Fourteenth Amendments was not offended by this arrangement. Because this question was reserved in *Committee for Public Education* v. *Nyquist* (1973), and because of a conflict between the decision of the Court of Appeals for the Eighth Circuit and that of the Court of Appeals for the First Circuit in *Rhode Island Federation of Teachers* v. *Norberg* (CA1 1980), we granted certiorari. We now affirm.

Minnesota, like every other state, provides its citizens with free elementary and secondary schooling. It seems to be agreed that about 820,000 students attended this school system in the most recent school year. During the same year, approximately 91,000 elementary and secondary students attended some 500 privately supported schools located in Minnesota, and about 95% of these students attended schools considering themselves to be sectarian.

Minnesota, by a law originally enacted in 1955 and revised in 1976 and again in 1978, permits state taxpayers to claim a deduction from gross income for certain expenses incurred in educating their children. The deduction is limited to actual expenses incurred for the "tuition, textbooks and transportation" of dependents attending elementary or secondary schools. A deduction may not exceed $500 per dependent in grades K through six and $700 per dependent in grades seven through twelve.

Petitioners — certain Minnesota taxpayers — sued in the United States District Court for the District of Minnesota claiming that [Minn. Stat.] § 290.09 (22) violated the Establishment Clause by providing financial assistance to sectarian institutions. They named as respondents the Commissioner of the Department of Revenue of Minnesota and several parents who took advantage of the tax deduction for expenses incurred in sending their children to parochial schools. The District Court granted respondent's motion for summary judgment, holding that the statute was "neutral on its face and in its application and does not have a primary effect of either advancing or inhibiting religion." On appeal, the Court of Appeals affirmed, concluding that the Minnesota statute substantially benefited a "broad class of Minnesota citizens."

Today's case is no exception to our oft-repeated statement that the Establishment Clause presents especially difficult questions of interpretation and application. It is easy enough to quote the few words comprising that clause — "Congress shall make no law respecting an establishment of religion." It is not at all easy, however, apply this Court's various decisions construing the Clause to governmental programs of financial assistance to sectarian schools and the parents of children attending these schools. Indeed, in many of these decisions "we have expressly or implicitly acknowledged that 'we can only dimly perceive the lines of demarcation in this extraordinarily sensitive area of constitutional law.'" *Lemon* v. *Kurtzman* (1971), quoted with approval in *Nyquist.*

One fixed principle in this field is our consistent rejection of the argument that "any program which in some manner aids an institution with a religious affiliation" violates the Establishment Clause. *Hunt* v. *McNair* (1973). . . . For example, it is now well-established that a state may reimburse parents for expenses incurred in transporting their children to school, *Everson* v. *Board of Education* (1947), and that it may loan secular textbooks to all schoolchildren within the state, *Board of Education* v. *Allen* (1968).

Notwithstanding the repeated approval given programs such as those in *Allen* and *Everson,* our decisions also have struck down arrangements resembling, in many respects, these forms of assistance. . . . In this case we are asked to decide whether Minnesota's tax deduction bears greater resemblance to those types of assistance to parochial schools we have approved, or to those we have struck down. Petitioners place particular reliance on our decision in *Committee for Public Education* v. *Nyquist,* where we held invalid a New York statute providing public funds for the maintenance and repair of the physical facilities of private schools and granting thinly disguised "tax benefits," actually amounting to tuition grants, to the parents of children attending private schools. As explained below, we conclude that § 290.09 (22) bears less resemblance to the arrangement struck down in *Nyquist* than it does to assistance programs upheld in our prior decisions and those discussed with approval in *Nyquist.*

The general nature of our inquiry in this area has been guided, since the decision in *Lemon* v. *Kurtzman,* by the "three-part" test. . . :

> "First, the statute must have a secular legislative purpose; second, its principle or primary effect must be one that neither advances nor inhibits religion. . . ; finally, the statute must not foster 'an excessive government entanglement with religion.'"

While this principle is well settled, our cases have also emphasized that it provides "no more than [a] helpful signpost" in dealing with Establishment Clause challenges. With this *caveat* in mind, we turn to the specific challenges raised against § 290.09 (22) under the *Lemon* framework.

Little time need be spent on the question of whether the Minnesota tax deduction has a secular purpose. Under our prior decisions, governmental assistance programs have consistently survived this inquiry even when they have run afoul of other aspects of the *Lemon* framework.... This reflects, at least in part, our reluctance to attribute unconstitutional motives to the states, particularly when a plausible secular purpose for the state's program may be discerned from the face of the statute.

A state's decision to defray the cost of educational expenses incurred by parents — regardless of the type of schools their children attend — evidences a purpose that is both secular and understandable. An educated populace is essential to the political and economic health of any community, and a state's efforts to assist parents in meeting the rising cost of educational expenses plainly serves this secular purpose of ensuring that the state's citizenry is well-educated. Similarly, Minnesota, like other states, could conclude that there is a strong public interest in assuring the continued financial health of private schools, both sectarian and nonsectarian. By educating a substantial number of students such schools relieve public schools of a correspondingly great burden — to the benefit of all taxpayers. In addition, private schools may serve as a benchmark for public schools....

... All these justifications are readily available to support § 290.09 (22), and each is sufficient to satisfy the secular purpose inquiry of *Lemon*.

We turn therefore to the more difficult but related question whether the Minnesota statute has "the primary effect of advancing the sectarian aims of the nonpublic schools." In concluding that it does not, we find several features of the Minnesota tax deduction particulary significant. First, an essential feature of Minnesota's arrangement is the fact that § 290.09 (22) is only one among many deductions — such as those for medical expenses, and charitable contributions, available under the Minnesota tax laws. Our decisions consistently have recognized that traditionally "[l]egislatures have especially broad latitude in creating classifications and distinctions in tax statutes," in part because the "familiarity with local conditions" enjoyed by legislators especially enables them to "achieve an equitable distribution of the tax burden." Under our prior decisions, the Minnesota legislature's judgment that a deduction for educational expenses fairly equalizes the tax burden of its citizens and encourages desirable expenditures for educational purposes is entitled to substantial deference.

Other characteristics of § 290.09 (22) argue equally strongly for the provision's constitutionality. Most importantly, the deduction is available for educational expenses incurred by *all* parents, including those whose children attend public schools and those whose children attend nonsectarian private schools or sectarian private schools....

In this respect, as well as others, this case is vitally different from the scheme struck down in *Nyquist*. There, public assistance amounting to tuition grants, was provided only to parents of children in *nonpublic* schools. This fact had considerable bearing on our decision striking down the New York statute at issue; we explicitly distinguished both *Allen* and *Everson* on the grounds that "In both cases the class of beneficiaries included *all* schoolchildren, those in public as well as those in private schools." (emphasis in original). Moreover, we intimated that "public assistance (*e.g.*, scholarships) made available generally without regard to the sectarian-nonsectarian or public-nonpublic nature of the institution benefited," might not offend the Establishment Clause. We think the tax deduction adopted by Minnesota is more similar to this latter type of program than it is to the arrangement struck down in *Nyquist*. Unlike the assistance at issue in *Nyquist*, § 290.09 (22) permits *all* parents — whether their children attend public school or private — to deduct their children's educational expenses. As *Widmar* and our other decisions indicate, a program, like § 290.09 (22) that neutrally provides state assistance to a broad spectrum of citizens is not readily subject to challenge under the Establishment Clause.

We also agree with the Court of Appeals that, by channeling whatever assistance it may provide to parochial schools through individual parents, Minnesota has reduced the Establishment Clause objections to which its action is subject. It is true, of course, that financial assistance provided to parents ultimately has an economic effect comparable to that of aid given directly to the schools attended by their children. It is also true, however, that under Minnesota's arrangement public funds become available only as a result of numerous, private choices of individual parents of school-age children. For these reasons, we recognized in *Nyquist* that the means by which state assistance flows to private schools is of some importance: we said that "the fact that aid is disbursed to parents rather than to ... schools" is a material consideration in Establishment Clause analysis, albeit "only one among many to be considered." It is noteworthy that all but one of our recent cases invalidating state aid to parochial schools have involved the direct transmission of assistance from the state to the schools themselves. The exception, of course, was *Nyquist,* which, as discussed previously is distinguishable from this case on other grounds. Where, as here, aid to parochial schools is available only as a result of decisions of individual parents no "imprimatur of State approval," *Widmar,* can be deemed to have been conferred on any particular religion, or on religion generally.

We find it useful, in the light of the foregoing characteristics of § 290.09 (22), to compare the attenuated financial benefits flowing to parochial schools from the section to the evils against which the Establishment Clause was designed to protect. These dangers are well-described by our statement that "what is at stake as a matter of policy [in Establishment Clause cases] is preventing that kind of degree of government involvement in religious life that, as history teaches us, is apt to lead to strife and frequently strain a political system to the breaking point." It is important, however, to "keep these issues in perspective":

> "At this point in the 20th century we are quite far removed from the dangers that prompted the Framers to include the Establishment Clause in the Bill of Rights. . . . The risk of significant religious or denominational control over our democratic processes — or even of deep political division among religious lines — is remote, and when viewed against the positive contributions of sectarian schools, such risk seems entirely tolerable in light of the continuing oversight of this Court."

The Establishment Clause of course extends beyond prohibition of a state church or payment of state funds to one or more churches. We do not think, however, that its prohibition extends to the type of tax deduction established by Minnesota. The historic purposes of the clause simply do not encompass the sort of attenuated financial benefit, ultimately controlled by the private choices of individual parents, that eventually flows to parochial schools from the neutrally available tax benefit at issue in this case.

Petitioners argue that, notwithstanding the facial neutrality of § 290.09 (22), in application the statute primarily benefits religious institutions. Petitioners rely, as they did below, on a statistical analysis of the type of persons claiming the tax deduction. They contend that most parents of public school children incur no tuition expenses . . . and that other expenses deductible under § 290.09 (22) are negligible in value; moreover, they claim that 96% of the children in private schools in 1978-1979 attended religiously-affiliated institutions. Because of all this, they reason, the bulk of deductions taken under § 290.09 (22) will be claimed by parents of children in sectarian schools. Respondents reply that petitioners have failed to consider the impact of deductions for items such as transportation, summer school tuition, tuition paid by parents whose children attended schools outside the school districts in which they resided, rental or purchase costs for a variety of equipment, and tuition for certain types of instruction not ordinarily provided in public schools.

We need not consider these contentions in detail. We would be loath to adopt a rule grounding the constitutionality of a facially neutral law on annual reports reciting the extent to which various classes of private citizens claimed benefits under the law. Such an approach would scarcely provide the certainty that this field stands in need of, nor can we perceive principled standards by which such statistical evidence might be evaluated. Moreover, the fact that private persons fail in a particular year to claim the tax relief to which they are entitled — under a facially neutral statute — should be of little importance in determining the constitutionality of the statute permitting such relief.

Finally, private educational institutions, and parents paying for their children to attend these schools, make special contributions to the areas in which they operate. . . . If parents of children in private schools choose to take especial advantage of the relief provided by § 290.09 (22), it is no doubt due to the fact that they bear a particularly great financial burden

in educating their children. More fundamentally, whatever unequal effect
may be attributed to the statutory classification can fairly be regarded as a
rough return for the benefits, discussed above, provided to the state and all
taxpayers by parents sending their children to parochial schools. In the
light of all this, we believe it wiser to decline to engage in the type of empirical inquiry into those persons benefited by state law which petitioners
urge.

Thus, we hold that the Minnesota tax deduction for educational
expenses satisfies the primary effect inquiry of our Establishment Clause
cases.

For the foregoing reasons, the judgment of the Court of Appeals is

Affirmed.

JUSTICE MARSHALL, with whom JUSTICE BRENNAN, JUSTICE
BLACKMUN and JUSTICE STEVENS join, dissenting.

The Establishment Clause of the First Amendment prohibits a State
from subsidizing religious education, whether it does so directly or
indirectly. In my view, this principle of neutrality forbids not only the tax
benefits struck down in *Committee for Public Education* v. *Nyquist*
(1973), but any tax benefit, including the tax deduction at issue here,
which subsidizes tuition payments to sectarian schools. I also believe that
the Establishment Clause prohibits the tax deductions that Minnesota
authorizes for the cost of books and other instructional materials used for
sectarian purposes.

I

The majority today does not question the continuing vitality of this
Court's decision in *Nyquist*. That decision established that a State may
not support religious education either through direct grants to parochial
schools or through financial aid to parents of parochial school students.
Nyquist also established that financial aid to parents of students attending
parochial schools is no more permissible if it is provided in the form of a
tax credit than if provided in the form of cash payments. Notwithstanding
these accepted principles, the Court today upholds a statute that provides
a tax deduction for the tuition charged by religious schools. The Court
concludes that the Minnesota statute is "vitally different" from the New
York statute at issue in *Nyquist*. As demonstrated below, there is no
significant difference between the two schemes. The Minnesota tax statute
violates the Establishment Clause for precisely the same reason as the
statute struck down in *Nyquist:* it has a direct and immediate effect of advancing religion.

A

In calculating their net income for state income tax purposes, Minnesota
residents are permitted to deduct the cost of their children's tuition,

subject to a ceiling of $500 or $700 per child. By taking this deduction, a taxpayer reduces his tax bill by a sum equal to the amount of tuition multiplied by his rate of tax. Although this tax benefit is available to any parents whose children attend schools which charge tuition, the vast majority of the taxpayers who are eligible to receive the benefit are parents whose children attend religious schools.

Like the law involved in *Nyquist,* the Minnesota law can be said to serve a secular purpose: promoting pluralism and diversity among the State's public and nonpublic schools. But the Establishment Clause requires more than that legislation have a secular purpose. . . .

As we recognized in *Nyquist,* direct government subsidization of parochial school tuition is impermissible because "the effect of the aid is unmistakably to provide desired financial support for nonpublic, sectarian institutions.". . . For this reason, aid to sectarian schools must be restricted to ensure that it may be not used to further the religious mission of those schools. While "services such as police and fire protection, sewage disposal, highways, and sidewalks," may be provided to parochial schools in common with other institutions, because this type of assistance is clearly " 'marked off from the religious function' " of those schools, *Nyquist,* quoting from *Everson* v. *Board of Education,* unrestricted financial assistance, such as grants for the maintenance and construction of parochial schools, may not be provided. . . .

Indirect assistance in the form of financial aid to parents for tuition payments is similarly impermissible because it is not "subject to . . . restrictions" which " 'guarantee the separation between the secular and religious educational functions and . . . ensure that State financial aid supports only the former.' " By ensuring that parents will be reimbursed for tuition payments they make, the Minnesota statute requires that taxpayers in general pay for the cost of parochial education and extends a financial "incentive to parents to send their children to sectarian schools.". . .

That parents receive a reduction of their tax liability, rather than a direct reimbursement, is of no greater significance here than it was in *Nyquist.* "[F]or purposes of determining whether such aid has the effect of advancing religion," it makes no difference whether the qualifying "parent receives an actual cash payment [or] is allowed to reduce . . . the sum he would otherwise be obliged to pay over to the State." It is equally irrelevant whether a reduction in taxes takes the form of a tax "credit," a tax "modification," or a tax "deduction." What is of controlling significance is not the form but the "substantive impact" of the financial aid. . . .

B

The majority attempts to distinguish *Nyquist* by pointing to two differences between the Minnesota tuition-assistance program and the program struck down in *Nyquist.* Neither of these distinctions can withstand scrutiny.

1

The majority first attempts to distinguish *Nyquist* on the ground that Minnesota makes all parents eligible to deduct up to $500 or $700 for each dependent, whereas the New York law allowed a deduction only for parents whose children attended nonpublic schools. Although Minnesota taxpayers who send their children to local public schools may not deduct tuition expenses because they incur none, they may deduct other expenses, such as the cost of gym clothes, pencils, and notebooks, which are shared by all parents of school-age children. This, in the majority's view, distinguishes the Minnesota scheme from the law at issue in *Nyquist*.

That the Minnesota statute makes some small benefit available to all parents cannot alter the fact that the most substantial benefit provided by the statute is available only to those parents who send their children to schools that charge tuition. It is simply undeniable that the single largest expense that may be deducted under the Minnesota statute is tuition. The statute is little more than a subsidy of tuition masquerading as a subsidy of general educational expenses....

That this deduction has a primary effect of promoting religion can easily be determined without any resort to the type of "statistical evidence" that the majority fears would lead to constitutional uncertainty. The only factual inquiry necessary is the same as that employed in *Nyquist* and *Sloan* v. *Lemon:* whether the deduction permitted for tuition expenses primarily benefits those who send their children to religious schools. In *Nyquist* we unequivocally rejected any suggestion that, in determining the effect of a tax statute, this Court should look exclusively to what the statute on its face purports to do and ignore the actual operation of the challenged provision. In determining the effect of the New York statute, we emphasized that "virtually all" of the schools receiving direct grants for maintenance and repair were Roman Catholic schools....

In this case, it is undisputed that well over 90% of the children attending tuition-charging schools in Minnesota are enrolled in sectarian schools. History and experience likewise instruct us that any generally available financial assistance for elementary and secondary school tuition expenses mainly will further religious education because the majority of the schools which charge tuition are sectarian. Because Minnesota, like every other State, is committed to providing free public education, tax assistance for tuition payments inevitably redounds to the benefit of nonpublic, sectarian schools and parents who send their children to those schools.

2

The majority also asserts that the Minnesota statute is distinguishable from the statute struck down in *Nyquist* in another respect: the tax benefit available under Minnesota law is a "genuine tax deduction," whereas the New York law provided a benefit which, while nominally a deduction, also had features of a "tax credit." Under the Minnesota law, the amount of the tax benefit varies directly with the amount of the expenditure. Under the New York law, the amount of deduction was not dependent upon the amount actually paid for tuititon but was a predetermined amount which depended on the tax bracket of each taxpayer. The deduction was designed to yield roughly the same amount of tax "forgiveness" for each taxpayer.

This is a distinction without a difference. Our prior decisions have rejected the relevance of the majority's formalistic distinction between tax deductions and the tax benefit at issue in *Nyquist*.... The deduction afforded by Minnesota law was "designed to yield a [tax benefit] in exchange for performing a specific act which the State desires to encourage." Like the tax benefit held impermissible in *Nyquist*, the tax deduction at issue here concededly was designed to "encourag[e] desirable expenditures for educational purposes." Of equal importance, as the majority also concedes, the "economic consequence" of these programs is the same, for in each case the "financial assistance provided to parents ultimately has an economic effect comparable to that of aid given directly to the schools." It was precisely the substantive impact of the financial support, and not its particular form, that rendered the programs in *Nyquist* and *Sloan* v. *Lemon* unconstitutional.

C

The majority incorrectly asserts that Minnesota's tax deduction for tuition expenses "bears less resemblance to the arrangement struck down in *Nyquist* than it does to assistance programs upheld in our prior decisions and discussed with approval in *Nyquist*." One might as well say that a tangerine bears less resemblance to an orange than to an apple....

As previously noted, the Minnesota tuition tax deduction is not available to *all* parents, but only to parents whose children attend schools that charge tuition, which are comprised almost entirely of sectarian schools. More importantly, the assistance that flows to parochial schools as a result of the tax benefit is not restricted, and cannot be restricted, to the secular functions of those schools.

II

In my view, Minnesota's tax deduction for the cost of textbooks and other instructional materials is also constitutionally infirm. The majority is simply mistaken in concluding that a tax deduction, unlike a tax credit or a direct grant to parents, promotes religious education in a manner that is only "attenuated." A tax deduction has a primary effect that advances religion if it is provided to offset expenditures which are not restricted to the secular activities of parochial schools.

The instructional materials which are subsidized by the Minnesota tax deduction plainly may be used to inculcate religious values and belief.... It follows that a tax deduction to offset the cost of purchasing instructional

materials for use in sectarian schools, like a loan of such materials to
parents, "necesarily results in aid to the sectarian school enterprise as a
whole" and is therefore a "substantial advancement of religious activity"
that "constitutes an impermissible establishment of religion."

There is no reason to treat Minnesota's tax deduction for textbooks any
differently. Secular textbooks, like other secular instructional materials,
contribute to the religious mission of the parochial schools that use those
books. . . .

III

There can be little doubt that the State of Minnesota intended to
provide, and has provided, "[s]ubstantial aid to the educational function of
[church-related] schools," and that the tax deduction for tuition and other
educational expenses "necessarily results in aid to the sectarian school
enterprise as a whole." It is beside the point that the State may have
legitimate secular reasons for providing such aid. In focusing upon the
contributions made by church-related schools, the majority has lost sight
of the issue before us in this case. . . .

In my view, the lines drawn in *Nyquist* were drawn on a reasoned basis
with appropriate regard for the principles of neutrality embodied by the
Establishment Clause. I do not believe that the same can be said of the
lines drawn by the majority today. For the first time, the Court has upheld
financial support for religious schools without any reason at all to assume
that the support will be restricted to the secular functions of those schools
and will not be used to support religious instruction. This result is flatly at
odds with the fundamental principle that a State may provide no financial
support whatsoever to promote religion. . . .

July

COURT ON SEX BIAS
IN PENSION PLANS
July 6, 1983

In a decision that had potentially far-reaching repercussions for the insurance industry and the women's rights movement, the Supreme Court adjourned its longest term since 1975-76 by striking down sex bias in employer-sponsored pension and retirement plans. The Court ruled July 6 that an employer's retirement plan may not provide smaller benefits to women workers than to comparably situated male employees.

The Court declared that Title VII of the 1964 Civil Rights Act prohibits employers from discriminating against "any individual with respect to his compensation, terms, conditions, or privileges of employment because of such individual's race, color, religion, sex or national origin." This meant that workers were to be treated as individuals, not members of groups. The fact that women as a group lived longer than men was not a permissible basis for paying them different monthly retirement benefits, the Court held.

Justice Thurgood Marshall wrote for the majority in the main decision involved in the case of Arizona Governing Committee for Tax Deferred Annuity and Deferred Compensation Plans *v.* Norris. *He was joined by Justices William J. Brennan Jr., Sandra Day O'Connor, John Paul Stevens and Byron R. White. Chief Justice Warren E. Burger, and Justices Harry A. Blackmun, Lewis F. Powell Jr. and William Rehnquist dissented.*

The case involved a life annuity plan made available by Arizona as one of several retirement options for its employees. The plan provided a fixed monthly benefit for as long as a retiree lived. Noting that the Court had ruled in the 1978 case of Los Angeles Department of Water & Power *v.* Manhart *that Title VII barred employers from requiring women to make larger contributions than men to a pension fund, Justice Marshall, writing for the majority, said: "The classification of employees on the basis of sex is no more permissible at the pay-out stage of a retirement plan than at the pay-in stage."*

On the question of whether the relief granted as a result of this decision should be retroactive, and thus available to current retirees, O'Connor switched sides. She joined Burger, Blackmun, Powell and William H. Rehnquist — who had dissented from the main decision — in ruling that only retirement benefits derived from contributions made after this decision must be calculated on a unisex basis.

Majority, Dissenting Opinions

The majority said the assumption that gender properly may be used to predict longevity "is flatly inconsistent with the basic teaching of Manhart*: that Title VII requires employers to treat their employees as individuals, not 'as simply components of a racial, religious, sexual, or national class.' "*

"The use of sex-segregated actuarial tables to calculate retirement benefits violates Title VII whether or not the tables reflect an accurate prediction of the longevity of women as a class," Marshall continued, "for under the statute 'even a true generalization about a class' cannot justify class-based treatment." Quoting from the Manhart *decision, Marshall noted that "actuarial studies could unquestionably identify differences in life expectancy based on race or national origin, as well as sex." If Arizona's reasoning in the* Norris *case were adopted, he said, "such studies could be used as a justification for paying employees of one race lower monthly benefits that employees of another race." Marshall pointed out that* Manhart *had stated that a person's life expectancy was based on a number of factors other than sex.*

Dissenters Powell, Burger, Blackmun and Rehnquist warned of the decision's "far-reaching effect on the operation of insurance and pension plans." Writing for the four, Powell said, "Employers may be forced to discontinue offering life annuities, or potentially disruptive changes may be required in long-established methods of calculating insurance and pensions. Either course will work a major change in the way the cost of insurance is determined — to the probable detriment of all employees." The focus on the individual mandated by Title VII could not be squared with the whole concept of insurance, Powell said. "Insurance and life annuities exist because it is impossible to measure accurately how long any one individual will live. Insurance companies cannot make individual determinations of life expectancy; they must consider instead the life expectancy of identifiable groups. . . . Explicit sexual classifications, to be sure, require close examination, but they are not automatically invalid. Sex-based mortality tables reflect objective actuarial experience. Because their use does not entail discrimination in any normal understanding of that term, a court should hesitate to invalidate this long-approved practice on the basis of its own policy judgment. Congress may choose to forbid the use of any sexual classifications in insurance, but nothing suggests that it intended to do so in Title VII," Powell concluded.

In a separate opinion, O'Connor explained the practical reasons for which she joined the dissenters to form a majority limiting the relief available as a result of the court's decision. To make the new system of calculating benefits retroactive would not be fair, she wrote. A court order that employers must now pay out larger annuity benefits each month to retired women workers than had been anticipated could jeopardize an entire pension fund. Should such a fund collapse, innocent people would be harmed, she said. "This real danger of bankrupting pension funds requires that our decision be made prospective," she concluded.

Reaction, Effects of Ruling

Women's groups and the insurance industry had mixed feelings about the decision. For the women's advocates, the ruling established that employers could not discriminate in retirement benefits because of a worker's gender. And, while the ruling applied only to employer-sponsored pension programs, representatives of women's groups predicted the decision eventually would result in the elimination of sex as a factor in all types of insurance that people purchased outside of work.

Judy Goldsmith, president of the National Organization for Women, called the ruling "a victory for women's rights." Some women activists, however, were critical of the Court's decision to require unisex benefit calculations only for contributions made after August 1, 1983, the effective date of the ruling. They contended that employers were on notice since at least the 1978 **Manhart** *ruling that benefits should not be calculated on the basis of sex. Goldsmith said that retirement plans for women were governed by a double standard as a result of the Court's ruling, because the decision did nothing to preclude insurance companies from continuing to sell sex-based individual policies.*

Insurance industry officials were pleased that the ruling did not require that benefits be recalculated for current retirees or for contributions made to retirement plans prior to August 1. Such retroactivity would have resulted in "devastating costs to employers," said Richard S. Schweiker, president of the American Council of Life Insurance (ACLI), representing 573 life insurance companies. Industry officials also pointed out that the decision did not bar the use of separate actuarial tables for men and women. The ruling would allow use of those tables in establish-

ing a group plan, but not in distributing individual payments.

It was not immediately clear from the Court's ruling whether companies that offered annuity plans would have the option of reducing men's benefits and increasing women's until they were equal, or whether they would have to raise women's benefits to the men's level. There was a third option as well — one that Arizona already had chosen. Employers could refuse to offer any kind of annuity plan for their retirees. Schweiker and other insurance industry officials said that annuities as a benefit alternative likely would be eliminated by many employers because of the cost of equalizing benefits. But he added that the ruling "did not revolutionize the business of insurance," because it applied only to employer-provided pension programs, not to insurance companies selling annuity policies to individuals. Also, insurance companies could consider the gender makeup of a company's work force in determining the price of a pension program, he said.

The impact of the ruling on pending legislation to outlaw sex-based discrimination in all forms of insurance was unclear. Unlike the Court decision, the bills would affect all types of insurance and pension policies — annuities, life, health, disability and auto — whether provided by employers or bought individually. Also, the legislation would require companies to increase the benefits of current retirees and others who already had begun paying premiums if their contracts provided for lower benefits or higher rates because of sex-based tables.

> *Following are excerpts from the Supreme Court's July 6, 1983, decision in* Arizona Governing Committee v. Norris, *barring sex bias in employer-sponsored pension and retirement plans, and from the dissenting opinions of Justices Lewis F. Powell Jr. and Sandra Day O'Connor:*

No. 82-52

Arizona Governing Committee for Tax Deferred Annuity and deferred Compensation Plans, etc., et al., Petitioners Nathalie Norris etc.	On writ of Certiorari to the United States Court of Appeals of the Ninth Circuit

[July 6, 1983]

... JUSTICE MARSHALL, with whom JUSTICE BRENNAN, JUSTICE WHITE, JUSTICE STEVENS, and JUSTICE O'CONNOR join as to Parts I, II, and III, concurring in the judgment in part, and with whom JUSTICE BRENNAN, JUSTICE WHITE, and JUSTICE STEVENS join as to Part IV.

In *Los Angeles Dept. of Water & Power* v. *Manhart* (1978), this Court held that Title VII of the Civil Rights Act of 1964 prohibits an employer from requiring women to make larger contributions in order to obtain the same monthly pension benefits as men. The question presented by this case is whether Title VII also prohibits an employer from offering its employees the option of receiving retirement benefits from one of several companies selected by the employer, all of which pay a woman lower monthly benefits than a man who has made the same contributions.

I

A

Since 1974 the State of Arizona has offered its employees the opportunity to enroll in a deferred compensation plan administerd by the Arizona Governing Committee for Tax Deferred Annuity and Deferred Compensation Plans (Governing Committee). Employees who participate in the plan may thereby postpone the receipt of a portion of their wages until retirement. By doing so, they postpone paying federal income tax on the amounts deferred until after retirement, when they receive those amounts and any earnings thereon.

After inviting private companies to submit bids outlining the investment opportunities that they were willing to offer State employees, the State selected several companies to participate in its deferred compensation plan. Many of the companies selected offer three basic retirement options: (1) a single lump-sum payment upon retirement, (2) periodic payments of a fixed sum for a fixed period of time, and (3) monthly annuity payments for the remainder of the employee's life. When an employee decides to take part in the deferred compensation plan, he must designate the company in which he wishes to invest his deferred wages. Employees must choose one of the companies selected by the State to participate in the plan; they are not free to invest their deferred compensation in any other way. At the time an employee enrolls in the plan, he may also select one of the payout options offered by the company that he has chosen, but when he reaches retirement age he is free to switch to one of the company's other options. If at retirement the employee decides to receive a lump-sum payment, he may also purchase any of the options then being offered by the other companies participating in the plan. Many employees find an annuity contract to be the most attractive option, since receipt of a lump sum upon retirement requires payment of taxes on the entire sum in one year, and the choice of a fixed sum for a fixed period requires an employee to speculate as to how long he will live.

Once an employee chooses the company in which he wishes to invest and decides the amount of compensation to be deferred each month, the State is responsible for withholding the appropriate sums from the employee's wages and channeling those sums to the company designated by the employee. The State bears the cost of making the necessary payroll deductions and of giving employees time off to attend group meetings to learn about the plan, but it does not contribute any monies to supplement the employees' deferred wages.

For an employee who elects to receive a monthly annuity following retirement, the amount of the employee's monthly benefits depends upon the amount of compensation that the employee deferred (and any earnings thereon), the employee's age at retirement, and the employee's sex. All of the companies selected by the State to participate in the plan use sex-based mortality tables to calculate monthly retirement benefits. Under these tables a man receives larger monthly payments than a woman who deferred the same amount of compensation and retired at the same age, because the tables classify annuitants on the basis of sex and women on av-erage live longer than men. Sex is the only factor that the tables use to classify individuals of the same age; the tables do not incorporate other factors correlating with longevity such as smoking habits, alcohol con-sumption, weight, medical history, or family history.

As of August 18, 1978, 1,675 of the State's approximately 35,000 employees were participating in the deferred compensation plan. Of these 1,675 participating employees, 681 were women, and 572 women had elected some form of future annuity option. As of the same date, 10 women participating in the plan had retired, and four of those 10 had chosen a life-time annuity.

B

On May 3, 1975, respondent Nathalie Norris, an employee in the Arizona Department of Economic Security, elected to participate in the plan. She requested that her deferred compensation be invested in the Lincoln National Life Insurance Company's fixed annuity contract. Shortly there-after Arizona approved the respondent's request and began withholding $199.50 from her salary each month.

On April 25, 1978, after exhausting administrative remedies, respondent brought suit in the United States District Court for the District of Arizona against the State, the Governing Committee, and several individual members of the committee. Respondent alleged that the defendants were violating § 703(a) of Title VII of the Civil Rights Act of 1964, by administering an annuity plan that discriminates on the basis of sex. Respondent requested that the District Court certify a class under Fed. Rules Civ. Proc. 23(b)(2) consisting of all female employees of the State of Arizona "who are enrolled or will in the future enroll in the State Deferred Compensation Plan."

On March 13, 1980, the District Court certified a class action and granted summary judgment for the plaintiff class, holding that the State's plan violates Title VII. The court directed petitioners to cease using sex-based actuarial tables and to pay retired female employees benefits equal to those paid to similarly situated men. The United States Court of

Appeals for the Ninth Circuit affirmed, with one judge dissenting. We granted certiorari to decide whether the Arizona plan violates Title VII and whether, if so, the relief ordered by the District Court was proper.

II

We consider first whether petitioners would have violated Title VII if they had run the entire deferred compensation plan themselves, without the participation of any insurance companies. Title VII makes it an unlawful employment practice "to discriminate against any individual with respect to his compensation, terms, conditions, or privileges of employment, because of such individual's race, color, religion, sex or national origin." There is no question that the opportunity to participate in a deferred compensation plan constitutes a "conditio[n] or privileg[e] of employment," and that retirement benefits constitute a form of "compensation." The issue we must decide is whether it is discrimination "because of . . . sex" to pay a retired woman lower monthly benefits than a man who deferred the same amount of compensation.

In *Los Angeles Dept. of Water & Power* v. *Manhart* (1978), we held that an employer had violated Title VII by requiring its female employees to make larger contributions to a pension fund than male employees in order to obtain the same monthly benefits upon retirement. Noting that Title VII's "focus on the individual is unambiguous," we emphasized that the statute prohibits an employer from treating some employees less favorably than others because of their race, religion, sex, or national origin. While women as a class live longer than men, we rejected the argument that the exaction of greater contributions from women was based on a "factor other than sex" — *i.e.,* longevity — and was therefore permissible under the Equal Pay Act:

> "[A]ny individual's life expectancy is based on a number of factors, of which sex is only one. . . . [O]ne cannot 'say that an actuarial distinction based entirely on sex is "based on any other factor than sex." Sex is exactly what it is based on.' "

We concluded that a plan requiring women to make greater contributions than men discriminates "because of . . . sex" for the simple reason that it treats each woman " 'in a manner which but for [her] sex would [have been] different.' " 435 U.S., at 710, quoting Developments in the Law, Employment Discrimination and Title VII of the Civil Rights Act of 1964.

We have no hesitation in holding, as have all but one of the lower courts that have considered the question, that the classification of employees on the basis of sex is no more permissible at the pay-out stage of a retirement plan than at the pay-in stage. We reject petitioners' contention that the Arizona plan does not discriminate on the basis of sex because a woman and a man who defer the same amount of compensation will obtain upon retirement annuity policies having approximately the same present actuarial value. Arizona has simply offered its employees a choice among

697

different levels of annuity benefits, any one of which, if offered alone, would be equivalent to the plan at issue in *Manhart,* where the employer determined both the monthly contributions employees were required to make and the level of benefits that they were paid. If a woman participating in the Arizona plan wishes to obtain monthly benefits equal to those obtained by a man, she must make greater monthly contributions than he, just as the female employees in *Manhart* had to make greater contributions to obtain equal benefits. For any particular level of benefits that a woman might wish to receive, she will have to make greater monthly contributions to obtain that level of benefits than a man would have to make. The fact that Arizona has offered a range of discriminatory benefit levels, rather than only one such level, obviously provides no basis whatsoever for distinguishing *Manhart.*

In asserting that the Arizona plan is nondiscriminatory because a man and a woman who have made equal contributions will obtain annuity policies of roughly equal present actuarial value, petitioners incorrectly assume that Title VII permits an employer to classify employees on the basis of sex in predicting their longevity. Otherwise there would be no basis for postulating that a woman's annuity policy has the same present actuarial value as the policy of a similarly situated man even though her policy provides lower monthly benefits. This underlying assumption — that sex may properly be used to predict longevity — is flatly inconsistent with the basic teaching of *Manhart:* that Title VII requires employers to treat their employees as *individuals,* not "as simply components of a racial, religious, sexual, or national class. *Manhart* squarely rejected the notion that, because women as a class live longer than men, an employer may adopt a retirement plan that treats every individual woman less favorably than every individual man.

As we observed in *Manhart,* "[a]ctuarial studies could unquestionably identify differences in life expectancy based on race or national origin, as well as sex." If petitioners' interpretation of the statute were correct, such studies could be used as a justification for paying employees of one race lower monthly benefits than employees of another race. We continue to believe that "a statute that was designed to make race irrelevant in the employment market could not reasonably be construed to permit such a racial classification. And if it would be unlawful to use race-based actuarial tables, it must also be unlawful to use sex-based tables, for under Title VII a distinction based on sex stands on the same footing as a distinction based on race unless it falls within one of a few narrow exceptions that are plainly inapplicable here."

What we said in *Manhart* bears repeating: "Congress has decided that classifications based on sex, like those based on national origin or race, are unlawful." The use of sex-segregated actuarial tables to calculate retirement benefits violates Title VII whether or not the tables reflect an accurate prediction of the longevity of women as a class, for under the statute "[e]ven a true generalization about [a] class" cannot justify class-based treatment. An individual woman may not be paid lower monthly benefits simply because women as a class live longer than men. . . .

We conclude that it is just as much discrimination "because of . . . sex" to pay a woman lower benefits when she has made the same contributions as a man as it is to make her pay larger contributions to obtain the same benefits.

III

Since petitioners plainly would have violated Title VII if they had run the entire deferred compensation plan themselves, the only remaining question as to liability is whether their conduct is beyond the reach of the statute because it is the companies chosen by petitioners to participate in the plan that calculate and pay the retirement benefits.

Title VII "primarily govern[s] relations between employees and their employer, not between employees and third parties." *Manhart*. Recognizing this limitation on the reach of the statute, we noted in *Manhart* that

> "Nothing in our holding implies that it would be unlawful for an employer to set aside equal retirement contributions for each employee and let each retiree purchase the largest benefits which his or her accumulated contributions could command in the open market."

Relying on this caveat, petitioners contend that they have not violated Title VII because the life annuities offered by the companies participating in the Arizona plan reflect what is available in the open market. Petitioners cite a statement in the stipulation of facts entered into in the District Court that "[a]ll tables presently in use provide a larger sum to a male than to a female of equal age, account value and any guaranteed payment period."

It is no defense that all annuities immediately available in the open market may have been based on sex-segregated actuarial tables. In context it is reasonably clear that the stipulation on which petitioners rely means only that all the tables used by the companies taking part in the Arizona plan are based on sex, but our conclusion does not depend upon whether petitioner's construction of the stipulation is accepted or rejected. It is irrelevant whether any other insurers offered annuities on a sex-neutral basis, since the State did not simply set aside retirement contributions and let employees purchase annuities on the open market. On the contrary, the State provided the opportunity to obtain an annuity as part of its own deferred compensation plan. It invited insurance companies to submit bids outlining the terms on which they would supply retirement benefits and selected the companies that were permitted to participate in the plan. Once the State selected these companies, it entered into contracts with them governing the terms on which benefits were to be provided to employees. Employees enrolling in the plan could obtain retirement benefits only from one of those companies, and no employee could be contacted by a company except as permitted by the State.

Under these circumstances there can be no serious question that petitioners are legally responsible for the discriminatory terms on which annuities are offered by the companies chosen to participate in the plan. Having created a plan whereby employees can obtain the advantages of using deferred compensation to purchase an annuity only if they invest in one of the companies specifically selected by the State, the State cannot disclaim responsibility for the discriminatory features of the insurers' options. Since employers are ultimately responsible for the "compensation, terms, conditions, [and] privileges of employment" provided to employees, an employer that adopts a fringe-benefit scheme that discriminates among its employees on the basis of race, religion, sex, or national origin violates Title VII regardless of whether third parties are also involved in the discrimination. In this case the State of Arizona was itself a party to contracts concerning the annuities to be offered by the insurance companies, and it is well established that both parties to a discriminatory contract are liable for any discriminatory provisions the contract contains, regardless of which party initially suggested inclusion of the discriminatory provision. It would be inconsistent with the broad remedial purposes of Title VII to hold that an employer who adopts a discriminatory fringe benefit plan can avoid liability on the ground that he could not find a third party willing to treat his employees on a nondiscriminatory basis. An employer who confronts such a situation must either supply the fringe benefit himself, without the assistance of any third party, or not provide it at all.

IV

We turn finally to the relief awarded by the District Court. The court enjoined petitioners to assure that future annuity payments to retired female employees shall be equal to the payments received by similarly situated male employees.

In *Albemarle Paper Co.* v. *Moody* (1975), we emphasized that one of the main purposes of Title VII is "to make persons whole for injuries suffered on account of unlawful employment discrimination." We recognized that there is a strong presumption that "[t]he injured party is to be placed, as near as may be, in the situation he would have occupied if the wrong had not been committed." [Q]uoting *Wicker* v. *Hoppock* (1867). Once a violation of the statute has been found, retroactive relief "should be denied only for reasons which, if applied generally, would not frustrate the central statutory purposes of eradicating discrimination throughout the economy and making persons whole for injuries suffered through past discrimination." Applying this standard, we held that the mere absence of bad faith on the part of the employer is not a sufficient reason for denying such relief.

Although this Court noted in *Manhart* that "[t]he *Albermarle* presumption in favor of retroactive liability can seldom be overcome," the Court concluded that under the circumstances the District Court had abused its discretion in requiring the employer to refund to female employees all contributions they were required to make in excess of the contributions demanded for men. The Court explained that "conscientious and intelligent administrators of pension funds, who did not have the benefit of the extensive briefs and arguments presented to us, may well have assumed that a program like the Department's was entirely lawful," since "[t]he courts had been silent on the question, and the administrative agencies had conflicting views." The Court also noted that retroactive relief based on "[d]rastic changes in the legal rules governing pension and insurance funds" can "jeopardiz[e] the insurer's solvency and, ultimately, the insureds' benefits," and that the burden of such relief can fall on innocent third parties.

While the relief ordered here affects only benefit payments made after the date of the District Court's judgment, it does not follow that the relief is wholly prospective in nature, as an injunction concerning future conduct ordinarily is, and should therefore be routinely awarded once liability is established. When a court directs a change in benefits based on contributions made before the court's order, the court is awarding relief that is fundamentally retroactive in nature. This is true because retirement benefits under a plan such as that at issue here represent a return on contributions which were made during the employee's working years and which were intended to fund the benefits without any additional contributions from any source after retirement.

A recognition that the relief awarded by the District Court is partly retroactive is only the beginning of the inquiry. Absent special circumstances a victim of a Title VII violation is entitled to whatever retroactive relief is necessary to undo any damage resulting from the violation. As to any disparity in benefits that is attributable to contributions made after our decision in *Manhart*, there are no special circumstances justifying the denial of retroactive relief. Our ruling today was clearly foreshadowed by *Manhart*. That decision should have put petitioners on notice that a man and a woman who make the same contributions to a retirement plan must be paid the same monthly benefits. To the extent that any disparity in benefits coming due after the date of the District Court's judgment is attributable to contributions made after *Manhart*, there is therefore no unfairness in requiring petitioners to pay retired female employees whatever sum is necessary each month to bring them up to the benefit level that they would have enjoyed had their post-*Manhart* contributions been treated in the same way as those of similarly situated male employees....

JUSTICE POWELL, with whom THE CHIEF JUSTICE, JUSTICE BLACKMUN, and JUSTICE REHNQUIST join as to Parts I and II, dissenting in part and with whom THE CHIEF JUSTICE, JUSTICE BLACKMUN, JUSTICE REHNQUIST, and JUSTICE O'CONNOR join as to Part III, concurring in part.

The Court today holds that an employer may not offer its employees life annuities from a private insurance company that uses actuarially sound, sex-based mortality tables. This holding will have a far-reaching effect on the operation of insurance and pension plans. Employers may be forced to discontinue offering life annuities, or potentially disruptive changes may be required in long-established methods of calculating insurance and pensions. Either course will work a major change in the way the cost of insurance is determined — to the probable detriment of *all* employees. This is contrary to our explicit recognition in *Los Angeles Dept. of Water & Power* v. *Manhart* (1978), that Title VII "was [not] intended to revolutionize the insurance and pension industries." . . .

II

. . . [T]he consequences of the Court's holding are unlikely to be beneficial. If the cost to employers of offering unisex annuities is prohibitive or if insurance carriers choose not to write such annuities, employees will be denied the opportunity to purchase life annuities — concededly the most advantageous pension plan — at lower cost. If, alternatively, insurance carriers and employers choose to offer these annuities, the heavy cost burden of equalizing benefits probably will be passed on to current employees. There is no evidence that Congress intended Title VII to work such a change. Nor does *Manhart* support such a sweeping reading of this statute. That case expressly recognized the limited reach of its holding — a limitation grounded in the legislative history of Title VII and the inapplicability of Title VII's policies to the insurance industry.

A

We were careful in *Manhart* to make clear that the question before us was narrow. We stated: "All that is at issue today is a requirement that men and women make unequal contributions to an *employer-operated* pension fund." And our holding was limited expressly to the precise issue before us. We stated that "[a]lthough we conclude that the Department's practice violated Title VII, we do not suggest that the statute was intended to revolutionize the insurance and pension industries."

The Court in *Manhart* had good reason for recognizing the narrow reach of Title VII in the particular area of the insurance industry. Congress has chosen to leave the primary responsibility for regulating the insurance industry to the respective States. . . . This Act reflects the long-held view that the "continued regulation . . . by the several States of the business of insurance is in the public interest." Given the consistent policy of entrusting insurance regulation to the States, the majority is not justified in assuming that Congress intended in 1964 to require the industry to change long-standing actuarial methods, approved over decades by state insurance commissions.

Nothing in the language of Title VII supports this preemption of state jurisdiction. Nor has the majority identified any evidence in the legislative history that Congress considered the widespread use of sex-based mortality tables to be discriminatory or that it intended to modify its previous grant by the McCarran-Ferguson Act of exclusive jurisdiction to the States to regulate the terms of protection offered by insurance companies. Rather, the legislative history indicates precisely the opposite. . . .

B

As neither the language of the statute nor the legislative history supports its holding, the majority is compelled to rely on its perception of the policy expressed in Title VII. The policy, of course, is broadly to proscribe discrimination in employment practices. But the statute itself focuses specifically on the individual and "precludes treatment of individuals as simply components of a racial, religious, sexual or national class." This specific focus has little relevance to the business of insurance. (BLACKMUN, J., concurring in part and concurring in the judgment). Insurance and life annuities exist because it is impossible to measure accurately how long any one individual will live. Insurance companies cannot make individual determinations of life expectancy; they must consider instead the life expectancy of identifiable groups. Given a sufficiently large group of people, an insurance company can predict with considerable reliability the rate and frequency of deaths within the group based on the past mortality experience of similar groups. Title VII's concern for the effect of employment practices on the individual thus is simply inapplicable to the actuarial predictions that must be made in writing insurance and annuities. . . .

C

. . . Explicit sexual classifications, to be sure, require close examination, but they are not automatically invalid. Sex-based mortality tables reflect objective actuarial experience. Because their use does not entail discrimination in any normal understanding of that term, a court should hesitate to invalidate this long-approved practice on the basis of its own policy judgment.

Congress may choose to forbid the use of any sexual classifications in insurance, but nothing suggests that it intended to do so in Title VII. And certainly the policy underlying Title VII provides no warrant for extending the reach of the statute beyond Congress' intent.

III

The District Court held that Arizona's voluntary pension plan violates Title VII and ordered that future annuity payments to female retirees be made equal to payments received by similarly situated men. The Court of Appeals for the Ninth Circuit affirmed. The Court today affirms the Court of Appeals' judgment insofar as it holds that Arizona's voluntary pension plan violates Title VII. But this finding of a statutory violation provides no basis for approving the retroactive relief awarded by the District Court. To approve this award would be both unprecedented and manifestly unjust.

We recognized in *Manhart* that retroactive relief is normally appropriate in the typical Title VII case, but concluded that the District Court had abused its discretion in awarding such relief. As we noted, the employer in *Manhart* may well have assumed that its pension program was lawful. More importantly, a retroactive remedy would have had a potentially disruptive impact on the operation of the employer's pension plan. The business of underwriting insurance and life annuities requires careful approximation of risk. Reserves normally are sufficient to cover only the cost of funding and administering the plan. Should an unforeseen contingency occur, such as a drastic change in the legal rules governing pension and insurance funds, both the insurer's solvency and the insured's benefits could be jeopardized.

This case presents no different considerations. *Manhart* did put all employer-operated pension funds on notice that they could not "requir[e] that men and women make unequal contributions to [the] fund," but it expressly confirmed that an employer could set aside equal contributions and let each retiree purchase whatever benefit his or her contributions could command on the "open market." Given this explicit limitation, an employer reasonably could have assumed that it would be lawful to make available to its employees annuities offered by insurance companies on the open market.

As in *Manhart,* holding employers liable retroactively would have devastating results. The holding applies to all employer-sponsored pension plans, and the cost of complying with the District Court's award of retroactive relief would range from $817 to $1260 million annually for the next 15 to 30 years. In this case, the cost would fall on the State of Arizona. Presumably other state and local governments also would be affected directly by today's decision. Imposing such unanticipated financial burdens would come at a time when many States and local governments are struggling to meet substantial fiscal deficits. Income, excise and property taxes are being increased. There is no justification for this Court, particularly in view of the question left open in *Manhart,* to impose this magnitude of burden retroactively on the public. Accordingly, liability should be prospective only. . . .

JUSTICE O'CONNOR, concurring.

. . . Despite JUSTICE POWELL'S argument, ultimately I am persuaded that the result in *Manhart* is not distinguishable from the present situation. . . .

. . . Title VII clearly does not allow an employer to offer a plan to employees under which it will collect equal contributions, hold them in a trust account, and upon retirement disburse greater monthly checks to men than women. Nor could an employer escape Title VII's mandate by using a third-party bank to hold and manage the account. In the situation at issue here, the employer has used third-party insurance companies to administer the plan, but the plan remains essentially a "privileg[e] of employment," and thus is covered by Title VII.

For these reasons, I join Parts I, II, and III of JUSTICE MARSHALL's opinion. Unlike JUSTICE MARSHALL, however, I would not make our holding retroactive. Rather, for reasons explained below, I agree with JUSTICE POWELL that our decision should be prospective. I therefore join Part III of JUSTICE POWELL's opinion. . . .

. . . I see no reason to believe that a retroactive holding is necesary to ensure that pension plan administrators, who may have thought until our decision today that Title VII did not extend to plans involving third-party insurers, will not now quickly conform their plans to ensure that individual employees are allowed equal monthly benefits regardless of sex. . . .

. . . A retroactive holding by this Court that employers must disburse greater annuity benefits than the collected contributions can support would jeopardize the entire pension fund. If a fund cannot meet its obligations, "[t]he harm would fall in large part on innocent third parties." This real danger of bankrupting pension funds requires that our decision be made prospective. Such a prospective holding is, of course, consistent with our equitable powers under Title VII to fashion an appropriate remedy. . . .

In my view, then, our holding should be made prospective in the following sense. I would require employers to ensure that benefits derived from contributions collected after the effective date of our judgment be calculated without regard to the sex of the employee. For contributions collected before the effective date of our judgment, however, I would allow employers and participating insurers to calculate the resulting benefits as they have in the past.

COURT ON DEATH PENALTY

July 6, 1983

In a decision that had an uncertain impact on the use of the death penalty in the United States, the Supreme Court July 6 held 5-4 that the courts could expedite the appeals process for prisoners awaiting execution. In another aspect of the same case, Barefoot v. Estelle, *the judges voted 6-3 to uphold the prosecutor's use of testimony by two psychiatrists who said the defendant might pose a danger to society if he were to remain alive.*

Federal law provides that prisoners may challenge their convictions either through direct appeal (involving filing a civil suit) or writs of habeas corpus, requesting federal courts to examine whether there was a constitutional violation of the prisoner's rights during the trial process.

In upholding the appeals court decision, Justice Byron R. White, delivering the Supreme Court majority opinion, held that while expedited procedures were "tolerable," they should not be "accepted as the norm or as the preferred procedure" and appeals courts should grant a stay of execution "where necessary to prevent the case from becoming moot by the petitioner's execution."

The decision came in the case of Thomas Andy Barefoot, who was awaiting execution in Texas for the murder of a police officer in 1978. Barefoot previously had entered a direct appeal to a state court, an appeal to the Supreme Court, habeas corpus proceedings in both a state court and a federal district court and then, when those appeals were turned down, had taken his case to the U.S. Fifth Circuit Court of

Appeals. Federal appeals courts could not accept a habeas corpus application until a U.S. district judge had issued a "certificate of probable cause" that the appeal was not frivolous. On January 20, 1983, the appeals court denied Barefoot's application for a stay of execution after hearing oral argument on the merits of his application but without dealing formally with the application itself. His execution was set for January 25. Barefoot then took his case to the Supreme Court, which January 24 agreed to hear the case.

Although there was no question that the appeals court had considered the merits of the case, it "would have been advisable" for the court to have issued a formal decision, White wrote. "It must be remembered that direct appeal is the primary avenue for review of a conviction or sentence, and death penalty cases are no exception. . . . [The] role of federal habeas corpus proceedings, while important in assuring that constitutional rights are observed, is secondary and limited. Federal courts are not forums in which to relitigate state trials. Even less is federal habeas a means by which a defendant is entitled to delay an execution indefinitely."

Previous Death Penalty Decisions

The Barefoot case was the latest in a series of Supreme Court decisions affecting the death penalty. In 1972 the Court held in Furman v. Georgia *that existing death penalty laws were unconstitutional because they were imposed arbitrarily and gave judges and juries too little guidance in deciding when to issue a death sentence. The decision voided all 631 death sentences then in effect. But many states rewrote their capital punishment laws, and sentencing began anew. (Historic Documents of 1972, p. 499)*

The Court addressed the issue again in 1976, holding that death was not always so cruel and unusual a punishment that it violated the Constitution. In the case of Gregg v. Georgia, *the Court upheld the type of capital punishment law adopted by Georgia. Under Georgia's new law, a person charged with murder was first tried to determine his innocence or guilt. Upon conviction, a sentencing hearing followed at which evidence was presented concerning any aggravating or mitigating circumstances with regard to the crime or the defendant. (Historic Documents of 1976, p. 489)*

In the 1978 case of Lockett v. Ohio, *the Court held that judges and juries charged with sentencing convicted murderers must consider any factors that might argue for a lesser punishment than death. (Historic Documents of 1978, p. 505)*

Two years later, the Court ruled in the case of Godfrey v. Georgia *that the state's courts had interpreted too broadly the Georgia capital punishment statute, which provided for imposition of the death sentence only if the crime were found beyond reasonable doubt to be "outrageously or wantonly vile, horrible or inhuman . . ."* (Historic Documents of 1980, p. 460)

In the 1982 case of Eddings v. Oklahoma, *the Court reversed the death sentence imposed on Monty Lee Eddings, who was 16 years old when he murdered an Oklahoma highway patrolman in 1977. The Court skirted the issue of whether a minor could be sentenced to death and ruled only on a procedural point, that the lower courts had not considered all mitigating factors offered by the defendant as a basis for a lesser sentence.* (Historic Documents of 1982, p. 51)

Guidelines for Federal Courts

In what was viewed as an attempt to ease some of the Supreme Court's burden in handling last-minute appeals, to expedite the appeals process in general and to tighten standards for considering habeas appeals, the majority used the Barefoot *case to propose a set of guidelines for federal courts in dealing with habeas corpus death penalty appeals:*

● *In considering whether to issue a "certificate of probable cause," judges should be careful to consider whether the appeal had merit and was not frivolous. "[T]he severity of the penalty does not in itself suffice to warrant the automatic issuing of a certificate," the Court wrote.*

● *Once a certificate of probable cause was issued, the federal court was "obligated to decide the merits of the appeal" and "should grant a stay of execution pending disposition of an appeal when a condemned prisoner obtains a certificate of probable cause on his initial habeas appeal."*

● *Courts of appeals "may adopt expedited procedures in resolving the merits of habeas appeals." However, courts should adopt rules "stating the manner in which such cases will be handled." White cautioned that "the issuance of a certificate of probable cause generally should indicate that an appeal is not legally frivolous."*

● *Appeals courts could automatically use expedited procedures on repeated habeas appeals by the same defendant.*

● *"Stays of execution are not automatic pending the filing and consideration of a petition for a writ of certiorari from this Court to the Court of Appeals that has denied a writ of habeas corpus," the majority held.*

Dissenting Views

Justices Thurgood Marshall, Harry A. Blackmun, William J. Brennan Jr., and John Paul Stevens dissented on the procedural aspect of the case. The first three justices also dissented on the decision regarding

709

admissibility of psychiatric evidence, while Stevens implicitly joined the majority by not signing the dissent. Writing for the minoity on the first point, Marshall argued, "I frankly do not understand how the Court can conclude that the Court of Appeals' treatment of this case was 'tolerable.'... The Court offers no justification for the procedure followed by the Court of Appeals because there is none. A State has no legitimate interest in executing a prisoner before he has obtained full review of his sentence.... In view of the irreversible nature of the death penalty and the extraordinary number of death sentences that have been found to suffer from some constitutional infirmity, it would be grossly improper for a court of appeals to establish special summary procedures for capital cases."

The procedural decision also was criticized by The New York Times, *which editorialized July 8, 1983, that "the Court approved procedures barely fit for protecting debtors against unlawful repossession of a car."*

On the question of psychiatric evidence, Blackmun, joined by Brennan and Marshall, noted that the two psychiatrists who testified during the Barefoot *trial had not actually examined the defendant or requested the opportunity to examine him but had testified on the likelihood that Barefoot would pose a future danger to society. The justices pointed out that the American Psychiatric Association (APA), participating in the case as* amicus curiae *(friend of the court), had stated that the "unreliability of psychiatric predictions of long-term future dangerousness is by now an established fact within the profession." The justices concluded, "Neither the Court nor the State of Texas has cited a single reputable scientific source contradicting the unanimous conclusion of professionals in this field that psychiatric predictions of long-term future violence are wrong more often than they are right." (APA statement, p. 25)*

Related Cases, Impact of Barefoot Decision

In two other decisions, also handed down July 6, the Court came out in support of the death penalty. In the case of California v. Ramos, *the Court ruled 5-4 (with Justices Marshall, Brennan, Blackmun and Stevens dissenting) that a California law was constitutional in allowing judges to inform juries that defendants in capital cases could have their sentences commuted by the governor if given life in prison.*

In the case of Barclay v. Florida, *the Court ruled 6-3 (with Justices Marshall, Brennan and Blackmun dissenting) that a Florida judge had not acted properly when he allowed personal recollections of Nazi atrocities to influence his decision to impose a death sentence in a murder case with racial overtones. The judge had overruled a jury recommendation of life in prison.*

Some observers said the Barefoot *and related decisions probably would bring about quicker executions for a few of the more than 1,000 prisoners on death row in mid-1983. But the expedited approach allowed by the* Barefoot *decision probably would not be applied beyond the Fifth Circuit Court of Appeals, according to Joel Berger of the Legal Defense and Education Fund in New York and other experts. The principal effect might be to reinforce existing American attitudes supporting executions, said Henry Schwarzchild of the American Civil Liberties Union.*

Public support for death sentences had almost doubled between the mid-1960s and 1983, according to polling by Louis Harris and Associates. In 1965 only 38 percent of the people who responded to a Harris Survey favored capital punishment. Forty-seven percent were opposed. By 1983, 68 percent were for it and 27 percent opposed.

While Schwarzchild did not expect a "tidal wave" of executions across the country, he said he "would not be surprised if we had 10 or 20 or 30" a year for several years. He predicted it would take a generation and a significant reduction in the crime rate before Americans again turned against the death penalty. The 1983 Supreme Court decisions on the death penalty seemed to reflect public sentiment that death sentences ought to be carried out. They "expressed the sense of frustration with delays, gave vent to the impatience of the public," Schwarzchild said.

> *Following are excerpts from the Supreme Court's July 6 ruling in* Barefoot v. Estelle *upholding a circuit court's refusal to grant a stay of execution, rejecting the defendant's argument that psychiatric testimony was not admissible and setting forth procedural guidelines for handling applications for stays of execution on habeas corpus appeals, and from the dissenting opinions of Justices Thurgood Marshall and Harry A. Blackmun:*

<u>No. 82-6080</u>

Thomas A. Barefoot, Petitioner
v.
W. J. Estelle Jr., Director,
Texas Department of Corrections

On writ of Certiorari to the United States Fifth Circuit Court of Appeals

[July 6, 1983]

JUSTICE WHITE delivered the opinion of the Court.

We have two questions before us in this case: whether the District Court erred on the merits in rejecting the petition for habeas corpus filed by the petitioner, and whether the Court of Appeals for the Fifth Circuit correctly denied a stay of execution for the death penalty pending appeal of the District Court's judgment. . . .

[Section I omitted]

II

With respect to the procedures followed by the Court of Appeals in refusing to stay petitioner's death sentence, it must be remembered that direct appeal is the primary avenue for review of a conviction or sentence, and death penalty cases are no exception. When the process of direct review — which, if a federal question is involved, includes the right to petition this Court for a writ of certiorari — comes to an end, a presumption of finality and legality attaches to the conviction and sentence. The role of federal habeas proceedings, while important in assuring that constitutional rights are observed, is secondary and limited. Federal courts are not forums in which to relitigate state trials. Even less is federal habeas a means by which a defendant is entitled to delay an execution indefinitely. The procedures adopted to facilitate the orderly consideration and disposition of habeas petitions are not legal entitlements that a defendant has a right to pursue irrespective of the contribution these procedures make toward uncovering constitutional error.... Furthermore, unlike a term of years, a death sentence cannot begin to be carried out by the State while substantial legal issues remain outstanding. Accordingly, federal courts must isolate the exceptional cases where constitutional error requires retrial or resentencing as certainly and swiftly as orderly procedures will permit. They need not, and should not, however, fail to give non-frivolous claims of constitutional error the careful attention that they deserve....

A

Petitioner urges that the Court of Appeals improperly denied a stay of execution while failing to act finally on his appeal. He suggests the possibility of remanding the case to the Court of Appeals without reaching the merits of the District Court's judgment. The heart of petitioner's submission is that the Court of Appeals, unless it believes the case to be entirely frivolous, was obligated to decide the appeal on its merits in the usual course and must, in a death case, stay the execution pending such disposition. The State responds that the Court of Appeals reached and decided the merits of the issues presented in the course of denying the stay and that petitioner had ample opportunity to address the merits.

We have previously held that "[i]f an appellant persuades an appropriate tribunal that probable cause for an appeal exists, he must then be afforded an opportunity to address the underlying merits.".... These decisions indicate that if a court of appeals is unable to resolve the merits of an appeal before the scheduled date of execution, the petitioner is entitled to a stay of execution to permit due consideration of the merits. But we have also held that the requirement of a decision on the merits "does not prevent the courts of appeals from adopting appropriate summary procedures for final disposition of such cases."... We emphasized that there must be ample evidence that in disposing of the appeal, the merits have been addressed, but that nothing in the cases or the applicable rules prevents a Court of Appeals from adopting summary procedures in such cases....

It appears clear that the Court of Appeals ... was fully aware of our precedents and that their requirements were fully satisfied....

The course pursued by the Court of Appeals in this case was within the bounds of our prior decisions. In connection with acting on the stay, the parties were directed to file briefs and to present oral argument. In light of the Fifth Circuit's announced practice ... it was clear that whether a stay would be granted depended on the probability of success on the merits. The parties addressed the merits and were given unlimited time to present argument. We do not agree that petitioner and his attorneys were prejudiced in their preparation of the appeal. The primary issue presented had been briefed and argued throughout the proceedings in the state courts and rebriefed and reargued in the District Court's habeas corpus proceeding. From the time the District Court ruled on the petition on November 9, 1982, petitioner had 71 days in which to prepare the briefs and arguments which were presented to the Fifth Circuit on January 19, 1983.

Although the Court of Appeals did not formally affirm the judgment of the District Court, there is no question that the Court of Appeals ruled on the merits of the appeal, as its concluding statements demonstrate....

Although the Court of Appeals moved swiftly to decide the stay, this does not mean that its treatment of the merits was cursory or inadequate. On the contrary, the court's resolution of the primary issue on appeal, the admission of psychiatric testimony on dangerousness, reflects careful consideration. For these reasons, to remand to the Court of Appeals for verification that the judgment of the District Court is affirmed would be an unwarranted exaltation of form over substance.

B

That the Court of Appeals' handling of this case was tolerable under our precedents is not to suggest that its course should be accepted as the norm or as the preferred procedure. It is a matter of public record that an increasing number of death-sentenced petitioners are entering the appellate stages of the federal habeas process. The fair and efficient consideration of these appeals requires proper procedures for the handling of applications for stays of executions and demands procedures that allow a decision on the merits of an appeal accompanying the denial of a stay. The development of these procedures is primarily a function of the courts of appeals and the rulemaking processes of the federal courts, but the following general guidelines can be set forth.

First. Congress established the requirement that a prisoner obtain a certificate of probable cause to appeal in order to prevent frivolous appeals from delaying the States' ability to impose sentences, including death sentences. The primary means of separating meritorious from frivolous appeals should be the decision to grant or withhold a certificate of probable cause.... In a capital case, the nature of the penalty is a proper consideration in determining whether to issue a certificate of probable cause, but the severity of the penalty does not in itself suffice to warrant the automatic issuing of a certificate.

Second. When a certificate of probable cause is issued by the district court, as it was in this case, or later by the court of appeals, petitioner must then be afforded an opportunity to address the merits, and the court of appeals is obligated to decide the merits of the appeal. Accordingly, a circuit court, where necessary to prevent the case from becoming moot by the petitioner's execution, should grant a stay of execution pending disposition of an appeal when a condemned prisoner obtains a certificate of probable cause on his initial habeas appeal.

Third. As our earlier cases have indicated, a court of appeals may adopt expedited procedures in resolving the merits of habeas appeals, notwithstanding the issuance of a certificate of probable cause. If a circuit chooses to follow this course, it would be advisable to promulgate a local rule stating the manner in which such cases will be handled and informing counsel that the merits of an appeal may be decided upon the motion for a stay. Even without special procedures, it is entirely appropriate that an appeal which is "frivolous and entirely without merit" be dismissed after the hearing on a motion for a stay.... We caution that the issuance of a certificate of probable cause generally should indicate that an appeal is not legally frivolous, and that a court of appeals should be confident that petitioner's claim is squarely foreclosed by statute, rule or authoritative court decision, or is lacking any factual basis in the record of the case, before dismissing it as frivolous.

If an appeal is not frivolous, a court of appeals may still choose to expedite briefing and hearing the merits of all or of selected cases in which a stay of a death sentence has been requested, provided that counsel has adequate opportunity to address the merits and knows that he is expected to do so....

Fourth. Second and successive federal habeas corpus petitions present a different issue. "To the extent that these involve the danger that a condemned inmate might attempt to use repeated petitions and appeals as a mere delaying tactic, the State has a quite legitimate interest in preventing such abuses of the writ."... The granting of a stay should reflect the presence of substantial grounds upon which relief might be granted.

Fifth. Stays of execution are not automatic pending the filing and consideration of a petition for a writ of certiorari from this Court to the Court of Appeals that has denied a writ of habeas corpus. It is well-established that there " 'must be a reasonable probability that four members of the Court would consider the underlying issue sufficiently meritorious for the grant of certiorari or the notation of probable jurisdiction; there must be a significant possibility of reversal of the lower court's decision; and there must be a likelihood that irreparable harm will result if that decision is not stayed.' ''...

III

Petitioner's merits submission is that his death sentence must be set aside because the Constitution of the United States barred the testimony of the two psychiatrists who testified against him at the punishment hearing. There are several aspects to this claim. First, it is urged that psychiatrists, individually and as a group, are incompetent to predict with an acceptable degree of reliability that a particular criminal will commit other crimes in the future and so represent a danger to the community. Second, it is said that in any event, psychiatrists should not be permitted to testify about future dangerousness in response to hypothetical questions and without having examined the defendant personally. Third, it is argued that in the particular circumstances of this case, the testimony of the psychiatrists was so unreliable that the sentence should be set aside. As indicated below, we reject each of these arguments.

A

The suggestion that no psychiatrist's testimony may be presented with respect to a defendant's future dangerousness is somewhat like asking us to disinvent the wheel. In the first place, it is contrary to our cases. If the likelihood of a defendant committing further crimes is a constitutionally acceptable criterion for imposing the death penalty, which it is, *Jurek* v. *Texas* (1976), and if it is not impossible for even a lay person sensibly to arrive at that conclusion, it makes little sense, if any, to submit that psychiatrists, out of the entire universe of persons who might have an opinion on the issue, would know so little about the subject that they should not be permitted to testify....

Acceptance of petitioner's position that expert testimony about future dangerousness is far too unreliable to be admissible would immediately call into question those other contexts in which predictions of future behavior are constantly made....

In the second place, the rules of evidence generally extant at the federal and state levels anticipate that relevant, unprivileged evidence should be admitted and its weight left to the fact finder, who would have the benefit of cross examination and contrary evidence by the opposing party. Psychiatric testimony predicting dangerousness may be countered not only as erroneous in a particular case but as generally so unreliable that it should be ignored. If the jury may make up its mind about future dangerousness unaided by psychiatric testimony, jurors should not be barred from hearing the views of the State's psychiatrists along with opposing views of the defendant's doctors....

... We are unconvinced ... at least as of now, that the adversary process cannot be trusted to sort out the reliable from the unreliable evidence and opinion about future dangerousness, particularly when the convicted felon has the opportunity to present his own side of the case. . . .

B

Whatever the decision may be about the use of psychiatric testimony, in general, on the issue of future dangerousness, petitioner urges that such testimony must be based on personal examination of the defendant and may not be given in response to hypothetical questions. We disagree. Expert testimony, whether in the form of an opinion based on hypothetical questions or otherwise, is commonly admitted as evidence where it might help the factfinder do its assigned job. . . .

Today, in the federal system, Federal Rules of Evidence . . . provide for the testimony of experts. The advisory committee notes touch on the particular objections to hypothetical questions, but none of these caveats lends any support to petitioner's constitutional arguments. Furthermore, the Texas Court of Criminal Appeals could find no fault with the mode of examining the two psychiatrists under Texas law. . . .

Like the Court of Criminal Appeals, the District Court, and the Court of Appeals, we reject petitioner's constitutional arguments against the use of hypothetical questions. Although cases such as this involve the death penalty, we perceive no constitutional barrier to applying the ordinary rules of evidence governing the use of expert testimony.

C

As we understand petitioner, he contends that even if the use of hypothetical questions in predicting future dangerousness is acceptable as a general rule, the use made of them in his case violated his right to due process of law. For example, petitioner insists that the doctors should not have been permitted to give an opinion on the ultimate issue before the jury, particularly when the hypothetical questions were phrased in terms of petitioner's own conduct; that the hypothetical questions referred to controverted facts; and that the answers to the questions were so positive as to be assertions of fact and not opinion. These claims of misuse of the hypothetical questions, as well as others, were rejected by the Texas courts, and neither the District Court nor the Court of Appeals found any constitutional infirmity in the application of the Texas Rules of Evidence in this particular case. We agree.

IV

In sum, we affirm the judgment of the District Court. There is no doubt that the psychiatric testimony increased the likelihood that petitioner would be sentenced to death, but this fact does not make that evidence inadmissable, any more than it would with respect to other relevant evidence against any defendant in a criminal case. . . .

The judgment of the District Court is

Affirmed.

JUSTICE MARSHALL, with whom JUSTICE BRENNAN joins, dissenting.

I cannot subscribe to the Court's conclusion that the procedure followed by the Court of Appeals in this case was "not inconsistent with our cases." Nor can I accept the notion that it would be proper for a court of appeals to adopt special "summary procedures" for capital cases. On the merits, I would vacate petitioner's death sentence.

I

I wholeheartedly agree that when a State prisoner has obtained a certificate of probable cause to appeal from the denial of a petition for a writ of habeas corpus, he "must then be afforded an opportunity to address the merits, and the court of appeals is obligated to decide the merits of the appeal." A prisoner who has made the showing necessary to obtain a certificate of probable cause has satisfied the only condition that Congress has placed on the right to appeal in habeas corpus cases. We have repeatedly held that once a certificate of probable cause has been granted, an appeal must be "duly considered" and "disposed of on the merits" by the court of appeals "in accord with its ordinary procedure." I likewise agree that "[a]pproving the execution of a defendant before his appeal is decided on the merits would clearly be improper," and that "a circuit court, where necessary to prevent the case from becoming moot by the petitioner's execution, should grant a stay of execution pending disposition of [his] appeal." A prisoner's right to appeal would be meaningless if the State were allowed to execute him before his appeal could be considered and decided. . . .

II

Given the Court's acceptance of these basic principles, I frankly do not understand how the Court can conclude that the Court of Appeals' treatment of this case was "tolerable." If, as the Court says, the Court of Appeals was "obligated to decide the merits of the appeal," it most definitely failed to discharge that obligation, for the court never ruled on petitioner's appeal. It is simply false to say that "the Court of Appeals ruled on the merits of the appeal." The record plainly shows that the Court of Appeals did no such thing. It neither dismissed the appeal as frivolous nor affirmed the judgment of the District Court. The Court of Appeals made one ruling and one ruling only: it refused to stay petitioner's execution. Had this Court not granted a stay, petitioner would have been put to death without his appeal ever having been decided one way or the other.

The Court is flatly wrong in suggesting that any defect was merely technical because the Court of Appeals could have "verif[ied] the obvious by expressly affirming the judgment of the District Court" at the same time it denied a stay. The Court of Appeals' failure to decide petitioner's appeal was no oversight. The court simply had no authority to decide the appeal on the basis of the papers before it. . . . Neither the Federal Rules of Appellate Procedure, nor the local rules of the Fifth Circuit, nor any decision of the Fifth Circuit, would have authorized an affirmance prior to the filing of briefs on the merits.

Nor could the Court of Appeals have dismissed petitioner's appeal as frivolous . . . for the simple reason . . . that it was *not* frivolous.

The Court offers no justification for the procedure followed by the Court of Appeals because there is none. A State has no legitimate interest in executing a prisoner before he has obtained full review of his sentence. A stay of execution pending appeal causes no harm to the State apart from the minimal burden of providing a jail cell for the prisoner for the period of time necessary to decide his appeal. By contrast, a denial of a stay on the basis of a hasty finding that the prisoner is not likely to succeed on his appeal permits the State to execute him prior to full review of a concededly substantial constitutional challenge to his sentence. If the court's hurried evaluation of the appeal proves erroneous, as is entirely possible when difficult legal issues are decided without adequate time for briefing and full consideration, the execution of the prisoner will make it impossible to undo the mistake.

Once a federal judge has decided, as the district judge did here, that a prisoner under sentence of death has raised a substantial constitutional claim, it is a travesty of justice to permit the State to execute him before his appeal can be considered and decided. If a prisoner's statutory right to appeal means anything, a State simply cannot be allowed to kill him and thereby moot his appeal.

III

Not content with approving the precipitous procedure followed in this case, the Court also proceeds to suggest in Part II-B of its opinion that a court of appeals might properly adopt special "summary procedures" for "all or . . . selected cases in which a stay of a death sentence has been requested."

It is important to bear in mind that the Court's suggestion is directed at cases in which a certificate of probable cause to appeal has been granted *and* the court of appeals has concluded that the appeal is not frivolous. If the prisoner had been sentenced to any punishment other than death, his appeal would therefore have been considered and decided in accord with the court of appeals' ordinary procedure. But since he has been sentenced to death, and since his scheduled date of execution is imminent, his appeal is to be decided under special truncated procedures. In short, an appeal that raises a substantial constitutional question is to be singled out for summary treatment *solely because the State has announced its intention to execute the appellant before the ordinary appellate procedure has run its course.*

This is truly a perverse suggestion. If full briefing and argument are generally regarded as necessary to fair and careful review of a nonfrivolous appeal — and they are — there is absolutely no justification for providing fewer procedural protections solely because a man's life is at stake. Given the irreversible nature of the death penalty, it would be hard to think of any class of cases for which summary procedures would be less appropriate than capital cases presenting a substantial constitutional issue....

If ... the Court's approval of summary procedures rests on an assumption that appeals by prisoners under sentence of death are generally frivolous, the conclusive answer is that this assumption is contrary to both law and fact.

It is contrary to law because we are dealing here with cases in which the federal judge most familiar with the case has concluded that a substantial constitutional claim is presented and in which the court of appeals has agreed that the appeal is not frivolous. It is contrary to fact because experience shows that prisoners on death row have succeeded in an extraordinary number of their appeals. Of the 34 capital cases decided on the merits by courts of appeals since 1976 in which a prisoner appealed from the denial of habeas relief, the prisoner has prevailed in no fewer than 23 cases, or approximately 70% of the time.... This record establishes beyond any doubt that a very large proportion of federal habeas corpus appeals by prisoners on death row are meritorious, even though they present claims that have been unsuccessful in the state courts, that this Court in its discretion has decided not to review on certiorari, and that a federal district judge has rejected.

In view of the irreversible nature of the death penalty and the extraordinary number of death sentences that have been found to suffer from some constitutional infirmity, it would be grossly improper for a court of appeals to establish special summary procedures for capital cases....

IV

Adhering to my view that the death penalty is under all circumstances cruel and unusual punishment prohibited by the Eighteenth and Fourteenth Amendments ... I would vacate petitioner's death sentence.

JUSTICE BLACKMUN, with whom JUSTICE BRENNAN and JUSTICE MARSHALL join in Parts I-IV, dissenting.

I agree with most of what JUSTICE MARSHALL has said in his dissenting opinion. I, too, dissent, but I base my conclusion also on evidentiary factors that the Court rejects with some emphasis. The Court holds that psychiatric testimony about a defendant's future dangerousness is admissible, despite the fact that such testimony is wrong two times out of three. The Court reaches this result — even in a capital case — because, it is said, the testimony is subject to cross examination and impeachment. In the present state of psychiatric knowledge, this is too much for me. One may accept this in a routine lawsuit for money damages, but when a person's life is at stake — no matter how heinous his offense — a requirement of greater reliability should prevail. In a capital case, the specious testimony of a psychiatrist, colored in the eyes of an impressionable jury by the inevitable untouchability of a medical specialist's words, equates with death itself.

I

To obtain a death sentence in Texas, the State is required to prove beyond a reasonable doubt that "there is a probability that the defendant would commit criminal acts of violence that would constitute a continuing threat to society." As a practical matter, this prediction of future dangerousness was the only issue to be decided by Barefoot's sentencing jury.

At the sentencing hearing, the State established that Barefoot had two prior convictions for unlawful possession of firearms. None of these convictions involved acts of violence. At the guilt stage of the trial, for the limited purpose of establishing that the crime was committed in order to evade police custody . . . the State had presented evidence that Barefoot had escaped from jail in New Mexico where he was being held on charges of statutory rape and unlawful restraint of a minor child with intent to commit sexual penetration against the child's will. The prosecution also called several character witnesses at the sentencing hearing, from towns in five States. Without mentioning particular examples of Barefoot's conduct, these witnesses testified that Barefoot's reputation for being a peaceable and law abiding citizen was bad in their respective communities.

Last, the prosecution called Doctors Holbrook and Grigson, whose testimony extended over more than half the hearing. Neither had examined Barefoot or requested the opportunity to examine him. In the presence of the jury, and over defense counsel's objection, each was qualified as an expert psychiatrist witness. . . .

II

A

The American Psychiatric Association (APA), participating in this case as *amicus curiae*, informs us that "[t]he unreliability of psychiatric predictions of long-term future dangerousness is by now an established fact with the profession." The APA's best estimate is that *two out of three* predictions of long-term future violence made by psychiatrists are wrong. The Court does not dispute this proposition, and indeed it could not do so; the evidence is overwhelming. . . . Neither the Court nor the State of Texas has cited a single reputable scientific source contradicting the unanimous conclusion of professionals in this field that psychiatric predictions of long-term future violence are wrong more often than they are right....

B

It is impossible to square admission of this purportedly scientific but actually baseless testimony with the Constitution's paramount concern for reliability in capital sentencing. Death is a permissible punishment in Texas only if the jury finds beyond a reasonable doubt that there is a probability the defendant will commit future acts of criminal violence. The admission of unreliable psychiatric predictions of future violence, offered with unabashed claims of "reasonable medical certainty" or "absolute" professional reliability, creates an intolerable danger that death sentences will be imposed erroneously....

Indeed, unreliable scientific evidence is widely acknowledged to be prejudicial. The reasons for this are manifest. "The major danger of scientific evidence is its potential to mislead the jury; an aura of scientific infallibility may shroud the evidence and thus lead the jury to accept it without critical scrutiny."... Where the public holds an exaggerated opinion of the accuracy of scientific testimony, the prejudice is likely to be indelible.... There is little question that psychiatrists are perceived by the public as having a special expertise to predict dangerousness, a perception based on psychiatrists' study of mental disease.... It is this perception that the State in Barefoot's case sought to exploit. Yet mental disease is not correlated with violence ... and the stark fact is that no such expertise exists....

Psychiatric predictions of future dangerousness *are not accurate;* wrong two times out of three, their probative value, and therefore any possible contribution they might make to the ascertainment of truth, is virtually nonexistent....

...Surely, this Court's commitment to ensuring that death sentences are imposed reliably and reasonably requires that nonprobative and highly prejudicial testimony on the ultimate question of life or death be excluded from a capital sentencing hearing.

III

A

Despite its recognition that the testimony at issue was probably wrong and certainly prejudicial, the Court holds this testimony admissible because the Court is "unconvinced ... that the adversary process cannot be trusted to sort out the reliable from the unreliable evidence and opinion about future dangerousness." One can only wonder how juries are to separate valid from invalid expert opinions when the 'experts' themselves are so obviously unable to do so. Indeed, the evidence suggests that juries are not effective at assessing the validity of scientific evidence.

There can be no question that psychiatric predictions of future violence will have an undue effect on the ultimate verdict. Even judges tend to accept psychiatrists' recommendations about a defendant's dangerousness with little regard for cross-examination or other testimony.... There is every reason to believe that inexperienced jurors will be still less capable of "separat[ing] the wheat from the chaff," despite the Court's blithe assumption to the contrary. The American Bar Association has warned repeatedly that sentencing juries are particularly incapable of dealing with information relating to "the likelihood that the defendant will commit other crimes," and similar predictive judgments....

B

The Constitution's mandate of reliability, with the stakes at life or death, precludes reliance on cross-examination and the opportunity to present rebuttal witnesses as an antidote for this distortion of the truth-finding process. Cross examination is unlikely to reveal the fatuousness of psychiatric predictions because such predictions often rest, as was the case here, on psychiatric categories and intuitive clinical judgments not susceptible to cross-examination and rebuttal. Psychiatric categories have little or no demonstrated relationship to violence, and their use often obscures the unimpressive statistical or intuitive bases for prediction....

Nor is the presentation of psychiatric witnesses on behalf of the defense likely to remove the prejudicial taint of misleading testimony by prosecution psychiatrists. No reputable expert would be able to predict with confidence that the defendant will *not* be violent; at best, the witness will be able to give his opinion that all predictions of dangerousness are unreliable. Consequently, the jury will not be presented with the traditional battle of experts with opposing views on the ultimate question. Given a choice between an expert who says that he can predict with certainty that the defendant, whether confined in prison or free in society, will kill again, and an expert who says merely that no such prediction can be made, members of the jury charged by law with making the prediction surely will be tempted to opt for the expert who claims he can help them in performing their duty, and who predicts dire consequences if the defendant is not put to death....

One searches the Court's opinion in vain for a plausible justification for tolerating the State's creation of this risk of an erroneous death verdict.... Ultimately, when the Court knows full well that psychiatrists' predictions of dangerousness are specious, there can be no excuse for imposing on the defendant, on pain of his life, the heavy burden of convincing a jury of laymen of the fraud....

Our constitutional duty is to ensure that the State proves future dangerousness, if at all, in a reliable manner, one that ensures that "any decision to impose the death sentence be, and appear to be, based on reason rather than caprice or emotion." Texas' choice of substantive factors does not justify loading the factfinding process against the defendant through the presentation of what is, at bottom, false testimony.

V

I would vacate petitioner's death sentence, and remand for further proceedings consistent with these views.

ETHICS COMMITTEE REPORT, HOUSE MEMBERS' CENSURE

July 14, 1983

In a dramatic move, the House of Representatives voted overwhelmingly to censure two of its members, Daniel B. Crane, R-Ill., and Gerry E. Studds, D-Mass., for sexual misconduct with teenage congressional pages. The action, which came after the ethics committee's July 14 report, marked the first time that a member ever had been censured for sexual misconduct and the first time since 1980 the House had censured one of its members. Prior to the July action, the House had instituted censure proceedings 33 times, resulting in the censure of 21 members.

The penalty associated with either a reprimand or censure is public condemnation. A censured member, however, must also appear in the well of the House to hear the charges read against him or her. In addition, under the rules of the House Democratic Caucus, a censured Democrat loses any chairmanship of a committee or subcommittee that he or she holds.

In voting on July 20 to censure the two representatives, the House overturned a recommendation by its ethics committee, the Committee on Standards of Official Conduct, which had called for a reprimand. A reprimand was the least severe form of punishment the House could impose. The ethics committee reported that both Crane and Studds had sexual relationships with teenage pages, and had thus committed a "serious breach of the duty owed by the House and its individual members to the young people who serve the House as its pages." But the panel said, "discovery of improprieties by a few should not be allowed unjustly to sully the reputations of their colleagues...."

Several members, though, felt a reprimand was too mild. Newt Ging-rich, R-Ga., said, "With no malice toward any individual, I cannot see how a reprimand is in any way adequate." Gingrich wanted the two expelled.

Floor Debate on Censure

The mood on the House floor was somber, and many members ex-pressed appreciation to the ethics committee for performing a function members would rather not do. Minority Leader Robert H. Michel, R-Ill., called the position "the most distasteful job in the House." When ethics Chairman Louis Stokes, D-Ohio, sat down after his final remarks, he received a standing ovation.

Those who felt Studds and Crane deserved only a reprimand insisted that the punishment was indeed severe. "The member must live with this condemnation forever," said Stokes.

Floyd Spence, R-S.C., ranking Republican on ethics, said, "The public disclosure of the facts of these cases has already placed an indelible stain on the reputations of these members."

But Gingrich insisted, "Our focus should not be on what [Crane and Studds] are going through and what has happened to them." Rather, Gingrich said, "Our decisions are made today about the integrity of freedom, about belief in our leaders, about the future of this country, about what we should become."

Before the vote on the ethics committee's recommendations, Michel moved to change the recommendation of reprimand to censure. Michel said he sensed that members wanted a more severe form of punishment.

Michel's motion in Crane's case (H Res 266) was adopted 289-136. The censure resolution was then agreed to by a 421-3 vote.

In Studds' case (H Res 265), Michel's motion was adopted 338-87, and the House voted to censure Studds by a 420-3 vote.

Crane voted for his own censure. Studds voted present when the House voted on his censure.

Crane, who admitted to having a sexual relationship with a 17-year-old female page, approached the well of the House, then faced his silent colleagues as Speaker Thomas P. O'Neill Jr., D-Mass., read the resolu-tion of censure to him. Studds, who the ethics committee found had a sexual relationship with a male page, faced the Speaker, hands clasped behind him, as O'Neill read his resolution of censure.

Ethics Committee Investigation

The House's action was the result of a year-long investigation by the ethics committee, led by special counsel Joseph A. Califano Jr., who was secretary of health, education and welfare during Jimmy Carter's administration.

Even while the ethics committee investigation was going on, Congress was quietly overhauling the page system, from how pages were appointed to how they were housed and educated. Most of the changes occurred in the House, which employed about 70 pages during the academic year, compared with about 30 Senate pages. More were hired during the summer.

The House was quicker to act because allegations of misconduct touched its members. During the Califano investigation, though, the committee heard allegations of drug use involving Senate employees.

In its report released July 14, the panel found that Studds in 1973 had a sexual relationship with a 17-year-old male page, who might have been 16 at the time the relationship began. In addition, the panel said Studds made sexual advances on two other male pages in 1973.

Crane, the panel said, had a sexual relationship with a 17-year-old female page in 1980. Since the legal age of consent in the District of Columbia is 16, the panel accused neither Studds nor Crane with a crime. Nevertheless, the panel felt that any sexual relationship, consensual or not, between a member and a page constituted improper sexual conduct.

In addition, the panel voted July 14 to initiate disciplinary proceedings against James Howarth, former majority chief page in the House Doorkeeper's Office. According to the report, Howarth had a sexual relationship in 1980 with a female page under his direct supervision, and he gave that page preferential treatment. The report also charged Howarth with purchasing cocaine in the House cloakroom from Robert Yesh, a former House employee.

In choosing an appropriate penalty for Crane and Studds, Califano cited as precedents the two most recent cases of censure and expulsion. In 1980 the House censured Charles H. Wilson, D-Calif. (1963-81) for bribery. The same year, the House expelled Michael "Ozzie" Myers, D-Pa., (1976-80), who was convicted on Abscam bribery charges. Califano concluded, "Measured against the precedents, neither expulsion nor censure is warranted." Califano added, though, "The institutional integrity of the House of Representatives requires that the House itself act." He recommended a reprimand, and the committee agreed by an 11-1 vote. (Wilson censure, Historic Documents of 1980, p. 485; Myers expulsion, p. 899)

But for some members, this was not enough. "I want to change the precedent," Gingrich said. "The precedent is ridiculous." He said if Studds or Crane were a teacher or police officer, he would be fired.

Supporting Gingrich, Chalmers P. Wylie, R-Ohio, said July 18 he would support a stiffer penalty unless both members resigned.

Without mentioning Wylie's suggestion, Studds announced July 19 he would stay in the House. "I look forward," he said, "to concentrating all my energies once again on the job my constituents expect me — and elected me — to do."

Page Scandal Background

The ethics probe came after published allegations of widespread sexual misconduct and drug use by members and pages during the period July 1981 to June 1982. In a preliminary report issued in December 1982, Califano found the charges groundless, although he did learn of misconduct before that period, and he continued his investigation. (Historic Documents of 1982, p. 729)

Referring to the charges that set off the investigation, Califano said most of the "allegations and rumors of misconduct were the product of teenage exaggeration, gossip, or even out-and-out fabrication that was often repeated mercilessly in a political capital that thrives on rumor."

On June 30 and July 1, 1982, CBS television aired news reports quoting former pages who said that pages had been the victims of sexual misconduct on the part of House members. Later news reports identified the accusers as Leroy Williams, 18, of Arkansas, and Jeffrey Opp, 16, of Colorado. Both later admitted that they had lied.

On July 13, 1982, the House authorized the ethics committee to investigate the charges, which eventually led to the censures. At the same time, the Justice Department began an investigation, only to close it August 31, 1982, when it was unable to corroborate Williams' allegations.

Page System Reforms

The House also decided, for the third time in 20 years, to undertake an extensive examination of the page system.

Speaker O'Neill set up a special commission to look at the page system. It recommended that the system be retained, but improved.

The commission rejected proposals to use college students and senior citizens as pages. It said pages should be 11th graders who were at least 16 years old and who would serve for only one semester. To monitor the program, the commission recommended the creation of a Page Board, which was created November 30. (The Senate Rules and Administration Committee July 22, 1983, approved a measure to establish a joint House-Senate page board.)

In addition, the House converted two floors of an office building to be used as a page dormitory. House pages were required to live in the residence hall; Senate pages could live there if space was available. The residence hall was staffed by a director and five resident assistants. There was a nightly curfew.

Joseph G. Minish, D-N.J., who chaired the Page Board, felt the changes made in 1982 and 1983 had "alleviated a great deal of the concern" members had about the system. Vic Fazio, D-Calif., a member of the Page Board and the ethics committee, said, "I don't think there is ever any foolproof way" to avoid problems, but added, "We will continue to do what we can to make the program more safe."

The changes were not enough to satisfy Gingrich, who felt that the system remained open to abuse. "If we do not expel Studds," Gingrich said July 19, "I would abolish the page system." Bill Frenzel, R-Minn., ranking Republican of the House Administration Committee, won a round of applause during the House debate on the Crane censure resolution by proposing to scrap the page system. "We are not and cannot be real parents," Frenzel said, adding that page duties should be taken over by regular employees.

Following are excerpts from the July 14, 1983, final report of the Special Counsel to the House Committee on Standards of Official Conduct into allegations of improper or illegal sexual conduct on the part of House members:

I. Introduction and Summary
A. BACKGROUND OF THE INVESTIGATION

On July 13, 1982, the House of Representatives, by a 407 to 1 vote, passed House Resolution 518, which authorized and directed the Committee on Standards of Official Conduct to "conduct a full and complete inquiry and investigation" into allegations of:

(1) improper or illegal sexual conduct by Members, officers, or employees of the House:

(2) illicit use or distribution of drugs by Members, officers, or employees of the House; and

(3) the offering of preferential treatment by Members, officers or employees of the House in exchange for sexual favors or drugs.

H. Res. 518, 97th Cong., 2d Sess. (1982).

On July 27, 1982, the Committee retained Joseph A. Califano, Jr., as independent Special Counsel to conduct the investigation. At the time of Mr. Califano's appointment as Special Counsel, Committee Chairman Louis Stokes stated that "his charge is clear and straightforward — to conduct the investigation that in his judgment is required and to advise the Committee of his findings and recommendations."

The Speaker, the Majority Leader, and the Minority Leader of the House joined Chairman Stokes and the Committee's Ranking Minority Member, Floyd Spence, in assuring the Special Counsel that he would have the independence and resources to conduct a full and impartial investigation — "whatever investigation is necessary to ascertain the truth about the allegations that have been made." On January 3, 1983, the House agreed to House Resolution 12, 98th Cong., 1st Sess., which authorized and directed the Committee to continue and complete the investigation begun pursuant to H. Res. 518.

This is the final report of the Special Counsel concerning allegations of improper or illegal sexual conduct. This report, together with the Special Counsel's Interim Report of December 14, 1982 ... details the complete results of the investigation into allegations of sexual misconduct. It responds to the Chairman's charge that the Special Counsel report to the Committee on his findings and recommendations. This report sets out (1) the investigative work completed with respect to allegations involving sexual misconduct. (2) the findings and conclusions of the Special Counsel regarding this work, and (3) the recommendations of the Special Counsel on actions the Committee should take.

The Special Counsel recommends that the Committee make this report public.

Pursuant to H. Res. 518 and H. Res. 12, the Special Counsel has sought to determine whether there is any responsible evidence of improper or illegal sexual conduct by Members, officers, or employees of the House of Representatives involving congressional pages. The focus of the investigation has been on the period from July 1981, through June 1982. To assure completeness, however, the Special Counsel sought to contact every page employed by the House of Representatives over the three year period from September 1979 to August 1982. The Special Counsel also investigated allegations of illegal or improper sexual conduct involving pages occurring before this time period which were brought to his attention.

The investigation carried out by the Special Counsel and this Committee sought out hundreds of past and present congressional pages, dozens of individuals who supervised and taught those pages, hundreds of congressional staff members, and many other individuals with knowledge of the page system. In all, the Special Counsel's office has conducted some 700 interviews, taken more than 125 depositions covering more than 6,000 transcript pages, tried to contact every House page who served since September 1979 and dozens who served earlier, travelled almost 100,000 miles to more than 50 cities, and devoted more than 50,000 hours of staff time to the investigation.

For the overwhelming majority of pages, their work in the House of Representatives ranks as one of the most important and rewarding experiences of their lives. The Special Counsel can report to this Committee, to the House, and to the Nation that he has found no evidence of widespread improper or illegal sexual conduct by Members, officers, or employees of the House involving congressional pages. The evidence developed in the course of this investigation has shown time and again that allegations and rumors of misconduct were the product of teenage exaggeration, gossip or even out-and-out fabrication that was often repeated mercilessly in a political capital that thrives on rumor.

In truth, the House as an institution can be rightfully proud of the experience it has provided to thousands of American youngsters who have served as pages over the years.

B. SUMMARY OF FINDINGS

Three central findings dominate the exhaustive investigation carried out by the Special Counsel.

● First, the Special Counsel received no credible evidence of sexual misconduct by Members, officers or employees of the House of Representatives involving congressional pages during the 1981-82 time period involved in the original charges that prompted this investigation.

● Second, as detailed in the Special Counsel's Interim Report of last December, the evidence obtained showed there was no merit whatsoever in any of the original allegations of sexual misconduct made by the two former pages, Leroy Williams and Jeffrey Opp, whose sensational charges received such intense publicity a year ago.

● With the exception of three cases, the investigation uncovered no evidence to support the dozens of allegations that the Committee received concerning improper sexual conduct involving congressional pages or of preferential treatment of congressional pages in exchange for sexual favors. To the contrary, with the three exceptions, the evidence showed conclusively that these allegations were not true, or there was no credible basis for them.

The improper sexual conduct which the Special Counsel has uncovered took place between three and ten years ago. Two current Members of the House and one current employee were involved in separate incidents. The evidence obtained indicates that these were isolated instances, not typical of Members of the House of Representatives, or its employees. During the ten year period in which these incidents occurred, or are alleged to have occurred, more than 850 men and women have served as Members of the House; more than 60,000 employees have worked in the House.

At a time when confidence in many of our government institutions is low, each of us has a particular responsibility to be precise and accurate when discussing allegations of misconduct by public officials. When improper behavior occurs, it should not be understated or excused. It must be rooted out vigorously, promptly and publicly. But discovery of improprieties by a few, should not be allowed unjustly to sully the reputations of their colleagues, who labor long and hard for the public interest.

Speaking as the Special Counsel who carried out the investigation, I believe it is clear that the House of Representatives *as an institution* has been vindicated by this investigation. The investigation developed no evidence of any widespread sexual misconduct involving pages, and no evidence of sexual relationships by Members with pages involving preferential treatment.

The House of Representatives has discharged fully and completely its constitutional duty to police itself. This investigation has been searching and exhaustive. There have been no holds barred. The necessary resources have been provided. The bipartisan House leadership and Committee members have supported without qualification a thorough and independent investigation of these matters. Rarely has an institution in our democracy subjected itself to such a penetrating ordeal. The evidence of three cases involving sexual misconduct should be seen in that perspective.

The evidence of improper or illegal sexual conduct involving pages indicates that this conduct took place between three and ten years ago. In the instances involving sexual relationships, the pages involved have testified that the relationships were consensual. The Special Counsel has obtained evidence that:

- Congressman Daniel B. Crane engaged in a sexual relationship with a 17-year-old female page in 1980.
- Congressman Gerry E. Studds engaged in a sexual relationship in 1973 with a 17-year-old male page (who may have been 16 when the relationship began); and made sexual advances in 1973 to two other male pages; one was 16 or 17 years old at the time, the other was 17 years old.
- James C. Howarth, Majority Chief Page in the House Doorkeeper's Office, who had supervisory responsibilities over pages, engaged in a sexual relationship with a 17-year-old female page in 1980 who was at the time under his direct supervision, and gave her preferential treatment. There is also evidence that Mr. Howarth purchased cocaine in the House Democratic cloakroom during the period January 1979 to December 1980.

C. CONGRESS' SPECIAL RESPONSIBILITY TO ITS PAGES

The legislative history of House Resolution 518, as well as the legislative history of other House actions involving pages, reflects a recognition by the House of the special responsibility the House has in relation to its pages. This legislative history clearly establishes that the House of Representatives has a special relationship, analogous to *in loco parentis,* to the teenage pages it employs. As the Doorkeeper of the House has testified, the pages are the "wards" of the House.

Under these circumstances, a sexual relationship between a Member of the House and a teenage House page, even if consensual, constitutes a breach of the official obligations of a Member of the House. A sexual relationship between a page supervisor and a page under that supervisor's authority constitutes a serious violation of the fiduciary duty such a supervisor owes to his teenage charges.

Any such sexual relationships are precisely the type of improper sexual conduct covered by H. Res. 518 and H. Res. 12 and constitute a violation of clause 1 of the Code of Official Conduct of the House of Representatives, which states:

A Member, officer, or employee of the House of Representatives shall conduct himself at all times in a manner which shall reflect creditably on the House of Representatives. . . .

E. SUMMARY OF RECOMMENDATIONS

Based on the evidence, it is my responsibility as Special Counsel to recommend that the Committee take action with respect to the conduct of Representative Crane, Representative Studds and Mr. Howarth.

Existing Committee rules provide for the issuance of a Statement of Alleged Violation by the Committee. Following the issuance of such a Statement, the Committee establishes a timetable for motions and briefs by counsel and for a public hearing with testimony and cross-examination of witnesses. But Section 8 of H. Res. 518, 97th Cong., incorporated by H. Res. 12, 98th Cong., provides that "the Committee is authorized to adopt special rules of procedure as may be appropriate."

The matters presently before the Committee involve questions of great sensitivity for everyone, particularly the former pages involved, if there are extended public proceedings. Under Section 8 of H. Res. 518 and based on this consideration, the Special Counsel recommended to the Committee that it adopt special procedures if any respondent did not wish to contest the factual findings of the Special Counsel and was willing to waive his rights to a Statement of Alleged Violation and to a public hearing. Under these special procedures the Committee would act on the basis of the Special Counsel's report and the statement made by the respondent to the Committee. The Special Counsel's report and the respondent's statement, if any, would be made public at the time the Committee acts. . . .

VIII. Conclusion

The Special Counsel recommends that the Committee accept this report as the Final Report on Improper or Illegal Sexual Conduct and make this report public.

The Special Counsel also recommends that the Committee take action in three cases:

First, the Special Counsel recommends that the Committee find that Representative Daniel Crane engaged in conduct in 1980 in violation of clause 1 of the Code of Official Conduct of the House of Representatives. As a sanction, Special Counsel recommends that the Committee recommend that the House reprimand Representative Crane.

Second, the Special Counsel recommends that the Committee issue a Statement of Alleged Violation in the case of Congressman Gerry Studds alleging that Congressman Studds engaged in a sexual relationship with a House page in 1973 and that Congressman Studds made sexual advances to two other House pages in 1973, in violation of the Code of Official Conduct.

Third, the Special Counsel recommends that the Committee issue a

Statement of Alleged Violation against James C. Howarth, Majority Chief Page in the Doorkeeper's Office, alleging that Mr. Howarth engaged in a sexual relationship with a 17-year-old House page under his direct supervision in 1980, that Mr. Howarth accorded this page preferential treatment as a consequence of their sexual relationship, and that Mr. Howarth purchased and possessed illegal drugs within the precincts of the House in 1979 and 1980, all in violation of applicable laws and standards of conduct.

Respectfully submitted,
Joseph A. Califano, Jr.

August

JUSTICE DEPARTMENT REPORT ON KLAUS BARBIE

August 2, 1983

A Justice Department report, submitted to the U.S. attorney general August 2, stated that after World War II U.S. Army intelligence officers recruited, protected and eventually arranged an escape for Klaus Barbie, a former Gestapo officer wanted by the French government on criminal charges. The report was the result of a four-month investigation by the department regarding "the relationship between Klaus Barbie and the United States government from the end of World War II to the present."

Background

On February 4, Barbie was expelled from Bolivia where he had been living for 32 years under the assumed name of Klaus Altmann. He was flown to France to face charges that during World War II he had committed "crimes against humanity," including murders, tortures and arbitrary seizures. A Gestapo officer in Lyon from 1942-1944, Barbie was accused of responsibility for the deaths of some 4,000 people and the deportation of 7,500 others to Nazi concentration camps; he became known as "the butcher of Lyon." After the war, Barbie disappeared. From that time on, the French government had been trying to bring him to trial. In 1952 and 1954 French courts convicted Barbie of war crimes and sentenced him to death in absentia, but the time expired for carrying out that sentence.

In 1972 French Nazi hunters Beate and Serge Klarsfeld announced that Barbie was living in Bolivia under the assumed Altmann name.

Attempts by the French to have him extradited failed, however, as Barbie enjoyed the protection of Bolivia's right-wing military regime. In 1982 civilian rule was restored, and Barbie lost that governmental protection; he was turned over to the French to face the charges against him. (At the end of 1983 Barbie was being held in a military prison in Lyon awaiting trial.)

Upon Barbie's extradition and return to France, charges surfaced that the United States had employed him as an intelligence source in Germany after the war, had protected him and provided for his escape from Europe. Public interest and indignation over the allegations grew, and the Justice Department decided a full investigation was in order. Allen A. Ryan Jr., head of the Justice Department's Office of Special Investigations, was detailed to conduct the investigation. Ryan and his staff had been involved in tracking down and prosecuting former Nazis living in the United States.

Report Findings

The 218-page Justice Department report, divided into six sections, examined:

- *Barbie's Gestapo career, particularly his years in Lyon, 1942-1944.*
- *The recruitment and use of Barbie as an intelligence source by the U.S. Army's Counter Intelligence Corps (CIC), 1947-1949.*
- *The French request for extradition of Barbie and CIC's decision not to hand him over.*
- *Barbie's escape to Bolivia and the U.S. role in that escape, 1951.*
- *Barbie's activities in Bolivia.*

The final section contained the Justice Department's conclusions and recommendations. Ryan and his unit found that the U.S. Army intelligence service had recruited and used Barbie, knowing that he had been a Gestapo officer. As the report pointed out, however, it was not unusual for the United States or its allies to employ former Nazis after the war. The political climate was such that the job of "understanding and countering Communist influence" became a priority because the Soviet Union had become a military and political threat to the West. Former Nazis were offered protection in exchange for their expertise and knowledge of Soviet activities.

The investigators found no evidence that the American officers who had recruited Barbie in 1947 knew that he was suspected of war crimes. However, in 1949, when charges were first publicized that Barbie had used torture and committed other brutalities during the war, the CIC continued to use him. In 1950, when the French were seeking Barbie as an alleged war criminal, CIC officials kept his whereabouts secret and falsely told U.S. civilian authorities in Germany that they were not in contact with him.

In 1951 CIC officers arranged for Barbie and his family to escape to South America through the "rat line." This underground escape route was operated by Father Dragonovic, a Croatian priest in Rome who was a known Fascist war criminal. In March Dragonovic provided Barbie with a false passport and Bolivian visa; the CIC paid Dragonovic for his services.

The report proposed two reasons why the CIC refused to turn Barbie over to the French: embarrassment over CIC's employment of a war criminal and worry that Barbie, if apprehended, would reveal information about the CIC's intelligence operations. Neither concern, the report stated, was a valid excuse for sheltering Barbie.

The investigation also covered Barbie's activities in Bolivia. According to the report, in the 1960s the U.S. Army again considered using Barbie as an intelligence source but rejected the idea in the face of Central Intelligence Agency (CIA) doubts about the scheme. Justice investigators found no evidence of further U.S. involvement.

The report concluded that the United States had erred in its decision to protect Barbie after the war and recommended that the U.S. government apologize to France for justice delayed. In line with this recommendation, the Reagan administration sent a formal note to the French government expressing "deep regrets" regarding U.S. involvement in the Barbie affair.

> *Following are excerpts from the Justice Department's report, "Klaus Barbie and the United States Government," dated August 2, 1983. (Boldface headings in brackets have been added by Congressional Quarterly to highlight the organization of the text.):*

[Ryan's Memo to Attorney General]

As the investigation of Klaus Barbie has shown, officers of the United States government were directly responsible for protecting a person wanted by the government of France on criminal charges and in arranging his escape from the law. As a direct result of that action, Klaus Barbie did not stand trial in France in 1950; he spent 33 years as a free man and a fugitive from justice, and the fact that he is awaiting trial today in France is due entirely to the persistence of the government of France and the cooperation of the present government of Bolivia.

It is true that the obstruction of efforts to apprehend and extradite Barbie were not condoned in any official sense by the United States government. But neither can this episode be considered as merely the unfortunate action of renegade officers. They were acting within the scope of their official duties. Their actions were taken not for personal gain, or to shield them personally from liability or discipline, but to protect what they believed to be the interests of the United States Army and the United

States government. Under these circumstances, whatever may be their personal culpability, the United States government cannot disclaim responsibility for their actions.

Whether Barbie is guilty or innocent of the crimes with which he is charged will be decided by a French court. But whatever the verdict, his appointment with justice is long overdue. It is a principle of democracy and the rule of law that justice delayed is justice denied. If we are to be faithful to that principle — and we should be faithful to it — we cannot pretend that it applies only within our borders and nowhere else. We have delayed justice in Lyon.

I therefore believe it appropriate, and I so recommend, that the United States government express to the government of France its regret for its responsibility in delaying the due process of law in the case of Klaus Barbie. We should also pledge to cooperate in any appropriate manner in the further investigation of the crimes for which Barbie will be tried in France.

This is a matter of decency, and of honorable conduct. It should be, I believe, the final chapter by the United States in this case.

Introduction

On February 4, 1983, Klaus Barbie was expelled from Bolivia, where he had been living for 32 years, to France, where he was under indictment for crimes he allegedly committed during World War II as chief of the Gestapo in Lyon.

Within a few days of his arrival in France, charges were raised both in the United States and France that Barbie had been employed by United States intelligence in Germany after the war, and that the United States had arranged Barbie's escape to South America in 1951 after France had requested his extradition. . . .

On March 14, the Attorney General authorized an investigation to determine the relationship between Klaus Barbie and the United States government from the end of World War II until the present. . . . The report that follows is the result of that investigation. It was delivered to the Attorney General on August 2, 1983. . . .

This report describes the relationship between Klaus Barbie and the United States government. That relationship began in April 1947, but this report cannot begin there. To draw intelligent and informed judgments on the history of Barbie's use by American authorities, one must have answers to two lines of questions. First, who was Klaus Barbie, and what did he do during the war? Second, what did the Americans who recruited and used Barbie after the war know about him and his record? What could they have known from the resources that were available to them?

The answers to these questions are important because the controversy that has developed over public allegations of U.S. involvement with Barbie has been based on the assumption that Barbie was "the butcher of Lyon," a man responsible for crimes against humanity: the deaths and deportations of hundreds, perhaps thousands, of Jews and other innocent victims of Nazi persecution. This controversy has also assumed that those who dealt with Barbie after the war must have known that he was a butcher. Barbie himself has maintained that he was the head of the SS counter-resistance operation in Lyon, attempting to ferret out and neutralize sabotage directed against the German occupation.

... Barbie was the head of the Gestapo in Lyon; considering the responsibilities of the SS detachment in Lyon in 1942-1944, this role could be consistent with persecution, counter-resistance operations, or both. This investigation has not attempted to establish Barbie's guilt or innocence of crimes against humanity, which are the subject of criminal charges in France. It has endeavored to establish, as far as possible, what American officers who recruited and used Barbie over a period of time knew or should have known about him at the time he was recruited, and also as time went by. The answers to these questions are important because the actions of American officers, to be judged fairly, must be judged according to what they knew or ought to have known about the man they were dealing with. ...

As far as the first question posed ... — who was Barbie and what did he do — the following facts may be stated with reasonable certainty:

1. After a series of assignments in the intelligence field for the SD [the *Sicherheitsdienst,* an arm of the *Schutzstaffel* or SS, the Nazi network of death camps, armed divisions, intelligence services and mobile slaughter commandos] Barbie was assigned to Lyon as head of Section VI, the intelligence branch of the Einsatzkommando [EK], an amalgam of elements from the Security Police (Gestapo and criminal police) and the SD.

2. At some point, and for some period of time between November 1942 and the summer of 1944, Barbie served both as deputy and number three man of the EK.

3. At some point, and for some period of time, Barbie also was the head of Section IV, the Gestapo.

4. Barbie's responsibilities with the EK as a whole included counter-resistance operations: infiltrating the French Resistance, headquartered in Lyon; gathering information on its members and operations; and disrupting those operations and neutralizing (turning or arresting) its members to the maximum extent possible.

As to the second question — what could post-war investigators have known or be expected to know — the following points must be kept in mind.

1. Barbie's personnel file contains no mention of assignments to Section IV (Gestapo); taken by itself it outlines the career of an intelligence officer in Section VI, the foreign intelligence section of the SD.

2. The evidence regarding Barbie's activities in Section IV, the actions of the EK in Lyon, and the role of the EK in anti-resistance actions and persecution, was gathered by French authorities from late 1944 through

1948. This evidence is largely in the form of affidavits from Lyon residents and resistance fighters gathered in preparation for war crimes trials to be held by permanent military tribunals in Lyon and Paris.

THE LISTING OF BARBIE IN CROWCASS

As the war drew to a close in the spring of 1945, the Supreme Headquarters, Allied Expeditionary Force (SHAEF) composed a central register of war criminal suspects wanted by the allied nations. This Central Registry of War Criminals and Security Suspects — universally known as "CROWCASS" — grew quickly. The first list, published in July 1945, contained 70,000 names, including that of "Barbier" (no first name was listed) whom the French had listed under two numerical codes as wanted for "murder (of civilians)" and "torture (of military personnel)." The list was distributed to all major echelons of the Allied occupation forces in Germany, including the United States Army Counter Intelligence Corps [CIC].

RECRUITMENT AND USE OF BARBIE, 1947-1949

There are two very forceful arguments on the question of whether the Army should have used Barbie after the war.

The first is pragmatic. After the war, the alliance forged against Nazi Germany and the Axis powers shifted abruptly. The Soviet Union became a military and political adversary: Europe was the central theater of confrontation and Germany, itself dismembered into four zones of occupation, was center stage. There was a legitimate and pressing need for the United States to recognize, understand and, where necessary, counteract Soviet actions that might pose a threat to the security of the United States and its allies and the interests of the Western alliance.

The Counter Intelligence Corps, the only U.S. intelligence agency in Europe in the immediate post-war years, had an enormous responsibility. In order to gather and analyze intelligence effectively, CIC, like all intelligence organizations before and since, had no choice but to depend upon experienced, knowledgeable and politically reliable persons to provide information. No one in CIC was soft on Nazism or Nazis, but the price of turning away otherwise valuable assets simply on the basis of past affiliations was a high one. The job of understanding and countering Communist influence was there, it was legitimate and important, and it had to be done. If a Klaus Barbie was available and effective and loyal and reliable — and those who worked with him found him to be all of those — his employment was in the best interests of the United States at the time.

In understanding this argument, it is important to realize that Klaus Barbie is far more notorious today than he ever was, except in Lyon, during or immediately after the war. Barbie was a captain in the SS and the chief of the Gestapo in a French city in the latter part of the war. What he did there may have been brutal, criminal and inhuman — that matter will be decided at his trial in France — but he was not known far and wide at the time. Whatever his crimes, he has never been in the same category as Adolph Eichmann, Heinrich Himmler, Reinhard Heydrich or other SS leaders.

The second argument is visceral. The United States had, with its allies, spent nearly four years waging war against the Nazi regimes of Europe. Two hundred thousand American lives had been lost. The enemy was the most vicious political power in history; they had murdered, well behind the lines of combat, eleven million — eleven million — innocent victims, six million of them Jews who had been systematically exterminated simply because they were Jews.

The SS had been the instrument of slaughter. It ran the death camps and in many important ways it ran the government of Germany. It recognized no law but the will of Adolf Hitler. In 1946, it had been judged a criminal organization at Nuremberg. Among its many tentacles beyond the death camps none was as dreaded, and with good reason, as the Gestapo, the secret police whose weapons were terrorism, torture and death.

For the United States Government to have collaborated in any way with former Gestapo officers was, at the least, a grave misjudgment that, however unwittingly, betrayed those who had died fighting Nazism or falling innocent victim to it. To actually employ a man who had been the leader of the Gestapo in a city in France, and to rely on him to advance the interests of the United States, was incomprehensible and shameful....

... I cannot conclude that those who made the decision to employ and rely on Klaus Barbie ought not to be vilified for the decision. Any one of us, had we been there, might have made the opposite decision. But one must recognize that those who did in fact have to make a decision made a defensible one, even if it was not the only defensible one. No one to whom I spoke in this investigation was insensitive to the horrors perpetrated by Nazi Germany, nor entirely comfortable with the irony of using a Gestapo officer in the service of the United States. They were, on the whole, conscientious and patriotic men faced with a difficult assignment. Under the circumstances, I believe that their choice to enlist Barbie's assistance was neither cynical nor corrupt.

It must also be said that no other nation in occupied Germany — France, Great Britain or the Soviet Union — is in any position to criticize the decision to use Klaus Barbie now that the United States Government has revealed the facts behind that use. Each of those governments made essentially the same decision at the time: to invoke the available resources of the former German regime to protect and advance what each government perceived to be its national interest....

THE ABSENCE OF EVIDENCE OF WAR CRIMES

My conclusion that the decision to employ Klaus Barbie — and in fact it was a continuing series of decisions throughout 1947, 1948 and 1949 — was a defensible one depends upon the fact that the persons who made those decisions cannot be charged with knowledge that Barbie committed, or likely committed, or was wanted for, war crimes or crimes against humanity. Whether he did in fact commit such crimes is an issue to be decided in a French court. But the decision to use a former Nazi, even a former Gestapo officer, is one thing; the decision to use a person wanted for war crimes is another. . . .

But I am persuaded as a result of this investigation that CIC personnel had no reliable indication until at least May 1949, some two years after Barbie was first employed, that he was suspected of war crimes or crimes against humanity. . . .

[THE VAGUENESS OF THE CHARGE]

The critical fact is that the French listed Barbie as wanted for "murder." No details were given; there is no indication of war crimes or crimes against humanity; there is no accusation of specific charges such as the deportation of Jews to Auschwitz. Given that CIC had reason to credit Barbie's consistent story that he had been in charge of actions against the resistance — a story that had some basis in fact — it is certainly possible that CIC . . . concluded that the charges of "murder" grew out of the deaths of resistance fighters, and that the French understandably wanted Barbie back to exact the proper retribution for the deaths of French patriots.

It is important to understand that resistance fighters were not in the same category as innocent victims of the Holocaust; they were combatants in the same category as soldiers. That distinction was reaffirmed this year in the Barbie case, when the Lyon prosecutor pointed out that Barbie was not being prosecuted for actions against resistance fighters. . . .

CONCLUSION

. . . I conclude that CIC's actions through May of 1949 in recruiting and using Barbie, though subject to valid criticism by those who find use of a Gestapo official under any circumstances reprehensible, did not amount to the knowing use of a war criminal. The decision to use Barbie was a defensible one, made in good faith by those who believed that they were advancing legitimate and important national security interests. . . .

Publication of the allegations of torture and brutality in May 1949 marked the beginning of a transitional period in CIC's protection of Klaus Barbie. CIC's actions during this period were indecisive and equivocal, but they eventually led to a calculated and indefensible decision to conceal CIC's own actions and to actively impede the lawful search for Barbie being conducted by HICOG [U.S. High Commission for Germany, the U.S. civilian authority in Germany, 1949].

. . . Headquarters' initially decisive reaction to published charges of brutality and torture in May 1949 degenerated as time went by. Region XII's response to Headquarters' order was that the charges of brutality were probably not true, and that Barbie was a valuable asset to the CIC in Augsburg. Faced with the region's palpable reluctance to lose Barbie's services, the absence of any hard evidence to support the charges, and perhaps most importantly the absence of any inquiry or directive from higher levels, Headquarters apparently decided not to take any decisive action on its own. This indecision reached its zenith in January 1950 when Headquarters issued its inscrutable order that Region XII should not alert Barbie to the fact that his "status with this organization has been altered" — an order that, as Headquarters must have realized, could be satisfied only by the continued use of Barbie.

This course of action comes extremely close, and may cross over, the line drawn above between use of a former Nazi and the conscious protection of a war criminal. While the charges of the Jura veterans were not official government allegations, and while CIC had not learned of them through official channels, it was sufficiently concerned with the matter in May 1949 to take action on it. As CIC's order to Region XII stated, "This headquarters is inclined to believe that there is some element of truth in the allegations, since a mass reaction as that indicated in the clipping would hardly stem from naught or from behavior in accordance with the rules of land warfare." But this initial concern dissipated in the months ahead, and CIC took no further action to determine if the charges had any basis in fact.

Whether its lethargy, or timidity, in this respect amounted to a conscious neglect of the possibility that Barbie may have been a war criminal is a close question. But the answer to that question need not detain us, for CIC's inaction was soon overtaken by a far more deliberate decision.

The uneasy situation that festered from May 1949 onwards was forced to an end in the last days of April and the first days of May 1950, when the reading of Barbie's evidence at the [René] Hardy trial in Paris elicited strong charges, and equally strong public reaction, that Barbie was a torturer and war criminal who was enjoying the continued protection of American authorities in Germany. Although CIC had not received any request from French or American authorities for the extradition of Barbie, it immediately recognized that such a demand could not be far off (in fact, it had already been made, albeit imperfectly, to HICOG) and that a decision would have to be made whether to surrender Barbie when it came.

These days were in fact the last opportunity that CIC had to bring an end to its involvement with Barbie with any degree of honor. It could have informed HICOG that it knew of Barbie's whereabouts and that it was prepared to cooperate with any action directed by HICOG in response to an extradition request. Under the law, HICOG, and not CIC or EUCOM [European Command], was responsible for determining whether and under what conditions extradition requests would be granted.

Instead, CIC officials decided on May 4, 1950 that Barbie "should not be placed in [the] hands of [the] French," and that decision irrevocably altered the future course of the Barbie affair. The decision was implemented on June 16, 1950, when CIC and EUCOM representatives met with HICOG's Director of Intelligence and told him — falsely — that CIC had had no contact with Barbie since just prior to the allegations raised in the Hardy trial. CIC certainly knew, on the occasion of that meeting if not before, that France was seeking the surrender of Barbie on war crimes charges and that HICOG was endeavoring to find out where Barbie was.

CIC was influenced by two factors: surrender of Barbie would "embarrass" CIC by revealing that it had used a former Gestapo official, and would risk the compromise of CIC procedures and information should Barbie decide to reveal what he had learned over three years of CIC employment.

The risk of embarrassment, real as it was, can be quickly dismissed as justification for CIC's decision. Fear of embarrassment cannot be a valid excuse for one government agency knowingly providing false information to another.

The second factor — risk of divulging CIC's operations — was also real, but under the circumstances it was not more valid. Every intelligence organization has a legitimate obligation to avoid the compromise of its operations, but that obligation cannot supersede its duty to obey the law.

As the facts discussed in the report make clear, HICOG did not know that Barbie's whereabouts were known to CIC officers, and had no reason to suspect that CIC was not telling the truth.

CONCLUSION

The evidence yielded in this investigation and discussed in the body of the report justifies the conclusion that, by its decision on May 4, 1950 not to cooperate with efforts to obtain Barbie's surrender, and by its false statements to HICOG on June 16, 1950 that Barbie's whereabouts were unknown, responsible officials of the Army interfered with the lawful and proper administration of justice. They knowingly obstructed the bona fide efforts of the office of the U.S. High Commission for Germany to carry out its lawful obligation to effect the extradition of war criminals.

Had those Army officials fully and honestly revealed to HICOG the information known to them concerning the whereabouts of Klaus Barbie, HICOG would have been able to provide to the French government the information necessary to perfect its extradition request and could then have been able to render a decision on whether extradition was required by law. By knowingly misleading HICOG to believe that Army officials did not know Barbie's whereabouts, those officials wrongfully impeded the due and proper administration of the law in a matter then pending before the official agency of the United States Government.

[THE ESCAPE OF BARBIE]

Throughout the summer of 1950, CIC's prolonged refusal to go to HICOG with the truth amounted to a continuation of its obstruction of ·

HICOG's efforts to carry out its duties. This course of conduct took a further concrete step in September 1950 when HICOG solicited EUCOM's formal extradition clearance of Barbie in the event he could be found. CIC advised EUCOM that it could inform HICOG that Barbie was no longer under the control of CIC. This representation was false, and its effect was to renew and revalidate the misrepresentations first made on June 16.

Although unquestionably a more dramatic episode than the events of May and June 1950, the December decision to provide Barbie's escape to South America was only the culmination of CIC's continued obstruction of HICOG's efforts to deal with the Barbie case....

... [T]he evidence establishes that the 430th CIC in Austria had been using Father Dragonovic's rat line for several years as a means of providing defectors and informants with a safe and secret passage out of Europe....

As the discussion of the rat line's operation makes clear, the 430th CIC and its parent command, G-2 United States Forces Austria (USFA), were operating on the edge of the law, if not over it: false documentation was obtained surreptitiously, information was withheld from United States agencies controlling travel, funds were transferred in unorthodox and perhaps illegal ways, and knowledge of the entire procedure was intentionally restricted to the persons actually involved in it.

The use of the rat line for informants and defectors raises troubling questions of ethical and legal conduct. The United States Army certainly had an obligation to protect from harm those informants who had assisted the Army at substantial risk, as well as defectors whose discovery in the American zone would have jeopardized their lives and safety. Furthermore, there was nothing inherently wrong in evacuating such persons from Europe to places of sanctuary in South America. But to carry out this obligation by relying on the intercession of a foreign national whose own background and interests were suspect, by concealing information from United States agencies, and by possibly violating lawful regulations on travel, currency and documentation, the Army did not act responsibly....

... This investigation examined all materials known to exist on the operation of the rat line and interviewed all persons now alive known to have been involved with it. No other case was found where a suspected Nazi war criminal was placed in the rat line, or where the rat line was used to evacuate a person wanted by either the United States Government or any of its post-war allies....

The decision to invoke the rat line to arrange Barbie's escape from Europe, under the circumstances, amounted to a further and final step in the 66th CIC's obstruction of HICOG's attempts to carry out its lawful obligation to decide the extradition of Klaus Barbie. By arranging his escape to South America, the responsible officials of the 66th CIC insured that Barbie would not be brought to justice in France....

JUSTICE DEPARTMENT REPORT ON EPA OFFICIALS

August 11, 1983

A *Justice Department report, released August 11, found no evidence of wrongdoing on the part of six former Environmental Protection Agency (EPA) officials, including the agency's former administrator, Anne McGill Gorsuch Burford. The investigation had been ordered by President Ronald Reagan in February in response to congressional charges that EPA officials might have used paper shredders to destroy documents subpoenaed by Congress. The investigators also examined whether Burford had engaged in political manipulation to withhold hazardous waste cleanup funds for the Stringfellow Acid Pits in California to avoid boosting the Senate election bid of Gov. Edmund G. Brown Jr., a Democrat. They found no evidence that Burford actually had engaged in such political manipulation.*

The Justice Department investigation was one of several probes into the activities of officials at the beleaguered agency during 1982 and 1983. Headline-grabbing congressional hearings led to the resignation of Administrator Burford and her top aides early in 1983. The investigations spotlighted charges of lax enforcement of hazardous waste programs under the "superfund" cleanup law. (Historic Documents of 1982, p. 965)

Background of Investigations

The congressional investigations and hearings into EPA actions grew out of earlier, more routine congressional oversight on how certain laws were being carried out by the executive branch. The House Energy and Commerce Subcommittee on Oversight and Investigations had begun looking into implementation of the 1980 "superfund" hazardous waste cleanup law as early as September 1980. Concerned about "the deliberate illegal dumping of hazardous substances and the involvement of organized crime in segments of the toxic waste industry," the subcommittee in a December 16, 1982, report urged "a strong, effective federal deterrent" to illegal disposal.

What the subcommittee found, however, was a "dramatic decline" in hazardous waste enforcement litigation by EPA and the Justice Department after 1981, when the Reagan administration came into office. That was due partly to a policy stressing voluntary industry compliance.

As other subcommittees joined in with their own investigations, the scope of inquiry widened to include additional charges, among them possible conflict of interest, as in the case of superfund director Rita M. Lavelle, who eventually legally removed herself from a California dumping case that involved her former employer, Aerojet-General Corp.

None of the panels probing EPA — five House subcommittees and a Senate committee — had issued any report on their findings as of the end of the 1983 session.

Management Shake-up

The congressional investigations led to a complete change in EPA's top leadership. Burford resigned March 9, saying, "I resigned because I felt I had become the issue." Congressional Democrats, however, said the issue had not been Burford but the environmental policies of the Reagan administration.

While scarcely a half-dozen of the agency's managers were actually accused of wrongdoing, some 20 major officials resigned in the management change. The Senate May 17 confirmed William D. Ruckelshaus to succeed Burford as EPA administrator. The unanimous confirmation of Ruckelshaus, who headed EPA when it was first formed in 1970, reflected Senate confidence in his professional qualifications and personal integrity. By the end of the session, the Senate had confirmed all 12 members of a new management team picked by Ruckelshaus.

Ruckelshaus succeeded in restoring morale at EPA and improving relations with Congress. But some on Capitol Hill questioned whether the change of faces was enough to bring the revisions they sought in the environmental policies of the Reagan administration.

Criminal Probes, Lavelle Verdict

Reagan announced February 16 that he was directing the Justice Department to probe all allegations of wrongdoing at EPA. While several congressional panels referred information they had developed to the Justice Department for possible prosecution, it brought criminal charges against only one individual: former assistant administrator Lavelle, who headed hazardous waste programs until she was fired by Reagan on February 7.

Lavelle actually was prosecuted twice: once for contempt of Congress and once on charges of perjury and obstructing a congressional investigation. The House voted 413-0 on May 18 to cite Lavelle for contempt for failing to appear in response to a subpoena from the subcommittee that was investigating charges of conflict of interest at EPA. Lavelle was indicted on the charge May 27, but a federal grand jury in Washington, D.C., acquitted her on July 22. On August 4, Lavelle was indicted a second time. And on December 1 a federal jury in Washington, D.C., found her guilty on three counts of committing perjury during congressional testimony and one count of obstructing a congressional investigation. Lavelle was sentenced January 9, 1984, to six months in prison and was fined $10,000. Defense lawyers said she had been made a "scapegoat."

The Justice Department decided not to prosecute Burford and at least five other EPA officials whose actions had been questioned and criticized on Capitol Hill. In addition to Burford, the former officials were general counsel Robert M. Perry, assistant administrators John A. Todhunter and John P. Horton, special assistant Louis J. Cordia and consultant James W. Sanderson. In its report the department said an FBI investigation had found insufficient evidence of criminal wrongdoing to justify criminal prosecution of the six former officials. On some charges, it said criminal intent could not be proved and the department "declined" to prosecute. However, the department said that four allegations regarding EPA operations remained under investigation. They involved charges that an EPA official ordered destruction of a record requested by Congress; that EPA documents might have been removed improperly from the agency; that illegal (politically motivated) hiring practices might have occurred; and that a former official might have committed perjury before a House committee.

The Justice Department's report was criticized by a number of House Democrats who were conducting congressional investigations into EPA activities. One of them, Rep. Elliott H. Levitas, Ga., said the report "smacks of whitewash and doesn't have much credibility" because the Justice Department officials involved in the EPA investigation were themselves Reagan political appointees.

> *Following are excerpts from the Justice Department's August 11, 1983, report regarding its investigation into allegations against current and former officials of the Environmental Protection Agency (EPA):*

Alleged Document Destruction

On February 10, 1983, in a letter to the Attorney General, Congressman James J. Howard, Chairman of the House Committee on Public Works and Transportation, alleged that EPA personnel had destroyed documents under subpoena to the House of Representatives. In response to this allegation, agents of the Federal Bureau of Investigation conducted approximately 200 interviews and other investigation.

The focus of the investigation was both the possible destruction of subpoenaed documents and the circumstances surrounding the procurement and November 1982 placement of paper shredders in the EPA Office of Solid Waste and Emergency Response (OSWER).

On February 16, 1983, the FBI took action to identify subpoenaed documents and to determine whether any of them had been destroyed by shredding or any other means. Responsible EPA officials uniformly stated that all subpoenaed documents were maintained in a highly secure fashion. These interviews revealed no knowledge by the EPA officials of document handling practices at EPA which would have resulted, in any way, in the destruction of subpoenaed documents.

Thereafter, interviews were conducted of all OSWER employees having knowledge of document destruction. While some of those interviewed had knowledge that documents had been destroyed, none had knowledge of subpoenaed documents being destroyed, and no evidence to the contrary was discovered. However, a number of employees had seen the Acting Chief of OSWER's Compliance Branch at EPA Headquarters on Saturday, February 5, 1983, shredding documents.

On February 16, 1983, the Acting Chief was interviewed by the FBI and denied knowing of any subpoenaed documents being shredded or destroyed. He was again interviewed on March 3, at which time he explained that he destroyed some of his personal working files as a matter of routine and that a month in advance he and other EPA employees had scheduled a meeting for Saturday, February 5, to discuss the "computerization" of office records. While there, he destroyed documents which were duplicates of originals on permanent file or documents irrelevant to permanent retention. . . . Further investigation failed to develop any evidence inconsistent with the Acting Chief's stated position. To the contrary, the statement of . . . witnesses were consistent with his statement. . . .

Congressman Howard's original referral was based upon an allegation that subpoenaed documents had been destroyed. Since the investigation did not develop any proof that subpoenaed documents had been destroyed, the investigation of this matter was closed. . . .

Anne M. Burford

By memorandum of March 4, 1983, Richard A. Hauser, Deputy Counsel to the President, informed the Department of Justice of an allegation that

Anne M. Burford, then EPA's Administrator, stated, during a luncheon held August 4, 1982, aboard the yacht *Sequoia,* that no money would be released for the Stringfellow (California) clean-up until after the November 1982 election. The memorandum further stated that Mrs. Burford had stated, "I'll be damned if I am going to let Brown [Governor of California] take credit for that [Stringfellow clean-up]." On March 7, 1983, the Criminal Division decided to ascertain whether the conduct of Mrs. Burford relative to the Stringfellow matter constituted a violation of 18 U.S.C. § 595.

The investigation into this matter included FBI interviews of the participants in the luncheon aboard the *Sequoia,* and interviews of the individuals who were the most involved in the Stringfellow matter.

The investigation established that a luncheon was held aboard the *Sequoia* on August 4, 1982. In addition to Mrs. Burford, persons aboard the *Sequoia* that day included the Secretary of the Interior, the Secretary of Energy, a former Secretary of Energy, the Deputy Secretary of Energy, the Chief of Staff for EPA, the Executive Assistant to the Secretary of the Interior, and the Chairman and a member of the Council on Environmental Quality. The FBI interviewed these individuals, and only two witnesses recalled Mrs. Burford's making comments of a political nature about Governor Brown; the other individuals on the *Sequoia* denied any recollection of Mrs. Burford's making such comments. One witness recalled merely that Mrs. Burford had said something to the effect that she was not going to do any political favors for Governor Brown. Likewise, another witness recalled that in the course of a discussion about Governor Brown's Senate campaign, Mrs. Burford referred to six million dollars which EPA was to pay to the State of California, and she said that she believed that Governor Brown would claim credit for California's receiving this money should it be paid. This witness expressed his opinion that Mrs. Burford clearly implied that she was going to hold back the six million dollars to avoid assisting Governor Brown's election efforts; however, he was unable to provide any evidence to support that opinion or that Mrs. Burford actually held back any EPA money from the State of California to avoid helping Governor Brown. . . .

The allegation against Mrs. Burford raised the possibility that she had committed a criminal misdemeanor violation of a federal election statute. As pertinent to this allegation, 18 U.S.C. § 595 prohibited Mrs. Burford from using her official authority for the purpose of interfering with, or affecting, the nomination or election of Governor Brown for the office of the United States Senator. Since no competent evidence was discovered that Mrs. Burford engaged in the prohibited conduct, the investigation of this matter was closed.

WOMEN AND REPUBLICANS:
THE 'GENDER GAP' ISSUE
August 21, 1983

The issue of the so-called "gender gap" was one that troubled the Reagan administration in 1983. Women, pollsters reported, were more likely to express dissatisfaction with Reagan's job performance than were men.

The disaffection of American women with Reagan's policies was somewhat evident in the 1980 elections. While men voted for Reagan over Democratic incumbent Jimmy Carter by a margin of 56 to 36, women chose Reagan by the smaller margin of 47 to 45. One of the most important reasons for the slim margin was a perception on the part of many women that Reagan did not care about issues of principal interest to them.

Many women also opposed the more general policies of the Reagan administration, primary among them its emphasis on higher defense spending and simultaneous cutbacks in social programs. They argued that the hefty defense budget was made possible largely at the expense of social welfare programs. According to government statistics, women were the major recipients of public welfare, Social Security, subsidized housing and Medicaid benefits. The administration sought to reduce funding for many of those programs.

In addition, the administration opposed one of the major causes espoused by the organized feminist movement — enactment of an Equal Rights Amendment (ERA) to the Constitution. Since 1940 Republican platforms had supported an ERA amendment. Reagan opposed ratification but in a gesture to ERA supporters suggested that the 1980

*Republican Party platform not take a position on the issue. During his
1980 campaign, Reagan often said he was for the "E" and the "R," but
not the "A," of the proposed constitutional amendment. He argued that
women already were protected by the 14th Amendment, which prohibited
states from denying to any person equal protection of the law. Instead of
enacting a constitutional amendment, existing laws prohibiting sex
discrimination should be enforced, he said, and discriminatory ones
should be eliminated or corrected.* (Failure of ERA, Historic Documents of
1982, p. 611)

*Women's rights groups also faulted Reagan for his stand against
abortion and his opposition to affirmative action programs in hiring and
education. The number of women appointed to positions in the administration disappointed women's and civil rights groups as well. They
observed that most of Reagan's female appointees held jobs on advisory
boards or panels with little power or influence. The handful of high
ranking appointees, such as Supreme Court Justice Sandra Day O'Connor and U.N. Ambassador Jeane J. Kirpatrick, were staunch conservatives criticized by feminists on the basis of their politics, even if welcomed
for their gender.*

*The administration countered feminist criticism by pointing to its
proposals that were of particular interest to women. Those included
efforts to raise tax credits for child care, legislate tax breaks for
individual retirement accounts (IRAs) for non-working women and
reduce delinquencies in child support payments by absent fathers. The
administration also endorsed the principle of equity in pension payments. But these and other efforts moved slowly through the legislative
process.* (Supreme Court pension decision, p. 691)

*To move forward on its promise to review discriminatory practices and
laws as an "ERA alternative," the administration established a Gender
Discriminatory Agency Review group within the attorney general's office.
On September 8 William Bradford Reynolds, the assistant attorney
general in charge of the Justice Department's Civil Rights Division,
announced proposals to eliminate sex discrimination language from a
number of federal laws. Reynolds conceded that many of the proposed
changes were cosmetic. Judy Goldsmith, president of the National
Organization for Women, called the report "a response that is so inadequate it is either arrogant or ignorant."*

*The Justice Department had been in the news since August 21, when a
disillusioned department aide, Barbara Honegger, presented a resounding indictment of the project in an article appearing on the opinion pages
of* The Washington Post. *The next day, Honegger resigned her job on the
"ERA alternative" effort. She charged that bureaucratic roadblocks and
lack of interest by the administration had so hobbled the effort to
identify and propose changes in discriminatory federal statutes that "not
a single law has been changed." She also denounced the administration's*

positions opposing abortion and its support for narrowing, rather than broadening, applications of existing law banning sex discrimination.

Surprised by the intensity of Honegger's diatribe, administration officials at first sought to discredit her, contending that she had inflated the importance of her position at Justice. But the issues her article raised caused considerable debate. In an appearance before the Women's Republican Leadership Forum in San Diego four days later, Reagan stood by his "ERA alternative." He cited again his administration's proposals on child care tax credits, IRAs for non-working women, pension payment equity and child support payment enforcement. He also said he had instructed the Justice Department to speed up the review of discriminatory laws and present "specific recommendations." But presidential aides acknowledged to reporters that Honegger's attack had exacerbated the gender gap problem, and they admitted concern over the impact of female dissatisfaction on Reagan's re-election effort.

> *Following is the text of an article on the Reagan administration's record on women's rights, written by Barbara Honegger, a special assistant in the Justice Department, appearing in the August 21, 1983,* Washington Post. *(Boldface headings in brackets have been added by Congressional Quarterly to highlight the organization of the text.):*

When Ronald Reagan backed off his party's 40-year-long commitment to the broadest constitutional protection for the civil rights of American women — support of the ERA — he gave three reasons. First, he said, women were already protected by existing constitutional provisions, in particular the 14th Amendment. Second, what was really needed was stronger enforcement of the laws against sex discrimination already on the books. And third, he pledged himself to a "better way" — a two-pronged effort systematically to identify and eliminate or correct remaining individual instances of sex discrimination a) in the federal and b) in the states' codes.

All three of these arguments implied certain actions on Reagan's part. But he has not taken them. He has reneged on his commitment. I know. I have been there from the start — at the Republican National Convention, in the room on the 68th floor of the Renaissance Center where the platform was hammered out, on the six-man fast-turnaround research team for the president's speechwriters in the campaign, on the transition team after Nov. 4, specializing in outreach to federal departments and agencies which had specific programs relevant to women, and in the West Wing of the White House, at the physical node of the Offices of Policy Development, Public Liaison and Intergovernmental Affairs, personally translating the president's campaign promise for an "ERA alternative" into tangible federal programs. For the past year and a quarter, I have been in the Justice Department, as project director of the Attorney

General's Gender Discrimination Agency Review, trying to carry out the president's "ERA alternative."

[The 14th Amendment]

Let's take the president's three reasons one by one. When asked specifically to state which existing constitutional provisions he has in mind that already protect women, the president generally refers to the 14th Amendment — as he did after signing the executive order creating his federal-level "ERA alternative" back on Dec. 21, 1981, in the Cabinet Room. But the fact is that women are not today and never have been fully or securely protected under the 14th Amendment against federal sex discrimination, state sex discrimination, or lack of federal enforcement of existing sex discrimination prohibitions — which, as we shall see, becomes especially important under Reagan.

The 14th Amendment wasn't even used to overturn laws which discriminated against women until just a little over a decade ago. This wasn't for lack of women's trying to get the Supreme Court to use it to strike down the vast numbers of laws that discriminated against them purely on the basis of gender. Women brought cases trying to get the Supreme Court to give them the vote under the 14th Amendment and were turned down; they tried to get permission to practice law under the 14th Amendment and were turned down; and they tried to get permission to work the same hours and the same kind of jobs as men and were turned down. And to this day the Supreme Court does not rule in sex-discrimination cases based on the same toughest standard of review it uses when considering racial discrimination or religious discrimination cases.

There is, however, one exception to this rule. The one category of gender-specific law the Supreme Court has consistently reviewed under its strictest 14th Amendment standard consists of laws that interfere with a woman's right to choose abortion. But this is the area Reagan is doing everything in his power to *remove* from the jurisdiction of the court altogether — anti-abortion law.

[Existing Laws]

The second of Reagan's reasons that American women don't need an equal rights amendment is that all America really needs is tougher enforcement of the laws against sex discrimination we already have. But it is the Reagan administration itself that is doing everything in its power to reduce the enforcement and narrow the interpretation of the existing statutes that forbid sex discrimination.

An example is the administration's attempt not to broaden or strengthen but rather to narrow radically the scope of application of Title IX — the federal law that bans discrimination against women in any school, university or educational program receiving federal funds. Most do receive such funds in some form or another. Earlier administrations, both Democratic and Republican, have interpreted this law against sex discrimination to apply very broadly. The Justice Department's Title IX brief in *Grove City* takes the position that only educational programs or activities that receive federal funds directly should be constrained by existing federal laws that prohibit sex discrimination, not the school, college or university as a whole. If this administration is successful in *Grove City,* I believe a precedent will be set to gut enforcement of dozens of federal laws that currently protect Americans against discrimination on the basis of sex, race, color, national origin, religion, creed or handicap in "programs or activities which receive federal funds."

Reagan also undermined the Women's Educational Equity Act Program at the Department of Education. Authorization for the program was slashed from $80 million a year to $6 million. And then, not long ago, the Department of Education testified in a House hearing on its plan to gut the program even further by abolishing jobs that the remaining $6 million would, in part, fund. One of the major reasons women who know give for the absolute necessity of an ERA is precisely the point Ronald Reagan's own administration makes raw: federal statutes can be repealed or, if technically still on the books, be effectively voided by a president who doesn't enforce or who narrows the scope of the law.

[Administration Approach]

The third reason Reagan has given for why women do not require an ERA is that his two-pronged part-federal law- and part-state-law-oriented ERA alternative will be more efficient in actually eliminating remaining sex-discriminatory federal and state laws and regulations one by one. I believed the president and his men when they said they would do these things. With great expectations I agreed to work to develop and implement these projects in the White House's Office of Policy Development and spent the first year of the administration, from January 1981 through early 1982, doing just that before I followed the project to the Justice Department.

The president's federal-level "ERA alternative" under his Executive Order 12336 calls for an exhaustive effort to identify and correct or eliminate remaining sex discrimination found in the U.S. Code, the Code of Federal Regulations, and any policy, practice or program of any federal department or agency. As implemented in practice, the order has three stages: 1) identification of the "problems" by a massive computer-assisted search; 2) seeking to change the problem laws and regulations, policies and programs that discriminate against women; and 3) implementing these changes in the departments and agencies.

This is an immense project. The identification effort alone took a year to complete just for the laws; our search was more complete and definitive than the previous Civil Rights Commission list in its report of 1977. The results of this effort at identification, which I have personally directed at the Department of Justice for the past year and a quarter, are forwarded periodically to the president and his Cabinet Council on Legal Policy for decision as to actions. They are to decide what laws to seek to change and what regulations to alter or eliminate through presidentially initiated action — that is the second stage of the process.

The third and last stage — if and when the president decides to make any changes in a regulation, policy or practice of an agency — is the implementation stage. This would be undertaken by another group, called the Task Force on Legal Equity for Women, which has a purely implementary role. This task force is the only feature of the ERA alternative that has received any media attention to date, which is ironic since, so far, it has had nothing to do. The original chairman of the task force, Carol Dinkins — assistant attorney general for land and resources — has left the government, and the White House has not bothered to replace her at the task force.

[First and Second Reports]

Now you know what the president's "ERA alternative" is supposed to do. Let's compare that with what has actually happened. The identification effort is known as the Gender Discrimination Agency Review project. Fifteen attorneys and professional staff in the Coordination and Review Section of the Civil Rights Division have been involved in the effort over the past year. To date, three Quarterly Reports of the Attorney General have gone forward to the president, over the signature of William Bradford Reynolds, assistant attorney general for civil rights, but not a single law has been changed.

The first of these three reports, "The First Quarterly Report of the Attorney General Under Executive Order 12336," went to the White House on June 28, 1982. The substantive part of that report is a partial listing of federal laws that still discriminate against women (or men), current only through 1976. This first report, however — like the third report, which was just delivered — contains no proposed corrections for the problem statutes. This is for two reasons. First, the working group that was organized under Martin Anderson, assistant to the president for policy development, to propose specific corrections was disbanded by the White House the moment it reported its first options for specific corrections. Ed Harper, Anderson's successor, wrote the members of the working group thanking them for completing their work — which had only just begun! Second, Assistant Attorney General Reynolds interpreted the executive order as requiring Justice to identify problems but not also to propose solutions. Eventually Sen. Bob Dole arranged for a Senate Judiciary subcommittee attorney to draft a bill, now S 501, to correct selected "noncontroversial" laws in the list (translation: those that won't make a major difference if they're changed anyway).

The Second Quarterly Report under the executive order was only a three-page memorandum to the White House alerting the president that the agencies involved in searching their laws, regulations, policies and practices for sex discrimination were taking longer than expected to report, and that the Third Quarterly Report would contain the "big" item — the final list of sex discriminatory laws.

This "Third Quarterly Report of the Attorney General Under Executive Order 12336" is at the White House and has been since July 14 when I hand-delivered it to the West Wing.

[Third Quarterly Report]

This report has several parts. The first and key section is what the president mentioned to the International Federation of Business and Professional Women's Clubs recently when he said he would "do penance" by personally reading the "computer printouts of laws" needing to be changed. This list is now finished, final, definitive and exhaustive (with a notable exception which I will mention in a minute). It is *the* list of all federal laws that substantively discriminate on the basis of sex and which also have a sex-related term or terms in their language that the president has been waiting for. He has it in hand.

The second section of the Third Quarterly Report consists of the initial submissions from the first 17 (of 41) agencies reporting on their own internal reviews of their regulations, policies and practices for sex discrimination. These reports are above and beyond and different from the separate and complete list of statutes in the first section of the report.

Finally, the third section of the Third Quarterly Report is a list of all known federal laws that already prohibit sex discrimination in programs or activities that receive federal funds. If the president gets his way in trying to cut back on the definition of what constitutes a "program or activity" that receives federal funds under Title IX, this would set the precedent for cutting back in the same manner on enforcement coverage of every statute on that list, of which there are dozens and dozens designed to protect women against sex discrimination.

Following the president's promise to do his "penance," Larry Speakes was quoted in The Post that the president has been "mistaken" when he told the International Federation of Business and Professional Women's Clubs that the "final report" had been received by the White House. He said the Justice Department would not be finishing up its reporting until April 19, 1984. This is untrue. The Fourth Quarterly Report, which will contain the vast majority of the remaining reports on regulations, policies and practices from the individual agencies will be completed no later than September. All that might still be outstanding by April 1984 would be a few insignificant odds and ends from at most one or two of 41 agencies.

This summary of the president's federal-level "ERA alternative" would not be complete if I didn't mention an event that happened in the summer of 1982. Shortly after moving to the Department of Justice to carry out the identification of laws and regulations under the executive order, I was called to the White House. A presidential aide had discovered that our computer review had been programmed to include a search for laws and regulations relating to pregnancy and abortion, and angrily told me that abortion and pregnancy have nothing to do with women's rights and therefore were to have no part in the identification effort. The final list of laws in the Third Quarterly Report therefore reflects this instruction.

[Fifty States Project]

What about the second prong of the president's "ERA alternative," which addresses not federal but state laws and regulations? This is called the "Fifty States Project" and was actually the "brainchild" of myself and Kevin Hopkins, now director of the Office of Policy Information at the White House. After Reagan rescinded his party's longtime commitment to the ERA at the Republican National Convention in 1980 and women were up in arms, the two of us stayed up all night drafting a memo proposing the rock-bottom minimum we thought Reagan might accept as a "compromise" with women. Even then, we reasoned, if he did win the election, having something would be better than having nothing.

Much to our surprise, the inner circle reviewed the memorandum and liked it. The promise to implement a Fifty States Project, which would assist the states in tangible ways, through the governors' offices, to identify and correct remaining sex discriminatory laws and regulations found its way, amazingly, into the first substantive paragraph of Reagan's acceptance speech at the convention. Even at that time, it was clear that, to work, the project would require, at minimum, at least one full-time staff person.

But the first special assistant to the president, appointed to head the project, Judy Peachee, was given lead responsibility for all liaison with 50 states in the Office of Intergovernmental Affairs and could hardly devote full time to the project. The original promise that the White House would actually do something to accelerate the process of identification and correction of sex-discriminatory laws and regulations in the 50 states became impossible as a matter of lack of priority.

The project was announced, with a sit-down luncheon and all-day briefing for representatives of the 50 governors' offices in October 1981. All that has resulted from the project to date is a pretty booklet listing what the 50 states had already done without there ever having been a so-called federally directed "ERA alternative."

In a last-ditch effort to salvage something of some lasting value from the president's two-part "ERA alternative," on July 22, after completing the Third Quarterly Report under the federal-law effort, I offered the White House Office of the Assistant to the President for Public Liaison the same exhaustive computer search using the same gender-term key-word program we had just used at Justice to search the federal laws — this time to help the states do the same for their own laws and regulations. (Some states have done a complete review of laws and regulations; most only a partial review, which automatically outdates itself; and some haven't done any review at all.)

Within a week of my offer, the White House called with its answer. This, I was informed, was "not something that the White House wants to expend any financial or political capital on." I was congratulated for being a "good advocate" and thanked for the generous offer.

"Advocate"? Generous offer? Curious. All I was "advocating" was action on something the president promised the American people over a year and a half ago.

When this piece is published, I suppose I shall be characterized as a disappointed job seeker on account of that offer. Well, let me be plain. I *was* seeking to do a job or at least to get someone to do a job to which I thought the White House was committed. But as with the other aspects of the president's so-called "ERA alternative" this too turned out to be a sham.

I don't know about you, but I am insulted when the president of my country haggles with the Civil Rights Commission over whether his record on appointment of women to top government jobs is 1 percent or 2 percent better or worse than Jimmy Carter's own lousy record. And I am insulted when the president of my country defends another all-male advisory commission claiming that "we never select individuals just because they're men or women ... or whatever." Yes, there are other aspects, mostly economic, of any effort to undo wrongs against women in this country. But frankly, my dear, I don't think Ronald Reagan gives a damn.

CONGRESSIONAL BUDGET OFFICE REPORT ON BUDGET CUTBACKS

August 25, 1983

In a study requested by House Speaker Thomas P. O'Neill Jr., D-Mass., the Congressional Budget Office (CBO) found that 40 percent of the savings from cuts in federal benefits programs since Ronald Reagan took office were the result of reductions affecting households with incomes of less than $10,000 a year. The 80-page CBO report, released August 25, indicated that the domestic budget cuts were impacting the hardest on the lowest income groups in the nation.

The report, "Major Legislative Changes in Human Resources Programs Since January 1981," was published at a time when questions of poverty and hunger in the United States were emerging as potentially major political issues. For example, a comment by presidential counselor Edwin Meese III on December 8 that he had not seen "authoritative" evidence of hungry children in the nation and that some allegations of hunger were "purely political" provoked strong criticism from opponents of the Reagan administration.

However, the CBO was quick to point out that its study merely attempted to determine the immediate effect of changes in the funding levels of social programs since 1981 and that it did not try to consider the overall macroeconomic effects of the budget cutbacks.

CBO Report

An office within Congress, the CBO was established by the 1974 Congressional Budget and Impoundment Control Act to provide the experts and computers the legislature needed to absorb and analyze information that accompanied the president's annual budget.

In its report on the budget cutbacks, the CBO estimated the effect of legislative changes on expenditures by comparing current projections with those that would have occurred under laws in effect in 1981. The report stressed that the CBO made no assumption that the program levels at the beginning of Reagan's term had been optimal.

The study found that federal spending on human services programs (retirement and disability and other income security programs and health care, education, social services and employment programs) would decline by $110 billion, or 7 percent, over the 1982-85 period. Households with incomes below $10,000 a year would lose an average of $430 in benefits compared with what they would have received at the previous level. The average loss over all income levels would be $250. The report said that spending cuts amounted to about 28 percent in child nutrition programs, 13 percent in food stamps, 17 percent in compensatory education and 60 percent in employment and training programs.

Other 1983 Studies

Rising concern about poverty in 1983 resulted in a spate of studies and reports. Two of the studies found wide economic gaps between white and black Americans. The reports, by the Joint Center for Political Studies and by the Center for the Study of Social Policy, were released on June 20 and July 17, respectively.

The federal Census Bureau on August 2 reported that the nation's poverty rate increased in 1982 to 15 percent, the highest level in 17 years. The congressional Joint Committee on Taxation reported on October 24 that the poverty level ($9,862 a year for a family of four) was substantially higher than the point at which people began paying income taxes.

President Reagan August 2 ordered a "no-holds-barred" study of hunger in the United States. The report had not been published as the year ended.

Following are excerpts from a report on the impact of legislative changes in federal human resources programs released August 25, 1983, by the Congressional Budget Office:

Summary

In the last two years, major changes have been enacted in many of the human resources programs. These changes have affected both total program outlays and the numbers and types of families served by particular programs. This memorandum summarizes the effects of these changes, both for the budget and for families and individuals.

The focus of this analysis is the effect of program changes enacted from January 1981 through July 1983 in five major areas of the human resources budget:

- Retirement and disability programs,
- Other income security programs,
- Health care programs,
- Education and social services, and
- Employment programs.

Overall, the programs considered here account for 96 percent of human resources spending. For each area, the impacts of legislative changes on program outlays have been estimated by comparing the Congressional Budget Office's current projections with those that would have occurred under the laws in effect at the beginning of 1981. It should be noted, however, that the 1981 spending levels are not intended to represent optimal amounts, but rather what would have occurred if no policies had been changed. Both sets of projections have been prepared using the CBO's February 1983 economic assumptions, so that the effects of legislative changes may be seen without complications introduced by changing economic factors.

In addition to summarizing the effects of changes in particular programs, this memorandum also examines the overall impact on households in different income categories of the changes in programs providing benefits for individuals. In this part of the analysis, only those changes directly affecting specific households have been included. Thus, for example, changes in such programs as Social Security and Food Stamps, which provide benefits to identifiable individuals and families in the population, have been included in the estimates, but changes in grants-in-aid to state and local governments (other than individual assistance grants) have not. Because most education aid, social services, and employment services are provided through grants to states and localities, changes in these programs are for the most part included in the first part of this study only.

To estimate the impacts of the changes in benefit programs on households in different income categories, federal benefits have been valued at the cost to the federal government of providing them, which may either exaggerate or understate their value to individuals. This is especially likely for benefits provided in kind as goods and services, rather than in cash. A reduction in federal outlays for a health-care program, for example, may not reduce the perceived well-being of the recipients by the same amount as a reduction in cash benefits with equivalent federal savings.

In addition, the estimates of changes in benefits for households in different income categories represent averages over the entire income group. Within each category, some households will actually be affected by

Composition of Federal Outlays, Fiscal Years 1982-1985

	1982	1983	1984	1985
	In Percents			
Benefit Payments for Individuals	47.9	48.3	47.5	46.3
Retirement and Disability Programs[a]	24.9	24.8	24.9	24.3
Other Income Security	11.1	11.6	10.2	9.4
Health	10.7	10.9	11.5	11.8
Higher Education	1.1	1.0	0.9	0.9
Grants to State and Local Governments[b]	6.5	6.1	6.1	5.9
Education, Employment and Social Services	2.3	2.1	2.0	1.9
Other	4.3	4.0	4.1	4.0
National Defense	25.7	26.7	28.5	29.9
Net Interest	11.6	10.9	11.2	11.6
Other Federal Operations	8.3	8.0	6.8	6.3
	In billions of dollars			
Total Outlays	728	800	850	929

SOURCE: Congressional Budget Office, based on February 1983 baseline budget projections.

NOTE: Components may not sum to totals because of rounding.

[a] Excludes military retirement which is shown in national defense.

[b] Excludes individual assistance grants, which are included in benefit payments for individuals.

changes in many programs, while others will experience no changes. Therefore, the impacts of benefit reductions or increases on those who are affected will generally be larger than the averages for the entire income group suggest.

Further, the estimates presented here are for changes in federal spending only; they do not include the effects of the tax reductions and increases enacted over the last two years, nor do they reflect any change in state and local spending or taxes in response to the federal program changes. The federal tax reductions would raise after-tax incomes for some households in all income categories. For some income groups, particularly the higher-income ones, the tax reductions would more than offset benefit reductions, on average, while for other groups, average tax reductions would only partially offset average benefit cuts. In any event, the tax reductions would not necessarily affect the specific households whose benefits had been cut.

Finally, an important caution that applies to both parts of the study is that the estimates of projected changes in spending presented here do not include any macroeconomic impacts of either the tax or the spending changes enacted over the last two years. If the program changes taken together significantly raise the rate of economic growth and reduce unemployment, for example, then they would provide higher incomes that would to some extent offset the reductions in benefits.

The major conclusions of this study are:

> ● **Spending for human resources programs has been reduced, in total, by about 7 percent** relative to what it would have been under the laws existing at the beginning of 1981.

> ● **Reductions differ markedly by program area.** In percentage terms, they are largest for the employment programs, which have been reduced by almost 60 percent compared to what they would have been under prior law. The largest dollar savings over the 1982-1985 period will result from deductions in retirement and disability programs, other income security programs, and employment programs.

> ● **Reductions in benefit payments for individuals will be greatest for households with incomes below $10,000.** In 1984, for example, such households will lose an average of $430 in benefits relative to what they would have received under prior law, as compared to an average loss over all income categories of about $250.

The impacts of the legislative changes in human resource programs are outlined in the Summary Table for the major programs in each area. Federal savings resulting from reductions in retirement and disability programs, other income security programs, and employment programs are about the same magnitude, with projected savings in 1982-1985 exceeding $25 billion in each of these areas. Total reductions in outlays for human resources programs relative to prior law are projected to be about $110 billion over the fiscal year 1982-1985 period.

The largest percentage reductions, other than those in the employment programs, are projected in the area of education and social services, outlays for which have been reduced by almost 20 percent overall relative to prior law. Projected outlays for income security programs, excluding retirement and disability programs, have been reduced by about 10 percent, while projected health-care outlays have been cut about 5 percent and projected outlays for retirement and disability programs have fallen about 3 percent overall.

Within each area, the relative size of the changes varies by program. In the employment area, for example, the Public Service Employment program was eliminated, reducing projected outlays by about $17 billion, while projected outlays for the Job Corps have been reduced by about $145 million relative to what they would have been for the 1982-1985 period — a reduction of about 6 percent. Similarly, projected outlays for child nutrition programs are about 28 percent lower than they would have been under prior law, while outlays for the Supplemental Feeding Program for Women, Infants, and Children (WIC) have been increased slightly. The only other major human resources program to experience a net increase in projected outlays as a result of legislative action in this period is the Supplemental Security Income (SSI) program, which provides means-tested benefits for aged, disabled, and blind persons. Its outlays are projected to be about 4 percent higher than they would have been under prior law, largely as a result of a benefit increase enacted as part of the Social Security Amendments of 1983.

The changes in projected outlays will also have different effects on households with different incomes. Overall, about 40 percent of the federal savings from changes in benefit programs are projected to result from reductions affecting households with 1982 incomes of less than $10,000 — who make up about 23 percent of the population — and another 30 percent will come from reductions affecting households with incomes between $10,000 and $20,000 — about 25 percent of the population. Reductions in cash benefits will account for about 60 percent of the total savings from reductions in benefits for individuals, with the remainder coming from in-kind benefits.

Average reductions in benefits per household are also projected to be greater for households in the below $10,000 income category than for any other group. In 1984, for example, the average reduction in benefits going to this group is projected to be about $430, compared to an average reduction of about $300 for those with incomes between $10,000 and $20,000. Reductions for the households in higher income categories are projected to range from $140 to $170 per household. . . .

Impact of Recent Legislative Changes in Human Resources Programs

Shifts in spending levels for different groups of programs within the budget result from legislative, economic, and technical estimating factors. . . . [T]he CBO has prepared estimates of what spending for human resources programs would have been under the laws in effect in January 1981, but using the economic and technical assumptions of February 1983. By comparing these estimates with current baseline projections, it is possible to calculate the total impact for each program of legislative changes enacted between 1981 and 1983. . . .

. . . [O]utlays for virtually all of the major programs serving families and individuals are lower than they would have been under 1981 law. Across all of the human resoures programs considered here, the reductions average about 7 percent. The only programs not reduced relative to the 1981 baseline are the Supplementary Feeding Program for Women, Infants, and Children (WIC) and the Supplemental Security Income (SSI) program.

The first of these programs, which had total outlays of about $930 million in 1982, received $100 million in additional funding as a result of the recently passed Emergency Jobs Appropriation Act (P.L. 98-8), which is expected to increase outlays by $70 million and $30 million in 1983 and 1984, respectively. Benefits for SSI, a program with outlays of about $7.7 billion in 1982 that provides cash benefits to low-income elderly and disabled persons, were increased about 4 percent under the Social Security Amendments of 1983.

Aside from these two programs, however, the reductions in human resources programs have been widespread, although some areas have been more affected than others. For example, projected 1982-1985 outlays for the retirement and disability programs have been reduced by about 3 percent, while those for employment programs have been cut by almost 60 percent. Percentage reductions in the other categories are between these extremes — about 18 percent for education and social services, about 10 percent overall for the "other income security" category, and about 5 percent in total for health-care programs.

Much of the reduction in funding for employment programs results from the elimination of the Public Service Employment (PSE) program under the Omnibus Budget Reconciliation act of 1981 (OBRA). This elimination reduced total expenditures for employment programs by almost $17 billion over the years 1982-1985 relative to what they would have been under the 1981 baseline. Other employment and training expenditures have also been substantially reduced — by a third or more in some programs — although additional funds were appropriated for employment programs under the Emergency Jobs Appropriation Act.

Social services programs have also experienced large reductions. The social services block grant, for example, is funded at a level 22 percent lower than the adjusted 1981 baseline projection for the programs it replaced, while the community services block grant is funded at about 39 percent less than the revised 1981 baseline estimate for the Community Services Administration programs it replaced.

Reductions in education programs have been almost as large. While it is difficult to forecast what the rate of applications for student loans would have been without program changes, legislative changes in the guaranteed student loan (GSL) program have reduced projected outlays by approximately 27 percent, for example. Similarly, funding for grants to college students under means-tested student financial assistance programs — principally, Pell Grants — has been reduced by about 13 percent. Programs serving elementary and secondary school students have also been affected; funding for compensatory education for disadvantaged students has been reduced by about 17 percent as a result of legislative changes, for example.

Although there were substantial reductions in some income security programs as a result of the legislative changes of the last few years, these changes on average have not been as large in percentage terms as the reductions in employment, social services, and education programs. In general, projected outlays for the means-tested income security programs, particularly those serving primarily a non-elderly population, have been reduced by a larger percentage than expenditures in the non-means-tested and retirement programs. In percentage terms, the largest reductions in this area — about 28 percent of outlays — took place in the child nutrition programs, which provide subsidies for school lunches and other meals for children. The Aid to Families with Dependent Children (AFDC) and Food Stamp programs were each reduced by about 13 percent as a result of program changes that restricted eligibility and lowered benefits for some recipients. Unemployment Insurance (UI) benefits were also reduced overall for the projection period, largely as a result of changes in the rules governing the provision of benefits after 26 weeks. Special Federal Supplemental Compensation (FSC) benefits were granted for UI recipients in 1983, however, increasing outlays for UI in 1983 by $3 billion compared to what they would have been under the revised 1981 baseline.

The health-care area experienced smaller reductions overall as a result of the legislative changes. The two biggest programs, Medicare and Medicaid, were each reduced by about 5 percent relative to the revised 1981 baseline. These changes generally affected hospitals, other health care providers, and states more than beneficiaries. Outlays for health services previously funded under the Health Services Administration, however, are about 22 percent below the revised 1981 baseline estimates.

Finally, the retirement and disability programs experienced the smallest percentage reductions, as a group, of those considered in this memorandum. Since total outlays for these programs, especially Social Security, are so large, however, the dollar amounts of the reductions in this area are as large as those in employment programs. Both Social Security and Civil Service Retirement (CSR) were reduced by about 3 percent relative to the revised 1981 baseline estimates, and the veterans' compensation and pension programs, which provide benefits for disabled veterans and for low-income elderly and disabled veterans respectively, were reduced by a total of about 1 percent. In spite of these small percentage reductions, however, net savings as a result of legislative changes in this area total nearly $26 billion over the years 1982-1985.

In considering the impacts of the legislative actions outlined above, it is important to bear in mind that the estimates shown here represent only the total differences between the revised 1981 baseline and the current baseline for each program or set of programs. In some cases, these differences may result from several sets of legislative changes, which may have had offsetting effects. Also, the 1981 baseline is simply an estimate of what total spending for each program would have been under the laws that existed in 1981; it does not in any sense represent an optimal spending level for these programs. . . .

September

STATEMENTS ON KOREAN AIRLINE TRAGEDY

September 1, 5, 1983

A Soviet jet fighter's heat-seeking missile downed a South Korean commercial airliner September 1 after it flew over strategically sensitive Soviet territory, killing all 269 people aboard from more than 10 nations. Korean Air Lines Flight 007, one of 12,000 commercial flights that skirt Soviet air space in the North Pacific each year, had deviated 300 miles from its assigned course on the last leg of its flight from New York to Seoul. Among the 61 American passengers killed was 48-year-old Rep. Larry P. McDonald, D-Ga., chairman of the right-wing John Birch Society and one of Congress' most conservative members.

A crisis atmosphere surrounded the incident. President Ronald Reagan said September 5, "There was absolutely no justification, either legal or moral, for what the Soviets did.... It was an act of barbarism, born of a society which wantonly disregards individual rights and the value of human life and seeks constantly to expand and dominate other nations." Reagan avoided any major retaliatory initiatives, however, announcing several minor punitive measures that were widely viewed as symbolic and unlikely to have any appreciable effect on U.S.-Soviet relations.

The incident was one of the most serious international aerial confrontations in years. In 1978 a Soviet plane shot down a South Korean commercial jetliner, killing two passengers and forcing it to land on a frozen lake in Siberia. Israeli fighter planes shot down a Libyan passenger jet in 1973; 108 people died. Bulgaria shot down an El Al Israel Airlines plane in 1955; 85 people died.

The downing of the Korean plane unleashed a public furor, with the

United States accusing the Soviets of knowingly shooting down an unarmed civilian aircraft and then failing to acknowledge or apologize for the act. The Soviets accused the United States of using the plane for a spy mission and of manipulating public opinion in support of militaristic policies. The Soviets also contended that the craft had attempted to elude intercepting Soviet planes and ignored warning signals.

Details of the Flight

KAL's Boeing 747 jet departed New York August 30 and made a scheduled refueling stop in Anchorage, Alaska. The flight left Anchorage with a new crew headed by an experienced former South Korean air force pilot who had flown the route for five years. Four hours after leaving Anchorage, Flight 007 notified Tokyo that it had passed a routine checkpoint south of Kamchatka Peninsula, site of several Soviet military installations, including a Soviet naval base with 90 nuclear submarines. It emerged later, however, that the plane actually had overflown Kamchatka. Soviet radar picked it up and tracked it for two and a half hours as it flew 1,000 miles toward Sakhalin Island, where other Soviet strategic bases were located.

The pilot of a SU-15 supersonic jet fired one or possibly two missiles at the plane. "I have executed the launch," the pilot said. "The target is destroyed." Shortly thereafter the jetliner disappeared from Japanese radar screens, crashing into the Sea of Japan.

The United States acknowledged the plane had flown over Soviet territory but could give no definite explanation why. The plane's two crash-resistant flight recorders, the so-called "black boxes," were believed irretrievably lost in 2,500 feet of water. They contained valuable in-flight data and cockpit voice transmissions and held the best chance of disclosing what happened in the final minutes of Flight 007 and why the Boeing 747 had strayed far off course.

The plane was equipped not only with three computerized navigation systems but also with radar that enabled pilots to follow coastline and other terrain features. The navigational computers were designed to keep the plane on course automatically without radio contact from the ground. They were completely self-contained and were known for their accuracy. Aviation experts said that a simultaneous failure of three individual computers was unlikely. They also dismissed the possibility that erroneous coordinates were inserted into the systems because it was standard practice for one crew member to check the entries of a colleague.

Conflicting Versions of Events

A statement from Tass, the official Soviet press agency, three days after the downing of the plane said its outlines resembled those of the

American electronic reconnaissance plane, RC-135, the military's version of the Boeing 747. The United States disclosed then that an RC-135 had been near Kamchatka. It had been flying a routine mission about 50 miles off the peninsula as it monitored Soviet transmissions concerning missiles. The closest the two planes had come to each other was 75 miles, the United States claimed. Perhaps confused, Soviet air defense personnel may have assumed that the new blip on their radar screens was another RC-135 coming to relieve the first. The United States discounted that assumption because, according to the U.S. transcript, the Soviet SU-15 fighter pilot had seen the airliner.

There were other major contradictions between the U.S. and Soviet versions of the incident. The Soviets said their pilot gave wing signals to the 747, which did not respond. Standard procedures for intercepting planes that stray illegally into another country's airspace are laid down in the rules of the International Civil Aviation Organization (ICAO), a United Nations affiliate, to which 152 countries, including the Soviet Union, belonged. Pilots of the interceptors are supposed to rock their wings and at night flash lights to say, "You have been intercepted. Follow me." The off-course plane should duplicate the procedure to signal "Understood, will comply." The State Department said there was no evidence to suggest the Korean pilot was aware of any such warning.

The Soviet pilot said he saw no navigation lights on the 747, but the tapes Americans supplied contained mention of such lights. The taped references were made by a second fighter pilot, behind the first, remarking on the lights of the first fighter, the Soviets countered.

Soviet defense commanders were convinced that there was "no doubt that a reconnaissance plane was in the air." American officials maintained the jetliner was not performing reconnaissance tasks and that the RC-135 was well away from the area before the missiles were fired. They said, "We do not think this was a case of mistaken identity." The Soviets contended cloud cover, darkness and distance prevented Soviet pilots from identifying the target as a 747. But President Reagan said in his televised address September 5 that the firing occurred on "a clear night with a half moon." On the U.S. tapes a Soviet pilot could be heard saying he was as close as 1.3 miles to the 747.

The United States completed its review of evidence October 5. U.S. intelligence experts said then they found no indication that Soviet air defense personnel knew it was a commercial plane before the attack.

A draft report of the results of an ICAO investigation rejected the Soviets' reconstruction of the events. The report, made public in December, concluded that the Soviets "did not make exhaustive efforts to identify the aircraft through inflight visual observations" and had not complied with procedures for warning intruders that they had flown into prohibited airspace.

*Following is the text of a statement made September 1,
1983, by Secretary of State George P. Shultz on the downing
of the Korean airliner and excerpts from a televised address
by President Ronald Reagan, September 5, 1983:*

SHULTZ STATEMENT

At 1400 hours Greenwich Mean Time yesterday, a Korean Air Lines
Boeing 747 en route from New York to Seoul, Korea, departed Anchorage,
Alaska. Two-hundred sixty-nine passengers and crew were on board,
including congressman Lawrence P. McDonald.

At approximately 1600 hours Greenwich Mean Time, the aircraft came
to the attention of Soviet radar. It was tracked constantly by the Soviets
from that time.

The aircraft strayed into Soviet airspace over the Kamchatka Peninsula
and over the Sea of Okhotsk and over the Sakhalin Islands. The Soviets
tracked the commercial airliner for some two and a half hours.

A Soviet pilot reported visual contact with the aircraft at 1812 hours.
The Soviet plane was, we know, in constant contact with its ground
control.

At 1821 hours the Korean aircraft was reported by the Soviet pilot at
10,000 meters. At 1826 hours the Soviet pilot reported that he had fired a
missile and the target was destroyed. At 1830 hours the Korean aircraft
was reported by radar at 5,000 meters. At 1838 hours the Korean plane disappeared from the radar screen.

We know that at least eight Soviet fighters reacted at one time or
another to the airliner. The pilot who shot the aircraft down reported after
the attack that he had in fact fired a missile, that he had destroyed the target and that he was breaking away.

About an hour later, the Soviet controllers ordered a number of their
search aircraft to conduct search and rescue activities in the vicinity of the
last position of the Korean airliner as reflected by Soviet tracking. One of
these aircraft reported finding kerosene on the surface of the seas. . . .

During Wednesday night, United States State Department officials,
particularly Assistant Secretary [Richard] Burt, were in contact with
Soviet officials seeking information concerning the airliner's fate. The
Soviets offered no information.

As soon as U.S. sources had confirmed the shooting down of the aircraft,
the U.S. on its own behalf and on behalf of the Republic of Korea called in
the Soviet chargé d'affaires in Washington this morning to express our
grave concern over the shooting down of an unarmed civilian plane
carrying passengers with a number of nationalities. We also urgently
demanded an explanation from the Soviet Union.

The United States reacts with revulsion to this attack. Loss of life
appears to be heavy. We can see no excuse whatsoever for this appalling
act.

REAGAN ADDRESS

My fellow Americans:

I'm coming before you tonight about the Korean airline massacre, the attack by the Soviet Union against 269 innocent men, women, and children aboard an unarmed Korean passenger plane. This crime against humanity must never be forgotten, here or throughout the world.

Our prayers tonight are with the victims and their families in their time of terrible grief. . . .

Let me state as plainly as I can: There was absolutely no justification, either legal or moral, for what the Soviets did. One newspaper in India said, "If every passenger plane . . . is fair game for home air forces . . . it will be the end to civil aviation as we know it."

This is not the first time the Soviet Union has shot at and hit a civilian airliner when it overflew its territory. In another tragic incident in 1978, the Soviets also shot down an unarmed civilian airliner after having positively identified it as such. In that instance, the Soviet interceptor pilot clearly identified the civilian markings on the side of the aircraft, repeatedly questioned the order to fire on a civilian airliner, and was ordered to shoot it down anyway. The aircraft was hit with a missile and made a crash landing. Several innocent people lost their lives in this attack, killed by shrapnel from the blast of a Soviet missile.

Is this a practice of other countries in the world? The answer is no. Commercial aircraft from the Soviet Union and Cuba on a number of occasions have overflown sensitive United States military facilities. They weren't shot down. We and other civilized countries believe in the tradition of offering help to mariners and pilots who are lost or in distress on the sea or in the air. We believe in following procedures to prevent a tragedy, not to provoke one.

But despite the savagery of their crime, the universal reaction against it, and the evidence of their complicity, the Soviets still refuse to tell the truth. They have persistently refused to admit that their pilot fired on the Korean aircraft. Indeed, they've not even told their own people that a plane was shot down.

They have spun a confused tale of tracking the plane by radar until it just mysteriously disappeared from their radar screens, but no one fired a shot of any kind. But then they coupled this with charges that it was a spy plane sent by us and that their planes fired tracer bullets past the plane as a warning that it was in Soviet airspace.

Let me recap for a moment and present the incontrovertible evidence that we have. The Korean airliner, a Boeing 747, left Anchorage, Alaska, bound for Seoul, Korea, on a course south and west which would take it across Japan. Out over the Pacific, in international waters, it was for a brief time in the vicinity of one of our reconnaissance planes, an RC-135, on a routine mission. At no time was the RC-135 in Soviet airspace. The Korean airliner flew on, and the two planes were soon widely separated.

The 747 is equipped with the most modern computerized navigation facilities, but a computer must respond to input provided by human hands. No one will ever know whether a mistake was made in giving the computer the course or whether there was a malfunction. Whichever, the 747 was flying a course further to the west than it was supposed to fly — a course which took it into Soviet airspace.

The Soviets tracked this plane for 2½ hours while it flew a straight-line course at 30 to 35,000 feet. Only civilian airliners fly in such a manner. At one point, the Korean pilot gave Japanese air control his position as east of Hokkaido, Japan, showing that he was unaware they were off course by as much or more than a hundred miles.

The Soviets scrambled jet interceptors from a base in Sakhalin Island. Japanese ground sites recorded the interceptor planes' radio transmissions — their conversations with their own ground control. We only have the voices from the pilots; the Soviet ground-to-air transmissions were not recorded. It's plain, however, from the pilot's words that he's responding to orders and queries from his own ground control.

Here is a brief segment of the tape which we're going to play in its entirety for the United Nations Security Council tomorrow.

[At this point, the tape was played.]

Those were the voices of the Soviet pilots. In this tape, the pilot who fired the missile describes his search for what he calls the target. He reports he has it in sight; indeed, he pulls up to within about a mile of the Korean plane, mentions its flashing strobe light and that its navigation lights are on. He then reports he's reducing speed to get behind the airliner, gives his distance from the plane at various points in this maneuver, and finally announces what can only be called the "Korean Airline Massacre." He says he has locked on the radar, which aims his missiles, has launched those missiles, the target has been destroyed, and he is breaking off the attack.

Let me point out something here having to do with this closeup view of the airliner on what we know was a clear night with a half moon. The 747 has a unique and distinctive silhouette, unlike any other plane in the world. There is no way a pilot could mistake this for anything other than a civilian airliner. And if that isn't enough, let me point out our RC-135 that I mentioned earlier had been back at its base in Alaska, on the ground for an hour, when the murderous attack took place over the Sea of Japan.

And make no mistake about it, this attack was not just against ourselves or the Republic of Korea. This was the Soviet Union against the world and the moral precepts which guide human relations among people everywhere. It was an act of barbarism, born of a society which wantonly disregards individual rights and the value of human life and seeks constantly to expand and dominate other nations.

They deny the deed, but in their conflicting and misleading protestations, the Soviets reveal that, yes, shooting down a plane — even one with hundreds of innocent men, women, children, and babies — is a part of their normal procedure if that plane is in what they claim as their airspace.

They owe the world an apology and an offer to join the rest of the world in working out a system to protect against this ever happening again. Among the rest of us there is one protective measure: an international radio wave length on which pilots can communicate with planes of other nations if they are in trouble or lost. Soviet military planes are not so equipped, because that would make it easier for pilots who might want to defect.

Our request to send vessels into Soviet waters to search for wreckage and bodies has received no satisfactory answer. Bereaved families of the Japanese victims were harassed by Soviet patrol boats when they tried to get near where the plane is believed to have gone down in order to hold a ceremony for their dead. But we shouldn't be surprised by such inhuman brutality. Memories come back of Czechoslovakia, Hungary, Poland, the gassing of villages in Afghanistan. If the massacre and their subsequent conduct is intended to intimidate, they have failed in their purpose. From every corner of the globe the word is defiance in the face of this unspeakable act and defiance of the system which excuses it and tries to cover it up. With our horror and our sorrow, there is a righteous and terrible anger. It would be easy to think in terms of vengeance, but that is not a proper answer. We want justice and action to see that this never happens again.

Our immediate challenge to this atrocity is to ensure that we make the skies safer and that we seek just compensation for the families of those who were killed.

Since my return to Washington, we've held long meetings, the most recent yesterday with the congressional leadership. There was a feeling of unity in the room, and I received a number of constructive suggestions. We will continue to work with the Congress regarding our response to this massacre.

As you know, we immediately made known to the world the shocking facts as honestly and completely as they came to us.

We have notified the Soviets that we will not renew our bilateral agreement for cooperation in the field of transportation so long as they threaten the security of civil aviation.

Since 1981 the Soviet airline Aeroflot has been denied the right to fly to the United States. We have reaffirmed that order and are examining additional steps we can take with regard to Aeroflot facilities in this country. We're cooperating with other countries to find better means to ensure the safety of civil aviation and to join us in not accepting Aeroflot as a normal member of the international civil air community unless and until the Soviets satisfy the cries of humanity for justice. I am pleased to report that Canada today suspended Aeroflot's landing and refueling privileges for 60 days.

We have joined with other countries to press the International Civil Aviation Organization to investigate this crime at an urgent special session of the Council. At the same time, we're listening most carefully to private groups, both American and international, airline pilots, passenger associations, and others, who have a special interest in civil air safety.

I am asking the Congress to pass a joint resolution of condemnation of this Soviet crime.

We have informed the Soviets that we're suspending negotiations on several bilateral arrangements we had under consideration.

Along with Korea and Japan, we called an emergency meeting of the U.N. Security Council which began on Friday. On that first day, Korea, Japan, Canada, Australia, the Netherlands, Pakistan, France, China, the United Kingdom, Zaire, New Zealand, and West Germany all joined us in denouncing the Soviet action and expressing our horror. We expect to hear from additional countries as debate resumes tomorrow.

We intend to work with the 13 countries who had citizens aboard the Korean airliner to seek reparations for the families of all those who were killed. The United States will be making a claim against the Soviet Union within the next week to obtain compensation for the benefit of the victims' survivors. Such compensation is an absolute moral duty which the Soviets must assume.

In the economic area in general, we're redoubling our efforts with our allies to end the flow of military and strategic items to the Soviet Union.

Secretary [of State George P.] Shultz is going to Madrid to meet with representatives of 35 countries who, for 3 years, have been negotiating an agreement having to do with, among other things, human rights. Foreign Minister [Andrei] Gromyko of the Soviet Union is scheduled to attend that meeting. If he does come to the meeting, Secretary Shultz is going to present him with our demands for disclosure of the facts, corrective action, and concrete assurances that such a thing will not happen again and that restitution be made.

As we work with other countries to see that justice is done, the real test of our resolve is whether we have the will to remain strong, steady, and united. I believe more than ever — as evidenced by your thousands and thousands of wires and phone calls in these last few days — that we do.

I have outlined some of the steps we're taking in response to the tragic massacre. There is something I've always believed in, but which now seems more important than ever. The Congress will be facing key national security issues when it returns from recess. There has been legitimate difference of opinion on this subject, I know, but I urge the Members of that distinguished body to ponder long and hard the Soviets' aggression as they consider the security and safety of our people — indeed, all people who believe in freedom.

Senator Henry Jackson, a wise and revered statesman and one who probably understood the Soviets as well as any American in history, warned us, "the greatest threat the United States now faces is posed by the Soviet Union." But Senator Jackson said, "If America maintains a strong deterrent — and only if it does — this nation will continue to be a leader in the crucial quest for enduring peace among nations."

The late Senator made those statements in July on the Senate floor, speaking in behalf of the MX missile program he considered vital to restore America's strategic parity with the Soviets.

When John F. Kennedy was President, defense spending as a share of the Federal budget was 70 percent greater than it is today. Since then, the Soviet Union has carried on the most massive military buildup the world has ever seen. Until they are willing to join the rest of the world community, we must maintain the strength to deter their aggression.

But while we do so, we must not give up our effort to bring them into the world community of nations. Peace through strength as long as necessary, but never giving up our effort to bring peace closer through mutual, verifiable reduction in the weapons of war.

I've told you of negotiations we've suspended as a result of the Korean airline massacre, but we cannot, we must not give up our effort to reduce the arsenals of destructive weapons threatening the world. Ambassador [Paul H.] Nitze has returned to Geneva to resume the negotiations on intermediate-range nuclear weapons in Europe. Equally, we will continue to press for arms reductions in the [strategic arms limitation] START talks that resume in October. We are more determined than ever to reduce and, if possible, eliminate the threat hanging over mankind.

We know it will be hard to make a nation that rules its own people through force to cease using force against the rest of the world. But we must try.

This is not a role we sought. We preach no manifest destiny. But like Americans who began this country and brought forth this last, best hope of mankind, history has asked much of the Americans of our time. Much we have already given; much more we must be prepared to give.

Let us have faith, in Abraham Lincoln's words, "that right makes might, and in that faith let us, to the end dare to do our duty as we understand it." If we do, if we stand together and move forward with courage, then history will record that some good did come from this monstrous wrong that we will carry with us and remember for the rest of our lives.

Thank you. God bless you, and good night.

MINIMUM WAGE REPORT

September 19, 1983

Congress should not increase the minimum wage and should reject proposals to adopt a subminimum wage for youth, a study commissioned by the National Chamber Foundation recommended September 19. The Foundation is the public policy research arm of the U.S. Chamber of Commerce.

The report, entitled Minimum Wage Regulation in the United States, *was the product of a two-year study by Belton M. Fleisher, professor of economics at Ohio State University. The purpose of Fleisher's study was to evaluate the relative costs and benefits of minimum wage regulation as "an antipoverty device." Fleisher concluded that the minimum wage costs, especially in terms of disemployment and an actual lowering of employee income, substantially outweighed any benefits. Fleisher also argued that creation of a youth subminimum wage would result in a loss of jobs for adult workers.*

Background

The merits and problems of the minimum wage have been a topic of debate since the rate's inception. State legislatures began enacting minimum wage laws in 1912. A federal minimum wage, confined largely to manufacturing industries, was established in 1938 under the Fair Labor Standards Act. Its purpose was to reduce poverty and establish a minimum standard of living without substantially reducing employment or earning power.

Over the years, particularly in the 1960s and 1970s, the minimum wage was increased and its coverage extended. The rate in 1983, set in January 1981, was $3.35 an hour for most workers. The Reagan administration opposed any increase in the rate.

In 1977 Congress created the Minimum Wage Study Commission to review the "social, political and economic ramifications of the minimum wage." That group was responsible for a large number of reports. Studies were undertaken by other groups as well, many of them commissioned by the American Enterprise Institute for Public Policy Research. Those studies served as the basis for much of Fleisher's report.

Report's Findings

Fleisher concluded that the minimum wage "has no place in a constructive labor market policy for the United States and is counterproductive as an element of a humane program of income transfers." The report cited a number of negative effects of the minimum wage, including reduced employment opportunities for low-wage workers, fewer fringe benefits in minimum wage jobs as employers tried to make up for their increased salary costs, a loss of jobs for younger or slower workers and a possible adverse impact on the nation's ability to control inflation. Indexation, that is, statutory increases in the minimum wage rate to keep pace with inflation or real growth, would only exacerbate all the problems caused by the existing rate, Fleisher stated.

Fleisher's opposition to the minimum wage and any increases in its rate was in line with the Chamber's position but conflicted with that of organized labor. Unions historically had supported a minimum wage rate as a base from which to begin collective bargaining.

Fleisher also rejected adoption of a subminimum wage for youth, a proposal favored by the Reagan administration. In a message to Congress March 11, 1983, Reagan recommended adoption of a "youth opportunity wage" of $2.50 an hour, to be paid to persons under age 21 and only from May through September of each year. Reagan said the adult minimum wage hampered youth employment, which he estimated constituted 30 percent of overall U.S. unemployment.

Labor unions, however, opposed a youth subminimum wage, fearing employers would replace more costly adult workers with younger ones. Administration officials argued that their plan, with its May through September restriction, should protect most adult workers from job losses. On that issue, Fleisher agreed with labor, contending that employment gains for young workers would come at the expense of older employees.

Fleisher's study, which was financed by a number of restaurant chains, also recommended full tip credit for restaurant workers and other employees who received tips. Under a full tip credit, all tips a worker received would be counted toward the minimum wage rate. In 1983 employers were required to pay 60 percent of the minimum wage to employees who could make more than that rate in tips. The tip credit savings realized by employers would allow them to add to their payrolls and create jobs for other low-wage workers, Fleisher said.

Following are excerpts from the September 19, 1983, report prepared by Belton M. Fleisher for the U.S. Chamber of Commerce, entitled Minimum Wage Regulation in the United States:

In this report, minimum wage regulation is evaluated in terms of its benefits and costs as an antipoverty device. . . .

. . . The principal beneficial effect of minimum wage legislation must arise from increasing the incomes of low-wage workers or poor families. The other effects of minimum wages on the economy are to be judged against this criterion.

Ideal public policy designed to improve the economic circumstances of those incapable of supporting themselves as an acceptable standard of living is not always politically feasible. Political support for minimum wage laws has been based on (1) regional economic interests (protecting high-wage areas of the United States from competition by lower-wage regions in the South and outlying areas such as Puerto Rico), and (2) labor union interests which include reducing the competitive advantage of nonunion employees.

A major proposition of this report is that the most serious impact of minimum wages is on employment. While employers can be forced to pay higher wages they cannot be restrained from laying off, or refusing to hire, workers whose productivity falls short of their pay. This is the *disemployment* effect of minimum wages, and it is both large and harmful to the economy. While it is popularly believed that a major impact of minimum wages is on inflation . . . the inflationary impact of minimum wages is both indirect and relatively minor. The reason is this: while it is true that an increase in the minimum wage raises the costs of firms who hire minimum wage labor and that these cost increases are followed by price increases, consumers have limited spending power. The additional amounts they spend on goods and services produced with minimum wage labor must be subtracted from expenditures elsewhere. Thus, increases in expenditures on goods and services using minimum wage labor will be offset by a decline in expenditures on other goods and services — forcing their prices down. Only if government increases spending power through increases in the money supply in response to increases in the minimum wage can the minimum wage be inflationary. . . .

. . . [E]mployer responses to the minimum wage can include reducing fringe benefits and altering working conditions in such a way that the value of minimum wage jobs to workers is actually reduced by increases in the minimum wage rate. There is evidence that such negative adjustments have occurred. Particular attention is devoted to the impact on the training value of jobs to young workers, and it is likely that the full wage (including the training value) of jobs has been reduced by imposition of minimum wages. . . .

. . . [T]he percentage reduction in employment of minimum wage labor is a useful criterion of whether minimum wages reduce poverty. Using this criterion, a necessary condition for minimum wage legislation to have this desired effect is that percentage reductions in employment be smaller than percentage increases in the minimum wage. Even if this condition should hold, the likelihood that some disemployed workers will have little or no access to minimum wage jobs because their value to employers falls short of the minimum necessitates that these workers' losses be compared to employed workers' gains for a complete evaluation of the benefits and costs of minimum wages. . . .

. . . The preponderance of evidence is that the economy-wide and industry-specific disemployment effects of minimum wages on minimum wage workers in general and on youth in particular are to reduce average earnings, contrary to the intent of the law. These adverse effects are particularly severe in low-wage manufacturing, retail trade, and restaurant industries. Extensions of minimum wage legislation during the 1960s have thus exacerbated the negative impact on the earning power of low-wage workers.

The conclusion that must be drawn . . . is that, on average, low-wage workers are harmed, not benefitted, by minimum wages, because their real incomes are lowered. . . .

. . . [T]he impact of minimum wages on the unemployment rate is uncertain. *Paradoxically, if minimum wages cause unemployment to rise, this does not mean that minimum wage workers are necessarily worse-off, and if unemployment should fall, they may actually be harmed by minimum wages.* The impact of minimum wages on inflation is . . . indirect. There is much confusion about this, because the relationship between movements in individual wages and prices and the overall price level is frequently confused in popular discussions of inflation. The best available evidence is that the minimum wage has both reduced total output below the potential of our economy and has contributed — modestly — to inflation. For example, about one-tenth of the inflation that occurred between 1974 and 1977 is attributable to increases in the minimum wage. . . .

. . . [T]he minimum wage cannot be an efficient antipoverty device because there is a very small correlation between the wage rates of individual workers and their family incomes. Moreover, nearly half of all poverty families and over a third of all unrelated individuals whose income is in the poverty range receive no earnings because they do not work at all (1977 data). Those poor unrelated individuals whose incomes do depend mainly on their earnings are probably the most likely among minimum wage workers to lose their jobs if employers are required by law to raise their wages, because adult males who receive the minimum wage or less are most likely than others to have relatively permanent employment disadvantages than are women and teenagers, whose principal disadvantage is usually lack of experience and on-the-job training. An extensive study of the effects of minimum wages on the wage rates and earnings of adult women shows only very minor effects on both hourly rates of pay and annual labor incomes of workers whose unregulated wage would be equal to or less than the legal minimum.

The costs of minimum wage legislation documented in this report substantially outweigh the modest benefits, if any, that can be claimed by supporters of the minimum wage. Indeed, disemployment of minimum wage workers is so large, a strong case can be made that minimum wages have lowered their average earnings. Sound public policy calls for using other mechanisms, many of which are already available and operative, to supplement the incomes of the needy in our society.

The body of research on minimum wage rates, which has grown quite large in recent years, is by no means homogeneous, and diversity in approaches, assumptions, and conclusions do exist. However, this report argues that the potential antipoverty benefits are so small that even if one chooses to ignore the preponderance of evidence on the size of disemployment effects, one need not worry about failing to adopt a beneficial and cost-effective policy to accomplish desired aims in the case of minimum wage legislation.

Therefore, the basic recommendation of this report is that Congress should do nothing to increase the minimum wage in the future. Then the unregulated wage growth that can reasonably be expected to occur in our economy will eliminate most of the harmful effects of existing minimum wages over the next several years. In the meantime, various proposals are likely to be considered, and the following are recommendations regarding them:

- **Tip Credit**

    The fact that tip income cannot be fully credited to payment of legal minimum wages has reduced job and earning opportunities for many restaurant workers and other tipped employees.

    It is urged that legislation be adopted to provide full credit for tip income against the minimum wage, applicable to all workers in service, retail, and eating and drinking establishments.

- **Indexation**

    Statutory upward adjustment of the minimum wage to reflect inflationary or real wage growth would magnify disemployment effects and could significantly increase the inflationary impact, which has up to now been modest. This is because inflation would no longer cause the minimum wage to "self-destruct" as price and wage levels rise in relationship to it.

    Arguments in favor of indexation which refer to the benefits business would derive because they could plan more easily for the future are specious. Planning stability can more easily be achieved by not changing the minimum wage at all, and its harmful effects will gradually wither away.

● **Youth subminimum wage**

Adopting a lower wage for teenagers would have a beneficial effect on their job prospects. Unfortunately, this gain would occur at the cost of an unknown number of lost job opportunities for adult men and women. Moreover, teenagers are reasonably likely to be able to rely on support from other (adult) family members, while low-wage adults, particularly men, are less likely to be able to depend on the economic support of other family members because they are living alone or with other low-wage earners.

Therefore, a teenage subminimum wage cannot be recommended on grounds of equity. Freezing the minimum wage at its current level for all workers is preferred to lowering the minimum for only teenagers.[1]

The minimum wage has no place in a constructive labor market policy for the United States, and it is counterproductive as an element of a humane program of income transfers. The recommendations set forth here will, if adopted, minimize the harmful effects of existing law and of frequently proposed legislative changes.

▼▼▼

[1] It is to be emphasized here that this position is not that of the Chamber of Commerce of the United States, which has supported and continues to support a youth differential. This report is the result of Professor Fleisher's independent research, and his conclusions are not to be interpreted as statements of the policies of the U.S. Chamber, the National Chamber Foundation, or any other organization.

REAGAN ADDRESS TO
U.N. GENERAL ASSEMBLY
September 26, 1983

President Ronald Reagan unveiled a new arms control offer to the Soviets in a September 26 address to the United Nations General Assembly in New York. The proposal was intended to demonstrate the administration's flexibility in the U.S.-Soviet negotiations to limit inter-mediate-range nuclear forces (INF) under way in Geneva.

The administration hoped that the show of U.S. flexibility would help modify its image of rigidity on strategic arms issues. That image had fostered congressional opposition to the administration's stance in the separate U.S.-Soviet strategic arms reduction (START) talks as well as calls for a U.S.-Soviet freeze on deployment of nuclear weapons.

Reagan clearly wished to offset the suggestion that his administration had little sense of urgency about arms control and little sensitivity to the threat of nuclear war. "A nuclear war cannot be won and it must never be fought," he declared. ("Nuclear winter" reports, p. 857)

Reagan's speech came at a time of increased U.S.-Soviet tension in the aftermath of the Soviet downing of a South Korean commercial jetliner September 1. World reaction to the tragedy was "a timely reminder of just how different the Soviets' conception of truth and international cooperation is from that of the rest of the world," Reagan said. "Evidence abounds that we cannot simply assume that agreements negotiated with the Soviet Union will be fulfilled." (Korean airline tragedy, p. 775)

The president also used the occasion to cite Soviet actions, including the construction of a possible anti-ballistic missile radar and the testing of an intercontinental-range missile, that appeared to violate existing arms control agreements.

Background of INF Talks

Members of the North Atlantic Treaty Organization had agreed in December 1979 to deploy 108 U.S. Pershing II ballistic missiles and 464 ground-launched cruise missiles (GLCMs) in Western Europe by December 1983.

In November 1981 the Reagan administration put forward a "zero option" INF proposal, whereby the United States would cancel the scheduled deployment of the missiles if the Soviet Union dismantled its SS-20s and its 200 or so older SS-4s and SS-5s targeted at Western Europe. (Historic Documents of 1981, p. 823)

Moscow rejected the proposal out of hand, insisting that there currently was a balance in INF weapons in Europe if 162 French and British missiles and hundreds of U.S. and other NATO planes equipped to carry nuclear bombs were included in the tally. In December 1982 the Soviet Union offered to reduce the number of its intermediate missile launchers to the 162 deployed by France and Britain but insisted that no new U.S. missiles be deployed. The NATO members, however, continued to oppose inclusion of the British and French missiles in the INF talks.

In March 1983, while reaffirming the zero goal, Reagan countered the Soviet position by proposing an interim agreement setting equal ceilings at any level between zero and 572 on the number of warheads on U.S. and Soviet intermediate-range missiles. Again, the Soviet reaction was negative.

Major Features of the INF Proposal

Deployment of the U.S. Pershing missiles was due to begin in West Germany, the United Kingdom and Italy by the end of 1983, and Western negotiators hoped that signals of a softened U.S. position would make it easier for the three European governments to fend off domestic pressure to block the deployments.

In his U.N. speech Reagan announced three modifications that had been proposed to Soviet negotiators in Geneva several days earlier:

• The United States still insisted on equal worldwide ceilings for INF missile warheads. But, Reagan said, the United States would not necessarily deploy in Europe the total number of warheads allowed under the ceiling.

• The United States would consider Soviet demands that the scope of the INF negotiations be expanded to cover nuclear bomb-carrying airplanes. (The inclusion of more types of weapons might allow negotiators

more room to maneuver, but the two sides remained far apart in their estimates of how many planes on each side would be covered by such an agreement.)

● The United States would consider reducing the deployment of Pershing IIs, which were the focus of the most intense Soviet objections, as well as the much slower GLCMs.

The United States "seeks and will accept any equitable, verifiable agreement that stabilizes forces at lower levels than currently exist," Reagan said. "We are ready to be flexible in our approach, indeed, willing to compromise. We cannot, however, especially in the light of recent events, compromise on the necessity of effective verification."

Soviet Reaction, Missile Deployment

In a statement published by the official Soviet news agency Tass, Soviet President Yuri V. Andropov September 28 delivered a stinging indictment of the speech, accusing the Reagan administration of following "a militarist course" and of practicing "deception" in its proclaimed posture of flexibility. Appealing to European anti-nuclear sentiment, the Soviet leader said the planned INF deployment would come "at the expense of Europe." He charged that the U.S. policy was "frank but cynical. . . . What is not clear is whether this thought occurs to those European political figures who, disregarding the interests of their peoples and the interests of peace, help implement the ambitious militarist plans of the United States administration."

On November 14 U.S. negotiator Paul Nitze presented details of the revised proposal, which Moscow immediately criticized. ". . . President Reagan has not relinquished his lunatic plans to make the Russians fear that the United States will resort to the use of nuclear weapons, naively counting in the process on its own impunity," said a Tass statement. "It goes without saying that the Soviet Union cannot and will not accept any agreement based on the American double standard."

The elaboration of the U.S. proposal came at a time of mounting international tension, with Moscow threatening to walk out of the INF talks. Nitze's announcement coincided with the delivery of the first Pershing missiles to Britain's Greenham Common air base, site of anti-nuclear protests November 14-16. It also came shortly before votes in the Italian and German parliaments on whether to approve the deployments. The Italian Chamber of Deputies November 16 voted to proceed with the deployments, and the West German Bundestag followed suit November 22, after a heated two-day debate.

The Soviet Union's response to the missile deployment was to walk out of the INF talks on November 23. Affirming the withdrawal the next day, Andropov announced a series of additional retaliatory measures, includ-

*ing cancellation of "the moratorium on the deployment of Soviet me-
dium-range nuclear weapons in the European part of the U.S.S.R." (The
fact that the announcement was read for Andropov over Soviet television
fueled mounting speculation about his health. Andropov's death was
announced on February 9, 1984.) Nitze issued a statement saying the U.S.
delegation "expressed its profound regret over the decision of the Soviet
Union to suspend the INF negotiations" and that the action was "as
unjustified as it was unfortunate."*

*Following are excerpts from the address delivered Septem-
ber 26, 1983, by President Ronald Reagan to the United
Nations General Assembly.* (Boldface headings in brackets
have been added by Congressional Quarterly to highlight the
organization of the text.):

*Mr. Secretary-General, Mr. President, distinguished delegates, ladies
and gentlemen of the world:*

Thank you for granting me the honor of speaking today, on this first day
of general debate in the 38th Session of the General Assembly. Once again
I come before this body preoccupied with peace. Last year I stood in this
chamber to address the Special Session on Disarmament. Well, I've come
today to renew my nation's commitment to peace. And I have come to
discuss how we can keep faith with the dreams that created this
organization.

The United Nations was founded in the aftermath of World War II to
protect future generations from the scourge of war, to promote political
self-determination and global prosperity, and to strengthen the bonds of
civility among nations. The founders sought to replace a world at war with
a world of civilized order. They hoped that a world of relentless conflict
would give way to a new era, one where freedom from violence prevailed.

Whatever challenges the world was bound to face, the founders intended
this body to stand for certain values, even if they could not be enforced,
and to condemn violence, even if it could not be stopped. This body was to
speak with the voice of moral authority. That was to be its greatest power.

But the awful truth is that the use of violence for political gain has
become more, not less, widespread in the last decade. Events of recent
weeks have presented new, unwelcome evidence of brutal disregard for life
and truth. They have offered unwanted testimony on how divided and
dangerous our world is, how quick the recourse to violence. What has
happened to the dreams of the U.N.'s founders? What has happened to the
spirit which created the United Nations?

The answer is clear: Governments got in the way of the dreams of the
people. Dreams became issues of East versus West. Hopes became political
rhetoric. Progress became a search for power and domination. Somewhere
the truth was lost that people don't make wars, governments do.

And today in Asia, Africa, Latin America, the Middle East, and the
North Pacific, the weapons of war shatter the security of the peoples who

live there, endanger the peace of neighbors, and create ever more arenas of confrontation between the great powers. During the past year alone, violent conflicts have occurred in the hills around Beirut, the deserts of Chad and the western Sahara, in the mountains of El Salvador, the streets of Suriname, the cities and countryside of Afghanistan, the borders of Kampuchea, and the battlefields of Iran and Iraq.

[Need for Arms Control]

We cannot count on the instinct for survival to protect us against war. Despite all the wasted lives and hopes that war produces, it has remained a regular, if horribly costly, means by which nations have sought to settle their disputes or advance their goals. And the progress in weapons technology has far outstripped the progress toward peace. In modern times, a new, more terrifying element has entered into the calculations — nuclear weapons. A nuclear war cannot be won, and it must never be fought. I believe that if governments are determined to deter and prevent war, there will not be war.

Nothing is more in keeping with the spirit of the United Nations Charter than arms control. When I spoke before the Second Special Session on Disarmament, I affirmed the United States Government's commitment, and my personal commitment, to reduce nuclear arms and to negotiate in good faith toward that end. Today, I reaffirm those commitments.

The United States has already reduced the number of its nuclear weapons worldwide, and, while replacement of older weapons is unavoidable, we wish to negotiate arms reductions and to achieve significant, equitable, verifiable arms control agreements. And let me add, we must ensure that world security is not undermined by the further spread of nuclear weapons. Nuclear nonproliferation must not be the forgotten element of the world's arms control agenda.

At the time of my last visit here, I expressed hope that a whole class of weapons systems, the longer range INF — intermediate nuclear forces — could be banned from the face of the Earth. I believe that to relieve the deep concern of peoples in both Europe and Asia, the time was ripe, for the first time in history, to resolve a security threat exclusively through arms control. I still believe the elimination of these weapons — the zero option — is the best, fairest, most practical solution to the problem. Unfortunately, the Soviet Union declined to accept the total elimination of this class of weapons.

When I was here last, I hoped that the critical Strategic Arms Reduction Talks would focus, and urgently so, on those systems that carry the greatest risk of nuclear war — the fast-flying, accurate, intercontinental ballistic missiles which pose a first-strike potential. I also hoped the negotiations could reduce by one-half the number of strategic missiles on each side and reduce their warheads by one-third. Again, I was disappointed when the Soviets declined to consider such deep cuts, and refused as well to concentrate on these most dangerous, destabilizing weapons.

Well, despite the rebuffs, the United States has not abandoned and will not abandon the search for meaningful arms control agreements. Last June, I proposed a new approach toward the START negotiations. We did not alter our objective of substantial reductions, but we recognized that there are a variety of ways to achieve this end. During the last round of Geneva talks, we presented a draft treaty which responded to a number of concerns raised by the Soviet Union. We will continue to build upon this initiative.

Similarly, in our negotiations on intermediate-range nuclear forces, when the Soviet leaders adamantly refused to consider the total elimination of those weapons, the United States made a new offer. We proposed, as an interim solution, some equal number on both sides between zero and 572. We recommended the lowest possible level. Once again, the Soviets refused an equitable solution and proposed instead what might be called a "half zero option" — zero for us and many hundreds of warheads for them. And that's where things stand today, but I still haven't given up hope that the Soviet Union will enter into serious negotiations.

[New U.S. INF Proposals]

We are determined to spare no effort to achieve a sound, equitable, and verifiable agreement. And for this reason, I have given new instructions to Ambassador Nitze in Geneva, telling him to put forward a package of steps designed to advance the negotiations as rapidly as possible. These initiatives build on the interim framework the United States advanced last March and address concerns that the Soviets have raised at the bargaining table in the past.

Specifically, first, the United States proposes a new initiative on global limits. If the Soviet Union agrees to reductions and limits on a global basis, the United States for its part will not offset the entire Soviet global missile deployment through U.S. deployments in Europe. We would, of course, retain the right to deploy missiles elsewhere.

Second, the United States is prepared to be more flexible on the content of the current talks. The United States will consider mutually acceptable ways to address the Soviet desire that an agreement should limit aircraft as well as missiles.

Third, the United States will address the mix of missiles that would result from reductions. In the context of reductions to equal levels, we are prepared to reduce the number of Pershing II ballistic missiles as well as ground-launched cruise missiles.

I have decided to put forward these important initiatives after full and extensive consultations with our allies, including personal correspondence I've had with the leaders of the NATO governments and Japan and frequent meetings of the NATO Special Consultative Group. I have also stayed in close touch with other concerned friends and allies. The door to an agreement is open. It is time for the Soviet Union to walk through it.

I want to make an unequivocal pledge to those gathered today in this world arena. The United States seeks and will accept any equitable, verifiable agreement that stabilizes forces at lower levels than currently exist. We're ready to be flexible in our approach, indeed, willing to compromise. We cannot, however, especially in light of recent events, compromise on the necessity of effective verification.

Reactions to the Korean airliner tragedy are a timely reminder of just how different the Soviets' concept of truth and international cooperation is from that of the rest of the world. Evidence abounds that we cannot simply assume that agreements negotiated with the Soviet Union will be fulfilled. We negotiated the Helsinki Final Act, but the promised freedoms have not been provided, and those in the Soviet Union who sought to monitor their fulfillment languish in prison. We negotiated a biological weapons convention, but deadly yellow rain and other toxic agents fall on Hmong villages and Afghan encampments. We have negotiated arms agreements, but the high level of Soviet encoding hides the information needed for their verification. A newly discovered radar facility and a new ICBM raise serious concerns about Soviet compliance with agreements already negotiated.

Peace cannot be served by pseudo arms control. We need reliable, reciprocal reductions. I call upon the Soviet Union today to reduce the tensions it has heaped on the world in the past few weeks and to show a firm commitment to peace by coming to the bargaining table with a new understanding of its obligations. I urge it to match our flexibility. If the Soviets sit down at the bargaining table seeking genuine arms reductions, there will be arms reductions. The governments of the West and their people will not be diverted by misinformation and threats. The time has come for the Soviet Union to show proof that it wants arms control in reality, not just in rhetoric.

Meaningful arms control agreements between the United States and the Soviet Union would make our world less dangerous; so would a number of confidence-building steps we've already proposed to the Soviet Union.

[Nonalignment]

Arms control requires a spirit beyond narrow national interests. This spirit is a basic pillar on which the U.N. was founded. We seek a return to this spirit. A fundamental step would be a true nonalignment of the United Nations. This would signal a return to the true values of the charter, including the principle of universality. The members of the United Nations must be aligned on the side of justice rather than injustice, peace rather than aggression, human dignity rather than subjugation. Any other alignment is beneath the purpose of this great body and destructive of the harmony that it seeks. What harms the charter harms peace.

The founders of the U.N. expected that member nations would behave and vote as individuals, after they had weighed the merits of an issue —

rather like a great, global town meeting. The emergence of blocs and the polarization of the U.N. undermine all that this organization initially valued.

We must remember that the nonaligned movement was founded to counter the development of blocs and to promote détente between them. Its founders spoke of the right of smaller countries not to become involved in others' disagreements. Since then, membership in the nonaligned movement has grown dramatically, but not all the new members have shared the founders' commitment of genuine nonalignment. Indeed, client governments of the Soviet Union, who have long since lost their independence, have flocked into the nonaligned movement, and, once inside, have worked against its true purpose. Pseudo nonalignment is no better than pseudo arms control.

The United States rejects as false and misleading the view of the world as divided between the empires of the East and West. We reject it on factual grounds. The United States does not head any bloc of subservient nations, nor do we desire to. What is called the West is a free alliance of governments, most of whom are democratic and all of whom greatly value their independence. What is called the East is an empire directed from the center which is Moscow.

The United States, today as in the past, is a champion of freedom and self-determination for all people. We welcome diversity; we support the right of all nations to define and pursue their national goals. We respect their decisions and their sovereignty, asking only that they respect the decisions and sovereignty of others. Just look at the world over the last 30 years and then decide for yourself whether the United States or the Soviet Union has pursued an expansionist policy.

[Peacekeeping Efforts]

Today, the United States contributes to peace by supporting collective efforts by the international community. We give our unwavering support to the peacekeeping efforts of this body, as well as other multilateral peacekeeping efforts around the world. The U.N. has a proud history of promoting conciliation and helping keep the peace. Today, U.N. peacekeeping forces or observers are present in Cyprus and Kashmir, on the Golan Heights and in Lebanon.

In addition to our encouragement of international diplomacy, the United States recognizes its responsibilities to use its own influence for peace. From the days when Theodore Roosevelt mediated the Russo-Japanese war in 1905, we have a long and honorable tradition of mediating or damping conflicts and promoting peaceful solutions. In Lebanon, we, along with France, Italy, and the United Kingdom, have worked for a cease-fire, for the withdrawal of all external forces, and for restoration of Lebanon's sovereignty and territorial integrity. In Chad, we have joined others in supporting the recognized government in the face of external aggression. In Central America, as in southern Africa, we are seeking to discourage reliance upon force and to construct a framework for peaceful negotiations. We support a policy to disengage the major powers from Third World conflict.

The U.N. Charter gives an important role to regional organizations in the search for peace. The U.S. efforts in the cause of peace are only one expression of a spirit that also animates others in the world community. The Organization of American States was a pioneer in regional security efforts. In Central America, the members of the Contadora group are striving to lay a foundation for peaceful resolution of that region's problems. In East Asia, the Asian countries have built a framework for peaceful political and economic cooperation that has greatly strengthened the prospects for lasting peace in their region. In Africa, organizations such as the Economic Community of West African States are being forged to provide practical structures in the struggle to realize Africa's potential.

From the beginning, our hope for the United Nations has been that it would reflect the international community at its best. The U.N. at its best can help us transcend fear and violence and can act as an enormous force for peace and prosperity. Working together, we can combat international lawlessness and promote human dignity. If the governments represented in this chamber want peace as genuinely as their peoples do, we shall find it. We can do so by reasserting the moral authority of the United Nations.

In recent weeks, the moral outrage of the world seems to have reawakened. Out of the billions of people who inhabit this planet, why, some might ask, should the death of several hundred shake the world so profoundly? Why should the death of a mother flying toward a reunion with her family or the death of a scholar heading toward new pursuits of knowledge matter so deeply? Why are nations who lost no citizens in the tragedy so angry?

The reason rests on our assumptions about civilized life and the search for peace. The confidence that allows a mother or a scholar to travel to Asia or Africa or Europe or anywhere else on this planet may be only a small victory in humanity's struggle for peace. Yet what is peace if not the sum of such small victories?

Each stride for peace and every small victory are important for the journey toward a larger and lasting peace. We have made progress. We've avoided another world war. We've seen an end to the traditional colonial era and the birth of a hundred newly sovereign nations. Even though development remains a formidable challenge, we've witnessed remarkable economic growth among the industrialized and the developing nations. The United Nations and its affiliates have made important contributions to the quality of life on this planet, such as directly saving countless lives through its refugee and emergency relief programs. These broad achievements, however, have been overshadowed by the problems that weigh so heavily upon us. The problems are old, but it is not too late to commit ourselves to a new beginning, a beginning fresh with the ideals of the U.N. Charter.

Today, at the beginning of this 38th Session, I solemnly pledge my nation to upholding the original ideals of the United Nations. Our goals are those that guide this very body. Our ends are the same as those of the U.N.'s founders, who sought to replace a world at war with one where the rule of law would prevail, where human rights were honored, where development would blossom, where conflict would give way to freedom from violence....

IMF FUNDING CRISIS

September 27, 1983

President Ronald Reagan November 30 signed into law a bill that increased the U.S. contribution to the International Monetary Fund (IMF) by $8.4 billion. That amount represented the U.S. share of a nearly $32 billion total increase in funding agreed to by the 146 member nations of the IMF. Uncertainty over whether or not Congress would approve the measure, which the president strongly backed, hovered over the annual meeting of the IMF and the International Bank for Reconstruction and Development (World Bank) that was held in Washington, D.C., September 26-30.

Most experts believed that a failure by Congress to approve the U.S. contribution to the international financial agency would have been a disastrous blow to the IMF and would have precipitated a calamitous debt-related crisis of unforeseeable consequences for developed and developing nations alike. However, the IMF legislation became embroiled in fierce partisan wrangling and did not clear Congress until shortly before it adjourned November 18.

Addressing the IMF and the World Bank on September 27, President Reagan drew a stark picture of the chain reaction that might result from congressional inaction. "If the Congress does not approve our participation," he said, "the inevitable consequence would be a withdrawal by other industrial countries from doing their share. At the end of this road could be a major disruption of the entire world trading and financial systems — an economic nightmare that could plague generations to come."

Latin American Debt

The financial crisis, which the IMF hoped to ameliorate, centered on Latin American nations that together owed $350 billion, two-thirds of it to commercial banks. The IMF alone did not have the resources to refinance that amount of debt. But commercial banks depended on the agency's credit agreements with underdeveloped countries as a basis for refinancing their own loans.

For the most part, the conditions that led to the skyrocketing debt in Latin America were considered to have been beyond the control of nations in that region. Only a few years earlier, most of the countries had been considered good credit risks. But the high price of oil and the world recession of 1981 and 1982, coupled with high interest rates in the industrialized countries, sharply eroded their economies. The industrialized nations reduced imports of a number of products from Latin American countries, and the lack of export-generated income made it even more difficult for them to repay the staggering debt.

The potential repercussions of the global financial imbalance had consequences that went beyond economics. The political stability of Brazil, in particular, was threatened by a stringent austerity program imposed as a condition for further loans.

IMF Meeting

It was with a sense of crisis that finance ministers and central bankers of the member IMF nations — some of them East European communist nations — gathered in Washington for the annual meeting of that organization and the World Bank.

Jacques de Larosière, the managing director of the IMF, said that "given the weight of [the United States] in the fund's quotas, it is essential that the U.S. Congress act decisively and urgently in this matter."

Moreover, the United States and other industrialized nations came under attack at the meeting for huge budget deficits that exacerbated developing nations' debt problems. Jesus Silva Herzog, the Mexican finance secretary, told reporters that as a result of the high deficits, "inflation-adjusted interest rates" were excessive, adding to the debt burden of his and other nations. "One additional percentage point in the financial cost of Latin America's debt involves some $3 billion," he said.

In his address, Reagan assured the finance ministers that the U. S. deficit was "coming down" as a result of economic growth in the United States. "Revenues are higher than anticipated," he said, "and we expect continued improvement."

Partisan Struggle

A bitter conflict between the Reagan administration and the Democratic members of the House of Representatives broke out over the IMF funding legislation. A politically unpopular measure from the start, it was seen by some members of Congress as a means of "bailing out" banks that had made what critics considered improvident loans to developing nations. Democrats in the House resented the fact that they were providing most of the support on the bill for the president while a majority of Republican members opposed it.

The struggle heated up when the Republican Congressional Campaign Committee sent out press releases attacking Democrats who had voted against an amendment requiring the United States to oppose IMF loans to "communist dictatorships." Rep. Phil Gramm, R-Texas, the amendment's sponsor, asked in the press release, "What gives them the right to vote to support communism?"

House Speaker Thomas P. O'Neill Jr., D-Mass., blocked further action on the bill until Reagan, who also opposed the amendment, thanked the Democratic legislators for their support. Weeks later, Reagan met the Speaker's condition by sending a thank you letter to 145 House Democrats who had voted in favor of the U.S. contribution.

Another hurdle was placed in the path of the legislation by Fernand J. St Germaine, D-R.I., who insisted that Reagan support an unrelated housing bill that had stalled in the Senate as a price for House approval of the additional IMF funding.

The IMF legislation that cleared Congress November 18 was part of a carefully crafted package that also included a $15.6 billion housing authorization measure. The Reagan administration opposed several key provisions of the housing proposal but agreed to swallow them to achieve passage of the IMF legislation.

Following are excerpts from speeches delivered September 27, 1983, at a joint meeting of the International Monetary Fund and the International Bank for Reconstruction and Development by President Ronald Reagan and by Jacques de Larosière, managing director of the IMF:

REAGAN REMARKS

Good morning. Mr. de Larosière, Governors of the World Bank, and its affiliates, and of the International Monetary Fund, distinguished colleagues and guests:

On behalf of my fellow Americans, I'm delighted to welcome you to the United States and to our Nation's Capital.

And I am honored to have this opportunity to speak again to your distinguished members. I say honored because I believe that your institutions, the World Bank and affiliates and the International Monetary Fund, serve noble purposes. There can be no higher mission than to improve the human condition and to offer opportunities for fulfillment in our individual lives and the life of our national and our world communities. . . .

. . . [A]s I said when I last spoke to you, the societies that achieved the most spectacular, broad-based economic progress in the shortest period of time have not been the biggest in size nor the richest in resources and, certainly, not the most rigidly controlled. What has united them all was their belief in the magic of the marketplace. Millions of individuals making their own decisions in the marketplace will always allocate resources better than any centralized government planning process. . . .

In the turbulent decade of the 1970's, too many of us, the United States included, forgot the principles that produced the basis for our mutual economic progress. We permitted our governments to overspend, overtax, and overregulate us toward soaring inflation and record interest rates. Now we see more clearly again. We're working and cooperating to bring our individual economies and the world economy back to more solid foundations of low inflation, personal incentives for saving and investment, higher productivity, and greater opportunities for our people.

Our first task was to get our own financial and economic house in order. Our countries are interdependent, but without a foundation of sound domestic policies, the international economic system cannot expand and improve. Merely providing additional official development assistance will not produce progress. This is true for all countries, developed and developing, without exception. As the 1983 development report of the World Bank notes, "International actions can greatly improve the external environment confronting developing countries but cannot supplant the efforts that the developing countries must make themselves."

I believe the United States is making real progress. Since we took office, we've reduced the rate of growth in our Federal Government's spending by nearly 40 percent. We have cut inflation dramatically, from 12.4 percent to 2.6 percent for the last 12 months. The prime interest rate has been cut nearly in half, from 21½ percent to 11 percent. Figures released last week reveal our gross national product grew at an annual rate of almost 10 percent in the second quarter, and about 7 percent is estimated for the third.

In the United States we still face large projected deficits which concern us, because deficit Federal spending and borrowing drain capital that would otherwise be invested for stronger economic growth. But as [Treasury] Secretary [Donald T.] Regan correctly pointed out . . . the deficit is coming down as a result of economic growth. Revenues are higher than anticipated, and we expect continued improvement. We'll continue to work for greater restraint in Federal spending, but we will not risk sabotaging our economic expansion in a short-sighted attempt to reduce deficits by raising taxes. What tax increases would actually reduce is economic growth, by discouraging savings, investment, and consumption.

One other point about the United States deficit: Let me make clear that it is caused in part by our determination to provide the military strength and political security to ensure peace in the world. Our commitment to military security is matched by our resolve to negotiate a verifiable nuclear arms reduction treaty. Only then can we safely reduce military expenditures and their drain on our resources. As I mentioned at the outset, there can be no lasting prosperity without security and freedom.

Turning more directly to economic development, all signs point to a world economic recovery gaining momentum. As early as last February, the Conference Board predicted that economic growth rates in the United States and six major industrial countries spell economic recovery in any language. Since then, industrial production in the OECD [Organization for Economic Cooperation and Development] countries has been moving up. Your own IMF economists are predicting growth in the world economy of at least 3 percent next year. This is the brightest outlook in several years.

As the U.S. economy picks up steam, our imports rise with it. When you consider that half of all non-OPEC [Organization of Petroleum Exporting Countries] developing country manufactured goods exported to the industrialized countries come to the United States, it's clear what a strong stimulus our imports provide for economic expansion abroad. And as other economies prosper, our exports in turn increase. We all gain.

Many nations are moving steadily forward toward self-sustaining growth. And like us, they're doing it by relying again on the marketplace. This period of adjustment has not been easy for us; in fact, it's been very painful. But it is the one way that does work, and it's beginning to pay dividends.

Economic recovery is spreading its wings and taking flight. We all know those wings have not spread far enough and, I would add, recovery alone is not good enough. Our challenge is far greater: lasting, worldwide economic expansion. Together, we must make the 1980's an historic era of transition toward sustained, noninflationary world growth. I have every confidence that we can, and with our combined leadership and cooperation, we will.

The IMF is the linchpin of the international financial system. Among official institutions it serves as a counselor, coaxing the world economy toward renewed growth and stability. At various times in its history, the IMF has provided important temporary balance of payments assistance to its member nations, including my own. At times it must play the "Dutch uncle," talking frankly, telling those of us in government things we need to hear but would rather not. We know how significant the IMF's role has been in assisting troubled debtor countries, many of which are making courageous strides to regain financial health. We warmly applaud the efforts of Mr. de Larosière and his staff.

My administration is committed to do what is legitimately needed to help ensure that the IMF continues as the cornerstone of the international financial system. Let me make something very plain: I have an unbreakable commitment to increased funding for the IMF. But the U.S. Congress so far has failed to act to pass the enabling legislation. I urge the Congress to be mindful of its responsibility and to meet the pledge of our government.

The IMF quota legislation has been pending for several months, and I do not appreciate the partisan wrangling and political posturing that have been associated with this issue during recent weeks. I urge members of both political parties to lay aside their differences, to abandon harsh rhetoric and unreasonable demands, and to get on with the task in a spirit of true bipartisanship. The stakes are great. This legislation is not only crucial to the recovery of America's trading partners abroad and to the stability of the entire international financial system, it is also necessary to a sustained recovery in the United States.

The sum we're requesting will not increase our budget deficit, and it will be returned with interest as loans are repaid to the IMF. What's more, it will keep the wheels of world commerce turning and create jobs. Exports account for one out of eight manufacturing jobs in our country, the United States. Forty percent of our agricultural products are exported. I'm afraid that even today, too few in the Congress realize the United States as interdependent with both the developed and the developing world.

Examine the record: The United States has been a dependable partner, reaching out to help developing countries who are laboring under excessive debt burdens. These major debtor countries have already undertaken difficult measures in a concerted effort to get their economic houses in order. Most of them are working closely with the IMF to overcome economic hardships. They continue to demonstrate a commendable willingness to make necessary adjustments. And that's why I can state that our participation in the IMF quota increase is not a government bailout of these debtor countries or of the banks which are sharing the burden. On the contrary, IMF plans to assist financially troubled countries call for the banks to put up more new money than the IMF itself.

This is by nature a cooperative enterprise. If the Congress does not approve our participation, the inevitable consequence would be a withdrawal by other industrialized countries from doing their share. At the end of this road could be a major disruption of the entire world trading and financial systems — an economic nightmare that could plague generations to come. No one can afford to make light of the responsibility we all share.

We strongly support the World Bank; in fact, the United States remains its largest single contributor. We recognize its key role in stimulating world development and the vital assistance it provides to developing nations. Here again, I have proposed legislation to meet our commitment for funding the World Bank and especially the International Development Association. It is important that these funds be available to help the people in the poorest countries raise their standards of living. Tomorrow, Secretary Regan will be discussing both the Fund and the Bank in more detail. Because our investment in the World Bank's operations is so large, we feel a special responsibility to provide constructive suggestions to make it even more effective.

Let me simply underscore again a fundamental point, and I say this as a spokesman for a compassionate, caring people. The heart of America is good, and her heart is true. We've provided more concessional assistance to developing nations than any other country — more than $130 billion in the last three decades. Whether the question at hand be Bank project financing or Fund balance of payments assistance, it must be considered a complement to, not a substitute for, sound policies at home. If policies are sound, financing can be beneficial. If policies are irresponsible, all the aid in the world will be no more than money down the drain.

As we work together for recovery, we must be on guard against storm clouds of protectionist pressures building on the horizon. At the recent economic summit in Williamsburg, my fellow leaders and I renewed our commitment to an open, expanding world trading system. The Williamsburg Declaration reads, "We commit ourselves to halt protectionism, and as recovery proceeds, to reverse it by dismantling trade barriers."

Whether such words will prove to be empty promises or symbols of a powerful commitment depends on the real day-to-day actions which each of our governments take. Everyone is against protectionism in the abstract. That's easy. It is another matter to make the hard, courageous choices when it is your industry or your business that appears to be hurt by foreign competition. I know; we in the United States deal with the problem of protectionism every day of the year.

We are far from perfect, but the United States offers the most free and open economy in the world. We import far more goods than any nation on Earth. There is more foreign investment here than anywhere else. And access to our commercial and capital markets is relatively free.

Protectionism is not a problem solver; it is a problem creator. Protectionism invites retaliation. It means you will buy less from your trading partners, they will buy less from you, the world economic pie will shrink, and the danger of political turmoil will increase. . . .

STATEMENT BY JACQUES DE LAROSIERE

Mr. Chairman, when we met last year in Toronto, the world economy was facing perhaps the most critical combination of circumstances of the postwar period. The recession was becoming increasingly severe. Inflation and interest rates remained very high. And the debt difficulties of several of the most important borrowing countries were in imminent danger of becoming unmanageable. The possibility existed of a failure of international financial mechanisms, setting in train a further contraction of trade and capital flows and threatening another twist in the downward spiral of economic activity.

Now, a year later, considerable progress has been made in dealing with this threat. Economic recovery is under way in the industrial world. Inflation, though still high, has receded, permitting some decline in interest rates. And a concerted strategy has been set in place for the adjustment and financing of the external position of borrowing countries. Much, however, remains to be done. The recovery in industrial countries is still limited geographically and is not broad enough in its composition. A long process of convalescence will be necessary before the economies of many heavily indebted countries are restored to health. Moreover, other difficulties have remained serious including most importantly the spread of protectionism and exchange market instability.

In my remarks today, I want to address in turn the twin issues of fostering a sustainable recovery and consolidating the progress made in dealing with the adjustment and financing problems of heavily indebted countries. In light of these observations, I shall then consider how, and under what conditions, the International Monetary Fund can contribute to a strengthening of the international monetary and financial system.

1. Recovery in the Industrial World

THE PRESENT SITUATION

Led by North America, the industrial world has begun to recover from the most severe and prolonged recession of the postwar period. Industrial production in the seven major industrial countries is estimated to have been some 6 percent higher in July than at its low point in December last year. Gross national product (GNP) in the industrial countries as a group is now estimated by the Fund staff to be expanding at an annual rate of 3 to 4 percent and to continue at broadly the same pace into next year.

The recovery of output and demand has been accompanied and facilitated by a continuing decline in inflation. The average annual rate of increase in the consumer price index in industrial countries, which as recently as the first quarter of 1980 had been some 13 percent, has been reduced to about 5 percent in the latest 12-month period. While this progress owes something to special and temporary factors, it is encouraging that the rate of increase in basic costs — particularly wages — has moderated and that productivity growth is picking up again after the long period of decline. These developments augur well for further progress toward price stability.

The recovery has also had a beneficial impact on commodity prices and the prospective growth of world trade. Commodity prices had by August 1983 risen about 14 percent from their very depressed levels of the final quarter of 1982. This should enable developing countries to enjoy a modest improvement in their terms of trade in 1983 after five years of continuous and pronounced decline. Also, it would increase their capacity to participate in, and eventually contribute to, global recovery. World trade, which actually contracted in volume by 2½ percent in 1982, is likely to increase moderately in the current year and more substantially in 1984.

Despite this improved outlook, however, there are aspects of the recovery that must continue to give policymakers cause for concern. To begin with, the recovery thus far is confined to relatively few countries. While demand is now increasing rapidly in the United States and Canada, many other countries have only just begun to experience an increase in economic activity and others are still caught in the down-phase of the cycle. Potentially even more disturbing is the lack of dynamism and balance in the structure of demand expansion. Demand has been fed so far by interest-sensitive consumers' expenditure and stock building. Fixed investment — which is the decisive element in boosting productivity and growth over the longer term — remains weak. This underlines the fact that business confidence has been slow to revive and that interest rates are still too high.

POLICIES FOR THE FUTURE

The central task of policy in present circumstances is to consolidate the recovery that is taking hold and to ensure that it is extended and sustained.... [T]his requires avoidance of short-term policy adaptations in the face of temporary changes in circumstances and, instead, steadfast pursuit of sound policies over the medium term. This is the strategy that has been espoused by most industrial countries, and it is showing signs of success. We must build on this initial success. Those elements of the medium-term strategy that have already been put in place must be maintained, while those aspects of present economic policy which remain unsatisfactory must be corrected. Let me now deal with what this implies in concrete terms.

First, it is essential that the progress that has been made toward greater price stability be safeguarded. Allowing inflationary expectations to gather strength again would be a damaging blow to the sustainability of recovery. To avoid this, rates of growth of monetary aggregates must be, and must be seen to be, consistent with a further deceleration in price increases. I know that some observers fear this may keep interest rates high and complicate the task of fostering a recovery in investment. I do not believe this is the case. If interest rates today are high — and they are — they reflect largely the fear that competition for funds in capital markets is likely to intensify in the period ahead. The way to deal with this situation is not to loosen the reins on monetary expansion but to reduce inflationary expectations and improve the balance between available savings and the demands that are placed on them.

This brings me to my second point: the need for a credible plan for reducing fiscal deficits in those several countries — including the United States — where structural budget deficits are high in relation to available savings. This is perhaps the most important policy element that remains to be set in place. Now that recovery has begun, early steps must be taken by these countries to implement a medium-term strategy for restoring fiscal balance. Such a strategy is really the only means of building public confidence in the determination of national authorities to put an end to inflation and to bring about a durable reduction in interest rates. Otherwise one of two undesirable outcomes would seem all too likely to ensue. On the one hand, continuation of such deficits in certain major countries in combination with continued monetary restraint, would keep upward pressure on interest rates and lead to a misuse of global saving, jeopardizing the prospects for a balanced and sustainable recovery. On the other hand, the persistence of large budget deficits in conjunction with a more accommodative monetary policy would have even graver consequences through reviving inflation and undermining growth. There is, unquestionably, a close association over the medium term between inflation and interest rates. To attempt to bring down interest rates by increasing the money supply is not only futile but counterproductive. In present conditions, determined action to deal with structural budget deficits would serve to dispel inflationary expectations and ease the pressures on capital markets. As long as such a budgetary policy is not declared and implemented monetary policy will continue to have to bear the brunt of the effort to contain inflation.

A third central element of policy will have to be the pursuit of structural reforms aimed at improving the climate for a sustainable expansion in private investment. Fiscal responsibility is part of this climate. So is the development of wage-setting procedures that allow the cost of labor to respond in a timely way to changes in the demand for it. The high cost of labor has been a factor inhibiting the growth in employment opportunities, especially in Europe. It contributed to a decline of almost one half in the return on capital in industrial countries since the late 1960s. Adequate profit levels are an essential condition for a revival of investment. They are at the heart of a durable revival of employment and income levels. Another aspect of structural policies calling for re-examination is the nature of government involvement in industry. In an age of rapid and widespread technological change, industrial structures and practices must be responsive to shifts in comparative advantage. Resistance to such shifts, whether in the form of regulation, protectionism, subsidies to declining industries, or other means, produces rigidities that ultimately work to the detriment of those they are intended to help.

Fourth, and closely connected with the need to maintain structural flexibility, is the importance of resisting protectionism. Recovery can only be considered firmly based when it is achieved in the context of an open and liberal trading system that allows countries to expand international sales of items in which they have a comparative advantage. The growth of protectionism has been an alarming feature of our recent experience. It poisons economic and political relationships among countries and prevents the full benefits of the recovery from being shared by those countries, particularly in the developing world, where the need for open foreign markets is greatest. I, therefore, welcome the special emphasis given to the need to halt protectionism by the leaders of the seven major industrial countries at the Williamsburg summit [held in May 1983] and their commitment to dismantle trade barriers as recovery proceeds. The Fund, for its part, will continue to collaborate closely with the GATT [General

Agreement on Tariffs and Trade] toward that end. Also, the Fund is ready to take every practical initiative that has the support of its members to encourage a more open trading environment.

2. Adjustment and Financing in the Developing World

The developing countries have not yet shared in the recovery that is beginning in the industrial world. Indeed, 1983 is shaping up as another year in which growth in non-oil developing countries will be under 2 percent. This will be the third consecutive year in which GNP [gross national product] per capita in these countries, taken as a group, has been stagnant if not falling. And of course this average conceals a diversity of experience in which many countries have actually had to endure substantial declines in economic welfare. In addition, many of these countries have been facing acute external financing problems. The origins of these problems have been the subject of considerable analysis and are by now well known to all of us. I shall, therefore, focus my remarks on the key issues for policy arising out of the current situation.

THE NEED FOR ADJUSTMENT

In the years up to 1982, many developing countries were accumulating debt at an excessive rate. From 1973 to 1981, the total outstanding debt of non-oil developing countries increased at an average annual rate of some 20 percent. Much of this increase represented lending by private financial institutions at floating rates of interest. It was sustained by the expectation that worldwide inflation would be allowed to continue and would facilitate the servicing of the growing volume of debt. This expectation, as is now realized, rested on a false assumption.

The rate of price increase that was reached in recent years could not have been allowed to continue unchecked without grave consequences for economic growth and employment. Indeed, the experience of the 1970s graphically demonstrated that inflation, when it gains hold, saps the economic strength and resilience of countries and breeds recession. It was clear that a stop had to be put to inflation and that adequate incentives to save had to be provided by restoring positive real interest rates. The disinflationary process was eventually set in place. Of course, such a process accompanied by high interest rates has had painful consequences for heavily indebted countries. They are, thus, forced to curtail their external borrowing and, to achieve this, to cut back their net absorption of resources from abroad.

THE MAGNITUDE OF ADJUSTMENT UNDER WAY

Thus, debtor countries had to adjust to the new realities. The results of that adjustment are becoming increasingly evident. Though there are still some countries that have yet to take serious action to deal with their payments problems, balance of payments adjustment is well advanced throughout the developing world. A considerable measure of external adjustment has already been achieved. The external current account deficit of the non-oil developing countries as a group in 1983 is projected at 14 percent of their exports of goods and services, down from 23 percent in 1981 and somewhat lower than the proportion recorded in the period 1976-78. Underlying this improvement is a massive reduction in the combined trade deficit of this group which, in 1983, is projected at $40 billion, or approximately half of its level two years ago.

The Fund has been playing a crucial role in assisting in the process of orderly balance of payments adjustment in the developing world. We are currently providing financial support for programs under stand-by and extended arrangements in 46 countries. Progress toward external adjustment by these countries has been particularly encouraging, given that many of them have been experiencing acute external financing difficulties. The combined current account deficit for those countries with stand-by or extended arrangements currently in effect with the Fund is projected at $34 billion in 1983, about half of its nominal level in 1981. Their trade deficit is projected at $17 billion in 1983 — one third of its level two years ago.

ADJUSTMENT AND GROWTH

The argument has been made that the adjustment measures required of debtor countries have the effect of slowing down their growth and, thereby, adding to recessionary influences in the world economy. This line of argument betrays a very fundamental misunderstanding and it offers no alternative solution. As soon as a country's external deficit begins to outstrip the availability of foreign financing, that country has no alternative but to retrench, and to bring its external deficit within the bounds that are dictated by the availability of foreign financing. That process cannot be said to impair recovery, since recovery cannot be based on trade which is beyond the ability of importing countries to finance.

Comprehensive adjustment programs, such as those supported by the Fund, facilitate a much smoother process of adjustment than would otherwise be the case. By providing financial resources to countries implementing adjustment programs and by unlocking or "catalyzing" by means of those programs access to substantial amounts of additional external finance — on average of the order of four times the amounts provided by the Fund itself — the Fund enables deficit countries to sustain larger imports than would be possible if those countries were left to themselves. Adjustment programs also help to moderate any cutback in imports by their effects in helping countries to exploit more fully their export potential. Ultimately, however, the extent to which export-led adjustment is possible pivots upon the strength and durability of world demand, and continued, if not expanded, access by developing countries to the markets of the industrial world....

NEED TO MAINTAIN FINANCING

I have already spoken of the magnitude of the adjustment that is now underway in the developing world. Impressive though it is, it must not divert attention from the fact that, in a number of countries, it involves considerable hardship in the short run and is being realized at high social and political cost. Some countries are already approaching the limits of social and political tolerance of their adjustment efforts. This underlines the crucial need for adequate financing flows to facilitate and underpin the adjustment process. If the present difficult situation is to be overcome, all parties involved in international financing will have to continue to cooperate closely, recognizing fully their mutual interest in preserving financial stability. Informed understanding by creditors is needed to complement the determined adjustment actions of debtors.

This understanding has already shown positive results. In the case of several major debtor countries, the immediate threat of crisis has been averted by concerted action on the part of the Fund, governments, central banks, the BIS [Bank for International Settlements], other multilateral agencies, and commercial banks. The danger is not over, however. Recent collaborative efforts will have to be extended over a period of years and need to be consolidated by ensuring (i) that all commercial bank creditors, small as well as large, participate in restructuring efforts; (ii) that credits to large countries do not pre-empt the flow of funds to smaller ones; (iii) that official lending plays an important role in capital flows and in restoring a more viable debt structure; and (iv) that credits are provided on reasonable terms.

While the Fund's resources form an important part of international financial flows, they are relatively small in comparison with those of private creditors. This year, for example, when the Fund will make available record amounts of finance, our net contribution will represent under 20 percent of the current account deficit of developing countries. Continued financing by the commercial banks will be needed in support of the adjustment programs now in place in many debtor countries, but net new bank lending in the period ahead will be on a much smaller scale than the unsustainable rates recorded as recently as 1981. It seems clear that the transmission mechanism involving heavy reliance on commercial banks, which has been a dominant feature of international financing flows to the developing countries during the past decade, will have to be improved. . . .

It is . . . of crucial importance that the ratification of the Eighth General Review of [IMF] Quotas and of the enlarged GAB [General Agreements to Borrow] be completed by member countries so that the new resources can become available to the Fund by the end of November. Given the weight of the United States in the Fund's quotas, it is essential that the U.S. Congress act decisively and urgently on this matter. Moreover, we must be confident that members in a position to lend to the Fund will continue to cooperate with the institution. This support will also be needed after the quota increase becomes effective. Indeed, the realities of the time require the continuation of a meaningful enlarged access policy, as has been agreed by the Interim Committee on Sunday last. The financing of such a policy will require further borrowing by the Fund over the next few years. This is all the more important because adjustment and debt problems will be with us for a number of years to come....

October

KENNEDY SPEECH
TO MORAL MAJORITY
October 3, 1983

Sen. Edward M. Kennedy was the guest speaker October 3 at a small Baptist college with ties to the Moral Majority, a largely Protestant religious-political movement that lobbied for conservative causes. It was an unusual audience for the Massachusetts Democrat. The Moral Majority's leadership had called Kennedy a leading "ultraliberal" and urged members to oppose his philosophy vigorously.

In his speech, Kennedy called for respect for the rights of others, despite political disagreements, and drew attention to the danger that religious zeal might lead groups advocating political causes to cross the constitutional line separating church and state. "I am an American and a Catholic; I love my country and treasure my faith," said Kennedy, whose brother, John F. Kennedy, was the first Roman Catholic elected president of the United States. "But I do not assume that my conception of patriotism or policy is invariably correct — or that my convictions about religion should command any greater respect than any other faith in this pluralistic society. I believe there surely is such a thing as truth, but who among us can claim a monopoly on it?"

The Audience and Its Reaction

Kennedy's remarks were directed at an overflow crowd of 5,000 at Liberty Baptist College in Lynchburg, Va. The college was founded by Rev. Jerry Falwell, a television evangelist and leader of the Moral Majority.

Falwell became nationally known during the election of 1980, when he set out to weld fundamentalist Protestants into a political force. Under Falwell's leadership the Moral Majority took stands on a number of political issues — abortion, the Equal Rights Amendment, government spending, the nuclear freeze and others — almost always diametrically opposed to Kennedy's position.

The senator's speech at the college came about largely because of a mailing error: Kennedy's office received a membership card from the Moral Majority, accompanied by a letter that urged the recipient to join the fight against "ultraliberals such as Ted Kennedy." Kennedy countered with an offer to speak to the group and was accepted.

Students and visitors at the college received Kennedy's speech with a mixture of politeness and restraint. Asked about the impact of Kennedy's visit to the campus, Falwell told a reporter from The Washington Post, *"I have a feeling he and I will be just as outspoken and descriptive in our denunciations of each others' positions. But we'll probably like each other more."*

The Moral Majority

The Moral Majority was founded in 1979 to launch, according to Falwell and other leaders, "a moral and conservative revolution" in American politics. The organization took credit for registering hundreds of thousands of voters who helped elect conservatives, including Ronald Reagan, to national and state offices in 1980. Members were encouraged, often from church pulpits, to support candidates who espoused social and political values that met with the Moral Majority's approval: endorsement of prayer in public schools, tuition tax credits, capital punishment and reduced government spending. The group was opposed to abortion, homosexuals' rights, the Equal Rights Amendment, sex education and other liberal causes. Ministers active in the movement sometimes gave speeches in behalf of favored candidates.

Branches of the Moral Majority also were established at the state level. In Alabama, members lobbied for teaching "scientific creationism" based on the Bible in the schools, and in Indiana they set out to amend the state child abuse law so it would not interfere with parents' rights to use "reasonable corporal punishment in disciplining their children." A Maryland state chapter tried to stop a local bakery from selling decorated "pornographic" cookies to minors — an episode that so embarrassed the national Moral Majority that it quietly disowned the state group.

The Moral Majority drew its strength from southern and midwestern states with a tradition of Protestant fundamentalism. Membership in 1983 was estimated at between 4.5 million and 5 million. From its inception, the organization used tactics that sparked controversy. In his speech at Liberty Baptist College, Kennedy alluded to a meeting between

Ronald Reagan and evangelical Christians in Dallas, prior to the 1980 elections, when Reagan said he privately welcomed the group's support. To Kennedy, this constituted a possible breakdown of the separation between church and state.

>*Following is the text of the speech Sen. Edward M. Kennedy of Massachusetts delivered October 3, 1983, at Liberty Baptist College in Lynchburg, Va. (Boldface headings in brackets have been added by Congressional Quarterly to highlight the organization of the text.):*

I have come here to discuss my beliefs about faith and country, tolerance and truth in America. I know we begin with certain disagreements; I strongly suspect that at the end of the evening some of our disagreements will remain. But I also hope that tonight and in the months and years ahead, we will always respect the right of others to differ — that we will never lose sight of our own fallibility — that we will view ourselves with a sense of perspective and a sense of humor. After all, in the New Testament, even the Disciples had to be taught to look first to the beam in their own eyes, and only then to the mote in their neighbor's eye.

I am mindful of that counsel. I am an American and a Catholic; I love my country and treasure my faith. But I do not assume that my conception of patriotism or policy is invariably correct — or that my convictions about religion should command any greater respect than any other faith in this pluralistic society. I believe there surely is such a thing as truth, but who among us can claim a monopoly on it?

There are those who do, and their own words testify to their intolerance. For example, because the Moral Majority has worked with members of different denominations, one fundamentalist group has denounced Dr. [Jerry] Falwell for hastening the ecumenical church and for "yoking together with Roman Catholics, Mormons, and others." I am relieved that Dr. Falwell does not regard that as a sin — and on this issue, he himself has become the target of narrow prejudice. When people agree on public policy, they ought to be able to work together, even while they worship in diverse ways. For truly we are all yoked together as Americans — and the yoke is the happy one of individual freedom and mutual respect.

But in saying that, we cannot and should not turn aside from a deeper, more pressing question — which is whether and how religion should influence government. A generation ago, a presidential candidate had to prove his independence of undue religious influence in public life — and he had to do so partly at the insistence of evangelical Protestants. John Kennedy said at that time: "I believe in an America where there is no (religious) bloc voting of any kind." Only twenty years later, another candidate was appealing to an evangelical meeting as a religious bloc. Ronald Reagan said to 15 thousand evangelicals at the Roundtable in Dallas: "I know that you can't endorse me. I want you to know that I endorse you and what you are doing."

[Church-State Separation]

To many Americans, that pledge was a sign and a symbol of a dangerous breakdown in the separation of church and state. Yet this principle, as vital as it is, is not a simplistic and rigid command. Separation of church and state cannot mean an absolute separation between moral principles and political power. The challenge today is to recall the origin of the principle, to define its purpose, and refine its application to the politics of the present.

The founders of our nation had long and bitter experience with the state as both the agent and the adversary of particular religious views. In colonial Maryland, Catholics paid a double land tax, and in Pennsylvania they had to list their names on a public roll — an ominous precursor of the first Nazi laws against the Jews. And Jews in turn faced discrimination in all the thirteen original Colonies. Massachusetts exiled Roger Williams and his congregation for contending that civil government had no right to enforce the Ten Commandments. Virginia harassed Baptist preachers — and also established a religious test for public service, writing into the law that no "popish followers" could hold any office.

But during the Revolution, Catholics, Jews and Non-Conformists all rallied to the cause and fought valiantly for the American commonwealth — for John Winthrop's "city upon a hill." Afterwards, when the Constitution was ratified and then amended, the framers gave freedom for all religion — and from any established religion — the very first place in the Bill of Rights.

Indeed the framers themselves professed very different faiths — Washington was an Episcopalian, Jefferson a deist, and Adams a Calvinist. And although he had earlier opposed toleration, John Adams later contributed to the building of Catholic churches — and so did George Washington. Thomas Jefferson said his proudest achievement was not the presidency, or writing the Declaration of Independence, but drafting the Virginia Statute of Religious Freedom. He stated the vision of the first Americans and the First Amendment very clearly: "The God who gave us life gave us liberty at the same time."

The separation of church and state can sometimes be frustrating for women and men of deep religious faith. They may be tempted to misuse government in order to impose a value which they cannot persuade others to accept. But once we succumb to that temptation, we step onto a slippery slope where everyone's freedom is at risk. Those who favor censorship should recall that one of the first books ever burned was the first English translation of the Bible. As President Eisenhower warned in 1953, "Don't join the bookburners ... the right to say ideas, the right to record them, and the right to have them accessible to others is unquestioned — or this isn't America." And if that right is denied, at some future day the torch can be turned against any other book or any other belief. Let us never forget: Today's Moral Majority could become tomorrow's persecuted minority.

The danger is as great now as when the founders of the nation first saw it. In 1789, their fear was of factional strife among dozens of denominations. Today there are hundreds — and perhaps thousands of faiths — and millions of Americans who are outside any fold. Pluralism obviously does not and cannot mean that all of them are right; but it does mean that there are areas where government cannot and should not decide what it is wrong to believe, to think, to read and to do. As Professor Larry Tribe, one of the nation's leading constitutional scholars has written, "Law in a nontheocratic state cannot measure religious truth" — nor can the state impose it.

[Public Policy and Private Conscience]

The real transgression occurs when religion wants government to tell citizens how to live uniquely personal parts of their lives. The failure of Prohibition proves the futility of such an attempt when a majority or even a substantial minority happens to disagree. Some questions may be inherently individual ones or people may be sharply divided about whether they are. In such cases — cases like Prohibition and abortion — the proper role of religion is to appeal to the conscience of the individual, not the coercive power of the state.

But there are other questions which are inherently public in nature, which we must decide together as a nation, and where religion and religious values can and should speak to our common conscience. The issue of nuclear war is a compelling example. It is a moral issue; it will be decided by government, not by each individual; and to give any effect to the moral values of their creed, people of faith must speak directly about public policy. The Catholic bishops and the Reverend Billy Graham have every right to stand for the nuclear freeze — and Dr. Falwell has every right to stand against it.

There must be standards for the exercise of such leadership — so that the obligations of belief will not be debased into an opportunity for mere political advantage. But to take a stand at all when a question is both properly public and truly moral is to stand in a long and honored tradition. Many of the great evangelists of the 1800s were in the forefront of the abolitionist movement. In our own time, the Reverend William Sloane Coffin challenged the morality of the war in Vietnam. Pope John XXIII renewed the Gospel's call to social justice. And Dr. Martin Luther King, Jr., who was the greatest prophet of this century, awakened our national conscience to the evil of racial segregation.

Their words have blessed our world. And who now wishes they had all been silent? Who would bid Pope John Paul [II] to quiet his voice about the oppression in Eastern Europe; the violence in Central America; or the crying needs of the landless, the hungry, and those who are tortured in so many of the dark political prisons of our time?

President Kennedy, who said that "no religious body should seek to impose its will," also urged religious leaders to state their views and give

821

their commitment when the public debate involved ethical issues. In drawing the line between imposed will and essential witness, we keep church and state separate — and at the same time, we recognize that the City of God should speak to the civic duties of men and women.

[The Line Between Church and State]

There are four tests which draw that line and define the difference.

First, we must respect the integrity of religion itself.

People of conscience should be careful how they deal in the word of their Lord. In our own history, religion has been falsely invoked to sanction prejudice and even slavery, to condemn labor unions and public spending for the poor. I believe that the prophecy — "the poor you have always with you" is an indictment, not a commandment. I respectfully suggest that God has taken no position on the Department of Education — and that a balanced budget constitutional amendment is a matter for economic analysis, not heavenly appeals.

Religious values cannot be excluded from every public issue — but not every public issue involves religious values. And how ironic it is when those very values are denied in the name of religion — for example, we are sometimes told that it is wrong to feed the hungry — but that mission is an explicit mandate given to us in the 25th chapter of Matthew.

Second, we must respect the independent judgments of conscience.

Those who proclaim moral and religious values can offer counsel, but they should not casually treat a position on a public issue as a test of fealty to faith. Just as I disagree with the Catholic bishops on tuition tax credits — which I oppose — so other Catholics can and do disagree with the hierarchy, on the basis of honest conviction, on the question of the nuclear freeze.

Thus, the controversy about the Moral Majority arises not only from its views, but from its name — which, in the minds of many, seems to imply that only one set of public policies is moral. Similarly, people are and should be perplexed when the religious lobbying group Christian Voice publishes a morality index of congressional voting records — which judges the morality of senators by their attitude toward Zimbabwe and Taiwan.

Let me offer another illustration. Dr. Falwell has written — and I quote: "To stand against Israel is to stand against God." Now there is no one in the Senate who has stood more firmly for Israel than I have. Yet I do not doubt the faith of those on the other side. Their error is not one of religion, but of policy — and I hope to persuade them that they are wrong in terms of both America's interest and the justice of Israel's cause.

Respect for conscience is most in jeopardy — and the harmony of our diverse society is most at risk — when we re-establish, directly or indirectly, a religious test for public office. That relic of the colonial era, which is specifically prohibited in the Constitution, has reappeared in recent years. After the last election, the Reverend James Robison warned President Reagan not to surround himself, as presidents before him had, "with the counsel of the ungodly." I utterly reject any such standard for any position anywhere in public service. Two centuries ago, the victims were Catholics and Jews. In the 1980s, the victims could be atheists; in some other day or decade, they could be the members of the Thomas Road Baptist Church. Indeed, in 1976 I regarded it as unworthy and un-American when some people said or hinted that Jimmy Carter should not be president because he was a born again Christian. We must never judge the fitness of individuals to govern on the basis of where they worship, whether they follow Christ or Moses, whether they are called "born again" or "ungodly." Where it is right to apply moral values to public life, let all of us avoid the temptation to be self-righteous and absolutely certain of ourselves. And if that temptation ever comes, let us recall Winston Churchill's humbling description of an intolerant and inflexible colleague: "There but for the grace of God — goes God."

Third, in applying religious values, we must respect the integrity of public debate.

[The Nuclear Freeze]

In that debate, faith is no substitute for facts. Critics may oppose the nuclear freeze for what they regard as moral reasons. They have every right to argue that any negotiation with the Soviets is wrong — or that any accommodation with them sanctions their crimes — or that no agreement can be good enough and therefore all agreements only increase the chance of war. I do not believe that, but it surely does not violate the standard of fair public debate to say it.

What does violate that standard, what the opponents of the nuclear freeze have no right to do, is to assume that they are infallible — and so any argument against the freeze will do, whether it is false or true.

The nuclear freeze proposal is not unilateral, but bilateral — with equal restraints on the United States and the Soviet Union.

The nuclear freeze does not require that we trust the Russians, but demands full and effective verification.

The nuclear freeze does not concede a Soviet lead in nuclear weapons, but recognizes that human beings in each great power already have in their fallible hands the overwhelming capacity to remake into a pile of radioactive rubble the earth which God has made.

There is no morality in the mushroom cloud. The black rain of nuclear ashes will fall alike on the just and unjust. And then it will be too late to wish that we had done the real work of this atomic age — which is to seek a world that is neither red nor dead.

I am perfectly prepared to debate the nuclear freeze on policy grounds, or moral ones. But we should not be forced to discuss phantom issues or false charges. They only deflect us from the urgent task of deciding how best to prevent a planet divided from becoming a planet destroyed.

And it does not advance the debate to contend that the arms race is more divine punishment than human problem — or that in any event, the final days are near. As Pope John said two decades ago, at the opening of the Second Vatican Council: "We must beware of those who burn with zeal, but are not endowed with much sense ... we must disagree with the prophets of doom, who are always forecasting disasters, as though the end of the earth was at hand."

The message which echoes across the years since then is clear: The earth is still here; and if we wish to keep it, a prophecy of doom is no alternative to a policy of arms control.

[Tolerance in the Face of Disagreement]

Fourth and finally, we must respect the motives of those who exercise their right to disagree.

We sorely test our ability to live together if we too readily question each other's integrity. It may be harder to restrain our feelings when moral principles are at stake — for they go to the deepest wellsprings of our being. But the more our feelings diverge, the more deeply felt they are, the greater is our obligation to grant the sincerity and essential decency of our fellow citizens on the other side.

Those who favor E.R.A. [Equal Rights Amendment] are not "anti-family" or "blasphemers" and their purpose is not "an attack on the Bible." Rather we believe this is the best way to fix in our national firmament the ideal that not only all men, but all people are created equal. Indeed, my mother — who strongly favors E.R.A. — would be surprised to hear that she is anti-family. For my part, I think of the amendment's opponents as wrong on the issue, but not as lacking in moral character.

I could multiply the instances of name-calling, sometimes on both sides. Dr. Falwell is not a "warmonger" — and "liberal clergymen" are not, as the Moral Majority suggested in a recent letter, equivalent to "Soviet sympathizers." The critics of official prayer in public schools are not "Pharisees"; many of them are both civil libertarians and believers, who think that families should pray more at home with their children, and attend church and synagogue more faithfully. Nor does it help anyone's cause to shout such epithets — or try to shout a speaker down — which is what happened last April when Dr. Falwell was hissed and heckled at Harvard. So I am doubly grateful for your courtesy here today. That was not Harvard's finest hour, but I am happy to say that the loudest applause from the Harvard audience came in defense of Dr. Falwell's right to speak.

In short, I hope for an America where neither fundamentalist nor humanist will be a dirty word, but a fair description of the different ways in which people of good will look at life and into their own souls.

I hope for an America where no president, no public official, and no individual will ever be deemed a greater or lesser American because of religious doubt — or religious belief.

I hope for an America where the power of faith will always burn brightly — but where no modern Inquisition of any kind will ever light the fires of fear, coercion, or angry division.

I hope for an America where we can all contend freely and vigorously —

but where we will treasure and guard those standards of civility which alone make this nation safe for both democracy and diversity.

Twenty years ago this fall, in New York City, President Kennedy met for the last time with a Protestant assembly. The atmosphere had been transformed since his earlier address during the 1960 campaign to the Houston Ministerial Association. He had spoken there to allay suspicions about his Catholicism — and to answer those who claimed that on the day of his baptism, he was somehow disqualified from being president. His speech in Houston and then his election drove that prejudice from the center of our national life. Now, three years later, in November, 1963, he was appearing before the Protestant Council of New York City to reaffirm what he regarded as some fundamental truths. On that occasion, John Kennedy said: "The family of man is not limited to a single race or religion, to a single city or country . . . the family of man is nearly 3 billion strong. Most of its members are not white — and most of them are not Christian." And as President Kennedy reflected on that reality, he restated an ideal for which he had lived his life — that "the members of this family should be at peace with one another."

That ideal shines across all the generations of our history and all the ages of our faith, carrying with it the most ancient dream. For as the Apostle Paul wrote long ago in Romans: "If it be possible, as much as it lieth in you, live peaceably with all men."

I believe it is possible; the choice lies within us; as fellow citizens, let us live peaceably with each other; as fellow human beings, let us strive to live peaceably with men and women everywhere. Let that be our purpose and our prayer — yours and mine — for ourselves, for our community, and for all the world.

RESIGNATION OF
INTERIOR SECRETARY WATT
October 9, 1983

Facing an almost certain no-confidence vote in the Republican-controlled Senate, where his support had ebbed steadily for the preceding two and a half weeks, Interior Secretary James G. Watt resigned from the Reagan administration Cabinet October 9. The president named his national security adviser, William P. Clark, as Watt's replacement October 13.

Watt's penchant for politically damaging remarks was what ultimately led to his downfall. In a September 21 speech he characterized his appointees to a commission on federal coal leasing policies as "a black, ... a woman, two Jews and a cripple." It was by no means the first of Watt's casual remarks to cause a storm of protest, but this one, which managed to offend four key voting blocs within as many seconds, proved to be the last.

Negative reaction mounted steadily despite Watt's apology to his appointees and to the president. Only with difficulty did Senate Republican leaders temporarily prevent a Senate vote on a resolution urging Reagan to fire Watt.

Senate Republicans had begun to desert Watt even before the September 21 remark. On September 20 Watt lost a key vote on a coal leasing moratorium, 63-33, although the Senate had backed him narrowly in two previous votes on the same question.

What stampeded Senate Republicans was concern that with an election year nearing, Watt was damaging not only the president but their *own political prospects as well. "There are other Republicans in this country who deserve to be protected," said Sen. Robert Dole, R-Kan. "We want to retain the Senate majority [in 1984].... We just can't stand, every two or three months, Mr. Watt making some comment to offend another 20 or 30 or 40 million people."*

As one GOP senator after another denounced Watt, the White House publicly stood behind him. The president made clear he had no intention of firing his embattled appointee, and when Watt finally quit, Reagan accepted his resignation "reluctantly."

Watt's Role: Lightning Rod

When Watt was named secretary of the interior in 1981, he told Reagan that he would have to "back me and back me and back me, and when he could no longer back me, he'd have to fire me...." In a letter to the president October 9, Watt began, "The time has come."

"It is my view that my usefulness to you in this administration has come to an end," Watt told Reagan.

Watt's pro-development actions at Interior had been vehemently criticized by environmentalists from the day he took office, and polls indicated growing public disapproval of his performance during his 32-month tenure.

Watt had uprooted the legacy of the Carter administration at his department. Scores of officials, both political appointees and civil service, were fired or transferred and replaced with what he called "good people," those who shared his mission. Virtually every major Interior Department program was reorganized or reoriented. The buffalo on the departmental seal was even shifted to face right instead of left.

Watt sought to tilt the balance in federal resource policy away from environmental protection, which Reagan felt had received too much emphasis in the previous decade, and toward resource development, which the president felt was being slowed to a dangerous degree by federal regulation. As head of the Interior Department, Watt controlled more than a fifth of the nation's land — and with it vast reserves of oil, gas, coal, minerals, metals, water, timber, grazing lands, fish and wildlife breeding and feeding grounds, recreation areas, historic sites and natural wonders.

The Watt-Reagan goal of "unlocking" some of those resources so that oil and mining companies, cattlemen, loggers and other developers could make use of them won early cheers in the West, where the economy was based on those resources and where the federal government's role as the dominant landlord conflicted with traditions of personal freedom. Watt also won plaudits from conservatives, who liked his commitment to free-market economic theory, his opposition to government regulation and the zeal with which he lambasted liberals and environmentalists. Both of these constituencies had been important elements in the voting coalition that brought Reagan victory in 1980. The White House encouraged Watt to take time for political fence-mending and fund-raising missions out West, but polls showed that even Watt's Western support was slipping.

Clark Appointment

Commenting on Clark's appointment, Reagan said he had "decided once again to turn to someone who has been a trouble-shooter and a result-oriented professional." He called Clark a "God-fearing Westerner, a fourth-generation rancher, a person I trust."

Reagan three times as president had turned to the 51-year-old California attorney to fill a politically sensitive position. First, Reagan appointed Clark deputy secretary of state in 1981. Then in 1982 Reagan named Clark as Richard V. Allen's replacement as national security adviser. Allen had resigned after he became enmeshed in controversy involving the acceptance of cash and gifts from a Japanese firm.

Clark, who was confirmed by the Senate November 18 by a vote of 71-18, had had a longtime association with Reagan. In Reagan's first term as governor of California Clark was Reagan's chief of staff. In 1969 Reagan appointed him to the first of several state judicial posts, culminating in a 1973 appointment to the state Supreme Court.

Reagan named Robert C. McFarlane October 17 to replace Clark as national security adviser. McFarlane had been Clark's deputy national security adviser.

Following are the texts of Interior Secretary James G. Watt's letter of resignation and President Reagan's reply, both issued October 9, 1983:

LETTER WRITTEN BY WATT TO REAGAN

Dear Mr. President,

The time has come.

At my confirmation hearings in January 1981, I outlined the major changes we knew were needed in management of our natural resources if we were to restore America's greatness.

With your undaunted support, those changes have been put in place. We confronted the neglect and the problems. We gave purpose and direction to management of our nation's natural resources. The restoration of our national parks, refuges and public lands is well under way.

In fact, all the Department of Interior lands are better managed under our stewardship than they were when we inherited the responsibility. Our actions to reduce the nation's dependency on foreign sources of energy and strategic materials are working. The balance is being restored.

It is time for a new phase of management, one to consolidate the gains we have made. It is my view that my usefulness to you in this Administration has come to an end. A different type of leadership at the Department of Interior will best serve you and the nation.

I leave behind people and programs — a legacy that will aid America in the decades ahead. Our people and their dedication will keep America moving in the right direction.

It has been a high honor to serve the nation under your leadership. You are the right man for America. My wife, Leilani, and I will continue to support you with our prayers and in any other way you may ask.

With this letter, I ask permission to be relieved of my duties as Secretary of the Interior as soon as a successor is confirmed.

ACCEPTANCE BY THE PRESIDENT

Today, Jim talked with me by telephone and delivered to me his letter of resignation. He feels that he has completed the principal objectives that he and I agreed upon when he became Secretary of the Interior.

I respect his decision to leave the Government and thus have reluctantly accepted his resignation. He will continue in office until his successor is confirmed.

Jim has done an outstanding job as a member of my Cabinet and in his stewardship of the natural resources of the nation. He has initiated a careful balance between the needs of people and the importance of protecting the environment.

His dedication to public service and his accomplishments as Secretary of Interior will long be remembered.

Nancy and I appreciate the contribution that Jim and Leilani have made to this Administration, and we wish them well in their future endeavors.

ISRAELI PRIME MINISTER
SHAMIR ADDRESS TO KNESSET
October 10, 1983

Ending seven years of controversial leadership by Menachem Begin, the Israeli Knesset (parliament) October 10 approved a new government headed by Yitzhak Shamir. Addressing the Knesset the same day, Shamir pledged to continue Begin's policies.

Begin had announced his intention to resign as prime minister August 28 in the midst of a severe economic crisis and growing public disillusionment with the progress of the war in Lebanon. Israeli newspapers had speculated for some time that he might step down on his 70th birthday, August 16. As head of the conservative ruling Likud coalition since 1977, Begin was a charismatic leader — stubborn and strong willed. Much of his thinking had been influenced by the Holocaust and the long struggle to establish a Jewish homeland. Fiercely patriotic, he was respected by critics and admirers alike.

Begin had made few public appearances in the interval between the death of his wife, Aliza, in November 1982 and his resignation. In ill health, he was said to be depressed over the course of the Israeli invasion of Lebanon as well as by his personal affairs. The prime minister's supporters in the Knesset pleaded with Begin to change his mind, but Begin was quoted as saying at a meeting with the leaders of the ruling coalition on August 30, "I cannot continue."

On September 2 Foreign Minister Yitzhak Shamir was elected to fill Begin's post as leader of the Herut Party, the central party in the ruling Likud coalition. However, it was not until September 12, after two weeks of backroom bargaining, that several minor parties in the coalition agreed to support Shamir. The new cabinet was virtually identical to the one headed by Begin. Shamir retained his post as foreign minister and appointed a new minister of agriculture, Pessah Grupper, to replace the deceased Simcha Ehrlich. The Knesset approved the new government on October 10 by a vote of 60-53.

In his speech before the vote, Shamir promised to support the 1978 Camp David accords signed by Israel, Egypt and the United States, laying the groundwork for a Middle East peace settlement. He had opposed the agreement at the time of its negotiation and had abstained from the vote to ratify the 1979 Israeli-Egyptian peace treaty. (Camp David accords, Historic Documents of 1978, p. 605; peace treaty, Historic Documents of 1979, p. 223)

Shamir also endorsed continued Jewish settlements in the occupied West Bank territories captured from Jordan during the 1967 war. The policy was a cause of continued strife not only with Israel's Arab neighbors but also with the United States. In 1982 President Ronald Reagan had asked Begin to halt the establishment of new settlements at least temporarily while peace negotiations on Lebanon were under way, but Begin refused. (Settlements, Historic Documents of 1980, p. 235)

Shamir's Background

Shamir's background was similar in many respects to that of his predecessor. Shamir, whose family name was Jazernicki, was born in eastern Poland on October 15, 1915. After studying law in Warsaw, he went to Palestine in 1935, where he adopted the Hebrew name of Shamir. In 1936, after attending the Hebrew University of Jerusalem, he joined the Jewish underground, which was fighting for independence from British rule. In 1940 the underground, called the Irgun Zvai Leumi (National Military Organization), which was headed by Begin, split into two factions. Shamir joined the more radical faction, the Lohamei Herut Yisrael (Israel Freedom Fighters), also known as the Stern Gang after its leader, Abraham Stern.

According to a September 3, 1983, article in The New York Times, *historians cited Shamir as responsible for planning both the attempted assassination of the British high commissioner for Palestine, Michael MacMillan, and the murder in Cairo of the British minister of state for the Middle East, Lord Moyne. In 1948 the Israel Freedom Fighters assassinated Count Folke Bernadotte of Sweden, a United Nations representative who advocated a plan to divide Palestine between the Jews and the Arabs.*

Shamir worked for the Mossad, Israel's intelligence agency, from 1955 to 1965. He joined the Herut Party in 1970 and became speaker of the Knesset in 1977. Begin appointed him foreign minister in 1980.

Economic Problems

The Shamir government immediately announced measures to shore up Israel's troubled economy, which had experienced an inflation rate of 135 percent in 1983. Just prior to the formation of the new government, the shekel underwent a series of devaluations, leaving it less than half of what it was worth in January 1983.

The public responded to rumors of an impending devaluation by cashing in bank shares to buy foreign currencies as a hedge against losses. Panicky investors bought 26 million in dollars during two days in October. On October 10 the government suspended trading in foreign currency. The next day the government announced the second devaluation in 24 hours and at the same time effected a series of cuts in subsidies for basic goods and services that increased the cost of living by 12 percent.

Divisions Over War in Lebanon

The economic crisis was not the only burden Shamir assumed when he entered office. Israel was deeply divided over the war in Lebanon. At the time of Begin's resignation, 520 Israeli soldiers had been killed and 3,300 wounded. The war had stretched on for 15 months, far longer than generally had been anticipated.

Critics charged that former defense minister Ariel Sharon and former chief of staff Raphael Eitan persuaded Begin to launch the invasion without regard for either the history of the Lebanese conflict or the fact that the causes of the terrorism Israel sought to eradicate were political as much as military. "Israel did not stand a chance of building a new Lebanon or of solving the Palestinian problem with bayonets," wrote Yoel Marcus, a columnist for the Tel Aviv newspaper **Haaretz**.

On May 17, 1983, Israel signed an agreement with Lebanon governing a pullout of Israeli troops on the condition that Syria and the Palestine Liberation Organization (PLO) simultaneously withdraw their forces. Because Syrian troops remained in Lebanon, both Begin and Shamir refused to effect the agreement. (Israeli-Lebanese agreement, p. 471)

The country's morale had been dealt a crushing blow in September 1982 by the murder of approximately 700 Palestinian civilians by Lebanese Christian Phalangist militiamen in refugee camps near Beirut. The massacre brought a torrent of criticism on the Begin government, both from the international community and from the Israelis themselves. Hours after the massacre, the press reported that the militiamen had entered the camps with the permission of the Israeli army. A state commission appointed by Begin to investigate the Israeli role held Begin, Sharon and other leaders "indirectly responsible" for the killings. (Massacre report, p. 163)

Begin's Legacy

The invasion of Lebanon and Israel's economic problems had cast a cloud over Begin's tenure in office, perhaps causing some to forget his crowning achievement, the signing of a peace treaty with Israel's historic enemy, Egypt, in 1979. The treaty provided for the return of the Sinai Peninsula, seized by Israel in the 1967 war with Egypt, including hotels, settlements and factories built by Israel worth millions of dollars. Begin and Egyptian president Anwar Sadat received the Nobel Peace Prize for their work in ending the 30-year conflict between the two nations. (Sinai withdrawal, Historic Documents of 1982, p. 337)

On the issue of other territory seized by Israel during various wars with its neighbors, Begin refused to negotiate. He undertook an intense campaign to establish Jewish settlements in the occupied territories on the West Bank of the Jordan River, saying that the territories were part of the ancient land of Israel. In 1981 Israel annexed the Golan Heights, captured from Syria in 1967. (Historic Documents of 1981, p. 899)

Begin often referred to the Holocaust to justify his actions. In June 1981, after Israeli pilots bombed an Iraqi nuclear reactor near Bagdad, he responded to international condemnation by saying, "There won't be another Holocaust in history. Never again." (Iraqi bombing, Historic Documents of 1981, p. 507; report on Holocaust, p. 143)

On the domestic front, Begin's term of office brought something of an internal political revolution to Israel. He ousted the Labor Party, which primarily represented an elite of more affluent Jews of European and U.S. descent, and brought the Sephardic Jews of North Africa and the Middle East into the political mainstream. Begin was one of the first political leaders to forge a following of Oriental Jews, who tended to be poorer and more excluded from the political process than their countrymen of European origin.

Although Begin and the U.S. government often were at odds, with both presidents Jimmy Carter and Reagan urging a more moderate path than the prime minister was willing to pursue, U.S.-Israeli relations remained firm.

Shamir's Visit to Washington

In November 1983 Shamir made his first visit as prime minister to Washington, D.C., and with Reagan announced a new agreement for military and political cooperation. Reagan promised substantial increases in military assistance for Israel and agreed to negotiate a free-trade agreement under which the United States and Israel would waive duties on each other's exports.

Both Reagan and Shamir said the two countries decided to draw closer *together militarily as a result of the continuing turmoil in Lebanon and the Soviet Union's staunch backing for Syria. In a statement upon Shamir's departure from the White House November 29, Reagan characterized the military agreements as a response to "increased Soviet involvement in the Middle East."*

Following is the text of Israeli Prime Minister Yitzhak Shamir's October 10, 1983, address to the Knesset announcing the formation of a new government:

On 21 September 1983 I was requested by the President of the State, in accordance with Paragraph 13 of the Basic Law: The Government, to form a government.

I am honoured to present to the Knesset today the government I have formed.

I feel today, the heavy burden of responsibility that I have taken upon myself, in view of the task and challenges that face the state and the people. The burden is infinitely heavier when I realize in whose place I am standing here today before the Knesset.

The resignation of Prime Minister Menachem Begin was a great shock to the people, in Israel and the Diaspora, and filled the hearts of many with anguish and sorrow.

For his friends and followers, it was as if their whole world had collapsed, and they have still not reconciled themselves to this harsh decision. To this day, the wound in their hearts has not healed. It was impossible to reconcile oneself to the departure of the man who for forty years had stood at the centre of Jewish History as it unfolded before our eyes, who led the war of resistance to British rule in Eretz Israel, who headed the parliamentary opposition and established the patterns of a genuine democratic struggle, who gained the confidence of the people and reached the premiership, who, during the last six years, led the state to its first peace treaty with a neighbouring Arab state, to courageous campaigns that have buttressed the security of Israel for generations to come, who initiated large-scale social projects that have revolutionized the lives of tens of thousands of families in Israel, and who laid the foundations of an Israeli policy based on the quest for peace combined with the energetic defence of the goals and the honour of the Jewish state.

Now that his resignation has become an irreversible fact, we have no alternative but to accept the decision, to take the helm in our hands and to gather all our strength and ability in order to continue along the course he charted — for the sake of the people and the state.

The government which I present to the Knesset today will operate in accordance with the same basic guidelines that were brought before the Knesset when the previous government was presented (5 August 1981). Only the paragraph regarding the Golan Heights has been omitted, because the need for this paragraph in the basic guidelines lapsed after the

Knesset decided, on 14 December 1981, to introduce Israeli law, jurisdiction and administration in that region.

The coalition agreement signed before the presentation of the previous government and brought before the Knesset on 5 May 1981 will continue to bind the present government. We have neither added nor omitted anything.

Bid for Unity Government

When I began the work of forming the government, I believed that, in view of the weighty tasks facing us, it was our duty to try to form a government of national unity which would comprise, in the first place, the two major parliamentary blocs. I was convinced that the prospects of such a government overcoming the economic and social problems of the state would be much better and that, moreover, such a government would contain the process of polarization among the people which has reached excessive proportions and which is threatening our unity; that it would contribute to a clearing of the air, restore the norms of democratic and civilized debate among the various schools of thought; enhance the deterrent image of Israel in the eyes of its enemies, who have begun to believe that Israel is becoming weaker because of the sharp and vocal differences of opinion; and raise our political prestige in the international arena — in the eyes of friends and enemies alike. As a result of this effort, we had the rare opportunity for a serious, profound and open-hearted dialogue between representatives of the Labour Party and of the Likud on a number of issues which today occupy a central place on our national agenda.

The discussions were frank and amicable and there was a desire to examine whether it was possible, on the basis of what the two camps have in common, to form a united government that would be able to function in accordance with an agreed plan of action. To my regret, it did not work out because of the profound differences of opinion over political issues, and because of the lack of willingness on the part of the Labour Party representatives to make an attempt to circumvent for a certain period the controversial problems.

I am still convinced that, objectively, it would have been possible to form a unity government, provided neither side sought to impose its views on the other. That would have been possible, for a defined period, until the next elections, always assuming that until then we would not be required to make crucial political decisions on matters on which we differ.

I regret that we did not succeed in forming a unity government, for which the overwhelming majority of the people is yearning. At the same time, however, I am convinced that the dialogue was not in vain. The friendly spirit that prevailed at the talks shows that the attempts to establish a dialogue should be continued, even if they do not lead to far-reaching political results. Our society, our needs and constraints, are crying out for greater mutual understanding, for a greater willingness to listen to each other; and there are several areas in which it is vital and useful for government and opposition to maintain close contacts in order to cooperate, in thought and deed, in vital matters for the common good.

It is my intention to follow this policy regularly in the future, and if an opportunity arises to resume the attempt at forming a government of national unity, I shall not hesitate to try again — even at the risk of failing again.

Needs of the Hour

The need for greater unity, for realizing that "all Jews are responsible for each other," for love of Israel that goes beyond all sectarian and factional affiliation, is the nation's need of the hour. It need not necessarily find expression in common political frameworks. But it should be felt in all spheres of life and society. Lest we forget: we are still at the stage of building a people and a society. We must be prepared to absorb millions of Jews who will come to our shores to lend their hearts and hands to the building of our country. The dangers still are many, both from within and from without. Let us not allow the cracks to widen and polarization to grow unchecked. There must be a comprehensive effort to bolster that which unites and binds us, for a daily demonstration of the simple precept, "We are one people," which appeals to, and is understood by, every Jew. There must be a return to the roots of Judaism and Zionism. We must call a halt to superfluous conflicts, and must encourage all elements in our midst that work for greater national and social solidarity, for respect for one's neighbour and for the love of Israel. Ensuring a wholesome social fabric is a task that should have first priority. The security, strength and prestige of the State of Israel depend on the inner strength of its people. The soldier serving in the army, the worker in the factory, the teacher in school — each in his own place and position — must be deeply aware that we are all part of one people that is building its country and society in spite of difficulties, dangers and differences of opinion. The happiness of every individual depends on the success of the totality. Therefore we must work together, having consideration for each other and responsibility for the nation at large. The accomplishments of every individual can have their due value and weight only if the totality to which he belongs is secured.

The Economy

Recently, economic shocks have inflicted themselves upon us, as is happening in many countries throughout the world. Fortunately, we have been able, in spite of this, to maintain full employment and even to step up the rate of investments. But we are still confronted with grave problems such as inflation, the restraining of private consumption, cuts in government spending, encouragement of exports and restriction of imports, reduction in the balance of payments deficit and progress towards economic independence. We will have to take special steps to deal with these problems, immediately and simultaneously. The government will conduct an economic policy which will include a cut in the budget, as was already discussed during the last days of the previous government, as well as additional measures designed to bring about a balanced budget and a solution of the major economic problems.

These measures will require a joint effort on the part of all sectors of the public. The standard of living and consumption will be reduced, excepting those of the lower income groups. We cannot carry a burden of consumption that is not based on our productive efforts. We should consume only what we are able to produce and reduce our dependence on outside loans. This programme will mean rejecting demands that are not in keeping with the good of the economy.

In its economic policy, the government will strive for renewed prosperity based on the expansion of production. At the same time, our economic policy will seek to restrain inflation by means of budget cuts. Resources will be allocated in such manner as to encourage investments and employment in the production branches, in accordance with the priorities to be determined. All this will be done in a way that will protect the lower-income groups.

In order to ensure an adequate allocation of resources for the encouragement of investments, industry and growth, the government will act to reduce government spending and to restrain private and public consumption. There will be a fair division of the burden, resulting from the priority given to economic growth.

Our economic policy will be applied to this goal, with an emphasis on just taxation, the reduction of subsidies to a reasonable level, more efficient collection of taxes and consideration for social needs. The government will take care to preserve the competitiveness of industry and exports, and give proper encouragement to productivity. To this end, we will maintain a credit policy that is in line with developments in the economy, and of a realistic exchange rate.

We will stand firm on an integrated policy of prices, wages, and income, that will advance our economic and social goals; we will maintain full employment, and see to the needs of the lower income groups, also within the framework of the neighbourhood renewal project.

Our economic development depends on us alone. This government, which will have a majority in the Knesset, is authorized, empowered and obliged to take the economic decisions required by the situation. We will make these decisions without hesitation — and will carry them out without fear. But all those who are calling for the implementation of economic decisions are requested to stand by us, not only in their demands and criticism, but also in their support for the process of implementation. Let no one make his neighbour bear the economic burden alone. We must bear it together, with understanding and goodwill, if we wish to see a solution of our economic problems.

We will make demands of ourselves — and we will make demands of the public. All will be joined in the effort. An integrated economic and social policy such as we will conduct will carry us forward both to economic independence and to social justice.

The public will be required to lower the level of its personal demands in order to make possible the normal development of the economy. Our actual standard of living has gone up in recent years beyond the capabilities of the country's economy. Therefore, we will have to accept the fact that the standard of living will stop rising for a certain period, until we achieve a balance and recovery of the economy.

Social Welfare

This government will continue with the worthy activity begun by the previous governments headed by the Likud, in the areas of eliminating the disadvantaged neighbourhoods; easing overcrowding in housing; insuring decent housing for every family and every young couple, at reasonable prices; and offering social services to mothers, to infants up to kindergarten age, and to senior citizens.

Reducing the social gap and dealing with the educational problems it creates, and continuing the advancement of the disadvantaged sectors of the population, are the greatest educational challenges of Israeli society. We will continue to work energetically in order to increase the number of high school graduates in all the high schools. In the age of advanced technology we must continue to develop our qualitative advantage by pursuing excellence in the sciences and technology. Above all, we will work on enhancing motivation by cultivating the fundamental values of Jewish culture.

The government will also continue with the project that is the political and social glory of the previous government, namely, the neighbourhood renewal project, which has already marked up impressive achievements. It is essential to continue this project and to bring it to a successful conclusion in order to complete the revolutionary change taking place in many towns and neighbourhoods throughout the country.

National Security

Our security is based, first and foremost, on the power and strength of the Israel Defence Forces (IDF) — the army of the people, the defender of our homeland, the glory and pride of the renewed State of Israel.

In the last year, the IDF was put to an additional test, that of eradicating the terrorists and their bases, and insuring the tranquility of the residents of Galilee and of our northern border. They stood the test with honour, and peace has been restored to the north of the country.

The government will persevere in attending to the needs of the IDF and arming it with the very best in advanced weapons so that it will always be ready to fulfill its double mission: to deter any element plotting against Israel's security, and to repel and overwhelm any enemy who would endanger the state and its inhabitants.

Israel's security situation is immeasurably better than it has ever been at any time since we renewed our independence. In the south we have a peaceful border with Egypt; in the north the threat of the terrorists has been removed from Lebanese territory; in the east the bridges over the Jordan are open and there is a desire to maintain quiet along the border. Only on the northeast border with Syria is there a security alert, stemming from the hostility and aggressiveness of the Syrian regime.

Despite the relatively calm reality, we must always remember that we are living in a region which is still unstable and full of surprises. This is due to the character of the regimes around us, and to the continuing hatred of Israel and the refusal to come to terms with the fact of our existence in the region. This reality requires us to maintain a constant superior defence capability, and to be ever on the alert. This will be one of the primary tasks on the government's list of priorities.

Towards Peace with Israel's Neighbours

The outgoing government, headed by Menachem Begin, has to its credit two agreements which are of great significance as regards Israel's position in the Middle East and its relations with its neighbours. The ring of total hostility towards Israel was broken for the first time with Egypt in 1978, and again with Lebanon in May of this year. The change which resulted from these agreements is not limited to the area of bilateral relations with Egypt and Lebanon. There has been a revolutionary change in Israel's position in the entire region. Israel has become a part of the region which surrounds it, not only on the map, but in the practical and actual dynamics of day-to-day developments. We have become more involved in what is going on around us, and are no longer a passive element, only paying close attention to the threats and dangers to our security. The horror and fear of contacts with Israel which characterized the years preceding the peace treaty with Egypt have largely dissolved, and there are a considerable number of signs of a desire for contact, for dialogue, for hearing our position, and at times, even for our assistance. We were recently witness to a frontal change which is not significant in itself, but which is of great symbolic value. During the speech of our representative at the UN General Assembly, the representatives of all the Arab states left the hall in accordance with their annual custom, except for two countries: Egypt and Lebanon. A year ago, only the representatives of Egypt remained in their places. The events in Lebanon in the past seven years, and especially since the beginning of Operation Peace for Galilee, accelerated this process, since Lebanon represents and embodies many of the phenomena and the power elements operating in the whole region.

It is important to realize and to emphasize that we have no intention of intervening militarily in events in the Arab states, whether nearby or further away. But Israel must be fully aware of developments there, in order to protect its own interests. Such involvement could be positive, because it can make possible the use of political tools for understanding developments, locating possible dangers and, at times, even avoiding the need for activating military means at a later stage. Israel is part of the Middle East and, if it is able to develop the ability and the means of being aware of what is going on in the region, it will be in a position to promote chances for mutual understanding, for achieving coexistence with its neighbours and for preparing the ground for truly peaceful relations with the nations living there.

The first government under the leadership of Mr. Menachem Begin achieved a breakthrough in the sphere of peace when it conducted negotiations with Egypt. Peace was achieved, though at a heavy price and with many sacrifices. The peace with Egypt, which was unimaginable six years ago, is a fact of life. Even though we are not happy with the contents of the peaceful relations — we will continue to cultivate them, to bolster the peace, and we will reply with peace even in the face of a chilly attitude. At the same time, we will not hesitate to protest the failure to keep the agreements.

As for relations with Jordan and with the Arabs of Judea, Samaria and the Gaza district — we have gone a long way towards solving the problems with our signing of the Camp David Accords. To our regret, they have not taken advantage of the opportunity and have rejected our outstretched hand. Egypt has also discontinued the autonomy talks, despite President Sadat's letter, according to which it was obliged to continue to conduct negotiations on this issue. We point out once again: if those involved had been willing, we could have been today at the stage of negotiations on the final status. We once again invite Egypt to return to negotiations on the autonomy arrangements, and Jordan to join them, as well as represen-tatives of the Arabs of Judea, Samaria and the Gaza district to join the delegations of either Egypt or Jordan.

It must be clear to all that the Camp David Accords are the only document agreed on by all and, therefore, the only way to continue the process. Complicated and complex negotiations were held on this docu-ment. There is no possibility of demanding that Israel take a different way. The Camp David Accords were a breakthrough of historic dimensions: a golden opportunity for the Palestinian Arabs, for the first time in their history. It would be a pity to let it slip.

For Jordan and representatives of the residents of Judea, Samaria and the Gaza district to join the negotiations would be an additional link in breaking the circle of the negatives of Khartoum, which to our regret still characterizes most of the Arab world, even if cosmetic changes in formula-tion lead the naive astray in thinking that there has been a change.

Lebanon: Israel's primary interest in embarking on Operation Peace for Galilee against the PLO was the security of our northern border. For that purpose, and in order to establish relations on a peaceful basis with

Lebanon — relations which are definitely an important component of security — we conducted negotiations for an agreement with Lebanon. This agreement, which was reached following complex negotiations between Israel and Lebanon, with the participation of the United States, is the basis for future arrangements. We agreed to the security arrangements included in it, not because they were ideal, but because with the addition of an arrangement of a political and civilian character, we saw in it a possible minimum. Let no one imagine that it will be possible to come to an arrangement with Lebanon without the fulfillment of the agreement. All parties must know this. If the agreement is put into effect by the Lebanese government and the conditions attached to it are carried out, it will be a good thing. We are interested in a sovereign and independent Lebanon, free of foreign forces on its soil, and able to act as it deems necessary to ensure its security and to live in proper relations with its neighbours. We will continue to work for this. We will not agree, and we cannot imagine, that any state of the "Rejection Front" will be granted a veto over an arrangement of proper relations between Israel and a neighbouring country. We will remove our forces from Lebanon when security conditions are assured.

It should be pointed out in this connection that Syria's massive military presence on Lebanese soil increases the danger that Lebanon will once more become a base for attacks on Israel. Therefore, the sooner Syria accedes to the Lebanese government's demand to remove its occupying army from Lebanon, the better will it be for Lebanon and for the chances of bringing peace and stability to the entire region. In concluding this section, it can be said: Since we destroyed the terrorist infrastructure in Lebanon, there is no need for our military presence on its soil, and we would be willing to return to our borders the moment the security of Galilee is assured. The presence of Syria, which supports the terrorist war against Israel from Lebanese soil, prevents our leaving Lebanon.

Towards Peace in the Middle East

We get news every day of new kinds of arms reaching the Middle East, and as usual, every import is more sophisticated, more deadly, more murderous than the one preceding it. And that is in addition to the unending stream of regular means of destruction which flow into this region from East and West: missiles from the east, airplanes from the west. Perhaps the time has come to turn to the nations in this region and to call on them to stop for a moment and ask themselves: for how much longer? Has the time not come to halt the deadly, mad race, which has no logic and no end? Are we lacking arms in the Middle East? Haven't we had enough of catastrophes and wars?

It is not arms we lack, but peace. Give a chance to the peoples of the region to live in peace and quiet, and resolve their differences and quarrels peacefully, without bloodshed. I do not only mean the conflict between Israel and the Arabs — there are wars and conflicts in this region which are far more cruel, and far more dangerous.

We appeal to all the peoples and governments of the Middle East to stop the mad and destructive race and come to the tables of negotiation and peace.

And to the great powers we say: Leave this war-ridden area alone. Grant its peoples and residents an opportunity to live their lives in peace and quiet, at least like your peoples in your spacious countries. Do not send the products of your advanced military technology here. Help this part of the world invest its manpower and natural resources in the development of its economy and the advancement of its culture.

Foreign Relations

The relations of trust, friendship and close cooperation between ourselves and the United States are vital for us and for the stability of the whole Middle East. This closeness stems from both common values and a tradition of mutual sympathy between the two peoples, as well as from a complex of shared interests which have stood the test of time and events in our region. The Government of Israel will do all it can to foster and deepen our ties with the United States in all fields of endeavour.

The differences in positions which appear at times between Israel and the United States are a natural and understandable phenomenon, and do not cloud the atmosphere of friendship and the strong alliance which characterizes the relations between the two states. The declarations by the President of the United States of the United States' friendship with Israel and its commitment to its security encourage the people of Israel and strengthen peace in the region.

Our connection to the European continent stems from many roots whose sources lie buried in the histories of its peoples, from the distant past until our generation, in which more than a third of our people, who lived on European soil, was destroyed in the terrible Holocaust during the Second World War. Nevertheless, there were ups and downs in our relations with the European states regarding the Middle Eastern conflict. It may be noted with satisfaction that lately there has been an improvement in our relations with the nations of the European community, relations which have both political and economic importance. We shall persist in our activity among these states and their peoples, in order to bring them closer to our positions, and expand our cooperation with them.

The Eastern European states, under the leadership of the Soviet Union, continue along the line of detachment from us and abstention from official contact with us. Romania is the only exception, and we have normal and positive relations with it, serving the interests of both states.

Moscow's boycott of us is illogical and serves no purpose, and contradicts the principles customary in relations between civilized peoples. We cannot understand what harm would befall the interests of the Soviet Union if it re-established normal relations with Israel, enabled its Jewish citizens to live as Jews, and allowed those among them who so desire to return to their historic homeland, Israel. We call on the Soviet authorities to reassess their attitude towards the State of Israel and the Jewish people. We are convinced that such an assessment, if made, will lead to historic justice, and will strengthen the chances for peace in the Middle East.

For a number of years we have been carrying on vigorous activity aimed at renewing ties with African and Asian states which were severed following the Yom Kippur War. Many governments in these parts of the world now recognize that this severance is no longer justified, and they should no longer yield to pressure from the Arab states. The re-establishment of ties will serve both them and us. We hope that this activity will produce positive results in the near future.

We have good relations with the overwhelming majority of the countries of the Latin American continent. However, the changes this continent is undergoing, and their implications for the Jewish communities throughout the continent, as well as the great potential for economic and political cooperation which exists in those countries, require that we strengthen and deepen our relations with them.

Diaspora Relations

Let us not forget for a moment that the State of Israel is not only the state of Israel's citizens. The Land of Israel is the land, and the State of Israel is the state, of all the Jews, wherever they may be. The State of Israel needs and cries out for millions of Jews still living in foreign lands, and the Jews of the Diaspora must, for the sake of their future and Jewish existence, return to their homeland. This is both a historic law and a national goal.

The settlement of the state and guaranteeing of its security cannot take place without bringing millions of Jews from their countries of residence. The existence of the Jewish Diaspora, in all its variety and diversity, both in countries where Jews are imperiled and where they are not, is not possible for long without a massive stream of emigration from there to here to ensure a strong and vital centre of Jewish life in Israel.

We must fight the inhuman policy that closes the gates of emigration to the Jews of the Soviet Union. The State of Israel and the whole Jewish people should not rest and be silent until the gates of the Soviet Union are thrown open and the masses of Jews who yearn for their homeland are allowed to leave for their country. But first we must free from prison the strugglers for aliyah, suffering for their desire to be united with their people.

To the fighters for aliyah and those suffering and persecuted in the Soviet Union for their desire to come to us, we send today our blessing: Be strong, we are with you, and your day of deliverance will soon come.

And to our brethren in nearby Syria, imprisoned by decree of cruel rulers and prevented from leaving and uniting with their families and people, we say: You are not alone in your yearning and suffering. The Government of Israel and the Jewish people throughout the world identify with you. We shall do all we can to come to your assistance: We say thus to all our brothers and sisters in the other countries of persecution, in which their freedom to leave and come to us has been denied them.

From other countries, where there exists absolute freedom to leave for Israel, only a thin trickle of immigrants arrives. There the battle is perhaps more difficult than in the countries of persecution; there the battle must be fought for every Jew in danger of assimilation and separation from the body of the Jewish people.

This is a battle of life and death; it is the battle for the existence of the Jewish people. It must be included at the top of the state's list of priorities. What is required here is wide-ranging and thorough activity, using every possible means, to win the hearts of the Jews of the Diaspora.

Jewish Settlement

Paths must also be opened and cleared for Jewish settlement in all parts of the Land of Israel. The previous governments led by Menachem Begin have great achievements to their credit in this area. Jewish settlement has planted its stakes and kindled lights in many new places, in Galilee and Samaria, in Judea, the Arava and the Golan. This sacred work must not stop; it cannot stop; it is the heart of our existence and life — and the heart of our life cannot stop.

Exaggerated figures are published about huge investments in settlement, which allegedly come at the expense of other national needs. There are many exaggerations in the figures, since settlement in general is not carried out with public money. We have been fortunate that private capital and ordinary Jews are building their lives in many places outside of the country's crowded coastal strip. But clearly this settlement needs the helping and energizing hand of the state. This hand will be extended wherever possible.

Conclusion

We often frighten ourselves. Superlatives of blackness and gloom are very common in our political lexicon. Let us not exaggerate. Let us see matters in the proper perspective. True, we are faced with problems which are not easy and which we must deal with. We are a small nation which must stretch its capability in order to meet all the tests and challenges it has set for itself.

But that is how it always was, since we became a nation, and with the strength of belief and historic inevitability we have succeeded and overcome. Our generation, which saw and experienced the steep passage from the depths of the Holocaust to the heights of liberation and deliverance, cannot but anticipate — with faith and confidence — a future of blessing and success. If we believe, we shall succeed, since the story of the State of Israel from its establishment to this day has proved to be an unparallelled success story.

REAGAN ADDRESS ON GRENADA INVASION

October 27, 1983

Early on October 25, a mostly American force of 2,200 troops invaded the island of Grenada, located approximately 90 miles north of Venezuela. President Ronald Reagan announced the surprise move later that day. United States' intervention was necessary, he said, to ensure the protection of approximately 1,000 Americans on Grenada and to respond to the request from five member nations of the Organization of Eastern Caribbean States (OECS) for U.S. aid in a joint effort to restore order and democracy on Grenada after a violent military coup the week before. U.S. troops quickly gained control of the island, despite heavy resistance from members of the Grenadian army and from Cuban troops. On November 2 the Defense Department announced that hostilities had ceased; the last American combat troops left the island December 15.

Background

Grenada is the smallest of the Windward Islands, which curve in a northwesterly direction from Venezuela toward Puerto Rico in the eastern Caribbean. Approximately 110,000 people, mostly blacks, live on the island. Agriculture and tourism are Grenada's primary economic activities.

Grenada gained independence from Britain in 1974 and became a member of the Commonwealth, with Sir Eric Gairy as prime minister. In 1979 Maurice Bishop, a Marxist with close ties to Cuba and the Soviet Union, overthrew Gairy's government and installed his own New Jewel

Movement as the People's Revolutionary Government. Under Bishop's regime, Grenada's relations with Cuba and the Soviet Union were strengthened, and relations with the United States were cool at best. In June, 1983, however, Bishop visited Washington in an apparently conciliatory move.

On October 12 a group of military hard-liners deposed Bishop and placed him under house arrest. A week later, a crowd of his supporters freed the prime minister and marched with him to army headquarters. There, troops opened fire, and Bishop was recaptured and later executed with at least 17 of his top officials.

A 16-member military council, headed by General Hudson Austin, took over as Grenada's new government. The council imposed a 24-hour "shoot-to-kill" curfew, closed the airport, banned foreign journalists and enforced a strict censorship.

American Concerns

On Grenada at the time of the coup were approximately 1,000 Americans, more than half of whom were students at St. George's University School of Medicine. Despite assurances from Grenadian authorities and from the Cuban government that the Americans were in no danger, the Reagan administration decided to divert to Grenada a 10-ship naval task force that was in the Caribbean en route to Lebanon. The administration did not want to risk another hostage crisis like the one that the Jimmy Carter administration faced in Iran in 1978-79. (Historic Documents of 1979, p. 867)

The Reagan administration was worried also about Grenada's construction of an airport with a 9,000-foot runway, which could accommodate Soviet and Cuban warplanes. In a March television address, Reagan showed aerial photos of an airport being built on Grenada with Cuban help. He suggested that the island was becoming a Soviet-bloc military base to threaten U.S. interests and provide support for guerrillas in nearby Central America.

Bishop denied Reagan's charges, maintaining that the airport would be used to boost Grenada's tourism trade. Nonetheless, the Reagan administration remained concerned about the growth of leftist movements in the region.

On October 23 the United States received a formal request from five member nations of OECS to participate in a joint effort to restore order on Grenada. Two days later Reagan announced the landing of U.S. and Caribbean troops on the island. Considering the safety of Americans and the request for help from the neighboring states, Reagan said, "I concluded the United States had no choice but to act strongly and decisively."

Invasion

Early on October 25, 1,900 U.S. Marines and Army Rangers and 300 Caribbean troops landed on Grenada. The Rangers (soldiers trained to fight in small groups and to make surprise raids) and Marines undertook most of the combat responsibilities, while the Caribbean troops served primarily as police and security forces. Approximately 2,000 Grenadian army troops and 800 Cubans offered resistance to the American forces. Many of the Cubans, who were reportedly well-trained and well-armed, were on Grenada in connection with the construction of the airfield on the island.

U.S. troops, under the command of Vice Admiral Joseph Metcalf III, quickly secured the international airport at the northern end of the island, the airfield under construction at the southern end and the campus of St. George's University School of Medicine. The evacuation of American citizens from Grenada began the following day. In one unfortunate incident, a U.S. Navy plane mistakenly bombed a civilian mental hospital, killing several Grenadians and injuring others.

U.S. officials reported that on October 26 American troops had overtaken a major Cuban installation; caches of weapons and supplies, communications equipment and documents, including "secret treaties" involving Grenada, Cuba, the Soviet Union and North Korea, had been discovered. The Reagan administration maintained that some of the documents indicated that the Cubans had planned to take over Grenada and hold U.S. citizens hostage.

Most of the heavy fighting was over by October 26. More American soldiers arrived on Grenada October 26 and 27, boosting the total number of U.S. forces there to almost 6,000. American troops spent several days following the invasion engaged in sporadic fighting, searching for Cuban and Grenadian fighters who had retreated to the hills, and generally securing the island. On October 29 Marines captured Bernard Coard, Bishop's deputy prime minister and a suspect in his violent overthrow. Austin, who had led the coup, was arrested the following day.

On November 2 the Defense Department announced that hostilities had ended and that U.S. troops were engaged in routine police duties. The number of American soldiers on Grenada was pared down to 3,000. The approximately 700 wounded and captured Cubans were returned to Havana by November 9. The struggle on Grenada left 18 American soldiers dead, 151 wounded. Forty-five Grenadians and 24 Cubans were killed.

By December 15 all but 300 U.S. soldiers had left Grenada. Those remaining were in a non-combat role, to support the efforts of Caribbean peacekeeping forces.

Press Restrictions

News reports on the Grenadian mission were vague and often contradictory. In a controversial move, the Reagan administration banned the press from the island. Reporters were forced to set up camp on the island of Barbados, some 150 miles from Grenada. Reports from ham radio operators, U.S. officials, and Radio Havana gave journalists conflicting and hazy accounts of the invasion. On October 27, 15 reporters were allowed to visit the island for a few hours, under strict military supervision. Two larger groups of journalists were allowed visits October 28 and 29. The total press restriction was not lifted until October 31.

Government spokesmen maintained that the press ban was necessary for two reasons: a need for surprise in the attack and concern for the safety of the journalists themselves. Reporters argued that the attack came as no surprise to Grenada, the Soviet Union or Cuba and that the press had accompanied U.S. troops during all major wars — with no safety guarantees.

Congress, concerned about possible free press violations and censored news reports, held hearings. Three separate congressional delegations made fact-finding missions to Grenada November 3-8 to evaluate the need for the invasion and the situation on the island.

Reactions

Initial international reaction to the U.S. invasion was generally negative. Even staunch allies such as Britain, France, West Germany and Canada expressed reservations and opposition. The Soviet Union, predictably, blasted the invasion as an "act of undisguised banditry and international terrorism." On October 26 a majority of delegates at a meeting of the Organization of American States (OAS) condemned the U.S. action. The United Nations Security Council on October 28 and the General Assembly on November 2 approved resolutions deploring the invasion.

Domestic response was mixed. On Capitol Hill, Democrats were quick to criticize the president's decision to intervene, while conservatives generally supported Reagan's move. Critics drew parallels between the U.S. action in Grenada and the Soviet invasion of Afghanistan in 1979. (Historic Documents of 1979, p. 965)

On October 28 and November 11, Congress voted to apply the War Powers Resolution to the U.S. military operation in Grenada, thereby requiring withdrawal of American troops within 60 days unless Congress authorized a longer stay. (Asserting its rights under the War Powers Resolution was the strongest action available to Congress.)

Members of the three congressional fact-finding missions to Grenada reported, with some exceptions, that their visits had persuaded them that a potential threat to Americans there had existed and that Reagan had acted properly. Congressional expressions of support for the invasion increased.

The American public, from the start, appeared to back the president's decision to send troops to Grenada; the swiftness and effectiveness of the mission reinforced this position. A Washington Post-*ABC* News *poll reported November 9, for example, that 71 percent of those surveyed approved of the invasion.*

Aftermath

Immediately following the U.S. invasion, Grenada's governor general, Sir Paul Scoon, took over as temporary head of government. On November 15 an interim advisory council was sworn in to govern the island; elections were promised within six months to a year. Scoon cut ties with Cuba and the Soviet Union. The United States announced that it would help pay for damage to the island. In late December, two months after the coup attempt and U.S. intervention, the Grenadian public was optimistic and supportive of the U.S. invasion and continued presence of American support troops on the island.

Following are excerpts from President Ronald Reagan's October 27, 1983, nationally broadcast address on U.S. involvement in Lebanon and Grenada:

. . . [In addition to Lebanon] another part of the world is very much on our minds, a place much closer to our shores: Grenada. The island is only twice the size of the District of Columbia, with a total population of about 110,000 people.

Grenada and a half dozen other Caribbean islands here were, until recently, British colonies. They're now independent states and members of the British Commonwealth. While they respect each other's independence, they also feel a kinship with each other and think of themselves as one people.

In 1979 trouble came to Grenada. Maurice Bishop, a protégé of Fidel Castro, staged a military coup and overthrew the government which had been elected under the constitution left to the people by the British. He sought the help of Cuba in building an airport, which he claimed was for tourist trade, but which looked suspiciously suitable for military aircraft, including Soviet-built long-range bombers.

The six sovereign countries and one remaining colony are joined together in what they call the Organization of Eastern Caribbean States. The six became increasingly alarmed as Bishop built an army greater than all of theirs combined. Obviously, it was not purely for defense.

In this last year or so, Prime Minister Bishop gave indications that he might like better relations with the United States. He even made a trip to our country and met with senior officials of the White House and the State Department. Whether he was serious or not, we'll never know. On October 12th, a small group in his militia seized him and put him under arrest. They were, if anything, more radical and more devoted to Castro's Cuba than he had been.

Several days later, a crowd of citizens appeared before Bishop's home, freed him, and escorted him toward the headquarters of the military council. They were fired upon. A number, including some children, were killed, and Bishop was seized. He and several members of his cabinet were subsequently executed, and a 24-hour shoot-to-kill curfew was put in effect. Grenada was without a government, its only authority exercised by a self-proclaimed band of military men.

There were then about 1,000 of our citizens on Grenada, 800 of them students in St. George's University Medical School. Concerned that they'd be harmed or held as hostages, I ordered a flotilla of ships, then on its way to Lebanon with marines, part of our regular rotation program, to circle south on a course that would put them somewhere in the vicinity of Grenada in case there should be a need to evacuate our people.

Last weekend, I was awakened in the early morning hours and told that six members of the Organization of Eastern Caribbean States, joined by Jamaica and Barbados, had sent an urgent request that we join them in a military operation to restore order and democracy to Grenada. They were proposing this action under the terms of a treaty, a mutual assistance pact that existed among them.

These small, peaceful nations needed our help. Three of them don't have armies at all, and the others have very limited forces. The legitimacy of their request, plus my own concern for our citizens, dictated my decision. I believe our government has a responsibility to go to the aid of its citizens, if their right to life and liberty is threatened. The nightmare of our hostages in Iran must never be repeated.

We knew we had little time and that complete secrecy was vital to ensure both the safety of the young men who would undertake this mission and the Americans they were about to rescue. The Joint Chiefs worked around the clock to come up with a plan. They had little intelligence information about conditions on the island.

We had to assume that several hundred Cubans working on the airport could be military reserves. Well, as it turned out, the number was much larger, and they were a military force. Six hundred of them have been taken prisoner, and we have discovered a complete base with weapons and communications equipment, which makes it clear a Cuban occupation of the island had been planned.

Two hours ago we released the first photos from Grenada. They included pictures of a warehouse of military equipment — one of three we've uncovered so far. This warehouse contained weapons and ammunition stacked almost to the ceiling, enough to supply thousands of terrorists.

Grenada, we were told, was a friendly island paradise for tourism. Well, it wasn't. It was a Soviet-Cuban colony, being readied as a major military bastion to export terror and undermine democracy. We got there just in time.

I can't say enough in praise of our military — Army rangers and paratroopers, Navy, Marine, and Air Force personnel — those who planned a brilliant campaign and those who carried it out. Almost instantly, our military seized the two airports, secured the campus where most of our students were, and are now in the mopping-up phase.

It should be noted that in all the planning, a top priority was to minimize risk, to avoid casualties to our own men and also the Grenadian forces as much as humanly possible. But there were casualties, and we all owe a debt to those who lost their lives or were wounded. They were few in number, but even one is a tragic price to pay.

It's our intention to get our men out as soon as possible. Prime Mnister Eugenia Charles of Dominia . . . she is Chairman of the OECS. She's calling for help from Commonwealth nations in giving the people their right to establish a constitutional government on Grenada. We anticipate that the Governor General, a Grenadian, will participate in setting up a provisional government in the interim.

. . . It is no coincidence that when the thugs tried to wrest control over Grenada, there were 30 Soviet advisers and hundreds of Cuban military and paramilitary forces on the island. At the moment of our landing, we communicated with the Governments of Cuba and the Soviet Union and told them we would offer shelter and security to their people on Grenada. Regrettably, Castro ordered his men to fight to the death, and some did. The others will be sent to their homelands.

You know, there was a time when our national security was based on a standing army here within our own borders and shore batteries of artillery along our coasts, and, of course, a navy to keep the sealanes open for the shipping of things necessary to our well-being. The world has changed. Today, our national security can be threatened in faraway places. It's up to all of us to be aware of the strategic importance of such places and to be able to identify them. . . .

November

'NUCLEAR WINTER': LONG-TERM BLAST EFFECTS

November 1, 1983

Although numerous scenarios had been devised to estimate the long-term effects of a nuclear war, a series of papers presented by physicists, ecologists and biologists at a conference held in Washington, D.C., October 31-November 1, suggested far more serious consequences for human life and global ecosystems than had been previously calculated.

The scientists contributing to the international conference, "The World After Nuclear War," including specialists from the Soviet Union, were in remarkable agreement on the disastrous effects even a limited exchange of nuclear weapons would have on the Earth. A major contribution to the conference, "Nuclear Winter: Global Consequences of Multiple Nuclear Explosions," painted a particularly grim picture of conditions that would follow a nuclear war. Prepared by scientists R. P. Turco, O. B. Took, T. P. Ackerman, J. B. Pollack and Carl Sagan (the group was called TTAPS, an acronym of the last initial of the contributors) and reprinted in the December 23, 1983, issue of Science *magazine, the paper provided a baseline scenario of a 5,000-megaton (MT) exchange of nuclear weapons — roughly 400,000 times greater than the bomb dropped on Hiroshima — with additional calculations considering total yields from 100 to 25,000 megatons. (A megaton is the equivalent of a million tons of TNT; the nuclear arsenals of the world have been estimated in excess of 12,000 megatons.)*

Basing their estimates on previous studies of volcanic eruptions on Earth and dust storms observed on Mars, the TTAPS group calculated that such an exchange would emit approximately 225 million tons of smoke into the atmosphere. The resulting dense clouds would blanket much of the Earth, effectively cutting off sunlight and heat and immediately plunging much of the Northern Hemisphere (where the exchange was assumed to occur) into subfreezing temperatures, a veritable "nuclear winter." Even three to four weeks after a major nuclear exchange, surface temperatures on large land areas in the Northern Hemisphere still could register as low as -23° C and remain subfreezing for months, killing food sources for immediate survivors.

Lethal Radiation Levels

The related effects of a major nuclear exchange were revised to include higher levels of radioactivity than had been estimated previously, with doses of 250 rads, half the human lethal dosage, blanketing approximately 30 percent of the Northern Hemisphere. Ultraviolet radiation levels also would be raised, because of damage to the Earth's protective ozone layer. And if the blast sites were concentrated on 100 urban areas, the burning of particularly lethal combustible materials would result in atmospheric pollution more severe than if rural areas were targeted. Even a relatively small exchange of 100 megatons, if centered on urban areas, was calculated to have a potentially severe climatic effect from increased smoke emissions.

The Southern Hemisphere, hitherto considered comparatively protected from nuclear threat, also was shown to be susceptible to exchanges occurring in the Northern Hemisphere because of global weather circulation patterns. Winds would spread the nuclear cloud coverage, reducing light and temperature and carrying lethal radioactive fallout, again having severe consequences on human and biological life.

Long-term Consequences

A second study presented at the conference and also reprinted in Science magazine, "[The] Long-Term Biological Consequences of Nuclear War," carried the conclusions of the TTAPS paper a step further to consider the long-term residual effects of a nuclear exchange. The paper acknowledged the work of earlier studies estimating that a 5,000-to 10,000-megaton exchange would result in the deaths of 1.1 billion people from the immediate effects and an additional 1.1 billion injured and unable to obtain medical treatment, making 30 percent to 50 percent of the human population immediate casualties. The report further suggested, however, that the "longer term biological effects resulting from climatic changes may be at least as serious as the immediate ones." Basing their calculations on a "severe case" of a 10,000 megaton-exchange rather than TTAPS's 5,000 baseline figure, the scientists said, "We believe...that decision-makers should be fully apprised of the potential consequences of the scenarios most likely to trigger long-term effects."

"[The] Long-Term Biological Consequences of Nuclear War" was the consensus of 40 biologists who met in April 1983 to discuss the issue. The scientists calculated that most terrestrial ecosystems would be severely damaged from the cold, lack of sunlight and unavailability of water. The projected state of these ecosystems one year after nuclear fallout (a year was considered to be the minimum amount of time necessary for light and temperature to return to previously normal levels) was that plant growth would be significantly depressed, and there would be intense competition among surviving animals, including tropical species affected by the temperature stress. The study predicted conditions after 10 years would be somewhat improved as the productive capability of plant and animal life gradually recovered. Nonetheless, there would be irreversible damage to most ecosystems and extinction of many species.

The predictions for the state of mankind were equally grim. For those humans who survived the initial blasts and radioactive aftermath, as well as the unrelenting cold and starvation that would result, the slow redevelopment of societal and human support systems would vastly limit population growth. The scientists did not exclude the possibility of total human extinction should a large-scale exchange eliminate a large number of plant and animal species.

Soviet scientists also contributed to the conference with a report confirming the drastic global climatic consequences outlined by the U.S. participants. The Soviets' report differed only in the severity of temperature drop, predicting an even greater loss of heat.

Policy-making Issue

Public awareness of the nuclear arms issue was heightened with the broadcast November 20 of "The Day After," an ABC-TV film depicting the immediate effects of a nuclear exchange in the Midwestern United States. The film, widely publicized in advance and viewed by an estimated 100 million Americans, was broadcast amid a growing debate over U.S. defense spending, especially the development of the MX missile, and the scheduled deployment of U.S. nuclear weapons in Europe. Despite widespread concern over the threat of nuclear war and demonstrations in West Germany and Britain protesting missile deployment, U.S. officials continued to insist that nuclear weapons were needed as a deterrent to Soviet aggression. (MX deployment, p. 365; U.S.-Soviet arms limitation talks, p. 791)

> *Following are excerpts from scientists' reports — "Nuclear Winter: Global Consequences of Multiple Nuclear Explosions" and "Long-Term Biological Consequences of Nuclear War" — presented at a Washington, D.C., conference held October 31-November 1, 1983:*

NUCLEAR WINTER: GLOBAL CONSEQUENCES OF MULTIPLE NUCLEAR EXPLOSIONS

—R. P. Turco, O. B. Toon, T. P. Ackerman
J. B. Pollack, Carl Sagan

Concern has been raised over the short- and long-term consequences of the dust, smoke, radioactivity, and toxic vapors that would be generated by a nuclear war. The discovery that dense clouds of soil particles may have played a major role in past mass extinctions of life on Earth has encouraged the reconsideration of nuclear war effects. Also, [P. J.] Crutzen and [J. W.] Birks recently suggested that massive fires ignited by nuclear explosions could generate quantities of sooty smoke that would attenuate sunlight and perturb the climate. These developments have led us to calculate, using new data and improved models, the potential global environmental effects of dust and smoke clouds (henceforth referred to as nuclear dust and nuclear smoke) generated in a nuclear war. We neglect the short-term effects of blast, fire, and radiation. Most of the world's population could probably survive the initial nuclear exchange and would inherit the postwar environment. Accordingly, the longer-term and global-scale aftereffects of nuclear war might prove to be as important as the immediate consequences of the war.

To study these phenomena, we used a series of physical models: a nuclear war scenario model, a particle microphysics model, and a radiative-convective model. The nuclear war scenario model specifies the altitude-dependent dust, smoke, radioactivity, and NO_x injections for each explosion in a nuclear exchange (assuming the size, number, and type of detonations, including heights of burst, geographic locales, and fission yield fractions). The source model parameterization is discussed below.... The one-dimensional microphysical model predicts the temporal evolution of dust and smoke clouds, which are taken to be rapidly and uniformly dispersed. The one-dimensional radiative-convective model (1-D RCM) uses the calculated dust and smoke particle size distributions and optical constants and Mie theory to calculate visible and infrared optical properties, light fluxes, and air temperatures as a function of time and height. Because the calculated air temperatures are sensitive to surface heat capacities, separate simulations are performed for land and ocean environments, to define possible temperature contrasts. The techniques used in our 1-D RCM calculations are well documented.

Although the models we used can provide rough estimates of the average effects of widespread dust and smoke clouds, they cannot accurately forecast short-term or local effects. The applicability of our results depends on the rate and extent of dispersion of the explosion clouds and fire plumes. Soon after a large nuclear exchange, thousands of individual dust and smoke clouds would be distributed throughout the northern mid-latitudes and at altitudes up to 30 km. Horizontal turbulent diffusion, vertical wind shear, and continuing smoke emission could spread the clouds of nuclear debris over the entire zone, and tend to fill in any holes in the clouds, within 1 to 2 weeks. Spatially averaged simulations of this initial period of cloud spreading must be viewed with caution; effects would be smaller at some locations and larger at others....

The present results also do not reflect the strong coupling between atmospheric motions on all length scales and the modified atmospheric solar and infrared heating and cooling rates computed with the 1-D RCM. Global circulation patterns would almost certainly be altered in response to the large disturbances in the driving forces calculated here. Although the 1-D RCM can predict only horizontally, diurnally, and seasonally averaged conditions, it is capable of estimating the first-order climate responses of the atmosphere, which is our intention in this study.

Scenarios

A review of the world's nuclear arsenals shows that the primary strategic and theater weapons amount to 2,000 megatons (MT) of yield carried by 17,000 warheads. These arsenals are roughly equivalent in explosive power to 1 million Hiroshima bombs. Although the total number of high-yield warheads is declining with time, about 7000 MT is still accounted for by warheads of > 1 MT. There are also 30,000 lower-yield tactical warheads and munitions which are ignored in this analysis. Scenarios for the possible use of nuclear weapons are complex and controversial. Historically, studies of the long-term effects of nuclear war have focused on a full-scale exchange in the range of 5000 to 10,000 MT. Such exchanges are possible, given the current arsenals and the unpredictable nature of warfare, particularly nuclear warfare, in which escalating massive exchanges could occur....

Our baseline scenario assumes an exchange of 5000 MT. Other cases span a range of total yield from 100 to 25,000 MT. Many high-priority military and industrial assets are located near or within urban zones. Accordingly, a modest fraction (15 to 30 percent) of the total yield is assigned to urban or industrial targets. Because of the large yields of strategic warheads generally [equal to or less than] 100 kilotons (KT), "surgical" strikes against individual targets are difficult; for instance, a 100-KT airburst can level and burn an area of $\simeq 50$ km^2, and a 1-MT airburst, $\simeq 5$ times that area, implying widespread collateral damage in any "countervalue," and many "counterforce," detonations.

The properties of nuclear dust and smoke are critical to the present analysis.... For each explosion scenario, the fundamental quantities that must be known to make optical and climate predictions are the total atmospheric injections of fine dust ([equal to or less than] 10 μm in radius) and soot.

Nuclear explosions at or near the ground can generate fine particles by several mechanisms: (i) ejection and disaggregation of soil particles, (ii) vaporization and renucleation of earth and rock, and (iii) blowoff and sweepup of surface dust and smoke. Analyses of nuclear test data indicate that roughly 1×10^5 to 6×10^5 tons of dust per megaton of explosive yield are held in the stabilized clouds of land surface detonations. Moreover, size analysis of dust samples collected in nuclear clouds indicates a substantial submicrometer fraction. Nuclear surface detonations may be much more efficient in generating fine dust than volcanic eruptions, which have been used inappropriately in the past to estimate the impacts of nuclear war.

The intense light emitted by a nuclear fireball is sufficient to ignite flammable materials over a wide area. The explosions over Hiroshima and Nagasaki both initiated massive conflagrations. In each city, the region heavily damaged by blast was also consumed by fire. Assessments over the past two decades strongly suggest that widespread fires would occur after most nuclear bursts over forests and cities. The Northern Hemisphere has $\simeq 4 \times 10^2$ of forest land, which holds combustible material averaging $\simeq 2.2 \text{g/cm}^2$ (7). The world's urban and suburban zones cover an area of $\simeq 1.5 \times 10^6$ km². Central cities, which occupy 5 to 10 percent of the total urban area, hold $\simeq 10$ to 40 g/cm² of combustible material, while residential areas hold $\simeq 1$ to 5 g/cm². Smoke emissions from wildfires and large-scale urban fires probably lie in the range of 2 to 8 percent by mass of the fuel burned. The highly absorbing sooty fraction (principally graphitic carbon) could comprise up to 50 percent of the emission by weight. In wildfires, and probably urban fires, [approximately equal to or greater than] 90 percent of the smoke mass consists of particles $< \mu$m in radius. For calculations at visible wavelengths, smoke particles are assigned an imaginary part of the refractive index of 0.3.

Simulations

The model predictions discussed here generally represent effects averaged over the Northern Hemisphere (NH). The initial nuclear explosions and fires would be largely confined to northern mid-latitudes (30° to 60°N). Accordingly, the predicted mean dust and smoke opacity could be larger by a factor of 2 to 3 at mid-latitudes, but smaller elsewhere. . . . The vertical optical depth is a convenient diagnostic of nuclear cloud properties and may be used roughly to scale atmospheric light levels and temperatures for the various scenarios.

In the baseline scenario (. . . . 5000 MT), the initial NH optical depth is $\simeq 4$, of which $\simeq 1$ is due to stratospheric dust and $\simeq 3$ to tropospheric smoke. After 1 month the optical depth is still $\simeq 2$. Beyond 2 to 3 months, dust dominates the optical effects, as the soot is largely depleted by rainout and washout. In the baseline case, about 240,000 km² of urban area is partially (50 percent) burned by $\simeq 1000$ MT of explosions (only 20 percent of the total exchange yield). This roughly corresponds to one sixth of the world's urbanized land area, one fourth of the developed area of the NH, and one half of the area of urban centers with populations $> 100,000$ in the NATO and Warsaw Pact countries. The mean quantity of combustible material consumed over the burned area is $\simeq 1.9$ g/cm². Wildfires ignited by the remaining 4000 MT of yield burn another 500,000 km² of forest, brush, and grasslands, consuming $\simeq 0.5$ g/cm² of fuel in the process.

Total smoke emission in the baseline case is $\simeq 225$ million tons (released over several days). By comparison, the current annual global smoke emission is estimated as $\simeq 200$ million tons, but is probably < 1 percent as effective as nuclear smoke would be in perturbing the atmosphere.

The optical depth simulations ... show that a range of exchanges between 3000 and 10,000 MT might create similar effects.... [Other cases,] while less severe in their absolute impact, produce optical depths comparable to or exceeding those of a major volcanic eruption. It is noteworthy that eruptions such as Tambora in 1815 may have produced significant climate perturbations, even with an average surface temperature decrease of [equal to or less than] 1 K.

... [In] a 100-MT attack on cities with 1000 100-KT warheads ... 25,000 km² of built-up urban area is burned (such an area could be accounted for by $\simeq 100$ major cities). The smoke emission is computed with fire parameters that differ from the baseline case. The average burden of combustible material in city centers is 20 g/cm² ... and the average smoke emission factor is 0.026 gram of smoke per gram of material burned (versus the conservative figure of 0.011 g/g adopted for central city fires in the baseline case). About 130 million tons of urban smoke is injected into the troposphere in each case.... In the baseline case, only about 10 percent of the urban smoke originates from fires in city centers.

The smoke injection threshold for major optical perturbations on a hemispheric scale appears to lie at $\simeq 1 \times 10^8$ tons.... [O]ne can envision the release of $\simeq 1 \times 10^6$ tons of smoke from each of 100 major city fires consuming $\simeq 4 \times 10^7$ tons of combustible material per city. Such fires could be ignited by 100 MT of nuclear explosions. Unexpectedly, less than 1 percent of the existing strategic arsenals, if targeted on cities, could produce optical (and climatic) disturbances much larger than those previously associated with a massive nuclear exchange of $\simeq 10,000$ MT.

... In the baseline 5000-MT case, a minimum land temperature of $\simeq 250$ K ($-23°$C) is predicted after 3 weeks. Subfreezing temperatures persist for several months. Among the cases ... [studied], even the smallest temperature decreases on land are $\simeq 5°$ to $10°$C, enough to turn summer into winter. Thus, severe climatological consequences might be expected in each of these cases. The 100-MT city airburst scenario produces a 2-month interval of subfreezing land temperatures, with a minimum again near 250 K. The temperature recovery in this instance is hastened by the absorption of sunlight in optically thin remnant soot clouds. Comparable exchanges with and without smoke emission show that the tropospheric soot layers cause a sudden surface cooling of short duration, while fine stratospheric dust is responsible for prolonged cooling lasting a year or more. (Climatologically, a long-term surface cooling of only 1°C is significant.) In all instances, nuclear dust acts to cool the earth's surface: soot also tends to cool the surface except when the soot cloud is both optically thin and located near the surface (an unimportant case because only relatively small transient warmings [equal to or less than] 2 K can thereby be achieved).

Predicted air temperature variations over the world's oceans associated with changes in atmospheric radiative transport are always small (cooling of [equal to or less than] 3 K) because of the great heat content and rapid mixing of surface waters. However, variations in atmospheric zonal circulation patterns might significantly alter ocean currents and upwelling, as occurred on a smaller scale recently in the Eastern Pacific (El Niño). The oceanic heat reservoir would also moderate the predicted continental land temperature decreases, particularly in coastal regions. The effect is difficult to assess because disturbances in atmospheric circulation patterns are likely. Actual temperature decreases in continental interiors might be roughly 30 percent smaller than predicted here, and along coastlines 70 percent smaller. In the baseline case, therefore, continental temperatures may fall to $\simeq 260$ K before returning to ambient.

Predicted changes in the vertical temperature profile for the baseline nuclear exchange are illustrated as a function of time.... The dominant features of the temperature perturbation are a large warming (up to 80 K) of the lower stratosphere and upper troposphere, and a large cooling (up to 40 K) of the surface and lower troposphere. The warming is caused by absorption of solar radiation in the upper-level dust and smoke clouds; it persists for an extended period because of the long residence time of the particles at high altitudes. The size of the warming is due to the low heat capacity of the upper atmosphere, its small infrared emmissivity, and the initially low temperatures at high altitudes. The surface cooling is the result of attenuation of the incident solar flux by the aerosol clouds during the first month of the simulation. The greenhouse effect no longer occurs in our calculations because solar energy is deposited above the height at which infrared energy is radiated to space.

Decreases in insolation for several nuclear wars are shown [in several cases].... The baseline case implies average hemispheric solar fluxes at the ground [equal to or lesser than] 10 percent of normal values for several weeks (apart from any patchiness in the dust and smoke clouds). In addition to causing the temperature declines mentioned above, the attenuated insolation could affect plant growth rates, and vigor in the marine, littoral, and terrestrial food chains. In the 10,000-MT "severe" case, average light levels are below the minimum required for photosynthesis for about 40 days over much of the Northern Hemisphere. In a number of other cases, insolation may, for more than 2 months, fall below the compensation point at which photosynthesis is just sufficient to maintain plant metabolism. Because nuclear clouds are likely to remain patchy the first week or two after an exchange, leakage of sunlight through holes in the clouds could enhance plant growth activity above that predicted for average cloud conditions; however, soon thereafter the holes are likely to be sealed.

Sensitivity Tests

A large number of sensitivity calculations were carried out as part of this study. The results are summarized here. Reasonable variations in the nuclear dust parameters in the baseline scenario produce initial hemispherically averaged dust optical depths varying from about 0.2 to 3.0. Accordingly, nuclear dust alone could have a major climatic impact. In the baseline case, the dust opacity is much greater than the total aerosol opacity associated with the El Chichón and Agung eruptions; even when the dust parameters are assigned their least adverse values within the plausible range, the effects are comparable to those of a major volcanic explosion.

... [This study compares] nuclear cloud optical depths for several variations of the baseline model smoke parameters (with dust included). In the baseline case, it is assumed that fire storms inject only a small fraction ($\simeq 5$ percent) of the total smoke emission into the stratosphere. ... As an extreme excursion, all the nuclear smoke is injected into the stratosphere and rapidly dispersed around the globe; large optical depths can then persist for a year. ... By contrast, when the nuclear smoke is initially contained near the ground and dynamical and hydrological removal processes are assumed to be unperturbed, smoke depletion occurs much faster. But even in this case, some of the smoke still diffuses to the upper troposphere and remains there for several months.

In a set of optical calculations, the imaginary refractive index of the smoke was varied between 0.3 and 0.01. The optical depths calculated for indices between 0.1 and 0.3 show virtually no differences. At an index of 0.05, the absorption optical depth is reduced by only $\simeq 50$ percent, and at 0.01, by $\simeq 85$ percent. The overall opacity (absorption plus scattering), moreover, increases by $\simeq 5$ percent. These results show that light absorption and heating in nuclear smoke clouds remain high until the graphitic carbon fraction of the smoke falls below a few percent.

One sensitivity test considers the optical effects in the Southern Hemisphere (SH) of dust and soot transported from the NH stratosphere. In this calculation, the smoke in the 300-MT SH case is combined with half the baseline stratospheric dust and smoke (to approximate rapid global dispersion in the stratosphere). The initial optical depth is $\simeq 1$ over the SH, dropping to about 0.3 in 3 months. Predicted average SH continental surface temperatures fall by 8 K within several weeks and remain at least 4 K below normal for nearly 8 months. The seasonal influence should be taken into account, however. For example, the worst consequences for the NH might result from a spring or summer exchange, when crops are vulnerable and fire hazards are greatest. The SH, in its fall or winter, might then be least sensitive to cooling and darkening. Nevertheless, the implications of this scenario for the tropical regions in both hemispheres appear to be serious and worthy of further analysis. Seasonal factors can also modulate the atmospheric response to perturbations by smoke and dust, and should be considered.

A number of sensitive tests for more severe cases were run with exchange yields ranging from 1000 to 10,000 MT and smoke and dust parameters assigned more adverse, but not implausible, values. The predicted effects are substantially worse. The lower probabilities of these severe cases must be weighed against the catastrophic outcomes which they imply. It would be prudent policy to assess the importance of these scenarios in terms of the product of their probabilities and the costs of their corresponding effects. Unfortunately, we are unable to give an accurate quantitative estimate of the relevant probabilities. By their very nature, however, the severe cases may be the most important to consider. . . .

With these reservations, we present the optical depths for some of the more severe cases. Large opacities can persist for a year, and land surface temperatures can fall to 230 to 240 K, about 50 K below normal. Combined with low light levels, these severe scenarios raise the possibility of widespread and catastrophic ecological consequences.

Two sensitivity tests were run to determine roughly the implications for optical properties of aerosol agglomeration in the early expanding clouds. (The simulations already take into account continuous coagulation of the particles in the dispersed clouds.) Very slow dispersion of the initial stabilized dust and smoke clouds, taking nearly 8 months to cover the NH, was assumed. Coagulation of particles reduced the average opacity after 3 months by about 40 percent. When the adhesion efficiency of the colliding particles was also maximized, the average opacity after 3 months was reduced by $\simeq 75$ percent. In the most likely situation, however, prompt agglomeration and coagulation might reduce the average hemispheric cloud optical depths by 20 to 50 percent.

Other Effects

We also considered, in less detail, the long-term effects of radioactive fallout, fireball-generated NO_x and pyrogenic toxic gases. The physics of radioactive fallout is well known. Our calculations bear primarily on the widespread intermediate time scale accumulation of fallout due to washout and dry deposition of dispersed nuclear dust. To estimate possible exposure levels, we adopt a fission yield fraction of 0.5 for all weapons. For exposure to only the gamma emission of radioactive dust that begins to fall out after 2 days in the baseline scenario (5000 MT), the hemispherically averaged total dose accumulated by humans over several months could be $\simeq 20$ rads, assuming no shelter from or weathering of the dust. Fallout during this time would be confined largely to northern mid-latitudes; hence the dose there could be $\simeq 2$ to 3 times larger. Considering ingestion of biologically active radionuclides and occasional exposure to localized fallout, the average total chronic mid-latitude dose of ionizing radiation for the baseline case could be [equal to or less than] 50 rads of whole-body external gamma radiation, plus [equal to or less than] 50 rads to specific body organs from internal beta and gamma emitters. In a 10,000-MT exchange, under the same assumptions, these mean doses would be doubled. Such doses are roughly an order of magnitude larger than previous estimates, which neglected intermediate time scale washout and fallout of tropospheric nuclear debris from low-yield ($<$ 1-MT) detonations.

The problem of NO_x produced in the fireballs of high-yield explosions, and the resulting depletion of stratospheric ozone, has been treated in a number of studies. In our baseline case a maximum hemispherically averaged ozone reduction of $\simeq$ 30 percent is found. This would be substantially smaller if individual warhead yields were all reduced below 1 MT. Considering the relation between solar UV-B [ultraviolet] radiation increases and ozone decreases, UV-B doses roughly twice normal are expected in the first year after a baseline exchange (when the dust and soot had dissipated). Large UV-B effects could accompany exchanges involving warheads of greater yield (or large multiburst laydowns).

A variety of toxic gases (pyrotoxins) would be generated in large quantities by nuclear fires, include CO and HCN. According to Crutzen and Birks, heavy air pollution, including elevated ozone concentrations, could blanket the NH for several months. We are also concerned about dioxins and furans, extremely persistent and toxic compounds which are released during the combustion of widely used synthetic organic chemicals. Hundreds of tons of dioxins and furans could be generated during a nuclear exchange. The long-term ecological consequences of such nuclear pyrotoxins seem worthy of further consideration.

Meteorological Pertubations

Horizontal variations in sunlight absorption in the atmosphere, and at the surface, are the fundamental drivers of atmospheric circulation. For many of the cases considered in this study, sizable changes in the driving forces are implied. For example, temperature contrasts greater than 10 K between NH continental areas and adjacent oceans may induce a strong monsoonal circulation, in some ways analogous to the wintertime pattern near the Indian subcontinent. Similarly, the temperature contrast between debris-laden atmospheric regions and adjacent regions not yet filled by smoke and dust will cause new circulation patterns.

Thick clouds of nuclear dust and smoke can thus cause significant climatic perturbations, and related effects, through a variety of mechanisms: reflection of solar radiation to space and absorption of sunlight in the upper atmosphere, leading to overall surface cooling; modification of solar absorption and heating patterns that drive the atmospheric circulation on small scales and large scales; introduction of excess water vapor and cloud condensation nuclei, which affect the formation of clouds and precipitation; and alteration of the surface albedo by fires and soot. These effects are closely coupled in determining the overall response of the atmosphere to a nuclear war. It is not yet possible to forecast in detail the changes in coupled atmospheric circulation and radiation fields, and in weather and microclimates, which would accompany the massive dust and smoke injections treated here. Hence speculation must be limited to the most general considerations.

Water evaporation from the oceans is a continuing source of moisture for the marine boundary layer. A heavy semipermanent fog or haze layer might blanket large bodies of water. The consequences for marine precipitation are not clear, particularly if normal prevailing winds are greatly modified by the perturbed solar driving force. Some continental zones might be subject to continuous snowfall for several months. Precipitation can lead to soot removal, although this process may not be very efficient for nuclear clouds. It is likely that, on average, precipitation rates would be generally smaller than in the ambient atmosphere; the major remaining energy source available for storm genesis is the latent heat from ocean evaporation, and the upper atmosphere is warmer than the lower atmosphere which suppresses convection and rainfall.

Despite possible heavy snowfalls, it is unlikely that an ice age would be triggered by a nuclear war. The period of cooling ([equal to or less than] 1 year) is probably too short to overcome the considerable inertia in the earth's climate system. The oceanic heat reservoir would probably force the climate toward contemporary norms in the years after a war. The CO_2 input from nuclear fires is not significant climatologically.

Interhemispheric Transport

In earlier studies it was assumed that significant interhemispheric transport of nuclear debris and radioactivity requires a year or more. This was based on observations of transport under ambient conditions, including dispersion of debris clouds from individual atmospheric nuclear weapons tests. However, with dense clouds of dust and smoke produced by thousands of nearly simultaneous explosions, large dynamical disturbances would be expected in the aftermath of a nuclear war. A rough analogy can be drawn with the evolution of global-scale dust storms on Mars. The lower martian atmosphere is similar in density to the earth's stratosphere, and the period of rotation is almost identical to the earth's (although the solar insolation is only half the terrestrial value). Dust storms that develop in one hemisphere on Mars often rapidly intensify and spread over the entire planet, crossing the equator in a mean time of 10 days. The explanation apparently lies in the heating of the dust aloft, which then dominates other heat sources and drives the circulation. [R. M.] Haberle *et al.* used a two-dimensional model to simulate the evolution of martian dust storms and found that dust at low latitudes, in the core of the Hadley circulation, is the most important in modifying the winds. In a nuclear exchange, most of the dust and smoke would be injected at middle latitudes. However, Haberle *et al.* could not treat planetary-scale waves in their calculations. Perturbations of planetary wave amplitudes may be critical in the transport of nuclear war debris between middle and low latitudes.

Significant atmospheric effects in the SH could be produced (i) through dust and smoke injection resulting from explosions on SH targets, (ii) through transport of NH debris across the meteorological equator by monsoon-like winds, and (iii) through interhemispheric transport in the upper troposphere and stratosphere, driven by solar heating of nuclear dust and smoke clouds. . . .

Discussion and Conclusions

The studies outlined here suggest severe long-term climatic effects from a 5000-MT nuclear exchange. Despite uncertainties in the amounts and properties of the dust and smoke produced by nuclear detonations, and the limitations of models available for analysis, the following tentative conclusions may be drawn.

1) Unlike most earlier studies . . . we find that a global nuclear war could have a major impact on climate — manifested by significant surface darkening over many weeks, subfreezing land temperatures persisting for up to several months, large perturbations in global circulation patterns, and dramatic changes in local weather and precipitation rates — a harsh "nuclear winter" in any season. Greatly accelerated interhemispheric transport of nuclear debris in the stratosphere might also occur, although modeling studies are needed to quantify this effect. With rapid interhemispheric mixing, the SH could be subjected to large injections of nuclear debris soon after an exchange in the Northern Hemisphere. In the past, SH effects have been assumed to be minor. . . .

2) Relatively large climatic effects could result even from relatively small nuclear exchanges (100 to 1000 MT) if urban areas were heavily targeted, because as little as 100 MT is sufficient to devastate and burn several hundred of the world's major urban centers. Such a low threshold yield for massive smoke emissions, although scenario-dependent, implies that even limited nuclear exchanges could trigger severe aftereffects. It is much less likely that a 5000- to 10,000-MT exchange would have only minor effects.

3) The climatic impact of sooty smoke from nuclear fires ignited by airbursts is expected to be more important than that of dust raised by surface bursts (when both effects occur). Smoke absorbs sunlight efficiently, whereas soil dust is generally nonabsorbing. Smoke particles are extremely small (typically < 1 μm in radius), which lengthens their atmospheric residence time. There is also a high probability that nuclear explosions over cities, forests, and grasslands will ignite widespread fires, even in attacks limited to missile silos and other strategic military targets.

4) Smoke from urban fires may be more important than smoke from collateral forest fires for at least two reasons: (i) in a full-scale exchange, cities holding large stores of combustible materials are likely to be attacked directly; and (ii) intense fire storms could pump smoke into the stratosphere, where the residence time is a year or more.

5) Nuclear dust can also contribute to the climatic impact of a nuclear exchange. The dust-climate effect is very sensitive to the conduct of the

war; a smaller effect is expected when lower yield weapons are deployed and airbursts dominate surface land bursts. Multiburst phenomena might enhance the climatic effects of nuclear dust, but not enough data are available to assess this issue.

6) Exposure to radioactive fallout may be more intense and widespread than predicted by empirical exposure models, which neglect intermediate fallout extending over many days and weeks, particularly when unprecedented quantities of fission debris are released abruptly into the troposphere by explosions with submegaton yields. Average NH mid-latitude whole-body gamma-ray doses of up to 50 rads are possible in a 5000-MT exchange; larger doses would accrue within the fallout plumes of radioactive debris extending hundreds of kilometers downwind of targets. These estimates neglect a probably significant internal radiation dose due to biologically active radionuclides.

7) Synergisms between long-term nuclear war stresses — such as low light levels, subfreezing temperatures, exposure to intermediate time scale radioactive fallout, heavy pyrogenic air pollution, and UV-B flux enhancements — aggravated by the destruction of medical facilities, food stores, and civil services, could lead to many additional fatalities, and could place severe stresses on the global ecosystem. . . .

Our estimates of the physical and chemical impacts of nuclear war are necessarily uncertain because we have used one-dimensional models, because the data base is incomplete, and because the problem is not amenable to experimental investigation. We are also unable to forecast the detailed nature of the changes in atmospheric dynamics and meteorology implied by our nuclear war scenarios, or the effect of such changes on the maintenance or dispersal of the initiating dust and smoke clouds. Nevertheless, the magnitudes of the first-order effects are so large, and the implications so serious, that we hope the scientific issues raised here will be vigorously and critically examined.

LONG-TERM BIOLOGICAL CONSEQUENCES OF NUCLEAR WAR

— Paul R. Ehrlich, John Harte, Mark A. Harwell, Peter H. Raven
Carl Sagan, George M. Woodwell, Joseph Berry
Edward S. Ayensu, Anne H. Ehrlich, Thomas Eisner
Stephen J. Gould, Herbert D. Grover
Rafael Herrera, Robert M. May, Ernst Mayr
Christopher P. McKay, Harold A. Mooney, Norman Myers
David Pimentel, John M. Teal

Recent studies of large-scale nuclear war (5000- to 10,000-MT [megaton] yields) have estimated that there would be 750 million immediate deaths from blast alone; a total of about 1.1 billion deaths from the combined effects of blast, fire, and radiation; and approximately an additional 1.1 billion injuries requiring medical attention. Thus, 30 to 50 percent of the total human population could be immediate casualties of a nuclear war. The vast majority of the casualties would be in the Northern Hemisphere, especially in the United States, the U.S.S.R., Europe, and Japan. These enormous numbers have typically been taken to define the full potential catastrophe of such a war. New evidence presented here, however, suggests that the longer term biological effects resulting from climatic changes may be at least as serious as the immediate ones. Our concern in this article is with the 2 billion to 3 billion people not killed immediately, including those in nations far removed from the nuclear conflict.

We consider primarily the results of a nuclear war in which sufficient dust and soot are injected into the atmosphere to attenuate most incident solar radiation, a possibility first suggested by [Paul R.] Ehrlich et al., and first shown quantitatively and brought to wide attention by [P. J.] Crutzen and [J. W.] Birks. In a wide range of nuclear exchange scenarios, with yields from 100 MT up to 10,000 MT, we now know that enough sunlight could be absorbed and scattered to cause widespread cold and darkness (these papers are also collectively referred to as TTAPS). In each of these cases the computations indicate very serious biological consequences. This is so even though all the scenarios are well within current capabilities and do not seem to be strategically implausible. Furthermore, the probability of nuclear wars of very high yield may have been generally underestimated. We also examine the consequences of the spread of atmospheric effects from the Northern to the Southern Hemisphere.

As a reference case, we consider [a] case of the nuclear war scenarios discussed in TTAPS. This is a 10,000-MT exchange in which parameters describing the properties of dust and soot aerosols are assigned adverse but not implausible values and in which 30 percent of the soot is carried by fire storms to stratospheric altitudes. . . .

As an average over the Northern Hemisphere, independent of the season of the year, calculated fluxes of visible light would be reduced to approximately 1 percent of ambient, and surface temperatures in continental interiors could fall to approximately $-40°C$. At least a year would be required for light and temperature values to recover to their normal conditions. In target zones, it might initially be too dark to see, even at midday. An estimated 30 percent of Northern Hemisphere mid-latitude land areas would receive a dose [approximately equal to or greater than] 500 R [rads] immediately after the explosions. This dose, from external gamma-emitters in radioactive fallout, would be comparable to or more than the acute mean lethal dose (LD_{50}) for healthy adults. Over the next few days and weeks, fallout would contribute an additional external dose of [approximately equal to or greater than] 100 R over 50 percent of northern mid-latitudes. Internal doses would contribute another [approximately equal to or greater than] 100 R concentrated in specific body systems, such as thyroid, bones, the gastrointestinal tract, and the milk of lactating mothers. After settling of the dust and smoke, the surface flux of near-ultraviolet radiation [UV-B] would be increased severalfold for some years, because of the depletion of the ozonosphere by fireball-generated NO_x. Southern Hemisphere effects would involve minimum light levels < 10 percent of ambient, minimum land surface temperatures $< -18°C$, and UV-B increments of tens of percent for years. The potential impacts from the climatic change that would be induced by nuclear war are outlined in [the] Table.

Thermonuclear wars that would be less adverse to the environment are clearly possible, but climatic effects similar to those just outlined could well result from much more limited exchanges, down to several hundred megatons, if cities were targeted. Even if there were no global climatic effects, the regional consequences of nuclear war might be serious. We believe, however, that decision-makers should be fully apprised of the potential consequences of the scenarios most likely to trigger long-term effects. For this reason we have concentrated in this article on the 10,000-MT severe case rather than the 5000-MT nominal baseline case of TTAPS. Because of synergisms, however, the consequences of any particular nuclear war scenario are likely to be still more severe than discussed below. We still have too incomplete an understanding of the detailed workings of global ecosystems to evaluate all the interactions, and thus the cumulative effects, of the many stresses to which people and ecosystems would be subjected. Every unassessed synergism is likely to have an incremental negative effect.

Temperature

The impact of dramatically reduced temperatures on plants would depend on the time of year at which they occurred, their duration, and the tolerance limits of the plants. The abrupt onset of cold is of particular importance. Winter wheat, for example, can tolerate temperatures as low as $-15°$ to $-20°C$ when preconditioned to cold temperatures (as occurs naturally in fall and winter months), but the same plants may be killed by $-5°C$ if exposed during active summer growth. Even plants from alpine regions, *Pinus cembra* for example, may tolerate temperatures as low as $-50°C$ in midwinter but may be killed by temperatures of $-5°$ to $-10°C$ occurring in summer. In the TTAPS calculations, temperatures are expected to fall rapidly to their lowest levels; it is unlikely under these circumstances that normally cold-tolerant plants could "harden" (develop freezing tolerance) before lethal temperatures were reached. Other stresses to plants from radiation, air pollutants, and low light levels immediately after the war would compound the damage caused by freezing. In addition, diseased or damaged plants have a reduced capacity to harden to freezing conditions.

Even temperatures considerably above freezing can be damaging to some plants. For example, exposure of rice or sorghum to a temperature of only $13°C$ at the critical time can inhibit grain formation because the pollen produced is sterile. Corn (*Zea mays*) and soybeans (*Glycine max*), two important crops in North America, are quite sensitive to temperatures below about 10°C.

While a nuclear war in the fall or winter would probably have a lesser effect on plants in temperate regions than one in the spring or summer, tropical vegetation is vulnerable to low temperatures throughout the year. The only areas in which terrestrial plants might not be devastated by severe cold would be immediately along the coasts and on islands, where the temperatures would be moderated by the thermal inertia of the oceans. These areas, however, would experience particularly violent weather because of the large lateral temperature gradient between oceans and continental interiors.

Visible Light

The disruption of photosynthesis by the attenuation of incident sunlight would have consequences that cascade through food chains, many of which include people as consumers. Primary productivity would be reduced roughly in proportion to the degree of light attenuation, even making the unrealistic assumption that the vegetation would remain otherwise undamaged.

Many studies have examined the effects of shading on the rate of photosynthesis, plant growth, and crop yield. Although individual leaves may be saturated by light levels below one-half of unattenuated sunlight, entire plants that have several layers of leaves oriented at different angles to the sun and partially shading each other are usually not light-saturated. Thus, while only a 10 percent reduction in light might not reduce photosynthesis in a fully exposed leaf, it might well reduce it in the entire plant because of the presence of unsaturated leaves within the canopy. Because plants also respire, most would, in fact, be unlikely to maintain any net growth if the light level fell below about 5 percent of the normal ambient levels in their habitats (the compensation point). At the levels expected in the early months following a substantial nuclear exchange, plants would be severely affected and many would die because of the substantial reductions in their net productivity caused by reduced light alone.

Ionizing Radiation

Exposures to ionizing radiation in a nuclear exchange would result directly from the gamma and neutron flux of the fireball, from the radioactive debris deposited downwind of the burst, and from the component of the debris that becomes airborne and circulates globally.

The degree of injury to organisms would depend on the rate and magnitude of the exposure, with higher rates and larger total exposures producing more severe effects. The mean lethal exposure for human beings

Potential impacts from climatic changes induced by a major nuclear war at various time periods after the war.

First few months	End of first year	Next decade
	Natural ecosystems: Terrestrial	
Extreme cold, independent of season and widespread over the Earth, would severely damage plants, particularly in mid-latitudes in the Northern Hemisphere and in the tropics. Particulates obscuring sunlight would severely curtail photosynthesis, essentially eliminating plant productivity. Extreme cold, unavailability of fresh water, and near darkness would severely stress most animals, with widespread mortality. Storm events of unprecedented intensity would devastate ecosystems, especially at margins of continents.	Many hardy perennial plants and most seeds of temperate plants would survive, but plant productivity would continue to be depressed significantly. As the atmosphere clears, increased UV-B would damage plants and impair vision systems of many animal species. Limited primary productivity would cause intense competition for resources among animals. Many tropical species would continue to suffer fatalities or reduced productivity from temperature stress. Widespread extinction of vertebrates.	Basic potential for primary and secondary productivity would gradually recover; however, extensive irreversible damage to ecosystems would have occurred. Ecosystem structure and processes would continue to respond unstably to perturbations and a long period of time might follow before functional redundancies would reestablish ecosystem homeostasis. Massive loss of species, especially in tropical areas, would lead to reduced genetic and species diversity.
	Natural ecosystems: Aquatic	
Temperature extremes would result in widespread ice formation on most freshwater bodies, particularly in the Northern Hemisphere and in mid-latitude continental areas. Marine ecosystems would be largely buffered from extreme temperatures, with effects limited to coastal and shallow tropical areas. Light reductions would essentially terminate phytoplankton productivity, eliminating the support base for many marine and freshwater animal species. Storms at continental margins would stress shallow-water ecosystems and add to sediment loadings. Potential food sources would not be accessible to humans....	Early loss of phytoplankton would continue to be felt in population collapses in many herbivore and carnivore species in marine ecosystems; benthic communities would not be as disrupted. Freshwater ecosystems would begin to thaw, but many species would have been lost. Organisms in temperate marine and freshwater systems adapted to seasonal temperature fluctuations would recover more quickly and extensively than tropical regions.	Recovery would proceed more rapidly than for terrestrial ecosystems. Species extinctions would be more likely in tropical areas. Coastal marine ecosystems would begin to contain harvestable food sources, although contamination could continue.

First few months	End of first year	Next decade

Agroecosystems

First few months	End of first year	Next decade
Extreme temperatures and low light levels could preclude virtually any net productivity in crops anywhere on Earth. Supplies of food in targeted areas would be destroyed, contaminated, remote, or quickly depleted. Nontargeted importing countries would lose subsidies from North America and other food exporters.	Potential crop productivity would remain low because of continued, though much less extreme, temperature depressions. Sunlight would not be limiting but would be enriched with UV-B. Reduced precipitation and loss of soil from storm events would reduce potential productivity. Organized agriculture would be unlikely, and modern subsidies of energy, fertilizers, pesticides, and so on, would not be available. Stored food would be essentially depleted, and potential draught animals would have suffered extensive fatalities and consumption by humans.	Biotic potential for crop production would largely be restored. Limiting factors for reestablishment of agriculture would be related to human support for water, energy, fertilizers, pest and disease protection, and so on.

Human-societal systems

First few months	End of first year	Next decade
Survivors of immediate effects (from blast, fire, and initial ionizing radiation) would include perhaps 50 to 75 percent of the Earth's population. Extreme temperatures, near darkness, violent storms, and loss of shelter and fuel supplies would result in widespread fatalities from exposure, starvation, lack of drinking water, and synergisms with other impacts such as radiation exposure, malnutrition, lack of medical systems, and psychological stress. Societal support systems for food, energy, transportation, medical care, communications, and so on, would cease to function.	Climatic impacts would be considerably reduced, but exposure would remain a stress on humans. Loss of agricultural support would dominate adverse human health impacts. Societal systems could not be expected to function and support humans. With the return of sunlight and UV-B, widespread eye damage could occur. Psychological stresses, radiation exposures, and many synergistic stresses would continue to affect humans adversely. Epidemics and pandemics would be likely.	Climatic stresses would not be the primary limiting factors for human recovery. Rates of reestablishment of societal order and human support systems would limit rates of human population growth. Human carrying capacities could remain severely depressed from prewar conditions for a very long period of time, at best.

is commonly thought to be 350 to 500 R received in the whole body in less than 48 hours. Most other mammals and some plants have mean lethal exposures of less than 1000 R. If the rate of exposure is lower, the mean lethal dose rises.

The area subject to intense radiation from the fireball would also be affected directly by blast and heat. The radius within which the pressure from the blast exceeds 5 pounds per square inch has been defined as the lethal zone for blast, and the area within which the thermal flux exceeds 10 cal/cm² as the lethal zone for heat. The radius within which ionizing radiation from the fireball would be expected to be lethal for human beings is less than the radii for mortality defined by pressure or heat. No special further consideration has been given here to the effects of ionizing radiation from the fireballs.

One estimate, based on the *Ambio* scenario and similar to the TTAPS baseline case, involves an exchange of 5742 MT and about 11,600 detonations without overlapping fallout fields; it suggests that about 5×10^6 km² would be exposed to 1000 R or more in downwind areas. About 85 percent of this total exposure would be received within 48 hours. Such an exposure is lethal to all exposed people and causes the death of sensitive plant species such as most conifers — trees that form extensive forests over most of the cooler parts of the Northern Hemisphere. If nuclear reactors, radioactive waste storage facilities, and fuel reprocessing plants are damaged during an exchange, the area affected and the levels of ionizing radiation could be even greater.

If we assume that approximately half of this area affected by fallout radiation in the range 1000 to 10,000 R is forested, there would be about 2.5×10^6 km² within which extensive mortality of trees and many other plants would occur. This would create the potential for extensive fires. Most conifers would die over an area amounting to about 2.5 percent of the entire land surface of the Northern Hemisphere.

The possibility that as much as 30 percent of the mid-latitude land area would be exposed to 500 R or more from gamma radiation emphasizes the scale and severity of the hazard. While 500 R of total exposure would have minor effects on most plant populations, it would cause widespread mortality among all mammals, including human beings. The unprotected survivors would be ill for weeks and more prone to cancer for the remainder of their lives. The total number of people afflicted would exceed 1 billion.

UV-B Radiation

In the weeks following the exchange, tropospheric and stratospheric dust and soot would absorb the UV-B flux that would otherwise be transmitted by the partially destroyed ozonosphere. But when the dust and soot cleared a few months later, the effects of O_3 depletion would be felt at the surface. In the Northern Hemisphere, the flux of UV-B would be enhanced for about a year by a factor of about 2 for the baseline TTAPS exchange and by a factor of 4 for the 10,000 MT war. As is the case for an undepleted ozonosphere, the UV-B dose would be significantly greater at equatorial than at temperate latitudes.

Even much smaller O_3 depletions are considered dangerous to ecosystems and to people. If the entire UV-B band is enhanced by about 50 percent, the amount of UV-B at the higher energy end of the band, near 295 nm, would be increased by a factor of about 50. This region has particular biological significance because of the strong absorption of energy at these wavelengths by nucleic acids, aromatic amino acids, and the peptide bond. In larger doses, UV-B is very destructive to plant leaves, weakening the plants and decreasing their productivity. Near-surface productivity of marine plankton is known to be depressed significantly by contemporary ambient UV-B levels; even small increases in UV-B could have "profound consequences" for the structure of marine food chains.

There are at least four additional ways in which increased levels of UV-B are known to be harmful to biological systems: (i) the immune systems of *Homo sapiens* and other mammals are known to be suppressed even by relatively low doses of UV-B. Especially under conditions of increased ionizing radiation and other physiological stress, such suppression of the immune systems leads to an increase in the incidence of disease. (ii) Plant leaves that reach maturity under low light intensities are two to three times more sensitive to UV-B than leaves that develop under high light intensities. (iii) Bacterial UV-B sensitivity is enhanced by low temperatures, which suppress the normal process of DNA repair, a process that is dependent on visible light. (iv) Protracted exposure to increased UV-B may induce corneal damage and cataracts, leading to blindness in human beings and terrestrial mammals. Thus the effects of increased UV-B may be among the most serious unanticipated consequences of nuclear war.

Atmospheric Effects

In a nuclear war, large quantities of air pollutants, including CO, O_3, NO_x, cyanides, vinyl chlorides, dioxins, and furans would be released near the surface. Smog and acid precipitation would be widespread in the aftermath of the nuclear exchange. These toxins might not have significant immediate effects on the vegetation that was already devastated, although, depending upon their persistence, they could certainly hinder its recovery. Their atmospheric transport by winds to more distant, initially unaffected ecosystems, on the other hand, might be an important additional effect. Large-scale fires coupled with an interruption of photosynthetic CO_2 uptake would produce a short-term increase in the atmospheric CO_2 concentration. The quantity of CO_2 now in the atmosphere is equivalent to that used by several years of photosynthesis and is further buffered by the inorganic carbon reserves of the ocean. Therefore, if the global climate and photosynthetic productivity of ecosystems recovered to near-normal levels within a few years, it is unlikely that any significant long-term change in the composition of the atmosphere would occur. It is not beyond the realm of possibility, however, that an event encompassing both hemispheres, with the ensuing damage to photosynthetic organisms, could cause a sudden increase in CO_2 concentration and thus long-term climatic changes. For comparison, the time scale for recycling of CO_2 through the biosphere is about 2000 years.

Agricultural Systems

There is little storage of staple foods in human population centers, and most meat and fresh produce are supplied directly from farms. Only cereal grains are stored in significant quantities, but the sites at which they are stored often are located in areas remote from population centers. Following a spring or early summer war, the current year's crops would almost certainly be lost. Cereal crops would be harvested before a fall or winter war, but since the climate would remain unusually cold for many months, the following growing season would also be unfavorable for crop growth.

After a nuclear war, in short, the available potential supplies of food in the Northern Hemisphere would be destroyed or contaminated, located in inaccessible areas, or rapidly depleted. For nations experiencing the nuclear war directly, food resources would become scarce in a very short time. Further, nations that now require large imports of foods, including those untouched by nuclear detonations, would suffer an immediate interruption of the flow of food, forcing them to rely solely on their local agricultural and natural ecosystems. This would be very serious for many less-developed countries, especially those in the tropics.

Most major crops are annuals that are highly dependent on substantial energy and nutrient subsidies from human societies. Further, the fraction of their yields available for human consumption requires excess energy fixation beyond the respiratory needs of the plants, depending on full sunlight, on minimization of environmental stresses from pests, water insufficiency, particulates, and air pollution, and so on. Providing these conditions would be far more difficult, if not impossible, over much, if not all, of the Earth following a nuclear exchange. Agriculture as we know it would then, for all practical purposes, have come to an end.

Since the seeds for most North American, European, and Soviet crops are harvested and stored not on individual farms but predominantly in or near target areas, seed stocks for subsequent years would almost certainly be depleted severely, and the already limited genetic variability of those crops would probably be reduced drastically. Furthermore, the potential crop-growing areas would experience local climatic changes, high levels of radioactive contamination, and impoverished or eroded soils. Recovery of agricultural production would have to occur in the absence of the massive energy subsidies (especially in the form of tractor fuel and fertilizers) to which agriculture in developed countries has become adapted.

Except along the coasts, continental precipitation would be reduced substantially for some time after a nuclear exchange. Even now, rainfall is the major factor limiting crop growth in many areas, and irrigation, with requirements for energy and human support systems for pumping ground water, would not be available after a war. Moreover, in the months after the war, most of the available water would be frozen, and temperatures would recover slowly to normal values.

Temperate Terrestrial Ecosystems

The 2 billion to 3 billion survivors of the immediate effects of the war would be forced to turn to natural ecosystems as organized agriculture failed. Just at the time when these natural ecosystems would be asked to support a human population well beyond their carrying capacities, the normal functioning of the ecosystems themselves would be severely curtailed by the effects of nuclear war.

Subjecting these ecosystems to low temperature, fire, radiation, storm, and other physical stresses (many occurring simultaneously) would result in their increased vulnerability to disease and pest outbreaks, which might be prolonged. Primary productivity would be dramatically reduced at the prevailing low light levels; and, because of UV-B, smog, insects, radiation, and other damage to plants, it is unlikely that it would recover quickly to normal levels, even after light and temperature values had recovered. At the same time that their plant foods were being limited severely, most, if not all, of the vertebrates not killed outright by blast and ionizing radiation would either freeze or face a dark world where they would starve or die of thirst because surface waters would be frozen and thus unavailable. Many of the survivors would be widely scattered and often sick, leading to the slightly delayed extinction of many additional species.

Natural ecosystems provide civilization with a variety of crucial services in addition to food and shelter. These include regulation of atmospheric composition, moderation of climate and weather, regulation of hydrologic cycle, generation and preservation of soils, degradation of wastes, and recycling of nutrients. From the human perspective, among the most important roles of ecosystems are their direct role in providing food and their maintenance of a vast library of species from which *Homo sapiens* has already drawn the basis of civilization. Accelerated loss of these genetic resources through extinction would be one of the most serious potential consequences of nuclear war.

Wildfires would be an important effect in north temperate ecosystems, their scale and distribution depending on such factors as the nuclear war scenario and the season. Another major uncertainty is the extent of fire storms, which might heat the lower levels of the soil enough to damage or destroy seed banks, especially in vegetation types not adapted to periodic fires. Multiple airbursts over seasonally dry areas such as California in the late summer or early fall could burn off much of the state's forest and brush areas, leading to catastrophic flooding and erosion during the next rainy season. Silting, toxic runoff, and rainout of radionuclides could kill much of the fauna of fresh and coastal waters, and concentrated radioactivity levels in surviving filterfeeding shellfish populations could make them dangerous to consume for long periods of time.

Other major consequences for terrestrial ecosystems resulting from nuclear war would include: (i) slower detoxification of air and water as a secondary result of damage to plants that now are important metabolic sinks for toxins; (ii) reduced evapotranspiration by plants contributing to a lower rate of entry of water into the atmosphere, especially over continental regions, and therefore a more sluggish hydrologic cycle; and (iii) great disturbance of the soil surface, leading to accelerated erosion and, probably, major dust storms.

Revegetation might superficially resemble that which follows local fires. Stresses from radiation, smog, erosion, fugitive dust, and toxic rains, however, would be superimposed on those of cold and darkness, thus delaying and modifying postwar succession in ways that would retard the restoration of ecosystem services. It is likely that most ecosystem changes would be short term. Some structural and functional changes, however, could be longer term, and perhaps irreversible, as ecosystems undergo qualitative changes to alternative stable states. Soil losses from erosion would be serious in areas experiencing widespread fires, plant death, and extremes of climate. Much would depend on the wind and precipitation patterns that would develop during the first postwar year. The diversity of many natural communities would almost certainly be substantially reduced, and numerous species of plants, animals, and microorganisms would become extinct.

Tropical Terrestrial Ecosystems

The degree to which the tropics would be subjected to the sorts of conditions described above depends on factors such as the targeting pattern, the prevalence of fire storms, the breakdown of the distinction between troposphere and stratosphere, and the rate of interhemispheric mixing as a function of altitude. The spread of dense clouds of dust and soot and subfreezing temperatures to the northern tropics is highly likely, and to the Southern Hemisphere at least possible, so that it is appropriate to discuss the probable consequences of such a spread.

For example, the seeds of trees in tropical forests tend to be much more short-lived than those of temperate zones. If darkness or cold temperatures, or both, were to become widespread in the tropics, the tropical forests could largely disappear. This would lead to extinction of most of the species of plants, animals, and microorganisms on the Earth, with long-term consequences of the greatest importance for the adaptability of human populations.

If darkness were widespread in the tropics, vast areas of tropical vegetation, which are considered very near the compensation point, would begin to respire away. In addition, many plants in tropical and subtropical regions do not have dormancy mechanisms that enable them to tolerate cold seasons, even at temperatures well above freezing. Even if the darkness and cold were confined mainly to temperate regions, pulses of cold air and soot could carry quick freezes well into the tropics. This would amount to an enhanced case of the phenomenon known as "friagem," which is used to describe the effects of cool temperatures spreading from temperate South America and entering the equatorial Amazon Basin, where they kill large numbers of birds and fish. One can predict from existing evidence on cooling effects during the Plestocene and their consequences that continental low-latitude areas would be severely affected by low air temperatures and decreased precipitation.

The dependence of tropical peoples on imported food and fertilizer would lead to severe effects, even if the tropics were not affected directly by the war. Large numbers of people would be forced to leave the cities and attempt to cultivate the remaining areas of forest, accelerating their destruction and the consequent rate of extinction. These activities would also greatly increase the amount of soot in the atmosphere, owing to improvised slash-and-burn agriculture on a vast scale. Regardless of the exact distribution of the immediate effects of the war, everyone on the Earth would ultimately be affected profoundly.

Aquatic Ecosystems

Aquatic organisms tend to be buffered against dramatic fluctuations in air temperature by the thermal inertia of water. Nevertheless, many freshwater systems would freeze to considerable depths or completely because of the climatic changes after a nuclear war. The effect of prolonged darkness on marine organisms has been estimated. Primary producers at the base of the marine food chain are particularly sensitive to prolonged low light levels; higher trophic levels are subject to lesser, delayed propagated effects. Moreover, the near-surface productivity of marine plankton is depressed significantly by present UV-B levels; even small increases in UV-B could have profound consequences for the structure of marine food chains. It is often thought that the ocean margins would be a major source of sustenance of survivors of a nuclear war; the combined effects of darkness, UV-B, coastal storms, destruction of ships in the war, and concentration of radionuclides in shallow marine systems, however, cast strong doubt on this.

Conclusions

The predictions of climatic changes are quite robust, so that qualitatively the same types of stresses would ensue from a limited war of 500 MT or less in which cities were targeted as from a larger scale nuclear war of 10,000 MT. Essentially, all ecosystem support services would be severely impaired. We emphasize that survivors, at least in the Northern Hemisphere, would face extreme cold, water shortages, lack of food and fuel, heavy burdens of radiation and pollutants, disease, and severe psychological stress — all in twilight or darkness.

The possibility exists that the darkened skies and low temperatures would spread over the entire planet. Should this occur, a severe extinction event could ensue, leaving a highly modified and biologically depauperate Earth. Species extinction could be expected for most tropical plants and animals, and for most terrestrial vertebrates of north temperate regions, a large number of plants, and numerous freshwater and some marine organisms.

It seems unlikely, however, that even in these circumstances *Homo sapiens* would be forced to extinction immediately. Whether any people would be able to persist for long in the face of highly modified biological communities; novel climates; high levels of radiation; shattered agricultural, social, and economic systems; extraordinary psychological stresses; and a host of other difficulties is open to question. It is clear that the ecosystem effects *alone* resulting from a large-scale thermonuclear war could be enough to destroy the current civilization in at least the Northern Hemisphere. Coupled with the direct casualties of over 1 billion people, the combined intermediate and long-term effects of nuclear war suggest that eventually there might be no human survivors in the Northern Hemisphere. Furthermore, the scenario described here is by no means the most severe that could be imagined with present world nuclear arsenals and those contemplated for the future. In any large-scale nuclear exchange between the superpowers, global environmental changes sufficient to cause the extinction of a major fraction of the plant and animal species on the Earth are likely. In that event, the possibility of the extinction of *Homo sapiens* cannot be excluded.

MARTIN LUTHER KING JR. HOLIDAY PROCLAIMED

November 2, 1983

On November 2, 1983, President Ronald Reagan signed into law a bill designating the third Monday in January as a federal holiday in memory of civil rights leader Dr. Martin Luther King Jr. King's widow, Coretta Scott King, her four children and many of King's aides in the civil rights movement attended the ceremony.

The president's action marked a historic day for black Americans and ended a long struggle to have King's birthday made a holiday. Legislation to make January 15 (King's birthdate) a national holiday had been introduced every year since his death in 1968.

King became the third individual in U.S. history to be honored with a federal holiday. George Washington and Christopher Columbus are similarly honored. Abraham Lincoln's birthday is a holiday in some states, but it is not recognized by the federal government.

President Reagan opposed the creation of a 10th holiday for government workers on grounds that it would be too expensive. However, after the House and Senate passed the measure by large margins, the president signed it, saying the symbolism of King's birthday was important enough to warrant a holiday.

Reagan had been criticized for remarks he made after a news conference held October 19, the day the Senate passed the bill. The president was asked whether he agreed with Sen. Jesse Helms, R-N.C., who had charged that King was a Marxist Leninist who had associated with members of the American Communist Party. "We'll know in about 35 years, won't we?" Reagan answered, referring to sealed documents on King prepared by the FBI that would not be released until 2027 under the terms of a suit brought by the King family against the government. Reagan later called Coretta King to apologize.

Helms had gone to court to have the documents released but was unsuccessful. On October 18 U.S. District Court Judge John Lewis Smith Jr. ruled that the judiciary did not have the power to intervene in the legislative arena. The judge told Helms that if he wanted to see the documents, he should ask his fellow lawmakers to vote to release them.

Congressional Debate, Action

Passage of the bill honoring King came after acrimonious Senate debate and several attempts to defeat it through parliamentary maneuvers. At one point, Sen. Daniel Patrick Moynihan, D-N.Y., threw to the floor a folder of material on King circulated by Helms, calling the contents "filth" and "obscenities."

Sen. Edward M. Kennedy, D-Mass., and Helms exchanged angry words after Helms charged that when John F. Kennedy was president and Robert F. Kennedy was attorney general, wiretaps on King were authorized. Kennedy called the remarks part of a "smear campaign." "If Robert Kennedy were alive today," Kennedy said, "he would be among the first to stand and speak for this holiday in honor of Martin Luther King — whom he regarded as the greatest prophet of our time and one of the greatest Americans of all time."

Kennedy later admitted that his brothers had authorized a wiretap on King in November 1963, a few weeks before President Kennedy's assassination. He pointed out that later congressional investigations into King's work had uncovered no evidence that the Nobel Peace Prize winner had been influenced by Marxists.

A majority of Republicans supported the holiday, with 37 voting for the bill and 18 against. The final vote, which came after two days of debate, was 78-22, with 41 Democrats voting for it and 4 against. After the final tally, Sen. Robert Dole, R-Kan., standing beside Mrs. King, declared, "I'm proud of my party today. We're in the mainstream."

Several representatives and senators who voted against the bill praised King's contribution to national life but said they opposed creating an additional federal holiday because of the lost working hours. Rep. William E. Dannemeyer, R-Calif., estimated the holiday would cost taxpayers $225 million a year in lost productivity in the federal work force and three times that much in the private sector. The Congressional Budget Office estimated that the holiday's cost to the government would be only $18 million in 1986, the first year it would be celebrated.

King's Background

King was born in Atlanta on January 15, 1929, and named Michael Luther after his father. When his son was six years old, the senior King, a minister, changed both their names to Martin Luther, after the author of the Ninety-Five Theses.

The junior King received a B.A. from Morehouse College in Atlanta, attended the Crozer Theological Seminary in Chester, Pa., and was awarded a Ph.D degree in theology from Boston University in 1955.

King galvanized the civil rights movement with his leadership of the Montgomery, Ala., bus boycott, which began December 1, 1955, and ended just over a year later. His success in achieving his aims without allowing his followers to resort to violence made him a national hero. King was elected president of the newly founded Southern Christian Leadership Conference in 1957.

King was influenced greatly by the teachings of Mahatma Gandhi, the pacifist leader of the Indian independence movement. Like Gandhi, King preached passive resistance and non-violence in the struggle against segregation. His peaceful sit-ins, marches and prayer services stood in sharp contrast to the often brutal practices of his opponents, who sometimes turned fire hoses and police dogs on the marchers. King frequently was arrested as he led sit-ins against segregation at theaters, lunch counters, stores and colleges.

King probably is best known for his "I have a dream" speech, which he gave on the steps of the Lincoln Memorial on August 28, 1963, before a quarter million people. The 1963 March on Washington was the largest civil rights demonstration in the history of the United States at that time.

In 1964, at the age of 35, King became the youngest man ever to win the Nobel Prize for Peace. But as he became more prominent, he was attacked from both the right and the left. More militant blacks called him an "Uncle Tom." FBI director J. Edgar Hoover called him "the most notorious liar in the country" and ran a secret campaign to discredit him.

King was assassinated in Memphis, Tenn., on April 4, 1968.

Following are the remarks of President Ronald Reagan and Coretta Scott King at the November 2, 1983, signing ceremony proclaiming into law a holiday honoring Martin Luther King Jr.:

REAGAN REMARKS

The President. Mrs. King, members of the King family, distinguished

Members of the Congress, ladies and gentlemen, honored guests, I'm very pleased to welcome you to the White House, the home that belongs to all of us, the American people.

When I was thinking of the contributions to our country of the man that we're honoring today, a passage attributed to the American poet John Greenleaf Whittier comes to mind. "Each crisis brings its word and deed." In America, in the fifties and sixties, one of the important crises we faced was racial discrimination. The man whose words and deeds in that crisis stirred our nation to the very depths of its soul was Dr. Martin Luther King Jr.

Martin Luther King was born in 1929 in an America where, because of the color of their skin, nearly 1 in 10 lived lives that were separate and unequal. Most black Americans were taught in segregated schools. Across the country, too many could find only poor jobs, toiling for low wages. They were refused entry into hotels and restaurants, made to use separate facilities. In a nation that proclaimed liberty and justice for all, too many black Americans were living with neither.

In one city, a rule required all blacks to sit in the rear of public buses. But in 1955, when a brave woman named Rosa Parks was told to move to the back of the bus, she said, "No." A young minister in a local Baptist church, Martin Luther King, then organized a boycott of the bus company — a boycott that stunned the country. Within 6 months the courts had ruled the segregation of public transportation unconstitutional.

Dr. King had awakened something strong and true, a sense that true justice must be colorblind, and that among white and black Americans, as he put it, "Their destiny is tied up with our destiny, and their freedom is inextricably bound to our freedom; we cannot walk alone."

In the years after the bus boycott, Dr. King made equality of rights his life's work. Across the country, he organized boycotts, rallies, and marches. Often he was beaten, imprisoned, but he never stopped teaching nonviolence. "Work with the faith," he told his followers, "that unearned suffering is redemptive." In 1964 Dr. King became the youngest man in history to win the Nobel Peace Prize.

Dr. King's work brought him to this city often. And in one sweltering August day in 1963, he addressed a quarter of a million people at the Lincoln Memorial. If American history grows from two centuries to twenty, his words that day will never be forgotten. "I have a dream that one day on the red hills of Georgia, the sons of former slaves and the sons of former slave owners will be able to sit down together at the table of brotherhood."

In 1968 Martin Luther King was gunned down by a brutal assassin, his life cut short at the age of 39. But those 39 short years had changed America forever. The Civil Rights Act of 1964 had guaranteed all Americans equal use of public accommodations, equal access to programs financed by Federal funds, and the right to compete for employment on the sole basis of individual merit. The Voting Rights Act of 1965 had made certain that from then on black Americans would get to vote. But most important, there was not just a change of law; there was a change of heart.

The conscience of America had been touched. Across the land, people had begun to treat each other not as blacks and whites, but as fellow Americans.

And since Dr. King's death, his father, the Reverend Martin Luther King, Sr., and his wife, Coretta King, have eloquently and forcefully carried on his work. Also his family have joined in that cause.

Now our nation has decided to honor Dr. Martin Luther King, Jr., by setting aside a day each year to remember him and the just cause he stood for. We've made historic strides since Rosa Parks refused to go to the back of the bus. As a democratic people, we can take pride in the knowledge that we Americans recognized a grave injustice and took action to correct it. And we should remember that in far too many countries, people like Dr. King never have the opportunity to speak out at all.

But traces of bigotry still mar America. So, each year on Martin Luther King Day, let us not only recall Dr. King, but rededicate ourselves to the commandments he believed in and sought to live every day: Thou shall love thy God with all thy heart, and thou shall love thy neighbor as thyself. And I just have to believe that all of us — if all of us, young and old, Republicans and Democrats, do all we can to live up to those commandments, then we will see the day when Dr. King's dream comes true, and in his words, "All of God's children will be able to sing with new meaning, '. . . land where my fathers died, land of the pilgrim's pride, from every mountainside, let freedom ring.' "

Thank you, God bless you, and I will sign it.

CORETTA SCOTT KING REMARKS

Thank you, Mr. President, Vice President Bush, Majority Leader Baker and the distinguished Congressional and Senatorial delegations, and other representatives who've gathered here, and friends.

All right-thinking people, all right-thinking Americans are joined in spirit with us this day as the highest recognition which this nation gives is bestowed upon Martin Luther King, Jr., one who also was the recipient of the highest recognition which the world bestows, the Nobel Peace Prize.

In his own life's example, he symbolized what was right about America, what was noblest and best, what human beings have pursued since the beginning of history. He loved unconditionally. He was in constant pursuit of truth, and when he discovered it, he embraced it. His nonviolent campaigns brought about redemption, reconciliation, and justice. He taught us that only peaceful means can bring about peaceful ends, that our goal was to create the love community.

America is a more democratic nation, a more just nation, a more peaceful nation because Martin Luther King, Jr., became her preeminent nonviolent commander.

Martin Luther King, Jr., and his spirit live within all of us. Thank God for the blessing of his life and his leadership and his commitment. What manner of man was this? May we make ourselves worthy to carry on his dream and create the love community.

Thank you.

SOUTH AFRICAN CONSTITUTIONAL CHANGES
November 2, 1983

Two-thirds of South Africa's almost three million white voters in a November 2 whites-only referendum endorsed the government's proposed constitution, which for the first time provided for non-white, but not black, representation and participation in the national government. The new constitution offered no political role for South Africa's approximately 21 million blacks, who made up 70 percent of the population. And the constitutional changes did not touch on the great body of legislation that consigned people to destinies predicated on race.

The referendum results were a major victory for Prime Minister Pieter W. Botha, who had risked his political career in a divisive two-month campaign to persuade the ruling white minority to recognize the political rights of other racial groups.

Framework of New Government

Under the revised constitution an executive white president, replacing the prime minister, would have potentially authoritarian powers over a three-chamber legislative structure that would be dominated by a white assembly but would include smaller chambers for the 850,000 South African Asians, mostly of Indian descent, and the 2.7 million coloreds of mixed racial descent. Each racial group was to elect its own members to the tricameral parliament. The largest chamber would be the 178-member House of Assembly, representing the country's 4.6 million white population. The House of Representatives would have 85 members representing Asians, and the House of Delegates would be composed of 45 members elected by mixed-race voters.

The individual chambers were to exercise authority over their own affairs, defined as housing, social welfare, health, education and local government. Joint standing committees made up of members from all three houses were to consider "general affairs" such as foreign policy, defense, taxes and law and order.

The president would be chosen by an 88-member electoral college selected by the three chambers and composed of 50 white, 25 colored and 13 Asian electors. The composition was likely to ensure election of a white president.

Prime Minister Botha said he hoped to implement the new constitution during the second half of 1984.

Reaction

The Reagan administration saw the revisions as a sign of change in South Africa's rigid segregation system. The U.S. State Department hailed the referendum as "a potentially significant date in the modern history of South Africa."

Botha said the results disclosed "a decisive majority in favor of the attempt to secure security, peace, stability and prosperity for South Africa," which in 1983 was the continent's strongest nation militarily and economically. The prime minister denied charges by right-wing critics that the constitutional revisions were a step toward enfranchising blacks.

Other opponents criticized the constitution because it made no provision for the overwhelming majority of citizens, blacks. They argued the measure simply further institutionalized apartheid. Enacted in the Population Registration Act of 1950, the system compartmentalized people by color. Once classified by race at birth — by such criteria as the parents' language and their hair and skin color — a person's future was preordained because race classification determined where he could live, his economic and educational prospects and his voice in the political system.

Apartheid required most blacks to live in so-called tribal homelands, or semi-autonomous nations, scattered over only 13 percent of the country. Blacks were denied South African citizenship and technically any right to influence their or the country's future. They condemned the new constitution because it did not change their circumstances. A prominent leader in the black township of Soweto outside Johannesburg said it was "designed to enlarge the white power base" and turn the colored and Indian communities into "a buffer between them and us," both politically and militarily. (Report on South Africa human rights violations, Historic Documents of 1982, p. 797)

There were doubts that the colored and Indian peoples were ready to participate in large numbers in a process that would give them a limited franchise in return for little perceptible influence on issues such as where they could live or how they were classified racially. The "new dispensation" would, they charged, eventually render them eligible for military conscription, which had applied only to white males. Botha confirmed that this was a consequence of their being given the vote. Many coloreds and Indians also were strongly opposed to the new constitution because they did not want to break ranks with the black African majority that was excluded from the new arrangements.

A confidential report by the secretive and influential society of Afrikaners (the 2.8 million Afrikaners were the dominant white group that controlled South Africa) warned that, because of demographic trends, "The whites will be placed in such a minority position within 20 years and the blacks, particularly under a stronger leader, will build up such a solidarity that the coloreds and Asians will have no option but to unite with blacks against a white minority government."

> *Following are excerpts from the South African constitution adopted by a referendum of white voters November 2, 1983, and from the explanatory memorandum.* (Boldface headings in brackets have been added by Congressional Quarterly to highlight the organization of the text.):

[Constitution]

52. Every White person, Coloured person and Indian who —
   (a) is a South African citizen in terms of the South African Citizen-ship Act, 1949; and
   (b) is of or over the age of 18 years; and
   (c) is not subject to any of the disqualifications mentioned in section 4 (1) or (2) of the Electoral Act, 1979,
shall, on compliance with and subject to the provisions of the Electoral Act, 1979, be entitled to vote at any election of a member of the House of Assembly, the House of Representatives and the House of Delegates, respectively, in the electoral division of the House in question determined in accordance with the last-mentioned Act.

[Explanatory Memorandum]

Section 52: Franchise

The section lays down uniform franchise qualifications for Whites, Coloureds and Indians. Each White, Coloured and Indian will be entitled to be registered as a voter for the House of Assembly, the House of Representatives and the House of Delegates respectively, and to vote in an election if he

— is a South African citizen;

— is 18 years of age or older; and

— has not been convicted of murder, treason, certain security and electoral offences, and offence in connection with drug abuse, or if he has not been declared to be of unsound mind or is being detained as a mentally ill person, or in a reform school.

[Constitution]

93. The control and administration of Black affairs shall vest in the State President, who shall exercise all those special powers in regard to Black administration which immediately before the commencement of this Act were vested in him, and any lands which immediately before such commencement vested in him the occupation of Blacks in terms of any law shall continue to vest in him with all such powers as he may have in connection therewith, and no lands which were set aside for the occupation of Blacks and which could not at the establishment of the Union of South Africa have been alienated except by an Act of the Legislature of a Colony which became part of the Union of South Africa in terms of the South Africa Act, 1909, shall be alienated or in any way diverted from the purposes for which they were set aside, except under the authority of an Act of Parliament.

[Explanatory Memorandum]

Section 93: Matters affecting Black people

The provision in the Constitution Act, 1961, with regard to the State President's control over and administration of matters affecting Black people is retained.

PRESIDENT REAGAN'S TRIP TO THE FAR EAST

November 8-14, 1983

Serious international policy issues were on the agenda during President Ronald Reagan's trip to the Far East November 8-14. In talks with the Japanese, Reagan pressed home two points that had been troubling Washington for the past two decades: the restrictiveness of Japanese trade policies and the need for Japan to assume a stronger defense posture. During his stop in South Korea, the president reaffirmed longstanding support for that nation's anti-communist government.

Throughout the trip, Reagan used his skill as a communicator to reach audiences outside the formal diplomatic circuit, taking his message to the Japanese people in a lengthy television interview and speaking to U.S. troops stationed at the demilitarized zone, a narrow, barren strip of land that had separated the heavily armed boundaries of South Korea and communist North Korea since the Korean War.

The president originally had planned to visit the Philippines, Thailand and Indonesia as well, but he cancelled this leg of the trip because of domestic turmoil in the Philippines. Benigno Simeon Aquino Jr., a leading political opponent of President Ferdinand E. Marcos, had been gunned down as he returned to the Philippines after several years of self-imposed exile. Because Aquino was under the protection of government security forces at the time, the Marcos government was suspected of neglect, if not complicity, in the assassination.

The Visit to Japan

The first American president to address the Japanese Diet, or parlia-

ment, Reagan told members that the United States welcomed Japan's emergence as a strong partner in the Pacific; ties between the two democracies were far more important than their differences.

Nonetheless, differences did exist. "Americans believe your markets are less open than ours," he warned. Emphasizing his own opposition to protectionism, he pointed to growing protectionist sentiment in Congress. "We need your help in demonstrating free trade to address concerns of my own people," Reagan told the Diet. He urged the Japanese to permit more imports of U.S. manufactured and agricultural products, to bring their currency more into line with its real value and to open Japan to wider foreign investment.

Reagan also called on the Japanese to enlarge their share of the defense burden in the Pacific and pledged he would work for arms control — a matter of great concern in Japan — and that he would never negotiate a nuclear arms agreement that sacrificed Asia's interests to those of Europe.

Reagan-Nakasone Statements

Joint statements issued by President Reagan and Japanese Prime Minister Yasuhiro Nakasone November 10 indicated some headway toward cooperation had been made. An accord was announced on measures to strengthen the yen against the dollar. Washington had cited undervaluation of the Japanese currency as a prime cause of the United States' massive trade deficit with Japan.

Nakasone also promised to continue efforts "toward further strengthening the credibility of the Japan-U.S. security arrangements," a point of great interest to Washington, which held that the Japanese should increase their defense spending, a move that was unpopular in Japan.

When Nakasone visited Washington in May 1983, he and Reagan had struck up a warm relationship, and progress on the defense issue seemed possible. Nakasone was more amenable to America's requests for a larger Japanese defense budget than other Japanese leaders had been, and he had committed his government to that course.

Losses by Nakasone's Liberal Democratic Party in elections held in December 1983, however, cast some doubt on how much cooperation he could offer, although the losses were attributed primarily to the effects of a bribery scandal rather than to discontent with Nakasone's policies.

The Trip to South Korea

President Reagan's visit to South Korea provided a show of support for that nation at a crucial time. The downing of a South Korean commercial airliner by the Soviet Union in September 1983 and a bombing in

Rangoon, Burma, that killed several members of the South Korean Cabinet, had shaken the country. South Korea blamed North Korea for the bombing, adding strain to the always-tense relations between the Korean regimes. (Airline incident, p. 775)

Speaking to the South Korean National Assembly on November 12, Reagan emphasized America's steadfast military support for South Korea, where more than 40,000 U.S. troops were then stationed. In a further symbolic gesture of support, the president visited troops at Camp Liberty Bell, a U.S. Army outpost on the demilitarized zone, within two and one-half miles of North Korean lines. South Korean President Chun Doo Hwan had expressed reservations about the Camp Liberty visit, fearing it might provoke action by North Korea, which had labeled Reagan's trip a "dangerous war junket."

While praising South Korea for its "economic miracle," Reagan also made it clear that Washington viewed further development of democratic institutions as a matter of priority for that nation. "We welcome President Chun's farsighted plans for a constitutional transfer of power in 1988," Reagan told the national assembly, a remark he repeated at a reception at the American Embassy for South Korean community leaders, including some who had criticized Chun's government.

Successive South Korean governments had justified political repression on the grounds that the constant threat from the north necessitated extreme measures. During President Reagan's visit, policemen were posted outside homes of some of the more outspoken dissidents, placing them under virtual house arrest. Former President Jimmy Carter had openly criticized the South Koreans for suppressing dissent, but Reagan said his administration preferred to confine its reservations to private diplomatic channels.

Ending his two day visit to South Korea, Reagan pledged "steadfast support" for the country and said he would strengthen the U.S. forces stationed there. In a joint statement with President Chun, Reagan called Northeast Asia a "region of critical strategic significance."

Following are excerpts from the joint statements of President Ronald Reagan and Prime Minister Yasuhiro Nakasone, November 10, 1983; from Reagan's address before the Japanese Diet, November 11, 1983; from Reagan's interview with NHK Japanese television, November 11, 1983; and from Reagan's address before the South Korean National Assembly, November 12, 1983. (Boldface headings in brackets have been added by Congressional Quarterly to highlight the organization of the texts.):

STATEMENTS OF PRESIDENT REAGAN
AND PRIME MINISTER NAKASONE

The Prime Minister. For the people and Government of Japan as well as for my wife and myself, it is indeed a great pleasure to welcome the President of the United States of America and Mrs. Reagan as state guests.

Yesterday and today, the President and I had very productive meetings covering a wide range of subjects. Through these meetings, we reconfirmed the importance for Japan and the United States, two countries sharing the common ideas and values of freedom and democracy of promoting further cooperation towards peace and prosperity of the world.

The President has a clear recognition of the importance of the Asian and the Pacific region. His present visit to Japan and the Republic of Korea and his planned visit to China next year amply testify this fact, together with his visit to the countries in Southeast Asia, which I am sure will be rescheduled in the future. The economic dynamism in the Asian and the Pacific region is one of central elements in the expansion of the world economy. Thus, the President and I are in full agreement that we should continue to make efforts for the further development of the Asian and the Pacific region.

[East-West Tension]

Mr. President, I issued on November 1st the Tokyo Statement jointly with Chancellor Kohl of the Federal Republic of Germany, in line with the spirit of the political statement adopted at the Williamsburg summit in May this year declaring that we should maintain the unity and solidarity among the Western countries in our joint endeavor in pursuit of freedom, peace, and stability of the prosperity of the world economy, and of the development in the Third World.

As I know the recent events of increasing tension in the East-West relations, as well as frequent occurrences of regional disputes and violence in various parts of the world, I am worried that the peace in the world could be gravely threatened if such trends continue and amplify themselves. Under such circumstances, I firmly believe that the countries of the world should renew their resolve for the maintenance of freedom, peace, and stability, for the revitalization of the world economy, and for the prosperity of the peoples of the world.

I further believe that the rational dialogs and negotiations should be conducted to solve such international conflicts and disputes, and that the parties concerned should spare no effort in taking step-by-step measures or gradual approach[es] in pursuit of ultimate goals, and should carry on steady and realistic endeavors. This I consider is particularly pertinent to the arms control negotiations.

The Western countries should stand firmly in unity and solidarity for freedom and peace and should not hesitate to bear any hardships in upholding this cause. All these points are included in the Tokyo Statement. It is, indeed, truly significant, Mr. President, that you have fully endorsed this statement in our meeting.

The President and I had exchanges of views on East-West relations with emphasis on the question of arms control and on the situation in such areas as Asia, the Middle East, and Central America.

With regard to the INF [Intermediate-range Nuclear Forces] negotiations in particular, it was reconfirmed that the negotiations should not be conducted at the sacrifice of the Asian region, but should be conducted on a global basis, taking the Asian security into consideration.

With respect to the recent bombing in Burma, the very act of terrorism, we agreed that it should be strongly condemned as . . . inexcusable conduct . . . [challenging] world peace and order and that continued efforts must be made to bring about lasting peace and stability on the Korean peninsula.

On the Middle East, I expressed my deep appreciation for the role played by the multinational forces for stabilizing the situation in Lebanon.

The Japan-U.S. security arrangements are the foundation of the peace and security of Japan and the Far East. I wish to express that Japan will continue her efforts towards further strengthening the credibility of the Japan-U.S. security arrangements. With respect to the improvement of our defense capability, I wish to continue to make further efforts along the lines of the joint communique of May 1981.

[International Trade]

As to the international economy, the President and I reconfirmed — in line with the declaration of the Williamsburg summit — the importance of obtaining sustained, noninflationary growth of the world economy, of rolling back protectionism, and of lowering the prevailing high interest rates. We consider them important, together with extending financial cooperation, in order to alleviate the plight of the developing countries, which are suffering from accumulated debts.

With regard to bilateral economic issues, we acknowledge the achievements made thus far and agree to continue our efforts for the solution of the remaining issues. In this context, I highly appreciated the pledge by the President to combat protectionism in the United States.

The President and I are in full agreement on the importance of the yen-dollar issue. We have agreed on establishing consultative fora on exchange rate issues and investment. In this connection, I asked for continued U.S. efforts to lower U.S. interest rates.

The President and I have also underscored the importance of greater two-way investment flows between our two countries, and I expressed my concern that the unitary method of taxation is becoming a serious impediment to the Japanese investment in the United States. I stressed the importance of promoting the preparations of a new round of multilateral trade negotiations in order to consolidate the free trading system and to inject renewed confidence in the world economy. I am very glad that the President has strongly supported my view. We intend to call on other countries to join in our efforts.

Mr. President, in the present international situation, you are shouldering enormous global responsibilities. I will, on my part, make as much contribution as possible to the peace and prosperity of the world.

Thank you very much.

The President. Well, on behalf of the American people and our government, I would like to thank His Imperial Majesty the Emperor, Prime Minister Nakasone, and the Government and people of Japan for the generous and warm reception that you have extended to my wife, Nancy, myself, and my staff during our trip to your country.

Prime Minister Nakasone . . . [and I] have just completed 2 days of very productive discussions on a wide range of bilateral issues and global affairs. As leaders of two great Pacific nations, we're guardians of a strong, rich, and diverse relationship. Japan and America are bound by shared values of freedom, democracy, and peace. We're committed to greater future cooperation across a broad spectrum of political, economic, security, educational, cultural, and scientific affairs.

I have come as a friend of Japan seeking to strengthen our partnership for peace, prosperity, and progress. I will leave Japan confident that our partnership is stronger than before and confident that we're giving birth to a new era in Japanese-American relations. We have agreed to move forward with an agenda for progress by drawing upon the great well of talent, drive, determination, and creativity of our free peoples. We welcome Japan's more assertive role as a fellow trustee of peace and progress in international economic and political affairs.

[Global Issues]

We have discussed global issues, and we hold many similar views on opportunities for cooperation. The principles that Prime Minister Nakasone has enunciated as the Tokyo Statement are principles that I fully endorse. Together we have no greater responsibility than to make our world a safer place.

There are serious threats to peace on the Korean peninsula, in the Middle East, in the Caribbean, and over the Northwestern Pacific. Also, the attitude on the part of our adversary at the negotiating table on arms talks is at odds with the will of the world to reduce the weapons of war and build a more stable peace.

I conveyed to the Prime Minister my satisfaction that our mutual security relationship is proceeding smoothly. Japan is host to 45,000 American troops, and our bases in Japan, made possible by the Treaty of Mutual Cooperation and Security, are essential not only to the defense of Japan but also contribute to peace and prosperity in the Far East. As for Japan's defense efforts, the United States remains convinced that the most important contribution Japan can make toward the peace and security in Asia is for Japan to provide for its own defense and share more of the burden of our mutual defense effort.

During our discussions on arms control, I assured Prime Minister Nakasone that we seek global reductions in the Soviet's intermediate-range SS-20's to the lowest level possible. The United States will take no action in the intermediate nuclear forces negotiations that adversely affects the security of Asia. We agreed on the urgency of achieving consensus on comprehensive international safeguards to prevent the spread of nuclear weaponry.

[Trade Issues]

Prime Minister Nakasone and I discussed Japan and America's compelling international economic responsibilities as spelled out at the Williamsburg summit. Together we must press for continuing liberalization of the international trade and financial system, fight protectionism, promote economic development without inflation by encouraging the growth of free enterprise throughout the world, and share the obligation of assisting developing countries, including those facing severe debt problems. We also agreed to enhance coordination in foreign assistance.

Trade issues figure prominently in the Japan-U.S. relationship. There's no simple, overnight solution to our trade problems, but we have agreed to exert our best and continued efforts to solve these issues. We welcome recent actions by your government to reduce trade barriers, and I've emphasized the importance of further measures to open the Japanese market to trade and investment.

I didn't come to negotiate specific trade issues, but I did indicate certain issues of immediate importance to us. Because of both their trade and consumer significance, for example, we're seeking reductions in Japan's tariffs on certain products in which the U.S. is highly competitive. Japanese quotas on agricultural products are a cause for concern. In return, the United States must combat protectionism in our country, and I have given the Prime Minister my pledge to do so.

Progress in Japan-U.S. trade issues can foster greater trade liberalization efforts worldwide, such as the Prime Minister's call for a new round of multilateral trade negotiations, which I heartily endorse.

I expressed confidence that the United States can be a reliable long-term supplier of energy, particularly coal, to Japan. And I was pleased that Prime Minister Nakasone shared this view. Expanded energy trade will mean more jobs for Americans and greater security for both our countries.

With the approval of Prime Minister Nakasone and myself, a joint press statement is being released today by Finance Minister Takeshita and Treasury Secretary ... Regan ... on the yen-dollar issue and other financial and economic issues of mutual interest. We agree that the commitments and steps outlined in that statement will further strengthen economic relations between the United States and Japan.

aspirations of men and women everywhere — to be free, to live in peace, and to create and renew the wealth of abundance and spiritual fulfillment.

I have come to Japan because we have an historic opportunity. We can become a powerful partnership for good, not just in our own countries, not just in the Pacific region but throughout the world. Distinguished ladies and gentlemen, my question is: Do we have the determination to meet the challenge of partnership and make it happen? My answer is without hesitation: Yes we do, and yes we will.

For much of our histories, our countries looked inward. Well, those times have passed. With our combined economies accounting for half the output of the free world, we cannot escape our global responsibilities. Our industries depend on the importation of energy and minerals from distant lands. Our prosperity requires a sound international financial system and free and open trading markets. And our security is inseparable from the security of our friends and neighbors.

The simple hope for world peace and prosperity will not be enough. Our two great nations, working with others, must preserve the values and freedoms our societies have struggled so hard to achieve. Nor should our partnership for peace, prosperity, and freedom be considered a quest for competing goals. We cannot prosper unless we are secure, and we cannot be secure unless we are free. And we will not succeed in any of these endeavors unless Japan and America work in harmony.

[Arms Control]

I have come to your country carrying the heartfelt desires of America for peace. I know our desires are shared by Prime Minister Nakasone and all of Japan. We are people of peace. We understand the terrible trauma of human suffering. I have lived through four wars in my lifetime. So, I speak not just as President of the United States, but also as a husband, a father, and as a grandfather. I believe there can be only one policy for preserving our precious civilization in this modern age. A nuclear war can never be won and must never be fought.

The only value in possessing nuclear weapons is to make sure they can't be used ever. I know I speak for people everywhere when I say our dream is to see the day when nuclear weapons will be banished from the face of the Earth.

In the strategic arms reduction talks, American negotiators continue to press the Soviet Union for any formula that will achieve these objectives. In the longer range INF [Intermediate-range Nuclear Forces] talks, we are pursuing the same course, even offering to eliminate an entire category of weapons. I'm very conscious of our negotiating responsibility on issues that concern the safety and well-being of the Japanese people. And let me make one thing very plain. We must not and we will not accept any agreement that transfers the threat of longer range nuclear missiles from Europe to Asia.

901

Our great frustration has been the other side's unwillingness to negotiate in good faith. We wanted to cut deep into nuclear arsenals, and still do. But they're blocking the dramatic reductions the world wants. In our good-faith effort to move the negotiations forward, we have offered new initiatives, provided for substantial reductions to equal levels, and the lower the level the better. But we shall wait. We still wait for the first positive response.

Despite this bleak picture, I will not be deterred in my search for a breakthrough. The United States will never walk away from the negotiating table. Peace is too important. Common sense demands that we persevere, and we will persevere.

We live in uncertain times. There are trials and tests for freedom wherever freedom stands. It is as stark as the tragedy over the Sea of Japan, when 269 innocent people were killed for the so-called cause of sacred airspace. It is as real as the terrorist attacks last month on the Republic of Korea's leadership in Rangoon and against American and French members of the international peacekeeping force in Beirut. And yes, it is as telling as the stonewalling of our adversaries at the negotiating table, and as their crude attempts to intimidate freedom-loving people everywhere.

[Japanese Security]

These threats to peace and freedom underscore the importance of closer cooperation among all nations. . . . The stronger the dedication of Japan, the United States, and our allies to peace through strength, the greater our contributions to building a more secure future will be. The U.S.-Japan Treaty of Mutual Cooperation and Security must continue to serve us as the bedrock of our security relationship. Japan will not have to bear the burden of defending freedom alone. America is your partner. We will bear that burden together.

The defense of freedom should be a shared burden. We can afford to defend freedom; we cannot afford to lose it. The blessings of your economic miracle, created with the genius of a talented, determined, and dynamic people, can only be protected in the safe harbor of freedom. . . .

To all those who lack faith in the human spirit, I have just three words of advice: Come to Japan. Come to a country whose economic production will soon surpass the Soviet Union's, making Japan's economy the second largest in the entire world. Come to learn from a culture that instills in its people a strong spirit of cooperation, discipline, and striving for excellence; and yes, learn from government policies which helped create this economic miracle — not so much by central planning, as by stimulating competition, encouraging initiative, and rewarding savings and risk-taking. . . .

Partnership must be a two-way street grounded in mutual trust. Let us always be willing to learn from each other and cooperate together. We have every reason to do so. Our combined economies account for almost 35 percent of the world's entire economic output. We are the world's two largest overseas trading partners. Last year Japan took about 10 percent of our total exports, and we bought some 25 percent of yours. Our two-way trade will exceed $60 billion in 1983, more than double the level of just 7 years ago.

[Protectionism]

At the Williamsburg summit last May, the leaders of our industrial democracies pledged to cooperate in rolling back protectionism. My personal commitment to that goal is based on economic principles, old fashioned common sense, and experience. I am old enough to remember what eventually happened the last time countries protected their markets from competition: It was a nightmare called the Great Depression. And it was worldwide. World trade fell at that time by 60 percent. And everyone — workers, farmers, and manufacturers were hurt.

Let us have the wisdom never to repeat that policy. We're in the same boat with our trading partners around the globe. And if one partner in the boat shoots a hole in the boat, it doesn't make much sense for the other partner to shoot another hole in the boat. Some say, yes, and call that getting tough. Well, forgive me, but I call it getting wet all over. Rather than shooting holes, let us work together to plug them up, so our boat of free markets and free trade and fair trade can lead us all to greater economic growth and international stability.

I have vigorously opposed quick fixes of protectionism in America. Anticompetitive legislation like the local content rule, which would force our domestic manufacturers of cars to use a rising share of U.S. labor and parts — now, this would be a cruel hoax. It would be raising prices without protecting jobs. We would buy less from you. You would buy less from us. The world's economic pie would shrink. Retaliation and recrimination would increase.

It is not easy for elected officials to balance the concerns of constituents with the greater interests of the nation, but that's what our jobs are all about. And we need your help in demonstrating free trade to address concerns of my own people. Americans believe your markets are less open than ours. We need your support to lower further the barriers that still make it difficult for some American products to enter your markets easily. Your government's recent series of actions to reduce trade barriers are positive steps in this direction. We very much hope this process will continue and accelerate. In turn, I pledge my support to combat protectionist measures in my own country.

If we each give a little, we can all gain a lot. As two great and mature democracies, let us have the faith to believe in each other, to draw on our long and good friendship, and to make our partnership grow. We are leaders in the world economy. We and the other industrialized countries share a responsibility to open up capital and trading markets, promote greater investment in each other's country, assist developing nations, and stop the leakage of military technology to an adversary bent on aggression and domination.

[The Yen]

We believe that the currency of the world's second largest free-market economy should reflect the economic strength and political stability that you enjoy. We look forward to the yen playing a greater role in international financial and economic affairs. We welcome the recent trend toward a stronger yen. And we would welcome Japan's increasingly active role in global affairs. Your leadership in aid to refugees and in economic assistance to various countries has been most important in helping to promote greater stability in key regions of the world. Your counsel on arms reduction initiatives is highly valued by us.

We may have periodic disputes, but the real quarrel is not between us. It is with those who would impose regimentation over freedom, drudgery over dynamic initiative, a future of despair over the certainty of betterment, and the forced feeding of a military goliath over a personal stake in the products and progress of tomorrow.

You and your neighbors are shining examples for all who seek rapid development. The Pacific Basin represents the most exciting region of economic growth in the world today. Your people stretch your abilities to the limit, and when an entire nation does this, miracles occur. Being a Californian I have seen many miracles hardworking Japanese have brought to our shores. . . .

As the years pass, our contacts continue to increase at an astonishing rate. Today some 13,000 of your best college and graduate students are studying in America, and increasing numbers of U.S. citizens are coming here to learn everything they can about Japan. Companies like Nissan, Kyocera, Sony, and Toshiba have brought thousands of jobs to America's shores. The State of California is planning to build a rapid speed train that is adapted from your highly successful bullet train. In 1985 the United States will join Japan in a major exhibition of science and technology at Tsukuba, another symbol of our cooperation.

For my part, I welcome this new Pacific tide. Let it roll peacefully on, carrying a two-way flow of people and ideas that can break from barriers of suspicion and mistrust and build up bonds of cooperation and shared optimism.

Our two nations may spring from separate pasts; we may live at opposite sides of the Earth; but we have been brought together by our indomitable spirit of determination, our love of liberty, and devotion to progress. We are like climbers who begin their ascent from opposite ends of the mountain. The harder we try, the higher we climb and the closer we come together — until that moment we reach the peak and we are as one. . . .

. . . Together there is nothing that Japan and America cannot do.

Thank you very much. God bless you.

REMARKS IN AN INTERVIEW
WITH NHK TELEVISION

... **Q.** Mr. President, listening to your statement, like many other people I find that you are indeed a great communicator. I say this not because you said very kind words about our famous city of drama, but because I think that your personal style on television is more relaxed and informal than that of many other politicians. That is why, with your approval, Mr. President, I would like to conduct this interview in a very informal way so that the Japanese people can get a clearer view of your personality. . . .

... Yesterday you gave us your official view of the visit, but I wonder if you could give us now a more personal view of this visit?

The President. Well, yes, I'm very pleased with what has taken place here. First of all the warmth of the reception from all your people, and I mean not just the people of diplomacy and government that I had dealings with, but your people there on the streets and their showing of hospitality and friendship has been very heartwarming. But I have always believed that we only get in trouble when we're talking about each other instead of to each other. . . . I think that we have established a human kind of bond, not just one that is framed in diplomacy, but an understanding of each other as people. And I think that the world needs more of this.

Q. Mr. President, I would like you to know, in the first place, that many of my compatriots will be surprised and very happily so at the inclusion of Hiroshima and Nagasaki on the list of places that you'd like to visit or you wish you could visit. And to this end, of course, you'll have to be a young — [*inaudible*] — sagacious man so that you'll be able to fulfill your and our common desire in this regard. Now, are you going to be one? Are you going to be a sagacious man?

The President. Well, I'm certainly going to try. This is too dangerous a world to just be careless with words or deeds. And if ever there was a need for the world to work toward peace and to work out of the dangerous situation that we're in, that time is now.

Q. On a more, a little more serious note, Mr. President, my question is exactly related to this point. And that is, because of the experience that we in Japan went through, we are very genuine in hoping even for a very minimum, limited progress in the arms control talks which are currently underway. And just as it took another Republican President with very conservative credentials to effect a rapprochement very successfully with China, there are Japanese who hope that, perhaps, your hard-line policy may lead to the relaxation of East-West tensions. And in light of these hopes and expectations, Mr. President, could you comment on these talks? And, also, I would appreciate it a greal deal if you would give us your assessment of the current state of and, perhaps, future prospects for U.S.-Soviet relations, particularly in the arms control area.

The President. ... Yes, we're working very hard to improve relations with [The People's Republic of China] and establish trust and friendship. And I think we've made great progress. I know there is a question that is raised sometimes with regard to our friends on Taiwan — the Republic of China. And I have to say, there, that I have repeatedly said to the leaders of the People's Republic of China that they must understand that we will not throw over one friend in order to make another. And I would think that that would be reassuring to them, that they, then, might not be thrown over at some time in the future.

But with regard to the Soviet Union . . . what is being called a hard line, I think, is realism.

And I feel that we have to be realistic with the Soviet Union. It is not good for us, as some in the past have, to think, well, they're just like us and surely we can appeal to, say, their kindliness or their better nature. No. I think they're very materialistic. They're very realistic. They have some aggressive and expansionist aims in the world. And I believe that, yes, you can negotiate with them; yes, you can talk to them. But it must be on the basis of recognizing them as the way they are and then presenting the proposals in such a way that they can see that it is to their advantage to be less hostile in the world and to try and get along with the rest of the nations of the world. And if this is hard-line, then I'm hard-line.

But it is important because of, also, your opening remarks with reference to the great nuclear forces in the world. We are going to stay at that negotiating table. We won't walk away from it. We're going to stay there trying, not as we have in the past to set some limits or ceilings on how many more missiles would be built, how much more growth they could take in those weapons, we want a reduction in the numbers. But really and practically, when we start down that road, and if we can get cooperation from them in reducing them, we should then continue down that road to their total elimination. . . .

. . . Once upon a time, we had rules of warfare. War is an ugly thing, but we had rules in which we made sure that soldiers fought soldiers, but they did not victimize civilians. That was civilized. Today we've lost something of civilization in that the very weapons we're talking about are designed to destroy civilians by the millions. And let us at least get back to where we once were — that if we talk war at all, we talk it in a way in which there could be victory or defeat and in which civilians have some measure of protection. . . .

Q. Mr. President, you referred to the current situation as being very dangerous. And in recent months we have witnessed one act of violence after another — the assassination of Mr. Aquino in the Philippines, and the shooting down of the Korean Airlines passenger jet, the terrorist bombing in Rangoon, and again in the bombing in Lebanon, Beirut, and the regional conflicts that persist at many different parts of the world, including the Middle East and the Caribbean. I think we certainly live in a very dangerous world, and your administration has advocated very strongly for building more effective defense capabilities of the United States and of its allies.

Now, . . . Mr. President, my question is that the kind of danger that the world faces today would be minimized if the United States and its partners, including Japan, become stronger militarily?

The President. Yes, . . . for a number of years now, recently, we have sat at the table in meetings with the Soviet leaders who have engaged in the biggest military buildup in the history of mankind. And they sat on their side of the table looking at us and knowing that unilaterally we were disarming without getting anything in return. . . .

I think realistically to negotiate arms reductions they have to see that there is a choice. Either they join in those arms reductions, or they then have to face the fact that we are going to turn our industrial might to building the strength that would be needed to deter them from ever starting a war. . . .

Now, if they know that they cannot match us — and when I say us, I mean our allies and Japan and the United States — they cannot match us if we are determined to build up our defenses. So they then face the fact that as we build them up, they might then find themselves weaker than we are. . . .

Q. . . . Some of the dangers that I refer to do not take place only in the context of the confrontation between the United States and the Soviet Union. I think some of the regional conflicts have indigenous roots for that. And I just wonder if we are not having the kind of crises and dangers that don't lend themselves to the military solutions, which might call for some other approach to solving these problems and thereby reducing the tension in the world as a whole.

The President. Well, if I understand your question correctly, what we're talking about is . . . the Middle East. Once upon a time, nations like our own with oceans around us . . . could have a defensive army on our own land, we could have coastal artillery batteries, and we knew that if a war came to us, it would come to our shores and we would defend our shores. Today there are strategic points in various places in the world. The Middle East is one. . . .

. . . We know that the strategic waterways of the world — the Soviet Union has now built up the greatest navy in the world, and the biggest part of that navy is here in the Pacific, in the vicinity of your own country. But they know, as anyone must know in world strategy, that there are a limited number of choke points, sea passages that are essential to your livelihood and to ours. You can start with the Panama Canal and the Suez Canal [and] the Straits of Gibraltar, but then right here in the passages that lead to your own island, the Malacca and the Makassar Straits. There are a total of no more than 16 in the whole world. And a nation that could dominate those narrow passages and shut them off to our shipping could secure victory without firing a shot at any of us. . . .

Q. Mr. President, you said that — in the National Diet this morning — that you have vigorously opposed the quick fix of protectionism in America. But there remains the danger of protectionist legislation to restrict Japanese imports to the United States. Do you believe such anticompetitive legislation will be passed? And in regard to this, what do you think of the steps which Japan has been taking to further open up its own markets?

The President. We heartily approve. And one of the things that we've been discussing are some of the points of difference that still remain between our two marketplaces. And I have pointed to the danger of those in our Congress who, because of the unemployment, think the answer could be protectionism. Well, I think that protectionism destroys everything we want. I believe in free trade and fair trade.... There probably have been 40 bills that have been brought up and proposed, all of which would have some elements in them of protectionism....

ADDRESS BEFORE THE
KOREAN NATIONAL ASSEMBLY

Speaker Ch'ae, Vice Speaker Yun, Vice Speaker Koh, distinguished Members of the National Assembly, and honored guests:

I'm privileged to be among such friends. I stand in your Assembly as Presidents Eisenhower and Johnson have stood before me. And I reaffirm, as they did, America's support and friendship for the Republic of Korea and its people.

Not long after the war on this peninsula, your President paid a visit to Washington. In his remarks at the state dinner, President Eisenhower spoke of the Korean people's courage, stamina, and self-sacrifice. He spoke of America's pride in joining with the Korean people to prevent their enslavement by the North. In response, your first President expressed his country's deep, deep appreciation for what America had done. He concluded by saying, "I tell you, my friends, if I live hundreds of years, we will never be able to do enough to pay our debt of gratitude to you."

Well, I have come today to tell the people of this great nation: Your debt has been repaid. Your loyalty, your friendship, your progress, your determination to build something better for your people has proven many times over the depth of your gratitude. In these days of turmoil and testing, the American people are very thankful for such a constant and devoted ally. Today, America is grateful to you...

[Korea's Tragedies]

Our world is sadder today, because ... [i]nstead of offering assistance to a lost civilian airliner, the Soviet Union attacked. Instead of offering condolences, it issued denials. Instead of offering reassurances, it repeated its threats. Even in the search for our dead, the Soviet Union barred the way. This behavior chilled the entire world. The people of Korea and the United States shared a special grief and anger.

My nation's prayers went out to the Korean families who lost loved ones even as we prayed for our own. May I ask you today to pause for a moment of silence for those who perished. . . .

In recent weeks, our grief deepened. The despicable North Korean attack in Rangoon deprived us of trusted advisers and friends. So many of those who died had won admirers in America as they studied with us or guided us with their counsel. . . . To the families and countrymen of all those who were lost, America expresses its deep sorrow.

We also pledge to work with your government and others in the international community to censure North Korea for its uncivilized behavior. Let every aggressor hear our words, because Americans and Koreans speak with one voice. People who are free will not be slaves, and freedom will not be lost in the Republic of Korea.

We in the United States have suffered a similar savage act of terrorism in recent weeks. Our marines in Lebanon were murdered by madmen who cannot comprehend words like "reason" or "decency." They seek to destroy not only peace but those who search for peace. We bear the pain of our losses just as you bear the pain of yours. As we share friendship, we also share grief.

I know citizens of both our countries as well as those of other nations do not understand the meaning of such tragedies. They wonder why there must be such hate. Of course, regrettably there is no easy answer. We can place greater value on our true friends and allies. We can stand more firmly by those principles that give us strength and guide us, and we can remember that some attack us because we symbolize what they do not: hope, promise, the future. Nothing exemplifies this better than the progress of Korea. Korea is proof that people's lives can be better. And I want my presence today to draw attention to a great contrast. I'm talking about the contrast between your economic miracle in the South and their economic failure in the North.

In the early years following World War II, the future of Korea and of all Asia was very much in doubt. Against the hopes of Korea and other new nations for prosperity and freedom stood the legacies of war, poverty, and colonial rule. In the background of this struggle, the great ideological issues of our era were heard: Would the future of the region be democratic or totalitarian? Communism, at that time, seemed to offer rapid industrialization. The notion that the people of the region should govern their own lives seemed to some an impractical and undue luxury. But Americans and the people of Korea shared a different vision of the future.

Then North Korea burst across the border, intent on destroying this country. We were a world weary of war, but we did not hesitate. The United States, as well as other nations of the world came to your aid against the aggression, and tens of thousands of Americans gave their lives in defense of freedom.

As heavy as this price was, the Korean people paid an even heavier one. Civilian deaths mounted to the hundreds of thousands. President Johnson said before this very Assembly, "Who will ever know how many children starved? How many refugees lie in unmarked graves along the roads south? There is hardly a Korean family which did not lose a loved one in the assault from the North."

In 1951, in the midst of the war, General Douglas MacArthur addressed a Joint Session of our Congress. He spoke of you, saying, "The magnificence of the courage and fortitude of the Korean people defies description." As he spoke these words, our Congress interrupted him with applause for you and your people.

After the war, Korean displayed that same fortitude. Korea faced every conceivable difficulty. Cities were in ruins; millions were homeless and without jobs; factories were idle or destroyed; hunger was widespread; the transportation system was dismembered; and the economy was devastated as a result of all these plagues. And what did the Korean people do? You rebuilt your lives, your families, your homes, your towns, your businesses, your country. And today the world speaks of the Korean economic miracle.

[The Korean Economic Miracle]

The progress of the Korean economy is virtually without precedent. With few natural resources other than the intelligence and energy of your people, in one generation you have transformed this country from the devastation of war to the threshold of full development.

Per capita income has risen from about $80 in 1961 to more than 20 times — $1,700 today. Korea has become an industrial power, a major trading nation, and an economic model for developing nations throughout the world. And you have earned the growing respect of the international community. This is recognized in your expanding role as host to numerous international events, including the 1986 Asian games and the 1988 Olympics. . . .

[Korean-American Relations]

The United States knows what you've accomplished here. In the 25 years following the war, America provided almost $5½ billion in economic aid. Today that amounts to less than 6 months' trade between us. That trade is virtually in balance. We are at once Korea's largest market and largest source of supplies. We're a leading source of the investment and technology needed to fuel further development. Korea is our ninth largest trading partner, and our trade is growing.

Korea's rapid development benefited greatly from the free flow of trade which characterized the 1960's and 1970's. Today, in many countries, the call for protectionism is raised. I ask Korea to join with the United States in rejecting those protectionist pressures to ensure that the growth you've enjoyed is not endangered by a maze of restrictive practices.

And just as we work together toward prosperity, we work toward security. Let me make one thing very plain. You are not alone, people of Korea. America is your friend, and we are with you.

This year marks the 30th anniversary of the mutual defense treaty between the United States and the Republic of Korea. The preamble to that treaty affirms the determination of our two countries to oppose aggression and to strengthen peace in the Pacific. We remain firmly committed to that treaty. We seek peace on the peninsula. And that is why United States soldiers serve side by side with Korean soldiers along your demilitarized zone. They symbolize the United States commitment to your security and the security of the region. The United States will stand resolutely by you, just as we stand with our allies in Europe and around the world.

In Korea, especially, we have learned the painful consequences of weakness. I am fully aware of the threats you face only a few miles from here. North Korea is waging a campaign of intimidation. Their country is on a war footing, with some 50 divisions and brigades and 750 combat aircraft. The North has dug tunnels under the demilitarized zone in their preparations for war. They are perched and primed for conflict. They attacked you in Rangoon, and yet, in spite of such constant threats from the North, you have progressed.

Our most heartfelt wish is that one day the vigil will no longer be needed. America shares your belief that confrontation between North and South is not inevitable. Even as we stand with you to resist aggression from the North, we will work with you to strengthen the peace on the peninsula.

Korea today remains the most firmly divided of the states whose division stemmed from World War II. Austrian unity was reestablished peacefully 10 years after the war. Germany remains divided, but some of the pain of that division has been eased by the inner-German agreement of a decade ago. I know the Korean people also long for reconciliation. We believe that it must be for the people of this peninsula to work toward that reconciliation, and we applaud the efforts you've made to begin a dialog. For our part, we would, as we've often stressed, be willing to participate in discussions with North Korea in any forum in which the Republic of Korea was equally represented. The essential way forward is through direct discussions between South and North.

Americans have watched with a mixture of sadness and joy your campaign to reunite families separated by war. We have followed the stories of sisters torn apart at the moment of their parents' deaths; of small children swept away in the tides of war; of people who have grown old not knowing whether their families live or have perished.

I've heard about the program that uses television to reunite families that have been torn apart. Today, I urge North Korea: It is time to participate in this TV reunification program and to allow your people to appear. I would say to them, whatever your political differences with the South, what harm can be done by letting the innocent families from North and South know of their loved ones' health and welfare? Full reunification of families and peoples is a most basic human right.

Until that day arrives, the United States, like the Republic of Korea, accepts the existing reality of two Korean States and supports steps leading to improved relations among those states and their allies.

We have also joined with you over the past 2 years in proposing measures which, if accepted, would reduce the risk of miscalculation and the likelihood of violence on the peninsula. The proposals we have made, such as mutual notification and observation of military exercises, are similar to ones negotiated in Europe and observed by NATO and the Warsaw Pact. These proposals are not intended to address fundamental political issues, but simply to make this heavily armed peninsula a safer place. For we must not forget that on the peninsula today there are several times more men under arms and vastly more firepower than in June of 1950. We will continue to support efforts to reduce tensions and the risks of war.

[Democratic Development]

I have spoken of the need for vigilance and strength to deter aggression and preserve peace and economic progress, but there is another source of strength, and it is well represented in this Assembly. The development of democratic political institutions is the surest means to build the national consensus that is the foundation of true security.

The United States realizes how difficult political development is when, even as we speak, a shell from the North could destroy this Assembly. My nation realizes the complexities of keeping a peace so that the economic miracle can continue to increase the standard of living of your people. The United States welcomes the goals that you have set for political development and increased respect for human rights for democratic practices. We welcome President Chun's farsighted plans for a constitutional transfer of power in 1988. Other measures for further development of Korean political life will be equally important and will have our warm support.

Now, this will not be a simple process because of the ever-present threat from the North. But I wish to assure you once again of America's unwavering support and the high regard of democratic peoples everywhere as you take the bold and necessary steps toward political development.

Over 100 years ago you asked earlier American travelers to make their wishes known. Well, I come today to you with our answer: Our wish is for peace and prosperity and freedom for an old and valued ally. . . .

REAGAN ADMINISTRATION ON REVAMPED CIVIL RIGHTS PANEL

November 30, 1983

The U.S. Commission on Civil Rights was given a reprieve November 30 when President Ronald Reagan signed into law a bill extending its life. The commission had gone out of existence two months earlier when Congress, displeased at the president's attempt to replace three members, refused to pass reauthorization legislation. After heated debate, however, a compromise finally was reached that reauthorized the panel for six years and expanded its membership to eight members from six, four of whom were to be appointed by the president, two by the President pro tempore of the Senate and two by the Speaker of the House of Representatives. But the controversy surrounding the commission and its role in formulating civil rights policy for the administration was not settled by the passage of the bill. Questions about Reagan's commitment to civil rights, which had plagued him since his inauguration, continued.

The original commission was created by the Civil Rights Act of 1957 to serve as a temporary advisory board. It was designed to research civil rights problems and to monitor law enforcement but was given no enforcement authority of its own. The new law did not change those functions.

Disagreement between the commission and the president centered on the commission's perception that the administration lacked a firm commitment to advance civil rights, especially in the area of affirmative action. This policy, backed by the majority of the commission, favored advantages in education, hiring and promotions for minorities and women to make up for years of discrimination. The administration

913

argued that affirmative action meant the use of quotas and created a new class of victim, white males. And the president found some members of the commission too outspoken in their views.

Criticism of Reagan Administration

During 1983 the commission added to its already lengthy list of reports and public statements critical of administration policies. In January, for example, the panel published a statement on incidents of racial and religious bigotry in the United States, noting that there was a "wide-spread perception that the Federal Government is relaxing its enforcement posture in the area of civil rights" and that this perception was leading to an attitude of permissiveness regarding the activities of hate groups. The same month the commission criticized positions the Justice Department had taken in two cases involving the hiring, retention and promotion of minorities. In one case the department had asked the federal appeals court to throw out a court-approved plan for New Orleans that would promote one black police officer for every white officer until the force had equal numbers of black and whites at every level. In Boston, where budget cuts required the firing of some police and fire fighters, the Justice Department defended the seniority system that protected mostly white personnel.

In March the commission charged the administration with a "lack of cooperation" in supplying documents it considered necessary to monitor civil rights enforcement by other government agencies. The commission threatened to subpoena the documents. The commission said in June it was "disappointed and concerned" that Reagan had not named more minorities and women to full-time, high-level positions in the federal government. It also charged the administration with making numerous "efforts to reduce federal civil rights enforcement in education."

During the summer the commission contended that a proposed 13 percent cut in education funds would seriously harm programs for minorities and the handicapped. Chairman Clarence M. Pendleton Jr., a Reagan appointee, endorsed this statement, although he usually disassociated himself from most reports that were highly critical of the administration. In another report the commission found fault with the administration's endorsement of a narrow interpretation of the law barring sex discrimination in schools and colleges receiving federal aid.

In October a New York Times story described a 190-page commission report, not made public, in which the commission said that two years of fiscal austerity and staff reductions had seriously eroded the government's enforcement of civil rights. The report cited what the commission considered noticeable declines in several departments, including Justice, Education, Health and Human Services, Labor and Housing and Urban

Development. The administration defended its record against each charge, saying that civil rights legislation was enforced vigorously.

Firing of Three Commissioners

Reagan in May attempted to replace three Democratic commissioners, Mary F. Berry, Blandina Cardenas Ramirez and Rabbi Murray Saltzman, with three whose views on affirmative action and busing were closer to his. When his nominees had not been approved by the Senate by mid-October, Reagan fired the three commissioners. In an interview November 3 he said, "Honestly, I fired them — first of all it is a presidential commission and they serve at the pleasure of the president. Well, I have to tell you, I wasn't getting much pleasure.... They seemed to be devoting their time to sniping at me...."

Dismissals on the commission, whose members served open-ended terms, were rare. In 1972 Richard Nixon asked the Rev. Theodore Hesburgh, the panel's longtime chairman, to resign. Before the 1983 firings, Reagan removed Arthur S. Flemming, who was chairman when Reagan took office, and nominated Pendleton. Under the new law members served six-year terms and could be removed only for cause.

Direction of Commission

Many in the civil rights community expressed fears that the White House would have too much control over the newly constituted commission. The commission on January 16, 1984, unanimously passed a resolution stating that it "will remain independent of all outside wishes or pressures, whether they come from the White House or any other group." The resolution came in response to newspaper report in which an unidentified White House official was quoted as saying, "Now that we have the Civil Rights Commission on our side, we can make use of them to run some interference for us."

Whether the commission would retain its independence was unclear, but in early 1984 the panel, under the guidance of its new staff director Linda Chavez, appointed by Reagan, seemed to take a decidedly conservative turn. Chavez, like Pendleton and the other conservative members, opposed mandatory busing and affirmative action. In a memorandum to the commission, Chavez expressed the view that social problems could not be solved by civil rights legislation and urged that research on certain topics then under way be stopped.

Following are the texts of statements by President Reagan and the Justice Department on the signing of the bill reconstituting the Commission on Civil Rights, November 30:

REAGAN STATEMENT

I have signed today H.R. 2230, establishing a new Commission on Civil Rights. I believe that the birth of this Commission can serve as another milestone in our long struggle as a nation to assure that individuals are judged on the basis of their abilities, irrespective of race, sex, color, national origin, or handicap.

I take this opportunity to reaffirm this administration's commitment to these ideals, which the civil rights laws of the United States were designed to implement and which it will be the central mission of this Commission to articulate and defend.

The bill I have signed today is, of course, a product of negotiation and compromise. While, as noted, I am pleased that the Commission has been recreated so that it may continue the missions assigned to it, the Department of Justice has raised concerns as to the constitutional implications of certain provisions of this legislation. I have appended a recitation of these reservations.

During the preceding 6 months there has been considerable debate on the past and the future of the Commission on Civil Rights, but all seem to agree that the Commission's best and most productive years were its earlier ones. I believe that it is no coincidence that those years were characterized by open debate and a devotion to the principle of equal treatment under the law. With the bill I have signed today and the quality of appointments that can be made to the Commission, there is cause for confidence that the Commission's best years are yet to come.

JUSTICE DEPARTMENT STATEMENT

Under the terms of H.R. 2230, four members of the Commission will be appointed by the President, two members by the President pro tempore of the Senate, and two members by the Speaker of the House of Representatives. The Commission itself is not placed clearly within any of the three branches of government created by the United States Constitution, and restrictions have been placed upon the power of the President to remove members of the Commission.

Agencies which are inconsistent with the tripartite system of government established by the Framers of our Constitution should not be created. Equally unacceptable are proposals which impermissibly dilute the powers of the President to appoint and remove officers of the United States. The Civil Rights Commission is, however, unique in form and function and should therefore not become a precedent for the creation of similar agencies in the future.

The new appointment procedure created by the Congress has effectively imposed constitutional limitations on the duties that the Commission may perform. The basic purpose of the old Commission on Civil Rights — to investigate, study, appraise, and report on discrimination — would be maintained, and most of its current authorities would remain intact. However, because half of the members of the Commission will be appointed by the Congress, the Constitution does not permit the Commission to exercise responsibilities that may be performed only by "Officers of the United States" who are appointed in accordance with the Appointments Clause of the United States Constitution (Article II, Section 2, clause 2). Therefore, it should be clear that although the Commission will continue to perform investigative and informative functions, it may not exercise enforcement, regulatory, or other executive responsibilities that may be performed only by officers of the United States.

December

JUSTICE DEPARTMENT REPORT ON ENDING OIL FIRMS PROBE

December 7, 1983

The Justice Department December 7 issued a report that officially terminated a six-year investigation of whether four U.S. oil companies had conspired to raise the price of Persian Gulf oil in the mid-1970s. The investigators found little evidence that the corporations had done so. Moreover, because by 1983 the companies' influence over world oil prices had decreased substantially, the issue had become somewhat moot.

In announcing the department's action, William F. Baxter, assistant attorney general for antitrust, said, "I concluded there wasn't anything there that justified the almost inevitable foreign policy costs of pushing this further." The 66-page memorandum also declared, "The investigation has not discovered any remediable violations of the antitrust laws and should be closed."

The protracted antitrust case involved a dispute between the Justice Department and the Saudi Arabian government over obtaining financial documents from the Saudis concerning Aramco, an oil consortium that included Exxon, Mobil, Texaco and Standard Oil of California. The Justice Department's suit, filed in 1977, concerned allegations that the major oil companies, and not the Organization of Petroleum Exporting Countries (OPEC), had been primarily responsible for the quadrupling of world oil prices in 1973-74 through illegal collusion to control prices.

The report said that during the mid-1970s Aramco might have had some incentive to curtail Saudi oil production and thereby raise prices, but that by 1983 there was "little, if any, reason to believe that, under current market conditions, the Aramco partners could exercise market power in the world crude oil market."

The probe, which was launched during a period of spiraling oil price rises, was one of the most intensive U.S. antitrust investigations undertaken in recent years. It involved more than 25 lawyers, economists and other department officials. However, by the late 1970s and early 1980s world oil prices had dropped sharply and were holding relatively stable. The vehement objections of the Saudi government to turning over documents it considered to involve internal affairs further militated against continuing the investigation. "The question always arises as to how much you are willing to pay in terms of diplomatic repercussions, perhaps changing the tone if not the balance of Middle East alignment," Baxter commented to reporters. However, he also said the decision to end the investigation was made "not because of the Saudi government's objection, but because after careful analysis the [Antitrust] Division discerned no analytical or factual basis for pursuing possible antitrust action.'

Reaction to the Justice Department's decision was mixed. A statement by Texaco said it was "gratified" and that it had "scrupulously adhered to the letter and spirit of the United States antitrust laws." Consumer groups criticized the decision. It was "but another example of the [Ronald] Reagan administration's refusal to enforce the nation's antitrust laws," said Edwin Rothschild, assistant director of the Citizen/Labor Energy Coalition.

Meeting in Geneva on the day the department issued the memorandum, the OPEC oil ministers agreed to maintain existing oil price and production levels. Confronting a global oil glut, the majority of oil ministers, led by Saudi Arabia's oil minister, Sheik Ahmed Zaki Yamani, resisted demands of some members to increase prices, arguing that a new price hike would lead them to lose even more customers. It was also hoped that an economic upturn might relieve pressures to cut the cost of oil below the $29 a barrel set by the organization. (Between 1971 and 1981 the price of oil had risen from $2 a barrel to between $35 and $36 a barrel.) (Related stories on OPEC and oil prices, Historic Documents of 1982, p. 979; Historic Documents of 1981, p. 799; Historic Documents of 1980, p. 995; Historic Documents of 1979, p. 251; Historic Documents of 1978, p. 789; Historic Documents of 1976, p. 937; Historic Documents of 1974, p. 221)

> *Following is the summary excerpted from the Justice Department's report, released December 7, 1983, terminating the Antitrust Division's international oil investigation:*

Although I am aware that both you and the Deputy Attorney General are recused in this matter, I thought it appropriate to send to you this factual report on action I have taken. In 1977 the Department instituted a civil antitrust investigation of the activities of the major international oil companies in connection with the supply and price of crude oil produced in the Persian Gulf area. After extensive study and analysis of the evidence it had gathered, the Antitrust Division concluded that the only area of potential antitrust interest lay in the possibility that the firms participating in the Arabian-American Oil Company ("Aramco") joint venture might have the incentive and ability, independent of the Saudi Arabian government, together to limit the production of Saudi crude, and thus to increase world crude prices. In late 1979, the Department issued a second round of civil investigative demands which included requests for documents directed to the Aramco firms, focusing on the Saudi production limitation possibility and designed primarily to update the information previously received. The Saudi Arabian government objected to production of the documents, which, although located in this country, relate to what the Saudi government perceived to be its internal affairs.

When I assumed direction of the Antitrust Division in March of 1981, the International Oil Investigation was thus in a state of suspension. The question was whether to insist upon compliance with the demands that had been issued and, if necessary, to seek judicial enforcement. The answer depended on whether the evidence the Division already had, together with other reliable information about the international oil market available to us, raised any significant possibility that the matters under investigation involved a violation of the antitrust laws. Moreover, because the only conceivable theory of violation that had emerged would, if it could be established at all, afford a basis only for civil, prospective relief, there was the further question of whether such relief made sense and, indeed, whether it could have any positive effect at all in light of the dramatic changes that have occurred and are occurring in the international oil market.

After studying memoranda on these issues from members of the Division staff, including lawyers and economists who have had key responsibility for the matter, I concluded that the investigation should not be pursued. My conclusion was based on the following principal points:

1. There is no evidence of any private agreements regarding crude oil production or prices beyond those in effect within the various oil company consortia operating in individual Persian Gulf countries, nor is there evidence of similar or parallel conduct between consortia that raises antitrust concern.

2. The evidence suggests that between 1974 and 1977, and perhaps until 1979, the Aramco partners may have had the ability, by controlling (within Saudi government-imposed limits) Saudi crude production to exercise market power in the world crude oil market. Such market power, however, was entirely derived from that of the Saudis themselves. If the Aramco partners held such power, therefore, they did so at the sufferance of the Saudi government and presumably exercised it, if at all, in ways that the Saudis regard as consistent with the Saudis' own self-interest. Application of the U.S. antitrust laws in these circumstances would do nothing about Aramco's market power. Assuming that the Saudis behave rationally —

and there is absolutely no reason to suppose that they do not — compelling the Aramco partners to act competitively would not mean that crude oil prices would fall. The Saudi government would only be forced to employ some other mechanism for serving what is, by necessary hypothesis, its self-interest. Even if this were not so as to the period before 1979, it is clearly so now.

3. The evidence does not suggest that the Aramco partners had any similar market power after 1977. Even if they did, however, it was most certainly limited to the ability to affect the world price of oil within a very narrow, if not insignificant, range.

4. There is little, if any, reason to believe that, under current market conditions, the Aramco partners could exercise market power in the world crude oil market. Indeed, even the ability to control Saudi output fully, which the Aramco partners never had, may not be enough in today's market.

In sum, there is no reason to believe that arrangements solely among the Aramco partners either create or facilitate the exercise of market power — an essential element of a violation under either Section 1 or Section 2 of the Sherman Act. Nor is there any reason to believe that prospective antitrust relief would improve world oil market conditions. While it is always possible that a response to the civil investigative demands would have provided evidence of an actionable antitrust violation, such a result would have been serendipitous and unrelated to the antitrust concerns that had led to the demands' issuance. In these circumstances, it appeared that the only reason to insist on compliance with the civil investigative demands was to avoid the inference that otherwise might be drawn that the Department had failed to pursue the matter because of the Saudi government's objections. I believe, however, that although the demands may have been fully proper on the information as it appeared at the time, the information they call for simply is not needed to conclude the investigation responsibly. And while it may be desirable to avoid an inference of bowing to a foreign government's pressure, that is no more a proper basis for insisting on enforcement than it would have been for issuing the demands in the first place.

I reached these conclusions some time ago, and accordingly have not undertaken enforcement of the civil investigative demands. The demands, however, remain extant, and the investigation, as a formal matter, remains open. The investigation, in its initial phases, received great public and congressional attention, and it seemed to me that it should finally be terminated only after the Department had provided a full account of the investigation's history, of the division's analysis of what it learned, and of the reasons I believe that the investigation should now be closed without further action. This memorandum provides that account....

WALESA PEACE PRIZE
ACCEPTANCE ADDRESS
December 11, 1983

Citing his "contribution, made with considerable personal risk, to ensure Polish workers the right to establish their own organizations," the Norwegian Nobel Committee October 5 announced that it would award the 1983 Nobel Peace Prize to Lech Walesa, leader of the Solidarity trade union, which had been outlawed by Poland's communist regime in a brutal crackdown in 1981. In announcing its selection, the committee noted that Walesa had tried to solve his country's problems peacefully, through negotiation and cooperation, and emphasized its view that "a campaign for human rights is a campaign for peace."

Walesa did not attend the awards ceremony, which took place in Oslo, Norway, on December 11. Although Polish authorities assured him that he was free to leave the country, Walesa feared he would not be permitted to return. Walesa's wife, Danuta, accepted the prize and read a short statement from him saying the award confirmed "the vitality and strength" of the trade union movement. Exiled Solidarity leader Bogdan Cywinski then delivered Walesa's Nobel Peace Prize lecture.

Reaction

Predictably, reaction to the Nobel committee's announcement was enthusiastic in the West. President Ronald Reagan called the award a "triumph of moral force over brute force." Labor and political leaders applauded the decision. Spokesmen for the International Labor Organization and the United States' AFL-CIO lauded Walesa's achievements on behalf of all workers. Pope John Paul II praised the "special eloquence" of the award and noted that "in this way are honored the will and the efforts undertaken with the intent of resolving the difficult problems of the workers and society in Poland."

The reaction of Poland's communist government, headed by Gen. Wojciech Jaruzelski, was, not surprisingly, notably cool. Communist authorities jammed radio broadcasts from both Radio Free Europe and Voice of America on October 5, and many Poles learned of the award only from Western journalists seeking reaction. Walesa himself first heard that he had been selected for the prize from a Western television crew while picking mushrooms in the woods outside Gdansk, birthplace of the union movement. State-controlled radio and television services finally broadcast the news in sullen evening programs, along with a critical commentary denouncing the prize as part of "a growing propaganda aggression campaign against Poland and other Socialist countries."

Many Polish citizens, however, seemed pleased that their countryman, a constant thorn in the side of the communist authorities, had been honored for his work with Solidarity. The New York Times *reported that crowds in Warsaw's main railway station burst into applause when the government finally announced the news. Poles interviewed at random by Western journalists seemed to feel that Walesa deserved the Peace Prize and hoped it would not bring him a new round of trouble with the government.*

Appeal for Government-Workers Dialogue

In accepting the prize, Walesa said, "the honor is bestowed not on me personally, but upon Solidarity, upon the people and ideas for which we have fought and shall continue to do so in the spirit of peace and justice." He went on to emphasize the willingness of Solidarity to pursue a dialogue with the Polish authorities to find solutions to the social unrest and economic problems confronting the country. Walesa quoted Pope John Paul II on the workers' right to begin that dialogue: "'...the working man is not a mere tool of production, but he is the subject which throughout the process of production takes precedence over the capital. By the fact of his labor, the man becomes the true master of his workshop, of the process of labor, of the fruits of his toil and of their distribution. He is also ready for sacrifices if he feels that he is a real partner and has a say in the just division of what has been produced by common effort.'" Walesa told of the "frustration, bitterness and the mood of helplessness" that prevailed in Poland because those feelings were absent among Polish workers after the government outlawed Solidarity. (Pope's visit to Poland, p. 577; workers' demands, Historic Documents of 1980, p. 793; imposition of martial law, Historic Documents of 1981, p. 881)

"The dialogue is possible, and we have the right to it," said Walesa.

"...My most ardent desire is that my country will recapture its historic opportunity for a peaceful evolution, and that Poland will prove to the world that even the most complex situations can be solved by a dialogue and not by force." He appealed to the Polish government to release imprisoned Solidarity members and cancel the scheduled trials of 11 union activists. "All those already sentenced or still awaiting trials for their union activities or their convictions should return to their homes and be allowed to live and work in their country," he said.

Need for Poland's Independence

Referring to the Soviet Union's heavy-handed pressure to quash the Polish trade-union movement, and echoing sentiments expressed by the pope during his June visit to Poland, Walesa said, "As a nation we have the right to decide our own affairs, to mold our own future. This does not pose any danger to anybody. Our nation is fully aware of the responsibility for its own fate in the complicated situation of the contemporary world...."

Shortly before the awards ceremony in Oslo, Walesa had appealed to Western nations to end the economic sanctions against his country. In his lecture, Walesa renewed that request, saying that Poland was "in the grips of [a] major economic crisis" that was "causing dramatic consequences for the very existence of Polish families.... Poland ought to be helped and deserves help."

Upon Danuta Walesa's return from Oslo with her husband's award, the couple traveled to Poland's most revered icon, the Black Madonna of Czestochowa, where the Peace Prize would be enshrined.

> Following are excerpts from Polish Solidarity leader Lech Walesa's address on receiving the Nobel Peace Prize, delivered in Oslo, Norway, December 11, 1983, by exiled Solidarity leader Bogden Cywinski, as published in the December 12 New York Times:

Ladies and gentlemen:

Addressing you, as the winner of the 1983 Nobel Peace Prize, is a Polish worker from the Gdansk shipyard, one of the founders of the independent trade union movement in Poland.

It would be the simplest thing for me to say that I am not worthy of the great distinction. Yet, when I recall the hour when the news of the prize spread throughout my country, the hour of rising emotions and universal joy of the people who felt that they have a moral and spiritual share in the award, I am obligated to say that I regard it as a sign of recognition that the movement to which I gave all my strength had served well the community of men.

I accept the award with my deepest respect for its meaning and significance, and, at the same time, I am conscious that the honor is bestowed not on me personally, but upon Solidarity, upon the people and the ideas for which we have fought and shall continue to do so in the spirit of peace and justice. And there is nothing I desire more than that the granting of the award should help the cause of peace and justice in my country and the world over.

My first words which I address to you, and through you to all people, are those which I have known since my childhood days: peace to men of good will — all and everywhere, in the north and south, east and west.

The Polish Hope

I belong to a nation which over the past centuries has experienced many hardships and reverses. The world reacted with silence or with mere sympathy when Polish frontiers were crossed by invading armies and the sovereign state had to succumb to brutal force. Our national history has so often filled us with bitterness and the feeling of helplessness. But this was, above all, a great lesson in hope.

Thanking you for the award I would like, first of all, to express my gratitude and my belief that it serves to enhance the Polish hope. The hope of the nation which throughout the 19th century had not for a moment reconciled itself with the loss of independence, and fighting for its own freedom, fought at the same time for the freedom of other nations. The hope whose elations and downfalls during the past 40 years, i.e., the span of my own life, have been marked by the memorable and dramatic dates: 1944, 1956, 1970, 1976, 1980.

And if I permit myself at this juncture and on this occasion to mention my own life, it is because I believe that the prize had been granted to me as to one of many.

The Ruins and Ashes

My youth passed at the time of the country's reconstruction from the ruins and ashes of the war in which my nation never bowed to the enemy, paying the highest price in the struggle.

I belong to the generation of workers who, born in the villages and hamlets of rural Poland, had the opportunity to acquire education and find employment in industry, becoming in the course conscious of their rights and importance in society. Those were the years of awakening aspirations of workers and peasants, but also years of many wrongs, degradations and lost illusions.

I was barely 13 years old when, in June 1956, the desperate struggle of the workers of Poznan for bread and freedom was suppressed in blood. Thirteen also was the boy — Romek Strzalkowski — who was killed in the struggle.

It was the Solidarity union which 25 years later demanded that tribute be paid to his memory. In December 1970, when workers' protest demonstrations engulfed the towns of the Baltic coast, I was a worker in the Gdansk shipyard and one of the organizers of the strike. The memory of my fellow workers who then lost their lives, the bitter memory of violence and despair, has become for me a lesson never to be forgotten.

Worker's Rights and Dignity

A few years later, in June 1976, the strike of the workers at Ursus and Radom was a new experience which not only strengthened my belief in the justness of the working people's demands and aspirations but also has indicated the urgent need for their solidarity. This conviction brought me, in the summer of 1978, to the free trade union — formed by a group of courageous and dedicated people who came out in the defense of the workers' rights and dignity.

In July and August of 1980 a wave of strikes swept through Poland. The issue at stake was then something much bigger than only material conditions of existence. My road of life had, at the time of the struggle, brought me back to that shipyard in Gdansk. The whole country joined forces with the workers of Gdansk and Szczecin. The agreements of Gdansk, Szczecin and Jastrzebie eventually were signed and the Solidarity union thus came into being.

The great Polish strikes of which I have just spoken were events of a special nature. Their character was determined on the one hand by the menacing circumstances in which they were held and, on the other, by their objectives. The Polish workers who participated in the strike actions in fact represented the nation.

When I recall my own path of life I cannot but speak of the violence, hatred and lies. A lesson drawn from such experiences, however, was that we can effectively oppose violence only if we ourselves do not resort to it....

Lying at the root of the social agreements of 1980 are the courage, sense of responsibility and Solidarity of the working people. Both sides then recognized that an accord must be reached if bloodshed was to be prevented. The agreement then signed has been and shall remain the model and the only method to follow, the only one that gives a chance of finding a middle course between the use of force and a hopeless struggle.

Our firm conviction that ours is a peaceful way to attain our goals gave us the strength and the awareness of the limits beyond which we must not go. What until then seemed impossible to achieve has become a fact of life. We have won the right to organize in trade unions independent from the authorities, founded and shaped by the working people themselves.

Our union — the Solidarity — has grown into a powerful movement for social and moral liberation. The people, freed from the bondage of fear and apathy, called for reforms and improvements. We fought a difficult struggle for our existence. That was and still is a great opportunity for the whole country. I think that it marked also the road to be taken by the authorities, if they thought of a state governed in cooperation and participation of all citizens.

Solidarity, as a trade union movement, did not reach for power, nor did it turn against the established constitutional order. During the 15 months of Solidarity's legal existence nobody was killed or wounded as a result of its activities.

Our movement expanded by leaps and bounds. But we were propelled to conduct an uninterrupted struggle for our rights and freedom of activity while at the same time imposing upon ourselves unavoidable self-limitations.

The program of our movement stems from the fundamental moral laws and order. The sole and basic source of our strength is the solidarity of workers, peasants and intelligentsia, the solidarity of the nation, the solidarity of people who seek to live in dignity, truth and in harmony with their consciences.

Let the veil of silence fall presently over what happened afterwards. Silence, too, can speak out.

Poles Not Subjugated

One thing, however, must be said here and now on this solemn occasion: The Polish people have not been subjugated, nor have they chosen the road of violence and fratricidal bloodshed.

We shall not yield to violence. We shall not be deprived of union freedoms. We shall never agree to sending people to prison for their convictions. The gates of prisons must be thrown open and persons sentenced for defending union and civil rights must be set free.

The announced trials of 11 leading members of our movement must never be held. All those already sentenced or still awaiting trials for their union activities or their convictions should return to their homes and be allowed to live and work in their country.

The defense of our right and our dignity, as well as efforts never to let ourselves be overcome by the feeling of hatred — this is the road we have chosen.

The Polish experience, which the Nobel Peace Prize has put into the limelight, has been a difficult, a dramatic one. Yet I believe that it looks to the future. The things that have taken place in human conscience and reshaped human attitude cannot be obliterated or destroyed. They exist and will remain.

We are the heirs of those national aspirations, thanks to which our people could never be made into an inert mass with no will of their own. We want to live with the belief that law means law and justice means justice, that our toil has a meaning and is not wasted, that our culture grows and develops freedom.

As a nation we have the right to decide our own affairs, to mold our own future. This does not pose any danger to anybody. Our nation is fully aware of the responsibility for its own fate in the complicated situation of the contemporary world.

Despite everything that has been going on in my country during the past two years, I remain convinced that we have no alternative but to come to an agreement, and that the difficult problems which Poland is now facing can be resolved only through a real dialogue between state authorities and the people.

During his last visit to the land of his fathers, Pope John Paul II had this to say on this point:

"Why do the working people of Poland, and everywhere else for that matter, have the right to such a dialogue? It is because the working man is not a mere tool of production, but he is the subject which throughout the process of production takes precedence over the capital. By the fact of his labor, the man becomes the true master of his workshop, of the process of labor, of the fruits of his toil and of their distribution. He is also ready for sacrifices if he feels that he is a real partner and has a say in the just division of what has been produced by common effort."

It is, however, precisely this feeling that we lack. It is hardly possible to build anything if frustration, bitterness and the mood of helplessness prevail.

He who once became aware of the power of Solidarity and who breathed the air of freedom will not be crushed. The dialogue is possible, and we have the right to it. The wall raised by the course of events must not become an insurmountable obstacle. My most ardent desire is that my country will recapture its historic opportunity for a peaceful evolution, and that Poland will prove to the world that even the most complex situations can be solved by a dialogue and not by force.

We are ready for the dialogue. We are also prepared, at any time, to put our reasons and demands to the judgment of the people. We have no doubts as to what verdict would be returned.

I think that all nations of the world have the right to live in dignity. I believe that, sooner or later, the rights of individuals, of families and of entire communities will be respected in every corner of the world.

Respect for civil and human rights in Poland and for our national identity is in the best interests of all Europe. For in the interest of Europe is a peaceful Poland, and the Polish aspirations to freedom will never be stifled. The dialogue in Poland is the only way to achieving internal peace, and that is why it is also an indispensable element of peace in Europe.

I realize that the strivings of the Polish people gave rise, and still do so, to feelings of understanding and solidarity all over the world. Allow me from this place to express my most profound thanks to all those who help Poland and the Poles. May I also voice my desire that our wish for dialogue and for respect of human rights in Poland should be strengthened by a positive thought.

My country is in the grips of a major economic crisis. This is causing dramatic consequences for the very existence of Polish families. A permanent economic crisis in Poland also may have serious repercussions for Europe.

Thus, Poland ought to be helped and deserves help.

I am looking at the present-day world with the eyes of a worker — a worker who belongs to a nation so tragically experienced by the war. I most sincerely wish that the world in which we live be free from the threat of a nuclear holocaust and from the ruinous arms race. It is my cherished desire that peace be not separated from freedom, which is the right of every nation. This I desire, and for this I pray.

May I repeat that the fundamental necessity in Poland is now understanding and dialogue. I think that the same applies to the whole world; we should go on talking, we must not close any doors or do anything that would block the road to an understanding. And we must remember that only a peace built on the foundations of justice and moral order can be a lasting one.

In many parts of the world the people are searching for a solution which would link the two basic values: peace and justice. The two are like bread and salt for mankind. Every nation and every community have the inalienable right to these values. No conflicts can be resolved without doing everything possible to follow that road. Our times require that these aspirations which exist the world over must be recognized.

Our efforts and harsh experiences have revealed to the world the value of human solidarity. Accepting this honorable distinction, I am thinking of those with whom I am linked by the spirit of Solidarity:

● First of all, of those who in the struggle for the workers' and civil rights in my country paid the highest price — the price of life;

● Of my friends who paid for the defense of Solidarity with the loss of freedom, who were sentenced to prison terms or are awaiting trial;

● Of my countrymen who saw in the Solidarity movement the fulfillment of their aspirations as workers and citizens, who are subjected to humiliations and ready for sacrifices, who have learned to link courage with wisdom and who persist in loyalty to the cause we have embarked upon;

● Of all those who are struggling throughout the world for workers' and union rights, for the dignity of the working man, for human rights.

Inscribed on the monument erected at the entrance to the Gdansk shipyard in memory of those who died in December 1970 are the words of the psalm: "The Lord will give power to his people, the Lord will give his people the blessing of peace."

Let these words be our message of brotherhood and hope.

We have noted the importance of the yen-dollar exchange rate, of free and open capital markets in each country. We stress the need for closer economic consultations between the two governments. A ministerial-level working group is being set up to monitor each side's progress in carrying out the agreed-upon actions to improve the yen-dollar exchange rate.

Our mutual commitment toward specific steps to achieve open capital markets will allow the yen to reflect more fully Japan's underlying political stability and economic strength as the second largest economy in the free world. In addition, we've agreed to instruct our economic sub-Cabinet members to form a committee to promote mutual investments.

Progress must come one step at a time, but Japan and America have begun taking those steps together. I've been heartened that beginning with our first meeting last January, continuing with the Williamsburg summit, and now again during our visit this week, Prime Minister Nakasone and I have agreed that our two great democracies share special responsibilities to each other and to the world. Let us continue to go forward, building on our progress step by step. We must set milestones to monitor the success of our agenda for progress and to assure the followthrough that is essential. And I will be discussing this matter in more detail with the Prime Minister tomorrow.

This visit has strengthened the bonds of friendship between our two great nations. We are now better prepared to work together as partners to build a more peaceful and prosperous future at home and throughout the world. We know what needs to be done; we know how it must be done. Let us have the faith to believe in each other, the courage to get on with the job, and the determination to see it through.

Thank you very much.

REAGAN ADDRESS TO THE JAPANESE DIET

Mr. Speaker, Mr. President, Mr. Prime Minister, distinguished Members of the Diet:

It is with great honor and respect that I come before you today, the first American President ever to address the Japanese Diet. . . .

Yes, we are 5,000 miles apart; yes, we are distinctly different in customs, language, and tradition; and yes, we are often competitors in the world markets. But I believe the people represented by this proud parliament and by my own United States Congress are of one heart in their devotion to the principles of our free societies. . . .

America and Japan speak with different tongues, but both converse, worship, and work with the language of freedom. We defend the right to voice our views, to speak words of dissent without being afraid, and to seek inner peace through communion with our God. . . .

Our two countries are far from perfect. But in this imperfect and dangerous world, the United States and Japan represent the deepest

REPORTS ON TERROR BOMBING OF U.S. MARINES IN BEIRUT

December 19 and 28, 1983

A truck loaded with explosives crashed into the Marine Corps head-quarters in Beirut, Lebanon, early October 23, killing 241 U.S. service-men. The heavy loss of American lives in the suicide terrorist attack exceeded the casualties produced by any single action of the Vietnam War. A report on the disaster issued December 19 by a House subcommit-tee and another published December 28 by a special Defense Department commission severely criticized security at the Marine compound.

The Marines were in Lebanon as part of a multinational force that included American, French, British and Italian troops. It was hoped that the presence of the force would discourage further military action and violence in the war-torn country. At almost the same time that the U.S. Marine compound was attacked, another TNT-laden truck blew up at a French barracks only two miles away. Forty-seven French troops were killed in that terrorist act.

The attack on the Marine compound presented Ronald Reagan's administration with a sharp challenge to its Middle East policy. Al-though the president October 24 said he would not withdraw the Marines so long as the American mission in Lebanon was incomplete, the administration reversed its policy February 7, 1984, announcing that most of the Marines would be redeployed to ships offshore. The an-nouncement came in the midst of a sharply deteriorating situation in Lebanon and the collapse of the government of Amin Gemayel.

Both the report of the House Armed Services Subcommittee on Investigations and the report of the special Defense Department commis-

sion pointed to critical failures on the part of Marine commanders in Beirut and officers in the military chain of command above them. But courts-martial apparently were ruled out when Reagan December 27 said, "If there is to be blame, it properly rests here in this office and with this president."

The Attack

Occurring at 6:22 a.m. on a Sunday morning, the attack on the Marine headquarters building, which also served as a barracks, found most of the servicemen inside the structure, sleeping. The bombing was carried out by a single suicide-bent terrorist at the wheel of a yellow Mercedes truck. After running over a barbed wire obstacle, the truck went through an open gate, passed around one sewer pipe obstacle and between two others, flattened a sandbagged booth used by the sergeant-of-the-guard, rammed into the interior lobby of the building, and detonated. The Defense Department report said that the truck "passed between two Marine guard posts without being engaged in fire."

In the days after the attack, Western diplomats said that intelligence assessments pointed to a militant pro-Iranian Shiite Moslem group known both as Islamic Amal and as the Party of God. A New York Times *report October 29 said the Reagan administration assumed the Iranian government played a key role in the bombing.*

Middle East Terror

The attack on the Marine compound at the Beirut International Airport was the most devastating of a rising number of deadly terrorist acts directed against the United States in the Middle East. Leading intelligence officials believed that the United States had become the primary target for terrorists in the region.

On April 18 explosives carried in a pickup truck blew up outside the U.S. Embassy in Beirut. In that explosion, 63 people including 17 Americans were killed. Another truck loaded with explosives smashed December 12 into the American Embassy and four other places in Kuwait, killing five persons. The blasts in Kuwait also were attributed by Western intelligence officers to the Islamic Amal.

In the wake of the Kuwait bombings, concrete barriers were put in place along some of the sidewalks at the White House and in front of entrances to the State Department in Washington, D.C.

House Subcommittee

The report of the House Armed Services Investigations Subcommittee was based on hearings held both in Washington, D.C., and aboard the Iwo

Jima *in waters off Beirut. The report faulted the Marine commander in Beirut, Col. Timothy J. Geraghty, for "misjudgment with the most serious consequences." But it said that Geraghty was not guilty of "dereliction of duty." The subcommittee also criticized Geraghty's superiors in the chain of command "for failing to exercise sufficient oversight." It said, "The subcommittee is startled that higher level commanders did not reevaluate the security posture in light of increasing vulnerability in the weeks before the bombing."*

The report also disputed aspects of the description of events related to the bombing presented by Gen. Paul X. Kelley, the Marine Corps commandant, in his testimony.

Pentagon Commission

Of perhaps even greater impact than the report of the House subcommittee was the 141-page report of a special five-member commission appointed by Secretary of Defense Caspar W. Weinberger. The commission's chairman was retired admiral Robert L. J. Long, and the commission came to be known as the Long Commission.

The report blamed the Marine commanders in Beirut, Col. Geraghty and his subordinate, Lt. Col. Howard L. Gerlach, for inadequate security at the compound and for the concentration of Marines in a single building. The two officers, the commission said, shared "the responsibility for the catastrophic losses." Like the House report, however, the Long Commission report also faulted officers in the chain of command above the Marine commanders in Beirut. The report referred to the officers by position but not by name. It also suggested that the administration's decision to expand U.S. military involvement in Lebanon might have been made without "clear recognition" that it "greatly increased the risk to, and adversely impacted upon, the security" of the Marines in Beirut.

> *Following is the text of the summary of findings and conclusions from the December 19, 1983, report entitled "The Adequacy of U.S. Marine Corps Security in Beirut," by the Investigations Subcommittee of the House Armed Services Committee and excerpts from the December 28, 1983, "Report of the Department of Defense Commission on the Beirut International Airport Terrorist Act, October 23, 1983":*

SUMMARY OF HOUSE REPORT

1. There were inadequate security measures taken to protect the Marine Unit from the full spectrum of threats. The truck bomb that transited and exploded in the Battalion Landing Team (BLT) headquarters building,

with the loss of 240 lives, rolled through a concertina wire fence that was primarily a personnel barrier; it went between guard posts where the guards had their guns unloaded and had no opportunity to fire before the truck got past them; it went through a gate that was generally left open and was almost assuredly open that morning; iron pipes in front of the building were not large enough to stop the vehicle and had an opening the vehicle could drive through. It is by no means certain that defenses protecting the BLT building would have been adequate to repel a car bomb attack.

2. While the subcommittee fully recognizes it is easy to be wise after the fact, it finds that the commander of the Marine Amphibious Unit (MAU) made serious errors in judgment in failing to provide better protection for his troops within the command authority available to him. As the commander, he bears the principal responsibility for the inadequacy of the security posture at the BLT headquarters.

3. The Amphibious Task Force commander, as the commanding officer of the amphibious sea and land forces in the area, shares responsibility for the inadequate security posture of the MAU.

4. The subcommittee found no evidence of the military chain of command or the diplomatic and political leadership denying any requests for material or assistance with regard to security of the Marine detachment at Beirut International Airport or attempting to influence the deployment and actions of the battalion for political/diplomatic reasons in a way that would limit the security precautions the unit might take.

5. While the higher elements of the chain of command did not deny any requests for support from the MAU, the subcommittee concludes that these higher command elements failed to exercise sufficient oversight of the MAU. Visits by higher level commanders were commonly familiarization briefings and appeared not to provide positive oversight, such as directions to improve security. The change in security effective with the guidance of higher headquarters since the bombing is indicative of what that higher command influence might have done before the bombing. The subcommittee is particularly concerned that the higher level commanders did not reevaluate the MAU security posture in light of increasing vulnerability of the unit in the weeks before the bombing.

6. While of necessity calling attention to the failures of local commanders within their area of responsibility, the subcommittee must also call to account the higher policy-making authority that adopted and continued a policy that placed military units in a deployment where protection was inevitably inadequate.

7. Both the Marine ground commanders who testified, consistent with the view of the Marine Corps leadership, interpreted the political/ diplomatic nature of the mission to place high priority on visibility and emphasized visibility to the extent of allowing greater than necessary security risks. The subcommittee was particularly distressed to find that the security of the MAU was less than that provided at the interim U.S. embassy in Beirut.

8. The individuals attached to the MAU performed their duties with skill, courage and extraordinary fortitude. The subcommittee believes these individual Marines are worthy of high commendation for outstanding performance under extremely adverse circumstances. Despite the fact that these are our most-ready fighters, they are functioning well in a role that is more political than military.

9. The MAU in Lebanon did not receive adequate intelligence support dealing with terrorism. Serious intelligence inadequacies had a direct effect on the capability of the unit to defend itself against the full spectrum of threat. The Marines did not possess adequate capability to analyze the massive amount of data provided them. The chain of command should have provided a special intelligence officer, with expertise in terrorism, capable of assembling all-source intelligence in a usable form for the commander.

Notwithstanding the inadequacy of intelligence support, the subcommittee believes the Marine command erred in failing to consider the possibility of a large bomb-laden truck as a significant threat while it was receiving information on, and attempting to be prepared for, numerous car bomb threats. The failure is particularly inexplicable in view of numerous other threats considered (such as bomb-laden speedboats or airborne kamikaze-type planes that might attack the fleet) and in view of the fact that an intelligence survey in the summer of 1983 recommended that trucks be visually inspected for explosive devices.

10. The information, complete with diagrams, provided by the Marine Corps in Beirut four days after the explosion, and the initial testimony given to the Armed Services Committee by the Marine Corps Commandant and other Marine Corps and administration witnesses eight days after the explosion, was found by the subcommittee to be often inaccurate, erroneous and misleading. While not intentionally misleading, this testimony hindered the subcommittee and delayed its inquiry. Further, this first explanation provided the Congress and the American people thus presented a misleading picture of what actually took place on October 23.

11. The rejection of an Israeli offer for medical assistance on October 23 was a decision made solely by the commander of Task Force 61, the Amphibious Task Force that include[s] the MAU and naval amphibious units. The subcommittee finds that the decision was based solely on operational and medical considerations and has found no evidence of political considerations. The subcommittee found no evidence that the death of any U.S. personnel could be attributed to the matter of providing medical evacuation and medical care.

The message offering assistance to the Task Force commander did not come to his attention until several hours after the explosion and after he had made decisions regarding medical evacuation and had aircraft on the way that had been requested hours earlier. When the Task Force commander needed body bags he had no hesitancy in requesting them from Israel and they were supplied. The subcommittee commends the Task Force commander for his decision and also for the manner in which the medical evacuation was carried out.

12. Most witnesses insisted that the policy in the Middle East and the mission of the Marines has [sic] not changed. But between objectives, policy, mission and conditions — something has changed. The subcommittee urges in the strongest terms that the administration review the policy in Lebanon from the standpoint of how the Marine mission fits into that policy to determine if continued deployment of the Marine unit, as part of the Multinational Force (MNF) of French, Italian, British and American units, is justified.

Sustained deployment of personnel in the situation of almost certain further casualties should only be undertaken if the policy objectives are visible, profoundly important and clearly obtainable. Failure of the administration to adequately reexamine its policy and relate it to present conditions will only mean that such reexamination will have to be done by Congress.

13. Diplomatic pressure of the most serious sort must be brought to bear on the [Amin] Gemayal government to reach an accord with the warring factions. The solution to Lebanon's problems will only be found at the bargaining table. We must not in any way encourage the perception that a solution can be found on the battlefield with the participation of U.S. armed forces.

DEFENSE DEPARTMENT REPORT

Executive Summary

INTRODUCTION

The *DOD Commission on Beirut International Airport (BIA) Terrorist Act of 23 October 1983* was convened by the Secretary of Defense on 7 November 1983 to conduct an independent inquiry into the 23 October 1983 terrorist attack on the Marine Battalion Landing Team (BLT) Headquarters in Beirut, Lebanon. The Commission examined the mission of the U.S. Marines assigned to the Multinational Force, the rules of engagement governing their conduct, the responsiveness of the chain of command, the intelligence support, the security measures in place before and after the attack, the attack itself, and the adequacy of casualty handling procedures.

The commission traveled to Lebanon, Israel, Spain, Germany, Italy and the United Kingdom, interviewed over 125 witnesses ranging from national policy makers to Lebanese Armed Forces privates, and reviewed extensive documentation from Washington agencies, including the Department of State, Central Intelligence Agency, National Security Council and the Federal Bureau of Investigation, as well as all echelons of the operational chain of command and certain elements of the Department of the Navy administrative chain of command.

The Commission focused on the security of the U.S. contingent of the

Multinational Force through 30 November 1983. Although briefed on some security aspects of other U.S. military elements in Lebanon, the Commission came to no definitive conclusions or recommendations as to those elements.

The Commission was composed of Admiral Robert L. J. Long, USN, (Ret), Chairman; the Honorable Robert J. Murray; Lieutenant General Lawrence F. Snowden, USMC, (Ret); Lieutenant General Eugene F. Tighe, Jr., USAF, (Ret); and Lieutenant General Joseph T. Palastra, Jr., USA.

BACKGROUND

U.S. military forces were inserted into Lebanon on 29 September 1982 as part of a Multinational Force composed of U.S., French, Italian and, somewhat later, British Forces. The mission of the U.S. contingent of the Multinational Force (USMNF) was to establish an environment that would facilitate the withdrawal of foreign military forces from Lebanon and to assist the Lebanese Government and the Lebanese Armed Forces (LAF) in establishing sovereignty and authority over the Beirut area. Initially, the USMNF was warmly welcomed by the local populace. The environment was essentially benign and continued that way into the spring of 1983. The operation was intended to be of short duration.

The destruction of the U.S. Embassy in Beirut on 18 April 1983 was indicative of the extent of the deterioration of the political/military situation in Lebanon that had occurred since the arrival of the USMNF. By August 1983, the LAF were engaged in direct conflict with factional militias and USMNF positions at Beirut International Airport began receiving hostile fire. Attacks against the Multinational Force in the form of car bombs and sniper fire increased in frequency. By September, the LAF were locked in combat for control of the high ground overlooking Beirut International Airport and U.S. Naval gunfire was used in support of the LAF at Suq-Al-Gharb after determination by the National Security Council that LAF retention of Suq-Al-Gharb was essential to the security of USMNF positions at Beirut International Airport.

Intelligence support for the USMNF provided a broad spectrum of coverage of possible threats. Between May and November 1983, over 100 intelligence reports warning of terrorist car bomb attacks were received by the USMNF. Those warnings provided little specific information on how and when a threat might be carried out. From August 1983 to the 23 October attack, the USMNF was virtually flooded with terrorist attack warnings.

On October [23] 1983, a large truck laden with the explosive equivalent of over 12,000 pounds of TNT crashed through the perimeter of the USMNF compound at Beirut International Airport, penetrated the Battalion Landing Team Headquarters building and detonated. The force of the explosion destroyed the building, resulting in the deaths of 241 U.S. military personnel.

The Federal Bureau of Investigation (FBI) Forensic Laboratory described the terrorist bomb as the largest conventional blast ever seen by the FBI's forensic explosive experts. Based upon the FBI analysis of the bomb that destroyed the U.S. Embassy on 18 April 1983, and the FBI preliminary findings on the bomb used on 23 October 1983, the Commission believes that the explosive equivalent of the latter device was of such magnitude that major damage to the Battalion Landing Team Headquarters building and significant casualties would probably have resulted even if the terrorist truck had not penetrated the USMNF defensive perimeter but had detonated in the roadway some 330 feet from the building.

SUMMARY OF GENERAL OBSERVATIONS

Terrorism

The Commission believes that the most important message it can bring to the Secretary of Defense is that the 23 October 1983 attack on the Marine Battalion Landing Team Headquarters in Beirut was tantamount to an act of war using the medium of terrorism. Terrorist warfare, sponsored by sovereign states or organized political entities to achieve political objectives, is a threat to the United States that is increasing at an alarming rate. The 23 October catastrophe underscores the fact that terrorist warfare can have significant political impact and demonstrates that the United States, and specifically the Department of Defense, is inadequately prepared to deal with this threat. Much needs to be done, on an urgent basis, to prepare U.S. military forces to defend against and counter terrorist warfare.

Performance of the USMNF

The USMNF was assigned the unique and difficult task of maintaining a peaceful presence in an increasingly hostile environment. United States military personnel assigned or attached to the USMNF performed superbly, incurring great personal risk to accomplish their assigned tasks. In the aftermath of the attack of 23 October 1983, U.S. military personnel performed selfless and often heroic acts to assist in the extraction of their wounded and dead comrades from the rubble and to evacuate the injured. The Commission has the highest admiration for the manner in which U.S. military personnel responded to this catastrophe.

Security following the 23 October 1983 Attack

The security posture of the USMNF subsequent to the 23 October 1983 attack was examined closely by the Commission. A series of actions was initiated by the chain of command to enhance the security of the USMNF, and reduce the vulnerability of the USMNF to further catastrophic losses. However, the security measures implemented or planned for implementation as of 30 November 1983 were not adequate to prevent continuing significant attrition of USMNF personnel.

Intelligence Support

Even the best of intelligence will not guarantee the security of any military position. However, specific data on the terrorist threats to the USMNF, data which could best be provided by carefully trained intelligence agents, could have enabled the USMNF Commander to better prepare his force and facilities to blunt the effectiveness of a suicidal vehicle attack of great explosive force.

The USMNF commander did not have effective U.S. Human Intelligence (HUMINT) support. The paucity of U.S. controlled HUMINT is partly due to U.S. policy decisions to reduce HUMINT collection worldwide. The U.S. has a HUMINT capability commensurate with the resources and time that has been spent to acquire it. The lesson of Beirut is that we must have better HUMINT to support military planning and operations. We see here a critical repetition of a long line of similar lessons learned during crisis situations in many other parts of the world. . . .

Accountability

The Commission holds the view that military commanders are responsible for the performance of their subordinates. The commander can delegate some or all of his authority to his subordinates, but he cannot delegate his responsibility for the performance of the forces he commands. In that sense, the responsibility of military command is absolute. This view of command authority and responsibility guided the Commission in its analysis of the effectiveness of the exercise of command authority and responsibility of the chain of command charged with the security and performance of the USMNF.

The Commission found that the combination of a large volume of unfulfilled threat warnings and perceived and real pressure to accomplish a unique and difficult mission contributed significantly to the decisions of the Marine Amphibious Unit (MAU) and Battalion Landing Team (BLT) Commanders regarding the security of their force. Nevertheless, the Commission found that the security measures in effect in the MAU compound were neither commensurate with the increasing level of threat confronting the USMNF nor sufficient to preclude catastrophic losses such as those that were suffered on the morning of 23 October 1983. The Commission further found that while it may have appeared to be an appropriate response to the indirect fire being received, the decision to billet approximately one-quarter of the BLT in a single structure contributed to the catastrophic loss of life.

The Commission found that the BLT Commander must take responsibility for the concentration of approximately 350 members of his command in the BLT Headquarters building, thereby providing a lucrative target for attack. Further, the BLT Commander modified prescribed alert procedures, thereby degrading security of the compound.

The Commission also found that the MAU Commander shares the responsibility for the catastrophic losses in that he condoned the concentration of personnel in the BLT Headquarters building, concurred in the relaxation of prescribed alert procedures, and emphasized safety over security in directing that sentries on Posts 4, 5, 6, and 7 would not load

The Commission found further that the USCINCEUR [Commander in Chief, U.S. Forces Europe] operational chain of command shares in the responsibility for the events of 23 October 1983.

Having reached the foregoing conclusions, the Commission further notes that although it found the entire USCINCEUR chain of command, down to and including the BLT Commander, to be at fault, it also found that there was a series of circumstances beyond the control of these commanders that influenced their judgement and their actions relating to the security of the USMNF....

Background

I. LEBANON OVERVIEW

A. Geography and History

Lebanon, a country approximately the size of Connecticut, contains three million people, seventeen officially recognized religious sects, two foreign armies of occupation, four national contingents of a multinational force, seven national contributors to a United Nations peace-keeping force, and some two dozen extralegal militias. Over 100,000 people have been killed in hostilities in Lebanon over the past eight years, including the 242 U.S. military personnel that died as a result of the terrorist attack on 23 October 1983. It is a country beset with virtually every unresolved dispute afflicting the peoples of the Middle East. Lebanon has become a battleground where armed Lebanese factions simultaneously manipulate and are manipulated by the foreign forces surrounding them. If Syrians and Iraqis wish to kill one another, they do so in Lebanon. If Israelis and Palestinians wish to fight over the land they both claim, they do so in Lebanon. If terrorists of any political persuasion wish to kill and maim American citizens, it is convenient for them to do so in Lebanon. In a country where criminals involved in indiscriminate killing, armed robbery, extortion, and kidnapping issue political manifestos and hold press conferences, there has been no shortage of indigenous surrogates willing to do the bidding of foreign governments seeking to exploit the opportunities presented by anarchy in Lebanon.

Yet a picture of Lebanon painted in these grim colors alone would not be complete. Lebanese of all religions have emigrated to countries as widely separated as the United States, Brazil, Australia, and the Ivory Coast, where they have enriched the arts, sciences, and economies of their adopted nations. Lebanon has, notwithstanding the events of the past eight years, kept alive the principle and practice of academic freedom in such institutions as American University Beirut and Saint Joseph University. No one who visits Lebanon can resist admiring the dignity and resiliency of the Lebanese people and their determination to survive.

There is no sense of national identity that unites all Lebanese or even a majority of the citizenry. What it means to be Lebanese is often interpreted in radically different ways by, for instance, a Sunni Muslim living in Tripoli, a Maronite Christian from Brummana, a Greek Orthodox Christian from Beirut, a Druze from Kafr Nabrakh, or a Shiite Muslim from Nabatiyah. This is because the Lebanon of antiquity was Mount Lebanon, the highland chain running north-south through the center of the country, where Maronite Catholicism had over 1,000 years of relative isolation to develop its own national identity. In 1920, France, which acquired part of the Levant from the defeated Ottoman Empire, added non-Maronite territory to Mount Lebanon in order to create Greater Lebanon, a new state in which Maronites comprised but 30 percent of the population rather than the 70 percent of Mount Lebanon that they had previously constituted.

B. Religious and Political Factions

Most politically-conscious non-Maronites, especially Sunni Muslims and Greek Orthodox Christians, were opposed to integration into the new state. The idea of being ruled by Maronites was particularly objectionable to the Sunni Muslims who had been preeminent in the Ottoman Empire; hence their attraction to the concept of a unified Greater Syria. When the French were prepared to leave Lebanon, however, the Maronite and Sunni elites were ready to strike a deal. The unwritten "National Pact" of 1943 stipulated that the Maronites would refrain from invoking Western intervention, the Sunnis would refrain from seeking unification with Syria, and Lebanon's political business would be premised on the allocation of governmental positions and parliamentary seats on the basis of the sectarian balance reflected in the 1932 census, i.e. confessionalism. . . .

Much has been made of the outward manifestations of Lebanese confessionalism. The President of the Republic and Armed Forces Commander-in-Chief are always Maronites; the Prime Minister must be a Sunni; the Speaker of the chamber of deputies will be a Shiite; and for every five non-Christian deputies there must be six Christians. This allocation reflects the recognition of the founders of independent Lebanon that sectarian cooperation was the key to the country's survival. Lebanese confessionalism was the mechanism which they hoped would facilitate compromise.

The central government rested not only on confessionalism, but on localism as well. Political power in Lebanon traditionally resides in the hands of local power brokers, i.e. Maronite populists, Druze and Shiite feudalists, and Sunni urban bosses. These local leaders draw their political power from grass-roots organizations based on sectarian and clan relationships. Local leaders periodically have come together in Beirut to elect presidents and form governments, but none of them are prepared to allow the central government to penetrate their constituencies unless it is to deliver a service for which they have arranged and for which they will take credit. They guard their turf jealously against unwanted encroachments by the central government, whether it is in the form of the civilian bureaucracy or the military. If one of their Maronite number becomes President, the rest tend to coalesce in order to limit his power. The basic institutions of government, i.e. the army, the judiciary and the bureaucracy, are deliberately kept weak in order to confirm the government's dependency. If the local chiefs argue among themselves, especially over issues that tend to pit the major sects against one another, the central government simply stops functioning.

This, in essence, is exactly what has happened. Lebanon had survived earlier crises, but the Arab-Israeli confrontation proved to be a fatal overload for this fragile system. . . .

On 6 June 1982, Israeli forces launched a massive operation against Palestinian forces based in southern Lebanon, an invasion which brought the Israel Defense Forces to the outskirts of Beirut within three days. The three considerations that prompted Israel's assault were (1) putting an end to the military capabilities and political independence of the PLO [Palestine Liberation Organization]; (2) putting Israeli population centers in Galilee beyond the threat of hostile actions emanating from Lebanon; and (3) breaking the internal Lebanese political paralysis in a manner that would facilitate official relations between Israel and Lebanon.

Notwithstanding the evacuation of PLO and Syrian forces from Beirut — an event made possible by American diplomacy backed by U.S. Marines acting as part of a Multinational Force — Lebanon slipped back into chaos and anarchy. No sooner had the PLO departed Beirut than the new Lebanese President-Elect, Bashir Gemayel, was assassinated. That tragedy was followed by the massacre of hundreds of unarmed civilians, Lebanese as well as Palestinians, by Christian militia elements in the Sabra and Shatila refugee camps; an atrocity which, along with similar acts perpetrated by all sides, has come to symbolize the nature of sectarian hatred in Lebanon. This bloodletting, as well as the outbreak of fighting between Druze and Maronite militias in the mountainous Shuf area overlooking Beirut, demonstrated that the reconciliation long hoped for by most ordinary Lebanese was not at hand. Exacerbating the political ills that have afflicted Lebanon over the past several years, a new element of instability and violence has been added: the ability of Khomeini's Iran to mobilize a small, but violently extremist portion of the Lebanese Shiite community against the government and the LAF.

In summary, the Government of Lebanon is the creature of confessionalism and localism. Without consensus, any controversial stand taken by the central government will be labeled as sectarian favoritism by those who oppose it.

II. Major Events

... At approximately 0622 on Sunday, 23 October 1983, the Battalion Landing Team (BLT) Headquarters building in the Marine Amphibious Unit (MAU) compound at Beirut International Airport was destroyed by a terrorist bomb. This catastrophic attack took the lives of 241 U.S. military personnel and wounded over 100 others. The bombing was carried out by a lone terrorist driving a yellow Mercedes Benz stakebed truck that accelerated through the public parking lot south of the BLT Headquarters building, crashed through a barbed wire and concertina fence, and penetrated into the central lobby of the building, where it exploded. The truck drove over the barbed and concertina wire obstacle, passed between two Marine guard posts without being engaged by fire, entered an open gate, passed around one sewer pipe barrier and between two others, flattened the Sergeant of the Guard's sandbagged booth at the building's entrance, penetrated the lobby of the building and detonated while the majority of the occupants slept. The force of the explosion ripped the building from its foundation. The building then imploded upon itself. Almost all the occupants were crushed or trapped inside the wreckage. Immediate efforts were undertaken to reestablish security, to extricate the dead and wounded from the building's rubble, and to institute a mass casualty handling and evacuation operation.

Almost simultaneously with the attack on the U.S. Marine compound, a similar truck bomb exploded at the French MNF headquarters....

Part One - The Military Mission

I. MISSION DEVELOPMENT

Principal Findings

Following the Sabra and Shatila massacres, a Presidential decision was made that the United States would participate in a Multinational Force (MNF) to assist the Lebanese Armed Forces (LAF) in carrying out its responsibilities in the Beirut area. Ambassador [Philip C.] Habib, the President's Special Envoy to the Middle East, was charged with pursuing the diplomatic arrangements necessary for the insertion of U.S. forces into Beirut....

The mission statement provided to USCINCEUR by the JCS [Joint Chiefs of Staff] Alert Order of 23 September 1983 read as follows:

"To establish an environment which will permit the Lebanese Armed Forces to carry out their responsibilities in the Beirut area. When directed, USCINCEUR will introduce U.S. forces as part of a multinational force presence in the Beirut area to occupy and secure positions along a designated section of the line from south of the Beirut International Airport to a position in the vicinity of the Presidential Palace; be prepared to protect U.S. forces; and, on order, conduct retrograde operations as required."

The wording ". . . occupy and secure positions along . . . the line . . ." was incorporated into the mission statement by the JCS on the recommendation of USCINCEUR to avoid any inference that the USMNF would be responsible for the security of any given area. Additional mission-related guidance provided in the JCS Alert Order included the direction that:

● The USMNF would not be engaged in combat.

● Peacetime rules of engagement would apply (i.e. use of force is authorized only in self-defense or in defense of collocated LAF elements operating with the USMNF).

● USCINCEUR would be prepared to extract U.S. forces in Lebanon if required by hostile action. . . .

Conclusion

The Commission concludes that the "presence" mission was not interpreted in the same manner by all levels of the chain of command and that perceptual differences regarding that mission, including the responsibility of the USMNF for the security of Beirut International Airport, should have been recognized and corrected by the chain of command.

II. THE CHANGING ENVIRONMENT

A. Principal Findings

The mission of the USMNF was implicitly characterized as a peace-keeping operation, although "peace-keeping" was not explicit in the mission statement. In September 1982, the President's public statement, his letter to the United Nations' Secretary General and his report to the Congress, all conveyed a strong impression of the peace-keeping nature of the operation. The subject lines of the JCS Alert and Execute Orders read, "U.S. Force participation in Lebanon Multinational Force (MNF) *Peace-keeping* Operations." (Emphasis added) Alert and Execute Orders were carefully worded to emphasize that the USMNF would have a non-combatant role. Operational constraint sections included guidance to be prepared to withdraw if required by hostile action. This withdrawal guidance was repeated in CINCEUR's OPREP-1.

A condition precedent to the insertion of U.S. forces into Beirut was that the Government of Lebanon and the LAF would ensure the protection of the MNF, including the securing of assurances from armed factions to refrain from hostilities and not to interfere with MNF activities. Ambassador Habib received confirmation from the Government of Lebanon that these arrangements had been made. These assurances were included by the Government of Lebanon in its exchange of notes with the United States.

It was contemplated from the ouset that the USMNF would operate in a relatively benign environment. Syrian forces were not considered a significant threat to the MNF. The major threats were thought to be unexploded ordnance and possible sniper and small unit attacks from PLO and Leftist militias. It was anticipated that the USMNF would be perceived by the various factions as evenhanded and neutral and that this perception would hold through the expected 60 day duration of the operation.

The environment into which the USMNF actually deployed in September 1982, while not necessarily benign was, for the most part, not hostile. The Marines were warmly welcomed and seemed genuinely to be appreciated by the majority of Lebanese.

By mid-March 1983, the friendly environment began to change as evidenced by a grenade thrown at a USMNF patrol on 16 March, wounding five Marines. Italian and French MNF contingents were the victims of similar attacks.

The destruction of the U.S. Embassy in Beirut on 18 April, was indicative of the extent of the deterioration of the political/military situation in Lebanon by the spring of 1983. That tragic event also signaled the magnitude of the terrorist threat to the U.S. presence. A light truck detonated, killing over 60 people (including 17 Americans) and destroying a sizable portion of the building. An FBI investigation into the explosion later revealed that the bomb was a "gas enhanced" device capable of vastly more destructive force than a comparable conventional explosive. Although the technique of gas-enhanced bombs had been employed by Irish Republican Army terrorists in Northern Ireland and, on at least two occasions, in Lebanon, the magnitude of the explosive force of the device used in the Embassy bombing was, in the opinion of FBI explosive experts, unprecedented.

During August, rocket, artillery and mortar fire began impacting at BIA. On 28 August 1983, the Marines returned fire for the first time. Following the deaths of two Marines in a mortar attack the following day, the USMNF responded with artillery fire. On 31 August, Marine patrols were terminated in the face of the sniper, RPG and artillery threats.

Fighting between the LAF and the Druze increased sharply with the withdrawal of the IDF from the Alayh and Shuf Districts on 4 September 1983. Two more Marines were killed by mortar or artillery rounds at BIA on 6 September 1983. By 11 September, the battle for Suq-Al-Gharb was raging. The USMNF, under frequent attack, responded with counter-battery fire and F-14 tactical air reconnaissance pod TARPS missions were commenced over Lebanon. . . .

By the end of September 1983, the situation in Lebanon had changed to the extent that not one of the initial conditions upon which the mission statement was premised was still valid. The environment clearly was hostile. The assurances the Government of Lebanon had obtained from the various factions were obviously no longer operative as attacks on the USMNF came primarily from extralegal militias. Although USMNF actions could properly be classified as self-defense and not "engaging in combat," the environment could no longer be characterized as peaceful. The image of the USMNF, in the eyes of the factional militias, had become pro-Israel, pro-Phalange, and anti-Muslim. After the USMNF engaged in direct fire support of the LAF, a significant portion of the Lebanese populace no longer considered the USMNF a neutral force.

B. Discussions

The inability of the Government of Lebanon to develop a political consensus, and the resultant outbreak of hostilities between the LAF and armed militias supported by Syria, effectively precluded the possibility of a successful peace-keeping mission. It is abundantly clear that by late summer 1983, the environment in Lebanon changed to the extent that the conditions upon which the USMNF mission was initially premised no longer existed. The Commission believes that appropriate guidance and modification of tasking should have been provided to the USMNF to enable it to cope effectively with the increasingly hostile environment. The Commission could find no evidence that such guidance was, in fact, provided.

III. THE EXPANDING MILITARY ROLE

. . . Conclusion

The Commission concludes that U.S. decisions regarding Lebanon taken over the past fifteen months have been to a large degree characterized by an emphasis on military options and the expansion of the U.S. military role, notwithstanding the fact that the conditions upon which the security of the USMNF were based continued to deteriorate as progress toward a diplomatic solution slowed. The Commission further concludes that these decisions may have been taken without clear recognition that these initial conditions had dramatically changed and that the expansion of our military involvement in Lebanon greatly increased the risk to, and adversely impacted upon the security of, the USMNF. The Commission therefore concludes that there is an urgent need for reassessment of alternative means to achieve U.S. objectives in Lebanon and at the same time reduce the risk to the USMNF.

Recommendation

The Commission recommends that the Secretary of Defense continue to urge that the National Security Council undertake a reexamination of alternative means of achieving U.S. objectives in Lebanon, to include a comprehensive assessment of the military security options being developed by the chain of command and a more vigorous and demanding approach to pursuing diplomatic alternatives. . . .

Part Three - The Chain of Command

I. EXERCISE OF COMMAND RESPONSIBILITY BY THE CHAIN OF COMMAND

... The Commission holds the view that military commanders are responsible for the performance of their subordinates.

The commander can delegate some or all of his authority to his subordinates, but he cannot delegate his responsibility for the performance of any of the forces he commands. In that sense, the responsibility of military command is absolute. This view of command authority and responsibility guided the Commission in its analysis of the effectiveness of the exercise of command authority and responsibility of the chain of command for the USMNF in Lebanon.

The Commission believes there was a fundamental conflict between the peace-keeping mission provided through the chain of command to the USMNF, and the increasingly active role that the United States was taking in support of the LAF. The Commission believes that as the political/military situation in Lebanon evolved, aggressive follow-up and continuing reassessment of the tasks of the USMNF and the support provided by the chain of command were necessary. As the environment changed, the unique nature of the "presence" mission assigned to the USMNF demanded continuing analysis and the promulgation of appropriate guidance to assist the USMNF Commander....

Conclusions

The Commission is fully aware that the entire chain of command was heavily involved in the planning for, and support of, the USMNF. The Commission concludes, however, that USCINCEUR, CINCUSNAVEUR, [Commander in Chief, U.S. Naval Forces Europe], COMSIXTHFLT [Commander, Sixth Fleet] and CTF 61 [Commander, Amphibious Task Force] did not initiate actions to effectively ensure the security of the USMNF in light of the deteriorating political/military situation in Lebanon. In short, the Commission found a lack of effective command supervision of the USMNF prior to 23 October 1983.

The Commission concludes that the failure of the USCINCEUR operational chain of command to inspect and supervise the defensive posture of the USMNF constituted tacit approval of the security measures and procedures in force at the BLT Headquarters building on 23 October 1983.

The Commission further concludes that although it finds the USCINCEUR operational chain of command at fault, it also finds that there was a series of circumstances beyond the control of these commanders that influenced their judgement and their actions relating to the security of the USMNF.

Recommendation

The Commission recommends that the Secretary of Defense take whatever administrative or disciplinary action he deems appropriate, citing the failure of the USCINCEUR operational chain of command to monitor and supervise effectively the security measures and procedures employed by the USMNF on 23 October 1983.

Part Four - Intelligence

I. THE THREAT

Principal Findings

Intelligence assessments available to the National Command authorities and the military chain of command, and produced in support of this Commission, divide the spectrum of threat to the USMNF into two broad categories: conventional military action, and terrorist tactics. These assessments highlight the complexity of the threat environment confronting U.S. military units in Lebanon.

The potential use of terrorist tactics against American targets in Beirut — the USMNF, U.S. Embassy offices in the Duraffourd Building and co-located with the British Embassy, the U.S. Ambassador's Residence, apartments housing U.S. military and Embassy personnel, hotels housing U.S. officials, and even American University Beirut — is not the exclusive province of Iranian-backed Shiite terrorists. Radical Palestinian and Lebanese groups, some in conjunction with or with the support of Syria, could also employ terrorist tactics against the USMNF or other American targets. Stockpiles of explosives, built up over a decade prior to the Israeli invasion of June 1982, are reportedly still in place and available for future terrorist operations in and around Beirut....

The Conventional threat to the USMNF — land, sea, and air — is largely a function of the progress (or lack thereof) toward an internal Lebanese political settlement acceptable to Syria. All data available to the Commission suggest that a strong relationship exits between Lebanon's steady slide back toward anarchy and the tendency of some parties to label the USMNF a belligerent. It is obviously not the intention of the United States to place its power and prestige at the disposal of one or more of Lebanon's sectarian-based political factions. It is undeniable, however, that the facts of political life in Lebanon make any attempt on the part of an outsider to appear nonpartisan virtually impossible. The Government of Lebanon is not an antiseptic instrument of a collective Lebanese will; nor is it a collection of disinterested public servants isolated from the forces of family, clan, religion, and localism that are fundamental to life in Lebanon. President Gemayel is a Maronite Phalangist who is the son of the Phalange Party's founder and the brother of the man who built the LF militia.

General Tannous is likewise a Maronite who has a history of close connections with the Phalange Party and the LF militia. Whatever their true intentions may be concerning the future of Lebanon, they are caught in the same tangled web of distrust, misunderstanding, malevolence, conspiracy, and betrayal that has brought Lebanon to political bankruptcy and ruin. . . .

The Commission views Lebanon as an ideal environment for the planning and execution of terrorist operations. For over eight years, Beirut has been an armed camp featuring indiscriminate killing, seemingly random acts of terror, and massive stockpiling of weapons and ammunition. We are told that it is difficult, if not impossible, to find a Lebanese household which does not possess firearms. Notwithstanding the opportunity presented the Government of Lebanon by the evacuation of the PLO and the dispersal of LNM militias in September 1982, there are still neighborhoods in and around Beirut's southern suburbs which the LAF dare not enter.

The Iranian connection introduces a particularly ominous element to the terrorist threat in that the incidence of Iranian-inspired terrorism need not be connected directly with the reconciliation process in Lebanon. Iranian operatives in Lebanon are in the business of killing Americans. They are in that business whether or not the USMNF trains the LAF or provides indirect fire support to the defenders of Suq-Al-Gharb. If the reconciliation process succeeds in restoring domestic order and removing foreign forces, it may be more difficult for Iranian inspired terrorists to avail themselves of the support mechanisms (personnel, basing, supply, training) now so readily available. It is clear, however, that progress toward reconciliation in Lebanon will not dissuade Iran from attempting to hit American targets; indeed, any evidence of such progress may spur new Iranian-sponsored acts of political violence as a means of derailing the process. The only development which would seriously impede the terrorist activities of Iranian-dominated Shia groups in Lebanon, short of a change of regime in Tehran, would be a decision by Syria to shut down the basing facilities in the Bekaa Valley and sever the logistical pipeline. . . .

II. INTELLIGENCE SUPPORT

Principal Findings

Intelligence provided over 100 warnings of car bombings between May and 23 October 1983, but like most of the warning information received by USMNF, specific threats seldom materialized. Seldom did the U.S. have a mechanism at its disposal which would allow a follow up on these leads and a further refinement of the information into intelligence which served for other than warning.

The National Command Authorities and the chain of command received regular updates on the broadening threat to the USMNF.

Although intelligence was provided at all levels that presented a great deal of general information on the threat, there was no specific intelligence on the where, how and when of the 23 October bombing.

It should be noted that the FBI report on the 18 April 1983 bombing of the U.S. Embassy in Beirut, a report which described the use of explosive-activated bottle bombs in that incident, stayed within FBI, CIA, and Department of State channels. The report demonstrated that the gas-enhancement process, which requires only small amounts of explosives to activate the explosion of ordinary gas bottles, introduces a sizeable blast multiplier effect, and is relatively simple to employ. The necessary materials are readily available throughout the world and are relatively easy to deliver to the target. Indeed, oxygen, propane and similar gas bottles are common in most parts of the world. With regard to the BLT Headquarters bombing, FBI forensic experts have stated that it was the largest non-nuclear blast that they have ever examined; perhaps six to nine times the magnitude of the Embassy bombing. . . .

In summary, the U.S. did not have the specific intelligence, force disposition or institutional capabilities sufficient to thwart the attack on the BLT Headquarters building on 23 October 1983. The USMNF commander received volumes of intelligence information, but none specific enough to have enabled the prevention of the attack or provide him other than general warning. There was no institutionalized process for the fusion of intelligence disciplines into an all-source support mechanism.

Conclusions

The commission concludes that although the USMNF commander received a large volume of intelligence warnings concerning potential terrorist threats prior to 23 October 1983, he was not provided with the timely intelligence, tailored to his specific operational needs, that was necessary to defend against the broad spectrum of threats he faced.

The Commission further concludes that the HUMINT support to the USMNF commander was ineffective, being neither precise nor tailored to his needs. The Commission believes that the paucity of U.S. controlled HUMINT provided to the USMNF commander is in large part due to policy decisions which have resulted in a U.S. HUMINT capability commensurate with the resources and time that have been spent to acquire it.

Recommendations

The Commission recommends that the Secretary of Defense establish an all-source fusion center, which would tailor and focus all-source intelligence support to U.S. military commanders involved in military operations in areas of high threat, conflict or crisis.

The Commission further recommends that the Secretary of Defense take steps to establish a joint CIA/DOD examination of policy and resource alternatives to immediately improve HUMINT support to the USMNF contingent in Lebanon and other areas of potential conflict which would involve U.S. military operating forces.

Part Five - Pre-attack Security

... The BLT Headquarters building was occupied from the outset for a variety of reasons. The steel and reinforced concrete construction of the BLT Headquarters building was viewed as providing ideal protection from a variety of weapons. The building also afforded several military advantages that could be gained nowhere else within the BLT's assigned area of responsibility. First, it provided an ideal location to effectively support a BLT on a day-to-day basis. Logistic support was centrally located, thus enabling water, rations and ammunition to be easily allocated from a single, central point to the rifle companies and attached units. The Battalion Aid Station could be safeguarded in a clean, habitable location that could be quickly and easily reached. Motor transport assets could be parked and maintained in a common motor pool area. A reaction force could be mustered in a protected area and held in readiness for emergencies. The building also provided a safe and convenient location to brief the large numbers of U.S. Congressmen, Administration officials, and flag and general officers who visited Beirut from September 1982 to October 1983. In sum, the building was an ideal location for the command post of a battalion actively engaged in fulfilling a peace-keeping and presence mission.

Second, the building was an excellent observation post. From its rooftop, a full 360 degree field of vision was available. From this elevated position, forward air controllers, naval gunfire spotters and artillery forward observers could see into the critical Shuf Mountain area. Also from this position, observers could see and assist USMNF units in their positions at the Lebanese Science and Technical University. Further, this observation position facilitated control of helicopter landing zones that were critical to resupply and medical evacuation for the MAU. In sum, many of the key command and control functions essential to the well-being of the USMNF as a whole could be carried out from the building. No other site was available within the bounds of the airport area which afforded these advantages.

Third, the building provided an excellent platform upon which communications antennae could be mounted. ...

In summary, the Commission believes that a variety of valid political and military considerations supported the selection of this building to house the BLT Headquarters. The fact that no casualties were sustained in that building until 23 October 1983 attested to its capability to provide protection against the incoming fire received by the BLT Headquarters, while simultaneously providing the best available facility to allow the USMNF to conduct its mission. ...

III. BLT HEADQUARTERS ORGANIZATION, OPERATION AND SECURITY

... The interior of the building was utilized in a manner that facilitated command, control, coordination and communication both within the battalion and to senior, subordinate and supporting units. Effective use was made of the rooftop by key supporting arms team members. The total number of personnel billeted and working in and around the building averaged approximately 350 out of an average BLT strength of 1250. Since the BLT Headquarters building contained the only field mess in the 24th MAU, the number of personnel in and around the building during meal hours may have exceeded 400.

Notwithstanding the utility derived from the use of the building in question, and acknowledging the fact that the building did provide protection to personnel from incoming fire, the BLT commander failed to observe the basic security precaution of dispersion. The practice of dispersion is fundamental and well understood by the military at every echelon. It basically is the spreading or separating of troops, material activities, or establishments to reduce their vulnerability to enemy action. The BLT commander did not follow this accepted practice and permitted the concentration of approximately one-fourth of his command in a relatively confined location thereby presenting a lucrative target to hostile elements. The MAU commander condoned this decision.

IV. SECURITY GUARD ORGANIZATION AND EXECUTION

... Every Marine interviewed expressed concern over the restrictions against inserting magazines in weapons while on interior posts during Alert Condition II, III, and IV. The most outspoken were the sentries on posts 6 and 7 where the penetration of the compound occurred on 23 October 1983. The MAU Commander explained that he made a conscious decision not to permit insertion of magazines in weapons on interior posts to preclude accidental discharge and possible injury to innocent civilians. This is indicative of the emphasis on prevention of harm to civilians, notwithstanding some degradation of security. The threat to the MAU/BLT compound was perceived to be direct and indirect fire, ground attack by personnel, stationary vehicular bombs and hand grenade/RPG attack. In accordance with existing ROE (White Card), instructions pertaining to moving vehicles involved search and access procedures at gates. Hostile penetration of the perimeter by cars or trucks was not addressed in these instructions provided by the BLT guards.

The testimony of the Marines who stood post at the MAU/BLT compound was consistently in agreement concerning the activities of the guard force. Guard duty appears to have been professionally performed. All sentries interviewed were knowledgeable of the unique requirements of the various posts where they had performed duty.

Whether full compliance with the actions prescribed for Alert Condition

II would have prevented, in full or in part, the tragic results of the 23 October 1983 attack* cannot be determined, but the possibility cannot be dismissed. . . .

V. COMMAND RESPONSIBILITY FOR THE SECURITY OF THE 24th MAU AND BLT 1/8 PRIOR TO 23 OCTOBER 1983

. . . Competing with the MAU commander's reaction to the growing threat to his force was his dedication to the USMNF mission assigned to his command and his appreciation of the significance of peace-keeping and presence in achieving U.S. policy objectives in Lebanon. He perceived his mission to be more diplomatic than military, providing presence and visibility, along with the other MNF partners, to help the Government of Lebanon achieve stability. He was a key player on the U.S. Country Team and worked closely with the U.S. leadership in Lebanon, to include the Ambassador, the Deputy Chief of Mission, the President's Special envoy to the Middle East and the Military Advisor to the Presidential Envoy. Through these close associations with that leadership and his reading of the reporting sent back to Washington by the Country Team, the MAU commander was constantly being reinforced in his appreciation of the importance of the assigned mission.

Given his understanding of the mission, coupled with the perception that the greatest real threat to the MAU and to the BLT Headquarters personnel was from conventional small arms, mortar, rocket, and artillery fire, the BLT Commander enacted security procedures concurred in by the MAU Commander which resulted in billeting approximately 350 personnel in the BLT Headquarters building. Similarly, guard orders and procedures were characterized by an emphasis on peaceful neutrality and prevention of military action inadvertently directed against the civilian population using the airport. The security posture decisions taken by the MAU and BLT Commanders were further reinforced by the absence of any expression of concern or direction to change procedures from seniors in the military chain of command during visits to the MAU prior to 23 October 1983.

Conclusions

The combination of a large volume of specific threat warnings that never materialized, and perceived and real pressure to accomplish a unique and difficult mission, contributed significantly to the decisions of the MAU and BLT commanders regarding the security of their force. Nevertheless, the Commission concludes that the security measures in effect in the MAU compound were neither commensurate with the increasing level of threat confronting the USMNF nor sufficient to preclude catastrophic losses such as those that were suffered on the morning of 23 October 1983. The commission further concludes that while it may have appeared to be an appropriate response to the indirect fire being received, the decision to billet approximately one-quarter of the BLT in a single structure contributed to the catastrophic loss of life.

The Commission concludes that the Battalion Landing Team Commander must take responsibility for the concentration of approximately 350 members of his command in the Battalion Headquarters building, thereby providing a lucrative target for attack. Further, the BLT Commander modified prescribed alert procedures, degrading security of the compound.

The Commission also concludes that the MAU Commander shares the responsibility for the catastrophic losses in that he condoned the concentration of personnel in the BLT Headquarters building, concurred in modification of prescribed alert procedures, and emphasized safety over security in directing that sentries on Posts 4, 5, 6, and 7 would not load their weapons.

The Commission further concludes that although it finds the BLT and MAU Commanders to be at fault, it also finds that there was a series of circumstances beyond their control that influenced their judgement and their actions relating to the security of the USMNF.

Recommendation

The Commission recommends that the Secretary of Defense take whatever administrative or disciplinary action he deems appropriate, citing the failure of the BLT and MAU Commanders to take the security measures necessary to preclude the catastrophic loss of life in the attack on 23 October 1983.

Part Six - 23 October 1983

I. THE TERRORIST ATTACK

... When the truck exploded, it created an oblong crater measuring 39' by 29'6" and 8'8" in depth. The southern edge of the crater was thirteen feet into the lobby. To create such a crater, the explosion penetrated and destroyed the concrete floor which measures 7 inches in thickness and which was reinforced throughout with 1 3/4" diameter iron rods. Because of the structure of the building — it had a large covered courtyard extending from the lobby floor to the roof — the effect of the explosion was greatly intensified. This was caused by the confinement of the explosive force within the building and the resultant convergence of force vectors. This "tamping effect" multiplied the blast effect to the point that the bottom of the building was apparently blown out and the upper portions appeared to have collapsed on top of it. The force of the explosion initially lifted the entire building upward, shearing the base off its upright concrete columns, each of which was 15 feet in circumference and reinforced throughout with 1 3/4" diameter iron rods. The building then imploded upon itself and collapsed toward its weakest pont — its sheared undergirding.

The Federal Bureau of Investigation (FBI) assessment is that the bomb employed a "gas-enhanced" technique to greatly magnify its explosive force which has been estimated at over 12,000 pounds effective yield equivalent of TNT.

The FBI Forensic Laboratory described the bomb as the largest conventional blast ever seen by the explosive experts community. Based upon the FBI analysis of the bomb that destroyed the U.S. Embassy on 18 April 1983, and the FBI preliminary findings on the bomb used on 23 October 1983, the Commission believes that the explosive equivalent of the latter device was of such magnitude that major damage to the BLT Headquarters building and significant casualties would probably have resulted even if the terrorist truck had not penetrated the USMNF defensive perimeter but had detonated in the roadway some 330 feet from the building.

II. THE AFTERMATH

Principal Findings

The aftermath of the attack left a scene of severe injury, death and destruction. The dust and debris remained suspended in the air for many minutes after the explosion, creating the effect of a dense fog. There was a distinct odor present, variously described as both sweet and acrid, which one individual remembered as being present after the bombing of the U.S. Embassy in April 1983. The carnage and confusion made it difficult to establish control immediately. The explosion had eliminated the entire BLT Headquarters command structure. The initial actions of individual survivors were in response to their first impression of what had happened.

In his headquarters, the MAU Commander thought the MAU COC had been hit and went downstairs to investigate. The sentries closest to the BLT Headquarters building thought the compound was being subjected to a rocket attack and tried to report by telephone to the Sergeant of the Guard. Some personnel at the MSSG Headquarters area thought an artillery attack was in progress and went to Alert Condition I.

Once it was realized that a catastrophe had occurred, the independent actions of individual Marines in various stages of shock and isolation began to meld into coordination, teamwork and cooperation. Lebanese civilians in the immediate area, the Lebanese Red Cross, Italian soldiers (engineers) from the Italian MNF, and Lebanese construction crews with heavy equipment converged on the scene and went to work, acting instinctively from their many previous experiences in Beirut....

Discussion

Many individuals of the USMNF performed selfless and often heroic acts to assist their fellow Soldiers, Sailors and Marines. The response of the Lebanese citizens and the Italian MNF was superb. An example of this spontaneous outpouring of help was the response of a Lebanese construction company, which arrived with more heavy equipment than could physically be employed at one time and began immediate salvage and rescue efforts. The Italian soldiers assisted by moving the wounded and dead to Lebanese ambulances for evacuation to Lebanese hospitals or to the helicopter landing zones.

The MAU Commander remained concerned with his depleted security posture until he was reinforced with an additional rifle company deployed from the United States several days later. The MAU Commander properly perceived that his command was extremely vulnerable to a follow-on attack during the rescue/salvage operation.

The Commission takes particular note that the monumental demands placed upon the MAU Commander in the immediate aftermath of the attack required virtually superhuman effort. His situation was not enhanced by the large number of important visitors who arrived at his command in the days that followed. Throughout, the MAU Commander carried these burdens with dignity and resolve. In short, he performed admirably in the face of great adversity.

Part Seven - Post-attack Security

. . . Conclusions

The Commission concludes that the security measures taken since 23 October 1983 have reduced the vulnerability of the USMNF to catastrophic losses. The Commission concludes, however, that the security measures implemented or planned for implementation for the USMNF as of 30 November 1983, are not adequate to prevent continuing significant attrition of the force.

The Commission recognizes that the current disposition of the USMNF forces may, after careful examination, prove to be the best available option. The Commission concludes, however, that a comprehensive set of alternatives should be immediately prepared and presented to the National Security Council.

Recommendation

Recognizing that the Secretary of Defense and the JCS have been actively reassessing the increased vulnerability of the USMNF as the political/military environment in Lebanon has changed, the Commission recommends that the Secretary of Defense direct the operational chain of command to continue to develop alternative military options for both accomplishing the mission of the USMNF and reducing the risk to the force.

Part Eight - Casualty Handling

. . . Conclusions

The Commission found no evidence that any of the wounded died or received improper medical treatment as a result of the evacuation or casualty distribution procedures. Nevertheless, the Commission concludes that the overall medical support planning in the European theater was deficient and that there was an insufficient number of experienced medical planning staff officers in the USCINCEUR chain of command.

The Commission found that the evacuation of the seriously wounded to U.S. hospitals in Germany, a transit of more than four hours, rather than to the British hospital in Akrotiri, Cyprus, a transit of one hour, appears to have increased the risk to those patients. Similarly, the Commission found that the subsequent decision to land the aircraft at Rhein Main rather than Ramstein, Germany, may have increased the risk to the most seriously wounded. In both instances, however, the Commission has no evidence that there was an adverse medical impact on the patients....

Part Nine - Terrorism

I. 23 OCTOBER 1983 - A TERRORIST ACT

Principal Findings

... The bombing of the BLT Headquarters building was committed by a revolutionary organization within the cognizance of, and with possible support from, two neighboring States. The bombing was politically motivated and directed against U.S. policy in Lebanon in the sense that no attempt was made to seize Marine positions....

The BLT Headquarters building provided the greatest concentration of U.S. military forces in Beirut. The lawless environment in Beirut provided ideal cover for collecting intelligence on the target and preparing the attack. The expertise to build a bomb large enough to destroy the BLT Headquarters building existed among terrorist groups in Lebanon, as did the necessary explosives and detonating device. The availability of a suicide driver to deliver the bomb significantly increased the vulnerability of the BLT Headquarters building.

For the terrorists, the attack was an overwhelming success. It achieved complete tactical surprise and resulted in the total destruction of the headquarters, and the deaths of 241 U.S. military personnel.

Discussion

...The use of terrorism to send a political or ideological message can best be understood when viewed from the mindset of a terrorist. The strength of that message depends on the psychological impact generated by the attack. This, in turn, largely depends on the nature and breadth of media coverage. The political message in the 23 October 1983 attack was one of opposition to the U.S. military presence in Lebanon. An attack of sufficient magnitude could rekindle political debate over U.S. participation in the MNF and possibly be the catalyst for a change of U.S. policy. There were ample military targets in Beirut that were vulnerable to terrorist attack, but the symbolic nature of the BLT Headquarters building, and the concentration of military personnel within it, made it an ideal terrorist target of choice. The building was extremely well-constructed and located inside a guarded perimeter. This apparent security, however, may have worked to the advantage of the terrorists because the target, in fact, was vulnerable to a very large truck bomb delivered by a suicidal attacker. The first challenge would be to gain access to the USMNF perimeter at the parking lot south of the BLT Headquarters building. Once there, the barbed wire barriers could not prevent a large truck from penetrating the perimeter into the compound. . . .

From a terrorist perspective, the true genius of this attack is that the objective and the means of attack were beyond the imagination of those responsible for Marine security. As a result, the attack achieved surprise and resulted in massive destruction of the BLT Headquarters building and the deaths of 241 U.S. military personnel. The psychological fallout of the attack on the U.S. has been dramatic. The terrorists sent the U.S. a strong political message.

Conclusion

The Commission concludes that the 23 October 1983 bombing of the BLT Headquarters building was a terrorist act sponsored by sovereign states or organized political entities for the purpose of defeating U.S. objectives in Lebanon.

II. INTERNATIONAL TERRORISM

. . . Discussion

Terrorism is deeply rooted in the Eastern Mediterranean region. Mr. Brian Jenkins, a recognized expert on terrorism, calls this area "the cradle" of international terrorism in its contemporary form. He notes that the ideological and doctrinal foundations for campaigns of deliberate terrorism, which exist today in Lebanon, emerged from the post-World War II struggles in Palestine and the early guerrilla campaigns against colonial powers in Cyprus and Algeria.

Certain governments and regional entities which have major interests in the outcome of the struggle in Lebanon are users of international terrorism as a means of achieving their political ends. Such nationally-sponsored terrorism is increasing significantly, particularly among Middle

Eastern countries. The State Department has identified 140 terrorist incidents conducted directly by national governments between 1972 and 1982. Of this total, 90 percent occurred in the three year period between 1980-1982. More importantly, 85 percent of the total involved Middle Eastern terrorists. As an integral part of the political/military landscape in the Middle East, international terrorism will continue to threaten U.S. personnel and facilities in this region.

Conclusions

The Commission concludes that international terrorist acts endemic to the Middle East are indicative of an alarming world-wide phenomenon that poses an increasing threat to U.S. personnel and facilities.

III. TERRORISM AS A MODE OF WARFARE

A. Principal Findings

... [T]he conflict in Lebanon is a struggle among Lebanese factions who have at their disposal regular armies, guerrillas, private militias and an assortment of terrorist groups. ...

In Lebanon, violence plays a crucial role in altering an opponent's political situation. Therefore, the solutions are political ones in which the losers are not defeated, but maneuvered into a politically untenable position. Terrorism is crucial to this process because it is not easily deterred by responsive firepower or the threat of escalation. Terrorism, therefore, provides an expedient form of violence capable of pressuring changes in the political situation with minimum risk and cost.

The systematic, carefully orchestrated terrorism which we see in the Middle East represents a new dimension of warfare. These international terrorists, unlike their traditional counterparts, are not seeking to make a random political statement or to commit the occasional act of intimidation on behalf of some ill-defined long-term vision of the future. For them, terrorism is an integrated part of a strategy in which there are well-defined political and military objectives. For a growing number of states, terrorism has become an alternative means of conducting state business and the terrorists themselves are agents whose association the state can easily deny.

The terrorists in Lebanon and the Middle East are formidable opponents. In general, they are intensely dedicated and professional. They are exceptionally well-trained, well-equipped and well supported. With State sponsorship, these terrorists are less concerned about building a popular base and are less inhibited in committing acts which cause massive destruction or inflict heavy casualties. Armed with operational guidance and intelligence from their sponsor, there are few targets beyond their capability to attack. Consequently, they constitute a potent instrument of State policy and a serious threat to the U.S. presence in Lebanon.

Discussion

The Commission believes that terrorism as a military threat to U.S. military forces is becoming increasingly serious. As a super power with world-wide interests, the United States is the most attractive terrorist target and, indeed, statistics confirm this observation. Terrorism is warfare "on the cheap" and entails few risks. It permits small countries to attack U.S. interests in a manner, which if done openly, would constitute acts of war and justify a direct U.S. military response.

Combating terrorism requires an active policy. A reactive policy only forefeits the initiative to the terrorists. The Commission recognizes that there is no single solution. The terrorist problem must be countered politically and militarily at all levels of government. Political initiatives should be directed at collecting and sharing intelligence on terrorist groups, and promptly challenging the behavior of those states which employ terrorism to their own ends. It makes little sense to learn that a State or its surrogate is conducting a terrorist campaign or planning a terrorist attack and not confront that government with political or military consequences if it continues forward.

U.S. military forces lack an effective capability to respond to terrorist attacks, particularly at the lower ends of the conflict spectrum. The National Command Authorities should have a wide range of options for reaction. Air strikes or naval gunfire are not always enough. The whole area of military response needs to be addressed to identify a wider range of more flexible options and planning procedures.

State sponsored terrorism poses a serious threat to U.S. policy and the security of U.S. personnel and facilities overseas and thus merits the attention of military planners. The Department of Defense needs to recognize the importance of state sponsored terrorism and must take appropriate measures to deal with it.

Conclusion

The Commission concludes that state sponsored terrorism is an important part of the spectrum of warfare and that adequate response to this increasing threat requires an active national policy which seeks to deter attack or reduce its effectiveness. The Commission further concludes that this policy needs to be supported by political and diplomatic actions and by a wide range of timely military response capabilities.

Recommendation

The Commission recommends that the Secretary of Defense direct the Joint Chiefs of Staff to develop a broad range of appropriate military responses to terrorism for review, along with political and diplomatic actions, by the National Security Council.

IV. MILITARY PREPAREDNESS

Principal Findings

Not only did the terrorist's capability to destroy the BLT Headquarters building exceed the imagination of the MAU and BLT Commanders responsible for the Marine security of the USMNF. The ROE [Rules of Engagement], and supporting instructions, were all written to guide responses to a range of conventional military threats. . . .

Discussion

Of great concern to the Commission is the military's lack of preparedness to deal with the threat of State sponsored terrorism. The Commission found two different mindsets in Beirut regarding the nature of the threat and how to counter it. The USMNF units at the airport, behind their guarded perimeter, perceived the terrorist threat as secondary and could not envision a terrorist attack that could penetrate their base and cause massive destruction. The Commission found nothing in the predeployment training provided to the MAU that would assist them to make such an assessment. In the Commission's judgment, the Marines were not sufficiently trained and supported to deal with the terrorist threat that existed. . . . At a minimum, the USMNF needed anti-terrorism expertise of the caliber that supported the OMC [Office of Military Cooperation].

OSASM [Office of the Special Assistant for Security Matters] conducted a responsive anti-terrorist campaign that tried to anticipate changes in the threat and take appropriate measures to counter them. Unfortunately, neither USCINCEUR, the MAU nor OSASM saw the need to coordinate their anti-terrorist efforts, nor did they seem aware that different approaches to security were being pursued by the MAU and by the OMC. Approximately 350 Marines were concentrated in the BLT Headquarters building on the premise that it offered good protection against shelling and other small arms fire, the primary threat. The OMC, however, was dispersing its people on the premise that a large concentration of Americans offered an attractive target which a determined terrorist would find a way to attack. The Commission does not suggest that coordination of the security efforts of the MAU and the OMC would have prevented the disaster of 23 October 1983 because there were many other considerations. It does, however, concur with DCINCEUR's recent decision to expand OSASM's anti-terrorism responsibilities to include all U.S. forces in Lebanon. . . .

Conclusion

The commission concludes that the USMNF was not trained, organized, staffed or supported to deal effectively with the terrorist threat in Lebanon. The Commission further concludes that much needs to be done to prepare U.S. military forces to defend against and counter terrorism.

Recommendation

The Commission recommends that the Secretary of Defense direct the development of doctrine, planning, organization, force structure, education and training necessary to defend against and counter terrorism.

Part Ten - Conclusions and Recommendations

All conclusions and recommendations of the Commission from each substantive part of this report are presented below.

1. PART ONE - THE MILITARY MISSION

A. Mission Development and Execution
    (1) Conclusion:
        (a) The Commission concludes that the "presence" mission was not interpreted the same by all levels of the chain of command and that perceptual differences regarding that mission, including the responsibility of the USMNF for the security of Beirut International Airport, should have been recognized and corrected by the chain of command.
B. The Expanding Military Role
    (1) Conclusion:
        (a) The Commission concludes the U.S. decisions as regards Lebanon taken over the past fifteen months have been, to a large degree, characterized by an emphasis on military options and the expansion of the U.S. military role, notwithstanding the fact that the conditions upon which the security of the USMNF were based continued to deteriorate as progress toward a diplomatic solution slowed. The Commission further concludes that these decisions may have been taken without clear recognition that these initial conditions had dramatically changed and that the expansion of our military involvement in Lebanon greatly increased the risk to, and adversely impacted upon the security of, the USMNF. The Commission therefore concludes that there is an urgent need for reassessment of alternative means to achieve U.S. objectives in Lebanon and at the same time reduce the risk to the USMNF.
    (2) Recommendation:
        (a) The Commission recommends that the Secretary of Defense continue to urge that the National Security Council undertake a reexamination of alternative means of achieving U.S. objectives in Lebanon, to include a comprehensive assessment of the military security options being developed by the chain of command and a more vigorous and demanding approach to pursuing diplomatic alternatives. . . .

4. PART FOUR - INTELLIGENCE

A. Intelligence Support
    (1) Conclusion:

(a) The Commission concludes that although the USMNF Commander received a large volume of intelligence warnings concerning potential terrorist threats prior to 23 October 1983, he was not provided with the timely intelligence, tailored to his specific operational needs, that was necessary to defend against the broad spectrum of threats he faced.

(b) The Commission further concludes that the HUMINT support to the USMNF Commander was ineffective, being neither precise nor tailored to his needs. The Commission believes that the paucity of U.S. controlled HUMINT provided to the USMNF Commander is in large part due to policy decisions which have resulted in a U.S. HUMINT capability commensurate with the resources and time that have been spent to acquire it. . . .

5. PART FIVE - PRE-ATTACK SECURITY

A. Command Responsibility for the Security of the 24th MAU and BLT 1/8 Prior to 23 October 1983
    (1) Conclusion:
        (a) The combination of a large volume of specific threat warnings that never materialized and the perceived and real pressure to accomplish a unique and difficult mission contributed significantly to the decisions of the MAU and BLT Commanders regarding the security of their force. Nevertheless, the Commission concludes that the security measures in effect in the MAU compound were neither commensurate with the increasing level of threat confronting the USMNF nor sufficient to preclude catastrophic losses such as those that were suffered on the morning of October 1983. The Commission further concludes that while it may have appeared to be an appropriate response to the indirect fire being received, the decision to billet approximately one quarter of the BLT in a single structure contributed to the catastrophic loss of life.
        (b) The Commission concludes that the BLT Commander must take responsibility for the concentration of approximately 350 members of his command in the BLT Headquarters building, thereby providing a lucrative target for attack. Further, the BLT Commander modified prescribed alert procedures, thereby degrading security of the compound.
        (c) The Commission also concludes that the MAU Commander shares the responsibility for the catastrophic losses in that he condoned the concentration of personnel in the BLT Headquarters building, concurred in the modification of prescribed alert procedures, and emphasized safety over security in directing that sentries on Posts 4, 5, 6, and 7 would not load their weapons.
        (d) The Commission further concludes that although it finds the BLT and MAU Commanders to be at fault, it also finds that there was a series of circumstances beyond their control that influenced their judgement and their actions relating to the security of the USMNF.
    (2) Recommendation:

(a) The Commission recommends that the Secretary of Defense take whatever administrative or disciplinary action he deems appropriate, citing the failure of the BLT and MAU Commanders to take the security measures necessary to preclude the catastrophic loss of life in the attack on 23 October 1983. . . .

U.S. WITHDRAWAL FROM UNESCO
December 28, 1983

The U.S. government December 28 announced its decision to withdraw from UNESCO effective December 31, 1984. State Department officials said in a statement released with the letter to UNESCO's director general that the United Nations agency had "extraneously politicized virtually every subject it deals with," "exhibited hostility toward the basic institutions of a free society..." and "demonstrated unrestrained budgetary expansion."

The U.S. decision to withdraw came after several years of growing discontent with both the management and the direction of the agency. Founded in 1945, UNESCO (the United Nations Educational, Scientific and Cultural Organization) was at first involved mainly in promoting educational exchanges between the United States and Europe. In the late 1950s and early 1960s, when the newly independent African countries began to join the United Nations, UNESCO supported efforts to promote literacy and increase the level of education in the Third World. It also undertook projects to help poor countries protect their artistic and archeological treasures.

Controversies and the 'New Order'

As Third World nations grew more numerous and vocal in the United Nations, UNESCO increasingly became a political battlefield for debates on ideological issues. In 1974 members voted to exclude Israel from the agency's European group and withheld cultural aid, saying that the

967

country had "altered the historical features of Jerusalem" through its excavations there. In protest, the United States in 1975 and 1976 refused to make its yearly contribution to the agency. Responding to U.S. pressure, UNESCO in 1976 ended the exclusion of Israel.

Another controversial undertaking was an attempt by Third World and Soviet-bloc nations to create a "new world information and communications order." The "new order" was intended to end what was perceived as the dominance of the Western press, which Third World countries viewed as a threat to their cultural identity.

Under the "new order," UNESCO planned to encourage poor countries to impose restrictions on the Western press. The order endorsed the idea that governments had a right to control information for their own ends.

In 1982 and 1983 UNESCO drew up an international "code of conduct" for journalists. The agency planned to issue identification cards that supposedly would ensure the journalists' safety. Member governments would respect the cards but could revoke them if the holders were found to have violated the ethics code.

Many Western journalists and governments saw the "new order" as a way for the Third World countries, many of whom were dictatorships, to control what was written about them and limit unfavorable news coverage.

In November 1983 the Western nations opposed to the plan were successful in deleting some passages of the proposed guidelines, but journalists continued to oppose them.

Critics of UNESCO included the U.S. delegate, Jean Gerard. She recommended that the United States withdraw from the agency, saying that the delegates had embraced the ideology of the Third World and Soviet-bloc countries so thoroughly that it hampered UNESCO's work. Gerard described the organization as "collectivist and statist" and said its philosophy was opposed to American ideals.

Budget Issues

The Reagan administration objected to the way UNESCO was managed. The United States was the only member country to vote against the agency's $374 million budget for 1984. The United States, which contributed one-fourth of UNESCO's budget, tried unsuccessfully to freeze its spending for 1984 and 1985. According to figures from UNESCO's budget office published in The New York Times *December 30, 1983, UNESCO employed 2,250 people at its Paris headquarters and 466 in the field offices in the Third World.*

The New York Times *described the agency's budget documents as "obscure," saying that the list of proposed outlays for 1984 was unclear about whether the director general, Amadou-Mahtar M'Bow, was asking for an increase of 6 percent, 10 percent or 30 percent.*

The U.S. decision to leave UNESCO was not irrevocable. If the agency modified some of its positions, the United States could rescind its withdrawal or rejoin the organization later.

Comparison with ILO Pullout

The United States took a similar position in 1975, when it withdrew from membership in another U.N. agency, the International Labor Organization (ILO). Secretary of State Henry A. Kissinger charged that the ILO was being used for political purposes by a coalition of the Third World, Soviet-bloc and Arab states. Kissinger said the situation created a "double standard" of ignoring labor violations in totalitarian countries and condemning activities in democratic countries, especially Israel.

The United States rejoined the ILO in 1980. Secretary of State Cyrus R. Vance wrote to the membership body that the Jimmy Carter administration was convinced the ILO member nations were "now intent on assuring that the organization will live up to its principles and promises."

The American pullout appeared to have had an impact. In June 1983 the Arab states sponsored a resolution condemning Israel for its policy of "settlements, expansion and racism." The resolution did not pass, although the vote was 225 to 8 in its favor. With 186 states abstaining, the measure fell short of the 244 votes it needed to pass.

At the time of the U.S. withdrawal from UNESCO, officials could not say what the impact of the American action would be. France's UNESCO delegate, Jean-Pierre Cot, was quoted by The New York Times *as saying, "If the Americans leave, UNESCO will only be able to function poorly." U.N. Secretary General Pérez de Cuéllar said he "very much hopes that, given the significance of UNESCO's work and objectives, a way will be found for the United States to remain a member of that organization."*

> *Following is the text of a December 28, 1983, letter from Secretary of State George P. Shultz to Amadou-Mahtar M'Bow, director general of the United Nations Educational, Scientific and Cultural Organization (UNESCO), informing him of the U.S. intention to withdraw from UNESCO:*

The purpose of this letter is to notify you, within the terms of Article II, paragraph 6 of the Constitution that my government will withdraw from the United Nations Educational, Scientific and Cultural Organization effective December 31, 1984.

You may be assured that the US will, within the terms of the Constitution, seek to meet fully all of its legitimate financial obligations.

The Government of the United States, along with the American people generally, believe in the great principles enunciated in the Constitution of UNESCO. Today, as in the early years of the Organization, these principles summon us to a commitment of effort, and resources, in the interest of building a stable and enduring framework for peace in the world. Today, as in the early years, we believe that education, science, culture and communication are significant, even essential, elements in building a peaceful world.

But while the United States continues to devote substantial resources to the attainment of these goals, it must choose carefully the precise methods and means through which these resources are to be used. There are many groups and organizations whose purposes we approve, but which are not effective at carrying out the kind of international cooperation which will contribute to the making of a peaceful world. Good intentions are not enough.

For a number of years, as you know from statements we have made at the Executive Board and elsewhere, we have been concerned that trends in the management, policy, and budget of UNESCO were detracting from the Organization's effectiveness. We believed these trends to be leading UNESCO away from the original principles of its Constitution. We felt that they tended to serve — wittingly or unwittingly, but improperly — the political purposes of a few member states. During this period we worked energetically to encourage the Organization to reverse these trends; to redirect itself to its founding purposes; to rigorously avoid becoming a servant of one or another national policy; and to manage itself in a way that rewarded efficiency, promoted fearless program evaluation, and followed priorities based on program value rather than on past habit, political expediency, or some other extraneous consideration.

At the same time, we also recognized, and expressed our strong concern about, those pressures to divert UNESCO to politically-motivated ends which emanated from member states, rather than from within the organization itself. We consistently worked in the Executive Board and General Conference to minimize or eliminate the resulting political content — tendentious and partisan — from UNESCO resolutions and programs.

Many of these efforts, yours and ours, have been productive, at least in relative terms. The results of the recent General Conference prove the point, and we appreciate the role you played in the outcome of that Conference.

Viewed in a large sense, however, the General Conference proves a different point: if the results of the Conference demonstrate the *best* that can be expected from the Organization as it is presently constituted, and as it presently governs itself, there can be little hope for a genuine and wholehearted return of the Organization to its founding principles.

For the United States, that conclusion has become inescapable. The responsibility to act upon it is equally inescapable.

You, Mr. Director General, have our esteem, our appreciation, and our pledge of the fullest cooperation to make the year intervening between this letter and the date of our withdrawal as harmonious as possible. We recognize that you will continue to do your best, in the difficult circumstances in which you operate, to make UNESCO activities productive, and relevant to the unmet needs of the world. For our part, we are convinced that we can develop other means of cooperation in education, science, culture and communication, which better embody the principles to which we subscribed in UNESCO many years ago. We are convinced that such cooperation need not be diminished by the injection of political goals beyond its scope; that its authority need not be weakened through the compromise of such simple and lofty goals as individual human rights, and the free flow of information. It may yet be appreciated that our shared aims could have been accomplished effectively through attention to the principle that a few things done well have more impact than superficial examination of all the world's ills.

It is likely that the resources we presently devote to UNESCO will be used to support such cooperation. Any alternative programs which the U.S. develops could, in principle, serve as a basis for future cooperation between the U.S. and UNESCO, should both parties find that advantageous. We would be pleased to consider that possibility at the appropriate time.

▼▼▼

CUMULATIVE INDEX, 1979-83